BOYLE & BIRDS' COMPANY LAW

GW00493059

BOYLE & BIRDS' COMPANY LAW

3rd Edition

Editors
John Birds LLM, FRSA
Dibb Lupton Broomhead Professor of Commercial Law
University of Sheffield

Eilís Ferran MA, PHD, Solicitor
Director of Studies in Law
St Catharine's College
University of Cambridge

Charlotte Villiers LLM, Solicitor
Lecturer in Law
University of Sheffield

Consultant editor
A. J. Boyle LLM, SJD, Barrister
Professor of Law
Queen Mary and Westfield College
University of London

JORDANS
1995

Published by
Jordan Publishing Limited
21 St Thomas Street
Bristol BS1 6JS

British Library Cataloguing-in-Publication Data
A catalogue record for this book is available from the British Library.

ISBN 0 85308 311 8

Typeset by Create Publishing Services Limited, Bath
Printed in Great Britain by Bookcraft (Bath) Ltd, Midsomer Norton

Preface to Third Edition

Despite the large number of, generally good, company law textbooks currently on the market, it is clear from the numerous comments made to us that *Boyle & Birds'* not only has a special appeal but that many readers would welcome a new edition. Fortified by such comments, we have sought in this third edition to satisfy the needs of those readers and, in so doing, we hope that the book continues to provide an accurate account of this complex legal subject. In spite of the substantive and structural changes mentioned below, and the gradual development away from its parent, the book remains the distinctive offspring of *Gore-Browne on Companies*.

In the eight years which have passed since the second edition was published, there have been significant legislative changes with the introduction of the Companies Act 1989 and the subsequent secondary legislation, as well as the ever-growing volume of case-law. Consequently, our principal task in writing this new edition has been to take account of all the changes and developments in the law, but we have also taken the opportunity to restructure the book so that it is 'friendlier' for those coming to the subject for the first time. As a result of this restructuring, some of the material which falls outside the purview of company law in the strict sense, such as the regulation of the financial services industry, has been deliberately omitted.

The established team of authors has been strengthened for the third edition by the added expertise of Eilís Ferran and Charlotte Villiers, who, together with John Birds who exercised overall editorial responsibility, revised the majority of the text. Tony Boyle updated Chapter 1 and provided wise and supporting counsel throughout.

Further to the changes and developments already referred to, it is evident that company law is a dynamic area of the law and is likely to remain so in the foreseeable future. The Department of Trade and Industry has a number of working parties investigating different aspects of the subject; the Law Commission also has an active interest, and European developments will continue to have an impact. In this new, fully updated edition of *Boyle & Birds'*, we have attempted to provide a comprehensive and reliable textbook with sufficient detail for practitioners as well as providing a thorough grounding in the complexities of company law for students. The law is stated as at 31 May 1995.

John Birds
Tony Boyle
Eilís Ferran
Charlotte Villiers
June 1995

Contents

3   The Memorandum and Articles of Association

4 Company Contracts – Capacity, Authority and Form

5 The Public Issue of Securities

6 Share Capital – Allotment and Maintenance

7 Rights and Liabilities Attached to Shares: Reorganisations of Capital

8   Transfer and Transmission of Shares

9   Debentures, Charges and Debenture Holders' Remedies

PART 1: DEBENTURES

PART 2: CHARGES

17   Corporate Reconstruction and Insolvency

PART 1: GENERAL

PART 2: VOLUNTARY ARRANGEMENTS

PART 3: ADMINISTRATION

PART 4: THE COMPULSORY LIQUIDATION OF COMPANIES

PART 5: THE VOLUNTARY LIQUIDATION OF COMPANIES

PART 6: THE CONDUCT OF LIQUIDATIONS

Table of Cases

Boyle & Birds' Company Law

Table of Statutes

Table of Statutory Instruments

Table of EC legislation

1 The Registered Company: Its Development and Legal Personality

1.1 Introduction

This chapter is concerned with issues which have a general bearing on the various specific aspects of company law examined in the chapters that follow. The first of these is to explain in a concise way how the body of legislation[1] and case-law which today governs the affairs of registered companies[2] first developed and came to take its present form. The second issue to be discussed is the bearing which the European Community's programme for the harmonisation of company law has upon recent company legislation in Britain as well as upon future developments. The third general issue broached in this chapter is that of the basic principle of corporate personality. It will be seen that the separate[3] personality of the company is an inevitable consequence for a company (or any other body) upon which the privileged status of incorporation has been conferred. This is a judicially created doctrine but the courts have nevertheless shown themselves prepared, when moved by sufficiently strong policy considerations, to depart from this fundamental principle. This process is usually termed 'lifting the veil of incorporation'. It will be seen that the difficulty is to discover by what principle or principles the courts are guided in determining whether to adhere to the safe rule of respecting the separate legal persona of the company or whether to 'lift the veil'. It will be seen that this is an area in which the legislature has intervened on an *ad hoc* basis, especially in the case of 'groups' of holding and subsidiary companies. This chapter concludes with a discussion of two linked topics of contemporary relevance: 'corporate governance' and 'the market for corporate control'.

The first topic, dealt with immediately below, is the development of modern company law. The account given is in no sense a history of company law as a whole – too large an undertaking for our purpose. Instead, it is intended to show how the unincorporated joint-stock company of the early nineteenth century was transformed by the legislation of the 1840s and 1850s into a registered company of recognisably modern shape. For an understanding of the earlier history of company law, which had its origins in the sixteenth and seventeenth centuries, the reader is referred elsewhere.[4] There he will find an account of how the scandal and financial collapse produced in the early eighteenth century by the 'South Sea Bubble', and the resulting Bubble Act of 1720,[5] not only put down an illicit trade in the charters of incorporated companies but also placed an already flourishing number of unincorporated joint-stock companies under a cloud of official

---

[1] i.e. the Companies Act 1985 and related legislation.
[2] As to other types of business organisation, see 1.6 below.
[3] i.e. separate from that of the company's directors, shareholders, creditors, etc.
[4] For a lively and stimulating summary of this earlier period see Gower, *Principles of Modern Company Law* (Stevens, 5th edn 1992), Chapter 2. See further: C. A. Cooke, *Corporation, Trust and Company* (Manchester, 1950); A. B. Dubois, *The English Business Company After the Bubble Act, 1720–1800* (New York, 1938); B. C. Hunt, *The Development of the Business Corporation in England, 1800–1867* (Harvard Economic Studies, 1936).
[5] 6 Geo. I c. 18.

disapproval for over a century. Until the repeal of the Bubble Act in 1825,[6] such companies had a shadowy legal existence. The more favourable legal opinion of them was that, so long as their shares were not freely transferable, they were not liable to prosecution under the Bubble Act. Even after the Act's repeal, the only hope for those forming a corporate business enterprise (however economically important and substantial its operations) was to form a 'statutory company' by means of a private Act of Parliament. This gave the obvious advantage of legal personality with the attendant privilege of limited liability. Only in the case of very major undertakings (such as the canal and railway companies and other early utilities) which needed to raise large amounts of capital from the public, would the delay, trouble and very great expense entailed by the private bill procedure be justified. By this period the modern practice of refusing to grant a royal charter of incorporation to those engaged in trade or commerce was becoming established.[7] It may be noted that, although the common law protected the members of trading corporations from liability, it was common for provisions in their charters to allow the corporation to make 'leviations' on members to pay its debts. The courts of equity permitted creditors direct action against the members.

1.2 The incorporation of joint-stock companies by registration

At common law, despite the repeal of the Bubble Act in 1825, there remained some doubt about the legality of unincorporated joint-stock companies with freely transferable shares. These doubts had been fostered by Lord Eldon, who succeeded in inserting in the repealing Act a provision that their position at common law (with the taint of possible illegality) should be as it was before the Bubble Act was repealed. In the boom of the 1830s there was, nevertheless, a proliferation of unincorporated joint-stock companies, which in turn produced a growing demand for their legal regulation. In particular, there was a need to clarify their right to sue and be sued. There was also a growing demand for limited liability as a protection for shareholders who invested in them. In the case of formal written contracts, this was often obtained by express terms in those contracts, but this was obviously not possible in the case of the everyday informal contracts of a growing number of industrial and commercial companies. It has been seen that incorporation by charter was now deemed unsuitable for industrial and commercial companies, and a private Act of Parliament was prohibitively expensive.

1.2.1 *Legislative control*
The Trading Companies Act 1834 and the Chartered Company Act 1837 made a half-hearted attempt to deal with the problems of joint-stock companies, but the first was very restrictively applied by the Board of Trade and the second had little more success. Without conferring incorporation, these Acts made available some of the incidents of that status (e.g. the right to sue and be sued) and even (in the 1837 Act) limited liability to those seeking and obtaining the appropriate letters patent.

Especially during the cyclical slumps that followed economic booms in the nineteenth century, fraudulent promotion and other abuses were frequently revealed. This led to the appointment of a Committee of Parliament (eventually chaired by Gladstone when he became President of the Board of Trade). He undoubtedly had a strong influence on the

---

[6] 6 Geo. IV c. 91.

[7] As to types of business organisation other than the registered company, see 1.6 below.

eventual report.[8] This seminal report produced what is still referred to as 'Gladstone's Act' – The Joint Stock Companies Act 1844.

It is this piece of legislation which laid the foundation of the modern registered company; but modern company law still owes very much to those principles of partnership and trust law which the courts had already developed to cope with the unincorporated joint-stock company. However, 'Gladstone's Act' set company law on what is still its modern course by conferring ready access to incorporation by a process of registration.[9] It set up the office of Registrar of Companies who had not only to supervise the original registration, but had to keep up-to-date information about each company's constitution, directors and annual returns and make it available on 'public file'. At this stage the company's constitution was expressed in a 'deed of settlement', essentially the same document used by unincorporated joint-stock companies. It had broadly the same function as the modern articles of association, but in its original form was a trust deed which provided, *inter alia*, for the trustees in whom the assets of the old-style unincorporated joint-stock company might be vested.

The new Act applied henceforth to all joint-stock companies with more than twenty-five members or which allowed shares to be transferred without the consent of all the members. Thus began the divorce of partnership law from company law and the origin of the legislative practice that limits the size of membership in a 'private partnership'. In the case of ordinary trading, a business partnership's limit is still twenty members.[10] Existing unincorporated joint-stock companies could gain the privileges conferred by the Act if they altered their existing deeds of settlement and registered in compliance with its provisions.[11]

1.2.2 Limited liability

Limited liability was not conferred by Gladstone's Act. This was still a hotly debated issue in 1844 both in respect of 'private partnerships' and joint-stock companies. Thus the new type of registered company was like a modern unlimited company. There were some hesitations in the legislature's policy on winding up these new registered companies. The earliest winding-up Acts applied the ordinary bankruptcy law to companies while producing a conflict of jurisdiction between the bankruptcy courts and the Court of Chancery. By 1857, this confusion was resolved by conferring sole jurisdiction on the Chancery.[12] At the same time, certain principles of bankruptcy law were carried over to a new corporate setting.

The question of conferring limited liability on the new registered companies (and also upon certain forms of partnerships) was a strongly debated issue in the mid-nineteenth century, both in Parliament, in officially appointed committees, and in the press and the business community. While there was a strong movement for introducing a form of 'limited partnership' (based on the French model of the *société en commandite*), this had to

---

[8] 1844 BPP Vol. VII.

[9] There was a system of 'provisional registration' prior to the filing of the appropriate deed of settlement. Only after a full registration was the company incorporated.

[10] However, since 1967 this has been dispensed with in the case of 'professional partnerships'. See now section 716 of the Companies Act 1985. See further *Gore-Browne on Companies* (Jordans, 44th edn, loose-leaf) 6.10.1. As to the practical choice to be made between the small private limited company and the modern partnership, see 1.8 below.

[11] Those that did not do so still had to file certain information.

[12] See the Joint Stock Companies Act 1856 and the Companies Winding Up (Amendment) Act 1857.

wait in limbo for eventual enactment in the Limited Partnership Act 1907, by which time it proved to be of little practical utility.[13] Instead, in the mid-nineteenth century, the Government chose to confer limited liability only upon registered companies[14] – or more exactly upon those registered companies who opted to register in compliance with the requirements for a company limited by shares (then, as today, the vast majority).

As at first introduced (in the Limited Liability Act 1855), there were a number of important safeguards attached to the concession of limited liability (some of which have a contemporary ring in that they have been reintroduced in fairly recent legislation). Thus there were requirements of at least twenty-five members as well as specified amounts in respect of issued and paid-up capital. The word 'limited' had to be added at the end of the company's name everywhere it was displayed as an awful warning of the new risks faced by creditors! There were also safeguards to maintain the capital raised against the hazard of improperly paid dividends or unjustified loans to directors. The company had to have auditors approved by the Board of Trade. However, within a very short time, what had been termed the first 'modern Companies Act' – the Joint Stock Companies Act 1856 – consolidated and reformed earlier legislation. It abolished the old system of registering deeds of settlement and introduced the twin constitutional documents which still govern the modern company – the memorandum of association and the articles of association.[15] Rather less happily, this Act removed most of the safeguards for limited liability in the 1855 Act. In somewhat different form, most of these safeguards have been reintroduced into company law in the legislation of recent years.[16]

Undoubtedly, the grant of the benefit of limited liability helped to make possible the growth of the large modern company which today dominates the private sector of the economy. At an earlier period in the nineteenth century, those enterprises which had need to raise share and loan capital on a grand scale (notably the railway companies) had enjoyed limited liability as statutory companies created by Act of Parliament. The conferment of the same privilege on the registered company made it available to entrepreneurs and investors in industry and commerce generally.

It can be argued that in the case of the old unincorporated joint-stock company, with large numbers of shareholders whose liability was unlimited, this was not (for procedural and practical reasons) of great use in satisfying the claim of the unpaid creditors. Nevertheless the absence of limited liability was undoubtedly a major deterrent to investors in large-scale enterprises under the management of others. This does not of course silence the past and present critics of the unrestricted availability of limited liability for every small private company (or indeed for the subsidiaries of groups of companies). Where such companies are seriously (and deliberately) under-capitalised, the possibilities of abuse are self-evident.

1.3 Developments in the late nineteenth and twentieth centuries

During the remainder of the nineteenth century the legislature made only minor changes in company law, but the courts were responsible for the development of a number of

---

[13] The more flexible form of the registered company was by then readily available to small private companies. This gave the advantage of limited liability for all members and much else besides.

[14] Banking and insurance companies were at first excluded.

[15] As to the distinctive functions of the memorandum and articles, see Chapter 3.

[16] See e.g. the provisions of Parts V and VIII of the Companies Act 1985. See Chapters 7 and 8.

important principles. As regards legislation, a general pattern began in 1862 of reforming legislation followed by a consolidating Act. The Companies Act 1862 was the first Act of that name. This process continued at regular intervals (1908 and 1929) until the Companies Act 1948. The courts were faced with the task of evolving a number of new principles to fill out the statutory structure. In many areas, they could elaborate upon an existing body of partnership, trust and agency law already evolved to meet the needs of the old unincorporated joint-stock companies.[17] Alternatively, they might draw wide inferences from hints dropped by the legislature. Thus, from a somewhat slender statutory foundation, a substantial body of new judge-made principle might be created. Two obvious examples are the ultra vires doctrine[18] and the principles governing the raising and maintenance of share capital.[19] In other areas of company law, new concepts owed their origin to commercial practice and the skills of conveyancing counsel. These in due course received the scrutiny and approval of the courts.[20]

In this present century two issues have continued to preoccupy those who write official reports on company law reform and shape the consequent legislation. These issues are the need to increase the disclosure requirements in the Companies Acts and the related question of how far to exempt private companies from the accounting and other publicity requirements which apply to public companies. While the expense and administrative burden of disclosure has continued to grow, the question of how to handle the small private company has produced different answers at different times.

As regards publicity in respect of company accounts, this started with an annual balance sheet and then moved to a profit and loss account, to consolidated accounts for groups of companies and certain information as to 'associated companies'.[21] Today it includes further refinements such as information as to turnover and details about methods of valuation of assets, as well as requiring the accounts to be based on a historical cost basis in tandem with a current cost basis (so as to account for inflation). A wide range of other information must also be given about the company's activities, relating to its members and to its share and loan capital. An area of particular growth in respect of disclosure requirements in recent years relates to directors and their various interests in their company (or group of companies) such as interests in its shares, material contracts with it, loans made to them, etc. All this information is usually disclosed on an annual basis via publicly filed annual returns (or the accounts, or the directors' report). Much of this information (in addition to being made available at the Companies Registry) must be made available on a more immediate basis by means of registers kept at the company's own registered office.[22]

A good deal of the information that must thus be disclosed is (and was) inappropriate in the case of those private companies whose small numbers of shareholders had the remedy in their own hands, and where outside investors (or lenders) could bargain for themselves. Only unsecured trade creditors need the disclosure of such accounting and other information as was appropriate to their needs. Although the private company as a distinct species with certain privileges of its own dates back to the Companies Act 1908, it was not until the Companies Act 1948 that the legislature decided that the burden of the

---

[17] See e.g. directors' duties (Chapter 14, below), minority shareholders' actions (Chapter 15, below).

[18] See Chapter 4, below.

[19] See Chapter 7, below.

[20] e.g. preference shares (see Chapter 7), debentures and floating charges (see Chapter 9).

[21] See Chapter 12, below.

[22] As to the registered office, see 3.8, below.

accounting obligations imposed on most companies should not apply to small family or
'closely held' companies. These were termed 'exempt private companies'[23] and were
exempt from the necessity to file public accounts (and were given certain other special
privileges).[24] The pendulum of policy swung the other way in the Companies Act 1967
which abolished the exempt private company, thus visiting most of the accounting and
auditing requirements (increased by that Act) on private limited companies of any size.[25]
In the Companies Act 1981 the policy of the 1948 Act was reverted to in some measure.
In line with the requirements of the EC Fourth Company Law Directive (on company
accounts), new categories of 'medium' and 'small' companies have been created with
publicity and accounting requirements appropriately scaled down.[26]

Despite these changes, the general burden of disclosure (both at the Companies
Registry and at each company's own registered office) has been the target of considerable
criticism both in the business community and in those learned professions concerned with
company administration, as well as by some academic writers.[27] The clear lines of
segregation between public and private companies first laid down in the Companies Act
1980[28] have already made it possible for the legislature to place a lesser burden on the
private company (or at any rate medium or small private companies). However, while
limited liability remains overwhelmingly the norm for private companies, and while they
are in most instances seriously under-capitalised for the risks involved, there must be a
limit on how far the burden of disclosure can be lifted. A recent consultative document
issued by the Department of Trade and Industry, based on work done by the Law
Commission, foresees little change in the legal regime affecting private companies.[28a]
There is unlikely to be much reduction on the burden placed on public companies either
by Parliament or by the self-regulating bodies such as The Stock Exchange.[29]

Another source of growing complaint among both commentators and the legal
profession at large is the complexity and obscure drafting of much recent company
legislation. This seems to have had a number of causes. One is undoubtedly the
obligation to implement the EC programme for the harmonisation of the company laws
of member states.[30] Particularly in the case of directives which emerged from the
Community's complex legislative machinery before the accession of the United Kingdom to the Community in 1973, it is not surprising to find such directives framed in very
different terms, and starting from somewhat different basic conceptions, than would be
the case with 'home-produced' proposals for law reform. In some instances, a directive
may contain a useful reform but may be grudgingly or inadequately implemented by the
Department of Trade and Industry and its draftsmen.[31] In other cases the directive

---

[23] See Schedule 7 of the 1948 Act as to the complex conditions that had to be met to retain exempt status.
[24] Loans could be made to directors, and the company's auditors did not need professional qualifications.
[25] Unlimited companies provided an escape hatch for those dismayed by the new burden imposed as well as the risk of exposure to competitors.
[26] See Chapter 12. Most recently, the statutory audit of the accounts of some small companies has been abolished; see 12.26.
[27] See L. Sealy, 'The Disclosure Philosophy and Company Law Reform', 2 Co. Law 51 (1981).
[28] See 2.2, below, and the Companies Act 1985, Part I, Chapter 1.
[28a] The document was issued in November 1994.
[29] As to the Stock Exchange requirements as to continuous disclosure, see Chapter 12.
[30] This growing body of directives (some in force but many still in the draft stage) is discussed below at 1.5.
[31] See e.g. the First Directive as originally implemented by section 35 of the Companies Act 1985 before the reform embodied by the Companies Act 1989; see Chapter 4.

provides a 'Continental' solution to a problem of fraud or abuse which is already quite effectively tackled in a different manner by our own company law.

Another source of legislative complexity has been the attempt of the Parliamentary draftsman to curb the ever-present possibility of fraud and self-dealing by the directors of the company. In a perhaps misguided attempt to strive for both comprehensive yet precise prohibitions, while retaining a wide range of 'exemptions' to permit legitimate activities, the result has been legislation far more complex and convoluted than was the case with earlier company legislation.[32] With the prospect of a growing body of harmonisation directives either implemented or yet to be approved by the Council of Ministers, Companies Acts[33] have grown and will grow in bulk and complexity.

1.4 The EC harmonisation programme

The constitutional basis of the programme for company law harmonisation (though much debated in the past) is now generally agreed to be founded upon[34] the Right of Establishment and in particular Article 54 (2) and (3) of the Treaty of Rome.[35] Although various terms broadly equivalent to 'harmonisation' are used (e.g. 'approximation' or 'co-ordination'), the past arguments have been settled to the effect that the harmonisation programme does not require that a directive be implemented on a uniform basis in every member country (i.e. directives are not identical to 'uniform laws' in the United States). Another area of dispute in the early days of the harmonisation programme was whether it should be confined to the 'minimum safeguards' (referred to in Article 54). The now widely held view, reflected in the drafting initiatives of the Commission, is that virtually any aspect of the company law of the member states may be the subject of a harmonisation directive, since any major difference in company law may inhibit the freedom of establishment and thus come within the 'safeguards' referred to in Article 54. However, with the advantage of hindsight, it may be that the more restricted view of the proper scope for harmonisation had an element of political wisdom.

1.5 The directives in force[36]

The various directives that have so far received the approval of the Council of Ministers will be discussed in their appropriate contexts in later chapters of this book.[37] Although it will be seen that there have been certain shortcomings in the legislation implementing them, on the whole their effect has been beneficial and the general thrust of the reforms

---

[32] A notable example is the 'directors' loan provisions' in Part X of the Companies Act 1985 (see Chapter 14), but note the recent move towards possible revision and simplification mentioned in 14.1.

[33] The consolidating legislation of 1985, and subsequent developments, are discussed at 1.14, below.

[34] The other possible basis was Article 100: 'The Council shall, acting unanimously on a proposal from the Commission, issue directives for the approximation of such provisions laid down by law, regulation or administrative action in member states as directly affect the establishment or functioning of the common market.'

[35] '... co-ordinating to the necessary extent the safeguards which, for the protection of the interests of members and others, are required by member states of companies or firms ... with a view to making such safeguards equivalent throughout the Community'. Unlike Article 100, which requires unanimity, instead a qualified majority is sufficient. See further Andenas and Kenyon-Slade (eds), *EC Financial Market Regulation and Company Law* (Sweet & Maxwell, 1993) at Chapter 2 (Gisbert Wolff).

[36] The Companies Division of the Department of Trade and Industry regularly issues an updated report on *The Single Market – Company Law Harmonisation*.

[37] As to the First Directive, see Chapter 4; the Second Directive, see Chapter 6; and the Fourth Directive, see Chapter 12.

they contain is not out of line with the direction in which internally generated company law reform would have gone in any event. In the case of the Fourth Directive, some of the original defects evident at the earlier draft stages were amended as a result of representations made by British professional accounting bodies who were able at an early stage to bring appropriate pressure to bear through official channels when Britain became (or was about to become) a member of the Community.[38]

In the last decade, a number of other company law directives have been brought into force by the decision of the Council of Ministers and were subsequently implemented by the United Kingdom Government. The Third Directive[39] regulates mergers between public companies where the assets of the acquired company are transferred to the acquiring company.[40] The related Sixth Directive[41] is concerned with the division of an existing public company into separate corporate entities.[42] The Seventh[43] and Eighth Directives[44] deal respectively with consolidated accounts prepared and published by companies with subsidiaries[45] and with the independence and professional qualification and control of auditors.[46] The Eleventh Directive[47] deals with disclosures to be made by branches set up in one member state of companies registered in another member state or a non-EU country.[48] The Twelfth Directive[49] introduces the single member limited company into the company law systems of every member state.[50]

There are also a number of other directives in force (not all implemented in the United Kingdom) which have some bearing on company law and which are examined in subsequent chapters of this book.[51]

1.5.1 Capital market directives

There are a number of directives already in force concerned with capital markets and securities regulation. Thus, there are directives in force and implemented in Britain

---

[38] The most important change was the adoption of the overriding principle of the 'true and fair view' which has long been an important requirement of British company law. See further as to the Fourth Directive, Nigel Savage, 'Law and Accounting – the Impact of the EEC Directives', 1 Co. Law 24 and 91 (1980).

[39] 78/855/EEC, O.J. 1978 L 295/36.

[40] The Third Directive was implemented by the Companies (Mergers and Divisions) Regulations 1987 (SI 1987 No. 199). See Chapter 16 below.

[41] 82/891/EEC, O.J. 1982 L 378/47.

[42] The Sixth Directive was also implemented by the Companies (Mergers and Divisions) Regulations 1987 (see above).

[43] 83/349/EEC, O.J. 1983 L 193/1.

[44] 84/253/EEC, O.J. 1984 L 126/20.

[45] This was implemented in the Companies Act 1989, Part I. See Chapter 12 below. There have been two amendments to both the Fourth and Seventh Directives. The first of these aims to prevent avoidance of certain provisions of those directives by the use of partnerships with limited liability membership: Council Directive of 8 November 1993: Directive 90/605/EEC, O.J. 1990 L 317/60. Another Council Directive seeks to amend the Fourth and Seventh Directives so as to reduce the burdens placed on small enterprises by burdensome accounting requirements: Directive 90/604/EEC, O.J. 1990 L 317/57.

[46] The Eighth Directive was implemented by the Companies Act 1989, Part II. See Chapter 12 below.

[47] O.J. 1989 L 124/8.

[48] The Eleventh Directive was implemented by the Oversea Companies and Credit Financial Institutions (Branch Disclosure) Regulations 1992 (SI 1992 No. 3179). See Chapter 12 below.

[49] 89/667/EEC, O.J. 1989 L 395/40.

[50] The Twelfth Directive was implemented by the Companies (Single Member) Private Limited Companies Regulations 1992 (SI 1992 No. 1195).

[51] See, for example, the Directive on Disclosure of Significant Shareholdings: 88/627/EEC, O.J. 1988 L 348/62. This directive was adopted in 1988.

concerning the admission of securities to Stock Exchange listing,[52] concerning the listing particulars to be published for such admissions[53] and concerned with the continuing disclosure of information after an initial listing.[54] There are also directives concerning offers of transferable securities to the public by companies not seeking Stock Exchange listing at that time.[55] There are also directives on the mutual recognition of public offer prospectuses as listing particulars[56] and on the mutual recognition of listing particulars as such.[57] The Insider Dealing Directive[58] has quite recently been implemented by Part V of the Criminal Justice Act 1993. This re-casts existing British legislation in the Insider Dealing Act 1985 to comply with the directive. A more recent development concerns the regulation of the operation of the securities markets in member states. The Investment Services Directive[59] and the related Capital Adequacy Directive[60] are intended to remove barriers to the single market in financial services as between member states. The basic idea is that an investment firm should receive authorisation from its home state which will, subject to certain safeguards, entitle it to do business, either on a cross border basis or by setting up branches in other member states.[61] These directives await implementation by the United Kingdom.

1.5.2 Draft directives

It has been observed that the Fifth Draft Directive is the controversial centrepiece of the whole harmonisation programme. The Fifth Directive consists in part of fairly pedestrian but important provisions on the structure and functioning of companies (general meetings, boards of directors and their respective powers, shareholders' rights and directors' duties). However, this directive also tackles the thorny subject of employee participation. In the original draft published by the Commission such participation was posited on the basis of a 'dual board' structure (i.e. a supervisory board and a board of management) of a type which had long been established in the law of the German Federal Republic. This was combined with 'one-third' employee participation on the supervisory board, again largely modelled on the system of co-determination found in the Federal Republic.[62] After a long delay, and much debate in the Legal Committee of the European Parliament and elsewhere, a proposed compromise would allow a variety of alternative methods of employee participation which could be combined with either a single board structure or a

---

[52] See Directive 79/279/EEC, O.J. 1979 L 66/21 (amended by Directive 80/390/EEC, O.J. 1980 L 100/1. For implementation by Part IV of the Financial Services Act 1988, see Chapter 5.

[53] See Directive 82/121/EEC, O.J. 1982 L 48/26, likewise implemented by the Financial Services Act 1986.

[54] See Directive 82/121/EEC, O.J. 1982 L 48/26, likewise implemented by the Financial Services Act 1986.

[55] Directive 80/390/EEC, O.J. 1980 L 100/1.

[56] Directive 80/390/EEC, O.J. 1980 L 100/1.

[57] Directive 87/345/EEC, O.J. 1987 L 188.

[58] Directive 89/592/EEC, O.J. 1989 L 334/30.

[59] Directive 93/22/EEC, O.J. 1993 L 141.

[60] Directive 93/6/EEC.

[61] See *Gore-Browne on Companies* (Jordans, 44th edn, loose-leaf), vol 2 at 41.15–041.20. See also Andenas and Kenyon-Slade (eds), *EC Financial Market Regulation and Company Law* (Sweet & Maxwell, 1993), Chapter 3 (Eva Lomnicka) and Chapter 4 (Pauline Ashall).

[62] But as an alternative the system of 'co-option' in Dutch company law was also allowed.

dual board structure.[63] These alternatives are so diffuse as to destroy any real impact the Fifth Directive might have had on employee participation, but they are clearly designed to accord with the varying national and political attitudes to this controversial subject.

Apart from the Fifth Directive there are several other draft directives on company law where little progress has been made in recent years. The Ninth Directive[64] on the conduct of groups of companies was intended to provide harmonised legal structure for the unified management of a public company and any other undertaking which had a controlling interest in it. It also prescribed rules for the conduct of groups of companies. This directive, although informally circulated as early as 1984, has met considerable objections and has not been finally adopted as a draft directive by the Commission. The Tenth Directive concerns cross-border mergers between public limited companies in different member states. It was intended to complement the Third Directive which is confined to mergers within those states. However, although adopted by the Commission as a Draft Directive in 1985, it has not made much progress. This is in part due to the opposition of the United Kingdom Government to the worker participation provision it contains.[65]

A more recent development is a draft Thirteenth Directive on Takeovers[66] which seeks to lay down minimum requirements for the conduct of takeover bids with the general aim of ensuring equality of treatment for shareholders. This directive has produced considerable debate as to its effectiveness, especially as compared with the City Code on Takeovers which is a long-established system of effective self-regulation of takeover activity in the United Kingdom.[67]

1.5.3 *Other company law developments*

Besides the harmonisation programme properly speaking (i.e. by directive and based upon Article 54 of the Treaty), the Commission has made several other forays into reforming company law. Article 220 of the Treaty requires member states to enter negotiation with a view to securing for the benefit of their nationals the mutual recognition of companies and firms.[68] After negotiation under the auspices of the Commission, the representatives of the original six member states signed a Convention on the Mutual Recognition of Companies in fulfilment of Article 220 on 29 February 1968.[69] This convention is concerned with the obligation of member states to recognise companies formed in other member states. Subject to some concessions to the civilian

---

[63] See *Bulletin of the European Communities*, Supplement 6/83: 'The Structure of Public Limited Companies'; and see Mark Clough, 'Trying to Make the Fifth Directive Palatable', 3 Co. Law 109 (1982). The directive's proposals on directors' duties and shareholders' remedies would still make a useful reform of the complex British case-law as to minority shareholder rights of action. The British Government have made it clear that they are opposed to the introduction of compulsory measures of employee involvement. See a consultative document issued by the Department of Trade and Industry in November 1983.

[64] O.J. 1985 28/11.

[65] See Company Law Harmonisation (DTI, March 1993) at p. 7.

[66] The amended Proposal for the Thirteenth Directive was issued in September 1990. See O.J. 1990 C 240/7. Further work on this directive has now been halted.

[67] See especially Andenas and Kenyon-Slade (eds), *EC Financial Market Regulation and Company Law* (Sweet & Maxwell, 1993) Chapters 9 (L. S. Sealy) and 10 (Stephen Kenyon-Slade and Mads Andenas). See also the DTI's Consultative Document on the Thirteenth Directive (April 1989).

[68] i.e. those within the meaning of Article 58.

[69] Although this Convention has not been fully ratified by the new members who have since joined the Community (and who are obliged to do so), it is in practice already widely observed.

concept of the 'real seat' of a company,[70] the basic rule is that recognition is to be accorded to any company which has its statutory registered office in a member state. Since this is the basis of recognition of foreign companies long adopted by the courts of the United Kingdom, the Convention poses no particular problems for this country.

The Commission originally invoked the wide-ranging and catch-all provisions of Article 235 of the Treaty as a legal basis for an innovative and imaginative proposal: the draft regulation for a 'European Company'. This would allow a new type of company whose existence would transcend the natural boundaries of member states. In the current version of this proposal, access to European Company status could be achieved by various forms of merger between two companies, including the formation of a joint subsidiary or a joint holding company.[71] The component companies in this process are no longer (as the original version of the European Company) required to combine companies in two member states. It is possible for a company in a single member state to set up a holding company or a joint subsidiary in the form of a European Company. The only requirement is that the companies concerned have a subsidiary or an establishment in a member state other than that of their central administration.[72] The company must be registered in the state where central administration and therefore control exists.

In its current form, the Commission proposes a regulation and a directive together known as the European Company Statute.[73] The greater part of the regime would be contained in a regulation under Article 100A of the Treaty of Rome, but a directive under Article 54(3)(g) would govern the workers' participation options that would apply to the European Company.[74] These options are broadly the same as those now proposed in the draft Fifth Directive.[75]

Until recently, the European Company project made very little progress. Its opponents argued that the real reason for the small number of 'Euro-Mergers' since the Community came into being lay elsewhere than in any supposed obstacles in the existing merger legislation in the company law of member states. It was argued that the real problem was failure to harmonise the structure of tax laws and in the nationalistic attitudes of those who control large businesses. Although the British Government still has considerable difficulty[76] with the employee participation proposals,[77] the Commission has recently placed great emphasis (in the context of the completion of the single market) on the utility of the European Company concept.[78] A more constructive approach on the part of the British Government now seems possible.[79]

Another imaginative idea advanced in the form of a regulation (under Article 235) is

---

[70] In Articles 3 and 4. See Stein, *Harmonization of European Company Laws* (Bobbs Merrill, 1971), at pp. 394–422.

[71] See Andenas and Kenyon-Slade (eds), *EC Financial Market Regulation and Company Law* (Sweet & Maxwell, 1993) Chapter 11 (Janet Dine), p. 194.

[72] ibid., p. 194.

[73] O.J. 1991 176/1 and COM (91) 174. See also the DTI Consultation Document (January 1992).

[74] See *Gore-Browne on Companies* (Jordans, 44th edn, loose-leaf) 39.3. See further Dine, op. cit. The proposal reserves a number of matters to the national law of registration.

[75] ibid., 39.18.

[76] See the House of Lords report on the European Company Statute (HMSO, 1990, HC paper 71).

[77] See the DTI Consultation Document (January 1992); The Single Market – Company Law Harmonisation (DTI, March 1993). See also the House of Lords Report on the European Company Statute (HMSO 1990, HL paper 71).

[78] See *Gore-Browne on Companies* (Jordans, 44th edn, loose-leaf) at 39.1.

[79] See Dine, op. cit., at pp. 207–8.

the European Economic Interest Grouping (EEIG).[80] This regulation was adopted on 25 July 1985 having made rapid progress since negotiation began in late 1981. This concept owed its inspiration to the Groupement d'Intérêt Economique (GIE) introduced into French law in 1967. In both cases the idea was a flexible corporate form for joint venture activities (e.g. for joint marketing or joint production). In the case of the Economic Co-operation Grouping it must be a joint venture between companies and firms in different member states. The EEIG is based on a regulation[81] and as such is directly applicable under Article 189 of the Treaty. In most respects, no implementing domestic legislation is required. Some aspects of the regime governing the EEIG require, however, further implementation by member states.[82] In Britain this was achieved by the European Economic Interest Grouping Regulations 1989.[83]

No attempt is made in this very brief account of the EU harmonisation programme (and other company law projects) to discuss those wider concepts, doctrines and procedures enshrined in the Treaty or evolved by the decisions of the European Court of Justice. These may have a bearing on the directives already approved by the Council of Ministers and on any implementing national legislation. The reader is referred to the standard works on Community law as to the distinction between directives and regulations, the 'direct effect' of directives, the status of Community law as a kind of supranational law in national courts, and finally as to the jurisdiction of the court under Article 177 to entertain appeals from the national courts. Where the interpretation of a directive or the question of its implementation by national legislation is raised, any or all of these issues may have a bearing on the matter.[84]

1.6 Other types of corporate business organisation

The brief historical account given in this chapter has concerned the development of the registered company, since that is the subject of this book. At the same period of time there also evolved a number of different types of association based not upon the principle of investment for profit by proprietors but on quite distinct principles of co-operation or mutual self-help. In this the archetype was originally the unincorporated friendly society. In the course of the nineteenth century, bodies and associations concerned with specialised activities of this kind came to be regulated by their own special legislation. This usually conferred corporate personality as well as limited liability. One feature common to this type of legislation is that the body for which it was intended might not register under the Companies Acts. This is true of co-operative societies, working men's clubs and other friendly societies. It also applied to trade unions, trustee savings banks and building societies.[85] In the case of trustee savings banks legislation brought their business activities within the sphere of company law. The 'privatisation' of trustee savings banks converted

---

[80] Council Regulation (EEC) 2137/85, O.J. 1985 L 199/1.

[81] See above.

[82] e.g. as to registration and as to winding up of EEIGs.

[83] SI 1989 No. 638. See further *Gore-Browne on Companies* (Jordans, 44th edn, loose-leaf) 6.11–6.15. See also Dine in Andenas and Kenyon-Slade (eds), *EC Financial Market Regulation and Company Law* (Sweet & Maxwell, 1993) at pp. 198–207, and Attree et al., *European Economic Interest Groupings, Commercial Legal and Tax Considerations* (Jordans, 1990).

[84] See in general, T. C. Hartley, *The Foundations of European Community Law* (Clarendon Law Series, 1981), Chapters 7 and 8. See further, Andenas and Kenyon-Slade (eds) *EC Financial Market Regulation and Company Law* (Sweet & Maxwell, 1993), in particular Chapter 1 (Paulo Clarotti) and Chapter 2 (Gisbert Wolff).

[85] As to the legislation applicable, see *Gore-Browne on Companies* (Jordans, 44th edn, loose-leaf) 6.10.3.

them into a public company offering its shares to the public as well as existing investors.[86] The building societies legislation made it possible for them to convert themselves into public limited companies. There are increasing signs that this opportunity will be taken up.[87]

1.7 The consequences of incorporation

Lord Justice Lindley gave this definition of the old unincorporated joint stock company: 'I understand by a company – an unincorporated company – some association of members, the shares of which are transferable. As distinguished from a partnership, I know of nothing else except the transferability of shares.'[88] But with regard to an *incorporated* company there are other important distinctions: e.g. that, while in an ordinary partnership each partner is personally responsible for all the debts contracted by the firm, in an incorporated company the members have no individual liability to its creditors for debts owing by the company, and their personal liability is satisfied if they pay the calls properly made upon them by the company or its liquidator. These calls may be limited in amount or unlimited, according as the company is limited or unlimited, but they are enforceable only by the company or its liquidator. The company, moreover, is a distinct legal personality,[89] can own and deal with property, sue and be sued in its own name,[90] and contract on its own behalf. The members are not personally entitled to the benefits or liable for the burdens arising thereby: their rights are confined to receiving from the company their share of the profits or, after a winding-up, of the surplus assets, and their liabilities to paying the amounts due from them to the company. The creditors of a limited company accordingly know that they cannot, as in the case of an ordinary partnership, look to the whole property of the individual members to pay them, but are restricted to the property of the company, including such further amounts (if any) as the members are liable to pay in respect of shares held by them in the capital, and in the case of companies limited by guarantee the sums payable in accordance with the guarantee contained in the memorandum of association.

An incorporated company is a 'person' within the meaning of the Interpretation Act 1978, unless the contrary intention appears.[91] A company cannot, however, be convicted under a section which inflicts only imprisonment as the penalty.[92]

---

[86] Savings Bank Act 1985.

[87] Building Societies Act 1986.

[88] *R v Registrar of Joint Stock Companies* [1891] 2 QB 598 at p. 610.

[89] Where a partnership of eight persons transferred their property to a company in exchange for shares in the same proportions as their interests in the partnership, this was held to be a sale to a distinct person. 'We have two parties, one party consisting of several individuals, and the other party consisting of a corporation.' *Per* Lindley LJ: *John Foster & Sons v Commissioners of Inland Revenue* [1894] 1 QB 516 at p. 528.

[90] A limited company can maintain an action for defamation: *South Hetton Coal Co. v North Eastern News Association* [1894] 1 QB 133, *D. & L. Caterers & Jackson v D'Ajou* [1945] KB 364. A company cannot appear in person, but must be represented in proceedings: *Tritonia Ltd v Equity and Law Life Assurance Soc.* [1943] AC 584 (HL) (except in the county courts: *Kinnell & Co. v Harding* [1918] 1 KB 405 (CA)). Further, a company cannot be subpoenaed to give evidence: *Penn-Texas Corp. v Murat Anstalt* [1964] 1 QB 40 (CA). Cf. ibid. (*No. 2*) [1964] 2 QB 647 (CA) as to the position under the Foreign Tribunals Evidence Act 1856.

[91] See section 5 and Schedule 1. This applies to Acts passed in or after 1889: Schedule 2, para. 4 (1) (*a*).

[92] *Hawke v E. Hulton & Co.* [1909] 2 KB 93. The criminal liability of companies is discussed further at 1.11–1.12, below.

It can be fined for contempt of court, although it cannot be attached.[93] Any judgment or order against a company wilfully disobeyed, may, by leave of the court or a judge, be enforced by sequestration against the property of the company, or by attachment against the directors or other officers thereof, or by writ of sequestration against their property.[94] A company may be convicted of offences where the punishment is a fine.[95] A company may be 'a respectable and responsible person' within the meaning of those words in a licence to assign leasehold property.[96]

1.8 The advantages of incorporation

It is conventional in a textbook on company law to say something about the advantages of incorporation. This involves essentially a comparison of the limited company and the partnership. Most of the more obvious advantages of the corporate form (limited liability, the vesting of the business assets in the company, suing and being sued in the company's name, perpetual succession and transferable shares) have already been indicated earlier in this chapter. Other advantages (such as the ability to create a floating charge over its assets or to make a public issue of its securities) will become apparent in later chapters.[97] There are also disadvantages in using the corporate form (especially in the case of the limited company). As compared with partnership there is a much greater degree of formality (as well as publicity and expense) attendant not only upon the formation of a limited company[98] but also required throughout its life.[99] Furthermore, the rules about directors' and shareholders' meetings (as well as resolutions and voting) are likely to be observed more in the breach than honoured in the observance in the case of the really small private company. The flexible rules about the internal conduct of partnerships are more realistic and appropriate for the small business. The advantage to partners in being able readily to withdraw their capital from a partnership is now to some extent available even in the case of limited companies under the provisions first introduced by the Companies Act 1981. These allow private companies considerable freedom to purchase or to redeem issued share capital.[100] It should also be noted that the modern partnership has many of the practical advantages of a corporate body. It can sue and be sued in its own name. With properly drafted articles, it can 'survive' over long periods of time despite the death or retirement of individual partners.[101]

---

[93] *R. v J. G. Hammond & Co.* [1914] 2 KB 866. As to the liability of a director for a contempt by his company, see *Biba Ltd v Stratford Investments* [1972] 3 WLR 390.

[94] RSC Order 45, rule 5, and see: *Benabo v William Jay & Partners* [1941] Ch 52; *Phonographic Equipment v Amusement Caterers (Peckham) Ltd* [1964] Ch 195. This does not apply in Scotland.

[95] *Pharmaceutical Society v London and Provincial Supply Association* (1880) 5 App. Cas. 857 at p. 869; *Chuter v Freeth & Pocock Ltd* [1911] 2 KB 832.

[96] *Ideal Film Renting Co. v Nielsen* [1921] 1 Ch 575; *Willmott v London Road Car Co.* [1910] 2 Ch 525. See also *In re Greater London Property Ltd's Lease* [1959] 1 WLR 503. See further 1.10, below.

[97] See Chapters 5 and 9, below.

[98] See Chapter 2.

[99] See Chapters 10 and 12. These deal with the annual accounts as well as the annual returns and directors' reports. Some relief, as regarding accounts, is now given to 'medium' companies and more to 'small' companies.

[100] The new provisions in Part V of the Companies Act 1989 for the 'de-regulation of private companies' are addressed to meeting this need. See Chapter 11.

[101] It does not of course enjoy limited liability, and the partners' separate estates are at risk to creditors during the continuance of the partnership – not just on winding up as in the case of an unlimited company. It has been seen that the Limited Partnership Act 1907 has been little used. The small private company is of much more utility.

Ultimately, the question of choice as between the company or partnership form will depend upon the impact of taxation. In the case of companies, corporation tax (and capital gains tax) applies. Income tax will apply to the salaries of directors and in respect of the dividends distributed to shareholders.[102] Partners are subject to income tax and capital gains tax on their trading profits. In the case of the small business the advice given by professional advisers will take into consideration the level of trading income of the business and the number of participants in the business, as well as their separate sources of earned or investment income. Obviously the larger the scale of any business enterprise the more likely it is that there will be tax advantages in the corporate form. At a certain level this will become essential.

1.9 The principle of corporate personality

The separate personality of a company and its entity as distinct from its shareholders was established by the House of Lords in *Salomon v Salomon & Co.,*[103] where it was held that however large the proportion of the shares and debentures owned by one man, even if the other shares were held in trust for him, the company's acts were not his acts, nor were its liabilities his liabilities; nor is it otherwise if he has sole control of its affairs as governing director.[104] It is important to note that the House of Lords found no evidence whatever of fraud or deliberate abuse of the corporate form. Indeed, Salomon did his best to rescue his company by cancelling the debentures he took and reissuing them to an outside creditor who provided fresh loan capital. The *Salomon* decision gave express recognition to what were even then called 'one man' companies. The modern practice of having undercapitalised private companies (with the founding shareholders as creditors in their own company) stems from this case. This is certainly a use of the corporate form not contemplated when limited liability was made generally available.

The principle of the *Salomon* case,[105] that a company is a legal entity distinct from its members, is strictly applied by the courts whenever it is sought to attribute the rights or liabilities of a company to its shareholders, or regard the property of a company as belonging in law or equity to the shareholders. Thus the fact that one shareholder controls all or virtually all the shares in a company is not a sufficient reason for ignoring the legal personality of the company.[106] Further, a company cannot be characterised as an agent of its shareholders unless there is clear evidence to show that the company was in fact acting as an agent in a particular transaction or series of transactions.[107] Likewise, the property of a company in no sense belongs to its members.[108] The company is not a trustee of its property for its shareholders even where the directors have been appointed

---

[102] See further *Gore-Browne on Companies* (Jordans, 44th edn, loose-leaf) Chapter 24. Note the effect of the 'close company' provisions in preventing abuse of the corporate form.

[103] [1897] AC 22.

[104] *Inland Revenue Commissioners v Sansom* [1921] 2 KB 492. See also *Re Hydrodam (Corby) (In Liquidation)* [1994] BCC 161. The fact that a body corporate was director of a company did not necessarily mean that that body corporate's directors were therefore directors of the company.

[105] [1897] AC 22. See *F. J. Neale (Glasgow) Ltd v Vickery* 1974 SLT 88 for an application of the *Salomon* principle.

[106] See e.g. *Tunstall v Steigmann* [1962] 2 QB 593 (CA); *Lee v Lee's Air Farming Ltd* [1961] AC 12 (PC).

[107] *Ebbw Vale U.D.C. v South Wales Traffic Area Licensing Authority* [1951] 2 KB 366 (CA); *Pegler v Craven* [1952] 2 QB 69 (CA).

[108] *Bank voor Handel en Scheepvaart N.V. v Slatford* [1953] 1 QB 248.

trustees of some or all of the shares in a company.[109] A shareholder does not have an insurable interest in the assets or business of the company.[110]

1.10 Lifting the veil of incorporation

Notwithstanding the principle of *Salomon's* case[111] there are certain situations where the courts have shown themselves willing to 'lift the veil of incorporation', that is to ignore or set aside the separate legal personality of a company. It is not possible to formulate any single principle as the basis for these decisions, nor are all the decisions, as to when the separate legal entity of the company must be respected or when it may be disregarded, entirely consistent with one another.[112]

It is well established that the courts will not allow the corporate form to be used for the purposes of fraud,[113] or as a device to evade a contractual or other legal obligation. Thus in *Gilford Motor Co. v Horne*[114] the respondent had contracted with the appellant company not to solicit its customers when he left their employment. On ceasing employment, Horne formed a company to carry on a competing business and this company started to solicit the Gilford Motor Co.'s customers. The court granted an injunction to enforce the covenant not to solicit against both Horne and the company he had formed as a cloak for his activities. In *Jones v Lipman*[115] the defendant had entered into a contract to sell his house. He sought to escape his obligation to complete by conveying the property to a company in which he and a nominee of his controlled all the shares and were the directors. Russell J, in granting a decree of specific performance, described the company as 'the creature of the first defendant, a device and a sham, a mask which he holds before his face in an attempt to avoid recognition by the eye of equity'.[116]

In some cases, the courts have found on the particular evidence before them that a holding company was in fact carrying on a business through the agency of its subsidiary company. It is important to note that the mere fact that one company is the subsidiary of another, even a 'wholly owned' subsidiary, is not by itself sufficient to make the subsidiary an agent of its holding company.[117] The activities of the subsidiary must be so closely controlled and directed by the parent company that the latter can be regarded as merely an agent conducting the parent company's business.[118]

For certain purposes, the courts, while respecting the separate legal personality of a company, have treated the conduct or characteristics of its directors, managers or members as attributable to the company itself. This attribution does not in the true sense involve 'lifting the veil of incorporation'. For example, where the courts have had to

---

[109] *Butt v Kelsen* [1952] Ch 197 (CA).

[110] *Macaura v Northern Assurance Co.* [1925] AC 619 (HL (Ir)).

[111] [1897] AC 22.

[112] See e.g. *Wurzel v Houghton Main Home Service Ltd* [1937] 1 KB 380 and *Trebanog Working Men's Club and Institute Ltd v Macdonald* [1940] 1 KB 576.

[113] *Re Darby* [1911] 1 KB 95. See also *Wallersteiner v Moir (No. 1)* [1974] 1 WLR 997 (CA) at p. 1013.

[114] [1933] Ch 935 (CA).

[115] [1962] 1 WLR 832. See also *H. & H. Elliott Ltd v Pierson* [1948] Ch 852.

[116] ibid., p. 836. See also *Re F. G. (Films) Ltd* [1953] 1 WLR 483 and *Merchandise Transport Ltd v B.T.C.* [1962] 2 QB 173.

[117] *Kodak Ltd v Clark* [1903] 1 KB 505 (CA); *Gramophone & Typewriters Ltd v Stanley* [1908] 2 KB 89. (CA); *I.R.C. v Sansom* [1921] 2 KB 492 (CA).

[118] See the judgment of Atkinson J, in *Smith Stone and Knight Ltd v Birmingham Corporation* [1939] 4 All ER 116 and the cases there cited. See also *Firestone Tyre and Rubber Co. v Llewellyn* [1957] 1 WLR 464 (HL). As to lifting the veil in the case of groups of companies, see 1.13.4 below.

determine the residence of a company, they look not to the place of registration but to the way the company is actually managed in order to find where the centre or centres of management are in fact located.[119] The cases examined in 1.12, below, on the attribution of *mens rea* to a company for the purposes of criminal or civil liability are another illustration of the same principle. Another example is *Re Greater London Property Ltd's Lease*[120] where a subsidiary company was held a responsible assignee of a lease despite the landlord's contention that it was not financially viable without the support of its holding company. Danckwerts J refused to disregard the real economic link between the holding and subsidiary company. Again, this is not a true case of 'lifting the veil of incorporation'. In *The Abbey, Malvern Wells Ltd v Ministry of Local Government and Planning*[121] a limited company was formed to run a school for the profit of its shareholders. Later it was converted into a non-profit-making body by vesting its shares in charitable trustees and altering its articles to provide that it should be run by the trustees. Danckwerts J held that the company could claim charitable status so as to exempt it from paying a development charge under the Town and Country Planning Act 1947. This decision is not inconsistent with the generally established rule that a company is not a trustee for its members. In determining whether for a particular statutory purpose it had charitable status, Danckwerts J realistically attributed the characteristics of its shareholders as trustees of a charitable trust to the company itself.

Where fraud or deliberate breach of trust can be shown, as a recent case once again demonstrates, the courts show a willingness to set aside the corporate form even where this involves a network of interlocking foreign and English companies. The plaintiff companies in this case[122] were in liquidation and had brought an action against the defendant alleging deceit and breach of trust. The defendant, in the knowledge that the plaintiff companies were insolvent, had disposed of his personal assets so that they were held by a network of interlocking foreign and English companies and trusts so that his true beneficial interests were concealed. This was intended to prevent the plaintiffs from recovering those assets in an action against the defendant alleging fraud and breach of trust. The court granted injunctions[123] restraining the defendant from disposing of shares in the foreign companies, or interests under trusts or shares in English or foreign companies entitled to those assets. The injunctions also restrained the defendant from procuring the disposition of English assets by the trusts or the companies. The Court of Appeal upheld the grant of these injunctions explicitly on the basis that in the circumstances the court should pierce the corporate veil in order to achieve justice. The only qualification was that the relief granted was restricted to those companies and trusts over which the defendant exercised substantial or effective control.[124] Once again fraudu-

---

[119] See e.g. *De Beers Consolidated Mining Ltd v Howe* [1906] AC 455 (HL) and *Unit Construction Co. Ltd v Bullock* [1960] AC 351 (HL).

[120] [1959] 1 WLR 503. A similarly realistic approach can be found in other cases concerning remedies for minority shareholders (e.g. *S.C.W.S. v Meyer* [1959] AC 324, and *Ebrahimi v Westbourne Galleries Ltd* [1973] 3 AC 360 (HL) and with the construction of the objects clause of the memorandum (*Charterbridge Corporation Ltd v Lloyds Bank Ltd* [1970] Ch 62.

[121] [1951] Ch 728. See also the Court of Appeal's interpretation of the term 'establish a place of business' in section 409 of the Companies Act 1985 in *Re Oriel Ltd* [1985] BCLC 343.

[122] *Re a Company Ltd* [1985] BCLC 333 (CA).

[123] It also granted discovery by interrogatories of an unusually extensive nature.

[124] ibid., p. 337.

lent[125] abuse opened doors that would otherwise be kept firmly closed in the absence of that factor. It can also be argued that the technical form of the injunctions respected the corporate form of the English and foreign companies concerned.

The question of how far the courts are prepared to lift the veil in groups of companies is separately considered below[126] in its own context. It will be seen that distinctive, if not wholly dissimilar principles have in the last decade been evolved where groups of companies are concerned.

Parliament is not of course bound by the principle laid down by the House of Lords in *Salomon*.[127] For varying reasons of policy the legislature can, for example, impose personal liability for the company's obligations in shareholders or directors in particular circumstances. This achieves the same result as judicial veil lifting but requires no doctrinal justification by the courts.

Section 24 of the Companies Act 1985 and provisions in the Insolvency Act 1986 create two departures from the principle which respects the separate corporate personality of the company. Section 24 may impose liability where the number of members in a company falls below the minimum required by law. The requirement of a minimum of two members is now confined in practice to public companies, because section 24 has ceased to have application to private companies limited by shares or by guarantee since the Companies (Single Member Private Limited Companies) Regulations[128] were brought into effect.[129] Private companies whose members have unlimited liability are not exempt from section 24 as the 1992 regulations do not apply to them.[130] In the case of private limited companies to which section 24 no longer applies, where a sole shareholder ceases to be a member (e.g. on death) no liability under the section is imposed. In the case of companies to which section 24 does apply where the company carries on business for more than six months, those who are members after this period has elapsed and who are aware that the company has less than the minimum number of members, become severally liable for 'the whole of the debts of the company contracted during this time'.

In the course of winding up a company[131] certain provisions[132] of the Insolvency Act 1986 impose personal liability on directors and others where 'fraudulent trading' or 'wrongful trading' can be established.[133]

---

[125] The Court of Appeal regarded the decision as a straightforward application of *Wallersteiner v Moir* [1974] 1 WLR 991.

[126] See 1.13, below.

[127] [1897] AC 22.

[128] SI 1992 No. 1699.

[129] On 15 July 1992. Transitional provision is made in respect of section 24 of the Companies Act 1985 by regulation 3. Persons liable under section 24 before the regulation came into effect 'shall not be so liable for the payment of the company's debts contracted on or after the day on which these regulations came into force'.

[130] See Schedule 3, para. 2.

[131] In the cases of fraudulent trading, criminal prosecution may be brought outside the context of a winding up (Companies Act 1985, section 458).

[132] See sections 213 and 214. 'Wrongful trading' is confined to directors and 'shadow directors'. 'Fraudulent trading' may cast responsibility upon others who may be said to have carried on the business of a company with intent to defraud creditors. See 13.17 below.

[133] See also section 349 of the Companies Act 1985 (company's correct name to appear in correspondence). Section 349(4) imposes personal liability in certain circumstances. See 3.5 below.

1.11 The criminal liabilities of companies

The proof of *mens rea* on the part of the accused is an essential element in most serious criminal offences. Since a company, or any other corporate body, is a legal abstraction without a real mind of its own, the courts at one time were unwilling to convict a company of an offence involving proof of mental state whether of intention, malice or dishonesty. At this period it was only possible to charge a company with criminal offences of strict liability. In a number of cases the courts were prepared to allow a company to be prosecuted for offences committed by its employees where the statutes creating the offence could properly be construed as imposing vicarious liability upon the company as employer.[134]

In order to hold a company liable for crimes involving proof of *mens rea*, the courts have had to develop a new principle of corporate liability which is sometimes referred to as the *alter ego* doctrine. This allows the law to attribute the mental state of those who in fact control and determine the management to the company itself as being its 'directing mind and will'. The criminal intentions of a company's ordinary servants and agents will not suffice for this purpose, since the company is not being called to answer simply on the principle of *respondeat superior*.

The question of whether the mental state of the directors or other officers, collectively or individually, can be attributed to the company as its own act must 'depend on the nature of the charge, the relative position of the officer or agent and other relevant facts and circumstances of the case'.[135] This test applies both as to whether there is evidence to go to the jury on the issue and as to how the jury should satisfy themselves that *mens rea* on the part of the company has been proved.[136] On this basis companies have been convicted of crimes involving dishonesty whether created by statute[137] or by common law.[138] Conduct after the occurrence of irregularities may supply grounds for inferring that persons in control of a company (and consequently the company itself) had knowledge or means of knowledge at the time of the irregularities.[139]

The court will investigate as a question of fact how the management of the company has in reality been conducted so as to determine who is the responsible officer in the area of activity in which the offence occurred. The 'directing mind and will' of the company need not, in an appropriate case, be in the exalted position of the board of directors or the managing director. Thus in *Moore v Bresler Ltd*[140] a company was convicted of an offence requiring proof of an intention to deceive where those responsible were its secretary and

---

[134] *Pearks, Gunston & Tee Ltd v Ward* [1902] 2 KB 1, *Chuter v Freeth & Pocock Ltd* [1911] 2 KB 832, *Moussell Bros. Ltd v L. & N. W. Rly* [1917] 2 KB 836.

[135] *R. v I. C. R. Haulage* [1944] KB 551 at p. 559 (CCA).

[136] [1944] KB 551 at p. 559. A similar principle has yet to be accepted by the Scottish courts. See *Dean v John Menzies (Holdings) Ltd* [1981] SLT 50 and Alan Paterson 3 Co. Law 30.

[137] *D.P.P. v Kent & Sussex Contractors Ltd* [1944] KB 146 (Div. Ct).

[138] *R. v I. C. R. Haulage*, above.

[139] *Knowles Transport v Russell* [1975] RTE 87 (Div. Ct).

[140] [1944] 2 All ER 515 (Div. Ct). Cf. *Tesco Supermarkets Ltd v Nattrass* [1972] AC 153 (HL): here it was held that a shop manager, one of several hundred employed by the company, could not be regarded as an organ of the company.

a branch manager.[141] 'It is not every "responsible agent" or "high executive" or "manager of the housing department" or "agent acting on behalf of a company" who can by his actions make the company criminally responsible. It is necessary to establish whether the natural person or persons in question have the status and authority which in law makes their acts in the matter under consideration the acts of the company, so that the natural person is to be treated as the company itself. It is often a difficult question to decide whether or not the person concerned is in a sufficiently responsible position to involve the company in liability for the acts in question according to the law as laid down by the authorities.'[142]

Where both the shareholders and directors (in a small private company) consented to various payments of money from the company's bank account for their private use, the Court of Appeal (Criminal Division) held[143] that such consent did not of itself create a defence to a charge of theft. The court found that (on the evidence) the various ingredients of a charge of theft under the Theft Act 1968 could still be satisfied, and the issue of the dishonesty of the payments of the company's money to the defendants might be left to a jury to decide. The Court of Appeal distinguished cases where the consent of shareholders, unanimously given, was held to bar a civil action for breach of fiduciary duty or for negligence.[144] Where fraud upon the company is alleged in a civil action (or a criminal offence is charged whether under the Theft Act or on the basis of conspiracy) the unanimous consent of shareholders will not bar such criminal proceedings.[145] The purpose of the *alter ego* principle is, in the appropriate circumstances, to impose criminal (or sometimes civil) liability on the company for the acts of those who are regarded in law as its 'deciding mind and will'.[146] Its purpose is not to give such persons a defence for their own wrongdoing at the company's expense.

1.12 Application to civil law

The same principle has been employed by the courts where in civil proceedings it is necessary to attribute a particular mental state to a company. In most civil actions against companies this question does not arise, since the company may be affixed with liability on some other basis. Thus in tort the ordinary principles of vicarious liability will as a rule

---

[141] However, where a statute creates an offence which distinguishes between the 'actual offender' and 'an employer or principal', the company cannot be convicted as 'actual offender': *Melias Ltd v Preston* [1957] 2 QB 380 (Div. Ct). Further, on a charge of conspiracy it was held that a company could not conspire with its sole director who was the directing mind of the company: *R. v McDonnell* [1966] 1 QB 233. Cf. *R v Robert Millar (Contractors) Ltd* [1970] 2 QB 54 (CA), *Richmond-upon-Thames L.B.C. v Pinn & Wheeler* [1989] RTR 354 (company cannot be convicted of driving a lorry without a permit). Certain offences (e.g. bigamy and sexual offences) cannot be committed by a company as an artificial person.

[142] *R v Andrews Weatherfoil Ltd* [1972] 1 WLR 118 at p. 124 *per* Eveleigh J.

[143] *Attorney General's Reference (No. 2)* [1984] 2 QB 456. The court also observed that the vires of a company may be of evidential relevance on the issue of a defendant's honesty, but the fact that the transactions in question were or were not ultra vires was not dispositive of the issue of the accused's honesty for the purpose of the Theft Act 1968. See also *R v Appleyard* [1985] 81 Cr. App. R 319; and see Suzanne Simmonds (1986) 7 Co. Law 206.

[144] The Court of Appeal distinguished *Salomon v Salomon & Co. Ltd* [1987] AC 22 and *Multinational Gas and Petrochemical Co. v Multinational Gas and Petrochemical Services Ltd* [1983] 2 All ER 653.

[145] *Belmont Finance Ltd v Williams (No. 1)* [1979] Ch 256; *R v McDonnell* [1966] 1 QB 233.

[146] On this basis the Court of Appeal distinguished *Tesco Supermarkets v Nattrass* [1972] AC 153.

determine the matter, and contractual liability will depend first on the capacity of the company under the ultra vires doctrine[147] and secondly on that special adaptation of the principles of agency known to company lawyers as the 'rule in Turquand's case'.[148]

Nevertheless in some cases it is necessary to attribute an intention or actual default to the company. Thus under section 502 of the Merchant Shipping Act 1894 the owner of a vessel has a defence which allows him to exempt himself from liability for injury which is caused without 'his actual default or privity'. But what, as will usually be the case, if the owner is a company? In the leading case of *Lennard's Carrying Company v Asiatic Petroleum Ltd*,[149] the House of Lords held that the default of Lennard, as the managing director and 'directing mind and will' of his company, could be attributed to it so as to deprive it of the defence which section 502 provided. Viscount Haldane's judgment articulated the *alter ego* doctrine peculiar to company law as one quite distinct from the ordinary principles of agency or vicarious liability.

In a justly celebrated passage he observes that

> . . . a corporation is an abstraction. It has no mind of its own any more than a body of its own; its active and directing will must consequently be sought in the person of somebody who for some purposes may be called an agent, but who is really the directing mind and will of the corporation, the very ego and centre of the personality of the corporation.[150]

As in criminal law, the *alter ego* of a company may, depending on the circumstances of the case, be found at a lower level in the managerial hierarchy than that of the board of directors or the managing director. Thus in *The Lady Gwendolen*[151] the marine superintendent, to whom the assistant managing director and the traffic manager had surrendered 'all the relevant powers of control'[152] over the operation of its ships, was held to be a directing mind for this purpose.

The same principle, identifying the state of mind of the senior management with that of the company itself, has been employed to determine whether a company intended to occupy premises for its own business under the Landlord and Tenant Act 1954,[153] and to decide whether an inducement to breach of contract operates upon the company itself – as opposed to its servants – to persuade it to break its contract.[154]

1.13 Groups of companies

It is a commonplace of commercial life today that businesses are conducted not only in the form of a single private or public company, but also in the form of a group of

---

[147] See Chapter 4, below.

[148] (1856) 5 E&B 248. See 4.25, below.

[149] [1915] AC 705 (HL). Applied in *El Ajou v Dollar Land Holdings plc* [1994] 1 BCLC 464 (CA).

[150] [1915] AC 705 at p. 713.

[151] [1965] P 294 (CA).

[152] ibid., at p. 355, *per* Winn LJ. The company sought to limit its liability under section 503 of the Merchant Shipping Act 1894 on the basis that a collision occurred without 'actual fault or privity' on the part of the owners. The Court of Appeal held that the company was not entitled to do so. In *Registrar of Restrictive Trading Agreements v W. H. Smith and Sons Ltd* [1969] 1 WLR 1460 (CA) a branch manager of a company was held not to be a 'manager' or 'officer' for the purposes of section 15 (3) of the Restrictive Trade Practices Act 1956 (power to interrogate on oath). See also *Tesco Supermarkets v Nattrass* [1972] AC 153.

[153] Section 30 (1) (g). *Bolton (Engineering) Co. Ltd v Graham & Sons* [1957] 1 QB 159. The 1954 Act does not apply in Scotland.

[154] *D. C. Thompson & Co. v Deakin* [1952] Ch 646 (CA).

companies consisting of a holding company (which may often be a public company listed on The Stock Exchange) and a number of usually wholly owned subsidiaries and possibly sub-subsidiaries. Nowadays the group form may be employed at quite a small level of private business for tax or other reasons. As with larger groups of companies, different branches of the business or different properties will be located in each subsidiary.[155]

1.13.1 *Statutory definition of the group relationship*

The Companies Act 1989 provides two quite distinct statutory concepts to govern holding and subsidiary company relationships. A wholly new definition of 'parent and subsidiary undertaking' was introduced as the basis for consolidated accounts for groups of companies.[156] This is to be distinguished from the general definition of holding and subsidiary company wherever these terms are used elsewhere in the Companies Acts (i.e. other than in Part VII of the Companies Act 1985 as amended by the 1989 Act). The 'new' general purpose definition replaced the 'old' section 736 by inserting new sections 736 and 736A into the Companies Act 1985. The 'parent and subsidiary undertaking' concept is examined in Chapter 12, whereas attention is given here to the more generally applicable provisions of sections 736 and 736A of the Companies Act 1985.[157] It should be noted that the 'parent and subsidiary undertaking' concept has a broader, more flexible and 'judgmental' dimension to it, compared with more traditional legal criteria still employed in sections 736 and 736A.[158]

Before examining the detailed criteria employed in section 736[159] it may be noted that, like the old section 736, it defines a company as a 'wholly owned subsidiary of another company' if it has no members except that other and that other's wholly owned subsidiaries or persons acting on behalf of that other or its wholly owned subsidiaries.[160] As to the wider test of holding and subsidiary (to be examined below) this includes sub-subsidiaries as well.[161] The term 'company' in section 736 (i.e. both as to holding and subsidiary companies) includes any body corporate.[162] It does not, therefore, have the wide reach of the term 'undertaking' in the new section 285.

Section 144 (2) of the 1989 Act gives the new definition of holding and subsidiary company a wider frame of reference than the Companies Act 1985. It deals with references in other legislation to 'a subsidiary' or 'holding company' within the meaning of section 736 of the 1985 Act. Such references are to be read as referring to the new section 736 subject to 'any express saving or amendment made by or under this Act.'[163]

---

[155] See further Hadden, *The Control of Corporate Groups* (IALS, 1983).

[156] See sections 21 and 22 inserting sections 259 and 260 into the Companies Act 1985. See 12.14.

[157] See Companies Act 1989, section 144.

[158] Thus 'parent and subsidiary undertaking' extends to partnerships and unincorporated associations. The provisions of section 258 contain somewhat 'broad brush' terminology, e.g. 'actually exercising dominant influence' or 'managed on a unified basis', see 12.14.2 below.

[159] The application of this general definition of the holding and subsidiary company relationship will be found in varying contexts in the later chapters of this book. Among the more important are to be found in Chapter 6 (financial assistance by a company in the acquisition of its shares) and Chapter 14 (statutory fiduciary duties).

[160] See section 736(2).

[161] 'Or if it is a subsidiary of a company which is itself a subsidiary of that company': see section 736 (1).

[162] Section 736 (3).

[163] As to which see Schedule 18 of the 1989 Act. As to similar references to 'subsidiaries' or 'holding company' in 'deeds or other instruments or documents' the position is less clear. See section 144 (6) of the 1989 Act and *Gore-Browne on Companies* (Jordans, 44th edn, loose-leaf) at 1.5.3.

1.13.2 Holding or controlling majority voting power

The most obvious change in the new section 736 is a much more precise statutory definition of control through the exercise of majority voting power. The old section 736 (2) required the putative holding company to hold more than half the nominal value of the issued equity share capital in the subsidiary. Since this ignored variations in the right to vote that might be attached to 'equity' shares (as well as to other classes of share), it had the result that a company could be treated in law as a subsidiary of a company which had no voting control over it. Likewise, a company which controlled the majority of votes might not meet the definition of holding and subsidiary company under the old section 736. The essential change in the new section 736 (1)[164] is that a company is 'a subsidiary' of another company, its holding company, if that other company 'holds a majority of the voting rights in it'. A further provision[165] is made to cover voting agreements with other shareholders or members.[166] The holding/subsidiary relation will exist under section 736 (1) (c) if the holding company is a member of the subsidiary and 'controls alone, pursuant to an agreement with other shareholders or members, a majority of voting rights in it'. This provision would be applicable to a shareholder's agreement between the company as a member (i.e. shareholder) and other shareholders to put their voting rights at the disposal of the holding company. The voting rights thus controlled would have to confer majority voting powers. Such an agreement might take the form either of an agreement to confer an irrevocable proxy on the holding company,[167] or by means of an agreement which results in the setting up of a voting trust,[168] whereby the shares in the subsidiary are transferred to the trust whose trustees are appointed by the controlling company. In both cases majority voting power would have to be put at the disposal of the company. If a trustee were a company, the legal ownership of majority voting rights would not make the trustee company a holding company since section 736A (5) provides that rights 'held by a person in a fiduciary capacity shall be treated as not held by him'.

It should also be noted that section 736A (6) provides that rights (here voting rights) 'held by a person as a nominee for another shall be treated as held by that other'. Section 736A (6) amplifies this: 'rights shall be regarded as held by a nominee for another if they are exercisable only on his instructions or with his consent or concurrence'. This is clearly of significance in respect of shareholders' agreements which put majority voting power over another company at the disposal of an alleged holding company whether by means of irrevocable proxy, voting trust or in any other way.

It should be noted that the test specified in section 736 (1) (c) requires that the alleged holding company must (in addition to controlling a majority of voting rights by agreement) 'be a member of it' (i.e. of the subsidiary). This requirement would seem to allow an obvious way to evade section 736 (1) in this respect. Dominant voting power can be exercised, even if this amounts to control of more than 50 per cent of the voting power, so long as the company which is in a position to exercise this power is not 'a member'[169] of record.

---

[164] This is substituted in the Companies Act 1985 for the old section 736 by section 144 of the Companies Act 1989.

[165] Section 736 (1) (c).

[166] This term will apply in the case of companies limited by guarantee.

[167] See Murray Pickering, (1965) 81 LQR 248 at p. 267. As to proxies, see 11.21.

[168] See Murray Pickering, ibid. at p. 527.

[169] i.e. a registered shareholder in the case of a company with share capital or a member of a company limited by guarantee.

It will be seen that the same lacuna exists in section 736 (1) (*b*) which relates to the right to appoint or remove a majority of the board of directors.

Section 736A(2), which seeks to define various terms used in section 736, thus defines the expression 'voting rights in a company' as used in section 736 (1) (*a*)–(*c*). These are to be understood as 'rights conferred on shareholders in respect of their shares, or in the case of a company not having share capital, on members to vote at general meetings of the company on all, or substantially all, matters'. This definition would exclude shares that conferred limited voting rights at a class meeting. It would also exclude shares (e.g. many types of preference shares) that could only be voted in general meetings on matters that directly concerned such shares.[170]

1.13.3 Power to control a majority of the board

Section 736 (1) (*g*) provides that a company is a subsidiary of another company if that other company (which thus becomes its holding company) 'is a member of it and has the right to appoint or remove a majority of its board of directors'. As noted above,[171] the requirement of being 'a member of it' (in addition to the power over appointment and removal of a majority of directors) provides a lacuna in this test of the holding and subsidiary company relationship, which might be exploited by appropriate arrangements.

It was seen that section 736A seeks to 'explain expressions used in section 736 and otherwise supplement that section'. Section 736A (3) provides that the reference (in section 736 (1) (*b*)) to 'the right to appoint or remove a majority of the board of directors is to the right to appoint or remove directors holding a majority of the voting rights at meetings of the board on all, or substantially all, matters.' This provision is designed to cope with particular provisions in the articles of private companies that might give weighted voting rights to some directors. The qualifying provision would seem to exclude a provision giving a veto to a named director (or any director holding particular shares) in respect of a certain type of transaction.

Section 736A(3) further explains the meaning of the expression 'has the right to appoint' to a directorship. A company is to be treated as having such a right 'if a person's appointment to it follows necessarily from his appointment as a director of the company'. This right might be provided by the terms of the articles of the alleged subsidiary or by the terms of a shareholders' agreement relating to votes which ensured the election of directors with majority voting power at board meetings. A company is also treated as having the right to appoint to a directorship if the directorship is held by the company itself.[172] The existence of such 'corporate directorships' is required to be treated as establishing the right to appoint to the board of the alleged subsidiary.[173]

---

[170] See further section 736A (4). See also section 736A (7) as to the treatment of 'rights attached to shares held by way of security'. See further as to the interpretative provision of section 736A in *Gore-Browne on Companies* (Jordans, 44th edn, loose-leaf) at 1.5.1.

[171] See 1.13.2 above.

[172] Section 736A (*a*) (ii).

[173] A right to appoint or remove which is exercisable only with the consent or concurrence of another is left out of account, see section 736A (3) (*b*). As to the general interpretative provisions in section 736A as they apply to the right to appoint or remove a director, see *Gore-Browne on Companies* (Jordans, 44th edn, loose-leaf) at 1.5.2.

1.13.4 The treatment of groups by the courts

In *D.H.N. Food Distributors Ltd v Tower Hamlets L.B.C.*[174] the Court of Appeal was prepared to go some way towards recognising the economic entity of a tightly controlled group of companies so as to ignore (or set aside for a particular statutory purpose) the separate legal entities of the companies within the group. This allowed a holding company to claim compensation for compulsory acquisition of premises owned by its wholly owned subsidiary but on which the holding company carried on its business. If the holding company had been treated as a bare licensee of the premises owned by its subsidiary it would not have been entitled to compensation for disturbance to its business. However, though the Court of Appeal were agreed as to the result, the degree of domination of the subsidiary by the holding company, or of unity in the enterprise conducted formally by them, is nowhere stated with precision. It is difficult to predict with any certainty when the separate legal personality of the companies within a group will be set aside by the courts. It will be seen that the courts will not ignore the limited liability of a subsidiary so as to allow the creditor of an insolvent subsidiary to seek redress from the holding company.

The decision of the House of Lords in *Woolfson v Strathclyde Regional Council*[175] threw some doubt on the soundness of the Court of Appeal's decision in *D.H.N. v Tower Hamlets*. Lord Frazer observed that he had 'some doubt whether in this respect the Court of Appeal properly applied the principle that it is appropriate to pierce the corporate veil only where special circumstances exist indicating that it is a mere façade concealing the true facts'.[176] The *D.H.N.* decision was not overruled but was distinguished on the basis that there the company that owned the land was the wholly owned subsidiary of the company that carried on the business. The latter was in complete control of the situation as respects anything that might affect its business. In *Woolfson*, by contrast, the company that carried on the business had 'no sort of control whatever over the owners of the land'. The owners were the appellant and a company in which he held two-thirds of the shares. Further, Woolfson was not shown to be beneficially entitled to his wife's single share but owned all the shares in the company that carried on the business. A legitimate response is that this seems a thin basis for distinguishing the case, and it would seem to reflect a different judicial philosophy relating to lifting the veil of incorporation in the case of groups of companies.[177] In *D.H.N. v Tower Hamlets L.B.C.*[178] (and in other cases where a holding company and its subsidiary has been treated as 'an enterprise entity')[179] the court has been persuaded to do so at the insistence of the holding company and consequently for its benefit. Where a stranger to the group wishes to lift the veil, the courts continue to show the greatest reluctance to do so. Thus in *Multinational Gas v Multinational Services*[180]

[174] [1976] 1 WLR 852. See especially the judgment of Lord Denning at p. 860, citing Gower, *Principles of Modern Company Law* (3rd edn, 1969) at p. 216. Somewhat surprisingly, the decision in *Smith, Stone and Knight Ltd v Birmingham Corporation* [1939] 4 All ER 116 was not relied upon. See also the judgment of Lord Denning in *Littlewoods Mail Order Stores Ltd v C.I.R.* [1969] 1 WLR 1241.

[175] [1978] SLT 159 at p. 161.

[176] Lord Frazer further observes that the decisions of the House of Lords in *Harold Holdsworth & Co. v Caddies* [1955] 1 WLR 352 and *Scottish Co-op v Meyer* [1959] AC 324, which were relied upon by Goff LJ (and by Denning MR as regards *Meyer*) 'do not with respect appear to me to be concerned with that principle'.

[177] A clearer basis for distinguishing the Court of Appeal's decision was found in the reasoning of Goff LJ and Shaw LJ in respect of the land held by the subsidiary, on the basis of an irrevocable licence or a resulting trust.

[178] [1970] 1 WLR 852.

[179] See e.g. *Prenn v Simmonds* [1971] 1 WLR 1381 (HL) and *Harold Holdsworth & Co. v. Caddies* [1955] 1 WLR 352 (HL); *Bird & Co. v Thomas Cook & Sons Ltd* [1937] 2 All ER 227. See *The Roberta* (1937) 58 Lloyds R 159.

[180] [1983] 3 WLR 493.

the Court of Appeal refused to allow the liquidator of an insolvent subsidiary to serve a writ out of jurisdiction on three international oil companies who had set up their jointly owned subsidiary. They were held to have a good defence in law for any claim of negligence based on the permitted misconduct of the directors of the subsidiary appointed by them. As shareholders they could consent to negligent conduct and owed no duties to any third parties (such as the creditors whose interests the liquidator represented).

In *Lonrho Ltd v Shell Petroleum Ltd*[181] the House of Lords rejected an attempt to compel a joint holding company to use its powers to compel a foreign subsidiary and its sub-subsidiaries to release documents in their possession to comply with an order for discovery of documents in the context of litigation against the holding company. It was held that there was no obligation to use the voting powers available to change the articles of the subsidiary or otherwise to override the discretion of its board of directors. In both the *Multinational* and *Lonrho* cases it was clear that other policy factors were present which influenced the court in refusing to extend its jurisdiction, or make available a procedural remedy, against an overseas subsidiary or a foreign multinational company. However, these decisions give scant support to the more optimistic views that the courts were more prepared to lift the veil in the case of groups of companies.[182]

1.13.5 *Adams v Cape Industries plc*

In its landmark decision in *Adams v Cape Industries plc*,[183] the Court of Appeal took the opportunity to attempt to bring some order to the rather confused body of case-law relating to the question of lifting the veil where groups of companies are concerned. The case was concerned with the enforcement in an English court of judgments obtained in a United States court. One aspect[184] of the question of the exercise of foreign jurisdiction involved the alleged presence of various subsidiaries[185] of Cape Industries in the United States. The respondent and its subsidiaries operated a business mining asbestos in South Africa and selling this product in various parts of the world including the United States. The judgments obtained in a Federal Court in Texas were concerned with the liability in tort for asbestos-related injuries. Counsel for the appellant raised three arguments as a basis for asserting that subsidiaries of Cape were present in the United States. The Court of Appeal structured its new and more restrictive approach to lifting the veil around these three possible arguments for the 'presence' of Cape Industries in America.

(1) The single economic unit argument
This concept of the group as a single economic entity found no support as an independent basis on which the corporate veil might be lifted. It could not justify any departure from the normal rule that 'each company in a group of companies . . . is a separate legal entity

---

[181] [1980] 1 WLR 627 (HL).

[182] Some decisions in the field of labour law have been even more hostile to such an approach, and have been prepared to follow the *Salomon* principle to the most artificial extreme. Here policy arguments in favour of the rigorous application of industrial relations legislation may have prevailed. See *Dimbleby v N.U.J.* [1984] 1 WLR 427 (HL) and *National Dock Labour Board v Pinn Wheeler Ltd.* [1989] BCLC 64.

[183] [1990] Ch 433.

[184] The Court of Appeal also considered whether the defendants had consented to a foreign court exercising jurisdiction over them.

[185] In the discussion below of the Court of Appeal's judgment two of these subsidiaries are referred (as in the judgment itself) as AMC and CPC.

possessed of separate legal rights and liabilities'.[186] The considerable number of cases where the court has been prepared to ignore the distinction in law between a group of companies on the basis that 'justice so demands' or if 'the business realities' require it were all explained by Slade LJ as being turning 'on the wording of particular statutes or contracts'.[187] While this may be a very satisfactory explanation of some of these cases which explicitly turn on the liberal interpretation of an agreement in *Re Mercatoria*,[188] or on the construction of the wording of a particular statutory provision,[189] it cannot satisfactorily explain all of them. It certainly gives a strained interpretation to *D.H.N. Food Distributors Ltd. v Tower Hamlets L.B.C.*[190] Whatever doubts were cast upon the Court of Appeal's decision in this case by the House of Lords in *Woolfson v Strathclyde Regional Council*,[191] its authority cannot be wholly dismissed. In particular, the judgment of Lord Denning MR clearly expounds a doctrine about the corporate group as an economic entity which is very different from that of Slade LJ in *Cape Industries*. The Court of Appeal in *Cape Industries* recognised that the rigid doctrine now espoused by the English courts differs markedly from that of the European Court of Justice[192] where a group of companies may be treated as a single economic entity. Clearly, English courts applying European Community Law to groups of companies must follow the lead of the European Court of Justice.

(2) Piercing the corporate veil

The Court of Appeal in *Cape Industries* accepted that there is 'one well recognised exception to the rule prohibiting the piercing of the "corporate veil".' This referred to Lord Keith's well-known observations in *Woolfson v Strathclyde Regional Council*[193] that it is appropriate to pierce the corporate veil only where special circumstances exist indicating that it is a mere façade concealing the true facts. Slade LJ in *Cape Industries*[194] cited *Jones v Lipman*[195] as illustrating this principle.[196] As applied to the case itself, the 'façade' principle was applicable to 'A.M.C.' which was not only a wholly owned subsidiary of Cape but had been used by Cape and its subsidiaries as a corporate name on their invoices.[197] This, however, did not help the appellants since the court found that A.M.C. was not in fact carrying on business in the United States. Another company, C.P.C., was incorporated and carrying on business in the United States but was held not to be a façade. It was an independent corporation which was carrying on its own business in the United States and not that of Cape or its subsidiaries. Significantly, its shares were wholly

[186] [1990] Ch at p. 532 citing Roskill LJ in *The Albazero* [1977] AC 774, 807.

[187] [1990] Ch at p. 530, *Revlon Inc. v Cripps Lee Ltd.* [1980] FSR 85 at p. 105. See [1990] Ch at pp. 534–5.

[188] e.g. *Harold Holdsworth & Co. (Wakefield) Ltd v Caddies* [1955] 1 WLR 352 at p. 367. See [1990] Ch at p. 537.

[189] *Scottish Co-operative Wholesale Soc. Ltd. v Meyer* [1959] AC 324 at p. 342. See [1990] Ch at p. 537.

[190] [1976] 1 WLR 852 at pp. 860 and 861. See [1990] Ch at pp. 533–4.

[191] 1978 SLT 159. See [1990] Ch at p. 536.

[192] See the discussion of *Institutu Chemioterapico SPA v The Commission* [1974] ECR 233 in *Cape Industries* at [1990] Ch 433 at p. 535. See further *SAR Schotte GmbH v Parfums Rothschild* SARL [1992] BCLC 235.

[193] 1978 SLT 159 at p. 161.

[194] [1990] Ch.433 at pp. 542–3.

[195] [1962] 1 WLR 832.

[196] Slade LJ found little help in other authorities in terms of reasoned principle. Even the dicta of Lord Denning MR in *Wallersteiner v Moir* [1974] 1 WLR 991 at p. 1013 and in *Littlewoods Mail Order Stores Ltd v Inland Revenue Commissioners* [1969] 1 WLR 124, 1254 were not supported by other members of the Court of Appeal.

[197] [1990] Ch 543.

owned by its chief executive even if it had been set up at the behest and with funding from Cape.[198]

At a more general level, the Court of Appeal stressed that it is legitimate to use a corporate structure 'to ensure that legal liability (if any) in respect of particular future activity of the group ... will fall on another member of the group rather than the defendant company. Whether or not this is desirable, the right to use a corporate structure in this manner is inherent in our corporate law.'[199] The Court of Appeal stressed that the *motive* with which a subsidiary was formed (or an existing subsidiary used) is crucial. Slade LJ stressed that the arrangements involving C.P.C. were not shown to involve actual or potential illegality, nor were they intended to deprive anyone of their existing rights.[200] No doubt future litigation will throw much-needed light upon what is now this crucial if limited basis for lifting the corporate veil.

(3) The agency argument

The Court of Appeal in *Cape Industries* was careful to confine the possibility that a subsidiary might be treated as the agent of its holding company to situations where such an inference was factually justified. It was made clear that in the absence of an express agreement[201] it will be difficult to establish such a relationship.[202] The fact that C.P.C. acted as agent for Cape in particular transactions was not sufficient to establish that Cape was present in the United States through its agent.[203]

It is still too soon to conclude that the judgment in *Cape Industries* has finally determined the application of the *Salomon* principles to groups of companies. Some quite recent authorities show that the court will readily intervene where dishonesty or abuse of the corporate forms are shown.[204]

1.13.6 The problem of insolvent subsidiaries

One area where the tendency of Parliament to put the obligations of a company on to a group basis has stopped short, is that of the liability of a holding company for the debts of its insolvent subsidiary. Here neither the legislature nor the courts are willing to depart form the strict corporate entity principle and its attendant privilege of limited liability.[205] The fact that all or a majority of the shares in a company are owned by a holding company makes no difference to the ordinary rule that the shareholders in a limited company are not liable for its debts beyond the amount paid up (or to be paid up) on the shares held by them. In the case of the holding/subsidiary relationship this of course ignores the common reality that the subsidiary may be very thinly capitalised or indeed grossly under-capitalised. Moreover, the subsidiary may be capitalised by a loan re-payable on demand which may also be secured on the assets of the subsidiary. This may make the holding company the principal creditor in the insolvent winding-up of its subsidiary and, moreover, a creditor with priority over the ordinary trade creditors. As

---

[198] ibid., pp. 543–4.

[199] [1990] Ch at p. 544.

[200] ibid.

[201] See, for example, *Southern v Watson* [1940] 3 All ER 439 (CA).

[202] [1990] Ch at pp. 545–9.

[203] [1990] Ch at pp. 548–9.

[204] See *Re a Company* [1985] BCLC 333 (CA). The same principle will apply to jointly owned and directed companies: *Creasey v Breachwood Motors Ltd.* [1993] BCLC 480. These cases illustrate the notion of 'façade' while not employing it specifically in their judgments.

[205] Unless fraudulent or wrongful trading can be shown. See 13.17.

the House of Lords decided in *Salomon v Salomon & Co.*,[206] this will not in the absence of fraud (or the statutory offence of fraudulent trading) be a ground for lifting the veil.[207] This is equally true of the relationship between a holding company and a subsidiary company.

In recent years the unenviable position of creditors in subsidiary companies has become a matter of increasing concern.[208] In the case of banks and other lending institutions, the lender can be relied upon to make the appropriate contractual arrangements (e.g. lending directly to the holding company, or obtaining a guarantee for a loan to the subsidiary). In the case of an economically powerful creditor (e.g. a nationalised industry or an oil company), the holding company may hesitate before evading its moral obligation and relying upon its strict legal rights, since it may still need to obtain credit for itself or for its other subsidiaries. However, the lot of small trade creditors who have supplied goods or services to an insolvent subsidiary remains an unhappy one. In the German Federal Republic the 'law of integration'[209] has imposed, in the appropriate conditions, the responsibility of the group for the obligations of subsidiaries. Likewise, the EC Ninth Draft Directive proposes a reform in the company law of the other member states on broadly the same lines.

The Cork Committee,[210] while recognising the deeply unsatisfactory nature of the present law, was also impressed by the difficulties in framing satisfactory proposals to make holding companies liable for the debts of insolvent subsidiaries.[211] These difficulties relate to questions both of legal definition and of policy.[212] The Committee also felt that a fundamental change would have to be made not only in the law governing the winding up of insolvent companies but also in many aspects of company law in general (e.g. the duties of directors in holding companies could no longer relate primarily to that company).[213] The Committee therefore shied away from so fundamental a change in company law: 'The matter is of such importance and such gravity that there should be the widest possible review of the different considerations, with a view to the introduction of

---

[206] [1987] AC 22.

[207] Although Parts I and II of the 1985 Act require that public companies registering (or re-registering) under that Act have a paid-up share capital of £50,000, this does not apply to the subsidiaries of public companies, save in the unlikely event that these are themselves public companies.

[208] Attempts were made to introduce clauses into the bill that became the Companies Act 1981 that would have made a holding company responsible for its subsidiary's debts in certain circumstances. See also the Cork Report, Chapter 51, paras. 1922–1929 and Templeman LJ in *Re Southard & Co.* [1979] 1 WLR 1198.

[209] See H. Würdinger, *German Company Law* (Oyez Publishing, 1975), Chapter 2, pp. 138–40. There is also a lesser degree of group liability where, though the conditions of 'integration' do not apply, there is nevertheless a 'control contract': ibid., pp. 148–9. See further Frank Wooldridge, *Groups of Companies: The Law and Practice in Britain, France and Germany* (IALS, 1981); Klaus Hopt (ed.), *Groups of Companies in European Laws*, vol. II (Walter de Gruyter, Berlin, New York 1982).

[210] Insolvency Law and Practice, Report of the Review Committee (Cmnd 8558) 1982. See as to the EC Ninth Draft Directive, ibid., para. 1936.

[211] It reviewed various possibilities which varied in the range of severity from the viewpoint of the holding company, ibid., paras. 1934, and 1947 to 1949.

[212] The Committee was particularly concerned with the problems of: 'partly owned' subsidiaries (para. 1942); *de facto* control; the danger of discouraging entrepreneurial activity through the creation of subsidiaries (para. 1940); the added complexity of winding up groups of companies (para. 1943); the impact of any change in the practice of buying and selling subsidiaries (para. 1944); and the application to foreign subsidiaries or a foreign holding company of any change in the law (para. 1945).

[213] ibid., para. 1951.

reforming legislation in the near future. We would wish to see such a review undertaken as a matter of urgency'.[214]

1.14 The Companies Acts: consolidation and reconsolidation

The unwieldy mass of legislation in the Companies Acts 1948–1983 was consolidated into the Companies Act 1985 and three much smaller related Acts. Two of these latter deal with topics which have a wider application than company law as it is usually conceived. These are the Business Names Act 1985 and the Insider Dealing Act 1985. The Companies Consolidation (Consequential Provisions) Act 1985 relates, as its title implies, to matters (like old public companies) which will not be of long-term significance.

Even at a technical level it can be argued that neither the timing nor the scope of the 1985 consolidating legislation[215] were entirely happily chosen. While this legislation was going through Parliament, the Bill that became the Insolvency Act 1985 was also being enacted. This process entailed amendment of substantial parts of the Companies Act 1985 in respect of the winding up of insolvent companies. Scarcely were these two Acts of 1985 on the statute book when a change of policy was made. This produced a reconsolidation of the parts of the Companies Act 1985 concerning the winding up of *solvent* companies with the recent legislation on insolvency. This has produced the Insolvency Act 1986. At the same time the Department of Trade and Industry decided to reconsolidate the legislation on the disqualification of directors.[216] In this same period the provisions in the Companies Act 1985 relating to public issues, insider dealing and the compulsory acquisition of shares, have been substantially changed by the Financial Services Act 1986. This Act, of course, breaks much new ground by introducing a long overdue system of 'securities regulation'. Many other parts of the 1985 consolidating legislation await amendment or complete alteration as a result of further proposed EC directives.[217]

Since the consolidating legislation of 1985 there has been one major legislative development. The Companies Act 1989 contains a mélange of significant legislative innovation and a great number of technical reforms. The 1989 Act implements the EC Seventh and Eighth Directives on group accounts and the appointment of auditors.[218] It also reforms the law on the registration of charges and contains a new regime for private companies.[219] This allows more scope for avoiding the formality of company meetings by means of written resolutions or by the adoption of a more generalised 'elective regime'. In addition to these major changes, the 1989 Act contains a great number of significant reforms of the Companies Act 1985 and the Financial Services Act 1986.[220]

There is much to be said in favour of the companies legislation of 1985. In terms of its simplicity and lucidity of style and the ordered clarity of the arrangement of subject matter in the principal Act, it represents a considerable achievement for the draftsman

---

[214] Para. 1952.

[215] Which came into force on 1 July 1985. A new Table A also came into force for companies registered after that date. See the Companies (Tables A to F) Regulations 1985.

[216] The Company Directors Disqualification Act 1986.

[217] See 1.5.2 above.

[218] See Chapter 12 below.

[219] See Chapters 9 and 11, respectively.

[220] See in particular Part III 'Investigations and Powers to Obtain Information' and Part VII 'Financial Markets and Insolvency'. For more detailed amendment of the Companies Act 1985 and the Financial Services Act 1985, see Part V.

and those who instructed him. Nevertheless, even the most dazzling skills of drafts-manship (in the case of a consolidating Act) cannot cure the substantive defects in the state of existing legislation to be consolidated.

The cogent criticism made of the unconsolidated Companies Acts 1948–1983 by, among others, Professor L. S. Sealy[221] went beyond matters of legislative style and arrangement. The general thrust of this criticism is that our company legislation (whether carried forward from the past or the subject of recent reform) is over-technical and over-'sanctioned'. It is not directed to enabling businesses large and small to be run honestly and efficiently in the real commercial world. It is law created by civil servants and company lawyers who have had insufficient regard for the real needs of the industrial and commercial world. Our legislation makes very out-of-date assumptions about how private companies are formed, how public companies develop and about the realities of shareholders' meetings and resolutions as a genuine way of expressing shareholders' consent or effectively restraining directors and others who manage companies. While increasingly influenced by the rigid, elaborate and often inappropriate example of the European Community harmonisation programme,[222] our legislation has ignored the more radical and simplifying reforms that have been successfully adopted in the Commonwealth and the United States.

There is much force in Professor Sealy's detailed critique of existing company legis-lation which is deployed to support this more general thesis. It is inevitable, however, that not everyone will agree that the general policy of those reforming company law (especially in regard to large public companies) should be how best to meet the insti-tutional needs of businessmen. The real political and social world will inevitably demand that company law reflect a more complex, if sometimes competing, range of interests. In that sense it is entirely understandable that the Department of Trade and Industry regard company law (like labour law) as too politically sensitive to be left to the Law Commission or to any other 'neutral' reforming body. The political priorities will inevitably change with the colour of the government in power. Thus, both in Britain and in the European Community, company law remains more than a matter of commercial law. This latter body of law may be well described as 'the totality of the law's response to the needs and practices of the mercantile community. This then is the essence of commercial law – the accommodation of principles, rules, practices and documents fashioned by the world of business: the facilitation, rather than the obstruction, of commercial development.'[223]

Company law, as part of a different body of law – the law of institutions – must inevitably have a different character from that governing the law of commercial trans-actions. It will retain this character, even when freed from the burden of history and the 'Chancery mentality'.

1.15 Corporate governance and the market for corporate control

The idea of the market for corporate control has gained increasing attention since the early 1980s. It obviously reflects the neo-liberal ideology which has prevailed in a period when the concept of 'markets' and 'market forces' has been at the centre of most political

---

[221] See *Company Law and Commercial Reality* (Sweet & Maxwell, 1984), especially Chapter 4.

[222] See 1.4, above.

[223] R. M. Goode, *Commercial Law* (Penguin, 1982), p. 984 cited by Professor L. S. Sealy in *Company Law and Commercial Reality* at p. 81.

as well as economic discussion. The undoubted pragmatic basis for this concept is to be found in the regularly occurring battle for control of large public companies by means of contested takeover bids. The conditions that make this possible in Britain (perhaps alone among the member states of the European Union)[224] require at least a majority of the voting equity shares in the target company to be widely distributed among institutional investors as well as individual shareholders. Institutional investors (such as pension funds, insurance companies and unit trusts) are 'key players' in the takeover market. Their role is an essential one not only in deciding the success or failure of a takeover bid (or rival bids) but in generating such bids in the first place.

There is a significant connection between an active takeover market and the efficient and honest management of large public companies. It has long been argued that in such Stock Exchange listed companies, with very widely distributed shareholding, pressure from stockmarket institutional investors performs a vital function in disciplining incompetent or corrupt boards of directors. It is the threat or actuality of a takeover bid which brings the main shareholders' voting power to bear.[225]

Until quite recently, the whole question of corporate governance was largely unregulated by company law or indeed by City self-regulation. The corporate governance issue describes the practices and committee structures by which boards of directors conduct their affairs and seek to monitor senior management so as to make them accountable to the board. Such questions were seen as being an internal matter for each listed public company and not one for the law maker or City regulator. As a matter of basic political policy the Government throughout the 1980s regarded the way boards of directors functioned as part of 'the prerogative of management to manage'. It was contended that the market for corporate control would provide the necessary corrective to any corporate abuses that might occur. In more recent years the massive collapse of a number of well-known public companies[226] has induced a fresh scrutiny of the reality of corporate governance and the need to regulate it. This need found expression in setting up the Committee on the Financial Aspects of Corporate Governance under the chairmanship of Sir Adrian Cadbury. The sponsors of the Committee were the Financial Reporting Council, The London Stock Exchange and the accountancy profession.[227] The resulting report[228] of the Cadbury Committee proposed a new system for the self-regulation of corporate governance in public companies listed in The Stock Exchange. As its title indicates, the report is directed principally to the financial aspects of corporate governance. The central concern is the adequacy and accuracy of a company's financial reporting system as well as the way this information is assessed by the board and its committees. Inevitably, the Cadbury Report had wider concerns than financial reporting. A number of its detailed proposals require well-informed and independently minded non-executive directors to counterbalance the traditional domination of the board of directors by the company's managerial hierarchy. A number of key committees of the board (the audit committee, the nomination committee which makes board appoint-

---

[224] See 1.15.1 below.

[225] For a variety of reasons, including the control of the proxy voting machinery, most general meetings of shareholders are dominated by the board. This includes the election and re-election of directors.

[226] e.g. Maxwell Communications Corporation, and Polly Peck International.

[227] See Appendix 1 to the Committee's report. The Committee's membership reflects the major institutions of the City, the business community and the professions. The Department of Trade and Industry had a supportive and observing role in this exercise in self-regulation.

[228] The Report of the Committee on the Financial Aspects of Corporate Governance, December 1992.

ments, and the remuneration committee) are required to have a majority of non-executive directors. Other proposals require major transactions to be approved by the board as a whole and seek to prevent the board being dominated by a single powerful individual. Combining the roles of chairman and chief executive is strongly discouraged though not wholly excluded.[229]

Although the Cadbury Code came into operation as recently as 30 June 1994,[230] questions have already been raised about how effective it will prove to be.[231] Commentators have noted that the central thrust of Cadbury is directed at financial reporting and accountability. This places at centre stage the professional auditor's view of sound corporate governance. It tends to overlook other dimensions of successful management of major corporate enterprises. The development of new products and new markets for those products demands high levels of long-term investment in research and development. Such essential corporate goals may suffer from the over-emphasis placed on financial reporting.

The Cadbury Code is yet another form of self-regulation affecting listed companies.[232] As such, it is prone to the defects of self-regulation as well as its advantages. It tends to operate from the point of view of City institutions and professional accountants rather than from a wider public interest standpoint.[233] Much reliance is placed in Cadbury on institutional investors taking a more active role in enforcing good governance by using their 'muscle' to ensure compliance with the spirit as well as the letter of the Cadbury Report. It is not yet clear that the institutions will regularly behave in this way.[234]

If, in the years immediately ahead, the implementation of the Cadbury Report is seen not to have adequately answered the continuing problems of corporate governance, further efforts to build up and amplify its recommendations are likely to be made. It is likely that the system introduced by Cadbury will be built upon and strengthened. Even if the principle of self-regulation is retained it may well be given a legal framework. The 'teeth' of enforcement may no longer be left to The Stock Exchange and institutional investors.

Both the Conservative and Labour parties have recently exhibited concern about the issue of 'short termism' in public companies and in the City generally. This phrase encapsulates both the attitude of institutional investors and the response of the boards of directors in seeking to retain a favourable price for their companies' shares. It is widely believed that the distribution of excessive dividends to keep the share price high prevents the more appropriate ploughing back of profits to produce long-term investment. It is widely recognised that such investment in technical research for new and improved products has lagged behind badly in British industrial companies. This is alleged to be a major cause of Britain's relative industrial decline.

Stephen Dorrell, when he was Financial Secretary to the Treasury, repeatedly ex-

[229] For a detailed discussion of the work of the Cadbury Committee and the differences between its interim and final reports, see Vanessa Finch [1992] JBL 581 and Janet Dine 15 Co. Law 73 (1994).

[230] Companies listed on The Stock Exchange were thereafter required to make a statement about their compliance with the Code in the report and accounts.

[231] See Vanessa Finch: Corporate Governance and Cadbury, [1994] JBL 51. See also Parkinson, *Corporate Power and Responsibility* (Oxford University Press, 1993).

[232] As to the function of The Stock Exchange and the Takeover Panel see Chapters 5 and 16.

[233] See Finch [1994] JBL at pp. 57–8.

[234] It may serve their interests better to sell their holding or to wait passively for a takeover bid to emerge.

pressed concern about this problem. He asked whether 'City shareholders' place too much emphasis on dividends and whether they can spot good investment opportunities. He also asked 'how effective The Stock Exchange is in keeping companies in check in terms of corporate governance'.[235] This stand has also been taken by the House of Commons Trade and Industry Committee.[236] In the area of corporate governance, they stressed the need for Government action to 'help eradicate City short termism by controlling hostile takeovers, restraining excessive dividend payouts and the need for steps to control overgenerous pay to directors.' Robin Cook, in a Labour Party policy document,[237] has also expressed similar concerns. These include the reform of company law to provide a legal standard for the composition of company boards. This would include seats for suppliers and a minimum number of non-executive directors. It also proposes that the rules governing takeovers be changed by requiring a company attempting a takeover bid to demonstrate that it would be in the public interest. The purpose of this proposal is to give 'security to industrialists that if they don't pay out dividends but instead re-invest they won't be taken over'.[238]

At the time of writing all the ideas being canvassed, or questions raised, are at the level of general political debate. Whatever the political colour of a future government, it seems likely that further intervention affecting the structure and procedures of corporate governance is likely to occur.

1.15.1 Barriers to takeovers in the European Community

The Coopers & Lybrand report on *Barriers to Takeovers in the European Community*[239] was both commissioned and published by the Department of Trade and Industry. Here again, the central question was the effective working of the market for corporate control,[240] but this time the focus of attention was the tension between the situation in Britain as compared with other member states of the European Community.

The essential issue is how a national economy which values and regularly experiences competitive takeovers can relate to those of other member states of the European Union where such takeover bids are rare to non-existent. This has come to be known as 'the lack of a level playing field', where takeover bids are made for British companies listed on the London Stock Exchange. The main thrust of the Coopers & Lybrand report explores the well-known difference between Britain, where contested takeovers are an essential part of a flourishing market for corporate control, and other European states (within the EC and beyond it) where that is not the case.

In most countries of the EC there are very few listed companies in which the majority of voting shares are not controlled by families or institutions closely linked to the existing

---

[235] See e.g. *The Guardian*, Thursday 10 March 1994.

[236] ibid., Friday 29 April 1994.

[237] 'Winning for Britain'. See *The Guardian*, Friday 3 June 1994.

[238] The possibility of two-tier boards and tax changes to encourage long-term holding of shares is also canvassed.

[239] 3 Vols. (HMSO, 1989). See further the DTI's *Barriers to Takeovers in the European Community: A Consultative Document* (January 1990). For commentary see A. J. Boyle 12 Co. Law 163 (1991) and Alec Burside 13 Co. Law 19 (1992).

[240] For the concept of the market for corporate control, see p. 31 above. For a critique of the functioning of the takeover market in Britain, see Alan Peacock and Graham Bannock's *Corporate Takeovers and The Public Interest* (Aberdeen University Press, 1991). See further Caroline Bradley, 'Corporate Control: Markets or Rules' (1990) 53 MLR 170. For treatment of the regulation of takeovers in Britain by the Takeover Code, see Chapter 16 below.

management. This must be related to cultural factors in the business community of the countries concerned. These are in turn closely related to what the report terms 'structural barriers'. This refers to the extent to which the general pattern of shareholding in listed companies allows a genuine market for control of listed companies to operate in a particular country. In short, to what extent is a contested takeover bid a realistic proposition? Essentially, a structural barrier is the formal expression of the underlying cultural attitude to corporate wealth and to openness and competition in regard to the control of such wealth.

In most member states of the EC the cultural and structural barriers are further reinforced by technical legal barriers in the company law systems or permitted legal practices of those countries.[241] These legal barriers (to those steeped in British business culture) are perceived as unethical and designed to maintain the interests of the existing management. As seen from the City of London, the need for management to be accountable to shareholders (in terms of dividend level, share price, etc.), and the right of shareholders by majority to sack ineffective management, are paramount. In many EC countries, where a different ideology of corporate governance prevails, contested take-overs are seen in a different light. They may regard the possibility of a predator seizing control of a limited company as itself being unethical, especially where this has an adverse effect on the existing managers and on other employees of the target company.

The Department of Trade and Industry reflected carefully on the Coopers & Lybrand report which it had commissioned. It carried out a subsequent consultation exercise and then published a consultative document in 1990. Efforts were made, principally through tabling proposed amendments to the Draft Fifth Directive and the Draft Thirteenth Directive on Takeovers, to tackle at least the legal barriers to competitive takeovers.[242]

In the consultative document itself the difficulties in removing even the legal barriers are recognised.[243] Removing the cultural and structural barriers is a much more formidable task which may well prove insurmountable. It is a task which lies beyond not only the Commission's company law harmonisation programme but would seem to be outside the jurisdiction of any of the institutions of the European Community.

---

[241] These can be described very briefly as: unequal voting rights; proxy voting linked with bearer shares; cross shareholdings; difficulties for the bidder identifying shareholders; and difficulties, after control of a majority of voting shares is obtained, in appointing a new board and removing the old directors. See Boyle 12 Co. Law at pp. 164–7.

[242] See *Barriers to Takeovers in The European Community: A Consultative Document*, January 1990.

[243] The Draft Fifth Directive seems a rather limp instrument since Britain continues to oppose its existing provisions on employee participation.

2 Registration and Formation of Companies

2.1 Introduction

This chapter is concerned with the different types of company which can exist and the mechanisms which are provided for their registration and, occasionally, re-registration. Although the vast bulk of registered companies are companies limited by shares, the legislation makes provision also for unlimited and guarantee companies. The nature of these is briefly explained later in this chapter.[1] It is appropriate also to consider the law which applies to those people, known as promoters, who are actually engaged in the business of forming a company, and, briefly, the law which applies to foreign companies doing business in Britain.

Historically, the registered company form was made available for enterprises wishing to involve a large or at least reasonable number of investors. However, as has been seen in Chapter 1, it was also adopted by small concerns, even where there was only one person really involved, a move that was sanctioned by the House of Lords in *Salomon v Salomon & Co*.[2] At the time of this decision, the law made no distinctions between different types of registered company; that happened in 1909 when the concept of the private company, as something distinct from the basic form, the public company, was introduced. Under the law then, the private company was a special category meeting particular requirements (e.g. as to the number of members). All companies not registered as private fell into the residual category of public company. In order to implement the provisions of the EC's Second Directive on Company Law,[3] a new way of classifying public and private limited companies was introduced by the Companies Act 1980. Many of the more onerous requirements first imposed by this Act (which stem from the directive)[4] apply only to public companies. To prevent evasion of these requirements it was necessary to introduce a more rigid and watertight dividing line between public and private companies.[5] Under this modern system of classification, which better reflects the reality of company registration, all proposed companies must be registered as private unless they are specifically registered as public companies and meet the special requirements of such. The most important of these are a minimum capitalisation for public companies and an addition to their name (public limited company) indicating a public company's special status.[6]

---

[1] A further registered business association is the European Economic Interest Grouping, described briefly in 1.5.3.

[2] [1897] AC 22; see 1.9.

[3] 77/91/EEC, O.J. 1977 L 26/1.

[4] As to these, see Chapter 6, *passim*.

[5] This applies to the original registration of public and private companies and also to the re-registration of a private company as a public company or vice versa.

[6] As discussed in Chapter 1, it may be questioned whether the registered company form is really appropriate for very many of the small concerns which use it. The prospect of a new form of incorporation for such concerns appears to be on the agenda once more.

2.2 The classification of public and private companies

Section 1 (3) of the Companies Act 1985 defines 'public company' as a company limited by shares (or limited by guarantee and having a share capital)[7] whose memorandum of association states that it is a public company and in relation to which the provisions of the 1985 Act or the former Companies Acts as to the registration or re-registration of a company as a public company have been complied with. The Registrar of Companies must register intended companies as public or private, and in the case of a company registered as public the amount of share capital stated in the memorandum must not 'be less than the authorised minimum',[8] which is defined by section 118 (1) to mean £50,000.[9]

A public company must have a minimum of two members, while a private limited company can now have just one member.[10] Section 25 (1) requires that the name of a public company must end with the words 'public limited company',[11] which can be abbreviated to 'plc'.[12] Section 1 (3) defines 'private company', as 'a company that is not a public company'. This obviously includes all companies limited by shares which, when they are registered under section 13, are not specifically registered as public companies. It also includes all companies already registered as private companies under earlier Companies Acts 1948–1976 and all unlimited companies or companies limited by guarantee, whatever their previous status.

Sections 43 to 47 provide for the various types of company to be re-registered as another type of company. These provisions are described below.

It is an offence for a public company (other than an old public company) 'to use a name which may reasonably be expected to give the impression that it is a private company in circumstances in which the fact that it is a public company is likely to be material to any person.'[13]

2.3 The memorandum of association

The fundamental document which must be prepared for the registration of a company is the memorandum of association. The purpose and drafting of the memorandum are examined in detail in Chapter 3, but we must note the contents here. Section 2 of the Companies Act 1985 requires the memorandum of a company limited by shares to contain the following clauses:[14]

(1) the Name Clause;
(2) the Registered Office Clause;

---

[7] Guarantee companies with a share capital cannot be formed as such now (section 1 (4)), but those existing prior to 1980 could re-register as public.

[8] Sections 11 and 13.

[9] Or 'such other sum as the Secretary of State may by order made by statutory instrument specify instead'.

[10] The Companies (Single Member Private Limited Companies) Regulations 1992 (SI 1992 No. 1699), implementing Directive 89/667 and amending section 1 of the 1985 Act.

[11] It is an offence for a 'person' (e.g. a private company) which is not registered as a public company to carry on any trade, profession or business under a name which includes as its last part the words 'public limited company' or their Welsh equivalent: section 33 (1).

[12] Section 27. In the case of companies whose registered office is stated by the memorandum to be in Wales, this may be rendered in Welsh as 'cwmni cyfyngedig cyhoeddus', which may be abbreviated as 'ccc'.

[13] Section 33 (2).

[14] See the model forms in the Companies (Tables A to F) Regulations 1985 at Table B (private company limited by shares) and Table F (public company limited by shares).

(3) the Objects Clause;

(4) the Limited Liability Clause;

(5) the Share Capital Clause.

In the case of a public company an additional clause, stating that it is a public company, must be inserted between (1) and (2), above.

The memorandum may contain optional provisions (which might otherwise be inserted in the articles).[15] It should then conclude with a formal declaration of association by the subscribers.[16] Section 2 (6) requires that the memorandum 'must be signed by each subscriber in the presence of at least one witness who must attest the signature'. In practice, subscribers usually sign for only one share each; but there is no reason why they should not sign for as many shares as they intend to take up and pay for. The fact that they have subscribed makes them members of the company from the date of registration.[17]

The name, address and occupation of each subscriber must be stated fully, giving the number, street, city or town, and county. The memorandum may be subscribed by or on behalf of a firm or corporation. Any signature for a firm should be followed by the signature of all the partners. Minors (i.e. persons under age) should not subscribe, although the Registrar's certificate is conclusive evidence that the company is duly registered.[18] An agent may sign the memorandum on behalf of his principal, and the authority to sign may be given orally. The execution will be good, whether the agent simply writes his principal's name or adds words showing that it is signed by an attorney.[19] The signatures must be attested by one or more witnesses. A witness should be a disinterested person, and not a subscriber. He should give his address and occupation in the same manner as the subscribers. The document may be signed at different times and different places, and be witnessed by different persons.

The memorandum should be in correct form when presented for registration, and any alterations and interlineations in it should be initialled by each subscriber, or the witness should certify that the alterations were made before the document was executed. For the purpose of registration, the memorandum may be either entirely typed upon a sheet or sheets of foolscap; or it may be typed upon the forms provided for that purpose, in which case it will be partly written and partly printed; or it may be entirely printed. As, however, every member is entitled to be supplied with a copy on payment of 5p (or any less sum the company may prescribe), printing is almost indispensable. Printing the document has the further advantage that every copy is an exact reproduction of the registered original.

2.4 The articles of association

The other document which must be prepared for registration is the articles of association. Articles must be printed and divided into numbered paragraphs.[20] The original articles must be signed by each subscriber to the memorandum and attested by a witness.[21] The

---

[15] e.g. as to the rights attached to shares. See Chapter 7.

[16] Note that there is no bar on all the subscribers to a British company being foreigners: *Re General Company for Promotion of Land Credit* (1870) 5 Ch App. 363.

[17] See further 10.2.1.

[18] Section 13 of the Companies Act 1985. In Scotland, however, a minor (in the Scots law sense) may subscribe.

[19] *In re Whitely Partners* (1886) 32 Ch D 337 (CA). In the latter case the Registrar will require production of a written authority, stamped as a power of attorney.

[20] Companies Act 1985 section 7 (3).

[21] ibid.

purpose, contents and drafting of the articles of association are considered further in Chapter 3.

Companies limited by guarantee and unlimited companies must register articles, but a company limited by shares need not register articles, in which case the articles of the company will be the regulations contained in Table A.[22] If a company limited by shares is to be registered without articles, the fact must be stated on the back of the memorandum. It is important in the case of a private company that the articles should be so drafted to meet the requirements of the particular 'corporate partners' as to the distribution of voting power attached to shares, the powers of the board of directors and that of managing directors, the power to issue further shares, pre-emptive rights, etc. The provisions of Table A (especially the 1985 Table A) may be far from suitable for preventing or resolving problems of deadlock, oppression, etc. and for controlling the transfer of shares.[23] Where an existing registered company is to be used, the articles should be appropriately amended.

2.5 Registration of memorandum, articles, etc.

Section 10 of the Companies Act 1985 requires that the memorandum and articles of association (if any) be delivered to the Registrar for registration.[24] Under section 12, the Registrar may not register the memorandum unless he is satisfied that all the requirements of the Act in respect of registration and of matters precedent and incidental to it have been complied with. Section 11 further requires that, where a memorandum delivered to the Registrar concerns a public company, the amount of share capital stated in the memorandum to be that with which the company proposes to be registered must not be less than the 'authorised minimum'.[25]

Section 12 (3) also requires a statutory declaration of compliance with the requirements of section 10 in respect of registration. This must be made by a solicitor engaged in the formation of the company or by a person named in the articles as a director or secretary of the company in the statement delivered under section 10 (2) of the 1985 Act.

With every memorandum delivered for registration under section 10 of the Act there must be delivered a statement containing particulars of the first director or directors and first secretary or joint secretaries of the company. In the case of an individual director, the particulars required by Schedule 1 to the Companies Act 1985 are his present name and any former name,[26] his usual residential address, his nationality, his business occupation (if any), particulars of any other directorships held by him or which have been held by him,[27] and his date of birth. The corporate name and registered or principal

---

[22] See section 8 (1) and, for companies registered since 1 July 1985, the Companies (Tables A to F) Regulations 1985. Unless it has resolved to alter its articles appropriately since then, a company registered prior to 1 July 1985 is governed by the then applicable version of Table A, which was always in a Schedule to the Companies Act, to the extent that it was adopted by that company.

[23] A variety of models is provided in the standard works on precedents. See for example Jordan's Model Forms, reproduced in *Secretarial Administration* (Jordans, loose-leaf), FP 2.3.

[24] This will be the English Registrar (in Cardiff) if the company is to registered in England and Wales or the Scottish Registrar (in Edinburgh) if the company is to be Scottish.

[25] See 2.2.

[26] 'Name' is defined in para. 4 of Schedule 1 to mean Christian name or forename and surname, with qualifications for peers. 'Former name' is further defined.

[27] Directorships last held more than five years before the statement and in dormant companies and companies 'grouped with' the company delivering the document do not have to be disclosed here.

office of a corporate director must be given. As far as the secretary is concerned, the particulars required are his present name, any former name and his usual residential address,[28] and the same is required of joint secretaries unless all the partners in a firm are joint secretaries, in which case disclosure of the name and principal office of the firm will suffice.

The statement delivered under section 10 must be signed by or on behalf of the subscribers to the memorandum,[29] and must contain a consent signed by each of the persons named as director or secretary. Those named are deemed, on the incorporation of the company, to have been appointed to the office in question,[30] and any appointment by any articles delivered with the memorandum is void if it does not accord with the statement.[31]

The section 10 statement must also contain a statement of the intended situation of the company's registered office. The matter of the registered office is considered below in 3.8.

The other requirement for registration of a company is payment of the appropriate fee. The amount of this is governed by regulations.[32]

2.6 The certificate of incorporation

Section 13 (1) of the Companies Act 1985 requires that on registration of the memorandum of a company, the Registrar shall certify that the company is incorporated and, in the case of a limited company, that the company is limited.[33] Where the memorandum of the company registered states that it is a public company, the certificate must state that it is a public company.[34] From the date mentioned in the certificate, the subscribers of the memorandum together with such other persons as may from time to time become members of the company shall be:

(1) a body corporate by the name contained in the memorandum;
(2) capable forthwith of exercising all the functions of an incorporated company;
(3) but with such liability on the part of the members to contribute to the assets of the company in the event of its being wound up as is provided by the Act and the Insolvency Act.

Section 711 of the 1985 Act requires the Registrar to publish in the *London Gazette* notice of the issue by him of any certificate of incorporation of a company. He must state in the notice the name of the company, a description indicating that it is a certificate of incorporation and the date of its issue.

Section 13 (7) deals with the problem of irregularities in the process of registration. It provides that a certificate shall be conclusive evidence that the requirements of the Act in respect of registration and matters precedent and incidental to it have been complied with, and that the association is a company authorised to be registered and is duly

---

[28] In the case of a corporation or Scottish firm, its corporate or firm name and registered or principal office.

[29] Where the memorandum is delivered by a person as agent of the subscribers of the memorandum the statement required by this section shall specify that fact and the name and address of that person: section 10 (4).

[30] Section 13 (5).

[31] Section 10 (5).

[32] See the Companies (Fees) Regulations 1991 (SI 1991 No. 1206), as amended.

[33] As to the rights to inspect and require a copy of the certificate, see sections 709 and 710.

[34] Section 13 (6). The certificate may be signed by the Registrar or authenticated by his official seal. Note that it is possible to obtain registration on the same day as the documents are handed in.

registered under the 1985 Act, and, if the certificate contains a statement that the company is a public company, that the company is such a company.

It has been held that the certificate of incorporation is conclusive evidence that there is a company, and that it is duly incorporated.[35] The certificate is also conclusive evidence that the registration and incorporation of the company were fully effected on the day mentioned in the certificate. The date mentioned in the certificate is the first day of the company's existence, and the company is deemed to have been incorporated on the first moment of that day.[36] However, section 13 (7) only deals with ministerial acts, and a certificate does not establish the fact that the company is not a trade union and therefore capable of registration.[37] The House of Lords has held that the certificate of the Registrar is conclusive that the terms of the memorandum are within the law, and that accordingly the court's only function is to construe the memorandum as it stands.[38] The Registrar will refuse registration if he is of the opinion that any object of the company is illegal, and an appeal from his decision can be brought to the High Court by way of judicial review seeking an order that he be required to register.[39] Where the Registrar permits registration, the Attorney-General may be given leave for judicial review where the objects of the company involve entering into contracts which are sexually immoral.[40]

2.7 Certificate for public companies

As a way of guaranteeing that a newly incorporated public company satisfies the requirement as to its authorised minimum capital, section 117 of the Companies Act 1985 provides an administrative safeguard. A company registered as 'a public company on its original incorporation' may not do business or exercise any borrowing powers unless the Registrar issues a certificate as to its authorised minimum capital. If he does not do so, the company must re-register as a private company.

In order for the Registrar to issue this certificate an application must be made to him by the company in prescribed form, signed by a director or secretary, which satisfies him that the nominal value of the company's allotted share capital is not less than the authorised minimum; further, there must be delivered to him a statutory declaration complying with the matters set out below.[41] Shares allotted in pursuance of an employees' share scheme may not be taken into account in determining the nominal value of the company's allotted share capital unless they are paid up at least as to one-quarter of their nominal value and the whole of any premium.[42]

The statutory declaration must state:

---

[35] *Hammond v Prentice Brothers* [1920] 1 Ch 201.

[36] *Jubilee Cotton Mills v Lewis* [1924] AC 958 (HL).

[37] *Edinburgh and District Aerated Water Manufacturers' Defence Association v Jenkinson* (1903) 5 F 1159 (Ct of Sess.); *British Association of Glass Bottle Manufacturers v Nettlefold* (1911) 27 TLR 527. Whether a certificate of incorporation is conclusive when a friendly society purports to register as a company but adopts an extended memorandum or otherwise offends against the law was left open in *Blythe v Birtley* [1910] 1 Ch 229.

[38] *Cotman v Brougham* [1918] AC 514 (HL).

[39] *R v Registrar of Companies* [1931] 2 KB 197 (C.A.). If the conditions laid down in the Act have been complied with (and the object is not illegal) the court will compel the Registrar to issue a certificate of incorporation: *R v Registrar of Companies, ex parte Bowen* [1914] 3 KB 1161.

[40] *R v Registrar of Companies, ex parte Attorney-General* [1991] BCLC 476.

[41] See section 117 (3).

[42] Section 117 (4).

(1) the nominal value of the company's allotted share capital is not less than the authorised minimum;

(2) the amount paid up, at the time of application, on the allotted share capital of the company;

(3) the amount, or estimated amount, of the preliminary expenses of the company and the persons by whom any of those expenses have been paid or are payable;

(4) the details of any amount or benefit paid or given or intended to be paid or given to any promoter of the company, and the consideration for the payment or benefit.

The Registrar 'may accept a statutory declaration as sufficient evidence of the matters stated therein',[43] which presumably still leaves him the discretion in an appropriate case to enquire further.

A certificate issued under section 117 (1) is 'conclusive evidence that the company is entitled to do business and exercise any borrowing powers'.[44] Where a company does business or exercises borrowing powers in contravention of the section, criminal penalties are imposed on the company and any officer in default. There are, however, two further sanctions. First, the Secretary of State may present a petition to wind up a company on the ground that it is a public company which was registered as such on its original incorporation but that it has not been issued with a certificate under section 117 and more than a year has expired since it was registered.[45] It may be noted that, unlike the criminal penalties, this sanction may be invoked against a company incorporated as public even though it has not otherwise infringed section 117 by doing business, etc. The fact that it has lain dormant for a year would be sufficient. However, section 117 (1) permits such a company (e.g. where it is unable to raise the authorised minimum capital) to re-register as a private company. An undertaking to do so might persuade the court not to grant a winding-up order.

The second additional sanction imposed by section 117 concerns transactions entered into by a company in contravention of its provisions.[46] It is important to note that such transactions are expressly declared to be valid. If, however, a company fails to comply with its obligations under such a transaction within twenty-one days of being called upon to do so (i.e. by the other party), the directors become jointly and severally liable to indemnify the other party to the transaction in respect of any loss or damage suffered by him by reason of the failure of the company to comply with those obligations.

2.8 Unlimited companies

So far in this chapter it has been assumed that a company is formed with the liability of its members limited, but it has long been possible to register a company with unlimited liability. However, before the Companies Act 1967 very few companies, other than estate companies, were registered with unlimited liability, and many banking and other companies originally constituted as unlimited companies were re-registered with limited liability. When the 1967 Act relieved unlimited companies from the disclosure require-

---

[43] Section 117 (5).

[44] Section 117 (6). In view of the protection given to third parties even where no certificate is issued (see below), this must be intended to protect the company and its officers.

[45] Insolvency Act 1986, sections 122 (1) (*b*) and 124 (4). This would not seem to exclude others entitled to present a petition under section 124 (1) doing so on this ground.

[46] Section 117 (8) states that 'the provisions of this section are without prejudice to the validity of any transaction entered into by the company'.

ments in respect of accounts that apply to limited companies (private or public),[47] some encouragement was provided for the registration or re-registration of unlimited companies. The members of an unlimited company are liable in a liquidation to contribute until the whole of the company's debts or obligations (however heavy they may be) are paid, but their primary liability is at an end once they have ceased to be members.[48] An unlimited company must always now be classified as a private company.

Unlimited companies may be registered either with or without a capital divided into shares. The memorandum of association must state the name of the proposed company, whether the registered office of the company is to be situated in England and Wales or Scotland, and the objects for which the company is to be established.[49] It must be accompanied by articles of association,[50] for which Table E may be used as a model.[51] The articles must be printed[52] and must state the amount of its share capital (if any).[53] The capital (if the company has a capital), being stated in the articles of association, may be varied at any time by special resolution without the sanction of the court, and, if the articles allow it, capital may be returned to members, and they may cease to be members on such terms as may be agreed upon.[54]

So far as regards the powers of an unlimited company and of its directors, the conduct of its business and proceedings, the alteration of its memorandum or articles of association, and its winding up, the same considerations apply as in the case of a limited company. The returns required to be made by unlimited companies are the same as those by other companies, except that an unlimited company with a share capital is under no obligation to lodge a return of allotments.

2.9 Companies limited by guarantee

Companies limited by guarantee are usually formed for the purpose of carrying on business as mutual insurance and trade protection societies, social, athletic and other clubs, and concerns in which it is not intended to make a profit. There are two kinds of guarantee company still provided for under the Companies Act 1985:[55] companies limited by guarantee and not having a share capital; and companies limited by guarantee and having a share capital. It is only the first kind that is considered here, since the hybrid variety was in practice rarely used. Furthermore, since the Companies Act 1980, it has not been possible to register any more such companies. It should be noted that there is no provision for a company limited by shares to re-register as a company limited by guarantee or vice versa.

The principle on which these companies are constituted is that each person who

[47] Although many private limited companies are now relieved from many of the disclosure requirements; see 1.3 and Chapter 12.
[48] Past members may in certain circumstances escape liability, e.g. if they have ceased to be members of the company a year or more before the commencement of the winding-up; see section 74 of the Insolvency Act 1986.
[49] Section 2 (1).
[50] Section 7 (1).
[51] See section 8 (4). Though the general form of the tables in the Companies (Tables A to F) Regulations 1985 must be followed, their contents may be changed: *Gaiman v National Association for Mental Health* [1971] 1 Ch 317.
[52] Section 7 (4).
[53] Section 7 (2).
[54] *Re Borough Commercial and Building Society* [1893] 2 Ch 242.
[55] See sections 3 and 8.

becomes a member 'undertakes to contribute to the assets of the company in the event of its being wound up while he is a member, or within one year after he ceases to be a member, for payment of the debts and liabilities of the company contracted before he ceases to be a member, and of the costs, charges, and expenses of winding up, and for adjustment of the rights of the contributories among themselves, such amount as may be required, not exceeding a specified amount'.[56] This amount has to be stated in the memorandum of association, and may be any sum the subscribers to that document think fit – £1 or £1,000, or any other sum, large or small. The amount is not part of the capital of the company, and cannot be mortgaged or charged by debentures.[57]

In the form which is usually adopted the amount of the guarantee of each member remains the same, whatever his pecuniary interest in the company may be, and (beyond that interest) is the utmost extent to which he can be a loser in the event of the company going into liquidation. The guarantee, moreover, is only so much per member, and accordingly, if the number of members is reduced, the aggregate amount guaranteed is also reduced. Thus the security of the creditor is lessened to that extent unless the memorandum provides for membership continuing until some other person takes the place of the member then on the register.

In all companies limited by guarantee, articles of association must be registered with the memorandum of association, and must be printed. Section 8 (4) requires that the memorandum and articles of a company limited by guarantee (and not having a share capital) shall be in accordance with the form set out in Table C of the Companies (Tables A to F) Regulations 1985. In *Gaiman v National Association for Mental Health*,[58] Megarry J held that the draftsman of the articles, provided that he followed the general form of the relevant Table was free to add to, subtract from or vary the model set out in the Table 'as the needs of the case suggest'.[59] Section 15 (1) provides that 'every provision in the memorandum or articles or in any resolution of the company purporting to give any person a right to participate in the divisible profits of the company otherwise than as a member shall be void'.

2.9.1 *Exemption from using 'limited' as part of the name*

A private guarantee company may take advantage of the procedure in sections 30 and 31 of the Companies Act 1985 to omit the word 'limited' from its name (while of course retaining limited liability).[60] The objects of the company must be (or will be in the case of a company about to be registered) the promotion of commerce, science, education, religion, charity or any profession and anything incidental or conducive to those objects. In addition the following restrictions on profits, dividends and capital must be contained in the company's memorandum or articles. The memorandum or articles must require that its profits, if any, or other income be applied in promoting its objects, and prohibit the payment of dividends to members. The memorandum or articles must also require all the assets (which would otherwise be available, on a winding-up, to its members generally) to be transferred on its winding up either to another body with objects similar

---

[56] Section 2 (2) and (3).

[57] *Re Pyle Works* (1890) 44 Ch D 534 at pp. 574 and 584; *Re Irish Club Co* [1906] WN 127.

[58] [1971] 1 Ch 317.

[59] ibid., p. 328.

[60] Before the original introduction of these provisions, in 1981, Department of Trade and Industry approval was required.

to its own, or to another body whose objects are the promotion of charity and anything incidental or conducive to it.

A statutory declaration must be made that the company complies with the requirements of section 30 (3). In the case of a company about to be formed, this may be made by a solicitor engaged in the formation of the company or by a person named as a director or secretary of the company in the 'statement of first directors and secretary' delivered under section 10 (2).[61] In the case of a company which is proposing to drop the word 'limited' from its name, the statutory declaration must be made by a director or secretary of the company. On the delivery of such a declaration to the Registrar, he may accept it as sufficient evidence of the matter stated in it. Companies to which section 30 applies are exempt not only from the use of the word 'limited' as part of their name, but also from the requirements of the 1985 Act as to the publishing of its name[62] and the sending of lists of members to the Registrar of Companies.[63] These practical advantages may be even more beneficial to companies qualifying for exemption under section 30.

A company so exempt may not alter its memorandum or articles 'so that it ceases to be a company to which this section applies.'[64] If it appears to the Secretary of State that a company exempt under section 30 is in fact ignoring the requirements, he may, in writing, direct the company to change its name (by resolution of the directors) so that the name ends with 'limited'. The directors must do so within such period as may be specified in the Secretary of State's direction. Such a resolution by the directors must be treated as one to be registered under section 380 of the 1985 Act.[65] A company which has received a direction under section 31 may not thereafter be registered with a name which does *not* include the word 'limited' without the approval of the Secretary of State.[66]

Section 351 (1) requires a company exempt under section 30 to display in legible characters on all its business letters and order forms the fact that it is limited.[67]

2.10 The re-registration of companies

The Companies Act provides for a number of ways in which a company may be re-registered, for example from private to public. The principal requirements are examined in the following paragraphs.[68]

2.11 The re-registration of private companies as public

Sections 43 to 47 of the Companies Act 1985 provide for the re-registration of private companies as public companies. Section 43 requires the company to pass a special resolution making the necessary changes in its memorandum and articles and then to

---

[61] See 2.5.
[62] See 3.5.
[63] See 10.7.
[64] Section 31 (1).
[65] See 11.18.
[66] Section 31 (3).
[67] See 3.5.
[68] In addition to those described, there is provision for 'old public companies', i.e. those incorporating before the Companies Act 1980 came into force and which have not hitherto re-registered as public companies, to re-register as private companies. These are described in *Gore-Browne on Companies* (Jordans, 44th edn, loose-leaf), 7.10–7.10.3.

make an application accompanied by certain required documents. It must also meet certain conditions specified in section 45 as to the nominal value of its share capital, as described in 2.11.1.

The special resolution that the company should be re-registered as a public company must alter the memorandum so that it states that the company is a public company. The resolution must also make such other alterations in the memorandum necessary to make it conform with the memorandum of a public company.[69] The special resolution must also 'make such alterations in the articles as are requisite in the circumstances'. For example, articles restricting the transfer or transmission of shares, or entrenching the position of the existing directors on the board, might have to be changed. This would certainly be necessary where a Stock Exchange listing was contemplated.

Section 43 (3) requires that, having passed the special resolution to re-register as a public company, an application in prescribed form, signed by a director or secretary of the company, be delivered to the Registrar. The application must be accompanied by the following documents:

(1) A printed copy of the memorandum and articles as amended by the special resolution required by section 43.

(2) A copy of a written statement by the company's auditors that, in their opinion, the 'relevant balance sheet' shows that at the balance sheet date the amount of the company's net assets was not less than the aggregate of its called-up share capital and 'undistributable reserves'. 'Relevant balance sheet' means a balance sheet prepared as at a date not more than seven months before the company's application for re-registration under section 43.[70] 'Undistributable reserves' has the same meaning as in section 264 (3).[71]

(3) A copy of the relevant balance sheet, together with a copy of an 'unqualified report by the company's auditors in relation to that balance sheet'.[72]

(4) A copy of the experts' report required where shares have been issued for non-cash consideration. This is further explained in 2.11.1, below.

(5) Finally, there must be a statutory declaration in the prescribed form by a director or secretary of the company as to the following. First, that the requirements of section 43 (1) as to the special resolution altering the company's memorandum and articles have been complied with; secondly, that the conditions specified in section 44[73] where this applies and in section 45 (as to authorised share capital, etc.)[74] have been complied with; thirdly, that between balance sheet date and the application of the company for re-registration, there has been no change in the financial position of the company that has resulted in the amount of the company's net assets becoming less than the aggregate of its called-up share capital and undistributable reserves. The Registrar may accept the statutory declaration called for by section 43 (3) (*e*) as sufficient evidence that the special resolution has been passed and that the other conditions have been satisfied.[75]

[69] See 2.2 as to the form of the memorandum of a public company as regards the *name clause* and the *share capital clause*.

[70] Section 43 (4).

[71] See 6.21.3.

[72] See section 46.

[73] See 2.11.1.

[74] ibid.

[75] Section 47 (2).

2.11.1 *Requirements as to share capital*

Section 45 (1) provides that a private company shall not be re-registered as a public company unless, at the time the special resolution required by section 43 is passed, the following requirements as to the company's share capital are satisfied:

(1) The nominal value of the company's allotted share capital is not less than the authorised minimum.

(2) Each of the allotted shares is paid up at least as to one-quarter of the nominal value of that share and the whole of any premium on it.

(3) Where any share in the company or any premium payable on it has been fully or partly paid up by an undertaking given by any person that he or another should do work or perform services for the company or another, the undertaking has been performed or otherwise discharged.

(4) Where any shares in the company have been allotted as fully or partly paid up as to their nominal value or any premium payable on them otherwise than in cash and the consideration for the allotment consists of or includes an undertaking (other than one to which para. (3) above applies) to the company, then either

   (a) that undertaking must have been performed or otherwise discharged, or

   (b) there must be a contract between the company and any person pursuant to which that undertaking must be performed within five years from that time.

A further condition that must be met by a private company seeking to re-register as a public one[76] applies only where shares are allotted by the company between the balance sheet date[77] and the passing of the special resolution as fully or partly paid up as to their nominal value or any premium on them otherwise than in cash. In this event section 44 (2) adapts the provisions of section 108 of the 1985 Act.[78] A private company may not make an application for re-registration unless before doing so consideration for the allotment has been valued in accordance with the provision of section 108. Further, a report with respect to its value must have been made in accordance with section 108 during the six months immediately preceding the allotment of the shares.

2.11.2 *The effect of re-registration under section 43*

If the Registrar is satisfied that a company may be re-registered as a public company, he must retain the application and accompanying documents. He must then issue the company with a certificate of incorporation stating that the company is a public company.[79] Upon the issue of this certificate, the company becomes a public company and the alteration in the memorandum (and any alteration in the articles) set out in the special resolution required by section 43 (1) take effect accordingly.[80]

---

[76] See section 43 (1) and (3) (*e*).

[77] i.e. the date when the balance sheet (required as part of the documents contained with the application under that section) was prepared.

[78] See 6.14.3.

[79] Section 47 (1). The Registrar may not issue such a certificate where it appears to him that the court has made an order confirming a reduction of capital and where this brings the nominal value of the issued capital below the authorised minimum: section 47 (3).

[80] Section 47 (5).

2.12 Re-registration of unlimited companies as public companies

In principle, where an unlimited company wishes to re-register as a *public* limited company, the procedure and requirements of section 43 of the Companies Act 1985 must be followed. However, this is subject to certain modifications appropriate to the change from unlimited to limited status.[81] It should be remembered that, under the modern system of classification, an unlimited company is a private company and may not, while it remains such, register as a public one.[82] However, section 48 allows it to change its status by re-registering as a public limited company. Where an unlimited company wishes to become a private limited company, then it should re-register under section 51.[83]

2.13 Public companies re-registering as private

Section 53 of the Companies Act 1985 allows companies registered under the Act as public companies to re-register as private companies. This can apply to companies registered on incorporation as public and also to private companies which have re-registered as public.

The procedure for re-registration follows the usual pattern in requiring a special resolution that the company be re-registered. This must alter the company's memorandum so that it no longer states that the company is a public company. It must also make such 'other alterations in the company's memorandum and articles as are requisite in the circumstances'.[84] The name of the company (ending 'public limited company') will of course be changed to simply 'limited'. The articles may take the form of specially drafted articles suitable to a private company.

This special resolution may be challenged by dissenting shareholders applying to the court to have the resolution cancelled under section 54. An application may be made to the court within twenty-eight days after the passing of the resolution 'on behalf of persons entitled to make the application by such one or more of their number as they may appoint in writing for the purpose'. The persons entitled to make the application are shareholders (or members) who meet any of the following criteria:

(1) holders of not less in aggregate than 5 per cent in nominal value of the company's issued share capital or any class thereof;
(2) if the company is not limited by shares, by not less than 5 per cent of the company's members; or
(3) by not less than fifty of the company's members.

Where an application is made by those entitled, the company must 'forthwith' give notice in the prescribed form to the Registrar. The company must also, where on the hearing of that application the court cancels or confirms the resolution, deliver an office copy of the court order to the Registrar within fifteen days from the making of the order or within such longer time as the court may at any time by order direct.[85]

---

[81] See sections 43 (1) and 48 (1).
[82] See 2.2, above.
[83] See 2.15, below.
[84] Section 53 (2).
[85] Penalties are imposed for failing to comply with these requirements on the company and any officer of the company who is in default.

The court which hears an application to cancel or confirm a resolution is given wide powers. It may make that order (either cancelling or confirming the resolution) 'on such terms or conditions as it thinks fit'. Further, the court may, if it thinks fit, adjourn the proceedings in order that an arrangement may be made to the satisfaction of the court for the purchase of the interest of dissentient members. It may give such directions and make such orders as it thinks expedient for facilitating or carrying into effect any such arrangement. The court is given the further power to provide for the company itself to purchase the shares of any member of the company. Where that is ordered, the company's capital will be reduced accordingly. Such an order may make the necessary alterations in the memorandum and articles that are required in consequence. Quite apart from the power to order the company to purchase dissenters' shares, there is a further power to require the company to make any, or any specified, alteration in the memorandum or articles of the company. The company will then require the leave of the court before it may further alter the memorandum or the articles in breach of what has been required. However, any alterations in, or additions to, the memorandum or articles, ordered by the court under section 54, have the same effect as if made by the resolution of the company. The provisions of the Companies Act are to apply accordingly.

The wide powers which section 54 confers on the court are similar to those conferred on a court hearing a petition by unfairly prejudiced minority shareholders under sections 459–61 of the Companies Act 1985.[86] It remains to be seen how the courts will exercise these new powers in this context, since the ground for giving relief is quite distinct from that of unfair prejudice under section 459. Since the complainants under section 54 will, if the resolution is confirmed, be deprived of a market for their shares (e.g. the company will cease to be a company listed on The Stock Exchange, where that had been the case), it is to be hoped the court will as a rule be prepared to grant some form of relief where it decides not to cancel the resolution. The most obvious solution is that indicated by section 54 – the purchase of the dissenter's shares by or on behalf of the majority shareholders or by the company itself.

2.14 Re-registration of private limited companies as unlimited companies

Section 49 allows the conversion of a limited company into an unlimited one on application to the Registrar for re-registration.[87] The conditions that must be met are:

(1) that the unanimous consent of the members has been obtained;[88]
(2) that the memorandum is altered to bring it, both in substance and form, into conformity with the requirements of the Companies Act 1985 as to the memorandum of an unlimited company with a share capital.[89]

If it is not to have a share capital, the memorandum must set out such alterations as are 'requisite in the circumstances'. If the company had previously registered articles and it is to have a share capital, then the application must set out such alterations to the articles as

---

[86] See 15.12.

[87] This procedure was first introduced by the Companies Act 1967 to enable private companies to escape the disclosure obligations imposed on them by that Act. Section 49 (3) provides that a public company cannot re-register as an unlimited company. It also provides that a company that has previously been registered as unlimited may not re-register under this section.

[88] Section 49 (8).

[89] Section 49 (5) (*a*).

'are requisite to bring them, both in substance and form, into conformity with the requirements' of the 1985 Act as to the substance and form of the articles required for an unlimited company with share capital.

A public company cannot re-register directly as an unlimited company, because section 53 (3) provides that a company cannot under this section be re-registered 'otherwise than as a company limited by shares or by guarantee'. Thus a public limited company seeking to become a private unlimited company will have first to re-register as a private limited company under section 53. There is nothing to prevent it then applying for re-registration as an unlimited company under section 49. However, the unanimous consent of the members will be required. At the stage of re-registration under section 53, dissenting shareholders might apply to the court under section 54. As already noted, the court may make an order for the purchase of the shares of the dissentient members.

2.15 Re-registration of unlimited companies as private limited companies

The converse procedure for re-registering an unlimited company as a private limited company follows broadly the same pattern. However, instead of the unanimous consent of all the members, section 51 requires the passing of a special resolution. This resolution must state whether the liability of members is to be limited by guarantee or by share capital and, if the latter, what the capital is to be. The resolution must also make appropriate alteration in the memorandum and articles to fit the requirements of the Companies Act 1985 as to the substance and form of the memorandum and articles suitable to the type of limited liability chosen.

Section 77 of the Insolvency Act 1986 provides that those who were members at the time of re-registration shall remain liable to contribute if the company is wound up within three years of the re-registration, even though they have become past members by the time the winding-up commences. Such past members remain liable to contribute to the company's debts and liabilities incurred before the re-registration as if the company had not been re-registered as limited. Further, where none of the members at the time of the re-registration remain members at the commencement of the liquidation, those who were existing or past members at the time of re-registration are liable to contribute without limit to the debts and liabilities incurred before re-registration. This is notwithstanding the fact that the existing members at the time of winding up have 'satisfied the contribution required to be made by them' under the Companies Act 1985 and the Insolvency Act 1986.

2.16 Prohibited forms of re-registration

Neither section 49 nor section 51 permits a limited company to change to a different form of limited liability (i.e. a company limited by share capital to one limited by guarantee or vice versa). However, section 51 permits an unlimited company to re-register as a company limited by shares or by guarantee. The prohibition on the use of these sections by a company which is or wishes to become a public company has already been noted. Furthermore, section 51 does not permit an unlimited company to re-register as a limited one if it has previously changed from a limited to an unlimited company under section 49. Likewise, section 49 prohibits the converse process when a limited company seeking to re-register as an unlimited one has previously changed from unlimited to limited.

2.17 Promoting companies

It is now appropriate to consider the legal position regarding those who are involved in the formation of a company, conventionally called promoters. The courts have always refused, rightly, to define what constitutes a 'promoter'. If a rigid definition were given, those who want to avoid the liabilities of the position would be careful to come very close to the line without crossing it. The best description is that of Bowen LJ: 'The term "promoter" is a term not of law but of business, usefully summing up in a single word a number of business operations, familiar to the commercial world, by which a company is generally brought into existence.'[90] To this there should probably be added 'and by which its original capital is provided'. The promotion does not necessarily cease with the registration of the company, for 'a person not a director may be a promoter of a company which is already incorporated but the capital of which has not been taken up'.[91]

In seeking to ascertain who are the promoters of a company it is useful to ask:

(1) Who started the idea of forming a company for the purpose in question?
(2) Who decided what was to be included in the memorandum and articles of association and in the prospectus, or gave the lawyers instructions to prepare them and information upon which they might be prepared?
(3) Who undertook the liability for the costs of preparing those documents, registering the company and making the preliminary agreements?
(4) Who sought out the persons who ultimately became the first directors, and induced them to undertake the office?
(5) Who procured the subscription of the capital?
(6) Who benefited by the formation of the company?

However, none of these questions is decisive. A person may have done one or more of these things, and yet not be a promoter; or a person may have kept in the background and have appeared to do none of these things, and yet be a promoter. Usually, however, persons who have busied themselves in procuring subscriptions or underwriting will find it very hard to escape from being held to be promoters. Further, a person may be a promoter who is only acting as agent for others, or as director of a promoting syndicate, if he has personally taken an active part in the promotion.[92]

Frequently, the vendors of property to a company are the promoters,[93] but if they have done no more than agree to sell, they will not be promoters; nor will the solicitors who, as part of their professional duty, prepared the contracts.[94] However, the courts will look at the substance of a transaction, and vendors or others who are in reality the promoters will not escape liability by the interposition of a nominal vendor or a nominal promoter, who professes to purchase and resell the property or to undertake the financial operations incidental to forming and floating a company.[95]

[90] *Whaley Bridge Calico Printing Co. v. Green* (1880) 5 QBD 109.
[91] *Emma Silver Mining Co. v Lewis* (1879) 4 CPD 396, 407.
[92] *Lydney and Wigpool Iron Ore Co. v Bird* (1886) 33 Ch D 85, 94.
[93] *Twycross v Grant* (1877) 2 CPD 469; *Gluckstein v Barnes* [1990] AC 240, 249 (HL).
[94] *Re Great Wheal Polgooth Co. Ltd* (1883) 53 LJ Ch 42.
[95] See *Twycross v Grant* (1877) 2 CPD 469; *Bagnall v Carlton* (1877) 6 Ch D 371; *Emma Silver Mining Co. v Lewis* (1879) 4 CPD 396; *Erlanger v New Sombrero Phosphate Co.* (1878) 3 App. Cas. 1218 (HL); *Emma Silver Mining Co. v Grant* (1879) 11 Ch D 918; *Nant-y-Glo and Blaina Co. v. Grave* (1878) 12 Ch D 738; *Lydney and Wigpool Iron Ore Co. v Bird* (1886) 33 Ch D 85.

2.18 Duties of promoters

The relation of a promoter to the company he is about to form, although not strictly that of a trustee to his *cestui que trust*, or of an agent to his principal, is of the same nature. It follows that he may not secretly make a profit for himself, nor otherwise benefit at the expense of the company. Thus Lindley LJ described the relationship between a promoter and his company as follows:

> Although not an agent of the company nor a trustee for it before its formation, the old familiar principles of the law of agency and of trusteeship have been extended, and very properly extended, to meet such cases. It is perfectly well settled that a promoter of a company is accountable to it for all moneys secretly obtained by him from it, just as if the relationship of principal and agent, or of trustee and *cestui que trust*, had really existed between him and the company when the money was so obtained.[96]

The fiduciary relationship extends, moreover, not only to the company as constituted at the time, but also to future allottees of shares. Thus disclosure of profits made by the promoters must be made not only to the subscribers to the memorandum.

The fiduciary position commences as soon as the promoter begins to act for or promote the company, but not earlier. The fact of acquiring a property with the intention of ultimately forming a company which shall acquire and develop it does not render the purchaser accountable for the profit he makes on the resale, so long as the company, on coming into existence, is informed that the person selling to the company and the promoter are identical.[97] The same rule applies even though the acquisition is only in the form of an option or uncompleted contract,[98] or where the promoter contracted to sell 'the benefit of a lease agreed to be granted', and in fact there was no agreement for the lease, but only negotiations which ultimately resulted in a lease which was assigned to the company.[99] But any profit which the promoter makes after he has begun to promote the company, and the benefit of any contracts into which he enters during the period, prima facie belong to the company.[100] It is, however, too much to say that what a promoter acquires after he has commenced the promotion *ipso facto* belongs to the company. The question whether the promoter is in fact acquiring as agent for the intended company or for himself is one of fact; but where the scheme throughout is that he shall resell at a profit, the natural inference is that he is not acting as agent for the company, and if there is no concealment of the fact that he is the vendor when he resells the company, the company cannot claim the profit.[101]

If the promoter was not at the time he bought in a fiduciary position, though subsequently and at the time of his resale of the company he is in a fiduciary position and does not disclose his interest, the company is entitled to rescind. If in such a case rescission

[96] *Lydney and Wigpool Iron Ore Co. v Bird* (1886) 33 Ch D 85, 94.

[97] *Cavendish Bentinck v Fenn* (1887) 12 App. Cas. 652 (HL); *Gover's Case* (1875) 1 Ch D 182; *Erlanger v New Sombrero Phosphate Co.* (1878) 3 App. Cas. 1218; *Ladywell Mining Co. v Brookes* (1887) 35 Ch D 400. Compare *Burland v Earle* [1902] AC 83 (PC): the case of a director purchasing privately and selling to his company.

[98] *Gover's Case* (1875) 1 Ch D 182, followed in *Ladywell Mining Co. v Brookes* (1887) 35 Ch D 400.

[99] *Omnium Electric Palaces v Baines* [1914] 1 Ch 332 (CA).

[100] *Ladywell Mining Co. v Brookes* (1887) 35 Ch D 400; *Re Cape Breton Co.* (1885) 29 Ch D 795, affirmed *sub. nom. Cavendish Bentinck v Fenn* (1887) 12 App. Cas. 652 (HL).

[101] *Omnium Electric Palaces v Baines* [1914] 1 Ch 332 (CA).

has become impossible, the company cannot recover from the promoter, as money had and received, the profit he has made, or damages.[102]

However, if an additional secret profit has been made under a separate transaction which it is still open to the company to rescind, or under an ancillary transaction to which it was not a party, such a profit may be recovered.[103] Furthermore, a promoter will be liable in deceit if it can be shown that he has caused loss to the company by making fraudulent statements.[104]

2.18.1 To whom disclosure must be made

Promoters will not be protected by disclosures made before the public have joined the company unless there is an independent board or body of shareholders to receive and act upon the information, and the directors who participate in the profits must not be counted as independent.[105] Thus mere communication to the subscribers to the memorandum of association who are clerks in the vendor's office is obviously a farce, even though they hold a meeting and are the only members of the company. Equally, disclosure to directors who are mere nominees of the vendors or promoters will not be sufficient.[106] In such a case the information should be given in the prospectus;[107] and even if all the facts are known to all the members of the company at the time the contract is made, but a misleading prospectus is subsequently issued by the promoters to the public inviting them to join the company, the promoters will be liable.[108] If, however, there is no intention of making a public issue of shares, and no such issue is in fact made, the knowledge by all the directors and members of the company of the facts will exonerate the promoters, even where the purchase price has been greatly inflated.[109]

Where a promoter has to account to the company for secret profits, the measure of recovery is the amount of profit made by the promoter,[110] but he is allowed to deduct from the amount all reasonable expenses he has been put to, and is liable only for the net profits made.[111]

---

[102] *Gover's Case* [1875] 1 Ch D 182; *Re Cape Breton Co.* (1885) 29 Ch D 795; *Ladywell Mining Co. v Brookes* (1887) 35 Ch D 400; *Re Lady Forrest (Murchison) Gold Mine* [1901] 1 Ch 582; *Burland v Earle* [1902] AC 83; *Re Jacobus Marler Estates v Marler* (1913) 114 LT 640 note; *Cook v Deeks* [1916] AC 554 (PC). But in *Cavendish Bentinck v Fenn* (1887) 12 App. Cas. 652 (HL) Lord Hershell, at p. 664, suggested there might be a remedy in damages.

[103] *Gluckstein v Barnes* [1900] AC 240 (HL); *Jubilee Cotton Mills v Lewis* [1924] AC 958 (HL).

[104] *Re Leeds & Hanley Theatre of Varieties* [1902] 2 Ch 809 (CA). Where misstatements are made negligently which induce the company to enter into a contract in reliance on them, there may now be liability under section 2 (1) of the Misrepresentation Act 1967 (this Act does not apply in Scotland, but the Law Reform (Miscellaneous Provisions) (Scotland) Act 1985, section 10, allows for the award of damages for a negligent misrepresentation). Where the promoter can establish a reasonable ground for belief, he will have a defence to an action under section 2 (1). However, the court under section 2 (2) may now award damages in lieu of rescission when this latter remedy would otherwise be available for innocent misrepresentation. Finally, the company may have an action for negligent misstatement at common law within the principle laid down in *Hedley Byrne & Co. Ltd v Heller & Partners Ltd* [1964] AC 465 (HL).

[105] *Re Leeds and Hanley Theatre of Varieties* [1902] 2 Ch 809 (CA); *Erlanger v New Sombrero Phosphate Co.* (1878) 3 App. Cas. 1218 (HL); *Re Olympia* [1898] 2 Ch 153, affirmed *sub nom. Gluckstein v Barnes* [1900] AC 240 (HL).

[106] *Re Olympia* [1898] Ch 153 affirmed *sub. nom. Gluckstein v Barnes* [1900] AC 240. Compare *Kaye v Croydon Tramways* [1898] 1 Ch 358 (CA) and *Lagunas Nitrate Co. v Lagunas Syndicate* [1899] 2 Ch 392 at p. 431 (CA).

[107] *Re Leeds and Hanley Theatre of Varieties* [1902] 2 Ch 809 (CA).

[108] *Lagunas Nitrate Co. v Lagunas Syndicate* [1899] 2 Ch 392 at p. 428 (CA).

[109] *Re Ambrose Lake Tin and Copper Mining Co.* (1880) 14 Ch D 390; *Re British Seamless Paper Box Co.* (1881) 17 Ch D 467; *Re Innes & Co.* [1903] 2 Ch 254; *Attorney-General for Canada v Standard Trust Co.* [1911] AC 498 (PC).

[110] *Re Leeds and Hanley Theatre of Varieties* [1902] 2 Ch 809 (CA).

[111] *Emma Silver Mining Co. v Grant* (1879) 11 Ch D 918; *Lydney and Wigpool Iron Ore co. v Bird* (1886) 33 Ch D 85.

2.19 The remuneration of promoters

The traditional way for promoters to obtain their reward was in the form of the profit made on property sold to the company or in some other ancillary transaction connected with its formation. It has been seen that if proper disclosure is made, such transactions are binding on the company.[112]

Promoters have no right to any remuneration simply because the articles state that the promoters are entitled to a certain sum for their services. This does not of itself create a contract between the promoter and the company.[113] The promoter must prove the existence of a binding contract with the company,[114] and, as will be explained below, a contract purporting to be made with a company before it is formed is not binding upon it. This applies even to a claim for the preliminary expenses connected with the formation, such as registration fees.[115]

2.20 Underwriting commission

The function at one time performed by the traditional promoter is now carried out in the case of public companies by a city issuing house. The remuneration of such a body will take the form of an underwriting commission[116] and there are a number of statutory provisions governing such commission. Section 97 of the Companies Act 1985 allows an underwriting commission of up to 10 per cent of the price at which the shares were issued to be paid if this is authorised by the company's articles and the commission paid or agreed to be paid does not exceed 10 per cent of the price at which the shares are issued or the amount or rate authorised by the articles,[117] whichever is the less. Section 98 (4) allows vendors or promoters the power to apply part of the money or shares received from the company in the payment of an underwriting commission which would have been lawful under section 97 if paid directly by the company.

Section 98 prohibits a company, save as authorised by section 97 (1), from applying any of its shares or capital money either directly or indirectly in payment of commission; this applies to private as well as public companies.[118] However, there is no prohibition against paying commission unconditionally *out of profits* and this would seem to be lawful unless contrary to any stipulation in the articles.[119] Section 98 is very wide in its language, subsection (2) extending the prohibition in the following way: 'whether the shares or money be so applied by being added to the purchase money of any property acquired by the company or to the contract price of any work to be executed for the company, or the money be paid out of the nominal purchase money or contract price, or otherwise'. Further, the court will look at the substance of the transaction, and will prohibit a pretended purchase and resale which is in fact only a device to cover payment of a

[112] Payments, etc., made to promoters must also be disclosed where admission to The Stock Exchange's Official List is sought; see *Listing Rules*, para. 6.C.21.

[113] *Re Rotherham Alum and Chemical Co.* (1883) 25 Ch D 103 (CA). Moreover the directors may not rely on such a clause authorising payment unless they have made proper enquiry: *Re Englefield Colliery Co.* (1878) 8 Ch D 388.

[114] *Re English & Colonial Produce Co.* [1906] 2 Ch 435 (CA).

[115] *Re National Motor Mail Coach Co.* [1908] 2 Ch 515 (CA).

[116] As to the standard terms of underwriting contracts, see *Gore-Browne on Companies* (Jordans, 44th edn, loose-leaf), 8.4.2.

[117] If the articles allow a commission at a specified rate. This is not satisfied by a commission consisting of a lump sum: *Booth v New Afrikander Gold Mining Co.* [1903] 1 Ch 295 (CA).

[118] *Dominion of Canada General Trading & Investment Syndicate v Brigstocke* [1911] 2 KB 648.

[119] In addition, the share premium account (see 6.15) can be applied to paying commission.

commission.[120] However, an agreement giving underwriters an option to subscribe for further shares as consideration for underwriting is not an application of shares in payment of commission within the section and is lawful.[121]

Commission paid in respect of shares[122] must be disclosed in the annual return filed with the Registrar,[123] and listed companies must disclose details in their listing particulars.[124]

2.21 Pre-incorporation contracts

Whether the company is formed to acquire a business, to work a mine, to develop a patent, to undertake financial business, or for any other purpose, it seldom becomes incorporated or issues a prospectus without having entered into preliminary agreements for the purchase of the property or rights to be acquired, or for securing the services and connection of some manager or expert.

As the promoters of the company will want to offer the benefit of such agreements or contracts as an inducement to the public to take shares, it becomes necessary that the contracts should be made before the formation of the company, or at least before the general allotment of shares. Accordingly, an agreement or contract is usually prepared. Where incorporation of the company has not been effected, the contract may be expressed to be made between the vendor and the company, the draft being initialled for the purpose of identification, or it may be made between the vendor and a trustee for the intended company and dated and executed. But in the latter case the company is not bound by the contract until it has entered into a direct agreement, after incorporation, to become so, since a company cannot ratify a contract made before it came into existence.[125]

A contract can be made with a trustee for the company before the company has any existence, in which case the trustee will be personally bound by the contract unless he expressly protects himself from liability by including a power to rescind it.[126] It is usual in such a case to make it one of the objects of the company mentioned in the memorandum, and also to provide in the articles of association that the directors shall adopt the preliminary agreement; but this will not lay the company under obligation unless a distinctly new contract is made by which the company agrees to be bound by the terms of the preliminary agreement.[127] Nor will a resolution of the board of the new company adopting the agreement create a contract between the new company and the vendor.[128] A new contract may, however, sometimes be inferred from the circumstances and the conduct of the parties.[129] But the mere fact that the directors of the company think they

---

[120] *Booth v New Afrikander Gold Mining Co.* [1903] 1 CH 295 (CA).

[121] *Hilder v Dexter* [1902] AC 474 (HL).

[122] And debentures.

[123] See Chapter 10.

[124] *The Listing Rules*, para. 6.B.15.

[125] *Rover International Ltd v Cannon Film Sales Ltd* [1987] BCLC 540.

[126] *Kelner v Baxter* (1866) LR 2 CP 174; *Re Empress Engineering Co.* (1880) 16 Ch D 125 at p. 129 (CA).

[127] *Kelner v Baxter* (1866) LR 2 CP 174: *Scott v Lord Ebury* (1867) LR 2 CP 255.

[128] *Re Olympia* [1898] 2 Ch 153 at p. 168; *Re Northumberland Avenue Hotel Co.* (1866) 33 Ch D 16; *Natal Land Co. v Pauline Colliery* [1904] AC 120 (PC); *Kelpongs Prospecting Ltd v Schmidt* [1968] AC 810 (PC).

[129] *Re Johannesburg Hotel Co.* [1891] 1 Ch 119; *North Sydney Investment Co. v Higgins* [1899] AC 263 (PC).

are bound by the contract with the trustee, and act accordingly, is not enough, even though large sums of money are expended and work is done in that mistaken belief.[130]

Where the contract is expressed to be made with the company itself, it is usually prepared before the incorporation of the company, and then referred to in the memorandum and articles of association as an 'agreement already prepared and intended to be executed', and, for identification, signed or initialled by some of the subscribers to the memorandum of association or by a solicitor. In this case the agreement must be executed by the company and this must be done after proper consideration by the directors and not merely *pro forma*; in fact, they must exercise their judgment upon it, and if they are not an independent board the company may repudiate the contract.[131]

A third party prepared to sell or lease property to the company may not be prepared to wait until the company is formed and the contract executed. Here an agreement can be made between the vendor and the promoters on identical terms to the draft contract which it is intended the company will execute. The agreement with the promoters will provide that their liability is to cease once the company is incorporated and the contract with it executed.

Although, therefore, a company is not bound by a contract made in its name before incorporation, where, subsequent to incorporation, it has made payments or rendered services on the basis of an invalid pre-incorporation contract, it may succeed in a claim made in restitution, for money had and received or *quantum meruit*.[132] The same principle would apply against a company that had received payments or enjoyed services.

2.22 The liability of promoters or other 'agents' to third parties

Even though a pre-incorporation contract is not, as such, binding upon the company, there may be a remedy against those who purported to act on behalf of the non-existent company. At common law the position was, however, unclear and unsatisfactory. In *Kelner v Baxter*,[133] promoters who signed an agreement 'on behalf of' a company about to be formed were held to be personally liable on the contract as principals in the place of the non-existent company.[134] By contrast, in *Newborne v Sensolid (GB) Ltd*[135] it was held that, where a contractual document is signed by the company and the 'agent's' signature is added simply to authenticate the signature of the company, then neither the 'agent' nor the company can sue on the contract. It was also stated, *obiter*, that the 'agent' would not be personally liable to be sued on the contract nor would he be liable for breach of warranty of authority as he had not acted in the capacity of an agent.[136] It is difficult to see why a claim for breach of warranty of authority would not lie in such a case.

[130] *Re Northumberland Avenue Hotel Co.* (1866) 33 Ch D 16; *Howard v Patent Ivory Co.* (1888) 38 Ch D 156; *Natal Land Co. v Pauline Colliery* [1904] AC 120 at p. 126 (PC). Nor can the company be bound by an estoppel based on facts occurring before it came into existence: *Rover International Ltd v Cannon Film Sales Ltd* [1987] BCLC 540.

[131] See the discussion of promoters' duties, above.

[132] *Rover International Ltd v Cannon Film Sales Ltd* [1988] BCLC 710 (CA), reversing in this respect [1987] BCLC 540.

[133] (1866) LR 2 CP 174.

[134] i.e. liability was not founded on breach of warranty of authority.

[135] [1954] 1 QB 45 (CA).

[136] This reasoning was applied in the Australian case of *Black v Smallwood* [1966] ALR 744 (Aust HC). In *Cumming v Quartz AG Ltd* [1981] SLT 205, an attempt to rely on the principle of a stipulation in favour of a third party (which may be effective under Scots contract law) was rejected because the promoter had signed as an agent and not as a principal. See MacQueen [1982] SLT 257.

What is now section 36C of the Companies Act 1985[137] made a change in the law as regards the liability of those who purport to act on behalf of the company before it is incorporated. It provides as follows:

> A contract which purports to be made by or on behalf of a company at a time when the company has not been formed has effect, subject to any agreement to the contrary, as one made with the person purporting to act for the company or as agent for it, and he is personally liable on the contract accordingly.[138]

This provision does not change the position of the company once it is formed. It is not bound by such contracts and cannot ratify them.

The purpose of section 36C is to remove the subtle distinction between *Kelner v Baxter* and *Newborne v Sensolid (GB) Ltd*. Its effect is that even if the defendant did not contract as agent *or* assume personal liability but (as in *Newborne*) his signature is appended to that of the company's name to authenticate it, he will nevertheless be personally liable. Here there will be a contract which 'purports to be made by the company' which 'shall have effect as a contract entered into by the person purporting to act for the company'. This interpretation was adopted by the Court of Appeal in *Phonogram Ltd v Lane*,[139] where it was held that 'purports' does not require that there should be a representation that the company is already in existence. The court also held that the section is not confined to the case where the company is already in the course of formation. In this case no steps had been taken to do so.[140]

It should be noted that where liability is imposed by section 36C, it will not be based on breach of warranty of authority but on the personal liability 'on the contract'. This will be so even where the contract has been made 'by a person as agent for a company'. Although this is not made explicit, it would seem to follow that anyone made 'personally liable on the contract' would also have a right to enforce it. Where he is a promoter he might in some circumstances have to account to the company for the fruits of the contract.[141]

The qualifying proviso to section 36C – 'subject to any agreement to the contrary' – appears to require, for the application of the section to be excluded, that there should be an express term to that effect in the contract, whether oral or written.[142]

---

[137] Section 36C was derived initially, as section 36 (4), from section 9 (2) of the European Communities Act 1972 implementing a provision of the EC First Directive on Company Law. The current version was inserted by the Companies Act 1989, with some improved wording, to extend its coverage to deeds. See further, Green, 'Security of transactions after Phonogram v Lane' (1984) 47 MLR 671. The Court of Appeal has held that in section 9(1) and (2) of the 1972 Act, 'company' meant registered company and not a foreign corporation created by its own special statute: *Janred Properties v Ente Nazionale Italiane Per Il Turismo* (1983) 14 July (unreported). See also *Rover International Ltd v Cannon Film Sales Ltd* [1987] BCLC 540 in respect of section 36 (4).

[138] By section 36C (2), the section applies to the making of a deed (obligation in Scotland) as it applies to the making of a contract.

[139] [1981] 3 WLR 736.

[140] The Court of Appeal rejected an argument which rested on the French text of the First EEC Directive on Company Law. The court observed that under Article 189 of the EEC Treaty a directive is binding in so far as its spirit and intent are concerned. Section 36C satisfied this requirement, and its plain meaning should be applied even if it went further than the scope of the directive.

[141] See 2.18.

[142] See *Phonogram Ltd v Lane*, above. See N. N. Green in (1984) 47 MLR 671 at pp. 677–82 as to the effect of the parol evidence rule where an oral 'agreement to the contrary' relates to a written contract.

The courts have imposed sensible limits on the protection afforded by section 36C. So, it has been held that it did not apply to save a contract in the name of a company which had not existed for five years by the registration of a new company, because there was no intention to form the new company when the contract was made.[143] It does not apply to a company awaiting a new certificate of incorporation on a change of name,[144] since that is not a company that 'has not been formed'.[145] Similarly, there is no basis for applying the section to a contract made by a company which has been formed but which is not accurately named.[146]

2.23 Oversea companies

It is appropriate to conclude this chapter with a brief examination of the law concerning companies which are not registered in Great Britain.[147] The law has long recognised the existence of companies incorporated abroad and as regards those which set up business in some way in Britain, imposes a number of formal requirements.

Part XXIII of the Companies Act 1985 applies to such oversea companies. Following amendments introduced pursuant to the Eleventh EC Directive,[148] the provisions now distinguish between companies which have established a place of business in Great Britain,[149] and those which have a 'branch' in Great Britain.[150] Curiously, neither the directive nor the regulations define the term 'branch', and it is probably proper to refer to relevant decisions of the European Court of Justice.[151] From these it seems that the concept of a branch implies the actual transaction of business to a greater extent than that of a place of business. So if the oversea company can enter into contracts, etc. through its office in Great Britain, it will be subject to the branch registration regime.[152]

The traditional place of business regime requires the delivery to the Registrar, within one month of establishment, of: a certified copy of the charter, statutes or memorandum and articles or other instrument constituting or defining the constitution of the company; and a return including details of the company's directors and secretary, the names and addresses of one or more persons resident in Great Britain authorised to accept, on the company's behalf, service of process and any notices required to be served on it and a statutory declaration stating the date on which the place of business was established.[153]

---

[143] *Cotronic (UK) Ltd v Dezonie, t/a Wendaland Builders Ltd* [1991] BCC 200 (CA).

[144] See 3.6.

[145] *Oshkosh B'Gosh v Dan Marbel Inc* [1989] BCLC 507 (CA).

[146] *Badgerhill Properties Ltd v Cottrell* [1991] BCLC 805 (CA).

[147] For detail on this and on how the Companies Act applies to unregistered companies and certain other associations, see *Gore-Browne on Companies* (Jordans, 44th edn, loose-leaf), Chapter 37. Of course, a British-registered subsidiary of a foreign company is not an oversea company.

[148] 89/666/EC, introduced by the Oversea Companies and Credit and Financial Institutions (Branch Disclosure) Regulations 1992, SI No 3179.

[149] 'Place of business' includes a share transfer or share registration office (section 744); otherwise it requires some degree of permanence or recognisability in addition to the setting up of a place of business at a specific location: see especially *Re Oriel Ltd* [1989] BCLC 343 (CA).

[150] Companies registered in Northern Ireland or Gibraltar can register only under the old place of business regime.

[151] Mentioned in *Gore-Browne on Companies* (Jordans, 44th edn, loose-leaf), 42.10.4, especially *Etablissements Somafer SA v Saar-Ferngas AG* [1979] 1 CMLR 490.

[152] In general, it may be that only Northern Irish and Gibraltarian companies (see note 150) will in practice still be subject to the old regime.

[153] Section 691.

Alterations to the appropriate details must also be filed. The Secretary of State can control the name used by an oversea company[154] in a similar way to the controls over the names of British registered companies,[155] and the name, country of incorporation and whether the liability of the members is limited must be disclosed at the place of business and on all billheads and letters.[156] Audited accounts must be filed,[157] and charges over British property registered. Companies registered in the Channel Islands or the Isle of Man must in addition file an annual return.[158]

The branch registration regime differs only relatively slightly.[159] There is a similar registration requirement within one month with the same basic details required, and the provisions regarding names, etc. apply to all oversea companies. One change relates to the registration of reports and accounts, so that, *inter alia*, accounts which are prepared, audited and disclosed according to the law of the country of incorporation can be filed in Great Britain, but if accounts are not required in that country, accounts meeting the requirements of the 1985 Act must be filed. In addition, letters, etc. of branches must disclose the place of registration and registered number of the branch, and branches of companies from outside the EC have to disclose further detail.[160]

---

[154] Section 694.

[155] See 3.2.

[156] Section 693.

[157] Section 700.

[158] Section 699.

[159] Although the Registrar has had to establish a new register of branches. The detail regarding the branch regime is contained in sections 690A, 690B and 692A and Schedule 21A.

[160] Section 694 (3) and (4).

3 The Memorandum and Articles of Association

3.1 The memorandum of association

The constitution of every registered company is embodied in its memorandum of association and articles of association. The memorandum of association is the more fundamental of the two documents.[1] In it the basic characteristics of the company's particular corporate personality are identified. Section 2 of the Companies Act 1985 requires the memorandum of every company to state its name, the situation of the registered office (i.e. whether in England and Wales or in Scotland) and its objects. A company limited either by share capital or by guarantee must have further clauses stating (a) that the liability of its members is limited and (b) the amount of the share capital or guarantee. Where a company is registered as a public limited company (plc), this must be stated in the memorandum, and the words 'public limited company' (or the abbreviation 'plc') must come at the end of its name.[2] The first part of this chapter examines the law concerning each one of these essential 'clauses' in the memorandum with the exception of the 'objects clause'. This clause is so important in defining the limits of the authority of the directors, officers and other agents to act on the company's behalf that it is treated separately in the next chapter. Other matters, at the option of those forming the company, may also be included in the memorandum. The legal effect of such provisions is also considered in this chapter. In the case of each type of clause the extent to which, if at all, it may be altered after the company is formed will be examined. The question of the subscription of the memorandum has been considered at 2.3, above.

3.2 Initial registration of a company name

Those forming a company can choose any name for the company provided it does not infringe certain prohibitions which are set out in section 26 of the Companies Act 1985. The principal prohibition is that the chosen name must not be the same as a name which already appears on the Registrar's index of company and corporate names.[3] The founders of a new company should search the index of names to ensure that the name they have chosen has not already been registered.[4] There is nothing to stop a new company being registered with a name that is very similar to one that is already registered but, under section 28, a company can be required within twelve months of registration of a name[5] to change its name if, in the opinion of the Secretary of State, it is too like a name

---

[1] The articles of association, and the contract of association formed by both the memorandum and the articles, are discussed at 3.16 to 3.23, below.

[2] Companies Act 1985, sections 1 (3) and 25 (1).

[3] Section 26 (1) (c). The index is maintained in accordance with section 714.

[4] Section 709 authorises inspection of any records kept by the Registrar for the purposes of the Companies Acts. Commercial bodies also provide search facilities: see, e.g., the service provided by Jordan & Sons Ltd – identical and similar names searches – from their own computerised index.

[5] If misleading information has been given for the purposes of registration with a particular name or undertakings or assurances have not been fulfilled, the Secretary of State can require a name change within five years of initial registration: section 28 (3).

which appeared in the Registrar's index of company names at the time of registration of the new company, or which should have appeared in the index at that time.[6] It could prove to be an expensive and time-consuming exercise to change all of the accounts, stationery and other materials in the event of the company being required to change its name and, ordinarily, this would deter the founders of a company from choosing a name that is very like a name that is already registered.[7]

There are also prohibitions on the registration of a company with a name whose use would constitute a criminal offence or which is offensive.[8] Except with the approval of the Secretary of State, a company cannot be registered with a name which would be likely to give the impression that it is connected in any way with HM Government or with any local authority.[9]

Section 32 gives the Secretary of State a power to direct a change of name by which a company is registered if he is of the opinion that the name gives so misleading an indication of the nature of the company's activities as to be likely to cause harm to the public. The company has the right to apply to the court to set the Secretary of State's direction aside.[10] The purpose of section 32 appears to be to prevent public mischief rather than to protect private rights.

3.3 'Limited'

Section 25 (2) of the Companies Act 1985 also requires that, in the case of a private company limited by shares or by guarantee, 'limited' must form the last word of its name as stated in the memorandum. Such companies may also use the abbreviation 'Ltd' or the Welsh equivalent. The name of a public company must end with 'public limited company' (or plc) or the Welsh equivalent of either of these terms. In certain circumstances companies limited by guarantee (and some other private companies) may be dispensed from the requirement to place 'limited' after their name.[11] Section 33 makes it an offence for a person who is not a public company to carry on any trade, profession or business under a name which includes, as its last part, the word 'public company'. Likewise, a public company is guilty of an offence, if in circumstances in which the fact that it is a public company is likely to be material to any person, it uses a name which may reasonably be expected to give the impression that it is a private company.[12]

---

[6] Under section 26 (3) certain matters are disregarded in determining whether names are too similar: section 28 (2).

[7] Those trading under a name that is like the name of another company would also risk incurring liability in tort for passing off.

[8] Section 26 (1) (*d*) and (*e*). In both cases, it is for the Secretary of State to decide whether the use of the particular name would be a criminal offence or would be offensive. The words or expressions 'Limited', 'Unlimited' or 'Public Limited Company', or abbreviations thereof, or Welsh equivalents, must not be included otherwise than at the end of a name: section 26 (1) (*a*) and (*b*).

[9] Section 26 (2). The Secretary of State has the same power in respect of any words or expressions specified in regulations made under section 29 (see The Company and Business Names Regulations 1981, as amended (1981/1685) (these regulations remain in force despite consolidation of the Companies Acts)). Section 29 also makes provision for a procedure for obtaining the consent of government departments and other bodies for the use of a name which suggests that there is some connection: section 29 (2).

[10] As to the procedure see section 32 (2) and (3).

[11] See 2.9.1, above.

[12] As to the sanctions imposed, see section 33 (3). If the 'person' guilty of an offence is a company, any officer of the company who is in default is also liable.

3.4 'Business names'

In addition to the restrictions imposed by the Companies Act 1985, the Business Names Act 1985 regulates the use, control and disclosure of business names. This Act is relevant where a company has a place of business in Great Britain and carries on business in Great Britain under a name which is not its corporate name.[13] It contains provisions, which mirror those of the Companies Act, regarding the use of certain names such as those which are likely to give the impression of a connection with HM Government or with a local authority. The Act also requires disclosure of the corporate name in business letters and other documents, and at business premises.[14]

3.5 The display and use of the company's name

There are various requirements concerning the use and display of the corporate name. Every company must have its name painted or affixed, and kept painted or affixed, 'in letters easily legible' in a conspicuous position on the outside of every office or place in which it transacts business.[15] The company's name must also be mentioned 'in legible characters' on its seal if it has one[16] and must appear 'in all business letters of the company and in all notices and other official publications of the company, and in all bills of exchange, promissory notes, endorsements, cheques, and orders for money or goods[17] purporting to be signed by or on behalf of the company, and in all bills of parcels, invoices, receipts, and letters of credit of the company'.[18]

If an officer of the company, or a person on its behalf, signs or authorises to be signed on behalf of the company any bill of exchange, promissory note, endorsement, cheque or order for money or goods in which the company's name is not correctly stated in legible characters, by virtue of section 349 (4), he is personally liable to the holder of any such bill of exchange, promissory note, cheque or order for money of goods for the amount in question unless this is duly paid by the company.[19] In the case of an order for goods, the 'holder' to whom the person signing is made liable by this section is the person to whom the order is given.[20]

Personal liability under section 349 (4) comes into existence on the date when a cheque (signed in breach of that section) is not duly paid. This liability cannot be affected thereafter in the way in which liability of a surety under a contract of guarantee might be affected under the law of principal and surety.[21] The fact that the company in question has been sued to judgment under dishonoured cheques is no bar to recovery under section 349 (4) since the remedies are concurrent and not alternative.[22]

---

[13] The Act also applies to partnerships and sole traders.

[14] See further *Gore-Browne on Companies* (Jordans, 44th edn, loose-leaf), 2.2.4–2.2.5.

[15] Section 348. Penalties for default are specified in section 348 (2) and Schedule 24.

[16] Section 350.

[17] This does not include services: *East Midlands Electricity Board v Grantham* (1980) 6 Current Law para. 35.

[18] Section 349. In the event of default the company and the responsible individuals are liable to a fine: section 349 (2) and (3).

[19] Section 349 (4). In *Penrose v Martyr* (1858) EB&E 499, which was decided upon a similar worded clause in the Act of 1856, the secretary, who had accepted on behalf of the company a bill directed to the company in which the word 'limited' as part of its name was omitted, was held personally liable on the bill, the same not having been paid by the company.

[20] *Civil Service Co-operative Society v Chapman* [1914] WN 369.

[21] *British Airways Board v Parish* [1979] 2 Lloyds Rep. 361 (CA).

[22] *Maxform S.p.A. v Mariani and Goodville* [1979] 2 Lloyds Rep. 385, affirmed Lloyd's Rep. 54.

In the case of *Atkin v Wardle*[23] it was decided that the directors of a company were personally liable for the amount of a bill of exchange accepted by them as directors of the company, because, although the word 'limited' appeared in the bill in one place, the name of the company was not correctly given in either the draft or the acceptance. Where a cheque was signed which omitted the ampersand in the company's name, it was held that the directors who had signed the cheque had not complied with what is now section 349 and were personally liable.[24] This decision was distinguished in a later case where one letter had been omitted from the spelling of the company's name: the omission of a letter in the middle of a word was not to be equated with the omission of a whole word and, therefore, the directors were not held personally liable.[25] The later decision is based on a less semantic approach than that which characterises some of the earlier authorities.

In another case, where a bill contained more than the correct name, the directors were held personally liable[26] but they escaped where the name of the company had been impressed with a rubber stamp and the word 'limited' had overlapped, and did not appear on the bill.[27] The use of the abbreviation 'Ltd' has been held not to render the statement of the name incorrect.[28]

It should be noted that the directors can be liable under section 349 even though the 'holder' was not misled by the misdescription.[29] However, the 'holder' may be estopped from suing under section 349 where he is responsible for the misdescription: *Durham Fancy Goods Ltd v Michael Jackson (Fancy Goods) Ltd*.[30]

3.6 Change of name of a company

A company can change its name by passing a special resolution to that effect.[31] As on initial incorporation, the new name must not be the same as a name which appears on the Registrar's index of names at the time of registration of the new name;[32] if, in the opinion of the Secretary of State, the new name is too like a name which was, or was entitled to be, registered earlier the company can be required to change its name again.[33] The other restrictions on the choice of name, discussed above, also apply.

When a company has resolved to change its name it must inform the Registrar of Companies. The Registrar will enter the new name in the register in place of the former name and issue 'a certificate of incorporation altered to meet the circumstances of the case': section 28 (6). The change of name will take effect from this date: section 28 (6).

[23] (1899) 58 LJ QB 377 and, on appeal, 5 TLR 734. An example of misspelling is provided by *Durham Fancy Goods Ltd v Michael Jackson (Fancy Goods) Ltd* [1968] 2 QB 839 at p. 846 where this case is mistakenly referred to as *Atkins v Wardle*.

[24] *Hendon v Adelman* (1973) *The Times* 16 June.

[25] *Jenice Ltd v Dan* [1993] BCLC 1349, [1994] BCC 43.

[26] *Nassau Steam Press v Tyler* (1894) 70 LT 376.

[27] *Dermatine Co. v Ashworth* (1905) 21 TLR 510.

[28] *F. Stacey & Co. v Wallis* (1912) 106 LT 544. See also *Banque de L'Indochine v Euroseas Group Finance Co.* [1981] 3 All ER 198.

[29] *Scottish and Newcastle Breweries Ltd v Blair* 1967 SLT 72 at p. 74; *Lindholst & Co. A/S v Fowler* [1988] BCLC 166. Compare *Jenice Ltd v Dan*, above.

[30] Compare *Blum v OCP Repartition SA* [1988] BCLC 170, (1988) 4 BCC 771 and *Rafsanjan Pistachio Producers Cooperative v Reiss* [1990] BCLC 352, [1990] BCC 730.

[31] Section 28 (1).

[32] Or which ought to have appeared in that index at the time of the registration under the new name: section 28 (2) (*b*).

[33] Section 28 (2).

A change of name does not affect the legal identity of the company. Thus section 28 (7) provides that it will not affect any rights or obligations of the company or render defective any legal proceedings by or against the company. Any legal proceedings that might have been continued or commenced against the company by its former name may be continued or commenced against it by its new name.[34]

A company which is in the process of changing its name and which is awaiting a certificate of incorporation with its new name is *not* a company that has not been formed. Accordingly, there can be no question of the contracts which it enters into at that time being 'pre-incorporation' contracts for which those who act on its behalf could incur personal liability under section 36C of the Companies Act 1985.[35]

3.7 'Phoenix companies'

The Insolvency Act 1986 attempts to stamp out the notorious practice of incorporating 'phoenix companies'. A phoenix company is one which is formed with a name which is the same as, or very similar to, the name of a company which has recently gone into liquidation. The reason for choosing the same, or a very similar, name is usually to try to hide the fact that the earlier company has gone into liquidation from its creditors and thus ensure that the new company can continue to enjoy the goodwill of the old business.[36] Under section 216 of the Insolvency Act 1986, the directors[37] of a company which has gone into insolvent liquidation are prohibited[38] for a period of five years from being involved in another company which has the same name as one by which the old company was known[39] at any time in the period of twelve months preceding its liquidation or a name which is so similar as to suggest some association with the old company. Contravention of this prohibition attracts civil and criminal penalties.[40]

3.8 The registered office

Section 2 (1) (*b*) of the Companies Act 1985 requires the memorandum of every company to state 'whether the registered office of the company is to be situated in England and Wales, or in Scotland'.[41] The precise location of the registered office is not stated in the memorandum but this address must be notified to the Registrar of Companies as part of the process of incorporation.[42] The clause of the memorandum stating the jurisdiction in

---

[34] Cf. *Lin Pac Containers (Scotland) Ltd v Kelly* 1983 SLT 422.

[35] *Oshkosh B'Gosh Incorporated v Dan Marbel Incorporated Ltd* [1989] BCLC 507, (1988) 4 BCC 795, [1989] 1 CMLR 94. The directors could incur personal liability under section 349 (4) if they use the new name before the process of changing the name is complete because the company would have been misdescribed: *Allied Irish Bank plc v GFT Sales and Service Ltd* 1993 GWD 28–1789.

[36] But section 216 is not limited in its application to this particular form of abuse: *Thorne v Silverleaf* [1994] BCC 109.

[37] That is the persons who were directors at the time of liquidation or at any time in the preceding twelve months. Shadow directors are also caught: section 216 (1).

[38] Except with the leave of the court or as permitted by the Insolvency Rules 1986 (rules 4.228–4.230): section 216 (3).

[39] This includes business names as well as corporate names: section 216 (6).

[40] Section 216 (4) and section 217. See *Thorne v Silverleaf*, above.

[41] Special provision is made for companies whose registered office is in Wales to state this fact in their memorandum: section 2 (2). On companies with a registered office in Wales see *Gore-Browne on Companies* (Jordans, 44th edn, loose-leaf), 2.3.2.

[42] Section 10 (6).

which the registered office is situated cannot ordinarily[43] be changed but, subject to that limit, a company can change the precise location of its registered office by giving notice to the Registrar of Companies.[44] As a measure to ensure that any change in the precise location of a company's registered office is brought to the attention of the wider public, the Registrar must give official notification of the change in the *London Gazette.*[45]

The registered office of a company is the office to which all communications and notices may be addressed[46], and any writ, notice, summons or order is well served if left at, or sent by post[47] to, the registered office.[48] Service at other places where the company carries on business is not sufficient.[49]

Section 351 of the Companies Act 1985 requires the place of registration (i.e. England or Scotland), the registration number and the address of its registered office to be mentioned in legible characters in all business letters and order forms of the company.

3.9 The objects of the company

This clause in the memorandum is dealt with separately in Chapter 4.

3.10 The liability of the members

In the cases of companies limited by shares or by guarantee, with or without share capital, the fourth clause of the memorandum must simply state that 'The liability of the members is limited'. Those are the words contained in the forms given in the regulations made under the Companies Act 1985[50] and they should not be departed from. It is wrong to insert 'The liability of the *company* is limited'. Such a variation, if passed by the Registrar, might produce results disastrous to the members.

The most usual course is to frame the memorandum of association so as to limit the liability of each member or shareholder to the amount of the shares held by him. The meaning of this is that at no time can he be called upon to pay, either for the purpose of carrying on the company's business or of satisfying the claims of its creditors, a larger sum than remains unpaid on the shares which at the time of the call, or within a year before the commencement of the winding up of the company, were registered in his name. For example, if a member holds fifty shares of £1 each, his utmost liability is £50. When he

---

[43] Except that a company with a registered office in Wales can alter its memorandum to state that its registered office is situated in Wales rather than 'England and Wales': section 2 (2). Otherwise the Companies Act 1985 does not authorise amendments to this clause of the memorandum. A company could seek to obtain a private Act of Parliament for this purpose but the more practical alternative may be to form a subsidiary in the desired jurisdiction and to transfer the business of the company to it.

[44] Section 287 (3). The change takes effect when registered by the Registrar but for a period of fourteen days thereafter a person may validly serve a document on a company at its previous registered office: section 287 (4).

[45] Section 711. The consequences of official notification are discussed further at 3.14 below.

[46] Section 287 (1).

[47] Section 725 (1).

[48] *Pearks, Gunston & Tee v Richardson* [1902] 1 KB 91. See further as to the service of writs at the registered office *Gore-Browne* (Jordans, 44th edn, loose-leaf), 2.3.1.

[49] *British and Foreign Gas Generating Apparatus Co.* (1865) 12 LT 368; *Re Fortune Copper Mining Co.* (1871) 10 Eq 390. This is subject to section 42 (official notification) and section 287 (4) (service at previous registered office).

[50] See the Companies (Tables A to F) Regulations 1985 (SI 1985 No. 805), Tables B to D.

has paid a part, the balance only can be recovered from him. No alteration of the memorandum or articles of association after he becomes a member can bind him either to take up more shares than he held at the date when the alteration was made, or in any way increase his liability as at that date to contribute to the share capital of, or otherwise to pay money to, the company, unless he agrees in writing, either before or after the alteration is made, to be bound thereby.[51] Should he transfer his shares before the full amount is called up, his unsatisfied liability passes to the person who acquires them; but a contingent liability still attaches to a former holder to the limited extent that, if the company should go into liquidation within one year from the time of his parting with his shares, he may be called upon to contribute towards the payment of any debts contracted before he ceased to be a member, in the event of the company being unable to meet its liabilities in full, and the person who has acquired his shares failing to pay the balance owing on them.

Under the provisions of sections 306 and 307 of the 1985 Act, the directors or managers may take upon themselves an unlimited liability, although the liability of the other members is limited, this being similar to the distinction between general and limited partners under the Limited Partnerships Act 1907. Since the protection of limited liability is the main reason for registering a limited company, it is almost unknown for resort to be had to these provisions.

The second way of limiting the liability of members is by so framing the memorandum of association as to make each member guarantee a certain sum, which he can only be called upon to pay in the event of the company being wound up, and which will remain the same whatever his pecuniary interest in the company may be.[52]

3.11 The nominal capital

In the case of companies limited by shares the capital must[53] be divided into shares of a certain fixed amount, and a statement to that effect included in the memorandum: e.g. 'The share capital of the company is ten thousand pounds, divided into ten thousand shares of one pound each'.[54]

In the case of a company registered as a public limited company, the share capital clause must state a minimum share capital complying with that required for a public limited company (i.e. £50,000).[55]

A company limited by shares or by guarantee and having a share capital, if so authorised by its articles, may increase its nominal share capital by new shares of such amount as it thinks fit or may diminish the nominal share capital by cancelling shares which have not been taken up.[56]

---

[51] Section 16.

[52] See 2.9, above. As to unlimited companies, see 2.8.

[53] Section 2 (5) (*a*).

[54] The share capital can comprise shares of fixed amounts expressed in varying currencies (but each individual share must be expressed in one currency only): *Re Scandinavian Bank Group Plc* [1988] Ch 87.

[55] Section 118; see 2.2, above.

[56] Section 121 (2) (*a*) and (*e*). Cancellation of shares which have not been taken up is not a reduction of capital within the meaning of section 135.

3.12 Optional conditions in the memorandum

Any matter which might be provided for in the articles of association can instead be inserted in the memorandum. This is not wholly unusual in regard to the special class rights attaching to preferred shares. It is possible in this way to entrench such rights more strongly than if they were contained in the articles. The general question of class rights and their variation is examined later in Chapter 7. Here the restricted power to alter such provisions in the memorandum is considered.

3.13 Alteration of optional conditions in the memorandum

Section 2 (7) of the Companies Act 1985 prohibits the alteration, except in accordance with the Act, of the conditions contained in a company's memorandum. This prohibition is partly relaxed by section 17 which provides that any such condition which could lawfully have been contained in the articles instead of in the memorandum may be altered by special resolution. This is not to apply where the memorandum itself provides for or prohibits the alteration of such conditions. Nor does it authorise any variation or abrogation of class rights, which accordingly, if contained in the memorandum and not thereby made alterable,[57] will require either the unanimous consent of all the members of the company[58] or a scheme of arrangement under section 425 to effect a variation.[59]

The power given by section 17 is, moreover, subject to any restriction on the alteration of the memorandum existing by virtue of an order of the court under Part XVII of the 1985 Act;[60] nor will an alteration made under section 17 imposing a monetary liability on existing members bind them without their consent.[61]

Apart from provisions declaring the rights attached to different classes of shares, the memorandum rarely provides for matters which can be dealt with in the articles. Accordingly, it would seem that section 17 will have only a limited application as, for example, in such cases as *Re Society for Promoting Employment of Women*,[62] where the memorandum contained a clause restricting the application of income of the society, and it was held that the court had no jurisdiction to sanction an alteration of the provision, not being a provision with respect to the objects of the society.

When an alteration is made under the section, the shareholders (but not debenture holders) have the same right to apply to the court to cancel the variation as they have under section 5 in the case of an alteration of objects.[63]

---

[57] Where the memorandum does contain a provision for the alteration of class rights, the procedure stated must be followed. In certain cases the requirements of section 125 must be met. See 7.7.3, below.

[58] Section 125 (5).

[59] See Chapter 16.

[60] This gives the court power to give relief to minority shareholders. See 15.13, below.

[61] See section 16.

[62] [1927] WN 145.

[63] The section 5 procedure for objecting to an alteration to the objects is examined at 4.15, below. Section 17 (3) states that section 5 (except subsections (2) (*b*) and (8)) and section 6 (1) and (3) apply in relation to any alteration and to any application under section 17 as they apply to applications made under sections 4 to 6 of the 1985 Act.

3.14 Requirements as to the alteration of memorandum or articles

Section 711 of the Companies Act 1985 requires various documents there described to be published by the Registrar in the *Gazette*. Section 711 (1) (*b*) includes among this category a 'document making or evidencing an alteration in the memorandum or articles of association of a company'. The Registrar is required to state in the *Gazette* notice the name of the company, the description of the document and the date of receipt.

A company which does not furnish the Registrar with such information is put under a disability. Section 42 (1) provides that a company shall not be entitled to rely against other persons on the happening of certain 'events' – which include the alteration of the memorandum or articles of association – if the 'event' had not been officially notified (i.e. in the *Gazette*) at the material time.

Section 42 (1) then goes on to provide, as a qualification to the requirement of official notification, 'and is not shown by the company to have been known at the time to the person concerned'. Since the section is there not for the protection of the company but of outsiders dealing with the company, an outsider who is shown to have actual knowledge of the relevant event cannot insist that the company may not rely on the event because it failed to '*Gazette*' it.[64] Furthermore, it has been held by the Court of Appeal[65] that official notification of an event in the *Gazette* (as required by section 42 (1)) does not give constructive notice of the event in question to third parties. Its effect is merely to prevent the company relying on such an event which has not been duly '*Gazetted*'.

The term 'other person' in section 42 (1) would appear to bear the same meaning as 'a person dealing with the company' in section 35A.[66]

Section 42 (1) further provides that a company will not be entitled to rely on an event 'if the material time fell on or before the fifteenth day after the date of official notification (or where the fifteenth day was a non-business day,[67] on or before the next day that was not) and it was shown that the person concerned was unavoidably prevented from knowing of the event at that time'.

3.15 Filing of amendments to the memorandum and articles

Section 18 makes provision for the forwarding to the Registrar of a printed copy of any Act or instrument which varies a company's memorandum or articles together with a printed copy of the memorandum or articles as altered. Members of a company have a right to request copies of the memorandum and articles (if any) on payment of a fee.[68]

3.16 The contents of the articles of association

The articles of association govern the internal affairs of the company, and may from time to time be altered by the members to an almost unlimited extent.

---

[64] See article 3 (5) of the First Company Law Directive and *Official Custodian for Charities v Parway Estates Developments* [1985] Ch 151.

[65] *Official Custodian for Charities v Parway Estates*, above.

[66] See the discussion of the latter term at 4.21, below. In appropriate circumstances this might include the shareholders.

[67] Defined by section 42 (2) (*b*).

[68] Section 19. This right extends to any Act of Parliament amending the memorandum.

The articles of association regulate a great range of matters affecting almost every aspect of company law as it applies to each individual company. Such internal regulations are of course subject to the requirements of the Companies Acts and the general principles of company law laid down by the courts. The following[69] are some of the important matters which are commonly governed by the articles: voting rights and proxies,[70] the status and the powers of management of the board of directors,[71] shareholders'[72] and directors' meetings,[73] the payment of dividends,[74] the capitalisation of profits,[75] the transfer and transmission of shares,[76] the alteration of capital.[77] Detailed provisions in the articles are discussed, in their proper context in later chapters, in terms of the relevant articles of Table A. The purpose of this chapter is to examine certain more general questions about the articles of association. These are:

(1) the status of the articles as a contract of membership as defined by section 14;
(2) the drafting of articles of association and the adoption of Table A; and
(3) the power to alter the articles under section 9 and the equitable doctrine whereby the court may restrain the exercise of this power.

3.17 The articles as a contract: section 14

Section 14 (1) of the Companies Act 1985 provides that the memorandum and articles of association when registered bind the company and its members to the same extent as if each member had signed and sealed them and they contained a covenant by him to observe all the provisions contained in them. The effect of this[78] is to create an obligation binding alike on the members in their dealings with the company,[79] on the company in its dealings with the members as members,[80] and on the members in their dealings with one another as members.[81] Thus where the articles impose a duty on shareholders to purchase the shares of a member who wishes to dispose of them, such an individual right of membership can be directly enforced against the other shareholders without making the company a party.[82] It is not clear how far the rule in *Foss v Harbottle*[83] permits a minority shareholder to enforce any provision in the articles, as part of his contract of

---

[69] As to companies registered before 1 July 1985, see the Table A in the 1st Schedule to the 1948 Act (as amended). As to companies registered thereafter (under the 1985 Act), see the Companies (Tables A to F) Regulations 1985. References in this chapter to articles are to articles contained in the Companies (Tables A to F) Regulations 1985 unless otherwise indicated.

[70] Articles 54–63.

[71] Articles 64–87.

[72] Articles 36–53.

[73] Articles 88–98.

[74] Articles 102–108.

[75] Article 110.

[76] Articles 23–31.

[77] Articles 32–34.

[78] For a full discussion of the earlier authorities see *Hickman v Kent or Romney Marsh Sheep-Breeders' Association* [1915] 1 Ch 881.

[79] *Bradford Banking Co. v Henry Briggs & Co.* (1886) 12 App. Cas. 29. (HL); *Wood v Odessa Waterworks Co.* (1889) 42 Ch D 636; *Quin & Axtens v Salmon* [1909] AC 442 (HL); *Hickman v Kent or Romney Marsh Sheep-Breeders' Association*, above.

[80] *Oakbank Oil Co. v Crum* (1882) 8 App. Cas. 65 (HL).

[81] *Eley v Positive Government Security Life Assurance* (1876) 1 Ex. D 88 (CA).

[82] *Rayfield v Hands* [1960] Ch 1.

[83] (1843) 2 Hare 461.

membership, where no individual right of membership is concerned.[84] A member may seek to challenge a failure to comply with the articles under Part XVII of the 1985 Act on the grounds that this failure amounts to unfairly prejudicial conduct. However, Hoffmann LJ has stated that trivial or technical infringements of the articles are not intended to give rise to petitions under this Part.[85]

Although section 14 uses the language of contract, the section 14 contract is of a special kind, as was noted by Steyn LJ in *Bratton Seymour Service Co. Ltd v Oxborough*.[86] Distinctive features of the section 14 contract include the following:[87]

(1) it derives its binding force not from a bargain struck between the parties but from the terms of the statute:

(2) it is binding only in so far as it affects rights and obligations between the company and its members acting in their capacity as members;[88]

(3) it can be altered by special resolution without the consent of all of the contracting parties;[89]

(4) it is not defeasible on the grounds of misrepresentation, common law mistake, mistake in equity, undue influence or duress;

(5) it cannot be rectified on the grounds of mistake.[90]

In *Bratton Seymour* the Court of Appeal refused to imply a term into articles on the grounds of business efficacy which would have had the effect of imposing on members an obligation to make a financial contribution to certain expenses incurred by the company. The Court of Appeal indicated that terms would not easily be implied into articles from extrinsic circumstances[91] because of the special nature of the contract. Steyn LJ and Sir Christopher Slade emphasised the importance of third parties (in particular potential shareholders) being able to rely on the articles as registered.[92]

3.18 Outsiders' rights and the articles as a contract

In accordance with normal contractual principles, those who are not members cannot enforce the provisions of the articles either against the company or its members.[93] A special feature of the section 14 contract is that even a member cannot enforce provisions for his benefit in some other capacity than that of member: e.g. he cannot assert a right to

---

[84] This question is further considered at 15.3, below.

[85] *Re Saul D Harrison & Sons plc* [1994] BCC 475.

[86] [1992] BCC 471, [1992] BCLC 693.

[87] [1992] BCC at p. 475, [1992] BCLC at p. 698.

[88] This feature is discussed further at 3.18 below.

[89] Discussed at 3.24 below.

[90] *Evans v Chapman* [1902] WN 78; *Scott v Frank F Scott (London) Ltd* [1940] 1 Ch 794.

[91] This would not preclude the implication of a term purely from the language of the document itself: *Stanham v NTA* (1989) 15 ACLR 87 at pp. 90–1.

[92] See also *Mutual Life Insurance Co. v The Rank Organisation* [1985] BCLC 11 where Goulding J refused to imply pre-emption rights into articles. Limited pre-emption rights are now provided by statute: see 6.5, below.

[93] *Re Rotherham Chemical Co.* (1883) 25 Ch D 103; *Melhado v Porto Allegre Co.* (1874) LR 9 CP 503; *Re Empress Engineering Co.* (1881) 16 Ch D 125 (CA); *Re English and Colonial Produce Co.* [1906] 2 Ch 435. These cases establish that a clause in the articles requiring the company to pay preliminary charges cannot be enforced unless some other contract has been made. Equally a contract made with a trustee before the company is formed does not become enforceable merely because the articles purport to adopt the contract: *Re Northumberland Avenue Hotel Co.* (1886) 33 Ch D 16 (CA).

be appointed solicitor, secretary, or director[94] by reason of provisions contained only in the articles. So an article providing for the reference of disputes to arbitration may be enforceable by or against a member in his capacity as such, but not in some other capacity, e.g. that of director.[95] On the other hand the shareholder is not bound in his personal capacity. 'The purpose of the memorandum and articles is to define the position of the shareholder as shareholder, not to bind him in his capacity as an individual.'[96]

This special feature has received substantial criticism from some academic commentators.[97] It is objected that it rests solely upon Astbury J's decision in *Hickman v Kent or Romney Marsh Sheep-Breeders' Association*.[98] It is argued that his decision conflicts with earlier decisions which do not recognise the principle which Astbury J attempted to elicit from them. Moreover, it is said that the *Hickman* principle appears to ignore the wording of what is now section 14 (1) of the 1985 Companies Act, which creates a contractual obligation in respect of 'all the provisions of the memorandum and of the articles'. The view contended for by these commentators is that an 'outsider', so long as he sues in his capacity as shareholder, can compel the company not to depart from the contract with him under the articles. This is so even if that results indirectly in the enforcement of 'outsider' rights vested in third parties or in the plaintiff shareholder.

The somewhat unclear wording of section 14 (and its predecessors, e.g. section 16 of the 1862 Act and section 20 of the 1948 Act) long gave rise to conflicting judicial interpretation. This stemmed in part from the fact that though the memorandum and articles 'shall, when registered, bind the company and the members' this is based on a putative statutory signing and sealing by the members and not by the company. Likewise, the memorandum and articles are deemed to contain 'covenants on the part of each member' (but not the company) to observe their provisions.[99] Until the end of the nineteenth century the courts were divided as to the parties to this statutory contract of association (i.e. parties in the sense of having rights of action and liabilities thereunder). There were authorities both for and against there being a contract between the members *inter se*,[100] as well as both for and against section 14 creating a contract between the company and its members.[101]

As indicated above, the modern law was eventually settled that the section 14 contract confers rights between the company and its members and between the members *inter se*. However, the still conflicting reasoning in the cases (considered by Astbury J in *Hickman*)

[94] *Eley v Positive Government Security Life Assurance Co.*, above; *Browne v La Trinidad* (1888) 37 Ch D 1.

[95] *Hickman v Kent or Romney Marsh Sheep-Breeders' Association*, above; *Beattie v E. and F. Beattie* [1938] Ch 708; *London Sack and Bag Co. v Dixon* [1943] 2 All ER 763 (CA).

[96] *Per* Buckley LJ, *Bisgood v Henderson's Transvaal Estates* [1908] 1 Ch 743 at p. 759 (CA). See also *Baring-Gould v Sharpington Combined Pick and Shovel Syndicate* [1899] 2 Ch 80 (CA).

[97] See Gregory, 'The Section 20 Contract' 44 MLR 526 (1981). This amplifies views earlier expressed by Lord Wedderburn: [1957] CLJ 194 at pp. 212–13.

[98] Above.

[99] The explanation of this omission lies in the conveyancing background to this section. See 44 MLR 526 at pp. 528–9. Under the Companies Act of 1844 each shareholder executed an indenture with a trustee for the company. This incorporated or referred to the company's constitution. This requirement was dropped in the Companies Act of 1856. The covenant was simply deemed to exist by the statute but no covenant with the company was expressed.

[100] Compare *Eley v Positive Government Security Life Association Co.* (1870) LR 1 Ex. 88 at p. 89, with *Welton v Saffery* [1897] AC 299 at p. 315 *per* Lord Herschell.

[101] Compare *Johnson v Lyttle's Iron Agency* (1877) 5 Ch D 687 at p. 693, with *Browne v La Trinidad* (1888) 37 Ch D 1 at pp. 12 and 15.

induced his attempt to provide a perhaps novel reconciling principle with regard to the scope of the contactual effect of the articles.[102] It must be readily conceded that the case-law is still in a state of some confusion and that in some situations the courts have allowed a member, suing as such, to enforce a non-shareholder right conferred by the articles. This has been done to protect shareholder-directors whose rights to hold office, or to participate in management, or to exercise a veto over board decisions or to commence litigation, have been brushed aside in breach of a provision in the articles.[103] However, it is a long step from this to conclude that every shareholder has a right to have all and every one of the articles enforced by declaration or injunction.[104] To do so is to ignore not only the authorities on the *Hickman* principle (which, whatever its questionable provenance, has never been overruled and has been applied by the Court of Appeal).[105] It also overlooks the rule in *Foss v Harbottle*[106] and the related question of the majority shareholders' right to ratify some, but not all, breaches of the articles.[107] The contemporary Court of Appeal has, on more than one occasion, indicated that the members' contract of association cannot be used to 'short-circuit' the rule in *Foss v Harbottle*, especially in the case of shareholders' actions to remedy directors' breaches of fiduciary duty to the company.[108] This is clearly of more significance than the confusion of the courts in the late nineteenth century as to the parties to the statutory contract of association.[109] The point is reinforced by Steyn LJ's comments in *Bratton Seymour* which indicate that it is incorrect to attach too much importance to the 'contractual' nature of the relationship formed by section 14 between a company and its members (and between the members *inter se*) since the normal incidents of a contract do not necessarily apply.

---

[102] The earlier cases were influenced by other grounds than the *Hickman* principle: e.g. the old view that members were not parties to the contract (*Baring-Gould v Sharpington Combined Pick and Shovel Syndicate* [1899] 2 Ch 80) or that the article in question was directory rather than mandatory (*Pritchard's Case* (1873) 8 Ch App. 956 at p. 960), or that the plaintiff, as a matter of procedural form, sued not as a member but in some external capacity (e.g. as a solicitor or promoter): *Eley v Positive Government Security Life Association Co.*, above. See 44 MLR 531–9.

[103] e.g. *Imperial Hydropathic Hotel v Hamson* (1882) 23 Ch D 1, *Pulbrook v Richmond Consolidated Mining Co.* (1878) 9 Ch D 610, *Quin and Axtens v Salmon* [1909] AC 442, *Hayes v Bristol Plant Hire* [1957] 1 All ER 688, *Breckland Group Holdings Ltd v London and Suffolk Properties Ltd* [1989] BCLC 100, noted Wedderburn (1989) 52 MLR 401. Attempts have been made by commentators to explain, on 'organic' or constitutional grounds, when the courts will allow 'non-shareholder rights' in the articles to be enforced. See Goldberg 35 MLR 362 (1972), Bastin [1977] JBL 17, Prentice 1 Co. Law 179 (1980).

[104] It is clear that (claims for arrears of dividend and the like aside) damages will not be awarded for breach of this very special contract. This alone may indicate its special character: a case perhaps of *ibi remedium, ubi jus*.

[105] *Beattie v E. and F. Beattie Ltd* [1938] Ch 708 at pp. 713–14. See also *London Sack and Bag Co. Ltd v Dixon* [1943] 2 All ER 763.

[106] (1843) 2 Hare 461.

[107] See *Grant v UK Switchback Railways* (1889) 40 Ch D 135 (CA).

[108] See *Bamford v Bamford* [1970] Ch 212, *Prudential Assurance v Newman Industries (No. 2)* [1982] Ch 204. See a further discussion of these issues at 15.3 and 15.4, below.

[109] See further R. R. Drury, 'The Relative Nature of a Shareholder's Right to Enforce the Company Contract'. [1986] CLJ 219. This is an interesting attempt to reconcile the cases on the basis that the courts weigh various factors in the balance in deciding whether to enforce the shareholder's 'relative right'. This is more satisfying than some earlier theories in coming to grips with the institutional reality produced by the shareholder's contract. It still remains open to the criticism levied at earlier theories that it is essentially an *ex post facto* rationalisation.

3.19 Contracts incorporating provisions in the articles

If individuals have been engaged in some capacity without an agreement setting out the terms of employment,[110] the articles may be looked at to see what these terms are. On this footing the directors may be sued for payment of their qualification shares or sue for the remuneration specified in the articles,[111] and in any other case where a contract is established, but the terms do not appear, the articles may be referred to for the purpose of supplying the terms.[112]

3.20 The character of obligations in the memorandum or articles

All money payable in pursuance of the memorandum or articles becomes in England a 'speciality debt' from the members to the company,[113] so that the debt remains enforceable for twelve years before the Limitation Act 1980 affords a good defence to proceedings. It has been held that money payable from the company to the members in pursuance of the articles is not a speciality debt so that the relevant limitation period is that which applies to actions based on simple contract, namely six years.[114] A restriction in the articles of a company on the distribution of dividends was not 'imposed by law' for the purposes of a taxing statute. Rather it was imposed by the company since it was free to alter its articles to remove the restriction.[115]

3.21 Drafting articles: invalid provisions

The articles cannot vary rights given by the Companies Act, and must be rejected if inconsistent with the Act or the general law.

Articles cannot deprive a company of the powers which are conferred on it by statute: thus a provision in the articles which purports to make them unalterable is invalid because a company is empowered by section 9 of the Companies Act 1985 to alter its articles by special resolution.[116]

Articles cannot free a member from paying in full for his shares, or deprive members of their right to petition for the winding up of the company or to dissent in a reconstruction under what is now section 110 of the Insolvency Act 1986,[117] nor can they validly provide for the transfer of shares without a written instrument of transfer contrary to section 183.[118]

---

[110] *Boston Deep Sea Fishing and Ice Co. v Ansell* (1888) 39 Ch D 339 (CA).

[111] *Re New British Iron Co., ex parte Beckwith* [1898] 1 Ch 324. On the relevance of the articles to directors' service contracts, see 13.4, below.

[112] *Pritchard's Case* (1873) 8 Ch App 956; *Swabey v Port Darwin Co.* (1889) 1 Meg. 385 (CA); *Boston Deep Sea and Ice Fishing Co. v Ansell* (1888) 39 Ch D 339 at p. 366 (CA).

[113] Section 14 (2).

[114] *Re Compania de Electricidad de la Provincia de Buenos Aires Ltd* [1980] 1 Ch 146.

[115] *Noble (Inspector of Taxes) v Laygate Investments Ltd* [1978] 1 WLR 1457.

[116] *Walker v London Tramways Co.* (1879) 12 Ch D 705; *Allen v Gold Reefs of West Africa* [1900] 1 Ch 656 at p. 671; *Southern Foundries (1926) Ltd v Shirlaw* [1940] AC 701 at p. 739; *Russell v Northern Bank Development Corporation* [1992] 3 All ER 294, [1992] 1 WLR 588, [1992] BCLC 1016, [1992] BCC 578. The power to alter articles and the extent to which (if it all) it can be fettered are discussed further at 3.24–3.25 below.

[117] *Welton v Saffery* [1897] AC 299 (HL); *Re Peveril Gold Mines* [18989] 1 Ch 122 (CA); *Payne v Cork Co.* [1900] 1 Ch 308.

[118] *Re Greene* [1949] Ch 333. See 8.3.3, below, which notes proposals for the trading of shares in uncertificated form.

3.22 Drafting articles: adoption of Table A

Companies limited by guarantee, and unlimited companies,[119] must register articles of association with the memorandum; but a company limited by shares may either be registered with special articles of association, or may, without registering articles, rely upon the regulations in Table A. When special articles are not adopted, the memorandum must be endorsed 'registered without articles of association', and every member of the company will be bound by the regulations contained in Table A.[120]

A new Table A (prescribed by regulations of the Secretary of State[121]) came into operation with the Companies Act 1985 and, unless excluded, this applies to all companies which register under that Act. The 1985 Act Table A will obviously apply to more and more companies as time goes by, but very many companies now in existence were registered under the Companies Acts 1948 and 1980, and for those companies the applicable Table A (so far as it is not excluded) is the Table A contained in Schedule 1 to the Companies Act 1948 or, depending on the date of incorporation, the 1948 Act Table A as amended by subsequent companies legislation.[122] There are still of course a number of companies registered under the Companies Acts of 1862, 1908 and 1929 and in each case the relevant Table A is applicable.

Large companies almost always adopt their own special regulations in which case the articles begin with a provision to the effect that the relevant Table A is excluded. Where a company is adopting new articles and excluding Table A, the Table A to be excluded is that in force at the date of the company's registration. Other companies, instead of wholly excluding Table A, may adopt the suitable parts of that Table, with a few special articles containing the desired modifications. In such cases, the articles will commence with a provision to the effect that the regulations contained in the relevant Table A are to apply to the company, save in so far as they are excluded or varied. In cases of this kind it is a good plan to attach copies of Table A to the articles, so that each member who obtains a copy may have the whole of the regulations before him. It may be observed that Table A, or such portions of it as are adopted, need not be registered.

The articles must be printed and divided into paragraphs numbered consecutively.[123] The original articles must be signed by each subscriber to the memorandum and attested by a witness.[124]

Every company is bound to supply any of its members, on request, with a copy of its memorandum and articles (if any), upon payment of a sum not exceeding 5p. Where alteration has been made in the memorandum every copy issued after the alteration must be in accordance with the alteration. There must also be supplied on request, at a charge

[119] Unlimited companies registering under the Companies Act 1985 may adopt the form of articles contained in Table E of the Companies (Tables A to F) Regulations 1985 (SI 1985 No. 805). See section 8 (4) of the Companies Act 1985. Likewise a private company limited by guarantee (and not having a share capital) may adopt Table C and a company limited by guarantee and having a share capital may adopt Table D of those Regulations.

[120] Section 8 (2).

[121] Section 8 (1) and the Companies (Tables A to F) Regulations 1985 (SI 1985 No. 805). Having Table A in regulations rather than as a Schedule to primary legislation (as was previously the position) provides greater flexibility because it means that amendments can be made without the need for primary legislation.

[122] Section 8 (3) makes it clear that companies registered before the Companies Act 1985 came into operation continue to be governed by the articles which were in force at the time of registration.

[123] Section 7 (3).

[124] For the procedure on registration of memorandum and articles see 2.5, above.

not exceeding the published price thereof, a copy of any Act of Parliament which alters the memorandum.[125]

When Table A was contained in a Schedule to the Companies Act of the day it clearly had statutory force, and accordingly companies could safely adopt any operative regulations it contained without fear of such regulations proving invalid.[126] It may still be argued that the Table A to the Companies Act 1985 (though contained in a statutory instrument and no longer a Schedule to the Act itself) has statutory force by virtue of the wording of section 8.

3.23 Table G

The Companies Act 1989 inserted a provision into the Companies Act 1985 which empowers the Secretary of State to prescribe by regulations a Table G containing articles of association for a partnership company. A 'partnership company' is defined for this purpose as a company limited by shares whose shares are intended to be held to a substantial extent by or on behalf of its employees.[127]

At the time of writing, regulations prescribing Table G have not yet been passed, but the Department of Trade and Industry is consulting on their possible scope and content.[127a]

3.24 Alteration of articles: section 9

Section 9 of the Companies Act 1985 provides that the articles of a company may, subject to the provisions of the Act and to the conditions in the memorandum, be altered by special resolution. The company can amend both its own tailor-made articles and the provisions of Table A which it has adopted in this way. That articles may be altered with the consent of three-quarters of those voting on the resolution (i.e. the majority required for a special resolution[128]) and unanimity is not required is one illustration of the way in which the statutory contract formed by the articles of association differs from a normal contract.[129] Where all of the members who would have been entitled to attend and vote at a meeting to consider a resolution to change the articles consent informally to an alteration, that is also effective[130] but altering the articles by unanimous consent is likely to be feasible only in the very smallest of companies. Exceptionally, a long period of acquiescence under particular articles may be held to be effective even though they have not been adopted as the articles of the company.[131] Articles may also be altered by statute.[132]

The company has power to adopt any new article which could lawfully have been included in the original articles.[133] However, it is clearly established that no majority of shareholders can by altering the articles retrospectively affect, to the prejudice of

---

[125] Sections 19 and 20.

[126] *Lock v Queensland Investment and Mortgage Co.* [1896] AC 461 (HL).

[127] Section 8A of the Companies Act 1985, inserted by section 128 of the Companies Act 1989.

[127a] See the consultative document *Model Articles of Association for Partnership Companies* (Table G), issued in March 1995.

[128] Section 378(2).

[129] *Bratton Seymour v Oxborough*, above.

[130] *Cane v Jones* [1981] 1 All ER 533, [1980] 1 WLR 1451.

[131] *Ho Tung v Man On Insce Co.* [1902] AC 232.

[132] Section 18 of the Companies Act 1985.

[133] *Sidebottom v Kershaw, Leese & Co.* [1920] 1 Ch 154.

non-consenting owners of shares, rights already existing under a contract,[134] nor take away rights already accrued: for example, after a transfer of shares is lodged the company cannot create a right of lien so as to defeat the transfer.[135]

Requirements as to the procedure for effecting an alteration of the articles were introduced by the European Communities Act 1972 and are now contained in sections 18, 42 and 711 of the Companies Act 1985. These are the same as for alterations of provisions in the memorandum. They are discussed under this heading at 3.14–3.15, above.

3.25 Agreements not to alter the articles and voting agreements

A company cannot deprive itself of the power to alter its articles by special resolution by a statement to that effect in its articles of association.[136] But can a company enter into a contract outside the articles whereby it undertakes not to alter its articles or some part of them? This question has given rise to conflicting case-law but in the most recent opportunity to consider the problem the House of Lords has finally provided a definitive ruling.

In principle, there are three possible answers to the question whether, or to what extent, an extrinsic contract by a company not to alter its articles is valid, namely:

(1) such a contract is entirely ineffective;
(2) such a contract cannot prevent a company from exercising its statutory power to alter the articles but in that event the company will be in breach of contract and may be liable to pay damages to the other contracting party;
(3) such a contract is effective and in a suitable case the company can be prevented by injunction from seeking to exercise the statutory power to alter its articles.

Which of these propositions is correct depends essentially on the extent to which the powers conferred by the Companies Act 1985 must be viewed as a mandatory code which cannot be modified, as opposed to a series of standard provisions which a company might ordinarily want to adopt but which it can depart from as it thinks fit.

The proposition that a contract not to alter articles is effective but only to the extent of giving rise to a claim for damages in the event of breach was supported by *Punt v Symons*.[137] This was subsequently considered in *British Murac Syndicate Ltd v Alperton Rubber Co. Ltd*[138] where it was held that a contract not to alter articles was capable of being enforced by way of injunction, *Punt v Symons* being treated as having been implicitly overruled by a later Court of Appeal decision. On closer examination the analysis in *British Murac* is questionable. In the Court of Appeal decision relied upon, *Baily v British Equitable Assurance Co.*,[139] the court actually granted a declaration rather than an in-

---

[134] *Per* Rigby LJ in *James v Buena Ventura Syndicate* [1896] 1 Ch 456 at p. 466; *per* Lord Watson in *Welton v Saffery*, above at p. 309; *per* Vaughan Williams LJ in *Allen v Gold Reefs of West Africa*, above at p. 676.

[135] *McArthur v Gulf Line* 1909 SC 732.

[136] *Walker v London Tramways Co.*, above; *Allen v Gold Reefs of West Africa*, above; *Southern Foundries (1926) Ltd v Shirlaw*, above; *Russell v Northern Bank Development Corporation*, above.

[137] [1903] 2 Ch 505 following an unreported case in the Court of Appeal. *Malleson v National Insurance Corp.* [1894] 1 Ch 200, in spite of the headnote, is not an authority for this proposition.

[138] [1915] 2 Ch 186.

[139] [1904] 1 Ch 373 (reversed by House of Lords [1906] AC 35 but not on grounds relevant to this point).

junction. Also, this decision was not precisely in point, because the Court of Appeal was mainly concerned with the wider principle (well established by other authorities) that a company cannot by altering its articles justify a breach of an extrinsic contract. In *Cumbrian Newspapers Group Ltd v Cumberland & Westmorland Herald Newspaper & Printing Co. Ltd*[140] Scott J put forward a different interpretation. In Scott J's view the power to alter articles belonged to the members rather than to the company.[141] Accordingly, a promise by a company not to alter the articles amounted to no more than a promise not to *initiate* the process of alteration. Scott J considered that in appropriate cases an injunction could be granted to prevent the company from breaching this contract.

In *Russell v Northern Bank Development Corporation*[142] the House of Lords finally clarified the issue. This case concerned a contract by a company not to alter the nominal capital clause in its memorandum but the principles discussed are equally applicable to contracts not to alter the articles. The House of Lords ruled that an extrinsic contract by a company not to alter its articles was as obnoxious as a provision to that effect contained in the articles themselves. It was entirely invalid and could not be enforced even by way of damages.

Despite this unequivocal rejection of the freedom of the company to contract out of its statutory powers, the House of Lords upheld the right of individual shareholders to enter into contracts regarding the exercise of their votes.[143] This right is consistent with the well-established principle that a vote attached to a share is a property right to be exercised as its owner thinks fit.[144] Thus, the position now is that a company may not contract not to alter its articles, but its shareholders may agree amongst themselves that they will not vote in favour of a proposal to alter the articles and in a suitable case this shareholders' agreement can be enforced by injunction.[145] This means that it may be possible to achieve the aim of ensuring that articles are entrenched by drafting the agreement in the form of a shareholders' agreement rather than a covenant by the company itself. However, it may not be practicable to enter into a shareholders' agreement which is effective for this purpose where the company has a large number of shareholders: a shareholders' agreement will only ensure that the articles cannot be changed where the parties to it have sufficient voting strength to block the passing of a special resolution, since, as a normal contract, a shareholders' agreement will of course not be binding on non-contracting shareholders. Even where a company has only a few shareholders, the entrenching effect of a shareholders' agreement not to vote in favour of an alteration to

---

[140] [1987] Ch 1.

[141] An interpretation which seems rather at odds with the wording of section 9: '. . . a *company* may by special resolution alter its articles' (emphasis added).

[142] Above. See further Ferran, 'The Decision of the House of Lords in *Russell v Northern Bank Development Corporation Limited*' [1994] CLJ 343. A narrower interpretation of the ratio in *Russell* is suggested by Davenport, 'What Did *Russell v Northern Bank Development Corporation Ltd* Decide?' (1993) 109 LQR 553. Other comments on the decision in *Russell* include Riley, 'Vetoes and Voting Agreements: Some Problems of Consent and Knowledge', (1993) 44 NILQ 34; Sealy, 'Shareholders' Agreements – An Endorsement and a Warning from the House of Lords', [1992] CLJ 437; Shapira, 'Voting Agreements and Corporate Statutory Powers', (1993) 109 LQR 210.

[143] Lord Jauncey of Tullichettle, who delivered the Opinion of the House, found support for this conclusion in *Welton v Saffery* at p. 331.

[144] Leading authorities are *Pender v Lushington* (1877) 6 Ch D 70; *Northern Counties Securities Ltd v Jackson & Steeple Ltd* [1974] 1 WLR 1133; *North-West Transportation Co. Ltd v Beatty* (1887) 12 App. Cas. 589.

[145] The possibility of a shareholders' agreement being enforced by injunction was accepted in *Russell*, although the only remedy sought and granted in that case was a declaration.

the articles may not survive when a new shareholder, who is not party to the agreement, joins the company.[146]

Shareholders' agreements are often encountered in the type of company which is commonly referred to as a 'quasi-partnership' company where, despite the corporate form, the individuals forming the company intend to run their operations on partnership lines. By entering into a shareholders' agreement each individual seeks to protect himself against the principle of majority rule, which is the normal hallmark of corporate decision making, and to ensure that the bargain which he reached with his 'partners' when they established the business cannot be changed without his consent.

3.26 Acting on altered articles

Although a company may not contract not to alter its articles, acting on altered articles may amount to a breach of an earlier contractual promise which the company has given. The distinction between the situations is illustrated by *Southern Foundries (1926) Ltd v Shirlaw*,[147] where the company altered its articles to remove directors from office and then used this power to remove Shirlaw, the managing director, from his office. The House of Lords held that this action breached Shirlaw's service contract and ordered the company to pay damages. Lord Porter summarised the approach of the House in the following terms:

> The general principle therefore may, I think, be thus stated. A company cannot be precluded from altering its articles thereby giving itself power to act upon the provisions of the altered articles – but so to act may nevertheless be a breach of contract if it is contrary to a stipulation in a contract validly made before the alteration.[148]

In a suitable case, an injunction might be granted to prevent a company acting on its altered articles in breach of an earlier contract.[149] Although the distinction may be quite fine, this does not infringe the principle that a company cannot fetter its power to alter the articles, because the company is not actually prevented from altering the articles and can rely on the altered articles against everyone apart from parties to the earlier contract in whose favour the court is persuaded to grant the discretionary remedy of an injunction.

The power to alter articles is subject to any class rights which may be attached to particular shares. Class rights are discussed in Chapter 7.

3.27 'Bona fide for the benefit of the company as a whole'

The power conferred by section 9 of the Companies Act 1985 to alter the articles by resolution may not be abused by a majority of shareholders so as to oppress the

---

[146] To bind the new shareholder, the agreement regarding voting rights would have to be in the articles but such a provision in the articles would be regarded as an invalid fetter on the statutory power: *Russell* [1992] 3 All ER at p. 167. But this would not preclude the formation of a new shareholders' agreement to which the new shareholder is a party.

[147] [1940] AC 701. *Baily v British Equitable Life Assurance Co.*, above, is also more concerned with the consequences of acting on altered articles than with a contract not to alter articles.

[148] At pp. 740–1.

[149] *Allen v Gold Reefs of West Africa* at p. 672 *per* Lindley LJ, quoted by Lord Wright in *Shirlaw* at p. 725. On this point see further Trebilcock, 'The Effect of Alterations to Articles of Association' (1967) 31 Con (NS) 95 at pp. 113–16.

minority.[150] Even though a special resolution, valid in all respects as to form, has been passed as required by section 9, the minority may have it set aside for 'fraud on a minority'.[151] The courts will intervene where it is established that the majority have *not* acted 'bona fide in the interests of the company as a whole'. This equitable principle was first clearly stated by Lord Lindley in *Allen v Gold Reefs of West Africa*.[152]

Later cases have sought to elucidate the precise meaning of the phrase 'bona fide for the benefit of the company as a whole.'[153] It is clear that a heavy burden of proof rests on those seeking to prevent alteration of the articles. It must be shown that the object of the majority in altering the articles is not capable of being for the benefit of the company as a whole.[154]

Some first instance decisions suggest that 'bona fides' and 'the interests of the company as a whole' are separate requirements so that, regardless of the view of the majority, an alteration can be held to be invalid where, on an objective assessment, the court concludes that it is not in the interests of the company.[155] These cases have not been overruled but the Court of Appeal has strongly criticised the reasoning in the earlier first instance judgments[156] and has repeatedly affirmed that corporate benefit is not an independent ground for intervention: 'bona fides in the interests of the company' is a single composite standard by which the majority decision is to be judged.[157] The better view is that it is primarily for the majority to decide what is in the interests of the company, since in principle the majority is best qualified to decide this question. It is thus a subjective rather than an objective test.

3.28 A malicious alteration

If it can be shown that the majority acted maliciously or fraudulently, the alteration will not be allowed to stand because it cannot be said that the majority has acted bona fide in the interests of the company.[158] Malice for this purpose is used in the sense of a desire to harm or injure the minority.[159] Even if, on objective grounds, the alteration would be justifiable as being for the benefit of the company, it will be tainted by the bad motive of the majority. In *Sidebottom v Kershaw & Leese* the articles were altered to allow the company compulsorily to acquire the shares of any member who was in competition with the

---

[150] The same principle would apply to a resolution altering shareholders' rights where these are set forth in the memorandum, though the decided cases have concerned the alteration of the articles.

[151] The principle considered here is only one form of the wider concept of 'fraud on a minority'. See further 15.4, below.

[152] [1900] 1 Ch 656 at p. 671 (CA). A provision in the original articles of association, which might be open to attack if introduced as an alteration, will not be set aside on this basis. *Borland's Trustee v Steel Bros. Co. Ltd* [1901] 1 Ch 279; *Phillips v Manufacturers' Securities Ltd* (1917) 86 LJ Ch 305 (a power of compulsory acquisition of shares).

[153] These cases are examined thoroughly by Rixon, 'Competing Interests and Conflicting Principles: An Examination of the Power of Alteration of Articles of Association', (1986) 49 MLR 446.

[154] *Dafen Tinplate Co v Llanelly Steel Co.* [1920] 2 Ch 124, 137; *Sidebottom v Kershaw, Leese & Co.* [1920] 1 Ch 154 at pp. 163–4 and p. 169 (CA); *Shuttleworth v Cox Bros. & Co.* [1927] 2 KB 9 at pp. 18, 23, and 27 (CA).

[155] *Brown v British Abrasive Wheel Co.* [1919] 1 Ch 290; *Dafen Tinplate Co. v Llanelly Steel Co.* [1920] 2 Ch 124.

[156] *Sidebottom v Kershaw, Leese & Co. Ltd*, above at p. 172 where Astbury J in *Brown* is said by Warrington LJ to have 'confused himself' by treating bona fides and corporate benefit as separate things; see also Lord Sterndale MR at p. 167. The reasoning in *Dafen* was criticised by the Court of Appeal in *Shuttleworth*, especially at pp. 19, 22 and 27.

[157] See *Sidebottom* at pp. 163 and 172; *Shuttleworth* at pp. 18 and 22; and *Greenhalgh v Arderne Cinemas Ltd* [1951] Ch 286 at p. 291.

[158] *Sidebottom* at p. 163.

[159] *Sidebottom*, above at p. 161 *per* Lord Sterndale MR.

company's business. The Court of Appeal considered that this alteration in fact benefited the company but indicated that it would not have stood if the evidence had shown that the alteration was directed at an individual for any malicious motive or with any dishonest intention.[160] In *Shuttleworth v Cox* the articles were altered to add an additional event which disqualified a director from office. In the circumstances the Court of Appeal concluded that there was no 'trace of any vindictiveness or bad motive'[161] or of the decision having been taken 'maliciously, or with any desire to spite the plaintiff, or from any motive but that of doing what they thought best in the interest of the company';[162] it can be inferred that the alteration would not have stood if there had been such evidence.

Those seeking to prevent an alteration to articles becoming effective may find it difficult to establish positive evidence of malice, especially since, in all but the very smallest of companies, what will be in issue will be the motives of the group of persons who comprise the majority of the shareholders, rather than that of one majority shareholder. An inference may be drawn where an alteration is so oppressive of the minority as to cast suspicions on the honesty of the majority[163] but it is important to note that the mere fact that an alteration is directed at a particular individual may not, in itself, constitute sufficient evidence of oppression for such an inference to be drawn.[164] In both *Sidebottom* and *Shuttleworth* the articles were altered to enable the company to rid itself of a particular individual but in both cases the Court of Appeal considered that in the circumstances the action of the majority was not suspicious: in *Sidebottom* the circumstances surrounding the alteration were that the individual against whom it was directed could exploit the information which came to him as a shareholder for the benefit of his own business and to the detriment of the company, whilst in *Shuttleworth* the individual had already been validly dismissed from his employment as managing director because of his laxity in running the company's affairs. Again, in *Allen v Gold Reefs of West Africa* the company altered its articles to impose a lien on fully paid shares. The background to the alteration was that one shareholder owed a particularly large debt to the company and the imposition of the lien was one way of giving the company some security for the debt. Although the alteration was thus directed at one particular individual, it was upheld.

3.29 An alteration outside the bounds of reasonableness

It is not for the court to impose its own view of what is reasonable on the company but if the alteration is such that no reasonable body of persons could consider it for the benefit of the company, it will not be allowed to stand.[165] In *Shuttleworth* Bankes LJ indicated that an apt analogy is that of the grounds on which an appellate court will quash the verdict of a jury.[166] Bankes LJ also stated an alternative test which could be suitable in some cases: whether the action of the majority is capable of being considered for the benefit of the company.[167]

The absence of any reasonable grounds for deciding that an alteration is for the benefit

---

[160] At p. 166 *per* Lord Sterndale MR and at p. 172 *per* Warrington LJ.
[161] At p. 17 *per* Bankes LJ.
[162] At p. 21 *per* Scrutton LJ.
[163] *Shuttleworth* at p. 18 *per* Bankes LJ and at p. 27 *per* Atkin LJ; *Rights & Issues Investment Trust Ltd v Stylo Shoes Ltd* [1965] 1 Ch 250.
[164] *Sidebottom* at p. 173 *per* Eve J.
[165] *Shuttleworth* at p. 18 *per* Bankes LJ.
[166] ibid. at p. 18.
[167] ibid. at pp. 18–19.

of the company does not necessarily indicate malice but the alteration can still be set aside because the majority has not considered the matters which it ought to have considered.[168] In this respect, the 'jury' test is slightly wider than the malice test. Nevertheless, as the decisions of the Court of Appeal in *Sidebottom* and *Shuttleworth* indicate, it is still extremely difficult to persuade a court to set aside an alteration on this ground. An example of a claim that might succeed is where the articles are altered to allow the majority an unlimited power to expropriate or acquire compulsorily the shares of the minority and there are no valid commercial reasons, as there were in *Sidebottom* and *Shuttleworth*, to explain that alteration.[169] Another is if the majority alter the articles so as to restrict the dividend that would otherwise be due to the minority.[170]

3.30 The discrimination test and the 'interests of the company as a whole'

In *Greenhalgh v Arderne Cinemas Ltd*[171] Lord Evershed MR formulated another way of testing whether an alteration is bona fide in the interests of the company as a whole: an alteration would be liable to be impeached 'if the effect of it were to discriminate between the majority shareholders and the minority shareholders, so as to give the former an advantage of which the latter were deprived'. Taken out of context, this comment may suggest that the circumstances in which the court can invalidate an alteration are judged on objective grounds but passages elsewhere in the judgment of the Master of the Rolls confirm that what is for 'the benefit of the company' is primarily for the majority of the shareholders to decide.[172] Also, the actual decision in *Greenhalgh* indicates that the discrimination test is not satisfied simply because, objectively, the alteration favours the majority over the minority: the articles were altered to allow existing members to sell their shares to outsiders provided they had the sanction of an ordinary resolution of the shareholders in general meeting; if the majority wanted to sell its shares to an outsider it would be assured of obtaining the necessary resolution but the minority would not; this objective discrimination against the minority did not invalidate the alteration. Unfortunately, the decision leaves open what type of discrimination is required for the court to intervene on this ground.[173]

Lord Evershed MR also formulated his test in this way:[174] 'the case may be taken of an individual hypothetical member and it may be asked whether what is proposed is, in the honest opinion of those who voted in its favour, for that person's benefit'. The concept of 'an individual hypothetical member' is difficult to grasp and this test has not proved to be easy to apply. In *Clemens v Clemens*[175] the company had two shareholders and, in

---

[168] *Shuttleworth* at p. 23 *per* Scrutton LJ. *Estmanco (Kilner House) Ltd v GLC* [1982] 1 All ER 437 at p. 444 *per* Megarry V-C: 'Where the majority shareholders genuinely believe that it is in the best interests of the company as a whole, ... that is decisive, unless no reasonable shareholder in their position could hold this belief'.

[169] *Dafen Tinplate v Llanelly Steel*, on its facts, could support the proposition in the text because the alteration went further than what was required in the company's interest.

[170] *Dafen* at p. 143.

[171] Above at p. 291.

[172] At p. 291.

[173] Discrimination as a basis for impeaching an alteration of articles is mentioned by Pennycuick J in *Rights & Issues Investment Trust Ltd v Stylo Shoes Ltd* [1965] 1 Ch 250 but the meaning of 'discrimination' for this purpose is not explained.

[174] At p. 291.

[175] [1976] 2 All ER 268.

purported reliance on the *Greenhalgh* hypothetical member test, Foster J considered whether in voting on a particular resolution the majority shareholder had honestly believed that it would benefit the plaintiff who was the minority shareholder. The representative member chosen by Foster J could hardly be described as hypothetical;[176] but how such a member could have been constructed from the circumstances of the dispute defies description since it is difficult to see what common benefit could have transcended the interests of the warring factions. A further criticism of the hypothetical member test is that it seems to require the majority to act altruistically; this does not sit easily with the principle that a vote attached to a share is a property right which can be used as the owner of the share thinks fit. Lord Evershed MR himself acknowledged that persons in the majority did not have to disassociate themselves from their own interests when voting on the resolution to alter the articles.[177]

An important aspect of the decision in *Greenhalgh* is what Lord Evershed MR had to say about the meaning of the phrase 'the company as a whole'. The company is of course an entity distinct and separate from its shareholders and in cases such as *Allen v Gold Reefs*, *Sidebottom* and *Shuttleworth* it may be sufficient to consider whether the alteration is capable of being in the interests of the company as a commercial entity. However, cases such as *Greenhalgh* involve alterations which affect groups of shareholders differently but which have little or no effect on the company as a commercial entity; accordingly, 'the phrase, "the company as a whole", does not (at any rate in such a case as the present) mean the company as a commercial entity, distinct from the corporators: it means the corporators as a general body'.[178]

In *Peter's American Delicacy Co. Ltd v Heath*[179] the High Court of Australia accepted the need to distinguish alterations to articles which affected the rights *inter se* of shareholders from those which affected the interests of the company as a separate entity.[180] In cases of alterations involving competing shareholders' interests, 'the interests of the company as a whole' was thought to be an inappropriate, if not meaningless, tests.[181] Inhuman altruism was not expected of the shareholders in the majority. According to Dixon CJ, provided the resolution to alter the articles involved no oppression, no appropriation of an unjust or reprehensible nature and did not imply any purpose outside the scope of the power, it would be allowed to stand.[182] Latham CJ expressed the test in slightly different language,

---

[176] The decision in *Clemens* can also be criticised on other grounds: see Joffe (1977) 40 MLR 71. The resolution in question did not relate to an alteration of the articles and the court's assertion of a general power to review shareholder decisions is questionable. The subjecting of majority power to equitable constraint on the basis of the decision in *Ebrahimi v Westbourne Galleries Ltd* [1973] AC 360 is doubtful because that case concerned a specific discretion conferred by statute in particular circumstances, see 15.17 below, (but note also *Pennell v Venida Investments* (1974) which is unreported but is discussed extensively by Burridge, (1981) 44 MLR 40). *Clemens* hints at a fiduciary relationship between majority and minority shareholders but, although this has been accepted in certain American and Commonwealth jurisdictions, it is not yet part of English company law: Sealy, 'Equitable and Other Fetters on the Shareholder's Freedom to Vote' in Eastham and Krivy (eds), *The Cambridge Lectures* (1981) p. 80. See also Rider [1978] CLJ 148; Prentice (1976) 92 LQR 502.

[177] At p. 291.

[178] *Greenhalgh* at p. 291 *per* Lord Evershed MR.

[179] (1939) 61 CLR 457.

[180] At p. 481 *per* Latham CJ; at pp. 512–13 *per* Dixon J.

[181] *Per* Dixon CJ at p. 513. Similarly, Latham CJ at p. 481: 'The benefit of the company cannot be adopted as a criterion which is capable of solving all the problems in this branch of the law. . . . In cases where the question which arises is simply a question as to the relative rights of different classes of shareholders the problem cannot be solved by regarding merely the benefit of the corporation'. Also Rich J at p. 495.

[182] At p. 513.

but to the same effect: a resolution altering articles would be held to be invalid if there was 'fraud or trickery' or 'evidence of oppression' or if the alteration could be 'described as extravagant, so that reasonable men could not regard it as a fair alteration'.[183]

The judgments of the High Court of Australia in *Peter's* explicitly address the considerations which underlie the court's assertion of a power to review decisions to alter articles of association and the factors which restrict the scope of this power of review. It is a well-established principle of company law that voting rights attached to shares are property rights which shareholders can in general use as they think fit. It would be impossible to investigate the thoughts and motives with which each shareholder casts his votes. However, the court must set some limit on the power of the majority because of, in the words of Dixon J, 'the fear or knowledge that an apparently regular exercise of power may in truth be but a means of securing some personal or particular gain, whether pecuniary or otherwise, which does not fairly arise out of the subjects dealt with by the power and is outside and even inconsistent with the contemplated objects of the power'.[184]

Emphasising misuse of power by the majority[185] as a trigger which allows the court to intervene seems in many ways a much more realistic and workable test than those outlined in *Greenhalgh*. It is becoming increasingly unlikely, though, that the courts will have much opportunity in the future to refine further the meaning of the 'bona fide in the interests of the company' test enunciated in *Allen v Gold Reefs* because a minority which objects to an alteration to the articles can now voice the complaint by petitioning the court under Part XVII of the Companies Act 1985 for relief from unfairly prejudicial conduct. This form of statutory relief is very flexible, both in terms of the conduct which can be regarded as 'unfairly prejudicial' and with regard to the remedies which the court can grant where a claim is made out. The section is discussed further at 15.12 et seq.

---

[183] At p. 491, and see also p. 482.

[184] At pp. 511–12.

[185] Or as it may be described in equity: 'fraud on a power' *Estmanco (Kilner House) Ltd v GLC,* above at p. 445.

4 Company Contracts – Capacity, Authority and Form

4.1 Introduction

This chapter is concerned with the ability of a company to effect legally binding contracts and to enter into other transactions with valid effect. In the past[1] this would have involved detailed examination of two quite distinct areas of law, namely the ultra vires doctrine and agency principles. The ultra vires doctrine is related to the capacity of the company: in its original and strictest form, the ultra vires doctrine meant that no transaction which was beyond the capacity of a company could ever be binding on it.[2] The strictness of the ultra vires doctrine was first ameliorated as a consequence of the United Kingdom's accession to the European Community because it was incompatible with Community law. The European Communities Act 1972 contained a provision[3] which allowed transactions which were beyond a company's capacity to be enforced against it in certain circumstances; this provision was consolidated as section 35 of the Companies Act 1985. The wording of section 35 proved to be unsatisfactory and with effect from February 1991 it was replaced by sections 35, 35A, 35B and 322A of the Companies Act 1985, as amended by the Companies Act 1989.

Broadly, the effect of the provisions which are now in force is to reduce very significantly the importance of the ultra vires doctrine. The underlying purpose of the provisions is to allow outsiders dealing with a company to assume that the company has unlimited capacity and, although there are some uncertainties because of the way the legislation is drafted, this purpose is almost certainly achieved. The ultra vires doctrine remains relevant as an internal control mechanism: the directors will be in breach of duty if they fail to observe limits on the company's capacity and shareholders may be able to obtain injunctions to restrain acts which would be beyond those limits. Lord Strathclyde, the Government spokesman who introduced the relevant clauses of the Companies Bill to the House of Lords, explained their purpose in the following terms:[4]

> The clause[s] will in practice abolish the effect of the ultra vires rule on relations between a company and other parties... The ultra vires rule will still operate internally; that is for the purpose of defining the directors' duties to their shareholders.

In 1986 the DTI published a report by Professor Prentice entitled *Reform of the Ultra Rule*. The proposals outlined in the Prentice Report went further than the provisions

---

[1] The reforms introduced by the Companies Act 1989 apply to transactions entered into as from 4 February 1991.

[2] It is now generally accepted that the courts will not apply the ultra vires doctrine to limit a company's liability in tort or crime: Welch, 'The Criminal Liability of Corporations' (1946) 62 LQR 345; Smith and Hogan, *Criminal Law* (Butterworths, 7th edn 1992), pp. 178–9; *Bowstead on Agency* (Sweet & Maxwell, 15th edn 1985), pp. 396–7.

[3] Section 9.

[4] *Hansard*, HL Debs, 21 February 1989, cols. 508–12, esp. at 512. As a result of the decision of the House of Lords in *Pepper v Hart* [1993] AC 593, [1993] 1 All ER 42, [1992] 3 WLR 1032, it may be possible to look to this statement to clarify any ambiguities in the drafting of the sections.

which were eventually enacted because that report advocated the entire abolition of the ultra vires doctrine. The retention of the doctrine for internal purposes means that all of the old learning on ultra vires cannot be jettisoned completely, and this is reflected in this chapter. It also means that the statutory provisions which now govern the position are rather more complex than might have been the case if the proposal to give companies unlimited capacity had been adopted instead.

Agency principles remain extremely important in determining when a company is bound by a transaction. As a legal, as opposed to a natural, person a company must act though others, but simply because someone purports to act on a company's behalf does not mean that it is bound: the authority of those who act on behalf of the company to bind it is governed by agency principles together with a special principle of company law known as the *Turquand* rule. Agency principles are derived mainly from case-law but the statutory reforms to the ultra vires doctrine have affected these principles to a certain extent.

4.2 The term 'ultra vires'

The term 'ultra vires' used in a strict sense in relation to a registered company means acts which are outside the scope of the objects of the company set forth in the objects clause of its memorandum.[5] Prior to the statutory reforms, the distinguishing feature of a trans-action which was ultra vires in the strict sense was that it was beyond the company's capacity and could not be ratified even by a unanimous vote of the shareholders.[6] The consequences of an act which is ultra vires in the strict sense (which is the sense in which the term is used in this chapter unless otherwise indicated) are now governed by statute.

In company law the term 'ultra vires' is sometimes used to describe acts which are not beyond the *capacity* of the company, but simply beyond the authority of either the board of directors or a simple majority of the shareholders. Such acts may be in breach of the articles of association, but they are not, strictly speaking, beyond the powers of the company. Acts of this type can be ratified and, once properly ratified, they become binding on the company. Another use of the term ultra vires in a wider sense is to describe transactions which, although within the scope of the powers of the company, are entered into for an unauthorised purpose. These transactions are not void and can confer rights on a third party who is unaware of the improper purpose.[7] In *Rolled Steel Products (Holdings) Ltd v British Steel Corporation*[8] Slade and Browne-Wilkinson LLJ commented on the potential for confusion caused by the use of the term 'ultra vires' in these wider senses and suggested that its use should be confined to its strict sense.

---

[5] In the case of statutory companies created by private Acts of Parliament, the Act itself will define the company's objects. This will usually be done in much narrower terms than the objects clause of a modern registered company. The ultra vires doctrine does not apply to companies incorporated by Royal Charter. A chartered company which fails to observe restrictions in its charter may find itself subject to proceedings in the nature of *scire facias* for the revocation of its charter: *British South Africa Co. v de Beers Mines* [1910] 1 Ch 354. A member may obtain an injunction to restrain the company from acting in a manner inconsistent with its charter: *Rendall v Crystal Palace Co.* (1858) 4 K & J 326; *Breay v Royal British Nurses Association* [1897] 2 Ch 272; *Jenkins v Pharmaceutical Society of Great Britain* [1921] 1 Ch 392.

[6] *Ashbury Railway Carriage & Iron Co. Ltd v Riche* (1875) LR 7 HL 653; *Rolled Steel Products (Holdings) Ltd v British Steel Corporation*, [1986] Ch 246, [1985] 3 All ER 52, [1985] 2 WLR 908, [1984] BCLC 466, (1983–1985) 1 BCC 99, 158.

[7] *Rolled Steel Products (Holdings) Ltd v British Steel Corpn* [1982] Ch 478, [1982] 3 All ER 1057, [1982] 3 WLR 715 (Vinelott J). See Birds, (1982) 3 Co. Law. 123.

[8] [1986] Ch 246.

An act may also be void on the ground of illegality as being contrary to the provisions of the Companies Acts. A company cannot take power to do something which is contrary to the Companies Acts so that an act which is illegal can also properly be described as being ultra vires.[9]

4.3 Drafting of objects clauses

By an amendment to the Companies Act 1985 effected by the Companies Act 1989, where the memorandum states that the object of the company is to carry on business as a general commercial company, the object of the company is to carry on any trade or business whatsoever and the company has power to do all such things as are incidental to the carrying on of any trade or business by it.[10] A company may be incorporated with this object, or may amend its objects clause to adopt it.[11] In practice, companies tend to adopt very long objects clauses which authorise a wide range of activities some of which may not be 'commercial' or fall under the umbrella terms 'trade or business'. Also, a well-drafted objects clause usually confers numerous powers on the company and authorises the company to exercise these powers regardless of whether the exercise is incidental or conducive to the specified activities.[12] It is also usual for the objects clause to include a subjective incidental powers provision whereby the company is empowered to do anything which, in the opinion of its directors, is incidental or conducive to the activities or powers stated in the other paragraphs of the objects clause. The 'short-form' general commercial company object was enacted as an alternative to the long-form objects normally encountered but because long-form objects can be (and usually are) more extensive than the short form, there is unlikely to be any significant change of practice. Some companies have chosen to adopt the general commercial company object but as an addition to, rather than instead of, the traditional long-form objects clause.

If the memorandum authorises an act to a limited extent, this by implication forbids any act outside the limit: for example a power to borrow up to £10,000 renders unlawful any greater borrowing,[13] and a power to supply water in a certain parish renders ultra vires any supply outside such parish.[14] Express restrictions are now uncommon as companies tend to prefer to draw up their objects in the widest possible terms.[15]

The articles cannot vary the memorandum by giving powers inconsistent with it.[16] However, if the memorandum is ambiguous or silent, contemporary articles may explain in it.[17] Thus it was held that where the memorandum of association did not make

---

[9] In *Aveling Barford Ltd v Perion Ltd* [1989] BCLC 626, (1989) 5 BCC 677 the term 'ultra vires' is used in respect of an illegal act. Because such acts are illegal as well as void, third parties will not be entitled to the same consequential relief that is open to a party to a contract that is ultra vires but not contrary to the Companies Acts. The rules as to illegal contracts are applied: *South Western Mineral Water Co. v Ashmore* [1967] 1 WLR 1110.

[10] Section 3A.

[11] Amendment of the objects clause is discussed at 4.14–18 below. The text assumes that it is possible to combine the general commercial company object with other objects. This point is discussed further in *Gore-Browne on Companies* (Jordans, 44th edn, loose-leaf), 3.7.

[12] Whether, or to what extent, a provision which purports to confer an independent 'power' is effective is discussed at 4.6–8 below.

[13] *Wenlock v River Dee Co.* (1885) 10 App. Cas. 354 (HL).

[14] *Attorney-General v West Gloucestershire Water Co.* (1909) 2 Ch 338.

[15] For example, restrictions on the power to borrow are now more likely to be contained in the articles rather than in the memorandum.

[16] *Guinness v Land Corporation of Ireland* (1882) 22 Ch D 349.

[17] *Angostura Bitters v Kerr* [1933] AC 550 (PC).

any reference to the division of the capital into preference and ordinary shares, the original articles of association might sanction such an arrangement.[18]

The Registrar of Companies can refuse to register a company which has illegal objects.[19] If the purpose of a company which has been registered is illegal, the Attorney-General, acting on behalf of the Crown, can have the registration quashed.[20]

4.4 Construction of objects clauses

The ultra vires doctrine was created by judges in the nineteenth century but companies soon realised that a way around the restrictions which it imposed was to draft the objects clause as widely as possible. Initially there was judicial hostility to the practice of drafting very wide objects but, with some reluctance, the key clauses which companies wanted to include in their objects were accepted by the courts. Eventually the attitude of the courts shifted and in the more modern cases they have tended to endorse companies' efforts to express their capacity in the widest possible terms.

The ultra vires doctrine was never so harshly applied as to make void everything which was not expressly authorised by the memorandum, because the courts accepted that whatever might fairly be regarded as incidental to or consequential upon the objects specified ought not, unless expressly prohibited, to be held to be outside the powers of the company.[21] Nevertheless, it soon became commonplace to insert into the objects clause some general words empowering the company to 'do all such other things as may be deemed to be incidental or conducive to the attainment of the above objects or any of them'. Such a clause has been treated as extending the powers of the company[22] but it must not be taken as giving powers much in excess of those expressly given or implied by law. The words will only be held to cover operations of a nature similar to the business previously mentioned, and will not include any wholly fresh business.[23]

The incidental powers which are implied by law will vary with every company according to its main objects. A trading company has an implied power to borrow,[24] but not a building society.[25] All companies have implied power to compromise bona fide disputes,[26] and trading companies having power to deal with their property have power

---

[18] *Harrison v Mexican Railway Co.* (1875) 19 Eq 358; see *Re South Durham Brewery Co.* (1886) 31 Ch D 261; *Anderson's Case* (1878) 7 Ch D 75; *Phoenix Bessemer Steel Co.* (1875) 44 LJ Ch 683 (division of capital). This canon of interpretation is not affected by the fact that the occasion for it is removed by *Andrew v Gas Meter Co.* [1897] 1 Ch D 361 (CA). It has since been followed in *Fisher v Black and White Publishing Co.* [1901] 1 Ch 174; and *Rainford v James Keith and Blackman Co.* [1905] 2 Ch 147 (power to lend money) (CA). See also *Sime v Coats* 1908 SC 751; *Evling v Israel and Oppenheimer* [1918] 1 Ch 101 at 110.

[19] *R v Registrar of Companies ex p More* [1931] 2 KB 197.

[20] *Bowman v Secular Society Ltd* [1917] AC 406; *R v Registrar of Companies, ex p Attorney-General* [1991] BCLC 476 (1980). The certificate of registration is conclusive against everyone other than the Crown.

[21] *Attorney-General v Great Eastern Rly Co.* (1880) 5 App. Cas. 473; *Small v Small* (1885) 10 App. Cas. 119; *Deuchar v Gas Light and Coke Co.* [1925] AC 691 (HL); *Attorney-General v Smethwick Corporation* [1932] 1 Ch 562.

[22] *Re Baglan Hall Colliery Co.* (1870) 5 Ch App 346; *Simpson v Westminster Palace Hotel Co.* (1860) 8 HLC 712; *Taunton v Royal Insurance Co.* (1864) 2 H & M 135; *Re Peruvian Railways Co.* (1867) LR 2 Ch 617.

[23] *London Financial Association v Kelk* (1884) 26 Ch D 107.

[24] *General Auction Estate Co. v Smith* [1891] 3 Ch 432.

[25] *Blackburn Benefit Building Society v Cunliffe Brooks* (1882) 22 Ch D 61 (CA).

[26] *Bath's Case* (1878) 6 Ch D 334; *Re Irish Provident Assurance Co.* [1913] 1 Ir R 352.

to mortgage it.[27] A company formed to work a patent may purchase it.[28] A hotel company not requiring the whole of its premises may let off part,[29] and a colliery company may sell off its surplus lands.[30] In *Attorney-General v Mersey Railway*[31] it was held not to be within the implied powers of a railway company to have a business of running buses. The question is not whether the business can be conveniently or advantageously conducted with the principal business authorised, but whether it is by necessary implication incidental or accessory to it.[32]

As well as including general incidental wording, companies began to include a wide range of objects (in the sense of types of business) and powers in the objects clause. The judicial response to this practice was to evolve the main object rule of construction: the main object rule involved identifying the main object of the company and then construing the other objects and the powers specified in the objects clause as being ancillary to that main object.[33] Thus, for example, if the company's objects clause commenced with a paragraph authorising it to acquire rubber and tobacco estates but a subsequent paragraph gave it the power to underwrite shares,[34] under the main object rule of construction, the underwriting power would be viewed as ancillary to, and to be exercisable only for the purposes incidental or accessory to, the acquisition of rubber or tobacco estates. With a view to avoiding the operation of the main object rule of construction altogether, companies then started to include wording in their objects clause to the effect that each paragraph of the clause was to be read separately and without limitation by reference to the other clauses.

The effect of this wording was considered by the House of Lords in *Cotman v Brougham*.[35] The House held that once a company was registered, its memorandum of association had to be viewed as a valid instrument and the provisions which it contained had to be given effect to accordingly.[36] Therefore, effect had to be given to an independent objects paragraph by treating every object and power specified in the objects clause as independent objects, and not as ancillary to the main object. On that basis, the underwriting of shares by a rubber company, as permitted by its objects clause, could not be held to be ultra vires even though the underwritten shares were in a company with a business which had no apparent connection with rubber.

Their Lordships expressed unhappiness with this result and suggested that the Registrar of Companies should refuse to register companies which had objects clauses containing multifarious objects, powers expressed as objects and independent objects provisions, on the grounds that this practice did not satisfy the statutory requirement to

---

[27] *Re Patent File Co.* (1870) LR 6 Ch 83.

[28] *Leifchild's Case* (1865) LR 1 Eq 231.

[29] *Simpson v Westminster Palace Hotel,* above.

[30] *Kingsbury Collieries and Moore's Contract* [1907] 2 Ch 259.

[31] [1907] AC 415, overruling [1907] 1 Ch 81.

[32] *Attorney-General v London County Council* [1901] 1 Ch 781; see also *Attorney-General v Manchester Corporation* [1906] 1 Ch 643.

[33] As explained in *Anglo-Overseas Agencies v Green* [1961] 1 QB 1 at p. 8. For cases considering whether to wind up a company on the grounds that its principal object had failed see *Re Haven Gold Mining Co.* (1882) 20 Ch D 151; *Re German Date Coffee Co.* (1882) 20 Ch D 169 (CA); *Re Kitson & Co.* [1946] 1 All ER 435; *Re Eastern Telegraph* [1947] 2 All ER 104.

[34] The factual situation is taken from *Cotman v Brougham,* [1918] AC 514 (HL).

[35] Above. This must be taken to overrule *Stephens v Mysore Reefs (Kangundy) Mining Co.* [1902] 1 Ch 745.

[36] But the Crown can bring proceedings to quash the registration of a company which is registered with illegal objects: 4.3 above.

state the objects of the company.[37] This course was not taken by the Registrar and it is now standard practice for registered companies to include an extensive range of businesses in their objects clause, as well as every conceivable power that they could ever wish to use, and to provide that each paragraph of the objects clause is to be interpreted independently.

Anglo-Overseas Agencies v Green[38] provides an illustration of an independent objects clause and its effect.[39] The plaintiff company's objects clause had the usual series of paragraphs setting forth various objects of the company and then concluded with the following provision:

> The intention is that the objects specified in any paragraph of this clause shall, except where otherwise expressed in this clause, be in no wise limited or restricted by reference to or reference from the terms of any other paragraph or the name of the company.

Salmon J upheld the contention that these concluding words had the effect of making each paragraph an independent main object. This allowed a company, whose apparent main objects set out in paras. (A) and (B) were the export and import of merchandise, to obtain a building lease of a site from a local authority by virtue of a widely drafted para. (E), even though there was no paragraph expressly permitting property development.[40]

4.5 'Subjective' provisions in the objects clause

This liberal policy of allowing the draftsman of the objects clause to defeat the apparent purpose of the ultra vires doctrine was carried a stage further by the Court of Appeal in *Bell Houses Ltd v City Wall Properties Ltd.*[41] In that case clause 3 (c) of the memorandum of association allowed the company to 'carry on any other trade or business whatever which can, *in the opinion of the board of directors*,[42] be advantageously carried on by, in connection with, or ancillary to, any of the above businesses or general businesses of the company.' The appellant company maintained that clause 3 (c) allowed them to charge a procuration fee for introducing a source of finance (which they did not wish to use themselves at the time) to another property company, even though there was no express power to do so. The Court of Appeal held that, provided the directors of the plaintiff company honestly formed the view that that particular business could be carried on advantageously

---

[37] Now contained in section 2 (1) (c) of the Companies Act 1985.

[38] [1961] 1 QB 1.

[39] See [1961] 1 QB 1 at p. 8, for a discussion of the effect of the 'main object' rule where no such provision is made.

[40] Paragraph (E) reads: 'To obtain the grant of, purchase, or otherwise acquire any concessions, contracts, rights, patents, privileges, monopolies, undertakings or businesses, or any right or option in relation thereto and to perform and fulfil the terms and conditions thereof, and to carry the same into effect, operate thereunder, develop, turn to account, maintain and sell, and dispose of and deal with the same.'

[41] [1966] 2 QB 656. For an application of this case in New Zealand, see *American Home Assurance Co. v Tjmonis Properties* [1984] NZLR 452 (CA). See also *H. & H. Logging Co. Ltd v Random Services Corp. Ltd* (1967) 63 DLR (20) 6 and *H. A. Stephenson & Sons Ltd v Gillanders, Arbuthnot & Co. Ltd* (1931) 45 CLR 476 (Aust. HC).

[42] Italics supplied.

in connection with, or as an ancillary to, the company's main business,[43] then the agreement to charge a procuration fee was within the company's powers by virtue of clause 3 (c).

The decision in *Bell Houses Ltd* also rested on the alternative ground that, apart from the subjective discretion conferred on the directors, the obtaining of the procuration fee was, as a matter of objective construction, reasonably incidental to certain specific objects of the company.[44] However, Salmon LJ made it quite clear that the discretion conferred on the directors may allow them in good faith to extend the company's activities in ways which, strictly as a matter of objective construction, are *not* reasonably incidental to the activities specified in the objects clause:

> As a matter of pure construction the meaning of these words seems to me to be obvious. An object of the company is to carry on any business which the directors genuinely believe can be carried on advantageously in connection with or as an ancillary to the general business of the company. It may be that the directors take the wrong view and in fact the business in question cannot be carried on as the directors believe. But it matters not how mistaken the directors may be. Providing they form their view honestly, the business is within the plaintiff company's objects and powers ...[45]

4.6 Objects and powers

The *Bell Houses* decision appeared to indicate a marked shift in the judicial attitude towards the value of the ultra vires doctrine. It permitted the draftsman by a simple and flexible drafting device to give the company's management reasonable freedom of manoeuvre in developing and diversifying the company's activities. However, in a later Court of Appeal decision a more rigorous approach was taken.

In *Introductions Ltd v National Provincial Bank Ltd*[46] a company originally formed for the purpose of offering services and information to overseas visitors to the Festival of Britain was taken over and, under new management, it began pig-breeding as its only business. A bank which had advanced money to finance this business was held unable to recover on the company's liquidation. The bank was fully aware of the purpose of the loan and that the objects for which the company was formed were those set out in its memorandum, of which the bank had a copy. It was contended for the bank that, even if pig-breeding were ultra vires,[47] it might rely on a sub-clause (N) of the objects clause that enabled this company 'to borrow or raise money in such manner as it thought fit'. This was linked with a provision (similar to that in *Anglo-Overseas Agencies v Green*) that each sub-clause 'should be construed independently of, and should be in no way linked by, reference to any other

---

[43] This is an important qualification to the discretion conferred on directors to determine what is within the objects clause of the company. It is clear that the courts would not accept an unqualified discretion which allowed the company to do anything the directors thought fit to decide: *Re Crown Bank* (1890) 44 Ch D 634: *Introductions Ltd v National Provincial Bank* [1970] Ch 199 at p. 209 *per* Harman LJ. This should be contrasted with a more expansive approach (to a less qualified discretion conferred upon the directors) taken by the Australian High Court in *H. A. Stephenson Ltd v Gillanders, Arbuthnot & Co.* (1931) 45 CLR 476. See the judgment of Dixon J at pp. 490–1.

[44] See [1966] 2 QB 656 at p. 680 (Danckwerts LJ) and pp. 692–3 (Salmon LJ).

[45] [1966] 2 QB 656 at p. 690.

[46] [1970] Ch 199 (CA).

[47] Buckley J had held that pig-breeding was ultra vires the company and this point was not contested on appeal: [1968] 2 All ER 1221.

sub-clause, and that the objects set out in each sub-clause were independent objects of the company'.

The Court of Appeal made a sharp distinction between *powers* as opposed to *objects* in the memorandum. On the true construction of the sub-clause conferring a general power to borrow, this was a power not an object. Thus the power to borrow had to be used for the legitimate intra vires objects of the company. Since the explicit purpose of the loan (pig-breeding) was ultra vires, the borrowing itself was ultra vires. Despite the final provision declaring all the objects set forth to be independent, the power to borrow on sub-clause (N) was not on its wording capable of being a wholly independent object. As a power it was necessarily ancillary to the objects of the company.

It should be noted that the Court of Appeal's decision in the *Introductions* case did not, so far as *objects* were concerned, in any way repudiate attempts to exclude the main objects principle of construction. It did, however, have a limiting effect in respect of *powers*. In the case of an ordinary trading company, whilst it could specify a number of different objects (in the sense of trades and businesses) in its objects clause, ranging, say, from acquiring rubber plantations through to promoting festivals or pig-breeding, and each of those objects would be construed independently provided there was an appropriate independent objects clause, the paragraphs of the objects clause containing true powers, such as the power to borrow or to give guarantees, would always be construed as ancillary to the objects, notwithstanding any independent objects clause.[48]

Attempts have been made to exclude the distinction drawn in *Introductions* between objects and powers by explicitly providing that no such distinction is to be made, but the effect of this wording has not been tested in the courts.[49] In any event, in retrospect it can be seen that *Introductions* was a high point of judicial antipathy to the practice of drafting very broad objects clauses. Since then, two important cases decided by the Court of Appeal have greatly reduced the significance of the distinction between objects and powers.[50]

4.7 Objects and powers: *Re Horsley & Weight* and *Rolled Steel*[51]

In *Re Horsley & Weight Ltd*[52] the objects clause of a company which carried on the business of shopfitters authorised it: 'to grant pensions to employees and ex-employees and directors and ex-directors'. There was also an independent objects clause. The Court of Appeal held that the granting of pensions was capable of subsisting as a substantive object rather than as an ancillary power and that, having regard to the independent objects clause, it was to be so construed in this case. The Court of Appeal thus confirmed the existence of a distinction between objects and powers but, by classifying a provision as an object when it might easily have been regarded as a power, sidestepped the need to

---

[48] For a Scottish case following the restrictive approach in *Introductions* see *Thompson v J Barke & Co. (Caterers) Ltd* 1975 SLT 67.

[49] See *Company Law Materials I* (Jordans, 4th edn 1980) model memorandum of association settled by Richard Sykes QC, as to the concluding paragraph of the model objects clause at p. 18.

[50] Note also *Re New Finance and Mortgage Co.* [1975] Ch 420 and *Newstead v Frost* [1980] 1 All ER 363, [1980] 1 WLR 135 (HL) where the courts did not adopt a restrictive approach in determining the scope of objects clauses.

[51] Notes on the decision of Vinelott J at first instance and of the Court of Appeal include Wedderburn (1983) 46 MLR 204; McMullen [1983] CLJ 58; Sealy [1985] CLJ 39; (1986) 102 LQR 169.

[52] [1982] Ch 442, [1982] 3 All ER 1045, [1982] 3 WLR 431.

consider whether a power had been exercised otherwise than in pursuit of the objects, and the consequences in that event.

Rolled Steel Products (Holdings) Ltd v British Steel Corporation[53] provided an opportunity for a more detailed examination of the distinction between objects and powers and its consequences because, despite an independent objects clause, the relevant provision authorising the giving of guarantees and debentures was classified by the first instance judge, Vinelott J, and by the Court of Appeal as a mere power. This led to the question: given that the power to give guarantees and debentures had been exercised otherwise than in pursuit of the substantive objects of the company, were the guarantee and debenture binding on the company? The Court of Appeal held that they were not and the judgments of Slade and Browne-Wilkinson LJJ contain a valuable restatement of the law relating to the use of a power in the objects clause otherwise than in pursuit of the objects.[54] The learned Lord Justices sought to explain earlier decisions such as *Introductions* so as to reconcile them with their own analysis of the position. When the judgments in some earlier cases are compared closely with those of Slade and Browne-Wilkinson LJJ in *Rolled Steel* it is questionable whether the reconciliation is entirely persuasive[55] but, consistent with legislative developments in this area of the law, the approach in *Rolled Steel* embodies the policy of not penalising innocent outsiders dealing with a company when those who act on the company's behalf fail to observe limits which are imposed by the company's constitution.

It is far from clear how far this line of argument can be pushed. It plainly applies to the self-interested abuse of a borrowing power in the circumstances of *Rolled Steel* itself. It is debatable whether *Rolled Steel* supports the use of any and every power in the memorandum to justify a wholly new area of activity which is to be conducted on a permanent basis (e.g. pig-breeding as the sole activity of a company whose express objects give no hint of this type of animal husbandry). If and when *Rolled Steel* comes to be further considered by the courts, the impact of the new section 35 in protecting third parties may make that aspect of the reasoning in the case redundant.

4.8 The use of powers in the memorandum for improper purposes

The essence of the restatement of the law in *Rolled Steel* is that if an act performed pursuant to an ancillary power stated in the memorandum is of a category which, on a true construction of the company's memorandum, is capable of being performed as reasonably incidental to the attainment or pursuit of its substantive objects, it will not be rendered ultra vires the company merely because in a particular instance its directors, in performing the act in its name, are doing so for purposes other than those set out in its

---

[53] Above.

[54] Lawton LJ gave a brief judgment in which he considered the misfeasance aspects of the case (and certain matters arising from the handling of the case by the trial judge) but otherwise he agreed with Slade LJ. Browne-Wilkinson LJ also expressed agreement with Slade LJ.

[55] It is particularly difficult to reconcile *Rolled Steel* with the decision of the House of Lords in *Sinclair v Brougham* [1914] AC 398. Their Lordships were mainly concerned with the consequences of ultra vires but accepted that the power to borrow money must be limited to borrowing for the purposes of the company, borrowing for any other purpose being ultra vires.

memorandum.[56] Thus, if the directors exercise a power in the memorandum to borrow money, provided borrowing money is *capable* of being reasonably incidental to the pursuit or attainment of the company's objects (a test that would ordinarily be satisfied) a particular borrowing by a company is not ultra vires even though the purpose for which the directors borrowed the money falls outside the scope of the company's substantive objects.

The only limitation put upon the protective shield thus thrown around the use of powers in the memorandum, is that 'due regard must be paid to any express condition attached to, or limitation on, powers contained in a company's memorandum' (e.g. a power to borrow only up to a specified amount).[57] However, the court will not ordinarily construe a statement in the memorandum that a particular power is 'exercisable for the purposes of the company' (or similar phraseology) as a condition limiting the company's corporate capacity to exercise the power (as opposed to limit on the authority of the director).[58] In the view of Browne-Wilkinson LJ such a limitation 'does not put the third party on enquiry as to whether the power is being so exercised, i.e. does not give constructive notice of excess or abuse of such power'.[59]

Some[60] earlier cases had suggested that the consequences of an exercise of a mere power specified in the objects for an improper purpose could depend on the state of mind of the person who dealt with the company: taking the borrowing power as an example, if the lender knew that the directors were borrowing the money for a purpose which was not authorised by the company's memorandum, the loan would be ultra vires, but the loan would be binding if the lender did not have the requisite knowledge.[61] In *Introductions* Harman LJ said: 'if the defendant bank did not know what the purpose of the loan was it need not enquire, but it did know, and I can find nothing ... to protect it notwithstanding that knowledge'; in that case the loan and related debenture were held to be not binding on the company.[62]

In *Rolled Steel* it was held that the knowledge of the person dealing with the company was generally irrelevant to the question of *corporate capacity* but that it was significant with regard to matters of *authority*. Slade LJ explained this on the basis that the directors of a company are held out as having ostensible authority to bind the company in any transaction falling within the express or implied powers in its memorandum.[63] Unless put on notice to the contrary, a person dealing in good faith with a company which is carrying on an intra vires business is entitled to assume that the directors are properly exercising these powers for the purposes of the company set out in the memorandum and can

[56] [1986] 1 Ch at 295 *per* Slade LJ and at 306–7 *per* Browne-Wilkinson LJ. For an application of *Rolled Steel* to a housing association registered under the Industrial and Provident Societies Act 1965, see *Halifax Building Society v Meridian Housing Association Ltd* [1994] 2 BCLC 540.

[57] Slade LJ at p. 295 summarising his conclusions.

[58] ibid.

[59] ibid. at p. 307.

[60] But not all: Pennycuick J's reasoning in *Charterbridge Corporation Ltd v Lloyds Bank Ltd* [1970] Ch 62 is similar to that of the Court of Appeal in *Rolled Steel*. See also *Re Halt Garage (1964) Ltd* [1982] 3 All ER 1016. Both of these cases are considered further at para 4.13 below.

[61] *Re David Payne & Co Ltd* [1904] 2 Ch 608; *Re Jon Beauforte* [1953] Ch 131; *Introductions*, above.

[62] Buckley J, at first instance, [1968] 2 All ER 1221 at p. 1225 described the loan and debenture as 'ultra vires'. This categorisation is not expressly stated in any of the judgments in the Court of Appeal but Harman and Russell LJJ both expressed agreement with Buckley J (the third Lord Justice, Karminski LJ, agreed with the dismissal of the appeal without giving reasons).

[63] At p. 295.

therefore hold the company to any transaction of this nature. However, if a person dealing with a company is on notice that the directors are exercising the relevant power for purposes other than the purposes of the company, he cannot rely on the directors' ostensible authority to hold the company to the transaction.

To explain the decision in *Introductions*, the Court of Appeal considered the various senses in which the term 'ultra vires' can be used in company law and reinterpreted certain passages in the relevant judgments as being concerned with 'ultra vires' in the wider sense of being beyond the authority of the directors rather than in its narrow and strict sense of being outside the company's capacity.[64] This interpretation made sense of the references in those judgments to the knowledge of the bank of the intended unauthorised purpose for which the loan was sought, because, in accordance with agency principles, such knowledge may displace the ostensible authority that the directors would otherwise have had to bind the company.

The vigorous restatement of the nature and proper scope of the ultra vires doctrine in *Rolled Steel* is to be welcomed both for its logical character and the evident judicial policy aimed at reducing the scope of possible harm it may cause to innocent third parties. The proposition that the capacity of the company could in some circumstances depend on the knowledge of persons dealing with it was always logically dubious.[65] However, certain queries and doubts about the Court of Appeal's decision arise when what is un-questionably a 'restatement' of a difficult and confused body of case-law, is related to well-established principles and authorities.

The distinction between substantive objects and ancillary powers will, sometimes at least, be difficult to draw, though it must be accepted that not only *Re Introductions*[66] but *Re Horsley & Weight Ltd*[67] and *Rolled Steel v British Corporation*,[68] too, are adamant that this distinction must be made.[69] Moreover, the doctrine enunciated by the Court of Appeal in *Rolled Steel* is not easy to square with the treatment of subordinate powers by Buckley LJ in *Horsley v Weight* or with that of Harman LJ in *Re Introductions*. The contention in *Rolled Steel* that in the latter case Harman LJ was not concerned with ultra vires acts beyond the company's corporate capacity (as regards the bank's reliance on the power to borrow) seems open to serious question.

4.9 Ultra vires at common law and ratification

At common law, a transaction which was ultra vires in the strict sense was void and could not be ratified even with the unanimous consent of all of the shareholders.[70] Thus, an act which was not authorised by the substantive objects or express powers stated in the

---

[64] At pp. 293 and 294 *per* Slade LJ and at p. 306 *per* Browne-Wilkinson LJ. The judgment of Russell LJ in *Introductions* was not susceptible to this interpretation; Slade LJ held that the judgment was confined to its own facts, at p. 293. *Re David Payne*, above was subjected to similar reinterpretation. *Re Jon Beauforte*, above was not separately considered by Slade LJ or Browne-Wilkinson LJ but the reasoning in that case is undermined by *Rolled Steel*.

[65] A perceptive article by Baxter, 'Ultra Vires and Agency Untwined' [1970] CLJ 280, made this point and interpreted the authorities in a way very similar to that subsequently adopted by the Court of Appeal in *Rolled Steel*.

[66] [1970] Ch 199 (CA).

[67] [1982] Ch 442 (CA).

[68] [1986] Ch 246.

[69] However, it is not beyond argument that it may still be possible to draft a way out of this distinction.

[70] *Ashbury Railway Carriage v Riche*, above.

memorandum, and which could not be regarded as falling within the scope of the company's implied powers, was entirely[71] void at common law. In contrast a transaction which went beyond the authority of the directors under the articles could normally be ratified by an ordinary resolution of the shareholders in general meeting. What of a transaction in which the directors used an ancillary power expressly or impliedly conferred by the memorandum for a purpose which was beyond the company's substantive objects? Such transactions were not ultra vires and void according to the decision of the Court of Appeal in *Rolled Steel*; but a further complication raised by that case was the suggestion (although the point was not fully explored) that ratification of such transactions required the unanimous consent of all of the shareholders rather than the normal principle of ratification by a majority.[72] It is possible that the Court of Appeal had in mind situations where ratification is given informally as opposed to ratification by resolution: informal corporate decision-making is only effective where it is unanimous but majority consent normally suffices where decisions are taken at properly convened company meetings.[73] As a result of statutory reforms, even an act which is ultra vires in the strict sense can now be ratified by a majority[74] and it would be illogical if the ratification of an act which is not ultra vires in that sense but which is tainted by an improper purpose is subject to a more rigorous procedure.

4.10 Other consequences of ultra vires at common law

This needs only a brief review by way of background to the present position which is governed by statute.

As against the company 'an ultra vires agreement could not become intra vires by reason of estoppel, lapse of time, ratification, acquiescence or delay'.[75] At common law a company could always plead in its defence that any contract or other transaction was ultra vires. A minority shareholder could prevent the company carrying out an ultra vires transaction by obtaining an injunction to restrain the company.[76] An ordinary creditor of the company had no such *locus standi* in seeking to prevent an ultra vires transaction.[77] This was somewhat at odds with the idea that one of the purposes of the ultra vires doctrine was to protect creditors.[78]

There was no unequivocal ruling on whether the other party to an ultra vires contract

---

[71] On the question of who can plead ultra vires, see 4.10 below.

[72] At p. 295 *per* Slade LJ.

[73] Sealy [1985] CLJ 39 at pp. 40–1. This suggestion gathers weight from the fact that the cases cited by Slade LJ in support of the need for unanimity were concerned with shareholders' informal decision-making rather than with decisions taken at shareholders' meetings.

[74] Section 35 (3) which is discussed further at 4.11 below. A special resolution, i.e. three-quarters majority (of those voting), is required.

[75] *Per* Russell J in *York Corporation v Henry Leetham & Sons Ltd* [1924] 1 Ch 557 at p. 583.

[76] *Parke v Daily News Ltd* [1962] Ch 806. An executed ultra vires transaction is one of the exceptions to the rule in *Foss v Harbottle* in respect of which a minority shareholder may bring a derivative action: *Russell v Wakefield Waterworks* (1875) LR 20 Eq 374, 481. It has been held that, to have standing to proceed with a derivative action, a minority shareholder must establish that the wrongdoers are in control of the company and that his action has the support of those who are not implicated in the wrongdoing: *Smith v Croft (No 2)* [1988] Ch 144; see 15.5, below.

[77] *Mills v Northern Rly of Buenos Ayres* (1870) 5 Ch App 621; *Lawrence v West Somerset Rly* [1918] 2 Ch 520. A debenture-holder holding security over the company's property was allowed to sue in *Cross v Imperial Continental Gas Assoc* [1923] 2 Ch 553.

[78] See 4.12 below.

could raise the issue of the company's capacity when sued by the company. The Court of Appeal in *Bell Houses* left open the question whether it was proper to allow ultra vires to be raised as defence against a company, but Salmon LJ cast some doubt on the propriety of this.[79] The objection in principle to allowing ultra vires to be pleaded as a defence against a company was that this would subvert a doctrine which was intended to protect companies, and their shareholders and creditors.

It was a breach of fiduciary duty for directors to engage in ultra vires acts and the directors were liable to make good any loss suffered by the company as a result of an ultra vires transaction.[80] The court could relieve the directors under section 727 of the Companies Act 1985 of liability arising from ultra vires acts if it was satisfied that they had acted honestly and reasonably and ought fairly to be excused.[81]

Ultra vires loans made to companies were subject to detailed rules. Lenders could not sue either on the contract or for money had and received but they had two more restricted forms of redress open to them. First, to the extent that their money had been used to satisfy the claims of intra vires creditors they were entitled to be subrogated to the position of intra vires creditors. Secondly, even if they had no claim to be subrogated, they were entitled to trace such of their funds as had not been dissipated in accordance with common-law or equitable principles of tracing. The leading authority on the consequences of making an ultra vires loan to a company was *Sinclair v Brougham*.[82] Statutory reforms mean that a lender to a registered company should not have occasion to have regard to the principles discussed in that case but it remains relevant to bodies which are still subject to the ultra vires doctrine. The House of Lords has held it to be ultra vires the powers of a local authority to participate in swap transactions[83] and this has given the courts the opportunity to consider these questions in a modern context and against the background of restitutionary principles.[84]

4.11 Consequences of ultra vires: section 35 of the Companies Act 1985

Section 35 (1) of the Companies Act 1985 (as amended by the Companies Act 1989) provides that 'the validity of an act done by a company shall not be called into question on the ground of lack of capacity by reason of anything in the company's memorandum'.[85] This clearly reverses the common-law rule that ultra vires could be raised as a defence to

---

[79] [1966] 2 QB 656 at p. 694. At first instance in the same case [1965] 3 All ER 427, Mocatta J suggested that, if the company had performed its side of an ultra vires contract, it could claim in quasi-contract. See also Lawson J in *International Sales and Agencies Ltd v Marcus* [1982] 3 All ER 551 at p. 561.

[80] *Re Sharpe* [1892] 1 Ch 154; *Cullerne v London & Suburban Building Society* (1890) 25 QBD 485, 490.

[81] *Re Claridge's Patent Asphalte Co.* [1921] 1 Ch 543. See further on section 727, 14.24.4, below.

[82] Above.

[83] *Hazell v Hammersmith and Fulham London Borough Council* [1992] 2 AC 1. A simple example of a swap transaction is where one party is contractually obliged to a lender to pay interest at a fixed rate and the other party is contractually obliged to a lender to pay interest at a floating rate; in the swap transaction, the two parties agree to swap their respective interest-paying obligations.

[84] *Westdeutsche Landesbank Girozentrale v Islington London Borough Council* [1994] 1 WLR 938 (CA); *Kleinwort Benson Ltd v South Tyneside Metropolitan BC* [1994] 4 All ER 972; *South Tyneside Metropolitan BC v Svenska International plc* [1995] 1 All ER 545.

[85] There are special rules in relation to charitable companies: section 35 (4) and section 65 (1) of the Charities Act 1993, and section 112 (3) of the Companies Act 1989 amending the Charities Act 1960. Also note section 322A which applies where the person dealing with the company is a director or an associate of a director: 4.23 below.

any contractual claim brought against a company. Subject to a query arising from the drafting of a later sub-section,[86] the effect of section 35 (1) is also to ensure that lack of capacity cannot be pleaded against a company by the other party. In other words, section 35 (1) is two-way in its effect, operating to protect both the company and those who deal with it from the consequences of ultra vires.

When is an act done by a company for the purposes of section 35 (1)? In contractual matters, English company law has not adopted an organic theory whereby the acts of the board and of the general meeting are treated automatically as acts of the company.[87] Whether a company is bound by a transaction or other act which purports to be done on its behalf is normally determined by reference to agency principles, as modified by the *Turquand* rule and by section 35A of the Companies Act 1985 which is discussed later in this chapter.[88] Nothing in section 35 (1) appears to displace or override these principles and, although this is not spelt out, it would therefore seem that they should determine what is an 'act of the company' for this purpose: so interpreted, section 35 (1) ensures that an act done on behalf of a company which would otherwise be enforceable against it does not cease to be so simply because it is not authorised by the company's memorandum.[89]

The reference in section 35 (1) to the company's *memorandum* is significant because if the provision had simply referred to the company's objects clause[90] that would have provided scope for companies to reintroduce the ultra vires doctrine via restrictive additional clauses in the memorandum. In *Re Cleveland Trust*,[91] where an additional clause in the memorandum restricted the funds available for the payment of dividends, dividend payments in breach of the restriction were held to be ultra vires. Although this restriction was not contained in the objects clause, it would now be subject to section 35 (1) and such payments could therefore no longer be challenged on the grounds of lack of capacity. However, dividend payments made in breach of the restrictions on distributions imposed by the Companies Acts would still be illegal and might be described as ultra vires for that reason.[92]

The memorandum of a company may seek to limit its capacity either by express restrictions or by failing to make provision for matters that would not otherwise be implied as incidental to the stated objects. Since the capacity problems in respect of acts which are not expressly or implicitly authorised by the company's memorandum have their roots in what is expressly provided for in the memorandum, it is suggested that

---

[86] Section 35 (3).

[87] See e.g. *Rolled Steel* at p. 295 *per* Slade LJ and at p. 304 *per* Browne-Wilkinson LJ. Article 9 of the First Company Law Directive (68/151/EEC), the underlying Community provision implemented into English law by section 35 and the immediately following sections, is based rather more on the organic theory: 'acts done by the organs of the company shall be binding on it even though those acts are not within the objects of the company'. A purposive construction is to be adopted in respect of domestic legislation implementing a directive so as to ensure, so far as practicable, compliance with Community obligations: *Pickstone v Freemans plc* [1989] AC 66; *Litster v Forth Dry Dock Engineering Co. Ltd* [1990] 1 AC 546.

[88] 4.20–4.22 below.

[89] This interpretation of the phrase 'act of the company' is explored further in Ferran, 'The Reform of the Law on Corporate Capacity and Directors' and Officers' Authority' (1992) 13 Co. Law 124. See also Poole, 'Abolition of the Ultra Vires Doctrine and Agency Problems' (1991) 12 Co. Law 43.

[90] An early version of the bill was couched in these terms but the wording was changed during its passage through Parliament.

[91] [1991] BCLC 424, [1991] BCC 33.

[92] See *Precision Dippings Ltd v Precision Dippings Marketing Ltd* [1986] Ch 447, [1985] 3 WLR 812, [1985] BCLC 385, (1983–1985) 1 BCC 99, 539 (CA).

section 35 (1) applies in cases where the memorandum is silent and that the reference in that provision to anything in the company's memorandum does not limit its application to situations where an express limitation in the memorandum is breached.[93]

Section 35 (2) and (3) preserve some of the common-law consequences of ultra vires. Section 35 (2) gives statutory force to the right of a minority shareholder to bring proceedings to restrain the doing of an ultra vires act. No such proceedings may be brought in respect of any act which is to be done in fulfilment of a legal obligation arising from a previous act of the company. Where, as is typical in larger companies, the shareholders are mainly passive investors and are not involved in the management of the company's affairs, they are unlikely to be able to take advantage of the right to seek an injunction because they will not know of what is proposed until such time as it is too late and the company has already incurred legal obligations.[94] The right is likely to be most useful in companies where all of the shareholders are also involved in management but, if relations in that type of company have broken down, proceedings to restrain the doing of an act which is not authorised by the company's memorandum may be only one aspect of a larger dispute.

Section 35 (3) preserves the common-law position in respect of directors' duties and corporate capacity: 'it remains the duty of the directors to observe any limitations on their powers flowing from the company's memorandum'. Section 35 (3) provides that the shareholders may by special resolution relieve directors from liability for failing to observe limits flowing from the company's memorandum. Section 35 (3) also refers to ratification by separate special resolution of action by directors which, but for subsection (1), would be beyond the company's capacity. The precise effect of this clause is obscure. To the extent that it prevents shareholders from being misled by a composite special resolution which simultaneously ratifies the transaction and relieves the directors from liability, it is sensible and uncontroversial. In circumstances where the company chooses to ratify a transaction which is beyond the limits of its memorandum,[95] the clause makes clear that the ratification must be effected by a separate special resolution. However, it is arguable that the clause has a wider effect.

The wide interpretation of section 35 (3) is that to enforce any act of the directors which is beyond the limits of its memorandum, a company must ratify the action by special resolution. The argument on which this interpretation is based is that, until ratification, the company cannot claim the act as one of its own because the directors had no authority to do the act on its behalf; although, by virtue of section 35A which is discussed later in this chapter, the person dealing with the company may be able to enforce it against the company despite the directors' lack of authority, that provision does not operate in favour of the company.[96] This interpretation, which has been described as

---

[93] See also a publication of the Legal Risk Review Committee (a precursor of the Financial Law Panel, a City body which provides guidance to practitioners on areas of legal uncertainty) entitled *Reducing Uncertainty, The Way Forward*, (1992), Annex to Appendix 1, para. 10.

[94] This point was discussed in the House of Lords during the passage of the Companies Bill through Parliament. See *Hansard*, HL Debs. col. 512, 7 November 1989, col. 681 and Poole (1991) 12 Co. Law 43.

[95] e.g. where the transaction is voidable under section 322A because the other party is a director or a person connected with a director.

[96] See Poole (1991) 12 Co. Law 43 at p. 45 and Ferran (1992) 13 Co. Law 124 at p. 128 where this argument is further considered.

'strained',[97] undermines the unqualified two-way wording of section 35 (1) that an act 'shall not be called into question'. It is also objectionable in principle because in effect it subverts what was the underlying principle of the ultra vires doctrine, namely, protection of the company and its creditors and shareholders. Even when the ultra vires doctrine was most vigorously enforced at common law, it was doubtful whether ultra vires could be pleaded against the company; it would run entirely counter to the purpose of the statutory reforms if, by arguing lack of authority, a plea which is to substantially the same effect could now succeed.

Reading section 35 as a whole, it is questionable whether the wide interpretation of the offending clause in section 35 (3) is correct but, until it is considered by a court, the matter cannot be regarded as entirely free from doubt. In theory it would be prudent for a company to ratify by special resolution any acts which fall outside what is authorised by its memorandum but this advice might well be outweighed by practical considerations. Obtaining a special resolution can be a time-consuming and expensive task since, unless the company is so small that it is possible for all of the shareholders to reach agreement by informal means, this will involve convening a general meeting for the purpose. The safest course remains to have an objects clause which is drafted in the widest possible terms, because this minimises the circumstances in which recourse will have to be had to the statutory provisions. This is reinforced by the fact that failure to observe the limitations imposed by the company's memorandum remains a breach of duty by the directors and, if discovered far enough in advance, can be restrained by an injunction obtained by a shareholder. The consequences of an act falling outside the scope of a company's memorandum are now much less severe than they were previously, but companies, or more particularly their directors, are still likely to appreciate the advantages of avoiding those consequences altogether by appropriate drafting of the company's memorandum.[98]

4.12 The decline of the ultra vires doctrine

When the ultra vires doctrine was first developed by the courts in the nineteenth century it was perceived to be a valuable protection to shareholders and creditors from risky and wasteful ventures by the directors: shareholders and creditors could be assured that their money would not be put to uses beyond those authorised by the company's memorandum. As companies began to draft their way around the restrictions of the doctrine by devising ever more extensive objects, the usefulness of the objects clause as a source of information to shareholders and creditors about the uses to which their money could be

[97] *Gore-Browne on Companies* (Jordans, 44th edn, loose-leaf), at 3.1.1. Commenting on the relevant clause of the Companies Bill during its passage through Parliament, Lord Strathclyde, the Government spokesperson, stated that ratification 'would, among other things, enable the company to enforce the contract if that is what the shareholders believe to be in the interests of the company', *Hansard*, HL Debs., 21 February 1989, col. 516. In similar vein is his Lordship's later statement that 'ratification by the company of an ultra vires act that would not otherwise bind the company on the grounds of the lack of authority of the directors does not affect any liability incurred by the directors', *Hansard*, HL Debs., 7 November 1918, col. 675. These comments tend to support the wider view.
[98] For persons dealing with the company an advantage of a widely drafted memorandum is that it minimises the possibility of becoming implicated in a breach of duty by the directors flowing from their failure to observe the limits of the memorandum.

put declined. Judicial antipathy to devices such as the independent objects clauses ultimately failed to prevent companies from ensuring, by suitable drafting, that they had capacity to do virtually anything.

At the same time, company law was developing alternative rules to protect share-holders and creditors against dissipation by the directors of the funds made available to the company. Throughout the twentieth century, the rules regarding the funds which could be used to pay dividends or make other distributions to shareholders were progressively tightened.[99] Provisions of the insolvency legislation attacking preferences or transactions at an undervalue also sought to prevent unwarranted disposals of corporate funds.[100] Accounting and reporting obligations imposed on directors by the companies legislation became more onerous thus giving those dealing, or considering dealing, with a company the opportunity to monitor the stewardship of its affairs by consulting its published financial information.[101] Fiduciary duties, as well as specific personal liabilities under the insolvency legislation for wrongful trading,[102] also served as deterrents against abuse of position by directors.

When Professor Prentice reviewed the ultra vires doctrine in 1986, he concluded that 'the doctrine of ultra vires no longer serves any useful purpose' because 'the doctrine is for all intents and purposes defeasible at the discretion of the draftsman'.[103] Virtually all of those consulted by Professor Prentice were of the view that the doctrine of ultra vires failed to provide any significant protection to the interests of shareholders[104] and were critical of its operation in relation to creditors.[105] Professor Prentice concluded that the published accounts and reports of a company were a more helpful source of information than its objects clause.[106] He thought[107] that the provisions of the insolvency legislation relating to wrongful trading, preferences and transactions at an undervalue provided adequate protection to creditors against dissipation of assets without the need in addition for the ultra vires doctrine[108] and that shareholders were also protected against gratuitous dispositions by fiduciary duties, rules about maintenance of capital and unlawful distri-butions, reporting requirements and the provisions of the companies and insolvency legislation entitling them to seek relief from unfair prejudice[109] or to have the company wound up on just and equitable grounds.[110]

The DTI chose not to accept Professor Prentice's recommendation that a company should have the capacity to do any act whatsoever and opted instead for the rather more complex position reviewed in this chapter. However, because companies have tended to

[99] See 6.21, below.
[100] See 17.59.2 and 17.59.3, below.
[101] See Chapter 12.
[102] See 13.17.2, below.
[103] DTI, *Reform of the Ultra Vires Rule*, Part II, Chapter 2, para. 6.
[104] ibid., Chapter 3, para. 3.
[105] ibid., Chapter 3, para. 9.
[106] ibid., Chapter 5, paras. 7 and 11. He recommended that this should be bolstered, in respect of both private and public companies, by a specific obligation to file an annual activities and business statement: Chapter 5, paras. 11, 19 and 26.
[107] ibid., Chapter 6, paras. 28–30.
[108] ibid., Chapter 6, para. 25.
[109] Section 459; see 15.12, below.
[110] Section 122 (1) (g) of the Insolvency Act 1986. See 15.17, below.

continue to adopt prolix objects clauses[111] and the short-form 'general commercial company' object has proved not to be an attractive alternative, the DTI may have occasion to return to this aspect of the ultra vires doctrine.

4.13 Corporate gifts

The topic of corporate gifts provides a good illustration of the way in which, historically, the courts used the ultra vires doctrine to control the application of corporate funds but how, with the decline of that doctrine, other rules have developed to serve that purpose. Glosses were added to the ultra vires doctrine to accommodate control of corporate gifts, but in recent years the courts have stripped away those glosses as being incompatible with ultra vires in its strict sense of outside corporate capacity. The need to have those glosses diminished as other forms of control were put in place.

In *Re Lee, Behrens & Co.*,[112] Eve J laid down three tests by which improper gifts, charitable or otherwise, might be distinguished from those which formed a legitimate intra vires expenditure by the company. To be valid, any payment had to be:

(1) for the benefit of the company;
(2) reasonably incidental to its business; and
(3) made bona fide in the interest of the company.

Charterbridge Corporation v Lloyds Bank[113] repudiated the principles set forth in *Re Lee, Behrens & Co.*, above, so far as they applied to the interpretation of express powers. Pennycuick J rejected the test of the 'benefit of the company' as placing a limit upon the use that may be made of an express provision in the objects clause. He indicated that the question of good faith[114] on the part of the directors related to their fiduciary duty to the company and not to the question of ultra vires.

In *Re Horsley & Weight Ltd*[115] the Court of Appeal endorsed the approach taken in *Charterbridge*. Where on its true construction a clause in the memorandum allowed for the payment of pensions as a separate object, and not merely as an ancillary power or object to the main object of the company, the purchase of a pension policy could not be challenged by the liquidator as ultra vires the objects of the company. Buckley LJ discarded Eve J's criteria as they applied to express powers as 'no more than *obiter dictum*'. The clause in this case also allowed the making of grants for charitable, benevolent or public purposes or objects. Buckley LJ observed that 'the objects of a company need not be commercial; they can be charitable or philanthropic; indeed, they can be whatever the original incorporators wish, provided that they are legal. Nor is there any reason why a company should not part with its funds gratuitously or for non-commercial reasons if to do so is within its declared objects'.

However, where a gift or gratuitous payment may not be challenged as ultra vires for

---

[111] Or have retained existing long-form objects which were in place before the short-form 'general commercial company' object was introduced.

[112] [1932] 2 Ch 46.

[113] [1970] Ch 62. Pennycuick J's reasoning in *Charterbridge* was followed in *Thomson v J. Barke & Co. (Caterers) Ltd* 1975 SLT 67 at pp. 70–1.

[114] As to the directors' duty of good faith, see 14.4, below. For an illustration of such lack of good faith, see *Re W & M Roith Ltd* [1967] 1 WLR 432.

[115] [1982] 3 All ER 108. See also *Re Halt Garage (1964) Ltd* [1982] 3 All ER 1016, where Oliver J adopted a similar approach. He regarded the test of 'good faith' and 'the benefit of the company' as irrelevant to express powers.

the reasons stated, it may still be impugned as an unlawful return of capital (e.g. where a payment is made under the guise of directors' remuneration where the real intention is to make a gift of capital to shareholders)[116] or as a transaction at an undervalue under section 238 of the Insolvency Act 1986.[117] Directors who authorise the making of corporate gifts at a time when, to their knowledge, the company's solvency is in doubt may also be liable for misfeasance under section 212 of the Insolvency Act 1986.[118] An argument based on misfeasance will not succeed where gifts are made with the knowledge and consent of all of the shareholders at their instigation and the company is fully solvent.[119] It has been held that in addition to rules prohibiting the return of capital to members, a company which has no distributable profits cannot make gifts to outsiders except for the advancement of the company's business.[120] The best explanation for this rule would appear to be that the making of such gifts amounts to a fraud on the company's creditors, which is something that the shareholders are powerless to authorise.[121]

Where no express power has been conferred by the memorandum, the extent of the company's implied powers to make gifts must be determined. In the early case of *Attorney-General v Great Eastern Rly*[122] it was said that whatever could fairly be regarded as incidental to, or consequential upon, the stated objects would be implied. Eve J's second test – reasonably incidental to its business – is no more than a restatement of this conventional test for implying powers into an objects clause and, to that extent, the reasoning in *Re Lee, Behrens* may still be regarded as authoritative.[123]

With regard to the element of benefit to the company, in *Charterbridge* Pennycuick J commented that this was appropriate in part to the scope of implied powers and in part, and perhaps principally, to the duty of directors.[124] Oliver J was more explicit in *Re Halt Garage* stating that the test of benefit to the company was, in his view, really only appropriate to the question of the propriety of an exercise of a power.[125] Pennycuick J in *Charterbridge* and Oliver J in *Re Halt Garage* had the same view of the bona fides test: that it was relevant to the fiduciary duties of the directors and did not affect the construction of the company's implied powers.[126]

Neither *Charterbridge* nor *Re Halt Garage* required the court to rule on the scope of a company's implied powers and the comments on implied powers were therefore strictly obiter. This was also the position in *Rolled Steel* where the actual decision of the Court of Appeal related to the company's express power in its memorandum to give guarantees. Nevertheless, the Court of Appeal took the opportunity to consider the *Re Lee, Behrens* tests generally and, although not formally overruled, the force of the criticisms voiced by Slade

---

[116] *Re Halt Garage* above; *Aveling Barford Ltd v Perion Ltd*, [1989] BCLC 626; *Barclays Bank plc v British and Commonwealth Holdings plc* [1995] BCC 19 (indirect return of capital).

[117] The company must have gone into liquidation or an administrator must have been appointed. The conditions which must be satisfied for section 238 to apply are discussed in chapter 17. Note also section 423 of the Insolvency Act 1986 (transactions defrauding creditors).

[118] *Re Horsley & Weight*, above.

[119] *Brady v Brady* [1989] AC 755 at p. 776.

[120] *Barclays Bank plc v British and Commonwealth Holdings plc*, above.

[121] *ANZ Executors & Trustee Co. Ltd v Qintex Australia Ltd* (1990) 8 ACLC 980; *Plain Ltd v Kilney & Royal Trust Co.* (1931) 1 DLR 468; *Re George Newman & Co.* [1985] 1 Ch 674.

[122] (1875) LR 7 HL 653. Note also *Hutton v West Cork Railway Co.* (1883) 23 Ch D 654 at p. 671 *per* Bowen LJ.

[123] *Charterbridge* at p. 71; *Re Halt Garage (1964) Ltd* [1982] 3 All ER 1016 at p. 1034.

[124] At p. 71.

[125] At p. 1034.

[126] *Charterbridge* at p. 71; *Re Halt Garage* at p. 1034.

and Browne-Wilkinson LJJ means that little of Eve J's reasoning in the earlier case can be regarded as still relevant to the question of construction of implied powers to make corporate gifts.

Without distinguishing between express and implied powers, Slade LJ stated simply that:[127]

> the three tests of ultra vires suggested by Eve J ... should, in my opinion, now be recognised as being of no assistance, and indeed positively misleading, when the relevant question is whether a particular gratuitous transaction is within a company's corporate capacity. To this extent, the tests should, I think, be finally laid to rest, though they may well be helpful in considering whether or not in any given case directors have abused the powers vested in them by the company.

Browne-Wilkinson LJ endorsed Pennycuick J's analysis in *Charterbridge* and regarded the reasoning in *Re Lee, Behrens* as 'wrong'.[128]

Three types of corporate gifts require special mention. These are pensions to former employees and their dependants, redundancy payments and charitable or political donations.

4.13.1 *Pensions*

Where the paying of pensions is an independent object of the company, pensions paid under that power in the company's memorandum cannot be ultra vires.[129] Where the memorandum authorises the paying of pensions but, as a matter of construction, that provision is only a power and is not a substantive object, provided that power is capable of being used in a manner which is reasonably incidental to the attainment or pursuit of its substantive objects, its use in particular cases will not be ultra vires although the directors may be liable for breach of their fiduciary duties if they have abused the power.[130] The power to pay pensions could be viewed as being capable of being exercised reasonably incidentally to the company's business on the grounds that it is conducive to business to seek to retain the workforce by being seen to be a generous employer.[131]

If there is no express power in the memorandum to pay pensions, the test is whether this can be implied as being reasonably incidental to the company's business.[132] In an ordinary trading company that test would normally be satisfied; thus Plowman J in *Re W & M Roith Ltd*[133] was 'disposed to agree' with counsel 'that a widow's pension is reasonably incidental to carrying on a company's business'. In *Roith* a pension granted under an express power in the memorandum was held to be ultra vires by application of the *Re Lee, Behrens* tests; in view of *Re Horsley & Weight* and *Rolled Steel*, *Roith* may now be better regarded as an instance where the directors abused the corporate powers in breach of their fiduciary duties.

---

[127] At p. 288.
[128] At pp. 304–5.
[129] *Re Horsley & Weight*, above.
[130] *Rolled Steel*, above.
[131] Similar arguments could be used to justify the provision of sporting and social welfare facilities.
[132] *Henderson v Bank of Australasia* (1888) 40 Ch D 170; *Normandy v Ind Coope & Co Ltd* [1908] 1 Ch 84, 104; *Cyclists' Touring Club v Hopkinson* [1910] 1 Ch 179.
[133] [1967] 1 WLR 432 at p. 437.

4.13.2 Charitable or political donations

Parliament requires that charitable and political donations which exceed £200 in any financial year must be disclosed in the directors' report.[134] This provision does not of itself validate gifts, being concerned simply with disclosure. In *Evans v Brunner Mond & Co.*[135] a chemical manufacturing company was allowed to distribute £100,000 from its reserves in grants to universities and scientific institutions to finance scientific research and the training of scientists. Eve J, applying a test of benefit to the company, held that the company would be directly benefited by the advance of scientific research and by the increase in the number of trained scientists. If there is no express power, the question of the company's capacity to make charitable donations would now depend on whether this is reasonably incidental to the company's business.

It is a common practice to make donations to a political party whose policies, in the view of the board of directors, it is in the interest of the company to advance. The generally held assumption that companies may make political gifts to the Conservative Party, or indeed any other political party, even in the absence of an express power to do so was finally tested in the courts in a case concerning gifts to the Labour Party by the League Against Cruel Sports Ltd, a charitable company. In *Simmonds v Heffer,*[136] Mervyn Davies J was dealing with a charitable company whose main object was to prevent and oppose cruelty to animals. The plaintiff first challenged a gift of £50,000 to the general election fund of the Labour Party. This gift had been made on the ground that the party was committed to introducing legislation to ban hare-coursing and stag-hunting. This gift was held to be ultra vires as it could be used for purposes unconnected with the League's purposes. This was despite an ancillary power 'to affiliate, to combine or co-operate with, subscribe to, aid or support any institution having objects similar to the main objects of the League or any of them'. This was because the Labour Party, by its constitution, had vastly wider aims than the League and therefore did not have aims similar to the League's main objects. However, another gift of £30,000, made on the understanding that it would be used specifically for activities advertising the Labour Party's commitment to animal welfare, was upheld as being within the League's main objects as supported by ancillary powers in its objects clause.

This case was decided before *Rolled Steel v British Steel Corporation,*[137] and it is not surprising that its reasoning is not consistent with the Court of Appeal's restatement of the principles applicable to powers (as opposed to objects) in the memorandum. *Rolled Steel,* however, was not concerned with political or charitable gifts and it is questionable how far the protection that the court sought to give third parties in commercial transactions should in any event apply to the voluntary recipients of political or charitable donations. Where a political or charitable gift is covered by an express provision, *Re Horsley & Weight Ltd*[138] makes it clear that like any other gift it is not open to challenge. By the same token there may be companies where such gifts are not a 'substantive object' of the company but are made under ancillary powers which (per Buckley LJ)[139] by their very

---

[134] See now the Companies Act 1985, Schedule 7, para. 3.

[135] [1921] 1 Ch 359.

[136] [1984] BCLC 298.

[137] Above. But see a similar decision by Mervyn Davies J in *Rosemary Simmons Memorial Housing Association v United Dominions Trust* [1985] 1 WLR 1440. Though *Rolled Steel* was taken into account, ultra vires was strictly applied to a charitable company.

[138] [1982] 3 All ER 1045.

[139] ibid., at p. 1052.

nature are incapable of standing as independent objects which can be pursued in isolation as the sole activity of the company. Mervyn Davies J rightly applied this distinction made by Buckley LJ in *Re Horsley and Weight*.[140]

Although the courts may be a little more liberal, despite the absence of an express power, in construing political gifts by commercial companies as incidental or conducive to their commercial activities, it may be wise in any litigation to be able to point to some aspect of a political party's policy which seems, in the opinion of the directors, advantageous to that company or generally to companies in the same area of commercial or industrial activity. (This assumes the memorandum contains the 'common form' powers of this nature.) It may not be sufficient simply to assert that all the directors are members of, or wish to support, say the Conservative Party or that a company may support any party which stands for free enterprise. The courts are unlikely to uphold criteria which are too blatantly political, in the sense that they favour one party rather than another.

The simple solution is to have an express power to make political gifts (or indeed gifts to a named party). Such a power may be added to existing objects in accordance with section 4 of the Companies Act 1985 but there could be circumstances where the board of directors would be unwilling to risk the attendant publicity arising from a proposal to adopt such a provision.

4.13.3 *Redundancy payments*

In *Parke v Daily News*[141] it was held that gratuitous redundancy payments paid to former employees were in breach of the *Lee, Behrens* principles since they were motivated by a desire to treat the employees generously, and were not made to benefit the company (which was to cease to be an employer in the newspaper industry). The categorisation of these payments as 'ultra vires' the powers of the company might now be reassessed because of the reliance placed by Plowman J on the discredited *Lee, Behrens* tests. In any event, two statutory innovations originally made by the Companies Act 1980 would mean that a different decision would now be made where employees are affected. Where the company is a going concern, section 309 of the Companies Act 1985 provides that the 'matters to which the directors of a company are to have regard in the performance of their function include the interests of the company's employees in general as well as the interests of its members.'[142] Further, section 719 states that the powers of the company shall be deemed to include a power to make provision 'for the benefit of persons employed or formerly employed by the company or any of its subsidiaries in connection with cessation or transfer to any person of the whole or part of the undertaking of that company or that subsidiary'.

The power conferred by section 719 may be exercised notwithstanding that its exercise is not in the best interests of the company.[143] Section 719 (3) makes it clear the section is concerned with extending the capacity of the company and freeing it from a restriction that the ultra vires doctrine might otherwise impose on such voluntary (i.e. non-statutory) redundancy or retirement payments. It does not dispense with the proper authorisation within the company itself. Section 719 (3) provides that the power it confers may be exercised, if so authorised by the company's memorandum or articles, by a resolution of

[140] See Ewing 'Company Political Donations and the Ultra Vires Rule', 47 MLR 57 (1984).
[141] [1962] Ch 927.
[142] See 14.6, below.
[143] Section 719 (2). See also section 187 of the Insolvency Act 1986.

the directors. If, however, the memorandum or articles require the exercise of the power to be 'sanctioned by a resolution of the company of some other description for which more than a simple majority of members voting is necessary', it must be exercised with the sanction of a resolution of that description: section 719 (3) (*b*) and (*c*). Where no provision for the exercise of the power conferred by section 719 is made in the memorandum or articles, it may be exercised by ordinary resolutions of the company: section 719 (3) (*a*). On the winding up of a solvent company (whether by the court or a voluntary winding up), the liquidator may make any payments which the company decided to make before commencement of the winding up. Provision is also made for the liquidator to exercise this power himself if the company's liabilities have been fully satisfied and provision made for the costs of winding up. He must also obtain the authorisation of the shareholders by a resolution.[144] In the case of payments made before commencement of winding up, these must be made out of the profits of the company available for dividend. In the case of payments made after the commencement of winding up, these must be made out of the assets of the company which are available to its members on its winding up.[145]

4.14 Alteration of objects

The companies legislation which was in force between 1856 and 1890 did not permit the objects of a company to be altered. Once it became possible to alter objects with the consent of only a majority of the shareholders and without the consent of the creditors (although dissident shareholders and creditors might, in limited circumstances, be able to raise objections), the idea that the objects clause was a safeguard against shareholders' and creditors' money being put to purposes which they had not authorised was undermined.

A company may by special resolution, under the power conferred by section 4, alter the provisions of its memorandum of association. This section does not authorise an alteration of the memorandum which does not relate to the objects of the company.[146] But the whole objects of a company are not necessarily contained in the objects clause of the memorandum;[147] and provisions not relating to the objects may, if they could lawfully have been contained in the articles, be alterable under section 17.[148] It will be observed that under section 4 a company now has unrestricted power of limiting or narrowing the scope of its objects and of increasing them.

4.15 The procedure for objecting to an alteration to the objects

Dissenting shareholders or, to a more limited extent, creditors are permitted by section 5 to apply to the court to have the alteration cancelled. An application by shareholders must be made by the holders of not less in the aggregate than 15 per cent of the company's issued share capital or of any class of shares. If the company is not limited by shares, not

---

[144] See section 187 of the Insolvency Act 1986. This may be an ordinary resolution or one by more than a simple majority if the memorandum or articles so require. A resolution of the directors will not suffice.

[145] Section 719 (4) and 187 (3) of the Insolvency Act 1986.

[146] *In Re Society for Promoting Employment of Women* [1927] WN 145; cf. *Re Scientific Poultry Breeders' Association* [1933] 1 Ch 227; *Re Scottish Special Housing Association* 1947 SC 17.

[147] *Incorporated Glasgow Dental Hospital v Lord Advocate* 1927 SC 400.

[148] See 3.13, above.

less than 15 per cent of the members must make the application. The creditors entitled to make the application are limited to the holders of debentures secured by a floating charge which were issued or first issued before 1 December 1947, or which form part of the same series as any debentures so issued; and an application by debenture holders must be made by the holders of not less than 15 per cent of such debentures.

A person – whether a shareholder or debenture holder – who has consented to or voted in favour of the alteration cannot make an application under the section.

The application must be made within twenty-one days after the date of the passing of the resolution, and the persons entitled to make it may in writing appoint one or more of their number for the purpose.[149]

4.16 The court's discretion

On the hearing of an application under section 5 (4), the court may confirm the alteration either wholly or in part and on such terms and conditions as it thinks fit. Moreover, it may adjourn the proceedings in order that an arrangement may be made to the satisfaction of the court for the purchase of the interests of dissentient members, and may give directions and make orders for facilitating or carrying into effect any such arrangement.

Section 5 (5) provides that, if the court thinks fit, an order under section 5 may provide for the purchase by the company of the shares of any members of the company and for the reduction accordingly of the company's capital. The court may make such consequent alterations in the memorandum and articles as are required in consequence of such provision. Quite apart from this, the court may require the company to make any, or any specified, alteration in the memorandum or articles of the company. The company will not then have power without leave of the court to make any further alteration in breach of what the court has required.[150] Alterations of the memorandum or articles required by the court have the same effect as if duly altered by resolution of the company.[151]

Section 4 was amended by the Companies Act 1989 to remove certain limitations on the power to alter the objects. Even before those limitations were removed (i.e. at a time when it was possible to object to an alteration on the grounds that it exceeded the scope of the statutory power), applications under what is now section 5 had become a very rare occurrence.[152] Shareholders who are aggrieved by an alteration to the objects have the option of seeking alternative relief under Part XVII of the Companies Act 1985 (the unfair prejudice remedy) or may even seek to have the company wound up under section 122 (1) (g) of the Insolvency Act 1986.[153] These alternative remedies are not subject to the strict time-limit imposed on section 5 applications and there is no minimum shareholding requirement which must be met.

---

[149] As to the necessity for obtaining within the twenty-one days the authority of the holders of the requisite number of shares or debentures cf. *Re Suburban & Provincial Stores* [1943] Ch 106; *Re Sound City (Films)* [1947] Ch 169.

[150] Section 5 (6).

[151] Section 5 (7). For similar powers conferred on the court under sections 459 to 461 (relief where members are unfairly prejudiced) and section 54 of the 1985 Act (cancellation of special resolutions by the court where a public company becomes a private company), see respectively 15.15, below, and 2.13, above.

[152] After an earlier relaxation made by the Companies Act 1948 there was only reported application under the relevant section: *Re Hampstead Garden Suburban Trust Ltd* [1962] Ch 806.

[153] Para. 4.18 below.

4.17 Publicity for alterations of the memorandum

The requirements imposed by sections 42 and 711 of the Companies Act 1985 in regard to alteration of the memorandum have been examined at 3.14–3.15, above. As regards the alteration of the objects clause certain additional points should be noted. Section 18 (regarding forwarding printed copies of the altered memorandum and the instrument of alteration to the Registrar) does not apply to a special resolution under section 4 of the Companies Act 1985. However, section 6 (1) of the Companies Act 1985 itself requires, *inter alia*, the delivery of a printed copy of the memorandum as altered.

Section 17, which is concerned with the alteration of optional conditions in the memorandum, gives dissenting shareholders the same right to apply to the court as is given by section 5 to those who dissent from an alteration of the objects clause (see 3.13, above). However, even though section 17 invokes the procedure laid down by certain subsections of section 5, the resolution altering optional provisions in the memorandum is a resolution under section 17. Consequently, it is not exempt from the requirements of section 18.

4.18 Just and equitable winding up

Shareholders who object to a company undertaking a new type of activity when its original business is abandoned may have a form of relief open to them other than invoking the ultra vires doctrine. They may petition the court under section 122 (1) (*g*) of the Insolvency Act 1986 for a compulsory winding-up order on the ground that it is just and equitable to do so. One basis on which the court will make a just and equitable winding-up order is that the substratum of the company, the main object for which it was incorporated, has ceased to exist.[154] Moreover, a winding-up order may be made even though the new activity is technically within the scope of an express power. Even if the memorandum provides that each of the powers conferred by the objects clause shall be a main object, the court may still find that the company has abandoned the real purposes for which it was founded.[155]

4.19 Authority to bind the company

Where the company possesses undoubted contractual capacity in respect of a particular contract, there still remains the question of whether those who purported to make a contract on the company's behalf had the authority to do so. The authority to bind the company must be conferred either directly by the articles of association or by delegation under a power contained in them. Almost invariably the general power to manage the company will be conferred upon the board of directors[156] and the board itself will usually have a power to delegate their power to manage the company's affairs (e.g. to one or more managing directors[157]). On some important matters the approval of the general meeting must be obtained in the form of an ordinary resolution.[158]

Lack of authority to bind the company is not so radical a defect as lack of capacity.

---

[154] For detailed treatment of the grounds on which a court will make a just and equitable order, see 15.17, below, where the cases on the disappearance of the substratum of a company are examined.

[155] *Cotman v Brougham* [1918] AC 514 at p. 520 *per* Lord Parker.

[156] Article 70 of the Companies (Tables A to F) Regulations 1985. References in this chapter to articles are to articles of the Table A contained in these regulations.

[157] e.g. Table A, articles 84 and 72.

[158] e.g. Table A, article 70, in respect of the directors' powers relative to the company's powers.

Consequently, any want of authority can be cured by ratification by a resolution of the shareholders in general meeting.[159] An ordinary resolution normally suffices but where the lack of authority results from the provisions of the company's memorandum, a special resolution is required.[160] Where a contract is neither originally binding upon the company nor subsequently ratified, the third party may be entitled to recover on a restitutionary basis if the company has received money or goods have been supplied or services have been rendered.

Moreover a director or other lesser agent who lacks the authority to bind the company that he claims, may be liable for breach of warranty of authority. Where a wilful or reckless misrepresentation on the part of the directors can be established, an action for deceit might be brought.[161]

A contract for which there is no actual authority (express or implied) may nevertheless become binding on the company under a number of principles. The directors or other officers of a company have no actual authority to bind the company in matters falling outside the constitutional limits imposed by its memorandum and articles. However, by virtue of section 35A of the Companies Act 1985 (as inserted by the Companies Act 1989), transactions which are outside the constitutional limits can sometimes be enforced against the company.[162] Under the doctrine of ostensible (or apparent) authority, a person who has no actual authority to act on the company's behalf may be able to bind the company if he has been held out by someone with appropriate authority as a duly authorised agent of the company. The doctrine of ostensible authority is part of the general law of agency and it applies irrespective of whether the principal is a company or a natural person. A special modification of the doctrine known as the 'rule in *Turquand's case*' applies only in relation to corporate principals.

4.20 The protection of persons dealing with the company in good faith: section 35A

It is through section 35A (and the surrounding sections) that the United Kingdom seeks to comply with its obligation to implement article 9 of the First Company Law Directive.[163] Article 9 seeks to protect third parties in transactions with a company from 'limitations upon the powers of the competent organs imposed by the Charter or by a decision of the competent organs'. Such limitations 'may never be invoked against third parties even if they have been published'. The First Directive was adopted before the United Kingdom joined the European Community and its language is unfamiliar because, in contractual matters, English law traditionally has not regarded the board and the general meeting as 'organs' of a company. Possibly because of differences in established terminology, article 9 was badly implemented by section 9 of the European Communities Act 1972 (which, on consolidation of the companies legislation became section 35 of the Companies Act

---

[159]   *Grant v United Kingdom Switchback Railway Co.* (1889) 40 Ch D 135 (CA); *Phosphate of Lime Co. v Green* (1871) LR 7, CP 43; *Campbell's Case* (1873) 9 Ch App. 1.

[160]   Section 35 (3).

[161]   Or an action for negligent misstatement under *Hedley Byrne & Co. v Heller Partners* [1964] AC 465.

[162]   See 4.20 below.

[163]   Directive 68/151 (EEC), O.J. 1968 L 65/8. As to the European Community's programme of company law directives generally, see *Gore-Browne on Companies* (Jordans, 44th edn, loose-leaf), Part VIII.

1985).[164] What is now contained in section 35A (and surrounding sections) is therefore the United Kingdom's second attempt to implement the directive. Section 35A meets many of the criticisms which were levelled at its predecessor but some points of uncertainty or difficulty remain.

Section 35A (1) provides that:

> In favour of a person dealing with a company in good faith, the power of the board of directors to bind the company, or to authorise others to do so, shall be deemed to be free of any limitation under the company's constitution.

Thus, if a person negotiates a contract with the board of directors of the company and it subsequently emerges that the board's authority to conclude that contract was in fact limited by the company's constitution, that person can nevertheless hold the company to the contract provided he is in 'good faith'. The limitation on the board's authority may stem from the company's memorandum where it is beyond the company's express (or implied) objects and powers to enter into contracts of that type. A limitation imposed by the company's articles is also a limitation under the company's constitution: thus section 35A applies where the board exceeds a limit imposed by the articles on its power to manage the company's affairs. By virtue of section 35A (3), limitations under the company's constitution also include limitations deriving from a resolution of the company in general meeting or a meeting of any class of shareholders, or from any agreement between the members of the company or any class of shareholders.

It is usually not practicable for the board of a company to play a significant role in the day-to-day contracts which are entered into in the ordinary course of the company's business. These contracts are normally the responsibility of individual directors and other corporate officers. Typically, the board of directors is only involved in major contracts such as acquisitions of new businesses, disposals of existing divisions of the company, or loans and other financing agreements. A criticism of section 9 of the European Communities Act 1972 was that it only applied in respect of 'transactions decided upon by directors'; although the courts did attempt to interpret this provision robustly,[165] it appeared that, in all but exceptional cases,[166] transactions which were authorised within the company at a level below that of the board fell outside the scope of the statutory protection.

In this respect, section 35A is more helpfully drafted because, as well as protecting outsiders who deal with the board directly, it also deems the power of the board to authorise others to bind the company to be free of any limitations under the company's constitution. But for section 35A, if the board purports to delegate, say to a managing director, in breach of limitations on its powers to delegate in the company's constitution, the managing director cannot be said to have authority to bind the company. Although, in a factual sense the managing director may have been held out by the board as having authority, the principle of ostensible authority does not apply because the board itself has

---

[164] Commentaries on the implementation of article 9 by the European Communities Act 1972 include: Prentice (1973) 89 LQR 518; Farrar & Powles (1973) 36 MLR 270; Sealy & Collier [1973] CLJ 1; Wyatt (1978) 94 LQR 182.

[165] *TCB v Gray* [1986] Ch 621 (informal consent of all directors to the granting of a debenture), affirmed [1987] Ch 458n; *International Sales and Agencies Ltd v Marcus*, above.

[166] In *International Sales and Agencies Ltd v Marcus*, above at p. 560 Lawson J observed that the statutory protection could apply where there was a 'sole effective director to whom all actual authority to act for the board had been delegated'.

no authority under the company's constitution to make the representation.[167] In favour of an outsider, section 35A deems the board to have that authority.

An apparent lacuna in section 35A is that it does not expressly protect an outsider against specific constitutional limitations on persons other than the board. If the articles limit the authority of the managing director to contracts of a particular type or impose a ceiling on the amounts involved, that is obviously not a limit on the board's power to bind the company and, read literally, it is not a limit on the board's power to delegate authority. Accordingly, this is not covered by section 35A unless it is possible to argue that section 35A, by deeming the board to have unlimited power to authorise others to bind the company, overrides any specific limitation whether expressed to apply to the board or to an individual.[168] In practice, it would be uncommon for the authority of individual directors or officers to be limited by the company's constitution; such limitations are more usually imposed in the contracts of employment of the relevant individuals. The effect of contractual limitations on outsiders falls outside the scope of section 35A and is governed by agency principles and the rule in *Turquand's* case.

The application of section 35A to an improperly constituted board was debated during the passage of the Companies Bill 1988 through Parliament. The view of the government spokesperson was that articles specifying the quorum for board meetings, voting rights at board meetings and the like were to be regarded as provisions which defined the board rather than limitations on the powers of the board.[169] If that interpretation is correct,[170] a transaction which is entered into by an inquorate board is not protected by section 35A. However, it is well established in English company law that the rule in *Turquand's* case protects outsiders against internal irregularities of which they are unaware. The fact of a board being improperly constituted is an internal irregularity and an outsider would not usually be aware of it in his dealings with the company. Accordingly, even if section 35A does not apply in this situation, the outsider could still be protected under the older *Turquand* rule.[171]

4.21 A person dealing with a company in good faith

A person deals with a company if he is a party to any transaction or other act to which the company is a party.[172] The reference to 'any other act' makes clear that the protection of the section extends beyond purely commercial matters and includes charitable gifts and other gratuitous distributions of assets. Under the predecessor section, this point was doubtful.[173] Shareholders, as such, are not excluded from the protection of section 35A

---

[167] See further 4.31 below.

[168] Note the robust interpretation of 'limitations' in *TCB v Gray*, above. Even if section 35A can be interpreted in this way, it would still be necessary to refer to agency principles to determine whether the company is actually bound by the acts of an individual.

[169] *Hansard*, HL Debs., 7 November 1989, cols. 685–7.

[170] It was challenged by Lord Wedderburn in the House of Lords in the debate on the relevant clauses of the Companies Bill: *Hansard*, HL Debs., 7 November 1989, cols. 685–7.

[171] Note that the protection afforded by the *Turquand* rule is more limited than that given by section 35A. Section 35A protects persons who are in good faith, and good faith is not incompatible with knowledge that a limitation under the constitution has been breached: 4.21 below. However, an outsider who knows of an internal irregularity or who is put on inquiry cannot rely on the rule in *Turquand's* case: 4.25 below.

[172] Section 35A (2) (*a*).

[173] In *Re Halt Garage*, above at pp. 1039–40, Oliver J took the view, without deciding the point, that section 9 of the European Communities Act only protected those who were in a contractual relationship with the company. See also *International Sales v Marcus*, above at p. 560.

but it is doubtful whether that section could be invoked in connection with a claim arising from the contract of membership under section 14 of the Companies Act 1985. Special provision is made for directors who deal with their company. This is discussed in 4.23 below.

Good faith is presumed so that the burden of proof lies with the person who asserts that the outsider did not deal in good faith.[174] The burden of proof would thus normally fall on the company. Section 35A (2) (*b*) expressly provides that a person is not to be regarded as acting in bad faith by reason only of his knowing that an act is beyond the powers of the directors under the company's constitution. This provision clarifies some doubts that were created by the wording of the predecessor section but it also gives rise to some new uncertainties. Section 9 of the European Communities Act 1972 protected those who dealt with a company 'in good faith' but gave no guidance as to the meaning of that phrase. In *International Sales v Marcus*[175] Lawson J judged lack of good faith to be found either in actual knowledge or where 'it can be shown that such a person could not in view of all the circumstances have been unaware'.[176] In *Barclays Bank Ltd v TOSG Trust Fund Ltd*[177] Nourse J rejected objective standards, stating that in his judgment a person acted in good faith if he acted 'honestly and genuinely in the circumstances of the case'. It is now clear from section 35A (2) (*b*) that even actual knowledge of the constitutional limits does not amount to bad faith. An example of the type of situation where an outsider might be held to be in good faith, notwithstanding its knowledge, is where the outsider is itself a large organisation which is deemed[178] to have technical knowledge of the company's constitutional limitations, because they are known to some of its departments, but the particular individuals within the organisation who are dealing with the company lack the relevant knowledge.[179] Another is where the outsider reads but fails to understand, or to interpret properly, the company's memorandum and articles.

However, what would now constitute bad faith cannot be stated with any certainty and this is likely to be a matter which will lead to litigation in the future. If, for example, the outsider knows that the directors are acting contrary to constitutional limitations and also that the transaction is part of a scheme by the directors to defraud the company, there could surely be no question of his sheltering behind a protection given only to those who are in good faith. It is not provided that lack of knowledge of the constitutional limitations automatically equates to good faith, so that it is conceivable (although perhaps unlikely) that there could be circumstances where a person could be held to be in bad faith despite not being positively aware of the constitutional limitations.

4.22 No duty to inquire

Section 35B adds to the burden which falls on a company which is trying to establish that an outsider who dealt with it did so in bad faith. Under this section a party to a

---

[174] Section 35A (2) (*c*).

[175] Above.

[176] At p. 559.

[177] [1984] BCLC 121. Nourse J's judgment was reversed on appeal but not on grounds relevant to this point: [1984] AC 626.

[178] Law Commission, *Fiduciary Duties and Regulatory Rules: A Consultation Paper* (No. 124) (HMSO, 1992), section 2.3 considers the ways in which a firm can acquire knowledge.

[179] This example was given by Lord Fraser of Carmyllie during the passage of the Companies Bill 1988 through Parliament: *Hansard* HL Debs., 7 November 1989, col. 683.

transaction[180] with a company is not bound to inquire whether it is permitted by the company memorandum or as to any limitation on the powers of the board of directors to bind the company or authorise others to do so. Failure to make these inquiries cannot therefore be regarded as evidence of bad faith.

An established judge-made rule states that outsiders dealing with a company are deemed to know the contents of its memorandum and articles of association (as registered documents open to public inspection).[181] The constructive notice rule, as it is known, extends to certain other documents which require registration such as the register of charges[182] and also, it is thought, to special resolutions and other resolutions requiring registration under section 380 and the particulars relating to directors which require filing under section 288. Section 142 of the Companies Act 1989 makes provision for the abolition of the constructive notice rule by inserting a new section 711A into the Companies Act 1985. Implementation of this section has not yet taken place because of the need to coordinate the change with developments in the law relating to the registration of charges which are still under consideration.[183]

When section 711A (1) comes into force, a person will not be taken to have notice of any matter merely because of its being disclosed in any document kept by the Registrar of Companies (and thus available for inspection) or made available by the company for inspection. This abolition of the constructive notice rule will, however, be qualified by the immediately following subsection which provides that 'this does not affect the question whether a person is affected by notice of any matter by reason of a failure to make such inquiries as ought reasonably to be made'. Section 35B[184] will be relevant to the question of the 'inquiries as ought reasonably to be made' for the purposes of section 711A (2): where section 35B applies, the party to the transaction with the company has no duty of inquiry in respect of the matters mentioned in that section and therefore cannot be penalised for failing to make such inquiries.[185]

4.23 Directors who deal with their company

Where the person dealing with the company is a director of the company or of its holding company (or is a person connected with such a director or a company with which such a director is associated[186]) special rules apply. Where a director, or a connected person or associated company, is a party to a transaction[187] with the company, in connection with which the board of directors exceeds any limitation under the company's constitution,[188]

---

[180] Section 35B does not expressly apply to 'other acts'. Whether this is a drafting slip or is intended to limit the protection afforded to recipients of gratuitous distributions is unclear.

[181] *Ernest v Nichols* (1857) 6 HL Cas 401; *Rolled Steel*, above.

[182] *Wilson v Kelland* [1910] 2 Ch 306 at p. 313 *per* Eve J.

[183] See Chapter 9.

[184] Section 35B is already in force and explicitly applies to 'any limitation on the powers of the board of directors to bind the company or authorise others to do so'. As to the meaning of similar phraseology in section 35A, see 4.20, above.

[185] Even though section 9 of the European Communities Act 1972 did not contain any provision akin to section 711A and section 35B it was held that the constructive notice rule was excluded in situations covered by that section: *TCB v Gray*, above.

[186] 'Connected' and 'associated' are defined by section 346.

[187] This includes any act: section 322A (8). A non-contractual payment, such as that which was in issue in *Guinness v Saunders* [1990] 2 AC 663, HL, is thus within the scope of the section; see 14.8, below. The remedy afforded by section 322A is in addition to any other claims which the company may have: section 322A (4).

[188] 'Constitution' has the extended meaning which it also has in section 35A: section 322A (8).

the transaction is voidable at the instance of the company and section 35A does not apply. Whether or not the transaction is avoided, the director or, as the case may be, the connected person or associated company is liable to account to the company for any gain which he has made directly or indirectly by the transaction, and to indemnify the company for any loss or damage resulting from the transaction.[189] The directors of the company who authorised the transaction are also liable to the company to the same extent.[190] Directors of the holding company, connected persons and associated companies, but not directors of the company itself, have a defence to the personal liability imposed by section 322A if they can show that at the time when the transaction was entered into they did not know that the directors were exceeding their powers.[191]

A transaction which is voidable under section 322A ceases to be voidable in any of the following circumstances:

(1) restitution of any money or other asset which was the subject-matter of the transaction is no longer possible;
(2) the company is indemnified for any loss or damage resulting from the transaction;
(3) rights acquired bona fide for value and without actual notice of the directors exceeding their powers by a person who is not a party to the transaction would be affected by the avoidance;
(4) the transaction is ratified by the company in general meeting, by ordinary or special resolution or otherwise as the case may require.[192]

If the limits exceeded are those imposed by the company's memorandum, section 35 (3) requires the ratification to be given by special resolution. Where the directors exceed limits imposed by the articles, ratification by ordinary resolution suffices.[193]

Section 322A (7) addresses the problem of multi-party transactions where some of the parties are protected by section 35A but others are not because they are caught by section 322A. In that case, either a party protected by section 35A or the company can apply to the court for an order affirming, severing or setting aside the transaction on such terms as appear to the court to be just.

4.24 The 'internal' aspects of section 35A

Section 35A (4) provides that section 35A (1) does not affect the right of a member of the company to bring proceedings to restrain the doing of an act which is beyond the powers of the directors; but no such proceedings shall lie in respect of an act to be done in fulfilment of a legal obligation arising from a previous act of the company. This is similar to section 35 (2) which has already been discussed, but there is a significant difference in the wording of the two provisions. Whereas section 35 (2) codifies the right of a member of a company to seek an injunction restraining the doing of an act which is outside the limits of the company's memorandum, section 35A (4) merely preserves such right as the member may have to seek to restrain acts beyond the powers of the directors. The extent to which a member has standing to enforce the provisions of the articles depends on the

---

[189] Section 322A (3).
[190] ibid.
[191] Section 322A (6).
[192] Section 322A (5).
[193] *Grant v United Kingdom Switchback Railway Co.*, above.

scope of statutory contract formed by section 14 of the Companies Act 1985 and on the rule in *Foss v Harbottle*. Both of these questions are explored elsewhere.[194]

The qualification contained in section 35A (4) preserves the binding nature of transactions with outsiders who are protected by section 35A but it means that shareholders can only seek to restrain contemplated transactions or those which are not binding on the company because the other party is not within section 35A. The practical effect of section 35A (4) is likely to be limited because shareholders will rarely discover the directors' plans at a time before a legal obligation has been incurred.

Section 35A (5) preserves any liability incurred by the directors, or any other person,[195] by reason of the directors' exceeding their powers. Entering into an unauthorised transaction may amount to a breach of the directors' fiduciary duties.[196]

4.25 The *Turquand* rule: the indoor management principle

The purpose of the rule first clearly set forth in *Royal British Bank v Turquand*[197] is to provide some measure of protection for those who enter into contracts with the company from the consequences of the complex internal organisation of companies. The essence of the *Turquand* rule is that those dealing with a company are not affected by what is called the 'indoor management' of companies. They are entitled to assume that the internal procedures of a company, both at directors' and shareholders' meetings, have been regularly conducted in the absence of actual notice to the contrary. Section 382 (4) of the Companies Act 1985 gives indirect support to this principle. It provides that where the minutes of shareholders' or directors' meetings are kept as the section requires, there is a presumption, until the contrary is proved, that all meetings have been regularly convened and conducted.[198] However, where it applies, the *Turquand* rule is conclusive and does not simply raise a rebuttable presumption.

It has been held by the Court of Appeal that the rule in *Turquand's* case is not a mere plea of law (which therefore does not have to be pleaded). It is a plea of mixed law and fact. It must therefore be pleaded and may not be raised if it has not been pleaded unless the court permits the pleadings to be amended.[199]

The rule in *Turquand's* case ameliorated the severity of the constructive notice rule whereby outsiders were deemed to know the contents of documents registered at the Companies Registry. With the (expected) abolition of the constructive notice rule[200] and the enactment of the wide-ranging protection afforded to those dealing with a company by sections 35 and 35A of the Companies Act 1985, the importance of the *Turquand* rule has decreased. In many circumstances it overlaps with section 35A: for example, if the articles cap the directors' borrowing power by requiring them to seek the approval of the shareholders in general meeting by ordinary resolution for borrowings over a certain

---

[194] See 3.18, above and 15.2, below.

[195] A person dealing with a company may become implicated in the directors' breach of duty and thus incur liability to the company as a constructive trustee. It is unclear whether a person who is in good faith for the purposes of section 35A could nevertheless be held to be a constructive trustee. In *International Sales v Marcus* Lawson J held that section 9 of the European Communities Act 1972 did not affect constructive trust liability.

[196] See Chapter 14, below.

[197] (1856), 6 E & B 327 (Exch. Ch).

[198] This presumption extends to all appointments of directors, managers and liquidators.

[199] *Rolled Steel Products v British Steel Corporation*, above.

[200] By the insertion (from a date which is yet to be announced) of section 711A into the Companies Act 1985. Note the uncertain effect of this abolition because of the qualification in section 711A (2): 4.22 above.

amount, the lender can either assume that the ordinary resolution has been obtained, because, under the *Turquand* rule, this is a matter of internal management, or can disregard the need for the resolution because this is a limitation on the directors' power which is overridden by section 35A.[201]

The rule in *Turquand's* case cannot be relied upon by an outsider who knows the true position or who is put on inquiry.[202] The very nature of a proposed transaction can be sufficient to put an outsider on inquiry.[203] In circumstances where there is an overlap between section 35A and the rule in *Turquand's* case, section 35A may thus offer greater protection because even actual knowledge of the irregularity does not amount to 'bad faith' putting the person dealing with the company outside the scope of that section.

One situation to which the *Turquand* rule applies but to which section 35A may have no application is in respect of decisions made by a body which purports to be the board of the company but which is improperly constituted. Although the issue has not yet been tested in the courts, one interpretation of section 35A is that it only applies to acts of a properly constituted board and has no relevance to the logically prior question of what constitutes the 'board'.[204] The facts of *Rolled Steel* demonstrate one way in which a board may be improperly constituted: the articles of the company provided that where a director had a personal interest in any matter under consideration by the board, he had to declare that interest in order to count in the quorum at the meeting and to vote on the matter; where a director failed to declare his interest before voting, the board meeting was improperly constituted and the decision was therefore defective.

4.26 'Outsiders'

The *Turquand* rule is designed to protect 'outsiders' dealing with the seemingly authorised agents of the company. If they are unaware of any irregularity, the rule will protect not only complete outsiders, such as creditors, but also the members of the company (at any rate *vis-à-vis* the conduct of board meetings). Even a director in some circumstances may be treated as an outsider. If a director has not acted on behalf of the company in connection with the transaction he seeks to enforce, he may invoke the *Turquand* rule in order to bind the company.[205] Where he has acted on behalf of the company and it is his duty to have knowledge of the true state of affairs, he will not be able to rely on the rule.[206]

Section 322A does not draw a distinction between insider and outsider directors. A contract between a director and his company which infringes constitutional limits is voidable irrespective of the director's involvement on behalf of the company. A director

---

[201] In practice, lenders may insist on seeing a copy of the resolution as a pre-condition of the loan especially if the amounts involved are significant.

[202] *B Liggett (Liverpool) Ltd v Barclays Bank Ltd* [1928] 1 KB 48; *Morris v Kanssen* [1946] AC 459; *Rolled Steel*, above.

[203] *AL Underwood Ltd v Bank of Liverpool and Martins* [1924] 1 KB 775; *Northside Developments Pty Ltd v Registrar-General* (1989–1990) 2 ACSR 161, (1990) 64 ALJR 427, noted [1991] CLJ 47.

[204] 4.20 above.

[205] *Hely-Hutchinson v Brayhead Ltd* [1968] 1 QB 549, *per* Roskill J. (The decision was confirmed on other grounds in the Court of Appeal.)

[206] *Morris v Kanssen* [1946] AC 459 (HL); *Howard v Patent Ivory Co.* (1888) 38 Ch D 156. Where the third party is a company, notice will not be binding unless given to an officer in the course of the company's business, or in such circumstances that it was his duty to communicate it to the company. Thus, one of two companies having directors, or a secretary, in common will not by reason of that fact be taken to have notice of the manner in which the acts of the other are carried out: *Re Hampshire Land Co.* [1896] 2 Ch 743; *Re Marseilles Extension Rly Co.* (1871) 7 Ch App. 161; *Re Fenwick, Stobart & Co.* [1902] 1 Ch 507; *Re David Payne & Co.* [1904] 2 Ch 608 (CA).

cannot rely on the *Turquand* rule in relation to a transaction which is voidable under section 322A.

4.27 General agency principles and the *Turquand* rule

Although the *Turquand* rule will protect an outsider in regard to internal procedures at general meetings and board meetings, when it comes to the powers of individual officers and agents of the company the outsider cannot rely solely on the internal management rule. Whether a company is bound by acts which are done on its behalf depends on whether the director, or other individual, who acted for the company had authority to do so.

There are two main types of authority, namely actual authority and ostensible (or apparent) authority. Actual authority is authority which the principal confers, either expressly or impliedly, on the agent. The board of directors of a company has express actual authority to exercise such powers of the company as are vested in it by the company's memorandum and articles; a managing, or other executive, director appointed under a written service contract has express actual authority to bind the company to the extent that this is authorised by his contract. Where the terms on which someone is appointed to an executive position within a company are not spelt out in an express service contract, actual authority to bind the company may nevertheless be implied from the circumstances. Such authority may also be implied where a person is allowed de facto to assume a position but is never expressly appointed. In *Hely-Hutchinson v Brayhead Ltd*[207] the Court of Appeal held that the de facto managing director of the company had implied actual authority to bind the company to contracts of guarantee and indemnity.

The crucial distinction between actual authority and ostensible authority is that actual authority is a relationship between the principal and agent[208] and ostensible authority is the authority of an agent as it *appears* to others.[209] Ostensible authority is created 'by a representation, made by the principal to the contractor, intended to be and in fact acted upon by the contractor, that the agent has authority'.[210] The agent is not a party to the relationship created by the principal's representation and the representation, when acted upon, acts as an estoppel preventing the principal from claiming that it is not bound.[211] Actual authority and ostensible authority can coincide[212] but an important feature of ostensible authority is that it can exist in circumstances where the agent has no actual authority. Thus, if the company restricts the powers of its managing director in some respect, the managing director has no actual authority, whether express or implied, to bind the company in matters covered by the restriction; but an outsider dealing with the managing director who is unaware of the restriction may be able to hold the company to the transaction on the basis of ostensible authority.

Ostensible authority can take one of two forms: either the directors and officers have a 'usual' authority attached to their office, giving a certain scope of authority implied by law; or the company may be estopped from denying that it held out its agent as having

---

[207] [1968] 1 QB 549.

[208] The scope of which is to be ascertained by applying ordinary principles of construction: *Freeman & Lockyer v Buckhurst Park Properties (Mangal) Ltd* [1964] 2 QB 480.

[209] *Freeman and Lockyer* [1964] 2 QB at p. 503 *per* Diplock LJ; *Hely-Hutchinson v Brayhead* [1968] 1 QB at p. 583 *per* Lord Denning MR.

[210] *Freeman & Lockyer* [1964] 2 QB at p. 503 *per* Diplock LJ.

[211] ibid. Also at p. 498 *per* Pearson LJ.

[212] *Freeman & Lockyer* at p. 502 *per* Diplock LJ; *Hely-Hutchinson* at p. 583 *per* Lord Denning MR.

authority to act in a particular transaction. If this representation by words or conduct is relied upon by an outsider, who acts to his detriment in entering into the contract, the company will be bound.

The ultra vires doctrine and the constructive notice rule (as ameliorated by the *Turquand* rule) have, in their time, complicated the application of the principles of ostensible authority in relation to companies. The complications have largely disappeared either through statutory developments or through judicial reassessment of the scope of the constructive notice rule, but it is important to have their earlier significance in mind when considering some of the relevant authorities.

4.28 Usual authority

Depending on the context in which it is used, the term 'usual authority' can denote a species of implied actual authority or, alternatively, a form of ostensible authority.[213] A person who is appointed to a particular office may be said to have usual authority by which it is meant that he has implied actual authority to do whatever falls within the usual scope of that office.[214] Implied actual authority to do whatever acts are necessarily incidental to the performance of the agency is a form of usual authority.[215]

When a person is appointed to an office, he may also be said to have usual authority meaning that he has ostensible authority to do whatever falls within the usual scope of the office.[216] In this case the company will be bound where the agent acts within the scope of his usual authority even though he may exceed specific restrictions which the company has imposed on his actual authority. Appointing someone to an office can be regarded as one form of 'holding out'[217] but it is helpful to distinguish ostensible authority in the form of usual authority from ostensible authority in the form of holding out. This is because where someone has been appointed to a position, there is no doubt that the factual element of holding out has been satisfied and the relevant issue of potential dispute is as to the scope of the usual authority attached to that position.[218]

4.29 Directors, managing directors and chairmen

The exact scope of the usual authority of individual directors, chairmen of boards, managing directors and other executive directors and officers of the company differs considerably. In the case of managing directors, most modern articles empower the board to delegate to them wide powers of management (under the general supervision of the board).[219] In consequence, the courts have held that a managing director's usual authority has a wide scope. It extends to the management of the ordinary business of the company.[220] It will be seen that, where no managing director has been appointed despite a power to do so, the courts will readily infer, on the basis of estoppel, that either a

---

[213] *First Energy UK (ltd) v Hungarian International Bank Ltd* [1993] BCLC 1409, [1993] BCC 533. In *Armagas Ltd v Mundogas SA* [1986] AC 717 (ostensible) usual authority is described as 'general ostensible authority'.

[214] *Hely-Hutchinson*, above.

[215] *First Energy* [1993] BCLC at p. 1418 *per* Steyn LJ.

[216] ibid.

[217] *Egyptian International Foreign Trade Co. v Soplex Wholesale Supplies Ltd, The Raffaella* [1985] BCLC 404 at p. 411.

[218] The courts often distinguish between ostensible authority in the form of usual authority and in the form of holding out: see, for example, *Freeman & Lockyer; The Raffaella; Armagas v Mundogas; First Energy*, above.

[219] Article 72 of Table A.

[220] *Freeman & Lockyer v Buckhurst Park Properties (Mangal) Ltd* [1964] 2 QB 480 (CA).

chairman of the board or another director, acting de facto as chief executive, has been held out by the company as managing director.[221] However, the better view is that a chairman, *qua* chairman, has no wider usual authority than a director.[222] Individual directors, as such, have almost no usual authority[223] beyond a power to execute documents to clothe a transaction with formal validity which has already been authorised by the board or the managing director.[224] It has been held that a single director has usual authority to sign cheques or other negotiable instruments on behalf of the company.[225] Where a director has a service agreement which requires him to perform a particular task (e.g. sales manager) then, like any other management executive, he will possess the usual authority that his function requires.[226] This is a matter of ordinary agency law but, in terms of general powers of management, directors must act collectively as a board, unless the articles give a power to delegate to individual directors.[227] This is subject to section 35A because, where that section applies, the board is deemed to have power to authorise others to act on behalf of the company free of any limitations under the company's constitution. For this purpose a 'limitation' should include a matter on which the constitution is silent as well as express restrictions.[228]

The position of company secretary has grown in importance over the years. In the nineteenth century the company secretary was described as a mere servant[229] but, by the 1970s, it was accepted by the Court of Appeal that the company secretary was the chief administrative officer of the company and that, as such, he had ostensible authority to bind the company in contracts of an administrative nature such as employing staff and hiring cars.[230]

Where three companies were controlled by one individual, who was the major shareholder in and chairman, managing director and the organiser of, each of the three companies, it was held that the affairs of these companies were so 'mixed up' that the

---

[221] *Freeman & Lockyer v Buckhurst Park Properties Ltd*, above; *Hely-Hutchinson v Brayhead* [1968] 1 QB 549, *per* Roskill J, affirmed by the Court of Appeal on other grounds.

[222] Some of the earlier cases appear to invest the chairman with a usual authority equivalent to a managing director: *British Thomson-Houston Co. v Federal European Bank Ltd* [1932] 2 KB 176 (CA) and *Clay Hill Brick Co. v Rawlings* [1938] 4 All ER 100, but the sounder view is that the company is liable because the chairman has been held out as managing director. See *Biggerstaff v Rowatts Wharf Ltd* [1986] 2 Ch 93 (CA); *Hely-Hutchinson v Brayhead Ltd* [1968] 1 QB 549 at p. 560 (Roskill J) and p. 586 (Lord Wilberforce in CA).

[223] *Rama Corporation Ltd v Proved Tin & General Investments Ltd* [1952] 2 QB 147; *Houghton & Co. v Nothard, Lowe & Wills* [1927] 1 KB 247 (CA) – affirmed on other grounds [1928] AC 1.

[224] The power to execute documents is discussed below.

[225] *Re Land Credit Co. of Ireland* (1869) LR 4 Ch App 460. See also section 37 of the Companies Act 1985 and *Dey v Pullinger Engineering Co.* [1921] 1 KB 77.

[226] But if an executive goes beyond the confines of his routine duties, he will lack authority: *Kreditbank Cassel GmbH v Schenkers* [1927] 1 KB 826 (CA); *British Bank of the Middle East v Sun Life Assurance Co. of Canada* [1983] 2 Lloyds Rep. 9 (HL). See *Harmond Properties Ltd v Gajdzis* [1968] 1 WLR 1858 (a director acting as general agent of his company in giving notice to quit).

[227] Article 72 of Table A. However, even though it is not uncommon for the articles to provide for this, delegation cannot be assumed (as in the case of the managing director), i.e. such an article does not add to a director's 'usual' authority.

[228] See 4.11 above.

[229] *Barnett, Hoares & Co. v South London Tramways Co.* (1887) 18 QBD 815 at p. 817, approved by Lord Macnaghten in *George Whitchurch Ltd v Cavanagh* [1902] AC 117 at p. 124 and supported by the decision in *Ruben v Great Fingall Consolidated* [1906] AC 439.

[230] *Panorama Developments (Guildford) Ltd v Fidelis Furnishing Fabrics Ltd* [1971] 3 All ER 16. See also *First Energy*, above at p. 1422.

individual controlling them must be regarded as having actual or ostensible authority to act for any of the companies: *Ford Motor Credit Co. v Harmack.*[231]

4.30 When an outsider cannot rely on usual authority

There are a number of general rules which limit the right of an outsider to rely on the usual authority of any agent of the company. As in agency law in general, if the third party has knowledge of a relevant restriction on a particular agent's authority, the company will not be liable.[232] The result will be the same if the circumstances surrounding the transaction are sufficiently suspicious to put the third party on inquiry as to the agent's authority.

Restrictions on an agent's usual authority which are contained in the company's articles give rise to special considerations. Historically, the constructive notice rule meant that outsiders dealing with a company were deemed to know of such restrictions and therefore could not rely on an agent's usual authority in respect of any matter within the scope of the restrictions. Where the restrictions were not absolute but required a particular use of power to be authorised by the shareholders in general meeting or by the board, sometimes the internal management could be invoked to mitigate the constructive notice rule and to enable the outsider to hold the company to the transaction. This was possible where the required authorisation took the form of an ordinary resolution of the shareholders or of a board resolution because these were matters of internal management.[233] It was not possible where the required authorisation took the form of a special resolution, because an outsider could discover from the Registrar of Companies whether a special resolution had been passed and was therefore fixed with constructive notice of the existence or otherwise of such a resolution.[234] The constructive notice rule is to be abolished by section 711A (1) of the Companies Act 1985 but this is to be without prejudice to the question whether a person is affected by notice of any matter by reason of a failure to make such inquiries as ought reasonably to be made.[235] What will be regarded as falling within the scope of the 'inquiries as ought reasonably to be made' is not clear and the qualified nature of the intended abolition of the constructive notice rule may undermine its practical value.[236]

It should be stressed, however, that, so far as the usual authority of directors and officers is concerned, an outsider need not have read the articles. The articles can have a negative effect in limiting usual authority but they need not have been read as a positive basis for the usual authority of a particular agent. Here it is the appearance of authority

---

[231] (1972) *The Times*, July 7 (CA).

[232] *AL Underwood Ltd v Bank of Liverpool*, above; *Rolled Steel*, above.

[233] *Mahoney v East Holyford Mining Co.* (1875) LR 7 HL 869. This was provided that the outsider did not know that the required internal authorisation had not been obtained and there was no ground for suspicion.

[234] *Irvine v Union Bank of Australia* (1877) 2 App. Cas. 366 at p. 379. Copies of special resolutions must be filed with the Registrar of Companies: section 380.

[235] Section 711A (2). Section 711A is not yet in force.

[236] On the possible application of section 35A to restrictions on the authority of individuals as opposed to limitations on the power of the board, see 4.20 above.

with which a particular agent is commonly vested that determines the scope of his usual authority.[237]

4.31 The 'holding out' principle

The classic statement of the principles of ostensible authority in the form of holding out as applied to companies is to be found in Diplock LJ's judgment in *Freeman & Lockyer*, where he summarised the conditions which had to be fulfilled for a contractor to be entitled to enforce a contract against a company in the following terms:[238]

(1) a representation that the agent had authority to enter on behalf of the company into a contract of the kind sought to be enforced must be made to the contractor;

(2) such representation must be made by a person or persons who had actual authority to manage the business of the company either generally or in respect of those matters to which the contract relates;

(3) the contractor must be induced by the representation to enter into the contract (i.e., in fact he must rely on it); and

(4) under the memorandum or articles of association of the company, the company must not be deprived of the capacity to enter into a contract of the kind sought to be enforced or to delegate authority to enter into a contract of that kind to the agent.

Section 35A modifies conditions (2) and (4). The board may make a representation of authority to a contractor which exceeds its actual authority under the company's memorandum and articles but, by virtue of section 35A, the contractor, provided he is in good faith, is entitled to assume that the board's authority is unlimited. The reference to lack of capacity in (4) must now be read in the light of section 35. It is now not a bar to a contract being binding on a company that it is outside the limits of the company's memorandum. Condition (4) is also affected by the (expected) abolition of the constructive notice rule. This condition stemmed from the wider principle, which is applicable to this form of ostensible authority as it is to ostensible authority in the form of usual authority, that an outsider cannot rely on ostensible authority if he knows of limitations restricting the agent's actual authority. The constructive notice rule deemed outsiders to know of limitations contained in the company's memorandum or articles. To the extent that section 711A will abolish the constructive notice rule, this condition will therefore cease to apply. The qualified effect of section 711A is discussed in paragraph 4.30 above.

The elements of holding out and reliance embodied in conditions (1) and (3), as stated by Diplock LJ in *Freeman & Lockyer* are essentially matters that will be determined by reference to the factual circumstances of each case. It is not essential for the body with actual authority to state expressly that the agent has authority, as the holding out may be

---

[237] *Freeman & Lockyer v Buckhurst Park Properties Ltd* [1964] 2 QB 480 at p. 496 (Willmer LJ). There was formerly some uncertainty on this point, which this case has dispelled. See the reporter's note appended to *British Thomson-Houston Co. v Federated European Bank* [1932] 2 KB 176, and the subsequent history of this note in *Clay Hill Brick Co. v Rawlings* [1938] 4 All ER 100 and in *Rama Corporation v Proved Tin & General Investments Ltd* [1952] 2 QB 147.

[238] At p. 506. Diplock LJ's analysis in *Freeman & Lockyer* has been applied in numerous subsequent cases including *IRC v Ufitec Group Ltd* [1977] 3 All ER 924; *British Bank of the Middle East v Sun Life Assurance of Canada*, above; *Rhodian River Shipping v Halia Maritime* [1984] 1 Lloyds Rep. 373; *The Raffaella*, above.

inferred from the circumstances.[239] The representation by which the company may be said to have held out the individual as having authority will usually take the form of knowingly permitting a director or officer to assume an authority he does not in fact possess. In a one-off transaction, however, an express holding out may be necessary for an estoppel to arise.[240]

Most of the cases illustrating this form of ostensible authority have concerned directors who were held out as managing directors, even though they had never been appointed to that office.[241] The estoppel principle overcomes the lack of valid appointment and confers on the director the same scope of usual authority as if he were a regularly appointed managing director. In accordance with the second of Diplock LJ's conditions the representation must have been made by an individual or organ of the company with actual authority to make the appointment. In the case of the appointment of the managing director, most articles (e.g. article 72 of Table A) confer this power on the board of directors. The board will be estopped by their conduct in knowingly allowing a director either expressly to represent himself as managing director, or by his conduct impliedly to represent that he has the powers of such. In *Freeman & Lockyer v Buckhurst Park Properties*,[242] for example, no managing director had been appointed, despite a power in the articles to do so, in a company formed to purchase and develop certain properties. Two directors allowed the third director, Kapoor, the whole management of the company's business. The Court of Appeal held that the company was estopped from denying that Mr Kapoor was managing director and that it was within the usual authority of such to engage a firm of architects to obtain planning permission for the development of certain properties.

4.32 Knowledge of the articles

As in cases involving usual authority, where liability is founded on the holding out principle, it is *not* essential that the third party should have read the articles. The conduct of the board in acquiescing in the pretensions of a self-styled managing director will bind the company, even though the articles conferring the power to appoint a managing director have not been read. Conversely, the existence of a power to delegate, e.g. to a managing director, will not of itself raise an estoppel where no managing director has been appointed. The *Turquand* rule cannot be invoked by a person who knows of the contents of the articles to raise an estoppel against the company in circumstances where the articles permitted delegation but there is no evidence of an individual having being held out. The significance of a power to delegate in the articles, if known, is simply that this may help to establish[243] that the company is estopped, but it can scarcely do so alone without more positive evidence that a particular individual was held out as managing director by an organ which had the authority to appoint him.

---

[239] See the remarks of Pearson LJ in *Freeman & Lockyer* at p. 498 as qualified by his later remarks in *Hely-Hutchinson* at p. 593.

[240] *Armagas v Mundogas*, above at p. 777.

[241] The holding out principle may also extend the scope of the actual authority of an agent of the company: *Mercantile Bank of India v Chartered Bank of India* [1937] 1 All ER 231. (Agents authorised to borrow by power of attorney. A limitation on the amount imposed by the directors did not appear in the power of attorney. A charge granted to secure an amount in excess of the limitation was held to estop the company, since it had held out the agents by the power of attorney as having unlimited power to borrow.)

[242] Above.

[243] See *Houghton & Co. v Nothard, Lowe & Willis Ltd* [1927] 1 KB 246 at p. 266 *per* Sargant LJ.

In *Freeman & Lockyer* the Court of Appeal was divided on whether the holding out principle could bind the company even where the articles did not specifically provide a power to appoint a managing director.[244] The point may now be covered by section 35A which, irrespective of the actual contents of the articles, allows a person dealing with the company in good faith to assume that the directors have unlimited powers to authorise others to act on the company's behalf.

4.33 'Self-authorising' agents

The second of the conditions of ostensible authority outlined by Diplock LJ in *Freeman & Lockyer* is that the agent must be held out by someone who has actual authority in the matter to which the representation relates. It follows from this that an agent should not be able to increase his own power to bind the company by holding himself out as having more authority than he actually has. Likewise, an agent who lacks authority should not be able to bind the company by over-representing someone else's authority. These propositions are supported by the decision of the House of Lords in *British Bank of the Middle East v Sun Life Assurance Co. of Canada (UK) Ltd*[245], where it was held that the general manager of a branch office of an insurance company had no authority to give an undertaking on the company's behalf and had no authority to represent that a more junior employee, a unit manager, had the requisite authority.[246]

A gloss on this is, however, indicated by *The Raffaella*[247] where Browne-Wilkinson LJ said:

> It is obviously correct that an agent who has no actual or apparent authority either (a) to enter into a transaction or (b) to make representations as to the transaction cannot hold himself out as having authority to enter into the transaction so as to affect the principal's position. But, suppose a company confers actual or apparent authority on X to make representations and X erroneously represents to a third party that Y has authority to enter into a transaction; why should not such a representation be relied on as part of the holding out of Y by the company? By parity of reasoning, if a company confers actual or apparent authority on A to make representations on the company's behalf but no actual authority on A to enter into the specific transaction, why should a representation made by A as to his authority not be capable of being relied on as one of the acts of holding out?

This was applied by the Court of Appeal in *First Energy (UK) v Hungarian International Bank*[248] where it was held that a bank manager who had no authority to make an offer on the bank's behalf had ostensible authority by virtue of his position (i.e. what has been described in this chapter as a form of usual authority) to communicate that head office approval had been given to the transaction in question. Whether it was possible to draw a distinction between authority to enter into a transaction and authority to represent that it had been approved at a higher level, had been put in some doubt by the decision of the

---

[244] Diplock LJ at pp. 505–6 thought that this was possible but Willmer LJ at p. 492 and Pearson LJ at p. 480 thought otherwise.

[245] Above.

[246] See also *Armagas v Mundogas*, above.

[247] Above.

[248] Above.

House of Lords in *Armagas v Mundogas*. However, the Court of Appeal distinguished the earlier House of Lords decision on two grounds: first, *Armagas* was not concerned with the ostensible authority of an agent arising from his position but with ostensible authority arising from holding out on specific occasions, and the evidence in that case did not establish that such authority existed; secondly, the House of Lords had not ruled out altogether the possibility of an agent who had no authority to conclude the transaction having authority to communicate decisions, but had merely decided that it would be somewhat rare for that situation to arise.[249]

The pragmatic commercial considerations that underlie agency principles, and also the rule in *Turquand's* case, were emphasised by the Court of Appeal in *First Energy*. On the one hand, a contractor who is dealing with an agent acting on behalf of a company cannot know, nor be expected to inquire into, all of the internal approval procedures within the company; on the other hand, merely because someone (who may have no other connection with the company) purports to act for a company should not necessarily mean that the company is bound, since this could facilitate fraud and operate to the detriment of the company's innocent creditors and shareholders. A balance has to be struck which allows a contractor to hold the company to a transaction, without having to go to the (usually impossible) lengths of ensuring that the transaction is approved at board level, in circumstances where the contractor acts reasonably in assuming that appropriate corporate approvals have been obtained. Normally, the contractor will rely on the authority of the agent to conclude the transaction, but the decision of the Court of Appeal in *First Energy* recognises that an agent who lacks the authority to conclude the transaction may, in limited circumstances, bind the company by communicating, within the scope of his authority, that it has been approved at a higher level.[250]

4.34 Forgery, the *Turquand* rule and agency principles

There is authority from the House of Lords for the proposition that a forgery as such is a *nullity* and cannot bind the company.[251] On the other hand, if an organ or official of the company with the authority to bind the company held out the person who committed the forgery as having authority to execute the document in question, the company may be estopped from denying the validity of the forgery. In *Ruben v Great Fingall Consolidated*,[252] a company secretary, without authority to do so, issued a share certificate with the company's seal attached and under his own signature and the forged signatures of two directors. The execution of the share certificate was therefore a nullity, and there was no ground for holding the company estopped from denying this. In other cases, a director or other official has been held to have 'forged' his own signature to a parol agreement.[253] This would seem to be a misuse of the word 'forgery' and such cases should have been decided instead on the basis of lack of authority (whether actual or ostensible).[254] Indeed,

---

249 *British Thomson-Houston Co. Ltd v Federated European Bank Ltd* [1932] 2 KB 176 can be explained as a case where the agent's authority to conclude transactions was not commensurate with his authority to communicate decisions.

250 For a criticism of the decision see Reynolds (1994) 110 LQR 21.

251 *Ruben v Great Fingall Consolidated* [1906] AC 439 (HL) *per* Lord Loreburn at p. 443.

252 [1906] AC 439 (HL); see further *Slingsby v District Bank* [1931] 2 KB 588, 605 *per* Wright J (Affd. by the CA [1932] 1 KB 544).

253 *Kreditbank Cassel GmbH v Schenkers Ltd* [1927] 1 KB 826; *South London Greyhound Racecourses v Wake* [1931] 1 Ch 496.

254 See *Northside Developments Pty Ltd v Registrar-General*, above, where this distinction is drawn.

it is difficult to see why even forgery, as in *Ruben*'s case, must be treated as being governed by a special rule. So far as actual authority is concerned a forgery is clearly a nullity. However, whether or not it binds the company should depend on the general principles. It is clear that under general agency law[255] forgeries are not treated differently from other fraudulent acts which may be binding on the principal if the agent acts within his usual or apparent authority.[256]

4.35 Statutory provisions affecting appointments

Section 285 of the Companies Act 1985 appears to give additional protection to an outsider dealing with a director or manager who has been invalidly appointed. This section provides that 'the acts of a director or manager are valid notwithstanding any defect that may afterwards be discovered in his appointment or qualification.'[257] However, the House of Lords in *Morris v Kanssen* gave a very restricted interpretation to this section. Lord Simonds distinguished 'between (a) an appointment in which there is a defect or, in other words, a defective appointment and (b) no appointment at all'.[258] Thus it will validate a mere slip or procedural defect in the appointment of a director, but it will not cover even an originally valid appointment which has been vacated by reason of a statutory provision[259] requiring qualification shares to be taken up within two months.[260] Thus the *Turquand* rule will normally give an outsider better protection in dealing with invalidly appointed officers than does section 285.[261]

The publicity that the Companies Act 1985 requires about the identity of directors may, in some circumstances, prevent the company from denying the validity of an appointment of a director or officer. Thus the company is required to keep a register of directors and file a copy of this with the Registrar of Companies.[262] Further, the names of the directors may have to be shown on the company's notepaper and other business documents.[263] Where names of invalidly appointed directors are publicised in this way, third parties who have read and relied on this information might hold the company liable if the company could be shown to have acquiesced in the registration or display of erroneous information as to the identity of any of the directors. It might then be argued that there was implied actual authority for their appointment even though there had been no formal election to the board. Such an argument is more likely to succeed in the case of a private company with a small number of members.

[255] *Uxbridge Building Society v Pickard* [1939] 2 KB 248 (CA).

[256] *Lloyd v Grace, Smith & Co* [1912] AC 716 (HL).

[257] A similar provision is found in the articles of most companies (e.g. article 92 of Table A). See also section 382 (4), discussed in 4.25, above as to presumption of regularity at meetings where proper minutes are kept.

[258] [1946] AC 459 at p. 471.

[259] Now section 291.

[260] *Morris v Kanssen*, above.

[261] Although section 285 includes members as well as outsiders, it will not protect anyone who knew or ought to have known of the defect: *Re Staffordshire Gas and Coke Co.* (1892) 66 LT 413; *Tyne Mutual Steamship Insurance Association v Brown* (1896) 74 LT 283. See also *John v Rees* [1969] 1 WLR 1294 at p. 1320.

[262] Section 288.

[263] Section 305. See 13.20, below.

4.36 Publication in the *Gazette* of returns relating to the register of directors

Section 711 of the Companies Act 1985 requires the Registrar to publish in the *Gazette* 'any return relating to a company's register of directors, or notification of a change among its directors'. Under section 42 of the 1985 Act 'any change among the company's directors' is an 'event' on which 'the company shall not be entitled to rely against other persons' if the event has not been officially notified at the material time. See further 3.14, above.

4.37 The form of contracts by companies

A company may make a contract in writing under its common seal and a contract may be made on its behalf by its duly authorised agent.[264] Any formalities required by law in the case of a contract made by an individual also apply, unless a contrary intention appears, to a contract made by or on behalf of a company.[265]

4.38 The execution of company documents

Certain special rules apply to the execution of documents. Here a distinction has to be drawn between *formal* authority to execute a document and *substantive* authority to enter into the transaction (which is then clothed with formal validity by the execution of the document). Although the substantive validity of a transaction may require a decision by the board of directors or a managing director, the execution of documents will usually be left to lesser officers of the company. So long as the requirements of the articles have been complied with, the outsider will not have to prove that there was actual authority to execute the document. Where a document has to be sealed, most articles provide that this may be done by a director and the secretary, or by two directors.[266] The cases establish that where a document is executed with the signature or signatures that the articles require, its formal validity cannot be contested by the company,[267] but where this is not the case the document is not binding on the company[268] unless section 35A of the Companies Act 1985 applies.[269]

Section 36A of the Companies Act 1985 provides that a document is executed by a company by the affixing of its common seal. It is not now obligatory for a company to have a common seal.[270] Whether or not a company has a common seal, a document signed by a director and the secretary of the company or by two directors of the company, and expressed (in whatever form of words) to be executed by the company has the same effect as if executed under the common seal of the company.[271] A document executed by a company which makes it clear on its face that it is intended by the person or

---

[264] Section 36 (as substituted by the Companies Act 1989).

[265] ibid.

[266] e.g. article 101 of Table A.

[267] *County of Gloucester Bank v Rudry Merthyr, etc., Colliery Co.* [1895] 1 Ch 629 (CA); *Duck v Tower Galvanizing Co.* [1901] 2 KB 314.

[268] *T.C.B. Ltd v Gray*, above.

[269] ibid., p. 125.

[270] Section 36A (3). Section 36A was inserted by section 130 (2) of the Companies Act 1989. Where a company has a common seal, the name of the company must be engraved on it in legible characters: section 350 (1).

[271] Section 36A (4).

persons making it to be a deed has effect, upon delivery, as a deed; and it is presumed, unless a contrary intention is proved, to have been delivered upon it being so executed.[272]

It is common practice for the common seal to be affixed to important documents which are not deeds such as share and stock certificates.[273]

4.39 Protection for purchasers

Section 36A (6) provides that in favour of a purchaser[274] a document is deemed to have been duly executed by a company if it purports to be signed by a director and the secretary of the company and, where it makes it clear on its face that it is intended by the person or persons making it to be a deed, to have been delivered upon its being executed. The meaning of 'purports to be signed' is not certain. It would presumably cover any lack of authority on the part of the signing officers but it is open to argument whether it would also encompass forged signatures. If this were the case, section 36A (6) would, in effect, repeal *Ruben v Great Fingall*[275] in respect of documents within its scope.

Section 36A (6) is in similar terms to a more limited protection for purchasers provided by section 74 of the Law of Property Act 1925.

[272] Section 36A (5).

[273] A share certificate is not a deed: *South London Greyhound Racecourses v Wake* [1931] 1 Ch 496 at p. 503 *per* Clausen J. See section 186 as to the effect of sealing a share certificate. A company which has an official seal may have a securities seal which is a facsimile of its common seal (with the addition of the word 'securities') specifically for use in sealing documents creating and evidencing securities: section 40.

[274] For this purpose a purchaser means a purchaser in good faith for valuable consideration and includes a lessee, mortgagee or other person who, for valuable consideration, acquires an interest in the property.

[275] See 4.34, above.

5 The Public Issue of Securities

5.1 A time of rapid change

In October 1986 a revolution took place in the United Kingdom's financial markets. This revolution, which came to be known as 'Big Bang',[1] brought about fundamental changes in the way securities are traded on the United Kingdom's major public market for dealing in securities, the London Stock Exchange.[2] Until Big Bang, dealings in securities had been conducted by brokers and jobbers, with brokers acting as agents on behalf of investors and jobbers acting as principals in transactions. There was complete separation of function between brokers and jobbers. Competition between brokers was impeded by a mandatory system of minimum commissions. Membership of The Stock Exchange by brokers and jobbers was strictly controlled, which served to exclude the major banks and financial institutions, domestic and international, from direct participation in trading in securities. Big Bang saw the abolition of the single-capacity rule and of mandatory commissions. Rules regarding the ownership of firms were relaxed in order to allow banks and financial institutions to acquire businesses engaged in the buying and selling of securities. This gave traders in securities access to much greater amounts of capital than they had enjoyed as independent businesses and helped to produce the now familiar large financial conglomerates which are able to offer a wide range of financial services from traditional merchant banking (such as advising on flotations, mergers and acquisitions, and underwriting), to investment management and market-making in securities.

The international bond market, based in London but not subject to the same restrictions as the market in domestic securities, had served to highlight ways in which the structure of the domestic market pre-Big Bang could have been regarded as unduly restrictive. Pressure for change also came from the Office of Fair Trading, which regarded some of the established practices of the domestic market as anti-competitive. At one point The Stock Exchange faced being brought before the Restrictive Practices Court to defend its rules and practices, but that threat was deflected by an agreement in 1983 between the Exchange and the DTI whereby the Exchange agreed to review some of its practices. That agreement set in train some of the reforms which culminated in Big Bang.

Developments in information technology played a very significant role in creating a climate for change in the United Kingdom's financial services industry. As computers and communication facilities made it increasingly easy to deal in securities on a world-wide basis at any time of day or night, the international competitiveness of the United Kingdom's financial markets was challenged. In response, Big Bang also heralded the adoption by the London Stock Exchange of a computerised dealing system.[3]

[1] Rider, Abrams and Ferran, *Guide to the Financial Services Act 1986* (CCH Editions Ltd, 2nd edn 1989), Chapter 2; McRae and Cairncross, *Capital City* (Eyre Methuen, 2nd (revised) edn 1985); Plender and Wallace, *The Square Mile* (Hutchinson, 1985); Thomas, *The Securities Market* (Philip Allan, 1989).

[2] The formal name of this market is The International Stock Exchange of the United Kingdom and the Republic of Ireland Limited but the London Stock Exchange is its trading name: *Listing Rules*, definitions.

[3] For a brief description of SEAQ, see Samuels, Wilkes and Brayshaw, *Management of Company Finance* (Chapman & Hall, 5th edn 1990), p. 281.

Developments in information technology continue to exert a powerful influence on the securities industry and to produce competitive pressures. At present, although transactions on the London Stock Exchange are based on computerised trading, the completion of bargains by the transfer of title to securities to purchasers is effected manually. Many of the London Stock Exchange's international rivals, and also the international bond market, can offer trading and settlement services which are entirely computerised, and in this respect the London Stock Exchange is at a competitive disadvantage. Attempts are being made to develop a fully computerised settlement facility for the Exchange. The first proposal, involving a system known as TAURUS, proved to be too complex but a more modest computerised settlement system, CREST, is now being developed by the Bank of England.[4]

Historically, public issues of securities were regulated by the companies legislation. The first move away from the companies legislation as the source of regulation resulted from the need to implement three EC directives on listed securities.[5] Listed securities are securities admitted to official listing in a member state which, in the United Kingdom, means admitted to the Official List of the London Stock Exchange.[6] These directives were first implemented into English law in 1984 by means of regulations.[7] The effect of these regulations was, broadly, to disapply the relevant provisions of the companies legislation in relation to listed securities. The companies legislation continued to apply to unlisted securities and, on consolidation of that legislation, the relevant provisions governing unlisted securities were contained in Part III and certain sections of Part IV of the Companies Act 1985.

While these events were occurring, a more thoroughgoing review of the whole body of securities law was undertaken on behalf of the Department of Trade and Industry by their adviser, Professor L. C. B. Gower.[8] On the basis of this report, but in a form inevitably altered by the usual consultation processes and the pressures of various interest groups affected, the Financial Services Act 1986 introduced a new 'securities law' to regulate most aspects of the financial markets in the United Kingdom. The wider implications of this important piece of legislation, as it affects dealing in securities and the conduct of securities market, would form the subject-matter of a book on securities regulation. Here we are only concerned with the new regimes for both listed and unlisted securities.

Part IV of the Financial Services Act 1986 regulates listed securities. Part IV was first brought into force in 1987 and it is through this Part that the United Kingdom now implements the relevant EC directives, the 1984 regulations having been repealed.[9] Some, relatively minor, amendments to Part IV have been made by later legislation. The latest changes to Part IV[10] are intended to implement the EC Prospectus Directive[11] in so far as it affects listed securities. Largely because Part IV is already based on Community

---

[4] Bank of England Quarterly Bulletin, August 1993, p. 357; Bank of England Quarterly Bulletin, November 1993, p. 474; Bank of England Quarterly Bulletin, February 1994, p. 32; Bank of England Quarterly Bulletin, May 1994, p. 130.

[5] The Admissions Directive (No. 79/279); The Listing Particulars Directive (No. 80/390); and The Interim Reports Directive (No. 82/121).

[6] See further 5.4, below.

[7] The Stock Exchange (Listing) Regulations 1984 (1984/716).

[8] *Review of Investor Protection*, Part I (Cmnd 9125) 1984. See also Part II (1985), Chapter 6.

[9] Financial Services Act 1986 (Commencement No. 3) Order 1986 (SI 1986 No. 2246).

[10] Made by the Public Offers of Securities Regulations 1995.

[11] No. 89/298.

law, the impact of this directive on the regime governing listed securities is not especially great, but the relevant changes are noted in context in this chapter.

The Prospectus Directive is much more significant in relation to the regulation of unlisted securities. The directive applies where securities are offered to the public for the first time in a member state irrespective of whether a listing is sought for the securities which are the subject of the offer. Its purpose is to establish Community-wide standards of disclosure of information with a view to encouraging the creation of a pan-European capital market. Part V of the Financial Services Act 1986 contained provisions governing public issues of unlisted securities. These provisions were intended to replace Part III and relevant sections of Part IV of the Companies Act 1985 and to provide a more appropriate and better thought-out system of regulation for public issues of unlisted securities. They were drafted before adoption of the Prospectus Directive. Part V was never brought into force, mainly because the approach embodied in the Prospectus Directive differs in a number of fundamental respects from that taken in Part V of the Act. Part V thus proved to be an unsuitable vehicle for implementation of the directive.[12] Instead, the Government decided to repeal Part V and to implement the directive so far as it relates to unlisted securities by means of regulations made under section 2 of the European Communities Act 1972.[13]

An advantage of implementing the Prospectus Directive through new regulations is that these regulations, unlike Part V, have been drafted with the requirements of the directive in mind and with a view to implementing fully the directive into domestic law. Because of pressures on the Parliamentary timetable, using regulations as the method of implementation has also enabled the United Kingdom to comply more speedily with its Community obligations than might have been possible if the government had sought to achieve implementation through new primary legislation.[14] However, this solution has also had its drawbacks. The power to make regulations under section 2 of the European Communities Act 1972 is limited[15] to regulations for the purpose of implementing Community obligations or of dealing with matters arising out of, or related to, any such obligations. The scope of Part III and the relevant sections of Part IV of the Companies Act 1985 was wider than that of the Prospectus Directive and, to the extent that the two regimes did not overlap, the limited nature of the power to make regulations under section 2 meant that the Government could not make amendments to the Companies Act 1985. Accordingly, there remains a rather untidy category of circumstances in which it is necessary still to have regard to the provisions of the Companies Act 1985.

5.2 The regulatory framework

The broad framework of the regulatory control of listed and unlisted securities is as follows:

---

[12] Ferran, 'The Public Offers Directive and Problems of Implementation', in Andenas and Kenyon-Slade (eds), *EC Financial Market Regulation and Company Law* (Sweet & Maxwell, 1993). Initially the DTI did suggest that the directive could be implemented through Part V: DTI Consultative Paper, *Listing Particulars and Public Offer Prospectuses – Implementation of Part V of the Financial Services Act 1986 and related EC Directives*, (July 1990).

[13] The Public Offers of Securities Regulations 1995.

[14] The due date for implementation of the Prospectus Directive was April 1991.

[15] The section 2 power also extends to enabling Treaty rights to be enjoyed but this aspect of the power is not relevant to the present discussion.

(1) Securities which are to be admitted to official listing are governed by Part IV of the Financial Services Act 1986.[16] The detailed requirements vary slightly depending on whether the securities for which a listing is sought are 'transferable securities' subject to the Prospectus Directive and on whether the listing is sought in connection with a public offer of the securities.[17]

(2) First-time public offers of unlisted securities which are within the scope of the Prospectus Directive are regulated by the Public Offers of Securities Regulations 1995.[18]

(3) Offers of securities falling outside both Part IV and the regulations are subject to the provisions of section 57 of the Financial Services Act 1986 and to the exemptions provided by or under section 58 of that Act. Section 57 regulates the issue in the United Kingdom of investment advertisements.

(4) Certain matters relating to the allotment of shares and debentures remain subject to the Companies Act 1985.

(5) Special rules apply where a company wants to make a simultaneous offer of its securities in two or more member states.

Offers of securities are brought within the regulatory framework irrespective of whether those securities are offered for cash or for a non-cash consideration. This point is notable because the relevant provisions of the Companies Act 1985 (and earlier companies legislation) only applied to securities offered to the public 'for subscription or purchase'. This phrase was interpreted by the courts to mean subscription or purchase for cash[19] which meant that, for example, an offer made by a bidder to acquire the shares of the target by means of a share-for-share exchange was not caught. The change of policy embodied in the current law was based on a sensible fundamental approach recommended by Professor Gower in *The Review of Investor Protection*.[20]

5.3 Private and public companies

A private company may not offer its securities to the public[21] nor may its securities be admitted to official listing.[22] The rule that a private company may not offer its securities to the public is one of the provisions of the Companies Act 1985 which has had to remain in force because of the limited nature of the rule-making power under section 2 of the European Communities Act 1972. The Companies Act 1985 does not contain a

---

[16] This account does not consider the residual category of sophisticated investment instruments (such as traded options) which are not 'securities' under the definition of that term contained in Part IV but which can be admitted to listing under the London Stock Exchange's own rules.

[17] The meaning of 'public offer' is considered at 5.22 below. Part IV also applies where securities are simply admitted to official listing without an accompanying offer of any sort. Introductions of this kind are not especially common but can occur where, for example, shares are already admitted to and traded upon a foreign market and are introduced onto the London Stock Exchange in order to enhance their international marketability and liquidity.

[18] Made under the European Communities Act 1972.

[19] *Government Stock and Other Securities Investment Co. Ltd v Christopher* [1956] 1 All ER 490, [1956] 1 WLR 237. See also section 744 of the Companies Act 1985.

[20] (1984) Cmnd 9125.

[21] Section 81 of the Companies Act 1985.

[22] Section 143 (3) of the Financial Services Act 1986.

complete definition of what is meant by an 'offer to the public' for this purpose.[23] Uncertainty as to the precise scope of the phrase 'an offer to the public' was one of the criticisms levelled at the regulatory regime contained in the Companies Act 1985 and it is unfortunate that the phrase has had to be retained even for the limited purpose of a prohibition imposed only on private companies.[24]

A business conduced through the corporate form is usually established as a private company. At a later stage, its proprietors may choose to convert it into a public company[25] precisely in order to be able to raise additional capital by offering its securities to the public. Starting life as a private company allows the proprietors to operate the business under more relaxed rules governing the maintenance, increase and reduction of share capital than those applicable to public companies.[26] At the early stages of its development, the business is unlikely to be hampered by the prohibition on offering its securities to the public because, in any event, few external investors are likely to be interested in investing in such an untested operation. If and when the business has established itself as a successful and profitable trading venture, the proprietors may consider it to be worthwhile subjecting the company to the more rigorous regulations imposed on public companies and their capital in return for acquiring the freedom to exploit the company's reputation by offering its securities to the public.

Because, as a matter of law, only public companies may market their securities to the public and, as a matter of practice, it is only companies with a successful and established trading record which are in a position to attract many external investors (although it may be possible for a company to compensate for its poor or inadequate record in some way, such as by offering to pay investors a higher return than that offered by comparable investments), the number of companies that can raise capital by making public issues of securities is relatively limited when compared to the overall number of incorporated companies.[27] However, the total amount of corporate finance raised in this way is large. For example, in 1993 over £17 billion was raised through public issues of shares, of which £6 billion was raised by companies coming to the market for the first time and £11 billion comprised rights issues.[28]

5.4 The London Stock Exchange

The 'Official List' is the main market of the London Stock Exchange and when a company's securities are admitted to this market they are said to be 'listed securities'. An applicant for listing must comply with the requirements of Part IV of the Financial Services Act 1986. It must also comply with the Exchange's own requirements for listing which are set out in a publication entitled the *Listing Rules*. This publication is commonly known as the *Yellow Book* because of the colour of its cover. The *Listing Rules* have statutory backing under Part IV of the Financial Services Act 1986.

To qualify for official listing, an applicant must satisfy certain criteria relating to the length of time it has been trading, the value of the securities for which listing is sought and

[23] Some guidance is provided by sections 58 to 60 of the Companies Act 1985.

[24] Note also the requirements of section 97 of the Companies Act 1985 relating to the disclosure of underwriting commissions in respect of unlisted shares: 5.12, below.

[25] The procedure for conversion is contained in sections 43–48 of the Companies Act 1985. See 2.11, above.

[26] See Chapter 6.

[27] On the problems of financing smaller firms, see: *The Interim Report of the Wilson Committee to Review the Functioning of Financial Institutions* (1979), Cmnd 7503; George, 'The Financing of Small Firms', Bank of England Quarterly Bulletin, February 1994, p.67.

[28] 'Financial Market Developments', Bank of England Quarterly Bulletin, February 1994, p.30.

the proportion of securities that will be held by the public once listing has taken place. These criteria mean that official listing can only be sought by established businesses of a certain size which have a substantial trading record. Also, the persons who have built up the business must accept some dilution of their formal[29] control of the company in order to satisfy the requirement for the appropriate percentage of the company's securities for which listing is sought to be in the hands of the public. The costs and expenses involved in seeking and maintaining an official listing are significant and this is an additional consideration which can dissuade smaller companies from taking this step.[30]

To meet the needs of smaller or newer companies in 1980 the London Stock Exchange established the Unlisted Securities Market (USM) as its second-tier market. This was followed in 1987 by the setting up of the Third Market intended for companies even less established than those on the USM. The admission criteria for the USM and Third Market were progressively more relaxed than those which had to be satisfied by applicants for full listing. The Third Market failed to attract sufficient applicants to sustain its business and it was phased out by the beginning of 1991. Initially the USM had some success but its viability was called into question when, in 1990, the London Stock Exchange relaxed certain of its admission requirements for a full listing. The reason why the listing requirements were relaxed was to maintain the competitive position of the London Exchange as against its rivals in the European Community; essentially, the London Stock Exchange brought its standards down to the minimum required by Community law in order to avoid putting United Kingdom companies at a disadvantage in comparison to their counterparts elsewhere in the Community and to ensure that applicants seeking a listing would not reject London in favour of more relaxed regulatory regimes offered by other Community securities markets.[31] The result of this relaxation was to bring the requirements for admission to the Official List and to the USM closer together.

---

[29] There is much discussion about the extent to which practical, as opposed to formal, control is lost when the ownership of a company's securities becomes dispersed via a flotation. The persons who built up the business will, more likely than not, remain in managerial control after the securities are listed. Outside shareholders, individually, are unlikely to own enough of the company's securities to be able to exercise much control over the managers and may be too widely dispersed to be able to act effectively as a collective group. Also, they may be disinclined to take collective action, preferring instead the simple option of selling their shares if the managers of the company underperform. See, *inter alia*, Hadden, *Company Law and Capitalism* (Weidenfeld and Nicholson, 2nd edn 1972), Chapter 6; Herman, *Corporate Control, Corporate Power* (CUP, 1st paperback edn 1982); Bearle and Means, *The Modern Corporation and Private Property* (Macmillan, 1932); Choper, Coffee and Morris, *Cases and Materials on Corporations* (Little, Brown and Co., 3rd edn 1989), Chapter 1, Part D; Dent, 'Towards Unifying Ownership and Control in the Public Corporation', (1989) Wisconsin Law Review 883. On the role of institutional investors, see Davies, 'Institutional Investors in the United Kingdom', in Prentice and Holland (eds), *Contemporary Issues in Corporate Governance*, (1993), Chapter 5; Cadbury, 'Highlights of the Proposals of the Committee on Financial Aspects of Corporate Governance' in Prentice and Holland (eds), *Contemporary Issues in Corporate Governance* (Clarendon Press, 1993) Chapter 3; Farrar and Russell, 'The Impact of Institutional Investment on Company Law', (1984) 5 Co Law 107; Farrar, 'Ownership and Control of Listed Public Companies in Revising or Rejecting the Concept of Control' in Pettet (ed.) *Company Law in Change* (Stevens, 1987); Dickins, 'A Voice, A Vote, A Veto', Corporate Finance (September 1991), 13; Coffee, 'Liquidity Versus Control: The Institutional Investor as Corporate Monitor', (1991) Columbia Law Review 1277; Black, 'Agents Watching Agents: The Promise of Institutional Investor Voice', (1992) 39 UCLA Law Review 811; Black, 'Shareholder Passivity Reexamined', (1990) 89 Mich L Rev 520.

[30] 'New Equity Issues', Bank of England Quarterly Bulletin, May 1990, p. 243.

[31] EC directives on mutual recognition of prospectuses and listing particulars (89/298 (prospectuses) and 87/345 (listing particulars)), which allowed a prospectus or set of listing particulars approved in one member state to be used as a 'passport' for an offer of securities in other member states and eliminated the need to comply with the domestic securities laws of those states, created a pressure on the London Stock Exchange to relax its requirements.

The London Stock Exchange has now announced the closure of the USM which will take place some time after the end of 1996. In its stead, the Exchange has established[32] a new 'Alternative Investment Market' (AIM) for smaller and growing companies. This new market begins operating in June 1995. The background to the establishment of the AIM was that research conducted by the Exchange indicated that, notwithstanding the decline in the use of the USM, there was still a demand for a new source of funding and trading for smaller companies as an alternative to the Official List. The Exchange expects the AIM to appeal to companies which cannot satisfy the requirements for full listing, and also to companies which are eligible for a full listing but which are attracted to the lower admission criteria and less onerous continuing obligations imposed on companies trading on the AIM. Also, the costs of obtaining and maintaining admission to this AIM should be considerably lower than those of the Official List.[33] As was the case with the USM, some companies may view admission to the AIM as the first step in the process leading to full listing.

5.5 Criteria for admission to the Official List of the London Stock Exchange

The conditions to be fulfilled by an applicant for listing and the listing procedure are set out in the *Listing Rules*. For an applicant seeking a listing for its shares, the important admission requirements are as follows.

(1) The market value of the shares to be listed must be at least £700,000[34] (but, in practice, an applicant may have difficulty in finding a broker or issuing house to sponsor the issue[35] and may find the costs involved make an official listing prohibitively expensive unless the value of the securities involved is substantially greater than this).

(2) The company must have a trading record of at least three years and must have audited accounts for those three years.

(3) The company must have had continuity of management over the period covered by the accounts.

(4) The company's directors must collectively have appropriate expertise and experience for the management of its business and must in general be free of conflicts between their duties to the company and their personal interests, or other duties.

---

[32] London Stock Exchange, *Consultative Document on the Alternative Investment Market*, September 1993; *AIM: Rules for Companies* (February 1995); *AIM: Changes to the Rules of the London Stock Exchange* (February 1995); *AIM: Transitional Arrangements* (May 1995).

[33] A particular area of saving is in relation to sponsors. Unlike applicants for official listing, applicants for admission to the Alternative Investment Market will not require a sponsor. Having a sponsor is an expensive requirement because, under the *Listing Rules*, sponsors must give a confirmation that, having made due and careful inquiries, they have satisfied themselves that the rules have been complied with. Sponsors must perform extensive (and expensive) due diligence exercises in order to be in a position to provide such confirmation. AIM companies must have nominated advisers, but nominated advisers are not required to give this confirmation.

[34] In an application for the admission of debentures the equivalent figure is £200,000. In April 1995 the London Stock Exchange issued a consultative document outlining proposed changes to the *Listing Rules*, in which it is indicated that these minimum market capitalisation figures (for both debt and equity) are under review with a view to possible increase.

[35] *Listing Rules*, Chapter 2 sets out the requirement to have a sponsor.

(5) If the company has a controlling shareholder (i.e. one who can exercise, or control the exercise of, 30 per cent or more of the rights to vote at general meetings or who can control the appointment of directors who are able to exercise the majority of votes at board meetings), the company must be capable of at all times operating and making decisions independently of the controlling shareholder.

(6) At least 25 per cent of the shares must be in the hands of the public after the flotation.

5.6 Criteria for admission to the Alternative Investment Market

The criteria for admission to the Alternative Investment Market are much more relaxed than those relating to the Official List. There is no requirement for a minimum (or maximum) market value of the securities for which listing is sought, there is no minimum trading record and no requirement for a minimum proportion of the securities to be in public hands. A company joining the market must satisfy the following requirements.

(1) The company must be duly incorporated or otherwise validly established according to the laws of its place of incorporation or establishment.

(2) The company must be permitted by its national law to offer its securities to the public. In the UK this means that it must be a public limited company.

(3) The securities to be traded on the market must be freely transferable.

(4) The company must appoint and retain a nominated adviser and a nominated broker.

(5) The company must accept continuing obligations with regard to such matters as preparation of accounts, completion of transfers of securities and dealings in securities by directors and employees.

5.7 Offers of securities otherwise than through the London Stock Exchange

A company is not obliged to seek admission to one of the markets of the London Stock Exchange in connection with an offer of its securities. Securities can be offered and traded without having been first admitted to an official market. This form of trading in securities is sometimes described as 'over the counter' trading (although in modern trading conditions, such transactions are more likely to be concluded via telephone and computer links than face to face). An advantage of having securities admitted to a formal market is that this can facilitate trading in them by the widest possible range of investors and thus enhance the liquidity of the securities. Admission of its securities to a formal market can also increase a company's status and make it easier for it to raise capital from other sources. In return for these advantages, however, the company is likely to have to agree to abide by certain continuing obligations imposed by the market and will certainly have to incur the expense of admission and membership fees.

A company which has had its securities admitted to an overseas market can offer those securities to investors in the United Kingdom without also seeking to have the securities admitted to dealings on the London Stock Exchange. For example, specialised debt securities which are targeted mainly at expert investors are commonly listed on the Luxembourg Stock Exchange but offered to investors in the City of London and elsewhere throughout the world without being formally admitted to any other market.

5.8 'Offers for subscription' and 'offers for sale'

A large-scale issue to the general investing public can take one of two forms. A direct offer to the public (known as an 'offer for subscription' or a 'prospectus offer') is the traditional method of making a large-scale public issue. Where it is used, investors subscribe for shares to be allotted directly by the company. The issuing house will advise and help to arrange the issue, including underwriting and sub-underwriting arrangements. Today, however, this method is rarely used when a company offers its securities to the public for the first time, although subsequent capital-raising exercises through rights issues commonly adopt this form. The more usual method of large-scale initial public issue takes the form of an 'offer for sale'. Here the whole of the shares in issue are normally taken up by an issuing house which then itself offers them to the public for purchase. The issuing house, not the company, takes prime responsibility for the success of the issue. Since the shares are allotted to it, the issuing house will need to arrange for its own risk to be underwritten. The issuing house does not become a registered holder of the shares it agrees to purchase. Indeed, it is common for the company to issue the renounceable allotment letters[36] not to the issuing house but directly to those who purchase the shares from the issuing house.

As a general rule, the London Stock Exchange requires an offer for subscription or an offer for sale to be used in respect of any initial public offering of shares where the total offer price of those shares is more than £50 million.[37] However, in a consultative document published in April 1995, the Exchange has indicated that it is considering whether to continue to regulate the method of initial public offers and/or whether the monetary limits should be revised or abolished.

5.9 Placings, intermediaries offers and rights issues

The incidental costs of making an offer for sale or for subscription (including underwriting fees, advertising expenses and publicity costs, and legal and financial advisers' fees) can be very large. For a company which wants to raise a relatively small amount of capital by way of an offer of shares, these costs may be prohibitive. An appropriate method of marketing for smaller offers may be a placing. A placing is a marketing of securities to a limited class of persons (e.g. clients of the issuing house which is sponsoring the issue).[38] It does not involve an offer to the public at large, with the result that publicity expenses and advertising costs can be kept relatively low in comparison to an offer for sale or for subscription. At present the *Listing Rules* authorise the use of a placing where the shares which are being offered have a value of not more than £25 million.[39] If the value of the shares is between £25 million and £50 million, a placing may be used in part, but it must be combined with an offer for sale or for subscription, or with an 'intermediaries offer'.[40] An intermediaries offer is essentially a variant form of placing involving the marketing of the securities to the clients of a number of financial intermediaries.[41]

Issues of debenture stock are very commonly marketed through placings. The *Listing*

---

[36] See 6.8, below.

[37] *Listing Rules*, Chapter 4, para. 4.2. But the Exchange does retain a discretion to permit securities to be brought to listing via some other method: Chapter 4, para. 4.4.

[38] *Listing Rules*, Chapter 4, para. 4.9.

[39] Chapter 4, para. 4.2.

[40] Chapter 4, para. 4.2.

[41] Chapter 4, para. 4.16.

Rules impose no restrictions on the use of placings for debenture stock issues, irrespective of the size of the issue.

A rights issue is an issue to the existing members of the company which gives them the right to subscribe in proportion to their existing holding of shares in the company (or of the class of shares involved). This is now the most common method for companies already listed to raise new capital, although the amounts raised by such issues individually are much less than in the case of initial public offers.[42] The costs of rights issues, in the sense of the expenses of the issue, are proportionally less than in the case of a general public offer, but, because it is customary to offer the new shares on more favourable terms than would be available under a public offer the company may raise less capital in proportion to the shares issued than would have been raised by an offer to the public generally.[43]

The shares are usually offered to the existing shareholders by means of renounceable letters or other negotiable instruments (this is a Stock Exchange requirement for rights issues of shares which are to be listed[44]). Existing shareholders may take up their rights or renounce them in whole or in part. A shareholder can choose to renounce the offer but still take advantage of the discount element normally included in the rights issue price. In effect, the renouncing shareholder sells the value of the right which was offered to him. Provided the sale price is still lower than the market price of the company's existing shares, a purchaser may be prepared to pay a premium to the existing shareholder for this right. Inexperienced investors may not appreciate that they can, by renouncing their rights, make a profit from a rights issue without putting up any new capital. To guard against this, the *Listing Rules* contain a protective provision requiring rights which are not taken up to be sold on the market for the benefit of the existing shareholders who were entitled to them.[45]

Where a listed company wants to raise new capital through an issue of its ordinary shares it is prima facie obliged, both by section 89 of the Companies Act 1985[46] and by The Stock Exchange's own requirements[47] to do so by means of a rights issue in favour of its existing shareholders. This obligation can be disapplied. A public company is permitted to disapply the statutory pre-emption requirement by special resolution for a period of up to five years.[48] However, under the *Listing Rules* the maximum period of a special resolution disapplying section 95 is fifteen months.[49] Under Pre-emption Guidelines agreed between representatives of companies, institutional investors and the London Stock Exchange, there are also limits on the amount of securities that may be included in a special resolution disapplying section 89. The Pre-emption Guidelines are not formal rules of the London Stock Exchange but companies have the assurance that a disapplication resolution which complies with those guidelines will be supported by their institutional shareholders.

[42] As to The Stock Exchange requirements, see the *Listing Rules*, Chapter 4, paras 4.25–4.30.
[43] See McRae and Cairncross, op. cit., p. 149. Samuels et al, op. cit., pp. 295–303.
[44] *Listing Rules*, Chapter 4, para. 4.25.
[45] *Listing Rules*, Chapter 4, para. 4.28. But if the premium obtained over the subscription price (net of expenses) does not exceed £3, the proceeds may be retained for the company's benefit.
[46] See 6.5, below.
[47] *Listing Rules*, Chapter 9, para. 9.18.
[48] Section 95.
[49] Chapter 9, para. 9.20.

5.10 Other types of issue

Certain other types of public issue are less commonly employed. An 'offer by tender' is a method very commonly used in the United States but it is not in common use in Britain. Instead of having a fixed price at which securities will be offered to the public, under this method investors are invited to tender on the understanding that the shares will be allotted to the highest bidder. To protect the issuing company a minimum price will be fixed but, subject to that, the shares will be allotted at the highest price at which all the shares will be taken up. The aim is to ensure that in the case of successful and often oversubscribed issues the company benefits, and not the type of speculator known as a 'stag'.[50]

The privatisation of some previously state-owned industries has been done by means of offers by tender but it is a complicated method of public offer and this is usually reflected in high attendant costs.

An open offer is an offer of new shares to existing shareholders in proportion to their existing shareholdings, which differs from a rights issue to the extent that the offer is not made by renounceable letters or other negotiable instruments.[51]

A 'convertible issue' is a term which relates not to the method of issue but to the hybrid type of security involved. In the usual form, convertible debenture stock is offered with the right to convert at a future date into ordinary shares. The attraction of this type of investment is that it gives the investor the security of a fixed interest security, which may be particularly important where the funding is sought to capitalise a new, and perhaps somewhat risky, venture, combined with the opportunity to convert into 'equity' shares when the success and profitability of the company is established.

5.11 The function of the sponsor

In major public issues[52] a crucial role is performed by the company's sponsor, who will normally be its corporate broker or investment bank.[53] The sponsor not only acts as financial adviser to the company but will have the task of directing the strategy of the issue and co-ordinating the activities of the other professional advisers concerned (stockbrokers, auditors, reporting accountants and solicitors). The sponsor also has specific obligations which it owes to the Exchange to ensure that the company satisfies the listing criteria and is guided through the listing process.[54] The name and good reputation of the sponsor has a considerable influence on the reception that will be given by the financial press and the stock market to the issue. This is linked with the understanding that the broker or issuing house, before it agrees to sponsor an issue, will be aware of the need to protect its reputation with the investing public, especially the institutional investors who will be involved both as underwriters and sub-underwriters and as straightforward investors.[55]

---

[50] See McRae and Cairncross, op. cit., p. 148 and Samuels et al., op. cit., pp. 290–292, where the reasons why offers by tender have not been popular with the issuing houses and their client companies are considered.

[51] *Listing Rules*, Chapter 4, para. 4.31.

[52] An applicant for admission to the Alternative Investment Market does not require a sponsor.

[53] *Listing Rules*, Chapter 2 sets out the requirements relating to sponsors.

[54] See further, *Listing Rules*, Chapter 2.

[55] See *Gore-Browne on Companies* (Jordans, 44th edn, loose-leaf) 10.13 as to the initial searching enquiry that will be given by the issuing house to a company 'coming to market'. As to the technique of making certain common types of public issue (offer for sale, debenture placing and rights issue) see *Gore-Browne* 10.12–10.33. This is considered from the point of view of the issuing house.

5.12 Underwriting

A contract of underwriting is an agreement that, if the whole or a certain proportion of the issue is not applied for by the public, the underwriters will themselves apply or find persons to apply for the balance or a certain proportion of the balance of the issue. Where the underwriters undertake merely to find persons to apply for shares the remedy of the company in case of breach is in damages only.[56] Where the underwriters undertake to apply for the shares themselves, the company can hold the underwriters to their promise by placing them on the register of members.

The consideration to the underwriters is the payment of a commission, to be received by them whether they are called upon to take up any securities or not.[57] The maximum amount of commission that can be paid to underwriters from the proceeds of an issue of shares is regulated by sections 97 and 98 of the Companies Act 1985.

5.13 Official listing: the function of The Stock Exchange as 'competent authority'

Part IV of the Financial Services Act 1986 applies to the listing of most types of security. Section 142 stipulates that no investment to which the section applies may be admitted to the Official List of The Stock Exchange except in accordance with the provisions of Part IV. The types of security to which section 142 refers[58] are shares and debentures in companies, and certain public authority securities. It also includes certificates representing such securities and 'warrants or other instruments entitling the holder to subscribe to shares or securities'.[59]

An application for listing has to be made 'to the competent authority in such a manner as the listing rules may require'. The term 'competent authority' (which is derived from a term of general application in the EC listing directive[60]) means The Stock Exchange.[61]

Section 142 (6) gives The Stock Exchange the power to make 'listing rules' and it is this

---

[56] See *Gorrissen's Case* (1873) 8 Ch App. 507.

[57] The meaning of 'underwriting' was declared by the Court of Appeal after hearing evidence in *Re Licensed Victuallers' Mutual Trading Association* (1889) 42 Ch D 1.

[58] Section 142 (1) refers to investment categories 1, 2, 4 and 5 in Schedule 1 to the Act. In the case of categories 1, 4 and 5 the securities of building societies, industrial and provident societies and credit unions are included for the purpose of section 142. It also includes loan stock, bonds and similar instruments issued otherwise than by a member state of the EC, or a local authority in such a state: Section 142 (3). The instruments and certificates in paras. 4 and 5 must relate to the investments in para. 1. The Secretary of State has power by order to extend the categories of investment: Section 142 (4).

[59] Part IV was brought into force generally on 16 February 1987 and for 'privatisation issues' on 12 January 1987: Financial Services Act 1986 (Commencement No. 3) Order 1986.

[60] Council Directive No. 79/279, Council Directive No. 80/390 and Council Directive No. 82/121. The Act designates The Stock Exchange: section 142 (6).

[61] Following an internal reorganisation of the London Stock Exchange, the functions of the competent authority were transferred from the Council of The Stock Exchange to the Exchange itself (Official Listing of Securities (Change of Competent Authority) Regulations 1991 (SI 1991 No. 2000)). These regulations also repealed the power, formerly contained in section 157 of the Financial Services Act 1986, to alter the competent authority. Any function of the competent authority may be exercised by committee, subcommittee or an officer or servant. This does not apply to the power to make listing rules which therefore must be made by the board of The Stock Exchange itself. See section 142 (8).

power which provides the statutory backing for the *Listing Rules*.[62] The Stock Exchange has a delegated power to make law by regulating applications for listing and specifying the detailed criteria for admission to the Official List within widely drawn enabling provisions of the Act. In performing this rule-making function, The Stock Exchange seeks to comply with the EC directives relating to listing.[63] The Act, however, does not say that The Stock Exchange must comply with the directives. This appears to have been done so that a question of ultra vires may not arise by reason of any failure to comply with the directives. It is intended that companies which comply with the listing rules should not be imperilled.[64]

Article 15 of the Admission Directive provides that a person refused admission by a stock exchange has the right to judicial review.[65] This would allow the High Court to annul the decision taken or to direct a different decision. The grounds would have to be (apart from bad faith or abuse of function) that The Stock Exchange had made an error of law in reaching its decision. There remains a question of whether Article 15 is confined to refusal on the basis of the mandatory requirements in the directives. The Stock Exchange is permitted to (and does) impose additional requirements of its own. It is arguable whether Article 15 requires judicial review where, for example, listing is refused on the ground that such an additional requirement has not been satisfied. Not to do so would seem to defeat the purpose and policy of Article 15.

The right to apply to court contained in Article 15 is conferred on the company alone, and shareholders do not have standing to seek judicial review under this provision.[66]

5.14 Application for listing

Section 143 deals with applications for listing. It stipulates that these must be made to The Stock Exchange 'in such manner as the listing rules may require'. Section 143 also prohibits an application for listing of any securities 'except by or with the consent of the issuer of the securities'. 'Issuer'[67] is defined as the person by whom the securities have been or are to be issued. Thus, for example, an investment institution which owns a substantial holding of shares or other securities in a public company may seek a listing for these securities, but this requires the consent of the company.

Section 144 defines the responsibilities of The Stock Exchange for 'vetting' applications for listing. It provides for admission to official listing only if The Stock Exchange's listing rules and other requirements are complied with and specifies the circumstances in which an application for listing may or must be refused.[68] It also empowers and, in some

---

[62] Note, however, that the *Listing Rules* can have a wider application because certain securities which can be admitted to listing are not 'securities' for the purposes of Part IV.

[63] *Listing Rules*, Introduction.

[64] The Secretary of State, however, has preserved a power to enable him to ensure that international obligations are complied with. See section 192.

[65] Article 15 requires that member states shall ensure decisions of the competent authorities refusing the admission of a security to the official listing, or discontinuing such a listing, shall be subject to the right to apply to the courts. In the context of British administrative law this must amount to judicial review. However, no actions for damages will lie against The Stock Exchange or its members, officers or employees for any thing done or omitted in good faith on discharge of their functions: section 187 (4).

[66] *R v International Stock Exchange etc. ex parte Else (1982) Ltd* [1993] BCC 11.

[67] As to the meaning of 'issuer' in the case of certificates representing securities, see section 142 (7).

[68] Section 114 (1) and (3).

circumstances, obliges The Stock Exchange to require the publication of a prospectus or
'listing particulars'.[69]

The Stock Exchange may refuse an application if it considers that the admission of the
securities would be detrimental to the interests of investors because of any matters
relating to the issuer.[70] An application may also be refused where the issuer has failed to
comply with listing obligations imposed by another member state where the securities are
already listed there.[71]

A decision must be notified to the applicant within six months of the date of its receipt.
Where the applicant has been required to give further information, the six-month period
will run from the time when the information is supplied.[72] Where The Stock Exchange
fails to notify within this period, it is 'taken to have refused the application'.[73] No express
provision is made to implement Article 15 of the Admissions Directive (so as to give a
right to apply to the court) but, as discussed in 5.13 above, it is clear that companies are
entitled to seek judicial review of the Exchange's decisions.

The Stock Exchange has always had the power to discontinue and suspend listing. This
is obviously an important weapon in enforcing compliance with its rules relating to
original admission to listing as well as to continuous reporting and dealing requirements.
These powers are now given statutory force.[74]

5.15 Part IV prospectuses and listing particulars

Section 144 of the Financial Services Act 1986, which has been amended by the Public
Offers of Securities Regulations 1995 in order to implement the Prospectus Directive so
far as it affects listed securities, empowers the London Stock Exchange to require as a
condition of admission of securities to listing the production and publication of a
prospectus or a set of listing particulars.[75] A prospectus is mandatory where the securities
for which the listing is sought are to be offered to the public in the United Kingdom for the
first time prior to their admission to the Official List, unless the offer is within one of the
exemptions provided by Schedule 11A to the Act.[76] The exemptions provided by
Schedule 11A mirror those relating to unlisted securities provided by the Public Offers of
Securities Regulations 1995 and they are considered further in that context.[77] For the
moment, it suffices to note that an offer of shares for sale or subscription would be unlikely
to fall within an exemption. With regard to placings, although there is an exemption
where securities are offered to no more than fifty persons, there will often be more than
that number of placees involved in a placing. That limit will certainly be exceeded where
a company adopts a placing as its method of raising capital the first time its securities are

---

[69] Section 114 (2) as amended by the Public Offers of Securities Regulations 1995.

[70] Section 144 (3).

[71] ibid.

[72] Section 144 (4).

[73] Section 144 (5).

[74] Section 145. Securities whose listing is suspended, etc., under this section are to be regarded as still listed
for the purposes of section 153 (obligation of issuer of listed securities) and section 155 (payment of fees). Section
145 (3). Directors may also be subjected to public censure for failure by their company to comply with the *Listing
Rules*.

[75] For certain exemptions from the requirement to produce listing particulars see *Listing Rules*, Chapter 5,
paras. 5.23–5.30.

[76] As inserted by the Public Offers of Securities Regulations 1995, Schedule 3.

[77] 5.22 below.

admitted to listing, because of the requirement in the *Listing Rules* that a placing of shares of a new applicant must involve at least 100 placees.[78] A typical rights issue made by a listed company will also usually be too large to benefit from any of the exemptions.[79]

For the purposes of Part IV it is expressly provided that a person is to be regarded as offering securities if he makes an offer relating to the securities which, if accepted, would give rise to a contract to issue or sell[80] the securities or if he invites a person to make such an offer.[81] Thus, an offer for this purpose means not only an offer in its strict contractual sense but also an invitation to treat. A person is to be regarded as offering securities to the public if he offers them to any section of the public, whether selected as members or debenture holders of a company, or as clients of the person issuing the prospectus, or in any other manner.[82] This precludes an argument that it is not necessary to produce a prospectus in respect of a placing of securities or a rights issue: it cannot be said that the offer, in either case, is not an offer to the public simply because it is made to a section of the public rather than to the public at large.

The detailed requirements concerning the contents of listing particulars are set out in Chapters 5 and 6 of the *Listing Rules*. Listing particulars relating to an application for admission of shares must include a mass of information about the applicant and its share capital, and financial information about the applicant as well as its recent development and prospects. Information is also required about the applicant's group structure and its management. These detailed requirements are to a large extent derived from the Listing Particulars Directive. At the time of writing, the *Listing Rules* do not contain equivalent provisions relating to prospectuses. However, Article 7 of the Prospectus Directive provides that the contents of a prospectus relating to a public offer of securities for which listing is being sought must be determined in accordance with the Listing Particulars Directive subject to adaptations appropriate to the circumstances of a public offer. Accordingly, the rules relating to the contents of prospectuses can be expected to mirror those relating to listing particulars.

Since listing particulars and prospectuses are to be subject to virtually the same rules governing their form and content, it can be seen that little of substance turns on the fact that in some cases where Part IV applies the applicant for listing must produce a prospectus whilst in others it must produce listing particulars. The consequences of failing to provide all of the required information, or of providing false or misleading information, are the same in either case.[83] The distinction relates more to terminology and form than to substance.

5.16 The issuer's general duty to disclose

In addition to the information specified by the listing rules or otherwise required by The Stock Exchange, section 146 imposes an overriding duty on the issuer of listing securities

---

[78] Chapter 4, para. 4.12.

[79] The *Listing Rules* already contain an exemption from the obligation to produce listing particulars in respect of new shares of a class which is already listed where the new shares would increase the class by less than 10 per cent: *Listing Rules*, Chapter 5, para. 5.27 (*e*).

[80] 'Sell' includes to dispose of for valuable consideration: section 142 (7A) as inserted by the Public Offers of Securities Regulations 1995.

[81] Section 142 (7A), as inserted by the Public Offers of Securities Regulations 1995.

[82] Section 142 (7A) (*b*) and Schedule 11A (1) as inserted by the Public Offers of Securities Regulations 1995.

[83] 5.29 below.

in respect of what must be contained in any listing particulars submitted under section 144. The overriding duty of disclosure also applies in relation to a prospectus required by section 144 and the *Listing Rules*.[84] The prospectus or, as the case may be, the listing particulars must contain 'all such information' as investors and their professional advisers would reasonably require, and reasonably expect to find there, for the purpose of making an informed assessment of (a) the assets and liabilities, financial position, profits and losses, and prospects of the issuer[85] of the securities, and (b) the rights attached to the securities involved in the issue.[86] A qualification to this general obligation is that what is required is information 'which is within the knowledge of any person responsible for the prospectus or, as the case may be, listing particulars or which it would be reasonable for him to obtain by making enquiries'.[87] As a further guide, it is provided[88] that in determining what information is required to be included in a prospectus or in listing particulars by virtue of section 146, regard is to be had to the following factors. These are, first, the nature of the securities and of the issuer; secondly, the nature of the persons likely to consider their acquisition (e.g. professional investment managers). The third factor is the fact that certain matters may reasonably be expected to be within the knowledge of professional advisers of any kind which those persons may reasonably be expected to consult.[89] It would seem that this provision is intended to indicate that if professional investment advisers receive more detailed documentation appropriate to their skills and level of understanding, the ordinary investors for whom they act may receive simpler documentation which they will be more likely to comprehend. This is reflected in the current practice of issuing investors at large with 'mini-prospectuses'.[90] The full documentation is made available to professional investors and advisers or those members of the public who ask for it.

Provision is made for The Stock Exchange to exempt from the obligation to disclose in the prospectus, listing particulars or supplementary documents on the ground that the disclosure of certain information would either be contrary to the public interest or would be seriously detrimental to the issuer of the securities.[91] In the latter case The Stock Exchange may not give its authority to exempt where non-disclosure would be likely to

---

[84] Section 154A of the Financial Services Act 1986 (as inserted by the Public Offers of Securities Regulations 1995).

[85] The issuer of the securities may not be the maker of the offer (e.g. where an investment trust is disposing of its investment in a company by way of a public offer of those securities).

[86] Section 146 (1). This implements Article 4 (1) of the Listing Particulars Directive and Article 11 (1) of the Prospectus Directive. Professor L. C. B. Gower has expressed the view that the implementation of Article 4 (1) has made the listing particulars subject to an obligation of utmost good faith requiring the disclosure of all material facts, and not merely those which the directive specifically requires. See *Review of Investor Protection*, Part II (1985) at p. 47. It is to be hoped that the courts in the United Kingdom so interpret section 144.

[87] Section 146 (2).

[88] Section 146 (3).

[89] Regard must also be had to information which The Stock Exchange has required to be made available (or itself made available) under section 153. This applies to recognised investment exchanges exercising powers conferred by Schedule 4 to the Act.

[90] The contents of a mini-prospectus are regulated by the *Listing Rules*, Chapter 8, paras. 8.12–8.13. The authorisation for the issue of a mini-prospectus is contained in Chapter 8, para. 8.24 where the Exchange exercises the statutory power conferred by section 154. See further, 5.19, below.

[91] Section 148 (1).

mislead a person considering the acquisition of the securities 'as to any facts the knowledge of which is essential for him to have in order to make an informed decision'.[92]

5.17 Supplementary Part IV prospectuses and listing particulars

In the United States federal securities law administered by the SEC there is a policy of 'continuous disclosure'[93] in respect of publicly issued prospectuses, on the ground that securities issued thereunder will continue to be sold and resold in a market influenced by the publicly issued prospectus. For reasons of costs and administrative burden, the Financial Services Act 1986 does not go that far, but it does in certain circumstances require a document called, as the case may be, a supplementary prospectus or supplementary listing particulars to be issued before the commencement of dealings in the securities (i.e. after their admission to the official list).[94] The circumstances are a significant change in any matter required to be in the prospectus or listing particulars or the emergence of a significant[95] new matter which would have been disclosed had it arisen at the time of preparation of the prospectus or listing particulars. The supplementary prospectus or listing particulars must be submitted in advance to The Stock Exchange for its approval in accordance with the *Listing Rules*.[96]

5.18 Pre-publication vetting of Part IV prospectuses and listing particulars

Independent pre-publication vetting of the information contained in a prospectus or set of listing particulars can be an important safeguard for investors.[97] It can help to ensure that all of the required information has been included and that the information has not been stated in a way which is likely to create a false impression. Knowing that the information will be subject to vetting may also serve to deter those who would otherwise have been tempted deliberately to mislead or to conceal information. Professor Gower has described the vetting role played by the London Stock Exchange as being 'in practice, a more effective protection to investors than the legal sanctions'.[98] Under section 144 (2) of the Financial Services Act 1986, as amended by the Public Offers of Securities Regulations 1995, and as supplemented by the *Listing Rules* (but at the time of writing only in relation to listing particulars), the documents must be submitted in draft to

---

[92] Section 148 (2). Special provision is made in respect of certain types of debenture (section 148 (1) (*c*)) and for exemption by the Secretary of State or the Treasury. This latter power is clearly intended to relate to 'privatisation' by public issue: section 148 (3).

[93] In the case of listed securities in Britain there is of course the Interim Reports Directive and The Stock Exchange's listing rules in that regard. See the *Listing Rules*, Chapters 9–11.

[94] Section 147.

[95] 'Significant' means significant for the purpose of making an informed assessment of the matters required to be disclosed under section 146 (1): see section 147 (2).

[96] Section 147 (3) provides defences where the issuer or the person responsible for the listing particulars is unaware of the change or the new matter, etc.

[97] Gower, *Review of Investor Protection*, (Cmnd 9123, 1984), Part I, paras. 9.16–9.23 and Part II, paras. 6.10–6.12.

[98] *Review of Investor Protection*, Part I, para. 9.12.

The Stock Exchange and must be formally approved by the Exchange prior to publication.[99]

5.19 The Stock Exchange's power to control information

As 'competent authority' The Stock Exchange is given a general power to specify in the *Listing Rules* the requirements to be complied with by the issuers of listed securities. It may also specify the sanctions or measures it will take in the event of non-compliance. This may include publishing the fact that the issuer has broken the rules. The issuer may be required to publish any information and The Stock Exchange itself may be authorised to do so if the issuer fails to do so.[100]

Section 154 gives The Stock Exchange the power to control advertisements[101] where there is the publication of a prospectus or listing particulars in connection with an application for listing. There may be no publication of an advertisement in the United Kingdom[102] unless the contents of the advertisement (or other information) have been submitted to The Stock Exchange. The latter may either approve the contents or authorise publication without such approval.[103]

Those who contravene section 154, if they are authorised persons, will be treated as having infringed the 'conduct of business rules' in Part I, Chapter V of the Financial Services Act. Authorised persons are persons who are authorised to carry on investment business in the United Kingdom. Issuing houses and corporate brokers would be among the category of persons who are required to seek authorisation. The Securities and Investments Board (SIB), which is the body charged with overseeing the regulatory regime for authorised persons established by the Financial Services Act 1962, is empowered under section 61[104] to seek an injunction to restrain a contravention of Conduct of Business Rules and to apply for restitution orders in respect of breaches which have occurred. Private investors[105] may also seek damages for losses resulting from contravention of the Conduct of Business Rules. A criminal sanction is provided for those who, not being 'authorised persons', infringe section 154.[106] Innocent publication 'in the ordinary course of business other than investment business' will not be an offence.[107] To bring himself within this defence, the accused must show that he had reasonable ground to believe The Stock Exchange had approved or authorised the advertisement.[108]

Where advertisements to which section 154 applies have been approved or authorised by The Stock Exchange no civil liability will be incurred by those responsible for publishing the information if 'that information and the listing particulars (or prospectus), taken together, would not be likely to mislead persons of the kind likely to

---

[99] The *Listing Rules*, Chapter 5.

[100] Section 153.

[101] This extends to other information of a kind specified by the listing rules.

[102] Section 154 (1).

[103] *Listing Rules*, Chapter 8, paras. 8.23–8.26 specify various documents for the purposes of section 154 and indicate whether The Stock Exchange's approval is required before publication or whether publication without prior approval is permitted.

[104] The section vests the power in the Secretary of State but it has been delegated, as is permitted, to SIB.

[105] See section 62.

[106] Section 154 (3).

[107] Section 154 (4).

[108] ibid.

consider the acquisition of the securities in question.'[109] This excludes the possibility of a civil remedy (under section 150 or at common law), where the information, publication of which has been officially sanctioned, is not misleading when read in conjunction with other information publicly available. However, this will not preclude a claim where the information is still misleading, even when taken together with the information in the prospectus or listing particulars and, where relevant, supplementary documents.

Where, under the *Listing Rules*, the publication of a prospectus is required, the securities must not be offered to the public in advance of publication of the prospectus. It is a breach of Conduct of Business Rules for an authorised person to contravene this requirement, whilst contravention by any other person is an offence.[110] Contravention is also actionable at the suit of any person who suffers loss as a consequence, subject to the defences and other incidents applying to actions for breach of statutory duty.[111]

5.20 Registration of Part IV prospectuses and listing particulars

On or before the date on which a prospectus or a set of listing particulars is published as required by the listing rules it must be delivered for registration to the Registrar of Companies.[112] A statement to this effect must be included in the prospectus or particulars.

5.21 Public offers of unlisted securities

Public offers of unlisted securities are regulated by the Public Offers of Securities Regulations 1995 which implement the Prospectus Directive into English law. Much of the directive is drafted in precise language, and to a considerable extent the regulations simply adopt the wording of the directive. The directive and the regulations do not draw a significant distinction[113] between public offers made through a formal market (such as the Alternative Investment Market of the London Stock Exchange) and other public offers.

The core requirement of the regulations is contained in regulation 4 (1)[114] which provides that:

> When securities are offered to the public in the United Kingdom for the first time the offeror shall publish a prospectus by making it available to the public, free of charge, at an address in the United Kingdom, from the time he first offers the securities until the end of the period during which the offer remains open.

Any person who makes a public offer of securities may be subject to this requirement since it is not limited in its application to offers made by the company which is the issuer of the securities. Thus a traditional offer for sale on behalf of a company is within the scope

---

[109] Section 154 (5). For this purpose, incurring civil liability includes a reference to any other person being entitled as against that person to be granted any civil remedy or to rescind or repudiate any agreement.

[110] Section 156B, as inserted by the Public Offers of Securities Regulations 1995.

[111] Section 156B (5). Failure to comply fully with the requirements as to the form and content of a prospectus does not necessarily constitute contravention of this section: section 156B (4).

[112] Section 149. Section 154A extends this requirement to prospectuses.

[113] Note regulations 8 (4), 8 (5) and 15 (1) (*d*) where the fact of securities being admitted to dealings on an approved exchange has some relevance.

[114] See Articles 4, 9, 15 and 16 of the directive.

of the regulations. An offer by a large investor of its shareholding in a particular company may also be covered by the regulations, provided that the offer is of sufficient magnitude to constitute an offer to the public and those securities have not been the subject of an earlier public offer.

The prospectus must be delivered to the Registrar of Companies for registration prior to publication.[115] There is, however, no requirement for mandatory pre-publication vetting of prospectuses relating to unlisted securities, which, given the widely acknowledged benefits of the vetting process, may be regarded as an unfortunate lacuna in the regulatory framework. The proposed structure of the Alternative Investment Market makes no provision for vetting, even though that function was performed by the USM.[116]

Contravention of regulation 4 by an authorised person is treated as a breach of the relevant Conduct of Business Rules, whilst contravention by any other person is an offence.[117] Contravention by an authorised or an unauthorised person is also actionable at the suit of any person who suffers loss as a result, subject to the defences and other incidents applying to actions for breach of statutory duty.[118]

5.22 An 'offer to the public' of 'securities'

The requirement to publish a prospectus is triggered by the making of an offer to the public in the United Kingdom of securities. The expression 'offer to the public' is not defined by the Prospectus Directive, which, in its preamble, explains that 'so far it has proved impossible to furnish a common definition of the term public offer and all of its constituent parts'. Regulations 5 and 6 attempt to define the expression in the same terms as are used in Part IV of the Financial Services Act. An 'offer' includes an invitation to treat as well as a strict contractual offer;[119] and under regulation 6 an offer to a section of the public, whether selected as members or debenture holders of a company, or as clients of the person issuing the prospectus, or in any other manner, constitutes an offer to the public. A person offers securities to the public in the United Kingdom if, to the extent that the offer is made to persons in the United Kingdom, it is made to the public.[120]

The Prospectus Directive exempts various types of offer from its scope.[121] These exemptions are reflected in regulation 7,[122] which deems certain offers of securities to be offers to the public. The exempted offers in regulation 7 include the following:

(1) Offers to persons in the contexts of their trades, professions or occupations.[123]
(2) Offers to no more than fifty persons.[124] Previously, English law did not specify a

---

[115] Regulation 4 (2), implementing article 14.

[116] The absence of vetting creates a particular problem with regard to mutual recognition of prospectuses throughout the European Community. See 5.27, below.

[117] Regulation 16. A person is not to be regarded as having contravened regulation 4 by reason only of a prospectus not having fully complied with the requirements of the regulations as to form and content of prospectuses.

[118] Regulation 16 (4).

[119] Regulation 5.

[120] Regulation 6.

[121] Article 2.1.

[122] These exemptions also apply to the requirement under Part IV to publish a prospectus instead of listing particulars. For the purposes of Part IV, the exemptions are contained in section 144 (2A) of and Schedule 11A to the Financial Services Act 1986 but, in substance, they are the same as those that apply to public offers of unlisted securities which are discussed in the text.

[123] Regulation 7 (2) (*a*) and (in respect of listed securities) Schedule 11A, para. 3 (1) (*a*).

[124] Regulation 7 (2) (*b*) Schedule 11A, para. 3 (1) (*b*).

threshold number of offerees below which an offer was not to be regarded as an offer to the public. This important exemption will enable small-scale offers to be made without excessive regulation.[125]

(3) Offers made to a restricted circle of persons whom the offeror reasonably believes to be sufficiently knowledgeable to understand the risks involved.[126]

(4) Offers in connection with underwriting.[127]

(5) Offers of securities by a private company to its existing members, employees or debenture holders, or to members of the families of existing members and employees.[128]

(6) Offers where the total consideration payable for all the securities offered does not exceed ECU 40,000.[129]

(7) Offers where the securities are denominated in amounts of at least ECU 40,000.[130]

The Prospectus Directive only applies to 'transferable securities', which are defined as including shares in companies and debt securities having a maturity of at least one year.[131] Accordingly, the Public Offers of Securities Regulations 1995 do not require the publication of a prospectus in respect of an offer of short-term debentures which will mature within one year.[132] Also reflecting the scope of the underlying directive,[133] there are exemptions from the requirement to publish a prospectus in respect of bonus shares, that is shares issued on a fully paid basis to existing shareholders,[134] shares or debentures offered in connection with a takeover bid or merger,[135] and shares or debentures offered by employers to employees or former employees or members of their families.[136]

5.23 Form and content of prospectuses

Where a prospectus is required, its form and content must comply with the requirements set out in Schedule 1 to the regulations. The information required to be included relates to the issuer and its capital, financial position, activities and organisation, the offeror (if different from the issuer), the persons responsible for the prospectus, the securities and the offer.[137] The information in a prospectus must be presented in as easily an analysable and comprehensible a form as possible.[138]

---

[125] They will be regulated by sections 57–58 of the Financial Services Act 1986.

[126] Regulation 7 (2) (*d*) and (7); and see also Schedule 11A, para. 3 (1) (*d*) and (4).

[127] Regulation 7 (2) (*e*); and see also Schedule 11A, para. 3 (1) (*e*).

[128] Regulation 7 (2) (*f*) and (8); this exemption does not have an equivalent in Schedule 11A because the securities of a private company may not be admitted to listing. Other 'restricted circle' exemptions are in respect of offers to members of a club or association (regulation 7 (2) (*c*); Schedule 11A, para. 3 (1) (*c*)) and of offers to governments or local or public authorities (regulation 7 (2) (*g*); Schedule 11A, para 3 (1) (*f*)).

[129] Regulation 7 (2) (*h*); see also Schedule 11A, para. 3 (1) (*g*).

[130] Regulation 7 (2) (*j*); see also Schedule 11A, para. 3 (1) (*i*).

[131] Article 3 (*e*). For 'securities' subject to the regulations see regulation 3, and for 'securities' subject to Part IV see section 142.

[132] Regulation 3 (2) (*a*); see also Schedule 11A, para. 1 (*t*).

[133] See Article 2.2.

[134] Regulation 7 (2) (*m*); see also Schedule 11A, para. 3 (1) (*l*).

[135] Regulation 7 (2) (*k*) and (*l*) and (10); see also Schedule 11A, para. 3 (1) (*j*) and (*k*) and (10).

[136] Regulation 7 (2) (*o*) and (12); see also Schedule 11A, para. 3 (1) (*n*) and (8).

[137] These detailed requirements are derived from Article 11.

[138] Regulation 8 (3), implementing Article 11.2.

There is an overriding duty of disclosure which is very similar to, but not precisely the same as, the duty of disclosure imposed by section 146 of the Financial Services Act 1986 in respect of listed securities. Under regulation 9 a prospectus relating to unlisted securities must contain all such information as investors would reasonably require, and reasonably expect to find there, for the purpose of making an informed assessment of the assets and liabilities, financial position, profits and losses and prospects of the issuer and of the rights attaching to the securities. In determining the information required to satisfy the overriding duty of disclosure, regard is to be had to the nature of the securities and of the issuer;[139] and the duty is qualified to the extent that it is only information which is within the knowledge of the persons responsible for the prospectus, or which it would be reasonable for them to obtain by making inquiries, that must be disclosed.[140] However, unlike section 146, in determining the information required to be included, there is no express provision permitting account to be taken of the nature of the persons likely to consider the acquisition of the securities, or the fact that certain matters may reasonably be expected to be already within the knowledge of professional advisers of any kind which likely investors could be reasonably expected to consult. This may have the effect of imposing a heavier onus of disclosure under the regulations than that under the Act.

As permitted by the directive, the regulations make provision for the modification of the information required to be included in a prospectus in particular circumstances.[141] For example, where a company makes a number of public offers in the United Kingdom of its securities within a year, it may be relieved of the obligation to publish a full prospectus each time. In respect of second and subsequent offers, the company may instead publish a prospectus which contains only the differences which have arisen since the publication of the full prospectus and which are likely to influence the value of the securities. This prospectus must be accompanied by the earlier full prospectus or must refer to it.[142] Where the person offering the securities is not the company issuing them, and is not acting in pursuance of an agreement with that company, he can omit information from the prospectus that would otherwise be required if that information is not available to him because he is not the issuer and he has been unable, despite making such efforts (if any) as are reasonable, to obtain it.[143] Provision is also made for applications to be made to the London Stock Exchange for permission to omit information that would otherwise be required to be included: this extends one of the advantages of the regime governing listed securities to unlisted securities.[144]

5.24 Supplementary prospectuses

Where a prospectus has been registered in respect of an offer of securities and an agreement in respect of those securities can still be entered into in pursuance of the offer, there may be a need to publish one or more supplementary prospectuses. This need arises if, during the relevant period, there is a significant[145] change affecting any matter

---

[139] Regulation 9 (3).

[140] Regulation 9 (2).

[141] Regulation 8 (2), (4), (6) and regulation 11. Regulation 8 (5) paves the way for an approved exchange to dispense altogether with the requirement to publish a prospectus, where the offer is of a class of securities which is already admitted to dealings on that exchange and will increase the class by less than 10 per cent.

[142] Regulation 8 (6).

[143] Regulation 11 (2).

[144] Regulation 11 (3).

[145] Defined by regulation 10 (2).

contained in the prospectus which was required to be included, a significant[146] new matter arises which would have been so required if it had arisen when the prospectus was prepared, or there is a significant inaccuracy in the prospectus.[147] However, where the person who delivered the prospectus for registration is unaware of the matter which gives rise to the need for a supplementary prospectus, he is under no duty to comply unless he is informed of it by a person who is responsible for the prospectus; any person who is responsible for the prospectus is under a duty to provide the relevant notification.[148] A supplementary prospectus must be delivered to the registrar of companies for registration.[149]

5.25 Control of information

Any advertisement, notice, poster or document (other than a prospectus) announcing a public offer of unlisted securities for which a prospectus is required must not be issued or caused to be issued to the public in the United Kingdom by the person making the offer, unless it states that a prospectus is or will be published and gives an address in the United Kingdom from which it can be obtained.[150] Contravention of this requirement by an authorised person amounts to a breach of the relevant Conduct of Business Rules. An unauthorised person who breaches this requirement is guilty of an offence. Contravention by an authorised or unauthorised person is also actionable at the suit of any person who suffers loss, subject to the defences and other incidents applying to actions for breach of statutory duty.[151]

5.26 Regulation of investment advertisements by the Financial Services Act 1986

Apart from the regulation of prospectuses and listing particulars, another way in which the regulatory structure seeks to filter out unsuitable investment information is through section 57 of the Financial Services Act 1986. Under this section, investment advertisements which are issued in the United Kingdom must be issued by, or with the approval of, authorised persons. Authorised persons must comply with the Conduct of Business Rules when issuing, or approving for issue, investment advertisements. The responsibility so imposed on authorised persons acts as a safeguard against advertisements containing false or misleading information or failing to provide adequate information. The expression 'investment advertisement' is very broadly defined[152] and it would certainly include an advertisement containing an offer of securities. Thus, an offer of unlisted securities which, for some reason relating either to the nature of the securities or the type of offer, is not subject to the Public Offers of Securities Regulations 1995 does not necessarily escape from the regulatory net, since it may be caught in any event by section 57. Contravention of section 57 is an offence and an agreement entered into in

---

[146] ibid.

[147] The last of these does not have an equivalent in section 147 of the Financial Services Act 1986.

[148] Regulation 10 (4).

[149] Regulation 10 (3).

[150] Regulation 12.

[151] Regulation 16.

[152] Section 57 (2).

breach of the section may be unenforceable, with the innocent party being entitled to recover any money or property he has parted with together with compensation.[153]

Section 57 is subject to a number of exemptions made by or under section 58. Particularly important exemptions in the context of public offers of securities are those which relate to prospectuses, listing particulars and associated documents. As well as catching advertisements that would not otherwise be regulated, section 57 also prima facie brings within its scope prospectuses and listing particulars which are subject to the requirements of Part IV of the Financial Services Act 1986 or, as the case may be, of the Public Offers of Securities Regulations 1995. A requirement to comply with section 57 as well as Part IV or the Public Offers Regulations could be regarded as amounting to excessive regulation and this result is prevented by appropriate exemptions: listing particulars, supplementary listing particulars, Part IV prospectuses, supplementary prospectuses and other advertisements relating to listed securities published with the approval of the London Stock Exchange or in accordance with the *Listing Rules* are exempt from section 57;[154] prospectuses, supplementary prospectuses and other advertisements relating to unlisted securities which are the subject of a public offer that is regulated by the Public Offers of Securities Regulations are also exempted from the scope of section 57 by regulations made under section 58 (3).[155]

5.27 Mutual recognition of prospectuses and listing particulars in member states of the European Community

With a view to encouraging the development of a pan-Community capital market, the member states of the Community have adopted mutual recognition provisions. These allow securities to be offered, or admitted to listing, in a number of member states on the basis of a prospectus or set of listing particulars which has satisfied the requirements imposed by one of those states. Satisfying the requirements of one state can thus be said to act as a passport for the offering or listing of the relevant securities in other member states. Under European law, mutual recognition is governed by Article 21 of the Prospectus Directive and Articles 24a and 24b of the Listing Particulars Directive. Schedule 4 to the Public Offers of Securities Regulations makes provision for the recognition in the United Kingdom of prospectuses and listing particulars approved in other member states.

To qualify for use as a passport throughout the Community, a prospectus or set of listing particulars must first be approved in one member state. This poses a difficulty in the United Kingdom in relation to prospectuses relating to unlisted securities, because they are not required to be vetted or approved by an independent authority prior to publication. To ensure that companies do not have to seek a listing solely in order to benefit from the mutual recognition provisions, section 156A makes provision for the submission to, and the approval of, the London Stock Exchange of prospectuses relating to offers of unlisted securities. The section 156A procedure can only be used where the United Kingdom is one of the member states in which the securities are to be offered, but it is not restricted to companies having their registered office in the United Kingdom or

---

[153] Section 57 (3) and (5)–(7). Note the defence provided by section 57 (4) and the powers of the court under section 57 (8).

[154] Section 58 (1) (*d*) as amended by the Public Offers of Securities Regulations 1995.

[155] The Financial Services Act 1986 (Investment Advertisements) (Exemptions) (No. 2) Order 1995, article 14.

another member state. An application under section 156A would not amount to an application for listing and, although the Exchange would obviously charge a fee for performing the vetting service, the costs involved should be much smaller than those incurred in seeking a full listing.

5.28 Remedies for false, misleading or incomplete statements in connection with offers of securities

Part IV of the Financial Services Act 1986 provides a single type of statutory remedy in respect of three distinct situations, namely:

(1) the inclusion of false or misleading information in a prospectus or set of listing particulars (including supplementary prospectuses and listing particulars);

(2) failure to disclose the information required to be included in a prospectus or set of listing particulars (including supplementary prospectuses and listing particulars); and

(3) failure to publish, when required, a supplementary prospectus or set of listing particulars.

A virtually identical statutory remedy in respect of unlisted securities is provided by regulation 14 of the Public Offers of Securities Regulations 1995. The Part IV remedy is considered below, with reference to the equivalent provisions in respect of unlisted securities.

Various other remedies for deceit, misrepresentation and negligence must also be considered since they are applicable to offers which fall outside Part IV and the Public Offers of Securities Regulations 1995 and to statements made otherwise than in prospectuses, listing particulars and related documents. These remedies are also potentially applicable in respect of false statements in prospectuses and listing particulars, but considerations such as the burden of proof or range of possible defendants may lead investors to favour the statutory claims. It would seem undeniable that the range of overlapping remedies can create unnecessary confusion in this area of the law.

5.29 The statutory remedy for false, misleading or incomplete statements

Section 150 of the Financial Services Act 1986 creates liability for loss as a result of any untrue or misleading statement in listing particulars or the omission from them of any matter required to be included by section 146 (overriding duty of disclosure) or section 147 (supplementary listing particulars). Section 154A, inserted by the Public Offers of Securities Regulations 1995, extends this to Part IV prospectuses and supplementary prospectuses. Failure to publish supplementary listing particulars or prospectuses when required is similarly actionable.[156]

The 'person or persons responsible'[157] for any prospectus or set of listing particulars[158] are made 'liable to pay compensation to any person who has acquired[159] any of the

[156] Section 150 (3), as extended by section 154A. See regulation 14 (3) for the equivalent provision in respect of unlisted securities.

[157] This expression is defined at length by section 152, examined below. Primarily it is the 'issuer' and its directors.

[158] Or, where appropriate, supplementary prospectuses or listing particulars. See section 150 (1).

[159] See the definition of 'acquisition' in section 150 (5). The question of who may seek relief on this basis is considered below.

securities in question and suffered a loss in respect of them as a result of any untrue or misleading statement', etc. As is appropriate to a misrepresentation and non-disclosure remedy[160] intended to protect investors in the context of a public issue, the elements of 'reliance' and 'inducement' (required by the common law of misrepresentation) have been abolished. The element of causation ('as a result of') naturally remains. Further, it is specifically provided that actual knowledge by the plaintiff when he acquired the securities that the statement was false or misleading, etc., may be raised and proved as a defence against an action based on section 150.[161] It is obviously important that in a public issue investor remedy of this type, those who acquire securities without reading the prospectus or listing particulars but nevertheless suffer a loss because of false or misleading statements (or the omission of information that is required to be disclosed[162]) should have a remedy. This is because the market price is affected by the responses of other investors when the truth becomes known. The original price those investors were in general prepared to pay can be properly said to relate to the accuracy of the information made available to the investing public.[163]

A less satisfactory feature of section 150 is the nature of the 'compensation' payable to a person who has acquired securities and 'suffered a loss'. Similar terminology employed in section 2 (1) of the Misrepresentation Act 1967 has generally been understood to give a tort measure of damages (i.e. based on 'out of pocket' losses) rather than losses based on 'loss of expectation of bargain' (the traditional[164] contractual measure). Although it is possible that the draftsman may have intended otherwise (or perhaps hoped to leave the matter to the courts), it is regrettable, especially in an investor protection Act, that the answer cannot be given with any certainty. It seems that, whatever the basis of awarding compensation, section 150 does not impose contractual liability. Like other remedies for false or misleading statements (where these cannot be regarded as incorporated in the terms of a contract) failure to carry out promises will not ground relief. Undertakings of various kinds are commonly given in both public issue and take-over documents.[165]

5.30 Who may be sued and who may sue under the statutory remedy?

To the first of these questions an ample answer is given by section 152 of the Financial Services Act 1986.[166] Primarily it is the 'issuer of the securities' and (where the issuer is a

---

[160] This is a common feature of such remedies in American and Commonwealth securities regulation legislation. See Rider and Leigh French, *The Regulation of Insider Trading* (Macmillan, 1979).

[161] Section 151 (8). Regulation 15 (5) is the equivalent provision of unlisted securities.

[162] Where the prospectus or listing particulars require that a statement be made that no information can or need be given on a certain matter, failure to do so also comes within this remedy. Section 150 (2) and, in respect of unlisted securities, regulation 14 (2).

[163] Welch, 'Breach of Prospectus Requirements' (1985) 6 Co. Law 247.

[164] It is true that in some respects the rules governing damages in contract and in tort have, in recent years, 'grown together'. This, however, does not affect the point made in the text.

[165] The 'row' in the City in the summer of 1986 concerning the Guinness bid for the Distillers Company is one example. It concerned an undertaking as to who should become chairman of the combined company resulting from a successful bid.

[166] Regulation 13 is the equivalent provision in respect of unlisted securities. In certain detailed respects, regulation 13 and section 152 differ: for example, regulation 13 excludes the issuer from the list of responsible persons where it has not authorised the offer; section 152 does not provide an equivalent exemption, but the situation cannot arise because securities cannot be listed under Part IV without the consent of the issuer.

body corporate) the directors of the issuer at the time the listing particulars were submitted to The Stock Exchange.[167] It also extends to those who accept, and are stated in the prospectus or particulars as accepting, responsibility for the document. That will include those who accept responsibility for 'any part' of the document. It also covers those who authorise the contents of all or part of the document. These provisions cast a wide net. They will clearly cover an issuing house performing its usual functions (whether or not the relevant prospectus relates to an offer for sale). They will also catch an 'expert'[168] (e.g. a valuer or reporting accountant) who is responsible for that part of the contents of the prospectus or listing particulars for which he has taken responsibility.[169] The liability imposed by section 150 does not extend to those giving advice as to the contents of the prospectus or particulars in a professional capacity (e.g. solicitors).[170]

Liability to pay compensation under section 150 is ignored in determining the amount to be paid on subscription for the shares in question or as to the amount paid up or deemed to be paid up.[171] This preserves the formal requirements as to the raising of share capital.

The provisions relating to those who may seek a remedy under section 150 are less clearly spelt out than is the case in regard to those made responsible for the prospectus or listing particulars. Section 150 (1) itself refers to 'any person who has acquired any of the securities in question'. Section 150 (5) then states that references in section 150 'to the acquisition by any person of securities include references to his contracting to acquire them or an interest in them'.[172] This phraseology is not wholly free from ambiguity. It obviously means that not only those who have become registered owners of the securities in question but also who have agreed to purchase or subscribe for them (or options in them) may resort to the relief provided by section 150. Does this extend to 'market purchasers'[173] who might obtain relief in an action for fraud or negligence? It would seem a likely construction of section 150 (1). In the case of an offer for sale (where deemed subscribers would have been given a remedy in respect of sections 67 to 69 by section 58 of the Companies Act 1985) the term 'acquire' should not create a problem since it does not necessarily import privity of contract between those who have acquired and the 'person or persons responsible'.

---

[167] Section 152 (1) (*a*) to (*b*). It also includes those named in the prospectus or listing particulars who have authorised their naming as present or future directors: section 152 (1) (*c*). 'Issuer' for this purpose extends to the person offering or proposing to offer the securities: section 154A. As to issues of securities concerned with a take-over by share exchange, see section 152 (4).

[168] See the definition of 'expert' in section 151 (7).

[169] Section 152 (3). See also section 152 (1) (*d*) and (*e*).

[170] Section 152 (8). Certain exemptions from the liability imposed by section 152 are provided for in the case of an issuer of 'international securities' and in the case of the director of issuers who are exempted by The Stock Exchange in appropriate circumstances. See section 152 (5) and (6). There are no equivalent exemptions in respect of unlisted securities.

[171] Section 152 (9). See Regulation 13 (5) in respect of unlisted securities.

[172] See regulation 14 (5) in respect of unlisted securities.

[173] This interpretation is borne out by the wording of section 151 (1) (*d*) which implies that liability may occur after the commencement of dealings.

5.31 Defences available to persons responsible

Section 151 sets out a series of defences.[174] The principal defence is that the person responsible can satisfy the court that he 'reasonably believed',[175] having made such enquiries (if any) as were reasonable, that the statement was true and not misleading.[176] It must also be shown he continued in that belief until the securities were acquired. Alternatively, he may show that the securities were acquired before it was reasonably practical for steps to be taken to bring a correction to the attention of persons likely to acquire the securities,[177] or before the securities were acquired he had taken all such steps as it was reasonable for him to have taken to secure that a correction was brought to the attention of those persons. Another alternative defence is that he continued to believe (that the statement was true, etc.) until after the commencement of dealings in the securities following their admission to the Official List. Here he must satisfy the court that the securities were acquired after such a lapse of time that he ought in the circumstances to be reasonably excused.[178]

Reasonable reliance on statements made on the authority of an expert is a further defence,[179] and there is a defence against liability for loss resulting from a statement made by an official or contained in an official document.[180] A defence to the failure to publish required supplementary prospectuses or listing particulars is available to a person who can establish that he reasonably believed that no such supplementary document was required.[181]

5.32 The relationship of the statutory remedy to the common-law remedies

Section 150 (4)[182] is careful to preserve 'any liability which any person may incur apart from this section'. An investor in securities is thus free to pursue claims based on misrepresentation or negligence.[183] There are good grounds for the retention of the remedy of rescission for misrepresentation because, whereas he can only seek compensation under section 150, rescission allows the investor to set aside the contract for the

---

[174] See regulation 15 in respect of unlisted securities.

[175] That is, at the time when he submitted the prospectus or listing particulars to the Exchange. For prospectuses relating to unlisted securities the relevant time is when the prospectus is delivered to the Registrar of Companies for registration: regulation 15 (1).

[176] Or that the matter that was omitted (where the omission of required information caused the loss) was properly omitted.

[177] Section 151 (1) (*b*) and (*c*). See also section 151 (3) as to reasonable steps to bring corrections to the attention of those likely to acquire the securities. See regulations 15 (1) (*b*) and (*c*) and 15 (3) in respect of unlisted securities.

[178] Section 151 (1) (*d*). The equivalent defence in respect of unlisted securities is contained in regulation 15 (1) (*d*). This defence bears out the inclusion of 'market purchasers' in the initial period of dealing as among those who may sue. Note section 156A (3) (*d*) which modifies the defence as it applies to prospectuses which do not relate to listing securities and which are brought within Part IV for mutual recognition purposes.

[179] Section 151 (2).

[180] Section 151 (4), i.e. where these statements, etc., are included in the prospectus or listing particulars. See regulation 15 (2) and (4) for the equivalent provisions in respect of unlisted securities.

[181] Section 151 (6). The equivalent provision in respect of unlisted securities is regulation 15 (6).

[182] See regulation 14 (4) for the equivalent provision in respect of unlisted securities.

[183] Or in contract in a suitable case. A contractual claim would enable an investor to seek compensation for breach of promise.

acquisition of the securities and thus to unwind completely the original bargain. Also rescission can be sought on the basis of a purely innocent (i.e. non-negligent) misrepresentation. However, otherwise (and in particular with regard to the right to damages under section 2 (1) of the Misrepresentation Act 1967) there appears still to be an unnecessary and confusing overlap in remedies. It is a matter of regret that in an Act designed to make such a radical departure from the old law on public issues the question of overlap was not tackled. Section 2 (1) of the 1967 Act is only available against the other party to the investment contract (e.g. the issuing house in the case of an offer of sale) and is thus more restricted in its 'target' than section 150 of the 1986 Act. Moreover, it would appear to require the proof of 'reliance' and 'inducement'. On the other hand, since the only defence is reasonable ground for belief (and not the other defences in section 150 (6)) it may sometimes be worth pleading in addition to section 150. However, none of these distinctions was worth preserving, and it would have been a simple matter to disapply section 2 (1) in the context of investment contracts within the scope of section 150.[184]

5.33 The common-law remedies: the right to rescind a contract of allotment for material misrepresentation

An allottee's right to rescind the contract of allotment may arise in the case of any allotment of shares by a company whether public or private. An action for rescission must be brought by the subscriber against the company as the other party to the contract of allotment. Where the shares are not allotted directly to subscribers by the company, a right of rescission may not be exercised against the company. In the case of an offer for sale the issuing house is the 'subscriber' and the investors who obtain securities from the issuing house do so by 'purchase'. Clearly, any remedy by way of rescission will be against the issuing house.

A contract to take shares, like other contracts, is voidable if induced by misrepresentation, whether such misrepresentation is fraudulent or innocent: that is to say the contract is valid until repudiation, but upon repudiation becomes void as from the date when the shareholder gives notice that he requires to be released of his shares. This is subject, however, to the rule discussed later that he must actually take proceedings to enforce his right (if it is not admitted) before the company goes into liquidation, and that he must come promptly for relief. Accordingly, if there is a material misrepresentation in the listing particulars or, as the case may be, the prospectus upon which a shareholder relied when applying for shares offered by way of subscription, he is entitled, if he seeks relief within a reasonable time after learning the truth, and before the company is in liquidation, to have his name removed from the register, and the amount he has paid upon the shares returned to him,[185] with interest from the time of payment.[186] But it must be noted that only the shareholder who applied for the shares on the faith of the

---

[184] Something similar to this has been done in regard to a promoter's duties of disclosure to his company in section 150 (6) as amended. This equitable duty is disregarded as regards the duty to disclose information in the prospectus or listing particulars.

[185] The best statement of the effect of the cases will be found in *Re Scottish Petroleum Co.* (1883) 23 Ch D 413 (CA).

[186] *Karberg's Case* [1892] 3 Ch 1 (CA) (where the rate of interest was fixed by the court at 4 per cent).

prospectus is entitled to relief; the remedy does not extend to a purchaser from another shareholder who is not a party to the misrepresentation.

5.34 Responsibility for statements

Questions can arise concerning the responsibility of the company, its directors and its professional advisers for statements made in connection with a public offering of securities. In the case of the statutory remedy under the Financial Services Act 1986, the Act itself sets out a code of responsibility.[187] In the case of the common-law remedies such as rescission, a company is responsible for the statements of its directors, general agents and special agents who are acting within the scope of their authority,[188] which includes persons whose acts are subsequently ratified;[189] a company is also responsible for statements which, to the knowledge of its directors, were made before the contract and which induced it or which formed the basis of it.[190] In each case the company's responsibility does not depend on whether the representations were known to be false or not.[191]

Representations made even before the company was in existence, or made by persons who are strangers to the company, may become, by the subsequent knowledge of the directors, the responsibility of the company, as where an application for shares was made before the company was incorporated upon the faith of a prospectus prepared by a promoter, and the company later adopted the prospectus and allotted the shares.[192]

If a statement is actually included in listing particulars or in a prospectus, the company may find it difficult to deny that the statement formed the basis of the contract to take the shares. The cases establish that the statement will be so treated unless the company expressly dissociates itself from the report and warns investors that they must take the report for what it is worth:[193] the distinction is between showing that it is repeating on hearsay what it has been told, and affirming the matter as a fact.[194] However, such disclaimers of responsibility must be read in the light of section 3 of the Misrepresentation Act 1967, which invalidates any unreasonable[195] contractual term that would exclude or restrict liability for misrepresentation. Also, such a disclaimer cannot be included in a prospectus or a set of listing particulars relating to securities which are to be listed, because The Stock Exchange specifically requires the directors (or, in some cases, the company itself) to state expressly that they take responsibility for the information

---

[187] Regulation 13 of the Public Offers of Securities Regulations provides an equivalent code in respect of unlisted securities.

[188] Thus where the directors know that one of their body is obtaining subscriptions for shares, the company is responsible for representations made by him; *Hilo Manufacturing Co. v Williamson* (1911) 28 TLR 164.

[189] *Lynde v Anglo-Italian Hemp Co.* [1896] 1 Ch 178.

[190] ibid.

[191] This last proposition is not accurately stated in the headnote to *Collins v Greyhound Racecourses* [1930] 1 Ch 1, but is correctly stated in the judgment.

[192] *Karsberg's Case* [1892] 3 Ch 1; *Tamplin's Case* [1892] WN 146.

[193] *Mair v Rio Grande Rubber Estates* [1913] AC 853; *Karsberg's Case*, above; *Lynde v Anglo-Italian Hemp Co.*, above; *Re Pacaya Rubber Co.* [1914] 1 Ch 542.

[194] *Re Reese River Silver Mining Co.* (1867) 2 Ch App. 604 at 615.

[195] Reasonableness is judged in accordance with section 11 (1) of the Unfair Contract Terms Act 1977. The burden of establishing that a term is reasonable is on the person who wishes to rely on it: section 11 (5).

contained in the listing particulars.[196] Also, under the Public Offers of Securities Regulations, a prospectus relating to an offer of unlisted securities which is made or authorised by the issuer of the securities must contain a declaration by the directors that, to the best of their knowledge, the information accords with the facts and that there is no omission likely to affect the import of the information.[197]

5.35 Loss of the right to rescind

It is a general principle of law that where a party having a right to rescind his contract, after having knowledge of such right, performs any act affirming his contract, he cannot afterwards set up his right to avoid the contract.[198] Therefore any act by a shareholder recognising his position as a member of the company after knowledge of the misrepresentation, such as by selling or trying to sell the shares,[199] attending meetings,[200] signing proxies, paying calls, or accepting dividends,[201] will prevent the member from obtaining rescission, even though performed under a mistake as to rights,[202] unless he has meanwhile definitely elected to rescind the contract, as by commencing proceedings.[203]

The shareholder must, moreover, come within a reasonable time after learning the truth; for the rights and interests of other persons intervene, and the aggrieved shareholder will not be allowed to wait and see whether the speculation turns out to be a favourable one, and then, according to the result, retain the benefit or repudiate the loss.[204] As the intervention of the rights of others prevents the right of the applicant to rescind, it may well be that even a charge on the uncalled capital in favour of debenture holders will prevent relief, but this has not been definitely decided.[205] The occurrence of a winding-up, whether the assets are sufficient to pay the creditors or not, brings in other rights (i.e. those of the creditors or contributories) so as to render rescission impossible;[206] for upon the commencement of a liquidation the creditors or other shareholders are the persons interested in retaining the name of the shareholder upon the register, and against them he has no claim to set aside his bargain.[207]

---

[196] *Listing Rules*, Chapter 5, paras. 5.2–5.5. Special provision is made for listing particulars relating to an issue of securities in connection with a takeover, where the directors of the target alone can take responsibility for information in the listing particulars relating to their company (para. 5.3.). Only the company, and not its directors, is required to take responsibility for information in listing particulars relating to international securities such as eurobonds: *Listing Rules*, Chapter 23, para. 23.11.

[197] Schedule 1, part III, para. 10 (1).

[198] *Clough v London and North-Western Railway* (1872) LR 7 Ex. 26 (Ex. Ch.).

[199] *Ex parte Briggs* (1866) LR 1 Eq. 483. Compare *Crawley's Case* (1869) LR 4 Ch App. 322.

[200] *Sharpley v Louth and East Coast Railway* (1876) 2 Ch D 663.

[201] *Scholey v Central Railway of Venezuela* (1869) LR 9 Eq. 266, note.

[202] *Re Dunlop-Truffault Cycle Co.* (1896) 66 LJ Ch 25.

[203] *Tomlin's Case* (1898) 1 Ch 104.

[204] *Downes v Ship* (1868) LR 3 HL 343; *Houldsworth v City of Glasgow Bank* (1880) 5 AC 317 (HL).

[205] For the principle see: *Re Scottish Petroleum Co.* (1883), 23 Ch D 413 (CA); *Tennent v City of Glasgow Bank* (1879) 4 App. Cas. 615 (HL).

[206] *Tennent v City of Glasgow Bank* (1879) 4 App. Cas. 615 (HL); *Burgess's Case* (1880) 15 Ch D 507, this being the case of a solvent company.

[207] *Tennent v City of Glasgow Bank* (1879) 4 App. Cas. 615; *Stone v City and County Bank* (1877) 3 CP 282 (CA); *Oakes v Turquand* (1867), LR 2 HL 325; *Burgess's Case* (1880) 15 Ch D 507; *Re Scottish Petroleum Co.* (1883) 23 Ch D 413.

It is not enough merely to serve the company with notice of repudiation. The complainant must either procure the company to remove his name from the register of members, or commence proceedings to compel it to do so,[208] subject to the exception, however, that if he has *agreed to be bound* by a test case brought by another shareholder, he may await the decision of such case,[209] or if in an action for calls he has set up a counterclaim for rescission, he is in time.[210] In an action for calls it is not a sufficient defence to set up misrepresentation and repudiation of the shares. The defence must be coupled with a counterclaim for rescission of the contract and rectification of the register, or, if the action is brought in a court where such counterclaim cannot be entertained, a statement must be made that relief is being claimed in the proper court. If the delay has been so long that rescission will not be granted, the defence will fail.[211]

'Where a person has contracted to take shares in a company and his name has been placed on the register, it has always been held that he must exercise his right of repudiation with extreme promptness after the discovery of the fraud or misrepresentation.'[212] What is a reasonable time is a question of fact, and will vary with the circumstances of each case, but in practice a shareholder should not delay at all after he knows the facts which entitle him to relief. 'The delay of a fortnight in repudiating the shares', said Baggallay LJ,[213] 'makes it to my mind doubtful whether the repudiation in the case of a going concern would have been in time. No doubt where investigation is necessary some time must be allowed, as in *Central Railway Co. of Venezuela v Kisch*.[214] But where, as in the present case, the shareholder is at once fully informed of the circumstances he ought to lose no time in repudiating.'

5.36 An action for deceit

Besides the right to rescission of his contract to take shares, the shareholder may also claim damages against the persons who fraudulently induced him to become a shareholder, and this right does not cease when the company goes into liquidation. The company itself may be sued for fraudulent statements made by those for whom it is vicariously responsible.[215] Those responsible for the prospectus, so long as they have knowledge of the falsity of the statements made, are liable in deceit whether or not rescission of the allotment is obtained. 'Those responsible' will clearly embrace promoters, directors and issuing houses (as well as experts in respect of reports made by them).

---

[208] *Re Scottish Petroleum Co.* (1883) 23 Ch D 413 (CA); *First National Reinsurance Co. v Greenfield* [1921] 2 KB 260; but see 10.9, below.

[209] *Re Scottish Petroleum Co.* (1883) 23 Ch D 413; *Pawle's Case* (1869) 4 Ch App. 497; *Hare's Case* (1869) 4 Ch App. 503. The pendency of other cases will not save him if there is no agreement to be bound by their result (see cases cited in this note).

[210] *Whiteley's Case* [1900] 1 Ch 365.

[211] *First National Reinsurance Co. v Greenfield* [1921] 2 KB 260.

[212] *Per* Lord Davey in *Aaron's Reefs v Twiss* [1896] AC 273 at p. 294. See also *Sharpley v Louth and East Coast Railway* (1876) 2 Ch D 663 at p. 685.

[213] *Re Scottish Petroleum Co.* (1883) 23 Ch D at p. 434. See also *Re Christineville Rubber Estates* [1911] WN 216 (four months); *Taite's Case* (1867) LR 3 Eq. 795 (a month sufficed).

[214] (1867) LR 2 HL 99. In this case two months was allowed, but it was stated that it was necessary that the complainant should come 'with the utmost diligence' (*per* Lord Romilly at p. 125).

[215] Section 111A of the Companies Act 1985, as inserted by the Companies Act 1989, which reverses the effect of the decision. *Houldsworth v City of Glasgow Bank* (1880) 5 App. Cas. 317 (HL Scot.).

There is a wide distinction between an action for deceit and an action for rescission of contract. In the latter case it is only necessary to show that the contract was induced by an untrue statement of a material fact, whether made innocently or not,[216] while to sustain an action for deceit it is necessary to show that the defendant acted fraudulently – i.e. made the untrue statement either knowing it to be false or without belief in its truth, or recklessly, not caring whether it were true or false.[217] Thus liability would attach if the defendant 'shut his eyes to the facts or purposely abstained from inquiring into them'. It would not be enough to show that the statement was made through want of care.[218]

The House of Lords has held that if the misrepresentation complained of was contained in the prospectus, only original subscribers, and not purchasers of shares, can obtain damages for deceit; for the function of the prospectus is exhausted when once the allotment is made,[219] unless the prospectus was in fact issued with a view of inducing persons to become purchasers of shares. The latter inference will be the natural one to draw today in the context of normal public issues accompanied by the publication of the prospectus or at least a 'mini-prospectus' in national newspapers. If this is the case the directors and other persons issuing it with this object will become liable for losses suffered by those who bought shares, even from strangers. It is not necessary that the representation should be direct to the person injured; it is sufficient if it be made to another (e.g. to a newspaper) with the intent that it shall be repeated to and acted upon by the person who is subsequently injured.[220] 'But to bring it within the principle, the injury must be the immediate and not the remote consequence of the representation thus made ... It must appear that such false representation was made with the direct intent that it should be acted upon by such third person in the manner which occasions the injury or loss.'[221]

The misstatement must be of an existing fact, and not merely an unduly sanguine expression of hope or an exaggerated view of the advantages the company offers. A general commendation of his wares by a trader is not a false statement, even if too highly coloured. 'Anticipation of future results is not a statement of fact.'[222] 'If you are looking to the language as only the language of hope, expectation, and confident belief, that is one thing: but you may use language in such a way as, although in the form of hope and expectation, it may become a representation of existing facts';[223] and to say that something is expected when in reality it is not expected, or that directors have an intention to do something when they have not, is a misstatement of fact.[224] For example, a statement that property has been acquired which has not in fact then been acquired will be ground for an action against directors, even if the property be acquired a few days after

[216] *Karberg's Case* [1892] 3 Ch 1 at p. 13 (CA); *Lagunas Nitrate Co. v Lagunas Syndicate* [1899] 2 Ch 392 at p. 423 (CA).

[217] *Derry v Peek* (1889) 14 App. Cas. 337, 374 (HL).

[218] *Derry v Peek* (1889) 14 App. Cas. at pp. 375 and 376; *Angus v Clifford* [1891] 2 Ch 449 (CA).

[219] *Peek v Gurney* (1873) LR 6, HL 377, 400, 411. A subscriber who has sold his shares and subsequently repurchased them cannot obtain relief: *In re Bank of Hindustan, China and Japan* (1873) LR 16 Eq. 417.

[220] *Andrews v Mockford* [1896] 1 QB 372 (CA); *Barry v Crosskey* (1861) 2 J and H 1.

[221] Cited from *Barry v Crosskey* with approval by Lord Cairns in *Peek v Gurney* (1873) LR 6, HL 377 at p. 413.

[222] *Per* Lord Esher MR, in *Bentley v Black* (1893) 9 TLR 580 (CA).

[223] *Per* Lord Halsbury LC in *Aaron's Reefs v Twiss* [1896] AC 273 at p. 284 (HL).

[224] *Edgington v Fitzmaurice* (1885) 29 Ch D 459 (CA); *Karberg's Case* [1892] 3 Ch 1 at p. 11 (CA).

the allotment of the shares.[225] A misrepresentation of law is not a misstatement of fact which will give any remedy against directors.[226]

If a false or misleading statement is made, it is no protection to the defendants to say that the plaintiff had means of ascertaining the truth and was negligent in failing to inspect documents referred to in the prospectus or to make other inquiries, for he is entitled to rely on the statements made to him.[227] If before allotment the directors discover a mistake in the prospectus, it is fraud to allow applicants to remain under the mistaken belief and accept an allotment.[228] It is the duty of the directors to point out the mistake in unambiguous terms, and not merely to send a new prospectus correctly stating the facts. 'Assuming a fraud to have been committed, it obviously lies on those who rely upon a subsequent explanation to show that such explanation was quite clear.'[229]

In an action for deceit, the motive with which the statement was made is immaterial, for a person is liable for a false statement knowingly made, even if he have no intent to defraud.[230] It is not necessary to show that the false statement was the sole inducing cause if it forms a substantial ground for taking the shares,[231] and the courts pay little attention to a cross-examination as to the weight attached by the applicant to each statement, holding that a material misrepresentation likely to induce the application is enough, unless the plaintiff admits that he did not act upon it.[232] If, however, the court comes to the conclusion that the particular misrepresentation did not affect the plaintiff's mind, and that he would still have taken the shares if he had known the truth, he will have suffered no damage, and cannot recover. The court may come to this conclusion either from the plaintiff's answers in cross-examination or from his conduct, or from the nature of the misrepresentation relied upon.[233]

If a statement is true at the time it is made, but becomes untrue before the allotment of the shares (e.g. if a director named in the prospectus has meanwhile resigned), it will be good ground for rescinding the contract,[234] and there is authority for the view that it may give a cause of action for deceit.[235]

---

[225] *McConnel v Wright* [1903] 1 Ch 546 (CA).

[226] *Beattie v Lord Ebury* (1872) 7 Ch App. 777 (1874) LR 7 HL 102; *Rashdall v Ford* (1865) LR 2 Eq. 750; *Bentley v Black* (1893) 9 TLR 580.

[227] *Reynell v Sprye* (1851) 1 De G. M. & G. 660; *Arkwright v Newbold* (1881) 17 Ch D 301; *Aaron's Reefs v Twiss* [1896] App. Cas. 273; *Gluckstein v Barnes* [1900] AC 240 at p. 251; *Redgrave v Hurd* (1881) 20 Ch D 1; *Alliance & Leicester Building Society v Edgestop* [1994] 2 All ER, [1993] 1 WLR 1462.

[228] *Brownlie v Campbell* (1880) 5 App. Cas. 925 at p. 950; *Davies v London and Provincial Co.* (1878) 8 Ch D 469 at p. 475.

[229] *Arnison v Smith* (1889) 41 Ch D 348, *per* Lord Halsbury at p. 370.

[230] *Derry v Peek* (1889) 14 App. Cas. 337 at p. 374; *Smith v Chadwick* (1884) 9 App. Cas. 187; *Arnison v Smith* (1889) 41 Ch D 348 (CA).

[231] *Edgington v Fitzmaurice* (1885) 29 Ch D 459.

[232] *Per* Lord Halsbury in *Arnison v Smith* (1889) 41 Ch D 348, 369 (CA). And see *Smith v Chadwick* (1884) 20 Ch D 27 (CA); 9 App. Cas. 187 (HL).

[233] *Smith v Chadwick* (1884) 9 App. Cas. 187; *Macleay v Tait* [1906] AC 24 (HL); *Nash v Calthorpe* [1905] 2 Ch 237.

[234] *Anderson's Case* (1881) 17 Ch D 373; *Re Scottish Petroleum Co.* (1883) 23 Ch D 413 (CA). This will also be the case if the other directors know that one of the directors is on the point of resigning when they go to allotment: *Re Kent County Gas Co.* (1906) 95 LT 756.

[235] *Brownlie v Campbell* (1880) 5 App. Cas. 924 at p. 950 (HL Scot.); *Briess v Woolley* [1954] AC 333 at pp. 353–4 (HL). Cp. *Arkright v Newbold* (1881) 17 Ch D 301 at pp. 325 and 329, and *Bradford Building Society v Borders* [1941] 2 All ER 205 at p. 228 (HL).

5.37 Misleading omissions – *suggestio falsi*

Either in an action for deceit or in an action for rescission the omission of material facts may amount to a misrepresentation.[236] Thus, in a prospectus describing land purchased by the company as 'eminently suitable' for its operations, the *innocent* omission to state that the land had been scheduled to a town planning resolution and that the company would not be entitled to compensation for the removal of buildings unless they had been erected with the previous consent of the local authority was held sufficient to entitle an allottee of shares to rescission against the company.[237] Again, the omission of the names of the real vendors and the interpolation of a nominal vendor to conceal the true facts may be sufficient to entitle subscribers to relief,[238] but this rule applies only if the omission renders the prospectus as it stands misleading,[239] or the omissions are (in the words of James LJ) 'omissions amounting in effect to false statements',[240] or if the omission is of something which there was a duty to disclose. Lord Cairns said: 'There must, in my opinion, be some active misstatement of fact, or, at all events, such a partial and fragmentary statement of fact, as that the withholding of that which is not stated makes that which is stated absolutely false.'[241] 'There must be something more than mere non-disclosure proved before misrepresentation is established: it must, I think, be shown that the non-disclosure is the non-disclosure of something the disclosure of which would falsify some statement in the prospectus.'[242]

Furthermore, 'if by a number of statements you intentionally give a false impression and induce a person to act upon it, it is not the less false although if one takes each statement by itself there may be a difficulty in showing that any specific statement is untrue'.[243] Thus the prospectus must be taken as a whole, 'and everybody knows that half a truth is no better than a downright falsehood'.[244]

As regards statements that are misleading in the sense that they can bear more than one meaning, the law used to be stated that it is not material in what sense the directors intended the words to be understood if they are in fact untrue or misleading.[245] However, this formulation was rejected by the Privy Council in *Akerhielm v De Mare*[246] in favour of a more subjective test of the defendant's honesty. The following passage from the opinion of the Privy Council shows that in an action for deceit the subjective state of mind cannot be ignored:

---

[236] *Central Railway Co. of Venezuela v Kisch* (1867) LR 2 HL 99; *Oakes v Turquand* (1867) LR 2 HL 325, 342; *Cackett v Keswick* [1902] 2 Ch 456. It has been suggested that a concealment may be a ground for rescission of the contract to take shares, which would not be sufficient to ground an action of deceit against directors (see *per* Lord Cairns in *Peek v Gurney* (1873) LR 6 HL 377 at p. 403), but later cases do not draw the distinction.

[237] *Coles v White City (Manchester) Greyhound Association* (1928) 45 TLR 230. See also *Ross v Estates Investment Co.* (1868) LR 3 CH 682.

[238] *Components Tube Co. v Naylor* [1990] 2 Ir. R 1.

[239] *McKeown v Boudard Peveril Gear Co.* [1896] WN 36 (CA); *New Brunswick and Canada Rail and Land Co. v Conybeare* (1862) 9 HL C711; *Peek v Gurney* (1874) LR 6, HL 403.

[240] *Gover's Case* (1875) 1 Ch D 182 at p. 189 (CA).

[241] *Peek v Gurney* (1873) LR 6, HL 377, 403.

[242] *Per* Eve J, in *Re Christineville Rubber Estates* [1911] WN 216, and see *R. v Bishirgian* (1936) 154 LT 499 (CCA).

[243] *Per* Halsbury LC, in *Aaron's Reefs v Twiss* [1896] AC 273, 281.

[244] *Per* Lord Macnaghten in *Gluckstein v Barnes* [1900] AC 240 at pp. 250, 251 (HL).

[245] See *Greenwood v Leathershod Wheel Co.* [1900] Ch 421; *Arnison v Smith* (1889) 41 Ch D 348 at p. 372, per Lindley LJ (CA); *Arkwright v Newbold* (1881) 17 Ch D 301 at pp. 322, 323 (CA).

[246] [1959] AC 789 (PC), where the Privy Council refused to follow *Arnison v Smith*, above.

The question is not whether the defendant in any given case honestly believed the representation to be true in the sense assigned to it by the court on an objective consideration of its truth or falsity, but whether he honestly believed the representation to be true in the sense in which he understood it albeit erroneously when it was made. This general proposition is no doubt subject to limitations. For instance, the meaning placed by the defendant on the representation made may be so far removed from the sense in which it would be understood by the reasonable person as to make it impossible to hold that the defendant honestly understood the representation to bear the meaning claimed by him and honestly believed it in that sense to be true.[247]

The qualification in the latter part of this passage accords with the view of Lord Blackburn in *Smith v Chadwick*[248] that 'if with intent to lead the plaintiff to act upon it they put forth a statement which they know may bear two meanings, one of which is false to their knowledge, and thereby the plaintiff, putting that meaning upon it, is misled, I do not think they can escape by saying he ought to have put the other'. It is essential, of course, that the plaintiff prove that he understood the statement in the sense in which it is false.[249] Further, in considering whether a statement is misleading, the prospectus must be considered as a whole and if the tendency is to deceive there is no need to point out some one or more statements which are absolutely untrue.[250]

5.38 The Misrepresentation Act 1967

The changes introduced into the English law of innocent misrepresentation by the Misrepresentation Act 1967 would allow a claim for damages against the company for a misrepresentation made by or on behalf of the company. As part of the general law, this Act will apply to any misrepresentation by or on behalf of the company which has induced subscribers to enter into a contract of allotment on the faith of it. It is not confined, as are the civil remedies now provided by the Financial Services Act 1986, to public issues of securities nor to written statements in a formal prospectus or set of listing particulars. This Act does not apply to Scotland.

Under section 2 (1) of the Misrepresentation Act 1967:

where a person has entered into a contract after a misrepresentation has been made to him by another party thereto, and as a result thereof he has suffered a loss, then, if the person making the misrepresentation would have been liable to damages in respect thereof had the misrepresentation been made fraudulently, that person shall be so liable notwithstanding that the misrepresentation was not made fraudulently, unless he proves that he had reasonable ground to believe and did believe up to the time that the contract was made that the facts represented were true.

It is clear that an action based on section 2 (1) of the Act must be brought against the other party to the contract. It has been seen that in an offer for sale this will be the issuing house.

Section 2 (2) of the Misrepresentation Act 1967 confers a discretion upon the court, in

[247] [1959] AC 789 at p. 805.
[248] (1884) 9 App. Cas. 187 at p. 201.
[249] *Smith v Chadwick* (1882) 20 Ch D 45, 73 (CA); (1884) 9 App. Cas. 187 (HL).
[250] *Aaron's Reefs v Twiss* [1896] AC 273; *R. v Kylsant* [1932] 1 KB 442 (CCA).

the case of an innocent misrepresentation, to award damages in lieu of a decree of rescission where in the circumstances of the case it is in the interest of justice to do so. It should be noted that there is no *right* to damages in lieu of rescission on the part of either party to the contract. Section 2 (2) allows for damages to be awarded in lieu of rescission from which it appears that the court may only award damages if the plaintiff has not lost his normal right to rescission.[251]

5.39 The measure of damages

The basic measure of damages in an action at common law for deceit or under section 2 (1) of the Misrepresentation Act 1967[252] is the difference between the value of the shares at the time of allotment and the price paid for them.[253] The Court of Appeal has held[254] that in determining the value of a share which is traded on a market the court must consider what would have been paid for that share in the market on the assumption that the market knew all it did know but was not influenced by the misrepresentation. Where information has been fraudulently concealed, the effect of that information on the value of the shares must be taken into account but other information relevant to the price of the shares which is not known to the market generally is not to be considered.[255]

Smith New Court v Scrimgeour Vickers arose from the sale of shares in a public company rather than from a public offer of securities but it nevertheless illustrates this approach. The defendants misrepresented to the purchaser that another party was interested in acquiring the shares and taking over the company. Some time after the sale was completed, it emerged that the target company had, before the sale, been the victim of a major fraud, and publication of this news caused the value of its shares to plummet. The Court of Appeal held that the problems arising from the fraud were latent at the time of the sale of the shares and were not known generally to the market at that time. Accordingly, in valuing the shares at the time of the sale, no account was to be taken of these latent problems. The only relevant misrepresentation was the false statement about the existence of another interested bidder.

5.40 An action for negligent misstatement

Since the leading decision of the House of Lords in *Hedley Byrne & Co. Ltd v Heller & Partners Ltd*,[256] it is possible to argue that the directors and others responsible for a

---

[251] Section 2 (3) is intended to prevent any possibility of 'double recovery' where claims under subsection (1) and subsection (2) are combined. On the measure of compensation under section 2 (2) see *William Sindall plc v Cambridgeshire County Council* 1 WLR 1026.

[252] *Royscot Trust Ltd v Rogerson* [1991] 2 QB 297; *East v Maurer* [1991] 1 WLR 461.

[253] *Peek v Derry* (1888) 37 Ch D 541; *Arnison v Smith* (1889) 41 Ch D 348 at p. 363; *McConnel v Wright* [1903] 1 Ch 546 at pp. 554–5 *per* Collin MR (CA). This corresponds to the normal measure of damages in the tort of deceit based on the loss caused to the plaintiff. However, this will include consequential losses flowing directly from the injury caused by the fraudulent misstatement: *Doyle v Olby (Ironmongers) Ltd* [1969] 2 WLR 673 (CA). See *Archer v Brown* [1984] 2 All ER 267, which illustrates well the types of damages that may be recovered in the sale of shares in a private company. The normal measure of damages is not, however, an absolute or rigid rule and it should not be followed where it would give rise to injustice: *Naughton v O'Callaghan* [1990] 3 All ER 191.

[254] *Smith New Court v Scrimgeour Vickers* [1994] 1 WLR 1271, [1994] 2 BCLC 212 explaining *Twycross v Grant* (1877) 2 CPD 469. Leave to appeal to the House of Lords has been granted: [1995] 1 WLR 384.

[255] ibid.

[256] [1964] AC 465. See also *W. B. Anderson Ltd v Rhodes* [1967] 2 All ER 850; *Mutual Life & Citizens Assurance Co. Ltd v Evatt* [1971] 2 WLR 23 (PC).

prospectus may owe a duty of care to those intended to rely on the prospectus in respect of negligent misstatements it contains. So long as the 'special relationship' giving rise to such a duty of care can be established, an action for the tort of negligence might lie. The special relationship may arise in pre-contractual negotiations, and those who may be held liable for negligent statements need not be persons who carried on, or held themselves out as carrying on, the business of advising: *Esso Petroleum Co. Ltd v Mardon*.[257] In many instances the remedies afforded by section 2 (1) of the Misrepresentation Act 1967[258] and section 150 of the Financial Services Act 1986 will provide better protection to investors in company securities than an action for common-law negligence. Both these statutory provisions place the burden of disproving negligence upon the defendant. In an action for negligent misstatement, as in any other action for negligence, the burden of establishing negligence rests upon the plaintiff. However, in contrast with the remedies in the Financial Services Act 1986, an action in tort will apply to the private as well as to the public issue of company securities.

It has been seen that an action for damages under section 2 (1) of the Misrepresentation Act 1967 will only lie as between the contracting parties. An action for the tort of negligent misstatement would allow a wider range of possible plaintiffs and defendants. However, the courts will not lightly extend the duty of care under *Hedley Byrne*.[259] *Al Nakib Investments (Jersey) Ltd v Longcroft*[260] concerned a prospectus issued in connection with a rights issue. The court held that, because the purpose of the prospectus was to invite subscriptions for shares, there was insufficient proximity for a duty of care to arise between the directors and those persons (including existing shareholders of the company) who used the prospectus for the different purpose of purchasing further shares in the market.

5.41 Criminal liability for false or misleading statements in prospectuses

The Financial Services Act 1986 contains, in section 47, a general 'all purpose' criminal sanction to deal with false and misleading statements. This section replaces the 'anti-fraud' provision in section 13 of the Prevention of Fraud (Investments) Act 1958, but the scope of section 47 is considerably wider than its predecessor. This section clearly applies to public issues but also 'underpins' many other provisions in the Act concerning transactions in securities.

Section 47 (1) makes it an offence for anyone to make a statement, promise or forecast which he knows to be misleading, false or deceptive. It also comprises dishonestly concealing any material facts and covers recklessly making (dishonestly or otherwise) a statement, promise or forecast which is misleading, false or deceptive. In this event there is no liability for concealment of material facts.[261] The offence is 'investment related' in

---

[257] [1976] 2 WLR 583 (CA).
[258] This Act does not apply in Scotland.
[259] *Caparo Industries plc v Dickman* [1990] 2 AC 605, [1990] 1 All ER 568, [1990] 2 WLR 358, [1990] BCLC 273, [1990] BCC 164.
[260] [1990] 3 All ER 321, [1991] BCLC 7, [1990] BCC 517.
[261] These criteria are derived from section 13 of the Prevention of Fraud (Investment) Act 1958. This was repealed by the Financial Services Act 1986.

that the accused must make the statement (or conceal the facts dishonestly) for the purpose of inducing, or be reckless as to whether it may induce, another person to enter into, or offer to enter into, or to refrain from entering into, an investment agreement.[262] The 'other person' need not be the person to whom the statement is made or from whom the facts are concealed.

It has been held that a statement which is superficially true but actually untrue because of the omission of relevant information can be a false statement.[263] Such a statement could also be described as misleading or deceptive.[264] The terms 'misleading, false or deceptive' are not mutually exclusive in scope but they do differ slightly in degree. For instance, it would not be possible to describe an over-optimistic profit forecast as 'false' until the actual profit figures are known,[265] but, even without the actual figures, it might be possible to establish that the forecast was a misleading interpretation of the information on which it is based.

The offence of dishonest concealment of any material facts requires more than merely the omission of information, and in order to establish an offence under this section it must be shown that what has been said is incorrect or inaccurate because of what has been omitted.[266] This means that there is a very considerable overlap between the *actus reus* of the 'concealment' offence and the 'making' offence. A person is dishonest if he realises that he would be so judged on the standards of ordinary honest people, even though he does not consider himself to be dishonest by his own standards.[267]

Another provision in section 47[268] goes beyond statements or concealments and is concerned with conduct which has the effect of market manipulation or market rigging. An offence is committed by someone 'who does any act or engages in any conduct which creates a false or misleading impression as to the market in, or the price or value of any investments'. This must be done for creating that false impression and thus inducing others to acquire, dispose of, subscribe for, or underwrite investments.[269] A defence of reasonable belief that the act or conduct in question will not create a false or misleading impression is available to the accused.[270]

Section 200 (1) of the Financial Services Act 1986 makes it a criminal offence to furnish, knowingly or recklessly, information which is false or misleading in a material particular for the purposes of or in connection with any application under the Act or in purported compliance with any requirement imposed by the Act. This would apply, for example, to an application for listing made in accordance with Part IV of the Act.

5.42 Section 19 of the Theft Act 1968

This Act, which does not apply in Scotland, contains, in section 19, a special provision to deal with dishonest statements in writing by officers of corporate bodies or unincorpor-

---

[262] Section 47 (1) also applies to inducing another to exercise or refrain from exercising, any rights (e.g. options) conferred by those investments.

[263] *R v Kylsant* [1932] 1 KB 442; *R v Bishirgian, etc.* [1936] 1 All ER 568.

[264] *Oakes v Turquand and Harding* (1867) LR 2 HL 325 at pp. 342–3.

[265] *R v Bates* [1952] 2 All ER 842, 845.

[266] *R v MacKinnon* [1959] 1 QB 150, 154.

[267] *R v Ghosh* [1982] QB 1053.

[268] Section 47 (2).

[269] Inducing others to refrain from investing in these ways is also within section 47 (2).

[270] Section 47 (3). As to the jurisdictional limits to section 47, see section 47 (4) and (5). As to the penalties for conviction on indictment or summarily, see section 47 (6).

ated associations. It provides that 'an officer or person purporting to act as an officer of a body corporate or unincorporated association who, with intent to deceive its members or creditors about its affairs, publishes or concurs in publishing a written statement or account which to his knowledge is or may be misleading, false or deceptive in a material particular' is liable to a maximum sentence of seven years' imprisonment. Even under the more narrowly worded section 84 of the Larceny Act 1861 (the predecessor of section 19), which referred simply to 'false' statements, the courts gave it a liberal interpretation so as to include misleading or deceptive statements or omissions. Thus, in *R v Kylsant*[271] a prospectus relating to the issue of debenture stock said that the company paid a dividend in every year between 1921 and 1927. This was literally true, but it gave the misleading impression that the company during this period had made trading profits, whereas in fact substantial trading losses had been made. It was only able to pay dividends from reserves earned in earlier years. The fact that the dividends were paid from these 'hidden reserves' was not disclosed in the prospectus. Lord Kylsant, who knew the true state of affairs and was responsible for the prospectus, was convicted.

Section 19 of the Theft Act 1968 must certainly be given at least as wide an interpretation by the courts so long as an intention to deceive can be established. However, it does not extend to false promises or forecasts nor to oral statements.

---

[271] [1932] KB 442 (CCA). See further, *R. v Bishirgian* (1936) 154 LT 499 (CCA).

6 Share Capital – Allotment and Maintenance

6.1 Introduction

This chapter is concerned with the capital which is raised by companies by means of issuing shares. All companies, of course, need capital and, although in practice share capital is often less important than other sorts of capital, company law has traditionally paid particular attention to share capital in two particular respects. The first concerns the actual allotment of shares,[1] where rules exist primarily to protect shareholders, while the second is the rules that seek to ensure that share capital is properly raised and maintained for the benefit of the company's creditors.

6.2 Methods of capitalising companies

The overwhelming majority of private companies are small businesses which have chosen for tax or other reasons to incorporate. They are 'small' both in their capitalisation and in the number of their participators. They frequently take the form of 'one-man companies' or small 'corporate partnerships'. Almost without exception they will register as a private company limited by shares. However, the number of shares they allot will usually bear a purely nominal relationship to even a small business's real capitalisation. The £100 or so of shares issued simply represents the allocation of voting control in the proportion already agreed (e.g. mostly to one dominant shareholder or equally among the corporate partners). The assets conveyed by the company after incorporation are not 'paid for' by the company by issuing the appropriate number of shares with the requisite nominal value. Instead the 'participators', while holding shares as an instrument of control, become major creditors in their own companies. In lieu of payment for newly acquired assets (or an existing business) the company will issue debentures secured, in some cases (if the company's bank does not object), by a floating or fixed charge.

This common form of initial capitalisation in the case of small companies has obvious tax advantages for the company. Interest payments are deductible,[2] whereas dividend payments out of the company's profits are not. In the kind of small company where all the shareholder/creditors are likely to be directors as well, and to be closely involved in working for and running their company, there are also tax advantages in participating in profits in the form of salaries (or other remuneration) and not in the form of dividends upon the shares they hold. When it comes to 'ongoing' finance for such companies this is most likely to take the form of bank borrowings[3] and ploughing back (instead of

---

[1] Note that, as recently confirmed by the House of Lords (*National Westminster Bank plc v IRC* [1994] 2 BCLC 239), the terms 'issue' and 'allotment' in relation to shares have different technical meanings. Shares are allotted when there is a contract to take them in accordance with the procedures described later in this chapter; they are issued only when the allottee has been entered in the register of members (as to which, see Chapter 10) to complete the title of the allottee.

[2] However, the shareholder/creditor who receives interest payments will be liable to tax on them.

[3] And other forms of commercial credit such as industrial hire-purchase and 'factoring' of debts owed to the company.

distributing) profits earned by the company.[4] Other factors may come into play as further finance is needed. Thus the company may seek 'venture' capital from institutions or individuals prepared to take an 'equity stake' in the company. As the business matures the original 'participators' may need to dispose of their interest in the company. These and other factors may lead to the company issuing a substantial share capital as it continues to grow in size. The ultimate stage of such development may be a public issue of some or all of the company's share capital.[5]

In the case of large public listed companies, share capital obviously has a much more significant role. Nevertheless, in terms of continuing sources of fresh finance, share capital[6] is nowadays less important than loan capital[7] and self-financing through retaining profits that have been earned. However, the concept of 'gearing' in the prudent financing of public companies will discourage companies being too highly geared. 'High gearing' means that the ratio between equity shares and loan capital (as well as preference shares on which there is a fixed return) is too high[8] in regard to proportion of the latter to the former. Such high gearing puts the owners of equity shares at risk in that it may increase the chances of insolvency. The owners of such shares will also suffer in a period of low profits or actual losses in the company's (or group's) trading operations. Thus, especially in a time of high interest rates, capital and income repayments in respect of loan capital may absorb much too high a proportion of the company's earnings from its business activities. Where fresh capital is still needed the proper 'gearing' can then be restored by a fresh issue of equity shares to the existing ordinary shareholders in the form of a rights issue.[9]

6.3 Allotment of shares

The next part of this chapter looks at the two forms of statutory protection for shareholders against the traditional power of control of the board of directors over the issue of a company's share capital and is followed by a brief examination of the common-law control. The statutory protection was first introduced in 1980 to implement what was required by the Second EC Directive on Company law. The first form requires the authority of the shareholders for the issue[10] of shares. Secondly, in the case of equity shares, the Companies Act 1985 confers what are known as 'pre-emptive' rights on holders of existing equity shares in proportion to their holdings of such shares.

There is an evident need to circumscribe the power of the directors of public companies and of larger private companies to issue share capital. They may be tempted to do this to resist external take-over bids, or to entrench themselves when threatened by internal struggles for control of majority voting power at shareholders' meetings. There is

[4] This is limited by the tax regime established for 'close' companies. See *Gore-Browne on Companies* (Jordans, 44th edn, loose-leaf) at 24.32.
[5] See Chapter 5.
[6] This is true of both ordinary and preference shares. See the Committee to Review the Functioning of Financial Institutions (the Wilson Committee) (Cmnd 7937 1980 Table 34 at p. 133).
[7] See Chapter 9. Today this takes the form of bank borrowings over a relatively short term rather than a public issue of debentures over a medium- to long-term period.
[8] What this ratio should be will depend on the current level of interest rates, the company's profitability and its need for fresh capital.
[9] See 5.9.
[10] Their prior authority for the company's 'authorised' but unissued share capital was always required. This, however, allowed the directors to have a 'bank' of unissued shares at their disposal.

also the problem of what is known as 'share watering' and 'vote watering'. 'Vote watering' means that the existing shareholders will lose their existing voting strength and this process, if carried far enough, may tip the balance of control. 'Share watering' is of most concern to existing equity shareholders.[11] The existing and future earnings of the company will be divided among a larger number of shareholders. Although fresh capital has been raised, for many years this may not sufficiently augment the company's 'profit stream' so as to prevent the 'earnings-per-share' of the existing equity shareholders being proportionately diminished. This will have obvious implications for the value of those shares on the stock market or their value in a private company.

The statutory provisions provide a somewhat less than satisfactory bulwark against both vote watering and share watering. Section 80, described below, has only limited criminal sanctions for breach, and the pre-emption provisions can be fairly easily disapplied.

6.4 Authority required to allot shares

Section 80 of the Companies Act 1985 restricts the power of directors of a company to allot 'relevant securities' unless, in accordance with that section, they are authorised to do so either by the company in general meeting or by the articles of the company.[12] 'Relevant securities' means shares in the company other than shares shown in the memorandum to have been taken by the subscribers to the memorandum, or shares allotted in pursuance of an employees' share scheme. It also includes any right to subscribe for, or to convert, any security into the kind of shares of the company defined above.[13]

Any authority (given in general meeting or by the articles) may be given for a particular exercise of that power or for its exercise generally.[14] It may be unconditional or subject to conditions. An authority must state the maximum amount[15] of shares that may be allotted under it and the date on which it will expire, which must not be more than the five years from the relevant date applicable. This date, in the case of an authority contained at the time of the original incorporation of the company in the articles, is the date of incorporation. In any other case it is the date on which the resolution is passed by which the authority required by section 80 is given.[16] Any authority may be renewed by the company in general meeting for further successive periods not exceeding five years. The resolution renewing such authority must state (or restate) the amount of shares which may be allotted or, as the case may be, remains to be allotted under its authority, and the date on which the renewed authority will expire.[17] Even though any authority required by section 80 has expired, the directors may allot shares if they are allotted in pursuance of an offer or agreement made by the company before the authority expired. However,

---

[11] It will usually also have the effect of vote watering but this need not be the case (e.g. where the fresh issue consists of non-voting equity shares).

[12] Section 80 (1). As to the relationship between section 80 and section 125 protecting class rights, see 7.7.3, below.

[13] Section 80 (2).

[14] Section 80 (3).

[15] Where the 'securities' are not shares but rights to subscribe for shares or to convert any security into shares, then the 'maximum amount' of relevant securities means the maximum which may be allocated pursuant to the rights: section 80 (6).

[16] Section 80 (4).

[17] Section 80 (5).

the authority must have allowed the company to make an offer or agreement which would or might require shares to be allotted after the authority expired.[18]

A company may give, vary, revoke or renew an authority by ordinary resolution even though it alters the articles of the company. However, the requirements of section 380 of the 1985 Act (registration of copies of certain resolutions) apply to such a resolution.[19] While criminal penalties are provided for any director who knowingly and wilfully contravenes, or permits or authorises the contravention of, section 80,[20] this will not affect the validity of any allotment of shares.[21]

A private company which has opted for the elective regime described in 11.4.6 below, may, instead of following the requirements of section 80, give the directors authority to allot shares for an indefinite period or for a fixed period longer than the five years permitted by section 80.[22] A fixed period authority may be renewed or further renewed by the company in general meeting.[23]

6.5 Pre-emption rights

As already noted, statute has, since 1980, conferred pre-emptive rights on existing equity shareholders when further shares are allotted.[24] This right applies to both public and private companies, but private companies may exclude it by a provision in their memorandum or articles.

The right conferred by section 89 (1) of the Companies Act 1985 may, subject to various qualifications and exemptions to be considered later, be stated as follows. A company proposing to allot any 'equity securities' shall not allot any of those equity securities on any terms to any person, unless it has made an offer to each person who holds 'relevant shares' or 'relevant employee shares' to allot to him, on the same or more favourable terms, a proportion of those securities which is as nearly as practical equal to the proportion in nominal value held by him of the aggregate of 'relevant shares' and 'relevant employee shares'.[25] 'Relevant shares', in relation to a company, means shares of the company *other than* (a) shares which as respects dividends and capital carry a right to participate only up to a specified amount in a distribution and (b) shares held or to be held by a person who acquired them in pursuance of an employees' share scheme.[26] Conversely, 'relevant employee shares' means shares of the company which would be relevant shares (as above) but for the fact that they are held under an employees' share scheme. Thus 'relevant shares' excludes preference shares which do not have rights to

---

[18] Section 80 (7).

[19] Section 80 (8). The provisions of section 711 (documents to be published by the Registrar in the *Gazette*) apply to such a resolution. See section 711 (1) (*d*).

[20] Section 80 (9) and Schedule 24.

[21] Section 80 (10).

[22] Section 80A.

[23] This requires only an ordinary resolution or the statutory written resolution procedure (see 11.4.1) can be used; the original elective resolution must be unanimous.

[24] It has been common for the articles of private companies to make such provision. The Stock Exchange rules confer what amounts to a right of pre-emption upon existing holders of equity shares in listed companies. Such rights do not exist at common law: *Mutual Life Insurance Co. v The Rank Organisation* [1985] BCLC 11. The common law in the United States evolved such rights at an early stage.

[25] Section 89 (1) (*a*).

[26] See Section 94 (5). As to the meaning of 'employees' share scheme', see section 743.

participate in both profits and capital.[27] 'Equity security', in relation to a company, means a relevant share in a company or a right to subscribe for, or convert any securities into, relevant shares of a company. 'Equity security' does not include, however, a bonus share or a share shown in the memorandum to have been taken by a subscriber thereto.[28]

Section 89 makes provision for a twenty-one-day period during which the pre-emptive rights may be taken up or refused. During this period, the company may not allot any securities subject to the pre-emptive rights conferred by section 89 to any other person, unless the period during which any such offer may be accepted has expired, or the company has received notice of the acceptance or refusal of every offer so made.[29] Every offer under section 89 must state a period of not less than twenty-one days during which the offer may be accepted. The offer may not be withdrawn before the end of that period.[30] Shares offered by virtue of section 89 (1) may be allotted either to the holders of relevant shares (or relevant employee shares) *or* to anyone in whose favour such a person has renounced his right to allotment.[31]

Special provision is made to meet the situation where a company's memorandum or articles confer pre-emptive rights which require a company proposing to allot equity shares of a particular class to offer those shares to the holders of relevant shares or relevant employee shares of that class. Section 89 (3) provides that where that is the case, an offer to allot in compliance with such a provision will prevent the application of section 89 (1) in the event that the recipient, or anyone in whose favour the recipient has renounced his right to allotment, accepts the offer. The twenty-one-day period during which an offer (implementing pre-emptive rights conferred by the memorandum or articles) must be made and the manner in which it must be served, is governed by section 90 and not by what the memorandum or articles may prescribe.[32]

Section 89 (1) does not apply to an allotment of equity securities if they are to be paid up (or are in fact paid up) wholly or partly otherwise than in cash.[33] Further, it does not apply in relation to the allotment of any securities which would, apart from a renunciation or assignment of the right to their allotment, be held under an employees' share scheme.[34] Subject to these exemptions and the provision described in 6.5.1, below, pre-emptive rights are mandatory in the case of public companies. However, the rights conferred by section 89 may be excluded by a provision contained in the memorandum or articles of a private company. Furthermore, a requirement or authority contained in the memorandum or articles of a private company, if it is inconsistent with the requirements of sections 89 (1), 90 (5) to (6) (mode of service) and 90 (6) (period of offer), shall have effect as a provision excluding the pre-emptive rights conferred by section 89 (1).[35]

Section 92 (1) provides a civil, but not a criminal, sanction for a contravention of

---

[27] See 7.4, below. So, for example, preference shares with a preferential right to dividend, but the same capital rights as ordinary shares, are within the definition and caught by section 89.

[28] Section 94 (2).

[29] Section 89 (1) (*b*).

[30] Section 90 (6). Section 90 (2) to (5) makes provision for the communication of pre-emption offers to shareholders (e.g. delivery personally or by registered post).

[31] Section 89 (4).

[32] Section 90 (7). In other respects the provisions of the memorandum or articles to which section 89 (3) applies will remain valid.

[33] Section 89 (4).

[34] Section 89 (5). As to the definition of 'employees' shares scheme', see section 743.

[35] Section 91 (1) and (2). The 'implied' exclusion referred to in the text does not of course extend to provisions in the memorandum or articles conferring pre-emptive rights of the kind contemplated by section 89 (2) and (3).

sections 89 and 90. The company, and every officer of the company who knowingly authorised or permitted the contravention, are jointly and severally liable to compensate any person to whom an offer should have been made[36] for any loss, damage, costs or expenses which that person has sustained or incurred by reason of that contravention.[37] However, no such proceedings may be commenced after the expiration of two years from the delivery to the Registrar of Companies of the return of allotments in question.[38] Section 92 (1) does not appear to invalidate any allotment not complying with share-holders' pre-emptive rights.[39] They are simply left to the civil remedy provided by the subsection. It has been left to the courts to determine the measure and scope of loss or damage that may be recovered. It is not clear whether the loss of 'control' of a company would be compensable over and above the market price for shares of that class.

6.5.1 *When authority under section 80 overrides pre-emptive rights*

Section 95 attempts to reconcile the requirements of section 80 with those of section 89. It does this by providing for the disapplication of section 89 in certain circumstances. Section 95 (1) provides that where directors of a company are *generally*[40] authorised for the purposes of section 80, they may be given power by the articles or by special resolution to allot equity securities pursuant to their section 80 authority as if section 89 (1) did not apply to the allotment. Alternatively, section 89 (1) may apply to the allotment with such modifications as the directors may determine.

The power conferred by section 95 will cease to have effect when the authority to which it relates is revoked or would, if not renewed, expire. However, if the authority required by section 80 is renewed, the power conferred by section 95 (in the articles or by special resolution) may also be renewed (for a period not longer than that for which the authority is renewed) by a special resolution of the company.[41]

As in the case of an authority for the purposes of section 80, the directors may allot equity securities in pursuance of an offer or agreement previously made by the company even though the power or resolution required by section 95 has expired at the time of the allotment. However, the power or resolution must have enabled the company to make an offer or agreement which would or might require equity securities to be allotted after it expired.[42]

A special resolution conferring the power given by section 95 (2) (which applies where the directors are authorised for the purposes of section 80 generally and *otherwise*[43]) may not be proposed unless it is recommended by the directors. In addition, there must be circulated with the notice of the meeting at which the resolution is proposed, to the

---

[36] i.e. an offer under section 89 (1) or (3).

[37] Section 92 (1).

[38] Where the equity securities other than shares are granted it is two years from the date of the grant: section 92 (2).

[39] This is probably so in the case of an allotment to a large number of shareholders, but an allotment in a small company where the twenty-one-day period was not allowed was declared invalid in *Re Thundercrest Ltd* [1994] BCC 857.

[40] Section 95 (2) specifies how this may be achieved (where the directors are authorised generally or otherwise for the purposes of section 80) by the company passing a special resolution to exclude section 89 applying to a specified allotment of equity securities or applying with such modifications as may be specified.

[41] Section 95 (3).

[42] Section 95 (4).

[43] Special resolutions required by section 95 must be gazetted under section 711.

members entitled to have that notice, a written statement by the directors. This must set out:

(1) their reasons for making the recommendation;
(2) the amount to be paid to the company in respect of the equity securities to be allotted; and
(3) the directors' justification of that amount.[44]

6.6 Common-law controls on allotments

The statutory controls on allotments have their limitations. The remedies for breach are limited and do not appear to include avoidance of an allotment even for a breach of the pre-emption provisions. Where the directors of a company are in control of the voting power at general meetings, there will still be the possibility of abuse notwithstanding section 80 of the Companies Act 1985. The observance of statutory pre-emption rights in a private company may amount to an indirect method of squeezing out minority shareholders who lack the means to take up their proportionate share of a new issue.[45] Further, as has been seen, pre-emption rights do not apply to certain types of issue, in particular issues of equity shares not paid for wholly in cash; this leaves a very wide gap in the statutory protection, as it seems that a minor amount of non-cash consideration will suffice. In all of these cases, the only possible remedies for abuse will be for breach of directors' duties in respect of an allotment and/or for breach of controlling shareholders' duties, perhaps by way of a petition under section 459. The latter is considered elsewhere,[46] but it is appropriate to look briefly here at the law regarding directors' duties in this area.[47]

In deciding upon the making of allotments, the directors 'must dispose of their company's shares on the best terms obtainable, and must not allot them to themselves or their friends at a lower price in order to obtain a personal benefit. They must act bona fide for the interests of the company'.[48] But this does not mean that when the market price is at a premium, shares cannot be issued at par. In *Hilder v Dexter* Lord Davey observed that he was not aware 'of any law which obliges a company to issue its shares above par because they are saleable at a premium in the market. It depends on the circumstances of each case whether it will be prudent or even possible to do so, and it is a question for the directors to decide'.[49] When the shares command a premium, the directors must not allot them at par to members of their own body or their friends, for they should either offer them equally to all the shareholders or obtain the benefit of the premium for the company.[50] However, an allotment to the directors sanctioned by a general meeting of the company has been held to be unimpeachable notwithstanding that the directors held the majority of the shares and voted in favour of the allotments of the shares to

---

[44] Section 95 (5). A criminal sanction is imposed in respect of misleading, false, or deceptive matters in the statement: section 95 (6).

[45] See the unreported decision in *Pennell v Venida Investments*, 25 July 1974, discussed in Burridge (1981) 44 MLR 40.

[46] See 3.27–3.30, above, for the common-law controls on majority shareholders' voting and 15.12, below, for section 459.

[47] For directors' duties in general, see Chapter 14.

[48] *Per* Swinfen Eady J, *Percival v Wright* [1902] 2 Ch 421.

[49] [1902] AC 474 at p. 480 (HL).

[50] *York and North Midland Railway Co. v Hudson* (1853) 16 Beav. 485; *Parker v McKenna* (1874) 10 Ch App. 96; *Shaw v Holland* [1900] 2 Ch 305 (CA).

themselves.[51] Directors, moreover, must not allot shares to themselves or their friends for the purpose of obtaining the control of the voting power in the company. If they do so, the court will declare the allotment invalid and rectify the register, and in the meantime will restrain the allottees from voting in respect of the shares thus allotted.[52] Directors may, however, purchase shares from existing members to increase their voting power.[53] But they must not, when allotting shares to themselves or their friends, make the terms or time of payment more favourable to themselves than to the general body of members or to the public unless the latter are expressly informed of the arrangement.[54] Any profit the directors make out of shares improperly allotted to themselves will belong to the company, or if they have retained the shares they will be liable for the difference between the nominal value and the market value at the time of allotment.[55]

6.7 The contract of allotment

The contract to take shares is generally made by application and allotment, and for this purpose a form of application for shares is usually issued with the prospectus, to be filled up by the applicant and left at the office of the company or with its bankers, accompanied by a deposit of a specified amount for each share applied for. In cases where shares are not offered to the public it is advisable to have these forms ready for applicants to fill up, in order to prevent dispute as to the conditions under which the shares were applied for. But it is not absolutely necessary to have a printed form, as a letter applying for shares, or even a verbal application, is sufficient.[56]

6.8 Letters of allotment

Public companies do not, in making an allotment in response to an application, immediately issue a share certificate to the allottee. Instead, the allottee receives a letter of allotment which will only be replaced by the share certificate when the full issue price has been paid.[57] The position of the allottee,[58] before his name is entered on the register of members and a share certificate is issued to him, is that he is a shareholder and enjoys the rights and is subject to the liabilities of such. However, he is not yet a member of the company and, unless the articles otherwise provide, he cannot exercise a membership right[59] such as the right to vote or attend meetings.[60] However, as a shareholder he is entitled to any dividends declared and must pay any calls that are made.[61] If the company

---

[51] *Ving v Robertson and Woodcock* (1912) 56 SJ 412.

[52] *Fraser v Whalley* (1864) 2 H & M 10; *Punt v Symons & Co.* [1903] 2 Ch 506; *Piercy v Mills & Co.* [1920] 1 Ch 77. *Hogg v Cramphorn* [1967] Ch 254; *Bamford v Bamford* [1969] 2 WLR 1107 (CA). See further, 14.7, below.

[53] *North-West Transportation Co. v Beatty* (1887) 12 App. Cas. 589 (PC).

[54] *Alexander v Automatic Telephone Co.* [1900] 2 Ch 56 (CA).

[55] *Shaw v Holland* [1900] 2 Ch 305 (CA).

[56] *Cookney's Case* (1859) 3 De G & J 170; *Bloxam's Case* (1864) 4 De G J & S 447.

[57] As to share certificates, see 8.10, below.

[58] Subscribers to the memorandum are members from the time of subscription: see 10.2, below.

[59] See the Companies Act 1985, sections 368 to 370 and 373, which refer to members.

[60] Section 370 (6), which confers the right on 'every member ... of one vote in respect of each share' in the case of companies 'originally having a share capital' in so far as the articles 'make no other provision'.

[61] See *McEuen v West London Wharves & Warehouses Co.* (1871) 6 Ch App. 655 at pp. 661–2.

is wound up he may be made a contributory if the contract of subscription is still enforceable against him.[62]

The Companies Act gives an allottee of shares the right to apply to the court to have his name entered on to the register[63] and to have a share certificate issued to him[64] when the date for the issue of the share certificate arises.[65] The company also has the right to register a subscriber if he (or his renouncee) does not apply for registration.[66]

Nowadays a letter of allotment issued by a public company will always have attached to it a blank letter of renunciation and a registration application form. The former allows the original allottee to renounce his right to allotment in favour of whoever completes the appropriate registration application form.[67] However, the allottee may not wish to renounce and will then himself complete his registration application form and surrender the letter of allotment to the company. Alternatively, the allottee may wish to renounce some shares in his allotment and retain others. He will do this by executing the letters of renunciation in respect of those shares he wishes to renounce and surrendering the letter of allotment to the company. The company will then issue 'split letters of allotment' to the allottee and the renouncee.[68]

It should be noted that where a public issue is made by way of 'offer for sale'[69] by an issuing house, the allotment is made by the issuing house and not the company. The applicant is sent in response to his application a 'letter of acceptance' (instead of an allotment letter). Until the allottee (or his renouncee) had his name entered on the register of members, his contract of subscription is with the issuing house which may sue him if he is in default.

The usual practice in the case of allotments of shares by private companies is to dispense with the letter of allotment and, on allotment, to proceed at once to the issue of a share certificate and entry of the allottee's name on the register of members.[70] Sometimes public companies issue 'renounceable share certificates'. Within the period provided the renouncee may send it to the company to be entered on the register of members. An ordinary share certificate will then be sent to him. If the original allottee decides not to renounce, he may retain the original share certificate as permanent evidence of title by cancelling or destroying the attached letters of renunciation.[71]

---

[62] See *Re Direct Birmingham, Oxford, etc., Rly Co., Ex parte. Capper* (1851) 20 LJ Ch 148, 151; *Re Pennant and Craigwen Mining Co., Fenn's Case* (1852) 1 Sm. & G 26 and the definition of contributories in section 79 of the Insolvency Act 1986.

[63] Section 359 (1).

[64] Section 185 (6) and (7).

[65] Section 185 (1).

[66] *McEuen v West London Wharves and Warehouses Co.* (1871) 6 Ch App. 655.

[67] The directors cannot refuse to accept a renouncee by relying on the article entitling them to refuse transfer: *Re Pool Shipping Co.* [1920] 1 Ch 251. An article might be so drawn as to allow the directors to refuse to register the renouncee, but this is not usually done.

[68] For specimen forms of allotment letter and split allotment letter, see *Secretarial Administration* (Jordans, 1984, loose-leaf), Part 6. The allotment letter will always state the last date on which it may be split or renounced.

[69] See 5.8, above.

[70] Since shares in private companies are not as a rule freely transferable, there is no reason to issue renounceable allotment letters.

[71] The reason for this practice is to save unnecessary expense, but it will only be used where the shares are to be paid in full at the time of allotment or in the case of a capitalisation issue.

6.9 Restrictions on allotment of shares by public companies

There are two restrictions on the power of public companies to make a valid allotment of shares. First, section 84 of the Companies Act 1985 imposes a restriction on the allotment of any share capital of a public company. Such an allotment may not be made unless either that capital is subscribed in full, or the offer states that, even if the capital is not subscribed for in full, the amount of that capital subscribed for may be allotted in any event or in the event of the conditions specified in the offer being satisfied. Where such conditions are imposed, no allotment must be made unless those conditions are satisfied. The 'offer' document will, in the normal case of a public company offering shares to the public, be listing particulars or a prospectus subject to the requirements described in Chapter 5.

Section 84 (2) and (3) provides for the consequences of allotting shares in breach of its provisions. Thus all money must be repaid to applicants within forty days from the first issue of the prospectus. Personal liability is imposed on directors if this money is not repaid within forty-eight days of the issue of the prospectus. The director has the defence open to him of proving that this was not due to any misconduct or negligence on his part. Such an allotment will also be voidable at the instance of the applicant under section 85. Section 84 applies in the case of shares offered as wholly or partly payable otherwise than in cash as well as to shares offered for subscription in cash.[72]

The second restriction is that a public company may not allot a share except as paid up at least as to one-quarter of the nominal value of the share and any premium on it.[73] Where a public company allots a share in contravention of this provision, the share will be treated as if one-quarter of its nominal value together with the whole of any premium had been received. However, the allottee shall be liable to pay the company the minimum amount which should have been received in respect of the share less the value of any consideration actually supplied in payment (up to any extent) of the share and any premium on it, and the interest at the appropriate rate on the amount so payable.[74] This liability will not apply in relation to an allotment of a bonus share unless the allottee knew or ought to have known the share was allotted in contravention of section 101.[75]

6.10 Return of allotments

Whenever a company limited by shares or limited by guarantee and having a share capital makes any allotment of its shares, either upon public subscription or otherwise, it must within one month thereafter lodge with the Registrar for registration the following documents:

(1) a return of the allotments in the prescribed form stating the number and nominal amount of the shares comprised in the allotment, the names and addresses of the allottees, and the amount (if any) paid or due and payable on each share whether on account of the nominal value of the shares or by way of premium;

(2) when shares are allotted as fully or partly paid up otherwise than in cash, a contract in writing constituting the title of the allottee to the allotment, together with any

---

[72] Section 84 (4).

[73] Companies Act 1985, section 101 (1). This section does not apply to shares allotted in pursuance of an employees' share scheme: section 101 (2).

[74] Section 101 (4). As to the liability of subsequent holders, see section 112; see 6.14.

[75] Section 101 (5).

contract of sale or for services or other consideration in respect of which the allotment was made, and a return stating the number and nominal amount of the shares so allotted, the extent to which they are to be treated as paid up, and the consideration for which they have been allotted.[76]

In the absence of a contract in writing, a document containing the prescribed particulars must be stamped with the same stamp as if it were a contract for the purpose, and must be lodged with the Registrar for registration.[77] The court may grant relief and extend the time for delivery of the document if the omission was accidental or due to inadvertence or if it is just and equitable to grant relief.[78]

6.11 Maintenance of capital

As we have seen earlier in this chapter, although the raising of finance by the issue of shares is often the least important method, company law has always paid special attention to share capital and has developed sophisticated rules relating to what is called 'the raising and maintenance of capital'. It should be noted that the term 'capital' here means only capital in the narrow sense of money raised by the issue of shares and the assets towards the acquisition of which that money is used. It bears no necessary relationship to the more normal use of that word in economic jargon, which is simply the net worth of a business, the amount by which the value of its assets exceeds its liabilities.[79] The purpose of the legal rules is primarily to protect the creditors of a company limited by shares, whose existence is of course quite independent of any individual members of it, so that the creditors can be sure that there is something they can look to for payment of their debts. The fact that share capital may play a very small role in a company's financing means that these rules often have less significance than their volume and complexity would prima facie suggest.

The artificiality of these rules is compounded by the fact that there is no minimum share capital required of private companies. Of course, public companies must have such a minimum,[80] but the figure of £50,000 is paltry indeed compared to the actual worth of the vast majority of public companies. Despite these points, detailed attention must be paid to the law relating to the raising and maintenance of capital. This was initially developed by the courts and the general principle established by the cases may be stated in general terms as requiring that a company with a share capital is bound to obtain a proper consideration for the shares which it issues and to refrain from handing back any or all of the fund so acquired to its members except by a lawful distribution of profits or a lawful reduction of capital. Although much of the detail is now consolidated and modified by statute, as will be seen in ensuing paragraphs, the common-law principle is by no means redundant. Recent case-law has illustrated its vitality: denying the validity of 'unearned' remuneration awarded to a director who was also a shareholder;[81] striking

---

[76] Section 88 (2). Fines may be imposed for default on an officer of the company 'knowingly a party to the default'. This means knowing of the default at the time, not subsequently: *Beck v Solicitor to Board of Trade* (1932) *The Times*, 23 April; see *Gore-Browne on Companies* (Jordans, 44th edn, loose-leaf), 9.9.

[77] Section 88 (3). As to payment for shares other than in cash generally, see 6.13 *et seq.* below.

[78] Section 88 (5).

[79] For more detail, see Gower's *Principles of Modern Company Law*, 5th edn, pp. 199–201.

[80] See 2.2, above.

[81] *Re Halt Garage (1964) Ltd* [1982] 3 All ER 1045; see also *Re George Newman & Co* [1895] 1 Ch 974 at p. 686 and the discussion of corporate gifts at 4.13, above.

down a sale of company A's assets to B, a company controlled by A's sole substantial shareholder, at a gross undervalue;[82] and holding unlawful an agreement which sought to impose a liability to make a gratuitous payment at a future date when it was likely that the company would have no distributable profits.[83]

The statutory provisions are contained in Part V of the Companies Act 1985. This Part is the consolidation of part of the Companies Act 1980 which implemented the Second EC Directive,[84] the measure which necessitated the statutory enactment of the rules. It must be said that some of the directive's provisions – and hence those of the statute – appear to be rather pointless in practice; this is considered, where appropriate, in the following description of the legal rules. The issues surrounding the nature and rights of shares themselves and the ways in which a company may reorganise its capital structure are considered in the next chapter.

6.12 Price of allotted shares

The principle of maintenance of capital requires that as a general rule the total consideration received by a company in return for each share allotted by it must not be less than the nominal amount, or 'par value', of the share; that is, shares must not be allotted at a discount.[85] This rule applies whether the shares are issued fully paid or partly paid in the first instance.[86] It is, however, relaxed by the Companies Act in one specific instance, namely where commission or brokerage is paid under section 97.[87] Except in this case, where shares are allotted at a discount, the allottee is liable to pay the company the amount of the discount and interest thereon at the appropriate rate.[88] A subsequent holder of the shares is jointly and severally liable with the allottee unless he is a purchaser for value without actual notice of the issue at a discount at the time of the purchase or he derived title, directly or indirectly, from such a purchaser.[89] Sections 100 and 112 impose this liability upon an actual allottee and the subsequent holders described. It seems, therefore, that a mere contract to issue or allot shares at a discount is void and unenforceable under previous authority.[90]

Any liability to pay the amount of a discount may be enforced in a winding-up for the benefit of creditors or other shareholders,[91] as the case may be, but the mere fact that some members received their shares at a discount does not entitle other members holding shares properly issued to bring a winding-up petition.[92] As an alternative to these remedies, the company may make the directors who were responsible for the share issue liable to pay the amount of the discount as damages for breach of duty.[93]

The rule that a proper consideration must be obtained for issued shares is applicable in

[82] *Aveling Barford Ltd v Perion Ltd* (1989) 5 BCC 677.
[83] *Barclays Bank plc v British & Commonwealth Holdings plc* [1995] BCC 19.
[84] *Official Journal of the European Communities for 1977*, No. L26/1.
[85] Section 100, confirming *Ooregum Gold Mining Co. of India v Roper* [1892] AC 125 (HL).
[86] As to the minimum price payable on allotment of a public company's shares under section 101, see 6.9, above. As to the minimum capital requirements for public companies, see 2.2, above.
[87] See 2.20, above.
[88] Section 100 (2). the appropriate rate for interest is 5 per cent per annum or such other sum as is specified by statutory instrument: section 107.
[89] Section 112 (1).
[90] *Re Almada & Tirito Co.* (1888) 38 Ch D 415, (CA).
[91] *Welton v Saffery* [1897] AC 299 (HL).
[92] *Re Pioneers of Mashonaland Syndicate* [1893] 1 Ch 731.
[93] *Hirsche v Sims* [1894] AC 654.

a wide range of situations which clearly survive the statutory confirmation of the principle. For example, the issue of £1 debentures at a discount with a provision that they may be exchanged for fully paid £1 shares immediately or at any time before a fixed date, is unlawful, as the shares would be issued at a discount.[94] A company cannot issue 200 £1 shares in satisfaction of a debt of £100,[95] nor can it allot 200 £1 shares for 50p each in consideration of the allottee making a loan of £100 to the company.[96]

The rule does not go so far as to require that shares must be paid for in cash. That payment in money's worth is sufficient is confirmed in respect of both nominal value and premium by section 99 (1).[97] Furthermore, section 738 provides that payment in cash includes the following: cash in foreign currency; cheques received by the company which the directors have no reason for suspecting will not be paid; the release of a liability of the company for a liquidated sum;[98] and an undertaking to pay cash to the company at a future date. However, apart from these cases, the Companies Act 1985 provides important qualifications in respect of the payment for shares in public companies by non-cash consideration. Thus, this question must be considered separately in respect of private and public companies respectively.

6.13 Allotments of shares for non-cash consideration by private companies

As far as private companies are concerned, any valuable consideration prima facie suffices – for example an agreement to render services, as by becoming manager for five years.[99]

However, a company cannot by a contract make that which is not a good consideration in law a valid payment for shares – for example past services for which the company was not liable to pay.[100] But if the consideration is in kind, the court will not inquire whether it was really of a value equal to the nominal amount of shares issued, unless the consideration was illusory or had an obvious money value showing that a discount had been allowed.[101] Thus, a private company can agree to purchase property and pay for services at any price it thinks proper, and may make the payment in shares, provided that it does so honestly and not colourably, and has not been so imposed as to be entitled to repudiate the bargain.[102] The bargain must, however, represent a real valuation of the property transferred as an equivalent for the shares issued. Thus, if the directors have not considered at all whether the property and the shares are of equivalent value, the issue is bad.[103]

---

[94] *Mosley v Koffyfontein Mines Ltd (No. 1)* [1904] 2 Ch 108 (CA).

[95] *Re Wragg Ltd* [1897] 1 Ch 796, 831 (CA).

[96] *Re James Pitkin & Co. Ltd* [1916] WN 112.

[97] 'Money's worth' is expressly stated to include goodwill and know-how.

[98] This does not cover the case where a price for property is stated to be satisfied by an allotment of shares: *Re Bradford Investments plc (No. 2)* [1991] BCLC 688.

[99] *Re Theatrical Trust Ltd, Chapman's Case* [1895] 1 Ch 771.

[100] *Re Eddystone Marine Insurance Co.* [1893] 3 Ch 9 (CA). In Scotland, past consideration may be good: *Park Business Interiors Ltd v Park* [1990] BCC 914.

[101] *Re Wragg Ltd* [1897] 1 Ch 796.

[102] ibid.

[103] *Tintin Exploration Syndicate Ltd v Sandys* (1947) 177 LT 412.

6.14 Allotments of shares for non-cash consideration by public companies

In accordance with the requirements of the Second EC Council Directive on Company Law, the Companies Act 1985 contains detailed provisions governing the payment for shares allotted by public companies otherwise than in cash.[104]

In one case payment other than in cash is totally prohibited. This is where shares are taken by a subscriber to the memorandum by virtue of an undertaking by him in the memorandum; the nominal value and any premium on the shares must be paid up in cash.[105]

In the other cases described below, the Act imposes various sanctions for breach.[106] Criminal liability to pay a fine may be imposed on the company and on every officer in default.[107] The recipient of the shares is immediately liable to pay in cash[108] the difference between any cash actually paid and the nominal value of, plus any premium payable on, the shares. A subsequent holder of the shares is jointly and severally liable with an original recipient, unless he is a purchaser for value from him without actual notice[109] of the contravention at the time of purchase, or unless he derived title, directly or indirectly, from such a purchaser.[110] The court can grant relief from civil liability subject to the conditions of section 113. Among other things,[111] these conditions impose a requirement to have regard to the principle of capital maintenance and to whether or not the company has benefited from the transaction which was in breach of the statute. It has been held that very good reasons will be required before the court can accept that it is just and equitable to exempt an applicant from liability, notwithstanding that the company has not received sufficient value,[112] but relief is more than likely to be given if the company has in fact received good value for shares, notwithstanding a failure to observe the valuation requirements described in 6.14.3.[113]

6.14.1 Prohibited non-cash consideration
One form of non-cash consideration is prohibited by section 99 (2). This is consideration which consists of an undertaking to do work or perform services for the company or any other person, whether in respect of payment of the nominal value of shares or any premium payable on them.

---

[104] As to what is payment in cash, see section 738, discussed in 6.12. The payment of, or an undertaking to pay, cash to any person other than the company is non-cash consideration.

[105] Section 106.

[106] Note that where the consideration is an undertaking caught by the provisions described in 6.14.1 and 6.14.2, the company can still enforce the undertaking: section 115 (1).

[107] Section 114.

[108] See *Re Bradford Investments plc* [1990] BCC 740, where it was held that as a result, until cash is paid or the recipient of the shares is relieved from liability, under standard articles the recipient will be disenfranchised in respect of the shares (see Table A, article 57).

[109] This means actual notice of the facts constituting the breach; ignorance of the statutory requirements is no defence: *System Control plc v Munro Corporate plc* [1990] BCLC 659.

[110] Section 112 (1) and (3).

[111] For details, see *Gore-Browne on Companies* (Jordans, 44th edn, loose-leaf), 13.4.6. The list of matters in section 113 to which the court should have regard is not exhaustive: *Re Bradford Investments plc (No 2)* [1991] BCLC 688.

[112] *Re Bradford Investments plc (No 2)*, above.

[113] *Re Ossory Estates plc* [1988] BCLC 213.

6.14.2 *Future non-cash consideration*

By section 102, it is prohibited for a public company to allot shares as fully or partly paid up, whether as to their nominal value or in respect of any premium payable on them, other than for cash, if the consideration for the allotment is or includes an undertaking which is to be or may be performed more than five years after the allotment.[114]

6.14.3 *Valuation of non-cash consideration*

In those cases where it is permissible for a public company to allot shares for a non-cash consideration, i.e. in cases other than those just described, section 103 imposes a general requirement of valuation of the consideration.

For the allotment to be valid, a report on the value of the consideration must have been made to the company within the six months preceding the allotment, and a copy of the report sent to the proposed allottee.[115] The requirement does not apply, however, to the following:

(1) a bonus or capitalisation issue of shares (section 103 (2));
(2) allotments in connection with take-overs and mergers falling within the terms of section 103 (3) and (4);
(3) allotments in connection with a proposed merger within the terms of section 103 (5).

The 'curious and arcane'[116] provisions of section 108 lay down the requirements for the valuation of and report on the non-cash consideration, which must be made by an independent person qualified at the time of the report to be appointed or to continue to be auditor of the company, whom the Act refers to as the valuer.[117] However, he may arrange for or accept a valuation of the consideration or part of it made by another person, e.g. a surveyor, where it appears to him to be reasonable for it to be made by that person and where that person appears to him to have the requisite knowledge and experience and is not an officer or servant[118] of the company or its subsidiary or holding company or of another subsidiary of the company's holding company or a partner or employee of such an officer or servant. If the valuation is thus delegated, the delegate must also make a report which will enable the independent person to make his own report and to provide a note in accordance with subsection 6, described below.[119]

The valuer's report must state:

(1) the nominal value of the shares to be wholly or partly paid for by the consideration in question;

---

[114] Section 102 (1). Any variation of a contract to allot shares, or an ancillary contract relating to payment in respect of those shares, which originally complies with subsection (1), which purports to vary its terms so that the subsection would have been broken had the variation been in the original contract, is void (section 102 (3)); and this applies to the variation by a public company of the terms of such a contract entered into before it was re-registered as a public company (section 102 (4)).

[115] This applies whether the shares are fully or partly paid up and the requirement also applies when an allotment of shares is mixed with other consideration given by the company in exchange for non-cash consideration: section 108 (2). Here the valuer must also value the other consideration to determine what proportion of the consideration provided by the allottee is attributable to the shares.

[116] Per Harman J in *Re Ossory Estates plc* [1988] BCLC 213 at p. 215.

[117] Section 108 (1). This can clearly be the company's own auditor. As to who is qualified to be an auditor, see Chapter 12.

[118] Other than an auditor; see section 108 (3).

[119] Section 108 (2).

(2) the amount of any premium payable on the shares;

(3) the description of the consideration and of that part of it which he himself has valued, the method used to value it and the date of the valuation; and

(4) the extent to which the nominal value of the shares and any premium are to be treated as paid up on allotment by the consideration and in cash.[120]

Where the valuation was made by a delegate, the report must also state this fact and the name of the delegate and the knowledge and experience he had to carry out the valuation, and must describe so much of the consideration as was valued by the delegate, the method used to value it and the date of valuation.[121]

In addition, the report must contain, or be accompanied by a note containing, statements to the following effect:

(1) in the case of a valuation made by a delegate, that it appeared to the valuer reasonable to arrange for it to be so made or to accept a valuation so made;

(2) that the method of valuation was reasonable in all circumstances;

(3) that it appears to the valuer that there has been no material change in the value of the consideration in question since the valuation; and

(4) that on the basis of the valuation, the value of the consideration, together with any cash by which the nominal value of the shares or any premium payable on them is to be paid up, is not less than so much of the aggregate of the nominal value and the premium as is treated as paid up by the consideration and any such cash.[122]

Any person making a valuation or report under section 103 is by section 110 given the right to require from the officers of the company such information and explanation as he thinks necessary.[123]

A copy of any report must be delivered to the Registrar of Companies for registration at the same time as the return of the allotment of the shares concerned is made under section 88.[124]

By way of comment, it may be thought that the provisions described in this section were a complex overreaction to a not very real problem, given that the shares of most public companies are or will be listed on The Stock Exchange or dealt in under the auspices of some other body recognised under the Financial Services Act 1986, the rules of which should ensure the full disclosure of all relevant information. Like some other measures emanating from the Second Directive, they have complicated company law without any apparent benefit thereto and it is a pity that these considerations were not in the minds of those negotiating or implementing the directive.[125]

6.14.4 *Non-cash assets acquired from subscribers and others*

Sections 104 and 105 deal with certain agreements which may be entered into by public companies which, although they are not necessarily confined to allotments of shares, will often be so concerned and which it is convenient to describe here.[126] The sections impose

---

[120] Section 108 (4).

[121] Section 108 (5).

[122] Section 108 (6).

[123] It is an offence for an officer to mislead the valuer, section 110 (2) and (3).

[124] Section 111; see 6.10, above.

[125] See, also, Sealy, *Company Law and Commercial Reality*, pp. 68 and 82.

[126] This is a very brief account of the provisions; for more detail, see *Gore-Browne on Companies* (Jordans, 44th edn, loose-leaf), 13.4.5.

valuation, report and public filing requirements similar to those just described[127], where a public company enters into an agreement with an appropriate person for the transfer by him to the company or another person of one or more non-cash assets[128] equal to one-tenth or more of the company's issued share capital within what is described as the 'initial period'.

Where a company is formed as a public company, the appropriate person is any subscriber to its memorandum and the initial period is two years from the issue of the company's trading certificate.[129] Where a joint stock company is registered as a public company, or a private company is re-registered as a public company, the appropriate person is any member of the company at the time of registration or re-registration and the initial period is two years from the date of registration or re-registration.

These sections are open to even more criticism than the related ones on valuation discussed above. Their purpose is presumably the prevention of fraud by promoters of public companies, but they can be easily evaded. Public companies are never in practice formed as such and hence the provision as to their subscribers to the memorandum is in effect redundant. When public companies are converted from private companies, the sections apply, as described above, only to members at the time of registration or re-registration; an intending fraudster need only ensure that he does not become a member of a company at the appropriate time.

6.15 Issue of shares at a premium

It is very common for shares in a company to be issued in return for a consideration greater than the par or nominal value of the shares, whether the company is a public company making a public issue or a private company formed with a £100 share capital which is issued in return for the transfer of property worth much more than £100. The fact that such a premium is obtainable does not of itself impose a duty on the company to demand it.[130] However, if shares are issued at a premium, whether for a cash or non-cash consideration,[131] prima facie section 130 of the Companies Act 1985 requires the company to transfer a sum equal to the aggregate amount or value of the premiums on those shares to a share premium account which, like issued share capital, must appear on the liabilities side of the balance sheet.[132] In certain cases where shares are issued in return for shares or in other consideration from another company, section 130 does not apply by reason of sections 131 to 134, which are described below.

Where section 130 does apply, the share premium account is to some extent treated as if it were share capital so that the provisions regarding reduction of capital apply to it and it cannot be used to finance a payment of dividends.[133] However, it may be applied:

---

[127] Note that both valuations will be required when a company is allotting shares as all or part of the consideration for the transfer of a non-cash asset to it.

[128] Property or interests in property: section 739.

[129] Under section 117; see 2.2, above.

[130] *Hilder v Dexter* [1902] AC 474 (HL). But it may be a breach of duty by the directors who fail to obtain such a premium; see 6.6, above.

[131] *Henry Head & Co. Ltd v Ropner Holdings Ltd* [1952] Ch 124; *Shearer v Bercain* [1980] 3 All ER 295.

[132] Schedule 4, Part I; see Chapter 12, below.

[133] Although, using the reduction of capital procedure (see Chapter 7), a company may be able to cancel the share premium account and in effect convert it into distributable profits: *Quayle Munro Ltd, Petitioners* 1991 GWD 35–2104.

(1) to finance an issue of fully paid bonus shares (though not a partly paid issue nor to finance an issue of debentures);

(2) in writing off preliminary expenses or the expenses of, or commission paid or discount allowed on any issue of shares or debentures; and

(3) in providing for the premium payable on redemption of any debentures.[134]

6.15.1 Relief from section 130

In *Shearer v Bercain Ltd*[135] it was clearly established that the obligation to create a share premium account applied wherever a company in fact acquired assets worth more than the par value of the shares issued, and particularly in the case of a merger of companies by exchange of shares where the shares acquired by the new holding company were worth more than the par value of the shares issued by it.[136] This decision, though logically unimpeachable on the construction of what is now section 130, was felt to cause unnecessary difficulties in certain contexts, and mergers by exchange of shares were frequently effected since the introduction of what is now section 130 (as section 56 of the 1948 Act) on the basis of a different interpretation.[137] As a result the Companies Act 1981 provided for exemptions from the need to establish a share premium account in mergers by exchange of shares which satisfied certain conditions. In one case relief was given retrospectively,[138] and there are two specific prospective exemptions as described in the following sections.[139]

6.15.2 Relief in respect of certain mergers

Section 131 provides for relief from section 130 in cases of mergers by exchange of shares effected on or after 4 February 1981 which satisfy the conditions therein and which do not fall within the provisions of section 132.[140] These conditions are as follows:

(1) There must be an arrangement[141] to allot equity shares in the prospective holding company (the issuing company) on terms that the consideration for those shares is to be provided by the issue or transfer[142] to the issuing company[143] of equity shares in the prospective subsidiary company (the other company) or by the cancellation of any such shares not held by the issuing company. Although the relevant wording is somewhat obscure, this requirement does not prevent the issuing company providing additional consideration, such as cash or loan capital, for the shares of the other company to be acquired by it. 'Equity shares' are shares comprised in a company's issued share capital excluding any part which, neither as respects

---

[134] Section 130 (2). It may also be used by private companies making a lawful purchase of shares out of capital under the provisions of the 1985 Act; see 6.17, below.

[135] [1980] 3 All ER 295.

[136] It was also decided that the pre-acquisition profits of the acquired company were to be treated as capital, not profit. As to pre-acquisition profits, see 12.15, below.

[137] For an account of the debate that *Shearer v Bercain* stimulated, see 1 Co. Law 293 (1980).

[138] See now section 12 of the Companies Consolidation (Consequential Provisions) Act 1985. As this was entirely retrospective, detail may be sought elsewhere, e.g. *Gore-Browne on Companies* (Jordans, 44th edn, loose-leaf), 13.5.2.

[139] Note that the Secretary of State has wide powers under section 134 to extend the relief by statutory instrument and that the reliefs extend to the value of shares on the balance sheet; section 133 (1).

[140] Section 132 (6).

[141] Defined widely in section 131 (7).

[142] See section 133 (3).

[143] Or its nominee: section 133 (2).

dividends nor as respects capital, carries any right to participate beyond a specified amount in a distribution.[144]

(2) As the result of the arrangement, the issuing company must secure at least a 90 per cent holding by nominal value of the equity shares of the other company, counting shares held prior to the arrangement, if any, and counting shares held by other members of the group of which the issuing company is part (if that be the case).

(3) If the equity share capital of the other company is divided into different classes of shares, the requirements as to the arrangement and the acquisition of at least 90 per cent must be satisfied in relation to each of those classes taken separately.

If as a result of such an arrangement the equity shares allotted in the issuing company are issued at a premium, section 130 does not apply to the premium on the shares.

Additionally, if the arrangement also provides for the allotment of any shares in the issuing company on terms that the consideration for those shares is to be provided by the issue or transfer to the issuing company of non-equity shares in the other issuing company, the relief from section 130 extends to any shares in the issuing company allotted on those terms in pursuance of the arrangement.

6.15.3 Group reconstructions

The second specific exemption from section 130 concerns group reconstructions effected on or after 21 December 1984 which fall within the terms of section 132.[145] Here the issuing company must be a wholly owned subsidiary and must allot shares to its holding company or to another wholly owned subsidiary of its holding company in consideration for the transfer to it of any assets other than cash[146] belonging to another member of the group (the transferor company). Only the amount, if any, by which the base value of the assets transferred by the transferor company[147] exceeds the nominal value of the shares allotted, which is referred to as the 'minimum premium value', need be transferred to the issuing company's share premium account.

6.16 Acquisition by a company of rights in respect of its own shares

One of the most fundamental common-law principles relating to the maintenance of capital was that which made it illegal for a limited company to purchase its own shares.[148] To have allowed otherwise would in many cases have permitted a company unilaterally to reduce the capital fund available for creditors. The prohibition is now in statutory form (Companies Act 1985, section 143 (1)) and applies to the acquisition by a company of its own shares by purchase, subscription or otherwise except, *inter alia*, when fully paid shares are acquired other than for valuable consideration. This exception permits, for example, a company acting as trustee to hold its own shares in that capacity, provided that someone

---

[144] Sections 131 (7) and 744.

[145] As to the more limited relief in respect of reconstructions between 4 February 1981 and 21 December 1984, see Schedule 25, which is discussed in *Gore-Browne on Companies* (Jordans, 44th edn, loose-leaf), 13.5.5.

[146] This could be shares or any other form of property.

[147] That is their cost or the amount at which they are stated in the transferor company's accounts, less any liabilities assumed by the issuing company as part of the consideration for the assets transferred.

[148] *Trevor v Whitworth* (1887) 12 App. Cas. 409 (HL).

else paid for them. An acquisition in breach of section 143 is void and the company and every defaulting officer is liable to a criminal penalty.[149]

However, shortly after the introduction of what is now section 143, the 1981 Act made substantial inroads into the prohibition and, as will be seen in the following sections, statute does permit the purchase by a company of its own shares under stringent conditions. There are other exceptions to section 143[150] covering reductions of capital,[151] purchases pursuant to court orders under various sections of the Companies Act 1985, and forfeitures and surrenders of shares for failure to pay calls.[152]

The basic prohibition in section 143 cannot be evaded by the issue of shares to someone acting as nominee for the company or by such a nominee acquiring partly paid shares in the company. In most cases, by section 144, the nominee is deemed to hold the shares on his own account and is liable to pay for them.[153] However, this does not apply where the company does not have any beneficial interest in such shares, for example because it did not provide or agree to provide any consideration. In addition, if the nominee of a public company acquires shares in the company with financial assistance given to him directly by the company, the shares must be disposed of or cancelled under section 146.[154]

A nominee for a company has always been able to acquire from a member, and hold, already issued fully paid shares in the company – provided that the company provides no consideration.[155] If, however, the company is a public company, the regime of section 146[156] applies and the nominee cannot exercise any voting rights attached to the shares.[157]

6.17 The redemption or purchase of a company's own shares

The Companies Act contains a number of important provisions[158] (first introduced in the 1981 Act) which allow companies to purchase their own shares and, in respect of private companies, permit this to be financed out of capital. Although in part these represent a considerable departure from traditional principles of maintenance of capital, they were to some extent only an extension of a longstanding provision which allowed companies to issue preference shares which would be redeemable by the company.[159]

There seems little doubt that the idea underlying these provisions was worthwhile, since there is no reason why a purchase of its own shares by a company should necessarily

[149] See section 143 (2).
[150] See section 143 (3).
[151] See 7.14, below.
[152] See 7.16, below.
[153] See Section 144 (2) which also provides that if the nominee fails to pay a call, then the subscribers to the memorandum or the directors, as the case may be, are liable to pay it.
[154] See 7.16.2, below.
[155] *Kirby v Wilkins* [1929] 2 Ch 444; *Re Castiglione's Will Trusts* [1958] Ch 549. This course is unnecessary now that section 143, as described above, permits the company itself to hold such shares.
[156] See 7.16.2, below.
[157] Section 146 (4).
[158] These are complemented by provisions in the Income and Corporation Taxes Act 1988 designed to encourage their use. The latter Act provides that, assuming its conditions are satisfied, the consideration provided by companies redeeming or purchasing their own shares is taxed as a capital gain rather than on the less favourable basis of a distribution. Note that, under section 179, the Secretary of State has broad powers to amend or extend the provisions by statutory instrument.
[159] Section 58 of the Companies Act 1948.

infringe the capital maintenance principle and this is certainly not the case if the consideration is not provided out of capital, and it may be economically advantageous for unwanted capital to be freed in this way. However, it may be wondered whether the legislature was not far too cautious. As will be seen, the provisions are complex and the exercise of the power to redeem or purchase is surrounded by restrictive requirements. Other common-law jurisdictions have permitted companies to purchase their own shares under a much more relaxed regime, apparently with no untoward consequences. We could perhaps have learnt more from them.[160]

6.17.1 Redeemable shares

By section 159, a company limited by shares or limited by guarantee and having a share capital may, if authorised to do so by its articles and subject to the conditions laid down, issue shares of any class which are to be redeemed or are liable to be redeemed at the option of the company or the shareholder. No redeemable shares may, however, be issued by a company unless it has at the time issued shares which are not redeemable. Subject to the relevant provisions of the Act, the redemption of shares may be effected on such terms and in such manner as may be provided by the articles of the company.[161]

The conditions of redemption are as follows:

(1) Redeemable shares may be redeemed only if they are fully paid.
(2) The terms of redemption must provide for payment on redemption.
(3) The redeemable shares of public companies may be redeemed only out of distributable profits[162] or out of the proceeds of a fresh issue of shares made for the purposes of the redemption, and except as described below, any premium payable on redemption must be paid out of distributable profits.

Private companies may additionally redeem shares out of capital.[163]

Where redeemable shares were issued at a premium, any premium payable on their redemption may be paid out of the proceeds of a fresh issue of shares made for the purposes of the redemption up to an amount equal to the lesser of (a) the aggregate of the premiums received by the company on the issue of the shares redeemed, and (b) the current amount of the company's share premium account (including any sum transferred to that account in respect of premiums on the new shares). In such a case, the amount of the company's share premium account must be reduced by a sum corresponding (or by sums in the aggregate corresponding) to the amount of any payment made under this provision out of the proceeds of the issue of the new shares.

Shares redeemed under section 160 must be treated as cancelled on redemption and the amount of the company's issued capital[164] is diminished by the nominal value of the shares. However, capital is maintained either because the proceeds of a fresh issue are used or by the requirement to create a capital redemption reserve.[165] Where in pursu-

---

[160] See further Sealy, *Company Law and Commercial Reality* (Sweet & Maxwell, 1984), pp. 9–12.

[161] Section 160. This last provision (section 160 (3)) was due to be replaced by a more prescriptive regime in section 159A (inserted by CA 1989, section 133 (2)), but section 159A has not yet been implemented and may be repealed; see *Gore-Browne on Companies* (Jordans, 44th edn, loose-leaf), 13.8.1.

[162] That is (section 181) profits distributable under section 263 (2), as to which, see 6.21 *et seq.*, below.

[163] As to private companies, see 6.17.10–6.17.13, below.

[164] But not its authorised capital.

[165] As to the capital redemption reserve, see 6.17.9, below.

ance of the section a company is about to redeem any shares, it has power to issue shares up to the nominal amount of the shares to be redeemed as if those shares had never been issued.

Notice of every redemption within section 159 must be given to the Registrar within one month, failing which, the company and every officer in default is liable to a default fine.[166]

6.17.2 *Purchase by a company of its own shares*

Section 162 gives companies limited by shares or limited by guarantee and having a share capital the power to purchase their own shares, including any redeemable shares, if authorised to do so by their articles, provided that a purchase must not result in there being no member holding other than redeemable shares in the company. Section 162 (2) incorporates all except one of the provisions of sections 159 and 160. Thus purchases of companies' own shares may take place on the same conditions and with the same consequences as the redemption of redeemable shares, as described above. The one distinction is that the terms and manner of purchase need not be determined by the articles.

However, the exercise of a purchase of a company's own shares is governed by strict additional requirements, in terms of the authority which must be obtained for particular purchases, the publicity which must be given and certain other matters. These are described in the following sections.

6.17.3 *Authority required for off-market purchases*

The Act draws a distinction between what are described as 'off-market purchases' and 'market purchases' of a company's own shares. Off-market purchases are governed by section 164 and defined (in section 163 (1)[167]) as purchases otherwise than on a recognised investment exchange and purchases on a recognised investment exchange but not subject to a marketing arrangement on that exchange. Shares are subject to such a marketing arrangement if either (a) they are listed under Part IV of the Financial Services Act 1986,[168] or (b) the company has been accorded facilities for dealings in those shares to take place on that investment exchange without prior permission for individual transactions from the authority governing that investment exchange and without limit as to the time during which these facilities are to be available. Principally, therefore, purchases by private and non-listed public companies and over-the-counter purchases by listed companies are within section 164.

An off-market purchase may be made only if the terms of the contract of purchase are authorised before the company enters into the contract by a special resolution of the company[169] or if the company has previously authorised a contingent purchase contract under section 165 (as described in 6.17.4, below). The authority can be varied, revoked or from time to time renewed by special resolution. In the case of a public company, the special resolution conferring or renewing authority must specify a date for its expiry which must be within eighteen months of the date of the resolution.

If a member (or his proxy) whose shares are the subject of a proposal to purchase them

---

[166] Section 122 (1) (*e*).
[167] As amended by the Financial Services Act 1986, Schedule 16, para. 17.
[168] See Chapter 5.
[169] The provisions are modified if authority is conferred by a statutory written resolution (see 11.4), rather than by special resolution.

votes on the special resolution, on a poll or otherwise, his votes must not be counted. Notwithstanding anything in a company's articles, any member of the company (or his proxy) may demand a poll on the question whether any such resolution shall be passed.

In addition to the notice which will be required for a special resolution under section 164,[170] no such resolution is effective unless a copy of the proposed contract of purchase, if it is in writing, or a written memorandum of its terms, if it is not in writing, is available for inspection by members of the company both at the registered office of the company for at least fifteen days before the date of the meeting at which the resolution is passed, and at the meeting itself.[171] Any memorandum must include the names of any members holding shares to which the contract relates, and any copy of the contract must have annexed to it a written memorandum specifying any such names which do not appear in the contract itself.

A variation of an existing approved contract may be made by the company but only if authorised by special resolution. The same requirements as described above apply to such a special resolution and a copy or memorandum of the original contract (and any previous variations) must be available for inspection as well as a copy or memorandum of the proposed varied contract.

No criminal or civil penalties are prescribed if the requirements of section 164 are not complied with. In view of the terms of section 164 (1), a contract purportedly entered into in pursuance of a resolution which is not effective according to the section is void as a contract to perform an unlawful act, namely an unauthorised purchase by a company of its own shares.

6.17.4 Contingent purchase contracts

An alternative procedure in respect of off-market purchases is provided for by section 165. This allows the company to enter into what is described as a contingent purchase contract for its own shares. This is a contract not amounting to an actual contract to purchase but under which the company may, subject to any conditions, become entitled or obliged to purchase its own shares, in other words, an option.

The purchase of shares pursuant to a contingent purchase contract may be made only if the terms of the proposed contract are authorised by special resolution before the company enters into the contract, and the relevant provisions of section 164 (described in 6.17.3, above) apply to such a resolution and to variations of existing contingent purchase contracts.

6.17.5 Authority required for market purchases

A market purchase is defined by section 163 (3)[172] as a purchase made on a recognised investment exchange other than a purchase on an investment exchange of shares not subject to a marketing arrangement. Most purchases by listed companies will be market purchases.

Section 166 requires such a purchase to have the prior authority of the company in general meeting, that is by ordinary resolution only. The resolution may confer general authority to purchase the company's own shares of any particular class or description, and the authority may be unconditional or conditional. By section 166 (3), the authorising resolution must do three things:

---

[170] Under section 380; see 11.18, below.
[171] The requirement here is modified where the statutory written resolution procedure is used.
[172] As amended by the Financial Services Act 1986, Schedule 16, para. 17.

(1) It must specify the maximum number of shares authorised to be acquired.
(2) It must determine both the maximum and minimum prices which may be paid for those shares either by specifying a particular sum or by providing a basis or formula for calculating the amount of the price in question without reference to any person's discretion or opinion.
(3) It must specify a date within eighteen months on which the authority is to expire. Note though that a purchase can be made outside the time-limit, where the contract was concluded before it and the terms of the authority permitted the company to make a contract which could or might be executed wholly or partly after the authority expires.

Subject to these requirements, any authority may be varied, revoked or renewed from time to time by the company in general meeting.

A printed copy of any resolution conferring, varying, revoking or renewing authority within section 166 must be forwarded to the Registrar within fifteen days.

6.17.6 Assignments and releases of a company's right to purchase its own shares

The rights acquired by a company under any contract to purchase its own shares, whether a contract for an off-market purchase approved under section 164 or section 165 or a contract for a market purchase authorised under section 166, cannot be assigned.[173]

If a company proposes to release its rights under a contract for an off-market purchase approved under section 164 or section 165, the terms of the proposed release agreement must be authorised by special resolution before the company enters into the agreement. In the absence of such a resolution, any such agreement to release rights is void.

6.17.7 Payments other than of the purchase price

Certain payments which may be made by companies in connection with a purchase of their own shares, other than payments of the purchase price for the shares, must be made out of distributable profits.[174] The payments in question are any payments made by a company in consideration of:

(1) acquiring any right to purchase its own shares under a contingent purchase contract;
(2) the variation of any contract or contingent purchase contract for an off-market purchase of its own shares;
(3) the release of any of the company's obligations to purchase any of its own shares under any contract for an off-market or market purchase of its own shares.

If any such payment is not made out of distributable profits, a purchase of shares within (1) above and a purchase of shares following a variation within (2) above is unlawful, and a release within (3) above is void.

6.17.8 Publicity for purchases

The requirements that companies disclose purchases of their own shares are contained in section 169. It should be noted that private companies taking advantage of the power to purchase out of capital are subject to the additional requirements described in 6.17.10,

---

[173] Section 167 (1).
[174] Section 168. As to distributable profits, see 6.21.2–6.21.4, below.

below. Within twenty-eight days of the date of delivery of the shares to the company, it must deliver to the Registrar a return in the prescribed form stating with respect to shares of each class purchased the number and nominal value of those shares and the date they were delivered to the company. A single return may cover shares delivered on different dates and under different contracts of purchase. The return sent by a public company must also state the aggregate amount paid by the company for all the shares covered by the return and the maximum and minimum prices paid in respect of shares of each class purchased.

In addition, the company must keep a copy of any contract to purchase its own shares (and any variation of it), or a memorandum of its terms if it was not in writing, at its registered office for the period from the conclusion of the contract to the date ten years after the date on which the purchase of the shares was completed. Every copy or memorandum must be open to the inspection of any member of the company without charge and, if the company is a public company, to the inspection of any other person without charge. Inspection must be permitted during business hours, subject to such reasonable restrictions as the company in general meeting may impose, but for at least two hours in each day.[175]

Failure to deliver the return, to keep copies or memoranda, or to permit an inspection may be punished by fines on the company and every officer in default, and the court may order immediate inspection of a copy or memorandum where an inspection has been refused.

6.17.9 *The capital redemption reserve*

Often when a company redeems redeemable shares or purchases its own shares, it will be obliged to transfer a sum to its capital redemption reserve under the provisions of section 170. This reserve, like share capital, appears on the liabilities side of the balance sheet[176] and is treated as capital. It can only be reduced by a proper reduction of capital.[177] However, it can be used to finance an issue to existing members of fully paid bonus shares.[178]

The requirement to transfer to this reserve applies only to the extent that the shares redeemed or purchased are not represented by new shares, that is when their redemption or purchase is financed wholly or partly by the use of distributable profits. So, when profits alone are used, the amount to be transferred is the nominal value of the shares redeemed or purchased. When a combination of profits and the proceeds of a new issue of shares is used, it is the amount, if any, by which the nominal value of the shares redeemed or purchased exceeds the amount of the proceeds of the new issue. Note, however, that by section 170 (3), this latter requirement does not apply when a private company makes an authorised payment out of capital to finance a redemption or purchase, as described in the next section; this is because when a company is permitted to use capital, there is obviously no point in having the same capital maintenance requirement.

---

[175] The right of inspection is governed by section 723A and the Companies (Inspection and Copying of Registers, Indices and Documents) Regulations 1991 (SI 1991 No. 1998).

[176] Details of any redeemable shares must be given in the notes to the accounts: Schedule 4, para. 38 (2).

[177] See 7.15, below.

[178] See 6.23, below. So far as the company at least is concerned, this really amounts to no more than a juggling around of the items on its balance sheet.

6.17.10 *Private companies redeeming or purchasing shares out of capital*

As has been mentioned earlier, section 171 permits private companies limited by shares or limited by guarantee and having a share capital, if authorised by their articles and subject to the stringent conditions laid down in the Act, to redeem redeemable shares and purchase their own shares out of capital. In effect the relevant provisions lay down an easier procedure whereby private companies may reduce their share capital,[179] as well as making it easier for them, for example, to satisfy the claims of a retiring member or the estate of a deceased member.[180]

The payment which may be made out of capital, described as 'the permissible capital payment for the shares', is such an amount as, taken together with any available profits and the proceeds of a fresh issue of shares made for the purpose of the redemption or purchase, is equal to the price of redemption or purchase. It seems that a company must use its 'available profits', the meaning of which is described below, before it can touch capital. This somewhat restricts the advantages of the section.

Where the permissible capital payment for any shares redeemed or purchased is not combined with the proceeds of a fresh issue, and it is less than the nominal amount of the shares redeemed or purchased, the amount of the difference must be transferred to the capital redemption reserve. If it is greater than the nominal amount of the shares redeemed or purchased, the amount of the difference may be used to reduce the amount of any capital redemption reserve, share premium account or fully paid share capital of the company and any amount representing unrealised profits of the company for the time being standing to the credit of any reserve maintained by the company in accordance with Schedule 4, para. 34 (the revaluation reserve).[181] In any case where the proceeds of a fresh issue of shares are applied in the redemption or purchase of a company's own shares, in addition to a payment out of capital, if the aggregate of the proceeds and payment is less than the nominal amount of the shares, the amount of the difference must be transferred to the capital redemption reserve.[182] If the aggregate is greater, the difference may be used to reduce any capital redemption reserve, share premium account or fully paid share capital of the company, together with any amount in the revaluation reserve, as described above.

For the purpose of section 171, available profits are profits available for distribution within the meaning of Part VIII[183] but determined in the way laid down in section 172 rather than in accordance with the accounts normally required[184] to determine a company's distributable profits. They must be determined within the period of three months before the date of the statutory declaration of the directors required by section 173[185] by reference to such accounts prepared within that period as are necessary to enable a reasonable judgment to be made of any of the company's profits, losses, assets, liabilities, provisions, share capital and reserves. For the purpose of determining the amount of the permissible capital payment for any shares, the amount of the company's

---

[179] As to reduction of capital otherwise, see 7.15 *et seq.*, below.

[180] For a full description of the circumstances where the power may be taken advantage of, see the 'Green Paper', *The Purchase by a Company of its own Shares*, 1980 Cmnd 7944.

[181] As to the revaluation reserve, see 12.7.1, below.

[182] This applies in place of section 176 (2); see 6.17.9, above.

[183] As described in 6.21.2–6.21.4, below.

[184] See 6.21.1, below.

[185] See 6.17.11, below.

available profits thus determined is to be treated as reduced by the amount of any distributions lawfully made by the company after the date of the relevant accounts and before the date of the statutory declaration.

Payments out of capital under section 171 must comply with the procedural requirements of sections 173 and 174 and the publicity requirements of section 175. In addition, there is provision for objecting members or creditors to apply to the court (sections 176 and 177), and liabilities may arise under the terms of section 76 of the Insolvency Act 1986 where a winding-up ensues within a year of payment out of capital. These matters are examined in the following sections.

6.17.11 *Procedure and publicity*

Sections 173 to 175 specify the following requirements to secure an effective payment out of capital:

(1) The directors must make a statutory declaration which states the permissible capital payment and is otherwise essentially a declaration of existing solvency and that, in the view of the directors, the company will continue to trade and be solvent for one year.

(2) The auditors of the company must make a report to the directors which confirms the permissible capital payment and that they are not aware of anything to indicate that the statutory declaration is unreasonable.

(3) A special resolution must be passed approving the payment out of capital on, or within a week of, the date of the statutory declaration, at a general meeting at which the statutory declaration and auditors' report are available for inspection and in respect of which resolution the votes of any member holding shares to which it relates cannot be counted.[186]

(4) The payment out of capital can be made only between five and seven weeks after the date of the resolution.

(5) The company must publish notice in the *Gazette* and either notice in a national newspaper or notice in writing to each of its creditors within one week of the special resolution. The notice must give the details specified in section 175, namely the fact and date of the resolution, the amount of the permissible capital payment, that the statutory declaration and auditors' report can be inspected at the company's registered office, and that any creditor can seek to restrain the payment out of capital by applying to the court under section 176. From the date of this notice the declaration and report must be kept at the registered office and be open to inspection by any member or creditor without charge until the end of the fifth week following the special resolution.

(6) Copies of the statutory declaration and auditors' report must be delivered to the Registrar by the date of the public notice.

Criminal penalties are specified for directors making a knowingly false declaration and for refusals to allow inspections of the declaration and report. The latter can also be remedied by court order.

---

[186] This requirement is appropriately modified when a company uses the statutory written resolution procedure (see 11.4).

6.17.12 Applications to the court

Within five weeks of a special resolution under section 173, any member of the company other than one who consented to or voted in favour of the resolution and any creditor may apply to the court for the cancellation of the resolution.[187] The court has wide powers.[188] It may adjourn proceedings so that arrangements can be made to purchase the interest of dissentient members or protect creditors. Failing this, it must confirm or cancel the resolution on such terms and conditions as it thinks fit. It has the specific power to provide for the company to purchase the shares of any member, reducing capital in consequence, and to make any necessary alterations in the memorandum and articles.

The Act does not spell out when the court might accede to such an application. It would obviously do so for a serious default in procedure or if available profits had not been fully utilised. However, it is not clear whether, for example, a minority shareholder would succeed if he could show that he was discriminated against because the chance to have his shares bought by the company was denied to him whereas the majority had caused the company to purchase some or all of theirs. Compare, for example, section 127 which gives the court power to disallow a variation of class rights[189] and expressly directs the court to consider fairness. It is thought that section 176 should not be used for such complaints, given the absence of any reference to fairness in section 177 and given the fact that the minority which has been unfairly treated can use the statutory remedy under sections 459 to 461.[190]

6.17.13 Liability of past shareholders and directors

Where, in redeeming or purchasing any of its own shares, a company has made a payment out of capital, and it is subsequently wound up, and is insolvent, the winding-up commencing within one year of the payment, liability to contribute to the assets of the company may be imposed under section 76 of the Insolvency Act 1986 upon the person from whom the shares were redeemed or purchased to the extent of the amount of capital he received and the directors of the company who signed the relevant statutory declaration who are jointly and severally liable with that person, except a director who shows that he had reasonable grounds for forming the opinion set out in the declaration.

6.17.14 Failure of a company to redeem or purchase its own shares

Section 178 contains provisions dealing with cases where a company has issued redeemable shares or agreed to purchase any of its own shares, under the provisions described in the preceding sections, and has failed to perform its obligations.

A company cannot be liable in damages for any failure to perform its obligations, but other remedies for a breach of contract are available to the shareholder, provided that the court must not grant an order for specific performance if the company shows that it is unable to meet the cost of redeeming or purchasing the shares in question out of distributable profits.

Where a company is being wound up and, at the commencement of the winding-up, has failed to meet an obligation to redeem or purchase its own shares which has already

[187] Section 176.
[188] Section 177.
[189] See 7.17.5, below.
[190] See 15.13, below.

accrued, the terms of redemption or purchase may be enforced by the shareholder, provided that, during the period between the due date for redemption or purchase and the date of the commencement of the winding-up, the company could have lawfully made a distribution equal in value to the price at which the shares were to have been redeemed or purchased.

Any money so owed is deferred to the claims of all creditors and preference shareholders having capital rights ranking in preference to those of the shares redeemed or purchased; but it ranks before the claims of other shareholders.

6.18 Financial assistance by a company for the acquisition of its own shares

Sections 151 to 154, which consolidate the replacement of section 54 of the Companies Act 1948, act as a reinforcement of the rule that a company may not, except subject to the strict conditions described in the preceding sections, purchase its own shares. Uncertainty surrounding the exact scope of the repealed section 54[191] led to the introduction in 1981 of what are now sections 151 to 154. The prohibitions in these sections are relaxed in respect of private companies which comply with the requirements of sections 155 to 158 as described in 6.18.3 below. Notwithstanding this relatively recent revision of the statutory provisions, there are still many uncertainties surrounding the operation of them which continue to cause difficulties in practice. A Department of Trade and Industry working group is currently looking at proposals to reform the law again; see the consultative document issued in October 1993.

6.18.1 Prohibited under section 151

The basic prohibition, which is subject to the exceptions discussed below, is twofold. First, where a person is acquiring or is proposing to acquire any shares in a company, it is unlawful for the company or any of its subsidiaries to give financial assistance directly or indirectly for the purpose of that acquisition[192] before or at the same time as the acquisition of the shares takes place.[193] Secondly, where a person has acquired any shares in a company and any liability has been incurred by him or any other person for the purposes of that acquisition, it is unlawful for the company or any of its subsidiaries to give any financial assistance directly or indirectly for the purpose of reducing or discharging the liability incurred.[194]

The reference above to a person incurring any liability includes the case of a person changing his financial position by making any agreement or arrangement (whether enforceable or unenforceable and whether made on his own account or with any other person) or by any other means.[195]

The reference to a company giving financial assistance to reduce or discharge a liability incurred by a person for the purpose of acquiring shares in the company includes the case

[191] See in particular the cases of *Belmont Finance Corp. Ltd v Williams Furniture Ltd (No. 2)* [1980] 1 All ER 393 (CA) and *Armour Hick Northern Ltd v Whitehouse* [1980] 1 WLR 1520, discussed in (1980) 1 Co. Law 99 and 145. Section 54 was notorious for often hitting the innocent and failing to deter the guilty; see the Jenkins Report (Cmnd 1749, paras. 170–176) for a general review.

[192] The equivalent words in section 54 were 'purchase or subscription'. 'Acquisition' is wider since it covers cases where the payment for shares is not in cash.

[193] Section 151 (1).

[194] Section 151 (2).

[195] Section 152 (3) (*a*).

where the company gives financial assistance for the purpose of wholly or partly restoring his financial position to what it was before the acquisition took place.[196]

Financial assistance is defined in section 152 (1) (*a*) as meaning any of the following:

(1) financial assistance given by way of gift;

(2) financial assistance given by way of guarantee, security or indemnity, other than an indemnity in respect of the indemnifier's own neglect or default, or by way of release or waiver;

(3) financial assistance given by way of a loan or any other agreement under which any of the obligations of the person giving the assistance are to be fulfilled at a time when, in accordance with the agreement, any obligation of any other party to the agreement remains unfulfilled or by way of the novation or assignment of any rights arising under the loan or such other agreement; or

(4) any other financial assistance given by a company the net assets[197] of which are thereby reduced to a material extent[198] or which has no net assets.

It is thought that 'assistance' necessarily involves the existence of at least two persons, one giving and one receiving the assistance. So where, for example, a company borrows money and gives security in order to finance a purchase of its own shares, this can hardly be regarded as the giving of financial assistance within section 151. A surrender of tax losses by a subsidiary company to another company within the same group, as part of a wider agreement for the sale of its shares to one of its directors, was held not to amount to the giving of financial assistance where there was no evidence that the surrender reduced the price which the director would otherwise have paid.[199] On the other hand, in the leading case of *Brady v Brady*,[200] in order to effect the reorganisation and division of a company, Brady Ltd, between the two principal shareholders (brothers who had fallen out), two new companies (A and B) were created which would ultimately each be owned by one brother and run one side of the previously merged businesses. Company A acquired the share capital of Brady in return for loan stock issued to company B. Subsequently A was to redeem the loan stock by arranging for Brady to transfer to B one half of Brady's assets. It was accepted that Brady would give financial assistance by this transfer when A redeemed loan stock to discharge the liability it had incurred in acquiring the shares in Brady.

Further examples of the sorts of transactions prohibited by section 151 can be found in some of the cases decided on its predecessor: a loan made by a company to finance the borrower's purchase of shares in the company;[201] the case of a purchaser of shares undertaking a liability as part of the consideration which he never discharges or causes the company to discharge;[202] or the purchase by a company of assets at an inflated price to enable the vendor of the assets to buy shares in the company.[203]

The company which is prohibited by section 151 from giving financial assistance must

---

[196] Section 152 (3) (*b*).

[197] That is, the current excess of assets over liabilities.

[198] 'Material extent' is not defined.

[199] *Charterhouse Investment Trust Ltd v Tempest Diesels Ltd* [1986] BCLC 1.

[200] [1989] AC 755, HL. The significance of the decision lies in the construction of the purpose exceptions, discussed below. See also *Plaut v Steiner* (1989) 5 BCC 352.

[201] See e.g. *Selangor United Rubber Estates Ltd v Cradock (No. 3)* [1968] 1 WLR 1555.

[202] See the 'circular cheque' transaction in *Wallersteiner v Moir (No. 1)* [1974] 1 WLR 991.

[203] See *Belmont Finance Corp. Ltd v Williams Furniture Ltd*, above.

be a company registered in Britain.[204] In addition, the phrase 'any of its subsidiaries' must be construed as limited to British companies.[205] So the section does not prohibit a foreign subsidiary of an English parent company from giving financial assistance for an acquisition of shares in its parent, nor, it seems, does it prohibit the giving of financial assistance by an English subsidiary to acquire shares in its foreign parent.[206]

A contravention of section 151 attracts severe criminal sanctions,[207] and the transaction itself is void and unenforceable.[208] However, the directors responsible and, possibly, any third parties involved, can be sued for breach of trust[209] to compensate the company for any loss suffered.

6.18.2 *Exceptions provided for by section 153*

It is important that, for financial assistance to be given unlawfully, it is given *for the purpose of* an acquisition or discharge of liability.[210] This requirement is reinforced by section 153 (1) and (2). Section 153 (1) provides that section 151 (1) does not prohibit a company from giving any financial assistance if:

(1) the company's principal purpose in giving it is not to give it for the purpose of an acquisition or the giving of it for that purpose is but an incidental part of some larger purpose of the company; and

(2) the assistance is given in good faith in the interests of the company.

Section 153 (2) contains similar provisions to cover the prohibition in section 151 (2). Thus, for example, a transaction under which a company buys from another a chattel or commodity it genuinely wants but with the intention also of putting the vendor in a position to acquire shares in the company is not prohibited provided that the latter purpose is not the principal purpose and the transaction is entered into in good faith in the interests of the company.[211] Whether the purpose exceptions have much more scope is doubtful following the House of Lords' decision in *Brady v Brady*.[212] Here they were said to contemplate two alternative situations. The first envisages a principal and a secondary purpose and was enacted to cover the sort of situation just described. The second situation is where it is not suggested that the financial assistance was intended to achieve any object other than the giving of assistance or the reduction or discharge of indebtedness, but where the result is merely incidental to some larger purpose of the company. Lord Oliver stated that in construing the word 'purpose' in the context of the fasciculus of sections regulating the provision of finance by a company in connection with the

---

[204] Section 735.

[205] *Arab Bank plc v Merchantile Holdings Ltd* [1994] 1 BCLC 330.

[206] ibid.

[207] See section 151 (3) and Schedule 24.

[208] See *Brady v Brady, above; Selangor United Rubber Estates Ltd v Cradock*, above.

[209] *Steen v Law* [1964] AC 287 (PC); *Selangor United Rubber Estates Ltd v Cradock*, above; *Wallersteiner v Moir (No. 1)*, above; *Belmont Finance Corp. Ltd v Williams Furniture Ltd (No. 2)*, above. On appropriate facts, an alternative cause of action is in the tort of conspiracy: see the *Belmont Finance* case.

[210] In section 54 of the 1948 Act, it was sufficient in the alternative that assistance was given 'in connection with' an acquisition, and this caught some otherwise legitimate transactions; see *Armour Hick Northern Ltd v Whitehouse*, above.

[211] This phrase is traditionally used to describe the fundamental duties of company directors (see 14.4, below) and in this context requires consideration of the interests of creditors: see *Brady v Brady* above.

[212] See above. It was correctly pointed out that the section is complex and not altogether easy to construe.

purchase of its own shares, there had always to be borne in mind the mischief against which section 151 was aimed. If this section was not to be deprived of any useful application, it was important to distinguish between a purpose and the reason why a purpose was formed. The reason for a scheme which involved the provision of financial assistance might be a needed reorganisation or take-over which was regarded as commercially desirable or even necessary, but that could not be regarded as a larger purpose:

> The purpose and the only purpose of the financial assistance is and remains that of enabling the shares to be acquired and the financial or commercial advantages flowing from the acquisition, whilst they may form the reason for forming the purpose of providing financial assistance, are a by-product of it rather than an independent purpose of which the assistance can properly be said to be an incident.[213]

So, in the case itself,[214] the purpose of the financial assistance was to enable the acquisition of shares and the commercial desirability of the reorganisation was not a larger corporate purpose. The scheme was not saved by section 153(2).[215] It has to be said that this construction leaves very little room for the operation of the second situation.[216]

Quite apart from the 'purpose' exception, section 153 (3) lists a number of things which are totally outside the prohibition in section 151. These are:

(1) a distribution of a company's assets by way of a dividend lawfully made or a distribution made in the course of the company's winding up;

(2) the allotment of bonus shares;

(3) any reduction of capital confirmed by order of the court under section 137;[217]

(4) a redemption or purchase of any shares made in accordance with the provisions described above;[218]

(5) anything done in pursuance of an order of the court made under section 425, that is a court-approved reconstruction,[219]

(6) anything done under an arrangement made in pursuance of section 110 of the Insolvency Act 1986, that is a reconstruction linked to a voluntary winding up;[220] and

(7) anything done under an arrangement made between a company and its creditors which is binding on the creditors by virtue of Part I of the Insolvency Act.[221]

Section 153 (4) provides for more exceptions, but so far as a public company is concerned, advantage can be taken of these only if they do not reduce the company's current worth according to the value of its assets and liabilities in its accounting records or, to the extent that they do reduce it, if the financial assistance is provided out of distributable profits.[222] The first section 153 (4) exception exempts the lending of money

---

[213] [1989] AC at 780.
[214] The facts are given briefly above.
[215] Although it was open to be saved by sections 155–158 (see 6.18.3, below).
[216] Which partly explains why the DTI may have yet another go at legislating; see above.
[217] See 7.15, below.
[218] See 6.17 *et seq.*, above.
[219] See 16.17, below.
[220] See 16.12, below.
[221] See Chapter 17.
[222] See section 154 (1) and (2) (*a*).

in the ordinary course of its business by a company whose ordinary business includes moneylending.[223]

The other three exceptions are all essentially concerned with the acquisition of or dealing in a company's shares by employees and are thus designed to encourage employee shareholding. First, a company can provide financial assistance for the purposes of an employees' share scheme[224] for the acquisition of fully paid shares in the company or its holding company. Secondly, it, or a subsidiary of it, can provide assistance for the purposes of or in connection with anything done by it, or by a company in the same group, to enable or facilitate transactions in its shares between or for the benefit of employees and others.[225] Thirdly, it can make loans to bona fide employees, other than directors, with a view to enabling them to acquire fully paid shares in it or its holding company to be held by way of beneficial ownership.[226]

6.18.3 *Exemption from section 151 for private companies*

Private companies are permitted to provide financial assistance for the acquisition of their shares and are thus wholly exempted from the prohibition in section 151, provided that they comply with the conditions prescribed in sections 155 to 158, which, broadly speaking, require a special resolution following a statutory declaration of solvency by the directors and a report by the auditors. The exemption covers in addition financial assistance given by a private company which is a subsidiary of another private company in connection with the acquisition of shares in that holding company, unless the company is also a subsidiary of a public company which is itself a subsidiary of that holding company.[227]

The statutory declaration and the auditors' report have to comply with broadly the same requirements, *mutatis mutandis*, as those required for a redemption or purchase of shares out of capital.[228]

However, by section 155 (2) a company may give financial assistance to any person within the exemption only if according to its accounting records the company has net assets which are not thereby reduced or, to the extent that these assets are thereby reduced, if the financial assistance is provided out of distributable profits.

A special resolution is required unless the company proposing to give the financial assistance is a wholly owned subsidiary.[229] In addition, where the financial assistance is to be given by a company in any case where the acquisition of shares in question is or was an acquisition of shares in its holding company, a special resolution is also required of the

---

[223] A loan made by a moneylending company for the specific purpose of financing a purchase of its shares is not made 'in the ordinary course of business'; *Steen v Law* [1964] AC 287 (PC); *Fowlie v Slater* (1979) 129 NLJ 465.

[224] Section 153 (4) (*b*). An employees' share scheme is defined in section 743 as a scheme for encouraging or facilitating the holding of shares or debentures in a company by or for the benefit of the bona fide employees or former employees of the company, its subsidiary or holding company or a fellow subsidiary, or the wives, husbands, widows, widowers or children or stepchildren under the age of eighteen of such employees or former employees.

[225] Section 153 (4) (*bb*). The 'others' are the same people as are mentioned in section 743; see footnote 224, above.

[226] Section 153 (4) (*c*).

[227] The exemption was partly designed to facilitate 'management buy-outs'.

[228] See 6.17.11, above. For more detail, see section 156.

[229] The requirements are modified when the company uses the statutory written regulation procedure (see 11.4).

holding company and any other company which is both the company's holding company and a subsidiary of that other holding company, except in the case of any company which is a wholly owned subsidiary.[230] Any such special resolution must be passed on the date of or within the week immediately following the date of the statutory declaration made by the directors, and the statutory declaration and the auditors' report must be available for inspection at the meeting.

There is a strict time-scale dictating when the financial assistance can be given. It must not be given until four weeks after the date of the special resolution (or the last of the resolutions, where appropriate). This allows for the expiry of the time within which a dissentient shareholder can apply to the court to cancel the resolution,[231] and naturally it does not apply if the resolution(s) was (were) passed by all members entitled to vote. In addition the assistance must not be given after the expiry of eight weeks from the date of the statutory declaration (or the earliest of the statutory declarations, where appropriate).[232]

6.19 The holding by a subsidiary of shares in its holding company

A further statutory reinforcement of the rule that a company may not purchase its own shares is contained in section 23. This section forbids a body corporate[233] from being a member (or having its nominee as a member) of its holding company, and any allotment or transfer of shares in a company to its subsidiary (or nominee) is void.[234] This would be tantamount to the holding company owning its own shares. The provision is of long standing, although it was revised in 1989, and these days appears somewhat inadequate because it is limited to situations where there is a holding company/subsidiary company relationship. Control of another company may be obtained by a holding of less than 50 per cent of voting shares, for example by the use of cross and circular holdings,[235] but section 23 will not apply in those cases.[236]

In any event, the section has no application where a subsidiary holds shares in its holding company as personal representative or as trustee, unless the holding company or a subsidiary thereof is beneficially interested[237] under the trust and is not so interested

---

[230] In this case, more than one statutory declaration will also be required.

[231] The relevant provisions governing the application to the court are similar to those concerning applications to cancel a payment for shares out of capital (see 6.17.12, above), save that dissentient shareholders must hold 10 per cent of the company's issued shares or of a class of issued shares and there is no provision for creditors to apply.

[232] Unless the court resolves otherwise following an unsuccessful application by a dissenting shareholder (in which case the eight-week limit is likely to have expired long before the issue is resolved).

[233] This term is defined in section 740 and comprehends all companies, including foreign companies, except for corporations sole and Scottish firms.

[234] For the definitions of 'holding company' and 'subsidiary company', see sections 736 and 736A discussed in 1.13, above.

[235] See the example cited in Gower, *Principles of Modern Company Law* (Sweet & Maxwell, 4th edn) p. 226, footnote 63: company A holds 45 per cent of the voting shares of company B and company B holds 45 per cent of the voting shares of company A. In effect the directors of both are irremovable and the companies are grouped together, but sections 736 and 736A will not apply. See also Pickering at (165) 81 LQR 248.

[236] The Jenkins Committee thought that it should, but that enacting the appropriate provision would be too difficult: Cmnd 1749, para. 153.

[237] The meaning of 'beneficial interest' is qualified by the provisions of Schedule 2, as to which see *Gore-Browne on Companies* (Jordans, 44th edn, loose-leaf), 13.10.1–13.10.4.

only by way of security for the purpose of a transaction entered into by it in the ordinary course of a business which includes the lending of money.[238]

6.20 Serious loss of capital by public companies

Section 142 consolidates a provision first introduced in the 1980 Act as a result of the Second EC Directive. It provides that where the net assets of a public company are half or less of the amount of the company's called-up share capital, the directors of the company must duly convene an extraordinary meeting of the company to consider whether any, and if so, what, measures should be taken to deal with the situation. The meeting must be convened not less than twenty-eight days after the earliest day on which a director learns of the fact, to take place at a date not later than fifty-six days after that day.[239]

Failure to comply with the section renders the director responsible liable to criminal sanctions,[240] but there are no civil consequences, nor does the section provide any specific guidance as to the position, if, following the meeting, the company resolves to do nothing. It is really a rather curious provision which looks like another example of an ill-thought-out implementation of the Second Directive. In fact it may be wondered whether it really does implement Article 17 of the directive, which requires the meeting 'to consider whether the company should be wound up or any other measures taken' and which thus at least has a more specific point in mind than section 142.

6.21 Dividends

The remainder of this chapter is concerned with profits and dividends, namely how profit is assessed and how it is distributed or otherwise dealt with. The differing entitlement of different classes of shares to such profits, where appropriate, is considered in the next chapter.

The common-law rule, in accordance with the general principle of maintenance of capital, was that dividends could not be paid out of capital,[241] but this rule has now been largely overtaken by statute.[242] The basic rule now is that a distribution, a generic term including a dividend,[243] can only be made out of profits available according to the rules laid down in Part VIII of the Companies Act 1985 and only by reference to properly prepared accounts. The latter point will be examined first.

---

[238] In addition, it does not apply where the subsidiary is concerned only as a market maker.

[239] The section does not dispense with the need for proper notices, etc., of any resolution which might be proposed: subsection (3).

[240] Section 142 (2).

[241] *Re Exchange Banking Co., Flitcroft's Case* (1882) 21 Ch D 519.

[242] The common-law rule was notoriously out of touch with good commercial and accounting practice; see Yamey 4 MLR 273 (1941).

[243] The full definition in section 263 (2) is every description of distribution of a company's assets to members of the company, whether in cash or otherwise, except distribution made by way of: (1) a fully or partly paid issue of bonus shares (see 6.23, below); (2) the redemption or purchase of any of the company's own shares under Chapter VII of Part V (see 6.17 *et seq.*, above); (3) the reduction of share capital by extinguishing or reducing the liability of any partly paid shares or by paying off paid-up share capital (see 7.15 *et seq*, below); and (4) a distribution of assets to members of the company on its winding-up. It might be argued that the width of this definition means that it covers such distributions as the payment of remuneration to directors of a small company, especially where they are its only members and this is the usual way in which profits are shared.

6.21.1 *The relevant accounts*

Section 270 requires that companies determine the question of whether a distribution can be made, and its amount, by reference to a list of items in the 'relevant accounts'. The items amount to the basic contents of accounts, that is profits, losses, assets, liabilities, provisions, share capital and reserves.[244] There are three descriptions of relevant accounts; in all cases they must have been properly prepared so as to give a true and fair view,[245] but only the first two descriptions must have been audited.[246] They are:

(1) the last annual accounts, that is the standard accounts prepared annually under Part VII of the Act;[247]

(2) initial accounts, that is accounts prepared to allow for a distribution to be made by a recently formed company, during the company's first accounting reference period or before accounts are laid in respect of that period;[248]

(3) interim accounts, that is accounts prepared by a public company which wishes to declare an interim dividend, as such companies frequently do in the course of the financial year.[249]

Where a company has made a distribution by reference to particular accounts and wishes to make a further distribution by reference to the same accounts, it must take account of the earlier distribution and of certain other payments made, if any, as listed in section 274.[250]

6.21.2 *Determination of profits*

The Act, consequent upon the need to comply with the Second EC Directive, lays down what can be termed the 'balance sheet surplus method' of determining profits available for distribution.[251] Under this, a company can distribute what is the net profit on both capital and revenue at the particular time, that is according to the relevant accounts.

Section 263 (3) lays down the basic rule, but it does not apply to investment companies[252] and is qualified in respect of public companies by section 264.[253] It states that a company's profits available for distribution are its accumulated, realised profits (on both revenue and capital)[254] not previously distributed or capitalised,[255] less its accumu-

[244] Section 270 (2).

[245] As to this classic formula, see 12.4, below.

[246] If the audit is qualified and the qualification does not state whether it is material to determining the legality of a distribution, a distribution thus in breach of the statute is unlawful: *Precision Dippings Ltd v Precision Dippings Marketing Ltd* [1985] 3 WLR 812 (CA). The same consequence must apply to any breach of the relevant accounts provisions. Certain small companies can dispense with the audit requirement, for this as well as general, purposes, see 12.26, below.

[247] See section 271 and, further, 12.2.3, below.

[248] Section 272.

[249] Section 273.

[250] These relate to various categories of financial assistance given for the purpose of an acquisition of a company's shares (see 6.18 *et seq.*, above) and various payments in respect of a company's purchase of its own shares (see 6.17 *et seq.*, above).

[251] For a very clear general account, see Renshall, 1 Co. Law 194 (1980).

[252] See *Gore-Browne on Companies* (Jordans, 44th edn, loose-leaf), 13.14.9.

[253] See 6.21.3, below.

[254] Section 280 (3).

[255] This means used to finance a bonus issue or the purchase or redemption of the company's own shares with a resulting transfer to the capital redemption reserve: section 280 (2).

lated realised losses (on both revenue and capital) not written off in a proper reduction or reorganisation of capital.[256]

The inclusion of 'accumulated' is important, making it clear that the current year's position cannot be taken in isolation. As indicated, realised profits include both trading profits and profits on the sale of capital assets,[257] but obviously not unrealised profit arising as a result of a revaluation of assets. An unrealised profit cannot be used to pay up debentures or amounts outstanding on partly paid shares.[258] However, such a profit can sometimes be capitalised,[259] and in certain circumstances can be treated as realised if made on a revaluation of fixed assets and a sum is set aside for depreciation of the assets.[260]

Under section 275 (1) realised losses to be taken account of in the calculation include amounts written off or retained for depreciation.[261] However, if a company revalues all its fixed assets, or all except goodwill, it can distribute profits thereon provided that the overall revaluation produces a profit.[262] Development costs must also prima facie be treated as a realised loss.[263]

6.21.3 Public companies

It is not sufficient that a public company has made a distributable profit under section 263. Section 264 imposes an additional capital maintenance requirement, to ensure that the net worth of the company is at least equal to the amount of its capital. A public company can only distribute profit if at the time the amount of its net assets, that is the total excess of assets over liabilities, is not less than the total of its called-up share capital and its undistributable reserves, and only if and to the extent that the distribution does not reduce the amount of the net assets to less than that total. Undistributable reserves are:

(1) the share premium account;
(2) the capital redemption reserve;
(3) the amount by which unrealised uncapitalised profits exceed unrealised losses not written off; and
(4) any other reserve which the company is prohibited from distributing by statute or its memorandum or articles.

6.21.4 Improperly paid dividends

The Act provides[264] that a member who knows or has reasonable grounds to believe that

---

[256] The ability to write off losses by a reduction of capital has led to an increased use of the reduction procedure under section 135 since these provisions were first introduced in 1980: see *Re Jupiter House Investments* [1985] 1 WLR 975 and *Re Grosvenor Press plc* [1985] 1 WLR 980, discussed in 7.15.2.

[257] 'Realised' is not defined and its application could cause difficulties in certain cases; see Renshall, op. cit., p. 195.

[258] Section 263 (4).

[259] Section 278; see 6.23, below.

[260] See Section 275 (2).

[261] These are 'provisions', as to which see 12.5, below.

[262] Note the exemption from the need for an actual revaluation in certain circumstances, in section 275 (5) and (6).

[263] But there are exceptions; see section 269.

[264] Section 277.

a distribution or part of it is unlawful is liable to repay it or that part of it,[265] but it does not specify any further consequences of an improper dividend.

It is clear, though, that the additional remedies provided by the common law in respect of a dividend out of capital will apply to a payment illegal under the Act. Thus directors are liable to compensate the company if they know or should know that a distribution is illegal.[266] Any member can restrain a proposed illegal distribution by injunction,[267] but a member who has knowingly received such a distribution cannot bring a derivative action against the directors,[268] and will be liable to account to the company as a constructive trustee.[269]

Rather curiously, perhaps, a creditor has no *locus standi* to restrain an illegal distribution, unless he has an enforceable security which is thereby put in jeopardy.[270] His only remedy is to seek a winding-up.

6.22 Reserves

Directors have power to set aside a proportion of profits, before a dividend is declared, to form a reserve.[271] Whether or not a company chooses to set aside profits in this way depends on its particular circumstances. A reserve generally remains undivided profit and can be used, for example, to pay dividends in bad years. However, it can be capitalised, and thus cease to be profit, as described in the next section.

Reserves in the sense described above must be distinguished from provisions, that is amounts written off or retained to provide, for example, for depreciation or bad debts.[272] It should also be noted that, despite its name and despite the fact that it is often funded from distributable profits, the capital redemption reserve required under section 170[273] is, for most purposes, a capital account.

6.23 Capitalisation of profits

In times of prosperity it is common practice for companies which have large undistributed profits to convert them into capital and distribute fully paid bonus shares representing the increased capital amongst the members in proportion to their right. This requires express sanction in the memorandum or articles.

Under the common-form article, article 110 of Table A, the directors may, with the authority of an ordinary resolution, capitalise any undivided profits not required for

---

[265] This remedy does not apply to any unlawful financial assistance given to members in contravention of section 151 (see 6.18.1, above) nor to payments in respect of the redemption or purchase of a company's own shares (see 6.17 *et seq.*, above).

[266] See e.g. *Flitcroft's Case* (1882) 21 Ch D 519. Where directors do not know, e.g. because they rely upon others, the question becomes one as to their liability for negligence, as to which see 14.23, below.

[267] See e.g. *Hoole v Great Western Railway Co.* (1867) 3 Ch App. 262.

[268] *Towers v African Tug Co.* [1904] 1 Ch 558. As to derivative actions, see 15.8–15.10.

[269] *Precision Dippings Ltd v Precision Dippings Marketing Ltd* [1985] 3 WLR 812 (CA).

[270] *Mills v Northern Railway of Buenos Aires* (1870) 5 Ch App. 621.

[271] This may be expressed in the articles, but is not in the modern Table A. If not, it is implied from the fact that, usually, no dividend can exceed the amount recommended by the directors (see 6.24, below).

[272] See further 12.5, below.

[273] See 6.17.9, above, and 6.23, below.

paying any preferential dividend, whether or not they are available for distribution,[274] or any sum standing to the credit of the share premium account[275] or capital redemption reserve.[276] They may then appropriate the capitalised sum to the members who would have been entitled to it by way of dividend, by issuing fully paid-up bonus shares to them.[277] A bonus issue may be declared void for mistake if it was made on the false premise that there were profits available for capitalisation.[278]

6.24 Mode of distribution of profits

Unless the memorandum or articles provide or imply otherwise, a dividend is not payable until it has been declared,[279] and any proceedings to recover it from the company before it has been declared are premature. However, it has been stated that members are entitled to have profits distributed so far as is commercially possible, and that directors who fail to make an appropriate recommendation are exercising their powers for an improper purpose.[280] Once a dividend is properly declared, it is a debt payable to the members. The articles generally state which organ of the company has the power to declare a dividend. Under Table A, article 102, this power is vested in the general meeting,[281] subject to the proviso that it may not declare a dividend exceeding the amount recommended by the directors. Under article 103 the directors also have power to pay 'interim dividends,' i.e. dividends on account of the 'final dividend' declared by the general meeting.[282] The general meeting cannot interfere with the directors' exercise of this power.[283] But the power to resolve that a distribution of profits should take some other form than that of a cash dividend is vested by article 105 in the general meeting.

Dividends can only be paid in cash, unless there are words authorising payment by the issue of shares or debentures in the company fully or partly paid up (i.e. capitalisation), or the distribution among the members of assets (as, for instance, shares in other companies) *in specie*.[284]

If the articles are silent as to the distribution of profit, or declare that it shall be divided among the shareholders 'in proportion to their shares', the division must be made in accordance with, not the amount paid up on the shares, but the nominal amount of the shares, so that a shareholder whose shares are fully paid up gets no more per share than one whose shares are only partly paid up.[285] However, section 119 (c) of the Companies Act 1985 authorises companies, if they so wish, to pay dividends in proportion to the amount paid up on the shares, where a larger amount is paid up on some shares than others and article 104 of Table A so provides.

---

[274] Thus including unrealised profits.

[275] See 6.15, above.

[276] See 6.17.9, above.

[277] If the capitalisation is of distributable profits, it can also be used to fund the issue of fully paid-up debentures and to pay up, wholly or partly, any amount owing on hitherto partly paid-up shares.

[278] *Re Cleveland Trust plc* [1991] BCC 33.

[279] *Bond v Barrow Haematite Steel Co.* [1902] 1 Ch 353.

[280] *Re a Company, ex parte Glossop* [1988] BCLC 570 at p. 577. Habitual abuse may justify a winding-up on the just and equitable ground (see 15.17) or a petition under section 459: *Re Sam Weller & Sons Ltd* [1989] 3 WLR 923.

[281] It is usually exercised at the company's annual general meeting.

[282] There must be a legitimate profit available according to the rules already set out.

[283] *Scott v Scott* [1943] 1 All ER 582.

[284] *Wood v Odessa Waterworks Co. Ltd* (1889) 42 Ch D 645; see Table A, article 105.

[285] *Oakbank Oil Co. v Crum* (1882) 8 App. Cas. 65 (HL).

Unless the articles otherwise provide, dividends and bonuses are payable to those who are registered holders at the time of the declaration.[286]

[286] The question of entitlement to dividends upon shares which have been transferred or transmitted is dealt with at 8.5 and 8.15, below.

7 Rights and Liabilities Attached to Shares: Reorganisations of Capital

7.1 Shares

The ways in which a company may raise capital were described in a general way at the beginning of the previous chapter. It now falls to consider the nature of shares, the rights and liabilities attached to them and different classes thereof, and the ways in which share capital may be reorganised.

Looking first at the nature of a share, we find that the Companies Act 1985 describes it as an item of personal property transferable in the manner provided by the company's articles.[1] A share is in fact a chose in action, one of those property interests which do not give the owner the right to possess anything physical. This bare description does not in fact seem to help very much. A more vivid description is provided by the oft-cited dictum of Farwell J, 'A share is the interest of a shareholder in the company, measured by a sum of money for the purpose of liability in the first place and of interest in the second, but also consisting of a series of mutual covenants entered into by all the shareholders *inter se* in accordance with section [14] of the Companies Act [1985] . . . A share is not a sum of money . . . but is an interest measured by a sum of money, and made up of various rights contained in the contract.'[2]

This illustrates how a share is both contractual and confers property rights on its holder. It distinguishes the share from the debenture, the other standard form of security issued by companies, the holder of which, a lender of money to the company,[3] simply has rights against the company and not in it.

In practice, however, as regards the securities of at least a public listed company, this distinction is to some extent illusory.[4] What is really important is to distinguish the security which gives real ownership rights in terms of votes at company meetings from that which does not. In practice only ordinary shares confer such rights and for this reason are known as 'equities'. As well as the debenture, the security which does not confer real ownership rights over a company is the preference share. The nature of the preference share is described below, as it is still conventional to compare and contrast it with the ordinary share, but it must not be forgotten that in practice it is lumped together with the debenture and the two are collectively referred to as preferred stock or securities. This is because, as well as having no or limited voting rights, the preference share usually shares the characteristic of the debenture of having the right to a prior, but fixed, rate of return.

---

[1] Section 182 (1); as to transfer, see Chapter 8. Shares must be of a fixed amount specified in the memorandum (section 2(4)), a requirement which persists despite occasional suggestions that shares with no par value be permitted, and they must be numbered unless all the issued shares or shares of a particular class are fully paid up and rank *pari passu* for all purposes: section 182 (2).

[2] *Borland's Trustee v Steel Bros. & Co. Ltd* [1901] 1 Ch 279 at p. 288. As to section 14, see 3.17, above.

[3] See Chapter 9.

[4] It will normally hold for private companies, since the issue by them of more than one class of share is unusual.

7.2 Classes of shares

As the above introductory remarks have indicated, a company may divide its share capital into different classes, although this would be relatively unusual for a private company. The power to create shares with varying rights is normally contained in the articles,[5] but occasionally it is found in the memorandum.[6]

Whatever preferences or postponements or other special rights are intended to be created for a class of shares should be clearly expressed in the memorandum or articles or in the resolution authorising the issue, and also in the prospectus inviting subscriptions for the shares. The mere use of a name such as 'preference shares' or 'preferred ordinary shares' is not enough of itself to indicate what special rights are to be attached to the shares. It is particularly important to express clearly what are the rights of the various holders in the case of a winding-up.

If there is any conflict between the memorandum and the articles as to what rights are conferred on a particular class of shareholders, the memorandum prevails.[7] Where, however, there is an ambiguity in the memorandum, resort may be had to the articles to resolve the ambiguity.[8] Prima facie, the memorandum, the articles, the resolution authorising the issue and, it is submitted, the share certificates express all the rights of the holders, and the prospectus cannot be looked at for the purpose of interpreting them.[9] This rule as to interpretation does not, however, exclude proof that the prospectus did, in fact, contain part of the contract, or constitute a binding collateral contract.[10]

7.3 Ordinary shares

Except in so far as the memorandum, articles or terms of issue provide otherwise, an ordinary shareholder is entitled to receive dividends when declared (subject to any priority as to dividend enjoyed by preference shareholders), to have his appropriate proportion of the company's assets after payment of creditors paid or transferred to him on a winding-up (subject again to any priority enjoyed by preference shareholders) and to exercise one vote for each share that he holds at the general meetings of the company.[11] It should be noted that these rights as to dividend and return of capital include a right to participate in any surplus; thus in a winding-up, the holder of a £1 ordinary share is not confined to receiving back his £1 if the value of the assets available for distribution among the ordinary shareholders exceeds the nominal amount of the issued ordinary shares.

These rights of an ordinary shareholder may be, and often are, varied in specific respects by express provision in the memorandum, articles or terms of issue. A company may, for instance, have two or more classes of ordinary shares, with each class carrying different voting rights, or indeed, with one such class having no voting rights at all.[12]

---

[5] See article 2 of Table A for the standard form.

[6] If necessary, a company can generally adopt the power by altering the memorandum or articles.

[7] *Re Duncan Gilmour and Co. Ltd* [1952] 2 All ER 871; *Guinness v Land Corp. of Ireland* (1883) 22 Ch D 349 (CA).

[8] *Angostura Bitters Ltd v Kerr* [1933] AC 550 (PC).

[9] *British Equitable Assurance Co. Ltd v Baily* [1906] AC 35 at pp. 38–41 (HL).

[10] *Jacobs v Batavia and General Plantations Trust Ltd* [1924] 2 Ch 329 (CA) (which related to an issue of short-term notes).

[11] See Companies Act 1985, section 370 (6).

[12] See 7.6, below.

7.4 Preference shares

Preference shares may give a preferential right as to dividend only, or as to return of capital only, or both as to dividend and to return of capital. In either case the preferential dividend may be cumulative, or it may be payable only out of the profits of each year.

In addition to their fixed preferential rights, preference shares sometimes give further rights to participate in profits or assets. In this case, they may be known as 'participating preference shares'.

In the last resort, the rights of a preference shareholder as to dividend and capital turn upon the construction of the relevant parts of the memorandum or articles, or of the terms of issue. The courts have developed certain rules to govern this task of construction, as it is not always an easy one. It is proposed now to examine these rights, first as regards dividend and secondly as regards capital.

7.4.1 Dividend

The dividend on a preference share is generally a fixed one: that is, it is expressed in terms of a fixed percentage of the par value of the share.[13]

A fixed preferential dividend is prima facie cumulative.[14] That is, arrears in one year must be made up from profits in subsequent years before any ordinary dividends are declared.[15] But this presumption may be rebutted, e.g. where the dividend is declared to be payable from 'yearly profits'[16] or 'out of the net profits of each year.'[17]

The holders of preference shares cannot prevent the company setting aside profits earned in any year to make good the losses sustained in previous years or to build up reserves if good faith is observed, even where they are entitled to a cumulative preferential dividend at a fixed rate. Their right to dividend is, in the absence of express bargain to the contrary, subject to the directors' right to carry sums to reserve, and as with ordinary dividends, it only accrues when the dividend is declared.[18]

When a winding-up supervenes, the question whether the holders of cumulative preference shares have a right to receive the whole or any part of undeclared arrears of dividend is often particularly difficult to determine. If neither the memorandum nor the articles nor the terms of issue provide expressly for these arrears to be paid, then prima facie they are not payable;[19] i.e. even the fact that the dividend might properly have been declared before the winding-up does not give a preference shareholder the right to claim it from the liquidator.[20] This presumption is, however, easily rebutted. The arrears will be payable, for instance, if the articles declare that the profits available for dividend 'belong' to the preference shareholders to the extent of their stipulated rate of dividend,[21] or that the preference shares have 'a preferential right to dividend' and (in a subsequent clause)

---

[13] The cash sum payable will have to take account of advance Corporation Tax; see Income and Corporation Taxes Act 1988, section 14.

[14] *Webb v Earle* (1875) LR 20 Eq. 556.

[15] However, the payment of such arrears is a dividend for the year in which it was declared, not in respect of the year when no payment was made: *Re Wakley* [1920] 2 Ch 205.

[16] *Adair v Old Bushmills Distillery Co.* [1908] WN 24.

[17] *Staples v Eastman Photographic Materials Co.* [1896] 2 Ch 303 (CA).

[18] See 6.24, above.

[19] *Re Crichton's Oil Co.* [1902] 2 Ch 86 (CA); *Re W. Foster & Son Ltd* [1942] 1 All ER 314; *Re Wood Skinner & Co. Ltd* [1944] Ch 323; *Re Catalinas Warehouses & Mole Co. Ltd* [1947] 1 All ER 51.

[20] *Re Odessa Waterworks Co. Ltd* [1901] 2 Ch 190n.

[21] See *Re Bridgewater Navigation Co. Ltd* [1891] 2 Ch 317 (CA).

'priority as to dividend and capital',[22] or if there is evidence that the dividend is payable irrespective of its being declared.[23]

Where the arrears are payable either by virtue of an express provision or as a result of implications such as have just been discussed, they must be paid in full even though under the articles dividends are expressly made payable only out of profits and the profits available do not measure up to the amount of the arrears.[24]

All these difficulties of construction may be avoided by careful draftsmanship. A common provision nowadays is to the effect that in a winding-up, arrears of preferential dividend, 'whether earned or declared or not', should be paid down to the date of the commencement of the winding-up[25] (or the date of payment, as the case may be) in priority to capital.

Where the memorandum, articles or terms of issue simply declare that the holders of such shares have the right to a preferential dividend (be it cumulative or not), this is all they will be entitled to receive; if it is intended that they should have any further participation in profits, their right must be expressly stated.[26] In other words, shares carrying a preferential dividend are non-participating as to surplus profits unless otherwise stipulated. The reasoning is that the provision conferring preference as to dividend is taken to have stated exhaustively what are the rights of the shares in respect of dividend.[27]

7.4.2 Capital

Provisions in the memorandum or articles or terms of issue of preference shares which give the holders priority in regard to dividend do not give them priority in regard to the division of capital unless it is expressly mentioned. Thus, in the case of a winding-up, or upon a reconstruction of the company, they may be reduced to the position of holders of ordinary shares as to return of capital. This follows from the presumption that prima facie all shareholders rank equally.[28]

If the memorandum or articles declare that the preference shares do confer priority in a winding-up, or that the surplus assets shall be applied first in repaying the preference shares, but do not further deal with the capital, it is in every case a question of construction whether the preferential rights are given by way of priority only or by way of delimitation. Generally speaking, however, such a provision will constitute an exhaustive declaration of the preference shareholders' rights in a winding-up,[29] so as to exclude them from participation in any surplus remaining after repayment of the ordinary

[22] *Re Walter Symons Ltd* [1934] Ch 308; *Re F. de Jong & Co. Ltd* [1946] Ch 211 (CA); *Re E. W. Savory Ltd* [1951] 2 All ER 1036; *Re Wharfedale Brewery Co. Ltd* [1952] Ch 913. The ground of these decisions is that the shareholder's priority as to dividend while the company was carrying on business was conferred by the first of these phrases, and therefore the second phrase must be taken to deal with his rights in a winding-up. Cf. *Re Wood Skinner & Co. Ltd*, above, where the omission of the word 'preferential' from otherwise similar provisions led the court to the opposite conclusion.

[23] *Bishop v Smyrna and Cassaba Rly (No. 1)* [1895] 2 Ch 285.

[24] *Re New Chinese Antimony Co. Ltd* [1916] 2 Ch 115; *Re Springbok Agricultural Estates Ltd* [1920] 1 Ch 563; *Re Wharfedale Brewery Co. Ltd*, above. The reasoning, namely that on a winding-up a company simply has 'assets' to which the capital/profits distinction is no longer relevant, is borne out also in *Dimbula Valley (Ceylon) Tea Co. Ltd v Laurie* [1961] Ch 353.

[25] *Re E. W. Savory Ltd* [1951] 2 All ER 1036.

[26] *Will v United Lankat Plantations Co.* [1914] AC 11 (HL).

[27] Cf. *Scottish Insurance Corporation Ltd v Wilsons & Clyde Coal Co. Ltd* [1949] AC 462 (HL (Sc.)).

[28] *Birch v Cropper* (1889) 14 App. Cas. 525 at pp. 543 and 546, *per* Lord Macnaghten.

[29] This question is also especially relevant in a reduction of capital: see 7.14.3, below.

capital.[30] Any preference shareholder who wishes to displace the presumption must shoulder the onus of so doing.[31] The fact that his shares carry a right of participation in any surplus profits available for dividend does not displace the presumption; indeed it strengthens it if anything.[32]

Where the preference shareholders do have a right to participate, it extends to all the available assets, including those representing profits which before the winding-up the company could have distributed as an ordinary dividend,[33] unless a provision in the memorandum or articles makes it clear that such profits 'belong to' the ordinary shareholders[34] or in some other way reserves them for such holders.

7.5 Other classes of shares

There is no limit to the classes of shares which can be created, even within a single company. Founders' shares, often issued to promoters, in respect of which the receipt of a dividend was deferred until after the preference and ordinary shares had been paid a dividend at a specified rate, used to be common but are now rare.[35]

Alternatively, a company may issue shares which, like preference shares, carry the right to a fixed preferential dividend, but, like ordinary shares, carry the right to participate in surplus profits after their own fixed dividend and a fixed dividend attached to the ordinary shares have been paid. Such 'hybrid' shares are sometimes labelled 'participating preference shares' or 'preferred ordinary shares'. Also commonly found in practice are employees' shares. Shares of any class may be issued as redeemable under the terms of section 159 of the Companies Act 1985.[36]

7.6 Voting rights

The holders of all classes of shares have equal rights of voting[37] unless restrictions are specifically imposed. But a provision in the articles that holders of any class of shares shall not have votes or shall only have limited rights of voting in respect of those shares is good; and resolutions passed by those having votes may be binding even when they affect the interests of all classes.[38] It has been suggested from time to time that voteless shares should be made illegal,[39] but this suggestion has never been implemented, and even The Stock Exchange accepts voteless shares provided that they are clearly designated as such.[40]

---

[30] *Scottish Insurance Corporation Ltd v Wilsons & Clyde Coal Co. Ltd* [1949] AC 462 (HL (Sc.)); *Re Isle of Thanet Electricity Supply Co. Ltd* [1950] Ch 161 (CA); *Re Saltdean Estate Co. Ltd* [1968] 1 WLR 1844.

[31] *Re Isle of Thanet Electricity Supply Co. Ltd,* above.

[32] ibid.

[33] *Dimbula Valley (Ceylon) Tea Co. Ltd v Laurie* [1961] Ch 353; *Re Saltdean Estate Co. Ltd,* above; cf. *Scottish Insurance Corp. Ltd v Wilsons & Clyde Coal Co. Ltd,* above (cf. footnote 24, above).

[34] *Re Bridgewater Navigation Co. Ltd* [1891] 2 Ch 317 (CA).

[35] As to these and the requirements of the Companies Act in respect of them, see *Gore-Browne on Companies* (Jordans, 44th edn, loose-leaf) 14.5.

[36] See 6.17.1, above.

[37] See also 11.19, below.

[38] *Re Barrow Haematite Steel Co. (No. 1)* (1888) 39 Ch D 582; *Re Mackenzie & Co. Ltd* [1916] 2 Ch 450. This proposition is, however, subject to the specific rules governing variation of class rights, discussed at 7.7 *et seq.,* below.

[39] See e.g. the Note of Dissent in the Report of the Jenkins Committee (Cmnd 1749), p. 207.

[40] *Listing Rules,* Chapter 13, Appendix 1, para. 2.

Often, by the provisions of the articles, the holders of preference shares are not entitled to receive notice of or to attend or vote at general meetings in respect of their preference shares; but it is desirable that they should have the right to vote on any resolution involving a variation of their rights or a reduction of capital or a winding-up, and usually cumulative preference shareholders are given voting rights during any period when their dividend is in arrears for longer than a specified period.[41]

Sometimes even the holders of debentures are given votes in pursuance of a provision to that effect in the articles of association, and accordingly have a voice in the management of the company; but such votes could not be counted upon a special or extraordinary resolution, for the Companies Act 1985 provides that such a resolution must be passed by the specified majority of *members* entitled to vote.[42]

The articles generally determine how joint holders of shares are to vote. Of course, only one of such holders can vote, and the right is usually (as in Table A, article 55) given to the senior who tenders a vote, seniority for this purpose being determined by the order in which the names stand in the register of members. Under articles in the usual form a joint holder can give a proxy without the concurrence of the other joint holders.

Every shareholder is entitled to vote in accordance with his own interests, although they may appear to be different from those of the company at large, unless the vote is given to him as a member of a class, in which case he must conform to the interest of the class itself when seeking to exercise the power conferred on him in his capacity of a member of that class,[43] or unless in so doing he infringes the broad principle, discussed elsewhere in this work,[44] that members must exercise their voting power in what they bona fide believe to be the interests of the company. Subject to this principle, a shareholder may, for example, vote in favour of property being purchased from himself even though he is also a director, and the resolution will be binding even though passed by the votes of such shareholder.[45] An agreement by a vendor of shares with the purchaser that until they are transferred he will vote in a particular way will be enforced by the court by a prohibiting injunction[46] (although it seems the company could not take notice of the fact that a vote was given in breach of such an agreement) and an agreement in a mortgage that the mortgagor should retain the right of voting has in fact been enforced by a mandatory injunction.[47] An agreement made for a money consideration to vote for the advantage of another person in the course of a winding-up is, however, void.[48]

If by transferring his shares into other names or altering the order of the names a member can increase his voting power, he is entitled to do so.[49]

---

[41] See e.g. *Re Bradford Investments plc* [1990] BCC 740, where it was held that the preference shareholders' right to vote if this dividend had not been paid for six months after the due date was exercisable, whether or not there were profits available to pay the dividend.

[42] See section 378 (1), (2), discussed at 12.15, below.

[43] *Re Holders Investment Trust Ltd* [1971] 1 WLR 583.

[44] See 3.27, above.

[45] *North-West Transportation Co. v Beatty* (1887) 12 App. Cas. 589 (PC); *Pender v Lushington* (1877) 6 Ch D 70; *Burland v Earle* [1902] AC 82, 94 (PC); *Dominion Cotton Mills Co. Ltd v Amyot* [1912] AC 546 (PC). See 17.4, below, for a more detailed discussion of the fiduciary aspects of voting at general meetings by directors.

[46] *Greenwell v Porter* [1902] 1 Ch 530. As to the duration of a voting agreement, see *Greenhalgh v Mallard* [1943] 2 All ER 234 (CA).

[47] *Puddephatt v Leith* [1916] 1 Ch 200.

[48] *Elliot v Richardson* (1870) LR 5 CP 744.

[49] *Pender v Lushington*, above; *Moffat v Farquhar* (1878) 7 Ch D 591; *Burns v Siemens Brothers Dynamo Works Ltd* [1919] 1 Ch 225.

7.7 Variation and abrogation of the class rights of shareholders

Special provisions exist in the Companies Act 1985, principally sections 125 to 127, to protect the 'class rights' of shareholders, so that they cannot simply be varied or altered or, indeed, removed by alteration of the documents in which they are contained, i.e. the memorandum or articles or a resolution passed under the authority of the articles. Where a company has only one class of shares, then variation of their rights would in general be effected by such alteration, though even in these circumstances, it seems that rights may be class rights.[50]

A number of questions arise, including:

(1) What is a 'class right'?
(2) What constitutes a 'variation' or 'abrogation' of such a right?
(3) What is the appropriate procedure for varying or abrogating class rights?

Further questions will arise once these have been considered.

7.7.1 The concept of a 'class right'

When Parliament enacted the statutory provisions protecting class rights,[51] it chose not to define what it meant by 'class rights' or, to use the statutory phase, 'rights attached to any class of shares', nor even what it meant by 'class'. This was probably because it was thought that there was no difficulty in determining what class rights were – if the shares in a company are divided into different classes according to the criteria set out earlier in this chapter, so that they have differing rights in respect of dividend, capital and voting or any of these, then the rights specifically conferred in contrast to one or more of the other classes are class rights.[52] The rights might be conferred by the memorandum, the articles, the terms of issue or the resolution authorising the issue (as originally framed or subsequently varied).[53] That such rights are class rights was confirmed in the only reported case properly to consider the meaning of the term, namely *Cumbrian Newspapers Group Ltd v Cumberland & Westmoreland Herald Newspaper & Printing Co. Ltd*,[54] although, as will be seen below, the actual decision in that case went somewhat further. It was also, clearly correctly, decided in that case that a right unrelated to any shareholding cannot by any stretch of imagination be a class right.[55]

In addition to rights conferred specifically on a class, it is thought that the basic rights of all the classes as to dividends, capital and voting should be treated as class rights even when on a particular aspect there happens to be no difference between the various classes. Thus, for example, where preference and ordinary shares are clearly demarcated as regards dividend, but both classes participate *pari passu* in the assets on a winding-up, a resolution giving the preference shareholders the normal position of priority without further participation on a winding-up should be treated as varying a class right of the

---

[50] See 7.7.1, below.

[51] Section 125 was introduced only in 1980, implementing part of the Second EC Directive. Section 127 was first introduced in 1929.

[52] *Re John Smith's Tadcaster Brewery Co. Ltd* [1953] Ch 308 at pp. 319–20 (CA), *per* Jenkins LJ.

[53] As in *Re Old Silkstone Collieries Ltd* [1954] Ch 169 (CA).

[54] [1986] 3 WLR 26.

[55] See also *Re Blue Arrow plc* [1987] BCLC 587 at p. 590 rejecting, in line with the reasoning of Scott J in *Cumbrian Newspapers*, the idea that a right in the articles to be 'president' of the company, unrelated to any shareholding, could be a class right.

preference shares. Furthermore, the right to insist upon a variation of rights clause[56] is a class right, not least since section 125 (7) provides that any alteration of a variation of rights clause in the articles or the insertion of such a clause into the articles shall be treated as a variation of class rights.

As well as rights of the sort already described which are clearly class rights, articles of association in particular often confer other sorts of rights on shareholders not attached to a conventional 'class' of shares, for example weighted voting rights in certain circumstances[57] or rights of pre-emption over shares. These will only normally be found in the articles of private companies. In the *Cumbrian Newspapers* case, the question arose as to whether such rights, even when not conferred on a shareholder as a member of a conventional class, could be class rights. Here, the plaintiff was given rights under the defendant's articles, including a pre-emptive right regarding the transfer of any shares in the defendant and the right to nominate a director to the board of the defendant so long as it held 10 per cent of the issued ordinary shares of the defendant. It was held that rights of this sort were class rights, provided that they were conferred on a shareholder as such,[58] and thus subject to the protection of section 125. The learned judge, Scott J, found no basis for this result in the wording of the statute and justified it by what he perceived to be the legislative purpose behind section 125, namely the protection of such rights lest they be subject to removal by simple alteration of the articles.

It is submitted, with respect, that this conclusion is open to question.[59] There are other bases for protecting minority shareholders, both at common law[60] and under statute.[61] The purpose of section 125 was to implement part of the Second EC Directive, whose purpose was the harmonisation of provisions relating to shares and share capital in *public* companies. Section 125(1) provides that the section is concerned with the variation of the rights attached to any class of shares in a company *whose capital is divided into shares of different classes*.[62] This seems to require conventionally different classes. If the decision is correct and followed, it has wide-ranging implications for rights often conferred by the articles of private companies, as already indicated. In effect these rights are unalterable save with the consent of the individual shareholder concerned, since that person alone would constitute the class for the purposes of section 125 which, as will be seen below, requires the consent of a proportion of the class by itself to a variation of class rights. It is submitted that, if it is thought proper that such rights should be unalterable, this should be provided for in the context of a properly thought-out code for private companies, not by a 'surprisingly wide'[63] construction of a provision which had its origins in a code for public companies.

---

[56] This is not contained in the modern Table A because of the existence of section 125, but will still be relevant to companies which have the former Table A, article 4 (see note 88, below).

[57] Cf. *Bushell v Faith* [1970] AC 1099 (HL), discussed in 13.7, below. The right which was the subject of this decision – weighted voting on a resolution to remove a director – was used as an example of a class right in the *Cumbrian Newspapers* case; see [1986] 3 WLR at p. 37.

[58] This limitation was not framed as narrowly as that which is often said to surround the statutory contract created out of the memorandum and articles by section 14; see 3.18, above.

[59] See also (1986) 7 Co. Law 202; [1986] CLJ 399. Sealy, *Cases and Materials in Company Law* (Butterworths, 5th edn 1992) at p. 424 refers to the decision as 'surprisingly wide'. Gower, *Principles of Modern Company Law* (Sweet & Maxwell, 5th edn 1992) at p. 538 welcomes it.

[60] See 3.27, above.

[61] Especially under section 459; see 15.12, below.

[62] Italics supplied.

[63] See note 59, above.

7.7.2 *The meaning of 'varying' or 'abrogating' class rights*

It is easy to discern that a class right is being 'varied' or 'abrogated'[64] when the proposed alteration directly conflicts with, and purports to override, the particular provision under which the right arises. Thus a resolution reducing a preferential dividend from 10 per cent to 5 per cent clearly involves the 'variation' of a class right, and a resolution depriving a class of preference shares of a right, guaranteed by a previous special resolution, to participate in compensation accruing to the shareholders under impending nationalisation legislation, has been held to involve the 'modification or abrogation' of a class right attached to the preference shares.[65]

This is not to say that variation or abrogation of a class right belonging to a particular class cannot arise in some other way, e.g. through a variation of the literal terms of the class rights of another class, or through some measure not on its face involving class rights at all. It would seem, for example, that a resolution raising the voting power of one class of shares from one vote to ten votes per share alters the class rights, not only of that particular class, but of all other classes carrying voting rights.[66] Equally, it has in general been assumed[67] that a reduction of capital under which the various classes are not treated in accordance with their capital rights on a winding-up involves a variation of class rights. Probably the removal of a modification of rights clause constitutes such a variation also. The articles can extend the meaning of a variation of class rights, for example by providing that any reduction of capital is deemed to be such.[68]

The general tendency of the courts has, however, been to rule that the class rights attached to (say) 'class X' of shares have not been 'varied' or 'abrogated', or even 'affected' or 'dealt with',[69] by a resolution which alters the literal terms of the class rights of another, 'class Y', or on its face does not bear upon class rights at all. The following measures have been held not to vary or abrogate the class rights attached in each case to 'class X' and therefore not to fall within the scope of a modification of rights clause:

(1) an issue of new shares ranking *pari passu* with class X;[70]

---

[64] These are the vital words in sections 125 and 127. Further by virtue of section 125 (8), in any provision for the variation of class rights, except where the context requires otherwise, references to variation include references to abrogation.

[65] *Re Old Silkstone Collieries Ltd* [1954] Ch 169 (CA).

[66] *Greenhalgh v Arderne Cinemas Ltd* [1946] 1 All ER 512 at p. 516 (CA); *Lord St David's v Union Castle Mail Steamship Co. Ltd* (1934) *The Times* November 24. But cf. the actual decision in the *Greenhalgh* case, referred to in the next paragraph, and cf. the approach of the Court of Appeal in *White v Bristol Aeroplane Co. Ltd* [1953] Ch 65 (CA) and *Re John Smith's Tadcaster Brewery Co. Ltd* [1953] Ch 308 (CA).

[67] See e.g. *Scottish Insurance Corp. Ltd v Wilsons & Clyde Co. Ltd* [1949] AC 462 (HL (Sc.)); *Re Old Silkstone Collieries Ltd*, above. The adjustment of rights as between different classes of shareholders on a reduction of capital is discussed more fully at 7.14.3, below.

[68] See *Re Northern Engineering Industries plc* [1993] BCC 267. As to reductions of capital and class rights generally, see 7.14.3, below.

[69] These extra terms are sometimes inserted in modification of rights clauses in an attempt to widen their scope, but no decision to date has shown them to have any substantial effect. In *Re Mackenzie & Co. Ltd* [1916] 2 Ch 450, they seem to have been ignored, but in *White v Bristol Aeroplane Co. Ltd*, above, and *Re John Smith's Tadcaster Brewery Co. Ltd*, above, they did come under discussion by the Court of Appeal.

[70] *Re Schweppes Ltd* [1914] 1 Ch 322 (CA) (a decision under the Companies (Consolidation) Act 1908).

(2) an issue ranking in priority to class X,[71] there being no extrinsic contractual promise to the holders of class X that this would not be done;[72]

(3) an issue of bonus shares (whether ordinary or preference) to the holders in class Y (ordinary shares), when it had the effect of greatly increasing their voting power as against that of the holders in class X (preference shares),[73] or of reducing the amount which would come in a liquidation, on a distribution of surplus assets, to the holders in class X (preference shares);[74]

(4) a subdivision of shares in class Y so that the holders in that class acquired a greatly increased voting power in comparison to class X;[75]

(5) the cancellation of paid-up capital to an equal extent on both class X (preference shares) and class Y (ordinary shares), with the result that the fixed preferential dividend payable to class X, though unaltered in percentage, was substantially reduced in amount, whereas the dividend for class Y remained at large;[76] and

(6) the alteration of the place of payment (and thus the currency) of dividends from England to Australia, causing the fixed preferential dividend payable to class X to be of lesser value because the Australian pound was worth less than the English pound sterling.[77]

Lord Evershed MR[78] suggested an explanation for such decisions, namely that it was not the class rights of the complaining class that were varied or abrogated or affected, but merely the 'enjoyment' of those rights. No doubt this is a valid theoretical distinction. It is submitted, however, that more than once minority classes have lost the benefit of their rights, without any class meeting being held, in circumstances where the relevant modification of rights clause seems clearly to have been intended to supply protection to them.[79] A narrow and literal approach to the concept of 'variation of rights' has in general been the cause.

7.7.3 Procedure for variation

Once it is clear that a 'class right' is being sought to be 'varied' or abrogated', the procedure to be adopted depends upon two factors in particular: whether the memorandum, articles or terms of issue contain an express provision for variation (i.e. a 'variation of rights clause') and whether the right in question has been set out in the memorandum, the articles, the resolution authorising the issue, or any other contractual document containing the terms of issue. The procedure is largely governed by section 125.

Where class rights are set out in the memorandum and no variation of rights clause exists, either in the memorandum or the articles, then they may be varied if all the members of the company agree,[80] or by a virtue of a scheme of arrangement under

---

[71] *Pulbrook v New Civil Service Co-operation* (1878) 26 WR 11; *Underwood v London Music Hall Ltd* [1901] 2 Ch 309; *Hodge v James Howell & Co. Ltd* [1958] CLY 446 (CA).

[72] See *Allen v Gold Reefs of West Africa Ltd* [1900] 1 Ch 656 at pp. 673–4, 679 (CA).

[73] *White v Bristol Aeroplane Co. Ltd*, above; *Re John Smith's Tadcaster Brewery Co. Ltd*, above.

[74] *Dimbula Valley (Ceylon) Tea Co. Ltd v Laurie* [1961] Ch 353.

[75] *Greenhalgh v Arderne Cinemas Ltd* [1946] 1 All ER 512 (CA).

[76] *Re Mackenzie & Co. Ltd*, above.

[77] *Adelaide Electric Co. Ltd v Prudential Assurance Co.* [1934] AC 122 (HL).

[78] In *White v Bristol Aeroplane Co. Ltd* [1953] Ch 65 at p. 74 (CA).

[79] Notably in *Greenhalgh v Arderne Cinemas Ltd*, above, and *Re Mackenzie & Co. Ltd*, above.

[80] Section 125 (5).

section 425.[81] Where the rights are set out in the memorandum which also provides for their variation, then clearly the procedure there laid down must be followed. However, more than this may be required if the variation proposed is concerned with the giving, variation, revocation or renewal of an authority to issue securities for the purposes of section 80,[82] or is concerned with a reduction of capital under section 135.[83] In these cases rights can only be varied by either the consent in writing of the holders of 75 per cent in nominal value of the issued shares of the class, or by an extraordinary resolution passed at a separate general meeting of the class,[84] together with any other requirement laid down in the memorandum in so far as it is not comprised in the statutory requirements.[85]

Where class rights are set out in the memorandum and a variation of rights clause exists in the articles, then, provided that the variation of rights clause was included in the articles at the time of the company's original incorporation, and subject to the qualification to be mentioned shortly, the rights may only be varied in accordance with the variation of rights clause.[86] The qualification is that, if the proposed variation concerns either an authority under section 80 or a reduction of capital under section 135, as described above, then the rights can only be varied by either the consent in writing of the holders of 75 per cent in nominal value of the issued shares of the class or by an extraordinary resolution passed at a separate general meeting of the class, together with any other requirement laid down in the memorandum in so far as it is not comprised in the statutory requirements.

Where class rights are set out in the articles or in some independent document, for example the resolution under which the shares were issued, and there is no variation of rights clause in the articles, then those rights may be varied but only if the holders of 75 per cent in nominal value of the issued shares of the class consent in writing to the variation, or the variation is sanctioned by an extraordinary resolution passed at a separate general meeting of the holders of the class.[87]

If the articles do contain a variation of rights clause,[88] then this must be complied with.[89] Further, if the proposed modification concerns either an authority under section 80 or a reduction of capital under section 135, as described above, then the requirements

---

[81] *Ashbury v Watson* (1885) 30 Ch D 376 (CA); *City Property Investment Trust Corp. Ltd* 1951 SC 571. As to schemes of arrangement, see 16.17, below.

[82] See 6.4, above.

[83] See 7.14 *et seq.*, below.

[84] See below for the statutory requirements relating to such meetings.

[85] Section 125 (3).

[86] Section 125 (4). Presumably if the variation of rights clause was not included in the articles at the time of incorporation, the previous law applies and the memorandum should expressly or impliedly refer to or contemplate variation of the rights according to the clause in the articles. If there is no such indication, variation of the rights in the memorandum must be carried out as if the clause in the articles did not exist, i.e. under section 125 (5) or by a scheme of arrangement under section 425, as described earlier.

[87] Section 125 (2). Any other requirement, however imposed, is automatically complied with.

[88] The common form clause was exemplified by Table A, Part I, article 4 in the Companies Act 1948, which provided that where the share capital was divided into different classes of shares, the rights attached to any class might be varied with the consent in writing of the holders of three-fourths of the issued shares of that class, or with the sanction of an extraordinary resolution passed at a separate general meeting of the holders of the shares of the class. There is no standard form clause in the modern Table A, because of the statutory protection afforded by section 125, first introduced in 1980.

[89] Section 125 (4).

as to 75 per cent class consent in writing or an extraordinary resolution at a class meeting as described earlier must be complied with if not imposed by the articles.[90]

7.7.4 Notice for class meetings and statement to the Registrar

If, under any of the circumstances described, a class meeting is held, whether required by the statute or by a variation of rights clause, then the requirements of section 369 as to the length of notice for calling meetings, section 370 concerning general provisions regarding meetings and votes,[91] and sections 376 and 377 regarding the circulation of members' resolutions,[92] and any relevant provisions in the articles must be complied with. In addition the quorum at any such meeting must be two persons at least holding or representing by proxy one-third of the issued shares of the class concerned, except at an adjourned meeting where one person holding shares of the class is sufficient; any holder of shares of the class concerned present in person or by proxy may demand a poll.[93]

Where a company allots shares with rights which are not stated in its memorandum or articles or in any resolution or agreement to which section 380 applies,[94] the company must (unless the shares are in all respects uniform with shares previously allotted) deliver to the Registrar of Companies within one month from allotting the shares a statement in the prescribed form containing particulars of those rights.[95] Where the rights attached to any shares of a company are varied otherwise than by an amendment of the company's memorandum or articles (or a resolution or agreement to which section 380 applies), the company must within one month from the date of the variation deliver to the Registrar a statement in prescribed form containing particulars of the variation.[96] A similar statement must be delivered to the Registrar where (without otherwise varying them) the company assigns a name or other designation (or a new name or other designation) to any class of its shares.[97] A criminal sanction is imposed upon the company and every officer who is in default if the company fails to comply with section 128.[98]

7.7.5 Protection for minority in class

Where a variation of rights clause in the memorandum or articles has been invoked to vary or abrogate class rights, or where there is no such clause but class rights have been varied or abrogated under section 125 (2), section 127 provides that the holders of not less than 15 per cent of the issued shares of the class affected, if they did not consent to or vote in favour of the variation, may apply to the court to have the variation cancelled. The court may, if satisfied that the variation would unfairly prejudice the shareholders of the class represented by the applicant, disallow the variation; if not so satisfied, it must confirm it. Application may be made by such one or more of the shareholders affected as

[90] Section 125 (3).
[91] See 11.10.1, below.
[92] See 11.15, below.
[93] Section 125 (6).
[94] Section 380 concerns registration of certain resolutions and agreements. See 11.18, below. Any statement or notice delivered under section 128 to the Registrar will be gazetted under section 711.
[95] Shares are not treated as being different by reason only of the fact that they do not carry the same rights to dividends for the first twelve months after allotment; section 128 (2).
[96] Section 128 (3).
[97] Section 128 (4).
[98] Section 128 (5). See section 129 for a similar obligation imposed on companies without a share capital, but with different classes of members, in respect of the creation or variation of class rights.

may be appointed by them in writing and must be made within twenty-one days after the appropriate consent was given or resolution passed.[99]

Section 127 does give a measure of protection to minorities within a class of shareholders who consider that their rights have been unjustly overridden by the majority. But its narrow scope must be noted. It only applies where there is (a) a variation of rights clause in the memorandum or articles or a variation under section 125 (2) and (b) a genuine 'variation' or 'abrogation' of a 'class right'. The narrow meaning of these terms has already been described. Further, there is no reported use of the section. On the other hand, there are House of Lords dicta[100] to the effect that a minority shareholder within the relevant class has a right at general law to challenge a class resolution on the ground of lack of good faith and that section 127 is not intended to deprive him of such right. To enforce this general law right, a holding of 15 per cent of shares of the class in question is not necessary.[101]

7.8 Liabilities on shares

The fact of becoming a member of a company renders the person liable to contribute to its assets to the extent and in the manner prescribed by the Companies Act 1985, taken along with the general law and the memorandum and articles of association, as outlined below.

In an unlimited company the members are liable while the company is a going concern to pay to it the nominal amount of the shares (if any) held by them as and when called up, together with any premium payable on issue, and upon winding up to pay whatever amount is necessary to satisfy the debts of the company and the expenses of liquidation,[102] but as far as possible all the members contribute rateably.

In a company limited by guarantee the members are liable while the company is a going concern to pay to it the amount payable on the shares (if any) held by them as and when called up, and on a winding-up they are liable for any balance of the amount of their shares unpaid and, in addition, the amount guaranteed by them in the memorandum of association, if required for the purpose of paying the debts of the company and the costs of liquidation, but no more.[103]

In the case of a company limited by shares each member is liable to pay only the nominal amount of the shares held by him (together with any premium which he may have agreed to pay);[104] and notwithstanding any provision of the memorandum or articles, no member is bound by any alteration thereof, to which he has not previously or at the time thereof given his assent in writing, which requires him to subscribe for more

---

[99] Section 127 (3). The court's decision is final (section 127 (4) and a copy of any order made must be lodged with the Registrar within fifteen days of the date thereof (section 127 (5)).

[100] *Carruth v Imperial Chemical Industries Ltd* [1937] AC 707 at pp. 756, 765; see too *British American Nickel Corp. v O'Brien* [1927] AC 369 (PC) and *Re Holders Investment Trust Ltd* [1971] 1 WLR 583. The latter case, which is described in 7.14.4, below and where the issue arose on a petition to confirm a reduction of capital, is perhaps the best reported example of what might be regarded as 'unfair prejudice' under section 127.

[101] The matter could also be litigated on a petition to confirm a reduction of capital (see footnote 100 above) or by a petition under section 459, the general remedy for unfairly prejudiced minority shareholders (see 15.13, below).

[102] Insolvency Act 1986, section 74 (1); and see section 1 (2) (*c*) of the Companies Act 1985.

[103] Insolvency Act 1986, section 74 (3); and see section 1 (2) (*b*) of the Companies Act 1985.

[104] Insolvency Act 1986, section 74 (2) (*d*); and see section 1 (2) (*a*) of the Companies Act 1985. In exceptional circumstances the liability of a member or a director may become unlimited: see 3.10, above.

shares than he then holds or in any way increases his liability to pay money to the company.[105]

In each of the above cases, until a liquidation takes place, the amounts are payable at the times and in the manner prescribed by the articles of association, which almost invariably declare that so much as is not paid on application and/or allotment may be called up by the directors as and when they think fit.[106]

7.9 Initial payments on shares

Payments on applications for shares and/or allotment are dealt with in connection with the general topics of public issues and allotment of shares.[107] For present purposes it is sufficient to note that, subject to certain specific statutory provisions relating to public companies only,[108] and to any provisions in the articles or any agreement between the company and the member, the mere fact of becoming a member, whether as a subscriber to the memorandum or otherwise, does not of itself impose any obligation on the member to make an immediate payment to the company in respect of his shares.[109] In practice, of course, at least part of the price of the shares will in any event be made payable on application where the process of application is resorted to. Similarly, all, or the balance outstanding, or a part, will be payable on allotment.

7.10 Calls

A call is the way in which amounts due on shares not fully paid up on application are raised.[110] These amounts can in general be called up by a proper authority at any time, subject to the articles.[111] In the early days of company law, when the holding of partly paid shares for a considerable time was common, calls would be made at regular intervals. This is infrequent, and perhaps unknown, these days, but the articles, as in Table A, article 15, usually deem any amount payable in respect of a share on allotment or at any fixed date in the future to be a call. The result is that, for example, a failure to pay the balance or an instalment due on allotment of shares, a sum having been paid on application, or to pay the balance due at a later specified date, will attract the prospect of the shares being forfeited.[112]

Article 12 of Table A proves that, subject to the terms of allotment, the directors may from time to time make calls upon the members in respect of any moneys unpaid on their

---

[105] Section 16 of the Companies Act 1985.

[106] See e.g. Table A, article 12. As to calls by a liquidator when a company is being wound up, see 17.56, below.

[107] See Chapters 5 and 6, above.

[108] Especially section 101, by which shares in a public company must not be allotted to any person unless not less than one-quarter of the nominal value of the shares together with the whole of any premium has been received by the company (see 6.9, above).

[109] *Alexander v Automatic Telephone Co.* [1900] 2 Ch 56 (CA).

[110] For more detail, see *Gore-Browne on Companies* (Jordans, 44th edn, loose-leaf), 14.10 *et seq.*

[111] A member cannot escape liability unless he shows that he has been wrongly made a member and has used all diligence to have his name removed from the register: see 10.5, below.

[112] As to forfeiture, see 7.15, below. Note that in the absence of a provision like article 15, payments on application or allotment are not calls (*Croskey v Bank of Wales* (1863) 4 Giff 314) and that in the absence of a provision to the contrary in the articles or in some other agreement, there is no obligation to make any payment on shares subsequent to allotment until a call is made; *Re Russian Spratt's Patent Ltd* [1898] 2 Ch 149 (CA).

shares (whether in respect of nominal value or premium),[113] and requires at least fourteen days' notice to be given to the members, who are then liable to pay at the time(s) and place(s) appointed by the directors.

If calls remain unpaid, the members liable should be sued for the amount. In England, a call is specialty debt,[114] and accordingly can be recovered by action at any time within twelve years of the date of the call.[115] In Scotland, five years is the equivalent period.[116]

Table A provides that calls in arrear shall bear interest.[117] Any dividends becoming payable upon the shares of defaulting members should be retained by the company, and in addition any rights of lien[118] or refusal to register a transfer of the shares[119] exercised. As a last resort (if the articles give the power) the shares should be forfeited.[120]

7.11 Liens on shares

Articles[121] generally give a company a lien on the shares of a member for the calls or any debts as are due to the company from such member. Such a lien is valid so far as private companies are concerned.[122] It can generally be enforced by sale[123] or forfeiture[124] of the shares concerned.[125]

As far as public companies are concerned, section 150 of the Companies Act 1985 restricts their right to take liens or other charges on their shares. Section 150 (1) provides that a lien or other charge of a public company is void unless permitted by the section.[126] This permits only the following categories of lien or charge:

(1) in respect of any public company, a charge on partly paid shares for any amount payable in respect of the shares;

(2) in respect of a public company whose ordinary business includes the lending of money or consists of the provision of credit or the bailment or (in Scotland) hiring of goods under a hire-purchase agreement, or both, a charge on any of its shares, fully or partly paid, which arises in connection with a transaction entered into by the company in the ordinary course of its business;

(3) in respect of a company which is re-registered as a public company or registered

---

[113] They must act in good faith and not for a collateral purpose. For example, it is prima facie improper to make calls on only some of a class of members: *Galloway v Hallé Concerts Society* [1915] 2 Ch 233. See further, as to directors' duties, Chapter 14.

[114] Companies Act 1985, section 14 (2) and Insolvency Act 1986, section 80.

[115] Limitation Act 1980, section 8.

[116] Prescription and Limitation (Scotland) Act 1973.

[117] Article 15.

[118] See 7.11, below.

[119] See 8.3, below.

[120] See 7.15, below.

[121] See e.g. Table A, article 8, in which a lien for calls or other moneys payable on the shares is given in respect of partly paid shares. Under the rules of The Stock Exchange, the articles of a company seeking quotation must not provide for any lien on fully paid shares.

[122] *Bradford Banking Co. Ltd v Henry Briggs & Co. Ltd* (1886) 12 App. Cas. 29 (HL); *Bank of Africa Ltd v Salisbury Gold Mining Co.* [1892] AC 281 (PC).

[123] See e.g. in Table A, articles 9–11.

[124] See 7.15, below.

[125] For more detail on liens, see *Gore-Brown on Companies* (Jordans, 44th edn, loose-leaf) 14.11 *et seq.*

[126] Or by section 6 of the Companies Consolidation (Consequential Provisions) Act 1985, which concerns 'old public companies', that is pre-1980 public companies which have not re-registered. See generally *Gore-Browne on Companies* (Jordans, 44th edn, loose-leaf), 7.10–7.10.3. *Quaere* whether there are any left.

under section 680[127] as a public company, a charge on its own shares in existence immediately before its application for re-registration or registration.

7.12 The reorganisation of capital

A company may reorganise its capital structure in various ways:

(1) It may increase its capital.
(2) It may reduce its capital.
(3) It may enforce forfeitures of shares and, under certain conditions, accept surrenders.
(4) It may consolidate its shares into shares of larger amount, and convert its paid-up shares into stock, and subsequently reconvert the stock into shares.
(5) It may subdivide its shares.

7.13 Increase of capital

The 'capital' referred to here is the nominal capital authorised by the memorandum of association, and must not be confused with the issued capital or the paid-up capital. It follows that to make an issue of shares already authorised, or to make a call upon the shares already issued, would increase the issued share capital or the paid-up capital respectively, but neither proceeding would be such an increase of capital as to fall within the provisions of the Companies Act described below.

By virtue of section 121 of the Companies Act 1985, a company limited by shares, or a company limited by guarantee and having a share capital, may, if authorised by its articles,[128] increase its share capital by new shares of such amount as it thinks expedient.[129] The increase must be effected by the company in general meeting.[130] The nature of the resolution – whether special, extraordinary, or ordinary – may be prescribed by the articles. If it is not, an ordinary resolution suffices. Notice of the increase must be given in the prescribed form to the Registrar of Companies within fifteen days after the passing of the resolution authorising the increase.[131]

7.14 Reduction of capital

The provisions as to reduction of capital are set out in sections 135 to 141 of the Companies Act 1985.

Under section 135 a company limited by shares or a company limited by guarantee and having a share capital,[132] may, if authorised by its articles, by passing a special

---

[127] These are old (pre-1862) joint stock companies.
[128] See e.g. Table A, Article 32.
[129] Section 121 (1) and (2) (*a*).
[130] Section 121 (4).
[131] Section 123.
[132] An unlimited company may reduce capital at will, without the confirmation of the court being required, as long as there is power in the articles: *Re Borough Commercial and Building Society* [1893] 2 Ch 242.

resolution[133] and obtaining the sanction of the court,[134] reduce its share capital 'in any way'. The words 'in any way' indicate that the power to reduce capital is unlimited, but section 135 (2) gives also special instances, providing expressly that such a company may:

(1) extinguish or reduce the liability on any of its shares in respect of share capital not paid up; or

(2) either with or without extinguishing or reducing liability on any of its shares, cancel any paid-up share capital which is lost or unrepresented by available assets; or

(3) either with or without extinguishing or reducing liability on any of its shares, pay off any paid-up share capital which is in excess of the wants of the company.

A further common use of the power to reduce capital is to reduce the share premium account. In addition a company may take power under section 121 (1) (*e*) to cancel shares which at the date of the passing of the relevant resolution have not been taken or agreed to be taken by any person and to diminish the amount of share capital to that extent; it may take power to issue redeemable shares and to purchase its own shares subject to the conditions of Chapter VII of Part V of the Act.[135] The fact that a private company can in certain circumstances purchase its own shares out of capital provides in effect for a much easier procedure for reducing capital. However, none of these measures is deemed to be a reduction of share capital within the meaning of the Act.[136] The court has power to make an order for reduction of capital under section 461.[137]

Section 135 deals with the reduction of *share capital*, so that, in cases under (3) above, a reduction may be confirmed, although the money to make the payment off is to be borrowed,[138] and even if it is to be borrowed (e.g. on the security of debentures) from the very persons whose shares are to be reduced.[139] The amounts by which the share capital is to be reduced may be satisfied by the distribution of assets in specie even though the value of those assets may exceed the nominal amount by which the share capital is reduced.[140]

7.14.1 *Matters incidental to a reduction*
In the course of reducing its capital with the court's confirmation, a company may do things which would otherwise be illegal, such as repurchasing its own shares.[141] A reduction may also be confirmed even though its purpose is one not apparently contemplated by the section provided that it has a discernible purpose; for example, where

---

[133] The requirement for a special resolution is not usually displaced by the unanimous agreement of all the shareholders: *Re Barry Artist Ltd* [1985] BCLC 283 but a private company can use the statutory written resolution procedure; see 11.4, below. The court can correct a trivial error in the resolution: *Re Willaire Systems plc* [1986] BCLC 67.

[134] The court can confirm a reduction of capital which does not actually exist, provided that the resolution is conditional on other resolutions which will increase the capital to the necessary amount: *Re TIP-Europe Ltd* (1987) 3 BC 647.

[135] See 6.17 *et seq.*, above.

[136] See sections 121 (5) and 160 (4).

[137] See 15.15, below.

[138] *Re Nixon's Navigation Co.* [1897] 1 Ch 872.

[139] *Re Thomas de la Rue & Co. Ltd* [1911] 2 Ch 361.

[140] *Ex parte Westburn Sugar Refineries Ltd* [1951] AC 625 (HL (Sc.)).

[141] *British and American Trustee Corp. v Couper* [1894] AC 399 (HL); of course it is not now always illegal to do so: see 6.17.2, above.

the company has ceased to carry on business and the only aim of the reduction is to distribute the assets,[142] where a holding company wishes to reduce its share premium account in order to eliminate goodwill arising on consolidation of the group's accounts,[143] or where the company wishes to convert ordinary shares into redeemable deferred shares.[144]

7.14.2 Matters relevant to confirmation

Once provision has, where relevant, been made for creditors,[145] the court's attitude to confirming a reduction of capital depends on three factors:

(1) that the reduction is fair and equitable between the different classes of shareholders in the company, where there is more than one class;
(2) that the proposal affects all shareholders of the same class in a similar manner, unless those treated differently have consented to it; and
(3) that the causes of the reduction were properly put to shareholders so that they could exercise an informed choice and that the cause is proved by evidence before the court.[146]

7.14.3 Shareholders' class rights

The first two of these factors have traditionally posed the most problems and merit examination here. There is no general rule that a reduction of capital must bear equally upon all the shares of the company, or even upon all the shares in a particular class, and reductions have been confirmed as fair and equitable where only some of the shares in a particular class have been wholly or partly paid off[147] or cancelled.[148] Where, however, different shareholders or classes of shareholders have different rights as to return of capital on a winding-up, there is a prima facie rule that a reduction of capital should be framed so as to conform with these rights, unless consent is obtained from the particular shareholders or classes of shareholders whose rights are prejudiced.[149]

The most important instance of this rule is that where there are preference shares having priority as to return of capital (but no rights of further participation in surplus assets) and there are ordinary shares as well, then in a reduction involving a return of

---

[142] See *Scottish Insurance Co. Ltd v Wilsons & Clyde Coal Co. Ltd* [1949] AC 462 (HL (Sc.)).
[143] *Re Ratners Group plc* (1988) 4 BCC 293; *Re Thorn EMI plc* (1988) 4 BCC 698.
[144] *Forth Wines Ltd, Petitioner* [1991] BCC 638.
[145] As to creditors, see 7.14.5, below.
[146] See the dictum of Harman J in *Re Jupiter House Investments (Cambridge) Ltd* [1985] BCLC 222, 224. This dictum actually omits the first factor, but its importance is well established by the cases cited in the next section. See also *Re Ratners Group plc* (1988) 4 BCC 293 and *Re Thorn EMI plc* (1988) 4 BCC 698, requiring that all shareholders be treated 'equitably'. Note that Harman J expressed disapproval of dicta to the effect that the public interest, in terms of people who might become shareholders in the future, was a relevant factor (*per* Lord Macnaghten in *Poole v National Bank of China Ltd* [1907] AC 229, 239 (HL)); see also *Re Grosvenor Press plc* [1985] BCLC 286, 290–1. It was clear, previously, that the public interest, if relevant, did not extend to the interests of the community at large: *Ex parte Westburn Sugar Refineries Ltd* [1951] AC 625 (HL).
[147] e.g. *British and American Trustee Corporation v Couper*, above; *Re Robert Stephen Holdings Ltd* [1968] 1 WLR 522 (but note that in this case the court suggested that a scheme of arrangement under section 425 would have been a more appropriate procedure, because minority interests would have been better protected thereby).
[148] e.g. *Re Gatling Gun Ltd* (1890) 43 Ch D 628; *Re Pinkney & Sons Steamship Co.* [1892] 3 Ch 125.
[149] *Bannatyne v Direct Spanish Telegraph Co.* (1887) 34 Ch D 287, 300 (CA).

capital in excess of the company's wants, the preference shares should be paid off first,[150] whereas in a reduction involving partial or total cancellation of shares on account of losses, it is the ordinary shares that should first be cancelled.[151] Sometimes the preference shareholders in a prosperous company may feel aggrieved at losing a favourable investment through being thus paid off at par in advance of the ordinary shareholders, but this of itself gives them no legal grounds of objection,[152] not even if under the articles they had a right of participation in distribution of surplus profits by way of dividend.[153] It is only when they have clearly defined[154] rights of participation in surplus assets on a winding-up (whether under the memorandum or articles or terms of issue, or under some special statutory provision),[155] or (perhaps) where there is an independent agreement between them and the company that capital will not be reduced without their consent,[156] that they can raise the objection that their rights are not being strictly observed. This vulnerability of preference shareholders who have no such rights of participation is sometimes overcome in quoted companies by the use of the so-called 'Spens formula', namely a provision in the memorandum or articles or terms of issue that where preference shares are paid off, the price should be tied to the quoted market value at the time and the preference shareholders should have voting rights on the resolution for reduction. An alternative method of protection is to provide that any reduction of capital is deemed to be a variation of class rights, so that the special procedure described in 7.7.3, above, must be complied with.[157]

7.14.4 *Reduction not in accordance with class rights*

In certain cases, the courts were prepared to confirm reductions which did not accord with class rights on a winding-up, even though the consent of the shareholders or classes affected had not been obtained. In such a case, however, the onus lay on the company to prove that the reduction was fair and equitable, and the court would examine its terms and effect with particular care.[158] It appears that this is no longer permissible owing to the provisions of section 125, providing that any variation of class rights in connection with a reduction of capital must be sanctioned by a three-quarters majority of the class.[159]

Even if the variation procedure has prima facie been complied with, the court can still disallow the variation and hence the reduction if the variation was improper. In one

---

[150] *Re Chatterley-Whitfield Collieries Ltd* [1948] 2 All ER 593, 596 (CA) affirmed sub. nom. *Prudential Assurance Co. Ltd v Chatterley-Whitfield Collieries Ltd* [1949] AC 512 (HL); *Re Saltdean Estate Co. Ltd* [1968] 1 WLR 1844; *House of Fraser plc v ACGE Investments* [1987] AC 387, HL and see *Scottish Insurance Corporation Ltd v Wilsons & Clyde Coal Co. Ltd* [1949] AC 462 (HL (Sc.)).

[151] *Re Floating Dock Co. of St Thomas Ltd* [1895] 1 Ch 691; *Re London and New York Investment Corporation* [1895] 2 Ch 860; *Poole v National Bank of China Ltd* [1907] AC 229 (HL).

[152] *Scottish Insurance Corporation Ltd v Wilsons & Clyde Coal Co. Ltd*, above.

[153] *Re Saltdean Estate Co. Ltd*, above; *House of Fraser plc v ACGE Investments*, above.

[154] Inchoate rights (e.g. an expectation of compensation under the Coal Industry Nationalisation Act 1946, section 25) will not suffice: *Scottish Insurance Corp. Ltd v Wilson & Clyde Coal Co. Ltd*, above; *Prudential Assurance Co. Ltd v Chatterley-Whitfield Collieries Ltd* [1949] AC 512 (HL).

[155] e.g. where their expectation of compensation under the Coal Industry Nationalisation Act 1946, section 25, has been confirmed by resolution, as in *Re Old Silkstone Collieries Ltd* [1954] Ch 169 (CA).

[156] See ibid.

[157] *Re Northern Engineering Systems plc* [1993] BCC 267.

[158] *British and American Trustee Corp. v Couper* [1894] AC 399, 406 (HL); *Carruth v Imperial Chemical Industries Ltd* [1937] AC 707 at 744, 749 (HL); *Re Holders Investment Trust Ltd* [1971] 1 WLR 583.

[159] As to section 125 in more detail, see 7.7.3, above.

case[160] the court refused to confirm a reduction whereby redeemable preference shares were cancelled and the holders received an equivalent amount of unsecured loan stock, it being conceded by the company that this entailed a modification of the class rights of the preference shareholders. The court found (a) that the resolution for class consent was ineffectual because the majority had not voted with a view to the interests of the class and (b) that, having regard to the terms of issue of the loan stock, the reduction had not been shown by the company to be fair and equitable.

Where class consent is obtained (which may be done under section 125, a 'modification of rights clause' or under an accompanying scheme of arrangement under section 425)[161] class rights may on a reduction be changed or overridden to a substantial degree: for example, the preference shareholders may agree to surrender their priority as to capital[162] or to forgo arrears of cumulative preferential dividend,[163] or the voting powers of the respective classes may be altered,[164] or the reduction may be accompanied by other arrangements reconstituting for the future the class rights of the different classes.[165]

7.14.5 *Rights of creditors*

Under section 136, if a reduction involves any diminution of liability or any repayment of capital, and in any other case if the court so directs, creditors are entitled to object. The court can, however, under section 136 (6), dispense with creditors' rights and will generally do so if there is obtained a guarantee of their debts from a bank or if satisfied that the company has cash and liquid assets exceeding the claims of the creditors and the amount of the capital to be returned.

A typical 'other case' where the rights of creditors are relevant is where a company is reducing capital in order to write off a loss, but the loss is not expected to be permanent, for example because the company has acquired a loss-making business which it is hoped will prove profitable in the future.[166] Here the reduction will be confirmed if the company undertakes to put into a capital fund not available for distribution any money received in respect of the business up to the amount of the reduction.[167]

If the rights of creditors are not dispensed with, section 137 requires the court to be satisfied on the hearing of the petition to confirm the reduction with respect to every creditor that either (a) his consent to the reduction has been obtained or (b) his debt or claim has been discharged or determined, or has been secured by setting apart and appropriating, in such manner as the court may direct, a sufficient sum.[168]

---

[160] *Re Holders Investment Trust Ltd*, above.

[161] As to section 425 see 16.17, below.

[162] *Re Hyderabad (Deccan) Co. Ltd* (1897) 75 LT 23; *Re National Dwellings Society Ltd* (1898) 78 LT 144; *Balmenach Glenlivet Distillery Ltd v Croall* (1907) 8 F 1135.

[163] *Oban and Aultmore Glenlivet Distillery Ltd* (1904) 5 F 1141.

[164] *Re James Colmer Ltd* [1898] 1 Ch 524.

[165] *Re Allsopp & Sons Ltd* (1903) 51 WR 644 (CA); *Re Welsbach Incandescent Gas Light Co. Ltd* [1904] 1 Ch 87 (CA).

[166] See *Re Jupiter House Investments (Cambridge) Ltd* [1985] BCLC 222 and *Re Grosvenor Press plc* [1985] BCLC 286, which illustrate that using the reduction procedure in this way can increase the amount of profits available for distribution under section 239 (as to which, see 6.21 *et seq.*, above).

[167] ibid. These authorities also make it clear that the interests of future creditors are irrelevant.

[168] For more detail as to procedure in respect of creditors, see *Gore-Browne on Companies* (Jordans, 44th edn, loose-leaf) 15.3.8. Note also the provisions of section 140 whereby a creditor ignorant of the reduction and who did not therefore object to it, may be entitled if the company is wound up insolvent, to receive payment from the shareholders whose shares were reduced up to the amount of the reduction.

7.14.6 Procedure on a reduction of capital

Detailed consideration of the procedure involved in the presentation of a petition to confirm a reduction of capital is unnecessary here.[169] If the court sanctions the reduction, the order and a minute, approved by the court, showing the particulars of the capital as reduced must be registered with the Registrar,[170] and notice of this registration must be published in such manner as the court directs. The reduction does not take effect until the registration has been carried out.[171] The Registrar than certifies the registration and his certificate is conclusive evidence that all the requirements of the Act have been complied with, and that the capital is as stated in the minute.[172] All future copies of the memorandum must contain the minute, which on registration is deemed to form part thereof,[173] in substitution for the original statement of the capital of the company.[174]

The court can require the company to publish the reasons for the reduction,[175] but rarely does so.

7.15 Forfeiture and surrender of shares

A forfeiture or surrender of shares is a reduction of capital and in consequence cannot usually be carried out without the confirmation of the court under section 135. It is, however, established that without such confirmation shares may be forfeited, but only for non-payment of calls and provided it is done under an express power in the articles.[176] In cases where such a forfeiture would be permissible the shares may be validly surrendered.[177] A company's articles may be altered so as to introduce a power of forfeiture,[178] subject to the general limitations upon alteration of articles.[179]

Where shares are forfeited in the absence of any such authorisation in the articles, or in a manner falling outside the relevant clause thereof, the forfeiture is invalid and cannot be ratified, even by a majority of shareholders.[180]

By the same token, a surrender of partly paid shares in circumstances not justifying a forfeiture is invalid, because the shareholder is purportedly released from his liability for uncalled capital.[181] A voluntary surrender of fully paid shares in such circumstances may perhaps be valid if it is authorised by the articles and new shares are issued in exchange so as to prevent diminution of the company's capital.[182] A surrender in return for any other

---

[169] See *Gore-Browne on Companies* 15.3.7–15.3.11.

[170] Section 138 (1) and (3).

[171] Section 138 (2).

[172] Section 138 (4).

[173] Section 138 (5).

[174] Section 138 (6). This constitutes an alteration of the memorandum within the meaning of section 20.

[175] Section 137 (2).

[176] *Lane's Case* (1862) 1 De GJ & Sm. 504; *Kipong v Todd* (1878) 3 CPD 350 (CA). See Table A, articles 18–22 permitting forfeiture and note the extended meaning of 'call' under Table A; see 7.10, above.

[177] *Trevor v Whitworth* (1887) 12 App. Cas. 409 at pp. 417, 429, 438 (HL).

[178] *Dawkins v Antrobus* (1881) 17 Ch D 615 (CA).

[179] See 3.24, above.

[180] *Spackman v Evans* (1868) LR 3 HL 171; *Houldsworth v Evans* (1868) LR 3 HL 263.

[181] *Bellerby v Rowland and Marwood's Steamship Co. Ltd* [1902] 2 Ch 14 (CA).

[182] *Re County Palatine Loan & Discount Co., Teasdale's case* (1873) 9 Ch App. 54.

form of valuable consideration is clearly invalid as being in substance a purchase by the company of its own shares.[183] On the other hand, a voluntary transfer of fully paid shares to a nominee to hold them as trustee for the benefit of the company is valid. In such a case the company pays nothing for the shares, and its capital is not reduced.[184]

The procedure specified by the articles for forfeiture must be strictly complied with,[185] and directors must exercise the power for a proper purpose, not, for example, simply to get rid of an obnoxious shareholder.[186]

If a forfeiture is invalid, the invalidity is not cured by lapse of time and the holder remains a member of the company as regards both liabilities and rights.[187]

7.15.1 Reissue of forfeited shares

The company usually has power to reissue forfeited shares (e.g. under Table A, article 20)[188] and on such reissue may treat them as paid up to any extent not exceeding the amount paid by the former holders. If in exercise of this power it reissues shares irregularly forfeited, it may be liable in damages to the original holder.[189] When forfeited shares have been reissued, the company may make a fresh call upon the new holder in respect of the amount remaining unpaid by the former holder upon which the forfeiture was made.[190]

7.15.2 Treatment of forfeited and surrendered shares in public companies

By section 146, shares in public companies[191] which are forfeited or surrendered for failure to pay calls and shares which are subject to the other circumstances described below are subject to a special regime. The other circumstances are:

(1) where shares in the company are acquired by the company other than as a result of a redemption or purchase under Chapter VII of Part V,[192] or a reduction of capital,[193] or of a court order under the various provisions whereby the court can

---

[183] *Trevor v Whitworth* (1887) 12 App. Cas. 409 at p. 438 (HL).

[184] *Kirby v Wilkins* [1929] 2 Ch 444. See further 6.16, above. However, as far as public companies are concerned, the consequences of a lawful acquisition by a nominee are the same as those of a forfeiture, by virtue of sections 146 to 149. See 7.15.2, below.

[185] See e.g. *Johnson v Lyttle's Iron Agency* (1877) 5 Ch D 687.

[186] As to directors' duty to act for the proper purpose, see 14.5, below.

[187] *Garden Gully United Quartz Mining Co. v McLister* (1875) 1 App. Cas. 39. However, a shareholder may be precluded from setting aside a forfeiture after acquiescing in it over a long period: *Jones v North Vancouver Land and Improvement Co.* [1910] AC 317.

[188] A public company is in effect obliged to reissue them by virtue of section 146, described in 7.15.2, below.

[189] *Re New Chile Gold Mining Co.* (1890) 45 Ch D 598.

[190] *New Balkis Eersteling Ltd v Randt Gold Mining Co.* [1904] AC 165 (HL) but any payment by the former holder goes to reduce this amount (*Re Randt Gold Mining Co.* [1904] 2 Ch 468) and, conversely, any payment by the new holder reduces the debt of the former holder (*Re Bolton* [1930] 2 Ch 48).

[191] Where a private company is re-registered as a public company (see 2.11, above), and shares in it have been forfeited, surrendered or otherwise acquired in circumstances to which section 146 applies, the provisions of the section apply, the relevant period for disposal or cancellation of the shares (see below) commencing with the date of re-registration; section 148.

[192] See 6.17 *et seq.*, above.

[193] See 7.14 *et seq.*, above.

    order a company to purchase its own shares[194] and it has a beneficial interest[195] in them;

(2) where the nominee of the company acquires shares in the company from a third person without financial assistance being given directly or indirectly by the company and the company has a beneficial interest[196] in those shares;[197]

(3) where any person acquires shares in the company with financial assistance given to him directly or indirectly by the company for the purpose of or in connection with the acquisition[198] and the company has a beneficial interest in those shares.[199]

If such shares are not disposed of within the relevant period of the date of forfeiture, surrender or acquisition, the company must cancel them and diminish the amount of its share capital by the nominal value of the shares concerned and, where the effect of the cancellation will be to bring the level of the company's allotted share capital below the authorised minimum,[200] apply for re-registration as a private company, stating the effect of the cancellation.[201] The relevant period in all cases except that described in paragraph (3) above is three years. In the cases of shares acquired in the circumstances described in paragraph (3), it is one year.[202] In addition, shares forfeited, surrendered or acquired in these circumstances cannot carry voting rights.[203] Failure to comply with either of the requirements mentioned renders the company and every officer in default liable to a fine.[204] Failure to comply with the requirement to apply to be re-registered as a private company within the relevant period means that the company is treated as a private company for the purpose of section 81;[205] i.e. it is unable to offer its securities to the public, but otherwise it continues to be treated as a public company until it is re-registered.[206]

    The cancellation procedure required may be effected by a resolution of the directors of the company without complying with the statutory procedures for a reduction of capital under sections 135 and 136[207] and a resolution of the directors can alter the memorandum of the company so that it no longer states that it is to be a public company and so as to make such other alterations as are required.[208]

    Where a public company or its nominee acquires shares or an interest in shares in the company, and those shares or that interest are shown in a balance sheet of the company as an asset, an amount equal to the value of the shares or the interest must be transferred

---

[194] That is, section 5 (see 4.16, above); section 54 (see 2.13, above); and section 461 (see 15.13, below).

[195] 'Beneficial interest' is subject to the qualifications in schedule 2; see *Gore-Browne on Companies* (Jordans, 44th edn, loose-leaf) below, 15.4.6.

[196] See footnote 195, above.

[197] On the acquisition of shares by a nominee, see 6.16, above.

[198] See 6.18, *supra.*

[199] Section 146 (1).

[200] See 2.2, above.

[201] Section 146 (3).

[202] Section 146 (3).

[203] Section 146 (4).

[204] Section 149 (2).

[205] See 5.3, above.

[206] Section 149 (1).

[207] Section 147 (1). As to these, see 7.14 *et seq.*, above.

[208] Section 147 (2). If the requirement to apply for re-registration applies, the conditions of section 147 (3) and (4) must be complied with.

out of profits available for dividend[209] to a reserve fund and is not available for distribution.[210]

7.16 Other capital alterations

'If so authorised by its articles', a company limited by shares or a company limited by guarantee and having a share capital can under section 121 (2) of the Companies Act 1985 consolidate and divide all or any of its share capital into shares of larger amount than its existing shares, convert all or any of its paid-up shares into stock and reconvert that stock into paid-up shares of any denomination or subdivide its shares into shares of a smaller amount. The power must be exercised by the company in general meeting.[211] Every copy of the memorandum issued thereafter must be in accordance with the alteration.[212] Notice of any such consolidation or conversion or of any reconversion must be given to the Registrar of Companies[213] on the proper form.

Stock is 'simply a set of shares put together in a bundle'.[214] It is in fact the holding of the stockholder expressed in pounds instead of in so many shares of so much each. Unless forbidden by the articles any fraction may be transferred, but it is usual to provide that the directors may fix the minimum amount of stock transferable, which minimum, however, is not to exceed the nominal amount of the shares from which the stock arose.

It should be noted that a company cannot make an original issue of stock. If it desires to have a capital held as stock it must first issue shares, and only when they are fully paid convert them into stock. Conversion of shares into stock is a very rare phenomenon these days.

[209] See 6.21.2, above.

[210] Section 148 (4).

[211] The form of resolution required depends on the articles, but a private company can use the statutory written resolution procedure.

[212] Section 20.

[213] Section 122.

[214] *Morrice v Aylmer* (1875) LR 7 HL: 717 at p. 725, *per* Lord Hatherley.

8 Transfer and Transmission of Shares

8.1 The transfer of shares

The original allottee of the shares of a company remains personally entitled to the benefits and subject to the obligations of the shares until he has got rid of them either:

(1) by transfer;
(2) by death or bankruptcy;
(3) by forfeiture or surrender; or
(4) on a reduction of capital or other form of capital reorganisation.

The last two processes have been considered in the previous chapter. The first two, which are commonly referred to as 'the transfer and transmission of shares', will be dealt with in this chapter. In cases of transfer the transferee takes the place of the transferor, and in cases of transmission the estate of the former holder takes his place as regards benefits and liabilities.

It should be noted that, unless the contrary is provided, the term 'transfer' in a company's articles refers only to a transfer of the legal title to shares, that is the registered membership,[1] and not to transfer of an equitable interest.[2] This can have important consequences as regards restrictions on the transfer of shares, as will be discussed in the following sections.

8.2 Transferability of shares

Subject to certain limited restrictions imposed by law,[3] a shareholder has prima facie the right to transfer his shares when and to whom he pleases.[4] This freedom to transfer may, however, be significantly curtailed by provisions in the articles. Restricting provisions are legal;[5] on the other hand, The Stock Exchange requires that the transfer of fully paid quoted shares should not be restricted by the articles in any way.[6] In determining the extent of any restriction on transfer contained in the articles, a strict construction is adopted; that is to say, the restriction must be set out expressly, or must arise by necessary implication, and any ambiguous provision is construed in favour of the shareholder wishing to transfer.[7]

---

[1] As to the register of members, see Chapter 10, below.

[2] *Theakston v London Trust plc* [1984] BCLC 390. As to the consequences of this, see 8.2.2, below; neither an allotment nor the renunciation of an allotment of shares is a transfer of them: *System Control plc v Munro Corporate plc* [1990] BCLC 659 at pp. 662–3.

[3] These are briefly discussed at 8.2.4, below.

[4] *Re Smith Knight & Co., Weston's Case* (1868) 4 Ch App. 20: *Re Bede Shipping Co.* [1917] 1 Ch 123 at pp. 132–3 (CA).

[5] Since 1980 there has not been any obligation on private companies (as existed previously) to restrict the right of transfer, although restrictions of the sort discussed below are still usual. Article 24 of Table A restricts certain transfers, including transfers of partly paid shares.

[6] *Listing Rules*, Chapter 13, Appendix 1, para. 6. This rule of The Stock Exchange does not prohibit the imposition of purely formal requirements as to transfer.

[7] *Re Smith & Fawcett Ltd* [1942] Ch 304 at p. 306 (CA); *Moodie v W. & J. Shepherd (Bookbinders) Ltd* [1949] 2 All ER 1044 (HL (Sc.)).

Two common forms of restriction found in articles of association are (a) provisions that the board of directors should have a power, general or limited in scope, to refuse to register transfers as they should deem fit, and (b) pre-emption clauses, i.e. provisions that a member wishing to transfer should first offer his shares to other specified persons, such as the directors or the other members. These two forms of restriction will now be discussed in turn, though it must be borne in mind that many other forms of restriction exist as well.

8.2.1 *Power to refuse registration*

Any discretionary power vested in the directors to refuse to register transfers of shares is a fiduciary power, which must be exercised bona fide in what the directors conceive to be the interests of the company.[8] If the transferor can show that the directors have acted wantonly or capriciously or from an improper motive or with a collateral purpose in refusing to register the transfer, the court will order the transfer to be registered.[9] Evidence that the directors were acting upon undertakings given to outsiders would be evidence that their discretion was being improperly exercised,[10] as too would evidence that they had an explicit policy of refusing to allow a particular shareholder to transfer his shares to anyone.[11]

If the directors, having a general and absolute power of refusal, decide to reject a transfer, the court will not interfere provided the requirements as to bona fides are satisfied.[12] Furthermore, it will not compel the directors to state their reasons for the rejection.[13] But the power will be construed strictly, in the sense that in the absence of clear words it will not be held to authorise the directors to refuse to register the executor of a deceased member on a transmission[14] or, in the case of shares being issued to members with a right to renounce, a person to whom a member has duly renounced his right to subscribe.[15] Neither of these transactions involves a 'transfer' strictly so-called.

Where the board's power of refusal is limited to grounds specified in the articles, the board's reasons for a particular refusal are again not examinable.[16] The court is, however, concerned to see that the refusal really is based on at least one of the specified grounds; accordingly, unless the articles stipulate otherwise,[17] the directors may be compelled to identify the particular ground on which their decision to refuse is based.[18] In general, the rule of strict construction applies again. Thus, if the directors' power is expressed to be a right to refuse to register a transfer to a person of whom they do not approve, or whose membership would, in their opinion, be contrary to the interests of the company, their objection must be to something personal to the transferee (for instance, that he cannot pay calls or is a quarrelsome person, or is acting in the interests of a rival business), and if their refusal is on the ground of something which relates only to the transferor (such as that the transfer is made only to increase his voting power), or is on the ground that the directors desire that only members of a particular family should be

---

8 *Re Smith & Fawcett Ltd* [1942] Ch 304 (CA); and see 14.4, below.
9 *Ex parte Penney* (1873) 8 Ch App. 446; *Re Coalport China Co.* [1895] 2 Ch 404 (CA).
10 *Clark v Workman* [1920] 1 Ir. R 107.
11 *Robinson v Chartered Bank* (1865) LR 1 Eq. 32.
12 *Re Smith & Fawcett Ltd* [1942] Ch 304 (CA); *Charles Forte Investments Ltd v Amanda* [1964] Ch 240 (CA).
13 *Ex parte Penney* (1873) 8 Ch App. 446; *Berry v Tottenham Hotspur Football and Athletic Co. Ltd* [1935] Ch 718.
14 See *Re Bentham Mills Spinning Co.* (1879) 11 Ch D 900 (CA).
15 *Re Pool Shipping Co. Ltd* [1920] 1 Ch 251.
16 *Re Coalport China Co.* [1895] 2 Ch 404 (CA).
17 *Berry v Tottenham Hotspur Football and Athletic Co. Ltd* [1935] Ch 718.
18 *Sutherland v British Dominions Land Settlement Corp.* [1926] Ch 746.

shareholders, or that there should not be a number of small holdings, this is in excess of the power, and the court will order registration of the transfer.[19]

Unless the articles expressly make the directors' approval of transfers a condition precedent to their registration, a transfer only fails if there is a positive decision by the directors to reject it; thus if the directors are equally divided on the matter, or there is no board at all, the transfer is entitled to registraton.[20] The same applies if a decision is not reached within a reasonable time after lodgment of transfer[21] and since section 183 (5) of the Companies Act 1985 requires that any company refusing to register a transfer must notify the transferee accordingly within two months of lodgment, it will normally be safe to say that once the two months' period has elapsed, the transfer can no longer be rejected.[22] Subject to these rules, mere silence on the part of the directors does not amount to acquiescence in the transfer.[23]

8.2.2 Pre-emption clauses

Pre-emption clauses constitute valid restrictions upon the transfer of shares.[24] They are enforceable against individual members by the company[25] and by the persons upon whom the rights of pre-emption are bestowed, at least if they are members of the company.[26] A pre-emption clause will be strictly construed; in particular, the court will be reluctant to hold that such a clause fetters the right of a member to transfer his shares to another member at any price that may be agreed upon between them.[27] On the other hand, the court will be prepared to construe a pre-emption clause with sufficient liberality to prevent its obvious purpose being thwarted.[28] Thus, in *Lyle & Scott Ltd v Scott's Trustees*[29] when a company's articles provided that any member 'desirous of transferring his shares' should serve a 'transfer notice' upon the company, thereby setting in train certain procedures whereby other members could exercise rights of pre-emption, the House of Lords held that a member who in return for a sale price executed a transfer of his shares to a non-member and gave him an irrevocable proxy in respect of the votes thereon was 'desirous of transferring' within the meaning of the article, even though both parties to

---

[19] These instances are taken from *Moffat v Farquhar* (1878) 7 Ch D 591; *Re Bell Brothers Ltd* (1891) 65 LT 245; *Re Bede Stream Shipping Co.* [1917] 1 Ch 123 (CA).

[20] See three cases on transmission: *Re Hackney Pavilion Ltd* [1924] 1 Ch 276; *Moodie v W. & J. Shepherd (Bookbinders) Ltd* [1949] 2 All ER 1044 (Sc.)); *Re New Cedos Engineering Co. Ltd* [1994] 1 BCLC 797.

[21] *Re Joint Discount Co., Shepherd's Case* (1866) 2 Ch App. 16.

[22] *Re Swaledale Cleaners Ltd* [1968] 1 WLR 1710 (CA). During the two months' period, the transferee has no rights, even if the company has no directors to exercise the right of refusal: *Re Zinotty Properties Ltd* [1984] 1 WLR 1249.

[23] *Re European Central Rly Co., Gustard's Case* (1868) LR 8 Eq. 468.

[24] Altering the articles to remove such a clause may be unfairly prejudicial conduct within section 459: *Re Kenyon Swansea Ltd* [1987] BCLC 514; see 15.12 *et seq.*, below.

[25] *Borland's Trustee v Steel Brothers & Co. Ltd* [1901] 1 Ch 279; *Lyle & Scott Ltd v Scott's Trustees* [1959] AC 763 (HL (Sc.)); *Jarvis Motors (Harrow) Ltd v Carabott* [1964] 1 WLR 1101.

[26] Cf. *Rayfield v Hands* [1960] Ch 1, where a clause entitling members who wished to sell their shares to require the directors (who were subject to a share qualification) to buy them out at a fair price was held to be enforceable against the directors without the company having to be joined as a party to the proceedings. See further 3.17 and 3.18, above.

[27] *Delavenne v Broadhurst* [1931] 1 Ch 234; *Greenhalgh v Mallard* [1943] 2 All ER 234 (CA).

[28] *Lyle & Scott Ltd v Scott's Trustees* [1959] AC 763 (HL (Sc.)); and see *Jarvis Motors (Harrow) Ltd v Carabott* [1964] 1 WLR 1101.

[29] Above.

the sale had sought to evade the article by refraining from requesting registration of the transfer. The member was accordingly directed to serve a 'transfer notice'.

This decision was distinguished in *Safeguard Industrial Investments Ltd v National Westminster Bank Ltd*.[30] Here, subject to certain exceptions, the articles required a 'proposing transferor' to give notice to the company to set in motion a pre-emption procedure. The bank, executor of a deceased member who had bequeathed his shares to two members of the company, was registered as holder of the shares which it would hold for the latter on completion of the administration of the estate. However, at their request, it did not propose to transfer the shares to the two members. It was held that the bank did not fall within the articles. It had no intention of transferring the shares and the word 'transfer' was apt to cover only the transfer of the legal title to the shares, not the transfer of beneficial interests.

The court left open the question of the effect of an uncompleted agreement to sell shares on the operation of the articles. It may be that, unless the articles are drafted to cover dispositions of equitable interests, nothing short of a declaration of trust or the execution of a transfer and the handing over of an irrevocable proxy, as in the *Lyle & Scott* case, would suffice to bring a member within the terms of standard-form pre-emption provisions such as these.[31]

Where a company's articles provided in essence that shares could not be transferred to any person not already a member of the company if any member was willing to purchase the same, it was held that a term would be implied requiring a member wishing to transfer to take reasonable steps to give notice of his wishes to existing members.[32]

Pre-emption clauses often provide that for the purpose of any sale carried out in accordance therewith the value of the shares should be determined by an accountant, who in performing this task is to act as an expert and not as an arbitrator. An accountant acting under such a clause cannot be compelled to state the basis on which he makes his valuation. If he does not, the valuation is referred to as 'non-speaking' and can be challenged only if not made honestly by the correct person. If the valuer does give reasons (a 'speaking' valuation), his valuation can also be challenged if its basis is significantly erroneous.[33] If the auditor or accountant reaches an incorrect valuation through negligence, he can be sued in damages by the aggrieved party; his function is not sufficiently akin to the judicial to render him immune from such proceedings.[34]

---

[30] [1982] 1 All ER 449 (CA).

[31] See the comments of Vinelott J at first instance, [1980] 3 All ER 849, 859. The *Safeguard* decision was followed in *Theakston v London Trust plc* [1984] BCLC 390, where a member had taken a transfer of shares (not restricted by the articles) with the aid of a loan, charging the shares to the lender as security. At the chargee's request, he was obliged to set in motion the pre-emption procedure in the company's articles. The loan was interest-free and only repayable if and when the member disposed of the shares. It was held that he was not a 'person proposing to transfer' as there was 'no unequivocal obligation to execute any instrument at all at present' (*per* Harman J at p. 401). See also *Re Ringtower Holdings plc* (1989) 5 BCC 82 at p. 99 and *Re Macro (Ipswich) Ltd* [1994] 2 BCLC 354. In the latter case, there had been declarations of trust and transfer documents completed and Arden J had no difficulty in holding (at pp. 401–3) that the members in question were 'desiring to sell'.

[32] *Tett v Phoenix Property Co.* [1986] BCLC 149 (CA). It was held on the facts that the transferor had failed to give such notice and thus the alleged transfer of his shares was void. However, the 'transferee' who had paid the price held the equitable interest in the shares. See also footnote 35, below.

[33] See, in particular, *Dean v Prince* [1953] Ch 590, [1954] Ch 409 (CA); *Burgess v Purchase & Sons Ltd* [1983] 2 All ER 4; for more detail, see *Gore-Browne on Companies* (Jordans, 44th edn, loose-leaf) 16.2.2.

[34] *Arenson v Casson, Beckman Rutley & Co.* [1977] AC 405 (HL).

If shares are sold in contravention of a pre-emption clause and the purchase price is paid, the purchaser acquires an equitable title to them, so that, for instance, a subsequent charging order purporting to bind them in the hands of the vendor is ineffective.[35] There is, of course, no transfer of the legal title while the vendor remains on the register. However, a person who is entitled under the pre-emption clause to have the shares first offered to him can sue to have the register rectified by insertion of his name as legal holder.[36]

8.2.3 Compulsory transfer

A clause to the effect that in the event of bankruptcy a member should sell his shares to particular persons at a particular price cannot be impeached by the member's trustee in bankruptcy, unless the price stipulated is shown to be less than the fair price which could otherwise be obtained. It is likewise not open to attack on the ground that such a restriction upon ownership is repugnant to the nature of personal property.[37]

A company's articles may furthermore contain a clause to the effect that a member infringing any specified regulation or regulations may be compelled by resolution to sell his shares to other members at a specified price. Any resolution passed in pursuance thereof will be valid and effective provided that it is passed bona fide in what the members conceive to be the interests of the company as a whole.[38]

8.2.4 Restrictions not arising out of the articles

Where the articles impose no restrictions upon the transfer of shares, the right to transfer fully paid shares is unlimited,[39] except as follows:

(1) the transferee must have capacity to hold the shares;[40]
(2) the principle of maintenance of capital must be observed;[41] and
(3) certain important restrictions come into operation once a winding-up has commenced.

There is thus nothing objectionable, for instance, in a member transferring some of his shares in order to increase his voting power,[42] and a misdescription of the transferee, even if intentional, gives no ground for setting a transfer aside.[43]

---

[35] *Hawks v McArthur* [1951] 1 All ER 22. Despite dicta to the contrary in *Hunter v Hunter* [1936] AC 222 at p. 261 (HL), *Hawks v McArthur* was followed in *Tett v Phoenix Property Co.* [1984] BCLC 599 by Vinelott J. The point was not argued and was left open by the Court of Appeal ([1986] BCLC 149), where the decision of Vinelott J was overruled on other grounds (see footnote 32, above), but it seems implicit in the Court of Appeal judgment that the purchaser obtains *an* equitable title and this is consistent with the notion that the question of title to property of any sort is relative: cf. Battersby and Preston (1972) 35 MLR 268 arguing in favour of the notion of relative title to goods, but whose argument is applicable, *mutatis mutandis*, to intangible personal property such as shares. See also Borrowdale [1988] JBL 307 and Luxton [1990] JBL 14.

[36] *Hunter v Hunter*, above. As to rectification of the register, see 10.6.3, below.

[37] *Borland's Trustee v Steel Brothers & Co. Ltd* [1901] 1 Ch 279.

[38] See *Phillips v Manufacturers' Securities Co.* (1917) 116 LT 290 (CA); *Sidebottom v Kershaw, Leese & Co.* [1920] 1 CH 154 (CA); *Gaiman v National Association for Mental Health* [1971] Ch 317. As to the application of the same test in determining whether the introduction or deletion of such a clause by an alteration of the articles is valid, see 3.27, above.

[39] Assuming of course that the transferor is the beneficial owner free from any encumbrance.

[40] See 10.5, below.

[41] See 6.11, above.

[42] *Re Stranton Iron and Steel Co.* (1873) LR 16 Eq. 559.

[43] *Re Smith, Knight & Co., Battie's Case* (1870) 39 LJ Ch 391; *Re Financial Insurance Co., Bishop's Case* (1872) 7 Ch App. 296n.

With regard to partly paid shares, the restrictions just mentioned apply, and in addition there are certain grounds upon which a liquidator may in a winding-up set aside transfers made before the commencement thereof.[44]

8.3 The mode of transfer of shares

The formalities of a transfer of shares are in general regulated by the articles and, when applicable, the Stock Transfer Act 1963. If the articles provide for the issue of share warrants to bearer, the transfer of shares comprised in any warrants that are issued is effected by delivery of the warrant.[45] In all other cases, however, section 183 (1) of the Companies Act 1985 provides that, notwithstanding anything in the articles, a 'proper instrument of transfer' must be delivered to the company. Otherwise the company is prohibited from registering the transfer.[46] This phrase means a written instrument 'such as will attract stamp duty under the relevant fiscal legislation'; it does not carry any further implication as to the form of the transfer.[47] As a result of section 183 (1), an oral transfer is ineffective even if the articles purport to make it effective. Furthermore, a clause in the articles purporting to effect an automatic transfer of shares in stipulated circumstances without any written instrument (e.g. from a deceased member to his widow as a beneficial holder) is invalid.[48]

Except where partly paid shares are involved, the actual form of the instrument of transfer may be one of those provided by the Stock Transfer Act 1963; as these are relatively short and simple, they are used in the vast majority of cases.[49]

It is proposed that a computerised system for the transfer of publicly listed shares and other securities be introduced some time in 1996. This will result in changes to the legal regime governing the transfer of such shares, including the modification of section 183. This question is considered further briefly in 8.3.3, below.

8.3.1 The Stock Transfer Act

Under section 1 of the Stock Transfer Act 1963, simplified forms are provided for the transfer of fully paid shares or stock[50] in any company within the meaning of the Companies Act 1985 except an unlimited company or a company limited by guarantee. The section provides for transfer by an instrument in the form set out in Schedule 1, called a 'stock transfer', or any form substantially corresponding thereto.[51] This instrument

[44] As partly paid shares are rare nowadays, no detail is given here; see *Gore-Browne on Companies* (Jordans, 44th edn, loose-leaf) 16.2.4.
[45] As to share warrants, see 8.12, below.
[46] Note, however, that the section expressly disclaims any effect on the power of the company to register as shareholder any person to whom the right to any shares in the company has been transmitted by operation of law: see 8.15, below. Under the Insurance Companies Act 1982, section 50 (4), and the Trade Union and Labour Relations Act 1974, section 4 (4), the requirements of what is now section 183 (1) are bypassed in certain limited situations as set out in the respective statutes.
[47] *Re Paradise Motor Co. Ltd* [1968] 1 WLR 1125 at p. 1141 (CA); *Nisbet v Shepherd* [1994] 1 BCLC 300 (CA).
[48] *Re Greene* [1949] Ch 333.
[49] When they are not used, the transfer must accord with the articles, of which article 23 in Table A is the standard example. As to this, see *Gore-Browne on Companies* (Jordans, 44th edn, loose-leaf), 16.3.1.
[50] The section also covers debentures and other specified forms of security: see section 4 (1).
[51] The relaxation in favour of 'forms substantially corresponding' is contained in section 3 (1). The forms of stock transfer and brokers' transfer contained in Schedules 1 and 2 respectively were amended by the Stock Transfer (Amendment of Forms) Order 1974 (SI 1974 No. 1214), so as to allow standard abbreviations of names of undertakings and descriptions of securities to be used in them.

must be executed by the transferor, execution under hand being sufficient, but need not be executed by the transferee. It must contain particulars of the transferor and of the description and number or amount of the shares or stock and, save where the transfer takes place in pursuance of a 'stock exchange transaction',[52] the nature and amount of the consideration and the full name and address of the transferee must be included. Attestation is unnecessary, and, where the transfer is in pursuance of a stock exchange transaction, these particulars of the consideration and of the transferee may be inserted either in the stock transfer or supplied by means of separate instruments in the form set out in Schedule 2, called 'broker's transfers', or in any form substantially corresponding thereto. Each of these instruments identifies the stock transfer and the particular shares to which it relates, and specifies the consideration paid for such shares.

Alternative forms to those specified in Schedule 1 are provided[53] for use when registered securities are transferred to or from a stock exchange nominee under the Talisman scheme.[54]

Section 1 of the Stock Transfer Act provides forms which are permissible alternatives to, and not in substitution for, those provided for by the articles. Furthermore, any instrument purporting to be in any form which was common or usual for the transfer of shares before the commencement of the Act, or in any other form authorised or required for that purpose save under section 1 itself, is sufficient to transfer shares falling within section 1, whether or not it is completed in accordance with such form, provided that it complies with the requirements as to execution and contents which apply to a stock transfer.[55]

Section 1 of the Act does not affect any right of the company to refuse to register a transfer on any ground other than the form of the transfer, nor does it affect the existing position as regards execution of documents by companies or other bodies corporate. It does, however, apply notwithstanding anything to the contrary in any enactment or instrument relating to the transfer of shares; thus its provisions cannot be excluded by a company's memorandum or articles.[56] Any enactment or instrument relating to the transfer of fully paid shares such as falls within section 1 applies, *mutatis mutandis*, in relation to stock transfers and broker's transfers authorised by that section.[57]

8.3.2 *Procedure on transfer of unlisted shares*

Provided that the share certificate currently issued in respect of unlisted shares being transferred does not also contain shares which are not transferred within the same transaction, the transferor normally delivers the certificate to the transferee along with the executed transfer, receiving in exchange any consideration that is payable. Where,

---

[52] 'Stock exchange transaction' is defined by section 4 (1), coupled with the Stock Transfer (Recognition of Stock Exchanges) Order 1973 (SI 1973 No. 536).

[53] The Stock Transfer (Addition of Forms) Order 1979 (SI 1979 No. 277) and the Stock Transfer (Substitution of Forms) Order 1990 (SI 1990 No. 18), made under section 3 (2) of the Stock Transfer Act (as amended by section 6 of the Stock Exchange (Completion of Bargains) Act 1976), amending section 1 of the 1963 Act.

[54] See 8.3.3, below.

[55] Section 1 (3).

[56] Section 2 (1).

[57] Section 2 (2). Where both a stock transfer and a broker's transfer are used, any reference in any enactment or instrument to the delivery or lodging of an instrument (or proper instrument) of transfer is to be taken as referring to the delivery or lodging of the stock transfer and the broker's transfer; any such reference to the date of lodgment is to be taken as referring to the date on which the later of the two forms of transfer to be lodged was lodged; and it is the broker's transfer that operates as the conveyance and transfer for stamp duty purposes.

however, the certificate contains more shares than those being transferred, an alternative procedure is adopted. The transferor lodges the certificate at the company's office and the fact of lodgment is certified by the company's secretary on the margin of the form of transfer.[58] The certified transfer is returned by the company to the transferor, who in due course delivers it to the transferee, receiving the consideration, if any, payable. After lodgment and registration, two new certificates are made out by the company: one in the name of the transferee, for the shares transferred, and the other in the name of the transferor, for the shares retained by him.

After execution and delivery of the form of transfer to the transferee, it must be stamped, and duty paid[59] within thirty days of execution.[60] Registration of an improperly stamped transfer cannot operate to bring about a legal transfer of the shares into the name of the transferee.

After stamping, the instrument of transfer is delivered to the company, with a request that a new certificate may be prepared and issued to the transferee. Either the transferor[61] or the transferee may be the party who delivers it. Except where the transfer has been certified, the old certificate should accompany the instrument of transfer for the purpose of being cancelled or destroyed, and a new certificate issued in its place. Indeed, the articles usually provide that unless the certificate is produced the transfer will not be passed,[62] and a company receiving the purchase money for shares, the certificate for which was, to the knowledge of the directors, in the hands of a stranger, has been held liable to pay over the amount to the holder of the certificate, who was, in fact, a mortgagee of the shares.[63]

Upon receiving a transfer[64] it is the secretary's duty to satisfy himself that the instrument is properly executed and bears the requisite stamp, and is correct in other particulars, such as the distinctive numbers (if any) of the shares, and that the transferor is the registered holder of the shares expressed to be transferred. If he is a responsible person, the directors are not personally liable to the transferee if they accept his investigations as sufficient.[65]

Before issuing the new certificate to the transferee the secretary may, for the company's protection, send notice of impending registration of the transferee to the transferor.[66]

If the transfer is in order, and no objection is received from the reputed transferor, the secretary should bring the document before the directors at the next board meeting.

On a transfer being brought before the board, the directors should consider whether or

---

[58] As to this, see 8.11, below.

[59] Generally a transfer on sale attracts *ad valorem* duty of 0.5 per cent. See further, *Gore-Browne on Companies* (Jordans, 44th edn, loose-leaf), 16.3.3.

[60] Stamp Act 1892, section 15. The Finance Act 1990 provides for the abolition of stamp duty on the transfer of shares and other securities, but this is not yet in force. It is linked to the creation of a new system for transferring listed securities: see 8.3.3, below.

[61] See Companies Act 1985, section 183 (4).

[62] See e.g. Table A, article 24.

[63] *Rainford v James Keith and Blackburn Co.* [1905] 2 Ch 147 (CA).

[64] The secretary's giving a receipt for the transfer is no warranty that the transfer will be accepted for registration: *Longman v Bath Electric Tramways Ltd* [1905] 1 Ch 646 (CA).

[65] *Dixon v Kennaway & Co.* [1900] 1 Ch 833, but note that the position of a director who actually signs the certificate in the transferee's favour was left open.

[66] But the sending of such a notice does not protect the company where the transfer is forged, even if the true owners makes no reply: *Baxton v London & North-Western Rly Co.* (1890) 24 QBD 77 (CA); *Welch v Bank of England* [1955] Ch 508.

not it should be passed for registration.[67] In addition, if they know that a transfer is made in breach of trust or in fraud of a person having equitable rights, they should not pass the transfer without notifying the person interested,[68] and if they do pass the transfer they may come under a personal liability, although the company is protected by section 360 of the Companies Act 1985[69] which forbids notices of trusts being entered in the register.

If the transfer is passed, a certificate in favour of the transferee must be prepared and ready for delivery to him within two months, unless the terms of issue of the shares otherwise provide.[70]

8.3.3 Procedure on transfer of listed shares

With a few exceptions,[71] the transfer of shares and other securities listed on The Stock Exchange takes place under the 'Talisman' system introduced in 1979. The essential point here is that, by the use of computers, all bargains are settled centrally and central accounts for member firms are maintained, facilitating both the transfer of and payment in respect of Talisman securities. The system works as outlined below.[72]

Listed securities within the system are never registered in the name of a member firm. A holder of securities who has contracted to sell them transfers them to SEPON Ltd (Stock Exchange Pool Nominees Ltd), a company owned by The Stock Exchange, under a 'Talisman Sold Transfer',[73] rather than on the form specified in the Stock Transfer Act. No stamp duty is payable on this transfer. SEPON thus acts as the nominee holder of all stock in the course of settlement and as such is trustee of all stock registered in its name.[74] There is no need for the company to issue a new share certificate to SEPON.[75] Stock thus sold is debited to the account of the selling member. His account is debited at the appropriate settlement date and the account of the buying member is credited.

The legal title to the stock remains vested in SEPON. As soon as a member has bought, his client obtains a beneficial interest but not in any particular stock. His interest is as tenant in common for the appropriate share of all the stock of the description in question held at that time by SEPON. The beneficial owner for the time being of stock in the course of transfer is entitled to receive dividends, take up rights issues and exercise other rights enjoyed by beneficial owners. The Stock Exchange determines who at any particular time is the beneficial owner entitled to these benefits. The ultimate purchaser receives his legal title by means of a 'Talisman Bought Transfer' from SEPON.[76]

It is the intention that dealings in listed securities, as well as the settling of transactions, will be computerised. To that end, The Stock Exchange invested a great deal of resources in seeking to develop a system called TAURUS, and the legislature obliged by passing regulations making some fairly significant changes to the legal regime surrounding the

[67] In accordance with the principles discussed in 8.2.1, above.

[68] Notification is mandatory when a 'stop notice' has been served on the company: see 8.8.1, below.

[69] *Société Générale de Paris v Walker* (1885) 14 QBD 424 (CA); (1886) 11 App. Cas. 20 (HL). As to section 360, see 10.6.1, below.

[70] Section 185; see further 8.10, below.

[71] As to these and the system for their transfer, see *Gore-Browne on Companies* (Jordans, 44th edn, loose-leaf), 16.3.4.

[72] For a fuller account, see Pennington, *Company Law* (Butterworths, 6th edn, 1990) pp. 390–9, and Abrams at 1 Co. Law 17 (1980).

[73] The form is prescribed in the Stock Transfer (Addition of Forms) Order 1979.

[74] The Stock Exchange has rules to protect the investing public from any loss caused by the default of members under the Talisman system.

[75] Section 185 (4).

[76] See footnote 73, above.

transfer of listed securities.[77] These complex regulations abolished the need for share certificates and allowed for title to securities to be evidenced and transferred without a written instrument. Unfortunately, TAURUS proved to be unworkable and was abandoned in May 1993. The Bank of England then took charge of the matter and began developing an alternative system – CREST – with the intention that this be operational in the second half of 1996. New regulations are being devised by the Treasury to replace the existing ones, although they will have a similar basic legal effect as already mentioned.[78] It seems, however, that shareholders will be able to veto their company joining CREST and individually have the option to retain their share certificates.

8.4 The position as between transferor and transferee

Quite apart from the effect of a proper transfer of shares as between the transferor or transferee and the company, questions may arise as to the legal relationship between the transferor and the transferee, particularly when the transfer is, quite properly, refused registration[79] or the parties choose not to seek registration of the transfer. The answers may vary depending on the nature of the transfer, namely whether it was a sale, a gift or a mortgage. These points are explored in the following sections.

8.5 Sales of shares

A contract for the sale of shares may be oral. If the shares are sold through a stock exchange, the usages of the exchange are incorporated into and form part of the contract;[80] an important effect of this principle is that once a vendor and a purchaser are brought together by the negotiations of their brokers on the exchange, the brokers 'drop out' and in general are not parties to the contract of sale ultimately formed.[81]

If the shares to be sold are not specified by the contract, they may be specified at a later stage by appropriation; in many cases (e.g. in sales on The Stock Exchange) this may not occur until the transfer form is filled in. Once the shares have been specified (whether by the contract, or subsequently) the contract becomes enforceable in most cases[82] by specific performance.[83]

A further effect of the shares being specified is that whilst the vendor remains the holder of the legal title to the shares, and is treated by the company as the owner thereof,[84] the beneficial ownership passes to the purchaser,[85] even though the sale is in breach of a pre-emption clause in the articles.[86]

Once the beneficial ownership thus passes, a number of consequences ensue. In the

---

[77] The Uncertificated Securities Regulations 1991 (SI 1991 No. 225), made under section 207 of the Companies Act 1989.

[78] A consultation document with draft regulations was issued in January 1995.

[79] In accordance with a restriction on transfer of the sort discussed earlier in this chapter.

[80] *Coles v Bristowe* (1868) 4 Ch App. 3; *Bowring v Shepherd* (1871) LR 6 QB 309.

[81] *Bowring v Shepherd*, above.

[82] An exception is where a winding-up supervenes, because a transfer would prima facie be void under what is now section 127 of the Insolvency Act 1986; *Sullivan v Henderson* [1973] 1 WLR 333.

[83] *Duncuft v Albrecht* (1841) 12 Sim. 189.

[84] See section 360, discussed at 10.6.1.

[85] *Re National Bank of Wales, Taylor, Phillips and Rickard's case* [1897] 1 Ch 298 at pp. 305–6 (CA); *Wood Preservation Ltd v Prior* [1969] 1 WLR 1077 (CA). As to the passing of beneficial ownership where an option is granted and exercised, see *Hare v Nicoll* [1966] 2 QB 131 (CA).

[86] *Hawks v McArthur* [1951] 1 All ER 22; and see 8.2.2, especially at footnote 35, above.

absence of express provision in the contract, the purchaser becomes entitled as against the vendor to any dividends subsequently declared in respect of the shares, even if such dividend relates back wholly or partly to a period prior to the passing of beneficial ownership.[87] Dividends declared before the beneficial ownership passes but paid thereafter may, however, be retained by the vendor.[88] In practice, where shares are sold on The Stock Exchange near the time of declaration of a dividend the contract normally provides whether the sale is to be *ex div.* or *cum div.* If after the beneficial ownership has passed a call is made or a contribution sought in a winding-up in respect of the shares, the vendor is the person liable to the company,[89] but he is entitled to an indemnity from the purchaser[90] (unless the contract of sale provides otherwise), or indeed against any sub-purchaser who has become beneficially entitled to the shares.[91] As to calls made before the beneficial ownership passes, the vendor has no indemnity, but if he fails to pay, the company may make a fresh call against the purchaser after registration of the transfer.[92]

Voting rights are subject to slightly different principles. The vendor, while he remains the registered holder, is from the company's point of view the person entitled to exercise the voting rights attached to the shares. The purchaser acquires the right to direct how the votes should be cast, not when the beneficial ownership passes to him, but when he has paid the full purchase price for the shares.[93] When the purchaser is in default in paying for the shares, a clause in the contract of sale providing that all rights pass to the vendor on a specified date before completion will be construed, in the absence of compelling language to the contrary effect, as not depriving the unpaid vendor of his right to vote.[94]

Upon a sale of shares the seller is only bound to execute a proper transfer and deliver it with the share certificate to the purchaser. He does not warrant that the company will accept the transferee,[95] and even if the company wrongfully refuses to register the purchaser he can, it seems, keep the purchase money.[96] He must not, however, do anything to hinder registration; if he does, he may be made liable in damages.[97]

Subject to the terms of the contract, the obligations of the purchaser are to prepare the form of transfer[98] (though often in practice the vendor takes over the task), to execute it (if this is necessary to obtain registration), to pay the purchase price and stamp duty and to lodge the transfer for registration.[99]

---

[87] *Black v Homersham* (1879) 4 Ex. D 24; *Re Wimbush* [1940] Ch 92. The vendor is, moreover, bound to take steps to collect the dividend so as to be able to pay it over to the purchaser: *Stevenson v Wilson* 1907 SC 445.

[88] *Re Kidner* [1929] 2 Ch 121.

[89] *Ex parte Hennessy* (1849) 2 Mac & C. 201.

[90] *Bowring v Shepherd* (1871) LR 6 QB 309; *Re National Bank of Wales Taylor, Phillips and Rickard's Case* [1897] 1 Ch 298 at pp. 305–6 (CA).

[91] *Spencer v Ashworth, Partington & Co.* [1925] 1 KB 589 (CA).

[92] *New Balkis Eersteling Ltd v Randt Gold Mining Co.* [1904] AC 165 (HL).

[93] *Musselwhite v C. H. Musselwhite & Son Ltd* [1962] Ch 964; see also *Re Piccadilly Radio plc* [1989] BCLC 683 at p. 696.

[94] *JRRT (Investments) Ltd v Haycroft* [1993] BCLC 401, applying the principle in *Alghussein Establishment v Eton College* [1988] 1 WLR 587, HL, that it is to be presumed that the parties did not intend that either should enjoy benefits between the contract date and completion arising from their own default.

[95] *Skinner v City of London Marine Corp.* (1885) 14 QBD 882 (CA).

[96] *London Founders Association v Clarke* (1888) 20 QBD 576 (CA).

[97] *Hooper v Herts* [1906] 1 Ch 549 (CA).

[98] *Birkett v Cowper-Coles* (1919) 35 TLR 298.

[99] *Re Stranton Iron and Steel Co.* (1873) LR 16 Eq. 559. The vendor may do this if the contract so permits; section 183 (4).

Where an unpaid vendor of shares executes a transfer and delivers it to the purchaser along with the share certificate, he has, unless the contract of sale otherwise provides, a lien upon the shares for payment of the purchase price. The company cannot, however, be required to accept notice of the lien, which may therefore be overridden if the shares are transferred to a bona fide purchaser for value without notice.[100]

8.6 Gifts of shares

Where shares are transferred by way of gift, the beneficial ownership does not pass to the donee until the donor has done all within his power to implement registration of the donee as transferee.[101] In the ordinary course, this means executing a transfer in the proper form and delivering it to the donee or to the company along with the relevant certificate, but if further requirements are imposed upon the donor by the articles or by statute these must also be complied with.[102] Until the donor has done all within his power to implement registration, the intended gift is revocable, the donee having no equity to compel the donor to perfect it and no right to ask the court to construe it as a declaration of trust.[103] On the other hand, if the donor has done everything that is required of him, but registration does not occur through some act or omission of one or more third parties (e.g. a refusal by the board to register the transfer, in exercise of a power in the articles), the donor is, it seems, treated as a trustee of the shares for the donee.[104]

8.7 Mortgages of shares

A legal mortgage of shares can only be implemented by registration of a transfer to the mortgagee, though the parties will, of course, agree between themselves that it is a transfer by way of security only. From the point of view of the company the transfer will operate as an out-and-out transfer, so that, if the shares are partly paid, the mortgagee will be personally liable for calls.[105] Equally, anyone inspecting the share register or the share certificate issued to the mortgagee will be induced, if he does not know the true position, to treat the mortgagee as the absolute owner of the shares at law and in equity. The mortgagor may accordingly protect his equity of redemption by serving a 'stop notice' on the company.'[106]

An equitable mortgage or charge upon shares can be created simply by deposit of the share certificate as security for the relevant advance.[107] Alternatively or in addition, the parties may execute and deliver to the mortgagee a transfer in blank. If the mortgagee receives both the share certificate and a transfer in blank, he may exercise his power of sale in the event of default by the mortgagor without having to apply to the court for an

---

[100] *Langen & Wind Ltd v Bell* [1972] Ch 685; and see the discussion of priorities at 8.8, below.

[101] *Re Rose* [1949] Ch 78; *Re Rose* [1952] Ch 499 (CA); *Re Paradise Motor Co. Ltd* [1968] 1 WLR 1125 (CA); *Vandervell v C.I.R.* [1967] 2 AC 291, 330 (HL).

[102] *Re Fry* [1946] Ch 312.

[103] *Milroy v Lord* (1862) 4 De G. F. & J. 264.

[104] *Re Rose* [1952] Ch 499 at p. 510 (CA) *per* Evershed MR. Doubts, however, have been expressed about this proposition (see e.g. Hanbury and Martin, *Modern Equity* (Sweet & Maxwell, 14th edn 1993), pp. 120–1), on the ground that it contradicts the general rule that an imperfect gift can never be construed as a declaration of trust because the donor has no intention to constitute himself a trustee (as to which, see e.g. *Jones v Lock* (1865) 1 Ch App. 25).

[105] *Re Land Credit Co. of Ireland, Weikersheim's Case* (1873) 8 Ch App. 831.

[106] See 8.8.1, below. This is not possible in a Scottish company.

[107] *Harrold v Plenty* [1907] 2 Ch 314. In a Scottish company, only registration of the mortgagee by the company will constitute a valid mortgage.

order for sale, just as a legal mortgagee may do.[108] Furthermore, subject to certain difficulties which arise when the transfer is required by the articles to be by deed,[109] he may at any time convert the mortgage into a legal mortgage by filling in his own name as transferee and procuring registration of the transfer.[110] While the mortgage remains equitable only, it is the mortgagee who should consider protecting his interest; this he may do by serving a stop notice.[111]

8.8 Priorities in England

Competing claims to the beneficial entitlement to shares sometimes arise in the context of share transfers in England.[112] Contests may arise between the registered holder of the shares and a claimant asserting a prior or a subsequent equity, or between two equitable claimants.[113]

Generally speaking, the registered holder, as legal owner, will prevail over a prior equitable claimant if he gave valuable consideration for the transfer through which he acquired his legal title[114] unless before the time of giving such consideration he had notice of the prior equity.[115] As against a subsequent equitable claim not created by his own act or with his authority, he will generally prevail, but not if his conduct has been such as to disentitle or estop him from asserting his rights against the person asserting the claim.[116]

As between two equitable claimants, the earlier in point of time prevails,[117] unless his conduct has been such to disentitle or estop him,[118] or, it has been said, the later claimant has acquired 'a present, absolute unconditional right to registration'.[119] It is not clear what this last phrase means, as in a later case a transferee for value who had lodged a transfer for registration was held not to have acquired such a right even though the directors had no power to refuse to register the transfer.[120]

Some authority is available as to the type of conduct that will disentitle or estop a legal or equitable claimant as against a subsequent equitable claimant. The mere fact that the beneficiaries under a trust of shares leave the share certificate in the hands of the trustees does not constitute such conduct,[121] but, according to an Irish case, a first mortgagee who fails to obtain the certificate relating to the mortgaged shares will be 'disentitled' as against a subsequent claimant who has acquired an equitable interest for value from the

---

[108] *Stubbs v Slater* [1910] 1 Ch 632 (CA). This is not possible in a Scottish company.

[109] See *Gore-Browne on Companies* (Jordans, 44th edn, loose-leaf), 16.14.

[110] *Re Tahiti Cotton Co.* (1874) LR 17 Eq. 273.

[111] See 8.8.1, below.

[112] The problems discussed here do not arise in Scottish law.

[113] It should be noted that particular problems can arise when transfers of shares are executed in blank. These are considered in *Gore-Browne on Companies*, 16.5.1.

[114] *Shropshire Union Railways and Canal Co. v R* (1875) LR 7, HL 496; *Guy v Waterlow Brothers and Layton Ltd* (1909) 25 TLR 515; *Langen & Wind Ltd v Bell* [1972] Ch 685. Where the articles give a company a 'first and paramount' lien over the shares of any shareholder indebted to it, this will prevail over an equitable charge over those shares given to a third party: *Champagne Perrier-Jouet S. A. v H. H. Finch Ltd* [1982] 3 All ER 713.

[115] See *Dodds v Hills* (1865) 2 H & M 424. *Sheffield v London Joint Stock Bank* (1888) 13 App. Cas. 333 (HL).

[116] *Fry v Smellie* [1912] 3 KB 282 (CA).

[117] *Roots v Williamson* (1888) 38 Ch D 485; *Peat v Clayton* [1906] 1 Ch 659.

[118] See *Shropshire Union Railways and Canal Co. v R*, above, in which disentitling conduct was said to comprise 'misconduct or fraud or negligence' (p. 514).

[119] *Société Générale de Paris v Walker* (1886) 11 App. Cas. 20 at p. 29 (HL).

[120] *Ireland v Hart* [1902] 1 Ch 522.

[121] *Shropshire Union Railways and Canal Co v R*, above.

mortgagor, bona fide believing him to have an unencumbered title because he held the certificate.[122]

8.8.1 *Notice to the company*

In cases involving questions of priority, the mere fact that the company has notice of an equitable claim is not enough of itself to give that claimant priority over other claims of which the company has no notice; in other words, the rule in *Dearle v Hall* has no application.[123] The company is bound by statute not to enter on the register notice of any trust, express, implied or constructive,[124] and this rule is often widened in the articles[125] to take in any equitable interest whatsoever. On receiving notice of an equitable claim, the company may, however, decide against registering a competing transferee,[126] or may even remove such a transferee from the register,[127] in which event this transferee's position may be weaker through being based on equitable rights only.

With the same purpose in mind – that of preventing a competing claimant from strengthening his position by obtaining registration of a transfer – any person claiming a beneficial interest in shares may apply *ex parte*, by summons or motion in the Chancery Division, for an order prohibiting the registration of any transfer of the shares.[128] This will serve to 'freeze' the position while the rights of the competing claimants are worked out.

A final form of protection for equitable claimants is the serving of a 'stop notice', a procedure which is regulated by the Rules of the Supreme Court, Order 50, rules 11–14. By the terms of these rules, any person who has such an interest may, upon making and filing an affidavit of his interest, and serving an office copy of the affidavit and a notice on the company, require it to stop the transfer of or the payment of dividends upon the shares in question. This notice is not enough to give the server priority over a claimant to whom, under the rules just discussed, he ranks subject.[129] However, it prevents the company from registering a transfer of the shares or paying the dividends without giving the server an opportunity of applying to the court to prevent the transfer or payment. But if the person in whose name the shares stand requests the company to transfer or pay, the company must notify the server of the notice, and if he does not within fourteen days obtain an order from the court, the company may proceed, despite the notice, to deal with the shares or pay the dividends as requested. This course is, in practice, very little resorted to; but it will be obvious that a very valuable method is provided for checking any anticipated or possible misappropriation of shares by a trustee or person whose title to them is not absolute. If such a notice is served on the company, it must be careful not to register any transfer or pay any dividend without referring to the server of the notice. If it does register a transfer, so as to cause the interest asserted by the server of the notice to be

---

[122] *Kelly v Munster and Leinster Bank* (1891) 29 LR Ir (Eq) 19.

[123] *Société Générale de Paris v Walker* (1886) 11 App. Cas. 20 (HL).

[124] Companies Act 1985, section 360. For an instance of the application of a similar provision in Commonwealth legislation, see *Simpson v Molson's Bank* [1895] AC 270 (PC). This rule apparently extends to notice of an unpaid vendor's lien: see *Langen & Wind Ltd v Bell* [1972] Ch 685. In this case Brightman J may, however, have been thinking of common-form provisions in company articles such as the provision referred to in the next footnote.

[125] See e.g. Table A, article 5.

[126] See e.g. *Roots v Williamson* (1888) 38 Ch D 485; and see 8.3.2, above.

[127] This was done in *Peat v Clayton* [1906] 1 Ch 659.

[128] RSC Ord. 50, rule 15.

[129] *Wilkins v Sibley* (1863) 4 Giff 442 at p. 446.

overridden, the directors,[130] and possibly also the company itself, will be liable to him in damages for the loss which he has suffered.

A judgment-creditor who has taken out a charging order in respect of shares does not thereby obtain the right to receive notice of and oppose the impending registration of any transfer presented by the registered holder. He does, however, have a sufficient interest in the shares to provide the basis for a stop notice, and if he proceeds to serve such a notice, he will be protected to the extent described.[131]

8.9 Forged transfers

A forged transfer is in law no transfer, and gives the alleged transferee no rights, not even if the company issues to him a certificate stating that he is the holder of the shares which the transfer purports to assign.[132] If the company, acting upon a forged transfer, removes the true owner from the register and substitutes the supposed transferee, it can be compelled to reinstate the true owner and replace or restore his shares.[133] In England, the Limitation Act only runs against the true owner as from the time when his demand for reinstatement to the register is refused.[134] He can claim any intervening dividends from the company, which can in turn claim them from the transferee.[135]

By reason of a general law principle of estoppel discussed in the next section, persons who suffer damage through relying on the share certificate issued pursuant to a forged transfer can in general recover compensation for their loss from the company.[136] But estoppel cannot be invoked by a person who has presented for registration a forged transfer in his favour. Indeed, such a person may instead be required by the company to reimburse it for any damages that it has been compelled to pay out to a third party under the estoppel principle.[137] Thus a transferee taking a forged transfer can only claim damages under the estoppel principle when two conditions are satisfied: (a) that someone other than him presented the transfer for registration, and (b) that he relied on the certificate to his detriment, e.g. in being 'put to rest' thereby so that he delayed in taking action against the forger until the forger, through becoming bankrupt or for some other reason, ceased to be able to satisfy the transferee's claim against him in respect of the forgery.[138]

The proposition, just stated, that a company can claim reimbursement for any damages it has had to pay out on a forged transfer, from the person who presented the transfer for registration, stems from the wider principle that a person presenting a transfer impliedly warrants that it is genuine and given with due authority. Thus a broker who deposits a forged transfer in good faith is liable to the company for loss it may suffer thereby,[139] and, if a broker represents, whether in good faith or not, that he has authority

---

[130] *Société Générale de Paris v Walker* (1884) 14 QBD 424 at p. 453 (CA) (affd (1885) 11 App. Cas. 20 (HL)).

[131] *Adams v Bank of England* (1908) 52 SJ 682.

[132] *Simm v Anglo-American Telegraph Co.* (1879) 5 QBD 188 (CA).

[133] *Barton v North Staffordshire Rly Co.* (1888) 38 Ch D 458. This applies even if the true owner has been notified of the transfer before its registration but has failed to make any objection to it: see 8.3, above.

[134] *Barton v North Staffordshire Rly Co.*, above; *Welch v Bank of England* [1955] Ch 508.

[135] *Foster v Tyne Pontoon and Dry Dock Co.* (1893) 63 LJQB 50.

[136] *Re Bahia and San Francisco Rly Co.* (1868) LR 3 QB 584; *Dixon v Kennaway & Co.* [1900] 1 Ch 833.

[137] *Sheffield Corp. v Barclay* [1905] AC 392 (HL); *Welch v Bank of England*, above; *Yeung v Hong Kong and Shanghai Bank* [1981] AC 787 (PC).

[138] *Dixon v Kennaway & Co.*, above.

[139] *Sheffield Corp. v Barclay*, above; *Yeung v Hong Kong and Shanghai Bank*, above. It may be, though, that this principle should be reviewed in the light of the Civil Liability (Contribution) Act 1978; ibid., pp. 799–800.

to act for the supposed transferor when in fact he has not, he is liable to the company upon an implied warranty that he has authority.[140]

8.10 Share certificates

The articles almost invariably give to each member a right, free of charge, to a certificate or certificates indicating the share or shares to which he is entitled;[141] indeed, by virtue of section 185 (1) of the Companies Act 1985, a member is entitled to a certificate unless this right is expressly excluded by the conditions of issue. The usual practice is to include in one certificate all the shares of the same class held by a member. The articles also generally state how such a certificate is to be signed. Table A, articles 6 and 101, require it to be under the seal of the company, and to be signed by a director and by the secretary or by a second director, unless the directors determine that some other or others shall sign it. The certificate is not a deed,[142] however, and it does not attract stamp duty.

Section 185 (1) requires every company, unless the conditions of issue otherwise provide, to complete and have ready for delivery the certificates of shares within two months after allotment or lodgment of any transfer of shares.[143] If notice has been served requiring the company to make good any default with respect to the issue of certificates and the default is not made good within ten days after service of the notice, the court may, on the application of the person entitled to have the certificate delivered to him, order the company and any officer of the company to make good the default within a specified time, and the order may provide that all costs of and incidental to the application shall be borne by the company or by any officer responsible for the default.[144] Where the shares are listed on The Stock Exchange, the two months' time is reduced to five business days,[145] but section 185 (1) does not apply to transfers to a 'stock exchange nominee' under the 'Talisman' system.[146]

8.10.1 Evidence of title

A certificate under the seal of the company is prima facie evidence of the title of the person named to the shares;[147] but it does not given the person an indefeasible right to the shares. If it can be shown that the holder obtained the shares from some person who could not give him a title to them, the name of the true owner will be retained upon or restored to the register, and the holder will lose the shares.[148] But if the holder acquired the shares in good faith and for value, relying upon an untrue certificate issued to his predecessor by the company, the company will be estopped from denying his title to the shares which he has been induced to buy or pay for by being shown the certificate.[149]

---

[140] *Starkey v Bank of England* [1903] AC 114 (HL).

[141] See e.g. Table A, article 6.

[142] *South London Greyhound Racecourses v Wake* [1931] 1 Ch 496; *R v Williams* [1942] AC 541 (PC).

[143] 'Transfer' here means a transfer duly stamped and otherwise valid, and does not include any transfer which the company is for any reason entitled to refuse to register and does not register.

[144] Section 185 (6) and (7).

[145] *Listing Rules*, 9.40.

[146] Section 185 (4); see 8.3.3, above. Note the comments in 8.3.3 regarding the future of share certificates.

[147] Section 186.

[148] See 8.9, above.

[149] *Re Bahia and San Francisco Rly Co.* (1868) LR 3 QB 584; *Re Ottos Kopje Diamond Mines Ltd* [1893] 1 Ch 618 (CA). This estoppel arises when the holder, having been refused registration or having been removed from the register to make way for the true owner, sues the company for damages for wrongful refusal or wrongful removal.

Similarly, if after acquiring the shares in good faith and for value, he makes a contract to resell them in reliance on an untrue certificate issued to him and is then compelled to pay damages to his purchaser or buy other shares in order to fulfil the contract, he may recover his loss from the company.[150] If, however, the certificate is a forgery, the company comes under no liability, even when the forgery was the act of its secretary.[151] Furthermore, if the certificate is in fact correct, stating that a certain person is the registered holder of the shares, the company will not be liable to a purchaser from him by reason of having certified a previous transfer of the shares to another person, even though the company has parted with the certificate to the registered holder after certifying the transfer, thus enabling the registered holder to deal with the shares again. The proximate cause of the loss by the purchaser is taken to be the fraud of the registered holder and not the negligence (if any) of the company, and in any event any duty of the company to ensure that the certificate in such circumstances is sent to the registered holder is owed to the registered holder only, not to third parties such as purchasers.[152]

Another form of estoppel may arise against the company if it issues a certificate which states that the shares comprised in it are fully paid when in fact they are only partly paid or have nothing paid up on them. If the shares come into the hands of a bona fide transferee for value who relied upon such a statement in the certificate held by his predecessor and had no knowledge of the true position, the company will be estopped as against him from denying that they are fully paid and thus will be prevented from claiming from him the amount unpaid on the shares or any part thereof.[153]

8.11 Certification of transfers

The act of certification of a transfer of shares is often a step in the process of transfer; its general nature and purpose have already been described.[154] The position of persons, such as transferees, who act on the faith of a certification by the company is dealt with in section 184:

> The certification by a company of any instrument of transfer[155] of shares in or debentures of the company is to be taken as a representation by the company to any person acting on the faith of the certification that there have been produced to the company such documents as on their face show a prima facie title to the shares or debentures in the transferor named in the instrument of transfer. However, the certification is not to be taken as a representation that the transferor has any title to the shares or debentures.

For the purposes of the section a transfer is to be deemed to be certified if it bears the words 'certified lodged', or words to this effect.[156]

The section further provides that when any person acts on the faith of a false

---

[150] *Balkis Consolidated Co. Ltd v Tomkinson* [1893] AC 396 (HL).

[151] *Ruben v Great Fingall Consolidated* [1906] AC 439 (HL); *South London Greyhound Racecourses Ltd v Wake* [1931] 1 Ch 496; but these cases may not be followed today – see 4.34, above.

[152] *Longman v Bath Electric Tramways Ltd* [1905] 1 Ch 646 (CA).

[153] *Burkinshaw v Nicholls* (1878) 3 App. Cas. 1004 (HL); *Re British Farmers' Pure Linseed Cake Co.* (1878) 7 Ch D 533 (CA).

[154] See 8.3.2, above.

[155] 'Instrument of transfer' includes a broker's transfer under the Stock Transfer Act 1963; see section 2 (2) of that Act.

[156] Section 184 (3) (*a*).

certification made negligently, the company is to be under the same liability to him as if the certification had been made fraudulently.[157]

Decisions[158] prior to 1948 established that where an agent of a company had authority to certify transfers but fraudulently did so without the share certificates having been lodged, he was not acting within the scope of his authority and accordingly his act was not the act of the company. These decisions were substantially overruled by what is now section 184 (3) (*b*), which provides that certification is to be deemed to be made by the company if (a) the person issuing the instrument is a person authorised to issue certificated transfers on the company's behalf, and (b) the certification is signed by a person authorised to certificate transfers on the company's behalf or by any officer or servant of the company or of another company which is so authorised. It would seem, however, that the old law still applies where the secretary or other officer fraudulently certifying the transfer had no authority to certify transfers at all.

A certification is to be deemed to be signed by a person if it purports to be authenticated by his signature or initials (whether handwritten or not), unless it is shown that the signature or initials were placed there neither by himself nor by a person authorised to use the signature or initials for the purpose of certificating transfers on the company's behalf.[159]

8.12 Share warrants

By virtue of the Companies Act 1985, section 188 (1), the articles of any company limited by shares may contain a power to issue 'share warrants' to bearer in respect of fully paid shares.[160] The effect of the issue of a share warrant is to make the bearer of it absolutely entitled to the shares named in it, and the ownership can accordingly be passed by mere delivery.[161] No person purchasing a share warrant need make any inquiry as to the title of the person who sells it, any more than if he were receiving a banknote, but if the holder has in fact stolen or fraudulently obtained a share warrant, he can, of course, be compelled to surrender it in the same way as a thief would have to give up a banknote.

The company may provide for the payment of dividends by coupons or otherwise.[162] It is usual to do this by coupons attached to the warrant, each stating that the bearer is entitled to the dividend for a certain year or half-year, or to the first, second, or third dividend declared, and in such case the bearer of the coupon, and not of the warrant, is entitled to the dividend.

Subject to the regulations of the company, the bearer of a share warrant can return it to the company, and be re-entered upon the register as a shareholder, the warrant being thereupon cancelled.[163] The company will be responsible for any loss incurred by any person if the name of a bearer of a share warrant is entered in the register without the warrant being surrendered and cancelled.[164]

---

[157] Section 184 (2).

[158] *George Whitechurch Ltd v Cavanagh* [1902] AC 117 (HL); *Kleinwort v Associated Automatic Machine Corp.* (1934) 50 TLR 244 (HL).

[159] Section 184 (3) (*c*).

[160] Table A contains no relevant article. Share warrants have not been popular, partly because of former exchange control legislation, but there is evidence of their increasing use: see *Gore-Browne on Companies*, (Jordans, 44th edn, loose-leaf), 16.9.

[161] Section 188 (2).

[162] Section 188 (1).

[163] Section 355 (2).

[164] Section 355 (3).

Without exception, the bearer of a share warrant may, if the articles of the company so provide, be deemed to be a member of the company, either to the full extent or for any purposes defined in the articles.[165] For the purpose, however, of any provision in the articles requiring a director or manager to hold a specified share qualification the bearer of a share warrant is not to be deemed to be the holder of the shares specified in the warrant.[166]

On the issue of a share warrant a company must strike out of its register the name of the holder of the shares represented, and enter particulars as to the date of issue of the warrant, and a statement of the shares represented by it, distinguishing each share by its number (if any). If the warrant is surrendered the date of the surrender must be entered in the register.[167]

Before a share warrant is signed, sealed or issued, it must be stamped, the duty being three times the amount which would be chargeable on a transfer of the shares specified in the warrant if the consideration for the transfer were the nominal value of such shares.[168]

8.13 The transmission of shares

A transmission of shares occurs upon the holder dying, becoming a patient under the Mental Health Act 1983, or becoming bankrupt. The persons or person with whom the company must deal in such a case are the executors or administrators of a deceased shareholder, the committee or receiver of a Mental Health Act patient, or the trustee of a bankrupt, all of whom may be described by the words 'the representatives of the former holder'.

8.14 Trustees in bankruptcy

The title of the trustee in bankruptcy to the shares of the bankrupt is conferred by the Insolvency Act 1986, which vests the property in the shares in him,[169] empowers him to exercise the right of transfer to the same extent as the bankrupt could have done,[170] and authorises him to disclaim the shares.[171] Thus, unless the articles otherwise provide, the trustee can take the shares into his own name, leave them in the name of the bankrupt, transfer them without first taking them into his own name, or disclaim them, but in each case the rights of third parties are left unaffected.[172]

When the trustee takes the shares into his own name he can insist upon a 'clean' certificate; i.e. he can object to an entry in the register or upon the certificate to the effect that he holds them as trustee or subject to a lien.[173] By taking partly paid shares into his own name, he becomes personally liable for calls on them.

If the trustee elects to leave the shares in the bankrupt's name, the bankrupt can vote upon the shares and give proxies, but he must exercise these powers in accordance with

---

[165] Section 355 (5), to which cf. section 22 (2).

[166] Section 291 (2).

[167] Section 355 (1) and (4).

[168] Finance Act 1963, section 59 (1). This provision will be abolished (under the Finance Act 1990) when stamp duty on the transfer of shares generally is abolished; see 8.3.2, above.

[169] Section 306.

[170] Section 314 and Schedule 5.

[171] Section 315. As to the trustee's power to disclaim, see *Gore-Browne on Companies* (Jordans, 44th edn, loose-leaf), 15.5.

[172] See *Re Cannock and Rugeley Colliery Co.* (1885) 28 Ch D 363 (CA); *Wise v Lansdell* [1912] 1 Ch 420.

[173] *Re W. Key & Sons Ltd* [1902] 1 Ch 467.

the trustee's directions.[174] He cannot sue the company to enforce his personal rights, but in appropriate cases he probably has the *locus standi* to bring a derivative action to redress a wrong done to the company.[175] The trustee for his part does not have the *locus standi* to present a petition to wind up the company.[176] The bankrupt estate, and not the trustee, is liable for calls on any partly paid shares, and the company can prove for the estimated value of any future calls.[177]

8.15 Executors and administrators

On the death of a shareholder other than a joint holder, even if he bequeaths his shares to a specific legatee, the executor or administrator is the person entitled to the shares so far as the company is concerned, because he has the legal title to them.[178] The title of the executor or administrator is shown by the probate or letters of administration, which must be produced to the company for registration.[179] Thereafter the executor or administrator is the person with whom the company must deal in all matters relating to the shares. His title cannot be bypassed by an article purporting on the death of the holder to vest the shares in someone else.[180] Equally, the directors cannot reject an executor's claim to be registered as the holder of shares held by the testator, relying upon an article which enables them to refuse transfers, because such an article does not apply to a transmission by operation of law.[181] There must instead be an express power of veto conferred by the articles to justify a refusal to enter the name of an executor on the register of members.[182] The articles may give the directors in such a case the same right to decline registrations they would have had in the case of a transfer of the share by the deceased. A provision in the articles that on the death of a member his shares must be offered to the other members at par can be enforced against the executors of a deceased member, and has been construed so as to operate even when there is only one member surviving.[183] Where the articles of a company permitted the transfer of shares to, among others, 'privileged relatives', while allowing the directors to refuse to register other transfers, and incorporated the provisions of Table A[184] providing for the same position to apply in the case of transmission by death or bankruptcy, it was held that the personal representatives of a deceased member could not be prevented from transferring the shares to his beneficiary who was within the class of privileged relative.[185]

Articles sometimes compel representative holders either to take the shares in their own names, assuming all the responsibilities of a member of the company, or to nominate

---

[174] *Morgan v Gray* [1953] Ch 83.

[175] *Birch v Sullivan* [1957] 1 WLR 1247; and see 15.8, below.

[176] *Re H. L. Bolton Engineering Co. Ltd.* [1956] Ch 677. There is nothing to prevent the bankrupt presenting a petition on the trustee's behalf: see *Re K/9 Meat Supplies (Guildford) Ltd* [1966] 1 WLR 1112.

[177] *Re McMahon* [1900] 1 Ch 173.

[178] See *Roberts v Letter 'T' Estates Ltd* [1961] AC 795 (PC). This is normally confirmed in the articles: see e.g. Table A, 85 article 29.

[179] See the Companies Act 1985, section 187. In a Scottish estate, confirmation is the equivalent.

[180] *Re Greene* [1949] Ch 333.

[181] *Re Bentham Mills Spinning Co.* (1879) 11 Ch D 900 (CA).

[182] *Scott v Frank F. Scott (London) Ltd* [1940] Ch 794 (CA).

[183] *Jarvis Motors (Harrow) Ltd v Carabott* [1964] 1 WLR 1101.

[184] The relevant Table A articles were articles 30 and 31 of the 1948 Table A, but in this respect the 1985 Table A has the same effect.

[185] *Re William Steward (Holdings) Ltd* [1994] BCC 284, CA.

some other person to take the shares. If such provisions are not in the articles, there is nothing to prevent representative holders from continuing to allow the shares to remain in the name of the deceased shareholder.[187] But in the absence of express provisions in the articles[188] the representatives are not entitled to have any notice sent to them or to the registered address of the deceased unless such representative holders become members by formal registration.[189] If the company has not been notified of the death of a member, it is entitled to assume that a notice sent to his registered address has been duly received.[190]

While the shares thus remain in the name of the deceased holder, his estate is prima facie entitled to any subsequent benefits deriving from the shares and is liable to pay any subsequent calls.[191] It follows that, if the articles require that new shares must be offered to the members, the estate of a deceased member must not be ignored when a new issue is made.[192] Similarly, in the event of reconstruction under section 110 of the Insolvency Act 1986, an executor or administrator can exercise the statutory right of dissent.[193] He has also the necessary *locus standi* to present a petition to wind up the company,[194] or to challenge a resolution for voluntary winding up,[195] or to institute proceedings under section 459[196] or section 653[197], but he is not to be counted in determining whether there is a sufficient quorum at a general meeting unless the articles otherwise provide,[198] nor in determining whether the company's membership has fallen below the statutory minimum prescribed by sections 1 and 24.[199]

Whether the personal representatives have taken the shares into their own names or not, they can transfer them.[200]

---

[187] *City of Glasgow Bank in Liquidation, Buchan's Case* (1879) 4 App. Cas. 549 at pp. 588–9 (HL (Sc.)).

[188] See e.g. Table A, article 38.

[189] See *Allen v Gold Reefs of West Africa Ltd* [1900] 1 Ch 656 (CA), where, however, the point was expressly covered by an article.

[190] *New Zealand Gold Extraction Co. (Newbery-Vautin Process) v Peacock* [1894] 1 QB 622 (CA).

[191] *James v Buena Ventura Syndicate Ltd* [1896] 1 Ch 446 at pp. 464–5 (CA); and see Table A, articles 29 and 31.

[192] *James v Buena Ventura Syndicate Ltd*, above.

[193] *Llewellyn v Kasintoe Rubber Estates Ltd* [1914] 2 Ch 670.

[194] See *Re Cuthbert Cooper & Sons Ltd* [1937] Ch 392; *Re Chesterfield Catering Co.* [1976] 3 WLR 879.

[195] *Howling's Trustee v Smith* (1905) 7 F. 390.

[196] Section 459 (2); see 15.12, below.

[197] *Re Bayswater Trading Co. Ltd* [1970] 1 WLR 343.

[198] *Re J. Franklin & Son Ltd* [1937] 4 All ER 43.

[199] *Re Bowling and Welby's Contract* [1895] 1 Ch 663 (CA); and see 10.6, below.

[200] Section 183 (3). See further as to the procedure to be adopted on a transmission of shares, *Gore-Browne on Companies* (Jordans, 44th edn, loose-leaf), 16.13.

9 Debentures, Charges and Debenture Holders' Remedies

9.1 Introduction

The immediately preceding chapters have been concerned with various aspects of share capital.[1] This chapter is concerned with loan capital raised by companies. When organised in a formal way this entails the issue of debentures or debenture stock. Such debentures[2] are commonly (but by no means always) secured by a charge secured upon the company's assets. The types of charge that can be issued by companies, and the distinction between fixed and floating charges, are then considered. This in turn leads to an examination of the relative priority of fixed and floating charges *inter se* and in respect of various other interests. This necessarily involves consideration of the system for the registration of charges created by companies.

In Part 4 of the chapter the remedies of debenture holders are explored. Principal attention is given to the enforcement of secured debentures. The appointment of an administrative receiver (in the case of a floating charge) is today the normal remedy.[3]

There are many defects in the existing system for the creation and registration of company charges. One is the complexity of the rules governing the relative priority of the floating charge in relation to fixed charges. Recent case-law has also made the task of distinguishing between fixed and floating charges more difficult. Another problem with the existing system is that some transactions commonly used by companies to obtain credit, such as industrial hire-purchase and leasing agreements, are not considered to involve the creation of a charge and therefore will not appear on the register of charges. Even certain types of undoubted charge (e.g. over shares in other companies) are not registrable. In 1986 Professor Diamond was appointed by the Department of Trade and Industry to undertake a 'review of security over property other than land'. The review, published in 1989, contained wide-ranging proposals for reform and, as an interim measure, suggestions for improvement in the system for registration of company charges.[4] Some of the suggested interim measures were enacted in the Companies Act 1989 but those provisions have not been brought into force (and it now appears that they will be replaced by revised legislation[4a]).

Radical proposals for the reform of the law relating to security interests have been

---

[1] As to the relationship between equity and loan capital, known as 'gearing', see 6.2 above.

[2] In Stock Exchange parlance the terms 'debenture' or 'debenture stock' may only be used where the issue is secured by a charge. Where that is not the case, they should be termed 'loan stock', etc. In legal usage, however, 'debenture' has a wider meaning. See 9.3, below.

[3] As to the treatment of fixed and floating charges in the context of administration under Part II of the Insolvency Act 1986, see 17.21, below. As to the effect of a Voluntary Arrangement (whether consequent upon an Administration Order or not) under Part I of the 1986 Act, see 17.8, below.

[4] In September 1987 the DTI published its own proposals for amendment of the statutory requirements governing the registration of company charges: *Outline Proposals for Amendment of Sections 395 to 424 Companies Act 1985*, noted (1988) 9 Co. Law 101 and (1988) 9 Co. Law 220.

[4a] See *Company Law Review: Proposals for Reform of Part XII of the Companies Act 1985* (DTI consultative document, November 1994).

made periodically but the general pattern has been that the reform process has not proceeded beyond the discussion stage. At the end of the chapter, there is a brief account of the main proposals which have been made and an attempt is made to assess why it has proved, thus far, to be impossible to convert those proposals into law.

PART 1: DEBENTURES

9.2 General borrowing powers

Besides raising capital by means of shares, companies frequently, either at the time of their incorporation or subsequently, raise money by borrowing.[5] This may be done in various ways – by an ordinary unsecured loan, by making bills of exchange or promissory notes, by a mortgage on the property of the company, or by the issue of debentures. In all these cases it is necessary to see, first, whether the company has power to borrow; secondly, whether the directors have authority to exercise the company's borrowing powers without a resolution of the company or, as is sometimes required, the consent of a class of shareholders; thirdly, whether there is any limit on the amount which may be borrowed, and, if so, whether that limit is reached; and, fourthly, whether the company or the directors have power to secure the repayment of the money borrowed by a mortgage or charge on all or any part of the assets of the company.

These general questions as to the capacity of a company and as to the authority of the directors and officers to bind the company have been examined in an earlier chapter.[6]

If a company has power (express or implied) to borrow, it can create mortgages or charges to secure the repayment of the loan;[7] but if the power is express, its directors must observe any limitations in the power. Thus, if the memorandum contains the necessary authority, the company can charge or mortgage all its property, of whatever nature, including future property, such as book debts not yet due.[8] It may also charge its uncalled capital,[9] although this is, 'strictly speaking, more in the nature of power than of property'.[10] Uncalled capital capable of being charged does not include capital which can only be called up in the event of a winding-up as provided by section 120,[11] nor the amount payable under the guarantee in the case of a company limited by guarantee, this not being part of the capital of the company nor at any time under the control of the directors.[12]

---

[5] For the exemption of borrowing by companies under the Consumer Credit Act 1974, see sections 8, 16 and 189.

[6] See Chapter 4, above.

[7] *Re Patent File Co.* (1870) LR 6 Ch App. 83; *Australian Auxiliary Steam Clipper Co. v Mounsey* (1858) 4 K & J 733; *Bryon v Metropolitan Saloon Omnibus Co.* (1858) 3 De G & J 123.

[8] *Illingworth v Houldsworth* [1904] AC 353 (HL); *Bloomer v Union Coal Co.* (1873) 16 Eq. 383: compare *Tailby v Official Receiver* (1888) 13 App. Cas. 523 (HL).

[9] *Newton v Anglo-Australian Investment Co.* [1895] AC 244 (PC): *Re Pyle Works (No. 1)* (1890) 44 Ch D 534 (CA).

[10] *Bank of South Australia v Abrahams* (1875) LR 6 PC 265 at p. 271.

[11] *Barlett v Mayfair Property Co.* [1898] 2 Ch 28 (CA).

[12] *Re Pyle Works (No. 1)* (1890) 44 Ch D 534 at pp. 574: but capital which can only be called up with the sanction of a special resolution may be charged, and the charge enforced in a winding-up even though no such resolution has been passed: *Newton v Anglo-Australian Investment Co.* [1895] AC 244 (PC).

9.3 Borrowing on debentures

The most usual form of borrowing by a company is on debentures. When the term 'debenture' is used in its familiar commercial sense it means a series of bonds which evidence the fact that the company is liable to pay the amount specified, with interest, and generally charge the payment of it upon the property of the company.[13] They may be offered to the public by means of a prospectus in the same manner as shares. The procedure governing the application for and allotment of debentures is similar to that in the case of shares; but, as a debenture holder is a creditor, and not a member of the company, widely different results follow.[14]

Although debentures are well-known instruments in the mercantile world and are the subject of various provisions in the Companies Act 1985, there is no complete legal definition of them. It was said by Chitty J that 'a debenture means a document which either creates a debt or acknowledges it, and any document which fulfils either of these conditions is a debenture'.[15] But this is possibly too wide a definition[16]: for example, a bank statement may be an acknowledgment of a debt, but it would not ordinarily be regarded as a debenture. At any rate, an acknowledgment of indebtedness fulfils the primary qualification of a debenture. It does not matter by what name the company calls the document. Thus an 'income stock certificate' containing such an acknowledgment but no charge has been held to be a debenture, having regard to the terms and conditions under which it was issued.[17] A document, with coupons attached, promising to 'pay the amount of this debenture to A. B. or order', has been held to be liable to duty as a debenture and not as a promissory note.[18] A document may be a debenture even though the debt to which it relates is not quantified at the date of its creation.[19]

Section 744 of the Companies Act 1985 states that for the purpose of the Act[20] 'debenture' includes debenture stock, bonds, and any other securities of a company, whether constituting a charge on the assets of the company or not. An ordinary mortgage of freehold land is a debenture within this section.[21] For the purposes of the Financial Services Act 1986 'debenture' includes debenture stock, loan stock, bonds, certificates of deposit and other instruments creating or acknowledging indebtedness save for certain instruments, such as cheques, bills of exchange, banknotes and bank statements, which are expressly excluded.[22]

In *Re SH & Co (Realisations) 1990 Ltd*[23] Mummery J acknowledged the absence of a

---

[13] For precedents see: *Encyclopaedia of Forms and Precedents* (Butterworths, 5th edn), Vol. 10, pp. 570–647.

[14] Companies, like individuals and partnerships, may resort to other means of obtaining credit (e.g. overdrafts on bank accounts, and the issue of negotiable instruments). Companies also obtain finance by means of hire-purchase agreements and commercial leasing arrangements. Such arrangements, however, have no special provision (e.g. as to registration) made for them in the Companies Act. For an account of the various forms of raising loan capital available to listed public companies, see *Gore-Browne on Companies* (Jordans, 44th edn, loose-leaf), Chapter 17.

[15] *Levy v Abercorris Slate and Slab Co.* (1887) 37 Ch D 260. See also *Edmonds v Blaina Furnaces Co.* (1887) 36 Ch D 215; *Knightsbridge Estates Trust v Byrne* [1938] Ch 741 at p. 769 *et seq.*; and *R. v Findlater* [1939] 1 KB 594 (CCA).

[16] See (*per* North J) *Topham v Greenside Co.* (1888) 37 Ch D 281 at p. 291.

[17] *Lemon v Austin Friars Investment Trust* [1926] 1 Ch 1 (CA).

[18] *British India Steam Navigation Co. v Commissioners of Inland Revenue* (1881) 7 QBD 165.

[19] *N. V. Slavenburg's Bank v Intercontinental Natural Resources* [1980] 1 All ER 955 at p. 976.

[20] And unless the contrary intention appears.

[21] *Knightsbridge Estates Trust v Byrne* [1940] AC 613 (HL).

[22] Schedule 1, para. 2.

[23] [1993] BCC 60.

precise definition of the term 'debenture' but commented that this rarely seemed to cause problems in practice.

Debentures may be either (a) a mere promise to pay, or (b) a promise to pay secured by a mortgage or charge. The mortgage or charge may be created by words in the debenture itself, or by a deed to the benefit of which the debenture holders are declared to be entitled or by a combination of these two methods.[24]

Debentures may be payable to the registered holder and those persons to whom he assigns or to bearer,[25] in which latter case they pass by delivery.

9.4 Main terms of debentures

The main terms of debentures relate to the payment of interest and the repayment of principal.

9.4.1 Principal

The debenture or the trust deed by which the bonds are constituted fixes the date when, or the circumstances in which, the principal is repayable. Debentures may be for a fixed term, or may be repayable on demand or on notice, or may be 'perpetual' or 'irredeemable'. The equitable rule which invalidates restrictions on a mortgagor's[26] right to redeem does not apply to debentures.[27] It may be slightly misleading to describe a debenture as 'irredeemable'[28] or 'perpetual' because closer examination of the terms will usually indicate that, although the holder has no right to redeem, the company has an option to redeem in given circumstances.[29]

As well as specifying a final redemption date or period, the terms of debentures may also give the company the power to make early repayment or may provide for the establishment of a sinking fund which the company is obliged to apply in repaying principal from time to time. Selection of the debentures which are to be repaid early may be done by drawings or the company may simply purchase its debentures in the market.

Section 194 of the Companies Act 1985 empowers a company which has redeemed debentures to re-issue the debentures, either by re-issuing the same debentures or by issuing other debentures in their place.[30] One reason for using this power is that the persons entitled to the re-issued debentures enjoy the same priorities as if the debentures had never been redeemed.[31] Thus, if the company has created a security, or issued a subsequent series of debentures, which ranks behind the original debentures, the secur-

[24] The extent of the company's indebtedness covered by the security given will depend in the proper construction of the debenture itself. It was held in *Re Quest Cae Ltd* [1985] BCLC 266, that even a widely drafted 'all moneys' debenture did not cover unsecured loan stock issued to a third party and subsequently acquired by the debenture holder.

[25] As to the issue of bearer debentures, see 9.10, below.

[26] For this purpose, this includes a company which has given a floating charge: *Kreglinger v New Patagonia Meat Co.* [1914] AC 25 (HL) dispelling doubts expressed in *De Beers Consolidated Mines v British South Africa Co.* [1912] AC 52.

[27] Section 193 of the Companies Act 1985. *Knightsbridge Estate Trust v Byrne*, above.

[28] 'Irredeemable' may mean, if the context so requires, 'not liable to be called in': *Willey v Joseph Stocks & Co* [1912] 2 Ch 134n (1909).

[29] Stock which is expressed to be 'redeemable at the option of the company' is not repayable on the demand of the holder: *Edinburgh Corporation v British Linen Bank* [1913] AC 133 (HL (Sc)).

[30] But this power can be excluded, expressly or impliedly, by the company's articles or by any contract entered into by the company: section 194 (1) (*a*); it is also excluded if the company manifests its intention, by resolution or otherwise, to cancel the original debentures: section 194 (1) (*b*).

[31] Section 194 (2).

ity, or subsequent series, does not take priority to the re-issued debentures, even though it would rank before an entirely new issue of debentures.[32]

Section 194 only authorises the re-issue of debentures having the same provisions in every respect as the original debentures, including the date (if any) for redemption.[33]

Section 194 (3) provides that where the company has (at any time) deposited any of its debentures to secure advances from time to time on current account or otherwise, the debentures are not deemed to have been redeemed by reason only of the company's account having ceased to be in debit whilst the debentures remain so deposited. Thus, if a company deposits, say, debentures for £10,000 to secure its overdraft of varying amount, and its account is for a while in credit, and then again in debit, the security will be good as against the new debit, and there will be no reissue.

9.4.2 *Interest*

At common law, interest is not payable on a debt except by agreement.[34] The debenture must therefore contain a covenant to pay interest, and should provide that if the capital is not paid at the due date, interest shall continue to be payable at the agreed rate. If there is no such provision, though interest may be recovered as damages for nonpayment of the principal, it will only be allowed at the 'merchantable rate', or at the rate previously paid, whichever is less.[35] The interest on debentures is a debt, and, although usually expressed to be payable half-yearly, accrues *de die in diem*.[36] It is payable whether or not there are profits. Sometimes, however, interest is declared to be payable only out of profits, in which case the company must apply all available profits for this purpose, and not set aside any part as reserve until the interest is paid in full.[37] Such debentures are usually called 'income bonds'.

9.5 The issue of debentures

A public issue of debentures must comply with the relevant provisions of the Financial Services Act 1986 or the regulations governing unlisted securities. If the debentures are to be admitted to dealings on a formal market such as the London Stock Exchange, the requirements of the relevant market must also be satisfied.[38] If any question arises as to the meaning of the terms of the debentures, no reference can, as a rule, be made to the prospectus by which they were marketed to the public: the provisions of the debentures alone must be considered.[39] But the offer by the prospectus will create an equitable charge in favour of those who have paid their money if it is clearly stated what property is to be charged, but not if this is left uncertain, as, for instance, by merely referring to

---

[32] *Fitzgerald v Persse* [1908] 1 Ir 279.

[33] *Re Antofagasta (Chile) and Bolivia Rly Co's Trust Deed* [1939] Ch 732.

[34] *Higgins v Sargent* (1823) 2 B & C 348; *Page v Newman* (1829) 9 B & C 378.

[35] *Price v Great Western Rly* (1847) 16 M & W 244; *In re Roberts* (1880) 14 Ch D 49 (CA); *Mellersh v Brown* (1890) 45 Ch D 225.

[36] Apportionment Act 1870, sections 2 and 5; *In re Rogers' Trusts* (1863) 1 Dr. & Sm. 338.

[37] *Heslop v Paraguay Central Rly* (1910) 54 SJ 234.

[38] See Chapter 5.

[39] *Re Tewkesbury Gas Co.* [1911] 2 Ch 279; [1912] 1 Ch 1 (CA); *British Equitable Assurance Co. v Baily* [1906] AC 35 at pp. 38, 41 (HL). A debenture prima facie contains the whole contract. As to the circumstances in which a prospectus may form part of the contract, or constitute a binding collateral contract, see *Jacobs v Batavia and General Plantations Trust* [1924] 2 Ch 329 (CA).

mortgage debentures.[40] This charge, however, will require registration and will be superseded by the debentures as soon as issued.

9.6 Debenture certificates

Section 185 (1) of the Companies Act 1985 requires debentures or certificates of debenture stock to be complete and ready for delivery, unless the conditions of issue of the debentures or debenture stock provide otherwise, within two months after allotment, and makes provision for the imposition of a penalty in case of default.[41]

9.7 Specific performance

Section 195 of the 1985 Act makes a contract with a company to take up and pay debentures of the company enforceable by an order for specific performance; but if under the conditions of allotment the company forfeits the debentures for nonpayment of an instalment, the right to enforce specific performance is lost.[42] Where a loan has been made, specific performance of the agreement to give security will be decreed,[43] and an agreement to issue debentures for money paid creates a charge, although the debentures are not actually issued.[44]

9.8 Debentures issued at a discount

Debentures may be issued at a discount: e.g. a debenture for £100 may be issued in consideration of £95 advanced to the company, the effect of the discount being an addition to the interest paid,[45] and commission may be paid to underwriters or others for placing or guaranteeing the taking up of debentures. However, convertible debentures must not be issued at a discount so as to evade the rule against issuing shares at a discount. In *Moseley v Koffyfontein Mines*[46] debentures issued at a discount entitled the holder to call for the allotment of fully paid up shares in satisfaction of the same nominal amount as the debentures. Since the debentures here were immediately convertible it was obviously a device for issuing shares at a discount. Cozens-Hardy LJ left open the question of whether an option to convert is valid if it is not exercisable until some time after the debentures are issued.[47] Although convertible debentures are frequently issued, there will usually be a premium element in the conversion terms so that a discount will not arise.

Equally, bonus shares must not be given to subscribers for debentures, at any rate to

---

[40] *Re New Durham Salt Co.* (1890) 7 TLR 13.

[41] The penalty is the same as in the case of default in having share certificates ready, as to which see 8.10, above.

[42] *Kuala Pahi Estates v Mowbrays* (1914) 111 LT 1072 (CA).

[43] *Hermann v Hodges* (1873) 16 Eq. 18.

[44] *Re Strand Music Hall* (1865) 3 De GJ & S 147; *Pegge v Neath Tramways* [1898] 1 Ch 183; *Re Queensland Land and Coal Co.* [1894] 3 Ch 181; *Simultaneous Printing Syndicate v Foweraker* [1901] 1 KB 771; *Re Perth Electric Tramways* [1906] 2 Ch 216.

[45] *Re Anglo-Danubian Steam Co.* (1875) 20 Eq. 339; *Campbell's Case* (1876) 4 Ch D 470; *Webb v Shropshire Rly Co.* [1893] 3 Ch 307 (CA).

[46] [1904] 2 Ch 108 (CA).

[47] ibid. at p. 120.

any greater amount than what may fairly be called commission. If they are given, the holder will be liable for calls.[48]

9.9 Transfer of registered debentures

Debentures are usually transferred by a form of transfer similar to that used for transferring shares, and executed in the same manner. A debenture to registered holder may be transferred in the manner specified in the endorsed conditions. Further, under the Stock Transfer Act 1963, fully paid debentures to registered holder (of any registered, statutory or chartered company)[49] may be transferred by the simplified method of stock transfer introduced by this Act.[50] There must be an instrument of transfer. Notwithstanding anything in the articles of a company, an oral transfer of debentures cannot be registered.[51] This was intended to prevent evasion of stamp duty. It does not prejudice any power of a company to register as debenture holder any person to whom the right to any debentures has been transmitted by operation of law. Indeed, upon the production of probate (or letters of administration or confirmation), the company is bound to register an executor (or administrator) with a clean title, no transfer being necessary.[52] In the case of listed securities, including listed debentures, the Stock Exchange 'Talisman' system has been in operation since 1979. It does not apply to bearer securities, but does apply to registered debentures. The system is examined in Chapter 8, above,[53] as are proposals for further reform.

It is common to provide that debentures may be transferred 'free from equities between the company and the original or any intermediate holder'. Without these words the holder of a chose in action can only transfer such rights as he has, and if the company has any set-off against the transferor, it can enforce it against the transferee.[54] These words will effectually negate any such right where the transfer is complete.[55] If the conditions authorise transfer, the company cannot refuse to register a transfer, and the transfer may be made after liquidation or judgment in a debenture holders' action as well as before, and the same rule as to equities will then prevail, for the claim of the general body of debenture holders under their charge is no greater than that of the company against the particular debenture holder who holds the transferred debenture.[56]

---

[48] In *Re Railway Time Tables* (1893) 62 LJ Ch 935, shares to the amount of £10 were issued as fully paid for each £10 debenture. Kekewich J held that the allottee was liable for the amount of the shares. There was an appeal, which went to the House of Lords on other points: *Welton v Saffrey* [1897] AC 29, but this point was not further discussed.

[49] See section 1 (4) and section 4 (1) for the definition of registered securities.

[50] See further, as to the Stock Transfer Act 1963, 8.3.1, above, and as to the 'Talisman' system of listed securities, see 8.3.3, above.

[51] Companies Act 1985, section 183 (1).

[52] *Edwards v Ransomes and Rapier* (1930) 143 LT 594.

[53] See 8.3, above.

[54] *Re Richard Smith & Co.* [1901] 1 Ir. R. 73; *In the matter of Gwelo Matebeleland Exploration Co.* [1901] 1 Ir. R. 38.

[55] An equitable mortgagee of debentures will still be subject to any equities existing at the time when he gives notice of his mortgage: *Christie v Taunton Delmard & Co.* [1893] 2 Ch 175. See also *Re Richard Smith & Co.* [1901] 1 Ir. R. 73 and *Re Brown and Gregory* [1904] 1 Ch 627, [1904] 2 Ch 448 (CA) (complete transfer but only upon a trust).

[56] *Re Goy & Co.* [1900] 2 Ch 149. *Hilger Analytical Ltd v Rank Precision Industries* [1984] BCLC 301. But see *Re Palmer's Decoration Co.* [1904] 2 Ch 743 where the 'free from equities clause' refers to 'registered holder'.

9.10 Debentures to bearer

According to the general law of England a debt cannot be assigned by delivery of the document which creates or evidences the debt. However, there is an exception in certain cases where the law merchant makes such an assignment valid (e.g. in the case of a bill of exchange). It has been held that the custom to treat debentures to bearer as negotiable by delivery is sufficiently proved to take effect under the law merchant, of which custom judicial notice will be taken without express evidence.[57] Even without reference to the law merchant it had previously been held that, by a doctrine of estoppel, a company may be prevented from denying its liability to pay a debenture if it has invited persons to accept a transfer by delivery, and has held out or represented that the debenture so transferred gives the bearer a right to be paid. Likewise a declaration in the debenture that the delivery of the bond to the company will be a valid discharge to it for payment will bind the original and intermediate holders. The case which deal with this subject are numerous: some of the most important are referred to in a footnote below.[58] Debentures can accordingly be framed so as in effect to be payable to bearer; and section 197 of the Companies Act 1985 expressly authorises the issue of debentures to bearer in Scotland, treating their validity in England as not requiring any mention.

9.11 Debenture stock

Debenture stock is of the same nature as ordinary debentures,[59] except that, instead of each bond securing a definite amount, the whole sum secured is treated as a single stock, and certificates are issued declaring the holder to be entitled to a definite sum, part of the stock. The sum is not necessarily a round sum but may be for any number of pounds, and may include fractions of a pound unless express limitation is made in that respect. The debenture stock may be repayable at a fixed date, or may be irredeemable according to the deed creating it, and may be secured in any manner in which a debenture may be secured.

The issue of debenture stock will, where the stock is secured by a charge, require the appointment of trustees under a debenture stock trust deed. The stockholders have a beneficial interest in equity in the legal contract of loan between the company and the trustees. Trust deeds for securing debenture stock, as well as for ordinary debentures, are discussed below.

Debenture stock may be irredeemable: that is to say, the money is raised by the sale of a perpetual annuity, and this again may be qualified by giving the company power at its option to repurchase such annuity.[60]

---

[57] *Bechuanaland Exploration Co. v London Trading Bank* [1898] 2 QB 658; *Edelstein v Schuler & Co.* [1902] 2 KB 144.

[58] *Re Agra and Masterman's Bank* (1867) 2 Ch App. 391; *Re Blakeley Ordnance Co.* (1867) 3 Ch App. 154; *Re Natal Investment Co.* (1868) 2 Ch App. 355; *Re Imperial Land Co.* (1871) 11 Eq. 478 at p. 487; *Goodwin v Robarts* (1876) 1 App Cas. 476; *Eaglesfield v Londonderry* (1876) 4 Ch D 693 (CA); *Re Romford Canal Co.* (1883) 24 Ch D 85.

[59] Debenture stock passes under a bequest of 'all my debentures'; *Morrice v Aylmer* (1875) LR 7 HL 717; *Re Herring* [1908] 2 Ch 493.

[60] *Edinburgh Corporation v British Linen Bank* [1913] AC 133 (HL (Sc.)).

9.12 Trust deeds for securing debentures[61]

Trust deeds have considerable advantages when debentures are issued to more than a very small number of persons. The effect of such a deed is to mortgage the property in favour of the trustees, and at the same time to provide persons who can act upon an emergency and take steps on behalf of all the debenture holders without delay. In such a deed there is also more scope than in the conditions printed on a debenture for setting out the terms and provisions of the mortgage and the manner and conditions of its enforcement. Further, foreign property, patents, ships, etc., can be mortgaged to trustees in a manner more satisfactory than by giving a charge in the debentures.

The deed should contain an express declaration that the trustees' remuneration shall be paid out of the mortgaged property; for a covenant by the company to pay, even if coupled with a power to the trustees to retain their remuneration out of moneys coming into their hands, will not suffice if the property is realised in an action.[62] If, however, the deed declares that the proceeds of sale by the trustees are to be applied in paying the remuneration first, and then the debenture debt, the remuneration will be payable out of such proceeds, even though by an order in a debenture holders' action they are paid direct into court. The date to which the remuneration is payable will be determined by the terms of the deed, and differences of judicial opinion have arisen as to the right of the trustees to remuneration after the appointment of a receiver.[63]

9.13 Powers and duties of trustees

A trust deed charging property in favour of trustees gives them the position of mortgagees of the property charged, so that, subject to any express provisions of the deed, they can exercise all the powers of mortgagees.[64] Thus, where shares form part of the security and are registered in the names of the trustees, they can exercise the voting power free from control by the company, whether or not there is any interest in arrear or any default.[65] Title deeds relating to the property charged will normally be in the trustees' custody, though if it be more convenient, the court may direct that a receiver have the custody, giving the trustees access to them when necessary.[66]

Except that they are usually paid for their services, trustees for debenture holders are in the same position as any other trustees, and a purchase by them of any of the debentures can only be supported under the stringent principles which apply to the purchase by a trustee of the interest of a beneficiary.[67]

Trust deeds used commonly to contain a clause exempting a trustee from liability for anything but his own wilful neglect or default. The effectiveness of such a clause[68] is considerably curtailed by what is now section 192 of the 1985 Act: any such provision is to

---

[61] See generally, *Gore-Browne on Companies* (Jordans, 44th edn. loose-leaf) 17.10. Trustees are normally appointed in respect of issues of domestic debt securities. The practice in relation to international debt securities (such as eurobonds) is less consistent and fiscal agents may be appointed instead of trustees.

[62] *Hodson v Accles* [1902] WN 164.

[63] *Re Piccadilly Hotel* [1911] 2 Ch 534; *Re Locke & Smith* [1914] 1 Ch 687 (CA); *Re Anglo-Canadian Lands* [1918] 2 Ch 287; *Re British Consolidated Oil Corp.* [1919] 2 Ch 81.

[64] For precedents see: *Encyclopaedia of Forms and Precedents* (Butterworths, 5th edn), Vol. 10, pp. 670–746.

[65] *Siemens Brothers & Co. v Burns* [1918] 2 Ch 324 (CA).

[66] *Fisher v Ind Coope* (1909) 26 TLR 11 (CA).

[67] *Re Magadi Soda Co.* (1925) 94 LJ Ch 217.

[68] As to which, see *Re City Equitable Fire Insurance Co.* [1925] Ch 407 (CA). On trustee exemption clauses generally see Mathews, 'The Efficacy of Trustee Exemption Clauses in English Law' [1989] Conv 42.

be void in so far as it would have the effect of exempting a trustee from or indemnifying him against liability for breach of trust where he fails to show the degree of care and diligence required of him as trustee, having regard to the provisions of the trust deed conferring on him any powers, authorities, or discretions.

This is not, however, to deprive a trustee of any exemption or right to be indemnified in respect of anything done or omitted to be done while any such provision was in force,[69] nor is it to invalidate either:

(1) any release otherwise validly given in respect of anything done or omitted to be done by a trustee before the giving of the release; or

(2) any provision enabling such a release to be given –

    (a) on the agreement of a majority of not less than three-quarters in value of the debenture holders present and voting at a meeting summoned for the purpose; and

    (b) either with respect to specific acts or omissions or on the trustee dying or ceasing to act.[70]

The trust deed usually declares that the principal money shall become payable in certain events, including the event of the company committing any breach of the covenants contained in the deed. This does not necessarily give each debenture holder a right to assert that the principal is payable because of some trivial default.[71]

Power is sometimes given to the trustees to settle disputed questions. In such case an exercise of their discretion is valid.[72]

9.14 Meetings of debenture holders – power to vary rights

It is common to provide, either in the trust-deed or in the conditions on the debentures, for meetings of debenture holders to be held, and to give power to a three-quarters majority to vary the terms of the security, or generally to sanction alterations. Such provisions are valid,[73] and the minority will be bound by the decision of the majority. But in such cases care must be taken that the provisions of the trust deed or the debentures are strictly complied with. A majority must not *give* away the rights of the whole body,[74] for there must be circumstances which bring the power into operation: that is to say, if the power is to compromise there must be a dispute, or if the power is a more general one (e.g. to make arrangements) there must be mutual concessions. Accordingly, the terms of the power must be carefully considered.

Generally speaking, debenture holders may vote according to their private interests, even if these conflict with those of the general body, and it is no objection that special advantages are given to one debenture holder or a class with special interests if they are given openly.[75] But while usually a holder of shares or debentures may vote as his interest

---

[69] See section 192 (3) and (4) as to provisions in force on 1 July 1948.

[70] Section 192 (2).

[71] *Re Melbourne Brewery and Distillery* [1901] 1 Ch 453.

[72] *Re Noakes v Noakes & Co.* [1907] 1 Ch 64.

[73] *Re Dominion of Canada Etc. Co.* (1886) 55 LT 347; *Follit v Eddystone Granite Quarries* [1892] 3 Ch 75.

[74] *Mercantile Investment and General Trust Co. v International Co. of Mexico* [1893] 1 Ch 484n.

[75] *Goodfellow v Nelson Line* [1912] 2 Ch 324.

directs, he is subject to the further principle that where his vote is conferred upon him as a member of a class he must conform to the interest of the class itself when seeking to exercise the power conferred on him in his capacity as a member. An undisclosed consideration for voting in any particular way, not forming part of the scheme to be voted for, would if the resolution depended upon that vote, invalidate the resolution.[76]

With regard to the convening of meetings of debenture holders, if the deed contains no provision for giving notice to the debenture holders, notice by advertisement is sufficient, and will be deemed to have been given on the day of the advertisement appearing.[77]

9.15 The register of debenture holders

There is no provision in the Companies Act 1985 requiring the keeping of a register of debenture holders as distinct from the register of charges; but the debentures or trust deed usually provide for such a register being kept, and the register is essential if the debentures are expressed to be payable to the registered holders thereof. If there is such a register, it is provided by section 190 that it must be kept at the registered office or at any other office of the company where the work of making it up is done; or where it is made up by an agent on behalf of the company, it may be kept at the agent's office.[78]

Under section 191 (1), every register of holders of debentures of a company must be open to the inspection of the registered holder of any such debentures or any shareholder without fee and of any other person on payment of a prescribed fee.[79] Every such debenture holder or shareholder or other person is entitled to a copy of all or part of the register on payment of a prescribed fee.[80]

PART 2: CHARGES

9.16 Fixed and floating charges

The charge created by a debenture may be either 'fixed' or 'floating'. When the charge is fixed it is like an ordinary mortgage and affects the title to the property, so that the company can only deal with the property affected, subject to the charge. But where the

---

[76] *British American Nickel Corporation v O'Brien* [1927] AC 369 (PC).

[77] *Sneath v Valley Gold Co.* [1893] 1 Ch 477 (CA).

[78] The register may now be kept in computerised form: see section 723 of the 1985 Act. If the register has not at all times been kept at the company's registered office, notice must be sent to the Registrar. See section 190 (1), (2) and (3) as to the keeping of duplicate registers, or parts of registers, where such are kept outside Great Britain; and as to companies registered in Scotland and in England and Wales, respectively, see ibid.

[79] This is subject to the proviso that the company may close the register in accordance with provisions contained in the articles or the debentures (or in the case of debenture stock in the stock certificates, or in the trust deed or other document securing the debentures or debenture stock), for any specified period of periods not exceeding thirty days in any year: section 191 (6).

[80] Section 191 (2). The fees are prescribed in the Companies (Inspection and Copying of Registers, Indices and Documents) Regulations 1991 (SI 1991 No. 1998).

charge is a 'floating' one the company may in the ordinary course of its business[81] deal with the property covered by the charge, mortgaging it so that the mortgage takes priority of the floating charge, or selling or disposing of it, free from the floating charge, or using it up as the business requires at any time before the charge attaches.[82]

It is common to create the security in such manner that the lands and immovable property of the company are covered by a fixed charge, while the stock-in-trade, chattels, and book debts of the company and its future property are included in a floating charge. In recent years, however, fixed charges on present and future book debts have become more common.[83] The debentures usually specify in what events (such as liquidation, default in payment of principal or interest for a stated period, etc.) the charge is to be enforceable, and in interpreting these the court will always lean against treating the charge on goods required for the business as being fixed while the business is going on.[84] Where an intention appears that the company should receive and deal with the property charged, it is assumed that only a floating security is intended.[85] A charge, though expressed in words which would otherwise suffice to create a fixed mortgage, will be treated as a floating charge if it appears that it was intended that the company should continue to use the articles charged and turn them over in its business.[86] The proper classification of a charge as fixed or floating depends on construction of the charging document in which the parties have expressed their intention.[87] Subsequent events are not relevant to this question of construction, although they may establish a variation in the terms of the charge.[88] The principal indicia of a floating charge have been stated by the Court of Appeal as follows: first, if it is a charge upon all of a certain class of assets, present and future; secondly, if the assets charged would in the ordinary course of

---

[81] *Re Old Bush Mills Distillery Co.* [1897] Ir. R. 488. What is within the 'ordinary course of business' will depend on the circumstances of each case. A specific mortgage to raise money for the purpose of carrying on the business of the company is within the words: *Cox Moore v Peruvian Corp.* [1908] 1 Ch 604. Some cases have equated the 'ordinary course of business' to what is permitted by the company's objects clause: *Re H. H. Vivian & Co. Ltd* [1900] 2 Ch 654; *Re Borax Co.* [1901] 1 Ch 326, 342; *Re Automatic Bottle Makers Ltd* [1926] Ch 412, 421; *Hamilton v Hunter* (1982) 7 ACLR 295. But intra vires transactions which would cause a cessation of the company's business may fall outside the ordinary course: *Hubbuck v Helms* (1887) 56 LJ Ch 536. The consequences of acting outside the ordinary course have been discussed more in Australia than in England: *Hamilton v Hunter*, above; *Torzillu Pty Ltd v Brynac Pty* (1983) 8 ACLR 52; see generally Worthington, 'Floating Charges – An Alternative Theory' [1994] CLJ 81 at pp. 99–102. The absence of relevant English authority suggests that this point rarely causes difficulty in practice. In England, because 'ordinary course' has been linked to issues of vires, there is a question concerning the effect (if any) of section 35 of the Companies Act 1985.

[82] *Re Florence Land Co.* (1878) 10 Ch D 530 (CA); *Wheatley v Silkstone etc. Coal Co.* (1885) 29 Ch D 715; *Re Hamilton's Windsor Ironworks* (1879) 12 Ch D 707; *Re Colonial Trusts Corporation* (1879) 15 Ch D 465 at p. 472; *In re H. H. Vivian & Co.* [1900] 2 Ch 654.

[83] See para. 9.18, below.

[84] *Government Stock Investment Co. v Manila Rly* [1897] AC 81 (HL); *Evans v Rival Granite Quarries* [1910] 2 KB 979 (CA).

[85] *Illingworth v Houldsworth* [1904] AC 355 (HL); *Re GE Tunbridge Ltd* [1995] 1 BCLC 34.

[86] *National Provincial Bank v United Electric Theatres* [1916] 1 Ch 132; *United Builders Pty Ltd v Mutual Acceptance Ltd* (1980) 33 ALR 1; *Boambee Bay Resort Ltd (in Liq.) v Equus Financial Services Ltd* (1991) 6 ACSR 532.

[87] As does the determination of the extent of the property covered by the charge: *Northern Bank Ltd v Ross* [1991] BCLC 504, [1990] BCC 883 (charge on book debts did not extend to bank account); *Re HiFi Equipment (Cabinets) Ltd* [1988] BCLC 65, (1987) 3 BCC 478 (machines were not 'fixed plant and machinery' and were therefore not caught by a fixed charge (not following *Tudor Heights Ltd v United Dominion Corporation Finance Ltd* [1977] 1 NZLR 532).

[88] *William Gaskell Group Ltd v Highley [1993] BCC 200; Re Armagh Shoes Ltd* [1984] BCLC 405; *Re Wogans (Drogheda Ltd); Jenkins v Hill Samuel Bank* (unreported 10 April 1992) (noted Fealy, 'Fixed Charges over Bookdebts: A Loosening of the Reins?' June 1993, Irish Law Times, 133).

business be changing from time to time; and, thirdly, if expressly or by necessary implication the company has the power, until some step is taken by the debenture holders or trustees, of carrying on its business in the ordinary way so far as regards the assets charged.[89]

It is important to bear in mind that these tests are descriptive and that they do not amount to a precise definition of a floating charge.[90] Thus, although there is a prima facie rule that the property secured by a floating charge on the company's undertaking includes future property as well as such property as is owned by the company when the charge is created,[91] it has been held that a charge on present property only can be a floating charge.[92] Equally a charge can be a fixed charge where the property secured includes future, as well as present, property.[93]

Land owned by a company which is not in the business of property trading would not be regarded as a class of asset changing from time to time in the course of the company's business. Nevertheless, in *Welch v Bowmaker (Ireland) Ltd*[94] the majority of the Irish Supreme Court[95] held that a charge secured on land could be a floating charge.

The essence of a floating charge is embodied in the third of the characteristics outlined in *Re Yorkshire Woolcombers*: if the charge allows the company to continue to deal with the assets secured as if they were not subject to the security, the charge will be floating; conversely, if the company is restricted in its dealings with the assets secured, the charge will be a fixed charge. The degree of control (or freedom) required to create a fixed (or floating) charge has been discussed extensively in cases concerned with the nature of charges on debts.[96] The principles which emerge from these cases are discussed at 9.18, below.

Precisely because it confers greater control, lenders might be expected to prefer fixed security and to take floating security only on assets where the frequency of turnover makes fixed security impracticable. An inherent risk in a floating charge is that the company will dissipate the subject-matter of the security through imprudent trading, leaving the lender with a security that is virtually worthless. Also, a lender who has taken only floating security, risks finding himself postponed to other creditors of the company who have themselves obtained fixed security or who are afforded a preferential status by the insolvency legislation.

---

[89] *Re Yorkshire Woolcombers' Association* [1903] 2 Ch 284 (CA), affirmed in the House of Lords *sub nom. Illingworth v Houldsworth* [1904] AC 355, where it was held that a general charge on book debts, present and future, was a floating charge, although not expressed to be so, and required registration under the Act of 1900.

[90] *Re Yorkshire Woolcombers* at p. 295 *per* Romer LJ and p. 298 *per* Cozens Hardy LJ; *Re Croftbell Ltd* [1990] BCLC 844, [1990] BCC 781.

[91] Re Panama, New Zealand and Australia Royal Mail Co. (1870) LR 5 Ch App. 318; *Illingworth v Houldsworth* [1904] AC 355; *Re Croftbell Ltd*, above. This rule can assist where there is some doubt about the extent of the security: *Re Alfred Priestman & Co. Ltd* [1936] 2 All ER 1340.

[92] *Re Bond Worth Ltd* [1980] 1 Ch 228 at p. 267; *Re Atlantic Medical Ltd* [1992] BCC 653 at p. 658 ('it is very unusual indeed that a floating charge would be limited to existing assets of a company'); *Re Cimex Tissues Ltd* [1994] BCC 626 at pp. 637–9.

[93] *Tailby v Official Receiver* (1883) 13 App. Cas. 583. See further para. 9.18, below.

[94] [1980] IR 251.

[95] Kenny J dissented precisely because the second characteristic of a floating charge, as outlined in *Yorkshire Woolcombers*, was not present.

[96] See also *Re Cimex Tissues Ltd*, above which concerned the classification of a charge (expressed to be a fixed charge) on certain plant and machinery.

The Insolvency Act 1986 provides a reason[97] why it can be important for a lender to take a floating charge, either on its own or in addition to fixed security. Under the Act, an administrator can be appointed by the court to administer the affairs of a company in financial difficulties. Administration is a collective insolvency procedure and no one creditor, or group of creditors, is entitled to control the administrator in the exercise of his powers. The administrator's statutory powers are extensive and include the ability to sell property which is subject to a charge without the consent of the holder of that security.[98] The significant restriction on the adminstration procedure is that an administrator may not be appointed where an administrative receiver has been appointed to the company unless the appointor of the administrative receiver consents.[99]

An administrative receiver is defined by section 29 (2) of the Insolvency Act 1986 as a receiver or manager of the whole (or substantially the whole) of a company's property, appointed by or on behalf of the holders of any debentures of the company secured by a charge which, as created, was a floating charge, or by such a charge and one or more other securities.[100] Lenders who want to be able to block the appointment of an administrator must thus ensure that their security includes an appropriately drafted floating charge.

Since the coming into force of the administration procedure contained in Insolvency Act 1986 there has emerged the concept of the 'lightweight' floating charge.[101] Where a company's assets consist wholly or mainly of property which is not expected to be the subject of rapid turnover, an example being a holding company with assets consisting almost entirely of shares in subsidiaries, the lender can take a fixed charge on the assets without unduly impeding the company's business affairs. This fixed charge will largely satisfy the lender's desire for control, save for the fact that it will not enable the lender to prevent the appointment of an administrator. This need can, however, be met by also taking a floating charge over the company's undertaking. This floating charge may be almost identical in scope to the fixed charge and the detailed covenants which would usually be required from the company if the floating charge stood alone can be dispensed with, thus making the charge 'lightweight'; but a floating charge tacked onto a fixed charge in this way is not an artificial device and it is effective for the purpose of allowing its holder to block the appointment of an administrator.[102]

9.17 The nature of a floating charge in England

A floating charge is a present charge, not a future one, but it does not specifically affect any item until some event happens which causes it to become fixed.[103] Thus the debenture holder has under his floating charge an immediate equity or charge on the

---

[97] Another reason, also provided by the Insolvency Act, is that an administrative receiver, but not an ordinary receiver, enjoys a wide range of implied statutory powers. See paragraph 9.61, below.

[98] The administrator requires the consent of the court to sell property which is subject to a fixed charge; the court's consent is not required where the security is a floating charge: section 15 (1) and (2).

[99] Section 9 of the Insolvency Act 1986.

[100] Or a person who would be such a receiver or manager but for the appointment of some other person as the receiver of part of the company's property: section 29 (2) (*b*).

[101] Oditah, 'Lightweight Floating Charges' [1991] JBL 49; Marks and Emmet, 'Administrative Receivers: Questions of Identity and Double Identity' [1994] JBL 1.

[102] *Re Croftbell Ltd*, above.

[103] See (*per* Buckley LJ) *Evans v Rival Granite Quarries* [1910] 2 KB at p. 999; *Mercantile Bank of India v Chartered Bank of India & Co.* [1937] 1 All ER 231.

property, but the company can continue to deal with the property charged in the course of its business until the charge attaches as a fixed charge, or, as it is often described, 'crystallises'.

Some of the earlier cases,[104] reasoning by analogy to the fixed charge, explained what was then a novel form of security as being like a specific mortgage plus a licence to the mortgagor to dispose of the company's assets in the ordinary course of business. Buckley LJ[105] repudiated this explanation of the floating charge in favour of the concept of 'a floating mortgage applying to every item comprised in the security, but not specifically affecting any item until some event occurs, or some act on the part of the mortgagee is done, which causes it to crystallize into a fixed security'. This notion of a floating charge, characterising it as a 'present security on a shifting fund of assets',[106] better accords with the detailed rules governing the functioning of the floating charge between the time of its creation and its crystallisation.

The nature of the lender's interest in the company's property created by a floating charge and the related question of the basis of the company's power to continue to deal with the assets are issues which have intrigued commentators and on which there is an extensive amount of literature. In his book on *Company Charges* (Butterworths, 1978), Gough argued that a floating charge gives the lender no proprietary interest in the company's property until such time as the charge crystallises into a fixed charge[107] but this view has been disputed by many other writers.[108] The cases are not consistent and whilst the argument that a floating charge confers a proprietary interest has support,[109] so too does the alternative view.[110] Although its true nature has proved to be somewhat elusive, this has not prevented the floating charge from becoming an important element of corporate financing. Bearing this in mind, it may be that it is unnecessary to attempt to pinpoint in an absolute sense the proprietary interest created by a floating charge and that a more fruitful line of inquiry is to consider whether in specific contexts, the floating charges give the lender an interest which, for the purpose in question, is to be regarded as 'proprietary'. In *Re Margart Pty*, the Supreme Court of New South Wales[111] held that a statutory provision[112] which invalidated dispositions of a company's property after the commencement of its liquidation did not apply to dispositions made to a debenture

[104] e.g. *Re Florence Land Co.* (1878) 10 Ch D 543; *Davey & Co. v Williamson* [1898] 2 QB 194 at p. 200.

[105] *Evans v Rival Granite Quarries* [1910] 2 KB 979 at p. 999. See also *Biggerstaff v Rowatts Wharf Ltd* [1896] 2 Ch 93 at p. 105 *per* Kay LJ.

[106] *Re Cimex Tissues*, above, at p. 635.

[107] A view reasserted by the same author in Chapter 9 of Finn (ed.), *Equity and Commercial Relationships* (Law Book Company, 1978).

[108] For example: Goode, 'It can now be taken as settled that the floating charge creates an immediate interest *in rem*' in *Legal Problems of Credit and Security* (Sweet & Maxwell, 2nd edn 1988), p. 46; Farrar, 'World Economic Stagnation Puts the Floating Charge on Trial' (1980) 1 Co. Law 83; Ferran, 'Floating Charges – the Nature of the Security' [1988] CLJ 213; and Worthington, 'Floating Charges – An Alternative Theory' [1994] CLJ 81. See also Pennington, 'The Genesis of the Floating Charge' (1960) 23 MLR 630.

[109] *Driver v Broad* [1893] 1 QB 744; *Wallace v Evershed* [1899] 1 Ch 891; *Landall Holdings Ltd v Caratti* [1979] WAR 97 at pp. 102–3; *Hamilton v Hunter* (1982) 7 ACLR 295 at p. 306; *Re Margart Pty Ltd, Hamilton v Westpac Banking Corp* (1984) 9 ACLR 269 at pp. 271–2; *Canadian Imperial Bank of Commerce v Coopers & Lybrand* (1989) 57 DLR (4th) 633.

[110] *Tricontinental Corp v FCT* (1987) 12 ACLR 421, citing, *inter alia, Evans v Rival Granite Quarries Ltd* [1910] 2 KB 979.

[111] Although an Australian decision, this was followed by Vinelott J in *Re French's Wine Bar Ltd* [1987] BCLC 499 and would seem to represent English law.

[112] The equivalent provision in the Insolvency Act 1986 is section 127.

holder who held an uncrystallised floating charge, because, for that purpose, the debenture holder had a beneficial interest in the property transferred. In *Re Goldcorp Exchange Ltd*[113] Lord Mustill, delivering the judgment of the Judicial Board of the Privy Council, stated that the chargor's freedom to deal with the secured assets prior to crystallisation did not mean that the chargee's right to the assets was circumscribed by an indebtedness of a purely personal nature and held that the floating charge gave its holder a sufficient proprietary interest to defeat a claim by a third party to an estoppel arising from statements made by the company.

9.18 Charges on book debts

The characteristics of fixed and floating charges have recently received close judicial scrutiny in a line of cases concerned with charges on book debts or other debts or receivables such as rental payments.[114] 'Book debts' are simply debts which, as a matter of accounting practice, would ordinarily be entered in the books of the company.[115]

In the landmark decision of *Siebe Gorman & Co Ltd v Barclays Bank Ltd*[116] the court held that a debenture effectively created a fixed charge on present and future book debts. The significant terms of the debenture obliged the company not to assign or charge its book debts without the lender's consent and required the company to pay the proceeds of book debts into an account held with the lender. The bank had a lien on the proceeds paid into the bank account and could assert this lien so as to prevent the company from making withdrawals in the course of its business. It was held that the restrictions on the book debts and on their proceeds together gave the lender a degree of control which was inconsistent with the freedom to the company that was the vital characteristic of a floating charge.

Despite condemnation from the Review Committee on Insolvency Law and Practice,[117] the decision in *Siebe Gorman* was not reversed by the 1980s' insolvency legislation and it has since been followed,[118] and distinguished.[119] In *Re New Bullas Ltd*,[120] at first instance, Knox J summarised the post-*Siebe Gorman* orthodoxy on the creation of fixed charges on present and future book in the following terms:

(1) the label attached to a charge by the parties is not conclusive; a charge described as 'fixed' will be treated as a floating charge if the description is a sham or where the stated characteristics of the charge compel the court to conclude that the parties have in fact created something different from that which they had intended;[121]

---

[113] [1994] 3 WLR 199 at pp. 212–13.

[114] For an explanation of the tendency of banks in recent years to move from a floating charge to a series of fixed charges giving a greater degree of protection, see Robbie and Gill, 'Fixed and Floating Charges. A New Look at the Banks' Position' [1981] JBL 95. For further analysis of the cases, see Pennington, 'Fixed Charges over Future Assets of a Company' (1985) 6 Co. Law 9; McCormack, 'Fixed Charges over Future Book Debts' (1987) 8 Co. Law 3; Pearce, 'Fixed Charges Over Book Debts' [1987] JBL 18.

[115] *Tailby v Official Receiver; Independent Automatic Sales Ltd v Knowles and Foster* [1962] 1 WLR 974; *Paul & Frank Ltd v Discount Bank (Overseas) Ltd* [1967] Ch 348.

[116] [1979] 2 Lloyd's Rep 142.

[117] Cmnd 8558 (1982), at paras. 1584–86.

[118] *Re Keenan Bros Ltd* [1986] BCLC 242 (Supreme Court (Ireland)); *William Gaskell Group Ltd v Highley* [1993] BCC 200.

[119] *Re Brightlife Ltd* [1987] Ch 200, [1986] 3 All ER 673, [1987] 2 WLR 197, [1986] BCLC 418, (1986) 2 BCC 99, 359.

[120] [1993] BCLC 1389, [1993] BCC 251.

[121] *Re Armagh Shoes Ltd; Re Brightlife Ltd; Hart v Barnes* [1983] 2 VR 347.

(2) fetters, or even a prohibition against factoring, assigning or selling the book debts, on their own, are insufficient to create a fixed charge;

(3) an obligation to pay the proceeds of book debts into a particular account can, in combination with appropriate restrictions on dealing with the debts themselves, be sufficient, provided that there are also sufficient restrictions on the company's powers to deal with the moneys in the account.

Re New Bullas was the subject of an appeal. The decision of the Court of Appeal[122] heralds a more flexible approach and establishes that control of the debts *and* of their proceeds is not the prerequisite of a fixed charge on book debts: the charging document can treat the debts and their proceeds as divisible and create a fixed charge on the debts, but only a floating charge on the proceeds of those debts.[123] The debenture in question was expressed to create a fixed charge over debts and provided for their proceeds to be paid into a current account or another designated account. In the absence of directions from the debenture holder, on payment into the account the proceeds were released from the fixed charge and became subject to a floating charge. Even though the proceeds of the debts could thus cease to fall within the debenture holder's control as soon as they were paid into the account, the charge on the debts themselves was held to be a fixed charge.

A theme which underlies the cases from *Siebe Gorman* to *New Bullas* is that charges are consensual securities and that, whilst there is a fundamental requirement for 'control' which must be satisfied in order for a charge to be a fixed charge as a matter of law, nevertheless the characteristics of a fixed or floating charge are not rigidly defined so that the parties to a charge therefore enjoy considerable licence to tailor the terms of their bargain as they think fit. These cases are an encouragement to ingenious companies and their advisers to devise security documentation which combines the advantages of fixed and floating charges. However, it is arguable that by supporting freedom of contract the courts are allowing secured creditors in effect to subvert the operation of the insolvency legislation.

Any relaxation of the requirements necessary to create a fixed charge has wide-ranging implications. In general, a fixed security ranks before a floating charge in terms of priority. More particularly, by virtue of the Insolvency Act 1986 certain 'preferential' debts rank for payment before debts secured by a floating charge but behind debts secured by a fixed charge.[124] Accordingly, a lender whose security is fixed has a considerable advantage over one whose security is merely floating.[125] An administrator appointed by the court under Part II of the Insolvency Act 1986 is permitted to sell property which is subject to a security as if it were not secured but, where the security is fixed rather than floating, this permission is conditional upon the consent of the court. Also, there is a specific provision in the Insolvency Act 1986 which invalidates charges in particular circumstances but its application is limited to floating charges.[126]

Also relevant in this context is the decision of the Court of Appeal in *Re Atlantic Computer*

---

[122] [1994] BCLC 485, [1994] BCC 36 noted (1994) 110 LQR 340, [1994] CLJ 225. See also Goode, 'Charges over Book Debts: a Missed Opportunity' (1994) 110 LQR 592.

[123] Compare *Waters v Widdows* [1984] VR 503, Victoria, Australia and *Re Holidair Ltd* [1994] ILRM 481 (Ireland, Supreme Court).

[124] Section 175 and schedule 6 of the Insolvency Act 1986.

[125] In Ireland, debts secured by fixed charges on book debts enjoy no priority over revenue debts: section 115 of the Finance Act 1986. This solution reconciles giving parties as much freedom as possible in structuring financing agreements and ensuring that preferential status established by statute has meaningful effect.

[126] Section 245 of the Insolvency Act 1986.

Systems plc.[127] Unlike the cases just discussed, this was concerned with a charge on present debts only which did not extend to future debts. The Court of Appeal held that the lender had a fixed charge on the debts by virtue of restrictions in the charging documentation on dealing with the debts. The charge did not restrict the company in its use of the proceeds of the debts but such restrictions were held to be unnecessary. This decision is clearly distinguishable on its facts from the *Siebe Gorman* line of authority in that it was not concerned with a charge on present and future assets. In *Re Atlantic Medical Ltd*[128] Vinelott J held that, in respect of a security which did extend to future debts, it was not necessary for him to decide whether the company was obliged to pay the proceeds of the debts into a separate account because, in any event, the charge was fixed. If *Atlantic Medical* is correctly decided and is widely interpreted, it may enhance further the freedom of contract allowed to the parties to a charge[129] in that it does not require the express separation of debts and proceeds as contemplated by *New Bullas* but it may be possible to confine the case by reference to its facts. The charge was on subleases in respect of equipment, and the future property in question comprised subleases and similar agreements entered into in respect of the same equipment in the event of the termination by passage of time or otherwise of the original subleases. This is a narrow category of future property and the situation is very different from a normal charge on present and future book debts, where the future book debts may have no connection with the debts which were in existence at the time of the charge.

9.19 Floating charges and the Bills of Sale Act

A debenture of a company formed under the Companies Act 1985 is not within the Bills of Sale Acts 1878 and 1882, and may therefore create a charge on chattels, without being in the form prescribed by or registered under the last-named Act.[130] It has been held that this exception does not apply to debentures of building societies and industrial and provident societies,[131] but extends to the debentures of foreign companies,[132] but it is difficult to reconcile these two rulings. It should be noted that the Bills of Sale Acts do not apply to Scotland where the floating charge is a statutory creation of what is now Part XVIII, Chapter 1 of the Companies Act 1985.

As a consequence of the requirements of the Bills of Sale Acts, it is not practicable for partners (or sole traders) to create an effective floating charge. This inability was made the greater by the 'reputed ownership' provision of the Bankruptcy Act 1914[133] (now repealed), which used to apply in the bankruptcy of partnerships and individuals but not

---

[127] [1992] Ch 505; [1992] 1 All ER 476, [1992] 2 WLR 367, [1991] BCLC 606, [1990] BCC 859. See also *Re CCG International Enterprises Ltd* [1993] BCC 580.

[128] [1992] BCC 653; [1993] BCLC 386. See also *Royal Trust Bank v National Westminster Bank* [1995] BC 128.

[129] Bridge, (1991) 107 LQR 394 at pp. 396–7.

[130] See section 17 of the Bills of Sale Act 1882. *Re Standard Manufacturing Co.* [1891] 1 Ch 627 (CA); *Richards v Overseers of Kidderminster* [1896] 2 Ch 212. Registration is, however, necessary under the Companies Act 1985, section 395.

[131] *Great Northern Rly Co. v Coal Co-operative Society* [1896] 1 Ch 187. Under section 1 of the Industrial and Provident Societies Act 1967, such a society in England and Wales may now execute a floating charge which will not be invalidated by the Bills of Sale Acts. As to recording such a charge, see section 1 (2).

[132] *Clark v Balm, Hill & Co.* [1908] 1 KB 667. Applied in *N. V. Slavenburg's Bank v International Natural Resources Ltd* [1980] 1 All ER 955, where Lloyd J preferred to follow *Clark v Balm*, above.

[133] Section 38 (c). This provision was repealed by what is now the Insolvency Act 1986.

in the liquidation of insolvent companies.[134] The report of the Review Committee on Insolvency Law and Practice[135] proposed the abolition of 'reputed ownership' together with 'appropriate amendments' of the Bills of Sale Acts so as to permit individuals (and partners) to create effective floating charges over their business undertaking.[136] This would not extend to assets not used in the debtor's business, trade or profession. Professor Diamond in his review of security interests in property other than land also proposed that the floating charge form of security should be made available to businesses generally, irrespective of the form in which the business was carried on.[137] There is no indication that repeal or reform of the Bills of Sale Acts is likely to be forthcoming in the immediate future.

9.20 Crystallisation of the floating charge

The charge crystallises or becomes fixed when the debenture holders or their trustees take possession or appoint a receiver on the occurrence of one of the events which under the provision of the debenture renders the security enforceable. Moreover, if the company goes into liquidation the charge will crystallise, even though the liquidation is for reconstruction purposes and the provisions of the debenture only stipulate that the principal shall become payable on the company going into liquidation otherwise than for the purpose of reconstruction.[138] But while the company continues in business[139] the charge does not crystallise merely by the happening of the events which entitle the debenture holder to intervene,[140] for 'unless something has occurred entitling the debenture holders to make such an application' (i.e. an application to the court for a receiver), 'and the application has in fact been made, or an action brought by them or on their behalf to realize their security, or unless something has happened which entitles the debenture holders to determine their licence to the company to carry on their business, and they have actually done so, the company is entitled to do all the things which the licence entitles them to do'.[141] If, therefore, the company assigns a book debt which is covered by the floating charge, it becomes the property of the assignee, and the receiver subsequently appointed cannot obtain priority by giving the debtor notice to pay him after the assignment.[142] A contractual lien will take priority over a floating charge where it arises from a contract made in the ordinary course of business before crystallisation. Where a carrier sought to exercise a lien (Condition 13 of the Conditions of Carriage of the Road Haulage Association) in respect of goods which came into their possession in carrying out their transport contract after the appointment of a receiver, it was held that

[134] See *Gorringe v Irwell Rubber Co.* (1886) 34 Ch D 128.

[135] Cmnd 8558, June 1982.

[136] ibid., paras. 1093 and 1569.

[137] *A Review of Security Interests in Property* (HMSO, 1989), para. 16.15.

[138] *Player v Crompton & Co.* [1914] 1 Ch 954.

[139] The 'cessation of the company's business' is preferable to 'ceasing to be a going concern' as a description of this crystallising event. *Re Woodroffes (Musical Instruments) Ltd*, [1986] Ch 366, [1985] 2 All ER 908, [1985] 3 WLR 543, [1985] BCLC 227.

[140] *Edward Nelson & Co. v Faber* [1903] 2 KB 367.

[141] *Evans v Rival Granite Quarries* [1910] 2 KB 979 *per* Vaughan Williams LJ at p. 986. At p. 993 Fletcher Moulton LJ says, 'Mere default on the part of the company does not change the character of the security; the debenture holder must actually intervene.' At p. 1002 Buckley LJ says, 'No equity arises in a debenture holder whose security is a floating charge from his merely giving notice to seize a particular asset of the company. He must do something to turn his security from a floating into a fixed charge.'

[142] *In re Ind, Coope & Co.* [1991] 2 Ch 223.

such an appointment did not prevent the carriers exercising their lien since their rights came into existence when the contract was made, not when they took possession of the goods. It was immaterial that the lien was exercised after the receiver's appointment.[143] It is uncertain whether the commencement of administration proceedings or the appointment of an administrator would cause a floating charge to crystallise in the absence of express provision to that effect in the charge. Since 1986, when the administration procedure was first introduced, it has become common for debenture terms to provide expressly for crystallisation in the event of administration.

The crystallisation of a floating charge over the undertaking of the company effects an equitable assignment to the debenture holders of the company's present assets which are comprised in the security[144] and also, unless excluded by the terms of the charge, of future assets accruing to the company as they arise. In *N. W. Robbie & Co. Ltd v Witney Warehouse Co. Ltd*[145] the majority of the Court of Appeal held that after the appointment of a receiver each future debt to the company became, as it arose, a chose in action belonging to the company subject to an equitable charge in favour of the debenture holder.

9.21 Notices of crystallisation

It has become increasingly common for debentures to include a provision whereby the holders are entitled to cause the charge to crystallise by serving a notice to that effect on the company. In *Re Woodroffes*, above, the effectiveness of a notice of crystallisation was assumed and in *Re Brightlife*, above, Hoffmann J decided the point. Hoffmann J held that crystallising events were not prescribed by law[146] and were to be determined by the parties to a charge as a matter of contract; crystallisation on winding up, receivership or cessation of business would be implied into a charge unless expressly excluded but it was open to the parties to agree upon additional crystallising events. A notice of crystallisation served in accordance with the terms of the charge would therefore be effective to cause the crystallisation of a floating charge.

9.22 Automatic crystallisation

Crystallisation on the service of a notice requires positive action by or on behalf of the debenture holders. Is it possible to dispense altogether with the need for positive action and to provide for crystallisation to occur automatically upon the occurrence of specified

---

[143] *George Barker (Transport) v Eynon* [1974] 1 WLR 462; (CA) (overruling Mocatta J [1973] 1 WLR 1461). (*Parsons v Sovereign Bank of Canada* [1913] AC 160; *Rother Iron Works Ltd v Canterbury Precision Engineers* [1973] 2 WLR 281 applied.) As to the priority of a floating charge over a *Mareva* injunction granted before the charge crystallises, see *Cretanor Maritime Co. Ltd v Irish Marine Management* [1978] 1 WLR 968.

[144] *George Barker (Transport) Ltd v Eynon* [1974] 1 All ER 900, [1974] 1 WLR 462, [1974] 1 Lloyd's Rep 65; *Leyland DAF Ltd v Automotive Products Ltd* [1993] BCC 389 at p. 392; *Re ELS Ltd, Ramsbottom v Luton Borough Council* [1994] 3 WLR 616, [1994] BCLC 743, [1994] BCC 449 (local authority precluded from levying distress on goods for non-payment of rates after charge had crystallised).

[145] [1963] 1 WLR 1324 (CA). The reasoning in *Witney Warehouse* was applied in *Rendell v Doors & Doors Ltd* [1975] 2 NZLR 199. See also *Security Trust v Royal Bank of Canada* [1976] 2 WLR 437 (PC) at p. 491 in respect of land acquired after a floating charge has crystalised by the appointment of a receiver.

[146] As suggested by *Edward Nelson & Co. Ltd v Faber & Co.* [1903] 2 KB 367, 376. Hoffmann J explained the statements in the earlier case by saying that the judge (Joyce J) was simply stating the crystallising events that would be implied unless expressly excluded by the parties.

events? It is established that an event which is of such magnitude as to lead to the cessation of the company's business is an implied automatic crystallising event: in that situation the raison d'être of the floating charge, namely continued freedom for the chargor company to use the charged assets in the course of its business, disappears. Greater controversy has in the past surrounded the possibility of providing for automatic crystallisation upon the happening of some lesser event which is not necessarily incompatible with continued trading by the company, such as the creation of a second mortgage or charge without the debenture holder's consent; but it is now clear that freedom of contract prevails in this area of the law.

The validity of an automatic crystallisation clause was upheld in New Zealand in *Re Manurewa Transport Ltd*.[147] The concept of automatic or 'self-generating' crystallisation has also been accepted in Australia,[148] although it has been rejected in Canada.[149] In England, dicta of Buckley LJ in *Evans v Rival Granite Quarries Ltd*[150] supported automatic crystallisation, but both Vaughan Williams and Fletcher Moulton LJJ stated in the same case (also obiter) that the debenture holder was required to intervene. The matter finally arose for decision in England in *Re Permanent House (Holdings) Ltd*[151] where, confirming views which he had expressed obiter in *Re Brightlife*, above, Hoffmann J held that an automatic crystallisation clause was valid and effective. In *Brightlife* Hoffmann J preferred the New Zealand authority to the approach taken in Canada and did not feel constrained by earlier English decisions to reach the opposite conclusion. In his view, automatic crystallisation was essentially a matter of explicit contractual provision. The rights and duties which the law might or might not categorise as a floating charge were derived from the agreement of the parties, as supplemented by implied terms, and merely because some terms deviated from what might be regarded as the 'standard' terms of a floating charge did not preclude the charge from being a floating charge. Hoffmann J considered that any policy objections to automatic crystallisation were matters to be settled by an appellate court or by Parliament.

Policy objections to automatic crystallisation clauses include the potential prejudice that they may cause to innocent third parties, who may be unaware (and have no means of knowing) that the charge has crystallised.[152] There is also the uncertainty that could result from a situation where a debenture holder tacitly waives a crystallisation which has occurred in accordance with an automatic crystallisation clause and allows the company to continue its business.[153]

---

[147] [1971] NZLR 909. See D. W. McLauchlan, 1972 *New Zealand Law Journal*, p. 330.

[148] *Stein v Saywell* (1969) 121 CLR 529; *DCT (Vic) v Horsburgh* [1984] VR 773; *Fire Nymph Products Ltd v The Heating Centre Pty Ltd (in liq)* (1991–1992) 7 ACSR 365. Cf. *Re Bismark Australia Ltd* [1981] VC 527. See also Burns, 'Automatic Crystallisation of Company Charges: Contractual Creativity or Confusion' (1992) 20 ABLR 125.

[149] *The Queen in Right of British Columbia v Consolidated Churchill Copper Corporation Ltd* (1978) 5 WWR 652.

[150] [1910] 2 KB 979.

[151] (1989) 5 BCC 151.

[152] The policy objections have been considered by various commentators and review bodies. The literature includes Farrar, 'The Crystallisation of a Floating Charge' (1976) 40 Conv 397; Gough, *Company Charges* (Butterworths, 1978), pp. 97–100 and 'The Floating Charge' in Finn (ed.), *Equity and Commercial Relationships* (Law Book Company, 1987) p 239; Boyle, 'The Validity of Automatic Crystallisation Clauses' [1979] JBL 231; Dean, 'Crystallisation of a Floating Charge' (1982–1984) 1–2 *Company and Securities Law Journal* 185; Review Committee on Insolvency Law and Practice, (Cmnd 8558) (1982) paras. 1577–80; Goode, *Legal Problems of Credit and Security* (Sweet & Maxwell, 2nd edn 1988) pp. 69–75; Pennington, 'Loans to Companies' in Pettet (ed.), *Company Law in Change* (Stevens, 1987) pp. 99–107.

[153] McLauchlan, [1972] *New Zealand Law Journal* 330. On 'decrystallisation' see Goode, op. cit. pp. 73–6 and Lightman and Moss, *The Law of Receivers of Companies* (Sweet & Maxwell, 2nd edn 1994), at paras. 3–41 to 3.45.

A particular objection, considered in *Re Brightlife* and *Re Permanent Houses*, above, but now, because of legislative developments, of no more than historical interest, was the effect of automatic crystallisation clauses on the position of preferential creditors. In a receivership or liquidation, preferential debts rank before debts secured by a floating charge[154], but before reforms enacted by the 1980s insolvency legislation, it was held[155] that the preferential status could only be claimed over debts secured by a floating charge which *was floating at the time of the receivership or liquidation*. If a floating charge had crystallised prior to the receivership or liquidation, the preferential debts ranked behind the debt secured by the charge. An automatic crystallisation clause could thus enable the holder of a floating charge to be repaid before the preferential debts. It may be noted that this objection could be levelled not just at automatic crystallisation clauses but also at clauses permitting crystallisation on the service of a notice and at crystallisation upon cessation of business prior to receivership or liquidation. However, automatic crystallisation clauses attracted particular criticism because they were thought to increase significantly the power of creditors lending money on the security of a floating charge to structure the lending to their advantage at the expense of the holders of preferential debts. This objection to automatic crystallisation has disappeared because, for the purposes of the relevant provisions of the Insolvency Act 1986, a floating charge is now defined as a charge which as created was a floating charge.[156] The status of the charge when it is created is all important and it now makes no difference that the charge may have crystallised before receivership or liquidation.

The possible ill effects of such clauses on innocent third parties remain.[157] A solution is offered by a provision of the Companies Act 1989[158], whereby the Secretary of State is empowered to make regulations requiring notice of the occurrence of crystallising events to be filed at the companies registry. These regulations can provide for the crystallisation to be ineffective until notified. This provision of the Companies Act 1989 is part of the extensive amendments to the requirements for the registration of company charges. At the time of writing, it is uncertain whether any of these amendments will ever be brought into force.

9.23 Crystallisation and rights of set-off

A right of set-off which accrues to a debtor of the company before crystallisation can be raised against a claim by the receiver against the debtor: in *Rother Iron Works Ltd v Canterbury Precision Engineers Ltd*[159] Russell LJ distinguished *Robbie v Witney Warehouse Co Ltd*,[160] where the cross claim was assigned to the debtor after the crystallisation of the

---

[154] Sections 40 and 175 of the Insolvency Act 1986. The categories of preferential debts are set out in Schedule 6 to the Act.

[155] *Re Griffin Hotel Co.* [1941] Ch 129; *Re Christionette International* [1982] 3 All ER 227; *Re Brightlife*, above; *Re Permanent Houses*, above; *William Gaskell v Highley*, above.

[156] Sections 40 and 251 contain the definition.

[157] Goode, op. cit. argues that potential unfairness to third parties disappears if the position is analysed on agency principles. He suggests that automatic crystallisation may terminate the company's actual authority to use the charged assets in the course of its business, but that, until the fact is brought to their attention, outsiders can continue to rely on the company's apparent authority.

[158] Section 100.

[159] [1973] 2 WLR 281 (CA).

[160] [1963] 1 WLR 1324 (CA).

charge. Moreover, there the claim made by the receiver arose out of a contract made by the receiver subsequent to his appointment. In *Rother Iron Works* the contract to sell goods, which the receiver was seeking to enforce, had been made before his appointment.[161]

9.24 Priorities and the floating charge

The rules as to priority between charges created by a company are basically the same as those governing legal and equitable charges generally. These rules are derived from the cases and they have not been codified in statutory form. The registration requirements of the Companies Act 1985 may affect the operation of the priority rules but it is important to note that they do not supplant those rules. The absence of clear statutory rules governing priority is open to criticism because it leads to some uncertainty. The position is different in Scotland where clear statutory rules are laid down as to priority.[162]

As between equitable charges, priority is governed by the order of creation, the charge created first ranking first in order of priority. A legal mortgage will rank before a previous equitable security where the legal interest is acquired by a bona fide purchaser for value without notice of the earlier interest. The special qualities of the floating charge mean that these general rules are modified in relation to a security of that type. In principle a floating charge will be postponed to any subsequently created fixed security (legal or equitable) regardless of notice, because the company is permitted to continue to deal with the assets which are the subject-matter of the floating charge and this dealing power includes the power to charge or mortgage them.[163]

As between two floating charges, the first created will prevail since there is no implied authority to create subsequent floating security ranking first. A second floating charge will only have priority if either: (a) the instrument creating the first floating charge gave an express power to create later floating charges ranking first;[164] or (b) the second floating charge is over part only of the company's assets and the court construes the express reservation in the general floating charge of the right to create prior charges as embracing particular types of floating charge.[165] Crystallisation of second floating charge before a first floating charge should not enable the second charge to move ahead of the first charge, because that result would be inconsistent with the bargain between the company and the holder of the first charge.[166]

To avoid the risk of being postponed to future charges by the creation of fixed mortgages or charges on all or part of the property of the company, it has become common in the case of floating charges to insert a declaration that the company shall not

---

[161] See further, as to the legal position of an 'administrative receiver' appointed under a general floating charge, Part 4 of this chapter.

[162] Sections 463–4 of the Companies Act 1985. For a recent example of the application of the statutory ranking provisions see *AIB Finance Ltd v Bank of Scotland* [1994] BCC 184.

[163] *Wheatley v Silkstone and Haigh Moor Coal Co.* (1885) 29 Ch D 715.

[164] *Re Benjamin Cope & Sons Ltd* [1914] 1 Ch 800.

[165] *Re Automatic Bottlemakers Ltd* [1926] Ch 412. The second floating charge must not affect substantially the whole of the company's property: ibid., p. 423.

[166] *Re Benjamin Cope & Sons Ltd*, above; *Re Household Products Co. Ltd* (1981) 124 DLR (3d) 325. But note *Griffiths v Yorkshire Bank* [1994] 1 WLR 1427, where a contrary view is taken. The statutory order of priority governing Scottish floating charges does not depend on, nor is it affected by, order of crystallisation.

have the power to mortgage the property in priority to or equally with the floating charge created by the debentures. This restriction is not incompatible with the nature of the floating charge.[167] The effect of inserting this restriction, which is sometimes referred to as a negative pledge, into a floating charge is that, if the equities are otherwise equal, it will bind a subsequent equitable fixed chargee even without notice.[168] Equities will not be equal where the debenture holder allows the company to retain the title deeds to the property which is the subject of the subsequent security.[169] In that event, the holder of the subsequent security will not be bound in the absence of notice of the restriction in the earlier floating charge.[170] The owner of a subsequent legal mortgage will only be bound where he has notice of the restriction.[171] Merely because a lender is aware of the existence of an earlier floating charge does not put the lender on inquiry or fix him with notice of a restriction that may be contained in that charge.[172]

9.25 The effect of registration on priorities

The requirement of registration under section 395 of the Companies Act 1985 affects the rules as to priorities in two ways. First of all, a charge which is not duly registered[173] within the twenty-one-day period is void and will lose all priority it would otherwise possess.[174] Secondly, registration, besides giving actual notice to those who search the register, has been held to give constructive notice to subsequent mortgagees or charg-ees.[175] Thus a registered fixed equitable charge will be protected as against a legal mortgage created after the time of registration of the equitable charge.

It should be noted that, subject to the effect of constructive notice, priority is based on the date of creation, not that of registration, though subsequent registration is necessary if the charge is to be effective.

It was held in *Wilson v Kelland*[176] that registration of a charge gave constructive notice of the charge, but not of the terms contained in the deed creating it. Thus registration of a floating charge will not by itself give constructive notice of the prohibition contained in that charge so as to postpone a subsequent mortgage.[177]

In order to give greater protection to floating charges, the practice has developed, which the Registrar has accepted, of including the prohibition in the trust deed among the registered particulars of the charge. It is widely assumed that this will give construc-

---

[167] *Re Brightlife* [1987] 1 Ch 200 at p. 209; *Re Cimex Tissues* at p. 635.

[168] *Re Castell & Brown Ltd* [1898] 1 Ch 315.

[169] As in *Castell & Brown*, above.

[170] ibid.

[171] *English & Scottish Mercantile Investment Co. v Brunton* [1892] 2 QB 700 at p. 707.

[172] *English & Scottish Mercantile Investment Co. v Brunton*, above, (where inquiries were in fact made); *Re Valletort Sanitary Steam Laundry Co Ltd* [1903] 2 Ch 654.

[173] See 9.42, below, as to the possibility of rectifying the register. But this will not be allowed so as to regain priority.

[174] *Re Monolithic Building Co.* [1915] 1 Ch 643.

[175] *Wilson v Kelland* [1910] 2 Ch 306; *Re Standard Rotary Machine Co.* (1906) 95 LT 829.

[176] [1910] 2 Ch 306.

[177] *Re Valletort Laundry* [1903] 2 Ch 654; *Re Standard Rotary Machine Co.* (1906) 95 LT 829.

tive notice of the prohibition, but this has not yet been tested in the courts in England,[178] and it has been rejected in New Zealand and Ireland.[179]

A provision enacted in the Companies Act 1989 is designed to clarify the position with regard to registration and notice. Under this provision[180] a person taking a charge over a company's property is deemed to have notice of any matter requiring registration and disclosed on the registration at the time the charge was created. Otherwise, a person is not to be taken to have notice of any matter by reason of its being disclosed on the register or by reason of his having failed to search the register in the course of making such inquiries as ought reasonably to have been made. Thus, under this provision, a chargee (which would include a mortgagee) is conclusively presumed to have notice of the matters which require registration and which are disclosed on the register but a purchaser is conclusively presumed not to have such notice.

The Companies Act 1989 provides for the matters requiring registration to be prescribed by the Secretary of State in regulations. When that legislation was enacted, it was expected that the Secretary would follow existing provisions governing registration of charges under Scottish law[181] and make the existence, or otherwise, of restrictions in floating charges a matter requiring registration, and hence bring such restrictions within the ambit of the notice provision.[182]

At the time of writing, the sections of the Companies Act 1989 on the registration of charges have not been brought into force.

9.26 Further advances and subsequent charges

A particular case should be noted. Mortgages and debentures are often created in favour of banks and others to secure a current account. In such a case if a subsequent mortgage is created on the same property and the bank entitled to the prior security has notice of such subsequent mortgage, it cannot make further advances upon its own security to the prejudice of the later mortgagee. Further, if it continues the current account, payments made by the debtor company will go in reduction of the debt existing at the time of the later mortgage,[183] so that in course of time the bank or lender on current account will become postponed to the later lender, for all subsequent advances will rank after the amount advanced by the later lender.[184] To meet this danger banks usually rule off and

---

[178] See also the effect of a clause providing for 'automatic crystallisation', discussed at 9.22, above. For an argument that constructive notice is not given by including the prohibition among the registered particulars, see Farrar, 38 Conveyancer 315 at p. 325 *et seq*. The author argues in favour of the different concept of 'inferred notice'. This inference would rest on the common practice but would be open to rebuttal; ibid. p. 319. This distinction was made in *Siebe Gorman v Barclays Bank* [1979] 2 Lloyd's Rep. 142.

[179] *Dempsey v The Traders Finance Corporation Ltd* [1933] NZLR 1258 (New Zealand); *Welch v Bowmaker (Ireland) Ltd* [1980] IR 251 (Ireland). The problem does not arise in Scotland, because the existence of a clause in a floating charge which prohibits, restricts or regulates the power of the company to grant further securities ranking in priority to or *pari passu* with the floating charge is a registrable particular: section 417 (3) (*e*) and section 413 (2) (*e*).

[180] Section 103 of the Companies Act 1989.

[181] Sections 417 (3) (*e*) and 413 (2) (*e*) of the Companies Act 1985.

[182] Section 103 of the Companies Act 1989 expressly mentions restrictions in floating charges as one of the matters which the Secretary of State can prescribe as a particular requiring registration.

[183] Under what is known as the rule in *Clayton's Case* (1816) 1 Mer. 572; see also next footnote.

[184] *Deeley v Lloyd's Bank* [1912] AC 756 (HL); *Hopkinson v Rolt* (1861) 9 HLC 514; *London and County Bank v Ratcliffe* (1881) 6 App. Cas. 722 (HL); *Bradford Banking Co. v Henry Briggs & Co.* (1886) 12 App. Cas. 29 (HL). *Siebe Gorman v Barclays Bank* [1979] 2 Lloyd's Rep. 142.

close the current account as soon as they learn of the subsequent mortgage, thus retaining their charge for the balance then due on current account.

9.27 Purchase money, security interests and floating chargees

If property is acquired subject to an existing charge or upon the terms of the purchase price being advanced on the security of the property, these charges will take priority over a floating charge on the company's undertaking or a fixed charge on the company's present and future assets of a description which covers the property so acquired. The implications of acquiring property on a mortgage and the priority position of the mortgagee as against others with competing interests in the same property were considered recently by the House of Lords in *Abbey National Building Society v Cann*.[185] This case concerned an individual acquiring residential property with the help of a mortgage, but the reasoning of their Lordships is equally applicable to corporate finance.

The House of Lords held that where a conveyance and a mortgage or charge take place at approximately the same time, in reality the purchaser never acquires more than an equity of redemption.[186] According to Lord Jauncey of Tullichettle:

> a purchaser who can only complete a transaction by borrowing money ... cannot in reality even be said to have acquired even for a scintilla temporis the unencumbered freehold or leasehold interest in the land whereby he could grant interests having priority over the mortgage ...

Thus a pre-existing charge must rank behind a later purchase-money security.

9.28 Postponement and avoidance of floating charges by statute

Certain special provisions affect the priority or validity of floating charges. The position of preferential debts has already been noted:[187] preferential debts which cannot otherwise be met have priority over debts secured by a charge which as created was a floating charge.[188] In *Re GL Saunders Ltd*[189] it was settled that where the realisation of a fixed charge produced a surplus (after satisfying the claims of the chargee) the surplus was not part of the assets subject to the floating charge. The company was in receivership and the significance of the decision was that it meant that the receiver had no obligation to pay preferential debts from the surplus because that obligation was limited to payment out of floating-charge assets. It has been held that the duty to meet the claims of preferential

---

[185] [1991] 1 AC 56, [1990] 1 All ER 1085, [1990] 2 WLR 832. Gregory, 'Romalpa Clauses as Unregistered Charges – a Fundamental Shift' (1990) 106 LQR 550; McCormack, 'Charges and Priorities – The Death of the Scintilla Temporis Doctrine' (1991) 12 Co. Law 11; de Lacy, [1991] LMCLQ 531; Bennett and Davis, 'Fixtures, Purchase Money Security Interests and Dispositions of Interests in Land' (1994) 110 LQR 448. Commentators note some uncertainty regarding the application of the Companies Act registration requirements to purchase money securities: e.g. [1991] LMCLQ 531 at pp. 535–7, (1994) 110 LQR 448 at pp. 479–83.

[186] Following *Re Connolly Brothers Ltd (No. 2)* [1912] 2 Ch 25 and *Security Trust Co. v Royal Bank of Canada* [1976] AC 503, [1976] 1 All ER 381, [1976] 2 WLR 437, and overruling the scintilla temporis approach favoured in *Church of England Building Society v Piskor* [1954] Ch 553.

[187] 9.22, above.

[188] Sections 40 and 175 of, and Schedule 6 to, the Insolvency Act 1986.

[189] [1986] BCLC 40.

creditors from floating-charge assets does not cease merely because the debenture holder has been paid, but is capable of having a separate life of its own.[190]

In a winding-up, section 245[191] of the Insolvency Act 1986 renders invalid certain floating charges created within twelve months of the winding-up in favour of persons not connected with the company. In the case of 'connected persons' this period is two years. The charge may be valid where value has been given to the company. All charges, fixed as well as floating, may be open to attack under section 239 of the Insolvency Act 1986 on the basis that the transaction has given one of the company's creditors (or a surety or guarantor of its debts) a preference.[192]

All these matters are examined at length in the context of the winding up of companies.[193]

9.29 Priority agreements

If a fixed charge is expressed to be subject to an earlier floating charge it will rank behind the earlier floating charge even though it would otherwise have taken priority.[194] Also, where there are two (or more) existing securities affecting the same property, the holders of the securities can agree amongst themselves to alter their priority and this does not require the company's consent.[195]

A priority agreement between the holders of fixed and floating charges can produce circularity problems concerning preferential debts: this problem arises where, under the insolvency legislation, the preferential debts rank behind debts secured by a fixed charge but before debts secured by a floating charge, whilst under the priority agreement, the debts secured by the floating charge rank before those secured by the fixed charge. How is this conundrum to be resolved?

The question was considered by Chadwick J in *Re Portbase (Clothing) Ltd, Mond v Taylor*.[196] Chadwick J held that the effect of the priority agreement was to postpone the fixed charge had been postponed to the floating charge. Preferring the approach taken in the Australian case of *Waters v Widdows*,[197] to the obiter views of Nourse J in *Re Woodroffes*,[198] he concluded that this postponement meant that the preferential debts ranked before the debt secured by the floating charge and also the debt secured by the fixed charge. If Chadwick J had followed the solution suggested in *Re Woodroffes* (where construction of a priority agreement did not arise for decision),[199] the debt secured by the floating charge would have ranked before the preferential debts to the extent of the fixed-charge security. Chadwick J noted that this solution might apply where the parties, by their agreement, exchanged their rights under their respective securities but that, as a matter of construction, it was not the effect of the agreement in question.

---

[190] *Re Pearl Maintenance Services Ltd* (judgment 2 March 1995, as yet unreported). See further 9.59 on the obligation of a receiver to pay preferential debts.

[191] See further 17.59.6, below.

[192] Sections 239 to 241. See 17.59.3 below.

[193] See Chapter 17, below.

[194] *Re Robert Stephenson & Co.* [1913] 2 Ch 201 (CA); *Re Camden Brewery Ltd* (1912) 106 LT 598.

[195] *Cheah Theam Swee v Equiticorp Finance Group Ltd* [1992] 1 AC 472, [1991] 4 All ER 989, [1992] BCLC 371, [1992] BCC 98.

[196] [1993] Ch 388, [1993] 3 All ER 829, [1993] 3 WLR 14, [1993] BCLC 796, [1993] BCC 96.

[197] [1984] VR 503.

[198] [1986] Ch 366. Nourse J adopted the analysis in Goode, *Legal Problems of Credit and Security* (Sweet & Maxwell, 1st edn 1982), pp. 54–5 (see also 2nd edn 1988, pp. 97–8).

[199] The solution adopted by Nourse J was conceded by counsel.

9.30 Retention of title clauses and floating charges

A receiver appointed on behalf of a debenture holder has no better title to goods in the company's possession whose ownership lies elsewhere than the company itself. Consequently, the owner of goods which are hired to the company or are the subject of a hire-purchase agreement may recover them from the receiver.[200] The same principle will apply to a 'title retention' clause in a sale of goods contract. Such clauses are known as *Romalpa* clauses from the leading case[201] in which their validity was upheld. They provide that the goods purchased shall remain the property of the seller until the purchase price is paid (as well, sometimes, as money outstanding in other contracts between the buyer and seller). In consequence the unpaid purchaser will be able to recover goods still in the company's possession against the claims of a receiver subsequently appointed under a floating charge. In *Romalpa*[202] there was a further provision that if the purchasing company resold any of the contract material it should do so as agent of the seller. It was held on that basis the buyer was accountable to the seller for the proceeds of the sub-sales. As agent a fiduciary duty was owed in respect of these proceeds which could be traced in equity.

Subsequent cases have tended to limit the protection which is afforded by a title retention clause to an unpaid seller who is in competition with the claims of a receiver appointed by a debenture holder.[203] The simplest type of clause where the seller retains title[204] to the very goods sold (as provided for in the Sale of Goods Act 1979, section 19 (1)) until specified debts are paid[205] is effective and it does not create a charge which must be registered so long as the goods supplied are identifiable and in the possession of the buyer.[206] If the goods supplied are subjected to a manufacturing process[207] with other materials, ordinarily a title retention clause does not vest title to the new product in the

---

[200] For the problems that arise where goods which are affixed to the company's land are still the subject of a hire-purchase agreement, see *Pennington's Company Law* (Butterworths, 6th edn 1990) pp. 459–61.

[201] *Aluminium Industrie Vaassen B. V. v Romalpa Aluminium Ltd* [1976] 1 WLR 676 (CA). The Scottish courts have also recognised title retention clauses: *Armour v Thyssen Edelstahlwerke AG* [1991] 2 AC 339, [1990] 3 All ER 481, [1990] 3 WLR 810, [1991] 1 Lloyd's Rep. 395, [1991] BCLC 28, [1990] BC 925.

[202] Above.

[203] There is a large amount of literature on retention of title clauses, including the following: Goodhart and Jones, 'The Infiltration of Equitable Doctrine into English Commercial Law' (1980) 43 MLR 489; Palmer, *Bailment* (Sweet & Maxwell, 2nd edn 1991), pp. 148–78; *Benjamin's Sale of Goods* (Sweet & Maxwell, 4th edn 1992), paras. 375 *et seq.*; Goode, *Proprietary Rights and Insolvency in Sales Transactions* (Sweet & Maxwell, 2nd edn 1989), Part V; Parris, *Effective Retention of Title Clauses* (Collins, 2nd edn 1989); McCormack, *Reservation of Title* (Sweet & Maxwell, 1990); Wheeler, *Reservation of Title Clauses: Impact and Implications* (Clarendon Press, 1991); Watts, 'Reservation of Title Clauses in England and New Zealand' (1986) 6 OJLS 456; Bradgate, 'Reservation of Title Ten Years On' [1987] Conv 434; Hicks, 'Retention of Title – Latest Developments' [1992] JBL 398; Ahdar, 'Romalpa's Empire: The Reception of Reservation of Title Clauses in New Zealand' [1993] LMCLQ 382; McCormack, 'Reservation of Title – Past, Present and Future' [1994] Conv 129.

[204] That is, legal title. 'Retention' of equitable ownership has been held to amount to a charge granted by the buyer in favour of the supplier: *Re Bond Worth Ltd* [1980] Ch 228, [1979] 3 All ER 919, [1979] 3 WLR 629; *Stroud Architectural Systems Ltd v John Laing Construction Ltd* [1994] BCC 18.

[205] The title retention clause in *Armour v Thyssen*, above, was an 'all monies' clause; title was retained pending payment of all debts between the parties. On 'all monies' retention of title clauses see further McCormack [1991] LMCLQ 154; Mance [1992] LMCLQ 35; McCormack [1994] Conv 129.

[206] *Clough Mill v Martin* [1984] 3 All ER 982, [1985] 1 WLR 111, [1985] BCLC 64 (CA), noted Goodhart, (1986) 49 MLR 96; *Armour v Thyssen*, above; *Hendy Lennox (Industrial Engines) Ltd v Grahame Puttick Ltd* [1984] 2 All ER 152, [1984] 1 WLR 485; *Re Andrabell Ltd* [1987] 3 All ER 407 at p. 414.

[207] The extent of the processing to which the goods are subjected may be significant. In *Armour v Thyssen* some of the goods supplied (steel strips) had been cut but this did not prejudice the claim of the original supplier.

supplier[208] and, furthermore, does not give a right to trace into the resulting new product.[209] Any rights[210] given by the contract in the newly created product would normally be a charge granted by the buyer to the seller and requiring registration under the Companies Act 1985.[211]

Despite the fact that such a claim was successful in *Romalpa* itself, suppliers' claims to the proceeds of resale of goods supplied on title retention terms (irrespective of whether those goods are processed before resale) have usually failed.[212] The obstacles are that the supplier must establish that there is a fiduciary relationship between himself and the buyer in respect of the proceeds of sale and that he has a beneficial interest in the proceeds of sale otherwise than by way of charge. The courts are reluctant to characterise the relationship between buyer and supplier as fiduciary. Instead, any interest of the supplier in the proceeds which is defeasible upon the payment of specified debts owing from the buyer to the supplier is usually characterised as a charge granted by the buyer to the supplier and, as such, it requires registration under the Companies Act 1985.[213]

9.31 Execution creditors and floating charges

If the debenture holders take steps promptly to enforce their security then their rights under a floating charge to the property comprised in their security take precedence over those obtained by an execution creditor where execution is incomplete. Execution is incomplete for this purpose where even though a sale by the sheriff has been avoided by the payment of money by the debenture holders, provided the money still remains in his hands;[214] but where money has been paid by the debtor company to the sheriff on the terms that he shall not sell the property seized, the title of the execution creditor to the money prevails as against the receiver.[215] If an execution is put in, or garnishee order obtained, the trustees or debenture holders ought at once to give the sheriff notice to withdraw, or to the debtor not to pay the garnishor, and proceed to the appointment of a

---

[208] In *Clough Mill v Martin* [1984] 3 All ER 982 at pp. 989–990, 993 Goff and Oliver LJJ thought that in principle it would be possible for parties to agree that title to manufactured goods would vest in the supplier of part of the goods used in the manufacturing process but that in practice it was unlikely that they would so agree. Goff LJ at p. 989 noted problems that would result from the conclusion that an agreement conferred absolute ownership of (or a right to trace in respect of manufactured goods) in a supplier: (1) buyer may have paid for some of the goods supplied; (2) buyer may have supplied part of the materials used in the manufacturing process and will have borne the cost of the manufacturing process; and (3) part of the materials used in the manufacturing process may have been supplied, subject to a title retention clause, by another supplier.

[209] *Borden (UK) Ltd v Scottish Timber Products* [1981] Ch 25, [1979] 3 All ER 961, [1979] 3 WLR 672 (CA); *Re Peachdart Ltd* [1984] Ch 131, [1989] 3 All ER 204, [1983] 3 WLR 878, [1983] BCLC 225 (1983) 1 BCC 98, 920; *Specialist Plant Services Ltd v Braithwaite* (1987) 3 BCC 119 and *Ian Chisholm Textiles Ltd v Griffiths* [1994] BCC 96.

[210] In *Borden* the court found that the seller had no interest whatsoever in the manufactured product.

[211] *Re Peachdart Ltd; Clough Mill; Modelboard Ltd v Outer Box Ltd* [1993] BCLC 623. Note *Hendy Lennox (Industrial Engines) Ltd v Grahame Puttick Ltd* (diesel engines supplied subject to title retention clause incorporated into generators but remained readily identifiable and easily disconnected; title retention effective despite incorporation).

[212] In *Tatung (UK) Ltd v Galex Telesure Ltd* (1989) 5 BCC 325 (noted McCormack [1989] LMCLQ 198; Wheeler (1989) 10 Co. Law 188) Phillips J questioned whether *Romalpa* had been correctly decided on the point.

[213] *Re Peachdart Ltd; Re Andrabell Ltd; E Pfeiffer Weinkellerei-Weineinkauf GmbH & Co. v Arbuthnot Factors Ltd* [1988] 1 WLR 150, [1988] BCC 608; *Tatung v Galex Leisure Ltd; Re Weldtech Equipment Ltd* [1991] BCC 16, [1991] BCLC 393, noted de Lacy (1991) 54 MLR 736; *Compaq Computers Ltd v Abercorn Group Ltd* [1991] BC 484, noted Hicks (1992) 13 Co. Law 217; de Lacy (1992) 13 Co. Law 164; *Modelboard v Outer Box*, above.

[214] *Re Opera* [1891] 3 Ch 260 (CA); *Taunton v Sheriff of Warwickshire* [1895] 2 Ch 319 (CA).

[215] *Robinson v Burnell's Vienna Bakery* [1904] 2 KB 624.

receiver, for if the security becomes a fixed one before the goods are sold or the debt paid the debentures will prevail.[216]

The equities of the debenture holder entitle him to oust the sheriff after he has seized if the security has crystallised before he has sold,[217] or to deprive the garnishor of his advantage if the crystallisation of the security has taken place before he has collected the money.[218] But if the debenture security is allowed to continue to float, the execution creditor's or garnishor's right will prevail, and a garnishee order *nisi* will be made absolute notwithstanding the opposition of the debenture holder or a claim made by him on the debtor to pay the money direct to the debenture holder,[219] for a debenture holder cannot single out and take a particular debt or piece of property while allowing the company to trade with the rest of its assets.[220]

Cases of considerable hardship have occurred where debenture holders have allowed a company to trade on credit, and have applied for a receiver only when the trade creditors were seeking to enforce their rights; but the rule that an execution creditor or garnishor takes precedent, subject to all equities affecting the debtor, is well established,[221] and the court has been compelled, sometimes with great reluctance, to appoint a receiver, who takes possession of all the assets and leaves the unsecured creditors unsatisfied.[222] The position of an execution creditor garnishing a debt owing to a company is not a favourable one, for if the debenture security has attached, not only is he postponed to debentures already issued,[223] whether a receiver has or has not been appointed at the time his order is made absolute,[224] but even after the service of the garnishee order absolute on the company it can, for good consideration, issue debentures which take priority over the rights of the garnishor.[225]

PART 3: THE REGISTRATION OF CHARGES

9.32 Legislative framework

Part XII of the Companies Act 1985 governs the registration of company charges. Details of most, but not all, charges created by companies must be delivered to the companies registry within twenty-one days of creation. The Registrar of Companies is required to maintain a register of charges and this is available for public inspection. Failure to deliver the requisite particulars to the companies registry results in the charge becoming void against certain categories of person. There is provision for late filing but this requires an order of the court. Where particulars are duly filed in accordance with the statutory requirements, the priority of the charge depends on the rules already dis-

---

[216] *Davey & Co. v Williamson & Sons Ltd* [1898] 2 QB 194, as explained in *Evans v Rival Granite Quarries* [1910] 2 KB 979 at p. 1000 (CA); *Norton v Yates* [1906] 1 KB 112.

[217] *Re Opera* [1891] 3 Ch 260; *Davey & Co. v Williamson & Sons Ltd* [1898] 2 QB 194; *Duck v Tower Galvanising Co.* [1901] 2 KB 314.

[218] *Norton v Yates* [1906] 1 KB 112.

[219] *Evans v Rival Granite Quarries* [1910] 2 KB 979 (CA).

[220] *Robson v Smith* [1895] 2 Ch 118; approved by CA [1910] 2 KB at pp. 989 and 998.

[221] *Re Standard Manufacturing Co.* [1891] 1 Ch 627 at p. 641 (CA); *Re Opera* [1891] 3 Ch 260.

[222] See the judgment of Buckley J in *Re London Pressed Hinge Co.* [1905] 1 Ch 576.

[223] *Norton v Yates* [1906] 1 KB 112.

[224] *Cairney v Back* [1906] 2 KB 746.

[225] *Geisse v Taylor and Hartland* [1905] 2 KB 658 (Div. Ct, Kennedy J, doubting).

cussed.[226] Priority of company charges is not governed by order of filing at the companies registry.

The system for the registration of company charges is open to criticism. The twenty-one-day period allowed for delivery of particulars means that the register may not give a searcher an accurate picture of the existing registrable charges on a company's property. The fact that not all charges which can be created by companies require registration further detracts from the register as a comprehensive source of information. The company also has to keep its own register of charges at its registered office and this register, which extends to all charges, can be searched to obtain a more complete picture; but a charge is not rendered void if it is not entered on this register which means that there is less incentive to ensure its accuracy. The existence of financing arrangements, such as conditional sales and hire purchase agreements, which are not in law regarded as charges will not be disclosed by either register. A further criticism of the existing system is that it preserves old, complex priority rules. A system of priority based on date of filing would be far more straightforward than a series of rules which depend on order of creation of competing securities, equality of equities and notice.

Professor Diamond in his *Review of Security Interests in Property* (HMSO, 1989) made various criticisms of the statutory regime for the registration of charges. The main thrust of Professor Diamond's report was directed at recommending a fundamental overhaul of the law relating to security interests generally, but he also made specific recommendations regarding company charges which were intended as interim measures pending the larger reform.[227] The proposed interim measures included amending the list of registrable charges, streamlining the registration procedure and, in particular, reducing the burden on the Registrar of Companies, making 'negative pledge' restrictions in floating charges registrable, introducing a system of priories related to the date of registration, eliminating the need to apply to court for an order authorising late registration, and removing anomalies in the law relating to the registration of charges by oversea companies.

Some of Professor Diamond's interim measures were included in the Companies Act 1989.[228] Part IV of that Act contains a set of provisions which are designed to replace in their entirety the existing sections of Part XII of the Companies Act 1985. Part IV of the Companies Act 1989 has not been brought into force. One difficulty with the new provisions is their relationship with other applicable registration requirements, in particular those relating to registered land. At the time of writing, it is uncertain whether the existing regime for the registration of charges will be reformed in the near future and whether, if it will be, the new provisions will bear much resemblance to those enacted in the Companies Act 1989. What is clear is that the DTI does not intend to bring Part IV of the Companies Act 1989 into force in its entirety. This is apparent from a consultative document, *Proposals for Reform of Part XII of the Companies Act 1985*, published by the DTI in November 1994. This paper outlines three options for reform, namely: (a) retention of the present legislation; (b) retention of the core provisions of the present legislation and incorporating improvements introduced by Part IV of the 1989 Act (but omitting some of

---

[226] See 9.24 above.

[227] *Review of Security Interests in Property*, Part III.

[228] In September 1987 the DTI had heralded the amendments by publishing its own proposals for amendment of the company charges requirements: 'Outline Proposals for Amendment of Sections 395 to 424 Companies Act 1985', noted (1988) 9 Co. Law 101 and (1988) 9 Co. Law 220.

the more controversial aspects of that Part); and (c) replacement of the present system with an entirely new one based on notice filing.

In view of the general uncertainty, the following account focuses mainly on the provisions which are currently in force. Brief mention is made of some of the ways in which the position would be different under the regime contained in the Companies Act 1989.[229] The more wide-ranging and fundamental reforms proposed by Professor Diamond, and also by previous review bodies, are considered at the end of the chapter.

Charges created by oversea companies may require registration at the English companies registry. Part IV of the Companies Act 1989 also includes new provisions which are designed to apply to charges created by oversea companies.[230]

9.33 Charges requiring registration

Every limited company must keep a register of charges, and enter therein particulars of all charges specifically affecting property of the company and of all floating charges.[231]

In addition to keeping such a register, sections 395 to 399 require particulars of certain mortgages and charges[232] created by companies registered in England to be delivered to the Registrar within twenty-one days after the date of their creation if they come within any of the descriptions mentioned below.

(1) a charge for the purpose of securing any issue of debentures;
(2) a charge on uncalled share capital of the company;
(3) a charge created or evidenced by an instrument, which if executed by an individual, would require registration as a bill of sale;
(4) a charge on any land, wherever situate, or any interest therein, but not including a charge for any rent or other periodical sum issuing out of land;
(5) a charge on book debts of the company;
(6) a floating charge on the undertaking or property of the company;
(7) a charge on calls made but not paid;
(8) a charge on a ship or aircraft or any share in a ship;
(9) a charge on goodwill or on any intellectual property.[233]

Anything which creates a charge in equity or law (being of any of the classes above described) therefore requires registration: that is to say, anything which would create a charge as between individuals will suffice. 'When there is a contract for value between the owner of a chose in action and another person which shows that such person is to have the benefit of the chose in action, that constitutes a good charge on the chose in action. The

---

[229] For more detailed examination of the 1989 Act see McCormack, 'Registration of Company Charges: The New Law' [1990] LMCLQ 520; Ferran and Mayo, 'Registration of Company Charges – The New Regime' [1991] JBL 152. The application of the requirements of the 1989 Act to various types of retention of title clauses is considered by McCormack, 'Reservation of Title and the Company Charges Registration System' in Palmer and McKendrick (eds), *Interests in Goods* (Sweet & Maxwell, 1993).

[230] This was recommended in the Diamond report: Chapter 27.

[231] Section 407, see 9.47 below.

[232] For the purposes of Chapter 1 of Part XII, 'the expression "charge" includes mortgage'; section 396 (4).

[233] 'Intellectual property' for this purpose is defined by section 396 (3A) which was inserted by the Copyright, Designs and Patents Act 1988.

form of words is immaterial so long as they show an intention that he is to have such benefit.'[234]

However, an absolute assignment (e.g. of book debts) is not a charge and will not require registration. Thus in *Lloyds and Scottish Finance Ltd v Cyril Lord Carpets Ltd*[235] the House of Lords held that assignments to a finance house of credit sale agreements, under a block discounting agreement, were absolute assignments and therefore did not require registration under section 93 of the Northern Ireland Companies Act 1960 (section 395 of the 1985 Act). Factoring arrangements are equally effective and do not require registration.[236] A company may enter into a complex financing arrangement, involving the sale of assets rather than a loan secured on those assets, specifically in order to avoid the need for registration (such arrangement may also fall outside the ambit of covenants in the company's existing loans whereby it has promised not to create any new security). This sale may be accompanied by an option in favour of the company allowing it to recover the assets at a later date so that, in economic terms, the arrangement may be indistinguishable from a secured loan. In *Welsh Development Agency v Export Finance Co Ltd*[237] a complex sale of this type was challenged by a debenture holder as amounting in substance to no more than a secured loan on the assets supposedly sold. The Court of Appeal rejected the claim on its facts but emphasised that the label attached to a financing arrangement is not conclusive and, if it is a sham or the substance of the arrangement does not accord with the label the parties have given it, the arrangement will not be allowed to stand.

Space does not permit even a cursory consideration of the special characteristics of various types of charge listed in section 396.[238] However, it should be noted that fixed charges over certain types of property are not included in the list in section 396.[239] The most important of these omissions is that of any fixed charge over shares held by the company in any other company. The Review Committee on Insolvency Law and Practice proposed[240] that charges over stocks and shares (and other marketable securities) be registrable under section 395. Professor Diamond reached the opposite conclusion and no provision for the registration of such charges is included in the Companies Act 1989. It is probable that a 'floating charge' (in section 396 (1) (*f*) includes such a charge over a class of the company's assets. This point is expressly covered in the Companies Act 1989. A charge 'for securing any issue of debentures' (in section 396(1) (*a*)) would not seem

---

[234] *Gorringe v Irwell India Rubber Works* (1886) 34 Ch D 128 at p. 134 *per* Cotton LJ (CA). In *National Provincial and Union Bank of England v Charnley* [1924] 1 KB 431 (CA) at pp. 449, 450, Atkin LJ expressed his view as follows: 'I think there can be no doubt that where in a transaction for value both parties evince an intention that property, existing or future, shall be made available as security for the payment of debt, and that the creditor shall have a present right to have it made available, there is a charge, even though the present legal right which is contemplated can only be enforced at some future date, and though the creditor gets no legal right of property, either absolute or special, or any legal right to possession, but only gets a right to have the security made available by an Order of the Court. ... If, on the other hand, the parties do not intend that there should be a present right to have the security made available, but only that there should be a right in the future by agreement, such as a licence to seize the goods, there will be no charge.'

[235] (1979) 129 NLJ 366; [1992] BCLC 609.

[236] *Re George Inglefield Ltd* [1933] Ch 1.

[237] [1992] BCLC 148, [1992] BCC 270; noted Oditah [1992] JBL 541.

[238] See further, *Gore-Browne on Companies* (Jordans, 44th edn, loose-leaf) 18.8–18.9.9, where the question of 'dual registration' under other legislation is also considered.

[239] Apart from charges upon shares referred to in the text, there are charges upon *non-book* debts and charges upon registered designs.

[240] Cmnd 8558 (1982), para. 1520.

to require a public issue of debentures (or debenture stock), but it would seem to require a series of debentures.

9.34 Effect of failing to register a charge

Any registrable mortgage or charge not registered within twenty-one days after the date of its creation is, 'so far as any security on the company's property or undertaking is conferred by the charge', void against the liquidator, the administrator and any creditor of the company,[241] and this is so even though the creditor is a second mortgagee who had notice of the prior unregistered mortgage.[242] It is to be noted that the charge is not avoided as against the company before liquidation or administration, and a chargee of goods who has seized the goods before liquidation, in pursuance of a licence to seize contained in the charge, is entitled to the benefit of the security as against the liquidator, despite non-registration of the charge.[243] An unregistered registrable charge is not avoided against purchasers, a point reversed in the registration regime of the Companies Act 1989. Section 395 does not invalidate the contract or obligation for repayment of the money thereby secured, which will accordingly, even if not registered, rank in a liquidation as an unsecured debt; and before liquidation the charge will be enforceable against the company by all the remedies of a mortgagee, although void against an execution creditor or a secured creditor. Section 395 (2), moreover, makes the money secured become immediately payable when the mortgage or charge becomes void. It has been held that an unregistered charge is void in a solvent liquidation as well as where the company is wound up insolvent. That interpretation of what is now section 395 (1) must be correct as a literal interpretation of the words 'void against any liquidator or creditor of the company'. It may, however, be doubted that that was the real intention of the draftsman in using the words 'liquidator and creditor' in conjunction. Where in the course of liquidation it is still unclear (as was here the case) whether the company is or is not insolvent, the validity of a charge will still be of great concern to the secured creditor.[244]

It is the duty of the company to effect the registration, and to supply the necessary particulars; but any person interested therein may, if he think fit, himself register the charge. Every person taking a mortgage or charge should protect himself by registering his security if the company has failed to do so. Section 399 (2) entitles him to recover from the company any fees he has to pay to the Registrar.

Failure to effect registration of a charge renders the company, and every officer in default, liable to a fine.[245]

9.35 The particulars of a charge to be registered

Under section 401 (1) the Registrar is to keep a register of all charges required to be registered, and to enter the following particulars:

(1) in the case of a charge to the benefit of which the holders of a series of debentures are entitled, the particulars as are specified in section 397 (1), namely:

[241] Section 395 (1). As to the similar provision made for Scotland, see section 410 (2).
[242] *Re Monolithic Building Co.* [1915] 1 Ch 643 (CA).
[243] *Mercantile Bank of India v Chartered Bank of India* [1937] 1 All ER 231. See also *Re Toomer: ex parte Blaiberg* (1883) 23 Ch D 254 (CA).
[244] *Re Oriel Ltd* [1984] BCLC 241.
[245] Sections 399 (3) and 400 (4). See Section 410 for the equivalent provision in Scotland.

(a) the total amount secured by the whole series;
(b) the dates of the resolutions authorising the issue of the series and the date of the covering deed, if any, by which the security is created or defined;
(c) a general description of the property charged; and
(d) the names of the trustees (if any) for the debenture holders;
(2) in the case of any other charge:
(a) if the charge was created by the company, the date of its creation, and if the charge was a charge existing on property acquired by the company, the date of the acquisition of the property;
(b) the amount secured;
(c) short particulars of the property charged; and
(d) the names of the persons entitled to the charge.

Any person may inspect such register.[246]

The registration of a series of debentures under this subsection protects all debentures properly issued in the series, and also agreements to issue such debentures, without separate registration, even when such agreements are only to be found in documents which were intended to be debentures, but from a technical defect can only be treated as agreements for debentures.[247]

Section 397 (2) requires the amount or rate of any underwriting commission paid, or any allowance or discount made on the placing or issue of debentures, to be included in the particulars filed; but omission to do this will not affect the validity of the debentures issued, and the deposit of debentures to secure a debt of the company is not, for the purposes of this subsection, an issue of the debentures at a discount.

9.36 The 'date of creation' for purposes of registration

Registration of a mortgage or charge under section 395 (1) is required to be effected within twenty-one days after the date of its creation. The 'date of creation' of a charge may differ from the 'date of issue' of the debenture it secures. The date of creation is the date when the trust deed or agreement creating the charge is executed or entered into.[248] This will be so even though no money is owing when the deed is executed.[249] Where a series of debentures is issued, the charge must be registered within twenty-one days after the date of issue of the first debenture.

Where, under a power in the debenture trust deed, other property of the company is substituted for the property originally charged, no new registration is required. No new charge requiring registration is thereby created.[250]

The charge created in equity by an agreement to issue debentures, if duly registered, will give an equal protection to the debenture holder as a complete debenture,[251] and so will a debenture informally issued if the holder had no notice of the informality.[252]

[246] Section 401 (3).
[247] *In re Fireproof Doors* [1916] 2 Ch 142.
[248] *Watson & Co. v Spiral Globe Co.* [1902] 2 Ch 209; *Re New London & Suburban Bus Co.* [1908] 1 Ch 621. Cf. *Re Harrogate Estates Ltd* [1903] 1 Ch 495. The Companies Act 1989 contains a specific provision dealing with the date of creation of a charge: section 103.
[249] *Esberger & Sons v Capital & Counties Bank* [1913] 2 Ch 366 and see *Transport & General Credit Corporation v Morgan* [1939] Ch 531.
[250] *Cunard S.S. Co. Ltd v Hopwood* [1908] 2 Ch 564.
[251] *Simultaneous Printing Syndicate v Foweraker* [1901] 1 KB 771.
[252] *Duck v Tower Galvanising Co.* [1916] 2 Ch 142.

9.37 The registration obligation

Prescribed particulars of the charge, together with any instrument creating or evidencing the charge, must be delivered to the Registrar of Companies within twenty-one days after the date of creation of the charge.[253] The duty to fulfil this registration requirements falls on the company but registration may instead be effected by any person who is interested in the charge.[254] It is in the lender's interest to take responsibility for registration, because the security will become void if it is overlooked. Section 399 (2) allows the lender to recover from the company any fee which has to be paid to the Registrar.

The Registrar of Companies is required to check the details of the prescribed particulars which are submitted against the charging document. When the checking process is complete, the Registrar registers the charge and issues a certificate of registration. Professor Diamond, echoing comments made previously by the Jenkins Committee,[255] thought that the obligation to check delivered prescribed particulars against charging documents was an unreasonable burden to impose on the Registrar. The registration regime contained in the Companies Act 1989 relieves the Registrar of Companies of this obligation submitted to the registry, but, as discussed in 9.38 below, this has implications with regard to one of the most controversial provisions of the 1989 Act, namely the abolition of the conclusive certificate of registration.

9.38 The Registrar's certificate as conclusive evidence

The Registrar must give a certificate of the registration of any mortgage or charge, stating the amount thereby secured, and the certificate will be conclusive evidence that the requirements of the Act as to registration have been complied with.[256] The company must cause a copy of the certificate so given to be endorsed on every debenture or certificate of debenture stock issued, the payment of which is secured by the charge so registered.[257] Where, however, the company has issued debentures or certificates of debenture stock, and further charges are created, to the benefit of which the holders are entitled, it will not be necessary for the company to endorse on the debentures or debenture stock certificates already issued a certificate of the registration of the charge.[258] Any person who knowingly and wilfully authorises or permits the issue of any debenture or certificate of debenture stock requiring registration without a copy of the Registrar's certificate being endorsed thereon incurs liability to a fine.[259]

The certificate of the Registrar is conclusive evidence that the requirements of the Act as to registration have been complied with, even if there is an omission in supplying the necessary particulars, e.g. the date of the resolution authorising the issue of the series,[260]

---

[253] Companies Act 1985, section 395. Note also section 397 which specifies the documents which must accompany particulars relating to a series of debentures.

[254] Section 399. If a charge is not registered the company and its responsible officers are liable to a fine: section 399 (3).

[255] *Report of the Company Law Committee*, 1965 Cmnd 1749, para. 302.

[256] Section 401 (2). This certificate will either be signed by the Registrar or authenticated by his official seal: section 401 (2) (*b*).

[257] Section 402 (1).

[258] Section 402 (2).

[259] Section 402 (3). As to the fine that may be imposed, see Schedule 24.

[260] *Cunard S.S. Co. v Hopwood* [1908] 2 Ch 564.

or of some class of property which is to be subject to the charge.[261] The court will refuse to go behind this certificate, and will not inquire whether there has been any irregularity.[262] Thus, where a creditor sent in defective particulars, omitting to state that the instrument conferred a charge over chattels, and the Registrar, by mistake or oversight, omitted to mention that charge in the register, his certificate was held to be conclusive that the document creating the charge was properly registered.[263] In the same case it was also decided that the requirement as to stating in the certificate 'the amount thereby secured' is sufficiently complied with by the words 'all sums now due or to become due'.

If the particulars submitted at the time the charge is registered do not give the true date of creation, and as a result the charge is registered and a certificate is issued by the Registrar, the charge will be valid even though more than twenty-one days have elapsed between the creation and registration of the charge.[264] The decision of the Court of Appeal in *In Re C. L. Nye Ltd*[265] illustrates the degree of protection afforded by section 401 (2). A company was granted loan and overdraft facilities by a bank against the security, *inter alia*, of its business premises. All the necessary documents for registration (including an undated charge) were delivered to the bank's solicitor on 28 February 1964. The charge was stamped on 19 March, but thereafter was mislaid in the office of the bank's solicitor, and was not discovered until 19 June 1964. The solicitor thereupon inserted that date as being the date when the charge was created, and lodged for registration on 3 July the prescribed particulars of the charge in accordance with section 395 (1). The Court of Appeal held that, notwithstanding that the date of the charge was incorrectly stated in the particulars delivered to the Registrar, once the certificate was granted section 401 (2) applied. The certificate was conclusive evidence that all the requirements of the Act as to registration had been complied with. The requirement for delivery of the particulars within twenty-one days in section 395 (1) was not a condition precedent to the Registrar's jurisdiction to register a charge or grant a certificate.[266]

In *R v Registrar of Companies ex parte Central Bank of India*[267] it was held that judicial review should not be allowed so as to challenge the Registrar's decision to register a charge where there were defects in the original registration of a charge in respect of the time allowed. What is now section 401 (2) did not exclude the jurisdiction of the court. It merely excluded the admission of evidence to challenge the decision of the Registrar in the exercise of his statutory duty. Only the Attorney-General could obtain judicial review of the Registrar's decision to register a charge because the Crown was not bound by section 401 (2).[268]

If inaccurate or incomplete particulars are delivered to the Registrar he is not obliged

---

[261] *National Provincial and Union Bank of England v Charnley* [1924] 1 KB 431 (CA); *Re Mechanisations (Eaglescliffe) Ltd* [1966] Ch 20.

[262] *Re Yolland, Husson and Birkett* [1908] 1 Ch 152 (CA); *National Provincial and Union Bank of England v Charnley*, above.

[263] *National Provincial and Union Bank of England v Charnley*, above; *Re Mechanisations (Eaglescliffe) Ltd*, above.

[264] *Re Eric Holmes (Property) Ltd* [1965] Ch 1052.

[265] [1971] 1 Ch 442.

[266] [1971] 1 Ch 442 (applying *National Provincial Bank v Charnley* [1924] 1 KB 431) *per* Harman LJ (p. 470), Russell LJ (pp. 472 and 474) and Megaw LJ (p. 476).

[267] [1986] QB 1114, [1986] 2 WLR 177 [1986] 1 All ER 105 (CA), overruling Mervyn Davies J, in *R v Registrar of Companies, ex parte Essal Commodities* [1985] 2 WLR 447.

[268] Except that the Court of Appeal left open the possibility of a challenge by someone other than the Attorney-General where the certificate disclosed an error on its face, or the challenge was based on fraud or duress.

to register the charge[269] and can return the particulars for correction.[270] Where defective particulars are returned, the obligation to file within twenty-one remains unfulfilled and the lender may have to move quickly to ensure that correct particulars are filed within the twenty-one-day period.

The registration regime contained in the Companies Act 1989 abolishes the conclusive certificate of registration. Instead, the Registrar is merely required to send to the company, the chargee and, if the particulars were delivered by another person, to that person a copy of the filed particulars and of the note made by him of the date of delivery.[271] The Registrar's note of the date of delivery does not constitute conclusive evidence of the date of delivery, but the Registrar can be required by any person to provide a certificate stating the date on which particulars were delivered to him and this certificate is conclusive evidence that they were delivered no later than that date.[272]

The abolition of the conclusive certificate of registration, although part of the streamlining measures advocated by Professor Diamond,[273] is one of the obstacles to implementation of the registration regime contained in the Companies Act 1989. Under the existing regime, the production of a certificate of registration gives a purchaser from a debenture holder (or a receiver acting on the debenture holder's behalf) the assurance that the charge under which the sale is made has not become void for want of registration. A purchaser would not have that assurance if the provisions in the Companies Act 1989 were to be implemented.[274] None of the options for reform outlined by the DTI in its consultative document published in November 1994 would include implementation of the Companies Act 1989 with regard to removal of the conclusive certificate of registration.

9.39 The transfer of charges

Where the benefit of a mortgage or charge on land owned by a company is transferred, and the company is a party to the transfer, the practice is to register the transfer as a new charge, but the question of registration does not arise if the company is not a party to the transfer.

The proper means of obtaining a decision of the court as to whether registration is necessary is by proceedings instituted for the purpose.[275]

9.40 Property acquired subject to a charge

Section 400 requires companies registered in England which acquire property already subject to a charge to register the charge within twenty-one days of the completion of the

---

[269] *Sun Tai Cheung Credits Ltd v AG* (1987) 3 BCC 357.

[270] The Registrar's practice of not accepting defective particulars in satisfaction of the filing obligation was endorsed by Lawton and Slade LJJ in *Central Bank of India.*

[271] Section 95 of the Companies Act 1989.

[272] Section 94. There is also a presumption that the particulars were delivered on the stated date, but that could be rebutted by evidence to the contrary.

[273] The Registrar would no longer be required to check filed particulars against original charging documents and would therefore no longer be in a position to determine whether the requirements as to registration have been complied with.

[274] The Land Registry is understood to oppose implementation for this reason *Company Law Review: Proposals for Reform of Part XII of the Companies Act 1985*, DTI consultative document, November 1994). Note section 99 which attempts to deal with the issue by providing that a chargee or receiver can give a good title to a purchaser (defined as a person who acts in good faith and who gives valuable consideration) even though the charge has become void but that the chargee must then hold the proceeds of sale on a statutory trust.

[275] *Re Cunard S.S. Co.* [1908] WN 160.

acquisition.[276] Though a penalty is provided for failure to register such charges on the register of charges kept by the Registrar, this failure does not render the charge void, as is the case with charges created by the company and not registered under section 395.[277] Where property was conveyed to a company, which created a legal mortgage in favour of the vendor for the unpaid balance of the purchase price, it was held that registration had to be effected under what is now section 395 and not under section 400.[278] Some doubt has been cast on this by the decision of the House of Lords in *Abbey National Building Society v Cann*[279] because it is now the case that there is never a moment when the purchaser of a property on a mortgage holds the property free of the security so that it is arguable that the purchaser does not create a charge over its own property for the purposes of section 395.[280]

9.41 Registration and priorities

Registration of a registrable charge 'perfects' the security against others who have competing interests in the same property and prevents the security becoming void. Registration, however, does not determine priority. Thus, the priority of two fixed charges on the same property, both of which are duly registered, is determined by order of creation, not by order of registration. Registration of a charge does give notice of the existence of that charge to subsequent chargees, so that where priority depends on notice (for example where a fixed charge is followed by a legal mortgage of the same property), compliance with the registration requirement can be a significant factor in establishing priority.[281]

Professor Diamond recommended a move to a priority system based on order of registration but this suggestion was not taken up in the Companies Act 1989.

9.42 Rectification of the register of charges[282]

Section 404 of the Companies Act 1985 provides that the register of charges may be rectified by supplying any omission or correcting any misstatement,[283] or the time for registration may be extended. Any such rectification or extension must be authorised by the court on the application of the company or any person interested.[284] But this will only be allowed if the court is satisfied that the omission to register a charge within the time required by the 1985 Act, or that the omission or misstatement of any particular with respect to any such charge, or in a memorandum of satisfaction, was accidental, or due to

---

[276] If the property charged is situated outside Great Britain the material date becomes twenty-one days after the copy of the instrument could in due course of post, if dispatched with due diligence, have been received in the United Kingdom: secton 400 (3).

[277] *Capital Finance Co. Ltd v Stokes* [1969] 1 Ch 261 (CA).

[278] ibid. Equivalent provision is made for Scotland by section 416.

[279] Above.

[280] The arguments against this view which are put forward in de Lacy [1991] LMCLQ 531 at pp. 536–7 are, however, persuasive.

[281] For a general discussion of the rules governing the priority of competing securities, see 9.24, above.

[282] McCormack, 'Extension of Time for Registration of Company Charges' [1986] JBL 282.

[283] e.g. cancelling a notice of satisfaction of a mortgage entered by mistake. *Re C. Light & Co.* [1917] WN 77. When once a certificate of registration has been given by the Registrar, it is, apparently, unnecessary for the secured creditor to take any steps to rectify the register, however defective or even misleading it may be: *National Provincial and Union Bank of England v Charnley* [1924] 1 KB 431 (CA).

[284] Swinfen-Eady J has held that it is not proper to apply for an extension of time as a means of determining whether or not registration is necessary: *Re Cunard S.S. Co.* [1908] WN 160.

inadvertence or to some other sufficient cause, or is not of a nature to prejudice the position of creditors or shareholders of the company, or that on other grounds it is just and equitable to grant relief: section 404 (1).[285] The court may impose terms as the condition of the grant of relief. Where a solicitor had advised that it was not necessary to register, that was held to be 'sufficient cause'.[286]

It is now[287] usual to make the order in the following form: 'That the time for registering the debentures [*or* mortgage] be extended until the   day of   19   ; and this order is to be without prejudice to the rights of parties acquired during the period between the date of creation of the said (charge) and the date of its actual registration).'[288]

Where a charge was created but not registered within the specified time, and leave to register was subsequently given, the charge was held to be postponed to a duly registered mortgage given before such registration to a director who had full knowledge of the earlier charge at the time he advanced his money.[289] Where, however, the only directors of a company learnt that the company had failed to fulfil its obligation to register a charge and then registered a charge in their own favour, the order extending time for registration of the earlier charge did not include the normal proviso which would have protected the rights of the directors.[290] The reasoning behind this is that the court will modify the order to exclude the proviso where its inclusion would facilitate an equitable fraud.[291] A chargee who discovers that, by mistake, he is unregistered, should act without delay. He should not deliberately defer action to see which course suits him best.[292]

The form of order that is now usual replaced the more traditional form, which was to the effect that the order was to be 'without prejudice to the rights of parties acquired prior to the time when such debentures [or mortgage] shall actually be registered'. The change in the form of the order resulted from the decision in *Watson v Duff Morgan & Vermont (Holdings) Ltd*,[293] which demonstrated that, under the old form, there could be circumstances when a charge registered out of time might regain the priority it had at the time of creation. Here, a company created first and second debentures on the same date, charging as security (by way of first and second floating charges, respectively) all its undertaking and property present and future (including its uncalled capital). The second charge was *expressly* made subject to, and ranked after, the charge created by the first debenture. The second was registered within twenty-one days, but by mischance the first debenture was *not* so registered (and thus initially became void under section 395 (1)). Templeman J held that, where the usual order had been made under section 404 (in an earlier application), the old form of the proviso in the order (see above) related only to rights acquired during the period when the first debenture was void, that is, rights acquired outside the original twenty-one day period for registration of the first debenture.

---

[285] *Re Chantry House Developments plc* [1990] BCC 646, [1990] BCLC 813 (relief granted by means of an interlocutory notice of motion).
[286] *Re S. Abrahams & Sons Ltd* [1902] 1 Ch 695.
[287] This contains the new form of proviso introduced as a result of *Watson v Duff Morgan & Vermont (Holdings) Ltd* [1974] 1 WLR 450, discussed below.
[288] *Re The Mendip Press* (1901) 18 TLR 38; *Re Joplin Brewery Co.* [1902] 1 Ch 79 as to the original form of the proviso. A more elaborate form is given for the case where there are duly registered debentures in *Re I. C. Johnson & Co.* [1902] 2 Ch 101 (CA).
[289] *Re Monolithic Building Co.* [1915] 1 Ch 643 (CA).
[290] *Re Fablehill Ltd* [1991] BCLC 830, [1991] BCC 590.
[291] *Re Telomatic Ltd, Barclays Bank plc v Cyprus Popular Bank Ltd* [1993] BCC 404.
[292] *Victoria Housing v Ashpurton Estates* [1982] 3 All ER 655; *Re Telomatic*, above.
[293] [1974] 1 WLR 450.

The rights of the holder of the second debenture had not been acquired during that period – but on the date when the second (as well as the first) debenture was executed. The mere expiration of the twenty-one day period allowed for registration had not conferred any rights on the holder of the second debenture.[294]

The decision in *Watson* was satisfactory on its facts because the holder of the second charge had express notice of subjection to a first charge. However, the general distinction which it implied, between a charge created within twenty-one days of an earlier charge and one created outside that period, was anomalous and open to objection in principle. The revised version of the proviso removes the anomaly but where, as in *Watson*, the second charge is expressly subject to the first charge, the court order will normally include specific provision preserving this postponement.

9.43 Effect of a winding-up

Except in very exceptional circumstances, an order extending the time for registration will not be made once a winding-up has commenced,[295] because a winding-up, whether compulsory or voluntary, is a proceeding for the benefit of the unsecured creditors, so as to establish their right not to be postponed to the holders of debentures subsequently registered.[296] It has been held that where a winding-up is imminent, the court may exercise its discretion to refuse registration out of time.[297] Alternatively, where liquidation appears to be imminent, the court may insert a proviso permitting the company to make an application to discharge the extension order within a specified period after a winding-up becoming effective on or before a specified date.[298]

Where there is no winding-up before the actual registration of the debentures, an order in the usual form does not prevent the debentures, when registered, from taking priority over existing unsecured creditors who have not levied execution or taken some effective step to enforce their debts before the registration of the debentures.[299] Thus it is clearly established that the order only protects creditors who have acquired a security or levied execution on the property which is the subject matter of the charge, and that the court will not insert any terms for the protection of the unsecured creditors of the company.[300]

The registration provisions of the Companies Act 1989 dispense with the need to apply to court for an extension order where a charge is not duly registered within twenty-one

---

[294] *Re Ehrmann Bros.* [1906] 2 Ch 691 and *Ramnarain v Rahda Kishen Moti Lal Chamaria* (1929) LR 57 Ind. App. 76 (PC), applied. *Re Monolithic Building Co.* [1915] 1 Ch 643, distinguished.

[295] *Re S. Abrahams & Sons* [1902] 1 Ch 695 (the order was refused on the ground that it would be of no value); *Re Anglo-Oriental Carpet Co.* [1903] 1 Ch 914; *Re Mechanisations (Eaglescliffe) Ltd* [1966] Ch 20 at pp. 36–7. *Re Spiral Globe Company* [1902] 1 Ch 396 and *Re R. M. Arnold & Co. Ltd* [1984] BCLC 535 are examples of exceptional cases where an order was granted after the commencement of winding up. In *Re Resinold and Mica Products Ltd* [1982] 3 All ER 677 the Court of Appeal did not accept any qualification to the general rule, but earlier authorities were not cited to the court.

[296] *Re Anglo-Oriental Carpet Co.* [1903] 1 Ch 914.

[297] *Re Ashpurton Estates* [1983] Ch 110.

[298] *Re L. H. Charles & Co. Ltd* [1935] WN 15; *Re Braemar Investments Ltd* [1989] Ch 54, (1988) 4 BCC 366, [1988] BCLC 556; *Exeter Trust Ltd v Screenways Ltd* [1991] BCLC 888, [1991] BCC 477.

[299] *Re Ehrmann Bros.* [1906] 2 Ch 697 (CA); *Re I. C. Johnson & Co.* [1902] 2 Ch 101; cf. *Re Cardiff Workmen's Cottage Co.* [1906] 2 Ch 627.

[300] *In re M. I. G. Trust* [1933] 1 Ch 542, *In re Kris Cruisers* [1949] Ch 138.

days. Under that regime, late filing[301] can be made at any time but, for a period of up to two years from the time of the late filing, the charge is vulnerable and liable to be avoided as against a liquidator or an administrator.[302] The priority of charges created before the late registration of an earlier charge is also preserved.

9.44 Memorandum of satisfaction

When a registered charge is paid or satisfied in whole or in part a memorandum of satisfaction in the prescribed form, verified by a statutory declaration by a director and the secretary, should be lodged with the Registrar. Registration of the satisfaction or partial satisfaction of the debt is optional and may be effected at any time[303] but it is obviously desirable to record the fact that the company's indebtedness has been discharged or reduced. A similar memorandum may be lodged with the Registrar where part of the property or undertaking charged has been released from the charge or has ceased to form part of the company's property or undertaking. Section 403 requires that the memorandum be recorded by the Registrar on his register.

Omissions or misstatements in a memorandum of satisfaction may be rectified by the court under section 404, discussed above.

9.45 Charges over foreign property

Section 398 (3) of the Companies Act 1985 provides that if the mortgage or charge is created within the United Kingdom[304] but comprises property outside the United Kingdom, the instrument purporting to charge such property must be lodged for registration. Registration must be effected even if further proceedings (e.g. registration in a foreign country) are necessary to make the charge valid in accordance with the law of the country in which such property is situate. Section 398 (1) provides that 'in the case of a mortgage or charge created out of the United Kingdom comprising property situate outside the United Kingdom', a copy verified in the prescribed manner, delivered to or received by the Registrar, with the proper particulars, within twenty-one days after the date on which the instrument or copy could in due course of post, if dispatched with due diligence, have been received, will be sufficient to comply with the requirements of the Act. Companies instructing their agents abroad to create a mortgage must therefore be careful also to instruct them to forward a verified copy of the mortgage by the earliest possible post.

When a charge comprises property situate in Scotland or Northern Ireland and registration in the country where the property is situate is necessary to make the charge valid or effectual according to the law of that country, the delivery to and the receipt by the Registrar of a copy, verified in the prescribed manner, of the instrument by which the charge is created or evidence, together with a certificate in the prescribed form stating that the charge was presented for registration in Scotland or Northern Ireland, as the case

---

[301] Or filing to correct incomplete or inaccurate particulars (section 96), a situation which, because of the conclusive nature of the certificate of registration and the Registrar's practice (post-*Esal*) of refusing to accept defective particulars, cannot occur under the existing registration requirements.

[302] Section 95.

[303] *Scottish & Newcastle plc, Petitioners* [1993] BCC 634 (on the equivalent Scottish provision).

[304] i.e. Great Britain and Northern Ireland. Equivalent provision for Scotland is made by section 411.

may be, on the date on which it was so presented is, for the purposes of section 395, to have the same effect as the delivery and receipt of the instrument itself.[305]

9.46 Charges on property in Britain created by an oversea company

By section 409, the provisions of Part XII, Chapter I of the Companies Act 1985 are extended to charges on property in England and Wales which are created, and to charges on property in England and Wales which is acquired, by a company (whether a company within the meaning of the Act or not) incorporated outside Great Britain which has an established place of business in England and Wales. The Court of Appeal has had to determine the meaning of 'established place of business' for the purposes of section 409 in the case of an Isle of Man company which had acquired seven petrol stations in Lancashire, and then created charges over these properties in favour of an oil company.[306] The charges had not been registered under what is now section 409. Oliver LJ (giving the judgment of the court) held that evidence that a company has 'carried on business' may not be substantial enough to show that the company has 'an established place of business'. 'The concept, as it seems to me, is of some more or less permanent location not necessarily owned or even leased by the company, but at least associated with the company and from which habitually or with some degree of regularity business has been conducted.'[307] On this basis only three of the seven charges were registrable under section 409 since, by the time they were created, the evidence showed that the company had established a business in the sense defined by Oliver LJ.

When an oversea company establishes a place of business or a branch in Great Britain, it is supposed to register under Part XXIII of the Companies Act 1985. Whether or not such registration has been effected, an oversea company which has an established place of business in Great Britain is subject to section 409 and must therefore register any charges on its property in England and Wales.[308] This creates an anomaly because it is the practice of the Registrar not to accept particulars of charges for registration under section 395 unless an oversea company is already registered under what is now Chapter I of Part XXIII of the 1985 Act.[309] In order to preserve the validity of the charge the owner of the charge must deliver particulars of the charge, together with the instrument (if any) by which it is created or evidenced. This will save the charge despite the lack of actual registration.[310] This divergence of the obligation imposed by section 409 from the Registrar's practice in administering section 395 would seem unsatisfactory both from the point of view of the owner of the charge and others who continue to deal with the company. Doubtless the policy of the Registrar is to provide further encouragement for oversea companies which establish a place of business in England to register under Chapter I of Part XXIII of the 1985 Act.

The Companies Act 1989 contains a new set of provisions governing the registration

---

[305] Section 398 (4).

[306] *Re Oriel* [1985] BCLC 343 at p. 347.

[307] Oliver LJ applied *Lord Advocate v Huron and Erie Loan and Savings Association* 1911 SC 612. See also *Deverall v Grant Advertising Inc.* [1955] Ch 111; *Act Dampskip Hercules v Grand Trunk Pacific Railway* [1912] 1 KB 222; *South India Shipping Corp. v Export Import Bank of Korea* [1985] 1 WLR 585.

[308] *NV Slavenburg's Bank v Intercontinental Natural Resources* [1980] 1 WLR 1076.

[309] See 2.23, above.

[310] [1980] 1 WLR 1076 *per* Lloyd J, following a dictum of Scrutton LJ in *National Provincial Bank v Charnley* [1924] 1 KB 431, 447.

of charges by oversea companies. Under these provisions (which are not in force) the anomaly highlighted by the *Slavenburg* decision would disappear.

It has also been held[311] that the term 'liquidator' in section 395 (as extended by section 409 to companies incorporated outside England) includes a liquidator appointed in a foreign winding-up where the foreign winding-up was similar in character to an English winding-up. In any event representative creditors may be joined, under Order 15, rule 6 (i), to plead the liquidator's case under section 395. Section 395 applies to floating charges as well as to fixed charges and when applied to oversea companies by virtue of section 409 includes a charge on future property in England. It is not confined to property existing in England when the charge was created. Further, if the charge initially came within section 395 by virtue of section 409, it remains within section 395 even if the company ceased to have a place of business in England before the commencement of the liquidation.[312]

9.47 The company's register of charges: section 407

In addition to registering with the Register those charges specified in section 396, section 407 of the Companies Act 1985[313] requires that every limited company must keep at its registered office a register of all charges specifically affecting property of the company and all of floating charges on the undertaking or any property of the company. In this register must be entered a short description of the property charged, the amount of the charge, and except in the case of securities to bearer, the names of the persons entitled to such charge. If any property of the company is charged[314] without such entry being made, every officer of the company who knowingly and wilfully authorises or permits the omission is liable to a fine.[315]

A person entitled to the benefit of a charge, however, even though a director of the company, does not lose his security by an omission to see that it is entered in the company's Register of Charges.[316] (It has been seen that he does so if the charge is one that requires registration under section 395 and is not registered with the Registrar.) The priority of charges is not affected by any imperfection of the register kept by the company.[317] Debentures containing a specific charge on the property of the company must be included in this register, and also those only containing a floating charge.

The company must also keep at its registered office a copy of every instrument creating a charge requiring registration.[318] In the case of a series of uniform debentures it will suffice to keep a copy of one of such debentures.[319]

Under section 408, the register of charges, and copies of all instruments creating charges which are required to be registered with the Registrar, must be open at all reasonable times to the inspection of any creditor or member of the company without

---

[311] [1980] 1 WLR 1076.

[312] ibid.

[313] Equivalent provision is made for Scotland by section 422. Section 422 is, however, not confined to limited companies. A floating charge is in principle assignable by the holder, and on due intimation of the assignation the particulars of the assignee must be entered in the company's own register of charges. Intimation of the assignation must be in writing, in such terms (on a reasonable interpretation) as to convey to the debtor company that the debt has been transferred to the assignee: *Libertas Kommerz GmbH* 1978 SLT 222.

[314] The expression 'charge' includes mortgage: section 396 (4).

[315] See now the Companies Act 1985, Schedule 24.

[316] *Wright v Horton* (1887) 12 App. Cas. 371 (HL).

[317] *Re General South American Co.* (1876) 2 Ch D 337 (CA).

[318] Section 406 (1). Equivalent provision is made for Scotland by section 423.

[319] Section 406 (2).

fee. The register of charges, but not copies of charging documentation, must be open to inspection by any other person on payment of a fee not exceeding 5p; but on a winding-up, the register cannot be inspected without an Order of Court.[320] The right to inspect the register of charges involves a right to take copies of it.[321] Any officer refusing to allow such inspection is liable to a penalty. In the case of such refusal in relation to a company registered in England the court may by order compel an immediate inspection.[322]

An advantage for a creditor, or prospective creditor, in searching the company's register of charges in addition to the register maintained by the Registrar of Companies is that this may disclose the existence of charges which do not require registration with the Registrar. Some idea of the amount of a company's existing secured debt can also be gleaned from its last annual return, but this is necessarily a historical record of the amount as at the date of the annual return, which may since have become out of date.

9.48 The reform of the law of security over personal property

The law of security over personal property has been the subject of two major reviews since the 1970s. The first review was conducted by the Committee on Consumer Credit, chaired by Lord Crowther (the 'Crowther Committee').[323] The Crowther Committee put forward a proposed new framework for the law relating to security over personal property. This framework was largely based on article 9 of the United States Uniform Commercial Code which governs all secured transactions over personal property.[324]

In a White Paper published in 1973[325] the Government accepted that aspects of the law caused difficulty and announced its intention to institute consultations to determine whether there was a need for a major recasting of the law on new principles and whether the proposed Crowther scheme commanded general support. Apart from a report relating to Scottish law[326] and limited reference to the Crowther scheme in the *Report of the Review Committee on Insolvency Law and Practice*,[327] thereafter there were few significant developments with regard to possible reform of personal security law until, in March 1986, the Department of Trade and Industry appointed Professor A. L. Diamond to undertake a 'review of security over property other than land'. Professor Diamond's final report was published in 1989.[328] Professor Diamond's main criticisms of the existing law were as follows:[329]

---

[320] *Somerset v Land Securities Co.* [1897] WN 29.

[321] *Nelson v Anglo-American Land, etc., Co.* [1897] 1 Ch 130. Note that, as these sections do not give the persons inspecting a right to have a copy supplied on payment, the case is different from that of the register of members. See 10.5.2, below.

[322] Section 408 (4).

[323] 1971, Cmnd 4596.

[324] Article 9 also formed the foundation of the Canadian Personal Property Security Act.

[325] *Reform of the Law on Consumer Credit* (Cmnd 5427).

[326] Halliday Working Party Report, published by the Scottish Law Commission in March 1986.

[327] 1982, Cmnd 8558.

[328] *Review of Security Interests in Property*. See also Diamond, 'The Reform of the Law of Security Interests' [1989] CLP 231.

[329] The Diamond Report is summarised by Lawson, 'The Reform of the Law Relating to Security Interests in Property' [1989] JBL 287 and the issues raised are discussed by Bridge, 'Form, Substance and Innovation in Personal Property Security Law' [1992] JBL 1.

(1) the law is too fragmented, treating transactions essentially equal in nature in different ways and complicating the legal issues quite unnecessarily;[330]
(2) the complexity and uncertainty of the law leads to expense and delay and hinders legitimate business activity;
(3) some of the rules operate unfairly and do not hold a just balance between the parties;
(4) the variations in the different legal rules cause problems in determining between competing interests and give rise to fortuitous differences in insolvency;
(5) it can be difficult to discover the existence of security interests until it is too late;
(6) purchasers of property subject to security interests of which they were unaware are put at risk and are inadequately protected; and
(7) the varieties of security interest that exist mean that it is more difficult for purchasers to obtain speedy legal advice.

An illustration of the fragmentation of the law is the fact that a genuine[331] sale of assets coupled with an option to repurchase which is entered into to enable the company to raise finance, although it may be economically indistinguishable from a loan secured on those assets, does not require registration at the companies registry because it is not, in legal terms, a 'charge'. The non-registrable status of retention of title clauses and hire-purchase agreements also illustrates the point.

Professor Diamond advocated[332] the introduction of a new simplified law which was similar to the Crowther scheme and which was based on the United States and Canadian models. Under the new law, substance would have precedence over form, and any arrangement, having as its true purpose the transfer or creation of rights over or interests in property other than land, as security for the provision of finance or the performance of any other obligation, would be treated as giving rise to a 'security interest'. Hire-purchase agreements and retention of title clauses, which are not presently registrable, would become security interests under this scheme, as could sales of assets entered into for financing purposes.

The creation of security interests enforceable against third parties would require a degree of formality in the form of a written financing agreement,[333] and as a general rule non-possessory securities interests would be required to be made public by some form of registration or filing.[334] Priority of competing securities would be governed by date of filing, not, as is presently the case, by date of creation and questions of notice.[335] One particular question raised by Professor Diamond at the consultive stage was the treatment of floating charges under a new scheme. In his final report, he recommended[336] the preservation of the essence of the floating charge, namely the freedom for the debtor to dispose of the property secured in the ordinary course of business, and the attachment of the charge to after-acquired property falling within the description of the security.

---

[330] Criticisms also voiced judicially by Browne-Wilkinson V-C (as he then was) in *Welsh Development Agency v Export Finance Co. Ltd* [1990] BCC 393 (decision reversed by the Court of Appeal).
[331] *Welsh Development Agency v Exfinco* (CA), above. Compare *Re Curtain Dream plc* [1990] BCLC 925 where a transaction which the parties designated a sale was held to be a registrable charge.
[332] Chapter 9 of the report sets out the main recommendations.
[333] Chapter 10 of the report.
[334] Chapter 11 of the report.
[335] ibid.
[336] Chapter 16.

Professor Diamond specifically recommended that the floating-charge form of security should be made available to all businesses, whether incorporated or not.

Reaction to Professor Diamond's final proposals was muted[337] and in 1991 the Secretary of State for Trade and Industry indicated that they would not be adopted.[338] The Minister stated that consultations had established that the majority of interested parties were opposed to major reform and that it could not be commercially justified. The main argument against reform is that, although it is widely accepted that the current law is complex and lacking in any functional basis, it is a system with which lenders, and their advisers, are familiar and which does allow lenders to achieve the object of obtaining adequate security for their loans.

At the time of writing it appears that limited reforms will be introduced in the relatively near future in order to remove some of the most obvious difficulties caused by the statutory provisions governing the registration of charges. However, it is likely that more radical reform initiatives will not be pursued until, perhaps, this becomes necessary in order to implement European Union harmonisation measures.[339] The DTI's consultative document published in November 1994 does include the option of fairly radical reform, but the Department itself seems not to favour this option, noting, as it does, that translation of any such proposal into workable legislation would be a task of some complexity which would take several years to complete.

PART 4: DEBENTURE HOLDERS' REMEDIES

9.49 Scope

This part is mainly concerned with the usual remedy employed when a debenture is secured by a floating charge, namely the appointment of a receiver under an express power in the debenture trust deed.

9.50 The categories of receiver

In English company law there have traditionally been two types of receiver (or receiver and manager): the receiver appointed by the court and the receiver appointed by debenture holders under a power in the debenture trust deed. The Insolvency Act 1986 has introduced a new category of receiver – the 'administrative receiver'.[340] Such a receiver is now subject to a distinct statutory regime over and above the rules that apply to

---

[337] The Company Law Committee of the Law Society and the Joint Working Party of the Bar and the Law Society on Banking Law were against implementation of the radical reforms: 'Comments on "A Review of Security Interests in Property"' (November 1989, Memorandum No. 211).

[338] *Hansard*, H. C. vol. 189, col. 482, 24 April 1991.

[339] The memorandum published by the Company Law Committee of the Law Society and the other bodies mentioned in note 337, above, cites possible European developments as a reason for not adopting the Diamond reforms at this stage: 'it would be unfortunate if a major change in the law were to be implemented and then followed by another major change to accommodate any EEC requirements', para. 8.2.10.

[340] See section 42 to 49.

receivers and managers generally.[341] An administrative receiver[342] is defined as a receiver or manager of the whole (or substantially the whole) of a company's property. He must be appointed by or on behalf of the holders of any debentures of the company secured by a floating charge, or by a floating charge and one or more fixed charges.[343]

The 'administrative receiver' should be distinguished from another institution, the 'administrator'.[344] Such an individual is appointed by the court making an 'administration order' under Part II of the Insolvency Act 1986 to help a company in financial difficulties. The court must be satisfied that the company is or will be insolvent. The aim is either to secure the survival of the company as a going concern or to secure a more advantageous realisation of the company's assets than would be effected in a winding-up. The petition for an administration order must be made either by the company or a creditor. However, the court cannot make an order if it is opposed by a secured creditor who has appointed, or is entitled to appoint, an administrative receiver. Since administration is not as such a remedy for secured creditors, it is discussed elsewhere in this book in the context of the law[345] of insolvent companies.

9.51 Unsecured debentures

Debenture holders, like any other creditors, may bring an action in debt if their principal or interest is in arrears. A debenture holder may, when his principal or interest is in arrears, petition for the winding-up of the company[346] and may also seek an administration order.

In the case of unsecured debentures (e.g. unsecured loan stock) these are the only remedies available to them.[347] The covenant to pay interest and repay capital, in the case of debenture stock, is made with the trustees of the debenture stock trust deed unless the trust deed otherwise provides. The trustees must commence any civil proceedings to enforce the covenant, but a debenture stock holder may compel them to do so by bringing proceedings in equity to enforce the execution of the trust. The debenture trust deed may

---

[341] References in the Companies Act 1986 or in the Insolvency Act 1986 to a receiver or manager of the property of a company include a receiver or manager of part of that property or of income arising from the property or part of it. This also includes references to a receiver who is not a manager. Likewise references to appointment of a receiver or manager under powers contained in an instrument includes appointment under powers which, by virtue of any enactment, are implied in and have effect as if contained in an instrument: section 29 (1).

[342] See section 29 (2) (*a*).

[343] This extends to a person who would be such a receiver or manager but for the appointment of some other person as the receiver of part of the company's property. On whether there can be more than one administrative receiver in office at the same time (apart from joint appointments) see Oditah, 'Lightweight Floating Charges' [1991] JBL 49; Marks and Emmet, 'Administrative Receivers: Questions of Identity and Double Identity' [1994] JBL 1. A receiver appointed to a foreign company can be an administrative receiver: *Re International Bulk Commodities Ltd* [1993] Ch 77; [1993] 1 All ER 361; [1992] BCLC 1074; [1992] BCC 463. Cf. *Re Devon and Somerset Farmers Ltd* [1993] BCC 410.

[344] See Part II of the Insolvency Act 1986.

[345] See Part 3 of Chapter 17.

[346] *Re Borough of Portsmouth & Tramways* [1892] 2 Ch 362.

[347] The court will not normally appoint a receiver unless the debentures are secured by a charge: *Harris v Beauchamp Bros.* [1896] 1 QB 801 (CA); *Re Swallow Footwear Ltd, The Times*, 23 October 1956. Moreover, in Scotland only the holder of a floating charge can appoint a receiver. The possibility of the court appointing a receiver on behalf of an unsecured lender has been considered in Australia: *Bond Brewing Holdings v National Australia Bank* (1990) 1 ACSR 445, noted (1991) 107 LQR 551, [1990] 8 JIBL 330, [1991] 10 JIBL 405.

impose a restriction on such proceedings by requiring them to be brought by a certain fraction of the debenture holders or debenture stock holders.[348]

9.52 Secured debentures

If default is made in the payment of the principal or interest secured by mortgage debentures,[349] the holders have all the remedies which mortgagees would have in like circumstances, i.e.: they may sue on the covenant to pay; they may obtain a receiver of the rents and profits, or apply for a sale of the mortgaged property;[350] they may, if the whole of the debenture holders are parties to the action,[351] proceed by way of fore-closure;[352] or, if they have legal estate or a power to enter, they may take possession.[353] In each case the debenture and trust deed (if any) must be consulted to see, first, whether there has really been a default, and, secondly, what remedies are available without the assistance of the court, and what remedies require an action to be commenced. The strict performance of all conditions is of the utmost importance, for without this the powers cannot be exercised nor will any order be made by the court for the appointment of a receiver or execution of the trust. For instance, if payment is stipulated to be made at a certain time and place, the condition is not broken unless demand is made by the debenture holder at that place;[354] but if the condition is only that the principal shall be paid at a named place, demand of the interest need not be made at such place.[355] So if the consent of a majority of the debenture holders is required by the deed before an action is brought, a debenture holder who has not obtained such consent cannot obtain the appointment of a receiver.[356]

The usual remedy today, where the debentures or debenture stock are secured by a charge, is to seek to enforce the powers given by the terms of the debentures in the trust deed to appoint a receiver out of court. The power to appoint a receiver may be either express or implied by reference to the Law of Property Act 1925;[357] but, as the power under that Act is very meagre, being primarily intended only to deal with real estate, there is usually an express power in elaborate terms to appoint a receiver without the need to resort to a debenture holder's action.[358] Where a debenture provides for the repayment of all moneys thereby secured on demand and for the debenture holder to become entitled to appoint a receiver in default of compliance with such demand, the debenture holder is required to give the debtor a reasonable opportunity of implementing the

---

[348] See *Pethybridge v Unibifocal Co.* [1918] WN 278.

[349] The company cannot by making default compel debenture holders to accept immediate repayment: *Re General Motor Cab Co. (No. 2)* (1912) 56 SJ 573.

[350] An action by one debenture holder for a receiver in the Chancery Division is no impediment to an action by another debenture holder in the Queen's Bench Division for the payment of arrears of interest: *Cleary v Brazil Rly Co.* [1915] WN 178.

[351] *Elias v Continental Oxygen Co.* [1897] 1 Ch 511.

[352] *Oldrey v Union Works* [1895] WN 77.

[353] The examples relate to English law, but the principle is true in Scotland also.

[354] *Thorn v City Rice Mills* (1889) 40 Ch D 357; *Re Escalera Silver Co.* (1908) 25 TLR 87.

[355] *Re Harris Calculating Machine co.* [1914] 1 Ch 920.

[356] *Pethybridge v Unibifocal Co.* [1918] WN 278.

[357] Sections 101 and 109.

[358] *Gore-Browne on Companies* (Jordans, 44th edn, loose-leaf), 19.3–19.6, contains a full account of the procedure governing debenture holders' actions.

mechanics of payment before appointing a receiver.[359] The 'mechanics of payment' test means that the debenture holder must allow the debtor time to effect the transfer from its account but it does not extend to giving the debtor time to raise new money to meet the demand.[360]

A receiver appointed out of court will usually be given wide powers, including a power of sale. The powers conferred on an administrative receiver are also deemed to include a wide range of statutory powers, except in so far as these are inconsistent with the terms of the debenture under which he was appointed.[361]

If the power to appoint a receiver is conferred on one or some of the debenture holders, it must be exercised as a trust for the benefit of all of the holders of the debentures: otherwise the court will intervene and itself appoint a receiver.[362]

Appointing a receiver under an express power in the trust deed avoids the trouble, delay and expense of applying to court. Nowadays it should rarely be necessary to resort to seeking an appointment of a receiver by the court unless there is some defect in the express power. One circumstance where the court may be asked to appoint a receiver is where the debenture holder's security is 'in jeopardy' and the debenture trust deed does not provide for the appointment of a receiver in that situation.[363]

On grounds of jeopardy, a receiver may be appointed, even before the principal or interest is in arrear if the assets are in danger[364] or a sale will be necessary in the near future.[365] Many appointments have been made under this power,[366] but if any opposition is offered, the court scans closely the circumstances, and will not allow a debenture holder to obtain a receiver merely because the security he has accepted is a risky one or the assets of the company are not sufficient to pay the debenture in full.[367] A receiver will, however, be appointed if the company's business is practically at an end, and the only asset remaining is a reserve fund created out of profits earned at an earlier date,[368] or if the business is about to be shut down and the premises let.[369] Indeed it now seems that the jeopardy must be from some act which would be wrongful as against the debenture holders or amounts or may amount to a destruction of his security.

If there is a specific charge on part of the assets and a floating charge on the rest, jeopardy, by reason of threatened executions on the specifically charged assets, will be a ground for the appointment of a receiver of them, without a receiver and manager of other assets not in jeopardy, the security being ample.[370]

---

[359] *Cripps (Pharmaceuticals) Ltd v Wickenden* [1973] 2 All ER 606, [1973] 1 WLR 944; *Bank of Baroda v Panessar* [1987] Ch 335, [1986] 3 All ER 751; *NRG Vision Ltd v Churchfield Leasing Ltd* [1988] BCLC 624, (1988) 4 BCC 56.
[360] ibid.
[361] Section 42 of the Insolvency Act 1986, see 9.61, below.
[362] *Stuart v Maskelyne Typewriter etc. Co.* [1898] 1 Ch 133 (CA).
[363] The court will not imply a term into a debenture trust deed entitling the debenture holder to appoint a receiver in the event of jeopardy: *Cryne v Barclays Bank plc* [1987] BCLC 548.
[364] *McMahon v North Kent Iron Works Co.* [1891] 2 Ch 148; *Edwards v Standard Rolling Stock Syndicate* [1893] 1 Ch 574; *Thorn v Nine Reefs* (1892) 67 LT 93 (CA); *Wissner v Levison & Steiner* [1900] WN 152; *Re London Pressed Hinge Co.* [1905] 1 Ch 576; *Re Braunstein and Marjolaine* [1914] WN 335.
[365] *Smith v Wilkinson* [1897] 1 Ch 158.
[366] The jeopardy is usually the danger of the assets charged being taken in execution by unsecured creditors under judgments. The right of the debenture holders thus to make their security attach was discussed by Buckley J in *Re London Pressed Hinge Co.* [1905] 1 Ch 576.
[367] *Re New York Taxicab Co.* [1913] 1 Ch 1.
[368] *Re Tilt Cove Copper Co.* [1913] 2 Ch 588.
[369] *Re Braunstein and Marjolaine* [1914] WN 335.
[370] *Grigson v George Taplin & Co.* (1915) 112 LT 985.

Since debenture holders rarely seek the assistance of the courts to enforce their security the remainder of this part is concerned only with receivers who are appointed out of court under powers contained in debentures or debenture trust deeds.[371]

9.53 Receivers and managers: capacity to act as a receiver

In England[372] a body corporate is not qualified for appointment as receiver of the property of a company; any body corporate acting as receiver is liable to a fine.[373]

If an undischarged bankrupt acts as receiver or manager of the property of a company on behalf of debenture holders, he is liable to imprisonment and/or a fine. This does not apply if the appointment was made by the court[374] but it is difficult to envisage circumstances where the court would be inclined to appoint a bankrupt as a receiver.

A receiver or manager may now be disqualified from 'managing' other companies by a court order under the Company Directors (Disqualification) Act 1986. Such an order may disqualify a person from acting as a receiver or manager where he has committed certain serious offences.[375]

An administrative receiver acts an 'insolvency practitioner'.[376] Insolvency practitioners, as a category, are regulated by the Insolvency Act 1986.[377] Persons must be qualified to act as insolvency practitioners, usually through membership of an appropriate authority such as the regulatory bodies of the accounting profession, and they must provide security for the performance of their functions.[378] It is an offence to act as an insolvency practitioner when not qualified to do so.[379]

An administrative receiver must vacate office of he ceases to be qualified to act as an insolvency practitioner in relation to the company. He may also resign office[380] but can only be removed from office by order of the court.[381] The fact that the debenture holder who appointed an administrative receiver cannot remove him from office without a court order gives an administrative receiver security against removal without cause (but note that the administrative receiver's freedom to act independently is curtailed by his duty to act in the interests of his appointor[382]). Where an administrative receiver vacates office (otherwise than by death) he must send notice to the Registrar of Companies within fourteen days.[383]

---

[371] *Gore Browne on Companies* (Jordans, 44th edn, loose-leaf), 19.9–19.13, considers court-appointed receivers.

[372] For receivers in Scotland, see ibid., 19.16–19.33.

[373] Section 30 of the Insolvency Act 1986.

[374] Section 31.

[375] See 13.16 *et seq.*, below.

[376] Section 388 of the Insolvency Act 1986.

[377] Part XIII.

[378] The details of the qualification requirements are fleshed out in the Insolvency Practitioners Regulations 1990 (SI 1990 No. 429).

[379] Section 389 (1). This does not apply to the official receiver: section 389 (2).

[380] Section 45. There is no statutory provision which entitles a receiver who is not an administrative receiver to resign and the matter is governed by the debenture under which the receiver is appointed.

[381] Section 45.

[382] See 9.59 below.

[383] Section 45 (4). See also the Insolvency Rules 1986 (SI 1986 No. 1925) which impose further notification requirements. When an administrative receiver vacates office the remuneration and expenses to which he is entitled are charged on the property of the company under his custody or his control at the time he leaves. This secures the payment of these claims. The same principle also applies to any indemnity to which he is entitled out of the assets of the company. See section 45 (3).

9.54 Notification of the appointment of a receiver

Within seven days after the appointment of a receiver or manager, the person making the appointment under the powers contained in any instrument must give notice of the fact to the Registrar, who must enter it in the register of charges.[384] If default is made, a fine may be imposed.[385] There is no statutory obligation on a receiver who is not an administrative receiver or on his appointor to notify the company of the appointment, but this would be done at an early stage in the ordinary course of events. On his appointment an administrative receiver must at once send notice of his appointment to the company. He must also publish this notice in the 'prescribed manner', that is in the *London Gazette* and in an appropriate newspaper. He must send notice of his appointment within twenty-eight days to all the creditors of the company (so far as he is aware of their addresses).[386]

Where any receiver or manager has been appointed, every invoice, order for goods or business letter issued on behalf of the company or the receiver or manager or the liquidator, being a document on which the name of the company appears, must state that a receiver or manager has been appointed.[387]

9.55 Defective appointments

Section 34 of the Insolvency Act 1986 deals with the consequences of invalid appointments of receivers or managers.[388] Whether this is caused by the invalidity of the instrument under which the appointment is made or otherwise, the court may order the person making the appointment, or the person on whose behalf the appointment was made, to indemnify the appointee against liability arising solely by reason of the invalidity of the appointment.[389] In practice receivers may prefer to ensure that their appointors give them a contractual indemnity to avoid the need to obtain a court order.

Also of note in this context is section 232 of the Insolvency Act 1986, which provides that the acts of an individual as administrative receiver are valid notwithstanding any defect in his appointment, nomination or qualifications.[390]

9.56 Application to the court to fix a receiver's remuneration

The court may, on application by the liquidator, fix the remuneration of a receiver or manager appointed under the powers contained in any instrument, and may from time to time, on the application of the liquidator, receiver or manager, vary or amend any order so made.[391] The power to fix the remuneration extends to fixing the remuneration for any period before the making of the order or the application, and is exercisable

---

[384] Section 405 (2) of the Companies Act 1985. The corresponding obligation to notify the Registrar of ceasing to act as a receiver or manager falls on the receiver or manager himself: section 405 (3).

[385] Section 405 (4).

[386] Section 46 and Insolvency Rules, rule 3.2.

[387] Section 39 (1) Insolvency Act 1986. See section 39 (2) as to the fine that may be imposed on those who have knowingly and wilfully authorised a default.

[388] *Shamji v Johnson Matthey Bankers Ltd* [1991] BCLC 36 is an example of an (unsuccessful) challenge to the appointment of a receiver.

[389] An invalidly appointed receiver may be liable as a trespasser on the company's property: *Re Goldburg (No. 2)* [1912] 1 KB 606.

[390] This is similar to section 285 of the Companies Act 1985, which deals with defectively appointed directors. On the limits of the protection afforded by that section, see *Morris v Kanssen* [1946] AC 459, which is discussed in 4.35, above.

[391] Insolvency Act 1986, section 36.

notwithstanding that the receiver or manager has died or has ceased to act before the making of the order or the application. Further, where the receiver or manager has been paid, or has retained for his remuneration for any period prior to the order any amount in excess of that fixed for that period, it extends to requiring him or his personal representatives to account for the excess or such part thereof as may be specified in the order. Such a requirement is not to be made in respect of any period before the making of the application unless there are special circumstances.[392]

A receiver is entitled to charge the property in his custody in respect of his right to remuneration.[393] Accordingly, the amount of remuneration paid to a receiver diminishes the amount remaining for the unsecured creditors. The power to apply to court is a safeguard against abuse and it is intended to protect unsecured creditors.[394] However, the courts will not interfere lightly: in *Re Potters Oils Ltd (No. 2)*,[395] it was said that the power of the court to fix a receiver's remuneration should be confined to cases in which the remuneration could clearly be seen to be excessive.

9.57 Receiver's right to indemnity

If a receiver and manager properly incurs expenses in carrying on business, he is entitled to be repaid out of the property in priority to the rights of the persons for whose benefit he acted, and where he is not declared to be the agent of the company he may sue the debenture holders who appointed him for his remuneration.[396] Receivers are now also given statutory indemnities.[397] The usual practice is for receivers to be appointed as agents of the company.[398]

9.58 Application to the court for directions

A receiver or manager appointed under the powers contained in any instrument may apply to the court for directions in relation to any particular matter arising in connection with the performance of his functions: and the court may give such directions or make such order declaring the rights of persons before the court or otherwise as it thinks just.[399] This power to apply is also given to those by whom or on whose behalf a receiver or manager has been appointed.

A receiver may apply for directions from the court in order to resolve disputes about entitlements to the secured property.[400] In *Tudor Grange Holdings Ltd v Citibank NA*,[401] Browne-Wilkinson V-C suggested that a receiver could use the power to apply to court for directions to cure any embarrassment involved in making a decision whether to

---

[392] Section 36 (2). Where a debenture incorporates section 109 of the Law of Property Act 1925, then the receiver is entitled to the 5 per cent commission allowed by section 109 (6) even though the debenture did not otherwise specify the remuneration. The receiver may fix this rate without applying to court unless he wants a higher rate: *Marshall v Cottingham* (1981) 125 SJ 411.

[393] Sections 37 (4) and 45 (3) of the Insolvency Act 1986.

[394] *Re Greycaine Ltd* [1946] Ch 269.

[395] [1986] 1 All ER 890, [1986] 1 WLR 201, [1986] BCLC 98, (1985) 1 BCC 99, 593.

[396] *Deyes v Wood* [1911] 1 KB 806 (CA).

[397] As to the statutory right of indemnity conferred by sections 37 and 44 of the Insolvency Act 1986, see 9.62 and 9.65, below.

[398] See 9.62 and 9.65, below.

[399] Insolvency Act 1986, section 35.

[400] As in *Re Ellis, Son & Vidler Ltd* [1994] BCC 532.

[401] [1992] Ch 53, [1991] 4 All ER 1, [1991] 3 WLR 750, [1991] BCLC 1009. Compare *Lascomme Ltd v UDT (Ireland) Ltd* [1994] 1 ILRM 227. See further 9.61, below.

commence proceedings on the company's behalf against the debenture holder who had appointed him.

9.59 Duties of a receiver

A receiver is subject to a statutory duty imposed by section 40 of the Insolvency Act 1986 to pay preferential debts in priority to any claims for principal or interest in respect of debentures secured by a floating charge. Preferential debts are specified in section 386 of and Schedule 6 to the Act, and they include certain debts due to tax authorities and certain payments to employees.[402]

If a receiver disposes of the assets, or allows them to be taken by others, without providing for claims having a right to preferential payment, with knowledge of the claims, he will be personally liable to those entitled to the extent to which they are prejudiced.[403] Once a receiver has collected assets he is liable to the extent of those assets to pay preferential creditors of whose claims he has notice. This is equally the case where payment is made to the company by the direction and on the indemnity of the debenture holder. A receiver is neither bound nor entitled, when he is removed from his appointment as a receiver, to account to the company for the moneys he has collected. Although those assets belong to the company, they are (in the case of a receiver appointed to enforce a floating charge) subject to a charge which has crystallised in favour of the debenture holder. The receiver cannot therefore pay the company and ignore the statutory rights of preferential creditors. A receiver so doing is liable to the preferential creditors for breach of statutory duty: *C.I.R. v Goldblatt*.[404]

Payments made to preferential creditors out of floating-charge assets can be recouped out of assets of the company available for payment of the general creditors.[405] This ensures that the burden of paying the preferential debts falls ultimately on the company's unsecured creditors, to the extent that the company's assets exceed what is owing to the debenture holder under the floating charge. Any other result would fail to give effect to the debenture holder's priority over unsecured creditors.

A floating charge is defined by section 40 as a charge which, as created, was a floating charge. Crystallisation of the floating charge prior to the appointment of the receiver does not take the situation outside the scope of that section.

Aside from the statutory duty to pay preferential debts, the primary duty of a receiver is to realise the security on behalf of his appointor.[406] The receiver is under no obligation to the company or to its other creditors to carry on the company's business at the expense of his appointor, nor need he delay realising the security even though he might have obtained a higher price at a later date.[407]

---

[402] See 17.55.1 below.

[403] *Woods v Winskill* [1913] 2 Ch 303; *Westminster City Council v Haste* [1950] Ch 442.

[404] [1972] Ch 498 (applying *Woods v Winskill*, above; *Westminster City Council v Haste*, above.

[405] Section 40 (3).

[406] *Re B Johnson & Co. (Builders) Ltd* [1955] Ch 634 at pp. 661–2 per Jenkins LJ, approved by Lord Templeman in *Downsview Nominees Ltd v First City Corporation* [1993] AC 295, [1993] 3 All ER 626, [1993] 2 WLR 86, [1993] BCC 46.

[407] ibid. Also *Cuckmere Brick Co. Ltd v Mutual Finance Ltd* [1971] Ch 949; *Bank of Cyprus (London) Ltd v Gill* [1980] 2 Lloyd's Rep. 51. Cf. *Standard Chartered Bank Ltd v Walker* [1982] 1 WLR 1410 at p. 1415 per Lord Denning: 'It is at least arguable that, in choosing the time, he must exercise a reasonable degree of care'. If a receiver sells at the worst possible time, this may be seen as evidence of bad faith.

A receiver is subject to equitable duties in his dealings with the company's property. He must not himself buy the property which he is appointed to realise, since such a purchase would infringe the self-dealing rule.[408] A sale of the property by a receiver to a company in which he has an interest infringes the fair-dealing rule and is liable to be set aside, unless he can show that the sale was made in good faith and that he took reasonable precautions to obtain the best price reasonably obtainable at the time.[409]

In *Downsview Nominees Ltd v First City Corporation*,[410] the Privy Council held that a receiver acting on behalf of a debenture holder[411] owes duties to second and subsequent debenture holders and to the company to use his powers for the sole purpose of securing repayment of the moneys owing under the debenture under which he was appointed, and to act in good faith. He also owes specific duties in equity to these persons, such as the duty to keep premises in repair and to avoid waste.[412] The Privy Council accepted that the receiver owes a specific equitable duty to take reasonable care to obtain a proper price for any assets he decides to sell.[413] However, the Privy Council denied the existence of a general duty of care in tort owed by a receiver to subsequent encumbrancers or to the company in respect of dealings with the security. Some earlier first-instance and appellate decisions of the English courts assume the existence of a duty of care in tort owed by debenture holders and their receivers to the company and subsequent encumbrancers, and also to guarantors of the company's debts.[414] The reasoning in these cases may now require reassessment if (as seems likely) the more restrictive approach adopted by the Privy Council in *Downsview* is indicative of how the House of Lords would decide the issue in an English case.[415]

A debenture holder who is contractually entitled to appoint a receiver is under no duty to refrain from doing so on the grounds that it might cause loss to the company or its creditors. The debenture holder is free to exercise his rights even if it is alleged that the appointment of a receiver is unnecessary because it would simply duplicate the efforts of the liquidator.[416]

---

[408] *Watts v Midland Bank plc* (1986) 2 BCC 98, 961; *Nugent v Nugent* [1907] WN 169; *Re Magadi Soda Co.* (1925) 94 LJ Ch 217.

[409] *Tse Kwong Lam v Wong Chit Sen* [1983] 1 WLR 1349; *Watts v Midland Bank* at pp. 98, 968.

[410] Above.

[411] Or the debenture holder itself.

[412] These equitable duties would also include those mentioned in the previous paragraph.

[413] This is consistent with *Cuckmere Brick Co. Ltd v Mutual Finance Ltd.*

[414] The existence of such a duty of care (extending to guarantors of the company's debts) was supported by *Standard Chartered Bank v Walker* [1982] 3 All ER 938, [1982] 1 WLR 1410 (CA), *American Express International Banking v Hurley* [1986] BCLC 52 (duty owed to guarantor of the secured debt) and *Knight v Lawrence* [1991] BCC 411; [1993] BCLC 215 (duty of care owed by a receiver to joint borrowers, which was breached when the receiver failed to put in motion rent review procedures contained in leases of properties owned by one of the joint borrowers); *Downsview* is consistent with other decisions of the House of Lords which have sought to restrict the ambit of the tort of negligence: *Caparo Industries plc v Dickman* [1990] 2 AC 605; *Murphy v Brentwood DC* [1991] Ac 398. See also *China & South Sea Bank Ltd v Tan* [1990] 1 AC 536 (no duty in tort to surety (PC)).

[415] The Court of Appeal has held that a mortgagee's duty arises in equity rather than tort: *Parker-Tweedle v Dunbar Bank* [1991] Ch 12. See further Berg, 'Duties of a Mortgagee and a Receiver' [1993] JBL 213; Nolan (1994) Co. Law 28; Grantham (1993) Conv 401; Fealy, 'Receivers' Duties: A Return to Orthodoxy' [1994] NILQ 61. Generally, on the development of receivers' duties, see Picarda, *The Law Relating to Receivers, Managers and Administrators* (Butterworths, 2nd edn 1990), Chapter 10 (this predates *Downsview*) and Meagher, Gummow and Lehane, *Equity Doctrine and Remedies* (Butterworths, 3rd edn 1992), Chapter 28.

[416] *Re Potters Oil Ltd (No. 2)*, above; *Shamji v Johnson Matthey Bankers Ltd* [1986] BCLC 278.

9.60 Powers of receivers and administrative receivers

It is in relation to their respective powers that the distinction between administrative and other receivers is most significant. An administrative receiver derives his powers from the Insolvency Act 1986 as well as from the instrument under which he is appointed, whereas other receivers must look to the terms on which they were appointed to determine the scope of their powers.[417]

Generally speaking, an administrative receiver is in a far more powerful position than a receiver who is not an administrative receiver. By definition, an administrative receiver takes charge of the whole (or substantially the whole) of the property of the company to which he is appointed, whereas an ordinary receiver or manager is concerned merely with a limited part of the company's assets. Where an administrative receiver is appointed, effective control of the company's business affairs passes from the board to the administrative receiver. Under the Insolvency Act 1986, an administrative receiver has power to deal with assets which are subject to other securities in ways which a debenture holder would never be competent to grant by contract to a receiver who is not an administrative receiver.

9.61 The administrative receiver's powers

Section 42 of the Insolvency Act 1986 provides that the powers conferred on an administrative receiver 'by the debentures by virtue of which he was appointed' shall be deemed to include a list of powers set out in Schedule 1 of the 1986 Act. These deemed powers are to operate 'except in so far as they are inconsistent with any of the provisions of those debentures'. The powers specified in Schedule 1 are as follows:

(1) Power to take possession of, collect and get in the property of the company and, for that purpose, to take such proceedings as may seem to him expedient.

(2) Power to sell or otherwise dispose of the property of the company by public auction or private contract.[418]

(3) Power to raise or borrow money and grant security therefor over the property of the company.

(4) Power to appoint a solicitor or an accountant or other professionally qualified person to assist him in the performance of his functions.

(5) Power to bring or defend any action or other legal proceedings in the name and on behalf of the company.

(6) Power to refer to arbitration any question affecting the company.

(7) Power to effect and maintain insurances in respect of the business and property of the company.

(8) Power to use the company's seal.

(9) Power to do all acts and to execute in the name or on behalf of the company any deed, receipt or other document.

(10) Power to draw, accept, make and endorse any bill of exchange or promissory note in the name and on behalf of the company.

---

[417] Subject to the specific statutory right already considered to apply to court for directions, and the limited powers which may be implied by the Law of Property Act 1925.

[418] 'or in Scotland, to sell, feu, hire out or otherwise dispose of property of the company by public coup or private bargain'. An English floating charge can affect property situated in Scotland.

(11) Power to appoint any agent to do any business which he is unable to do himself or which can more conveniently be done by an agent, and power to employ and dismiss employees.

(12) Power to do all such things (including the carrying out of works) as may be necessary for the realisation of the property of the company.

(13) Power to make any payment which is necessary or incidental to the performance of his functions.

(14) Power to carry on the business of the company.

(15) Power to establish subsidiaries of the company.

(16) Power to transfer to subsidiaries of the company the whole or any part of the business and property of the company.

(17) Power to grant or accept a surrender of a lease or tenancy of any of the property of the company, and to take a lease or tenancy of any property required or convenient for the business of the company.

(18) Power to make any arrangement or compromise on behalf of the company.

(19) Power to call up any uncalled capital of the company.

(20) Power to rank and claim in the bankruptcy, insolvency, sequestration or liquidation of any person indebted to the company and to receive dividends, and to accede to trust deeds for the creditors of any such person.

(21) Power to present or defend a petition for the winding-up of the company.

(22) Power to change the situation of the company's registered office.

(23) Power to do all other things incidental to the exercise of the foregoing powers.

The powers to establish subsidiaries and to transfer to those subsidiaries the whole or any part of the business and property of the company enable an administrative receiver to effect what is commonly known as a 'hive-down'.[419] A hive-down involves the transfer of the viable parts of a company's business to a new subsidiary with a view to selling the subsidiary to a purchaser. A 'clean' subsidiary which is not saddled with bad debts and unprofitable contracts is likely to be far more attractive to potential purchasers than the old business would have been. A hive-down can thus lead to the continuation of at least part of the business, where the only other alternative would have been to break up and sell separately the assets of the company. A sale of a going concern tends to be more profitable than a sale of assets on a 'break up' basis so that, as well as facilitating repayment of the debenture holder's debt, a hive-down may produce a surplus from which unsecured creditors can be paid. Employees can also benefit from a hive-down where their employment is transferred to the new subsidiary.

The Committee on Insolvency Law and Practice has this to say about the role of a receiver appointed under a floating charge over the whole of a company's undertaking:[420]

> There is, however, one aspect of the floating charge which we believe to have been of outstanding benefit to the general public and to society as a whole; we refer to the power to appoint a receiver and manager of the whole property and undertaking of a company. This power is enjoyed by the holder of any well-drawn floating charge, but by no other creditor. Such receivers and managers are normally given extensive

---

[419] A hive-down may cause the company to cease to carry on business and a floating charge to crystallise: *William Gaskell Group Ltd v Highley* [1993] BCC 200.

[420] 1982, Cmnd 8558, at para. 495.

powers to manage and carry on the business of the company. In some cases, they have been able to restore an ailing enterprise to profitability, and return it to its former owners. In others, they have been able to dispose of the whole or part of the business as a going concern. In either case, the preservation of the profitable parts of the enterprise has been of advantage to the employees, the commercial community and the general community.

The Committee suggested the codification of the extensive powers normally given to receivers appointed under floating charges; this was done.[421] The Committee also recommended that the advantages of floating-charge receivership should be made more widely available. The administration procedure now contained in the Insolvency Act 1986 was the legislative response to this suggestion. This procedure is based on the model of floating-charge receivership.[422]

The directors must not interfere with the administrative receiver in the discharge of his functions.[423] In view of the wide range of powers conferred on an administrative receiver, this means that the directors can play little active role in the company's affairs whilst it is in receivership, although they do remain in office despite the appointment of an administrative receiver. The directors retain certain residual powers, one of which, it was held by the Court of Appeal in *Newhart Developments Ltd v Co-operative Commercial Bank Ltd*, is that of bringing proceedings in the company's name against the person who appointed the administrative receiver.[424] Browne-Wilkinson V-C (as he then was) has since doubted whether *Newhart* was correctly decided, and has held that its scope is limited to the comparatively unusual situation where the company has been indemnified from outside sources not only for its own costs but also for costs that it might be ordered to pay to the other party. Only in these circumstances, can it be said that the costs of the directors' action would not in any way prejudice the property for which the receiver was responsible.[425]

It has been held that the directors are entitled to reasonable information about the assets remaining in the company's hands, in addition to a redemption statement showing how much is still owing, provided that they show a bona fide intention and ability to redeem the security.[426]

Section 42 (3) provides that a person dealing with an administrative receiver 'in good faith and for value' is not concerned to enquire whether the administrative receiver is acting within his powers. This provision is clearly intended to increase the protection which would in any event be given by conferring the powers set out in Schedule 1. For

---

[421] Section 42 and Schedule 1.

[422] See Part 3 of Chapter 17.

[423] *Newhart Developments Ltd v Co-operative Commercial Bank Ltd* [1978] QB 814, [1978] 2 All ER 896, [1978] 1 WLR 636.

[424] *Newhart Developments v Co-operative Commercial Bank*, above. See also *Watts v Midland Bank plc* (1986) 2 BCC 98, 961, where Peter Gibson J canvasses the possibility of the company (acting through its directors or shareholders) bringing an action against the administrative receiver himself where he is alleged to be acting improperly.

[425] *Tudor Grange Holdings Ltd v Citibank NA*, [1992] Ch 53, [1991] 4 All ER 1, [1991] 3 WLR 750, [1991] BCLC 1009. Compare the Irish decision, *Lascomme Ltd v UDT (Ireland) Ltd* [1994] 1 ILRM 227.

[426] *Gomba Holdings UK Ltd v Homan & Bird* [1986] 3 All ER 94, [1986] 1 WLR 1301, [1986] BCLC 331, (1986) 2 BCC 99, 102; *Rottenberg v Monjak* [1992] BCC 688, [1993] BCLC 374.

example, in the event of a conflict between the powers in the debenture and the Schedule 1 powers (which would be caught by the phrase in section 42 (1) 'except in so far as they are inconsistent with any provisions in those debentures'), a third party acting in good faith, etc., would not be required to investigate the powers in the debenture (or in the Schedule) unless such a problem were brought expressly to his attention.

Section 43 of the Insolvency Act 1986 confers a power on an administrative receiver, with the consent of the court, to sell company property free of the fixed charge or security to which it is subject. On the application of the administrative receiver, the court may so authorise him if it is satisfied that the disposal (with or without other assets) of any property of the company, subject to a fixed charge or security, would be likely to promote a more advantageous realisation of the company's assets than would otherwise be effected. The court may then authorise the receiver to dispose of the asset as if it were not subject to the security. It must be a condition of the court's authorisation under section 43 that the net proceeds of sale shall be applied towards discharging the sums secured by the fixed charge or security.[427] Where these proceeds are less than the amount, as may be determined by the court, which would have been realised on a sale of the property in an open market by a willing vendor, the deficiency must be made up.[428] The power conferred by section 43 does not apply to securities held by those who have appointed the administrative receiver. This is also true of any security to which such security (i.e. held by the person appointing) has priority.[429]

The power conferred by section 43 is analogous to that given to administrators by section 15 of the Insolvency Act 1986.[430]

9.62 The administrative receiver's agency and liability for contracts

Section 44 of the Insolvency Act 1986 provides that an administrative receiver of a company is deemed to be the company's agent unless and until the company goes into liquidation. The consequences of this is that he is personally liable on any contract entered into by him in the carrying out of his functions except in so far as the contract otherwise provides. In the case of employment contracts he is liable for those contracts adopted by him in the carrying out of those functions. However, he is not to be taken to have adopted a contract of employment by reason of anything done or omitted to be done within a fortnight of his appointment.[431] This provision allows the receiver to use the essential services of the company's employees in this initial period before he commits himself to their continued employment.

What amounts to 'adoption' was considered by the House of Lords in *Powdrill v Watson, Re Paramount Airways Ltd (No. 3)*.[432] An administrative receiver cannot avoid adoption by

---

[427] See section 43 (4) as to when there are two or more fixed charges and a sale is ordered. The proceeds of sale must be applied so as to respect priorities.

[428] Section 43 (3).

[429] Section 43 (2).

[430] See 17.21, below.

[431] See section 44 (1) and (2).

[432] [1995] 2 All ER 65, [1995] 2 WLR 312.

merely informing employees that he does not intend to adopt their contracts, because adoption is a matter of fact rather than words. Continuing, after the fourteen-day grace period, to employ staff and to pay them in accordance with the terms of their previous contracts, amounts to implicit adoption. The effect of adopting employment contracts is that the administrative receiver assumes personal liability for all liabilities incurred under the adopted contracts while he is in office.[433]

The Insolvency Act 1994 amended section 44 of the Insolvency Act 1986 with effect from 15 March 1994. The effect of the amendments is to limit the administrative receiver's personal liability in respect of contracts of employment adopted on or after that date, to sums payable by way of wages or salary[434] for services rendered after adoption of the contracts.

Section 44 gives the administrative receiver a right to an indemnity out of the assets of the company to recoup the liability to which the section exposes him. The section does not limit any other right of indemnity he may have. It also preserves the receiver's liability on contracts entered into (or adopted) without authority. Here he has no right of indemnity.[435]

An administrative receiver does not incur any personal liability in respect of contracts of the company (apart from employment contracts) which are already in existence when he is appointed. This principle is consistent with the administrative receiver's position as the company's agent and it has been explained in the following terms: an administrative receiver 'is not personally liable for the rent payable under an existing lease, or for the purchase charges under an existing hire-purchase agreement. This is not a surprising conclusion. It does not offend against basic conceptions of justice or fairness. The rent and hire charges were a liability undertaken by the company at the inception of the lease or hire-purchase agreement. The land or goods are being used by the company even when an administrative receiver is in office. It is to the company that, along with other creditors, the lessor and the owner of the goods must look for payment.'[436]

The appointment of an administrative receiver does not terminate existing contracts of the company,[437] but the administrative receiver may decide not to continue or complete contractual performance, thereby placing the company in breach of its obligations. There is some uncertainty in the case-law as to whether a receiver can repudiate a contract where this would damage the trading position of the company, but the minimalist formulation of a receiver's duty espoused by the Privy Council in *Downsview*

---

[433] *Re Leyland Daf* [1994] 4 All ER 300, [1995] 2 WLR 316 varied to this extent by the House of Lords in *Powdrill*.

[434] Or by way of contribution to an occupational pension scheme: section 44 (2A). The position regarding wages and salary payable during sickness or holidays clarified by section 44 (2C) and (2D).

[435] See section 44 (3).

[436] *Re Atlantic Computer Systems plc* [1992] Ch 505 at p. 524, [1992] 1 All ER 476 at p. 486, [1990] BCC 859 at p. 866 *per* Nicholls LJ.

[437] This includes employment contracts: *Re Mack Trucks Ltd; Foster Clark's Indenture Trusts* [1966] 1 WLR 125 at p. 132 *per* Plowman J. But there can be special circumstances where receivership does operate to terminate contracts of employment, such as where the continuation of a particular employee's employment is inconsistent with the role and function of the receiver and manager: *Griffiths v Secretary of State for Social Services* [1974] QB 468 (continued employment of managing director held not to be inconsistent with receivership).

would suggest that there is no such duty.[438] A third party who interferes with contractual relationships would ordinarily risk liability in tort, but this does not apply where, as is the case with an administrative receiver, the interferer is acting as an agent of one of the contracting parties.[439]

The proposition that a receiver can repudiate an existing contract of the company is justifiable in principle, because obliging the administrative receiver to perform the company's existing contracts would mean that contractors would be paid before the debenture holder who made the appointment, which would be inconsistent with the debenture holder's priority.[440]

9.63 The effect of liquidation on administrative receivership

A company which is in administrative receivership can go into liquidation. On liquidation, an administrative receiver ceases to be an agent of the company. It has been held, in relation to receivers, that a receiver does not automatically become his appointor's agent upon termination of the agency relationship with the company,[441] but that he may become so if his appointor treats him as such.[442]

9.64 Statements of affairs, investigations and reports

Section 47 of the Insolvency Act 1986 requires the company's officers to submit a report to the administrative receiver showing particulars of its assets, debts and liabilities. It must also include the names and addresses of the company's creditors and information about the securities over the company's property held by them.

This statement will assist the administrative receiver in forming a picture of the state of the company to which he has been appointed. An administrative receiver is an 'office-holder' for the purposes of the Insolvency Act 1986 and, as such, has powers to take control of the company's books, to compel co-operation from those who were involved in its formation or management, and to invoke the assistance of the court in conducting

[438] In *Airlines Airspares Ltd v Handley Page Ltd* [1970] Ch 193, [1970] 1 All ER 29, [1970] 2 WLR 163, Graham J suggested that a receiver could only decline to perform a contract where this would not affect the realisation of the assets or seriously affect the trading prospects of the company. This limitation is also supported by *R v Board of Trade* [1965] 1 QB 603 and *Astor Chemicals Ltd v Synthetic Technology Ltd* [1990] BCLC 1 at p. 11, [1990] BCC 97 at p. 105. The contrary view is supported by a passage in Jenkins LJ's judgment in *Re B. Johnson & Co. (Builders) Ltd*, [1955] Ch 634 at p. 661 (approved by the Privy Council in *Downsview*), where it is stated that a receiver commits no breach of duty to the company by refusing to carry on the company's business, even though discontinuance may be detrimental from the company's point of view. Commentators also disagree on this point: see Stewart, *Administrative Receivers and Administrators* (CCH, 1987) at p. 45; Picarda, *The Law Relating to Receivers, Managers and Administrators* (Butterworths, 2nd edn 1990), Chapter 11. (All of these predate the decision in *Downsview*.); Lightman and Moss, *The Law of Receivers of Companies* (Sweet & Maxwell, 2nd edn 1994), para. 8–14, notes that in the light of Downsview a duty to trade cannot be maintained.
[439] *Said v Butt* [1920] 3 KB 497; *Re Walter J Jacob & Co. Ltd* (1987) 3 BCC 532; *Lathia v Dronsfield Bros Ltd* [1987] BCLC 321; *Welsh Development Agency v Export Finance Co. Ltd*, above. See also *Airlines Airspares v Handley Page Ltd*, above and *Telemetrix v Modern Engineers of Bristol (Holdings) plc* [1985] BCLC 213, (1985) 1 BCC 99,417.
[440] *Airlines Airspares*, above, at p. 199. The administrative receiver cannot, however, interfere with any equitable right which ranks before the debenture holder's security: *Freevale v Metrostore (Holdings) Ltd* [1984] Ch 199; *Astor Chemical Ltd v Synthetic Technology Ltd* [1990] BCLC at p. 11, [1990] BCC at p. 105; *Ash & Newman v Creative Devices Research Ltd* [1991] BCLC 403 at p. 404.
[441] *Gosling v Gaskell* [1897] AC 575; *Thomas v Todd* [1926] 2 KB 511.
[442] *American Express International Banking Corp v Hurley* [1985] 3 All ER 564 at p. 568, citing *Re Wood* [1941] Ch 112. See further para. 9.65, below.

inquiries into the company's dealings.[443] The powers of office-holders are considered further in the context of liquidations.[444]

Within three months[445] of his appointment, an administrative receiver must send to the Registrar of Companies, to the debenture holder by whom, or on whose behalf, he was appointed, and to any trustee for those debenture holders, a report as to the following matters:

(1) the events leading up to his appointment;
(2) the disposal or proposed disposal by him of any property of the company and the carrying on, or proposed carrying on, by him of any business of the company;
(3) the amounts of principal and interest payable to the debenture holders by whom or on whose behalf he was appointed, and the amounts payable to preferential creditors;
(4) the amounts (if any) likely to be available for the payment of other creditors.[446]

Within the same three-month period the administrative receiver must make available this report to all the creditors.[447] He must also lay a copy of the report before a meeting of the company's creditors summoned for that purpose on not less than fourteen days' notice. Where a meeting of creditors is summoned under section 48, the meeting may, if it thinks fit, establish a creditors' committee to supervise the administrative receiver in carrying out his functions. If such a committee is established, it may require the administrative receiver to appear before it and furnish such information (as it may reasonably require) which relates to his functions.[448]

The court is given a power to release the administrative receiver from laying his report before a creditors' meeting. The court may *not* give a direction releasing the administrative receiver from an obligation to lay his report before a meeting of the company's creditors, unless the report states that it is his intention to apply for such a direction and the report has been made available[449] to creditors not less than fourteen days before the application.[450]

9.65 The status of a receiver appointed by the debenture holders who is not an administrative receiver

For the purpose of ascertaining the status of a receiver who is not an administrative receiver, the debentures and trust deed must be consulted to find out whether there are words declaring him to be the agent of the company or incorporating the provision of the Law of Property Act 1925 to that effect.[451] If these words are found, then, the receiver

[443] Sections 234–7 of the Insolvency Act 1986.
[444] See 17.15–17.60, below.
[445] Insolvency Act 1986, section 48. The court may allow a longer period.
[446] The report must also include a summary of the statement of affairs submitted to the administrative receiver under section 47. See section 48 (5).
[447] Section 48 (4). He may do this *either* by sending copies to all the creditors (so far as he is aware of their addresses) *or* publishing a notice stating an address where creditors may write for a copy.
[448] Section 49.
[449] By either of the methods allowed by section 48 (2).
[450] Section 48 (3). For the administrative receiver's obligation where the company goes into liquidation, see section 48 (4).
[451] *Central London Electricity Ltd v Berners* [1945] 1 All ER 160.

being appointed under the power declaring him to be agent for the company, his dealings will (subject to the provisions of what is now section 37 of the Insolvency Act 1986, referred to below) be governed by the ordinary principles relating to the acts of an agent, the company being his principal[452] until liquidation, whether compulsory or voluntary, when it ceases to hold that position.[453] But the receiver does not then become the agent of the debenture holders (or their trustees) who appointed him, nor are they liable for the debts incurred by him upon the company going into liquidation, unless they perform some act authorising him to pledge their credit or otherwise treat him as their agent.[454] In the unlikely event that there are no words declaring the receiver to be agent of the company, the debenture holders who appoint him are his principals and are liable for his faults or omissions, as well as upon the contracts he makes on their behalf, and to indemnify him against any liabilities he incurs as their agent, and to pay him his remuneration.[455] If appointed under powers in the debentures authorising him to carry on the business, but not declaring him to be agent of the company, he may even pledge the personal credit of the debenture holders.[456]

The agency relationship between a receiver and the company to which he is appointed is an unusual form of agency.[457] It is not a true agency. Essentially it is a device to protect the debenture holder from liability in respect of the receiver's actions and instead, to make the company, whose agent he is, is liable. Section 44 of the Insolvency Act 1986, in making an administrative receiver the agent of the company until liquidation, codifies what was in any event the usual practice for all receivers prior to that Act and what remains the practice with regard to receivers who are not administrative receivers. One aspect of the unusual nature of a receiver's agency relationship with the company is that the duties normally owed by an agent to his principal do not apply. A receiver owes his duties primarily to his appointor and not to the company.[458]

The position of a receiver in respect of the company's existing contracts (other than employment contracts) is the same as that of an administrative receiver. With regard to new contracts entered into by him, section 37 of the Insolvency Act 1986 provides that a receiver or manager of the property of a company appointed under the powers contained in any instrument is, to the same extent as if he had been appointed by the court, personally liable on any contract entered into by him in the performance of his functions, except in so far as the contract otherwise provides. He is also personally liable in any

---

[452] *Owen & Co. v Cronk* [1895] 1 QB 265 (CA); *Bissel v Ariel Motors* (1910) 27 TLR 73; *Gosling v Gaskell* [1897] AC 575 (HL); *Central London Electricity Ltd v Berners*, above.

[453] *Thomas v Todd* [1926] 2 KB 511; *In re S. Brown & Son (General Warehousemen)* [1940] Ch 961; but see *Re Northern Garage* [1946] Ch 188.

[454] *Gosling v Gaskell* [1897] AC 575 (HL); *Jeffereys v Dixon* (1866) 1 Ch App. 183 at p. 190; *Cox v Hickman* (1860) 8 HLC 268. As to when receivership will be regarded as being 'rateable occupation', see *Ratford v Northampton DC* [1986] BCLC 391.

[455] *Deyes v Wood* [1911] 1 KB 806 (CA); *Re Vimbos* [1900] 1 Ch 470. Since the decision in *Deyes v Wood*, a common form of debenture previously in use has been altered by the addition of the following words: 'and the holder of this debenture shall not in making or consenting to such appointment (i.e. of a receiver) incur any liability to the receiver for his remuneration or otherwise.' These additional words protect the debenture holder not only from liability to the receiver, but also from liability for debts incurred in the course of the carrying on by the receiver of the company's business: *Cully v Parsons* [1923] 2 Ch 512.

[456] *American Express International Banking Corp. v Hurley* above.

[457] *Lawson v Hosemaster Machine Co. Ltd* [1965] 1 WLR 1399; *Gomba Holdings UK Ltd v Minories Finance Ltd* [1989] BCLC 115.

[458] 9.59, above.

contract of employment adopted by him in the performance of those functions, but he is entitled in respect of that liability to an indemnity out of the assets.[459] This is not to limit any right of indemnity which he would otherwise have or to limit his liability on contracts entered into without authority or to confer any right to indemnity in respect of that liability.

Where a receiver is appointed in such circumstances as to be agent of the company, and the company subsequently goes into liquidation, the receiver ceases to be the agent of the company.[460] Although a winding-up deprives a receiver, appointed under a debenture, of power to bind the company personally, because he ceases to be its agent, this does not affect the exercise of his powers given by the debenture to hold and dispose of the property charged.[461]

9.66 Powers of a receiver

A receiver who is not an administrative receiver derives his powers from the instrument under which he is appointed. Under a debenture in common form which declares the receiver to be agent of the company, and confers on him power 'to take possession of and get in the property hereby charged', he is not limited to the right to take proceedings to get in the income of the property charged given by section 109 (3) of the Law of Property Act 1925. He can bring, without the consent of the company, an action in its name to recover any of the property charged.[462] Even when the words declaring the receiver to be the agent of the company are omitted he is agent of the company 'to such an extent as may be necessary to enable him to exercise the powers conferred on him by the debenture'.[463]

A receiver duly appointed under a debenture, which has the usual clause to take possession of all assets charged and to perform such acts as are incidental or conducive thereto, may present a winding-up petition on which an order will be made at the court's discretion.[464] The protection and preservation of assets is incidental to their possession, and where a winding-up order in respect of an insolvent company would achieve this aim, the receiver had power to petition.[465]

9.67 Receivership accounts

Section 38 of the Insolvency Act 1986 imposes an obligation on a receiver or manager appointed out of court (other than an administrative receiver, for whom separate provision is made) to deliver accounts to the Registrar on a periodic basis.

It should be noted that these statutory obligations are not exhaustive of a receiver's duty to provide accounts or other information to a debtor company. The extent of this obligation can be deduced from the nature of the receivership and the express or implied terms of the debenture. A company's right to such information depends upon it being

---

[459] Section 37 was not amended by the Insolvency Act 1994 but in May 1994 the government announced a consultation exercise on whether to extend that Act to receivers or managers who were not administrative receivers.

[460] *Gosling v Gaskell* [1897] AC 575; *Thomas v Todd* [1926] 2 KB 511; cf. *Re Northern Garage* [1946] Ch 188.

[461] *Sowman v David Samuel Trust* [1978] 1 WLR 22.

[462] *M. Wheeler & Co. v Warren* [1928] 1 Ch 840 (CA). *Gough's Garages v Pugsley* [1930] 1 KB 615.

[463] *Per* Warrington J *Robinson Printing Co. v Chic Ltd* [1905] 2 Ch 123, approved by Vaughan Williams LJ in *Deyes v Wood* [1911] 1 KB 806 at p. 821.

[464] See 17.33, below.

[465] *In Re Emmadart Ltd* [1979] 2 WLR 868 at p. 875.

shown that the information is needed to enable the board of directors to exercise its residual powers or perform their duties. However, this right is qualified by the receiver's primary responsibility to the debenture holder who appointed him. Thus the receiver may withhold information where he forms the opinion that this would be contrary to the interests of the debenture holder.[466]

---

[466] *Gomba Holdings UK Ltd v Homan* [1986] BCLC 331. Here the receiver was on the facts held not obliged to furnish additional information. See also *Smiths Ltd v Middleton* [1979] 3 All ER 842.

10 Membership of a Company

10.1 Introduction

A number of varied issues arise under the heading of a company, including some which have already been considered in earlier chapters, particularly the effect of the contract of membership under section 14 of the Companies Act 1985[1] and the transfer of shares by members.[2] This chapter is concerned with the general characteristics of membership of a company, with the register of members which every company must maintain, with the obligation to file an annual return and with the disclosure of interests by substantial shareholders of voting shares in public companies. It is, however, appropriate to introduce the chapter with a brief discussion of who in effect owns and/or controls companies, that is, who are the real members. This relates closely to some issues discussed below, not least the disclosure provisions described in 10.8 *et seq.*, below.

It has long been recognised that the control of a company with a widely held shareholding[3] may in fact be obtained by the holding of considerably less than a majority of the company's issued voting shares.[4] As long ago as 1932, Berle and Means[5] found that the ownership of shares in typical large American corporations was so widely dispersed that no individual or group was in a position to control the corporation; instead management was in control. This was probably not quite so true of British public companies, where at least a substantial proportion were controlled by their owners.[6] In recent years the crucial factor in the United Kingdom has been the level of institutional shareholding, which has risen considerably while the level of individual shareholding has fallen dramatically.[7] This complicates the question of control even more. While institutions are likely, at least together, to be in a position to have actual control of a majority of voting power in many large public companies, the fact is that they very rarely appear to use this control openly.[8] Of course their decision will be crucial in a take-over battle and there is no doubt a considerable amount of behind-the-scenes lobbying and discussion, but it is probably safe to say that on the whole the management of large public companies

---

[1] See 3.17, above.

[2] See Chapter 8, above.

[3] That is, the typical public company. Much of this discussion is irrelevant to the numerically much more common private company.

[4] For a much more detailed discussion of this question, see Farrar's *Company Law* (Butterworths, 3rd edn 1991) Chapter 34.

[5] *The Modern Corporation and Private Property*, revised in 1968.

[6] See Florence, *Ownership, Control and Success of Large Companies* (1961) and *The Logic of British and American Industry* (3rd edn 1972).

[7] See 11.1, below, and Farrar and Russell (1984) 5 Co. Law 107. Note the attempts by the present government to reverse this trend, particularly in respect of nationalised industries which have been 'privatised'. *Quaere* how successful these will be in the long term.

[8] Institutions often prefer to 'vote with their feet'. i.e. sell out rather than interfere. Perhaps this is inevitable given that the principal institutions are pension funds and insurance companies which have duties to their beneficiaries and policyholders. See for information on the role of Institutional Shareholders: *The Responsibilities of Institutional Shareholders in the UK*, Institutional Shareholders' Committee, 1991. See also Finch (1992) 55 MLR 179 and Prodham, Management Research Paper, Templeton College, Oxford No. 92/13 (1993).

is in de facto control.[9] The law's response to these factors has generally been piecemeal.[10] It could well be argued that the problem of supervising management remains a critical and important one and that present practices leave much to be desired.[11]

10.2 The members of a company

The law defines the members of a company in section 22 of the Companies Act 1985 as comprising first the subscribers to a company's memorandum, who are deemed to have agreed to become members and on registration must be entered on the register of members, and secondly every other person who agrees to become a member of a company and whose name is entered in its register of members. These two categories must be examined in more detail.

10.2.1 Subscribers to the memorandum

As section 22 provides, a subscriber to the memorandum is a member whether he has otherwise agreed to become so or not, and whether or not his name is entered in the register, and he is bound to take and pay for the number of shares written opposite his name,[12] although if he subsequently applies for and receives an allotment of an equal or greater number of shares this may be treated as a satisfaction of his obligation under the memorandum.[13] The directors have no power to release a subscriber from his obligation to take shares,[14] and he can therefore escape only by taking up and transferring the shares. He will, however, be relieved from liability if the whole of the shares are allotted to other persons, so that no shares are left in respect of which he can be registered.[15] When the liability is thus extinguished, it does not revive on a forfeiture of shares putting shares at the disposal of the directors.[16]

10.2.2 Entry in the register of members

As stated above, the other persons who are members are those who have agreed to take shares *and* whose names are entered in the register. Even if they are not so entered, if there is complete agreement between them and the company, subject to the possibility of

---

[9] See also 11.1, below. The law generally recognizes this; see 13.11, below.

[10] Attempts can be made, as in Farrar's *Company Law* Chapter 34, to bring together various themes in the case-law regarding control and the duties of institutional investors, but it seems clear that in this country there are no coherent principles, and it is not certain that there is much likelihood of these being developed, however desirable that might be. There is no doubt, though, that the concept of control can be relevant at common law, especially regarding the 'fraud on a minority' exception to the rule in *Foss v Harbottle*; see 15.2. below. As far as statute is concerned, there are isolated provisions in the Companies Act which recognise that control of a company can be obtained by a holding of less then 50 per cent of voting shares, for example, section 314 (1) (*c*) (see 14.20, below) and section 346 (4) (see 14.14, below), and there are the disclosure provisions in Part VI described in detail in 10.8 *et seq.*, below. The question of control of a company may also arise in other areas of law, especially in relation to taxation and employment law. Regarding the latter, see especially section 153 (4) of the Employment Protection (Consolidation) Act 1978 and the discussion by McMullen [1986] *Law Society's Gazette* 2923.

[11] See especially the report of the Wilson Committee, Cmnd 7937, Chapter 19; Boyle 24 ICLQ 487 (1978).

[12] *Re Tyddyn Sheffrey Slate Co.* (1869) 20 LT 105; *Drummond's Case* (1869) 4 Ch App. 772; *Pell's Case* (1869) 5 Ch App. 11. See further, Smith, 'Subscribers: their status on incorporation', 3 Co. Law 99 (1982) which, after an exhaustive examination of the cases, comes to the same conclusion as that expressed in the text.

[13] *Gilman's Case* (1886) 31 Ch D 420.

[14] *Re London and Provincial Consolidated Coal Co.* (1877) 5 Ch D 525.

[15] *Tufnell and Ponsonby's Case* (1885) 29 Ch D 421 (CA).

[16] *Mackley's Case* (1875) 1 Ch D 247.

that agreement being rescinded by mutual consent,[17] they will not escape liability, for the register can be amended under section 359 while the company is a going concern,[18] or under section 148 of the Insolvency Act 1986 when the company is in liquidation.[19] However, the entry in the register of the name of a person does not make him a member if he never agreed to become one, and his name can be removed in the same way. It is possible for the court to make an order for removing his name retrospectively in order to free him from liability as a contributory, if that name has remained on the register when it should have been removed.[20]

A corporation may be a member if authorised by its constitution to hold shares,[21] but an English partnership should not be entered in the firm name, as the firm is not a 'person', and the names of the individual holders of the shares must be entered in the register.[22] If, however, the firm name is in fact entered with the consent of the partners, they become liable as members.[23] A Scottish firm is a 'person' and may be entered in its firm name.

The simplest and most usual form of agreement to become a member is an application for and an allotment of shares.[24] But an agreement may be made in other ways.[25] For instance, it may be part of the preliminary contract with the vendor that he shall take shares; persons may by underwriting letters bind themselves to take any shares not subscribed for by the public; or there may be contracts to take shares which are not in writing, for a man may agree with the company by word of mouth, or even by conduct, to become a member. An agreement for value to take up shares in a company if called upon is enforceable notwithstanding the death of the person making the contract.[26] 'A formal agreement is not necessary ... If the substance of an agreement is made out the form is not material.'[27] Thus, if a man who has not previously agreed to take shares knows that they have been allotted to him, and afterwards acts as a member of the company (for instance, by attending meetings, giving proxies, or selling or attempting to sell some of the shares), he will be held to have accepted the allotment and to be a member in respect of the shares. Or a person accepting the office of director when the articles make it a condition of his office that he shall take shares from the company may be held to have agreed to become a member.[28]

A statement in the prospectus that directors or others have agreed to take shares will not alone be sufficient to render them liable.[29]

---

[17] *Nicol's Case* (1885) 29 Ch D 421 at p. 444, *per* Bowen LJ (CA).

[18] See 10.5.3, below.

[19] *Winstone's Case* (1879) 12 Ch D 239; compare *Portal v Emmens* (1877) 1 CPD 664 (CA).

[20] *Nation's Case* (1866) 3 Eq 77; compare *Re Sussex Brick Co.* [1904] 1 Ch 598 (CA).

[21] *Bath's Case* (1878) 8 Ch D 334; *Re Barned's Banking Co., ex parte Contract Corporation* (1867) 3 Ch App. 105.

[22] A purported transfer to a firm in its firm name may be rejected: *Re Vagliano Anthracite Collieries* [1910] WN 187.

[23] *Weikersheim's Case* (1873) 8 Ch App. 831.

[24] This is dealt with at 6.7, above.

[25] See section 22 (2) and *Re Nuneaton Borough Association Football Club* [1989] BCLC 454, where the Court of Appeal held that the phrase 'agrees to become a member' in section 22 (2) is satisfied where someone assents to become a member. It does not require that there be a binding contract between the person and the company. Thus, where a person is entered on the register of members with his consent, he is a member of the company.

[26] *William Beardmore v Park's Executrix* 1927 SLT 143. See also *Warner Engineering Co. v Brennan* (1913) 30 TLR 191 at p. 196.

[27] *Per* James LJ in *Ritso's Case* (1877) Ch D 782.

[28] See 13.2.2, below.

[29] *Re Moore Bros. & Co.* [1899] 1 Ch 627; *Todd v Miller* 1910 SC 869.

An agreement to take shares may be made through an agent.[30] The authority of the agent must be considered under the ordinary doctrines of principal and agent.

If an agreement to take shares (not arising merely by subscribing the memorandum) is brought about by misrepresentation, made either by the company or its agents, the member can, before a winding-up, obtain rescission of the contract, repayment of what he has paid, and removal of his name from the register. However, a contract procured by misrepresentation being only voidable and not void, if the company has gone into liquidation and other interests have come into existence, it is too late to set the contract aside, and the person remains a member.[31] If, however, there was in fact no contract to take shares, the supposed member can at any time have his name removed from the register, for he was never really a member.[32]

10.3 The termination of membership

A person ceases to be a member of a company upon a transfer of his shares being made and the name of the transferee being entered in the register of members,[33] but he remains liable to a limited extent in the event of a liquidation occurring within one year after the transfer. On the death of a shareholder his membership, of course, ceases, but his estate remains entitled to the benefits and subject to the burdens arising from his membership until some other person is entered in the register in respect of his shares. An executor or administrator, however, does not become a member unless he consents to be treated as such and to be entered in the register:[34] subject to the provisions of the articles, he is entitled, if he desires, to have his name entered in the register.[35] A person may also cease to be a member by a surrender or forfeiture of his shares properly made; and in the case of unlimited companies the articles may provide for a person ceasing to be a member in any manner which may be agreed, for in such cases the company has power to reduce its capital without reference to the court.[36] Thus in the case of mutual ship insurance companies, it is often provided that a person is a member only so long as he has ships insured in the company. It would seem, however, that in a company limited by shares a person cannot cease to be a member in any manner which would reduce the capital of the company other than in the ways referred to above. Therefore, as a company cannot purchase its own shares, except in the ways provided by Chapter VII of Part V of the Companies Act,[37] a transfer purporting to be made to the company will not relieve the transferor from liability.[38]

The fully paid shares of a company can be bequeathed or transferred to a nominee of the company.[39] The shares of a company can also be held on trust for it.[40]

---

[30] *Levita's Case* (1870) 5 Ch App., 489; *Fraser's Case* (1871) 24 LT 746; *Barrett's Case* (1864) 4 De GJ & S 416. See further, *Gore-Browne on Companies* (Jordans, 44th edn, loose-leaf), 20.3.

[31] On the effect of misrepresentation on a contract to subscribe for shares see 5.33 *et seq.* above.

[32] *Oakes v Turquand* (1867) LR 2 HL 325; *Alabaster's Case* (1869) 7 Eq 273.

[33] The rights and liabilities of the transferor and transferee of shares, both *inter se* and in relation to the company, are discussed in Chapter 8, above.

[34] *Bowling and Welby's Contract* [1895] 1 Ch 663 at p. 670 (CA).

[35] *Scott v Frank F. Scott (London)* [1940] Ch 794. The executor can (subject to the provisions of the articles of association) insist on being entered as a member in his own right: *Re T. H. Saunders & Co.* [1908] 1 Ch 415.

[36] See *Re Borough Commercial and Building Society* [1893] 2 Ch 242.

[37] See 6.16 *et seq.*, above. As to reduction of capital, see 7.14, above.

[38] *Trevor v Whitworth* (1877) 12 App. Cas. 409 (HL).

[39] See 6.16, above.

[40] *Re Castiglione's Will Trusts* [1958] Ch 549; *Kirby v Wilkins* [1929] 2 Ch 444.

The representatives of a deceased or bankrupt member are entitled to receive on behalf of the estate any dividends, bonuses, or benefits attaching to the shares, and are liable to contribute in respect of the estate in their hands and to be put on the list as representative contributories (see section 81 of the Insolvency Act 1986), but are not themselves members unless they take the shares into their own names.[41] Until they do this, however, they are not entitled to receive notices from the company,[42] unless the articles expressly so direct.

A shareholder who is bankrupt may continue to use his right to vote at shareholders' meetings while his name remains on the register, but he is obliged to do so in accordance with the instructions of his trustee in bankruptcy.[43] Such a shareholder may also bring a minority shareholders' action.[44]

The company cannot refuse to enter executors in the register or insist on inserting a notice that they hold in a representative capacity unless the articles contain some authority to do so,[45] and must enter the names in the order desired by the executors – a matter which often affects the right to vote and receive notices. Moreover, where articles allowed only the person first named upon the register to vote, as such person might be unable to attend meetings, the court, with a view to protecting the voting rights of the joint holders, ordered the company to enter the names in its register so that one name came first in respect of some of the shares and another name came first in respect of other of the shares.[46]

10.4 Minors as members

The following refers to persons domiciled in England who are 'minors' in English law in reference to their membership of a company. The Scots law in relation to minors is now contained in the Age of Legal Capacity (Scotland) Act 1991.

A minor[47] may become a member of a company and hold shares either by subscribing to the memorandum of association[48] or by taking a transfer of shares,[49] but the company has power to refuse to accept a minor as a shareholder or transferee of shares,[50] and should always do so in any case where a liability is attached to the shares, for the minor can, on or before attaining his majority, repudiate the shares if they are then burdensome.[51]

---

[41] *James v Buena Ventura Syndicate* [1896] 1 Ch 456 (CA); *New Zealand Gold Extraction Co. v Peacock* [1894] 1 QB 622 (CA); compare *Bowling and Welby's Contract* [1895] 1 Ch 633.

[42] *Allen v Gold Reefs of West Africa* [1900] 1 Ch 656 (CA).

[43] *Morgan v Gray* [1953] Ch 83.

[44] *Birch v Sullivan* [1957] 1 WLR 1247.

[45] *Re T. H. Saunders & Co.* [1908] 1 Ch 415; *Scott v Frank F. Scott (London)* [1940] Ch 794.

[46] *Burns v Siemens Brothers Dynamo Works* [1919] 1 Ch 225; see also *In re Hobson, Houghton & Co.* [1929] 1 Ch 300.

[47] At common law the age of majority was twenty-one. By the Family Law Reform Act 1969, section 1, the age of majority was reduced to eighteen. Section 12 of the Act authorises the use of the term 'minor' to describe those not of full age in place of the term 'infant' previously used. See also the Minors' Contracts Act 1987 which would appear to have little application in this area. As to Scotland see the Age of Majority Act 1969, section 1.

[48] *Re Laxon & Co. (No. 2)* [1892] 3 Ch 555; *Re Nassau Phosphate Co.* (1876) 2 Ch D 610.

[49] *Lumsden's Case* (1868) 3 Ch App. 31.

[50] *Symon's Case* (1970) 5 Ch App. 298; *Castello's Case* (1869) 8 Eq 504.

[51] *Dublin and Wicklow Rly Co. v Black* (1852) 8 Ex. 181: *Ebbett's Case* (1870) 5 Ch App. 302; *Re Laxon & Co. (No. 2)* [1892] 3 Ch 555. See further, as to the legal position of minors who become members by allotment or transfer, *Gore-Browne on Companies* (Jordans, 44th edn, loose-leaf) 20.5.

10.5 The register of members

Every company is required to keep a register of its members and section 352 of the Companies Act 1985 prescribes that the following particulars shall be entered therein:

(1) the names and addresses of the members, and in the case of a company having a share capital a statement of the shares held by each member distinguishing each share by its number so long as the share has a number,[52] and, where the company has more than one class of issued shares, by its class, and of the amount paid or agreed to be considered as paid on the shares of each member;[53]

(2) the date on which each person was entered in the register as a member; and

(3) the date at which any person ceased to be a member.

In the case of a private company limited by shares or by guarantee, if the number of members falls to one, on that event occurring a statement that the company has only one member (and the date on which this happened) must be entered into the register of members.[54]

By section 353, the register is to be kept at the registered office of the company, except that it may instead be kept at any office of the company where the work of making it up is done or, where it is made up by some other person on behalf of the company, at the office of that person at which the work is done.[55] It is not, however, to be kept, in the case of a company registered in England and Wales, at a place outside England and Wales, or in the case of a company registered in Scotland, at a place outside Scotland.[56]

Notice is to be sent to the Registrar of the place where the register of members is kept and of any change in that place. Such notice need not, however, be given where the register has, at all times during its existence or since 1 July 1948, been kept at the company's registered office.[57]

In the case of joint holders it is their right to determine in what order their names shall be entered, a matter which will under most articles affect the right of attending meetings and voting.[58] An article declaring that only the first named shall be entitled to attend and vote will not be so construed as to prevent shareholders from fairly and reasonably exercising their powers as members of the company. Accordingly, where shares were registered in the joint names of two trustees, and the first-named holder might not be able to attend meetings and the second-named holder could neither vote nor be appointed a proxy for a poll, the court rectified the register and directed the company to have the names of the holders entered as to some of such shares in one order and as to other of such shares in the reverse order.[59]

There are special provisions in section 362 and Schedule 14 relating to what are now

---

[52] As to when shares have to be numbered, see section 182 (2) and 7.1, footnote 1, above.

[53] As to the entries to be made on the register in relation to share warrants, see 8.12, above. As to when shares have been converted into stock, see section 352 (3) (*b*).

[54] Section 352A, inserted by the Companies (Single Member Private Limited Companies) Regulations 1992 (SI 1992 No. 1699), Schedule, para. 4.

[55] See the Companies (Registers and Other Records) Regulations (SI 1985 No. 724) as to the keeping of the register of members in computerised form.

[56] Section 353 (1).

[57] As to when an index to the register must be kept, see section 354.

[58] *Re T. H. Saunders & Co.* [1908] 1 Ch 415; see also Table A, article 55.

[59] *Burns v Siemens Brothers Dynamo Works* [1919] 1 Ch 225; see also *In re Hobson, Houghton and Company* [1929] 1 Ch 300.

known as 'overseas branch registers' (formerly they were 'dominion registers'). These allow the keeping in a particular country or territory of a register of members resident in that country or territory by a company with a share capital transacting business there in accordance with its objects.[60]

10.5.1 The register, equitable interests and notice

The register of members is prima facie (but not conclusive) evidence of any matters directed or authorised to be inserted therein.[61] By section 360, it is provided that no notice of any trust shall be entered on the register or be receivable by the Registrar in the case of English companies,[62] and the company may not enter particulars of a lien it may claim to have on the shares.[63] 'It seems to me extremely important', said Lord Coleridge in the Court of Appeal, 'not to throw any doubt on the principle that companies have nothing whatever to do with the relation between trustees and their *cestuis que trust* in respect of the shares of the company.'[64] But the court will intervene to protect equitable rights by injunction if application is made before a transfer is complete.[65]

The rule does not mean that the company, with knowledge of the rights of other people, can make advances to the registered holder on the security of the shares, ignoring the rights of which it has knowledge, for the company is not relieved from the obligation of giving effect to equitable rights of which it in fact has notice: e.g. its own lien will not take precedence of charges prior in date of which it has notice at the time of making the advance which gives rise to the lien.[66] Nor can it enforce its own lien against the holder upon shares held by trustees if at the time of making the advance it knew that the shares were held in trust.[67] Where a company had notice of a transfer to trustees for creditors or others, it was held that it was justified in refusing to give effect to a subsequent transfer by the debtor to a purchaser for value.[68] When a company upon receiving a transfer has notice of an adverse claim, it usually gives notice to the claimant that it will register the transfer unless he takes proceedings within a specified time. But a company is not concerned to inquire whether trustees who are registered as shareholders are acting within their powers in dealing with the shares,[69] and can enforce its own rights against the

---

[60] For more detail, see *Gore-Browne on Companies* (Jordans, 44th edn, loose leaf), 20.11. The countries and territories in question are Northern Ireland, any part of Her Majesty's Dominions outside the United Kingdom, the Channel Islands and the Isle of Man and any in the list in Part I of Schedule 14.

[61] Section 361.

[62] *Société Générale v Tramways Union Co.* (1884) 14 QBD 424 (CA), affirmed sub nom. *Société Générale de Paris v Walker* (1885) 11 App. Cas. 20 (HL), where it was held that the company is not liable, though the directors may be, for ignoring notices of trust. See also *Simpson v Molson's Bank* [1895] AC 270 (PC). Scottish companies may recognise trusts (although this is excluded for most purposes by the articles if article 5 of Table A applies), and this discussion of equitable rights relates only to English law.

[63] *Re W Key & Son* [1902] 1 Ch 467.

[64] *Re Perkins* (1890) 24 QBD 613 (CA). In a case, however, where it was alleged that an irregular disposition of the company's property by the directors had been authorised or approved by all the shareholders, the Privy Council seem to have thought it material to consider whether the shareholders were the beneficial owners of the shares; see *E. B. M. v Dominion Bank* [1937] 3 All ER 555 (PC).

[65] *Binney v Ince Hall Coal Co.* (1866) 35 LJ Ch 363.

[66] *Bradford Banking Co. v Henry Briggs & Co.* (1886) 12 AC 29 (HL); *Rearden v Provincial Bank of Ireland* [1896] 1 Ir. R. 532 (CA); *Binney v Ince Hall Coal Co.* (1866) 35 LJ Ch 363.

[67] *Mackereth v Wigan Coal and Iron Co.* [1916] 2 Ch 293.

[68] *Peat v Clayton* [1906] 1 Ch 659; *Roots v Williamson* (1888) 38 Ch D 485; *Moore v North-Western Bank* [1891] 2 Ch 599.

[69] *Simpson v Molson's Bank* [1895] AC 270 (PC).

actual holders of shares irrespective of the rights of the persons for whom they are trustees.[70] Nor does priority in giving notice to the company affect the priority of two charges one against another.[71] If a person having equitable rights in shares desires protection he should serve a notice under RSC Order 50, rules 11–15.[72]

If an official of the company, under a mistake, strikes out the name of a member properly registered, this is a nullity and must be disregarded, and if disputes arise as to the propriety of the act the court will, on being satisfied that a mistake was made, order rectification of the register so as to 'restore and retain' the name of the person entitled to the shares.[73]

The register of members gives particulars of the shares as they were originally issued, with the changes from time to time made. A register of transfers which is usually kept, though not specifically required by the Companies Act 1985, gives particulars of the changes which take place in the ownership of shares.

A company not entering in the register the name of a person entitled to be put therein is liable to pay him damages for any loss he may have sustained by its neglect or refusal to do its duty.[74] By section 352 (7), any liability incurred by a company from the making or deletion of any entry in its register of members or from a failure to make or delete any such entry, is not enforceable more than twenty years after the date on which the entry was made or deleted or, in the case of any such failure, the failure first occurred. This provision is 'without prejudice to any lesser period of limitation'.

Section 352 (6) allows any entry relating to a *former* member of the company to be removed from the register of members after the expiration of twenty years from the date on which he ceased to be a member.

10.5.2 *Inspection and copies of the register*

The register of members, and the index (where required to be kept) must, except when the register is duly closed, be open for a period of at least two hours a day to the inspection of any member gratis, and to the inspection of any other person on payment of a fee not exceeding £2.50 per hour or part thereof during which the right of inspection is exercised.[75] Further, the company must permit a person inspecting the register and index to copy any information therein by means of the taking of notes, the transcription of the information, or photographic reproduction (by means provided by that person). The obligation to permit copying does not oblige the company to provide any facilities additional to those provided for the purpose of facilitating inspection. The person

---

[70] *London and Brazilian Bank v Brocklebank* (1882) 21 Ch D 302 (CA). But it would seem that if the company had notice of the trust before the debt to itself was incurred, the doctrine of *Bradford Banking Co. v Henry Briggs & Co* (1886) 12 AC 29 would apply, and the company would be postponed.

[71] *Société Générale de Paris v Walker* (1886) 11 AC 20 (HL).

[72] See 8.8.1, above.

[73] *Re Indo-China Steam Navigation Co.* [1917] 2 Ch 100. If the company loses its register if should apply to the court before compiling a new one: *Re Data Express Ltd* (1987), *The Times*, 27 April.

[74] Section 359 (2). See *Re Ottos Kopje Diamond Mines* [1893] 1 Ch 618 (CA); *Tomkinson v Balkis Consolidated Co.* [1893] AC 397 (HL).

[75] Sections 356 and 723A and the Companies (Inspection and Copying of Registers, Indices and Documents) Regulations 1991 (SI 1991 No. 1998). The penalties for failing to comply with section 356 are imposed upon the company and 'every officer in default', which includes any person at whose office the register is kept as permitted by section 353 (1) (*b*) (section 357).

inspecting may require a copy or extract on payment of the prescribed fee.[76] The company is not obliged to present the register or index for inspection in a manner which groups together entires by reference to whether a member has given an address in a particular geographical location, is of a particular nationality, has a holding of a certain size, is a natural person or not, or is of a particular gender.[77]

The court is given powers where inspection is refused or copies of the register are not supplied to order an immediate inspection or direct copies required to be sent to the persons requiring them.[78]

A person desiring to inspect cannot be required to give the reason for his desire,[79] and even if it be known that the object of inspecting the register or of requiring a copy thereof is antagonistic to the company, it is illegal to refuse such inspection or copy.[80] But the right to inspect ceases upon the commencement of a winding-up,[81] and if inspection is required after liquidation an order of the court must be obtained under section 155 of the Insolvency Act.[82] Such an order entitles the party to inspect and take copies himself. He need not pay the liquidator a fee for having them made.[83]

A company may close its register for a period not exceeding thirty days in each year, upon giving notice thereof by advertisement in some newspaper circulating in the district in which the registered office is situate.[84] The main objects of closing the register are that entries of transfer may be deferred until after dividends have been declared and paid, and that lists of members may be made out in the event of polls being demanded, and the like. But closing the register is sometimes resorted to with the object of preventing hostile action, in which case the courts will usually grant relief, as this is not a proper use of the power.

10.5.3 Rectification of the register

It is of the greatest importance that the register of members should be promptly and accurately entered up, as delay or inaccuracy may lead to an expensive lawsuit. Section 359 prescribes that if the name of any person is without sufficient cause entered in or omitted from the register of members of any company, or if default is made or unnecessary delay takes place in entering in the register the fact of any person having ceased to be a member, the person aggrieved, or any member of the company, or the company itself, may apply for the order of the court[85] that the register be rectified, and the court may 'either refuse the application or may order rectification of the register, and payment by the company of any damages sustained by any party aggrieved'.[86] Such an

---

[76] Not more than £2.50 for the first 100 entires (or part thereof), £20 for the next 1000 entries (or part thereof) and £15 for every subsequent 1000 entries (or part thereof).

[77] The Companies (Inspection and Copying of Registers, Indices and Documents) Regulations 1991, reg 4. Nor is it obliged to extract entries from the register by reference to any of these criteria.

[78] Section 356 (6).

[79] *Holland v Dickson* (1888) 37 Ch D 669.

[80] *R v Wilts and Berks Canal Navigation Co.* (1874) 29 LT 922 (CA); *Mutter v Eastern and Midlands Railway* (1888) 38 Ch D 92 (CA); *Davies v Gas Light and Coke Co.* [1909] 1 Ch 708 (CA).

[81] *Re Kent Coalfields Syndicate* [1898] 1 QB 754 (CA).

[82] This section in terms applies only to a winding-up by the court, but in the case of a voluntary winding-up, section 112 allows an order to be made under section 155 (*per* Chitty LJ in *Re Kent Coalfields Syndicate*, above).

[83] *Re Arauco Co.* [1899] WN 134.

[84] Section 358.

[85] 'The court' means the court having jurisdiction to wind up the company (section 744).

[86] As to the measure of damages see *Re Ottos Kopje Diamond Mines* [1893] 1 Ch 618.

order must be notified to the Registrar of Companies.[87] Where the issue is not rectification but damages, the court cannot give damages upon a motion made under section 359, the proper course being for the person aggrieved to bring an action.[88] The court has power to determine any question relating to the title of any party to the application.[89] If no dispute arises as to the rights of the person who seeks to have his name entered in or removed from the register, this section presents no difficulty. But as the inclusion or exclusion of a person's name in or from the register determines his right to the benefit of the shares or his liability to pay calls upon them, a number of cases have arisen under the similar section in the earlier Acts.

The court will interfere and rectify the register, upon a motion made under section 359, where the error is due to the neglect or default of the company, and generally when the question arises between the company and a member or alleged member whether his name is properly included or excluded.[90] The power of the court is discretionary, and regard must be had to the 'justice of the case'.[91] In a dispute between two individuals as to which ought to be registered as a member of the company, if the matter is a simple one the court will decide it upon a motion under this section, and will make the necessary order for rectifying the register. But if the question is complicated, or if the rights of third parties intervene, the court will not make an order upon a motion, but will allow the party aggrieved to seek his remedy by an action.[92]

There is authority for the proposition that where a person on the register has a right to rectification and the company recognises that right, the register may be rectified without an application to the court.[93] It has been said, however, that 'the protection of the court's order is in the ordinary case essential to any rectification of the register by the removal of the name of a registered holder of shares'.[94]

10.6 Carrying on business with less than the minimum number of members

If a public company carries on business without having at least two members and does so for more than six months, a person who, for the whole or any part of the period that it so carries on business after those six months (a) is a member of the company and (b) knows that it is carrying on business with only one member, is liable (jointly and severally with the company) for the payment of the company's debts contracted during the period (or, as the case may be, that part of it).[95] This no longer applies to a private company limited by shares or by guarantee since the Companies (Single Member Private Limited

---

[87] Section 359 (4).

[88] See *Re Ottos Kopje Diamond Mines* [1893] 1 Ch 618 (CA).

[89] Section 359 (3).

[90] *Ward and Henry's Case* (1867) 2 Ch App. 431; *Reese River Silver Mining Co. v Smith* (1869) LR 4 HL 64 at p. 57.

[91] *Sichell's Case* (1868) LR 3 Ch App. at p. 122; *Re Dronfield Silkstone Co.* (1880) 17 Ch D 76 at p. 97 (CA); *Trevor v Whitworth* (1888) 12 App. Cas. 409 (HL), *per* Lord Macnaghten at p. 440.

[92] *Ward and Henry's Case* (1867) 2 Ch App. 431; *ex parte Shaw* (1877) 2 QBD 463; *ex parte Sargent* (1874) 17 Eq 273; *Re Greater Britain Products Development Corp.* (1924) 40 TLR 488.

[93] *Reese River Silver Mining Co.* (1869) LR 4 HL 64 at p. 74; *Re Poole Firebrick Co.* (1875) 10 Ch App. 157; *First National Reinsurance Co. v Greenfield* [1921] 2 KB 260 at pp. 278–80.

[94] *Re Derham and Allen* [1946] Ch 31 at p. 36. For a further discussion of the procedure under section 359 and the cases decided on application under this section (and its predecessors), see *Gore-Browne on Companies* (Jordans, 44th edn, loose-leaf), 20.10.

[95] Section 24.

Companies) Regulations 1992 came into effect on 15 July 1992. The company may also be wound up by the court.[96]

In *Jarvis Motors (Harrow) Ltd v Carabott*,[97] the articles of a private company provided that in the event of the death of a member, his shares were to be offered to the other members at par. There were only two members of the company, one of whom died. The surviving member was entitled to compel the personal representative to sell the deceased's shares to him. It is not, therefore, per se illegal for a company to have less than the minimum number of members.

10.7 The annual return

Companies are required to file annual returns with the Registrar of Companies at least once each year. The rules relating to this requirement were changed substantially by Section 139 of the Companies Act 1989, which inserted new sections 363 to 365 in place of the existing sections in Part XI of the Companies Act 1985.[98]

Section 363 (1) requires every company to deliver to the Registrar successive annual returns, each of which is made up to the company's return date. The return date is defined as the anniversary of the company's incorporation or the anniversary of the date to which the company's last annual return was made if that date is different. Section 363 (2) requires the return to be in the prescribed form[99] containing the information required by section 364 (and 364A where applicable) and that it must be signed by a director or the company secretary.

The return must be delivered within twenty-eight days from the date on which it is made up.[100] The company and its officers face penalties for failure to comply and a daily default fine is imposed for continuous contravention.

10.7.1 The contents of the annual return

Section 364 sets out the required contents of annual returns in respect of every type of registered company. Companies which have a share capital where further particulars of share capital and shareholders are required are dealt with by section 364A. Section 364 requires:

(1) Information about the company[101]
    (a)   the address of the company's registered office;
    (b)   the type of company it is and its principal business activities.
(2) Information about officers
    (a)   the name and address of the company secretary;
    (b)   the name and address of every director of the company;
    (c)   in the case of each individual director

---

[96] Section 122 (1) (*e*) of the Insolvency Act 1986. For the purposes of these sections, it seems that past members and persons who are merely representatives of deceased members, without having put themselves on the register, must not be counted: *Re Bowling and Welby's Contract* [1895] 1 Ch 663 (CA).

[97] [1964] 1 WLR 1101.

[98] For details on the old law see *Gore-Browne on Companies* (Jordans, 44th edn, loose-leaf), 22.2–22.6 The new law simplifies the information that must be given about shareholders.

[99] See the Companies (Forms) (No. 2) Regulations 1991 (SI 1991 No. 1259).

[100] Section 363 (2), (3).

[101] Including the date to which the annual return is made up.

       (i)   his nationality, date of birth and business occupation, and

      (ii)   such particulars of other directorships and former names as are required to be contained in the company's register of directors;

  (d)   in the case of any corporate director, such particulars of other directorships as would be required to be contained in that register in the case of an individual.

(3) Information as to registers

  (a)   if the register of members is not kept at the company's registered office, the address of the place where it is kept;

  (b)   if any register of debenture holders (or a duplicate of any such register or a part of it) is not kept at the company's registered office, the address of the place where it is kept.

(4) Elective resolutions – if the company has elected to dispense under section 252 with the laying of accounts and reports before the company in general meeting, or to dispense under section 366A with the holding of annual general meetings, a statement to that effect must be made.

(5) Particulars of share capital and shareholders (section 364A) – a company having a share capital is required to supply the following information in its annual returns

  (a)   the total number of issued shares of the company at the date to which the return is made up and the aggregate nominal value of those shares;

  (b)   with respect to each class of shares in the company

      (i)   the nature of the class, and

      (ii)   the total number and aggregate nominal value of issued shares of that class at the date to which the return is made up;

  (c)   the names and addresses of every person[102] who

      (i)   is a member of the company on the date to which the return is made up, or

      (ii)   has ceased to be a member of the company since the date to which the last annual return was made up (or since the incorporation of the company if the first return);

  (d)   the number of shares of each class held by each member of the company at the date to which the return is made up; and

  (e)   the number of shares of each class transferred since the date to which the last return was made up (or in the case of the first return, the date of incorporation of the company) by each member, or person who has ceased to be a member, and the dates of registration of the transfers.

Regarding (c), (d) and (e), if either of the two immediately preceding annual returns still provide accurate information at that date, the current return need only give changes in membership[103] since the date of the last annual return and shares transferred since that date.[104]

Finally, Section 365 allows the Secretary of State by regulation to add to the information that must be given in the annual returns. These regulations may amend or repeal the existing disclosure requirements of sections 364 and 364A.[105]

---

[102] If the names are not arranged in alphabetical order the return shall be annexed with an index sufficient to enable the name of any person in the list to be easily found.

[103] i.e. 'persons ceasing to be or becoming members': section 364A (6).

[104] Section 364A (6).

[105] See also section 139(3), (4) and (5) of the Companies Act 1989.

10.8 Disclosure of interests in the voting shares of public companies

While, as we have seen in 10.5.1, above, a company with a share capital is prima facie concerned only with the registered ownership of its shares, there have long been felt to be good reasons why the true beneficial ownership of the shares in public companies should be discoverable.[106] Otherwise, for example, the real identity of persons building up an interest, perhaps with a view to obtaining control by a cheaper means than the making of a takeover bid, may be concealed. The Secretary of State has wide powers to investigate the beneficial ownership of companies.[107] Our present concern is with the provisions which require the disclosure of interests in the voting shares of public companies. These provisions are contained in Part VI of the Companies Act 1985 which consolidated provisions, first introduced in 1967, which were beefed up considerably by the 1981 Act. The latter for the first time required the notification of group interests of persons acting together and gave a minority of members the right to require their company to exercise its powers to compel the disclosure of information about interests in its voting shares.

10.9 The obligation of disclosure

Any person who has certain interests in the shares with voting rights in a public company may, on the occurrence of certain events, come under an obligation to notify the company. If such a person to his knowledge acquires an interest in shares 'comprised in a public company's relevant share capital' or ceases to be interested in such shares, or becomes aware that he has acquired such an interest or that he has ceased to have such an interest, he is under the 'obligation of disclosure' of his interests.[108]

Section 198 (3) extends the obligation to notify beyond the knowledge of acquisition or loss of interests specified in section 198 (1). Where a person is aware at the time when it occurs of any change of circumstances affecting facts relevant[109] to the application of the notification requirement to an existing interest of his in shares comprised in a company's share capital of any description, then he comes under the obligation of disclosure. This will also apply if such a person 'otherwise becomes aware of any such fact (whether or not arising from any such change of circumstances)'.

'Relevant share capital' means issued share capital of a public company of a class[110] carrying rights to vote in all circumstances at general meetings of the company.[111]

The obligation of disclosure arises in the following events:[112]

(1) under section 198 (1) or (3), if a person has a notifiable interest[113] immediately after the 'relevant time', but did not have such an interest immediately before that time;
(2) under section 198 (1),
    (a) if he had a notifiable interest immediately before the 'relevant time' but does not have such an interest immediately after it, or

[106] See also the discussion in 10.1, above.
[107] See 15.28, below.
[108] Section 198 (1).
[109] e.g. full voting rights becoming exercisable in respect of shares on the satisfaction of a condition.
[110] Where the relevant share capital is divided into different classes, a percentage (the relevance of which is discussed below) means a percentage of the nominal value of the issued shares in each class taken separately.
[111] Section 198 (2); any temporary suspension of voting rights does not affect the application of Part VI.
[112] Section 199 (4) and (5).
[113] As to the meaning of this, see 10.9.3, below.

(b) if he had a notifiable interest immediately before that time and has such an interest immediately after it, but the percentage levels have changed.

The 'relevant time' for these purposes is the time of the event or change of circumstances or the time at which the person becomes aware of the facts in question, as appropriate.[114]

10.9.1 *The percentage level*

The obligation of disclosure arises when a person is interested in a prescribed percentage of relevant share capital. Section 199 (2) states that a person has a 'notifiable interest' at any time when he is interested in shares, comprised in relevant share capital of a company, of an aggregate nominal value equal to, or more than, the percentage of the nominal value of the share capital[115] which is 'for the time being the notifiable percentage'.[116] This percentage is 3 per cent or such other percentage as may from time to time be prescribed by regulations under Section 201.[117] The percentage level is found by expressing the aggregate nominal value of the shares, comprised in the share capital concerned, in which a person is interested, immediately before or (as the case may be) after the relevant time, as a percentage of the nominal value of that share capital. The figure must be rounded down if it is not a whole number, to the next whole number.[118] Where the nominal value of the share capital is greater immediately after the relevant time than it was immediately before, the percentage level of the person's interests immediately before (as well as immediately after) that time is determined by reference to the larger amount.[119]

10.9.2 *The form of notification required*

A notification required by section 202 (1) must be in writing and must specify the share capital to which it relates.[120] Such notification must also state the number of shares in that share capital in which the person making it knows he was interested immediately after the time when the obligation to make the notification arose. In the event that a person making notification no longer has a notifiable interest, the notification must state that he no longer has such an interest. Notification must be given within two days after the obligation to notify arises.[121]

A notification must give[122] particulars of the identity of each registered holder of any shares to which the notification relates and the number of those shares held by each registered holder.[123] Any person who has a notifiable interest must notify the company in

---

[114] Section 198 (4).

[115] When the 'relevant share capital' is divided into different classes of shares, the 'percentage level' means the percentage level of the nominal value of the issued shares in each of these classes taken separately (section 198 (2)).

[116] 'All the facts relevant to determining for the purposes of this section whether a person has such an interest at any time (or the percentage level of his interest) shall be taken to be what he knows them to be at the time.'

[117] Section 210A, inserted by the Companies Act 1989, section 134.

[118] Section 200 (1).

[119] Section 200 (2).

[120] Section 202 (2).

[121] Excluding Saturdays, Sundays or bank holidays; sections 202 (1) and 220 (1). See the amendment of section 202 (1) by section 134 (3) of the Companies Act 1989.

[122] So far as this is known to the person making the notification at the date of the notification. Section 202 (3) does not apply to a notice stating that there is no longer a notifiable interest.

[123] Section 202 (3).

writing within two days of any particulars in relation to those shares (or any change in those particulars) of which he becomes aware after the 'interest notification date' and before the first occasion following that date on which he becomes subject to any further obligation to make notification.[124] The term 'interest notification date' is defined as being either (a) the date of any notification made by him with respect to his interest under Part VI, or (b) where he has failed to make any such notification, the date on which the period allowed for making it came to an end. A person who at any time has an interest in shares is regarded for the purposes of section 202 (4) as continuing to have an interest in those shares subject to that requirement, unless and until he becomes subject to an obligation to make notification that he no longer has such an interest: section 202 (6).

10.9.3 'Notifiable interest in shares'

The meaning of 'notifiable interest in shares' for the purposes of section 198 to 202 is defined in sections 203, 208 and 209. Under section 203 (1), a person is 'taken to be interested in any shares' in which his spouse or any infant[125] child or stepchild of his is interested. A person is also so taken if a body corporate is interested in shares and (a) that body or its directors are accustomed to act in accordance with his directions or instructions, or (b) he is entitled to exercise, or control the exercise of, one-third or more of the voting power at general meetings of that body corporate.[126] It should be noted that a corporation (controlled in either of these ways) need not be the registered holder; it need only have an interest in accordance with the rules discussed below. Furthermore, where a person is entitled to exercise, or control the exercise of, one-third or more of the voting power at general meetings of a body corporate, and that body corporate is entitled to exercise, or control the exercise of, any of the voting power at general meetings of another body corporate (the 'effective voting power'), then for the purposes of section 203 (2) (*b*), the effective voting power is taken as exercisable by that person.[127] Here the degree of control of the first body corporate over the second would be insufficient to make it a holding and subsidiary relationship within section 736.[128]

Section 208 lays down certain general rules for determining, for the purposes of sections 198 to 202, whether a person has a notifiable interest in shares. These rules are subject to section 209 (discussed below) which provides for certain interests to be disregarded.

Section 208 (2) casts a wide net by providing that 'a reference to an interest in shares is to be read as including an interest of any kind whatsoever in the shares, and accordingly there are to be disregarded any restraints or restrictions to which the exercise of any right attached to the interest is or may be subject'. Section 208 (3) then provides that where any

---

[124] i.e. 'with respect to his interest in shares comprised in that share capital': section 202 (4). A person who at any time has a notifiable interest in shares is regarded under section 202 (4) as continuing to have an interest in those shares subject to that requirement unless and until he becomes subject to an obligation to make notification that he no longer has such an interest: section 202 (6).

[125] In Scotland, a person under the age of eighteen (Age of Legal Capacity (Scotland) Act 1991, Schedule 1, Section 202 (5)).

[126] Section 203 (2).

[127] Section 203 (3). For the purposes of section 203 (2) and (3), a person is entitled to exercise or control the exercise of any voting power if he has a right (whether subject to conditions or not) the exercise of which would make him so entitled, or is under an obligation (whether so subject or not) the fulfilment of which would make him so entitled: section 203 (4).

[128] See 1.14.1, above.

property is held on trust, any beneficiary of that trust who apart from the subsection does not have an interest in the shares is to be taken as having such an interest.

A person is also taken to have an interest in shares if he enters into a contract for their purchase by him (whether for cash or other consideration).[129] Section 208 (4) (*b*) also casts a wide net by providing that a person is taken to have an interest in shares if (not being the registered holder) he is entitled to exercise any right conferred by the holding of those shares, or is entitled to control the exercise of any such right. A person is entitled to exercise, or control the exercise of, any right conferred by the holding of shares if he has a right (whether subject to conditions or not) the exercise of which would make him so entitled, or if he is under an obligation (whether so subject or not) the fulfilment of which would make him so entitled.[130] However, section 208 (4) (*b*) does not apply to someone appointed a proxy to vote at a specified meeting of a company,[131] nor to corporate representatives at *any* meeting of a company or any class of its members.[132] The reference to 'specific meeting' (in respect of the appointment of proxies) clearly indicates that not only irrevocable proxies but the grant of a proxy for more than one meeting would be caught by section 208 (4) (*b*). Section 208 (6) would also catch 'voting trust' or 'voting pool' agreements (see also the wide terms of section 208 (2), as already discussed).

A person is taken to have an interest in shares if (otherwise than by virtue of having an interest under a trust) he has a right to call for delivery of the shares to himself or his order (a call option).[133] This will also be the case where he has a right to acquire an interest in shares or is under an obligation to take an interest in shares.[134] Persons having a joint interest are taken each of them to have that interest.[135] It is immaterial that the shares, i.e. the precise shares, in which a person has an interest are unidentifiable.[136]

The Secretary of State has amended the original Section 209 exempting disclosure of certain interests in shares.[137] The new regulations distinguish between material and non-material interests. Material interests must be disclosed if they represent at least 3 per cent of the company's nominal share capital, whereas non-material interests must be disclosed if they represent at least 10 per cent or if the various interests of the shareholders (whether or not material) when aggregated are at least 10 per cent.[138] The regulations also state the interests which may be disregarded for the purposes of disclosure under section 209 as amended. The Secretary of State has been given wide powers to amend, where it appears to him necessary and expedient to achieve the following three purposes:

(1) for enabling orders to be made in a form protecting the rights of third parties;
(2) with respect to the circumstances in which restrictions may be relaxed or removed;
(3) with respect to the court making interim orders.

---

[129] Section 208 (4) (*a*).
[130] Section 208 (6).
[131] Including class meetings or adjourned meetings: section 209 (2).
[132] Section 209 (2).
[133] Section 208 (5) (*a*).
[134] Section 208 (5) (*b*). Here 'interest' will have the meaning indicated by the other provisions of section 208.
[135] Section 208 (7).
[136] Section 208 (8).
[137] Under powers conferred by section 210A of the 1985 Act, inserted by section 134 (5) of the 1989 Act.
[138] SI 1993 No. 1819. The regulations have been further amended by the Disclosure of Interests in Shares (Amendment) (No.2) Regulations 1993 (SI 1993 No. 2089).

10.9.4 Sanctions to enforce notification of interests

If a person authorises an agent to acquire or dispose of interests in shares comprised in the relevant share capital of a public company, he must secure that the agent notifies him immediately of acquisitions and disposals which may give rise to an obligation of disclosure under Part VI.[139] A notification of disclosure is not adequate unless it identifies the person obliged to give it and his address, and if the person notifying is a director of the company, states that the notice is given in fulfilment of the obligation.[140] An offence is committed by a person who:[141]

(1) fails to fulfil an obligation of disclosure under Part VI;
(2) gives a notification containing a false statement made knowingly or recklessly;
(3) fails to give a notification to other parties to an 'acquisition agreement' within the time allowed under section 206; or
(4) fails to comply, without reasonable excuse, with section 210 (1).

However, it is a defence to a charge under (3) that it has not been possible to give the notification, or that the notification was given as soon as it became possible to do so.[142] If a person is convicted of any of the above offences (other than failing to give notification of ceasing to be interested in shares) the Secretary of State may impose restrictions under Part XV[143] (restrictions on transfer, voting, payment of dividends and issue of further shares) on the shares in respect of which the offence was committed.[144]

10.9.5 The register of interests in shares

A public company must keep a register in which it must record contents of notifications received by it under sections 198 to 202 in chronological order within three days after receipt of notifications, and where notification is that any person has ceased to be a party to an acquisition agreement within section 204, the company must record that fact against the name of the person concerned in every place in the register where his name appears as a party to the agreement.[145] The company is not affected by notice of any matter or put on inquiry as to rights of any person by reason of anything done for purposes of keeping the register.[146] Unless the register is in the form of an index, an index of names entered in the register must be kept by the company.[147] If a public company is converted into a private company, it must keep the register kept by it under section 211 for a further six years.[148] The register and index must be kept at the same place as its

---

[139] Section 210 (1). As to the liability of the directors and officers where bodies corporate commit offences under section 210, see section 733. Members who manage a body corporate's affairs may also be liable under section 733.

[140] Section 210 (2).

[141] Section 210 (3) and (4). As to the power to prosecute, see section 732.

[142] Section 210 (5). The accused must show that it was not possible for him to give the notice required by section 206 within the proper time period, and either (a) that it has not since become possible for him to give the notice so required, or (b) that he gave the notice as soon after the end of that period as it became possible for him to do so.

[143] Section 210 (5). See as to Part XV, 15.29, below.

[144] These provisions apply notwithstanding any provisions in the articles or memorandum imposing a similar restriction. Increasing concern about nominee shareholdings may lead to more drastic sanctions, particularly automatic disenfranchisement, if interests are not notified.

[145] Section 211 (1) to (3).

[146] Section 211 (4).

[147] Section 211 (6).

[148] Section 211 (7).

register of directors' interests in shares and debentures is kept and must be available for inspection by members and others.[149] The register and index shall not be open to inspection in respect of information about a company's interests in shares of a public company which need not be disclosed in the shareholding companies' annual accounts.[150]

10.9.6 'Acquisition agreements'

Sections 204 to 206 make provision for the notification of 'group interests of persons acting together'. For brevity such agreements are hereafter referred to as 'acquisition agreements'. Section 204 is the statutory equivalent of the City Code rules in respect of 'concert parties' in the context of a takeover bid. These provisions are intended to provide some sanction against the practice of 'warehousing' and the more recent development of 'dawn raids' as a method of takeover, or a preliminary to a takeover bid.

Section 204 applies to an agreement between two or more persons which includes provisions for the acquisition, by any one or more of them, of interests in shares in a particular company (the target company)[151] where the following conditions are met. To be caught, the acquisition agreement must include provisions imposing obligations or restrictions on any one or more parties to it with respect to their use, retention or disposal of interests in that company's shares acquired in pursuance of the agreement,[152] and any interests in that company's shares must *in fact* be acquired by any of the parties in pursuance of the acquisition agreement. The reference to 'the use of interests in shares in the target company' is to the exercise of any rights or of any control or influence arising from those interests. This includes the right to enter into any agreement[153] for the exercise, or for control of the exercise, of any of those rights by any other persons.[154] Once any interest in shares in the target company has been acquired in pursuance of an acquisition agreement, section 204 will still apply despite certain changes in the parties to, or terms of, the agreement. Likewise the section will continue to apply 'whether or not any further acquisitions of interests in that company's shares take place in pursuance of the agreement'.[155] Furthermore, references to 'the agreement' include any agreement having effect (whether directly or indirectly) in substitution for the original agreement.

This is the first of a number of subsections to section 204 containing 'catch-all' provisions designed to defeat the common legal techniques of statutory evasion. Their far-reaching character may in practice place difficult evidential burdens upon the prosecution. Thus, by section 204 (5), references in section 204 (and elsewhere in Part VI)

---

[149] See section 211 (8) and section 219 as to the inspection of the register 'during business hours' by members and other persons and their right to obtain copies. See 10.9.10, below.

[150] Section 211 (9). The exemption referred to is conferred by paras. 3 and 10 of Schedule 5 (exemption of a company from requirement to disclose in its accounts particulars of substantial shareholdings in subsidiaries or other bodies corporate incorporated or carrying on business outside the United Kingdom in circumstances where disclosure would be harmful to business), ibid.

[151] In relation to acquisition agreements, references to 'target company' elsewhere in sections 205 or 206 are to the company which is the target company for that agreement in accordance with section 204 (1) and (2).

[152] Whether or not together with any other interests of theirs in that company's shares to which the agreement relates.

[153] e.g. an option agreement giving the right referred to in section 204 (2). But such an 'agreement' need not necessarily be a legally binding contract. See section 204 (5) and (6).

[154] Section 204 (3).

[155] Section 204 (4). 'So long as the agreement continues to include provisions of any description mentioned in section 204 (2) (*a*).'

to the term 'agreement' include any agreement or arrangement. The reference in section 204 to the 'provisions' of an agreement accordingly includes 'undertakings, expectations or understandings operative under any arrangement'. The term 'provision' extends to 'any provisions whether express or implied and whether absolute or not'. However, section 204 'does not apply to an agreement which is not legally binding unless it involves mutuality in the undertakings, expectations or understanding of the parties to it'.[156]

One consequence of section 204 applying to an acquisition agreement is that each party to such an agreement shall be taken to be interested in all the shares in the target company in which any other party to the agreement is interested *apart* from the agreement. This is so whether or not the interest of the other party in question was acquired, or includes, any interest which was acquired, in pursuance of the agreement.[157]

Thus a reporting shareholder must notify the company not only as to his own interests (under the agreement or otherwise), but also as to all the interests of other parties to the agreement. This may include interests (in shares in the same target company) arising under separate agreements to which other parties to the agreement are party.[158]

Section 205 (4) defines the contents of the notification of interests required by Part VI as this applies to acquisition agreements. Any notification must state that the person making the notification[159] is a party to an agreement to which this section applies. It must indicate the name and (so far as known) the addresses of the other parties to the agreement, 'identifying them as such'. It must also state whether or not any of the shares to which the notification relates are shares in which he is interested by virtue of section 204 and, if so, the number of those shares.[160]

It should be noted that section 204 does not apply to any agreement to underwrite or sub-underwrite any offer of shares (not just public issues) so long as the agreement is confined to that purpose and matters incidental to it.[161]

10.9.7 'Persons acting together' to keep each other informed

Section 106 imposes an obligation 'on persons acting together' (i.e. parties to an acquisition agreement within section 204) to keep each other informed of relevant particulars of their interests (if any) apart from the agreement, in shares comprised in the 'relevant share capital'[162] of the 'target company'.[163] This obligation arises only when the target company is a public company, and the shares in that company to which the agreement relates consist of, or include, shares comprised in relevant share capital of that company. The person liable to the obligation[164] imposed by section 206 must know the

---

[156] Section 204 (6).

[157] Section 205 (1).

[158] See section 205 (2) as to the meaning of 'an interest apart from that agreement'.

[159] The Department of Trade and Industry seems to envisage that a single notification could be made by the member of a section 204 'acquisition agreement' as agent for all its members: Department of Trade consultative document, May 1981, *The Disclosure of Interests in Shares*, Annex B, Clause E.

[160] If a person ceases to be interested in shares because he or another person ceases to be a party to the agreement, the notifications must where appropriate give particulars of that person and the fact that he has ceased to be a party: section 205 (5).

[161] Section 204 (6).

[162] See 10.9, above.

[163] See as to the meaning of 'target company' footnote 151, above.

[164] An obligation to give notice imposed by section 206 must be performed within two days 'next following the day on which the obligation arises': section 206 (8) (as amended by section 134 (3) of the Companies Act 1989).

facts which make the agreement one to which section 204 applies, the status of the target company and the type of share capital affected.

The 'relevant particulars' that must be notified in writing[165] are (a) the number of shares (if any) comprised in the relevant share capital in which he would be required to state his interest if he were under an obligation of disclosure with respect to his interest in those shares, apart from the agreement immediately after the time when the obligation to give notice under section 206 (2) arose; and (b) the relevant particulars with respect to the registered ownership of those shares,[166] so far as it is known to him at the date of the notice.

A person for the time being subject to section 206 is also under an obligation to notify in writing each party to the agreement of relevant particulars,[167] and of changes therein, of which he becomes aware at any time after any 'interest notification date',[168] and before the first occasion following that date on which he becomes subject to any further obligations to give notice under section 206 (2) with respect to his interest in shares comprised in that share capital.[169]

Anyone who is a party to a section 204 acquisition agreement is under an obligation to notify each other party to the agreement, in writing, of his current address. He must do this on first becoming subject to the requirements of section 206, and on any change of address while he is still subject to those requirements.[170]

10.9.8 *The investigation by a company of interests in its shares*

Section 212 gives a public company the power to require information with respect to interests in its voting shares. Such a company may by notice in writing require any person whom the company knows, or has reasonable cause to believe, to be interested in shares comprised in 'relevant share capital'[171] of that company to confirm the fact or (as the case may be) to indicate whether or not it is the case. The company has the like power where it knows, or has reasonable cause to believe, that a person has been interested in shares at any time during the three years immediately preceding the date on which the notice was issued. The notice may also require, where the person holds (or has held during the three-year period) any interest in shares (in relevant share capital), the further information specified in section 212 (2):

(1) He must give particulars of his own past or present interest in shares, comprised in relevant share capital of the company, held by him at any time during the three-year period referred to above.

(2) Where his interest is a present interest, and any other interest in the shares subsists, or, in any case, where another interest in the shares subsisted during that three-year

---

[165] This must be done '(a) on his first becoming subject to the requirements [of section 206], and (b) on each occurrence after that time, while he is still subject to those requirements, of any event or circumstances within section 198 (1) as it applies to his case otherwise than by reference to interests treated as his under section 205 as it applies to that agreement': section 206 (2).

[166] This has the same meaning as in section 203 (3) (*a*) and (*b*): section 206 (7).

[167] i.e. with respect to the registered ownership of any shares comprised in relevant share capital of the target company in which he is interested apart from the agreement, and changes in these particulars: section 208 (4).

[168] See section 206 (5) as to the meaning of 'interest notification date' for the purpose of section 206 (4).

[169] Section 206 (4).

[170] Section 206 (6).

[171] See 10.9, above as to the meaning of 'relevant share capital' for Part VI; see sections 198 (2) and 220 (1).

period at any time when his own interest subsisted, he must give (so far as lies within his knowledge) such particulars with respect to that other interest as may be required by the notice.

(3) Where his interest is a past interest, he must give (so far as lies within his knowledge) particulars of the identity of the person who held the interest immediately upon his ceasing to hold it.

The particulars required by section 212 (2) include particulars of the identity of persons interested in the shares in question. They also include whether persons interested in the same shares are, or were, parties to a section 205 'acquisition agreement', or to any agreement or arrangement relating to the exercise of any rights conferred by the holding of shares.[172]

A recipient of a notice under section 212 must provide the information requested in writing, and within such reasonable time as may be specified in the notice.[173] The question of what is meant by 'reasonable time' in a notice served under section 212 (4) was explored by Vinelott J in *Re Lonrho plc*[174] in which he came to the conclusion that where such a notice is served on a person outside the United Kingdom, two clear working days should be allowed. The same concept of 'interest in shares' and 'persons interested in shares' applies to section 212 as it does to sections 198 to 201.[175] Thus section 203 (family and corporate interests)[176] and section 205[177] (group interests of persons acting together) apply, as do the general rules about 'interests to be notified' laid down in section 208.[178] However, the effect of section 209 (interests to be disregarded) is excluded for the purpose of section 212.

Section 212 also applies to a person 'who has or previously had, or was entitled to acquire, a right to subscribe for shares in a public company which would on issue be comprised in relevant share capital of that company'. References to 'interest in shares' in section 212 are to be construed accordingly.[179]

Section 214 allows a certain fraction of the members of a public company a right of requisition so as to enforce the powers conferred on the company under section 212. A company may be required to exercise its powers under section 212 on the requisition of members of the company holding, at the date of the deposit of the requisition, not less than one-tenth of such of the paid-up capital of the company as carries at that date the right of voting at general meetings of the company.[180]

The requisition must state that the requisitionists are requiring the company to exercise its powers under section 212, and must specify the manner in which they require those powers to be exercised. They must also give 'reasonable grounds' for requiring the company to exercise those powers in the manner specified.[181] Who is to determine (short of litigation) whether the grounds are 'reasonable' (in the event of dispute between the company and the requisitionists) is not made clear. A requisition must be signed by the

---

[172] Section 212 (3).
[173] Section 212 (4).
[174] [1989] BCLC 315.
[175] But not the 3 per cent requirement.
[176] See 10.9.3, above.
[177] See 10.9.6, above.
[178] See 10.9.3, above.
[179] Section 212 (6).
[180] Section 214 (1).
[181] Section 214 (2).

requisitionists and deposited at the registered office of the company. However, it may consist of several documents 'in like form each signed by one or more of the requisitionists'.[182]

On the deposit of a requisition complying with these requirements, it then becomes the duty of the company to exercise its powers under section 212 in the manner specified in the requisition.[183] Seemingly the company can argue that the grounds given are not reasonable and this affects the validity of the requisition (see above). On the conclusion of an investigation by the company, in consequence of a requisition under section 214, it is 'the duty of the company to cause a report of the information received in pursuance of that investigation to be prepared'. This report must be available at the company's registered office within a reasonable period after the conclusion of the investigation.[184]

By section 213 a public company (to which section 212 applies) must include information obtained as a result of an enquiry under section 212 in a separate part of the register of interests in shares it must keep under section 211.[185] The company may not enter on the register information acquired about the ownership of its shares other than under section 212.[186]

Section 216 provides sanctions for the failure to provide information under section 212. If a person who is or was interested in shares of a public company fails to give the information required in response to a notice served on him by the company (under section 212), then the company may apply to the court for an order imposing restrictions on the shares (to which the notice relates) under Part XV.[187] The company is entitled to its costs on an application for a 'freezing' order under section 216. The costs will be paid by those who have failed to do their best to provide the information.[188]

Such an order may be made notwithstanding any power in the articles or memorandum to make similar restrictions.[189] A person who fails to comply with a notice under section 212, or who knowingly or recklessly makes statements false in a material particular in response to such a notice, is guilty of an offence. However, it is a defence to a charge of failure to comply with a notice under section 212 that the requirement was frivolous or vexatious.[190] The Secretary of State may (after consultation with the Governor of the Bank of England) exempt a person from complying with notices under

---

[182] Section 214 (3).

[183] Section 212 (4).

[184] Section 215 (1). Section 215 makes further provision for interim reports where the investigation takes more than three months (section 215 (2)); for the period of making the report available (section 215 (3)); for exempting substantial holdings in bodies incorporated, etc., outside the United Kingdom (section 215 (4)); and for informing the requisitionists of the availability of the report (section 215 (5)). Further provision is made as to when an investigation is to be regarded as concluded (section 215 (6)); as to where reports prepared under section 215 are to be kept (section 215 (7)), and for sanctions in the event of default in complying with section 215; section 215 (8).

[185] Section 211 (3) to (10) applies correspondingly to information so recorded: section 213 (3). See also the definition of 'register of interests in shares' in section 220 (1).

[186] *Re TR Technology Investment Trust plc* [1988] BCLC 256.

[187] Section 216 (1). See *House of Fraser, Petitioners* [1983] SLT 500. As to the provisions of section 445 (giving a power to impose restrictions on transfer, voting rights, payment of dividends and issue of further shares) see 15.29, below. See also *Gore-Browne on Companies* (Jordans, 44th edn, loose-leaf), note 6 to 20.24.

[188] *Re The Bestwood plc* (1989) 5 BCC 620.

[189] Section 216 (2).

[190] Section 216 (4). Where a body corporate is guilty of an offence under section 216 (3), directors, managers and other officers involved may incur liability (as may members where they manage the company's affairs): section 733 (2) and (3).

section 212. However, he must be satisfied that, having regard to the undertaking given by that person with respect to the shares held or to be held by him, there are special reasons why that person should not be subject to section 212. A person fails to give information under section 216 if he fails to give a full and truthful answer to a section 212 inquiry.[191]

10.9.9 *Removal of entries from the register*

Section 217 makes provision for the removal of certain entries from the register of interests in shares (kept in accordance with section 211)[192] The company may remove an entry in the register after more than six years have elapsed since the entry was made if the entry in question either (a) related to a person ceasing to be interested in shares or (b) has been superseded by a later entry against the same person's name.

Where anyone, 'in pursuance of an obligation imposed upon him by any provision' of Part VI, notifies the company that another person is interested in shares, the company must, within fifteen days of the date on which it was given the information, notify that person and give him particulars of the entry made in the register in consequence of the information given to the company. He must also be informed of his right to apply to have the entry removed (i.e. if it is incorrect) in accordance with the provisions of section 217 (discussed immediately below).[193] A person thus notified may apply to the company for the removal of the entry relating to him. The company must then remove such an entry if satisfied that it is incorrect.[194] Where a person, shown in the register of interests in shares as being a party to a section 204 acquisition agreement,[195] ceases to be such a party, he may apply to the company in writing for the inclusion of that information in the register.[196] The company, if satisfied that he has ceased to be a party to the agreement, must record that information, if it has not already done so, 'at every place where his name appears as a party to that agreement in the register'. If a company refuses an application, made under section 217 (3) or (4), the applicant may apply to the court for the appropriate order.[197] The court may if it thinks fit make such an order.[198]

Entries in the register of interests in shares, kept under section 211, may not be deleted except in accordance with the provision of section 217 (set out above).[199] An entry deleted in contravention of this provision must be restored as soon as reasonably practicable. Sanctions are provided for default in compliance with sections 217 and 218.[200]

---

[191] *Re TR Technology Investment Trust plc* [1988] BCLC 256. See further *Gore-Browne on Companies* (Jordans, 44th edn, loose-leaf), 20.24.

[192] As to the register of interests in shares kept in accordance with section 211, see 10.9.5, above.

[193] Section 217 (2).

[194] Section 217 (3).

[195] See 10.9.6, above.

[196] Section 217 (4).

[197] i.e. for an order directing the company to remove the entry in question from the register or (as the case may be) to include the information in question in the register.

[198] Where names are removed from the register by the company or under court order, the company must alter the 'associated index' within fourteen days: section 217 (6).

[199] Section 218.

[200] See sections 217 (7) and 218 (3).

10.9.10 *Inspection of the register and of reports*

Section 219 regulates the right of inspection afforded both in respect of the register of interests in shares kept by virtue of section 211 and of any reports by the company under section 215. Both the register and reports (if any) must be available for inspection without charge by members of the company and other persons.[201] Any person may require the company to provide a copy of the register and any reports (or a part of them) on payment of the prescribed fee.[202] If either an inspection or the provision of copy required is refused, a court order may be obtained requiring the company to comply.[203]

---

[201] Section 219 (1). As to the detailed rights of inspection, see the Companies (Inspection and Copying of Registers, Indices and Documents) Regulations 1991 (SI 1991 No. 1998).

[202] Section 219 (2). The fee is prescribed in the 1991 Regulations (note 201, above).

[203] For the criminal sanction for refusal of inspection or the right to obtain copies, see section 219 (3).

11 Shareholders' Meetings

11.1 Introduction

This chapter is concerned with what is sometimes called the 'machinery of corporate democracy' – i.e. the legislation and case-law which regulates the summoning and conduct of meetings (including voting, proxies and quorums). There is a certain artificiality about the way this machinery works in respect of the modern company, even if it worked well enough in the world of Victorian shareholders and their companies.

In the case of small private companies (by far the most numerous type of company) the formal rules about holding shareholders' meetings (and directors' meetings) wear an awkward air of unreality. A handful of 'corporate partners' (i.e. shareholders/directors) will tend to meet perhaps every day just to run the company's business. In practice they may often forget the formalities of shareholders' and directors' meetings and may be unsure which corporate 'hat' they are wearing on any particular occasion. To some extent modern company law (in the Companies Act 1985, in Table A and in the case-law) recognises this problem. The provisions allowing waiver of notice, and permitting resolutions to be passed by circulating for signature a document so as to avoid the need for a meeting, go some way in this direction, as does the case-law on 'informal agreements'.[1] More important in this respect are the provisions of the Companies Act 1989 which provided for the de-regulation of private companies (see 11.4, below).[2] However, company law nowhere approaches the ease and informality of partnership law in respect of the conduct of internal affairs by partners.

In the case of large public companies (which will inevitably be listed on The Stock Exchange or quoted on the Unlisted Securities market) the law of meetings, voting, etc., operates in a somewhat unreal context of a different order from that affecting small private companies. Of course, shareholders' meetings will be summoned and conducted, and votes counted, with scrupulous regard for what the law requires. The problem is that such public company meetings are extremely poorly attended (even where every effort is made to encourage good attendance). Although there may be thousands (or hundreds of thousands) of shareholders, research has shown that about one in a thousand bothers to attend.[3] This stems in part from the obvious trouble and time involved in travelling to company meetings, where individual shareholders have a small interest at stake.

The use of what is called the 'proxy voting machinery' by the board of directors ensures that where an issue is contested at a company meeting (and the vote goes beyond

---

[1] See 11.2 and 11.3, below.

[2] These changes followed debate concerning the requirements and their effect on small firms. See e.g. L. C. B. Gower *A New Form of Incorporation for Small Firms*, 1981 Cmnd 8171; a consultative document, *A Code for Incorporated Firms*, Annexe A [Department of Trade and Industry]; and an Institute of Directors' paper, 'The Deregulation of Small Companies', December 1986.

[3] See K. Midgley, 114 *Lloyds Bank Review* 24 (1974). Even where a company has well-advertised problems and stormy shareholders' meetings, the average attendance only rises to 1 per cent. See further K. Midgley, *Companies and Their Shareholders: The Uneasy Relationship* (The Institute of Chartered Secretaries and Administrators, 1975).

a show of hands to a poll)[4] the board is extremely likely to win. This stems from the power of the board to 'solicit proxies'[5] at the company's expense. The evidence of experience is that the vast number of individual shareholders, who do not attend company meetings, either return a proxy vote in favour of the board's proposal (or counter proposal) or remain passive. It is true that the growth of 'institutional shareholders' (pension funds, unit trusts, etc.) has in recent decades tended to redress the balance somewhat.[6] However, as was pointed out in 10.1, above, it is not the usual practice of institutional shareholders to contest issues at company meetings. It is much more common for a prestigious institution to raise a matter 'behind the scenes' by approaching the chairman of the board (or other senior executive) directly. This may be done either by a number of institutional investors individually, or through various shareholder protection committees to which they belong.[7] This can sometimes be quite successful in rectifying the abuses or inadequacies of management, or in preventing what are thought to be undesirable initiatives by the board.

It must be conceded that the unstated threat behind such pressure by the institutions obviously comes from the proportion of voting shares held by them. This can be used to override the de facto control exercised by the boards of most large public companies. Thus, at the end of the day, the 'machinery of corporate democracy' has a vital role to play but rather through the implied threat it presents than in its actual use.[8]

11.2 Informal agreement

It is well established that if all the shareholders are present at a meeting and unanimously give their assent to a proposal, it does not matter that no formal resolution was put to the vote.[9] Likewise, any requirements as to the length of notice for a meeting (or for a resolution thereat), whether imposed by the Companies Act 1985 or by the articles, may be waived by the consent of all the members of a company.[10] It would also appear that, if all the shareholders have given their consent to a proposal, it is not necessary that they should have held a meeting. Although in *Re George Newman Ltd*[11] the Court of Appeal held

---

[4] See 11.19, below.

[5] See 11.20.1, below.

[6] About two-thirds of the shares in listed companies are now owned by institutional investors. See L. C. B. Gower, *Review of Investor Protection* (HMSO, 1982), 4.02–4.03, which cites *Shareholder Analysis* (published by The Stock Exchange in December 1980) as indicating that individual shareholders now own between 35 and 36 per cent of listed shares.

[7] See the Wilson Committee, Cmnd 7937, Chapter 19 at paras. 909–913. The institutions each have their own Investment Protection Committee as well as the collective body for all types of institution – the Institutional Shareholders' Committee.

[8] See also the discussion in 10.1, above.

[9] *Re Express Engineering Works* [1920] 1 Ch 466 (CA). Here the meeting consisted of directors who were also all the shareholders. See also *Baroness Wenlock v River Dee Company* (1883) 36 Ch D 675n at p. 681. This has been applied to unanimous agreement to vary a provision in the articles: *Cane v Jones* [1980] 1 WLR 1451, and to a reduction of capital: *Re Barry Artist plc* [1985] BCLC 283 (although only here 'with great reluctance' and with a warning that this procedure would not be accepted in future reductions).

[10] *Re Oxted Motor Co.* [1921] 3 KB 32. There is also provision in section 369 (4) permitting notice to be waived by 95 per cent in value of the shares carrying a right to vote at the meeting (or if the company has no share capital 95 per cent of the total voting rights): section 369 (3) requires unanimous consent in the case of twenty-one days' notice for an annual general meeting. See 11.10.1, below.

[11] [1895] 1 Ch 674 (CA). A possible explanation of this decision is that it concerned acts beyond the powers of the company.

that 'for the purpose of binding a company in its corporate capacity individual assents given separately are not equivalent to the assent of a meeting',[12] more recent decisions have come to a different conclusion. In two cases the members of a company were held to have informally ratified acts by directors beyond their powers even though no share-holders' meeting had been held. In *Parker and Cooper v Reading*[13] it was held that all the members had informally ratified a debenture granted by the directors even though no meeting had been held. In *Re Duomatic Ltd*[14] directors' salaries had been paid without the authority of a shareholders' resolution. It was held by Buckley J that the agreement of the two directors who held all the voting shares, even though they had not constituted themselves as a shareholders' meeting, amounted to an informal ratification of the payment of unauthorised salaries. This decision also establishes that all that is required is the unanimous assent of the shareholders with the right to vote.[15] It is of course only in small private companies that the informal agreement of all the shareholders is likely to occur.[16] In *Cane v Jones*[17] it was held that by unanimous agreement the members might without passing a special resolution alter the articles so that the chairman should no longer have the casting vote. Such an agreement will be registrable under section 380 of the Companies Act 1985.[18]

A single person cannot normally constitute a general[19] meeting[20] – a rule may have considerable importance now that a company may consist of only two persons, of whom one may be absent or ill – except that, where the court makes an order under section 371 for a meeting to be held,[21] or the Department of Trade and Industry calls or directs the calling of a general meeting under section 367,[22] it may direct that one member present in person or by proxy shall be deemed to constitute a meeting.[23]

11.3 Resolutions in writing signed by all members

The articles of association usually provide for written resolutions signed by all members to be as valid and effective as if they had been passed at a general meeting. The standard

---

[12] ibid., p. 686, *per* Lord Lindley, who noted, however, that such assents would preclude those who had given them from complaining of what had been sanctioned.

[13] [1926] Ch 975.

[14] [1969] 2 Ch 365.

[15] In *Re Duomatic Ltd* [1969] 2 Ch 365, the company had a share capital of 100 £1 ordinary shares and 80,000 £1 non-voting preference shares. The shareholder who held all the preference shares had not been consulted. But a different conclusion was reached as to disclosure to 'members' for the purposes of section 312.

[16] See *Attorney General for Canada v Standard Trust Co.* [1911] AC 498 (PC); *Re Innes & Co.* [1903] 2 Ch 254 (CA). These cases suggest that as a matter of legal principle the rule as to the effect of unanimous consent is confined to such companies. *Sed quaere.*

[17] [1980] 1 WLR 1451.

[18] See 11.19, below.

[19] *Secus* as regards class meetings: see *East v Bennett Brothers* [1911] 1 Ch 163.

[20] *Sharp v Dawes* (1876) 2 QBD 26 (CA); *Re Sanitary Carbon Co.* [1877] WN 233; *Prain & Sons* 1947 SC 325; *Re London Flats* [1969] 1 WLR 711.

[21] See 11.5, below.

[22] ibid.

[23] See *Re El Sombrero Ltd* [1958] Ch 900. A private company with one member is catered for by statute; see 11.22, below.

model, applicable to all companies limited by shares, is article 53 of Table A to the Companies Act 1985.[24]

> A resolution in writing executed by or on behalf of each member who would have been entitled to vote upon it if it had been proposed at a general meeting at which he was present shall be as effectual as if it had been passed at a general meeting duly convened and held and may consist of several instruments in the like form each executed by or on behalf of one or more members.

11.4 De-regulation of private companies

Sections 113–17 of the Companies Act 1989 provide for the de-regulation of private companies, and were intended to simplify company procedures in respect of small private companies where unanimous consent can be obtained for a particular proposal without the necessity for a general meeting (the written resolution procedure) or where such consent can be obtained to disapply a Companies Act requirement for a particular type of resolution (the elective resolution procedure).

11.4.1 Written resolutions of private companies

The purpose of Section 113 of the Companies Act 1989 (which inserted new sections 381A, 381B and 382A into the Companies Act 1985) is to allow more effective and widespread use by small private companies of written resolutions so as to avoid company meetings. The statutory power has a more extensive scope than the provisions in article 53 of Table A. Section 381A allows the replacement not only of ordinary resolutions in general meetings, and resolutions in class meetings, but also special and extraordinary resolutions.[25] It also extends to an 'elective resolution'[26] by a private company to apply the 'elective' regime provided by sections 115 and 116 of the Companies Act 1989.[27]

The new written resolution procedure will apply even in those cases where the existing provisions in the Companies Act 1985 insist on a special resolution passed at a shareholders' meeting.[28]

11.4.2 The procedure

This requires 'without a meeting and without any previous notice', a 'resolution in writing by or on behalf of all the members of the company who at the date of the resolution would be entitled to attend and vote at such meeting'.[29] The signature need not be in a single document so long as each signature is on a document which accurately states the terms of the resolution.[30] The date of the resolution is deemed to be the date when the resolution is signed by or on behalf of the last member.[31] This date will in general be

---

[24] A similar provision appeared (though with the addition of words making it subject to the Companies Acts) in the 1948 Act Table A. Originally it was article 5 in Part II of Table A (and thus applicable automatically only to private companies). Following the Companies Act 1980, which abolished Part II, it became article 73A and applicable to all companies adopting it.

[25] See section 381A (4) and (6).

[26] See section 379A.

[27] See 11.4.6, below.

[28] e.g. section 4 (alteration of the memorandum) or section 135 (reduction of capital). As to the necessity of a special resolution under the old law, see *Re Barry Artists Ltd* [1985] BCLC 283. In the case of amendment of the articles, unanimous agreement would suffice: *Cane v Jones* [1981] 1 All ER 533.

[29] Section 381A (1).

[30] Section 381A (2).

[31] Section 381A (3).

regarded as 'the date of the passing of the resolution', but this is subject to the provisions of section 381B which defined the rights of auditors in relation to written resolutions.[32]

11.4.3 Rights of auditors

Section 381B stipulates that 'a copy of any written resolution proposed to be agreed in accordance with section 381A (1) shall be sent to the company's auditors'. If the resolution 'concerns the auditors as auditors' they may, within seven days of receiving their copy of the resolution, give notice to the company 'stating their opinion that the resolution should be considered by the company in general meeting'.[33] The phrase 'concerns the auditors as auditors' is not defined and appears to confer a subjective discretion to be exercised in good faith rather than implying a precise concept.[34] A written resolution is not to have effect unless the auditors notify the company that in their opinion the resolution, (a) does not concern them as auditors, or (b) does so concern them but need not be considered at a general meeting. If the seven-day period expires without the auditors notifying the company of their opinion then the written resolution may also take effect.[35]

The various provisions of sections 381A and 381B 'have effect notwithstanding any provision of the company's memorandum or articles'.[36] This is important in that the 'rights of auditors' requirements (in relation to written resolutions) might appear to apply even if the company purports to act under a power in the articles. The language of section 381C (1) on its own would appear to have this effect. However, section 381C has a saving provision to cover tacit informal consent by the shareholders not amounting to a written resolution.[37] It provides that nothing (in sections 381A and 381B) 'affects any enactment or rule of law as to (a) things done otherwise than by passing a resolution, or (b) cases in which a resolution is treated as having been duly passed or a person is precluded from alleging that a resolution has not been duly passed'. Section 381C (2) covers both the cases on informal consent or an argument based on acquiescence by lapse of time.[38] It is debatable whether para. (b) in section 381C (2) prevents section 381C (1) overriding an article such as article 53 of Table A. It is likely that the rights of auditors will be repealed before this issue is resolved.[38a]

11.4.4 Minuting written resolutions

Section 382A makes provision for recording written resolutions. The company 'shall cause a record of the resolution (and of the signatures) to be entered into a book in the same way as minutes of a general meeting of the company'.[39] Such a record, if purporting to be signed by a director or secretary, is 'evidence of the proceedings in agreeing the resolution'. Where a record is made in accordance with section 382A then,

---

[32] See section 381A (5) and section 381B.

[33] Section 381B (2). This will also apply, in the case of class resolutions, to a class meeting.

[34] This view is supported by the reference in section 381B (2) to 'a notice to the company stating their opinion' and by the procedure in section 381B (3) and (4) which gives various options to the auditors.

[35] See section 381B (3) and (4).

[36] See section 381C (1).

[37] See *Re Duomatic Ltd* [1969] 2 Ch 365 and *Cane v Jones* [1981] 1 All ER 533.

[38] Any attempt to organise acquiescence or informal consent would be open to attack as infringing sections 381A and 381B.

[38a] See the consultative document, *Resolutions of Private Companies* (DTI, February 1995).

[39] Section 382A (1).

until the contrary is proved, the requirements of the Act with respect to the proceedings is deemed to be complied with.[40]

Section 382B applies to private companies limited by shares or by guarantee which have only one member.[41] Where such a member takes a decision 'which may be taken by the company in general meeting and which has effect as if agreed by the company in general meeting' he must[42] provide the company with a written record of that decision. A criminal sanction[43] is provided for failure to comply, but this does not affect the validity of the decision taken by the single member.[44]

11.4.5 Additional requirements for particular types of written resolution

The procedure set out in section 381A for written resolutions is specifically subject to Schedule 15A.[45] Part I of the Schedule bars the use of a written resolution altogether in two cases. These are a resolution under section 303 (removing a director before the expiration of his office) and a resolution under section 391 (removing an auditor before the expiration of his term of office). In these cases the person to be removed has a right to speak in his own defence at the meeting to consider the resolution, making the written resolution procedure inappropriate. Part II of the Schedule deals with resolutions (mostly concerning share capital) that are for a particular statutory purpose which has a specific statutory requirement not applicable to company resolutions generally.

Part II adapts certain procedural requirements to the written resolution procedure. This may relate to specific statements or documents to be circulated with the notice of meeting, which by virtue of Part II are to be supplied to each member 'by whom or on whose behalf the resolution is required to be signed in accordance with that section'.[46] This applies to resolutions concerned with disapplication of pre-emption rights under section 95,[47] with financial assistance for the purchase of a company's own shares,[48] with authority for off-market purchases, or contingent purchase contracts of a company's own shares.[49] It also applies to resolutions under section 319 (approval of a director's service contract),[50] and section 337 (funding of a director's expenditure in performing his duties).[51] In some cases members holding shares to which the resolution relates are disqualified from voting. This has likewise been adapted to the written resolution procedure.[52]

---

[40] The penalties for failing to comply with section 382A are carried over from those applicable to section 382. The same applies to the right of inspection of minute books given by section 383: see section 382A (3).

[41] See the Companies (Single Member Private Limited Companies) Regulations 1992 (SI 1992 No. 1699), Schedule, para. 6.

[42] 'Unless that decision was taken by written resolution': section 382B (1).

[43] Section 382B (2), Schedule 24, as amended.

[44] Section 382B (3).

[45] See section 381A (7).

[46] Schedule 15A, para. 2.

[47] Schedule 15A, para. 3; see 6.5.1, above.

[48] i.e. under section 155 (see 6.17.3). See Schedule 15A, para. 4.

[49] i.e. under sections 164, 165 and 167 (see 6.17.4). See Schedule 15A, para. 5.

[50] Schedule 15A, para. 7. See 14.15, below.

[51] ibid., para. 8. See 14.17.3.

[52] i.e. in respect of sections 164 and 174. See Schedule 15A, paras. 5 and 6.

11.4.6 The elective resolution procedure

The elective resolution procedure under section 379A of the Companies Act 1985 allows certain requirements to pass resolutions to be disapplied. The elective resolution may take the form of the written resolution procedure. The matters subject to elective resolution[53] are authority to issue shares, laying accounts before a general meeting, consent to short notice of meetings, and the appointment of auditors. The Secretary of State has power to extend this by statutory instrument.[54] Generally speaking the elective regime will be confined to matters of internal administration and will not impinge upon the protection of creditors or other outsiders.

A private company which has acted by elective resolution may, instead of following the requirements of section 80 of the Companies Act 1985, give the directors authority to issue shares for an indefinite period, or for a fixed period which does not have to be limited to five years.[55] Authority given for a fixed period may be renewed or further renewed by the company in general meeting,[56] the written resolution procedure being possible in these cases.

A private company may dispense with the requirement to lay accounts before the general meeting except where a member or the auditors demand this to be done.[57] The same procedure can be used by a private company to dispense with the need to hold an annual general meeting unless a member requires one to be held.[58] A private company can also reduce the 95 per cent majority of shareholders required to consent to short notice to 90 per cent.[59] A private company may free itself by elective resolution from the need to make annual appointments of its auditors. The auditors are then automatically reappointed.[60]

11.4.7 Procedure for elective resolutions

The procedure for an elective resolution is set out in section 379A (2).[61] Such a resolution requires twenty-one days' notice in writing given of the meeting, stating that an elective resolution is to be proposed and the terms of the resolution.[61a] It must then be agreed to at the meeting, in person or by proxy, by all the members entitled to attend and vote.[62] The elective resolution may be revoked by ordinary resolution.[63] The passing or revoking of elective resolutions under section 379A have effect notwithstanding any contrary

---

[53] Section 379A (1).

[54] See section 117 of the Companies Act 1989. Such regulations may make different provisions for different cases. They may also amend or repeal provisions of the Companies Act 1985 and 'may provide for such provisions to have effect, where an election is made, subject to such adaptions and modifications as appropriate': section 117(2), (3).

[55] Section 80A.

[56] Section 80A (4).

[57] Section 252.

[58] Section 366A.

[59] See section 119 of the Companies Act 1989 amending sections 369(4) and 378 (3) of the Companies Act 1985.

[60] Section 379A.

[61] Such a resolution can of course be passed as a written resolution.

[61a] It is proposed to dispense with the need for twenty-one days' notice if all the members entitled to attend and vote agree; see the DTI consultative document referred to in footnote 38a, above.

[62] Section 379A (3).

[63] Section 379A (5). If a private company re-registers as a public one, an elective resolution ceases to have effect: section 389A (4).

provision in the articles.[64] An elective resolution must be registered under section 380 within fifteen days.[65]

11.5 Annual general meetings

Every company must in each year hold a general meeting as its annual general meeting in addition to any other meetings in that year, and must specify the meeting as such in the notices calling it. Not more than fifteen months must elapse between the date of one annual general meeting and the next. But so long as a company holds its first annual general meeting within eighteen months of its incorporation it need not hold it in the year of its incorporation or the following year.[66]

If default is made in holding such a meeting the Secretary of State may, on the application of any member, call or direct the calling of a general meeting, and give such ancillary or consequential directions as he thinks expedient. These may include directions modifying or supplementing[67] the operation of the company's articles, including a direction that one member present in person or by proxy shall be deemed to constitute a meeting.[68] Failure to hold a meeting in accordance with section 366 or in complying with any directions of the Department of Trade and Industry under section 367, renders the company and every officer in default liable to a fine.[69]

A general meeting held under section 367 is (subject to any directions of the Secretary of State) deemed to be an annual general meeting, but, where a meeting so held is not held in the year in which the default in holding the company's annual general meeting occurred, such meeting is not to be treated as the annual general meeting for the year in which it is held unless at that meeting the company resolves that it shall be so treated.[70] Where a company does so resolve, a copy of the resolution must, within fifteen days after its passing, be forwarded to the Registrar of Companies and recorded by him.[71]

It is customary to provide in the articles[72] that all business except such as is therein mentioned (e.g. declaring a dividend, considering the accounts, balance sheets, and the reports of the directors and auditors, and electing directors and appointing auditors and fixing their remuneration)[73] shall be deemed special, and that notice must be given of the general nature of all special business. Without such a provision in the articles it seems that no business could be transacted of which previous notice had not been given,[74] and where such provisions are included, any business not specially mentioned as an exception can only be transacted if notice has been given.

---

[64] Section 379A (5).

[65] Section 380 (4) (*bb*).

[66] Section 366. As to the sanctions, see section 366 (4), Schedule 24.

[67] '... in relation to the calling, holding and conducting of the meeting'. Where a meeting is held after the prescribed time, voting rights are determined as of the actual time of the meeting, not as they would have been if the meeting had been held at the proper time: *Musselwhite v C. H. Musselwhite Ltd* [1962] Ch 964.

[68] Section 367 (1) and (2).

[69] Sections 366 (4) and 367 (3). As to the fines that may be exacted, see Schedule 24 to the 1985 Act.

[70] Section 367 (4).

[71] For the sanctions for failure to send a copy to the Registrar, see section 367 (5).

[72] The 1948 Table A, Part I, article 52 so provided, but, rather curiously, there is no equivalent provision in the 1985 Table A.

[73] As to the special requirements when an auditor other than the retiring auditor is proposed, see 12.21.2, below.

[74] *Per* Littledale J in *R v Hill* (1825) 4 B&C 444.

11.6 Requisitioning extraordinary general meetings

In addition to annual general meetings, a company may also from time to time hold other general meetings, which are usually called extraordinary general meetings. Under all usual forms of articles only the special business of which notice has been given can be transacted. Extraordinary meetings can be convened by the directors whenever they think proper[75] and in certain circumstances may be convened by the members themselves, subject to the conditions contained in section 368 of the Companies Act 1985 which overrides any regulations of the company. By this section the directors are bound forthwith to convene an extraordinary general meeting on the requisition of

> ... (a) members of the company holding at the date of the deposit of the requisition not less than one-tenth of such of the paid-up capital of the company as at that date carries the right of voting at general meetings of the company, or (b) in the case of a company not having a share capital, members of the company representing not less than one-tenth of the total voting rights of all the members having at the date of deposit of the requisition a right to vote at general meetings.[76]

The requisition (which may consist of several documents in like form each signed by one or more requisitionists) must state the objects of the meeting and must be signed by the requisitionists and deposited at the registered office of the company. If joint holders of shares join in the requisition all must sign, unless the articles specifically authorise one to sign for all: the signature of one on behalf of all is of no avail.[77] If the directors do not within twenty-one days from the date of the requisition being deposited proceed duly to convene a meeting,[78] to consider the matters specified in the requisition,[79] the requisitionists, or any of them representing more than one-half of the voting rights of all of them, may themselves convene the meeting; but it must be held within three months from the date of the deposit of the requisition.[80] Any meeting convened by requisitionists is to be convened as nearly as possible in the same manner as that in which meetings are to be convened by directors.[81] Unreasonable and unjustifiable delay may, however, amount to 'unfair prejudice' for the purposes of section 459.[82]

A meeting requisitioned by members under section 368 cannot deal with a resolution

---

[75] As to the directors' duty of good faith in respect of their power to call meetings, see *Pergamon Press Ltd v Maxwell* [1970] 1 WLR 1167.

[76] If the articles allow a smaller number to requisition a meeting, this, being an additional power not inconsistent with the Act, will be effective.

[77] *Patent Wood Keg Syndicate v Pearse* [1906] WN 164.

[78] The twenty-one-day period refers to the time by which the directors must have decided to *convene* the extraordinary general meeting. The meeting so convened need not be held within this period so long as it has been convened and this will prevent the requisitionists themselves convening a meeting: *Re Windward Islands Enterprises* [1983] BCLC 293. This decision of Nourse J allows extensive delay by the directors. It indicates a need to tighten the wording of section 368; see (1983) 4 Co. Law 219. See also *McGuinness v Bremmer plc* [1988] BCLC 673, Ct of Sess.

[79] If the directors convene a meeting to consider part only of the specified matters, the requisitionists may ignore it, and call their own meeting: *Isle of Wight Rly Co. v Tahourdin* (1883) 25 Ch D 320 (CA). If the requisition contains matters which, though apparently irregular, may be carried out in a lawful manner, the court will not restrain the holding of the meeting (same case).

[80] The secretary cannot without the sanction of the board summon the meeting on receipt of the requisition. Whether the requisitionists can employ him to give the notice after the twenty-one days have elapsed is still an open question: *Re State of Wyoming Syndicate* [1901] 2 Ch 431.

[81] Section 368 (5).

[82] *McGuinness v Bremmer plc*, above.

not included in the objects for which the meeting was requisitioned. Unless the articles otherwise provide, the requisitionists will not be able to insist on any matter not in the requisition being included in the notice of meeting sent out by the company.[83]

Any reasonable expenses incurred by the requisitionists by reason of the failure of the directors duly to convene a meeting shall be repaid by the company, and the company must deduct any sum so repaid from any sums due or to become due from the company by way of fees or other remuneration in respect of their services to such of the directors as were in default.[84] For the purposes of the section directors are, in the case of a meeting at which a resolution is to be proposed as a special resolution, deemed not to have duly convened the meeting if they do not give such notice thereof as is required by section 378 (2).[85]

There is no provision in the Companies Act 1985 similar to that usually inserted in articles, that at a meeting convened by requisitionists no business is to be done other than that mentioned in the requisition. However, this is perhaps implied in the provision that the requisition must state the objects of the meeting. In any case due notice must be given of any business to be transacted.

The directors have a duty, as well as a right, to circularise the members for the purpose of advising them as to the prudence or propriety of any proposed resolution, and may use the company's money for this purpose or for procuring proxies in their own favour.[86]

If there are no directors,[87] or no special provisions in the articles to meet the case, any two or more members holding not less than one-tenth of the issued share capital or, if the company has not a share capital, not less than 5 per cent in number of the members of the company, may call a meeting.[88] The court may also order a meeting to be held if it is impracticable otherwise to call or conduct it.[89]

A minority shareholder seeking an order that an extraordinary general meeting of the company be convened under section 371 must fail if the claim cannot be brought within an exception to the rule in *Foss v Harbottle*.[90] Such a claim should be brought not by way of originating summons but in a contentious action with pleadings.[91]

Where the hearing of an unfair prejudice claim under section 459 is pending, and quorum requirements and refusal to attend meetings by a minority shareholder prevent the holding of shareholders' meetings, the court will order a meeting under section 371 so as to allow directors to be appointed and accounts to be approved.[92] However, to protect the minority shareholder until the section 459 petition is heard, restrictive provisions will be placed upon what could be done or in consequence of the meeting ordered by the court. For example, directors could not effect any alteration in the constitution or capital

---

[83] *Ball v Metal Industries* 1957 SC 315.

[84] Section 368 (6).

[85] Section 368 (7).

[86] *Peel v London and North-Western Rly* [1907] Ch 5 (CA); *Campbell v Australian Mutual Provident Society* (1909) 77 LJPC 117; *Wilson v L.M.S. Rly Co.* [1940] Ch 393 (CA); but if invitations to appoint proxies are issued at the company's expense, they should be sent to all the members entitled to be sent a notice of the meeting and to vote thereat by proxy: section 372 (6); see 11.21.1, below.

[87] See *Re Brick & Stone Co.* [1878] WN 140, a decision under the Act of 1862.

[88] Section 370 (3).

[89] Section 371.

[90] (1843) 2 Hare 461.

[91] *Re Downs Wine Bar* [1990] BCLC 839 at p. 842.

[92] *Re Sticky Fingers Restaurant Ltd* [1992] BCLC 84.

of the company.[93] The existence of a section 459 petition at the date of hearing of the section 371 application is a matter which bears upon the discretion of the court but does not prevent it exercising its discretionary powers under section 371.[94]

11.7 Representatives of corporate members

Only members of the company (and the auditors)[95] are, in the absence of express provisions in the articles, entitled to be present. A member cannot insist on his solicitor or other agent being allowed to accompany him, though a solicitor or other agent may be appointed proxy, as a proxy need not be a member of the company.[96] Section 375 empowers any corporation (whether a company within the meaning of the Companies Act 1985[97] or not), if it is a member of another corporation which is a company within the meaning of the Act, to authorise, by resolution of its directors or other governing body, such person as it thinks fit to act as its representative. A representative of a corporate member may attend any meeting of the company or of any class of members of the company, and, if a creditor, any meeting of any creditors of the company held in pursuance of the Act or of any rules made thereunder, or in pursuance of the provisions contained in any debenture or trust deed, as the case may be. Such person need not be a member. A person so authorised is entitled to exercise the same powers on behalf of the corporation which he represents as that corporation could exercise if it were an individual shareholder, creditor, or holder of debentures, of the other company. Such representative must be counted in estimating the quorum present.[98] If the chairman allows the vote of a person claiming to represent a company, it is no objection that no proxy has been produced if it subsequently appears that such person was duly appointed by resolution;[99] but there is no authority as to whether the chairman can insist upon evidence of the appointment before receiving the vote. Unless the articles deal with the matter, a chairman should allow a person claiming to represent a company to attend, but specially note how he votes, and require evidence subsequently of his appointment by resolution of the directors.[100]

11.8 Class meetings

Meetings of a class of shareholders will often be held in order to vary the rights of the class by extraordinary resolution. Provision for this may be made by the articles,[101] but in

---

[93] ibid. at pp. 89–90.

[94] *Re Whitchurch Insurance Consultants* [1994] BCC 51 at p. 56. *Re Sticky Fingers* was distinguished on the ground that there the hearing of the section 459 petition was imminent: *Re Opera Photographic* [1989] 5 BCC 601 followed.

[95] Section 387.

[96] Section 372 (1). As to the appointment and powers of proxies at general meetings, see 11.21, below.

[97] The word 'company', when used in the Act, is defined in section 735: 'company' means a company formed and registered under this Act or an existing company.

[98] *Re Kelantan Coco Nut Estates* [1920] WN 274.

[99] *Colonial Gold Reef v Free State Rand* [1914] 1 Ch 382.

[100] As to the appointment of a corporate representative by a company in liquidation, the power conferred by section 375 may be exercised by the liquidator: *Hillman v Crystal Bowl Amusements* [1973] 1 WLR 162 (CA).

[101] See e.g. article 4 in the 1948 Table A. There is no equivalent provision in the 1985 Table A because of the statutory provisions, first introduced in 1980, referred to below.

practice it is usually regulated by the provisions of section 125 of the Companies Act 1985.[102] If a class of shareholders consists of only one person (e.g. holding all the preference shares), clauses in the memorandum or articles requiring the consent of a meeting of such class may be satisfied by a resolution in writing signed by that one person.[103] Class meetings may also be summoned by order of the court under section 425.[104]

Prima facie a separate meeting of a class should be attended only by members of that class, but if, the presence of strangers being known, no objection is taken at the meeting to their presence, the members present must be taken to have assented to the meeting being so conducted.[105]

11.9 Adjourned meetings

In the absence of express directions in the articles the chairman of a general meeting can, on proper grounds, adjourn the meeting,[106] but usually the articles only give him power to do so with the consent of the meeting, in which case he cannot, by leaving the chair before the business is completed, bring the meeting to a close; if he purports to do so, the meeting may appoint another chairman and proceed with the business.[107] If the articles provide that 'the chairman, with the consent of the meeting, may adjourn', the majority cannot compel the chairman to adjourn the meeting if he thinks it ought to proceed.[108] But Table A (article 45) requires the chairman to adjourn the meeting if so directed by the meeting, further providing (by article 51) that a poll demanded on the question of adjournment shall be taken forthwith.[109]

An adjourned meeting is merely a continuation of the original meeting,[110] and all the requirements as to the original meeting must have been complied with to make the adjourned meeting valid. In the absence of special regulations no further notice is necessary, and if any notices have to be given before 'the meeting' this will be read as being before the commencement of the original meeting.[111] The same quorum will be required as for the original meeting unless the articles otherwise provide.[112] Proxies given for the original meeting are available for an adjourned meeting; but where articles require proxies to be lodged so many hours before a meeting, they have to be lodged that number of hours before the commencement of the original meeting.[113] To avoid this it is

---

[102] See 7.7 *et seq.*, above.
[103] *East v Bennett Bros.* [1911] 1 Ch 163.
[104] See 16.18, below.
[105] *Carruth v Imperial Chemical Industries* [1937] AC 707 (HL).
[106] *R. v D'Oyly* (1840) 12 A & E 139; *R. v Wimbledon Local Board* (1882) 8 QBD 459 (CA).
[107] *National Dwellings Society v Sykes* [1894] 3 Ch 159; *John v Rees* [1969] 2 WLR 1294.
[108] *Salisbury Gold Mining Co. v Hathorn* [1897] AC 268 (PC).
[109] As to the chairman's power to adjourn a meeting, see *Byng v London Life Association Ltd* [1989] BCLC 400, which stated that where there is a meeting at which the views of the majority cannot be validly ascertained, the chairman has a residual common-law power to adjourn.
[110] *Wills v Murray* (1850), 4 Ex. 843; *Scadding v Lorant* (1851) 3 HLC 418; *McLaren v Thomson* [1917] 2 Ch 261. As to the date of a resolution passed at an adjourned meeting, see section 381 described below.
[111] See further, as to notice in respect of adjourned meetings, at 11.11, below.
[112] Table A, article 41 requires the same quorum for an adjourned meeting.
[113] *McLaren v Thompson* [1917] 2 Ch 261.

often provided that proxies must be lodged not less than so many hours[114] before 'the meeting or adjourned meeting', as in Table A, article 62.[115]

Section 381 provides that where a resolution is passed at an adjourned meeting of a company, or the holders of any class of shares in a company, or the directors of a company, the resolution shall for all purposes be treated as having been passed on the date on which it was in fact passed, and shall not be deemed to have been passed on any earlier date. It must be remembered, however, that the taking of a poll is not an adjournment of a meeting.[116]

11.10 Notices of general meetings

Notice of all general meetings must be given to the members entitled thereto[117] in manner prescribed by the company's articles or by Table A, and also to the auditors.[118] If all the members do not attend, a company is not 'corporately assembled', so as to be able to do business, unless the meeting is held upon notice given to every member entitled thereto, and complies with the provisions of the articles as to stating the objects for which the meeting is held.[119] If the registered address of a member entitled to notice under the articles is situate in enemy territory or enemy occupied territory, or the right to receive notices is otherwise suspended by operation of law, the company can conduct its business without serving notices upon such members.[120]

A provision in the articles that the accidental omission to give notice to or the non-receipt of notice by any person entitled to receive notice shall not invalidate the proceedings (see Table A, article 39) will prevent any such omission being relied upon as a ground for questioning any resolutions or proceedings of a meeting of which a member did not receive notice. It has been held that such a provision in the articles will validate a meeting where some members did not receive notice of a meeting because their addressograph plates had been separated from the rest. This had been done because their dividend warrants had previously been returned undelivered and uncashed.[121] Presumably, this would also cover a situation where the whereabouts of a shareholder was unknown to the company (e.g. communications had been returned from an old address and where no later address was known). However, it has been held that an article such as article 39 of Table A will not cover a deliberate omission even if based on a mistaken belief that a member is not entitled to notice.[122] Where all the shareholders attend a meeting of which no notice or insufficient notice has been given, they can waive the informality, and pass valid resolutions.[123] A member who is in fact present and has

---

[114] *Spiller v Mayo (Rhodesia) Co.* [1926] WN 78, and 11.21, below. For some purposes the date of the original meeting may be the governing date: see *Cousins v International Brick Co.* [1931] 2 Ch 90. See further, 11.21, below.

[115] This must not exceed forty-eight: section 372 (5).

[116] As to the court's power to adjourn a meeting which it has previously ordered to be held, see *Northern Counties Securities v Jackson* [1974] 1 WLR 1133.

[117] Where restricted voting rights are conferred on a class (see 7.6, above) the entitlement to receive notice of or to attend at the meeting is usually expressly made to depend on the same circumstances as the right to vote. Even if it is not, the same result may follow: *Re Mackenzie & Co.* [1916] 2 Ch 450.

[118] Section 387.

[119] *Baillie v Oriental Telephone Co.* [1915] 1 Ch 503 (CA); cf. *Young v Ladies' Imperial Club* [1920] 2 KB 523.

[120] *Re Anglo-International Bank* [1943] Ch 233.

[121] *Re West Canadian Collieries Ltd* [1962] Ch 370. See also *Royal Mutual Benefit Society v Sharman* [1963] 1 WLR 581.

[122] *Musselwhite v C. H. Musselwhite & Sons Ltd* [1962] Ch 964.

[123] See the cases discussed at 11.2, above.

allowed the business determined upon to be carried out for a long period cannot subsequently set up an irregularity in summoning the meeting.[124]

11.10.1 *Length of notice*

By section 369 (1), any provision of a company's articles is void in so far as it provides for the calling of a meeting of the company (other than an adjourned meeting) by a shorter notice than

(1) in the case of the annual general meeting, twenty-one days' notice in writing; and
(2) in the case of a meeting other than an annual general meeting or a meeting for the passing of a special resolution, fourteen days' notice in writing in the case of a company other than an unlimited company and seven days' notice in writing in the case of an unlimited company.

By section 369 (2), a meeting of the company (other than an adjourned meeting) may (unless the company's articles make some other provision not being a provision invalidated by section 369 (1)) be called

(1) in the case of the annual general meeting, by twenty-one days' notice in writing; and
(2) in the case of a meeting other than an annual general meeting or a meeting for the passing of a special resolution, by fourteen days' notice in writing in the case of a company other than an unlimited company and by seven days' notice in writing in the case of an unlimited company.

These provisions are confirmed in article 38 of Table A, which also adds to the twenty-one days' notice requirement notice of a meeting to pass a resolution appointing a director, and refers to the periods being 'clear days', i.e. exclusive of the day of giving the notice and the day of the meeting. Article 111 requires that the notice is in writing and article 115 provides that proof that an envelope containing a notice was properly addressed, prepaid and posted is conclusive evidence that the notice was given, and that a notice is deemed to be given at the expiration of forty-eight hours after the envelope containing it was posted.

It has been seen that the articles may provide for giving longer notice than specified, but not shorter notice. Section 369 (3) and (4) do, however, go on to provide some latitude, by saying that a meeting shall, although called by shorter notice than that specified in subsection (2) or in the company's articles, be deemed to have been duly called if it is so agreed

(1) in the case of a meeting called as the annual general meeting, by all the members entitled to attend and vote;
(2) in the case of any other meeting, by a majority in number of the members having a right to attend and vote at the meeting, being a majority together holding not less than 95 per cent in nominal value of the shares giving a right to attend and vote at the meeting, or, in the case of a company not having a share capital, together

[124] *Re British Sugar Refining Co.* (1857) 3 K & J 408.

representing not less than 95 per cent of the total voting rights at that meeting of all the members.[125]

A private company may elect to reduce the percentage to anywhere between 90 and 95 per cent.[126] In general, no notice is required to be given of adjourned meetings, if held within the limits prescribed by the articles of association, as they are merely continuations of the previous meetings, at which, if notice was properly given, all the members have had the opportunity of being present, and those who were present have agreed to the time and place of adjournment. But under Table A, article 45 if the adjournment is for fourteen days or more, fresh notice is required.

Although the adjourned meeting is only a continuation of the original meeting,[127] if notice to propose a director is required to be given so many days before 'the day of election', and the election takes place at an adjourned meeting, the notice is sufficient if given the specified time before the day of holding the adjourned meeting.[128] It would be otherwise if the article required notice before the meeting at which the election is to take place.[129]

When notice has been duly given of a meeting, the meeting cannot be postponed by a subsequent notice;[130] the proper course is for the meeting to be held and adjourned.

In the absence of some special provision in the articles it is not necessary to give notice to the representatives of deceased shareholders unless such representatives have become members by formal registration.[131] Under article 38 of Table A such notice is required to be given to representatives of deceased shareholders: the use to which they can put this notice is not clear, since article 31 prevents them attending the meeting, and, of course, voting thereat. Even if the articles allowed them to attend and vote, their votes could not be counted on an extraordinary or special resolution, because under section 378 the votes to be counted are those of members.

A notice of meeting, to be good, must be given by persons authorised to summon the meeting. Resolutions passed at a meeting convened by the secretary without the authority of the board are invalid; not will the consent of directors separately given suffice.[132] But if the notice purports to be issued by the authority of the directors and is subsequently ratified by them at a board meeting it will be valid.[133] A statement in the report of the directors sent with the notice of meeting that certain business will be proposed is a sufficient notice.[134]

---

[125] Provision to the same effect is contained in article 38 of Table A. Section 378 (3) allows a special resolution to be validly passed without the usual twenty-one-day period of notice where a majority in number of the members having the right to attend and vote at the meeting, and holding 95 per cent in nominal value of the shares giving that right, agree to accept a lesser period of notice. But the members must, in giving their consent, have knowledge of the special resolution which it is proposed to pass on a shorter period of notice: *Re Pearce Duff & Co. Ltd* [1960] 1 WLR 1014. See 11.16–11.17, below, as to special and extraordinary resolutions.

[126] As to elective resolutions generally, see 11.4.6, above.

[127] *Wills v Murray* (1850) 4 Ex. 843; *Scadding v Lorant* (1851) 3 HLC 418.

[128] *Catesby v Burnett* [1916] 2 Ch 325.

[129] See *McLaren v Thomson* [1917] 2 Ch 261.

[130] *Smith v Paringa Mines* [1906] 2 Ch 193.

[131] *Allen v Gold Reefs of West Africa* [1900] 1 Ch 656 (C.A).

[132] *Re Haycraft Gold Reduction Co.* [1900] 2 Ch 230; *Re State of Wyoming Syndicate* [1901] 2 Ch 431.

[133] *Hooper v Kerr Stuart & Co.* (1900) 83 LT 729.

[134] *Boschoek Proprietary Co. v Fuke* [1906] 1 Ch 148.

11.10.2 Misleading notices

The articles usually provide that notice must be given of the general nature of any special business to be transacted,[135] and by section 378 (1) notice must be given of the intention to propose an extraordinary or special resolution. In the absence of provisions in the articles of association, and if Table A be excluded, no business can be brought on without notice. The notice must 'give at any rate a fair, candid, and reasonable explanation' of the business proposed, and if something is wrapped up or kept back it will invalidate the proceedings.[136] Thus Kekewich J held that a notice of a meeting to adopt new articles which might be seen at the company's office was not sufficient where the new articles increased the directors' remuneration and borrowing power, and made other important changes.[137]

Directors who are to derive some benefit under resolutions have sometimes attempted to cover it up in the notice of meeting in such a way that it shall not be fully understood by the shareholders. Such a notice is insufficient, and a resolution passed in pursuance of it will be invalid.[138] Thus, where in a reconstruction directors did not state that they were participating in the purchase consideration to be received by the selling company,[139] or where in seeking the sanction of the company to the retention by the directors of remuneration they had received irregularly no proper statement was made as to the amount,[140] the resolutions passed were held to be invalid. The holding of extraordinary general meetings without sufficient notice, where this results in the ineffective creation of new shares, may amount to unfairly prejudicial conduct of the company's affairs within section 459 of the Companies Act 1985.[141]

11.11 Minutes of business done at meetings

Every company must, pursuant to section 382 of the Companies Act 1985, cause minutes of all proceedings of general meetings, and of meetings of its directors or managers, to be entered in books kept for the purpose. Such minutes if purporting to be signed by the chairman of the meeting or of the next succeeding meeting are evidence of the proceedings. Until the contrary is proved every meeting of the company, or of the directors or managers, of which minutes have been so made, is deemed duly held and convened, and all proceedings thereat duly had, and all appointments of directors, managers, or liquidators are deemed to be valid.[142]

---

[135] Table A has this provision (Table A of 1862, article 35; Table A of 1908, article 49; Table A of 1929, article 42; Table A of 1948, article 50; Table A of 1985, article 38).

[136] *Kaye v Croydon Tramways* [1898] 1 Ch 358 (CA); cf. *Young v Ladies' Imperial Club* [1920] 2 KB 523 (CA), where in a club case the rules required that the expulsion of a member should only be effected at a meeting of the committee specially convened for that purpose. A notice 'to elect directors' constitutes a sufficient notice to elect directors up to the maximum number authorised by the articles: *Choppington Collieries v Johnson* [1944] 1 All ER 762 (CA).

[137] *Normandy v Ind Coope & Co.* [1908] 1 Ch 84.

[138] *Pacific Coast Coal Mines v Arbuthnot* [1917] AC 607 (PC).

[139] *Kaye v Croydon Tramways* [1898] 1 Ch 358 (CA); *Tiessen v Henderson* [1899] 1 Ch 861. See also *Clarkson v Davies* [1923] AC 100 (PC).

[140] *Baillie v Oriental Telephone Co.* [1915] 1 Ch 503 (CA).

[141] *Re a Company, ex parte Shooter* [1990] BCLC 385 at p. 394.

[142] Section 382, and see Table A, article 100. This must of course mean in regard to matters properly entered in the minutes, and the evidence will only be that such and such proceedings were had, and not that the statements of fact contained therein are true.

The absence of any reference to a matter in the minutes is treated as evidence that it was not brought before the company or the board, but express evidence may be given to prove what was in fact done and what resolutions have been passed.[143] Where the articles provide that the minutes of meetings when signed shall be conclusive evidence of the facts therein stated, as between members of the company, the minutes are in the absence of fraud conclusive, and unless bad faith or fraud is alleged, evidence tendered for the purpose of contradicting the facts set forth in the minutes is inadmissible.[144]

Directors present when the minutes of a previous meeting are read and signed are not thereby made responsible for the resolutions passed at the previous meeting, although they thus are fixed with notice of what has been done.[145] If any matter is debated afresh, this should be the subject of a separate minute. It is improper to remove a page from the minute book. If it requires rewriting, a line should be drawn through it, leaving the page in its place. The mutilation of any book gives rise to suspicion of bad faith.[146] The minutes should be full and accurate because they are constantly referred to in legal proceedings.

It is advisable to have separate minute books for general and board meetings. Under section 383 (1), the books containing minutes of proceedings of general meetings are required to be kept at the registered office of the company and to be open to the inspection of members for not less than two hours during the period between 9 am and 5 pm on each business day free of charge;[146a] but the directors' minute book, containing as it does a record of the private affairs of the company, should not be accessible to any but the directors, secretary, and auditors, who will be entitled to see it for purposes of the audit. The covers of the directors' minute book are frequently secured by a lock. While carrying out an inspection of the minutes under section 383 (1) a member is entitled to be accompanied by an adviser of his own choice.[147]

11.12 The conduct of general meetings

It is only at general meetings that the shareholders can exercise any control over the affairs of the company. The Companies Act 1985 requires the directors to lay before the company in general meeting profit and loss or income and expenditure accounts, balance sheets and directors' and auditors' reports.[148] Subject to the articles, the chairman of directors, or, if there be no such chairman, the person elected by the meeting, takes the

---

[143] *Knight's Case* (1867) 2 Ch App. 321; *Re Great Northern Salt Co.* (1890) 44 Ch D 472; *Re Pyle Works (No. 2)* [1891] 1 Ch 172; *In re Fireproof Doors* [1916] 2 Ch 142.

[144] *Kerr v John Mottram* [1940] Ch 657, and see *In re Hadleigh Castle Gold Mines* [1900] 2 Ch 419, and *Arnot v United African Lands* [1901] 1 Ch 518 (C.A.).

[145] See 13.12, below.

[146] In *Hearts of Oak Assurance Co. v Flower & Sons* [1936] Ch 76, Bennett J held that loose leaves fastened between two covers in such a way that leaves could be taken out by any person and fresh ones substituted was not a book within the meaning of section 120 of the 1929 Act: but what is now section 722 (1) of the 1985 Act reverses this.

[146a] Members also have the rights to copies and to take notes, conferred by section 383 (3) and the Companies (Inspection and Copying of Registers, Indices and Documents) Regulations 1991 (SI 1991 No. 1998).

[147] *McCusker v McRae* 1966 SC 253. A director has a common-law right to inspect the minutes of directors' meetings, even though the Companies Act 1985 makes no provision for this. The director is entitled to be accompanied by an adviser of his choice: ibid. Although a Scottish decision, this is true of English law. As to the director's right to inspect his company's books of account, see the English cases discussed at 13.13, below.

[148] The Companies Act no longer requires that the auditors' report be read before the general meeting: see section 241 (1), as amended by the Companies Act 1989, section 11.

chair. It is his duty to preserve order, conduct proceedings regularly, and take care that the sense of the meeting is properly ascertained with regard to any question before it.[149] The conduct of a meeting is largely in the hands of the chairman with the assent of the persons properly present.[150] Under the general law of meetings, if the person appointed does not attend, those present may appoint someone else to chair the meeting.[151] The articles may sometimes provide that, where there is no chairman of the board of directors and no directors present, the members may choose a chairman of the general meeting from one of their number.[152] Prima facie every member has a right to be heard and to advocate or oppose any resolution before the meeting;[153] but if a matter has been fairly debated, the chairman, with the sanction of the majority, can stop the discussion, or, in modern phrase, 'the closure may be adopted' after resolutions have been reasonably debated.[154]

11.13 Publication of reports of meetings

As has been seen, minutes must be taken; but there is no obligation upon the company to print and publish a report of the proceedings at general meetings, although such a report is sometimes circulated among the shareholders by large companies. On the ground that members have a common interest in the affairs of the company, speeches at a meeting and circulars sent by directors or shareholders to the members are privileged, and in the absence of malice will not support an action for slander or libel.[155] The Defamation Act 1952, section 7, extends the defence of privilege to reports in the press of the meetings of public companies. These must be fair and accurate reports of the proceedings at general meetings of companies registered or certified under any Act of Parliament or incorporated by Royal Charter not being a private company[156] within the meaning of the Companies Act 1985.[157]

11.14 Notices of resolutions and amendments

Only such motions can be submitted to a meeting as fall within the notice given of business to be transacted;[158] but if all the members of the company are present they can

---

[149] *Per* Chitty J in *National Dwellings Society v Sykes* [1894] 3 Ch 159.

[150] *Carruth v Imperial Chemical Industries* [1937] AC 707 (PC) at p. 767 *per* Lord Maugham: see also the observations of Lord Russell of Killowen in the same case at p. 761. See *John v Rees* [1969] 2 WLR 1294 in respect of the chairman's power to adjourn the meeting in the event of disorder. He must act in good faith and should only exercise this power in the last resort. He should not adjourn the meeting for longer than is necessary.

[151] *Re Salcombe Hotel Development Corporation Ltd* (1989) 5 BCC 807.

[152] See *Re Bradford Investments Ltd* [1991] BCLC 224 for an illustration of this rule and the authority of the chairman's ruling at such a meeting.

[153] *Const. v Harris* (1824) Turn & R. 496 at p. 525. A proxy appointed to attend and vote instead of a member of a private company has the same right as the member to speak at the meeting: section 372 (1).

[154] *Wall v London and Northern Assets Corp.* [1898] 2 Ch 469 (CA); *Carruth v Imperial Chemical Industries* [1937] AC 707 *per* Lord Maugham at p. 767 (HL).

[155] *Lawless v Anglo-Egyptian Co.* (1869) LR 4 QB 262; *Quartz Hill Co. v Beall* (1882) 20 Ch D 501 (CA).

[156] See the definition of a private company at 2.2 above.

[157] The Faulk's Committee on Defamation (Cmnd 5909, 1975) proposed extending the defence of qualified privilege to reports on documents issued by the board of directors (or auditors) to shareholders and to documents circulated to shareholders concerning the appointment, resignation, retirement or dismissal of directors.

[158] See 11.10.2, above.

waive any irregularity.[159] By section 378 (3) of the Companies Act 1985 a resolution may be passed as a special resolution at a meeting of which less than the twenty-one days' notice prescribed by the section has been given, if it is so agreed by a majority in number of the members having the right to attend and vote, being a majority together holding not less than 95 per cent in nominal value of the shares giving that right, or in the case of a company not having a share capital, together representing not less than 95 per cent of the total voting rights at that meeting. It would seem that this proviso would be ineffective in a case where a special resolution was sought to be passed at an annual general meeting, because section 369 (3) requires, as a prerequisite to the meeting being deemed to have been duly called, agreement of all the members entitled to attend and vote. Where all the members agree, and the transaction is honest and intra vires, and entered into for the benefit of the company, they can waive the formality of a meeting.[160] The chairman usually proposes the resolutions necessary for the business brought forward by the board, and if notice has been given of other resolutions calls upon the giver of the notice to bring forward his motion. If a member during the meeting proposes a motion, then in cases where notice is required, and has not been given, or where insufficient notice has been given, the chairman should refuse to put the motion to the meeting. But an amendment of which notice has not been given may be proposed to a motion properly moved, so long as it is within the scope of the notice originally given.[161] If the notice of meeting is accompanied by the directors' report, stating that certain business will be proposed, this is a sufficient notice.[162] It has been held that where the notice was of a resolution to appoint as directors three persons named in the notice, it was competent for the company to add three others by way of amendment.[163] If the chairman improperly refuses to submit an amendment to the meeting, the resolution actually carried will be invalidated.[164]

11.14.1 Special notice
The Act requires special notice of certain resolutions. These are

(1) a resolution at the annual general meeting appointing as auditor a person other than a retiring auditor or providing expressly that a retiring auditor shall not be reappointed (section 388);

(2) a resolution to remove a director under section 303 or to appoint somebody instead of a director so removed at the meeting at which he is removed; and

(3) a resolution appointing or approving the appointment of a director over the age limit of seventy for the purposes of section 293 (5).[165]

Section 379 deals with special notice. It provides that where special notice is required of a resolution, the resolution is not to be effective unless notice of the intention to move it has been given to the company not less than twenty-eight days before the meeting at

---

[159] *Re Express Engineering Works* [1920] 1 Ch 466 (CA); *Re Oxted Motor Company* [1921] 3 KB 32. See further at 11.2, above.

[160] *Parker and Cooper v Reading* [1926] 1 Ch 975.

[161] *Torbock v Lord Westbury* [1902] 2 Ch 871; *Henderson v Bank of Australasia* (1890) 45 Ch D 330 (CA). The latter case also decided that an amendment need not be submitted in writing, but is good if its effect be made reasonably clear to the meeting orally.

[162] *Irvine v Union Bank of Australia* (1877) 2 App. Cas. 366 at p. 376 (PC); *Boschoek Proprietary Co. v Fuke* [1906] 1 Ch 148.

[163] *Betts & Co. v Macnaghten* [1910] 1 Ch 430.

[164] *Henderson v Bank of Australasia* (1890) 45 Ch D 330 (CA).

[165] See 13.2.1, below.

which it is moved. Then the company must give its members notice of any such resolution at the same time and in the same manner as it gives notice of the meeting or, if that is not practicable, must give them notice thereof, either by advertisement in a newspaper having an appropriate circulation or in any other mode allowed by the articles, not less than twenty-one days before the meeting. But if, after notice of the intention to move such a resolution has been given to the company, a meeting is called for a date twenty-eight days or less after the notice has been given, the notice though not given within the time required by the section is to be deemed to have been properly given for the purposes thereof.

Section 379 does not give to any individual shareholder a right (which he does not otherwise possess) to compel the inclusion of a resolution in the agenda for a company meeting.[166] To do so a member must either be given such a right by the articles or enjoy sufficient support to make a requisition under section 376. This section is discussed immediately below.

11.15 Members' resolutions and circulars

Section 376 of the Companies Act 1985 confers certain rights on members in regard to resolutions to be moved at annual general meetings and to the circulation of statements in relation to any general meeting.[167] Section 376 (1) requires the company on written requisition of the specified number of members and (unless the company otherwise resolves) at the expense of the requisitionists:

(1) to give to members of the company entitled to receive notice of the next annual general meeting notice of any resolution which may properly be moved and is intended to be moved at that meeting; and

(2) to circulate to members entitled to have notice of any general meeting sent to them any statement of not more than 1000 words with respect to the matter referred to in any proposed resolutions or the business to be dealt with at that meeting.

These, it will be observed, are quite separate and distinct matters: (a) resolutions to be moved at an annual general meeting and (b) circulars relating to *any* general meeting. With regard to (a), section 376 (6) provides that, notwithstanding anything in the articles, the business which may be dealt with at an annual general meeting is to include any resolution of which notice is given in accordance with the section.[168] There is no restriction on the nature of the resolution (except that it must not seek to achieve anything beyond the powers of the company), but if it seeks to do something which by law or under the articles is required to be done, for example, by special resolution, it would be prudent that the requisition should indicate what type of resolution it is to be.

The specified number of members necessary for an effective requisition is either any number representing not less than one-twentieth of the total voting rights of all the members who have at the date of the requisition a right to vote at the meeting to which the requisition relates, or not less than 100 members holding shares on which there has been paid up an average sum per member of not less then £100.

Notice of any such resolution is to be given, and any such statement is to be circulated,

---

[166] *Pedley v Inland Waterways Association* [1977] 1 All ER 209.

[167] As to the sanctions imposed for default, see Schedule 24.

[168] Notice is to be deemed to have been so given 'notwithstanding the accidental omission, in giving it, of one or more members' (*sic*): section 376 (6).

to members of the company entitled to have notice of the meeting sent to them, by serving a copy of the resolution or statement on each such member in any manner permitted for service of notice of the meeting, and notice of any such resolution shall be given to any other member of the company, by giving notice of the general effect of the resolution in any manner permitted for giving him notice of meetings of the company. The copy must be served, or notice of the effect of the resolution given, in the same manner and, so far as practicable, at the same time as notice of the meeting. Where this is not practicable, it must be served or given as soon as practicable thereafter.[169]

But the company is not bound to give notice of a resolution or to circulate a statement unless:[170]

(1) a copy of the requisition signed by the requisitionists (or two or more copies which between them contain the signatures of all the requisitionists) is deposited at the registered office of the company

   (a) in the case of a requisition requiring notice of a resolution, not less than six weeks before the meeting but if, after a copy of such a requisition has been so deposited an annual general meeting is called for a date six weeks or less after the copy has been deposited, the copy though not deposited within this time is deemed to have been properly deposited; and

   (b) in the case of any other requisition, not less than one week before the meeting; and

(2) there is deposited or tended with the requisition a sum reasonably sufficient to meet the company's expenses in giving effect thereto.

The company is also not bound to circulate any statement if, on the application either of the company or of any other person who claims to be aggrieved, the court is satisfied that the rights conferred by the section are being abused to secure needless publicity for defamatory matter.[171] The court may order the company's costs on an application under this section to be paid in whole or in part by the requisitionists, notwithstanding that they are not parties to the application.

11.16 Extraordinary resolutions

For certain acts of the company an ordinary resolution does not suffice, and either an 'extraordinary resolution' or a 'special resolution' must be passed. The requirements of section 378 of the Companies Act 1985 which govern such resolutions must be carefully followed, for any departure from the procedure there laid down will render the resolution void.

By section 378 (1) a resolution is an extraordinary resolution 'when it has been passed by a majority of not less than three-fourths of such members, as being entitled so to do, vote in person or, where proxies are allowed, by proxy, at a general meeting, of which notice specifying the intention to propose the resolution as an extraordinary resolution has been duly given.'[172] Notice of a meeting is to be deemed to be duly given and the meeting to be duly held when the notice is given, or the meeting is held in the manner

---

[169] Section 376 (3) to (5).

[170] See section 377 (1) and (2).

[171] Section 377 (3).

[172] As to the substantial identity required between the notice and the resolution, see *Re Moorgate Mercantile Holdings Ltd* [1980] 1 WLR 227 discussed at 11.17, below.

provided by the Act or the articles.[173] A notice will therefore be 'duly given' if given and served in accordance with the articles so long as the provisions in the articles are not avoided by section 369 (1).[174] If the articles make no valid provision as to the giving of notices, the length of notice will be that prescribed by section 369 (2), namely fourteen days for companies other than unlimited companies and seven days in the case of unlimited companies.[175] The method of giving it will be that prescribed by the articles, or if they do not prescribe a method, the method prescribed by section 370 (2). This provides that where no provision in that behalf is made in the articles the notice shall be served on every member in the manner required by the Table A for the time being in force, i.e. at present as set out in articles 111, 112, 115 and 116 of Table A. The number of days required by the Act is that number of *clear* days.[176] If the meeting is convened by the court under section 371, the court will give directions as to notice and service.

11.17 Special resolutions

A resolution is a special resolution 'when it has been passed by such a majority as is required for the passing of an extraordinary resolution and at a general meeting of which not less than twenty-one days' notice, specifying the intention to propose the resolution as a special resolution, has been duly given'.[177]

A notice of intention to propose a special resolution for the purpose of section 378 (2) of the Companies Act 1985 is valid only if it identifies the intended resolution by specifying either the text or the entire substance of the resolution it was intended to propose. Thus a special resolution is validly passed in accordance with the subsection only if it is the same resolution as that identified in the preceding notice.

In *Re Moorgate Mercantile Holdings Ltd*[178] Slade J reaffirmed the need for substantial concordance between the notice of a special resolution and the terms of the resolution passed. There is no room for the application of the *de minimis* principle in deciding whether there is complete identity between the substance of the resolution as passed and the substance of the intended resolution as notified. However,

> . . . a resolution as passed can properly be regarded as 'the resolution' identified in the preceding notice even though (i) it departs in some respects from the text of a resolution set out in such notice (for example by correcting those grammatical or clerical errors which can be corrected as a matter of construction, or by reducing the words to more formal language) or (ii) it is reduced into the form of a new text which was not included in the notice, provided only that in either case there is no departure whatever from the substance.[179]

A departure from the rigour of this rule can only be made with the unanimous consent of

---

[173] Section 378 (6).

[174] A resolution may be a good special resolution if the terms of the section are complied with, even though the articles contain further requirements which have not been complied with: *Etheridge v Central Uruguayan Northern Extension Rly* [1913] 1 Ch 425.

[175] As to the shorter period of notice allowed by section 369 (3) and article 38 of Table A, see 11.11, above.

[176] *Re Hector Whaling Co.* [1936] Ch 208. *Secus. Neil McLeod & Sons Ltd, Petitioners* 1967 SC 16.

[177] Section 378 (2).

[178] [1980] 1 WLR 227 at p. 242.

[179] ibid. However, so long as there is identity, no court can, under its inherent jurisdiction, correct insignificant errors in the resolution: *Re Willaire Systems plc* [1987] BCLC 67.

the shareholders concerned.[180] Slade J observed that propositions (expounded above) in respect of notices of special resolutions were intended to include circulars accompanying notices. In those cases where notices are so accompanied, the notices and circulars can and should ordinarily be treated as one document.[181] What is said about special resolutions will also apply to extraordinary resolutions.

At any meeting at which an extraordinary or a special resolution is submitted to be passed, a declaration of the chairman that the resolution is carried is, unless a poll is demanded, conclusive evidence of the fact without proof of the number or proportion of the votes recorded in favour of or against the resolution.[182]

Failure either to set out the resolution or to specify that it is to be an extraordinary or a special resolution will invalidate the resolution if passed,[183] and the result of the requirement as to giving notice of 'the resolution' is that no amendment can be made to any proposed extraordinary or special resolution.

As to the requisite majority on a show of hands, it will be observed that there must be in favour of the resolution not less than three-quarters of such members as, being entitled so to do, vote in person, or, where proxies are allowed, by proxy, and, accordingly, any member present but not voting should be ignored.[184] On a poll the requisite majority is three-quarters of the total number of votes cast.[185]

An irregularity in an ordinary resolution may be cured by a subsequent ratification by the company, but for a resolution to be good as a special resolution it must be carried *modo et forma* as required by the Act: that is to say, on proper notice, and by the requisite majority. Accordingly the company cannot by an ordinary resolution or by conduct make good an invalid special resolution, nor is it an objection to an action by a single shareholder to say that the company ought to be plaintiff on the ground that it can ratify the resolution, for this is not the case.[186]

11.18 Registration of resolutions

Within fifteen days after the passing of a special or extraordinary resolution, section 380 (1) of the Companies Act 1985 requires that a copy[187] must be lodged with the Registrar of Companies.[188] This obligation of forwarding copies of resolutions to the Registrar applies, in addition to special and extraordinary resolutions, to the following:

(1) resolutions or agreements[189] which have been agreed to by all the members of a

---

[180] ibid. See further, 11.2, above.

[181] ibid.

[182] Section 378 (4). As to demanding a poll, see 11.20.1, below.

[183] *MacConnell v E. Prill & Co.* [1916] 2 Ch 57.

[184] Section 378 (1).

[185] Section 378 (5).

[186] *Baillie v Oriental Telephone Co.* [1915] 1 Ch 503 (CA). But the articles may be varied by unanimous agreement of the members: *Cane v Jones* [1980] 1 WLR 1451; see 11.2, above.

[187] Either printed or in a form approved by the Registrar.

[188] A fine may be imposed on the company and every officer of the company in default.

[189] The inclusion of 'agreements' here resulted from an amendment to the Companies Act 1948 made, by the Companies Acts (Pre-Consolidation Amendments) Order 1984, at the same time as consolidation. It brings within the ambit of section 380 such things as an agreement of all members effecting an alteration in the articles (as in *Cane v Jones* [1980] 1 WLR 1451). Note though that a failure to register under section 380 does not affect the validity of any resolution or agreement.

company, but which, if not so agreed to, would not have been effective for their purpose unless passed as special resolutions or extraordinary resolutions;

(2) resolutions or agreements which have been agreed to by all the members of some class of shareholders but which, if not so agreed to, would not have been effective for their purpose unless passed by some particular majority or otherwise in some particular manner, and all resolutions or agreements which effectively bind the members of any class of shareholders though not agreed to by all those members;

(3) a resolution passed by the directors of the company in compliance with a direction under section 31 (2) (change of name on the Secretary of State's direction);

(4) a resolution giving, varying, revoking or renewing an authority to the directors under section 80 (allotment of securities);

(5) a resolution of the directors under section 147 (2) (alteration of the memorandum following a company ceasing to be a public company following an acquisition of its own shares);

(6) a resolution conferring, varying, revoking or renewing authority under section 166 (market purchase of a company's own shares);

(7) resolutions requiring a company to be wound up voluntarily passed under section 84 (1) (*a*) of the Insolvency Act 1986 (i.e. ordinary resolutions which are effective to wind up a company, as where the period fixed for the duration of the company, or the event in which it is to be wound up, is specified in the articles);

(8) a resolution of the directors of an old public company (under section 2 (1) of the Companies Consolidation (Consequential Provisions) Act 1985) that it should be re-registered as a public company.

The Registrar requires the copy to contain particulars of the date and place of passing the resolution, and to be authenticated by the signature of the chairman, a director, or the secretary of the company. A copy of every resolution or agreement, a copy of which is required to be forwarded to the Registrar and which is for the time being in force must, where articles have been registered, be annexed to or embodied in every copy of the articles issued after the passing of the resolution or the making of the agreement. Where articles have not been registered every member of the company is entitled to a printed copy of every such resolution or agreement upon request and payment of 5p or such lesser sum as the company may direct.[190] Any company not complying with these provisions of the Act is liable to a penalty, and every officer in default is alike liable.[191]

11.19 Votes at general meetings

A right to vote is property, and the courts will intervene to protect a member from being deprived of this right.[192] Where shares are mortgaged, but the mortgagor's name remains on the register of members, he alone can vote, but he must do so in accordance with the dictation of those entitled to the beneficial interest in the shares unless[193] it is otherwise agreed. However, an unpaid or partly paid vendor of shares remaining on the register after a contract of sale retains, *vis-à-vis* the purchaser, the right to decide how to

---

[190] Section 380 (2) and (3).

[191] A liquidator is deemed to be an officer for the purpose of liability under section 380. See section 380(7).

[192] *Pender v Lushington* (1877) 6 Ch D 70; *Osborne v Amalgamated Society of Railway Servants* [1911] 1 Ch 540 at p. 567 *per* Buckley LJ (CA).

[193] *Wise v Lansdell* [1921] 1 Ch 420; *Puddephatt v Leith* [1916] 1 Ch 200.

exercise the voting rights.[194] The company, however, is not concerned to inquire as to the beneficial interest and must accept the vote of the registered holder of the shares, and where shares are mortgaged and placed in the names of trustees for the mortgagee, these trustees may vote contrary to the wishes of the mortgagor even though no interest is in arrear and the principal is not payable.[195]

The articles of association usually provide how many votes each shareholder shall have. If the articles are silent and Table A of the Companies Act 1985 does not apply, every member has, in the case of a company originally having a share capital, one vote in respect of each share or each £10 of stock held by him, and in any other case every member has one vote.[196] Special articles of association frequently provide for a different apportionment of votes,[197] but a vote for every share on a poll is usual and is adopted in Table A, article 54. The register of members should be in readiness at the meeting to refer to for the number of shares held by each member, and the consequent number of votes to which he is entitled on a poll. Under Table A, article 50, and most special articles, the chairman has a second or casting vote in the case of an equality of votes, but he has no such right at common law.[198]

Where there is a mode of voting known to the community, that mode should be followed unless a binding rule is found in the articles to the contrary, and likewise any common-law rule as to voting will prevail unless inconsistent with the articles.[199] Thus, votes in the first instance are taken by a show of hands, each shareholder having a single vote for himself, but none for any persons whose proxies he holds.[200] But if a sufficient number of shareholders are dissatisfied with the result of the count of hands, they can demand a poll.

11.20 Polls at general meetings

11.20.1 The right to demand a poll

The right to demand a poll depends on the company's articles, but section 373 of the Companies Act 1985 contains provisions which in effect fix the maximum which can be

---

[194] *Musselwhite v C. H. Musselwhite & Son* [1962] 1 Ch 965. See also 8.5, above.

[195] *Siemens Brothers Dynamo Works v Burns* [1918] 2 Ch 324 (CA).

[196] Section 370 (6).

[197] See 7.6, above, as to the voting rights attached to shares. An article which gives a director three votes for every share held by him only in respect of a resolution to remove him from office is perfectly valid. It is not an infringement of section 303, which provides that 'a company may by ordinary resolution remove a director before the expiration of his period of office notwithstanding anything in its articles or in any agreement between it and him': *Bushell v Faith*, [1970] AC 1099 (HL). For comment on this decision, see 13.7, below. Where the Act confers a power to do a particular thing by special resolution, an article which purports to require a larger majority than that prescribed by the Act for a special resolution is ineffective: see *Ayre v Skelsey's Adamant Cement Company Ltd* (1904) 20 TLR 587 (affirmed on other grounds at (1905) 21 TLR 464). The above rule is not affected by the decision in *Bushell v Faith* (above).

[198] If the chairman has not voted in the first instance he can, upon an equality appearing, give an original vote and so determine the question in issue, but if he has voted, and as a result an equality arises, the common law has provided no way out of the difficulty. *Nell v Longbottom* [1894] 1 QB 767.

[199] *Per* Jessel MR, *Re Horbury Bridge Coal Co.* (1879) 11 Ch D 109 at pp. 113, 115 (CA).

[200] *Ernest v Loma Gold Mines* [1897] 1 Ch 1 (CA); but if a person not a member is allowed to be a proxy, it seems he can vote on a show of hands (see [1897] 1 Ch at p. 8). But most articles in modern form expressly confer a vote on a show of hands only on a member present in person. If the articles require a vote by show of hands on any resolution, this must be taken even though there is no opposition: *Citizens Theatre* 1946 SC 14; *Fraserburgh Commercial Co.* 1946 SC 444.

imposed by the articles. This section invalidates any provision in articles of association in so far as it would have the effect of either

(1) excluding the right to demand a poll at a general meeting on any question other than the election of the chairman of the meeting or the adjournment of the meeting; or
(2) making ineffective a demand (including a demand by a person as proxy) for a poll on any such question which is made
  (a) by not less than five members having the right to vote at the meeting; or
  (b) by a member or members representing not less than one-tenth of the total voting rights of all the members having the right to vote at the meeting; or
  (c) by a member or members holding shares in the company conferring a right to vote at the meeting, being shares on which an aggregate sum has been paid up equal to not less than one-tenth of the total sum paid up on all the shares conferring that right.

Article 46 of Table A follows the requirements of section 373 in defining who may demand a poll. However, it allows a minimum of two persons present in person or by proxy to demand a poll.

The section also provides that the instrument appointing a proxy is to be deemed also to confer authority to demand or join in demanding a poll. It would seem that section 373 (1) (*b*) (ii) and (iii) refer to the potential voting rights irrespective of whether or not those rights are in fact represented at the meeting.

Where the articles gave the right to demand a poll to 'members holding' a specified number of shares, it was held that two trustees holding that number could demand the poll without the support of any other member. But in this case there was also an article that words importing the plural include the singular.[201]

11.20.2 *The conduct of a poll*

The chairman must decide whether a poll is properly demanded, having regard to the articles (which usually require a poll to be demanded before or on the declaration of the result of the show of hands), and the Act. The chairman has generally also to determine how the poll is to be taken (see e.g. article 49 of Table A). At common law there is no requirement of confidentiality for poll votes. Those who organise a poll vote are entitled to know how people voted so that the validity of the votes can be scrutinised.[202]

If there is a question of much importance to be decided, the chairman may well fix a future day, and notice should be given to all the shareholders of the appointed place and time. If the matter is not of great importance, or if there is a representative gathering of shareholders present, the poll may be taken at once.[203] In any case the votes should be taken in writing, and an entry made of how many votes each shareholder is entitled to give and actually does give. Each shareholder should sign his name as a guarantee that there is no personation. A shareholder who has not voted at the meeting may vote on the poll. A member entitled to more than one vote need not, if he votes, use all his votes or cast all the votes he uses in the same way.[204] This provision, which at first sight may be

---

[201] *Siemens Brothers & Co. v Burns* [1918] 2 Ch 324 (CA): see Law of Property Act 1925, section 61.
[202] *Haarhus & Co. GmbH v Law Debenture Trust Corporation plc* [1988] BCLC 640.
[203] *Re Chillington Iron Co.* (1885) 29 Ch D 159.
[204] Section 374.

thought to be of a somewhat eccentric character, is designed principally for the benefit of trust corporations and the like, which may (and often do) hold precisely similar shares under totally different trusts. The chairman should fix the hours during which the poll is to be held. If he does not do so he cannot close the poll as long as votes are coming in;[205] but after waiting a reasonable time, if no more voters present themselves, he may declare the poll closed.[206] If he improperly excludes a voter it will invalidate the poll. The chairman must declare the result of the poll, but it is most desirable that there should be scrutineers present on each side at the counting. If there are several resolutions, the poll must be taken on each separately, though all may be included in one sheet of paper, to be marked by the voters.[207] If the vote be taken on a number of resolutions together, they cannot be validly passed.[208]

Where a poll takes place at a later date than the meeting, the resolution will not be deemed to have been passed until the result of the poll is declared, and the meeting will be regarded as continuing until then. Thus in *Holmes v Keyes*,[209] where the articles required the directors to acquire qualification shares within two months of election, their election dated from the declaration of the poll. It is a question of construction as to whether, under the relevant articles, a poll can be demanded before there has been a vote on a show of hands. In *Holmes v Keyes*[210] the articles stated (as does Table A, article 47) 'a resolution put to the vote of the meeting shall be decided on a show of hands unless a poll is (before or on the declaration of the show of hands) demanded' etc. The Court of Appeal held that under such an article a poll could be demanded without going through a vote by show of hands.

Under the common form of articles or under Table A a poll cannot be taken by sending voting papers to the members to be returned by post. They or their proxies must attend and give the votes personally.[211]

Unless a poll is demanded by the proper number of persons, the chairman's declaration of the result of the voting on a special or extraordinary resolution will be conclusive.[212]

Table A, article 47 extends this effect of the chairman's declaration, if accompanied by an entry in the minute book, to other resolutions. This will prevent the question being reopened in legal proceedings, even if evidence is tendered that the declaration by the chairman was wrong,[213] unless an error appears n the face of the declaration, for example where it states the number of votes given and they are insufficient,[214] or error is plain on the face of the proceedings,[215] or bad faith or fraud in writing up the minutes is proved.[216]

The right of bearers of share warrants to vote depends on the regulations of the

[205] *R v St Pancras* (1839) 11 A & E 15.
[206] *R v Lambeth* (1838) 8 A & E 356.
[207] *In re R. E. Jones Ltd* (1933) 50 TLR 31.
[208] *Patent Wood Keg Syndicate v Pearse* [1906] WN 164.
[209] [1959] Ch 199 (CA).
[210] ibid. See also *Carruth v ICI* [1937] AC 707 (HL).
[211] *McMillan v Le Roi Mining Co.* [1906] 1 Ch 331.
[212] Section 378 (4).
[213] *Arnot v United African Lands* [1901] 1 Ch 518 (CA); *Re Hadleigh Castle Gold Mines* [1900] 2 Ch 419, not agreeing with Kekewich J in *Young v South African Development Syndicate* [1896] 2 Ch 268.
[214] *Re Caratal (New) Mines* [1902] 2 Ch 498.
[215] *Clark & Co.* 1911 SC 243.
[216] *Kerr v John Mottram* [1940] Ch 657.

company.[217] When the articles give this privilege they usually contain special terms under which the power of voting is to be exercised, for example on depositing the warrants with the company.

11.21 Proxies at general meetings

When a company is governed by the regulations of Table A 'on a poll votes may be given either personally or by proxy'[218] (Table A, article 59), and special articles of association generally have a similar provision. In the absence of this provision there was at one time no legal right of a member to have his vote by proxy accepted.[219] Now, however, the Companies Act confers upon any member of a company having a share capital who is entitled to attend and vote at a meeting of the company or of a class of members of the company the right to appoint a proxy to attend and vote instead of him.[220] The proxy need not be a member. In the case of a private company the proxy has the same right as the member to speak at the meeting.[221] These provisions do not apply to a company not having a share capital unless the articles otherwise provide. In the absence of a provision in the articles, a member of a private company is not entitled to appoint more than one proxy to attend on the same occasion and a proxy is not entitled to vote except on a poll.

Some explanation is required of the reference to appointing more than one proxy to attend on the same occasion. It has been suggested that a form of proxy appointing X, or failing him, Y, appoints more than one proxy to attend on the same occasion, but it is arguable that an alternative appointment such as that is not what the section is referring to. One inference to be drawn is that a member of a company not being a private company is entitled to appoint more than one proxy as of right.

Notices convening the meetings have to indicate these statutory rights in respect of proxies.[222] Table A, article 62 requires the instrument of proxy and the power of attorney or other authority, if any, under which it is signed, or a notarially certified copy, to be deposited at the registered office not less than forty-eight hours before the meeting or adjourned meeting at which it is to be used. But special articles sometimes reduce the time to twenty-four hours. The Act prevents the time being more than forty-eight hours.[223]

It has been held that a 'resumed meeting' is not an adjourned meeting for the purpose of an article such as article 62 of Table A. In *Jackson v Hamlyn*[224] a motion to adjourn was lost, but shortly afterwards the hall where the meeting was being held had to be vacated. It was held that new proxies could not be lodged before the resumption of the meeting,

---

[217] Section 355 (5): 'The bearer of a share warrant may, if the articles of the company so provide, be deemed to be a member of the company ... either to the full extent or for any purposes defined in the articles.' Thus, if the articles provide that bearers of warrants shall be members, and do not exclude the right to vote, they will have votes; but if the articles state that they shall have the rights of members in respect of defined objects, and do not include the right to vote, they will have no votes.

[218] The appointment of a proxy is to be distinguished from a corporation which is a member of another company appointing a corporate representative under section 375. See 11.7, above.

[219] *Harben v Phillips* (1883) 23 Ch D 14 (CA). No such right exists at common law (*per* Bowen LJ at p. 35).

[220] Section 372 (1).

[221] ibid.

[222] Section 372 (3).

[223] Section 372 (5).

[224] [1953] Ch 577.

because a resumed meeting after such an unavoidable interruption was not an adjourned meeting.[225]

A proxy may in the first instance be given with a blank left for the name of the person entitled to vote if there is an authority to some person to fill in the blank,[226] and if stamped at the time of execution it is no objection that the blanks are subsequently filled up.[227] Where a member had notice that a requisition had been lodged to summon a meeting, and gave authority to another member to fill up a proxy for him, but the requisition was withdrawn and another lodged, the authority was held to extend to the meeting called on the later requisition.[228] The proxy need not be actually named if he is sufficiently described to be identified.[229] Sometimes the form of proxy authorises 'the chairman of the meeting' to vote for the absent shareholder; but this is very inadvisable.

It is the duty of the secretary to examine the instruments of proxy that may be sent in, and to report any irregularity to the directors.

Where articles required that proxies should be lodged two days before the day for holding the meeting, and the meeting was adjourned, proxies lodged after the original day and before the adjourned meeting were invalid.[230] It would be different if the article said 'not less than forty-eight hours before the time for holding the meeting or adjourned meeting,' as is now usually the case (see e.g. Table A, article 62).

As a poll is a continuance of the meeting, which is not at an end until the poll is taken, a proxy vote at the meeting includes authority to vote on the poll.[231] But if the articles require the proxies to be lodged so many hours 'before the meeting or adjourned meeting', it is not sufficient that they should be lodged this length of time before the taking of the poll, for the occasion of taking the poll is not an adjournment of the meeting.[232] The taking of a poll is not a meeting of the company in the strict sense, but a mere continuation of the meeting at which the poll was directed to be taken. So that if the articles provide that a proxy is to be valid notwithstanding the death of the principal or revocation of the proxy or transfer of the share, unless intimation of the death, revocation, or transfer is received at the office before the meeting, a revocation of the proxy between the date of the meeting and the taking of the poll is inoperative. It is given 'during' and not 'before' the meeting.[233] It seems also that, where a meeting is adjourned, the adjourned meeting is not a separate meeting, but a continuation of the original one.[234] It follows that, under articles to the above effect, a revocation between the dates of the original and adjourned meetings is equally inoperative. But a shareholder who has given a proxy can, unless the articles otherwise expressly provide, attend the meeting and

---

[225] As to stamp duty in respect of proxies, see *Gore-Browne on Companies* (Jordans, 44th edn, loose-leaf), 21.20.

[226] *Re Lancaster* (1877) 5 Ch D 911 (CA). The authority may be oral only.

[227] *Sadgrove v Bryden* [1907] 1 Ch 318.

[228] *Bombay Burmah Trading Co. v Shroff* [1905] AC 213 (PC).

[229] ibid.

[230] *McLaren v Thomson* [1917] 2 Ch 261.

[231] Section 372 (1).

[232] *Shaw v Tati Concessions* [1913] 1 Ch 292.

[233] *Spiller v Mayo (Rhodesia) Co.* [1926] WN 78.

[234] So held by Luxmoore J in *Cousins v International Brick Co.* [1931] 2 Ch 90. His view was not dissented from in the Court of Appeal, although the Master of the Rolls (at p. 99) indicated the possibility that an adjourned meeting might be treated as a separate meeting. Inasmuch as the articles in common use (see e.g. article 45 in Table A) provide that no business may be transacted at an adjourned meeting other than the business left unfinished at the meeting from which the adjournment took place, the circumstances under which an adjourned meeting can be treated as a separate meeting must be very special.

vote personally. He has an option to vote either personally or by proxy, which he can exercise at any time up to the moment when the vote must be given. By thus attending and voting he supersedes the proxy, and it does not matter whether he has revoked it or not.[235] Where the revocation is out of time and the shareholder who has given the proxy does not attend the meeting, the person to whom the proxy has been given may commit a breach of duty if he uses the vote after notice of the withdrawal of his authority.[236]

'The right of a shareholder to vote by proxy depends on the contract between himself and his co-shareholders, . . . and all the requisitions of the contract as to the exercise of the right must be followed.'[237] Accordingly, proxies which are not in accordance with the regulations of the company must be rejected as invalid: for example if the articles of association require an instrument of proxy to be witnessed, it is invalid if not so witnessed.[238] It is for the chairman of the meeting to receive or reject proxies, and his decision is binding, unless it is proved to the court to be wrong.[239] A proxy holder may assume the position of temporary chairman to supervise the election of a proper chairman. This applies where the articles provide that, where there is no chairman of the board of directors and no directors present, the members should choose a chairman of a general meeting from one of their own number.[240]

Unless the articles of association or other document governing the meeting so require, it is not essential that the proxies should be produced at the meeting, and if duly lodged at the place required by the regulations the result of the proxies may be communicated by telegram or letter.[241]

11.21.1 Solicitation of proxies

The directors may employ the company's funds in printing or sending out to shareholders proxy forms filled up with the names of the directors or their nominees as the proxies, and in stamping the forms (when required) or the envelopes in which to return them. Indeed it is their duty thus to advocate the policy which they believe to be in the interests of the company.[242] But if at the company's expense they invite appointments of proxies they must send the invitations to all members entitled to be sent notice of the meeting and to vote thereat by proxy.[243]

Two alternative forms of proxy are contained in Table A, articles 60 and 61, the latter

---

[235] *Cousins v International Brick Co.* (above).

[236] *Cousins v International Brick Co.* (above) at p. 104, *per* Romer LJ.

[237] *Per* Cotton LJ, *Harben v Phillips* (1883) 23 Ch D 14 at p. 32. While the first phrase of this quotation no longer represents the law, having regard to section 372 it is submitted that, subject to the provisions of the Act, the second phrase remains apposite.

[238] *Harben v Phillips* (1883) 23 Ch D 14 (CA).

[239] *Re Indian Zoedone Co.* (1884) 26 Ch D 70. But the chairman is not entitled to reject properly executed proxy forms because he believes them to have been obtained by misrepresentation: *Holmes v Jackson, The Times*, 3 April 1957. Nor can the chairman reject proxies because of some minor misstatement in them: *Oliver v Dalgleish* [1963] 1 WLR 1274.

[240] *Re Bradford Investments Ltd* [1991] BCLC 224 at pp. 229–30. This is so even if the temporary chairman then has to rule on the admissibility of the votes of all the shareholders present.

[241] *Re English, Scottish and Australian Chartered Bank* [1893] 3 Ch 385 (CA).

[242] *Peel v London and North-Western Rly* [1907] 2 Ch 5 (CA). *Campbell v Australian Mutual Society* (1908) 77 LJPC 117. *Wilson v L.M.S. Rly Co.* [1940] Ch 393 (CA), where it was held to be in order for directors to send stamped proxies at the expense of the company to the larger shareholders only, is now overruled on this point by section 372 (6).

[243] Section 372 (6).

being what is known as a 'two-way' proxy, to enable members to instruct their proxies whether to vote for or against a resolution.

It has been held that if one proxy represents a number of members, some of whom have given proxy forms for and some against a particular resolution, and he votes for the resolution without indicating how many votes he is casting, his vote is valid to the extent of the shares in respect of which he has been given affirmative proxy forms.[244] It would seem that a proxy is not, in the absence of a contractual obligation or a special fiduciary relationship, obliged to use the proxy he has been given. It should be noted that those who solicit proxies (whether it is the board of directors or others) are *not* obliged by law to use 'two-way' proxy forms (which enable members to vote for or against a resolution). It became common practice for the board of directors to use proxy forms in their own favour. However, The Stock Exchange requires that the directors must undertake to send out 'two-way' proxy forms with notices calling meetings of shareholders or debenture holders.[245]

11.22 Quorum at general meetings

No business can be done at a meeting unless a quorum is present.[246] By section 370 (4) of the Companies Act 1985, two members personally present are a quorum, unless the articles otherwise provide.[247] Since the Companies (Single Member Private Limited Companies) Regulations 1992[248] came into force (on 15 July 1992), in the case of private companies limited by shares or by guarantee having only one member, one member present in person or by proxy is a quorum. This is so 'notwithstanding any provision to the contrary in the articles'.

Apart from requirements as to quorum under the articles, it is well established that there must be at least two members present who remain throughout the meeting.[249] However, under Table A to the 1948 Act (article 53), it is sufficient if a quorum exists at the beginning of the meeting.[250] The 1985 Table A, article 41, requires a continuing quorum.[251]

Unless the articles provide otherwise, 'presence' at a meeting for the purpose of a quorum means presence in person and not by proxy.[252] However, it has also been held that a member present in two capacities (e.g. as an individual member and as a trustee) counts as two members personally present.[253]

Where a company is represented under section 375, its representative must be counted in estimating the quorum.[254] An executor or administrator is not a member until he has

---

[244] *Oliver v Dalgleish* [1963] 1 WLR 1274.

[245] *Admission of Securities to Listing*, section 9, para. 12.1.

[246] *Howbeach Coal Co. v Teague* (1860) 5 H & N 151; *Re Romford Canal Co.* (1883) 24 Ch D 85.

[247] Table A, article 40, is to the same effect.

[248] Section 370A, inserted into the Companies Act 1985 by the Companies (Single Member Private Limited Companies) Regulations 1992 (SI 1992 No. 1699), Schedule, para. 5.

[249] *Sharp v Dawes* (1876) 2 QBD 76 (CA); *Re Sanitary Carbon Co.* [1877] WN 223; *Prain and Sons* [1947] SC 325; *Re London Flats* [1969] 1 WLR 711.

[250] *Re Hartley Baird Ltd* [1955] Ch 143.

[251] This could be awkward for small private companies, which would be well advised not to adopt this aspect of the 1985 Table A.

[252] *M. Harris Ltd* 1956 SC 207.

[253] *Neil M'Leod & Sons Ltd, Petitioners* 1967 SC 16. This was decided in respect of what is now section 370 (4), which makes provision for quorum in the absence of provision by the articles.

[254] *Re Kelantan Coco Nut Estates* [1920] WN 274.

taken the shares of the deceased into his own name;[255] he cannot therefore be counted in estimating a quorum, unless the articles expressly allow it.[256]

[255] *Re Bowling & Welby's Contract* [1895] 1 Ch 663 at p. 670 (CA).

[256] The court (by using its powers to order a meeting under section 371) will prevent a minority abusing the quorum requirement to frustrate the desire of a majority shareholder to hold a meeting: *In re H. R. Paul & Son Ltd, The Times,* 17 November 1973. See also *Re Opera Photographic Ltd* [1989] BCLC 763.

12 Accounts and Reports

PART 1: COMPANY ACCOUNTS

12.1 Introduction

Limited companies have for many years been required to produce annual accounts for circulation to members.[1] The basic purpose of such accounts is to provide an account of the stewardship of the directors to the shareholders and creditors, rather than to provide information to the investing public generally. It was at one time acceptable practice deliberately to understate the value of a company's assets. Investors required assurance that their investment was safe and creditors that the company could pay its debts. Now, however, greater accuracy is expected in accounts, and the deliberate understatement of assets or overstatement of liabilities is considered to be incompatible with the fundamental requirement of the Companies Act that accounts should give a true and fair view.[2]

Accounting standards are governed by an independent Accounting Standards Board[3] with the assistance of an Urgent Issues Task Force,[4] which endeavours to reach a consensus where unsatisfactory or conflicting interpretations have developed in respect of accounting treatment. The Accounting Standards Board issues Statements of Standard Accounting Practice (SSAP) and Financial Reporting Standards, the latter being based on the Statement of Principles for Financial Reporting, which provides a framework for the consistent and logical formulation of accounting standards. SSAPs do not have direct legal effect but they may have indirect effect on the interpretations that the courts would give to true and fair concepts.[5]

The adoption of the European Community's Fourth Company Law Directive in July 1978 foreshadowed new legislation in the United Kingdom governing the format and content of limited companies' accounts. The provisions of this directive, which were initially implemented by the Companies Act 1981 and were then consolidated in the Companies Act 1985, represented a major departure from previous United Kingdom practice in that, for the first time, the basic rules for the presentation and accounting measurement of income, expenditure, assets and liabilities were laid down by law. Before that, United Kingdom company law had been more concerned with the disclosure of accounting information than with precise methods of presentation or with measurement. The Companies Act 1989 extended the influence of the EC legislation by implementing the European Community's Seventh Company Law Directive, which includes detailed rules for preparing consolidated financial statements. This largely reflected existing accounting standards, but also changed the emphasis in defining a subsidiary undertak-

---

[1] Companies were first compelled to publish a balance sheet by the Companies Act of 1908. The Act of 1929 required them additionally to circulate to their members a copy of the profit and loss account.

[2] See 12.4, below.

[3] This replaced the Accounting Standards Committee in August 1990. For a brief history of the developments in this context, see *Gore-Browne on Companies* (Jordans, 44th edn, loose-leaf), 23.1.

[4] Created in March 1991.

[5] See *Gore-Browne on Companies*, 23.1.

ing from legal ownership to effective control. The 1989 Act[6] also implemented the Eighth Company Law Directive on the qualification and supervision of auditors. All references in this chapter to the Companies Act 1985 are, where appropriate, references to that Act as amended by the 1989 Act.

12.2 The directors' obligation to keep accounting records

12.2.1 *The definition of accounting records*

The directors of a company are required to ensure that accounting records sufficient to show and explain the company's transactions are kept. The accounting records must be such as to disclose with reasonable accuracy, at any time, the financial position of the company at that time and enable the directors to ensure that any balance sheet or profit and loss account of the company, prepared in accordance with the Companies Act, gives a true and fair view of its state of affairs or of its profit or loss. In particular, the accounting records must contain entries from day to day of all sums of money received and expended by the company and the matters in respect of which the receipt and expenditure takes place, a record of the assets and liabilities of the company and (where the company's business involves dealing in goods) information relating to stock and to purchases and sales. This information comprises statements of stock held by the company at the end of each financial year, all statements of stocktaking from which these statements have been or are to be prepared and (except in the case of goods sold by way of ordinary retail trade) statements of all goods sold and purchased, showing the goods and the buyers and sellers in sufficient detail to enable those goods and those buyers and sellers to be identified.[7]

Accounting records may be kept in non-legible (e.g. computerised) form so long as the recording is capable of being reproduced in a legible form.[8]

12.2.2 *The custody of accounting records*

The accounting records must be kept either at the company's registered office or at such other place as the directors think fit and must be open to inspection by the company's officers at all times. Shareholders have no statutory right to inspect accounting records. If the accounting records are kept outside Great Britain, accounts and returns must be sent to and retained in Great Britain, where they must be open to inspection by the company's officers.

Subject to any direction under the insolvency rules, the accounting records which companies, as a minimum, are required to keep by law must be preserved for at least six years (or, in the case of a private company, three years) from the date on which they are made.[9]

12.2.3 *The preparation of accounts*

The directors of every company are responsible for the regular preparation of accounts for presentation to the shareholders. The period covered by these accounts (the 'financial year') must coincide with the company's accounting reference period or, for the benefit of companies which prefer to make up their accounts for a fifty-two- or fifty-three-week

---

[6] Especially Part II.

[7] Section 221.

[8] For VAT purposes, the Customs and Excise must approve the form of any accounting records kept in non-legible form. See also FRAG 5/92, a statement issued in March 1992 by the Council of the Institute of Chartered Accountants in England and Wales, which gives guidance on the contents of such accounts.

[9] Companies Act 1985, section 222.

period, may end at a date within seven days of the accounting reference date.[10] For this purpose, the accounting reference period means the period between two successive accounting reference dates and the accounting deference date means the date registered as such with the Registrar of Companies. Initially a company may select and register its own accounting reference date but, if it does not avail itself of the opportunity to do so, then its accounting reference date will be 31 March for a company incorporated before 1 April 1990, and the last day of the month in which the anniversary of its incorporation falls for a company incorporated after that date.[11]

A company may alter its accounting reference date (and thereby its accounting reference period) by giving notice to the Registrar of Companies in prescribed form. Notice must normally be given before the end of the accounting reference period affected, but retrospective notice may be given if the company is the holding company or a subsidiary of another company and the new accounting reference date coincides with the accounting reference date of that other company – provided that the period for laying and delivering accounts[12] has not expired. If the change in accounting reference date will have the effect of increasing the length of an accounting reference period, the period so increased may not exceed eighteen months. An application to increase the length of an accounting reference period must also meet one of the further conditions that the period is being extended for the first time, or that it was last extended more than five years previously, or that the change is being made to make the date coincide with the accounting reference date of a holding company or a subsidiary, or that the Department of Trade and Industry has given its consent.[13]

The accounts required consist of a balance sheet, a profit and loss account and notes, all complying with the requirements of the Companies Act 1985, Schedule 4.[14]

As from 21 July 1993 limited companies which form partnerships with other companies are responsible for preparing accounts for the partnership and for causing them to be audited.[15]

12.2.4 *Laying and delivering accounts*
It is the duty of the directors to lay before the company in general meeting a copy of every document required to be comprised in the accounts for each financial year[16] and to deliver a copy of them to the Registrar of Companies[17] within a specified period after the accounting reference date. The documents required to be comprised in the accounts are

---

[10] Companies Act 1985, section 223 (3).

[11] Companies Act 1985, section 224 (3) The Companies (Forms) Regulations 1985 Form G224 prescribes the form to be used by companies when giving notice to the Registrar of their accounting reference date.

[12] Companies Act 1985, section 225 (3).

[13] Companies Act 1985, section 225 (7). As to the form of notice of a new accounting reference date given during the course of an accounting reference period, see Form G225 (1) as specified in the Companies (Forms) Regulations 1985 as amended. For notice given after the end of an accounting reference period, see Form G225 (2).

[14] Companies Act 1985, section 226. Besides this statutory requirement, it is customary for accounts to include a statement of source and application of funds, in accordance with SSAP No, 10 – Statements of source and application of funds – applicable only to enterprises with a turnover of gross income of not less than £25,000 per annum. See 12.4, below.

[15] The Partnerships and Unlimited Companies (Accounts) Regulations 1993 (SI 1993 No. 1820).

[16] Companies Act 1985, section 241 (1).

[17] Companies Act 1985, section 242 (1).

those specified in 12.2.6, below, and, where appropriate, group accounts.[18] A private company may elect to dispense with the laying of accounts before the company in general meeting,[19] but must send copies of the accounts to members and others entitled to receive them whilst an election is in force. A shareholder has the right to require the laying of accounts.[20]

Although the accounts laid before the shareholders must comply with the requirements of the Companies Act 1985, Schedule 4, small and medium-sized companies (see 12.17.1, below) are permitted to deliver to the Registrar (or otherwise publish) abbreviated accounts. The accounts that a company is permitted to deliver to the Registrar (whether they are in the normal format specified by the Companies Act, or whether they are in one of the abbreviated formats appropriate to small or medium-sized companies) are referred to in the Act (together with the report of the directors) as the 'statutory accounts'.[21]

Where any of the documents comprising the accounts are in a foreign language, there must be annexed to the copy delivered to the Registrar a translation into English which is certified to be a correct translation.[22] Since 16 November 1992 the amount set out in the annual accounts of a company may also be shown in the same accounts translated into ECUs. Alternatively the directors of a company may deliver to the Registrar an additional copy of the company's annual accounts in which the amounts have been translated into ECUs.[23]

The period allowed for laying and delivering accounts is, in the case of private companies, ten months and, in the case of other companies, seven months after the end of the relevant accounting period. A company which carries on business or has interests abroad and gives notice in prescribed form[24] to the Registrar of Companies within the periods mentioned above may obtain an extension of these periods by three months to thirteen months and ten months respectively. The Secretary of State may further extend them in special circumstances.[25]

If the company fails to deliver its accounts to the Registrar within the period of time allowed, the company and every person who was a director of the company immediately before the end of that period may be liable to a fine. The Registrar also now has the right under section 242A to obtain fixed penalty fines from companies that are late in filing accounts (SI 1991 No. 2945).

Certain unlimited companies are not required to deliver accounts to the Registrar.[26]

12.2.5 Signing of accounts

Every balance sheet of a company and every copy of such a balance sheet which is laid before the company in general meeting or delivered to the Registrar of Companies must be signed on behalf of the board by two of the directors or by one if there is only one

---

[18] Companies Act 1985, section 227 (1).
[19] Companies Act 1985, section 252 (1).
[20] Companies Act 1985, section 253 (2).
[21] Companies Act 1985, section 240.
[22] Companies Act 1985, section 242 (1). See also SI 1990 No. 572.
[23] Companies Act 1985, section 242B, as inserted by SI 1992 No. 2452.
[24] See Form G242 as specified in the Companies (Forms) Regulations 1985.
[25] Companies Act 1985, section 244 (5).
[26] Companies Act 1985, section 254 (1). However, such companies must still file an annual return.

director.[27] There is no legal requirement that the directors should also sign the consolidated balance sheet, although this is usually done. Section 238 (4), however, requires the board to approve the group accounts.

12.2.6 Documents to be annexed or attached to the balance sheet
The profit and loss account and any group accounts must be annexed to the balance sheet, these documents together comprising the accounts. The board must approve the profit and loss account and group accounts before the balance sheet is signed on their behalf. The auditors' report and the directors' report must be attached to a company's full individual (or group) accounts.[28]

12.2.7 Persons entitled to receive copies of the accounts
A copy of every balance sheet which is laid before the company in general meeting, together with the documents required to be annexed thereto and a copy of the auditors' and directors' reports, is to be sent to every member and debenture holder, except as stated in a footnote below,[29] and every other person entitled to receive notices of general meetings of the company not less than twenty-one days before the meeting. If they are sent less than twenty-one days before the meeting, they shall nevertheless be deemed to have been duly sent if it is so agreed by all the members entitled to attend and vote at the meeting. Any member of a company and any debenture holder is entitled to be furnished on demand and free of charge with a copy of the most recent balance sheet of the company including every document required to be annexed thereto and a copy of the auditors' report and directors' report.[30]

12.3 The publication of accounts

The full individual accounts of any company (see 12.2.4, above) may not be published otherwise than with the relevant auditors' report. In addition, where a company is required to produce group accounts, any full individual accounts that the company publishes must be accompanied by full group accounts. Similarly, full group accounts of any company may not be published otherwise than with either the company's full individual accounts for the period or the relevant auditors' report: section 254 of the Companies Act 1985.

Accounts that are neither statutory individual accounts nor statutory group accounts are called 'non-statutory accounts' (previously 'abridged'). Where a company chooses to publish non-statutory accounts, they must be accompanied by an explanatory statement

[27] Companies Act 1985, section 233.

[28] As to the penalties for failing to attach the auditors' report to the full individual accounts and the position with regard to the publication of abridged accounts, see 12.3, below.

[29] Except that it need not be sent to: a member or debenture holder who is not entitled to receive notices of general meetings and of whose address the company is unaware; to more than one of the joint holders of any shares or debentures none of whom are entitled to receive such notices; or in the case of joint holders of shares or debentures some of whom are and some of whom are not entitled to receive such notices, to those who are not so entitled. In the case of a company not having a share capital, it need not be sent to a member or debenture holder who is not entitled to receive notices of general meetings.

[30] Companies Act 1985, sections 238 and 239. See 12.18, below, for the penalties for the failure to comply with these provisions. Where the accounts of a company fail to comply with what is now Schedule 9, a shareholder may not sue the directors of a company on the basis that the accounts distributed to the members did not conform with Schedule 9 (previously 8A). *Devlin v Slough Estates Ltd*, [1983] BCLC 497. See 2 Co. Law 261 (1982).

that indicates that the abridged accounts are not the statutory accounts, and states whether the statutory accounts have been delivered to the Registrar of Companies, whether the auditors have made a report under section 235 in respect of the statutory accounts to which the non-statutory accounts relate, and whether that report was qualified. However, that report may not be published with the non-statutory accounts.

If the accounts or directors' report do not comply with the provisions of the Companies Act, the directors may prepare revised accounts or reports.[31]

12.4 The contents of accounts

Every balance sheet of a company must give a true and fair view of the state of affairs of the company as at the end of its financial year, and every profit and loss account a true and fair view of the profit or loss of the company for the financial year. A financial year is the period for which the accounts are made up and need not be a calendar year, or a period of twelve months.[32]

The balance sheet and profit and loss account must comply with the Companies Act 1985 Schedule 4. There are, however, some exceptions to this general rule.[33] The requirement that the accounts must comply with Schedule 4 is, with certain exceptions,[34] without prejudice to the requirement that a true and fair view be shown and to any other requirements of the Companies Act. The Secretary of State may add to or alter the requirements of the Companies Act in respect of balance sheet, profit and loss account and group accounts.[35] Any reference to a balance sheet or profit and loss account includes any notes to the accounts in question which give any information required by the Act.

Most of the detailed requirements of information to be disclosed in a company's accounts are set out in the Companies Act 1985, Schedule 4, which provides a company with a choice of two fixed formats for the balance sheet and four fixed formats for the profit and loss account. These formats specify the information that must be given on the face of the accounts and the information that may be given in a note to the accounts.[36] When a company has adopted a particular format, that format may not generally be changed in subsequent years. Regardless of where in the accounts an item is disclosed, assets and income may not be set off against liabilities and expenditure, or vice versa (immaterial items need not be disclosed).[37] Unless otherwise stated, the corresponding amounts for the preceding financial year for all items required to be disclosed in the balance sheet or profit and loss account should be shown on the face of those accounts. Where an amount for the previous year is not comparable with the amount shown for the current year, the prior year amount must be adjusted.

---

[31] Companies Act 1985, sections 245, 245A and 245B.

[32] As to the method of determining the financial year, see 12.2.3, above.

[33] See *Gore-Browne on Companies* (Jordans, 44th edn, loose-leaf), 23.6.

[34] For holding companies see 12.14.6, below. For exemptions provided by Part III of Schedule 9, see 12.17 below.

[35] Companies Act 1985, section 256 – for purposes of adapting them to the circumstances of the company.

[36] Banking companies must comply with the requirements of Schedule 9 (sections 255 and 255A, as amended by the Companies Act 1989, section 18, and further amended by the Companies Act 1985 (Bank Accounts) Regulations 1991 (SI 1991 No. 2705)). Insurance companies may choose to comply with the requirements of Schedule 9A, as amended by SI 1991 No. 2705. No detail is given in this book of these particular rules.

[37] Companies Act 1985. Schedule 4, paras. (2) and (5).

Schedule 4 contains a number of fundamental accounting principles which must be observed in drawing up the accounts. The company must be presumed to be carrying on business as a going concern (but this presumption is, of course, rebuttable if the facts do not support it). There must be consistency in accounting policies from one year to the next. The amounts included in the accounts must be arrived at on a prudent basis; in particular, only profits realised at the balance sheet date may be included in the profit and loss account[38] and provision must be made for all liabilities and losses relating to the financial year, or to a previous financial year, even if they do not become apparent until a date between the end of the financial year and the date when the directors sign the balance sheet. All income and expenditure relating to the financial year must be taken into account, regardless of when it is received or paid. In arriving at the amounts to be included in the accounts, each individual asset and liability must be considered separately.[39]

Where, in special circumstances, the directors consider that it is appropriate to depart from any of the above principles, they may do so, but particulars of the departure, the reasons for it, and its effect on the accounts must be explained in a note.[40]

It is a requirement of the Act that the accounting policies adopted in determining the company's profit or loss should be stated in the notes to the accounts.[41] These policies may vary from one company to another. It must also be stated whether applicable accounting standards have been complied with and particulars of and reasons for any material departures from them must be given.[42]

12.5 The balance sheet: share capital, reserves and provisions

A company that is required to prepare its accounts in accordance with Schedule 4 of the Companies Act 1985 must use one of two fixed formats for the balance sheet.[43] Every balance sheet must show the capital and reserves of the company, categorised as specified in these standard formats. The amount of the allotted share capital and the amount of the called-up share capital that has been paid up must be shown separately on the face of the balance sheet under the heading 'Called-up share capital' (Schedule 4, Part I, note 12 to the balance sheet formats). In addition a company must show, either on the face of the balance sheet or in the notes, the amount of the company's authorised share capital and where shares of more than one class have been allotted, the number and aggregate nominal value of the shares of each class so allotted (Schedule 4, para. 38(1)). If a company has allotted shares during the financial year, information must be given about the reasons for making the allotment, the class of shares allotted and (for each class) the number allotted, their aggregate nominal value and the consideration received for each class respectively (Schedule 4, para. 39). Where any part of the allotted share capital consists of redeemable shares, there must be shown the earliest and latest dates on which the company has power to redeem such shares, whether they must be redeemed in any

---

[38] The United Kingdom accounting bodies have issued their interpretation of realised profits in guidance statement TR81 (September 1982), which interprets 'principles generally accepted' for a definition of 'principles', for which see *Associated Portland Cement Manufacturers Ltd v Price Commission* [1975] ICR 27.

[39] Schedule 4, paras. 10–14. These principles follow closely those set out in SSAP No. 2 – Disclosure of accounting policies.

[40] Schedule 4, para. 15.

[41] Schedule 4, para. 36. This is also a requirement of SSAP No. 2 – Disclosure of accounting policies.

[42] Schedule 4, para. 36A.

[43] Section 226 (3): see *Gore-Browne on Companies* (Jordans, 44th edn, loose-leaf), 23.7.

event or are redeemable at the option of the company and any premium payable on redemption or the fact that no premium is payable (Schedule 4, para. 38 (2)).

The number, description and amount of any shares in the company for which any person has an option to subscribe are required by para. 40 of Schedule 4 to be shown, as are the periods during which the option is exercisable and the price to be paid for the shares when the option is exercised.

If a company holds any of its own shares among its investments the nominal value of the shares must be shown separately (Schedule 4, Part I, note 4 to the balance sheet formats).[44]

Provisions may not be shown under the heading of capital and reserves and, except for provisions for depreciation or diminution in the value of assets, should be shown under the heading of provisions for liabilities and charges. A provision is any amount written off or retained by way of providing for depreciation, renewals or diminution in value of assets or retained by way of providing for any known liability of which the amount or the date cannot be determined with substantial accuracy (Schedule 4, paras. 88 and 89). Reserves are not defined in Schedule 1, but it is generally accepted that they do not include any amounts which fall within the definition of a provision, or any sum set aside to prevent undue fluctuations in taxation charges.

In respect of each category of reserves and provisions for liabilities and charges, particulars must be given of the opening and closing balances and the source and amount of any increase or decrease during the financial year. Particulars must also be given of any transfer from provisions for liabilities and charges made otherwise than for the purpose for which the provision was established, and of any material provision included under the balance sheet heading of 'other provisions': Schedule 4, para. 46.

The amount of any provisions for taxation, other than deferred taxation, shall be stated separately in the notes to the balance sheet: (Schedule 4, para. 47).[45]

All movements on reserves should be accounted for through the profit and loss account, except for prior year adjustments and unrealised surpluses on valuation of fixed assets, which should be taken directly to reserves, and capital gains and losses of investment trust companies (whether realised or unrealised) which may be, and in practice are, dealt with in the same way. Prior year adjustments are defined for this purpose as material adjustments applicable to prior years arising from changes in accounting policies and from the correction of fundamental errors.

While there is no legal requirement to do so, it is good practice to state in the accounts the respective amounts of distributable and non-distributable reserves. In effect, this practice is encouraged by Financial Reporting Standard No. 2 – Accounting for subsidiary undertakings.[46]

As regards the need to create a revaluation reserve and the use to be made of it, see 12.7.1, below.

12.6 Liabilities

There are various kinds of liabilities that must appear separately in the accounts under the headings 'Creditors and Accruals' and deferred income. For each category of

[44] Further information of a similar nature must be given in the directors' report. See 12.26.1, below.

[45] However, disclosure of any provision for deferred taxation is required by SSAP No 15 (revised) – Deferred taxation.

[46] See 6.21.2, above, regarding what are distributable and non-distributable profits.

creditor, amounts falling due within one year and amounts falling due after more than one year must be stated separately, as also must convertible debenture loans and creditors for taxation and social security (Schedule 4 of the Companies Act 1985, Part I, notes 7, 9 and 13 to the balance sheet formats).[47]

Where a company has issued debentures during the financial year, the following information must be given either on the face of the accounts or in the notes: the reason for making the issue, the classes of debentures issued and, as respects each class of debenture, the amount issued and the consideration received for the issue (Schedule 4, para. 41 (1)).

Particulars of any redeemed debentures which the company has power to reissue must also be given (Schedule 4, para. 41 (2)). When a debenture is given, for example, to a bank to secure an overdraft, the debenture is not deemed to have been redeemed only because the account has ceased to be in debit while the debenture remains so deposited. If any of the company's debentures are held by a nominee or trustee for the company, the nominal amount of the debentures and the amount at which they stand in the company's books must be stated (Schedule 4, para. 41 (3)). The number, description and amount of its debentures held by subsidiaries or their nominees must also be shown (Schedule 5, para. 6).

In respect of each item shown under the heading 'Creditors' there should be stated the aggregate amount of any debts included under that item which are payable or repayable otherwise than by instalments and fall due for payment or repayment more than five years after the balance sheet date or are repayable by instalments any of which fall due after that date.[48] For each such item the payment or repayment terms and rates of interest must be given, except that if the number of loans is such that, in the opinion of the directors, compliance would result in a statement of excessive length, a general indication of such payment or repayment terms and interest rates may be given (Schedule 4, para. 48 (1) to (3)).

In respect of each item shown under the heading 'Creditors' there must be stated the amounts of any liabilities included under that item in respect of which any security has been given and an indication of that security: (Schedule 4, para. 48(4)).[49] Particulars must be given of any charges on the assets of the company to secure the liabilities of another person and the amount secured must be stated. Particulars must also be given of the amount or estimated amount and legal nature of any other material contingent liability not provided for, and of any valuable security that the company may have provided in connection with such a contingent liability (Schedule 4, para. 50 (1) and (2)).

The amount recommended for distribution as a dividend and the amount of any arrears of fixed cumulative dividends must be stated separately for each class, as must the periods to which such arrears relate (Schedule 4, para. 49).

Where practicable, the amount of any contracts for capital expenditure which have not been provided in the accounts and the amount of capital expenditure authorised by the directors but not contracted for should be stated (Schedule 4, para. 50 (3)).

The amount of any pension commitments included in the balance sheet, and any such

---

[47] For these purposes a loan is treated as falling due for repayment on the earliest date on which the lender could require repayment: Schedule 4, para. 85.

[48] For the more detailed analysis of maturity dates of borrowings required under the continuing obligations of companies whose securities are admitted to listing on The Stock Exchange, see *Gore-Browne on Companies* (Jordans, 44th edn, loose-leaf), 23.21.5.

[49] See Chapter 9, above, as to the creation and registration of charges under the Companies Act 1985. All charges required to be entered in a company's own register of charges here apply.

commitments that have not been provided for, must be stated. Where those commitments relate wholly or partly to pensions payable to past directors of the company, separate particulars must be given (Schedule 4, para. 50 (4)). Particulars must also be given of any other material financial commitments not provided for in the accounts (Schedule 4, para. 50 (5)).

12.7 Fixed assets

The fixed formats of balance sheet contained in Schedule 4 of the Companies Act 1985 require assets to be classified as fixed or current (with the exception that, at the company's option, called-up share capital not paid and prepayments and accrued income may be treated as separate categories). A fixed asset is defined as one that is intended for continuing use in the company's activities.[50]

12.7.1 *Types of fixed asset and general rules for their treatment in accounts*

Three main categories of fixed asset are recognised in the standard balance sheet formats in Schedule 4: intangible assets; tangible assets; and investments held for the long term.

Fixed assets with a limited useful economic life must be wholly written off, or written down to their estimated residual value (if any), by systematic charges for depreciation spread over the asset's useful economic life (Schedule 4, para. 18). In addition, if a fixed asset has diminished in value and diminution in value is expected to be permanent, the value of the asset concerned must be written down accordingly. If a fixed asset investment has diminished in value (but the diminution is not expected to be permanent) the value of the asset concerned may (but need not) be similarly written down. Any such provision for diminution in the value of a fixed asset must be disclosed separately or in aggregate, either in the profit and loss account or the notes. If it subsequently transpires that a provision for diminution in value of a fixed asset is no longer required, any surplus provision must be written back and the amount written back must be disclosed either in the profit and loss account or in the notes: (Schedule 4, para. 19). However, investment companies may account for profits and losses arising on the valuations of investments through reserves (Schedule 4, para. 71 (2)). The accounting policies adopted which relate to the depreciation and diminution in value of assets must be disclosed in a note to the accounts (Schedule 4, para. 36).

As an alternative to the historical cost accounting rules discussed above, companies may include certain fixed assets in their accounts on the basis of alternative accounting rules. These alternative accounting rules in general allow certain assets to be included in the accounts on the basis of their market value, or their current cost, instead of on the basis of their purchase price or production cost.

Where any of the alternative accounting rules are adopted, the assets affected and the basis of valuation used for determining the amounts at which those assets are stated in the accounts must be disclosed in a note. There must also be shown (except in the case of stocks), either separately on the face of the balance sheet or the notes, the comparable amounts determined according to the historical cost accounting rules, or the differences between the two amounts (Schedule 4, para. 33).

If fixed assets (other than listed investments) are included in the accounts on the basis of one of the alternative accounting rules, there must be shown the years (to the extent

[50] Section 262 (1).

known) in which the assets were valued, their respective values and, in respect of any valuation taking place during the financial year, the names or qualifications of the persons who undertook the valuation (Schedule 4, para. 43).

Where, as a result of adopting the alternative accounting rules, a profit or loss arises, it must be either credited or debited to a separate reserve called the 'revaluation reserve'. This reserve may be subsequently reduced to the extent that amounts standing to its credit are, in the opinion of the directors, no longer necessary. Transfers from the reserve to the profit and loss account may, however, be made only if either the amount transferred was previously charged to that account, or if the transfer represents a realised profit. The amount of the revaluation reserve must be shown on the face of the balance sheet. The taxation effect of any movements on the reserve must be disclosed in a note unless the company is an investment company (Schedule 4, para. 34).

Regardless of the method used for determining the value of a fixed asset for inclusion in the accounts, there must be shown for each category of fixed assets, either on the face of the balance sheet or in the notes, the cost at valuation of that item at the beginning and the end of the financial year, together with any revaluation adjustment and the amounts of any acquisitions, disposals or transfers that have taken place during the year. There must also be shown the cumulative amount of all provisions for depreciation or diminution in value of each such category of fixed assets, the amount of such provisions made in the financial year, the amount of any adjustments to such provisions arising from the disposal of any fixed assets and the amount of any other adjustments made to such provisions during the year (Schedule 4, para. 42).

12.7.2 *Intangible assets*

The categories of intangible asset that must be disclosed in the accounts are set out in Schedule 4.

Development costs may be included in the balance sheet only in special circumstances and, if they are so included, the notes to the accounts must state the period over which they are being written off and the reason why they were not written off in the year in which the expenditure took place.

Goodwill may be included in a company's balance sheet only if it has been purchased for valuable consideration. Its treatment is also covered by SSAP 22.[51]

As an alternative to the historical cost accounting rules, intangible assets (other than goodwill) may be included in the accounts at their current cost (Schedule 4, para 31 (1)).

The following items may not be treated as assets in a company's balance sheet: preliminary expenses; expenses of and commission on any issue of shares or debentures; and costs of research (Schedule 4, para. 3 (2)).

12.7.3 *Tangible assets*

The categories of tangible fixed asset that must be disclosed in the accounts are set out in Schedule 4.

In contrast to the general rule for accounting for fixed assets, tangible assets whose overall value is not material and whose quantity, value and composition are not subject to material variation, may be included in the accounts at a fixed quantity and value (Schedule 4, para. 25 (1) (*a*) and (2)).

---

[51] Schedule 4, Part I, Note (3) to Balance Sheet format, but SSAP 22 requires it to be written off immediately against reserves or amortised over its economic life against the profit and loss account. See also ASB paper on goodwill, November 1993.

As an alternative to historical cost accounting rules, tangible fixed assets may be included in the accounts at a market value, determined as at the date of their last valuation, or at their current cost (Schedule 4, para. 31 (2)).

Regardless of the accounting rules adopted, there must be shown, in respect of the land and buildings, either on the face of the balance sheet or in the notes, the amounts ascribable to freehold property and leasehold property respectively. This latter amount must be further subdivided between the amounts ascribable to long leases (fifty years' unexpired term or more) and those held on short leases.

Where the market value of the land differs substantially from the value at which it is stated in the balance sheet and the difference is, in the opinion of the directors, of such significance as to require that the attention of members or debenture holders should be drawn to it, it should be shown in the directors' report (Schedule 7, para. 1 (2)).[52]

12.7.4 *Investments (other than in group companies)*

The categories of investments that must be disclosed in the accounts, either as fixed or current assets, are set out in Schedule 4.

The accounts must show how much of the value of the investments is ascribable to listed investments (i.e. investments that have been granted listing on a recognised stock exchange or any stock exchange of repute outside Great Britain (Schedule 4, para. 84).

The aggregate market value of any listed investment must be given where it differs from the amount stated, and, if the market value of any investments is taken as being higher than the Stock Exchange value, both the Stock Exchange value and the market value must be shown (Schedule 4, para. 45).

If, at the balance sheet date, a company holds more than 10 per cent of the allotted shares of a class of equity capital in a company other than a subsidiary, it must show the name of the company in which it holds shares, the country of incorporation or regis- tration,[53] the identity of the class of shares held, the proportion of the shares held in the total of the allotted shares of that class, and similar details of shares of other classes which it holds in the same company (Schedule 5, para. 7). Similar particulars must be given if the company's holding of shares of all classes in another company exceeds 10 per cent of that company's allotted share capital. There is, however, no requirement to refer separately to different classes of shares held in the same company. These particulars need not be given if the company in which shares are held is either incorporated outside the United Kingdom or incorporated in the United Kingdom but carries on business abroad, if, in the opinion of the directors, to give them would be harmful to the business of the shareholding company or the other company, and the Secretary of State agrees that the information need not be disclosed.

If, under the provision described above, information has to be given about a company in which the investing company owns more than 10 per cent of the allotted share capital and if, furthermore, that holding exceeds 20 per cent, further particulars of that other company must be given in a note to the accounts. These further particulars are the aggregate amount of that other company's capital and reserves as at the end of its financial year ending with, or last before, the financial year of the investing company and

---

[52] See 12.26, below.

[53] The country of incorporation must be shown if it is incorporated outside Great Britain. The place of registration must be shown if the company holding shares is registered in England and the other in Scotland (or vice versa).

its profit or loss for that year.[54] These further particulars need not be given, however, where the investment in that other company is accounted for by the equity method of accounting.[55]

A further exemption from disclosure of the information referred to above in respect of holdings in excess of both 10 and 20 per cent is available if the directors are of the opinion that so many companies are involved that particulars of excessive length would have to be given; in that event, the information need be given only in respect of those investments that principally affect the company's assets and profit or loss. However, if any particulars are omitted from the accounts for that reason, that fact must be stated, and the full particulars must be given in the annual return.[56]

12.8 Current assets

A current asset is defined as one that is not intended for use on a continuing basis in the company's activities.[57]

Four main categories of current assets are recognised in the standard balance sheet formats in Schedule 4: stocks; debtors; investments[58] and bank balances and cash in hand.

Loans made under the authority of section 153 (4) (*b*) or (*c*) or section 155 of the Companies Act 1985 are to be disclosed either on the face of the balance sheet or in the notes (Schedule 4, para. 51 (2)). These provisions enable companies in limited circumstances to provide financial assistance for the purpose of purchasing their own shares.[59]

The requirements of the Act as regards disclosure in the accounts of information relating to loans to directors and officers are set out in 12.12–12.13, below.

12.9 The profit and loss account

A company that is required to prepare its accounts in accordance with Schedule 4 of the Companies Act 1985 must use one of four fixed formats for the profit and loss account.[60] Any of the information contained in these formats may be combined where either their individual amounts are not material, or their combination permits a readier appreciation of the company's profit or loss, but where any of these items are combined on the face of the profit and loss account for the latter of these reasons, they must be disclosed separately in a note (Schedule 4, para. 3 (4)).

[54] Schedule 5, paras. 15 and 16.
[55] Schedule 5, para. 17. Companies falling within this definition will normally be associated companies, within the meaning of SSAP No. 1 – Accounting for the results of associated companies – and the investments in such companies will normally be accounted for, therefore, by the equity method of accounting. Under this method of accounting, the investing company's share of profits less losses of associated companies for the financial year is included as a separate item in the profit and loss account; and the investing company's share of cumulative profits less losses of associated companies since acquisition is included as an addition to the cost of such investments in the balance sheet.
[56] Schedule 5, paras. 11 and 12. Section 231 provides that the company and every officer in default should be liable to a fine for failure to give the particulars in the annual return.
[57] Section 262.
[58] See 12.7.4, above.
[59] See 6.18, above.
[60] Section 226.

12.10 Directors' emoluments

The aggregate amounts of directors' emoluments, directors' or past directors' pensions and compensation to directors for loss of office must be shown separately in a note to the accounts.[61] In each case amounts in respect of service as a director must be distinguished from other amounts.

The amounts for emoluments must include emoluments paid to or receivable by a director for his services as a director of the company, for his services while a director of the company or any of its subsidiaries, and for other services in connection with the management of the company or its subsidiaries. For these purposes, if a director is, by virtue of the company's nomination, also a director of another company, the other company is deemed to be a subsidiary. Emoluments include fees and percentages, any expense allowance which is chargeable to United Kingdom income tax, any contribution to a pension scheme paid in respect of him and the estimated money value of any benefit in kind, and any emoluments paid in respect of accepting office as director ('golden hellos').

Pensions payable to a director or former director do not include pensions under a pension scheme if the contributions to the scheme are substantially adequate for the maintenance of the scheme. Pensions payable to another person on the nomination of, or by virtue of his dependence on or connection with, the director, for example to the widow of a former director, must be included.

Compensation for loss of office includes compensation for the loss of the office of director or of any other office connected with the management of the company or of any subsidiary. Compensation for the loss of the office of director must be distinguished from that for the loss of any other office. Any sum for which a director must account by reason of sections 314 and 315[62] need not be included (Schedule 6, para. 10).

The amounts to be shown include sums paid by or receivable from the company, its subsidiaries and any other person. In the case of compensation for loss of office the aggregate amounts received from sources in each of these categories must be shown separately. The relevant amounts are any amounts receivable in respect of the year, whenever paid, and sums that are not receivable in respect of any particular period but are paid in the year. If any sums are omitted from one year's figures because they are sums for which directors must account by virtue of sections 314 and 315 and the liability is subsequently released or is not enforced within two years, or if any expense allowances are not charged to income tax until after the end of the relevant year, these must be shown in the first accounts in which it is practicable to do so, and must be shown separately. The directors may make such an apportionment as they consider necessary.

Schedule 6, para. 4 requires there to be shown in a note to the accounts in respect of all directors, except those whose duties as such are wholly or mainly discharged outside the United Kingdom during the year, the number who receive emoluments in each of several bands of £5,000, the first such band being for those whose emoluments are either nil or an amount not greater than £5,000, the next for those whose emoluments exceed £5,000 but not £10,000 and so on. For the purposes of this and the two following paragraphs, the relevant emoluments are those required to be disclosed as directors' emoluments by the provisions of Schedule 5, para. 22 (which excludes directors' pensions and compensation

---

[61] Companies Act 1985, section 232, and Schedule 6, Part I.
[62] See 14.20, below.

to directors in respect of loss of office), except that contributions paid under any pension scheme are also to be excluded.[63]

Unless his duties as such are wholly or mainly discharged outside the United Kingdom during the financial year, the chairman's emoluments for the year must be shown. If more than one person acts as chairman, the emoluments of each for the period during which he so acts must be shown. The chairman is the person elected by the directors to be chairman of their meetings or who, though not so elected, holds any office which carries substantially similar functions.[64]

If the emoluments of any of the directors, other than those who during the year discharge their duties as such wholly or mainly outside the United Kingdom, exceed the aggregate of those of the chairman, or chairmen, for the year, the emoluments of the highest-paid such director must be disclosed.[65]

Section 232 obliges the directors to give certain information to the company. If any of the information required by Schedule 6, Part I, paras. 1–14 to be disclosed is omitted from the accounts, the auditors must give it in their report. A company which is neither a holding nor a subsidiary company is exempt from the provisions of the section if the total of the directors' emoluments shown in the accounts does not exceed £60,000.[66]

Schedule 6, para. 6 requires that a note to the accounts must show the number of directors who have waived their rights to receive emoluments which would otherwise be included under Schedule 5, para. 22 (see above) and the aggregate amount of such emoluments. An amount waived should be included in the year in respect of which it is receivable or, if it is payable on demand, in the year during which it is waived. The directors have the same duty to give information to the company, the auditors have the same duty to give it in their report if it is not given in the accounts, and the same exemptions are available to certain companies as were outlined in the previous paragraph.

12.11 Staff costs

Staff costs must be disclosed either in the accounts under the separate headings of 'Wages and salaries', 'Social security costs' and 'Other pension costs', or under such separate headings in the notes to the accounts depending on the format of accounts chosen.[67] In addition all companies must show in the notes to their accounts the average number of employees during the financial year and the average number of persons employed in each category of employees.[68] Self-employed persons should not be included in calculating staff costs.

---

[63] Companies Act 1985, Schedule 6, para. 2.

[64] Schedule 6, paras. 3 and 4.

[65] ibid., Schedule 6 para. 4 (3) and (5).

[66] Schedule 6, para. 2.

[67] Statement of Standard Accounting Practice No. 24 – Accounting for Pension Costs – requires further details to be disclosed.

[68] The Companies Act 1985 does not define what is meant by a 'category of person' but states that the directors may determine these categories by reference to the manner in which the company's activities are organised: Schedule 4, para. 56 (5).

12.12 Transactions with directors

Particulars must be given in the notes to the accounts of any of the following transactions: a loan, quasi-loan or credit transaction or a guarantee, security assignment or arrangement relating thereto, which is of the type described in section 330 of the Companies Act 1985 (see 14.17, below), and which the company has entered into for anyone who was a director of the company or its holding company or who was connected with such a director at any time during the financial year; an agreement by the company to enter into such a transaction or arrangement; and any other transaction or arrangement with the company in which a person who at any time during the financial year was a director of the company or its holding company had a material interest. If a director of the company or its holding company, or a person connected with him, is a party to a transaction or an arrangement, he is presumed to have an interest in it and his interest is presumed to be material unless a majority of the other directors who are preparing the accounts considers it not to be material. Where a director or his connected person is not a party to the agreement with the company, there is no presumption of interest. If the company is itself a holding company, the particulars given must relate to any transaction, arrangement or agreement made by a subsidiary, as well as any such arrangements made by the company itself.[69]

The particulars which must be given are the principal terms of the transaction or arrangement concerned, including, without limitation, the following: a statement that the arrangement was made, or existed, during the financial year; the name of the person with whom it was made and (if applicable) the name of the director with whom that person was connected or of the director who had a material interest; in respect of a loan or an arrangement relating thereto, the liability for principal and interest at the beginning and end of the financial year, the maximum amount of the liability during that period, the amount of any unpaid interest and the amount of any provision made in the accounts for failure or anticipated failure to repay; in respect of any guarantee or security or arrangement relating thereto, the amount for which the company was liable at the beginning and end of the financial year, the maximum amount for which it could become liable, and any amount paid or liability incurred in connection therewith; and (in respect of any other transaction, arrangement or agreement) the value of the transaction or arrangement concerned.[70] Corresponding amounts need to be given in the notes to the accounts. If the particulars required to be given are omitted from the accounts, the auditors must give them in their report, so far as they are reasonably able to do so.[71]

12.13 Transactions with officers (other than directors)

Summarised particulars must be given in the notes to the accounts (except in the accounts of banking companies) of loans, quasi-loans and credit transactions and guarantees, securities and agreements relating thereto, which are of the type described in section 330 of the Companies Act 1985 (see 14.17, below) and which the company has entered into for any persons who were officers of the company (other than directors) at any time

---

[69] Companies Act 1985, sections 232 and 233, and Schedule 6, Parts I and II. Schedule 9, Part IV, para. 2 exempts recognised banks from a part of these provisions, as to which see *Gore-Browne on Companies* (Jordans, 44th edn, loose-leaf), 23.12. Schedule 4, para. 63 (*b*) exempts companies from sections 232 and 234 where they are producing consolidated accounts that are not group accounts.

[70] Schedule 6, Part II.

[71] Section 237 (4).

during the financial year. If the particulars required to be given are omitted from the accounts, the auditors must give them in their report, so far as they are reasonably able to do so.[72]

12.14 Holding and subsidiary companies

12.14.1 Group accounts

A company which, at the end of its financial year, is a parent company is, with certain exceptions, required to produce group accounts, which must be consolidated accounts dealing with the state of affairs and profit or loss of the parent company and its subsidiary undertakings.[73] Group accounts are to be approved by the board of directors before the balance sheet is signed on their behalf and must be included in the documents which the company lays before its members and delivers to the Registrar. The exceptions are that:

(1) Where a parent company is itself a subsidiary undertaking and its immediate parent undertaking is established in the EC it need not produce group accounts if the company is a wholly owned subsidiary of that parent or the parent holds more than 50 per cent of the shares, provided that no notice has been received from minority shareholders requesting group accounts. Certain other conditions must be complied with including the requirements that the company is included in consolidated accounts of an EC group drawn up in accordance with the Seventh Directive and that a copy of these accounts is delivered to the Registrar of Companies. This exemption is not available to companies listed on The Stock Exchange.

(2) Some subsidiary undertakings may be excluded from consolidation by the effect of section 229.[74]

(3) In certain circumstances, the parent companies of small and medium-sized groups may be exempt from preparing group accounts.

12.14.2 The definition of a subsidiary

The Companies Act 1989 changed the definition of a subsidiary, for accounting purposes,[75] to include all undertakings which are controlled by a parent company rather than considering only legal ownership.

A subsidiary undertaking is defined as one where there is a parent undertaking that:

(1) holds a majority of the voting rights; or

(2) is a member and has a right to appoint or remove directors holding a majority of the voting rights at meetings of the board;

(3) has the right to exercise a dominant influence by virtue either of provisions in its memorandum or articles or a control contract; or

(4) is a member and controls a majority of the voting rights; or

---

[72] Section 237 (4).

[73] Section 227, implementing the Seventh EC Directive. The ASB issued Financial Reporting Standard No. 2 – Accounting for subsidiary undertakings – in July 1992, which requires that group accounts should in all circumstances take the form of a single set of consolidated accounts, covering the holding company and all its subsidiaries except those which are required to be excluded, see 12.14.4, below.

[74] See further *Gore-Browne on Companies* (Jordans, 44th edn, loose-leaf) 23.15.1A.

[75] As to the general definition of a parent–subsidiary relationship, see 1.14.1, above.

(5) has a participating interest and actually exercises a dominant influence over the undertaking or is managed on a full basis with it.[76]

An undertaking need not be a company and may be a partnership or unincorporated body. A participating interest is an interest in shares held by an undertaking on a long-term basis to secure a contribution to its activities by the exercise of control or influence arising from that interest. A holding of 20 per cent or more is presumed to be a participating interest unless the contrary is shown.

12.14.3 The financial year of a subsidiary

Unless there are special reasons to the contrary, the financial year of a company should coincide with that of its parent company.[77] If the financial year of a subsidiary does not coincide with that of the parent company, the group accounts must deal with the state of affairs of the subsidiary, as at the end of its latest financial year ending before that of the parent company and the profit or loss of the subsidiary for that year.[78]

12.14.4 Form of group accounts

Group accounts should normally take the form of a consolidated balance sheet and profit and loss account dealing with the accounts of the parent company and those of all the companies to be included in the group accounts. The 1985 Act, Schedule 4A, permits that if, in the directors' opinion, it is better for the purpose of presenting the same or equivalent information in such a way that it may be readily appreciated by the members of the company, the group accounts may be prepared in some other way.

12.14.5 The profit and loss account of a parent company

Certain modifications to the normal disclosure requirements apply to the accounts of parent and subsidiary companies. If a parent company's profit and loss account is framed as a consolidated profit and loss account dealing with the company and all or any of its subsidiaries, it need not comply with the requirements of the Companies Act relating to profit and loss accounts, so far as concerns the company itself, provided that the consolidated profit and loss account complies with the relevant requirements of the Companies Act and shows how much of the consolidated profit or loss for the year is dealt with in the accounts of the company.[79] Where a separate profit and loss account is not prepared, that fact must be disclosed in a note to the group accounts.[80] In practice, a separate profit and loss account in respect of the parent company itself is seldom published. However, the company must prepare a profit and loss account, although it need not contain the supplementary information required by Schedule 4, paras. 52–7. The profit and loss account must be approved by the board of directors but need not be filed with the Registrar of Companies.

---

[76] Companies Act 1985, section 258.

[77] Companies Act 1985, section 223 (5). Contrary to the general rule, companies are permitted to change their accounting reference date after the accounting reference period has ended, if the object is to make the date coincide with that of a holding company or subsidiary. See 12.2.3, above.

[78] See Schedule 4A para. 2 (2) and Schedule 5, paras. 4 and 19.

[79] Section 228 (7).

[80] Companies Act 1985, section 230 (4).

12.14.6 *A parent company's balance sheet*

A parent company is required to show separately, either on the face of its balance sheet or in a note, the aggregate amounts attributable to dealings with, or interests in, any ultimate parent company, subsidiary, or fellow subsidiary.[81]

There must be stated in the company's accounts, or in a note thereto, the name and country of incorporation or registration[82] of every subsidiary and the identity of each class of shares held and the proportion to the total of the issued shares of each class of the shares in the subsidiary held.

12.14.7 *A subsidiary company's balance sheet*

A subsidiary company is required to show separately the aggregate amounts attributable to dealings with, or interests in, any parent company, subsidiary or fellow subsidiary.[83] For these purposes, a company is deemed to be a fellow subsidiary of another if both are subsidiaries of the same company and neither is a subsidiary of the other.[84]

The subsidiary is required to state in its accounts or in a note thereto the name and, if known, the country of incorporation of the company regarded by the directors as being the company's ultimate parent company. This information need not be given by a company which carries on business outside the United Kingdom if the directors are of the opinion, and the Secretary of State agrees, that to give it would be harmful to the parent company, the subsidiary in question or any other of the parent company's subsidiaries.[85]

12.14.8 *Group accounts to give a true and fair view*

Group accounts must give a true and fair view of the state of affairs and profit or loss of the company and the subsidiaries dealt with in the group accounts, so far as concerns the members of the parent company. Group accounts that are required to be prepared in accordance with Schedule 4 of the Companies Act 1985 must, so far as is practicable, give the same information as that required by the balance sheet and profit and loss formats for individual companies.

12.14.9 *Consolidated accounts*

With certain exceptions, consolidated accounts, which are the most usual form of group accounts, are required to combine the information which has to be shown in the individual balance sheets and profit and loss accounts of the parent company and subsidiaries, with such adjustments as the directors deem necessary, and consolidated accounts are to comply, as far as possible, with the requirements of Schedule 4 of the Act, together with the other requirements of the Act as if they were the accounts of a single company.[86]

Consolidated accounts are required to show, in respect of subsidiaries not consolidated, the same information, relating to amounts attributable to dealings with, or interests in, any subsidiary and the number, description and amount of shares and

---

[81] Schedule 4, paras. 59 and 59A.

[82] The country of incorporation must be shown if the subsidiary is incorporated outside Great Britain. The place of registration must be shown if the holding company is registered in England and the subsidiary in Scotland (or vice versa). See Companies Act 1985, Schedule 5, para. 1.

[83] Schedule 4, paras. 59 and 59A.

[84] Schedule 4, para. 80.

[85] Companies Act 1985, section 231, Schedule 5, Part IV.

[86] Schedule 4, paras. 61 and 62.

debentures of the company held by the subsidiary, as a parent company is required to show in respect of its subsidiaries in its own accounts. There must also be shown in a note to the accounts, in respect of subsidiaries not consolidated, the same information, relating to the profits and losses of subsidiaries, qualifications contained in audit reports, and notes to the accounts, as a parent company must give when group accounts are not submitted. The same information as is required when there are no group accounts, in respect of subsidiaries with financial years ending on a different date from that of the parent company, must also be given in respect of subsidiaries not consolidated when group accounts are produced.[87]

12.15 Pre-acquisition profits

Any balance on a company's profit and loss account or other revenue reserves at the time the company becomes a subsidiary of another represents undistributed profits earned or losses incurred before the date of the acquisition of shares in the company by the parent company. Such profits or losses, adjusted as appropriate, are referred to as pre-acquisition profits or losses.[88]

12.16 Summary financial statements of listed public companies

A listed public company may send to its members what is called a 'summary financial statement', in place of a copy of the full accounts and reports.[89] This concession was introduced as a cost-saving measure following a great increase in the number of shareholders to whom otherwise full copies of all the documents would have to be sent, particularly in privatised companies. Shareholders have to make a conscious election to receive the full accounts and reports instead of the summary financial statement, but they must be alerted to this right on the summary financial statement and be issued with a pre-paid card or form on which they can notify the company of their wish to receive the full set of accounts and reports for the current and/or future years.

Summary financial statements must be derived from the full accounts and reports and contain a statement that they are only a summary. They must be approved by the board of directors and signed on their behalf by one director. The detail of what they must contain is prescribed in the Companies (Summary Financial Statements) Regulations 1992.[90]

---

[87] Companies Act 1985, Schedule 5, Part I. Standard No. 2 – Accounting for subsidiary undertakings.

[88] See *Gore-Browne on Companies* (Jordans, 44th edn, loose-leaf), 23.16 as to the treatment of dividends paid by a subsidiary out of pre-acquisition profits and their availability for distribution by the parent company. See 6.15.1–6.15.3, above, as to the relief from section 130 of the 1985 Act provided by sections 131 and 132 of the Act in the case of certain mergers. See also *Gore-Browne on Companies*, 23.16A.

[89] Section 251, as amended by the Companies Act 1985 (Amendment of Sections 250 and 251) Regulations (SI 1992 No. 3003). As well as summarising the accounts, the statement summarises the directors' and auditors' reports, described below.

[90] SI 1992 No. 3075. See further, *Gore-Browne on Companies*, 23.16B. The Department of Trade and Industry is consulting on simplifying the procedures; see the document, *Simpler Procedures for Summary Financial Statements*, March 1995.

12.17 Exemptions

12.17.1 Small and medium-sized companies

The requirements of Schedule 4 of the Companies Act 1985 may be modified in respect of accounts that are delivered to the Registrar of Companies under section 241 of the Act[91] by companies that are defined in section 248 of the Act as either 'small' or 'medium-sized'. This concession is not available, however, to any company that is, or was at any time during the financial year in question, a public company, a banking, insurance or shipping company, or a member of an ineligible group (that is, a group which includes such a company within it or which includes within it a body corporate, other than a company, that has powers to offer its shares and debentures to the public or is a recognised bank or licensed deposit taker, or an insurance company) or is a banking or insurance company.[92] A company qualifies to be treated under the amended rules as a small or medium-sized company if it satisfies, both for the financial year in question and the preceding year, two of the three following criteria. For a small company: the turnover (or its annual equivalent) must not exceed £2.8 million; the balance sheet total must not exceed £1.4 million; the average number of employees during the financial year must not exceed fifty. For a medium-sized company: the turnover (or its annual equivalent) must not exceed £11.2 million; the balance sheet total must not exceed £5.6 million; the average number of employees during the financial year must not exceed 250.[93] In determining whether a company satisfies the qualifying conditions for a preceding financial year for which the accounts are not drawn up in accordance with Schedule 4, amounts corresponding with those set out above should be aggregated.

Once a company's category has been established, it remains in that category until it has failed to meet the criteria, or has met a new set of criteria, for two consecutive years.

Where a company qualifies as either a small or medium-sized company, the directors may deliver modified accounts to the Registrar of Companies.

In the case of small companies, the accounts delivered to the Registrar may group together certain of the items required to be shown separately in the balance sheet in the standard form, and may omit the profit and loss account and the directors' report entirely.

The modifications permitted to the accounts delivered to the Registrar of Companies by a medium-sized company relate mainly to the format of the profit and loss account.

It should be clearly understood that the modifications referred to above relate only to the accounts that small and medium-sized companies may deliver to the Registrar of Companies. The accounts of small and medium-sized companies that are laid before the shareholders in general meeting must be in the normal, unmodified form.

Where the directors propose to deliver modified accounts to the Registrar of Companies in accordance with the provisions referred to above, the auditors must report to the directors whether in their opinion the requirements for exemption are satisfied. All

---

[91] See the Companies (Modified Accounts) Amendment Regulations 1986 (SI 1986 No. 1865). The amendment applies to financial years ending on or after 30 November 1986. It increased the qualification thresholds and contained transitional provisions to facilitate the use of the new thresholds as soon as possible.

[92] Section 246 (4).

[93] The method used for determining the average number of employees must be that prescribed by Schedule 4, para. 56 (2) and (3). The turnover threshold must be proportionately adjusted where a company does not prepare its accounts for a full year: section 247 (4). The amounts for turnover and balance sheet total were increased with effect from 16 November 1992 by SI 1992 No. 2452, regulation 5, and can be retrospectively applied to determine the size of a company for years ended after that date, subject to certain limitations.

modified accounts delivered to the Registrar of Companies must contain the report specified above, together with a copy of the company's balance sheet or modified balance sheet signed in accordance with section 238 (1) and (2) of the Companies Act 1985. Immediately above their signature, the directors must state that they have relied on the exemptions for small or medium-sized companies on the grounds that the company is entitled to the benefit of those exemptions as either a small or medium-sized company, as the case may be. All abbreviated accounts delivered to the Registrar of Companies must be accompanied by a special audit report, which states that, in the opinion of the auditors, the requirements for exemption are satisfied and which reproduces in full the text of the audit report that was given to the shareholders on the normal, unabbreviated accounts.[94]

A parent company that is required to produce group accounts may take advantage of the exemptions available to small or medium-sized companies only if both the company itself meets the appropriate criteria specified above and the group as a whole also meets those criteria. No company preparing group accounts can any longer file abbreviated group accounts.

12.17.2 Dormant companies

A company which meets the size criteria for treatment as a small company but which would otherwise be unable to claim the relevant exemptions because it is a member of an ineligible group may nevertheless have the benefit of the relevant exemptions if it is a dormant company within the meaning of the 1985 Act, if it has been so since its formation or since the beginning of the financial year, and if it has taken advantage of the provisions available to dormant companies under section 250 not to appoint auditors (see 12.20.1, below). For these purposes a company is regarded as dormant when no transaction of any accounting significance takes place during the period under review. Where the directors of a company take advantage of this exemption they must include in the balance sheet a statement that the company was dormant throughout the financial year ending with the date of that balance sheet.[95]

12.18 Penalties in respect of accounting requirements

The Companies Act imposes penalties for failure to comply with certain requirements. If a company fails to keep the required accounting records, every officer who is in default is liable to imprisonment or a fine or both. Likewise a person who dishonestly falsifies accounting information is liable to imprisonment. The penalty for other offences is confined to a default fine.[96]

12.19 Stock Exchange requirements

Companies listed on The Stock Exchange must comply with the rules made by The Stock Exchange in the *Listing Rules*, effective since 1 December 1993.[97] The continuing obligations of companies after admission to listing impose a general requirement to notify

---

[94] Schedule 8, Part I. For details of exemptions for small companies, see *Gore-Browne on Companies* (Jordans, 44th edn, loose-leaf), 23.17A.

[95] Section 250. A transaction is a significant accounting transaction if it would fall to be entered in the company's accounting records under section 221 and does not arise from the taking of shares in the company by a subscriber to the memorandum in accordance with an undertaking therein.

[96] See further, *Gore-Brown on Companies* (Jordans, 44th edn, loose-leaf), 23.20.

[97] See Chapter 5.

The Stock Exchange of any information necessary to enable holders of the company's listed securities and the public to appraise the position of the company and to avoid the establishment of a false market in its listed securities.[98]

The main requirements as to information to be disclosed under the continuing obligations are summarised below.

(1) *Particulars of any company (not being a subsidiary) in which the group has an interest in the equity of 20 per cent.*

The requirement is additional to that required by Schedule 5, Part II of the Companies Act 1985. In addition to particulars of share and loan capital, the principal country of operation must be shown.

(2) *Borrowing and interest.*

Interest capitalised must be stated and bank and other borrowings must be separately analysed over repayment periods.

(3) *The tax status of the company.*

It is necessary to state whether the company is within the close company provisions of the Income and Corporation Taxes Act 1988, or, if an investment trust, any change in its status for taxation purposes.

(4) *Standard accounting practices.*

The directors must state their reasons for any significant departure from standard accounting practice.

(5) *Interests of directors and substantial shareholders in share capital.*

A listed company must give a statement showing the interests of each director appearing in its register of directors' interests[99] and a similar statement concerning the interests of substantial shareholders.[100]

(6) *Waiver of emoluments or dividends.*

Particulars must be given of any arrangement under which a director has waived or agreed to waive any emoluments from a company or any of its subsidiaries, and of any arrangement under which a shareholder has waived or agreed to waive any dividends.

(7) *Interests of directors and substantial shareholders in contracts.*

Particulars must be given of any contract of significance between the company (or any of its subsidiaries) and a controlling shareholder,[101] or such a contract in which a director had a material interest. Where a director had no such interest, a negative statement is required. A contract of significance is, broadly, one worth 1 per cent or more of the company's share capital and reserves. In addition, particulars are required of contracts for the provision of services to the company by a controlling shareholder.

(8) *Purchase by the company of its own shares.*

More details are required than under the Companies Act of these purchases.[102]

---

[98] See further, *Gore-Browne on Companies*, 23.21.

[99] i.e. under section 325; see 13.22.5, below.

[100] i.e. under section 211; see 10.9.5., above.

[101] A controlling shareholder is one who is entitled to exercise or control the exercise of 30 per cent or more of the voting power at general meetings, or who is able to control the appointment of directors who are able to exercise a majority of votes at board meetings.

[102] See *Gore-Browne on Companies*, 23.21.8.

(9) *Non-executive directors.*

The company must identify its independent non-executive directors, and give a short biographical note on each.

(10) *Earnings per share.*

A company which issues summary financial statements[103] must include in them the earnings per share.

PART 2: AUDITORS

12.20 The appointment, qualifications and remuneration of auditors

12.20.1 Appointment

With the exceptions noted below, every company is required to appoint at each general meeting before which accounts are laid an auditor or auditors to hold office from the conclusion of that meeting until the conclusion of the next such general meeting.[104] Reappointment of a retiring auditor is not automatic and a resolution concerning the appointment or reappointment of auditors should therefore be put before each meeting held to consider the accounts.

Special notice[105] is required of a resolution concerning the appointment of the auditors, unless the resolution is for the continuation of the appointment of auditors whose appointment was approved at the previous general meeting held to consider the accounts.[106]

The first auditors of a company may be appointed by the directors at any time before the first general meeting held for consideration of the accounts, to hold office until the conclusion of that meeting. If the directors fail to do so, the company in general meeting may appoint them.[107]

A private company which has elected to dispense with the laying of accounts before the company in general meeting must appoint auditors at a general meeting held at least twenty-eight days before copies of the company's annual accounts are sent to members. It may, however, elect to dispense with the annual appointment of auditors, in which case the auditors are deemed to be reappointed in each succeeding year unless a resolution is passed ending their appointment.[108]

The directors or the company in general meeting may fill any casual vacancy.[109] If no auditors are appointed or reappointed at a general meeting held to consider the accounts, the Secretary of State may appoint a person to fill the vacancy. Within a week of the power becoming exercisable the company must give notice to him of that fact. The company and every officer in default are liable to a fine for failure to give the required notice.[110]

---

[103] See 12.16, above.

[104] Section 384 (1).

[105] See 11.14.1. Section 379 provides that at least twenty-eight days' notice of the intention to move such a resolution must be given to the company and that the company must give at least twenty-one days' notice to its members.

[106] Sections 388 (1) and 391A.

[107] Section 385 (3) (4).

[108] Sections 385A and 386.

[109] Section 388 (1).

[110] Section 387. As to the fines that may be imposed, see Schedule 24.

The first exception mentioned above to the general rule is that a dormant company (see 12.17.2, above) that is not required to prepare group accounts, may by special resolution exclude the obligation to appoint auditors. Such a resolution may be passed, either at any general meeting of the company at which copies of the accounts are laid before the company under section 241 in the normal way, or at any time before the first general meeting of the company, provided that the company has been dormant from the time of its formation. Where the resolution is passed at a general meeting that is not the first such meeting, the company must, in addition, be entitled to the benefit of the accounting exemptions available to small companies, or must be ineligible for those exemptions by reason only of the fact that it is a member of an ineligible group (see 12.17.1, above); it must also have been dormant since the end of that financial year.[111]

The second exception is that a private company exempt from the audit requirement as described in 12.24, below, is also exempt from the obligation to appoint an auditor.[112]

12.20.2 *Removal or resignation*

A company may remove an auditor by ordinary resolution before the expiration of his term of office, notwithstanding any previous agreement to the contrary. The Registrar of Companies must be informed within fourteen days of any such resolution having been passed.[113]

If a company receives special notice of a resolution proposing the removal of an auditor before the expiration of his term of office, or proposing a change of auditor when the present auditor's term of office expires, it must forward a copy of that notice to the retiring auditor, or to the auditor who is to be removed. The auditor may make representations in writing to the company and, if he so requests and the representations are not received too late, the company must, in any notice of the resolution given to members of the company, state that representations have been received and send a copy to every member to whom notice of the meeting is sent.

If an auditor wishes to resign his office, before its term expires, he may do so by depositing a notice in writing to that effect at the company's registered office, containing either a statement that there are no circumstances connected with his resignation which he considers should be brought to the notice of the members or creditors of the company, or a statement of any such circumstances as may exist. The company must, within fourteen days of receipt, send copies of the notice to the Registrar of Companies and, if the notice contains a statement of circumstances connected with the resignation as described above, to the members of the company and to any other persons who are entitled to receive a copy of the company's accounts.[114] If the notice of resignation states that there are circumstances which the auditor considers should be brought to the notice of members or creditors, he may call on the directors to convene an extraordinary general meeting of the company to consider his explanation. He may also require the company to circulate to the members a written statement of the circumstances connected with his resignation (of reasonable length) and to state in the notice of the meeting that such a statement has been issued.[115]

---

[111] Section 250, as amended by the Companies Act 1985 (Amendment of Sections 250 and 251) Regulations 1992 (SI 1992 No. 3003), regulation 2.

[112] Section 388A.

[113] Section 391 (1) (2).

[114] Section 392.

[115] Section 392A.

If the company does not, within fourteen days, circulate an auditor's notice of resignation, or does not, within twenty-one days, convene an extraordinary general meeting which has been requisitioned by the auditor then, unless the company has obtained a court order excusing it from so doing, the company and every officer who is in default will be liable to a fine.[116]

An auditor who has been removed or who has resigned is entitled to attend the general meeting of the company at which his appointment would otherwise have expired and any general meeting at which it is proposed to fill the vacancy caused by the removal or resignation, to receive notices relating to those meetings and to be heard on any business which concerns him as former auditor.[117]

12.20.3 *Qualifications*

The Companies Act 1989 implemented the Eighth EC Company Law Directive on the qualifications and training of auditors. The stated purposes of the Act are 'to secure that only persons who are properly supervised and appropriately qualified are appointed as company auditors, and that audits by persons so appointed are carried out properly and with integrity and with a proper degree of independence'.[118]

To qualify for appointment as a company auditor, a person, either an individual or a firm, must be[119] a member of a recognised supervisory body; and eligible for appointment under the rules of that body.

To be eligible, the auditor must hold an appropriate qualification, which may be:

(1) by virtue of membership immediately before 1 January 1990 of a body recognised for the purposes of section 389 (1) (*a*) of the Companies Act 1985;[120] or
(2) a recognised professional qualification obtained in the United Kingdom from a qualifying body; or
(3) an overseas qualification approved by the Secretary of State, provided that the person also satisfies any additional educational qualifications that the Secretary of State may require.[121]

Certain classes of person are disqualified from appointment as auditors. They are officers or servants of the company, persons who are partners or employees of an officer or servant of the company and bodies corporate. Not may a person be appointed auditor of a company if he is disqualified from appointment as auditor of its parent or subsidiary company. Any person who acts as auditor of a company when he knows he is disqualified, or who fails to vacate his office and to give notice of that fact to the company when to his knowledge he becomes disqualified, is liable to a fine.[122] Section 28 (5) of the Companies Act 1989 now provides that it is a defence for a person to show that he did not know and had no reason to believe that he was, or had become, ineligible for appointment.

---

[116] Sections 392 (3) and 392A (5).
[117] Sections 391 (4) and 392A (8).
[118] Companies Act 1989, section 24.
[119] Companies Act 1989, section 31.
[120] The Institute of Chartered Accountants in England and Wales, The Institute of Chartered Accountants of Scotland, the Chartered Association of Certified Accountants, the Institute of Chartered Accountants in Ireland and the Association of Authorised Public Accountants.
[121] Companies Act 1989, section 33.
[122] Section 28.

12.20.4 *Remuneration*

The remuneration of the auditors of a company is normally fixed by the company in general meeting or in such a way as the company in general meeting may decide.

A company's profit and loss account must show the remuneration of the auditors, including expenses.[123] A consolidated profit and loss account must show the remuneration of the auditors of all the companies included in the consolidated accounts. Disclosure of remuneration including expenses paid to the auditors or their associates in respect of services other than audit must also be made.[124]

12.21 The rights and duties of an auditor

12.21.1 *Right of information*

An auditor[125] has a right of access at all times to the books and accounts and vouchers of the company and a right to require from the officers of the company such information and explanations as he thinks necessary for the performance of his duty.[126]

An officer of a company who makes to an auditor (orally or in writing) a misleading statement which conveys, or purports to convey, any information or explanation which the auditor requires, or is entitled to require in his capacity as auditor, may be liable to imprisonment or to a fine or both.

A company's articles may not limit the auditor's statutory right to information. 'Any regulations which preclude the auditors from availing themselves of all the information to which under the Act they are entitled as material for the report which under the Act they are to make as to the true and correct state of the company's affairs are, I think, inconsistent with the Act.'[127]

The auditor of a parent company also has the right of access to information about the subsidiaries.[128]

---

[123] Schedule 4, para. 53 (7).

[124] Section 390B and the Companies Act 1985 (Disclosure of Renumeration for Non-Audit Work) Regulations 1991 (SI 1991 No. 2128).

[125] In March 1976 the major professional accounting bodies set up an Auditing Practices Committee to develop standards to which all audits should be carried out. In 1980 the Committee published a series of auditing standards and guidelines which, although they do not have legal backing, are intended to be followed by all members of the professional accounting bodies concerned. They apply to the audits of the accounts of all enterprises and not only to the audits of accounts of limited companies. The standards, which simply codify current good practice, consist of an operational standard and two standards relating to the audit report and are effective for the audit of accounts relating to periods starting on or after 1 April 1980. The operational standard requires an auditor adequately to plan, control and record his work; to ascertain the enterprise's system of recording and processing transactions and assess its adequacy as a basis for the preparation of accounts; to obtain relevant and reliable audit evidence sufficient to enable him to draw reasonable conclusions therefrom; to ascertain, evaluate and test the operation of any internal controls on which he wishes to place reliance in his work; and to carry out such a review on the accounts as is sufficient, in conjunction with the conclusions drawn from the other audit evidence obtained, to give him a reasonable basis for his opinion on the accounts. In April 1991 the APC was replaced by a new body called the Auditing Practices Board (APB), which is committed to leading the development of auditing practice in the United Kingdom and the Republic of Ireland so as to: establish the highest standards of auditing; meet the developing needs of users of financial statements; and ensure public confidence in the auditing process. See Statement of Objectives, Scope and Authority, May 1993, and SAS 600 – Auditors' reports on financial statements, May 1993. See *Gore-Browne on Companies* (Jordans, 44th edn, loose-leaf), 23.23.1.

[126] Section 389A.

[127] *Newton v B.S.A.* [1906] 2 Ch 378 at p. 389 *per* Buckley J.

[128] Section 389A.

Boyle & Birds' Company Law

Boyle & Birds' Company Law

12.21.2 Attendance at meetings

The auditors of a company are entitled to attend any general meeting of the company and to receive notice of, and other communications relating to, any general meeting which any member of the company is entitled to receive. They also have a right to be heard at a general meeting on any part of the business of the meeting which concerns them as auditors.[129] A similar right is available where a company is proposing a resolution as a written resolution.[130]

12.21.3 The auditors' report

The auditors of a company are required to make a report to the members on the accounts examined by them and on every balance sheet and profit and loss account and all group accounts, a copy of which is laid before the company in general meeting during their tenure of office. A copy is to be attached to the accounts and sent with them to every shareholder and debenture holder who is entitled to receive a copy of the accounts.[131]

12.21.4 The contents of the auditors' report

Section 235 of the Companies Act 1985 sets out the statutory requirements for the auditors' report.

When preparing a report under section 235 the auditors must consider whether the information given in the directors' report is consistent with the accounts. Where the information so given is inconsistent, that fact must be noted in their report.[132]

In the case of a small company that has availed itself of the new (1992) exemptions from disclosure in Part I of Schedule 8, the report should state whether the accounts have been properly prepared in accordance with the provisions of the Companies Act 1985 applicable to small companies.[133]

The auditors must carry out such work as to enable them to form an opinion as to (a) whether proper books of account have been kept by the company and adequate returns received from branches not visited by them and (b) whether the company's balance sheet and profit and loss account (unless it is framed as a consolidated profit and loss account) are in agreement with the books of account and the returns from branches.

If the requirements imposed by Parts V and VI of Schedule 5 and Parts I to III of Schedule 6 for the disclosure in the accounts of certain information about the emoluments of directors and certain employees and transactions with directors and officers are not observed, the auditors are required to give in their report the information which has been omitted.[134]

Where the audit report is qualified, the auditors must state whether in their opinion the qualification is material for the purpose of determining whether a proposed distribution would contravene section 271.[135]

Auditors who are not satisfied that the accounts comply with the Companies Act or

---

[129] Section 390.
[130] See section 390 and 11.4.3, above.
[131] Section 238 (1).
[132] Section 235 (3).
[133] See 12.17.1, above.
[134] Section 237 (4).
[135] Section 273 (4).

show a true and fair view of the state of affairs or of the profit or loss of a company must refer to those matters explicitly in their report.[136] They may not just hint at them.

In addition to their obligation to report on the accounts, the auditors have a duty to examine the register of directors' loans and similar transactions maintained by a recognised bank in accordance with section 343 before it is made available to the members of the company and to report to the members on that statement, stating whether in their opinion it contains the particulars required; if, in their opinion, it does not, they must include the missing particulars in their report, so far as they are reasonably able to do so.[137]

The form and content of the auditors' report has been changed and expanded with effect for accounting periods ending on or after 30 September 1993 by Statement of Auditing Standards – Auditors' report on financial statements (SAS 600).[138]

12.22 The auditor as an officer of the company

The Companies Acts do not make it clear wither or not an auditor is an officer of the company. Section 385 (2) of the 1985 Act refers to an auditor holding office. The Companies Act 1989, section 27(1), by excluding an auditor from its provisions, implies that, but for the exclusion, he might be considered an officer: 'For this purpose an auditor of the company is not to be regarded as an officer or employee of the company'. Further doubt arises from sections 434 (4) and 310 of the 1985 Act, which indicate that they apply to auditors whether or not they are officers of the company.

The court has held that an auditor is an officer for the purposes of section 212 of the Insolvency Act 1986 (a misfeasance summons in a liquidation).[139] He is also an officer for the purposes of the other sections dealing with offences antecedent to or in the course of winding up and may, therefore, be liable under, for example, section 206 of the 1986 Act for making, or being party to the making of, a false entry in the books or section 207 for fraud.[140]

It seems that an auditor appointed under the provisions of section 384 of the 1985 Act will be considered by the court to be an officer of the company. If, however, he is appointed for a more limited purpose, he may not be so considered.[141]

12.23 Liability for negligence

The auditor's potential civil liability[142] for negligence, which may arise in contract or tort, merits brief examination here.

12.23.1 Liability in contract

An auditor performs his duties under a contractual relationship with his company. If he is negligent in the performance of his contractual duties he may be liable to the company for loss arising from his negligence. If the company is in liquidation, proceedings may be

---

[136] *Newton v B.S.A.* [1906] 2 Ch 378.

[137] Section 343 (6).

[138] See *Gore-Browne on Companies* (Jordans, 44th edn, loose-leaf), 23.24.1.

[139] See e.g. *Re London and General Bank Ltd* [1895] 2 Ch 166, and *Kingston Cotton Mill Co. (No. 1)* [1895] 1 Ch 6. See 13.17.4, below.

[140] *R. v Shacter* [1960] 2 QB 252.

[141] See *Re Western Counties Steam Bakery & Milling Co. Ltd* [1897] 1 Ch 617 and *R. v Shacter*, above.

[142] As to potential criminal liability, see *Gore-Browne on Companies*, 23.27.

brought by way of misfeasance summons under section 212 of the Insolvency Act 1986.[143] The duties of an auditor were discussed extensively in *Re London and General Bank Ltd (No. 2)*,[144] *The Kingston Cotton Mill Co.*[145] case and *Re City Equitable Fire Insurance Co.*[146] Lopes LJ defined an auditor's duties as follows:[147]

> It is the duty of an auditor to bring to bear on the work he has to perform that skill, care and caution which a reasonably competent, careful and cautious auditor would use. What is reasonable skill, care and caution must depend on the circumstances of each case. An auditor is not bound to be a detective,or, as was said, to approach his work with suspicion. He is a watchdog, but not a bloodhound. He is justified in believing tried servants of the company in whom confidence is placed by the company. He is entitled to assume that they are honest, and to rely upon their representations, provided he takes reasonable care. If there is anything calculated to excite suspicion, he should probe it to the bottom, but in the absence of anything of that kind he is only bound to be reasonably cautious and careful.[148]

12.23.2 Liability in tort for negligent misstatement

The possibility of an auditor being held liable in negligence to persons relying on his report and with whom he does not stand in a contractual or fiduciary relationship has been raised by the decision of the House of Lords in *Hedley Byrne and Co. Ltd v Heller and Partners Ltd*.[149] The Court of Appeal in the earlier case of *Candler v Crane Christmas*[150] had held that a firm of accountants was not liable in negligence to someone who had relied on a report negligently prepared by them and which they had known would be acted on by him, and suffered loss as a result, because there was no contractual relationship between the parties. The House of Lords in *Hedley Byrne v Heller*[151] held that a duty of care could arise when there was no contractual relationship.

A landmark decision in the context of the law on negligent statements by professional people which cause economic loss was given by the House of Lords in *Caparo Industries plc v Dickman*.[152] The directors of a public limited company announced results for the financial year end which fell short of the predicted figure, and the share price dropped dramatically. The accounts had been audited by the auditors and approved by the directors before the results were announced. Caparo was an investor which had relied on the

---

[143] See 13.17.4, below.

[144] [1895] 2 Ch 673.

[145] [1896] 2 Ch 279.

[146] [1925] Ch 407.

[147] *Kingston Cotton Mitl Co. (No. 2)* [1896] 2 Ch 279 at pp. 288, 289.

[148] See also *Henry Squire (Cash Chemist) Ltd v Ball, Baker & Co.* [1911] 106 LT 197. Cf. *Fomento (Sterling Area) Ltd v Selsdon Fountain Pen Co.* [1958] 1 WLR 45 at p. 61 *per* Lord Denning. See also *Re Thomas Gerrard & Son Ltd* [1968] Ch 455.

[149] [1964] AC 465 (HL). See also *W. B. Anderson Ltd v Rhodes* [1967] 2 All ER 850. *Mutual Life & Citizens' Assurance Co. Ltd v Evatt* [1971] 1 All ER 150 (PC). There is no ground for excluding liability for negligence in relation to statements made in the course of negotiations which culminate in the making of a contract (though such statements may also create liability under the contract or the Misrepresentation Act 1967: *Esso Petroleum Company v Mardon* [1976] 2 WLR 587 (CA)).

[150] [1951] 2 KB 164 (CA).

[151] See footnote 149, above.

[152] [1990] 2 AC 605. For a review of the earlier case law see *Gore-Browne on Companies* (Jordans, 44th edn, loose-leaf), 23.26.3.

auditor's report on the company accounts and consequently suffered considerable financial loss. The Court of Appeal ruled that there was no sufficiently proximate relationship between an auditor and a potential investor to give rise to a duty of care at common law, but that an auditor had a duty of care to individual shareholders, entitling an individual shareholder to recover in tort where he suffered loss by acting in reliance on negligently prepared accounts. On appeal the House of Lords ruled that the auditors did not owe a duty of care to individual shareholders and agreed with the Court of Appeal that the auditors did not owe a duty of care to potential investors. Foreseeability alone was not sufficient to impose such a duty and the requisite relationship of proximity should also be present to limit what would otherwise be an unlimited duty of care owed by the auditors for the accuracy of their accounts to all who may foreseeably rely on them. The conclusion was that auditors owe no duty of care to members of the public at large who rely on the accounts to buy shares as, if it did, the duty would then extend to all who rely on the accounts such as investors deciding to buy shares, lenders or merchants extending credit. It was necessary to prove that the defendant knew that his statement would be relied upon by the plaintiff in deciding whether or not to enter upon a particular transaction. Thus even if reliance was probable, it was also necessary to have regard to the transaction for the purpose of which the statement was made. In the view of their Lordships the purpose of the statutory requirement for an annual audit was to enable shareholders to review the past management of the company and to exercise their rights to influence future management. They saw nothing in the statutory duties of an auditor to suggest that they were intended to protect the interests of the public at large or investors in the market. The statutory duty was owed to shareholders as a body and not as individuals, and this meant also that they did not owe duties to potential investors. It is still not clear whether there is a duty to protect individuals from losses in the value of the shares they hold.[153]

12.23.3 *Duty of auditor valuing shares*

Where an auditor of a private company is called upon to value shares in the company in the knowledge that his valuation would determine the price to be paid on the sale of such shares, the auditor owes a duty of care to those affected by his valuation. The House of Lords (overruling the Court of Appeal) has held that an auditor valuing shares has no general immunity from an action for negligence. In order to establish such an immunity, the auditor acting as valuer must show that a formulated dispute between at least two parties has been remitted to him to resolve in such a manner that he was called upon to exercise a judicial (i.e. arbitral) function, and that the parties had agreed to accept his decision.[154]

A valuer must also be seen to be truly independent of the company whose shares he has to value. If the valuer is independent then the valuing of the shares might reasonably be left to him.[155] It is also only possible to challenge a certificate of valuation of shares for

---

[153] See *Morgan Crucible Co. plc v Hill Samuel & Co. Ltd & Ors* [1990] BCC 686, [1991] BCC 82, and *James McNaughton Paper Group Ltd v Hicks Anderson & Co.* [1990] BCC 891.

[154] *Arenson v Casson, Beckman, Rutley & Co.* [1975] 3 WLR 815 (overruling *Arenson v Arenson* [1973] 2 WLR 553 (C.A.)); *Suttcliffe v Thackrah* [1974] All ER 859 applied. However, even if an action against the auditors in negligence would lie, the purchaser is still entitled to buy the shares at the price certified by the auditors. In the absence of fraud, collusion or error on the face of the certificate, it cannot be challenged: *Baber v Kenwood Manufacturing Co.* [1978] 1 Lloyd's Rep. 175 (C.A.).

[155] *Re Boswell & Co. (Steels) Ltd* (1989) 5 BCC 145.

mistake when the mistake is of such a nature that the expert has not performed what he was appointed to do.[156] Where a company's articles provide for shares to be valued by an auditor, the standard of care is that of a reasonable auditor, not that of a specialist valuer.[157]

12.23.4 *The limitation or exclusion of liability*

The Limitation Act 1980, as amended by the Latent Damage Act 1986, serves to limit the auditor's civil liability in England for negligence to losses arising within six years before the commencement of an action. Any provision contained either in a company's articles or in a contract to exempt an auditor from or to indemnify him against any liability which would otherwise attach to him in respect of any negligence, default or breach of duty or trust in relation to the company is void. The company may, however, indemnify him in respect of costs incurred in a successful defence of a civil or criminal action or in connection with an application for relief under section 727.[158] In Scotland the prescriptive period is five years: Prescription and Limitation (Scotland) Act 1973.

12.24 Small company exemption from audit

As a part of the Government's policy of deregulation and 'lifting the burdens' on small businesses, the Companies Act 1985 (Audit Exemption) Regulations 1994[159] remove the requirement for audit from private companies which qualify as 'small companies',[160] are not part of a group, have a balance sheet total of not more than £1.4 million, and comply with the further requirements specified.[161] There are two possible exemptions, the difference between them depending on the amount of the company's turnover. First, an appropriate company with a turnover of not more than £90,000 in respect of the year in question is in effect totally exempt from the audit requirement.[162] Secondly, a company with a turnover between £90,000 and £350,000 is exempt if the directors cause a report to be prepared in accordance with section 249C and sent to the company's members. The requirements for the second exemption are referred to as the 'report conditions'.

The effect of the second exemption[163] is that the report under section 249C is substituted for the auditors' report for the purposes of delivery to the Registrar, members and so on, and in all cases where the Act refers to the auditors' report. This report, often referred to as a compilation report, must be prepared by an eligible 'reporting accountant',[164] named therein, be signed by them and state the following:

---

[156] *Jones v Sherwood Computer Services Plc* [1992] 2 All ER 170.

[157] *Whiteoak v Walker* (1988) 4 BCC 122.

[158] Section 310. As to relief under section 727, see 14.24.4, below.

[159] SI 1994 No. 1935, inserting new sections 249A to 249E into the Companies Act 1985.

[160] See 12.17.1, above.

[161] Section 249A. The further requirements include the need for an appropriate statement by the directors on the balance sheet. A banking or insurance company, a registered insurance broker or an authorised person or appointed representative under the Financial Services Act 1986 cannot claim exemption.

[162] No copy of an auditors' report need be delivered to the Registrar or laid before the company in general meeting, and members' rights to receive or demand copies of accounts and reports do not extend to the right to a copy of the auditors' report. In addition, distributions of profits may be made without reference to an auditors' report: section 249E (1).

[163] Section 249E (2).

[164] Essentially someone qualified to be an auditor.

(1) whether in their opinion the accounts of the company for the financial year in question are in agreement with the company's accounting records;

(2) whether in their opinion, having regard only to, and on the basis of, the information in the accounting records, those accounts have been drawn up in a manner consistent with various provisions of the Act,[165] so far as applicable to the company; and

(3) that in their opinion, having regard only to, and on the basis of, the information in the accounting records, the company satisfied the requirements necessary to take advantage of the exemption and did not fall within the types of company ineligible to take advantage of the exemption.

Neither of the exemptions can be taken advantage of if a member or members of the company, holding not less in the aggregate than 10 per cent in nominal value of the company's issued share capital or any class thereof, or, in the case of a company without a share capital, being not less than 10 per cent in number of the members of the company, require the company to obtain an audit of its accounts for a particular financial year. The only formality is that a written requisition is deposited at the registered office during the year in question and at least one month before the end of the year.[166]

PART 3: THE DIRECTORS' REPORT

12.25 Introduction

Section 235 of the Companies Act 1985 requires that there must be attached to every balance sheet[167] a report by the directors and sets out the information which the directors' report must contain, which includes that detailed in Part I of Schedule 7.[168] Small companies which take advantage in relation to their accounts of the exemptions contained in section 247 and Part I of Schedule 8[169] are not required to deliver to the Registrar a copy of the directors' report.[170]

12.26 The information required in the directors' report

Section 235 (1) of the Companies Act 1985 requires that there be laid before the company in general meeting 'a report by the directors (a) containing a fair review of the development of the business of the company and its subsidiaries during the financial year and of their position at the end of it and (b) stating the amount, if any, which they recommend should be paid by way of dividend, and the amount, if any, which they propose to carry to reserves'. The additional matters of a general nature required to be stated are listed below:

(1) The report must state the names of those persons who at any time during the financial year were directors of the company, the principal activities of the

---

[165] Including the basic obligation under section 226 to prepare a balance sheet and profit and loss account.

[166] Section 249B (2) and (3).

[167] As to the requirements in respect of balance sheets, see 12.2, above.

[168] A director who fails to comply is guilty of an offence and liable to a fine, subject to the defence that he took all reasonable steps to secure compliance: section 235 (7).

[169] As to these, see 12.17, above.

[170] Schedule 8, para. 14.

company and its subsidiaries in the course of the year and any significant changes in those activities in the year: section 235 (3) to (6).

(2) The report must contain particulars of any significant changes in the fixed assets of the company or of any of its subsidiaries. In respect of those assets which consist of interests in land, if their market value at the end of the year differs substantially from the amount at which they are included in the balance sheet and the difference is, in the directors' opinion, of such significance as to require that the attention of members of the company or holders of its debentures should be drawn to it, the report must indicate the difference with such degree of precision as is practicable: Schedule 7, para. 1 (1) and (2).

(3) As respects each person who was a director at the end of the financial year, the report must state whether or not he was interested in shares in or debentures of the company or its subsidiary or holding company or fellow subsidiary, and, if he was, the number and amount of shares in and debentures of each company (specifying it) according to the company's register of directors' interests.[171] The same information must be given in relation to the beginning of the year or, if he was not then a director, when he became a director: Schedule 7, paras. 2, 2A and 2B.[172]

(4) The report must contain:
   (a) particulars of any important events affecting the company or any of its subsidiaries which have occurred since the end of the financial year;
   (b) an indication of likely future developments in the business of the company and of its subsidiaries; and
   (c) an indication of the activities (if any) of the company and its subsidiaries in the field of research and development: Schedule 7, para. 6.

(5) If a company employs an average number of persons exceeding 250,[173] the report must state such policy as the company has applied during the financial year for:
   (a) giving fair consideration to applications for employment by disabled persons;
   (b) continuing the employment of, and arranging appropriate training for, disabled persons;
   (c) training, career development and promotion of disabled persons employed by the company (Schedule 7, para. 9).

(6) The report must contain information about the arrangements in force for securing the health, safety and welfare at work of the employees of the company and its subsidiaries (Schedule 7, para. 10). However, no regulations necessary to bring this requirement into effect have yet been made.

(7) If the company during the financial year has had an average weekly number of at least 250 employees,[174] the report must contain a statement describing the action

---

[171] As to this register, see 13.22.5, below.

[172] 'Interest in shares or debentures' is defined in Schedule 13, Part I and has the same meaning as in sections 324 to 328, as to which see 13.22.2, below; references to a person 'becoming a director', in the case of a person who became a director on more than one occasion, are to be construed as a reference to when he first became a director: Schedule 7, para. 2 (2). The information required by this paragraph can be given by way of notes to the accounts instead of in the directors' report: Schedule 7, para. 2 (3).

[173] Excluding those employed to work wholly or mainly outside the United Kingdom: Schedule 7, para. 11 (4).

[174] Excluding those employed to work wholly or mainly outside the United Kingdom: Schedule 7, para. 11 (4).

that has been taken during the financial year to introduce, maintain or develop arrangements aimed at:

(a) providing employees systematically with information on matters of concern to them as employees;

(b) consulting employees or their representatives on a regular basis so that the views of employees can be taken into account in making decisions which are likely to affect their interests;

(c) encouraging the involvement of employees in the company's performance through an employees' share scheme or by some other means; and

(d) achieving a common awareness on the part of all employees of the financial and economic factors affecting the performance of the company: Schedule 7, para. 11.

(8) Listed companies incorporated in the United Kingdom are required to include in their directors' report a statement as to whether or not the company has complied throughout the relevant accounting period with the Code of Best Practice devised by the Committee on the Financial Aspects of Corporate Governance (the 'Cadbury Report'). A company which has not complied with the Code, or complied with only part of it, must specify which parts have not been complied with and give reasons for the non-compliance.[175]

12.26.1 *Particulars of acquisition of a company's own shares*

Section 235 (4) requires the directors' report to include the information specified in Schedule 7, Part II, where shares in the company are:

(1) purchased by the company by forfeiture or surrender, or in pursuance of section 143 (3) of the Act;[176]

(2) acquired by another person in circumstances where para. (*c*) or (*d*) of section 146 (1) applies;[177] or

(3) made subject to a lien or other charge taken (whether expressly or otherwise) by the company and permitted by section 150 (2) or (4) of the Act and section 6 (3) of the Consequential Provisions Act.[178]

The information required is:

(1) the number and nominal value of shares so purchased, the aggregate amount of the consideration paid by the company for such shares and the reasons for their purchase;

(2) the number and nominal value of the shares so acquired by the company, acquired by another person in such circumstances and so charged respectively during the financial year;

(3) the maximum number and nominal value of such shares which are held at any time by the company or the other person during the year;

(4) the number and nominal value of such shares which are disposed of by the company or that other person or cancelled by the company during the year;

---

[175] *Listing Rules*, 12.43 (*j*). The Code and the notes to it contain provisions for a nomination committee, a remuneration committee and an audit committee. It also contains requirements as to the chairman and chief executive and as to the minimum number of non-executive directors. See generally 1.15, above.

[176] As to forfeiture and surrender, see 7.15, above; as to section 143 (3), see 6.16, above.

[177] As to this, see 7.15.2, above.

[178] As to this, see 7.11, above.

(5) where the number and nominal value of the shares of any particular description are stated in pursuance of any of the above paragraphs, the percentage of the called-up share capital which shares of that description represent;

(6) where any of the shares have been so charged, the amount of the charge in each case;

(7) where any of the shares have been disposed of by the company or the person who acquired them in such circumstances for money or money's worth, the amount or value of the consideration in each case.

12.26.2 Charitable and political gifts

Schedule 7, paras. 3–5 provide that if a company, other than a wholly owned subsidiary[179] of a company incorporated in Great Britain, has given more than £200 during the financial year for either political or charitable purposes, the directors' report must state the amount given under each category and, in the case of political gifts, (a) the name of each person to whom more than £200 was given and the amount of the gift and (b) if more than £200 is given by way of donation or subscription to a political party, the identity of the party and the amount of the gift.

By para. 5 (2), a company is to be treated as giving money for political purposes if, directly or indirectly: (a) it gives a donation or subscription to a political party of the United Kingdom or of any part thereof; or (b) it gives a donation or subscription to a person who, to its knowledge, is carrying on, or proposing to carry on, any activities which can, at the time of the donation or subscription, reasonably be regarded as likely to affect public support for such a political party.

Money given for charitable purposes means purposes which are exclusively charitable,[180] the latter presumably having the technical meaning as it does in the general law of charities. Money given for charitable purposes to a person ordinarily resident outside the United Kingdom is to be ignored.[181]

In the case of companies which at the end of the financial year have subsidiaries, Schedule 7, para. 4 (2) provides for the disclosure on a group basis of political and charitable gifts if the amount given by the company and its subsidiaries exceeds £200 in total.

12.27 Duty of the auditors

Section 237 (6) of the Companies Act 1985 provides that in preparing their report on the accounts[182] the auditors are under a duty to consider whether the information given in the directors' report relating to the financial year in question is consistent with those accounts. If they consider that it is not, they must state that fact in their report.

12.28 Distribution of the directors' report

Section 239 of the Companies Act 1985 includes the directors' report in the definition of a company's accounts and thus confers the same right to receive the directors' report as is given by section 246 in respect of copies of the accounts and the auditors' report.

---

[179] Defined in section 736, as to which see 1.13.1, above.
[180] Schedule 7, para. 5 (4).
[181] Schedule 7 para. 5 (3).
[182] As to the auditors' report under section 236, see 12.21.3, above. See also Cadbury Code of Best Practice, 12.26, above.

Generally[183] this means all members and debenture holders (whether or not they have a right to receive notices of general meetings) and anyone else entitled to receive notices of general meetings.

[183] As to the exact requirements of section 246, see 12.2.7, above.

13 Management of a Company

13.1 Introduction

Although the Companies Act 1985 requires that every company must have a director or directors,[1] and although it attributes many functions to and casts many obligations on directors, it does not itself prescribe how the business of a company is to be managed.[2] This and some other aspects of the law relating to directors and other officers and managers of a company are left to the articles, which in practice will adopt or follow, with modifications, the relevant parts of Table A. Thus the articles will, among other things, determine the number of directors, the power of the board *vis-à-vis* the shareholders in general meeting, and the ability of directors to delegate their powers. In this permissive respect, British company law contrasts with the law in some other member-states of the EC. This situation is threatened by the EC Draft Fifth Directive which would impose a formal legal structure on public companies, including the representation of a company's employees on its board of directors or in some other formal way. The draft directive is also concerned to make directors more responsible to shareholders, something which relates to the issue of who really controls companies; this issue has been touched on in earlier chapters.[3]

Although, however, there appears to be little immediate prospect of this draft directive,[4] or indeed of other proposals for 'employee directors',[5] being implemented, steps have recently been taken to strengthen the supervision of the management of public companies, in particular, by a clear recognition of the distinction between executive and non-executive directors. This is part of the issue of 'corporate governance', which was considered in Chapter 1.[6] This chapter is henceforth concerned with the present law applying to directors and other officers. This includes their appointment, removal, functions and procedures, remuneration and service contracts, and the complex rules laid down to ensure that members (and often the public) are aware of the interests directors have in their companies. This chapter is also an appropriate place to examine the law regarding the disqualification of directors and their potential responsibility for fraudulent or wrongful trading. Although some of these issues touch on the duties of directors,

---

[1] Section 282; see 13.2.1, below.

[2] Nor, surprisingly, does it define the term 'director'; see 14.2 below.

[3] See especially 10.1 and 11.1, above.

[4] It was first produced, heavily influenced by the German law relating to public companies, in 1972 and has been the subject of argument and revision ever since. For a useful review of its history and contents, see Clough 3 Co. Law 109 (1982) and see further 1.5.2, above.

[5] The most controversial proposals were those of the Bullock Committee on Industrial Democracy, Cmnd 6706 (1977). The whole question of 'industrial democracy' has given birth to many different proposals and reactions over the last twenty years. It should not be forgotten in this context that a number of changes have been made to company law which reflect increasing recognition of employees' interests; see in particular section 309 of the 1985 Act, discussed in 14.4.2, below, Part V of Schedule 7, discussed in 12.26, above, and the fiscal and other measures introduced to encourage employee share ownership: see, e.g., 6.18.2, above.

[6] See 1.15. Note that this is another topic where the law and practice relating to public company is clearly different from that applying to private companies.

consideration of these duties in general is deferred to the next chapter. The other important question not considered here is the extent of directors' agency powers, namely when liability for their dealings will be attributed to their companies; this question has already been considered in Chapter 4.

13.2 Appointment of directors

The articles usually provide how the directors are to be appointed (see Table A of the Companies Act 1985, articles 73 to 80), and in practice the first directors are normally either named in the articles or directed to be appointed by the subscribers to the memorandum. If appointment lies with the subscribers, then, until they have made the appointment, a general meeting of the company must be held to perform any acts. A majority of the subscribers must act at a meeting in making the appointment of directors[7] but the appointment may be made in writing by all the subscribers without a meeting.[8]

The provisions for the appointment of future directors usually declare that vacancies[9] may be filled, or additional directors appointed, by the board of directors and that a certain proportion of the directors (usually one-third) must retire at each annual general meeting and the places be filled by the company at the meeting;[10] further, a director retiring by rotation is deemed to be reappointed if his place is not filled, unless it is expressly resolved not to reappoint him or not to fill the vacated office.[11]

A company has an inherent power to fill vacancies,[12] unless restricted by its articles, and even where this is restricted, the general meeting has a residual power if the directors cannot or will not act, for example because of deadlock or the failure of the directors to meet or if the directors are equally divided.[13]

If the articles authorise it, but not otherwise,[14] the directors may delegate the power to appoint directors to a third party.[15] If the appointment of directors requires the confirmation of the company at the next general meeting, the directors cannot by appointing a managing director for a fixed period dispense with this confirmation nor give him a right to damages for breach of contract.[16]

13.2.1 Statutory requirements

There are a number of statutory requirements relating to the appointment of directors. Section 282 requires that every private company and every public company registered before 1 November 1926 should have at least one director, and that every other public company should have at least two directors. Subject to this, the number of directors may be varied from time to time within the limits (if any) specified in the articles. In practice,

---

[7] *John Morley Building Co. v. Barras* [1891] 2 Ch 386.

[8] *Re Great Northern Salt and Chemical Works Co.* (1890) 44 Ch D 472.

[9] That is, all vacancies occurring other than through retirement by rotation, such as by death, resignation, disqualification or failure to accept office. The power to fill vacancies continues even if a general meeting has been held, if the vacancy has not been filled: *Re Munster v Cammell Co.* (1882) 21 Ch D 187.

[10] See 13.5 below.

[11] Table A, article 75.

[12] *Worcester Corsetry v Witting* [1936] Ch 640.

[13] *Barron v Potter* [1914] 1 Ch 895; *Foster v Foster* [1916] 1 Ch 532; see 13.11, below.

[14] *James v Eve* (1873) LR 6 HL 335.

[15] *British Murac Syndicate v Alperton Rubber Co.* [1915] 2 Ch 186.

[16] *Bluett v Stutchbury's Ltd* (1908) 24 TLR 469 (CA).

the articles often specify the minimum and maximum number of directors.[17] Section 10 requires the directors of all companies to sign a statement giving their consent to act at the time the company is registered.[18]

As far as public companies are concerned, section 292 prohibits the appointment of two or more persons as directors by a single resolution unless this procedure has been approved by the meeting without dissent.[19] A resolution contravening section 292 is void, but section 285[20] will apply to validate the acts of the improperly appointed 'directors' and such a resolution will prevent the operation of a provision in the articles (e.g. article 75 in Table A) for the automatic reappointment of retiring directors in default of another appointment. Section 293 provides that a person who has attained the age of seventy cannot be appointed director of a public company or a private company which is a subsidiary of a public company, and a director reaching that age must vacate office at the conclusion of the next annual general meeting, unless the articles provide otherwise or the director is appointed or approved by a resolution of which special notice[21] stating his age has been given.[22]

13.2.2 *Directors' qualification shares*

The Companies Act does not require that a director be a shareholder, but articles may require it.[23]

Where the articles prescribe a share qualification, section 291 requires directors to acquire it within two months after appointment, or such shorter time as may be fixed by the articles,[24] and declares that the office of any director not acquiring his qualification within such time, or ceasing to hold it after such time, shall be vacated, and that the disqualified person shall not be capable of reappointment as director until he has obtained his qualification.[25]

Articles sometimes provide that the holding of the necessary shares is a condition precedent to election,[26] but it is more usual to require the obtaining of the qualification after appointment. The articles may also require that a director cannot act before acquiring his qualification. In this case he must qualify before he acts and within a reasonable time (not more than two months) after his appointment, even though he has not acted in the meantime.[27]

---

[17] The articles of many private companies appoint a person, e.g. the vendor of a business to the company, as a director. He may be styled a 'governing director' with extensive powers, e.g. the right to appoint a successor and to appoint and remove other directors. As to whether the exercise of such powers may amount to an assignment of office and thus be subject to the requirement of a special resolution under section 308, see *Gore-Browne on Companies* (Jordans, 44th edn, loose-leaf), 25.1.2.

[18] See further, 2.5, above.

[19] 'Appointment' includes approving a person's appointment or nominating a person for appointment.

[20] See further 4.35, above.

[21] See 11.14.1, above.

[22] Under section 294, a person appointed or proposed to be appointed a director of such a company at a time when he has reached seventy (or the retiring age under the articles) must give notice of his age to the company, unless he is a retiring director reappointed, when the register of directors will give his date of birth.

[23] There is no reference at all to share qualifications in the modern Table A.

[24] Where directors are elected on a poll, the time runs from the date of the declaration of the poll: *Holmes v Keyes* [1959] Ch 199 (CA).

[25] A criminal penalty is imposed by subsection (5). Bearing a share warrant is not compliance: subsection (2).

[26] See e.g.: *Barber's Case* (1877) 5 Ch D 963 (CA); *Jenner's Case* (1877) 7 Ch D 132 (CA).

[27] *Molineaux v London, Birmingham and Manchester Insurance Co.* [1902] 2 KB 589 (CA).

If the articles do not prescribe that a director must take his qualification shares from the company, he may purchase them or obtain them from any person possessed of shares.[28] Shares held jointly with another person are a sufficient qualification unless the articles require a sole holding.[29]

A director may pay for his qualification shares out of the purchase money owing to him from the sale of property to the company, or in any acceptable form of money's worth.[30] It is a breach of duty to accept the shares as a gift from a promoter or any person having contracts with the company,[31] in respect of which the director will be liable to account to the company for the value of the shares, but shares so acquired will suffice to form his qualification.[32]

Section 285[33] and (usually) the articles provide that the acts of an unqualified director are valid until the defect is discovered, but an appointment vacated by reason of section 291 is not validated by section 285.[34]

13.3 Remuneration of directors

Directors *qua* directors are not entitled as of right to any remuneration, whether upon a *quantum meruit* or otherwise.[35] A 'director is not a servant; he is a person doing business for the company, but not upon ordinary terms. It is not implied from the mere fact that he is a director that he is to be paid for it.'[36] However, this proposition may be, and of course, normally is, qualified.[37] First the articles may provide for director's fees.[38] Second there may be a service contract between a director and his company which entitles him to a salary or other remuneration, in other words a director is often an employee as well as holding the office of director. Further, if a director performs services which are not comprehended by the terms of any service contract (or where there is no service contract), he may claim in *quantum meruit*. This applies to a director who continues to perform services for the benefit of his company after he ceases to be qualified as a director.[39] However, where a managing director is appointed under article 84 (of Table A, or a similar article) which confers on the board of directors the power to determine the managing director's remuneration, and the board have not determined his remuneration, the managing director will have no claim in *quantum meruit*; since he has agreed to

---

[28] *Brown's Case* (1873) 9 Ch App. 102; *Miller's Case* (1876) 3 Ch D 661.

[29] *Dunster's Case, Re Glory Paper Mills* [1894] 3 Ch 473 (CA).

[30] *Dent's Case* (1873) 8 Ch App. 768 at p.776. As to payment for shares in money's worth, see 6.12 *et seq.*, above.

[31] *Eden v Ridsdale's Railway Lamp and Lighting Co.* (1889) 23 QBD 368 (CA).

[32] *Re Hercynia Copper Co.* [1894] 2 Ch 403 (CA).

[33] See further 4.35, above.

[34] *Morris v Kanssen* [1946] AC 459 (HL).

[35] *Re Geo. Newman and Co.* [1895] 1 Ch 674 (CA).

[36] *Per* Bowen LJ in *Hutton v West Cork Rly* (1883) 23 Ch D 654 at p.671 (CA).

[37] 'Excessive' remuneration for executive directors of public companies has been the subject of public concern in recent years: see Ramsay [1993] JBL 351; Villiers, 'Executive Pay: Beyond Control' (1995) 14 LS (forthcoming).

[38] See Article 82 of Table A, described below.

[39] *Craven-Ellis v Canons* [1936] 2 KB 403 (CA).

serve the company on the basis of this provision in the articles, this excludes a quasi-contractual claim in *quantum meruit*.[40]

In practice the articles usually declare that directors shall receive remuneration and fix the amount, in which case when earned it becomes a debt for which the directors can sue.[41] Their own right in such cases arises from the contract to employ them as directors, and the articles must be looked at to see what are the terms agreed upon for their remuneration.[42] If the articles provide that a director is to be paid such remuneration as the board of directors determines, and the company is wound up before the board has passed any such resolution as to remuneration, then a director will *not* be entitled to recover for any services he has performed on a contractual basis (since the contractual amount has not been determined in the way the article required). Further, as described above, a claim on a *quantum meruit* is also excluded by the terms of the articles.[43] If the articles are silent, the company in general meeting may vote remuneration; but in such case the remuneration is a gratuity, and not a matter of right.[44] So in an operative company a general meeting may vote a gratuity beyond the amount prescribed by the articles, but upon liquidation this cannot be done.[45] Standard articles[46] provide that the directors are entitled to such remuneration as the company may by ordinary resolution determine.[47] Where the remuneration of the directors is governed by such an article, it is incompetent for the board to fix it.[48]

Liquidation puts an end to a director's service,[49] but the appointment of a receiver and manager does not determine the director's right to remuneration.[50] If remuneration is payable 'at such time as the directors may determine', one of the directors cannot sue for fees until the board have fixed the time for payment.[51]

If a director's appointment is not validly made he cannot recover remuneration as a director, either under the articles or under a *quantum meruit*, although he may have served for a long period,[52] and if it be discovered that fees have been paid for a period after the director has vacated office under the terms of the articles, the company, in a case where the facts negate the probability of an intention to grant remuneration, can recover the amount paid by mistake.[53] It should, however, be noted that a person purported to be appointed *managing director* by the supposed board may recover remuneration as such on

---

[40] *Re Richmond Gate Property Co.* [1965] 1 WLR 335. The contract of service in this case was not constituted by the articles but was a contract of service created by the conduct of the parties based on, or incorporating, the articles – 'those were the terms on which he accepted office'.

[41] *Nell v Atlanta Gold and Silver Consol Mines* (1895) 11 TLR 407 (CA); *New British Iron Co., Ex parte Beckwith* [1898] 1 Ch 324; *Re Dover Coalfields Extension Co.* [1908] 1 Ch 65 (CA).

[42] *Molineaux v London, Birmingham, and Manchester Insurance Co.* [1902] 2 KB 596 (CA).

[43] *Re Richmond Gate Property Co.* [1965] 1 WLR 335.

[44] *Re Geo. Newman & Co.* [1895] 1 Ch 674 (CA); see generally the discussion of 'corporate gifts' in 4.13. above.

[45] *Hutton v West Cork Rly Co.* (1883) 23 Ch D 654.

[46] See article 82 of Table A.

[47] As to variations on this method of calculation which may be found in articles of association, see *Gore-Browne on Companies* (Jordans, 44th edn, loose-leaf), 25.3.2.

[48] *Kerr v Marine Products* (1928) 44 TLR 292. But a formal resolution in general meeting may be dispensed with if *all* the shareholders entitled to attend and vote at a general meeting have approved the remuneration: *Re Duomatic* [1969] 2 Ch 365. See further 11.2, above.

[49] *In Re Central de Kaap Gold Mines* [1899] WN 216; *Re T. N. Farrer* [1937] Ch 352.

[50] *Re South Western of Venezuela Rly* [1902] 1 Ch 701.

[51] *Caridad Copper Mining Co. v Swallow* [1902] 2 KB 44 (CA).

[52] *Woolf v East Nigel Gold Mining Co.* (1905) 21 TLR 660.

[53] *Re Bodega Co.* [1904] 1 Ch 276.

the basis of a *quantum meruit*, notwithstanding that such appointment was altogether void, neither he nor any person constituting such board being a director, through failure to qualify.[54]

The remuneration of a director as such covers travelling expenses, and unless specially authorised by the articles (see Table A, article 83) or by resolution of a general meeting, expenses of travelling to or from board meetings must not be paid in addition.[55]

Section 311 contains provisions prohibiting the payment to a director of tax-free remuneration, whether paid to him as a director or otherwise. The prohibition extends to the payment of remuneration calculated by reference to or varying with the amount of his tax, or the rate of income tax. Provisions in any other contract or in the articles or any resolution for payment of remuneration tax-free or calculated by reference to tax are to have effect as if they provided for payment, as a gross sum subject to tax, of the net sum actually provided for.

13.4 Directors' service contracts and the articles

Where a managing director or other director has a service contract with the company and he is dismissed in breach of his service contract, a provision in the articles which enables the general meeting or the board to dismiss him from the office of director or managing director will not prevent him from suing for damages for breach of contract.[56] Thus, where, as in *Southern Foundries v Shirlaw*,[57] a director is appointed managing director for a term of years, and the articles provide that a managing director shall be subject to the same provisions for removal as any other director 'subject to the provisions of any contract between him and the company', it is an implied term of the contract that the company will not remove the managing director from his office as director. In *Nelson v James Nelson & Sons*[58] it was held that even without such a phrase the directors could not revoke an appointment otherwise than in accordance with the terms of the service agreement.

Although section 303 of the Companies Act 1985 allows the company in general meeting to dismiss a director by ordinary resolution,[59] section 303 (5) specifically provides that nothing in the section deprives a director removed under it 'of compensation or damages payable to him in respect of the termination of his appointment or of any appointment terminating with that as a director' (e.g. as managing director). In *Shindler v Northern Raincoat Co*[60] the plaintiff was appointed a managing director of the defendant company for ten years. The company's articles included article 68 of Table A of the 1929 Act, which gave the company in general meeting a power to determine the appointment of a managing director.[61] As a result of a change in the control of the defendant's holding company, resolutions were passed at a general meeting removing the plaintiff from office

---

[54] *Craven-Ellis v Canons* [1936] 2 KB 403 (CA). See also *Re Richmond Gate Property Co.* [1965] 1 WLR 335 (see 13.3, above, at footnote 40).

[55] *Young v Naval and Military Co-operative Society* [1905] 1 KB 687.

[56] It is most unlikely that he will have any prospect of obtaining an injunction: see, e.g., *Walker v Standard Chartered Bank plc* [1992] BCLC 535 (CA).

[57] [1940] AC 707 (HL). See further as to the powers and status of managing directors, 13.14.1, below.

[58] [1913] 2 KB 471 (CA).

[59] See further as to section 303, 13.7, below.

[60] [1960] 1 WLR 1038.

[61] The equivalent article in respect of the appointment of managing directors in the 1985 Act (article 84) does not give this power. The general meeting can, however, act under section 303.

as director and terminating his service agreement as managing director. It was held that the plaintiff could sue for damages for wrongful dismissal since it was an implied term in his service agreement that the defendant company would do nothing of its own motion to put an end to the circumstances which enabled the plaintiff to continue as managing director. In another case,[62] where a managing director was appointed under an identical article, his service contract was held to incorporate article 68 (which allowed the company to dismiss him without notice by a resolution in general meeting). Here the plaintiff was not appointed for any specific period. It was held that in the absence of a contract independent of the articles there was no ground for implying a term as to reasonable notice.

Where a director has a claim for damages for wrongful dismissal, he is of course subject to the general contractual rule that he must seek to mitigate his loss. It has been held, however, that where a managing director is dismissed and is offered the position of assistant managing director at the same salary, he is entitled to refuse the offer because of the loss of status involved.[63] In estimating the amount of damages, the court must apply the principle of *British Transport Commission v Gourlay*[64] and take into account what would have been his liability for income tax.

In addition to, and as apart from, any common-law claim for wrongful dismissal, a director who has a service contract and is therefore an employee of his company may bring a claim for unfair dismissal before an industrial tribunal.[65]

13.5 Vacating the office of director

Table A, article 73 provides that at the first annual general meeting all the directors shall retire from office, and that at the annual general meeting in every subsequent year one-third of the directors for the time being, or, if their number is not three or a multiple of three, then the number nearest to one-third, shall retire. Most articles of public companies have similar provisions for the retirement of a certain proportion of the directors by rotation, although most private companies will not provide for this.

Articles usually provide too[66] that the office of director is to be vacated if he does or suffers certain things, such as becoming bankrupt or insolvent, and on grounds such as failure to acquire or hold the necessary share qualification, absence from meetings for a long period or disqualification under the statutory provisions. The vacation of office is automatic,[67] but unless the cause of disqualification is a continuing one, or is bankruptcy, the director may be re-elected.

As far as bankruptcy is concerned, section 11 of the Company Directors Disqualification Act 1986 (consolidating a long-established provision in the companies legislation) provides that it is a criminal offence for an undischarged bankrupt to act as a director of, or directly or indirectly take part in or be concerned in the promotion, formation or management of, a company, without the leave of the court by which he was adjudged

---

[62] *Read v Astoria Garage* [1952] Ch 637 (CA). Cf. *James v T. Kent & Co. Ltd* [1951] 1 KB 551 (CA) where a term as to reasonable notice was implied.

[63] *Yetton v Eastwoods Froy Ltd* [1967] 1 WLR 104. As to the measure of damages in respect of various 'heads' (loss of salary and commission, reduction in pension, loss of life insurance cover, etc.), see *Bold v Brough, Nicholson and Hall Ltd* [1964] 1 WLR 201.

[64] [1956] AC 185 (HL).

[65] i.e. under the Employment Protection Act 1978, Part V, as amended.

[66] See article 81 of Table A.

[67] *Re Bodega Co.* [1904] 1 Ch 276.

bankrupt. In England the court may not give leave unless notice of the application is served on the Official Receiver, who may attend and oppose it.

The provisions under which directors (and others) may be disqualified from management are considered later in this chapter at 13.16 *et seq.*

13.6 Resignation

Articles usually permit a director to resign. Even in the absence of such a power, unless the articles contain conditions, he may resign, and his resignation is complete when notice is given to the secretary, and cannot subsequently be withdrawn,[68] even though no acceptance has taken place. Notwithstanding that the articles contemplate a written resignation, a verbal notice of resignation given and accepted at a general meeting of the company is binding.[69]

13.7 Removal by ordinary resolution

Section 303 of the Companies Act 1985 provides that a company may, by ordinary resolution, remove a director before the expiration of office, notwithstanding anything in its articles or in any agreement between the company and the director.[70] Even assuming that a director may be entitled, having been removed under section 303, to petition for a just and equitable winding-up on the principles laid down by the House of Lords in *Ebrahimi v Westbourne Galleries Ltd*,[71] this does not affect the validity of the removal under the section and the court will not grant an injunction.[72] The director's only remedy is to petition for a winding-up or, perhaps more likely now, for an order under sections 459 to 461.[73]

An important limitation on the effectiveness of section 303 may arise, however, as the result of the decision in *Bushell v Faith*.[74] Here the articles of a private company provided that 'in the event of a resolution being proposed at any general meeting for the removal from office of any director any shares held by that director shall on a poll in respect of such resolution carry the right of three votes per share.' The House of Lords, affirming the Court of Appeal, upheld this provision for weighted voting in resolutions under section 303. The House held that this was not an infringement of the requirement imposed by section 303 to the effect that, despite any contrary provision in the articles, any director may be removed by ordinary resolution. The following passage[75] from Lord Upjohn's judgment stresses the distinction between voting rights attached to shares and the scope of section 303.

---

[68] *Maitland's Case* (1853) 4 De GM & G 769.

[69] *Latchford Premier Cinema Ltd v Ennion* [1931] 2 Ch 409.

[70] The only exception, which is unlikely to be relevant today, is in the case of a director of a private company holding office for life on 18th July 1945: section 14, Companies Consolidation (Consequential Provisions) Act 1985.

[71] [1973] AC 360; see 15.17, below.

[72] *Bentley-Stevens v Jones* [1974] 1 WLR 638. *Quaere*, though, whether on exceptional facts if the removal was a breach of a contract with the company, e.g. between it and a debenture holder, an injunction might be awarded: see the discussion in 3.25, above.

[73] The remedy for 'unfair prejudice', fully discussed in 15.13 *et seq.*, below.

[74] [1970] AC 1099; see Prentice (1969) 32 MLR 693.

[75] ibid., p.1109.

Parliament has never sought to fetter the right of the company to issue a share with such rights or restrictions as it may think fit. There is no fetter which compels the company to make the voting rights or restrictions of general application and it seems to me clear that such rights or restrictions can be attached to special circumstances and to particular types of resolution. This makes no mockery of section [303]; all that Parliament was seeking to do thereby was to make an ordinary resolution sufficient to remove a director. Had Parliament desired to go further and enact that every share entitled to vote should be deprived of its special rights under the articles it should have said so in plain terms by making the vote on a poll one vote one share.

There was a strong dissent by Lord Morris[76] to the effect that this construction made a mockery of what Parliament really intended and it is possible that in future legislation[77] section 303 will be strengthened to prevent evasion in this manner. On the other hand, an article of the kind considered by the House of Lords arguably is legitimate in the context of small private companies where majority rule may work to the prejudice of a minority shareholder-director.[78]

A resolution to remove a director under this section, or to appoint a director in his place at the meeting at which he is removed, requires special notice;[79] and on receipt of notice of an intended resolution to remove a director under section 303 the company must send a copy to the director, who has then the right to make representations and have them notified to the members: if this is not done, the representations must be read out at the meeting. The obligation of the company to circularise the representations or have them read at the meeting may, if the representations contain defamatory matter, be avoided by an application to the court.[80]

A director removed under the section does not lose any right to compensation or damages he may have for the termination of his appointment as director or of any other appointment (e.g. that of managing director) which terminates with his directorship.[81]

If the vacancy created by the removal of a director is not filled at the meeting at which he is removed, it may be subsequently filled as a casual vacancy. A person appointed to the vacancy is to be treated, for purposes of retirement by rotation or otherwise, as if appointed on the day on which his predecessor was last appointed.[82]

It should be noted that the provisions of the section do not affect or apply to any other power (e.g. under the articles) to remove a director. Prior to the Companies Act 1948, which first introduced what is now section 303, articles commonly contained a power to remove a director by extraordinary resolution, and such a power may still be taken with advantage, since proceeding under the articles will not involve the complication of special notice or the statutory rights in regard to making representations. It should also be noted that the administrator of a company appointed under Part II of the Insolvency Act 1986[83] has, under section 14 (2) of that Act, power to remove any director of the company.

---

[76] [1970] AC 1099 at p.1106.
[77] See the lapsed Companies Bill 1973, clause 44 (1).
[78] See the speech of Lord Donovan in [1970] AC 1099 at pp. 1110–11.
[79] As to which see 11.14.1, above.
[80] Section 304.
[81] See 13.4, above.
[82] Section 303 (3) and (4).
[83] See Chapter 17.

13.8 Alternate directors

It is a fairly common practice for the articles to provide for the representation of a director who will be absent from board meetings for a lengthy period by enabling him to appoint an 'alternate' or 'substitute' director. Such an appointment is not an 'assignment' of the office under section 308 of the Companies Act 1985, because the appointing director continues in office. Under the model form in Table A (articles 65 to 69), an alternate director is regarded as a director 'for all purposes'.

13.9 Directors' meetings

Directors must obviously meet as a board to transact the business vested in them by the Companies Act or the articles of association. The common law has developed a number of rules, in many cases drawing on common-form articles, relating to the conduct of and jurisdiction of directors' meetings. These are examined in the following sections.

13.9.1 Quorum

The presence of all the directors at a board meeting is not required if, as is usually the case (e.g. article 89 of Table A), the articles provide that a specified number of directors shall form a quorum. If a quorum is not so prescribed, a majority of the board is required to attend,[84] unless a quorum can be established by the practice of the board.[85] If the articles so provide, questions may be decided by a majority of the directors present; but where such provision is made and controlling powers are vested in joint governing directors, those powers must be exercised by all of them.[86] If there is a clause in the articles stating that the continuing directors may act notwithstanding vacancies, a number less than the minimum number of directors prescribed by the articles is capable of binding the company.[87] Article 90 in Table A so provides, but with the qualification that if the number of directors is below that fixed as the quorum, the continuing directors may act only for the purpose of filling vacancies or of summoning a general meeting. In reckoning a quorum, directors not entitled to vote (e.g. as being interested in the contract under discussion) must not be counted.[88]

13.9.2 Notice

Notice of the meeting must be given to all the directors, for business done at a meeting of which some directors had no notice is invalid even though the latter are in a minority, and a director has no power to waive his right to notice,[89] but if a director is abroad and out of reach of notices, a meeting held without notice to him is valid.[90] There is a conflict of judicial opinion as to whether it is necessary to give notice of a board meeting to a director who, under the articles, has no vote thereat: for example an ordinary director, when all

---

[84] *York Tramways Co. v. Willows* (1882) 8 QBD 685.

[85] *Re Regent's Canal Ironworks* [1867] WN 79; *Lyster's Case* (1867) LR 4 Eq. 233.

[86] *Perrott & Perrott Ltd v Stephenson* [1934] Ch 171. But see *Bersel Manufacturing Co. v Berry Ltd* [1968] 2 All ER 552 (HL) where a husband and wife were the two permanent life directors who had the power under the articles to terminate the directorship of the ordinary directors. It was held, on the construction of the article in question, that the power was exercisable by the husband after the wife's death.

[87] *Re Scottish Petroleum Co.* (1883) 23 Ch D 413 (CA).

[88] *Yuill v Greymouth-Point Elizabeth Rly* [1904] 1 Ch 32; *Victors v Lingard* [1927] 1 Ch 323; *Re Cleadon Trust* [1939] Ch 286 (CA). See further 14.8, below, as to this and the provisions of Table A, article 94 and 95.

[89] *Re Portuguese Copper Mines* (1889) 42 Ch D 160 (CA); *Young v Ladies Imperial Club* [1920] 2 KB 523 (CA).

[90] *Halifax Sugar Refining Co. Ltd v Franklyn* (1890) 59 LJ Ch 591.

the powers of the directors are vested in permanent directors.[91] The notice may be a very short one; even a few minutes' notice will suffice if the director can attend, and where he objects to the shortness of the notice he should make his objection at once, or it will not prevail.[92] A verbal notice is also sufficient.[93] It is not necessary that the notice should state what business is to be transacted, unless the articles require that certain business shall only be transacted at a meeting specially convened for that purpose, in which case the notice must sufficiently indicate the business to be considered.[94] A casual meeting of the two directors, even at the company's office, cannot be converted into a board meeting if one of them denies that it is a board meeting and has not received notice calling such a meeting.[95]

Articles (e.g. article 88 of Table A) usually declare that the chairman shall have a casting vote in case of the directors being equally divided upon any question.[96]

13.10 The validity of directors' acts

If the articles authorise it, but not otherwise,[97] the board may delegate any of its powers to a committee, which may consist even of a single director,[98] but the board does not by making such delegation lose its power to act in the matter,[99] and the board cannot deprive itself of power to control the company's business.[100] Each director has not alone power to bind the company unless he has had this power specially delegated to him. By section 284 of the Companies Act 1985 a provision requiring or authorising a thing to be done by or to a director and the secretary is not satisfied by its being done by or to the same person acting both as director and as, or in place of, the secretary.

Articles (e.g. Table A, article 93) often provide that a resolution in writing signed by all or a majority of the directors shall have the same effect as a resolution passed at a meeting of the board. In the absence of such a provision the directors cannot act without meeting.[101]

The directors must not exclude any of their body from their meetings, and unless the company has by resolution declared that it does not desire a director to act,[102] an excluded director can obtain an injunction restraining his continued exclusion.[103] However, it is possible for the articles to confer a power to remove a director on the board.

The directors are the proper persons to perform any act in the name of the company,

---

[91] *John Shaw & Sons (Salford) v Shaw* [1935] 2 KB 113; *per* Greer LJ at p.133 and *per* Slesser LJ at pp.138–41 (CA).

[92] *Browne v La Trinidad* (1888) 37 Ch D 1 at p.9 (CA).

[93] *La Compagnie de Mayville v Whitley* [1896] 1 Ch 788 (CA).

[94] *Young v Ladies' Imperial Club* [1920] 2 KB 523 (CA).

[95] *Barron v Potter* [1914] 1 Ch 895.

[96] But this does not validate the casting vote of an improperly appointed chairman: *Clark v Workman* [1920] IR. R. 107.

[97] *Howard's Case* (1886) 1 Ch App. 561.

[98] *Re Taurine Co.* (1884) 25 Ch D 118 (CA). See Table A, article 72.

[99] *Huth v Clarke* (1890) 25 QBD 391.

[100] *Horn v Faulder & Co.* (1908) 99 LT 524.

[101] *D'Arcy v Tamar Hill Rly Co.* (1867) LR 2 Ex. 158; *Re Haycraft Gold Reduction Co.* [1900] 2 Ch 230; *Re Homer District Gold Mines* (1888) 39 Ch D 546 (CA).

[102] *Bainbridge v Smith* (1889) 41 Ch D 462 at p.474 (CA); *Harben v Phillips* (1883) 23 Ch D 14 at p.40 (CA).

[103] *Pullbrook v Richmond Consolidated Mining Co.* (1878) 9 Ch D 610. *Hayes v Bristol Plant Hire Ltd* [1957] 1 WLR 499.

and in particular to commence actions in the name of the company, to make contracts, and to affix the seal of the company to deeds.

13.11 The relationship between board and general meeting

The question whether the company in general meeting has any power to direct the directors in their management of the company's business is one that has been much discussed over the years. The answer depends upon the construction of the appropriate article of association vesting powers of management in the directors.[104] It has long been established that in principle it is perfectly acceptable for the board to have powers quite free from interference by the shareholders. Thus the court has refused to allow the general meeting to take the conduct of the business out of the directors' hands or to compel them to adopt a particular line of action, such as sealing a draft deed or effecting a sale of the company's property[105] or discontinuing legal proceedings commenced in the name of the company on the instructions of the board[106] or to interfere in the exercise of the directors' power to appoint a managing director.[107] In most of these cases, the article in question was based on the standard article in Table A, which in the 1948 Act was article 80, and this was generally thought to permit interference only by special resolution. However, the wording of articles based on article 80 was not free from difficulty[108], one particularly contentious area concerning the question of the use of the company's name in litigation.[109]

While companies registered prior to 1 July 1985 adopting this part of Table A will continue to have article 80 as their regulation in this respect, unless and until they amend their articles appropriately, the matter has been clarified in respect of companies adopting Table A to the 1985 Act.[110] Article 70 of this Table A makes it clear that, subject to the provisions of the Act and to any special provisions in a company's memorandum or articles, the general meeting can interfere only by 'any directions given by special

---

[104] There is no doubt in law that this 'contract-based' view is the correct one. Whether it should be or not is another matter.

[105] *Automatic Self-Cleansing Filter Co. v Cunninghame* [1906] 2 Ch 34 (CA); *Gramophone and Typewriter v Stanley* [1908] 2 KB 89 at p.105 (CA); *Salmon v Quin & Axtens Ltd* [1906] AC 442 (HL).

[106] *John Shaw & Sons (Salford) Ltd v Shaw* [1935] 2 KB 113 (CA); *Scott v Scott* [1943] 1 All ER 582 (CA); compare *Marshall's Valve Gear Co. v Manning, Wardle & Co.* [1909] 1 Ch 267, which may be explained as authorising the shareholders to commence proceedings when the board refuses to do so.

[107] *Thomas Logan v Davis* (1911) 104 LT 914, 105 LT 419.

[108] It conferred on the directors 'all such powers of the company as are not by [the legislation] or by these regulations, required to be exercised by the company in general meeting, subject, nevertheless, to any of these regulations, to the provisions of the [legislation] and to *such regulations, being not inconsistent with the aforesaid regulations or provisions, as may be prescribed by the company in general meeting*' (emphasis added). The judicial construction put on the word 'regulations' was that throughout article 80 it meant 'articles' or 'new or amended articles', but this made the passage in italics somewhat tautologous and led certain writers to take a different view as to its meaning: see, especially, Goldberg, 33 MLR 177 (1970), and Sullivan, 93 LQR 569 (1977). In *Breckland Group Holdings Ltd v London & Suffolk Properties Ltd* (1988) 4 BCC 542, Harman J ignored these difficulties.

[109] In *Marshall's Valve Gear Co. v Manning, Wardle & Co.* [1909] 1 Ch 267, it was held that the majority shareholder had the right to commence proceedings in the company's name, even where general management powers were vested in the directors. While this right has been confirmed in situations of deadlock or where there are no directors (see *Alexander Ward v Samyang Navigation Co.*, below, and *Re Argentum Reductions (UK) Ltd* [1975] 1 WLR 191), it was totally swept aside in the *Breckland Group Holdings* case, above. See further Wedderburn (1976) 39 MLR 327 and (1989) 52 MLR 401.

[110] i.e. in the Companies (Tables A to F) Regulations 1985.

resolution' and further that no such direction (or alteration of the memorandum or articles) can operate retrospectively to validate any prior act of the directors.

However, if the directors are unable or unwilling to exercise the powers conferred upon them, whether by reason of there being no independent quorum or by reason of disputes among the directors, the company in general meeting can perform the duties which the directors fail to carry out.[111] In addition, the general meeting has wide powers to ratify an excess of power by directors, i.e. an act beyond the authority vested in the directors under the articles,[112] or to ratify or cure an abuse of power by directors, i.e. an act in breach of duty though not necessarily beyond the directors' powers.[113]

Further, the House of Lords has held that the absence of validly appointed directors does not prevent a company taking proceedings to recover its debts.[114] Lord Kilbrandon had this to say about an article similar to article 70 (and article 80 in the 1948 Table A) in respect of the management of the company's business:

> I think the article probably means no more than this, that the directors, and no one else, are responsible for the management of the company, except in the matters specifically allotted to the company in general meeting. This is a term of the contract between the shareholders and the company. But it does not mean that no act of management, such as instructing the company's solicitor, can validly be performed without the personal and explicit authority of the directors themselves.[115]

Article 70 of Table A is concerned with the board's powers of *management*. Thus it does not, for example, confer authority on a board to present a winding-up petition[116] or to apply to set aside an order restoring the company's name to the register.[117]

The court can appoint a receiver and manager where the company is in a condition in which there is no properly constituted governing body, or there is such dissension in the governing body that it is impossible to carry on the business with advantage to the parties interested. Such an appointment would only be made for a limited time, i.e. until a meeting of the company could be held and a governing body appointed.[118]

13.12 Minutes of directors' meetings

Minutes must be kept of all proceedings at every meeting of directors. Such minutes, when kept in a proper book[119] and signed by the chairman of that or the next succeeding meeting, are evidence of the proceedings. Where minutes have been made in accordance with the provisions of the section, then, until the contrary is proved, every such meeting is deemed to have been duly held and convened, and all proceedings to have been duly had, and all appointments of directors, managers, or liquidators shall be deemed to be valid.[120]

---

[111] *Barron v Potter* [1914] 1 Ch 895; *Foster v Foster* [1916] 1 Ch 532.

[112] *Irving v Union Bank of Australia* (1877) 2 App. Cas. 366.

[113] See 14.24.1, below, as to which breaches of duty are ratifiable.

[114] *Alexander Ward v Samyang Navigation Co.* [1975] 1 WLR 673.

[115] ibid., p.683.

[116] *Re Emmadart Ltd* [1979] Ch 540.

[117] *Re Regent Insulation Co. Ltd*, *The Times*, 5 November 1981.

[118] *Featherstone v Cooke* (1873) LR 16 Eq. 298.

[119] By section 722, a minute book may be kept either by making entries in bound books or by recording the matters in question in any other manner.

[120] Section 382.

The adoption of minutes at a subsequent meeting of directors does not make those taking part in such adoption responsible for the acts of the earlier meeting if such acts were complete before the minutes came up for consideration.[121]

13.13 A director's right to inspect company books

A director has the right to inspect the company's books either at a board meeting or elsewhere. This right extends both to the minutes of directors' meetings,[122] and to the company's accounting records,[123] but the court has a discretion as to whether or not to order an inspection which is conferred on a director not for his own advantage but to enable him to carry out his duties as a director.[124]

13.14 The officers of a company

For the purposes of the Companies Act 1985, 'officer' includes a director, manager or secretary.[125] The position of directors in general has already been discussed; the position of the other usual officers of a company will now be dealt with.[126] The terms of their employment depend upon their contract, whether written or verbal, with the company, though the position of a managing director may in some respects be governed by the articles.[127]

13.14.1 The manager or managing director

Most companies, even small private companies, are actually managed on a day-to-day basis by one or more people who will be described as 'managing director' or 'chief executive'. Perhaps surprisingly, the general law is that the directors cannot appoint one of themselves to an office of profit or delegate power to a managing director unless expressly empowered by the articles or by a resolution of the company.[128] It is therefore usual to insert in the articles power for the directors to appoint one or more of their body to be managing director or directors, and to pay him or them special remuneration, delegating to him or them such powers as are necessary.[129]

Modern articles, as exemplified by article 84 of Table A, allow the directors to appoint a managing director (and other executive directors) on such terms as they determine, and, by article 72, to delegate to such persons such of their powers and on such conditions as they consider desirable; such delegation may be altered or revoked. These articles do not, however, permit revocation of the appointment.[130] A managing or other executive

---

[121] *Re Lands Allotment Co.* [1894] 1 Ch 616 at p. 634 (CA).

[122] See *McCusker v McRae* 1966 SC 253. Note that the Scottish court held that the director was entitled to be accompanied by an adviser of his choice. English authorities (see below), which established the directors' right to inspect accounting records, do not discuss that point.

[123] *Burn v London and South Wales Coal Co.* [1890] WN 209.

[124] *Conway v Petronius Clothing co.* [1978] 1 WLR 72. Here an immediate order was refused because misconduct was alleged against the two plaintiff directors and a meeting to consider their removal was held.

[125] Section 744.

[126] The auditor may or may not be an 'officer'. As to him, see 12.22 above.

[127] A mere statement in the articles that someone shall be secretary, manager or other officer is not a contract with that person: *Eley v Positive Government Assurance Co.* (1876) 1 Ex. D 88 (CA); *Browne v La Trinidad* (1888) 37 Ch D 1 (CA); see 3.18 above.

[128] *Boschoek Proprietary Co. v Fuke* [1906] 1 Ch 148 at p. 159; *Nelson v James Nelson & Sons* [1914] 2 KB 770 at p.779 (CA).

[129] Such a power is conferred by Table A, articles 72 and 84.

[130] Compare article 107 of Table A to the Companies Act 1948.

director is not usually subject to retirement by rotation.[131] If a managing director is removed from his office of managing director, where the articles permit the directors to do this,[132] or from his directorship by the company in general meeting,[133] before the expiry of the term of his contract of service, the removal is valid, but he will have a claim to damages for breach of contract if he complied with his part of the bargain.[134]

There is very little case-law as to the nature of the relationship between the board and a managing or other executive director. In *Harold Holdsworth & Co. (Wakefield) Ltd v Caddies*,[135] the House of Lords held that the board of Holdsworth were entitled to direct Caddies to confine his attention to a subsidiary company. Under his contract of employment Caddies had been appointed a managing director of Holdsworth itself. The contract provided that he should perform the duties and exercise the powers in relation to the business of the company and the business of its existing subsidiaries 'which may from time to time be assigned to or vested in him by the board of directors of the company'. Up until the time when a dispute arose between Caddies and his fellow directors, he had managed Holdsworth itself and a subsidiary of it. The decision of the House of Lords (that Caddies could be so demoted without a breach of his contract of employment) turned on the particular wording of this contract. This conferred a discretion on the board as to the mode or extent of his employment in managing the company and any of its subsidiaries. Thus under the more usual terms of employment of a managing director this option would not be available to the board without committing a breach of contract.[136]

Thus the exact status and powers of a managing director depend both upon the articles which confer a power on the board to appoint a managing director and upon the terms of the contract by which he is employed. Although he must be a director, his status as managing director derives from his appointment by the board to this office. He is thus both a director and, as managing director, an employee of the company.[137]

13.14.2 *The secretary*

The secretary is the other important officer of a company. Every company must have a secretary, and a sole director of a company, or a corporation the sole director of which is

---

[131] See article 84 of the modern Table A. If the articles do not so provide, a managing director not reappointed by the general meeting will lose his office even though expressed to be appointed for a term of years: *Bluett v Stutchbury's* (1908) 24 TLR 469 (CA).

[132] As under article 107 of the 1948 Table A.

[133] Under section 303; see 13.7, above.

[134] *Nelson v James Nelson & Sons* [1914] 2 KB 770 (CA); see 13.4, above. An appointment for an indeterminate period may be determined, however, at any time, without the company being liable for breach of contract: *Foster v Foster* [1916] 1 Ch 532.

[135] [1955] 1 WLR 352 (HL).

[136] See also *Yetton v Eastwoods Froy* [1967] 1 WLR 104, where a managing director was dismissed and then offered the position of assistant managing director at the same salary; he was held entitled to refuse the offer because of the loss of status involved.

[137] See *Anderson v James Sutherland (Peterhead) Ltd* 1941 SC 203, where Lord Carmont relied upon *Southern Foundries Ltd v Shirlaw* [1940] AC 701 (HL) and *Fowler v Commercial Timber Co.* [1903] 3 KB 1. See also *Trussed Steel Concrete v Green* [1946] Ch 115; *Lee v Lees Air Farming Ltd* [1961] AC 12 (PC); *Boulting v A.C.T.A.T.* [1963] QB 600 (CA). Although a managing director was held (*Re Newspaper Proprietary Syndicate Ltd* [1990] 2 Ch 349) not to be a 'clerk' or 'servant' when these were the relevant persons described as preferential creditors on a winding-up in the former legislation (consolidated in Schedule 19 of the Companies Act 1985), the appropriate legislation now (Schedule 6, para. 9 of the Insolvency Act 1986) refers simply to 'employee' and there seems no reason why this should not include a managing director. As to preferential debts, see 17.55.1 below.

a sole director of a company, may not be the secretary of the company.[138] A provision requiring or authorising anything to be done by or to a director and the secretary is not satisfied by being done by or to the same person acting both as director and as, or in the place of, the secretary.[139] However, if at any time the office of secretary is vacant, or there is no secretary capable of acting, his functions may be carried out by any assistant or deputy secretary or, if there is no such, by an officer duly authorised by the directors.

The importance of the office of secretary is recognized by the fact that secretaries of public companies must since 1980 have been qualified. Under section 286, it is the duty of the directors of a public company, when appointing the secretary, to take all reasonable steps to secure that he is a person who appears to them to have the requisite knowledge and experience to discharge the functions of secretary, and such a person must have one of several possible types of experience or professional qualification. The professional qualifications include chartered secretaryship, accountancy and the legal profession. Sufficient experience is provided by the person having been secretary (or assistant or deputy secretary) of the company on 22 December 1980, by his having been secretary of a public company for at least three of the previous five years or, by virtue of his holding or having held any other position, or his being a member of any other body, by his appearing to the directors capable of discharging the function of secretary.[140]

Case-law has also recognised the important position that the secretary holds in respect of a company's administrative affairs.[141] He is wholly or partly responsible for the accuracy of documents lodged with the Registrar, and if the company defaults in this respect, the liability to a fine is almost invariably incurred by the secretary. He is the agent through whom the clerical work of the company is done. He must obey the orders of the directors and give effect to their resolutions by issuing notices, sending circulars, writing letters, etc. He will also prepare the agenda for directors' meetings and general meetings, and usually write up the minutes, either from his own notes of from those of the chairman.[142]

13.15 Disqualification and other sanctions against miscreant directors and others involved in company management

Legislation contains various provisions under which directors and others may be disqualified from office or subjected to personal liability for the debts of their companies or under which other forms of sanction may be imposed.[143] These are essentially aimed at situations where the privileges of corporate personality and limited liability have been abused. The provisions are a mixture of ones which have existed for some years and ones

---

[138] Section 283. Particulars of the secretary must be notified to the Registrar: see 13.19, below.

[139] Section 284. 'Provision' is not expressed to be limited to 'statutory provision', and the enactment presumably applies to provisions in the articles, e.g. an article requiring the presence and signature of a director and the secretary for the affixing of the seal.

[140] The date is the date when the previous section (in the 1980 Act) came into force. The last qualification by experience is rather odd, since it seems to negate the general purpose of section 286.

[141] *Panorama Developments (Guildford) Ltd v Fidelis Furnishing Fabrics Ltd* [1971] 2 QB 711 (CA); the company was held liable to pay car hire charges incurred by the secretary in the company's name, but where the cars were fraudulently used by the secretary for his own pleasure, on the ground that the hiring fell within the apparent authority of a company secretary; see 4.29, above.

[142] For more detail as to the secretary's functions, see *Gore-Browne on Companies* (Jordans, 44th edn, loose-leaf), 26.10.

[143] In addition to those reviewed here, see also 3.7, above.

which were introduced relatively recently.[144] Others were first introduced by the Insolvency Act 1985.[145] They are now all consolidated in the Company Directors Disqualification Act 1986 and the Insolvency Act 1986.

13.16 Disqualification of directors and others

The powers of the court to make disqualification orders[146] are contained in the Company Directors Disqualification Act and the statutory references in this and the following sections are to that Act.[147]

13.16.1 The meaning of disqualification

'Disqualification order' is defined as follows.[148] It is an order that a person shall not, without leave of the court, be a director of a company, or a liquidator or administrator of a company, or a receiver or manager of a company's property or, in any way, whether directly or indirectly, be concerned or take part in the promotion, formation or management of a company, for a specified period beginning with the date of the order. Being concerned or taking part in management has been widely construed to cover the position of management consultant or the giving of advice on the financial management and reconstruction of a company.[149]

The various sections provide for maximum penalties of five years' disqualification in respect of persistent default (see below) and in all disqualifications by courts of summary jurisdiction, and of fifteen years in any other case. 'Tariffs' have been established, particulary for disqualification on the ground of unfitness, so that there are three 'brackets': ten or more years for serious cases, six to ten years for middling cases, and two to five years for minor cases.[150] The period of any subsequent disqualification imposed against a person already subject to an order runs concurrently with the existing period.[151] An order may be made on grounds which are or include matters other than criminal convictions, notwithstanding that the person in question may be criminally liable in respect of those matters.[152] There are heavy penalties for breach of a disqualification order.[153]

---

[144] In the Companies Acts of 1976 and 1981. For a useful survey, see Leigh (1986) 7 Co. Law 179.

[145] There was a considerable amount of controversy surrounding these. Originally, the Government introduced provisions providing for the automatic disqualification of directors of insolvent companies, with the onus on such directors to prove to the court reason why they should not be disqualified. These were based on, but not identical to, proposals recommended by the Review Committee on Insolvency Law and Practice (the Cork Committee), Cmnd 8558 (1982), Chapter 45. Opposition from such influential bodies as the CBI and the Institute of Directors, as well as in Parliament, led to the dropping of these provisions and their replacement by the provision relating to 'unfitness' described in 13.16.3, below.

[146] As to the nature of disqualification proceedings regarding admissible evidence, the applicability of natural justice, etc., see *Re Churchill Hotel (Plymouth) Ltd* [1988] BCLC 341; *Re Rex Williams Leisure plc* [1993] BCLC 568; *Re Polly Peck International plc* [1993] BCLC 886; *Re Moonbeam Cards Ltd* [1993] BCLC 1099; *Re Polly Peck International plc* [1994] BCC 15.

[147] See generally Dine (1991) 12 Co. Law 6, [1994] JBL 325.

[148] Section 1.

[149] *R v Campbell* [1984] BCLC 83.

[150] See e.g. *Re Sevenoaks Stationers (Retail) Ltd* [1991] BCLC 325 and the other cases referred to in *Gore-Browne on Companies* (Jordans, 44th edn, loose-leaf), 25.7.4.

[151] Section 1 (3).

[152] Section 1 (4).

[153] Section 13.

13.16.2 Application for disqualification

An application to a court with jurisdiction to wind up companies to obtain a disqualification order under sections 2 to 5 may be made by the Secretary of State or the Official Receiver, or the liquidator or any past or present member or creditor of any company in relation to which the person in question has committed or is alleged to have committed an offence or default.[154] In respect of disqualification on the ground of unfitness, only the Secretary of State, or the Official Receiver acting under the direction of the Secretary of State, has *locus standi* to apply.[155]

13.16.3 Grounds for disqualification

The grounds for disqualifying a person from acting as a director, etc., are as follows:

(1) *Conviction of an offence.* The court can disqualify a person convicted of an indictable offence (whether on indictment or summarily) in connection with the promotion, formation, management or liquidation of a company or with the receivership or management of a company's property.[156] This ground is very wide as there is no requirement that the offence be committed in the course of the internal management of a company's affairs. So, for example, convictions for theft or other offences of dishonesty against outsiders are sufficient.[157]

(2) *Persistent default.* Disqualification can be imposed if it appears to the court that a person has been 'persistently in default' in relation to provisions of the companies legislation requiring any return, account or other document to be filed with, delivered or sent, or notice of any matter to be given, to the Registrar.[158] There is a presumption of persistent default where the person has been convicted of relevant offences or default orders have been made against him on three or more occasions. Otherwise, there is no need to show culpable disregard, merely a need to show some degree of continuance or repetition.[159] Under section 5, disqualification on this ground can be imposed by a magistrates' court (in England and Wales) at the same time as a person is convicted of an offence relevant to the filing of returns etc.

(3) *Fraud.* The court can disqualify if, in the course of winding up a company, it appears that a person

    (a) has been guilty of an offence for which he is liable (whether or not he has been convicted) under section 458 of the Companies Act 1985, that is the offence of fraudulent trading;[160] or

    (b) has otherwise been guilty, while an officer or liquidator of the company, of any fraud in relation to the company or of any breach of his duty as such officer, liquidator, receiver or manager.[161]

---

[154] Section 16; the other procedural aspects are also prescribed in this section and section 17. The courts are prepared to be flexible regarding these aspects where feasible; see e.g. the treatment of the 'requirement' for ten days' notice of an application for a disqualification order by the Court of Appeal in *Secretary of State for Trade and Industry v Langridge* [1991] BCLC 543.

[155] Section 7 (1).

[156] Section 2.

[157] *R v Corbin* (1984) 6 Cr. App. R (S) 17, see 6 Co. Law 183 (1985); *R v Austen*, above, see 7 Co. Law 68 (1986). See also *R v Georgiou* (1988) 4 BCC 322 (CA); *R v Goodman* [1992] BCC 625.

[158] Section 3.

[159] *Re Arctic Engineering Ltd* [1986] BCLC 253; see 7 Co. Law 27 (1986).

[160] See 13.17.1 below.

[161] Section 4.

The reference to any breach of duty in (b) above obviously makes this potentially a very wide ground for disqualification.

(4) *Unfitness.* This ground for disqualification, and the next, are the most recent and this is potentially the broadest of all. It arises under sections 6 to 9 and its introduction (in the Insolvency Act 1985) gave rise to considerable controversy.[162] Because of its importance, it is dealt with separately in the next section.

(5) *Wrongful and fraudulent trading.* The concepts of wrongful and fraudulent trading are examined below, but it is appropriate to note at this stage that any person found liable under the relevant provision to contribute to a company's assets may also be disqualified under section 10.

13.16.4 Disqualification for unfitness

As has already been pointed out, only the Secretary of State (or the Official Receiver in most cases)[163] can apply for disqualification on the ground of unfitness, and he can do so if he thinks that 'it is expedient in the public interest,'[164] but liquidators and others[165] are under a duty to report what can be described as suspected cases of unfitness to the Secretary of State, and the latter (and the Official Receiver) can require those persons to produce information and documents which he 'may reasonably require for the purpose of determining whether to exercise, or of exercising, any function of his' under the section.[166] Except with the leave of the court,[167] an application under section 6 may not be made more than two years after the company in question becomes insolvent.[168]

Section 6 allows the court to disqualify only a director or shadow director[169] for unfitness, and is thus narrower in this respect than the other disqualification provisions. The court must be satisfied of two things: (a) that the person in question is or has been a director of a company which has at any time become insolvent[170] (whether while he was a director or subsequently); and (b) that his conduct as a director of that company (either taken alone or taken together with his conduct as a director of any other company or companies)[171] makes him unfit to be concerned in the management of a company.[172]

---

[162] See footnote 145, above.

[163] Only the Secretary of State can act in respect of a director of a company in voluntary liquidation; section 7 (1); see *Re Probe Data Systems Ltd* [1989] BCLC 561.

[164] Section 7 (1).

[165] The Official Receiver in respect of a company being wound up by the court, the liquidator (company being otherwise wound up), the administrator (company in administration) and the receiver (company in receivership).

[166] Section 7 (4).

[167] See further *Re Tasbian Ltd (No. 3)* [1991] BCLC 792; *Re Copecrest Ltd* [1993] BCC 844; *Re Polly Peck International plc, Secretary of State for Trade and Industry v Ellis (No. 2)* [1993] BCC 890.

[168] Insolvency is widely defined for these purposes as when either (a) a company goes into liquidation at a time when its liabilities and the expenses of winding up exceed its assets, (b) an administration order (not an interim administration order: *Secretary of State for Trade and Industry v Palmer* [1993] BCC 650) is made in relation to the company or (c) an administrative receiver of the company is appointed: section 6 (2). The period runs from when the first one of these events occurs: *Re Tasbian Ltd (No. 1)* [1991] BCLC 54 (CA).

[169] As to the meaning of this, see 14.2, below.

[170] As to the meaning of insolvency, see footnote 168, above.

[171] There is no territorial limit on the conduct that may be considered: *Re Seagull Manufacturing Co. Ltd (No. 2)* [1993] BCC 833.

[172] Section 6 (1). References to conduct include, where a company has become insolvent, references to a person's conduct in relation to any matter connected with or arising out of the insolvency of that company: section 6 (2).

Under section 8, an application for disqualification for unfitness may be made by the Secretary of State from a different route, namely where he thinks it expedient to apply following an inspection under the provisions of the Companies Act 1985.[173]

Obviously the concept of 'unfitness' is central to applications under both sections 6 and 8. Section 9 directs the court to determine the question by reference to the matters listed in Schedule 1. These matters are divided into those applicable in all cases, and those applicable where the company has become insolvent. The first head comprises misfeasance or breach of duty as a director, the responsibility of the director for a transaction liable to be set aside as a fraud on creditors,[174] and the extent of his responsibility for any breaches of many of the filing requirements of the Companies Act 1985. The second includes the extent of the directors' responsibility 'for the causes of the company becoming insolvent' and for failing to supply paid-for goods or services, the extent of his responsibility for any voidable preference[175] or failure to summon a creditors' meeting in a creditors' voluntary winding-up[176] and any failure to comply with any obligations to deliver statements of affairs to the liquidator, administrator or receiver.[177]

The extent to which these provisions are successful in curbing the abuses at which they are directed depends upon a number of factors. These include the willingness of insolvency practitioners to report suspected cases, made more likely by their obligation to make appropriate returns to the Department of Trade and Industry and the willingness of the DTI to pursue individual cases. Also of crucial importance is the attitude of the court when faced with applications for disqualification. We now have a large volume of case-law on the unfitness provisions, which is summarised in the following paragraph.

Basically, what must be shown to justify disqualification is conduct that is dishonest, is in breach of standards of commercial morality or is grossly incompetent, such as to convince the court that it would be a danger to the public to allow the person in question to continue to be involved in the management of companies.[178] On the other hand, commercial misjudgment by itself does not constitute unfitness. What constitutes dishonesty does not need to be considered further here. It is clear that commercial morality and competence are separate matters, so that a director can be shown to have been grossly incompetent even if his conduct was 'commercially moral.' Even if, for example, it is regarded as moral to use money owed to the Crown in respect of taxes (especially PAYE, VAT and national insurance) to finance the company's trading activities,[179] and the director in question knows or ought to know what is happening, this can still be sufficiently incompetent.[180] So also, incompetence is evidenced by failure to file accounts

---

[173] Sections 437 and 447 or 448; see Part 3 of Chapter 15.

[174] Under Part XVI of the Insolvency Act 1986; see 17.59 *et seq.*, below.

[175] Under Insolvency Act 1986, sections 127, 238 or 241.

[176] ibid., section 98.

[177] ibid., sections 22, 47, 66, 99, 131, 234, or 235.

[178] This was first clearly set out by Hoffmann J in *Re Dawson Print Group Ltd* [1987] BCLC 601. Other leading cases include *Re Stanford Services Ltd* [1987] BCLC 607; *Re Lo-Line Electric Motors Ltd* [1988] Ch 477; *Re Bath Glass Ltd* [1988] BCLC 329; *Re Churchill Hotel (Plymouth) Ltd* [1988] BCLC 341; *Re Majestic Recording Studios* [1989] BCLC 1; *Re McNulty's Interchange Ltd* [1989] BCLC 709; *Re C U Fittings* [1989] BCLC 556; *Re Ipcon Fashions Ltd* (1989) 5 BCC 773; *Re Cladrose Ltd* [1990] BCLC 204 and *Re ECM Europe Electronics* [1991] BCLC 268.

[179] It will not always be such.

[180] The use of Crown money to continue trading has on the balance of the cases been viewed as a much more serious matter than the failure to pay ordinary creditors.

and returns as required by the Companies Act 1985, pressure of work being no excuse.[181] A clear illustration of conduct contrary to commercial morality is provided by *Re Ipcon Fashions Ltd*.[182] The director had carried on business in the clothing trade for fifteen years through a succession of companies which had become insolvent. In the four months before Ipcon Fashions was wound up, knowing it was insolvent, he abandoned it to its fate and transferred the business to a new company, while still incurring liabilities to suppliers and paying himself and his wife salaries without accounting for tax.

The court's refusal to regard mere incompetence as revealing unfitness has been criticised, on the ground that the courts seem to view the policy behind section 6 as punitive rather than as protecting the public against incompetent directors.[183] Judicial reluctance to disqualify without blameworthiness may be influenced by the mandatory nature of the duty under section 6,[184] and it has been observed on a number of occasions that the court must use its jurisdiction to protect the public against those who abuse limited liability, but must be careful not to stultify all enterprise. It may not be easy to resolve what exactly is or should be the dominant purpose of disqualification, and consideration of this cannot be divorced from looking at the impact of other measures such as the wrongful trading provision.[185] What cannot be denied is that the law seems much more effective than it used to be at penalising rogue directors and thus protecting the public from them.

13.16.5 Register of disqualification orders

Under section 18 and regulations made thereunder,[186] the Secretary of State maintains a register of disqualification orders on the basis of information which it is the duty of the officers of the courts making the orders to supply. Entries must be deleted on the expiry of any order. The register is open to public inspection on the payment of a fee of 5p.

13.17 Liability of directors (and others) to contribute to the assets or for the debts of their companies

There are now three provisions under which directors and, in certain cases, others may be made liable by the court in effect for the debts of their companies. A person may be made liable for fraudulent trading, for wrongful trading or for acting while disqualified. All these situations provide for statutory exceptions to the principle of the separate legal personality of a company from its members.[187]

13.17.1 Fraudulent trading

Section 213 of the Insolvency Act 1986 provides that if in the course of winding up a company it appears that any business of the company has been carried on with intent to defraud creditors of the company or creditors of any other person, or for any fraudulent

---

[181] See in particular *Re Churchill Hotel (Plymouth) Ltd*, above, and *Re Cladrose Ltd*, above, referring to Schedule 1 which, as indicated above, directs the court to have regard to the extent of a director's responsibility for a failure to comply with a duty.

[182] Above. See also on the 'Phoenix syndrome', *Re Travel Mondial (UK) Ltd* [1991] BCC 224; *Re Swift 736 Ltd* [1992] BCC 93; *Re Linvale Ltd* [1993] BCLC 654.

[183] Finch (1990) 53 MLR 385.

[184] In contrast to its predecessor, section 300 of the Companies Act 1985, which afforded a discretion.

[185] See 13.17.2, below.

[186] The Companies (Disqualification Orders) Regulations 1985 (SI 1985 No. 829).

[187] See 1.9, above.

purpose, the court, on the application of the liquidator, may declare that any persons who were knowingly parties to the carrying on of the business in that manner are to be liable to make such contributions (if any) to the company's assets as the court thinks proper. This is the provision which has existed the longest, and it should be noted that it is also, under section 458 of the Companies Act 1985, a criminal offence to trade fraudulently, an offence which can be prosecuted whether or not the company is being wound up.[188]

Despite the propounding of a somewhat looser test in an early case on the predecessor to section 213[189] it is clear that the words 'defraud' and 'fraudulent purpose' connote 'real dishonesty involving, according to current notions of fair trading among commercial men at the present day, real moral blame.'[190] It is sufficient if directors allow the company to incur credit at a time when it is clear that the company will never be able to pay its creditors. It may be sufficient if they so allow it at a time when they know the company is unable to meet all its liabilities as they fall due.[191]

It does not matter for the purpose of the section that only one creditor is defrauded and by a single transaction, if it is shown that the transaction can properly be described as a fraud on the creditor perpetrated in the course of carrying on business.[192] The phrase 'carrying on business' is not necessarily synonymous with actively carrying on trade. The collection in and distribution of assets in payment of debts can constitute a carrying on of business. However, where the only allegation is that a company or its officers preferred one or more creditors over others, that cannot constitute fraud within the meaning of the section.[193]

The expression 'parties to' in section 213 involves some positive step. Mere omission by a company secretary to give certain advice to the directors was held not to render the secretary liable under the section,[194] though this is not to say that a secretary who does more than the duties appropriate to his office might not be liable, and it is clear that given the necessary evidence, a creditor[195] or a parent company could fall within the expression.[196] In this respect, section 213 contrasts with the wrongful trading provision, discussed next, under which only directors and shadow directors can be found liable.

Under section 215 (2), the court, on making a declaration, may also provide that the liability of a person is to be a charge on any debt or obligation due from the company to him, or on any mortgage or charge on any assets of the company held by or vested in him,

---

[188] Note that until the amendment of the fraudulent trading provision by the Insolvency Act 1985, liability under the section was 'for all or any of the debts or other liabilities of the company', and that the official receiver and any creditor or contributory could make application. The amendments were to bring what is now section 213 into line with the wrongful trading provision, discussed below.

[189] *Re William C. Leitch Bros.* [1932] 2 Ch 71.

[190] *Per* Maugham J in *Re Patrick and Lyon* [1933] Ch 786. The need to show dishonesty was more recently stressed in *R v Cox and Hedges* (1982) 75 Crim. App. R 291 and *Re Augustus Barnett & Son Ltd* [1986] BCLC 170. See also *Re L Todd Swanscombe Ltd* [1990] BCLC 454. The dishonesty involved in fraudulent trading may justify an order which includes a punitive element: *Re a Company* [1990] BCC 526.

[191] *R v Grantham* [1984] 3 All ER 166 (CA), disapproving the decision to the contrary in *Re White and Osmond (Parkstone) Ltd*, unreported, 30 June 1960. See also *R v Lockwood* (1986) 2 BCC 99, 333 (CA).

[192] *Re Gerald Cooper Chemicals Ltd* [1978] 1 Ch 262. It does not matter that the creditor is not owed a present debt at the time of the fraud: *R v Kemp* [1988] BCLC 217 (CA).

[193] *Re Sarflax Ltd* [1979] 1 Ch 529.

[194] *Re Maidstone Building Ltd* [1971] 1 WLR 1085.

[195] *Re Sarflax*, above.

[196] Note that by section 215 (4), if a creditor is found liable, his debt can be deferred to rank for payment after all the other debts owed by the company.

or any company or person on his behalf. It can from time to time make such further orders as may be necessary to enforce any such charge. By section 215 (5), the section applies notwithstanding that the person concerned may be criminally liable in respect of the matters on the ground of which a declaration is made.

13.17.2 *Wrongful trading*

Section 214 of the Insolvency Act 1986 (first introduced as section 15 of the Insolvency Act 1985) was enacted, pursuant to the recommendations of the Review Committee on Insolvency Law and Practice,[197] to eliminate the need to prove fraud, under the fraudulent trading provision just described, in order to make someone contribute to the assets of an insolvent company in liquidation. It is an alternative to alleging fraudulent trading under section 213.[198] It should be noted though, that the section imposes liability for ommissions and goes beyond the examples given by the Review Committee regarding continuing to trade while insolvent.

Application under section 214 may only be made, as now in respect of section 213,[199] by the liquidator of a company, and only in respect of a person who is or has been a director or shadow director[200] of the company. The court may declare that person liable to make such contribution (if any) to the company's assets as it thinks fit if:

(1) the company has gone into insolvent liquidation,[201]
(2) at some time before the commencement of the winding-up, that person knew or ought to have concluded that there was no reasonable prospect that the company would avoid going into insolvent liquidation; and
(3) that person was a director (or shadow director) of the company at that time.

However, the court must not make a declaration in relation to any person if satisfied that, after he first realised the likelihood of insolvent liquidation, i.e. the time in (2) above, he took every step with a view to minimising the potential loss to the company's creditors as (assuming him to have known that there was no reasonable prospect that the company would avoid going into insolvent liquidation) he ought to have taken.[202] In respect of this point and (2) above, the facts which a director of a company ought to know or ascertain, the conclusions which he ought to reach and the steps which he ought to take are those which would be known or ascertained, or reached or taken, by a reasonably diligent person having both (a) the general knowledge, skill and experience that may reasonably be expected of a person carrying out the same functions as are carried out by that director in relation to the company, and (b) the general knowledge, skill and experience which that director has.[203]

The subjective criterion will work against, rather than in favour of, the director; the function of (b) is to catch a director who fails to live up to his own standards when those are higher than would usually be expected, having regard to his functions within the

---

[197] 1982 Cmnd 8558, paras. 1758–60 and Chapter 44.
[198] See section 214 (8).
[199] See footnote 188, above.
[200] As to shadow directors, see 14.2.
[201] i.e. its assets are insufficient to pay its liabilities and the expenses of winding up: section 214 (6).
[202] Section 214 (3). For an argument that the burden of proof in this aspect continues to lie on the liquidator, see *Gore-Browne on Companies* (Jordans, 44th edn, loose-leaf), 35.4.2.
[203] Section 214 (4).

company. Conversely, (a) will catch those who simply fail to match the standards of performance 'reasonably expected' of directors having similar functions. In particular cases, the scope of a director's 'functions in relation to the company' will be of decisive importance. A director may be an executive or non-executive director, full-time or part-time; he may be elected for his financial acumen or business experience, for his knowledge of particular products or services, or to provide, for example, technical expertise.[204] All these are matters which may be relevant in determining what a particular director's 'functions' are, although it will also be necessary to examine the 'functions' which are actually conferred upon him. This is made clear by section 214 (5), which provides (as might well have been implied) that a director's functions include those 'which he does not carry out but which have been entrusted to him'.[205]

The courts have recognised that the degree of competence found among directors will vary from company to company,[206] and the criterion of 'functions ... in relation to the company' may reflect this to some extent. The nature of the company must be relevant, since the standards reasonably to be expected of directors of a large public company cannot be the same as those of directors of an incorporated family business. The courts will no doubt recognise this, but cannot be expected to allow the argument to be pressed too far; the function of section 214 is to protect the company's creditors against neglect and incompetence, and even a small family concern will have creditors whose position, relatively speaking, may be as vulnerable to such neglect and incompetence on the board as that of the creditors of a much larger company. Even within a small company, therefore, there will inevitably be one or more directors whose functions include monitoring the company's solvency.[207] In any event, and in any company, there must come a point when a director ought to realise from information which he has received[208] that the company faces solvency problems, and it seems that the effect of section 214 must be that, at that point, his duties include the function of ascertaining the true position and, if necessary, taking action. There will, therefore, be a duty to supervise under section 214, and that duty may be broken either by individual directors, or by the whole body of directors in failing to institute or to operate an adequate monitoring process. In *Re Produce Marketing Consortium Ltd (No. 2)*[209] the company's accounts were prepared some considerable time after the statutory periods had expired. The court imputed to the directors the knowledge that timely delivery of the accounts would have given them. It is clear that directors will usually, if not invariably, be taken for the purposes of section 214 to have knowledge of the accounts, at the latest by the time when they should have been delivered. The director's position will be even weaker if the failure to prepare accounts is accompanied by obvious warning signs, such as a supplier's refusal to make further deliveries, or pressure for payment from the company's creditors. In *Re DKG Contractors*

---

[204] e.g. in a 'high-tech' company.

[205] The word 'entrusted' may raise nice questions. The court may feel itself free to disregard formal requirements as to delegation of functions and pay attention instead to the company's actual working arrangements. It may also feel that it may look at what actually occurred by way of 'entrusting' functions even if it was in complete disregard of the articles. This would mean, in all probability, that there might be liability both in a director to whom a function was in fact entrusted and in a director who should, strictly speaking, have been exercising that function. Further, it seems likely that it will be a 'function' of all directors to some extent to oversee the activities of the company, including those of other directors.

[206] *DHSS v Evans* [1985] 2 All ER 472.

[207] *Re DKG Contractors Ltd* [1990] BCC 903.

[208] Or ascertained or, indeed, ought to have ascertained: section 214 (4).

[209] [1989] BCLC 520.

Ltd[210] the company was a small works contractor managed by the two directors, a husband and wife team. The wife kept a 'black book' recording payments and invoices received, which was a basis on which proper accounts might have been prepared, but this was never done. It was held that, given the warning signs referred to above, the directors should have instituted some form of financial control. That would have revealed that there was no reasonable prospect of avoiding liquidation. The two directors had thus failed to satisfy the standards set by subsection (4) (*a*). The 'hopeless inadequacy' of their knowledge, skill and experience could not protect them. It is the duty even of the directors of an incorporated family business to acquire some basic knowledge of their legal obligations and financial responsibilities. Nor, in this case, was it sufficient answer to say that the directors had relied on assurances that money would come into the company; although these come from a quantity surveyor, his task had been merely to supervise contract income, and he had no information about the company's finances.

It has already been mentioned that section 214 of the 1986 Act goes far beyond the active trading to which the Review Committee on Insolvency Law and Practice addressed its recommendations. In covering the whole area of a company's financial affairs, and in attaching liability to omission as well as commission, the section imposes a potentially limitless duty on the director to pay constant attention to all aspects of his company's affairs, for fear that with hindsight a court may find that a reasonably diligent person in his position would have been able to evaluate the company's performance and prospects.[211] This will no doubt be mitigated in practice by allowing a measure of 'business judgment' to the board, but it seems unlikely that this can excuse complete omission. Further, a duty to inquire is clearly placed upon a director by judging him in the light of facts which he ought to know or *ascertain*: section 214 (4). At the least, this means that when a director feels, or, it seems, ought to feel, that the information available to him is inadequate he must press for more. This may place an individual director in some difficulties since (apart from provoking hostility, which section 214 presumably expects him to suffer rather than avoid) a failure to obtain satisfactory answers seems itself to be a ground upon which a liquidator might later rely. In order to assess his own and the company's position, a director may have to seek advice and assistance from outside the company.[212] Section 214 may also produce a certain amount of 'defensive management', since an alert director will wish to keep very clear records of his own activities.

Section 214 (3) is equally and deliberately imprecise in requiring the director, on actual or imputed foresight of insolvent liquidation, to take 'every step ... with a view to minimising the potential loss to the company's creditors[213] as ... he ought' to take, the only limitation being that he is liable only for failure to take steps which a reasonably diligent person in his position would have taken. The director is, subject to that

---

[210] [1990] BCC 903; see also *Re Purpoint Ltd* [1991] BCC 121 at pp.127–8, where Vinelott J clearly contemplates that there may be companies which no prudent director would allow to begin trading.

[211] In *Re Produce Marketing Consortium Ltd (No. 2)* [1989] BCLC 520 the judge stressed in making the order under section 214 that the case was not one of deliberate wrongdoing but of 'failure to appreciate what should have been clear'. It is the nature of this liability which prevents a director from claiming relief under section 727 of the Companies Act 1985; *Re Produce Marketing Consortium Ltd* [1989] 1 WLR 745; *Re DKG Contractors Ltd* [1990] BCC 902 (see 14.24.4).

[212] It is a moot point whether his duties under section 214 will in all cases override obligations of confidentiality.

[213] Presumably those who are likely to be creditors in an insolvent liquidation, and not merely those who happen at present to be creditors.

qualification, expected to follow the course of conduct which will not merely reduce but reduce as far as possible the potential loss, and it appears to follow that, given a range of possible actions, he must take that course which satisfies that criterion; he may use his business judgment in evaluating the consequences of each course which is open, but once that is done he has no choice but to follow the course which minimises the loss. Resignation from the board is manifestly not such a course,[214] and it is difficult to avoid the conclusion that the section will, whatever its true intentions, make insolvency proceedings the likeliest outcome. The director is still, however, required to decide what form of proceedings (i.e. receivership, administration or liquidation) will in fact minimise the creditors' losses, and for this purpose the preliminary step of seeking advice[215] may not be only permissible but necessary. There is a real risk that section 214 will actually precipitate insolvency proceedings which in some cases may have been avoidable, particularly as directors face possible disqualification if held liable under the section.[216] Even if some form of insolvency proceedings is the step which the section itself contemplates, however, there may be cases where a decision to trade on, albeit for a limited period, may be justified insofar as it appears reasonably likely to increase the assets available to creditors, although it may be wondered whether directors or their advisers will in practice be prepared to support such a decision. Conversely, if the directors have properly considered the possible courses of action open to them, concluded reasonably that some form of insolvency proceedings are inevitable, and honestly and reasonably begun the process of realising assets by sale, they are probably not to be judged by the standards of an insolvency practitioner; provided that they obtain a reasonable price, they are not required to conduct a full-scale investigation of other offers which might produce a better price.[217]

What is absolutely clear from section 214 (2) to (4) of the 1986 Act is the vital importance of the time element. It must be established at what moment the conditions set out in section 214 (2) first applied to a particular director before the question of complying with section 214 (3) can arise. In a wider sense, the impact of the section may be determined by the willingness or unwillingness of the court, with hindsight, to trace a company's affairs backwards in time from an insolvent liquidation to the first warning signs.

13.17.3 Liability for acting while disqualified

Section 15 of the Company Directors Disqualification Act 1986 contains a further provision under which a person can be liable for the debts of a company, and in this case liability is for those debts as such,[218] rather than, as in the cases of fraudulent and wrongful trading just described, liability to contribute to a company's assets.

A person is 'personally responsible' for all the relevant debts of a company if at any time either (a) he is involved in the management of a company in contravention of a disqualification order[219] or section 11 of the Act (i.e. acting as a director while an

---

[214] Still less, of course, abandoning the company while seeking fresh starts elsewhere: *Re Purpoint Ltd* [1991] BCC 121 at p. 125.

[215] As expeditiously as possible.

[216] See 13.16.3, above.

[217] Cf. *Welfab Engineers Ltd* [1990] BCC 600 (directors' duties at common law).

[218] Jointly and severally with the company and any other person who, whether under the section or otherwise, is liable: section 15 (2).

[219] Made under any of the provisions described above.

undischarged bankrupt),[220] or (b) as a person involved in management he acts or is willing to act on instructions given without the leave of the court by a person whom he knows at that time to be disqualified or to be an undischarged bankrupt.

'Relevant debts' are those debts and liabilities incurred at a time when the person was involved in management or those incurred when he acted or was willing to act on the instructions of a person disqualified, etc.[221] Involvement in management is given a wide meaning, namely being a director or being concerned, directly or indirectly, or taking part in the management of a company.[222] For the purposes of situation (b), a person who has acted at any time on instructions as described above is presumed, unless the contrary is shown, to have been willing at any time thereafter to act on instructions.[223]

The attraction of section 15 to creditors of a company is that it can be used by them directly without the need for action by a liquidator or even for the company in question to be in liquidation. It should also therefore prove a strong deterrent to those disqualified.

13.17.4 *Summary remedy*

Finally, it is convenient to note the summary remedy available against directors and others in a liquidation, provided for by section 212 of the Insolvency Act 1986, and available not just to the liquidator or the official receiver, but also to any creditor and, subject to the leave of the court, contributory. This provision replaced and extended what was section 631 of the Companies Act 1985.

13.18 Publicity about directors and their interests

The Companies Act 1985 and associated legislation contains many provisions designed to ensure that the members of companies, and in some instances creditors and others dealing with companies, are protected from abuse by directors of their position. Some of these provisions have already been considered earlier in this chapter.[224] Some require disclosure in the accounts of certain transactions entered into by directors and have been considered in Chapter 12. Others relate directly to the duties of directors and are considered in the next chapter. The remainder of this chapter is devoted to those provisions which require publicity to be given to directors and others and to the interests which they may hold in their companies.

13.19 The register of directors and secretaries

Under sections 288 to 290 of the Companies Act 1985, every company is required to keep a register of its directors[225] and secretaries, and to file copies thereof or of any changes therein with the Registrar of Companies within fourteen days of the appointment of the first directors or any change, as the case may be.[226]

---

[220] See 13.5 above.

[221] Section 15 (3).

[222] Compare the wide construction of the similar words in section 1; see 13.16.1, above.

[223] Section 15 (5).

[224] e.g. section 303 and the disqualification provisions.

[225] Including shadow directors (see 14.2).

[226] Any notification of a change must contain a signed consent to act by the new director or secretary. Any change must also be notified in the *Gazette* under section 711. The register may be computerised: the Companies (Registers and Records) Regulations 1985 (SI 1985 No. 724).

Under section 289, the register must contain the following particulars with respect to each director:

(1) in the case of an individual, his present name[227] any former name,[228] his usual residential address, his nationality, his business occupation (if any), particulars of any other directorships held by him or which have been held by him[229] and the date of his birth; and

(2) in the case of a corporation, its corporate name and registered or principal office.

The register must contain the following particulars with respect to the secretary or where there are joint secretaries, with respect to each of them: (a) in the case of an individual, his present name, any former name and his usual residential address; and (b) in the case of a corporation or a Scottish firm, its corporate or firm name and registered or principal office. Where all the partners in a firm are joint secretaries, the name and principal office of the firm may be stated.[230]

The register must be open to the inspection of any members of the company without charge, and of any other person on payment of the prescribed fee.[231] If inspection of the register is refused, the court may by order compel an immediate inspection of it.[232]

The annual return required by sections 363 to 365[233] must also state the same particulars as to the persons who are the directors and secretary of the company at the date of the return as are required to be inserted in the register.

13.20 Business letters

Section 305 of the Companies Act 1985 contains provisions as to the names of directors on business letters which apply to every company registered under the Companies Acts on or after 23 November 1916, and to every company incorporated outside Great Britain with an established place of business in Great Britain if such place of business was established on or after the said date.

Section 305 (1) provides that a company to which the section applies shall not state in any form the name of a director[234] otherwise than in the text or as a signatory on any business letters on which the company's name appears, unless it states on the letter in legible characters the Christian name or the initials thereof and surname of every director of the company who is an individual, and the corporate name of every corporate director. Prior to the Companies Act 1981, the obligation to state the names of directors applied without qualification to those companies subject to the equivalent section. It is

---

[227] 'Name' throughout the section means Christian or other forename and surname, with qualifications regarding titles: see section 289 (2).

[228] See section 289 (2) (c).

[229] Subject, in the case of past directorships, to the exceptions in section 289 (3) which, broadly speaking, refer to directorships not held for five years or more and directorships in dormant companies (as to which see 12.17.2, above) or companies which are part of the same group of companies where all the subsidiaries and sub-subsidiaries are wholly owned.

[230] Section 290.

[231] Section 288 (3). As to the fee and the detailed rights of inspection and copying, see the Companies (Inspection and Copying of Registers, Indices and Documents) Regulations 1991 (SI 1991 No. 1998).

[232] Section 288 (5). As to the penalties for breach of section 288, see section 288 (4).

[233] See 10.7 above.

[234] 'Director' includes shadow director, as to which see 14.2, below.

surprising that Parliament should choose to amend the requirement, given that it was some, albeit small, protection against small company fraud.[235]

13.21 Directors' service contracts

Section 318 (1) of the Companies Act 1985 requires every company to keep copies of each director's service contract, or where such contract is not in writing, a written memorandum setting out the terms of the director's contract of service.[236] In the case of each director who is employed under a contract of service with a subsidiary of the company, a similar obligation is imposed. Section 318 (2) requires copies and memoranda of service contracts to be kept in one place. Section 318 (3) states that the following are 'appropriate places' for this purpose:

(1) its registered office;
(2) the place where its register of members is kept (if other than its registered office);
(3) its principal place of business, provided that it is situated in that part of Great Britain in which the company is registered.

The company must give notice to the Registrar as to the place where these copies and memoranda are kept and any change of place, except where this has always been the registered office. These documents are to be open to inspection by any member of the company. Section 318 provides for heavy penalties for the company and every officer in default, and empowers the court by order to compel an immediate inspection where this has been refused.

Section 318 does not apply in relation to a director's service contract with the company, or with a subsidiary of the company, if that contract requires him to work wholly or mainly outside the United Kingdom. However, even in such a case the company must keep, in the case of a contract of service with the company, a memorandum setting out the names of the director and the provisions of the contract relating to its duration. In the case of a contract of service with a subsidiary of the company, the company must keep a memorandum, setting out the names of the directors, the name and place of incorporation of the subsidiary and the provisions of the contract relating to its duration.

13.22 Directors' interests in shares or debentures

Section 324 and Schedule 13 of the Companies Act 1985 place anyone who becomes a director[237] under an obligation to notify the company in writing of his interest in shares in or debentures of the company, or its subsidiary, holding company or co-subsidiary within five days of his becoming a director or, if he is ignorant of his interest, within five days after it comes to his knowledge. He is required to give notice of his interests in terms of the number of shares of each class and the amount of debentures of each class in the

---

[235] See 2 Co. Law (1981), pp.125–6.

[236] This obligation applies also to a variation of a director's service contract: section 318 (10). As to the statutory controls on the length of directors' service contracts, see 14.10 below.

[237] This includes a shadow director: section 324 (8).

company or its subsidiary, etc. The meaning of being 'interested in shares in or debentures of the company' is defined in Schedule 13, Part I, which will be considered below.

While he remains a director of a company a director is under an obligation to notify the company of the occurrence of any of the following events:[238]

(1) any event in consequence of whose occurrence he becomes, or ceases to be, interested in shares in, or debentures of, the company or any other body corporate, being the company's subsidiary or holding company or a subsidiary of the company's holding company;[239]

(2) the entering into by him of a contract to sell any such shares or debentures;[240]

(3) the assignment by him of a right granted to him by the company to subscribe for shares in, or debentures of, the company;[241] and

(4) the grant to him by another body corporate, being the company's subsidiary or holding company or a subsidiary of the company's holding company, of a right to subscribe for shares in, or debentures of, that other body corporate, the exercise of such a right granted to him as aforesaid and the assignment by him of such a right so granted.[242]

In each case he must state the number or amount, and class, of shares or debentures involved.

13.22.1 *Duty to notify an investment exchange*

Section 329 (1) imposes upon a company a duty, in certain cases, to notify an investment exchange[243] of information obtained from directors in compliance with section 324. The obligation arises where the company has shares or debentures listed on a recognised investment exchange and it is notified by a director, in compliance with section 324, in respect of the acquisition, etc., of an interest in the securities of a company and those securities are listed on the investment exchange. This obligation must be fulfilled before the end of the next day following that on which it arises (i.e. the day on which the company was notified by the directors). The period allowed to the company excludes Saturdays, Sundays or Bank Holidays.[244] The investment exchange 'may publish, in such manner as it may determine, any information received' under section 329 (1).

---

[238] The same five-day period as above applies.

[239] He must state the price to be paid under the contract: Schedule 13, para. 17 (1). 'Price' includes 'any consideration other than money'.

[240] He must state the price received under the contract: Schedule 134, para. 17 (2). 'Price' includes 'any consideration other than money'.

[241] He must state the consideration for the assignment or that there is none: Schedule 13, para. 18 (1).

[242] Where he assigns such a right he must state the consideration: Schedule 13, para. 18 (2). Where he is granted a right to subscribe for shares or debentures he must state (a) the date on which the right was granted, (b) the period during which or time at which the right is exercisable, (c) the consideration for the grant (or the absence of it), and (d) the price to be paid for the shares or debentures. Where he *exercises* such a right to subscribe for shares, etc., he must state the number of shares or amount of debentures in respect of which the right was exercised, and the names of those in whose name the shares are registered: Schedule 13, para. 19.

[243] In most cases this will be The Stock Exchange.

[244] Section 329 (2).

13.22.2 *The meaning of 'interest' in shares and debentures*

Part I of Schedule 13 contains elaborate provisions as to what is meant by 'interest' in shares or debentures for the purposes of a director's disclosure obligations under section 324.

Paragraph 1 starts with the wide proposition that interest includes a reference to any interest of any kind whatsoever in shares or debentures. Accordingly, there must be disregarded any restraints or restrictions to which the exercise of any right attached to the interest is or may be subject. Where trust property includes any interest in shares or debentures, any beneficiary of the trust who, apart from this provision, does not have any interest in the shares or debentures, is taken to have such an interest (without prejudice to the later provisions of Part I).[245]

The entering into a contract to purchase shares, for cash or other consideration, gives a person an interest for these purposes,[246] as does the right, when a person is not the registered holder, to exercise or to control the exercise of any rights conferred by the holding of shares or debentures.[247]

Paragraph 4 deals with interest in shares or debentures held through 'controlled' companies. A person is taken to be interested in shares or debentures if a body corporate is interested in them and either of the following two criteria is met: (a) that body corporate or its directors are accustomed to act in accordance with his directions or instructions, or (b) the person in question is entitled to exercise or control the exercise of one-third or more of the voting power at a general meeting of the body corporate. When condition (b) is met and the body corporate in question is entitled to exercise or control the exercise of *any* of the voting power at general meetings of another body corporate (the 'effective voting power'), then for the purposes of condition (b) the effective voting power is taken to be exercisable by the person in question.

A person is taken to have an interest in shares or debentures if, otherwise than by virtue of having an interest under a trust, he has a right to call for delivery of the shares or debentures to himself or his order (a call option), or if he has a right to acquire an interest or is under an obligation to acquire an interest.[248] However, rights or obligations to *subscribe* for shares or debentures do not for these purposes amount to rights or obligations to acquire (but this is without prejudice to the general concept of interest in shares or debentures in paragraph 1).[249]

Those who have a joint interest are each deemed to have that interest,[250] and it is immaterial that shares or debentures in which a person has an interest are unidentifiable.[251]

[245] Schedule 13, para. 2.

[246] ibid., para. 3 (1) (*a*).

[247] ibid., para. 3 (1) (*b*). This includes the cases when a person has an option, conditional or not, to exercise or control the exercise of such rights and when he is under an obligation, conditional or not, the fulfilment of which would make him so entitled. However, appointment as a proxy at a *specified* company meeting or class meeting or the appointment of someone as the representative of a corporation at *any* company meeting or class meeting does not amount to an interest.

[248] ibid. para. 6 (1).

[249] ibid., para. 6 (2).

[250] ibid., para. 7.

[251] ibid., para. 8.

13.22.3 Types of interest disregarded

Certain types of interest in shares or debentures are disregarded, including an interest in reversion or remainder[252] so long as someone is entitled to receive, during the lifetime of himself or another, income from trust property comprising shares or debentures.[253] A person who holds shares or debentures as a bare trustee or custodian trustee[254] is treated as uninterested in them.[255]

Those who invest in an authorised unit trust scheme are not regarded as having an interest in the underlying investments.[256] Certain statutory investment schemes are also exempted.[257] The Secretary of State has power by regulation to except other categories of interest in shares or debentures.[258]

13.22.4 Spouses and children of directors

Section 327 and 328 extend section 324 by treating the interests of the spouses or children of directors as being those of the director. 'Spouse' means a husband or wife of a director, not being herself or himself a director of that company. Likewise 'children' means the infant son or daughter of a director, not being himself or herself a director of that company. 'Son' includes stepson and adopted son, and 'daughter' includes stepdaughter and adopted daughter. A contract, assignment or right of subscription entered into, exercised or made by, or grant made to, such a spouse or child (in respect of shares or debentures) is treated, for the purpose of section 324, as having been entered into, etc., by the director.

Consequently a director of a company is under an obligation to notify the company in writing of the occurrence (while he or she is a director) of either (a) the grant to his wife or her husband or to his or her infant son or infant daughter, by the company, of a right to subscribe for shares in, or debentures of, the company; or (b) the exercise by his wife or her husband or by his or her infant son or infant daughter of such a right.

In either case he must report the same information as section 324 requires where a director is granted a right to subscribe or exercises it. The five-day period during which written notice must be given runs from 'the day next following that on which the occurrence of the event that gives rise to it comes to his knowledge'.

13.22.5 The register of directors' interests

Section 325 requires every company to keep a register to record the information about those interests in shares and debentures which section 324 requires directors to notify to the company. Under the Companies (Registers and other Records) Regulations,[259] this register may be kept in non-legible (e.g. computerised) form. Every company is also under

---

[252] Or as regards Scotland, in fee.

[253] Schedule 13, para. 9.

[254] i.e. under English law. The same applies to a simple trustee in Scottish law.

[255] Schedule 13, para. 10.

[256] ibid., para. 11.

[257] See ibid., paras. 11 and 12.

[258] Section 324 (3). See the Companies (Disclosure of Directors' Interests) (Exceptions) Regulations 1985 (SI 1985 No. 802). These except, *inter alia*, disclosure to a company which is the wholly owned subsidiary of a body corporate incorporated outside Great Britain of interests in that body corporate or any other body corporate so incorporated, and disclosure by a director of a wholly owned subsidiary of his interests in the subsidiary when he is also a director of its holding company and the latter is obliged to keep a register of directors' interests.

[259] SI 1985 No. 724.

an obligation, without such notification, to record on this register the grant of a right to subscribe in shares in or debentures of the company to a director. It must inscribe:

(1) the period during which or the time at which the right is exercisable;
(2) the consideration for the grant (or the fact that there is no consideration);
(3) the description and the number and amount of shares or debentures involved;
(4) the price or other non-monetary consideration to be paid for them.

Whenever such a right to subscribe is exercised, the company must inscribe this fact on the register as well as the following information:

(1) the number or amount of shares or debentures in respect of which a right is exercised;
(2) if they are registered in his name, that fact;
(3) if they are not registered in his name, the name or names of those in whose name they are registered.[260]

Part IV of Schedule 13 makes detailed provision as to the way in which this register must be maintained.[261] This register must be kept at the company's registered office if the company's register of members is kept there. If the company's register of members is not so kept, it may be kept at the company's registered office or at the place where its register of members is kept.

This register must be open to inspection by members free of charge, and by members of the public on payment of the prescribed fee.[262] The company is required to send notice to the Registrar of Companies as to the whereabouts of the register and of any change of place (unless it has at all times been kept in the company's registered office). Any member of the company or other person may require a copy of the register or part of it. The company is required to send such a copy within ten days. The register must be produced at the company's annual general meeting and remain open and accessible throughout it to any person attending.

Section 326 provides penalties for failing to maintain the register properly or for refusing a request for inspection or copying. Further, a court order compelling compliance can be obtained where an inspection is refused or there is a failure to send a copy.

13.22.6 *Powers of inspection by Secretary of State*

By section 446 (1), where it appears to the Secretary of State that a contravention of section 324 may have occurred in relation to shares in, or debentures of, a company, he may appoint one or more competent inspectors. The latter will carry out such investigations as are necessary to establish whether or not contraventions have occurred. The procedure and purpose of this and other powers to appoint inspectors will be considered in Chapter 15 below.

---

[260] Together with (if they are registered in the name of two or more persons) the number or amount registered in the name of each of them.

[261] See para. 21 (entries for each director in chronological order); para. 28 (index of names); para. 22 (obligation to inscribe to be fulfilled within three working days). The index of names may, like the register itself, be kept in non-legible form. See the Companies (Registers and Other Records) Regulations 1985.

[262] As to the fee and the detailed rights of inspection and copying, see the Companies (Inspection and Copying of Registers, Indices and Documents) Regulations 1991 (SI 1991 No. 1988).

14 The Duties of Directors

14.1 Introduction

This chapter is concerned with the scope and content of various duties which the law imposes upon a director of a company by virtue of his holding office as such. Broadly speaking, the duties discussed fall into two categories, fiduciary duties (i.e. duties of good faith and honesty) and duties of skill and care. Their general purpose is the protection of present and future shareholders and (to a lesser extent) creditors, though, as will be seen,[1] they are generally expressed as being owed to 'the company'. Much of the content of the duties to be discussed has been developed by way of analogy with rules governing legal relationships comparable to that between a director and his company, a point which is briefly discussed in the next section. In part these have been supplemented by often complex statutory provisions. The result is a large number of heads of duty, many of which overlap with one or more others. Partly because of this complexity, the Department of Trade and Industry has a working party looking at the whole of directors' duties. A consultative document is expected to be issued in 1995 and it may be that a more straightforward legislative code of duties will result at some future date.

14.2 The legal nature of the office of director

The Companies Act 1985 does not define directors. There is, however, a general provision that, for the purposes of the Act, the expression 'director' includes 'any person occupying the position of director by whatever name called'.[2] The meaning of 'director' is to be derived from the words of the Act as a whole and varies according to the context in which it is found. In respect of certain provisions, someone who acts as a director but is not actually appointed as such, i.e. a de facto as opposed to a de jure director, will be treated as a director.[3] Furthermore, in respect of certain provisions, obligations are cast on any 'shadow director', who is 'a person in accordance with whose directions or instructions the directors of a company are accustomed to act'.[4] It should be noted that the concept of de facto director is quite different from that of shadow director.[5]

The absence of a definition of 'director' renders it somewhat difficult to ascertain the exact nature of the director's office. He is certainly an agent of the company but is rather more than that as in practice he is not subject to much control by his principal, the

---

[1] See 14.3, below.

[2] Companies Act 1985, section 741 (1). This means persons described as governors or managers rather than as directors, but performing the same function.

[3] *Re Lo-Line Electric Motors Ltd* [1988] BCLC 698. This will be particularly so in respect of the disqualification provisions (see 13.16).

[4] Section 741 (2). These provisions are noted in the appropriate parts of the text. A person is not deemed a shadow director by reason only of the fact that the directors act on advice given by him in a professional capacity, and the definition does not catch a holding company, which could clearly fall within it in some situations, in respect of the sections listed in section 741 (3).

[5] *Re Hydrodan (Corby) Ltd* [1994] BCC 161.

company acting through the shareholders in general meeting.[6] In certain respects the director is a trustee[7] and there is no doubt that many of his duties developed from the law of trusts, but he is certainly not a full trustee, not least because his very function is an entrepreneurial one and he may properly take risks with the company's funds which a trustee in the strict sense cannot. If a director performs more than the tasks of a director pure and simple, such as attending board meetings and the like, he may well also be an employee of the company and as such subject to a stricter duty of care and skill[8] and the beneficiary of important statutory rights if he is declared redundant or unfairly dismissed.[9]

In short, the director's office is *sui generis*, although for certain purposes the analogies of agency, trusteeship and employment may be useful.

It should be noted that a director need not be an individual person and another company may even, if it has the requisite power, be appointed the sole director.

14.3 The scope of directors' fiduciary duties

It is an established general rule that, in so far as a director of a company is bound by fiduciary duties at general law, these duties are owed to the company only. Thus they are now owed to other companies or bodies corporate with which the company is associated, e.g. its holding company[10] or subsidiary,[11] nor do they operate in favour of any person simply because he is a person to whom the company itself stands in a fiduciary relationship.[12] More significantly, they are not owed to the individual shareholders of the company. This proposition stems from *Percival v Wright*,[13] in which a group of shareholders in a company approached the directors with a request that the directors purchase their shares; some of the directors did so without disclosing that a purchase of the company's undertaking was imminent, this being a piece of information which was known to them and to the other members of the board, though not to any of the shareholders who were not directors. It was held that the directors in question were not under any duty to the shareholders to disclose this information, even though the price being offered for the undertaking represented a substantial amount more per share than they paid to the shareholders on the purchase, and that accordingly the shareholders could not have the purchase set aside. The judgment does, however, stress that there was no 'unfair dealing' by the directors and seems to suggest that it was significant that the initial approach in the matter was made by the shareholders.[14] The possibility that fiduciary duties would have arisen between the directors and the shareholders if the directors had instigated the purchase is thus not entirely ruled out.

Furthermore, directors, in supplying information to their shareholders regarding a

---

[6] The 'separation of ownership and control', recognised by Berle and Means in *The Modern Corporation and Private Property* (Harcourt, Brace & World Inc, revised edn 1967). See also 10.1 and 11.1, above.

[7] See 14.8, below.

[8] See 14.23, below.

[9] See further, 13.4, above. In acting as an employee, a director can bargain as he wishes over the terms of his service contract, provided that there is compliance with the articles; in practice these remove any possibility of conflict of duty and interest. See further 14.15 and 14.16 and *Jackson v Invicta Plastics Ltd* [1987] BCLC 329.

[10] *Bell v Lever Bros. Ltd* [1932] AC 161 at p. 228 (HL).

[11] *Lindgren v L. & P. Estates Ltd* [1968] Ch 572 (CA); but note the effect of *Scottish Co-operative Wholesale Society Ltd v Meyer* [1959] AC 324 (HL (Sc.)), discussed at 14.22 below.

[12] *Wilson v Bury (Lord)* (1880) 5 QBD 518 (CA).

[13] [1902] 2 Ch 421. See also *Dawson International plc v Coats Paton plc* (1988) 4 BCC 305.

[14] ibid., at pp. 426–7.

takeover offer and expressing a view as to whether the offer should be accepted, have 'a duty towards their own shareholders which ... clearly includes a duty to be honest and a duty not to mislead'.[15] It has also been laid down that if in a particular transaction a director expressly or by his conduct constitutes himself as agent for one or more of the shareholders, he thereby become subject to fiduciary duties to the shareholder or shareholders concerned.[16] Such duties arise, however, by virtue of his agency, not his directorship. In the decision of the New Zealand Court of Appeal in *Coleman v Myers*,[17] a fiduciary relationship between directors and shareholders was held to have arisen where, in a private company with the shareholding spread over a few associated family groups, the directors had a high degree of inside knowledge which they failed to disclose to the other shareholders when the shares in the company were the subject of a takeover offer from a company owned by one of the directors. The court stressed, however, that the existence of such a relationship depended entirely on the facts of any particular case and dissented from the view expressed by the trial judge[18] that the decision in *Percival v Wright* was wrong and should be ignored.[19] A further example of a duty which may be owed directly to shareholders is the duty to allot shares for a proper purpose.[20]

The time at which a director's fiduciary duties to the company arise is the time when he becomes a director. He is not bound by them when he is merely a 'director-elect'.[21]

The form in which a director's fiduciary duties are expressed is that of a number of general law and statutory rules, varying greatly in their range of application and at many points overlapping with each other. The lack of any precise and logical pattern makes orderly exposition of these rules difficult, but what follows is an attempt to summarise and explain them with as much coherence as the subject-matter permits. Except where the text expressly indicates otherwise, it is assumed that the conduct of the directors being dealt with is within the literal terms of the powers conferred on them by the memorandum and articles. It is arguable, of course, that merely to act in excess of those powers is *ipso facto* a breach of fiduciary duty; such conduct is certainly invalid unless and until effectively ratified.[22] But for the purposes of the present discussion it is treated as a breach of fiduciary duty only when, through causing loss to the company, it involves the relevant director or directors in liability to the company.

14.4 Duty to act bona fide in the interest of the company

As Lord Greene MR said in the case of *Re Smith & Fawcett Ltd*[23] directors are bound to exercise the powers conferred upon them 'bona fide in what they consider – not what a court may consider – is in the interests of the company ... '. This duty of honesty and

---

[15] *Gething v Kilner* [1972] 1 WLR 337 at p. 341, *per* Brightman J. See also *Dawson International plc* v *Coats Paton plc*, above, at pp. 310, 312.

[16] *Allen v Hyatt* (1914) 30 TLR 444 (PC); and see *Briess v Woolley* [1954] AC 333 (HL).

[17] [1977] 2 NZLR 297; See Rider 41 MLR 585 (1978). This decision was followed by the British Columbia Court of Appeal in *Dusik v Newton* (1985) 62 BCLR 1 and by the New South Wales Court of Appeal in *Glandon Pty Ltd v Strata Consolidated Ltd*, September 1993; see *Gore-Browne on Companies* (Jordans, 44th edn, loose-leaf), 12.17.

[18] [1977] 2 NZLR 22.

[19] These cases involved what is generally known as 'insider dealing'. The statutory prohibitions against such dealing are described below at 14.21.

[20] See *Re a Company* [1987] BCLC 82; *John Crowther Group plc v Carpets International plc* [1990] BCLC 460 at p. 464. This relates in particular to the question of minority shareholders' remedies; see 15.6, below.

[21] *Lindgren v L. & P. Estates Ltd* [1968] Ch 575 (CA).

[22] Although third parties dealing with the directors are protected: see Chapter 4.

[23] [1942] Ch 304 (CA) at p. 306.

good faith in the exercise of his powers is in fact the primary duty of a director. As Lord Greene's formulation indicates, the duty is subjective, in that the court will not consider it broken merely because, in the court's own opinion, the particular exercise of power was not in the company's interests;[24] *a fortiori* the court will not take it upon itself to order that a particular power vested in directors should be exercised in a particular way.[25] On the other hand, the court will insist that, save in so far as the articles expressly permit, it should be the directors, and not some other person or body to whom they have purported to delegate their powers, who determine how the powers vested in the directors are best used to serve 'the interests of the company'.[26]

14.5 The interests of the company

This last phrase merits some special consideration. Modern management often takes the view that the interests to be taken into account by directors in running a company should include the interests of not only the present and future shareholders, but also the company's employees, its customers and its creditors and, in the case of large public companies at least, the State and the general public. No doubt this represents an adequate practical guide for most decisions that a director has to take. It is, however, thought that from the point of view of strict law, while the 'interests of the company' may now include the interests of the company's employees,[27] and in certain situations the interests of its creditors,[28] it otherwise means the interests of the company as a commercial entity, to be judged in most cases by reference to the interests of present and future shareholders alone. Thus the only circumstances in which the directors may legitimately promote the interest of any other groups or entitles are those where to do so ultimately advances the interests of the shareholders.[29]

Where a particular decision to be taken by the directors bears differently upon different classes of shareholders, their duty is to act fairly having regard to the interests of all classes;[30] similarly, they should, in appropriate circumstances, seek to balance short-term considerations, affecting the present shareholders only, against long-term considerations which involve future shareholders as well.[31] In contrast, where a company is to be taken over and the only issue is as to which of competing bids is to succeed, the interests of the company are the interests of its current shareholders only,[32] but this does not necessarily

[24] No doubt it will hold, however, that a breach has occurred if the relevant exercise of power could not possibly be considered by a reasonable man to be in the interests of the company; cf. *Shuttleworth v Cox Bros. & Co. (Maidenhead) Ltd* [1927] 2 KB 9 (CA), and other authorities on the fiduciary duties of the shareholders in general meeting, cited at 3.27, above.

[25] *Pergamon Press Ltd v Maxwell* [1979] 1 WLR 1167.

[26] *Re County Palatine Loan and Discount Co., Cartmell's Case* (1874) 9 Ch App. 691.

[27] Under section 309 which is discussed in 14.6, below.

[28] See below.

[29] *Hutton v West Cork Rly Co.* (1883) 23 Ch D 654 (CA); *Parke v Daily News Ltd* [1962] Ch 927. Although these decisions were concerned with gratuitous payments, where the matter may concern the validity of a resolution of shareholders as well as or rather than a decision of the directors, it is submitted that the same meaning of the 'interests of the company' applies when an issue is solely one of the duties of directors; see further Birds (1980) 1 Co. Law 67; *contra* Instone [1979] JBL 221. As to the statutory reversal by what is now section 719 of the Companies Act 1985 of the actual decision in *Parke v Daily News Ltd*, see 4.13.3, above, where the topic of gratuitous payments is also discussed more fully.

[30] *Henry v Great Northern Rly* (1857) 1 De G & J 606 at p.638.

[31] See the report of the Inspector, Mr E. Milner-Holland QC, in the Savoy Hotel Investigation (HMSO, 1954); see Gower (1955) 68 Harv. LR 1176.

[32] *Heron International Ltd v Grade* [1984] BCLC 244, esp. at pp. 264–5 (CA).

mean that the directors are under a positive duty to recommend the higher bid nor that they cannot agree to recommend a particular bid or agree not to encourage or co-operate with another would-be bidder.[33] The mere fact that, in a particular transaction, the directors of a company having a holding company and/or subsidiaries and/or co-subsidiaries looked to the interests of the group as a whole does not of itself mean that they are in breach of duty, provided that an 'intelligent and honest man' in the position of the directors could have reasonably believed the transaction to be in the interests of the company.[34]

When a company is insolvent or on the verge of insolvency, but not otherwise, it is the creditors' interest that become paramount.[35] This recognition of creditors' interest by the common law is a relatively recent development, and has probably been heavily influenced by the same factors as led to the introduction of statutory provisions designed to give more effective protection to creditors.[36] Although it has been said that a duty is owed by the directors to the company and to the creditors of the company to ensure that the affairs of the company are properly administered and that its property is not dissipated or exploited for the benefit of the directors themselves to the prejudice of the creditors,[37] it is submitted that this is not a duty owed directly to creditors, but rather a duty to the company, which in the event of liquidation can be enforced by the liquidator for the benefit of the creditors.[38]

If a power is found not to have been exercised by the directors bona fide in the interests of the company, the exercise may be declared void. Any agreement made with a third party is voidable against the third party if he was aware of the lack of bona fides,[39] and if the exercise of the power causes loss to the company, the directors responsible may be liable to make good the loss.

14.6 The interests of the employees

By section 309,[40] the matters to which the directors of a company are to have regard in the performance of their functions include the interests of the company's employees in general as well as the interests of its members. This welcome acknowledgement of the fact that modern management does often take into account the interests of employees[41] is based upon a recommendation of the Committee of Inquiry on Industrial Democracy

---

[33] See *Re a Company* [1986] BCLC 382 at pp. 389–90 and *Dawson International plc v Coats Paton plc* (1989) 5 BCC 405.

[34] *Charterbridge Corporation Ltd v Lloyds Bank Ltd* [1970] Ch 72 at p. 74.

[35] See especially *Lonrho Ltd v Shell Petroleum Ltd* [1980] 1 WLR 627 at p. 634 (HL) *per* Lord Diplock; *West Mercia Safetyware Ltd v Dodd* [1988] BCLC 250 at pp. 252–3 (CA) *per* Dillon LJ. See also *Brady v Brady* [1989] AC 755 (HL).

[36] Especially the wrongful trading provision (section 214 of the Insolvency Act 1986); see 13.17.2.

[37] *Winkworth v Edward Baron Development Co. Ltd* [1987] BCLC 193 at p. 197 (HL) *per* Lord Templeman.

[38] *Re Horsley & Weight Ltd* [1982] 3 All ER 1045 at p. 1055 (CA) *per* Buckley LJ; *Kuwait Asia Bank EC v National Mutual Life Nominees Ltd* [1990] BCLC 868 at p. 888 (PC) *per* Lord Lowry. In practice it seems more likely that the matter will be litigated and decided under the statutory wrongful trading provision rather than as a common-law duty.

[39] ibid. at pp. 69, 75; *Lindgren v L & P Estates Ltd* [1968] Ch 572 (CA); *Rolled Steel Products Ltd v British Steel Corporation* [1984] BCLC 466 (CA). See also *John Crowther Group plc v Carpets International plc* [1990] BCLC 460, holding invalid an agreement by directors to recommend a course of action or to propose a resolution which was entered into in breach of duty. See also *Rackham v Peek Foods Ltd* [1990] BCLC 895.

[40] See also section 719, which is discussed at 4.13.3, above.

[41] See also 14.5, above.

(the Bullock Report).[42] However, this duty is, by subsection (2), owed only to the company, and not to employees individually, and is enforceable in the same way as any other fiduciary duty.[43]

It is submitted that the full import of this section is not entirely clear.[44] Before the enactment of its predecessor in 1980, directors were entitled to take account of the interest of employees provided that in so doing they ultimately advanced the interests of the shareholders. Section 309 goes further and requires them to have regard to those interests.[45] So if it could be shown that in taking a decision directors failed to consider the interests of employees, they would be in breach of duty. Whether, however directors are entitled to subordinate the interests of shareholders to those of employees must be open to doubt, because section 309 does not alter the legal meaning of 'interests of the company'[46] which must ultimately be paramount. For example, a board might be faced with a decision whether or not to close down a factory that is unprofitable but employs a considerable number of people who would lose their jobs if the decision to close were taken. Provided that the directors considered this latter point, it is submitted that they would not be in breach of section 309 if they decided to close the factory. Indeed if they did not so decide they might be liable for not acting bona fide in the interests of the company, if it could clearly be shown that they had acted against the interests of the shareholders.

14.7 Duty to act for proper purposes

In the judgment of Lord Greene MR in *Re Smith & Fawcett Ltd*, the principle already cited is supplemented by the statement that directors' powers must not be exercised for any 'collateral purpose'.[47] Thus, if the directors exercise a power conferred by the articles for a purpose other than that for which, upon its proper interpretation, it was so conferred, their conduct is open to challenge, and in such a case it is no answer for them to maintain that they bona fide believed their conduct to be in the interests of the company. The court will not substitute its own view for that of the board as to the correctness of the board's exercise of its management powers, but where, on an objective review of the situation, it finds that a requirement allegedly underlying the board's action was not urgent or critical, it may have reason (particularly where the action taken was unusual or extreme) to doubt or discount the assertions of the directors that they acted solely to deal with this requirement.[48] To this limited extent, their assessment of the company's interests in the exercise of their powers is open to review, on an objective basis, by the court.[49]

This principle was brought into prominence in the cases, described in the next paragraph, dealing with a power vested in the directors of a company to allot the company's shares. Since the introduction of what are now sections 80 and 89 to 96 of the

---

[42] Cmnd 6706 (1977), Chapter 7, para. 12, and Chapter 8, para. 38.

[43] See 14.25, below. *Quaere* whether a minority shareholder's derivative action would lie, particularly if the shareholder is also an employee; see 15.7, below.

[44] See also 1 Co. Law (1980) at pp. 72–3.

[45] See *Fulham Football Club Ltd v Cabra Estates plc* [1992] BCC 863 at p. 876 (CA).

[46] See 14.5, above.

[47] [1942] Ch 304 at p. 306 (CA).

[48] *Howard Smith Ltd v Ampol Petroleum Ltd* [1974] AC 821 at p. 823 (PC).

[49] For an argument that this test is not objective enough, see Birds 37 MLR 580 (1974); compare Sealy [1967] CLJ 33 and *Cases and Materials in Company Law* (Butterworths, 5th edn 1992), pp. 290–1. The proper purposes duty has been held to be one owed to shareholders directly rather than to the company (see 14.3) and as such may be relevant in an unfair prejudice petition (see 15.12).

Companies Act 1985, which restrict directors' powers of allotment,[50] the principle is of less importance thereto. However, those provisions may in certain cases be excluded and thus the common-law principle can be relevant. Further, as the cases discussed below reveal, the principle has often been used in modern times to question the validity of defensive tactics used by directors fighting a takeover bid for their company or of another means of maintaining directors' control. Thus it can be used in respect of any power exercised with these aims in mind whose purpose can clearly be discerned from the articles, as for example in the Savoy Hotel case, where it was the directors' power to lease the company's property as a means of forestalling an anticipated takeover bid which was in issue.[51] A further example concerned the directors entering into a management agreement which had the effect of depriving the shareholders of their constitutional right to appoint new directors with full managerial powers.[52]

In *Hogg v Cramphorn Ltd*,[53] the directors of the defendant company, fearing a takeover bid and their own dismissal from the board, allotted shares to persons who would support them in office. They honestly believed that, in acting to preserve their position on the board, they were serving the company's best interests, but it was held that they had used the power of allotment for a purpose for which it was not intended to be used and that the allotment was accordingly voidable. However, the court ruled that if a meeting of the shareholders existing prior to the allotment approved the allotment by a majority it would thereby be rendered valid, and ordered that such a meeting be held. In *Howard Smith Ltd v Ampol Petroleum Ltd*,[54] two shareholders holding between them 55 per cent of the shares in a company announced that they would jointly reject any offer from a particular intending takeover bidder, or from any other source. The board of directors then allotted new shares to the intending bidder. Although the company did need new capital at the time, the primary purpose of the directors in making this allotment was to reduce the proportionate shareholding of the two majority shareholders to below 50 per cent and thus enable the bidder to make an effective bid. In proceedings brought by one of the two majority shareholders against, *inter alia*, the directors and the bidder, it was held by the Privy Council that the board had acted with an improper purpose, albeit honestly and within their powers, and that the issue of shares to the bidder (which was on notice of the impropriety) should accordingly be set aside. Giving the Privy Council's judgment, Lord

---

[50] See 6.3–6.5, above.

[51] This *cause célèbre*, which was never litigated, was the subject of a Board of Trade Inspector's Report in 1954; see footnote 31, above. For reported examples of the use of a proper purposes principle outside the context of a struggle for control and unrelated to an allotment of shares, see *Stanhope's Case* (1866) 1 Ch App. 161 (power to forfeit shares), *Bennett's Case* (1867) 5 De GM & G 284 (power to approve transfers of shares), *Galloway v Hallé Concerts Society* [1915] 2 Ch 233 (power to make calls) and *Gaiman v N.A.M.H.* [1971] Ch 317 (power to expel members).

[52] *Lee Panavision Ltd v Lee Lighting Ltd* [1992] BCLC 22 (CA).

[53] [1967] Ch 254. The principles adopted in this case, which was actually decided in 1963, were approved of and applied in *Bamford v Bamford* [1970] Ch 212 (CA). Earlier authorities are *Punt v Symons & Co. Ltd* [1903] 2 Ch 506 and *Piercy v S. Mills & Co. Ltd* [1920] 3 Ch 77. It is clear that some Commonwealth authorities reject the breadth of the principle confirmed in *Hogg v Cramphorn Ltd* and in effect deny the existence of this objective restraint on directors' powers, despite Lord Wilberforce's valiant attempt in *Howard Smith Ltd v Ampol Petroleum Ltd* [1974] AC 821 (see below) to explain them as consistent with *Hogg v Cramphorn Ltd*; see in particular *Harlowe's Nominees Ltd v Woodside (Lake Entrance) Oil Co.* (1968) 121 CLR 483 (Australian HC) and *Teck Corporation Ltd v Millar* (1972) 33 DLR (3d) 288 (Sup. Ct. BC): see also the unreported English decision in *Pennell v Venida Investments Ltd*, discussed in Burridge, 44 MLR 40 (1981). Compare, however, for example, *Winthrop Investments Ltd v Winns Ltd* [1975] NSWLR 666 (New South Wales CA).

[54] [1974] AC 821 (PC).

Wilberforce said that a decision of directors to issue shares could be set aside on the ground of improper purpose even though there was no element of self-interest involved, and that while it might in some circumstances be proper to issue shares for purposes other than raising capital for the company, 'it must be unconstitutional for directors to use their fiduciary powers over the shares in the company purely for the purpose of destroying an existing majority, or creating a new majority which did not previously exist'. Further he said that the case was all the stronger against the directors where there was 'an ulterior purpose to enable an offer for shares to proceed which the existing majority was in a position to block'.[55]

It is submitted that, except as regards the possibility of ratification by the general meeting,[56] the consequences of infringement of this principle are the same as apply in relation to the principle of bona fides just discussed. Thus, where a power of forfeiture was exercised for improper purposes, the members concerned, who knew of the impropriety, could not rely on the forfeiture as a defence to an action for payment of the balance due on the shares.[57]

14.8 Trusteeship of the company's assets

Directors are regarded as trustees of company property which is in their hands or under their control. The primary consequence of this principle of trusteeship is that a director is answerable as a trustee for any misapplication of the company's property in which he participated and which he knew or ought to have known to be a misapplication.[58] A misapplication in this context means any disposition of the company's property which by virtue of any provision of the company's constitution or any statutory provision or any rule of general law the company or the board is forbidden or incompetent or unauthorised to make, or which is carried out by the directors otherwise than in accordance with their duty to act bona fide in the interests of the company and for the proper purposes. This second limb covers not only misappropriations of the company's property, but also dispositions in favour of third parties which do not satisfy the test of bona fides.

14.8.1 The scope of the trusteeship

Provided that the directors have possession or control of the property beneficially owned by the company, their trusteeship will arise whether the property is legally vested in the company, in one or more of the directors, or in a third party.

A director's trusteeship has been held to cover funds standing to the company's credit in a bank account.[59] Its scope is, moreover, widened by the fact that property which can be misapplied can include property which is not yet vested in the company or in any person on its behalf, but which comes to the directors in circumstances where they are in duty bound, for example through some express or implied mandate, to acquire and hold

[55] ibid. at p. 837. This is analogous to '*Wednesbury* unreasonableness' in public law cases; see *Re a Company, ex parte Glossop* [1988] BCLC 570.

[56] See 14.24.1, below.

[57] *Re London and Provincial Starch Co., Gower's Case* (1868) LR 6 Eq. 77.

[58] For a full statement of the nature of the director's liability, see *Selangor United Rubber Estates Ltd v Cradock (No. 3)* [1968] 1 WLR 1555 at pp. 1575–6. Third parties who participate in such a breach of trust may themselves be liable to the company as constructive trustees: see *Gore-Browne on Companies* (Jordans, 44th edn, loose-leaf), 27.6.3.

[59] *Selangor United Rubber Estates Ltd v Cradock (No. 3)*, above.

it for the company's benefit.[60] Furthermore, the term 'property' in this context may cover confidential information of a special and valuable nature (such as secret manufacturing processes and patents, but not mere 'know-how')[61] and also business advantages such as the opportunity to enter into a favourable contract within the company's existing line of business.[62] Thus, a director who makes an invention or other valuable technical discovery in the course of performing active duties as an employee of the company holds the benefit of his discovery (including any patent rights that he has acquired in respect thereof) on trust for the company; it would not matter that he was not specifically commissioned by the company to make the relevant discovery, provided that it fell within the company's line of business.[63] It is equally a breach of trust for a director to make use of 'trade secrets' to the company's detriment, and in appropriate cases he can be prevented by injunction from so doing.[64]

In *Cook v Deeks*[65] three directors of a private company, holding a majority of the shares, appropriated to themselves an opportunity to enter into a highly favourable business contract, it being evident that the opportunity was only presented to them because they were directors of the company and that the company's business would have greatly benefited from having the contract. They purported to ratify this breach of duty by using the votes attached to their shares to pass an ordinary resolution, but were nonetheless held liable to account to the company for the profits derived from the contract, on the basis that the contract 'belonged in equity to the company'.[66] An alternative remedy for the company in such a situation may be damages for breach of the director's contract of service (assuming that he has one); in the assessment of these damages the court will take into account the extent to which the company was likely to obtain the business contract for itself.[67] If misapplied assets have already been returned to the company, the director will be under no further liability,[68] but the director who is accountable cannot claim to set off against this anything owed to him under a contract of employment.[69]

14.8.2 *Further examples of misapplications*
Many further instances of directors' liability for losses resulting from the misapplication of company property are to be found in the case-law. Examples are:

---

[60] *Benson v Heathorn* (1842) 1 Y & CCC 326; *Burland v Earle* [1902] AC 83 at pp. 98–9 (PC); *Cook v Deeks* [1916] 1 AC 554 (PC). For a detailed discussion of when such a duty arises, see the South African case of *Robinson v Randfontein Estates Gold Mining Co. Ltd* [1921] AD 168 (South African SC).

[61] See e.g. *Saltman Engineering Co. Ltd v Campbell Engineering Co. Ltd* [1963] 3 All ER 413n (CA); *Heyting v Dupont* [1964] 1 WLR 843 (CA); *Cranleigh Precision Engineering Ltd v Bryant* [1965] 1 WLR 1293; *Phipps v Boardman* [1967] 2 AC 46 (HL). In relation to such 'property', the positions of directors, ordinary employees and other fiduciary agents are virtually the same, though the duty not to misuse confidential information 'applies with particular force as between a director and his company': *Baker v Gibbons* [1972] 1 WLR 693 at p. 700. See also *Thomas Marshall (Exports) Ltd v Guinle* [1979] Ch 227, especially at p. 248, for a discussion of what constitutes confidential information; cf. *Island Export Finance Ltd v Umunna* [1986] BCLC 460.

[62] *Burland v Earle*, above, at p. 93; *Cook v Deeks*, above.

[63] *Cranleigh Precision Engineering Ltd v Bryant*, above; and see *British Syphon Co. Ltd v Homewood* [1956] 1 WLR 1190.

[64] *Measures Bros. Ltd v Measures* [1910] 1 Ch 336 (affirmed in [1910] 2 Ch 248 (CA)); *Cranleigh Precision Engineering Ltd v Bryant*, above; and see *Printers & Finishers Ltd v Holloway* [1965] 1 WLR 1.

[65] [1916] 1 AC 554 (PC). See too *Canadian Aero Service Ltd v O'Malley* [1973] 40 DLR (3d) 371 (Canadian SC).

[66] ibid., at p. 564. As to the ratification issue, see 14.24.1, below.

[67] *Industrial Development Consultants Ltd v Cooley* [1972] 2 All ER 162 (discussed further at 14.9, below).

[68] *Re Derek Randall Enterprises Ltd* [1990] BCC 749 (CA). No doubt this assumes no further loss by the company.

[69] *Zerco Ltd v Jerrom-Pugh* [1993] BCC 275 (CA).

(1) the application of funds in breach of what is now section 151 of the Companies Act 1985;[70]

(2) the payment of compensation to a director in breach of section 312;[71]

(3) the making of a loan to a director in breach of what is now section 330;[72]

(4) the payment or recommendation to pay dividends out of capital;[73]

(5) the unlawful issue of bonus shares or shares at a discount;[74]

(6) the payment of unauthorised commission to a broker for placing shares;[75]

(7) the allotment of shares by directors to themselves or their friends at par when they would be able to find purchasers willing to take them at a premium;[76]

(8) any ultra vires disposition of a company's assets,[77] unauthorised payment of remuneration to a director,[78] or bribe paid to a third party;[79]

(9) the execution of a guarantee and debenture in breach of the articles and not bona fide in the interests of the company;[80]

(10) the signing of blank transfer forms in respect of securities owned by the company which were transferred without consideration and without the authority of the full board of directors.[81]

Where directors are liable for misapplication of a company's funds, they may be charged compound interest.[82]

14.9 Avoidance of conflict of interest and duty

Directors are in general bound by the broad principle, affecting all persons who are subject to fiduciary duties, that 'no-one, having such duties to discharge, shall be allowed to enter into engagements in which he has, or can have a personal interest conflicting, or which possibly may conflict, with the interests of those whom he is bound to protect.'[83] This principle equally applies if the director has an 'outside' duty which clashes or may

---

[70] *Steen v Law* [1964] AC 287 (PC); *Selangor United Rubber Estates Ltd v Cradock (No. 3)* [1968] 1 WLR 1555; *Wallersteiner v Moir (No. 1)* [1974] 1 WLR 991 (CA). *Belmont Finance Corp. Ltd v Williams Furniture Ltd* [1980] 1 All ER 393 (CA).

[71] *Re Duomatic Ltd* [1969] 2 Ch 365.

[72] *Wallersteiner v Moir (No. 1)*, above.

[73] *Flitcroft's Case* (1882) 21 Ch D 536 (CA).

[74] *Hirsche v Sims* [1894] AC 654 (PC).

[75] *Re Faure Electric Accumulator Co.* (1889) 40 Ch D 141.

[76] *Parker v McKenna* (1875) 10 Ch App. 96.

[77] *Russell v Wakefield Waterworks Co.* (1875) LR 20 Eq. 474. This is expressly preserved by section 35 (3) of the Companies Act 1985.

[78] *Re George Newman & Co.* [1895] 1 Ch 674 (CA). See also *Guinness plc v Saunders* [1990] 2 AC 663 (HL), discussed in 14.9, although the House of Lords did not use the language of misapplication.

[79] *E. Hannibal & Co. Ltd v Frost* (1988) 4 BCC 3 (CA).

[80] *Rolled Steel Products v British Steel Corporation* [1985] 2 WLR 908 (CA); see further as to this case, 4.7–4.8 above.

[81] *Bishopsgate Investment Management Ltd v Maxwell* [1993] BCC 120 (CA).

[82] *Wallersteiner v Moir (No. 2)* [1975] QB 373 (CA), applying principles established in relation to defaulting trustees. See further, *Gore-Browne on Companies* (Jordans, 44th edn, loose-leaf), 27.6.2.

[83] *Aberdeen Rly Co. v Blaikie* (1854) 1 Macq. 461 at pp. 471–2 (HL (Sc.)), *per* Lord Cranworth LC; see too *North-West Transportation Co. Ltd v Beatty* (1887) 12 App. Cas. 589 at p. 593 (PC); *Bray v Ford* [1896] AC 44 at pp. 51–2 (HL); *Regal (Hastings) Ltd v Gulliver* [1942] 1 All ER 378 at p. 381; [1967] 2 AC 134n at p. 137 (HL); *Boulting v A.C.T.A.T.* [1963] 2 QB 606 at p. 635 (CA); *New Zealand Netherlands Society 'Oranje' Inc. v Kuys* [1973] 1 WLR 1126 at p. 1129 (PC); *Queensland Mines Ltd v Hudson* (1978) 52 ALJR 399 (PC); *Guinness plc v Saunders* [1990] 2 AC 663 (HL).

clash with his fiduciary duties to the company.[84] It is a principle that may be invoked by the company only, and not by the director by way of a defence to proceedings instigated to compel performance of the conflicting duty.[85] It has at times been suggested that it is too broad a principle to be strictly applicable in all situations,[86] but it is nonetheless the underlying basis of the more specific fiduciary duties discussed in the following sections, as well as being a distinct principle in its own right.[87]

This last point is illustrated by *Industrial Development Consultants v Cooley*.[88] Here the managing director of a design and construction company, being himself a successful architect, failed in an attempt to obtain for the company a valuable contract to do work for a local gas board. He was subsequently approached by the board with an offer to take up the contract in his private capacity, the board still indicating that it was not interested in letting the company have the contract. He concealed this offer from the company and, by misrepresenting that he was in poor health, procured the company to release him from his service contract, in order that he could take up the contract for himself. It was held by Roskill J that he was liable to account to the company for the profit which he obtained from performing the contract, on the footing that he should have informed the company of the board's offer to him and that, after the offer was made, he 'embarked on a deliberate policy and course of conduct which put his personal interest as a potential contracting party with the [gas board] in direct conflict with his pre-existing and continuing duty as managing director of the [company].'[89]

A further example is provided by the recent House of Lords' decision in *Guinness plc v Saunders*.[90] Here a director of Guinness, which was engaged in making a takeover bid for the shares of another company, agreed to provide services to Guinness in connection with the bid for a substantial fee, the size of which was dependent on the value of the bid. In the absence of a properly authorised contract,[91] it was held by the House of Lords that the director had put himself into a position where there was an irreconcilable conflict between his personal interests and his duty, in consequence of which he had no claim to an equitable allowance for his services.

14.10 Disclosure of interests in contracts at general law

Subject to modification by the articles, the requirement to avoid a conflict of duty and interest means that a director is under a duty to disclose to the shareholders in general

---

[84] *Transvaal Lands Co. v New Belgium (Transvaal) Land and Development Co.* [1914] 2 Ch 488 (CA); and see further 14.22, below.

[85] *Boulting v A.C.T.A.T.*, above.

[86] See e.g. ibid.; *Phipps v Boardman* [1967] 2 AC 46 at p. 124, *per* Lord Upjohn, dissenting; *New Zealand Netherlands Society 'Oranje' Inc. v Kuys*, above, at p. 1130. For a brief comment as to the fairness of the principle as it applies to 'secret profits', see 14.18.3 below, and the sources cited there.

[87] See *Phipps v Boardman*, above, at pp. 103, 111. This principle is clearly more aptly described as a 'principle' rather than as a 'duty', although its application may lead to duties imposed on directors, e.g. duties of disclosure. See Vinelott J in *Motivex Ltd v Bulfield* (1986) 2 BCC 99, 403 (following *Tito v Waddell (No. 2)* [1977] 3 All ER 129); this case is discussed further in 14.24.3, below.

[88] [1972] 2 All ER 162.

[89] [1972] 2 All ER 162, at pp. 173–4.

[90] [1990] 2 AC 663.

[91] The articles of Guinness would have permitted such a contract provided that it had been approved by the full board of directors (along the lines of standard articles referred to in the following sections). Instead it was only the sub-committee of the board charged with facilitating the takeover which had purported to enter into a contract. This 'contract' was void.

meeting the nature of any interest which he has in a contract to which the company is or is to be a party.[92] In the event of the director failing to disclose his interest to the meeting, or of the meeting refusing to sanction his interest, two consequences follow.[93] In the first place, the contract is voidable at the option of the company against any party thereto who has notice of the breach of duty,[94] though its right of avoidance will lapse if it affirms the contract, or it delays unduly before rescinding, or the rights of bona fide third parties intervene.[95] Secondly, any profit which the director derives from the contract is recoverable from him by the company,[96] even if he can show that it is unfair for the company to have the profit and/or that the transaction was fair and reasonable and/or that he could have made the same amount of profit after disclosure.[97] It should be noted, however, that when all that he has done is to fail to disclose his interest in a sale to the company of property which he acquired in his own right free from any duty to hold it on trust for the company, his profit on the resale is not accountable and the company's only remedy is to rescind (which makes it particularly important that the company should rescind quickly before anything happens to bar this right).[98] If the general meeting sanctions the director's interest in the contract, the contract ceases to be voidable and the director may retain any profit arising out of it. On the resolution for approval, the director may vote in his own interests on any shares of which he is the holder, except where to do so constitutes fraud or 'oppression'.[99]

14.11 Statutory duty to disclose interests in contracts

These duties imposed by general law are supplemented by a number of provisions in the Companies Act 1985.[100] As a general provision, section 317 makes it the duty of every director interested directly or indirectly in any way in any contract, proposed contract, transaction or arrangement with a company of which he is a director to declare the nature of his interest at a meeting of directors,[101] and an unlimited fine on conviction on indictment may be imposed for default. The section does not prejudice any rule of law restricting directors of a company from having any interest in a contract with the company;[102] in other words, the general law described in 14.10 must be complied with.[103]

In the case of a proposed contract the declaration must be made at the meeting of the

---

[92] *Aberdeen Rly Co. v Blaikie* (1854) 1 Macq. 461 (HL (Sc.)).

[93] Under some articles, the director may in addition be liable to disqualification.

[94] *Hely-Hutchinson & Co. Ltd v Brayhead* [1968] 1 QB 549 (CA); *Cowan de Groot Properties Ltd v Eagle Trust plc* [1991] BCLC 1045 at pp. 1116–7.

[95] ibid. *Victors Ltd v Lingard* [1927] 1 Ch 323. It is submitted that only the general meeting, and not the board, should have the right to affirm the contract: see *Re Cardiff Preserved Coke and Coal Co.* (1862) 32 LJ Ch 154; *North-West Transportation Co. Ltd v Beatty* (1887) 12 App. Cas. 589 at p. 600 (PC).

[96] *Aberdeen Rly Co. v Blaikie* (1854) 1 Macq. 461 (HL (Sc.)); *Imperial Mercantile Credit Association v Coleman* (1873) LR 6 HL 189.

[97] *Costa Rica Rly Co. v Forwood* [1901] 1 Ch 746 at p. 761 (CA); *Gray v New Augarita Porcupine Mines Ltd* [1952] 3 DLR 1 at p. 15 (PC).

[98] *Cavendish-Bentinck v Fenn* (1887) 12 App. Cas. 652; *Re Lady Forrest (Murchison) Gold Mines Ltd* [1901] 1 Ch 582; *Burland v Earle* [1902] AC 83; *Jacobus Marler Estates Ltd v Marler* (1913) 114 LT 640n (PC).

[99] *North-Western Transportation Co. Ltd v Beatty*, above; *Burland v Earle*, above, at p. 94; *Harris v A. Harris Ltd* 1936 SC 183; *Baird v Baird & Co. (Falkirk) Ltd* 1949 SLT 368; and see 14.24 and 15.4, below.

[100] In addition to that described here, see those discussed in 14.14 *et seq.*, below.

[101] Section 317 (1).

[102] Section 317 (9).

[103] Save in so far as it is modified by the articles as described in 14.12, below.

directors at which the question of entering into the contract is first taken into consideration, or if the director was not at the date of that meeting interested in the proposed contract, then at the next meeting of the directors held after he became so interested. Where the director becomes interested in a contract after it is made, the declaration must be made at the first meeting of the directors held after the director becomes so interested.[104] A general notice given to the directors of a company by a director to the effect that (a) he is a member of a specified company or firm and is to be regarded as interested in any contract which may, after the date of the notice, be made with that company or firm, or (b) he is to be regarded as interested in any contract which may after the date of the notice be made with a specified person who is connected with him,[105] is a sufficient declaration of interest in relation to any contract so made, provided that it is given at a meeting of the directors, or the director takes reasonable steps to ensure that it is brought up and read at the next meeting of the directors after it is given.[106]

Section 317 requires disclosure to a duly convened meeting of the full board of directors,[107] and where the director is already interested, the contract must be presented for consideration and approval, not as a *fait accompli*.[108] A failure formally to declare an interest common to all members of the board and, *ex hypothesi*, known to all, is unlikely to be regarded as a breach of the section.[109] Similarly, it has been held that a company could not rely upon the section where the failure to declare an interest, a variation of a director's service contract, was a purely technical breach since all the directors were aware of the variation.[110] It is important to bear in mind that this amounts to a dispensation on equitable grounds, where any other result would have been unjust.[111] It does not support any general dispensing with the requirements of section 317,[112] since there appear to be sound policy reasons for, in general, requiring formal declarations of interest, in particular that they draw the attention of the directors specifically to the duties that the law imposes on them and that they will be minuted and permanently recorded.[113]

Section 317 also applies to a 'shadow director'.[114] Such a person obviously cannot declare his interest at a meeting of the directors. He is required to inform the directors by notice in writing, which must be either a specific notice before the date of the meeting if the matter relates to an existing or proposed contract and section 317 (2) would have required disclosure at that meeting had the person been a director, or a general notice under section 317 (3).

14.12 The effect of releasing provisions in the articles

The outcome of these rules is that no less than three distinct duties of disclosure exist: direct disclosure to the general meeting (at general law) and disclosure to the board (under

---

[104] Section 317 (2).

[105] The relevance of 'connected person' is with regard to the provisions regarding substantial property transactions and loans. It is defined in section 346 and discussed in 14.16, below.

[106] Section 317 (3) and (4).

[107] *Guinness plc v Saunders* [1988] BCLC 607 (CA), affirmed on other grounds [1990] 2 AC 663.

[108] *Re Nuneaton Borough AFC Ltd (No. 2)* [1991] BCLC 44 at pp. 59–60.

[109] *Lee Panavision Ltd v Lee Lighting* [1992] BCLC 22 at p. 33 (CA).

[110] *Runciman v Walter Runciman plc* [1992] BCLC 1084.

[111] ibid. at pp. 1093 and 1097.

[112] And article 85 of Table A, with which in practice it will often have to be read. See 14.12.

[113] [1992] BCLC 22 at p. 1095. See also *Neptune (Vehicle Washing Equipment) Ltd v Fitzgerald*, 10 February 1995, where it was held that a sole director was obliged to make a section 317 declaration of interest.

[114] Section 317 (8). See 14.2, above.

section 317 of the Companies Act 1985); there is also a requirement of disclosure to the general meeting and the public through the accounts (under sections 232 and 233 and Schedule 6).[115] In practice, however, the articles almost invariably contain provisions which release directors from the first of these duties,[116] provided that section 317, which is mandatory in operation, is complied with and (in most cases) that, with some specified exceptions, the interested director does not vote upon any board resolution by which the contract or his having an interest therein is approved, and is not counted in the quorum for such resolution.[117] Such provisions are valid and, provided they are strictly complied with, neither of the two remedies prescribed at general law for breach of the general law duty of disclosure – i.e. rescission of the contract and an account of profits – can be invoked by the company.[118] On the other hand, any failure to comply with the relevant provisions of the articles renders both remedies available to the company,[119] subject to the limitations thereon which have already been mentioned. A breach of section 317 does not of itself render the contract voidable, although that result may follow from the general law principles described above.[120]

Article 85 of Table A is the current standard provision. It provides that: 'Subject to the provisions of the Act, and provided that he has disclosed to the directors the nature and extent of any material interest of his, a director notwithstanding his office ... may be a party to, or otherwise interested in, any transaction ... with the company...'. The drafting of this article has been judicially criticised, but it has been held that its effect is that the whole thrust of the Act, and in particular the specific requirements for disclosure under section 317, must be read into it.[121] On that basis, disclosure under article 85 had to be 'to the board at a meeting and at the meeting when the relevant contract first comes to be considered.[122]

14.13 Interpretation of the rules as to disclosure

Various decisions have been given as to the meeting of 'interest' in this context, though in considering them it should be remembered that most of them are decisions on particular provisions in company articles and are thus not necessarily applicable directly to other such provisions or to section 317 of the Companies Act 1985.[123] A director has been

---

[115] See 12.12, above.

[116] See e.g. Table A, articles 85 and 86 described below and see further 14.24.3, below.

[117] See articles 94 and 95 of Table A.

[118] *Imperial Mercantile Credit Association v Coleman* (1871) 6 Ch App. 558 (revd on other grounds (1873) LR 6 HL 189).

[119] *Imperial Mercantile Credit Association v Coleman* (1873) LR 6 HL 189; *Hely-Hutchinson & Co. Ltd v Brayhead* [1968] 1 QB 549 (CA).

[120] *Hely-Hutchinson & Co. Ltd v Brayhead*, above; *Guinness plc v Saunders* [1990] 1 All ER 653 at pp. 664–5 *per* Lord Goff of Chievely. Lord Templeman (ibid. at p. 662) seemed to think that the *Hely-Hutchinson* decision decided the contrary, but it is thought that the view of Lord Goff is to be preferred. See also *Lee Panavision Ltd v Lee Lighting Ltd* [1991] BCLC 575 at p. 583 and *Cowan de Groot Properties Ltd v Eagle Trust plc* [1991] BCLC 1045 at p. 1113.

[121] *Lee Panavision Ltd v Lee Lighting* [1991] BCLC 575. This decision was upheld by the Court of Appeal ([1992] BCLC 22) on other grounds (see 14.7, above) and the CA expressly declined to express a view on this point.

[122] ibid. at pp. 583–84, *per* Harman J. As to the construction of a slightly different article, see *Cowan de Groot Properties Ltd v Eagle Trust plc*, above, at pp. 1113–4.

[123] Note in particular that the modern Table A (14.12) refers to 'material interest', which is clearly narrower than the reference to 'interest' in the 1948 Table A, and might well not comprehend the situations in the cases in the next two footnotes.

held to be interested in a contract with another company in which he was a share-holder[124] or a firm of which he was a member,[125] in a contract to allot shares or debentures to him,[126] and in a debenture granted to release him from a personal guarantee of a debt.[127] It goes without saying that a director is 'interested' in an agreement whereby he provides services to the company (whether as chairman of directors, managing director, executive director or otherwise) for a remuneration; on the other hand, an agreement whereby he is appointed chairman or managing director without any (or any additional) remuneration is merely a delegation of power and not a contract in which he is 'interested'.[128] It is expressly provided by section 317 (6) that a transaction or arrangement within section 330, i.e. loans and related dealings,[129] made by a company for a director or for a person connected with a director[130] is to be treated as a contract in which that director is interested for the purposes of section 317, if it would not otherwise be so treated, and whether or not the transaction or arrangement is prohibited by section 330.

Under section 317, 'the nature' of the director's interest must be disclosed by him, and the articles cannot reduce this obligation. It has been said in addition that disclosure must be 'full and frank'.[131] The result is that generally speaking it will not be enough for the director merely to say 'I am interested' in the relevant contract; however, there is no hard and fast rule as to how far disclosure must go. 'The amount of detail must depend in each case upon the nature of the contract or arrangement proposed and the context in which it arises.'[132] It has been held[133] that directors negotiating an agreement whereby their contracts of service are terminated in return for compensation for loss of office are not bound to disclose past breaches of duty which would entitle the company to dismiss them without compensation, but this is somewhat difficult to accept, and the opposite view has more recently been taken.[134]

14.14 Specific rules regarding directors' interests in contracts

Even if the above rules as to disclosure are complied with, a contract in which a director is 'interested' will be voidable if it is not made bona fide in the company's interests, and for the proper purposes, in accordance with the first two fiduciary principles discussed above. If the director is actually a party, he will most likely not have a defence to an action for

---

[124] Even as a trustee (*Transvaal Lands Co. v New Belgium (Transvaal) Land and Development Co.* [1914] 2 Ch 488), though not if he is a bare trustee without duties to perform (*Cowan de Groot Properties Ltd v Eagle Trust plc* [1991] BCLC 1045 at p. 1115).

[125] *Imperial Mercantile Credit Association v Coleman* (1873) LR 6 HL 189.

[126] *Neal v Quin* [1916] WN 223; *Cox v Dublin City Distillery (No. 2)* [1915] 1 Ir. R. 145.

[127] *Rolled Steel Products Ltd v British Steel Corporation* [1984] BCLC 466 (CA). See also *Lee Panavision Ltd v Lee Lighting Ltd* [1991] BCLC 575 (contract including indemnity for director).

[128] *Foster v Foster* [1916] 1 Ch 532; *Runciman v Walter Runciman plc* [1992] BCLC 735.

[129] See 14.17.1, below.

[130] 'Connected person' is defined in section 346 and discussed in 14.14, below.

[131] *Fine Industrial Commodities Ltd v Powling* (1954) 71 RPC 253 at p. 262, *per* Danckwerts J. Standard articles following article 85 of Table A require disclosure of the nature *and extent* of any material interest.

[132] *Gray v New Augarita Porcupine Mines Ltd* [1952] 3 DLR 1 at p. 14, *per* Lord Radcliffe.

[133] *Healey v SA Française Rubastic* [1971] 1 KB 946, approved in *Bell v Lever Bros. Ltd* [1932] AC 161 at pp. 228, 231 (HL).

[134] *Horcal Ltd v Gatland* [1983] BCLC 60, esp. at pp. 65–7. Compare, however, the view of Robert Goff LJ on appeal, obiter: [1984] BCLC 549 at p. 554.

rescission because he will be aware of the relevant breach of duty. Furthermore, certain types of contract in which a director is 'interested' are subject to special rules and restrictions in the Companies Act 1985 over and above those just mentioned. These rules and restrictions relate particularly to directors' service contracts, substantial property transactions involving directors, and loans to and related deals with directors. These are examined in the following sections.[135]

It should be noted that most of these rules and restrictions apply to shadow directors as much as to directors.[136] Further, many of them also apply to 'persons connected' with directors, so that avoidance of them is not easily effected. It is appropriate to describe such persons at this stage.

By section 346, a connected person is someone who is not a director of the company who falls within one of the following categories.[137]

(1) A director's spouse or infant child or step-child.[138]
(2) An associated body corporate; this is basically a body corporate[139] in which a director and any person connected with him has a 20 per cent interest. The interest may be either an interest in equity share capital[140] or the control of one-fifth or more of the voting power at general meetings.[141]
(3) The trustee (other than under an employees' share scheme or a pension scheme) acting in that capacity of any trust under which a director, his spouse or infant children or an associated body corporate are or may be a beneficiary.
(4) A partner of a director or connected person, acting as such.
(5) A Scottish firm in which a director or connected person is a partner.

14.15 Directors' service contracts

It should be noted first that these have their own special rules in Table A, article 84 of the Companies Act 1985, and in the articles commonly adopted by public companies in imitation of Table A. Further, the articles are usually more liberal in respect of voting and quorum requirements[142] than the articles governing directors' contracts in general.

Secondly, section 319 contains important restrictions on the length of service contracts.[143] The section applies to the employment[144] of a director by a company and, where the company is a holding company, to the employment of any of its directors within the group,[145] provided that the company is a company within the meaning of the Act or registered under section 680, and except where the company is the wholly owned

---

[135] Note also the controls where directors exceed their powers: section 322A, discussed in 4.23, above.
[136] As to shadow directors, see 14.2, above.
[137] For a fuller explanation, see *Gore-Browne on Companies* (Jordans, 44th edn, loose-leaf), 27.11.
[138] Including an illegitimate child.
[139] This expression, defined in section 740, is used to catch foreign as well as British companies.
[140] 'Interest' is defined widely by reference to Schedule 13, as to which see 13.22.2, above.
[141] Note the qualifications in section 346 (6) regarding this category of connected person.
[142] See article 97 of Table A.
[143] For other provision controlling service contracts, see 13.21, above. There seems to be a growing feeling that the five years allowed by section 319 without general meeting approval is now too long for directors of public companies.
[144] Whether under a contract of service or a contract for services; section 319 (7) (*a*).
[145] i.e. that company and its subsidiaries; section 319 (7) (*b*).

subsidiary[146] of any body corporate, wherever incorporated.[147] It is prohibited for any company thus falling within section 319 to incorporate in any agreement providing for such a director's employment[148] a term whereby that employment may continue, other than at the instance of the company, for more than five years, if during that time it cannot be terminated by the company by notice or can be terminated by notice only in specified circumstances, unless that term is first approved by a resolution of the company in general meeting or, in the case of a director of a holding company, by a resolution of that company in general meeting.

Where a director is, or is to be, employed under an agreement with similar restrictions on its being terminated, and, more than six months before the end of this agreement, a further agreement is entered into under which he is to be employed with the company, or with the group where he is a director of a holding company, the unexpired part of the old agreement must be added to the period of the new agreement. If the result is a term of more than five years, general meeting sanction as above must be obtained. However, this does not apply where the new agreement was entered into in pursuance of a right conferred on the party to the agreement other than the company.[149]

Before a resolution approving a term longer than five years can be passed, a written memorandum setting out the proposed agreement containing the term must be available for inspection by members of the company at the company's registered office for at least fifteen days before the relevant meeting, and at the meeting itself.[150]

A term which contravenes section 319 is void to the extent that it contravenes the section, and the agreement is deemed to contain a term entitling the company to determine it at any time by reasonable notice.[151] In other words, the agreement is deemed to be made for five years subject to its being determinable at any time within that period by reasonable notice.

14.16 Substantial property transactions

Any contract by which a company sells to or buys from a director property of any sort, and any other property dealings between directors and their companies, are subject to the general rules already described. The provisions of sections 320 to 322 of the Companies Act 1985 reinforce these general rules, in particular by imposing a requirement of general meeting approval similar to that required by the general law[152] which had in practice been modified by articles of association[153] until the introduction (in 1980) of what are now sections 320 to 322. Further, the sections do not catch only contracts between

---

[146] See section 736 (2), by which a company is deemed to be the wholly owned subsidiary of another if it has no members except that other and the latter's wholly owned subsidiaries or persons acting on behalf of that other or its wholly owned subsidiaries.

[147] Section 319 (4).

[148] Section 319 does not therefore apply just to a contract directly between a director and his company, and cannot be evaded by, e.g., the use of a contract between the company and another company which the director controls.

[149] Section 319 (2).

[150] Section 319 (5).

[151] Section 319 (6).

[152] See 14.10, above.

[153] See 14.12, above.

directors and their companies, since they apply to 'arrangements', a deliberately broad word, and to deals with shadow directors[154] and connected persons.[155]

The statute applies to an arrangement for the acquisition[156] from a company[157] of one or more non-cash assets[158] of the requisite value by a director of the company or its holding company or a person connected with such a director, and conversely, to an arrangement for the acquisition by a company of one or more non-cash assets of the requisite value from such a director or connected person. To fall within the section, the value of the asset or assets must be more than £10,000 or 10 per cent of the company's asset value, subject in the latter case to a minimum of £2,000.[159] The amount of a company's asset value is the value of its net assets as determined by reference to its last annual accounts prepared and laid under Part VII,[160] or its called-up share capital if no such accounts have been prepared and laid at the relevant time.[161]

However, section 320 does not apply in the following circumstances:

(1) where the company is the wholly owned subsidiary of any body corporate, wherever incorporated;[162]

(2) to an arrangement for the acquisition of a non-cash asset, if the asset in question is to be acquired by a holding company from any of its wholly owned subsidiaries or from a holding company by any of its wholly owned subsidiaries or by one wholly owned subsidiary of a holding company from another wholly owned subsidiary of that same holding company;[163]

(3) to an arrangement for the acquisition of a non-cash asset entered into by a company which is being wound up, unless the winding-up is a members' voluntary winding-up;

(4) to an arrangement whereby a person is to acquire an asset from a company of which he is a member if the arrangement is made with him in his character as such member;[164]

(5) to a transaction on a recognised investment exchange which is effected by a director or connected person through the agency of an independent broker.[165]

An arrangement to acquire an asset in the circumstances described is forbidden unless it is first approved by a resolution of the company in general meeting and, if the director

---

[154] See 14.2, above.

[155] See 14.14, above.

[156] This clearly includes any dealing, whether by way of sale, gift, exchange or whatever. By section 739 (2), the acquisition of a non-cash asset includes the creation of an estate or interest in, or a right over, any property and the discharge of any person's liability, other than a liability for a liquidated sum.

[157] Within the meaning of the Act (see section 735) or registered under section 680.

[158] 'Non-cash asset' is defined in section 739 (1) as 'any property or interest in property other than cash (including foreign currency)'. This clearly includes a lease: *Niltan Carson Ltd v Hawthorne* [1988] BCLC 298.

[159] Reading section 320 (2) as if it included the words 'whichever is the lesser': *Niltan Carson Ltd v Hawthorne*, above. The onus is on the party alleging breach of the section to prove that the value exceeded the requisite value.

[160] See 12.2, above.

[161] Section 320 (2).

[162] Section 321. A body corporate is deemed to be the wholly owned subsidiary of another if it has no members except that other and the latter's wholly owned subsidiaries or persons acting on behalf of that other or its wholly owned subsidiaries: section 736 (2).

[163] Section 321 (2).

[164] Section 321 (3).

[165] Section 320 (4).

or connected person is a director of its holding company or a person connected with such a director, by a resolution of the holding company in general meeting. By section 322, a breach of this requirement renders the arrangement and any transaction entered into in pursuance of it voidable at the instance of the company,[166] except in the following circumstances:

(1) if restitution of any money or other asset which is the subject-matter of the arrangement or transaction is no longer possible, or the company has been indemnified in respect of loss or damage suffered by it under section 322;

(2) if avoidance would affect rights acquired for value by a third person not a party to the transaction or arrangement who acted in good faith and without actual notice of the contravention; or

(3) if the arrangement is within a reasonable time affirmed by the company in general meeting, and by a resolution in general meeting of its holding company if it involves a director of the holding company or a person connected with such a director.

In addition the party to an arrangement not so approved and any director of the company not a party to it who authorised it or a transaction entered into in pursuance of it are liable, whether or not the arrangement has been avoided, to account to the company for any gain made directly or indirectly by the arrangement or transaction, and are jointly and severally liable to indemnify the company for any loss or damage resulting from it. However, a connected person and a director not a party are excused from liability if they can show that at the time the arrangement was entered into, they did not know the relevant circumstances constituting the contravention, and where the arrangement is with a person connected with a director, that director is not liable if he shows that he took all reasonable steps to secure the company's compliance with the section. These statutory liabilities are expressly stated to be without prejudice to any liability imposed otherwise, i.e. under the common-law rules already discussed in 14.10, above.

14.17 Loans to directors and others

The Companies Act 1985 contains comprehensive prohibitions on companies making loans to and entering into equivalent transactions on behalf of directors and persons connected with directors. These replaced a prohibition in the Companies Act 1948 which was both easily avoided and, it seems, often evaded. As loans and similar transactions must be disclosed in the accounts,[167] the task of ensuring compliance with the provisions falls to some extent on the auditors. Subject to the general exceptions described below, the prohibitions fall into two categories: first those applying to all companies, and secondly those applying only to 'relevant companies'. The sections concerned are some of the most complex to be found in the companies legislation.

---

[166] But not illegal: *Niltan Carson Ltd v Hawthorne*, above.
[167] See 12.12, above.

14.17.1 Prohibitions on all companies

By section 330 (2), no company may lend money[168] to any of its directors or to a director of its holding company, nor may it guarantee[169] or provide security in connection with a loan made by a third person to such a director. In addition a company must not assume or have assigned to it any rights, obligations or liabilities under a transaction which, if it had been entered into by the company, would have contravened section 330 (2),[170] nor must it take part in any arrangement whereby another person enters into a transaction which, if it had been entered into by the company, would have contravened section 330 (2), and under the arrangement that person has obtained or is to obtain any benefit from the company or its holding company or a subsidiary of the company or its holding company.[171]

14.17.2 Prohibitions on relevant companies

A 'relevant company' is basically a public company or a company within a group which contains a public company.[172]

The prohibitions on relevant companies extend in particular to dealings with 'connected persons',[173] to what are termed 'quasi-loans', and to 'credit transactions'. The last two terms are dealt with below.

By section 331 (4) a 'quasi-loan' is a transaction under which a creditor pays, whether by agreement or otherwise, a sum for a borrower, or reimburses expenditure incurred by a third party for the borrower, on the terms that the borrower or someone on his behalf will reimburse the creditor, or in circumstances giving rise to a liability on the borrower to reimburse the creditor. For the purpose of the prohibitions, the company will be the creditor who pays money or reimburses expenditure to a third party for the director or connected person, the latter being the 'borrower' in the statutory definition liable to repay the sum to the company.[174]

A 'credit transaction' is defined as a transaction under which one party (the creditor)

(1) supplies any goods or sells any land under a hire-purchase or conditional sale agreement;[175]

(2) leases or hires any land or goods in return for periodical payment; or

---

[168] 'Loan' must be construed in its ordinary sense as a straightforward lending of money to be returned in money or money's worth — see *Champagne Perrier SA v H. H. Finch Ltd* [1982] 3 All ER 713, a case concerned with the predecessor to section 330 (section 190 of the 1948 Act). The arrangement in this case was what under the Act is a 'quasi-loan' (see 14.17.2 below).

[169] Or indemnify: section 331 (2).

[170] Section 330 (6). If a company does arrange for this in contravention of the prohibition, the transaction is treated as having been entered into on the date that the company enters into the arrangement.

[171] Section 330 (7).

[172] The full definition in section 331 (6) refers to a company which (a) is a public company, (b) is a subsidiary of a public company, (c) is a subsidiary of a company of which another subsidiary is a public company, or (d) has a subsidiary which is a public company.

[173] See 14.14.

[174] Any reference to the person to whom a quasi-loan is made is a reference to the borrower, and a borrower's liabilities under a quasi-loan include the liability of any person who has agreed to reimburse the creditor on behalf of the borrower: section 331 (4). A good example of a quasi-loan is to be found in *Champagne Perrier SA v H. H. Finch Ltd*, above, where a company paid bills for a director, on the basis that he would repay at a future date. Another example would be the provision of a credit card on similar terms.

[175] These bear the same meaning as in the Consumer Credit Act 1974 (see section 189 thereof): section 331 (10).

(3) otherwise disposes of land or supplies goods or services[176] on the understanding that payment (whether in a lump sum or instalments or by way of periodical payments or otherwise) is to be deferred.[177]

The prohibitions on relevant companies fall under five heads. Such a company must not:

(1) make a loan or quasi-loan to a director of it or of its holding company;
(2) make a loan or quasi-loan to a person connected with such a director; or
(3) enter into a guarantee or provide any security in connection with a loan or quasi-loan made by any other person for such a director or a person so connected.[178]

There are two qualifications to these first three prohibitions. First, where a relevant company is a member of a group of companies (meaning a holding company and its subsidiaries), heads (2) and (3) do not apply to prohibit the relevant company from making a loan or quasi-loan to another member of that group or entering into a guarantee or providing any security in connection with a loan or quasi-loan made by any person to another member of the group by reason only that a director of one member of the group is associated[179] with another member.[180] Secondly, a relevant company may make a quasi-loan to one of its own directors provided that it contains a term requiring the director or a person on his behalf to reimburse the company incurring the expenditure and provided that the amount of the quasi-loan and of any existing outstanding relevant[181] quasi-loans does not exceed £5,000.[182]

The fourth and fifth prohibitions rule that a relevant company must not:

(4) enter into a credit transaction as creditor for a director of it or of its holding company or a person connected with such a director; or
(5) enter into any guarantee or provide any security in connection with a credit transaction made by any other person for such a director or connected person.[183]

By section 335, there are two exceptions to heads (4) and (5). The first allows a relevant company to enter into, or guarantee, a credit transaction of the sort described so long as the aggregate of the value of that transaction and existing ones outstanding does not exceed £10,000.[184] Secondly, a relevant company whose ordinary course of business includes such transactions can enter into one with a director or connected person if it does so on its usual terms, i.e. the director, etc., is treated no differently from the way in which the company would treat an unconnected person of the same financial standing.[185]

---

[176] Services means anything other than goods or land: section 331 (8).

[177] Section 331 (7).

[178] Section 330 (3).

[179] Association is defined in section 346 (4), discussed in 14.14, above.

[180] Section 333.

[181] A quasi-loan is relevant if it was made to the director by virtue of this exception by the company or by its subsidiaries or, where the director is a director of the company's holding company, any other subsidiary of that company.

[182] Section 332.

[183] Section 330 (4).

[184] Section 335 (1). The full definitions, which are quite complex, of 'value' etc. are contained in sections 339 and 340. For a full description, see *Gore-Browne on Companies* (Jordans, 44th edn, loose-leaf), 27.14.3.

[185] Section 335 (2).

14.17.3 General exceptions

In addition to the limited exceptions already discussed, sections 334, 336, 337 and 338 provide for a number of general exceptions to the prohibitions on loans and related dealings in section 330. These are as follows:

(1) *Loans of small amounts.* Section 334 exempts entirely loans made to a director of the company or of its holding company if the aggregate of such loans outstanding does not exceed £5,000.

(2) *Transactions in favour of a holding company.* By section 336, none of the prohibitions against loans, quasi-loans and credit transactions applies where the deal is with or in favour of a company's holding company; in the absence of this exception, a holding company might well be caught as a director or connected person.

(3) *Directors' expenditure.* Under section 337, a company can provide its directors with funds (but only up to £20,000 in respect of relevant companies) to enable them to perform their duties or to meet expenditure incurred or to be incurred for the purpose of their duties. This is subject to a requirement of disclosure to and approval by the general meeting, or, failing such approval, to repayment within six months of the conclusion of the meeting.[186]

(4) *Moneylending companies.* These companies[187] can, by section 338, make loans, etc., to directors, etc. (but only up to £100,000 in the case of relevant companies which are not authorised institutions under the Banking Act 1987), if they are made on the ordinary terms, i.e. the director, etc., is treated no differently from the way in which the company would treat a person of the same financial standing without a connection with the company.[188]

14.17.4 Remedies and criminal penalties

The Companies Act 1985 makes express provision for civil remedies and criminal penalties[189] in respect of contraventions of section 330. By section 341, a transaction or arrangement in breach is voidable at the instance of the company unless:

(1) restitution of any money or other asset which is the subject-matter of the transaction or arrangement is no longer possible;

(2) the company has been indemnified under section 341 (2) (b)[190] for the loss or damage suffered by it; or

(3) any rights acquired bona fide for value and without actual notice of the contravention by a person other than the person for whom the transaction or arrangement was made would be affected by its avoidance.

In addition, or alternatively, and without prejudice to any other liability,[191] where a

---

[186] Section 337 (3) and (4).

[187] Defined in section 338 (1).

[188] More generous provision may be made for loans for house purchase and improvement if such loans are ordinarily made on similar terms to employees and do not exceed £100,000.

[189] The criminal penalties under section 342 are restricted to relevant companies, their directors, etc.

[190] Presumably, if the company relies on general law to recover any loss or damage (see footnote 191, below), this bar to avoidance will not apply.

[191] i.e. under the general law. In *Wallersteiner v Moir (No. 1)* [1974] 1 WLR 991, it was held that a director receiving a loan in breach of section 190 of the 1948 Act (the predecessor to the provision consolidated in section 330) was liable for misfeasance and to compensate the company for any loss. It is submitted that the same result would follow a breach of section 330. In addition, profit recoverable under section 341 (2) (see below) would be recoverable as a matter of general law.

prohibited transaction or arrangement has been made by a company with a director of it or of its holding company or with a person connected with such a director, any of these persons and any other director who authorised the transaction or arrangement is liable to account to the company for any gain made directly or indirectly by the transaction or arrangement, and jointly and severally liable to indemnify the company for any loss or damage resulting from it. However, a connected person or an authorising director is excused from civil liability if he shows that, at the time the arrangement or transaction was entered into, he did not know of the relevant circumstances constituting the contravention, and where an arrangement or transaction is with a person connected with a director, that director is not liable if he shows that he took all reasonable steps to secure the company's compliance with section 330.

14.18 Secret profits

There is a broad principle, developed from the law as to trustees and agents that any profit acquired by a director through holding the office of director must as a matter of law be accounted for to the company, unless the director has disclosed the profit and the circumstances in which he acquired it to the company in general meeting and his retention of it has been sanctioned by an ordinary resolution or by the acquiescence of all the individual members entitled to vote thereon, or unless he is protected by an appropriately worded provision of the articles.[192] This principle overlaps considerably with, but does not fully embrace, the rule that directors must not misapply the assets of the company[193] and also the rule that directors must disclose any interest in a contract involving the company as a party.[194]

14.18.1 Various types of secret profit

In the leading case of *Regal (Hastings) Ltd v Gulliver*,[195] the plaintiff company had formed a subsidiary company which was to take up a lease of two cinemas, but the owner of the cinemas insisted that the subsidiary should have a paid-up capital which, in the honest opinion of the plaintiff's board, was greater than the plaintiff could afford to subscribe. The ordinary directors accordingly subscribed at par for part of the balance themselves, the remainder being taken up by 'outsiders' in the name of the chairman of directors and by the plaintiff's solicitor. The whole transaction had been carried out with a view to a sale of the two cinemas, together with another cinema which the plaintiff itself owned, as a going concern, but ultimately the shares of the plaintiff and of the subsidiary were purchased instead at a price substantially above par. The plaintiff company sued the ordinary directors, the chairman and the solicitor for an account of their profits on the resale. It was found that they had all acted honestly throughout, but nonetheless the ordinary directors, who had taken their shares as beneficial owners, were held liable to account to the plaintiff, it being said that only disclosure to and approval by the general meeting would have saved them. On the other hand, the chairman escaped liability

---

[192] See further as to these matters, 14.24.3, below.

[193] Misapplications do not necessarily involve profit to the director, but may do so; conversely, the making of a secret profit does not necessarily involve loss to the company (which is of the essence of a misapplication), but may do so.

[194] An interest in a contract of the company does not necessarily produce a profit for the director, but may do so; conversely, the making of a secret profit does not necessarily involve having an interest in a contract of the company, but may do so.

[195] [1942] 1 All ER 378; [1967] 2 AC 134n (HL).

because the 'outsiders' who beneficially owned the shares for which he had subscribed owed no fiduciary duties to the company. The solicitor escaped also, on the ground that, although owing fiduciary duties to the company as its solicitor, his breach thereof could be and was effectively sanctioned by the board.

The effect of this decision is sometimes reversed, or substantially modified, by a provision in the articles,[196] but it submitted that its scope is wide enough to render a director liable to account when, through being aware of confidential information which comes to him because he is a director – an example is information as to an impending takeover – he makes a profit through buying and selling the company's own shares. The party entitled to claim the account would, of course, be the company; the decision in *Percival v Wright*[197] substantially curtails, if not totally bars, any claim by an individual shareholder in such a case unless he can establish some material misrepresentation by the director.

This general prohibition against the acquisition of secret profits is applicable to, *inter alia*, any secret commission or 'bribe' received by a director in the course of negotiating business transactions on the company's behalf,[198] any secret benefit coming to him in the course of any takeover bid for the company's shares or any reconstruction or amalgamation involving the company,[199] and profit derived through the use of confidential information which comes to the director's knowledge through his position on the board.[200]

14.18.2 *Remedies available to the company*

The *Regal (Hastings)* decision[201] establishes that, in an action for account of profits based upon his principle, it is no answer for the director to allege by way of defence that the company could not itself have acquired the relevant profit, or had bona fide decided not to try to acquire it, or in any event had not suffered any loss by virtue of the director having acquired it. However, evidence that an opportunity to enter into the transaction out of which the profit arose had been offered to and rejected by the company, then subsequently offered to the individual directors after a reasonable period of time had elapsed, may be enough to persuade the court that the profit was not derived by virtue of the director's position as such. It will be a question of fact in each case.[202] But it would seem that no defence is furnished by establishing any of the following matters:

---

[196] As to this, see 14.24.3, below. In the Table A to the 1948 Act, the decision was reversed (article 78). In the modern Table A it is instead modified by article 85.

[197] [1902] 2 Ch 421. See 14.3, above.

[198] *Boston Deep Sea Fishing and Ice Co. Ltd v Ansell* (1888) 39 Ch D 339 (CA). For a discussion of the law relating to bribes in a company law context, see Birds, Chapter 6 in Birks (ed.), *The Frontiers of Liability*, vol. 1 (Oxford University Press, 1994). As to the remedial consequences, see Millett J., ibid., Chapter 5 and *Attorney-General for Hong Kong v Reid* [1994] 1 All ER 1 (PC).

[199] *General Exchange Bank v Horner* (1870) LR 9 Eq. 480. The Companies Act 1985 reinforces this position: see sections 313 to 316, described in 14.20, below.

[200] This case may also, if the information is property and is misused to the company's detriment, amount to a misapplication of company property as described in 14.8, *supra*.

[201] [1942] 1 All ER 378; [1967] 2 AC 134n (HL). See also e.g. *Industrial Development Consultants Ltd v Cooley* [1972] 2 All ER 162, discussed in 14.9, above.

[202] See the Canadian case of *Peso Silver Mines Ltd v Cropper* (1966) 58 DLR (2d) 1 (Canadian SC); and the decision in *Queensland Mines Ltd v Hudson* (1978) 52 ALJR 399 (PC), where it was clear that the company had given up all interest in the transaction and was fully informed, albeit informally, of the director's intention to take up the opportunity himself. It was held therefore that the director was not accountable for the profit he made.

(1) that the director acted honestly and in good faith throughout;[203]

(2) that the profit was acquired through the use of the director's own property and/or skill as well as through his directorship;[204]

(3) that disclosure to the general meeting would have been a mere formality because at a general meeting the director had or could have summoned sufficient votes to pass a resolution approving his retention of the profit;[205]

(4) that none of the shareholders at the time of the proceedings for an account was a shareholder at the time when the profit was made.

If a director employed under an express contract of service makes a secret profit without due authorisation, the company can not only recover the profit, but also dismiss him without compensation, even though this breach of duty does not occur more than once. It does not matter that the company in fact effects the dismissal on some other insufficient ground and only finds out about the secret profit after the dismissal.[206] However, a director entering into an agreement to terminate his contract of service is not bound to disclose an intention to commit a breach of fiduciary duty. So non-disclosure does not make the agreement void for mistake, nor is any compensation paid recoverable.[207]

14.18.3 Comment on the secret profits rule

It is clear that the English courts may apply the secret profits rule strictly and it has been argued that it is applied too strictly. It has been said that it penalises the honest and leads to absurd results, especially in that the company may receive a windfall.[208]

While such criticisms appear at first sight to be well founded, and it has been further argued that the courts should move away from the strict accountability of the director who benefits secretly from his position towards the notion of whether he took advantage of a genuine corporate opportunity,[209] it is thought that there is merit in the strict rule at least as respects directors of large companies and of companies with widely dispersed

---

[203] *Regal (Hastings) Ltd v Gulliver*, above; and see *Phipps v Boardman* [1967] 2 AC 46.

[204] See ibid.; *Industrial Development Consultants v Cooley*, above.

[205] *Regal (Hastings) Ltd v Gulliver*, above.

[206] *Boston Deep Sea Fishing Co. v Ansell* (1888) 39 Ch D 339 (CA).

[207] *Horcal Ltd v Gatland* [1984] BCLC 549 (CA). Neither is any salary paid while the director is working out his contract recoverable, though he would, as admitted in that case, be accountable for any secret profit made. *Quaere* whether a director is under a duty to disclose a breach of duty already committed; see footnote 134, above. But a director's fiduciary duty does not necessarily come to an end when he ceases to be a director: *Island Export Finance Ltd v Umunna* [1986] BCLC 460.

[208] For the most persuasive criticism, based at least partly on the courts' failure to require a genuine conflict of duty and interest, see Jones, 84 LQR 472 (1968), attacking particularly the *Regal (Hastings)* case, above and the subsequent decision in *Phipps v Boardman* [1967] 2 AC 46 (HL) concerning a solicitor in a fiduciary position. The same cannot easily be said of a case like *Industrial Development Consultants Ltd v Cooley* [1972] 2 All ER 162, where the director certainly did not act honestly and where, it is thought, there was a real conflict of duty and interest; see 14.9, above. The same certainly cannot be said where the profit has resulted from a misapplication of company property, i.e. a breach of trust of the sort involved in *Cook v Deeks* [1916] 1 AC 554 (PC); see 14.8, above. For consideration of the economic aspects, see Bishop and Prentice (1983) 46 MLR 289.

[209] For suggestions along these lines, see the Canadian Supreme Court decision in *Canadian Aero-Service Ltd v O'Malley* (1973) 40 DLR (3d) 371, and the discussion in *Farrar's Company Law* (Butterworths, 3rd edn 1991), pp. 420–6. For an application of the reasoning in this case in an English case, see Hutchinson J in *Island Export v Umunna* [1986] BCLC 460 at pp. 478–9.

shareholders.[210] After all,[211] such directors are generally well-paid fiduciaries;[212] a strict rule can have the positive effect of encouraging them to do all they can for their companies in terms of pursuing opportunities and, last but by no means least, the prohibition is only against *secret* profits, so that if disclosure is made to and approval obtained of the company in general meeting, the director is relieved of any possibility of a breach of duty.[213]

14.19 Prohibition on option dealings

The 'secret profits' rule has been reinforced by a number of statutory provisions.[214] Section 323 of the Companies Act 1985 makes it a criminal offence for a director to buy either

(1) a right to call for delivery at a specified price and within a specified time of a specified number of 'relevant shares' or a specified amount of 'relevant debentures'; or

(2) a right to make delivery of 'relevant shares' or 'relevant debentures' on such terms; or

(3) a right at his election to call for or make delivery of 'relevant shares' or 'relevant debentures' on such terms.[215]

'Relevant shares' and 'relevant debentures' are shares and debentures respectively in the company of which the director is a director, or in any body corporate which is the company's subsidiary or holding company or a fellow subsidiary of the company's holding company, provided that they are listed on a stock exchange, whether in Great Britain or abroad. The section applies to shadow directors,[216] and 'price' includes any consideration other than money.[217] The section does not, however, prohibit a director from buying convertible debentures or options to subscribe for shares or debentures.[218]

Section 327 applies section 323 to the wife or husband or infant child (including a stepchild and adopted child) of a director who is not himself or herself a director, but it is a defence for such a person charged to show that he or she had no reason to believe that his or her spouse or parent (as the case may be) was a director of the company.

---

[210] As far as small companies are concerned, breaches of the duty must often in practice be waived either by the articles or by the consent of the members (who, of course, will often be the same people as the directors).

[211] For this sort of argument in full, see Prentice (1967) 30 MLR 450 and (1974) 50 Can. Bar. Rev. 623, and Beck, 'Corporate Opportunity Revisited', *Studies in Canadian Company Law*, vol. 2, p. 224.

[212] As opposed to, e.g., the solicitor in *Phipps v Boardman*, above. Even if they are not, the court can allow them such remuneration, in effect allowing them to retain part of their profits, as in *Phipps v Boardman*, above, and *O'Sullivan v Management Agency and Music Ltd* [1985] 3 WLR 448 (CA).

[213] Further, the articles may lessen or even possibly exclude the obligation of disclosure (see 14.24.3, below) and the director can also seek relief if he has acted honestly and reasonably under section 727 of the Companies Act 1985 (see 14.24.4, below, especially the comment in footnote 332).

[214] In addition to those described in this and the following section, note also the statutory obligation of directors and members of their families to disclose any interests they have in shares or debentures (see 13.22 *et seq.*, above).

[215] No civil consequences are indicated, but presumably the law as to illegal contracts applies to any prohibited option.

[216] Section 323 (4); see 14.2, above.

[217] Section 323 (3) (*c*).

[218] Section 323 (5).

14.20 Payments in connection with loss of office

Sections 312 to 315 of the Companies Act 1985 require the disclosure to and approval by the general meeting of certain types of payment made to directors connected with the loss of their office.

Section 312 prohibits the making of any payment by a company to a director of the company by way of compensation for loss of office or as consideration for or in connection with his retirement from office, unless particulars of the proposed payment, including the amount thereof, have been disclosed to the members[219] of the company and the proposal has been approved by the company. A director receiving such a payment in breach of the requirements is liable to repay it, and the directors responsible for its being made are also liable. It seems, however, that the section covers only payments made to compensate for the loss of the office of director. It does not cover payments made to compensate for the loss of a position as employee or payments which the company is contractually obliged to make, for example compensation payable under the terms of a managing director's service contract.[220]

Section 313 imposes the same requirements in respect of payments made to a director by the company or any other person in connection with the transfer of the whole or any part of the undertaking or property of the company. A payment in breach of section 313 is unlawful and the director is deemed to have received it in trust for the company.

Section 314 deals with similar payments when made in connection with the transfer to any persons of all or any of the shares in the company resulting from any of the following types of takeover bid:

(1) an offer made to the general body of shareholders;
(2) an offer made by or on behalf of some other body corporate with a view to the company becoming its subsidiary or a subsidiary of its holding company;
(3) an offer made by or on behalf of an individual with a view to his obtaining the right to exercise or control the exercise of not less than one-third of the voting power at any general meeting of the company;
(4) any other offer which is conditional on acceptance to a given extent.

When such a payment is to be made to a director, the director is under a duty to take all reasonable steps to secure that particulars of it, including its amount, are included in or sent with any notice of the offer made for their shares which is given to any shareholders.[221] If this duty is not discharged or the making of the proposed payment is not approved as described below, any sum received by the director on account of the payment is deemed to have been received by him in trust for any persons who have sold their shares as a result of the offer, and the expenses incurred by him in distributing that sum among those persons must be borne by him and not retained out of that sum. The approval must be given, before the transfer of any shares in pursuance of the offer, by a

---

[219] Including members with no or restricted voting rights: *Re Duomatic Ltd* [1969] 2 Ch 365.

[220] *Taupo Totara Timber Co. v Rowe* [1978] AC 537, a Privy Council decision on the identically worded section 191 of the New Zealand Companies Act 1955.

[221] A fine may be imposed on a defaulting director and on any person who fails to include or send the particulars, having been properly required to do so by the director: section 314 (3).

meeting, summoned for the purpose, of the holders of the shares to which the offer relates and of other holders of shares of the same class as any of those shares.[222]

Section 316 supplements the above sections in important ways. First, in relation to all the sections, the payments referred to do not include any bona fide payment by way of damages for breach of contract or by way of pension in respect of past services.[223] Secondly, avoidance of section 313 to 315 is prohibited by the following provisions. Where, in proceedings for the recovery of any payment received by any person on trust by virtue of the sections, it is shown that (a) the payment was made in pursuance of any arrangement entered into as part of the agreement for the transfer in question, or within one year before or two years after that agreement or the offer leading thereto, and (b) the company or any person to whom the transfer was made was privy to the arrangement, the payment is deemed, except in so far as the contrary is shown, to fall within the relevant section.[224] In addition, if, in connection with a transfer within either section, (a) the price to be paid to a director whose office is to be abolished or who is to retire from office for any shares held by him in the company is in excess of the price which could at the time have been obtained by other holders of the like shares, or (b) any valuable consideration is given to any such director, the excess or the money value of the consideration is deemed to be a payment made to him by way of compensation for loss of office or as consideration for or in connection with his retirement from office.[225] Finally, section 316 (4) provides that nothing in sections 313 to 315 prejudices the operation of any rule of law requiring disclosure to be made of any payments within the sections or any other like payments.[226]

Even if a payment falling within these sections is duly approved, it can still be invalid if made gratuitously and not for the benefit of the company as a whole, in the absence of an express power in the memorandum.[227]

14.21 Insider dealing

A further statutory provision relating to 'secret profits' is the prohibition against insider dealing. It is very important to note that the rules in question are not confined in their application to company directors. However, directors are among the people most likely to be within the rules and this is the most convenient place to describe them. Essentially, insider dealing involves the deliberate exploitation of unpublished price-sensitive information, obtained through or from a privileged relationship, to make a profit or avoid a loss by dealing in the securities of a company, when the price of the securities would be materially altered if the information were disclosed. For some years the balance of

---

[222] Section 315 (1). If these are not all the members of the company and the articles make no provision for such a meeting, the provisions of the Act and of the articles relating to general meetings apply to this meeting, with, if appropriate, such modifications as the Secretary of State may direct: section 315 (2). If the meeting is not quorate, and the adjourned meeting is similarly not quorate, the payment is deemed to have been approved for the purposes of the section: section 315 (3).

[223] Section 316 (3).

[224] Section 316 (1).

[225] Section 316 (2).

[226] e.g. disclosure in the accounts of compensation payments (see 12.10, above).

[227] *Gibson's Executor v Gibson* 1980 SLT 2. This is merely a particular application of the law as to corporate gifts (see 4.13, above).

opinion has supported the view that such dealing is wrong and should be the subject of legal sanctions.[228]

If a director or other person in a fiduciary relationship with a company makes a profit from insider dealing, it is clear that he is accountable for that profit under the principles described in 14.18. However, it seems equally clear that, in the absence of a special relationship, there is no fiduciary relationship requiring the disclosure of information between the director and shareholders individually. So a contract to buy or sell securities between a director and a shareholder will not in general be voidable for non-disclosure.[229] In essence this remains the civil-law position. However, there are now several regulatory and criminal-law provisions in place which seek to control insider dealing.[230] Whether or not they are successful is another matter, but not something which can be explored here. This section is hereafter concerned with the specific criminal-law provisions concerning insider dealing.

These are now contained in Part V of the Criminal Justice Act 1993, implementing the EC Directive on Insider Dealing.[231] This directive had a tortuous history, but has a philosophy firmly based on the importance of maintaining and fostering confidence in the integrity of the EC's securities markets by promoting 'smooth markets' where there is equality of information.[232] The United Kingdom had first made insider dealing a specific criminal offence in 1980,[233] and re-enacted the provisions with minor amendments in the Company Securities (Insider Dealing) Act 1985. The 1993 Act, completely replacing the 1985 Act, retains many of the central elements of the former law, but has refashioned and modified them in important respects.[234] Essentially there is one offence of insider dealing, although it can be committed in three ways:

(1) by dealing in securities the price of which will be affected by the inside information which is in that person's possession,[235]
(2) by encouraging another person so to deal;[236] and
(3) by disclosing the inside information to another person.[237]

---

[228] There has, nonetheless, been much debate over the morality or immorality of insider dealing, particularly in the United States where controls have existed since the 1930s, and the subject has spawned a voluminous literature. A dated although comprehensive guide to the position in many countries is Rider and Leigh (Ffrench's *Regulation of Insider Trading* (Macmillan, 1979). For a detailed account of the new law, see Rider and Ashe, *Insider Crime* (Jordans, 1993). See also Lomnicka [1994] JBL 173 and, for an interesting critique, Alcock (1994) 15 Co. Law 67.

[229] *Percival v Wright* [1902] 2 Ch 421; see 14.3, above. Note the qualifications to this principle discussed earlier.

[230] Two particular sets of provisions in the Companies Act 1985, namely those requiring disclosure of directors' interests in a company's securities and that criminalising options dealing by directors, are examined elsewhere; see 13.22 *et seq.* and 14.19, respectively. There are also provisions in The Stock Exchange's *Listing Rules* and in the *City Code on Takeovers and Mergers*. See generally, *Gore-Browne on Companies* (Jordans, 44th edn, loose-leaf), 12.14–12.16.

[231] 89/592/EEC. The statutory references in this section are to the 1993 Act.

[232] In contrast, the North American controls are based more on notions of abuse or misappropriation of information obtained in a relationship funded on trust or confidence.

[233] Part V of the Companies Act 1980.

[234] Note that not all the provisions concerning insider dealing are in the 1993 Act; e.g., the provisions regarding investigations remain in the Financial Services Act 1986; for a detailed consideration of these, see *Gore-Browne on Companies*, 12.31. The Government has been criticised for the way in which it implemented the directive; see *Gore-Browne on Companies*, 12.18.

[235] Section 52 (1).

[236] Section 52 (2) (*a*).

[237] Section 52 (1) (*b*).

The scope of this offence is examined in the following sections.

There have been relatively few prosecutions for insider dealing since 1980. This partly reflects the difficulties in detecting the crime but also the prevailing view that prosecutions should be brought only when there can be little doubt as to the individual's lack of integrity. The somewhat special nature of this crime is also reflected in the requirement that prosecutions can be brought only by or with the consent of the Secretary of State or the Director of Public Prosecutions.[238] On conviction on indictment, a person can be imprisoned for up to seven years and/or receive an unlimited fine,[239] indicating that the legislature regards the offence as a very serious one,[240] but the courts have not imposed punishments which might operate as a substantial deterrent. The Act expressly provides, by section 62 (2), that 'no contract shall be void or unenforceable by reason only' that it is entered into in contravention of the Act. However, the courts may well use well-established principles of public policy to deny specific performance of an executory contract entered into in breach of the Act.[241]

14.21.1 *Securities covered*

A wide range of securities is covered by the insider dealing law. The provisions first define the securities, then define the circumstances and conditions which will bring those securities within the parameters of the insider dealing law, and then set out the circumstances of dealing in those securities with which the law is concerned.

The list of securities includes shares and debentures in companies, and rights and options under contracts in relation to such shares and debentures.[242] Dealing in these securities is within the Act if (a) the transaction occurs on a regulated market or (b) the person dealing either relies on, or is himself acting as, a professional intermediary. Regulated markets are prescribed by Order[243] and include The Stock Exchange, other recognised investment markets in the United Kingdom and some major investment exchanges in the European Economic Area (EEA).[244] In addition the security must satisfy one of a number of conditions, in particular that it is officially listed in a state within the EEA or that it is admitted to dealing on, or has its price quoted on or under the rules of a regulated market.[245] A professional intermediary is defined[246] as a person who carries on a business of acquiring or disposing of securities, whether as an agent or principal, or a business of acting as an intermediary between persons taking part in any dealing in

---

[238] Section 61 (2).

[239] On summary conviction the punishment is restricted to the usual limits of magistrates' courts.

[240] It is also an extraditable offence and one to which the provisions for the seizure and forfeiture of profits in the Criminal Justice Acts of 1988 and 1993 apply.

[241] See *Chase Manhattan Equities v Goodman* [1991] BCLC 897. This decision was concerned with the previous legislation where the equivalent to section 62 (2) used 'voidable' rather than 'unenforceable'. As to whether this might make a difference, see *Gore-Browne on Companies*, 12.20, where other potential civil consequences are also discussed.

[242] See Sch 2 to the 1993 Act. Public sector debt securities and various other financial instruments are also covered; see *Gore-Browne*, 12.21.

[243] The Insider Dealing (Securities and Regulated Markets) Order 1994 (SI 1994 No. 187).

[244] Note though that the criminal offence is territorially limited by section 62 so that dealing must either take place on United Kingdom markets or with or through professional intermediaries based in the United Kingdom. The encouragement and disclosure offences can be committed if either the insider or the recipient was in the United Kingdom at the time. Of course offences of similar scope should now exist in most European countries in any case.

[245] Section 54 (1) and the 1994 Order.

[246] Section 59 (1).

securities.[247] The purpose of these provisions is to exclude from the scope of criminal liability a truly private deal executed off the market without the involvement of a market professional.

14.21.2 *Inside information*

By section 56, information must satisfy four characteristics in order to be inside information for the purposes of the Act. First, it must relate to particular securities or to a particular issuer, or particular issuers, of securities and not to either securities or issuers in general. Thus information is inside information even if it does not relate to a particular issuer but does relate to the industry within which that issuer operates, so it may come from within or without the issuer. A classic example of information relating to a particular issuer is a decision to make a takeover bid for that issuer. Further, 'information shall be treated as relating to an issuer not only where it is about the company itself, but also where it may affect the company's business prospects'.[248] The exclusion of 'general information' would appear to exclude information, like unpublished information regarding government economic policy or the bank rate, which might be expected to impact on the market in a general way.[249]

Secondly, the information must be either specific or precise. The directive requires only that information be precise, so it seems that United Kingdom law is wider in this respect. An example of specific information is that a takeover bid is to be made; an example of precise information is the price at which the bid is to be made: either is within the definition. The essential point is that rumours or casual remarks will not satisfy the requirement.

Thirdly, the information must not have been made public. Section 58 provides four specified situations where information is deemed to have been made public, but these are not exhaustive. The specified situations are:

(1) when information is published in accordance with the rules of a regulated market for the purpose of informing investors and their advisers;
(2) when information is placed in records which, by virtue of any enactment, are open to inspection by members of the public;
(3) if information can be readily acquired by those who are likely to deal in any of the securities to which it relates or of an issuer to which the information relates; or
(4) if the information is derived from information which has been made public.

Further, information may[250] be treated as having been made public even though it can be acquired only by persons exercising diligence or expertise, or where it is communicated to a section of the public rather than the public at large, or where it can be acquired only by observation, or it is communicated only on payment of a fee, or it is published outside the United Kingdom. It is notable that the law does not require a period for information to be digested. It is public as soon as, among other things, any of the four events listed above occurs.

Fourthly, the information must be such that if it were made public, it would be likely to

---

[247] This will generally correspond to persons regulated in this respect by the Financial Services Act 1986.

[248] Section 59 (4).

[249] As to whether or not this is consistent with Article 1 of the directive, see *Gore-Browne on Companies* (Jordans, 44th edn, loose-leaf), 12.22.

[250] It does not have to be so treated.

have a significant effect on the price[251] of any securities. The purpose of this requirement seems self-evident and sensible, and its application should not cause many difficulties.[252]

14.21.3 Who is an insider?

It is in respect of the definition of who is an insider that the structure of the 1993 Act is significantly different from that of the previous United Kingdom law.[253] Under the way the previous law defined the term, an insider had to be a director, officer or employee of, or professional adviser to, the company in question, in other words someone who almost inevitably stood in a fiduciary position or under a duty of confidentiality. The 1993 Act does not require a nexus of the same sort. Under section 57, a person has information as an insider if, and only if, it is, and he subjectively knows that it is, inside information, and he has it, and subjectively knows that he has it, from an inside source. This latter phrase is further qualified so that a person has inside information from an inside source if, and only if (a) he has it through being a director, employee or shareholder of an issuer of securities or through having access to the information by virtue of his employment, office or profession or (b) the direct or indirect source of his information is a director, employee or shareholder. So anyone can be an insider, even if they have had no previous connection with the issuer, provided that they get inside information from an inside source; the latter though has to be a director, officer, employee, shareholder or professional adviser.[254]

It is conventional in this area to distinguish by description between the types of insider in paras. (a) and (b) above. The first, who must have the connection with the company, is the primary insider. The second is the secondary insider or tippee.[255]

14.21.4 The offences in detail

As indicted earlier, there are three separate offences under Part V of the 1993 Act. The first is the dealing offence (section 52 (1)) and its two essential elements are (a) an individual has information as an insider, and (b) he must then deal in securities that are price-affected securities in relation to the information. 'Dealing' is comprehensively defined in section 55 as the acquisition or disposal of securities, whether as principal or agent, or the direct or indirect procurement of an acquisition or disposal by any other person. A person is considered as dealing if he procures an acquisition or disposal of a security if the security is acquired or disposed of by a person who is his agent or nominee or is acting at his direction in relation to the acquisition or disposal. Contracts to acquire or dispose of securities which are never executed are nonetheless caught, because of the wide definition of the terms 'acquire' and 'dispose'.[256]

The second offence is the encouragement offence (section 52 (2) (*a*)), involving an individual who has information as an insider encouraging another to deal in securities that are (whether or not that other knows it) price-affected securities in relation to the information, knowing or having reasonable cause to believe that the dealing would take place.[257] It should be noted that the offence fastens solely on the conduct and state of

---

[251] 'Price' includes value. Section 56 (3).

[252] Provided that complex disputes of the sort discussed in *Gore-Browne on Companies*, 12.22.3 do not occur.

[253] The effect may not be significantly different.

[254] The inclusion of shareholders, as required by the directive, is quite a new departure for United Kingdom law. For a detailed discussion of who is an insider, see *Gore-Browne on Companies*, 12.23.

[255] There was an unsuccessful attempt in Parliament to have the description 'tippee' enshrined in the legislation.

[256] Section 55 (2) and (3).

[257] This replaced the former, very similar, counselling and procuring offence.

mind of the insider who encourages another; it matters not whether the other person knows what is going on nor whether in fact that other deals. Whether 'encouragement' for this purpose covers only an explicit recommendation or goes further and covers mere 'hints' such as by a nod or a wink is not clear.[258]

The third offence is that of unauthorised disclosure of inside information by an individual (section 52 (2) (*b*)), that is disclosure otherwise than in the proper performance of the functions of his employment, office or profession. It is irrelevant whether or not the insider intends or suspects that the other will deal on the basis of the information.[259]

14.21.5 Defences

Section 53 contains a number of defences to the section 52 offences.[260] The first three apply to both the dealing and the encouragement offences.[261] It is a defence to these if the defendant shows:[262]

(1) that he did not, at the relevant time, expect the dealing to result in a profit which was attributable to the fact that the information was price-sensitive information in relation to the securities; for this purpose, 'profit' includes the avoidance of a loss;[263]

(2) that at the time he believed on reasonable grounds that the information had been disclosed widely enough to ensure that none of those taking part in the dealing would be prejudiced by not having the information;

(3) that he would have done what he did even if he had not had the information.

There are two defences to the offence of disclosing information. The first is if the defendant shows that he did not, at the time he disclosed the information, expect any person, because of the disclosure, to deal in the securities on a regulated market, or through or with a professional intermediary. The second is if he shows that although he had such an expectation at the time, he did not expect the dealing to result in a profit (or avoid a loss) attributable to the fact that the information was price-sensitive information in relation to the securities. Note that in both these instances, it is not necessary to show, in contrast to the second defence (above) to the dealing and encouragement offences, that the expectations were reasonable.

---

[258] For more detailed consideration, see *Gore-Browne on Companies*, 12.26.

[259] In this respect the offence is wider than the old law. What is not clear is the position of what are called multiple-function fiduciaries, who may in one capacity hold information which it is improper to disclose but who have another capacity in respect of which it would be appropriate to disclose, e.g. someone acting as a trustee of a fund including certain shares who is also a director of the company in question. As an insider he cannot disclose information which may cause the value of the shares to drop, but as a trustee it may be his duty to act on the information. This problem is not confined to the context of insider dealing laws: e.g. many of the regulatory rules effected under the auspices of the Financial Services Act 1986 may clash with traditional fiduciary duties. It raises the issue of the effectiveness of so-called 'Chinese walls' and is an issue under consideration by the Law Commission (Consultation Paper No. 124, 1992). For further consideration, see *Gore-Browne on Companies*, 12.30 and the sources there cited.

[260] There are also a number of specific defences in Schedule 1 relating to market making, stabilisation and market information; for more detail, see *Gore-Browne on Companies*, 12.29.

[261] With minor differences in wording for the second defence.

[262] This clearly imposes the burden of proof on the defendant.

[263] Section 53 (6).

14.22 Duty with regard to competing

Despite the general strict rule that a director must avoid positions of conflict between his duty to the company and his own interest, there is no general prohibition against a director competing with his company, whether on his own account or by virtue of his being director of another company in the same field of business.[264] This, however, is subject to any express agreement to the contrary between the director and the company, and, if the director is also an employee of the company, the court may in appropriate circumstances be prepared to imply into his contract of employment a term that he should not perform services for a competitor, even in his spare time.[265] In addition, of course, freedom to compete does not comprehend licence to disclose confidential information belonging to his company.[266]

It is not uncommon for a director to undertake, formally or informally, to act in accordance with the instructions of an 'outsider' or as representative of such an 'outsider'. This can arise when a holding company has nominee directors on the board of its subsidiary, or when the right to appoint a director is given to a class of shareholders or a debenture holder or class of debenture holders. It is not necessarily unlawful for a director to be in such a position, provided that he does not conceal his position, has the consent of the company,[267] preserves a substantial degree of independent discretion as to how he shall exercise his powers,[268] and, if a divergence occurs between the interests of the company and those of the 'outsider', does not subordinate the former to the latter as a means of resolving the conflict.[269] Directors cannot validly contract with an outsider as to how they will vote at future board meetings, but this does not preclude them from agreeing, in a contract entered into bona fide in the interests of the company, that they will take such further action as is necessary to carry out that contract.[270]

The potential responsibility of the 'outsider' for the acts of the directors was in issue in *Kuwait Asia Bank EC v National Mutual Life Nominees Ltd*,[271] where a bank held a beneficial interest in 40 per cent of the issued shares of a company and had nominated two of its employees to be directors of the company. It was held that in the performance of their duties, the directors were bound to ignore the interests and wishes of the bank and could not plead any instruction from the bank as an excuse for any breach of their duties. In the absence of evidence that the bank had exploited its position and interfered with the affairs of the company, it was neither vicariously nor personally liable for any negligence of the directors.

---

[264] *London v Mashonaland Exploration Co. Ltd v New Mashonaland Exploration Co. Ltd* [1891] WN 165, approved in *Bell v Lever Bros Ltd* [1932] AC 161 at pp. 195–6; but compare *Scottish Co-operative Wholesale Society Ltd v Meyer* [1959] AC 324 at p. 368 and, for a detailed analysis and trenchant criticism, see Christie, 'The Director's Fiduciary Duty Not to Compete' (1992) 55 MLR 506.

[265] See in particular *Hivac Ltd v Park Royal Scientific Instruments Ltd* [1949] Ch 169. Such a term will not always be implied; ibid.

[266] As to confidential information, see 14.8.1, above.

[267] See *Kregor v Hollins* (1913) 109 LT 225 at p. 231.

[268] *Boulting v A.C.T.A.T.* [1963] 2 QB 606 at pp. 626–7; *Clark v Workman* [1920] Ir. R. 107.

[269] See in particular *Scottish Co-operative v Meyer*, above. For useful comments on the position of nominee directors, see Boros (1989) 10 Co. Law 211 and (1990) 11 Co. Law 6, and Crutchfield (1991) 12 Co. Law 136.

[270] *Fulham Football Club Ltd v Cabra Estates plc* [1992] BCC 863 (CA), following the decision of the High Court of Australia in *Thorby v Goldberg* (1964) 112 CLR 597.

[271] [1990] BCLC 868 (PC).

14.23 Directors' duties of skill and care

The second major aspect of directors' duties concerns the standard of skill and care expected of a company director. The reported cases on this question were all decided around the end of the last century or in the early years of this century and hence really before the existence of 'professional' company directors. For this reason, perhaps, the standards imposed thereby are surprisingly low.[272] While a legal account of the duties of care and skill must still pay particular attention to these decisions, there are a number of reasons why they may not in fact be taken to represent the present law as and when the opportunity to consider the matter arises in a modern context. This matter is considered further in 14.23.1

With this qualification in mind, the starting-point is the judgment of Romer J in *Re City Equitable Fire Insurance Co. Ltd*,[273] which contains a useful review of the early authorities and which reduced the principles found therein to three general propositions.

First, 'a director need not exhibit in the performance of his duties a greater degree of skill than may reasonably be expected from a person of his knowledge and experience.'[274] Thus there is no objective standard of the reasonable director. In one case,[275] a 'country gentleman' director failed to study a set of accounts and subsequently proposed a dividend which in fact was paid out of capital. He was absolved from liability for negligence because he could not be expected to realise the significance of the accounts. Such an extreme result seems unlikely nowadays, and if a director is also employed under a contract of service, it will in any event contain an implied term requiring him to show objectively reasonable skill in the performance of his duties.[276]

Secondly, 'A director is not bound to give continuous attention to the affairs of his company. His duties are of an intermittent nature to be performed at periodical board meetings. ... He is not, however, bound to attend all such meetings, though he ought to attend whenever, in the circumstances, he is reasonably able to do so.'[277] Clearly this proposition, like the first, will often be expressly or impliedly displaced. In accordance with it, in one early case,[278] a 'figurehead' director, who never attended board meetings and who therefore failed to prevent the active director conducting the company's affairs improperly, was held not to have been negligent. Such a result is perhaps unlikely these days.[279]

Thirdly, 'In respect of all duties that, having regard to the exigencies of business, and the articles of association, may properly be left to some other official, a director is, in the absence of grounds for suspicion, justified in trusting that official to perform such duties honestly.'[280] Thus directors have escaped liability where subordinates to whom they

---

[272] For a general critique, see Finch, 'Company Directors: Who Cares about Skill and Care?' (1992) 55 MLR 179.

[273] [1925] Ch 407 (affirmed ibid. on other grounds by CA).

[274] ibid at p. 428. It was often said that a director was liable only for 'gross negligence'.

[275] *Re Denham & Co.* (1883) 25 Ch D 752.

[276] Cf. *Lister v Romford Ice & Cold Storage Co. Ltd* [1957] AC 555, where a term of this nature was read into the service contract of an ordinary employee. See also *Jackson v Invicta Plastics Ltd* [1987] BCLC 329 at p. 347, comparing the duty of care owed by a director with that owed by an employee.

[277] [1925] Ch 407 at p. 429.

[278] *Re Cardiff Savings Bank, The Marquis of Bute's Case* [1892] 2 Ch 100.

[279] See *Dorchester Finance Co. Ltd v Stebbing* [1989] BCLC 498, where failure to participate in the company's activities and the resulting failure to discover the defaults of the managing director on the part of the directors in question were regarded as negligent. See 14.23.1.

[280] [1925] Ch 407 at p. 429.

properly delegated functions relating to the company's finances misrepresented the company's financial position, with the result that the directors paid or recommended the payment of dividends out of capital.[281] It must be stressed, however, that there must be no grounds for suspicion, and the director who, having delegated a function, keeps an eye on its performance, cannot maintain that he did not know what was going on.[282]

It should be noted that a director is not the agent of his co-directors,[283] and the other officers of the company are not the agents of the directors.[284] Thus the mere fact that a director or officer is liable for breach of duty does not of itself render the remaining directors liable. Their liability can be established only if it can be shown that they were negligent in accordance with the standards of skill and care expected of them, or if they participated, however slightly,[285] in the breach, or sanctioned the conduct constituting the breach.

14.23.1 Modern developments in respect of the duties of care and skill

There are echoes of the propositions found in *Re City Equitable Fire Insurance Co. Ltd*[286] in more recent authorities, but it seems that the law is moving towards a more objective and thus demanding standard of care and skill for company directors, although the position cannot yet be regarded as settled. As already mentioned, an objective standard of care and skill will be required in any event of a director employed under a contract of service, that is an executive director, so that the discussion here is concerned solely with the position of non-executive directors.

In *Dorchester Finance Co. Ltd v Stebbing*,[287] Foster J applied the propositions laid down in *Re City Equitable Fire Insurance Co. Ltd*, but held that non-executive directors who were either qualified accountants or who had considerable accountancy and business experience had been negligent in signing blank cheques which allowed the managing director to misappropriate the company's money. This indicates a recognition of the concept of the professional director, although, in contrast, the legislature declined the opportunity to impose an objective standard on some company directors,[288] and more recently the Privy Council[289] cited *Re City Equitable Fire Insurance Co. Ltd* with approval.[290]

On the other hand, section 214 of the Insolvency Act 1986[291] requires a director to

---

[281] See in particular *Dovey v Cory* [1901] AC 477.

[282] Cf. *Department of Health and Social Security v Wayte* [1972] 1 WLR 19.

[283] *Cargill v Bower* (1878) 10 Ch D 502; *Re Denham & Co.* (1883) 25 Ch D 752.

[284] *Weir v Barnett* (1877) 3 Ex. D 32; *Weir v Bell* (1878) 3 Ex. D 238 (CA).

[285] See especially *Re Lands Allotment Co.* [1894] 1 Ch 617 (CA), where a chairman of directors, who signed the minutes relating to an ultra vires investment of company funds and announced the investment to the company in general meeting in terms indicating his assent thereto, was held liable as a participant in this misapplication of company funds. See also *Ramskill v Edwards* (1885) 31 Ch D 100 and *Bishopsgate Investment Management Ltd v Maxwell* [1993] BCC 120 (CA).

[286] [1925] Ch 407.

[287] [1989] BCLC 498 (decided in 1977, although unreported until 1989).

[288] The Supply of Goods (Exclusion of Implied Terms) Order 1982 (SI 1982 No. 1771) excludes from section 13 of the Supply of Goods and Services Act 1982, which lays down a generally objective standard of skill and care in contracts for the supply of a service, the services rendered to a company by a director of the company is his capacity as such. Section 13 would have applied anyway only to directors appointed under a contract. The exclusion cannot affect the duties owed by a director in some other capacity, e.g. as employee (see above).

[289] *Kuwait Asia Bank EC v National Mutual Life Nominees Ltd* [1990] BCLC 868 at p. 892.

[290] Even repeating the proposition that directors were only liable for gross negligence.

[291] Especially subsection (4) (a); see 13.17.2.

display a higher standard of skill and care lest he be found liable for wrongful trading. The section refers to the conduct of 'a reasonably diligent person having both – (a) the general knowledge, skill and experience that may reasonably be expected of a person carrying out the same functions as are carried out by that director in relation to the company, and (b) the general knowledge, skill and experience that that director has'. Although of course liability for wrongful trading can be imposed only when the company is in insolvent liquidation, this provision has been cited in two recent decisions[292] as an accurate statement of the director's common-law duty of care and skill. This does not mean, though, that, for example, a director will not be able to rely upon others. In the first of these cases,[293] it was held that, provided he observed the standard laid down in section 214, a director was entitled to trust people in positions of responsibility until there was reason to distrust them. So a director was not liable for the theft of company money by someone who was a senior partner in an eminent firm of solicitors when he had no reason to doubt the other's honesty. In contrast, in *Re D'Jan of London Ltd*,[294] a director who signed an insurance proposal form without checking its contents was regarded as negligent.

Although, as indicated, the position cannot be regarded as settled, it is submitted that there are clear signs that the courts are increasingly likely to impose a higher standard of care and skill on directors than as simple reading of the old authorities would suggest.

14.24 Factors relieving a director from liability for breach of duty

There are a number of ways in which a director who is prima facie liable for a breach of directors' duties may be relieved from such liability. These are examined in the following sections.

14.24.1 Ratification by the general meeting

As already indicated at various stages of this chapter, a breach of duty by a director may often, but not always, be 'cured' through his conduct being disclosed to the general meeting and ratified thereat by the passing of an ordinary resolution.[295] The notice summoning a meeting for this purpose should make it clear that the purpose or one of the purposes of the meeting is to sanction the relevant conduct of the director; if it does not, the notice may be held insufficient and the resolution ineffective.[296] However, the

---

[292] *Norman v Theodore Goddard* [1991] BCLC 1028 at pp. 1030–31, Hoffmann J; *Re D'Jan of London Ltd* [1993] BCC 646 at p. 648, Hoffmann LJ.

[293] *Norman v Theodore Goddard*, above.

[294] Above.

[295] Ratification should be distinguished from an exercise of power by the general meeting where the meeting validly performs the relevant act itself, as opposed to approving its prior performance by the board. The distinction is brought out in a comparison between the first instance judgment of Plowman J and the judgments of the Court of Appeal in *Bamford v Bamford* [1970] Ch 242. The *locus standi* of a minority shareholder to challenge the validity of the resolution may well turn upon the distinction; see 15.6, below. For an interesting article challenging the conventional view of ratification and arguing that, as opposed to a prospective release from liability, it can only bind the minority and not the company unless the director provides consideration or it is given under seal, see Partridge 46 CLJ 122 (1987).

[296] *Kaye v Croydon Tramways Co.* [1898] 1 Ch 358 (CA).

director may vote upon any shares that he holds in favour of his conduct being sanctioned, provided that this does not constitute 'fraud' or 'oppression'.[297]

The dividing line between those breaches of duty which are capable of ratification and those which are not is not at all easy to draw. Some types of breach have been expressly established as ratifiable,[298] namely failing to disclose an interest in a contract to which the company is a party,[299] obtaining a secret profit not involving a misapplication of company property,[300] negligence,[301] and using a power for an improper purpose.[302] In all cases there is an overriding qualification that the director must have acted bona fide in the interest of the company.[303]

The following breaches of duty are not capable of ratification by the general meeting:[304]

(1) one involving a lack of bona fides on the part of the director;[305]
(2) one resulting in the company performing an illegal or ultra vires act;[306]
(3) one resulting in the company performing an act which, though lawful and intra vires, cannot be done under the articles without some special procedure such as a special resolution;
(4) one bearing directly upon the 'personal rights' of individual shareholders, as defined in the articles;[307]
(5) one involving a 'fraud on the minority', that is whereby a majority of the shareholders or the directors succeed in expropriating at the expense of the minority the 'money, property, or advantages' of the company.[308]

---

[297] See in particular *North-West Transportation Co. v Beatty* (1887) 12 App. Cas. 589 (PC); *Burland v Earle* [1902] AC 83 at p. 94 (PC); *Northern Counties Securities Ltd v Jackson & Steeple Ltd* [1974] 1 WLR 1133 at p. 1146. Compare, however, the views of Vinelott J in *Prudential Assurance Co. Ltd v Newman Industries Ltd (No. 2)* [1980] 2 All ER 841 at pp. 862–3. The question of 'fraud on the minority' is discussed in more detail at 15.4, below.

[298] In addition, acting in excess of power, though intra vires the company, is ratifiable, whether a breach of duty or not: *Irvine v Union Bank of Australia* (1877) 2 App. Cas. 366 (PC); *Grant v United Kingdom Switchback Railways* (1880) 40 Ch D 135 (CA).

[299] *North-West Transportation Co. v Beatty*, above.

[300] *Regal (Hastings) Ltd v Gulliver* [1967] 2 Ac 134n (HL).

[301] *Pavlides v Jensen* [1956] Ch 565.

[302] *Alexander v Automatic Telephone Co.* [1990] 2 Ch 56 at p. 67 (CA); *Hogg v Crampton Ltd* [1967] Ch 254; *Bamford v Bamford*, above. If the impropriety was an improper allotment of shares, as in the latter two cases, the votes on the improperly allotted shares should not be used on the resolution.

[303] This is expressed in most of the cases cited above and is supported by *Daniels v Daniels* [1978] Ch 406 in respect of liability for negligence.

[304] For a fuller discussion in the context of minority shareholders' actions where the question is of paramount importance, see 15.2–15.4, below.

[305] *Attwool v Merryweather* (1867) LR 5 Eq. 464n; *Mason v Harris* (1879) 11 Ch D 97 (CA).

[306] *Re Exchange Banking Co., Flitcroft's Case* (1882) 21 Ch D 519 (CA).

[307] E.g., refusal to register a transfer of shares for an improper purpose.

[308] *Burland v Earle* [1902] AC 83 at p. 93 (PC). See too especially *Cook v Deeks* [1916] 1 AC 554 (PC), the facts of which were given at 14.8.1, above. Compare *Regal (Hastings) Ltd v Gulliver*, above, discussed in 14.18.1, above, where the opportunity to make the profit was not 'expropriated' from the company and the breach was ratifiable. There are, however, difficulties with this analysis: see *Gore-Browne on Companies* (Jordans, 44th edn, loose-leaf) 27.21.1; Gower, *Principles of Modern Company Law* (Sweet & Maxwell, 5th edn 1992), pp. 594–5; Wedderburn [1957] CLJ 194 and [1958] CLJ 93; Sealy [1967] CLJ 83 at pp. 102 *et seq.*; Beck, in Ziegel (ed.), *Canadian Company Law*, vol. II, pp. 232–8.

14.24.2 Ratification by the consent of all members

It is clear that any breach of duty by directors which is ratifiable by ordinary resolution, as described above, is equally ratifiable by the informal approval of every member who would have the right to vote on such a resolution.[309] However, there are dicta in recent cases indicating that the principle of unanimous approval goes further than this and that, whether given before or following the breach, it is effective to relieve a director from liability for *any* breach of duty, provided only that the breach is not ultra vires the company and does not involve a fraud on its creditors.[310] Such a fraud[311] seems likely to arise only when a company is in danger of going out of business in an insolvent state.

This principle seems acceptable in theory, given that ratification in this context means simply the company's waiving of its right to sue a director. It is obviously perfectly proper for a fully informed company to take such a decision in respect of any breach of duty, subject to the qualifications mentioned.

As regards breaches of duty which are beyond the capacity of the company, account must also be taken of section 35.[312] Although section 35 (1) abolishes the effect of ultra vires as far as third parties are concerned, section 35 (3) expressly preserves the duty of directors 'to observe any limitations on their powers flowing from the company's memorandum'. Further, action which but for subsection (1) would beyond the capacity of the company may be ratified by special resolution, but such ratification does not affect any liability incurred by the directors; relief from such liability must be agreed to separately by special resolution. It is clear therefore that a breach of duty which consists only of directors exceeding their powers under the memorandum is ratifiable (or can be relieved, to use the statutory language) by special resolution. It seems arguable that another effect of the statute is to make such breaches ratifiable by the consent of all members.[313] It would be odd for the law to require the formality of a special resolution in the face of the fully informed consent of all members and the subsection does not expressly contain the requirement of a general meeting. On the other hand, the first part of section 35 (3), referring to ratification in the sense of approval of an act rather than relief from liability, does state that such ratification can only be given by special resolution, and the second part uses the word 'must'.

It is submitted, however, that if the directors' breach of duty involves more than merely an excess of their powers under the memorandum, it is not necessarily ratifiable by special resolution. If the breach is otherwise ratifiable by ordinary resolution,[314] then clearly the ultra vires nature of it can be cured under section 35 (3). However, if it is not so ratifiable, it is thought that only the unanimous consent of the members will suffice.

14.24.3 Provisions in the articles

Section 310 makes void any provision, whether contained in the articles of the company or any contract with the company or otherwise, for exempting any officer of the company

---

[309] *Re Duomatic Ltd* [1969] 2 Ch 365; *Re Gee & Co. (Woolwich) Ltd* [1975] Ch 52; see 11.2, above.

[310] *Re Horsley and Weight Ltd* [1982] Ch 442 (CA) at p. 454; *Multinational Gas and Petrochemical Co. v Multinational Gas and Petrochemical Services Ltd* [1983] Ch 258 (CA) at p. 269 and pp. 289–90; *Rolled Steel Products Ltd v British Steel Corporation* [1984] BCLC 466 (CA) at pp. 508–9.

[311] e.g., the taking of excessive remuneration by directors as in *Re Halt Garage (1964) Ltd* [1982] 3 All ER 1016.

[312] See 4.11, above.

[313] A statutory written resolution (see 11.4.1, above) could be used by private companies.

[314] As described in 14.24.1.

or any person (whether an officer or not) employed by the company as auditor from, or indemnifying him against, any liability which by virtue of any rule of law would otherwise attach to him in respect of any negligence, default or breach of duty or breach of trust of which he may be guilty in relation to the company. Until an amendment made by the Companies Act 1989,[315] it was arguable that section 310 rendered void policies of professional indemnity insurance effected by companies on behalf of their directors and officers.[316] To cure the uncertainty in the face of a growing demand and market for this type of insurance,[317] section 310 (3) (*a*) now provides that the section does not prevent a company from purchasing and maintaining for any officer or auditor insurance against the liabilities in subsection (1).[318] Further, a company is permitted to indemnify any officer who is a successful defendant in civil or criminal proceedings or who successfully applies for relief under section 144[319] or section 727.[320]

Exactly what provisions in articles section 310 covers has been the subject of much academic debate,[321] but until recently there was no relevant case-law. The problem arose because Table A, the model form of articles of association, contains provisions, in both its 1948 and 1985 versions, which do appear to modify and even in part exclude the duties of directors; in the 1985 Table A, these are articles 85 and 94; in the 1948 Table A, which will continue to apply to many registered companies, they are articles 78 and 84. Clearly these articles must be valid as they have statutory authority.[322] The problem is whether, and if so to what extent, articles adopted by companies which do not follow them exactly are valid.

The problem arose for the first time judicially in *Movitex Ltd v Bulfield*.[323] Here the company in question had articles similar to but slightly more extensive than article 84 of the 1948 Table A. These allowed a director to have interests in and profit from transactions in which the company was interested, provided that he disclosed his interest to his fellow director and, in most instances, did not vote on the matter or, if he did vote, that his presence was not to be counted in the quorum.[324] However, in certain circumstances, a director could vote and be so counted.[325]

Vinelott J held that the articles were valid and did not infringe section 205 of the 1984 Act (now section 310). In doing so, he recognised that there was a difficult point of construction to be resolved in reconciling the articles with the section. He rejected the

---

[315] Section 137.

[316] There has never been any concern about liability insurance effected and paid for by directors themselves.

[317] For a very useful review, see Finch, 'Personal Accountability and Corporate Control: the Role of Directors' and Officers' Liability Insurance' (1994) 57 MLR 880.

[318] This does not automatically validate all such insurances so that, e.g., indemnity against the deliberate commission of a breach of duty could be unenforceable on public policy grounds; see Birds, *Modern Insurance Law* (Sweet & Maxwell, 3rd edn 1993), Chapter 12. The existence of any insurance of this sort must be disclosed in the directors' report: Schedule 7, Part I, para. 5A.

[319] See 6.16, above.

[320] See 14.24.4, below.

[321] See Baker [1975] JBL 181; Birds (1976) 39 MLR 394; Parkinson [1981] JBL 335; Gregory (1982) 98 LQR 413.

[322] This point was not, however, made in *Movitex Ltd v Bulfield*, discussed below, where Vinelott J was at pains to reconcile what is now section 310 and the relevant articles in Table A, implying that if he could not do so, the articles in Table A would be invalid: *sed quaere*.

[323] (1986) 2 BCC 99, 403; for a fuller discussion, see Birds (1987) 8 Co. Law 31.

[324] See 14.12, above.

[325] Cf. article 84 (2) of the 1948 Table A and article 94 of the 1985 Table A. The difference from these provisions was that the number of circumstances where voting was allowed was greater.

argument that articles could rewrite the content of directors' duties so long as they did not purport to exempt directors from liability for breaches of duty not ratifiable by the general meeting or from breaches of duties stemming from a mandatory rule of statute. He reasoned, applying dicta of Megarry V-C in *Tito v Waddell*[326] that the general principle forbidding directors (and others in fiduciary positions) from putting themselves in a position where their duty to the company might conflict with their own interest was not a *duty* in the strict sense of the word, but simply a disability. It thus did not fall within the wording of section 310. The company could exclude the general principle in its articles, providing in effect that specified situations did not give rise to a conflict of duty and interest, provided that it did not exclude the duties of directors properly so-called.

On this analysis, it would seem that the non-excludable *duties* of directors are those obligations which seek to prevent a director from damaging the interests of the company. These probably comprehend the primary duties of good faith and proper purpose,[327] the duty to show proper care and skill, the duty not to misappropriate company property, and any statutory duty imposed on directors. However, the general rule imposing accountability for secret profits, as well as that avoiding a transaction involving a conflict of duty and interest, would, on Vinelott J's analysis, be excludable, so long as the director acts in good faith.[328] Many would probably feel that this result is acceptable.[329]

14.24.4 *Discretionary relief from liability by the court*

Section 727 (1) of the Companies Act 1985[330] allows the court which has found a director or other officer[331] liable for negligence, default, breach of duty or beach of trust to relieve him from liability, wholly or partly, on such terms as it thinks fit, provided and only provided that the director establishes the three distinct matters specified in the section, namely

(1) that he acted honestly;
(2) that he acted reasonably; and
(3) that, having regard to all the circumstances, he 'ought fairly to be excused'.

---

[326] [1977] 3 All ER 129 at p. 247.

[327] Though as the proper purposes doctrine (see 14.7, above) is derived from the articles, it must in principle be excludable in the sense that the articles can define the range of purposes in respect of which a power is properly exercisable; see Birds 39 MLR at p. 400.

[328] Indeed, Vinelott J expressly held that article 78 of the 1948 Table A, which excludes accountability for secret profits in a particular situation, was consistent with what is now section 310. He seems to have assumed that liability for secret profits (as to which see 14.18 *et seq.*, above) is imposed only when there is a conflict of duty and interest, but this is not the case as the speeches in *Regal (Hastings) Ltd v Gulliver* [1942] 1 All ER 378 make clear; simply, a director is under a duty to account for a secret profit obtained by use of his position. It could be argued that this is a duty which is subject to section 310 and thus non-excludable. Article 78 was perhaps a statutory aberration; it was not replaced in exactly the same form in the 1985 Table A – instead of excluding a duty to account totally, part of article 85 of the 1985 Table A excludes it only if the director has disclosed his profit to his fellow directors, thus making the subject-matter of the former article 78 subject to the same requirement as directors' interests in contracts, etc., (see 14.12, above).

[329] It may also accord with the intentions of the Greene Committee (Cmnd 2627, 1925, paras. 46 and 47), who recommended the introduction of what is now section 310, although it is somewhat difficult to discern their intention other than that clauses excusing directors' liability for negligence should be outlawed. Vinelott J's conclusion, though not his reasoning, is similar to that reached by Parkinson, op. cit., footnote 321.

[330] Cf. the equivalent section 61 of the Trustee Act 1925, from which this provision was adapted.

[331] Or an auditor.

It is possible for a director to succeed on the first two points, yet fail on the third, which is a matter for the court's discretion in each case.[332]

14.24.5 Limitation of actions

After the lapse of six years, section 21 of the Limitation Act 1980 bars proceedings against a director for breach of duty, unless the claim is founded upon any fraud or fraudulent breach of trust, or is to recover trust property or the proceeds thereof still retained by the director or previously received by him and converted to his own use.

14.25 Enforcement of civil liabilities against directors

It is all very well for the law to impose what are generally strict duties on company directors, as described in the previous pages of this chapter. What may well be much more important in practice is that the law provides effective ways in which breach of those duties can be remedied. While the company can always take action, that is, for obvious reasons, not likely in many cases in practice. For that reason, and despite the fact that, as we have seen,[333] a director's duties are generally owed only to the company itself, in certain circumstances a minority shareholder may be able to institute proceedings. These circumstances are fully explored in the next chapter.

When a company is in liquidation, a breach of duty will be much easier to litigate since the liquidator will in general have the conduct of the action in the company's name. Further, if the breach falls within section 212 of the Insolvency Act 1986,[334] he, or the official receiver, or any creditor or contributory, may instead be able to invoke the simpler procedure of a summons in the liquidation.

If a director dies, his estate remains liable for any breach of duty he may have committed, including any wrongful dealing with the company's property such as a payment of dividend out of capital or sale of its assets at an undervalue.[335] A discharge in bankruptcy does not release a director from liability for a fraudulent breach of duty[336] or a claim for a refund of secret profits, for the retention of them is a breach of trust.[337] The company can prove in the bankrupt estate for the secret profit.

If two or more directors are implicated in the same breach of duty, their liability is joint and several: accordingly, if in the same transaction they have each misappropriated company assets, each of them is liable for the total amount so misappropriated by himself and his co-directors.[338] If one of them has been rendered liable, he can usually recover contribution from any of the other directors who were responsible also.[339]

---

[332] *Re J. Franklin & Son Ltd* [1937] 2 All ER 32. See further as to section 727, *Gore-Browne*, 27.21.5. It is curious that the section was not at least pleaded in *Regal (Hastings) Ltd v Gulliver* [1967] 2 AC 134n (HL) (see 14.18.1, above), the facts of which look like the sort of case where relief should be considered: see Birds 39 MLR 394 (1976) at p. 397.

[333] See 14.3, above.

[334] See 13.17.4 above.

[335] *Ramskill v Edwards* (1885) 31 Ch D 100; *Re Sharpe* [1892] 1 Ch 154 (CA).

[336] Insolvency Act 1986, Section 281 (3).

[337] See *Emma Silver Mining Co. v Grant* (1881) 17 Ch D 122.

[338] See e.g. *Re Carriage Co-operative Supply Association* (1884) 27 Ch D 322.

[339] See generally *Ramskill v Edwards*, above.

15 Minority Shareholders' Remedies

15.1 Introduction

This chapter is concerned with various remedies available to minority shareholders. Such remedies are in practical terms the only effective way of enforcing directors' and controlling shareholders' duties (outside the context of the company's liquidation). It will be seen that these remedies are also very much concerned with actions or conduct by the company or its officers which infringe the rights, or prejudice the interests, of individual shareholders or groups of shareholders. The first part of this chapter is concerned with the rule in *Foss v Harbottle*[1] and the minority shareholders' actions which are allowed by exception to it.

The second part of this chapter deals with two interrelated statutory remedies. A member of a company may petition on the ground of unfair prejudice under Part XVII of the Companies Act 1985 or petition to have the company wound up on the 'just and equitable' ground now contained in section 122 (1) (*g*) of the Insolvency Act 1986.

It will be seen that well-justified minority shareholders' complaints are still thwarted by the undue technicality and doctrinal obscurity of the *Foss v Harbottle* rule. It is true that the statutory minority remedies now rest upon a broader and more liberal judicial discretion, the use of which has much improved the lot of minority shareholders in small or medium-sized private companies. However, their beneficial effect is largely confined to such companies, as these remedies are not an appropriate way of coping with corporate abuse or gross incompetence in public listed companies. In response to many criticisms over the years, the Department of Trade and Industry referred the issue of the enforcement of shareholders' rights and remedies to the Law Commission in December 1994. It will no doubt be some time before any changes to the law are made.

The last part of this chapter is concerned with the Department of Trade and Industry's range of powers to investigate companies. This may be done informally by civil servants or by the formal appointment of inspectors. The Department is also given the power to follow up its investigation by bringing various types of civil proceedings. While these powers are more than ample in terms of the letter of the law, their use has been much restrained by the customary bureaucratic caution and inertia. These habits tend only to be set aside where a clear prima-facie case of serious corporate abuse, already publicised in the press, affects the affairs of a public listed company. Even then it is the power to investigate the affairs of the company (or the ownership of or dealings in its shares) that are likely to be employed. The powers to bring civil proceedings are almost never used. The power to wind up already failed or defunct public companies is occasionally resorted to.

---

[1] (1843) 2 Hare 461.

PART 1: MINORITY SHAREHOLDERS' ACTIONS

15.2 The rule in *Foss v Harbottle*

There is a general principle of company law[2] that minority shareholders cannot sue for wrongs done to their company or complain of irregularities in the conduct of its internal affairs. This principle has come to be known as the rule in *Foss v Harbottle*[3] from the decision in which it was first clearly established. The cases[4] show that this rule rests upon two related propositions: (a) the right of the majority to bar a minority action whenever they might lawfully ratify alleged misconduct; and (b) the normally exclusive right of the company to sue upon a corporate cause of action. In *Edwards v Halliwell*[5] Jenkins LJ elucidated the relationship between these two propositions by contending that the will of the majority, *vis-à-vis* the minority, is to be identified with that of the company. Consequently, to say that the company is prima facie the proper plaintiff in actions concerning its affairs is only another way of saying that the majority, within the limits of their power to ratify, have the sole rights to determine whether or not a dispute shall be brought before the courts.

The courts have justified the policy expressed by the rule by certain practical arguments of convenience. In *Gray v Lewis*[6] James LJ justified the principle, that any body corporate is the proper plaintiff in proceedings to recover its property, by pointing to the obvious danger of a multiplicity of shareholders' suits in the absence of a rule such as *Foss v Harbottle*. 'There might be as many bills as there are shareholders multiplied into the number of defendants.' This situation would be aggravated where suits were discontinued at will, or dismissed with costs against plaintiff shareholders unable to meet these costs.[7] In *MacDougall v Gardiner*[8] Mellish LJ observed the futility of ignoring the majority's power to ratify. If 'something has been done irregularly which the majority are entitled to do regularly, or if something illegally which the majority of the company are entitled to do legally, there can be no use having litigation about it if the ultimate end of which is that a meeting is called and then ultimately the majority gets its wishes'. In this case the Court of Appeal refused to allow a minority shareholder to complain of the refusal by the

---

[2] In *Hodgson v NALGO* [1972] 1 WLR 130, Goulding J held that the rule in *Foss v Harbottle* did not apply to the case of an *unregistered* trade union since it was incapable of suing in its own name. Dicta in *MacDougall v Gardiner* [1875] 1 Ch 13 at p. 25, *Cotter v N.U. Seamen* [1929] 2 Ch 58 at p. 71 and *Edwards v Halliwell* [1950] 2 All ER 1064 at p. 1066 were applied. The two latter cases established that the *Foss v Harbottle* rule *does* apply to unions that have been given the statutory right to sue in their own name. See further *Taylor v NUM* [1985] BCLC 237.

[3] (1843) 2 Hare 461. As to the historical development of the rule, see Wedderburn (1957) Camb. LJ 194 and (1958) Camb. LJ 93; Boyle 28 MLR 317 (1965); Baxter (1987) 38 NILQ 6; see also Drury (1986) 45 CLJ 219.

[4] *Foss v Harbottle* (1843) 2 Hare 461 at pp. 492–3 and 494–5; *Mozley v Alston* (1847) 1 Ph. 790 at p. 800; *Burland v Earle* [1902] AC 83 at p. 93 (PC); *Pavlides v Jensen* [1956] 1 Ch 565 at p. 575.

[5] [1950] 2 All ER 1064 at p. 1066. However, this does not provide an explanation for 'wrongdoer control' in actions based on the 'fraud on a minority' exception to the rule.

[6] (1873) 8 Ch App. 1035 at p. 1051. This problem of abuse of procedure could of course be handled by the courts in other ways (e.g. the power to stay or consolidate actions). See Boyle 28 MLR 327.

[7] See *La Compagnie de Mayville v Whiteley* [1896] 1 Ch 788 at p. 807; *Mozley v Alston* (1847) 1 Ph. 790 at p. 799; *Lord v Copper Miners* (1848) 2 Ph. 740.

[8] (1875) 1 Ch D 13 at p. 25. See also James LJ at p. 22.

chairman of a shareholders' meeting to call a poll.[9] It is well established that a mere breach of the fiduciary duties that directors owe to their company is ratifiable and hence cannot be the subject of a minority shareholder's action.[10] The same is true of an act by directors beyond the authority conferred upon them by the articles, or an irregularity in the appointment of directors.[11] The rule has also been applied to allegations by a minority shareholder that the directors have been engaged in practices in breach of the competition rules in Articles 85 and 86 of the Treaty of Rome, with the intention of damaging the company.[12]

15.3 The exceptions to the rule

The rule does not extend to a case where the act complained of is either illegal or ultra vires, or is a fraud upon the minority,[13] and there is also an exception in cases where the act done, although regular in form, is unfair and oppressive as against the minority.[14] This will include acts by directors which are an abuse of powers contained in the memorandum and while not beyond the capacity of the company (and therefore void) may only be approved by the unanimous consent of the shareholders.[15] It does not apply to a case where the matter in question requires, by virtue of a provision either in the Companies Act 1985 or in a company's memorandum or articles, a special or extraordinary resolution,[16] for to allow a company to ratify an act requiring the sanction of a special or extraordinary resolution by refusing to be party to proceedings would be to enable a bare majority to do that which can only be done by a three-quarters majority. A unanimous though informal agreement by the shareholders will effectively amend the articles without a special resolution.[17]

A single shareholder may sue in his own name to restrain an act which is an

---

[9] This decision is not easy to reconcile with *Pender v Lushington* (1877) 6 Ch D 70, which established that the right to vote at shareholders' meetings is a personal right for which a shareholder may sue. It would be idle to pretend that all the cases on shareholders' 'individual' rights (as an exception to the rule) can be reconciled. For an exploration of the difficulties and a suggested solution, see Baxter, 'The Role of the Judge in Enforcing Shareholder Rights', 1983 Camb. LJ 96.

[10] *Burland v Earle* [1902] AC 83 (PC); *Dominion Cotton Mills v Amyott* [1912] AC 546 (PC); *Pavlides v Jensen* [1956] Ch 565; *Heyting v Dupont* [1961] 1 WLR 843 (CA); *Bentley-Stevens v Jones* [1974] 1 WLR 638; *Lee v Chou Wen Hsien* [1984] 1 WLR 1202 (PC). As to directors' fiduciary duties, see Chapter 14, above.

[11] *Grant v UK Switchback Railways* (1888) 40 Ch D 135 (CA); *Mozley v Alston* (1847) 1 Ph. 790.

[12] *O'Neil v Ryan* [1990] 2 IR 200.

[13] *Alexander v Automatic Telephone Co.* [1900] 2 Ch (CA); *Hope v International Financial Society* (1877) 4 Ch D 327; *Simpson v Westminster Palace Hotel* (1860) 8 HLC 712; *Clinch v Financial Corp.* (1868) 4 Ch App. 117. See the cases on 'fraud on a minority' discussed at 15.4, below. As to the ultra vires doctrine, see Chapter 4, above.

[14] See the cases establishing the principle that the majority in general meeting must act bona fide in the interests of the company as a whole (e.g. in altering the articles to the prejudice of a shareholder or class of shareholders). These cases are examined in 3.27, above.

[15] *Rolled Steel Products Ltd v British Steel Corporation* [1985] 2 WLR 908 (CA).

[16] *Baillie v Oriental Telephone Co.* [1915] 1 Ch 503 at p. 515 (CA); *Cotter v N.U. Seamen* [1929] 2 Ch 58 at pp. 69–70; *Edwards v Halliwell* [1950] 2 All ER 1064 at p. 1067 (CA). Further, the notice of such a resolution must give a fair and reasonably full statement of the facts if the resolution is to bind the minority: *Kaye v Croydon Tramways* [1898] 1 Ch 538 (CA); *Tiessen v Henderson* [1899] 1 Ch 861; *MacConnell v E. Prill & Co.* [1916] 2 Ch 57. CF. *Normandy v Ind Coope & Co. Ltd* [1908] 3 Ch 84.

[17] *Cane v Jones* [1980] 1 WLR 1451. However, such an agreement requires registration under section 380; see 11.18, above.

infringement of his individual rights,[18] for example a wrongful refusal to accept his vote at a general meeting of the company[19] or a wrongful exclusion of him from the board of directors.[20] The rule of *Foss v Harbottle* has, of course, no application to any statutory right conferred by the Companies Act 1985 on individual shareholders or a minimum number of them.[21] There is also judicial authority for the view that the rule has no application to any individual right conferred by the articles or memorandum.[22] However, whether such rights are an exception to the rule or are beyond its scope is largely a matter of language.

It is sometimes said that a minority shareholder has the right to have any provision in the articles enforced as part of his contract of membership. This proposition has received some support in judicial dicta,[23] but it appears contrary to two principles of company law. The first of these is that a member of a company is only entitled to enforce rights conferred upon him by the contract of membership, as defined by section 14 (1) of the Companies Act 1985, in his capacity as a member *qua* member.[24] The second principle, which such a general right to enforce articles would appear to offend, is the *Foss v Harbottle* rule itself. This rule prevents actions by minority shareholders for internal irregularities, such as breaches of the articles. Where such a breach does not involve the infringement of the individual rights conferred upon a shareholder, it has been held that a breach of the articles may be ratified by the majority.[25]

15.4 The 'fraud on a minority' exception to the rule

The 'fraud on a minority' exception to the rule demands more extensive consideration than do the other exceptions to the rule, as it has occasioned considerable litigation. The scope of this exception to the rule is important in determining the extent to which minority shareholders may enforce the duties owed by directors to their company,[26] by way of a 'derivative action' (see 15.8, below).[27]

The relationship between the *Foss v Harbottle* rule and the fraud on a minority exception

---

[18] *Johnson v Little's Iron Agency* (1877) 5 Ch 687 (CA); *Wood v Odessa Waterworks Co.* (1881) 42 Ch D 636; *Clark v Workman* [1920] 1 Ir. R. 107 at p. 112; *Davis v Commercial Publishing Co. of Sydney* [1901] NSW (Eq.) 37 at pp. 47–8; *Edwards v Halliwell* [1950] 2 All ER 1064 (CA). As to difficulties about this 'exception', see footnote 9, above.

[19] *Pender v Lushington* (1877) 6 Ch D 70 at p. 81.

[20] *Pullbrook v Richmond Consolidated Co.* (1878) 9 Ch D 610; *Harben v Phillips* (1883) 23 Ch D 14 (CA).

[21] As to the rights of members (in respect of meetings) as to notice of resolutions, the requisitioning of meetings, circulating resolutions, etc., see Chapter 11, *passim*. As to the right of shareholders to petition under Part XVII of the 1985 Act, see 15.12, below.

[22] *Edwards v Halliwell* [1950] 2 All ER 1064 at p. 1067 *per* Jenkins LJ (CA).

[23] *Wood v Odessa Waterworks* (1889) 42 Ch D 636; *In Re Harmer* [1959] 1 WLR 62 at p. 87 *per* Harmer LJ (CA) (but this was a case of a petition under section 210 of the 1948 Act); and *Bamford v Bamford* [1968] 3 WLR 317 *per* Plowman J. In the Court of Appeal Plowman J's decision was affirmed on other grounds and his remarks as to the right to enforce the articles as a contract received no support: *Bamford v Bamford* [1969] 2 WLR 1107.

[24] See *Hickman v Kent and Romney Marsh Sheepbreeders' Association* [1915] 1 Ch 881. The decision in *Hickman* has been the subject of some criticism by academic writers on the ground that its reasoning is not consistent with all the other authorities on the shareholders' contract. This much-debated issue is examined at 3.18, above. These arguments, however, do not dispose of the problem posed by the *Foss v Harbottle* rule itself.

[25] *Grant v UK Switchback Railways* (1888) 40 Ch D 135 (CA).

[26] Where the *Foss v Harbottle* issue is raised by motion at the outset of the proceedings, the court may not, on the one hand, 'assume as fact every allegation in the statement of claim as in a true demurrer'. On the other hand, the plaintiff is not required to prove 'fraud' and 'control' before he can establish his title to prosecute the action: *Prudential Assurance Co. Ltd v Newman Industries (No. 2)* [1982] Ch 204.

[27] A shareholder does not necessarily have to be strictly a minority shareholder; a 50 per cent shareholder has been held entitled to bring a derivative action: *Barrett v Duckett* [1993] BCC 778.

to it was considered by Lord Davey in 1902[28] in a passage which has frequently been quoted, and was adopted by the Privy Council in 1912.[29] Lord Davey notes that an exception would be made to the principle of the company as proper plaintiff where 'the persons against whom relief is sought themselves hold and control the majority of shares in the company and will not permit an action to be brought in the name of the company'. This has come to be known as the element of 'wrongdoer control' and is discussed at 15.5, below. As regards the kind of wrongful conduct for which the minority may maintain an action,[30] these are 'confined to those in which the acts complained of are of a fraudulent character or are beyond the powers of the company. A familiar example is where the majority are endeavouring directly or indirectly to appropriate to themselves money or property, or advantages which belong to the company, or in which the other shareholders are entitled to participate . . .'.

The earlier case of *East Pant Du Mining Co.* illustrates the difference between the right to bring an action in the company's name and the right to bring a minority shareholders' action on its behalf. In this first instance an action was brought in the name of the company to set aside an agreement alleged to have been procured through a fraud upon the company practised by some of the directors, but upon it appearing that a majority of the shareholders (including those whose conduct was impugned) disapproved of the action, it was stayed.[31] Thereupon, another action was commenced by one of the minority in his own name, 'suing on behalf of himself and all the other aggrieved shareholders', and the company was made a defendant, and it was held that this action would lie,[32] the court laying down the rule that where justice cannot be done in any other manner this form of action will be allowed to proceed.[33] It used to be essential in such a case that the plaintiff should show that he has exhausted all reasonable means of obtaining the institution of an action by the company before commencing proceedings himself[34] but for this purpose it will be enough to show that the persons of whose wrongful conduct he complains either control a majority of the votes in the company or are sufficient to turn the scale in the voting.[35] The question of 'wrongdoer control' is further considered at 15.5, below.

An instructive comparison is to be found in cases where an act is authorised by the votes of interested directors given at a general meeting. In the absence of fraud or oppression such votes in general meeting are valid, and a minority suing to set aside the transaction

---

[28] *Burland v Earle* [1902] AC 83 at p. 93 (PC).

[29] *Dominion Cotton Mills v Amyot* [1912] AC 546 (PC); see also *Cook v Deeks* [1916] AC 554 (PC); *Foster v Foster* [1916] 1 Ch 532 at p. 547.

[30] i.e. an action in their own names, as a 'mere matter of procedure in order to give a remedy for a wrong which would otherwise escape redress, and it is obvious that in such an action the plaintiffs cannot have a larger right to relief than the company itself would have if it were plaintiff . . .'.

[31] *East Pant Du Mining Co. v Merryweather* (1864) 2 H & M 234.

[32] *Atwool v Merryweather* (1868) 5 Eq. 464n.

[33] See also *Russell v Wakefield Waterworks Co.* (1875) 20 Eq. 474 at p. 482 *per* Jessel MR; *Heyting v Dupont* [1964] 1 WLR 843 (CA).

[34] *Morris v Morris* [1877] WN 6, and cases in next note.

[35] *Atwool v Merryweather* (1868) 5 Eq. 464, note; *Duckett v Gover* (1877) 6 Ch D 82; *Mason v Harris* (1878) 11 Ch 97 (CA); *Alexander v Automatic Telephone Co.* [1990] 2 Ch 56 (CA); *Russell v Wakefield Waterworks Co.* (1875) 20 Eq. 474.

will fail;[36] but if the directors are seeking to appropriate to themselves property which belongs to the company as a whole, a resolution of the company in general meeting carried by their votes cannot validate the transaction, and a single shareholder or a minority of shareholders can obtain relief.[37] Misappropriation of corporate property extends to property (or contracts) which 'belong in equity' to the company.[38] Here the directors are accountable for a non-ratifiable breach of trust and not merely for a breach of their fiduciary duty.

In *Daniels v Daniels*,[39] Templeman J reviewed the authorities referred to above in an application to strike out the plaintiff's statement of claim (in a minority shareholder's action) on the ground that no cause of action was shown because no fraud was alleged. For the plaintiffs it was argued that any breach of fiduciary duty by directors could be a ground of action. The defendants contended that no cause of action was shown because the statement of claim did not allege fraud, and in the absence of fraud minority shareholders are unable to maintain a claim on behalf of the company against the majority.[40] Templeman J rejected this proposition as not consistent with the authorities, including *Pavlides v Jensen*.[41] The principle that he 'gleaned' from these authorities is 'that a minority shareholder who has no other remedy may sue where directors use their powers, intentionally or unintentionally, fraudulently or negligently in a manner which benefits themselves at the expense of the company'.[42] The cases which Templeman J particularly relied upon (as demonstrating that the word 'fraud' in this context does not mean literal or 'common-law fraud') are *Cook v Deeks*[43] and *Alexander v Automatic Telephone Co.*[44] His decision is valuable in clarifying the meaning of 'fraud on a minority' and restricting the scope of *Pavlides v Jensen*. The court's reasoning was clearly intended to be within the principles earlier laid down by higher courts. The facts alleged in the pleadings could well have led to the conclusion at a full hearing that the defendants had either appropriated property belonging in equity to the company (*Cook v Deeks*) or had acted in bad faith in exercising their power to sell the company's property (*Automatic Telephone*). As Templeman J was at pains to demonstrate, neither of these propositions amounts to an allegation of fraud.[45]

---

[36] *North-West Transportation Co. v Beatty* (1887) 12 App. Cas. 589 (PC); *Burland v Earle* [1902] AC 82 (PC); *Baird v Baird & Co. (Falkirk)* 1949 SLT 368. As to the distinction between the duty of directors in respect of circulating notices of meetings (and accompanying circulars), and their right to vote at the meeting which results, see *Northern Securities v Jackson Steeple* [1974] 1 WLR 1133. See also *Clemens v Clemens Bros. Ltd* [1976] 2 All ER 268 applying dicta of Sir Richard Baggallay in *North-West Transportation v Beatty*, above, at p. 593.

[37] *Cook v Deeks* [1916] 1 AC 554 (PC); *Menier v Hoopers Telegraph Co.* (1874) 9 Ch App. 350.

[38] *Cook v Deeks*, above. See 14.8.1–14.8.2, above, as to the distinction between a mere breach of fiduciary duty and the misappropriation of property which 'belongs in equity' to the company.

[39] [1978] Ch 406.

[40] ibid., p. 408.

[41] [1956] Ch 565.

[42] ibid., p. 414.

[43] [1916] 1 AC 554 (PC).

[44] [1900] 2 Ch 56.

[45] For further discussion of this case in the periodical literature, see Wedderburn 41 MLR 569 at p. 57 (1978), Rider [1978] Camb. LJ 270, Prentice 41 Conveyancer 47 (1979); Boyle 1 Co. Law 3 (1980). In *Prudential Assurance v. Newman Industries (No. 2)* Vinelott J's attempt at a radical restatement of the principle behind the 'fraud on minority cases' received no support in the Court of Appeal: [1982] Ch 204. See Boyle 2 Co. Law 264 (1981). A similar approach was taken by Megarry V-C in *Estmanco (Kilner House) Ltd v Greater London Council* [1982] 1 WLR 2. See Birds 2 Co. Law 31 and 77 (1982); see also, most recently, *Barrett v Duchett* [1995] 1 BCLC 73.

15.5 'Wrongdoer control'

In *Pavlides v Jensen*[46] the directors of a company did not, in the strict legal sense, control the company they were alleged to have harmed by their negligence. They were, however, a majority of the directors on the board of its holding company. Danckwerts J held that the action failed on two grounds. First, because the sale of the company's mine at a gross undervalue was not alleged to be fraudulent or an ultra vires act, but merely negligent and therefore open to ratification. Secondly, he held that there was not sufficient control exercised by the alleged wrongdoers to enable them to stifle any attempt to institute proceedings in the name of the company. The 'shareholders of the shareholding company could in general meeting decide differently and disagree with the directors of that company'.[47] Such a rigorous approach to this second aspect of 'fraud on a minority' does not appear to be entirely consistent with the cases discussed above.[48]

Vinelott J, in *Prudential Assurance Co. Ltd v Newman Industries (No. 2)*,[49] was prepared to extend the concept of 'wrongdoer control' so that it would apply not only where the wrongdoers were a majority, but also where it could be shown that unless the minority could be allowed to sue on the company's behalf, the interests of justice would be defeated in that an action which ought to be pursued on behalf of the company could not be pursued. Thus, in Vinelott J's view, 'wrongdoer control' comprehends 'de facto control' as well as de jure control (of the kind insisted upon by Danckwerts J in *Pavlides v Jensen*). It would, on this view, also comprehend a situation where a majority of the board of directors are deceived by the wrongdoers so that the question of bringing civil proceedings will never be put to the shareholders.

Unfortunately the Court of Appeal[50] (on appeal from Vinelott J) would have none of this. First of all, the court repudiated the whole 'justice of the case' principle as ground for departing from the rule in *Foss v Harbottle* and therefore as the theoretical basis employed by Vinelott J. The court was fully aware of the policy problem caused by de facto control of public companies,[51] but remained unconvinced that Vinelott J's test of 'de facto control' was a practical test, particularly as it involves a full dress trial before the test is applied. Instead the court suggested that 'it may well be right' for the judge trying the preliminary issue[52] to grant a sufficient adjournment to enable a meeting of shareholders to be convened by the board. This is to enable the judge to reach a conclusion (i.e. as to wrongdoer control) in the light of the conduct of, and proceedings at, the meeting. Where the company has an independent board with adequate information, then the board is entitled to make a commercial assessment of the advantage to the company in taking civil proceedings (whether that assessment be sound or unsound). Where a shareholders'

---

[46] [1956] Ch 565.

[47] ibid., at p. 577.

[48] See especially *Heyting v Dupont* [1964] 2 WLR 843 (CA) which accepted the following observation of Jessel MR in *Russell v Wakefield Waterworks* (1875) 20 Eq. 474 at p. 480, which had been rejected by Danckwerts J in *Pavlides v Jensen*, above, '... that is not a universal rule; that is, it is a rule subject to exceptions, and the exceptions depend very much on the necessity of the case; that is the necessity of the court doing justice'. See also *Hodgson v NALGO* [1972] 1 WLR 130 at p. 140.

[49] [1980] 2 All ER 841 at pp. 871–7.

[50] [1982] Ch 204. See Boyle 2 Co. Law 264 (1981).

[51] The court observed that the term 'control' embraces a broad spectrum extending from an overall absolute majority of votes at one end to a majority of votes at the other end made up of those likely to be cast by the delinquent himself plus those voting with him as a result of influence and apathy.

[52] As to the procedural basis on which this issue may be raised by the defendants, see *Smith v Croft (No. 2)* [1988] Ch 114, see below.

meeting is held, it seems that its function is not (as in *Hogg v Cramphorn*[53]) to ratify or approve an exercise of power by directors. Instead their function, in the event that they do not adopt the proceedings initiated by the minority, is to help clarify the judge's mind as to whether or not wrongdoer control exists. This ignores the difficulty of determining the motivation and conflicting interests of various shareholders at a company meeting.[54]

In *Smith v Croft (No. 2)*,[55] Knox J stressed the need for an appropriate independent organ of the company to decide that it was not in the commercial interest of the company to pursue the action. In that case, a majority within the minority was allowed so to decide. Such an independent majority within the minority must reach its conclusions on grounds genuinely thought to advance the company's interests. Its decision is then treated as that of a 'corporate independent organ' which can properly prevent the plaintiff minority shareholders from suing. It is for the judge to determine whether the 'majority within the minority' has fairly reached its decision. It is not his function to say whether its decision is right or wrong. This approach is certainly a judicial innovation which will make a derivative action extremely difficult to bring except in the smallest private companies.[56]

15.6 The exercise of directors' powers for improper purposes

It is well established that if directors exercise their powers *mala fide* or for an improper purpose this is not only a breach of duty to the company, but is a matter of which the minority are entitled to complain.[57] Thus, where the directors use their power to issue shares to retain control by giving themselves a majority voting power at the expense of those rightly entitled to a majority of votes, a shareholder may seek an injunction to protect the rights of the majority.[58]

In *Hogg v Cramphorn*,[59] Buckley J held that, where shares were issued to trustees for the benefit of the company's employees as part of an elaborate scheme to defeat a takeover bid, this was an improper use of the power to issue shares even if it was done in good faith for the benefit of the company. Although a minority shareholder was entitled to sue despite the *Foss v Harbottle* rule, the court directed a meeting to be held at which defendants undertook that the wrongly issued votes would not be used.[60] Thus the success of the minority's action depended upon whether or not the director's misconduct would

---

[53] [1967] Ch 254. See 15.6, below.

[54] The incomplete and unsatisfactory character of the Court of Appeal's observations stems from the fact that, on appeal, the *Foss v Harbottle* rule became irrelevant because the defendant company, Newman Industries, had 'adopted' the action against the real defendants. Thus the court's observations were entirely obiter and indeed the court refused to hear argument from counsel on the question.

[55] [1988] Ch 114.

[56] For a general comment, see Sealy, in Pettet (ed.), *Company Law in Change* (Stevens, 1987), Chapter 1.

[57] *Alexander v Automatic Telephone Co.* [1900] 2 Ch 56 (CA): *Re Smith & Fawcett Ltd* [1942] Ch 304 (CA). See 14.7, above, as to the duty of directors to act in good faith in the interests of their company. Where bad faith takes the form of a bribe, a constructive trust may be imposed on the proceeds of the bribe: *A. G. for Hong Kong v Reid* [1994] 1 AC 324 (PC).

[58] *Punt v Symons* [1903] 2 Ch 506; *Piercy v Mills* [1920] 1 Ch 77. In both these cases the 'majority and minority were already arrayed for battle on a specific issue when the latter attempted to create reinforcements by issuing additional shares': Buckley J in *Hogg v Cramphorn* [1967] 2 Ch 254 at p. 269 (decided in 1963).

[59] [1967] Ch 254. For a fuller discussion of this case in the context of directors' duties, see 14.7, above.

[60] It is not clear whether Buckley J would have allowed a general meeting to ratify if the directors had acted *mala fide*.

in fact be ratified in general meeting.[61] In *Bamford v Bamford*,[62] the Court of Appeal adopted a similar approach where the majority had ratified an improper issue of shares shortly after proceedings commenced. The natural inference to be drawn from these decisions is that the use of directors' powers for an improper or collateral purpose may be the subject of a minority shareholder's suit even though such conduct is open to ratification. Further, a minority action will be defeated if such ratification takes place. Both these propositions appear at first sight to be contrary to the well-established principles on which the *Foss v Harbottle* rule and the exceptions to it rest.[63] It is possible to regard the reasoning in Buckley J's judgment in *Hogg v Cramphorn* as primarily directed to the issue before the court, namely the improper issue of shares. The minority shareholder complained of a wrong neither to himself nor primarily to the company. It was, as Buckley J pointed out,[64] an attempt 'to deprive the majority of their constitutional rights', which attempt would 'cease to have any force' if (leaving aside the wrongly issued shares) the majority in fact approved of what had been done. If a minority are allowed to vindicate the rights of the majority, it is obvious that if the majority agree to what has been done, then *cadit quaestio*. Alternatively, it may be that the duty to exercise powers for a proper purpose, especially the power to allot shares, is owed directly to shareholders.[65]

15.7 The enforcement of statutory 'fiduciary' duties

Certain provisions in Part X of the Companies Act 1985 impose statutory duties upon directors and 'connected persons'.[66] These duties are intended to avoid a conflict of duty and interest arising. In the case of section 320 (substantial property transactions involving directors) and section 330 (prohibition of loans, etc., to directors) there are statutory civil remedies following the pattern of those already available under the rules of equity which apply in the case of a breach of fiduciary duty on the part of directors. Any transactions or arrangements which infringe section 320 or 330 are voidable (on certain conditions) at the instance of the company.[67] In addition there is both liability to account for gains (profits) made in breach of those sections and liability to indemnify the company for any loss or damage resulting.[68]

It was seen that these provisions in principle overlay the long-established rules laid down by the courts of equity and the remedies already afforded. However, it is clear that Parliament was seeking to do more than duplicate the existing law and thus intended to provide more effective civil remedies against the more flagrant forms of abuse of their fiduciary duty by directors. These remedies will be more effective in that they may not be

---

[61] It should be noted that the majority and minority were not already 'arrayed for battle on a specific issue'. See Buckley J in [1967] Ch 254 at p. 269.

[62] [1969] 2 WLR 1107.

[63] See e.g. *MacDougall v Gardiner* (1875) 1 Ch D 13 (CA); *Burland v Earle* [1902] AC 83 (PC); *Edwards v Halliwell* [1950] 2 All ER 1064 (CA);

[64] [1967] Ch 254 at p. 269. In *Bamford v Bamford* [1969] 2 WLR 1107 (CA) this passage from Buckley J's judgment was cited with approval. However, the judgment of Harman LJ appears to assume a minority shareholder's action could not have been brought in any event.

[65] See *Re a Company* [1987] BCLC 82, *John Crowther Group v Carpets International plc* [1990] BCLC 460 at p. 464, and 14.3, above.

[66] See 14.16 and 14.17, above.

[67] See sections 322 (1) (as to substantial property transactions) and 341 (1) (loans).

[68] See sections 322 (3) and 341 (2) (in respect of section 330).

modified in any way by provisions in the articles[69] nor by ratification by the general meeting (except in so far as section 322 (2) (*c*) expressly provides for this by making affirmation within a reasonable period a bar to the statutory form of recission at the instance of the company provided by section 322 (1)). It should be noted that the company's right to an accounting for gains and to an indemnity for losses (section 322 (3) (*b*)) is not barred by loss of the statutory right to recission by reason of affirmation by the shareholders in general meeting or otherwise.[70] In the case of the prohibition on loans, quasi-loans, etc., to directors and connected persons in section 330, the right to avoid transactions and arrangements in breach of the section cannot be barred by affirmation by the shareholders.[71] Again, the right to an accounting for gains and to an indemnity for losses may be pursued by the company 'whether or not' the company is still able to, or chooses to, seek to avoid transactions or arrangements in contravention of section 330.[72]

It is at least open to argument that these new statutory remedies might be the basis of a derivative action by a minority shareholder even though he cannot bring his case within the fraud on a minority exception to the *Foss v Harbottle* rule. Obviously there would have to be a contravention of either section 320 or 330 which was not within any of the exceptions provided[73] or for which any particular defendant had no defence under the relevant statutory provision. It is true that various civil remedies are expressed to be available to the company ('voidable at the instance of the company', 'to account to the company', 'to indemnify the company'), but it is of the nature of derivative proceedings that corporate rights are enforced for the company's benefit.[74] There is nothing in these sections which expressly excludes a minority action. This might well be brought under the 'ultra vires and illegality' exception to the *Foss v Harbottle* rule[75] which has always been understood to include not only acts ultra vires the objects clause but acts which are prohibited by provisions of the Companies Acts or otherwise illegal.[76] Furthermore, it is possible, where recovery is sought for the company's benefit, to bring a derivative action under this exception to the rule.[77] No doubt in this event 'wrongdoer control' of the company must be shown as one of the conditions for allowing a derivative action to proceed (i.e. even though it is not founded upon fraud on the minority).[78]

Where a minority shareholder seeks only a declaration or injunction for a breach of a statutory duty,[79] it is questionable whether the proceedings should be properly classified as derivative and that, therefore, the issue of 'wrongdoer control' has any relevance. A minority shareholder may therefore have more difficulty in establishing *locus standi*.

---

[69] See 14.24.3, above. Thus disclosure to and approval by an independent board of directors is not a ground of relief.

[70] See section 322 (4): 'whether or not it has been avoided in pursuance of subsection (3) above'.

[71] See section 341 (1).

[72] See section 341 (2).

[73] Sections 331 and 333 to 338.

[74] See 15.10, below.

[75] See 15.3, above.

[76] Thus the infringement of what was then section 54 of the 1948 Act can be regarded as one ground for allowing a minority action in *Wallersteiner v Moir (No. 1)* [1974] 1 WLR 991, and see *Smith v Croft (No. 3)* [1987] BCLC 355.

[77] See 15.8, below and *Russell v Wakefield Waterworks* (1875) 20 Eq. 474. See *Taylor v NUM* [1987] BCLC 237.

[78] See 15.5, above.

[79] This form of relief would be more appropriate to an alleged contravention of section 309 (directors to have regard to the interests of employees) and section 319 (contracts of employment of directors – see section 319 (5)). See *Devlin v Slough Estates* (1982), *The Times*, June 16.

Where a member of a company successfully petitions under Part XVII of the 1985 Act (15.13, below), the court may make an order authorising civil proceedings to be brought 'in the name and on behalf of the company' (see 15.16, below). Where such an order is obtained, then it is clear that any remedy available to the company in respect of sections 320 and 330 might be pursued.[80]

15.8 Procedure in minority shareholders' actions in England

In American law a representative action by shareholders to enforce corporate rights, by seeking the recovery of damages for or property belonging to their corporation, is termed a 'derivative' action (i.e. one derived from the corporation's right of action). Lord Denning first adopted this usage,[81] and the courts have long recognised that certain special rules apply to a minority shareholder's action brought for this purpose. The rules now to be discussed apply[82] where, under the 'fraud on a minority' or ultra vires exceptions to the rule in *Foss v Harbottle*, the plaintiff shareholder seeks to recover damages for breach of duty from directors (or third parties) or the restitution of property for the company. Such an action must be brought in the representative form[83] by the plaintiffs 'on behalf of themselves and all the other shareholders of the company other than the defendant.'[84] 'The reason the action takes this form is that the minority shareholder is not in a position to see that the action is brought in the name of the company itself to enforce the company's rights.[85] Although this type of shareholder's action is brought for the benefit of the company, the company must be joined as a nominal defendant as well as the real defendants against whom relief is sought. The reasons for this are succinctly explained in the judgment of Chitty LJ in *Spokes v Grosvenor Hotel Company*.[86]

> To such an action as this the company are necessary defendants. The reason is obvious: the wrong alleged is done to the company, and the company must be a party to the suit in order to be bound by the result of the action and to receive the money recovered in the action. If the company were not bound they could bring a fresh action for the same cause if the action failed, and there were subsequently a change in the board of directors and in the voting power. Obviously, in such an action as this, no specific relief

---

[80] However, in *Re Carrington Viyella plc* (1983) 1 BCC 98, 751, a breach of what was then section 47 of the Companies Act 1980 was held not to amount to unfair prejudice in a petition under section 75 of that Act.

[81] See *Wallersteiner v Moir (No. 2)* [1975] QB 373 at p. 391, citing Gower, *Modern Company Law* (Stevens, 3rd edn 1969), at p. 587. Such an action is not available to a shareholder seeking declaratory relief in respect of a statutory right: *Devlin v Slough Estates* (1982) *The Times,* June 16. See 3 Co. Law 261 (1982).

[82] The procedural points discussed in 15.8–15.10 do not apply in Scotland. See Paterson 2 Co. Law 155 (1981).

[83] Under RSC Order 15, rule 12.

[84] *Spokes v Grosvenor Hotel Co.* [1897] 2 QB 124 at pp. 128–9 (CA). See also *Mosely v Koffyfontein Mines Ltd* [1911] 1 Ch 73 (CA) at p. 81, where the distinction between shareholders' actions to enforce the rights of the company and other shareholders' actions is clearly expressed in the judgment of Fletcher Moulton LJ. See also *Prudential Assurance v Newman Industries (No. 2)* [1982] Ch 204; *Heron International v Lord Grade* [1983] BCLC 244 (CA).

[85] *Beattie v Beattie Ltd and Beattie* [1938] Ch 708 at p. 718 *per* Greene MR. See also *Burland v Earle* [1902] AC 83 at p. 93 *per* Lord Davey (PC). See, however, the judgment of Denning MR in *Wallersteiner v Moir (No. 2)* [1975] 2 QB 373 at p. 391 where the representative form is treated as a 'formula' that may be 'discarded'. See also *Taylor v NUM* [1985] BCLC 237. However, this does not appear to be consistent with earlier authority. Moreover, such a practice might harm the right of other minority shareholders to intervene where the proceedings are not being properly prosecuted.

[86] [1897] 2 QB 124 p. 128 (CA).

is asked against the company; and obviously, too, what is recovered cannot be paid to the plaintiff representing the minority, but must go into the coffers of the company.

This type of action can be brought by a shareholder even in respect of wrongs committed against the company before he became a shareholder,[87] but such an action if commenced by a member may not be continued by him when he ceases to be a member, although the court may allow the action to be continued by another member.[88] The conduct of a shareholder may debar him from bringing this type of shareholder's action. If he has participated in the wrongful act of which he complains, the application of the 'clean hands' doctrine will result in his suit being dismissed.[89] Further, such an action must be brought genuinely in the interests of the company and not for the benefit of a rival company which has fostered the litigation and indemnified the plaintiff against costs.[90] The distinctive characteristic of a shareholder's 'derivative' action is that 'what is recovered cannot be paid to the plaintiff representing the minority, but must go into the coffers of the company'.[91] Hence, such an action should not be combined with a claim for a wrong done to the plaintiff shareholder personally.[92] As in other representative suits, the plaintiff, as *dominus litis* until judgment, can discontinue or settle an action at his pleasure.[93] However, unless the settlement is embodied in a formal judgment, a second action may be brought by another shareholder.[94] In a representative action an unnamed but represented plaintiff was a 'party' within the definition of section 225 of the Supreme Court (Consolidation) Act 1925. Thus where the named plaintiff withdraws from the proceedings, the name of a previously unnamed but represented plaintiff may be added and the pleadings amended accordingly (RSC Order 15, rule 6 and Order 20, rule 5).[95]

A minority shareholder's derivative action cannot be pursued (even if otherwise well grounded) once the company is in liquidation. This is because the corporate cause of action is then vested in the liquidator. The shareholder should seek redress from the liquidator. If the liquidator refuses unreasonably, the shareholder can then apply to the court.[96]

---

[87] *Seaton v Grant* (1867) LR 2 Ch App. 459; *Bloxham v Metropolitan Rly* (1868) LR 4 Ch App. 337.

[88] *Birch v Sullivan* [1957] 1 WLR 1247. Such an action may not be brought if the company has been dissolved: *Coxon v Gorst* [1891] 2 Ch 73; *Clarkson v Davies* [1923] AC 100 (PC).

[89] *Towers v African Tug Co.* [1904] 1 Ch 558 (CA); *Nurcombe v Nurcombe* [1984] BCLC 557.

[90] *Forrest v Manchester, Sheffield & Lincolnshire Rly* (1861) 4 De GF & J 126.

[91] *Spokes v Grosvenor Hotel Co.* [1897] 2 QB 124 (CA).

[92] *Stroud v Lawson* [1898] 2 QB 44 (CA). Another view was expressed by Vinelott J in *Prudential Assurance v Newman Industries (No. 2)* [1980] 2 All ER 841. However, the Court of Appeal (in the same case: [1982] Ch 204) took a very different view of the possibility of combining representative actions in tort with derivative actions for breach of fiduciary duty. Such a possibility was rejected by the Court of Appeal. See Boyle 2 Co. Law 264 at p. 266.

[93] *Re Alpha Co.* [1903] 1 Ch 203.

[94] See *Gray v Lewis* (1869) LR 8 Ch App. 1035 at p. 1051. At an earlier stage in the proceedings the court has power to remove a plaintiff from control of a representative action where another of the class represented intervenes on the ground that the action is not being adequately prosecuted: *Re Services Club Estates Syndicate* [1930] 1 Ch 78 (a debenture holder's action).

[95] *Moon v Atherton* [1972] 2 QB 435.

[96] *Fargro Ltd v Godfrey* [1986] 1 WLR 1134, applying *Ferguson v Wallbridge* [1935] 3 DLR 66. See footnote 88, above.

15.9 Minority shareholders' right to an indemnity in a derivative action

The Court of Appeal has recognised[97] that a minority shareholder who brings a derivative suit[98] may have a right to an indemnity against the company is respect of his costs. This right was held to be closely analogous to the indemnity which a trustee is entitled to in respect of proceedings on behalf of the trust property or in the execution of the trust.[99] Fundamentally, the right will depend on whether the minority shareholder acted in good faith and reasonably in bringing proceedings. The Court of Appeal modelled the procedure for applying to the court to claim the indemnity on that already established in the case of a trustee.[100] This procedure in the case of a trustee is well established and Buckley LJ refers[101] to a useful summary in a note to RSC Order 85, rule 2.[102]

After the writ is issued the plaintiff can apply by summons in the action for directions as to whether he should proceed in the action and, if so, to what stage without further directions. This application by summons would come before the Master on an *ex parte* basis (at least in a relatively simple case) without the joinder of any other party. The Master in the exercise of his discretion can give approval for the continuance of the action to various stages: 'until close of pleadings, or until after discovery or until trial (rather like a legal aid committee does)'.[103] Indeed, this might extend to the plaintiff's costs down to judgment. Assuming that on the hearing of the summons the plaintiff was authorised to proceed, he would 'be secure in the knowledge that, when the costs of the action should come to be dealt with, this would be on the basis, as between himself and the company, that he had acted reasonably and ought prima facie to be treated by the trial judge as entitled to an order that the company should pay his costs.[104] Moreover, the Court of Appeal adds the extremely important rider that these costs would normally be taxed on a basis not less favourable than the common fund basis, and should indemnify him against any costs he may be ordered to pay to the defendants.[105]

In a more recent decision,[106] Walton J gave a somewhat cautious and restrictive interpretation of the Court of Appeal's decision in *Wallersteiner*. He indicated that, in order to hold the balance fairly between plaintiffs and defendants, it is incumbent on the

---

[97] *Wallersteiner v Moir (No. 2)* [1975] QB 373.

[98] A *Wallersteiner* order will not be made in a shareholders' action which is not a derivative one, but at the end of the proceedings an order for costs may be made on a common fund basis if the result of the case is beneficial to members generally: *Marx v Estates and General Ltd* [1976] 1 WLR 380 at p. 392. See also *Re a Company* [1987] BCLC 82.

[99] See *Hardoon v Belilios* [1901] AC 118 (HL).

[100] See *Beddoe, Doenes v Cottam* [1893] 1 Ch 557.

[101] [1975] 1 QB 373 at p. 404, where he cites the *Supreme Court Practice* (1973), at p. 1236. See now the *Supreme Court Practice* (1985), vol. 1, at p. 1194.

[102] ibid.

[103] ibid. at p. 392 *per* Denning MR.

[104] ibid. at p. 405 *per* Buckley LJ.

[105] ibid. at p. 405 *per* Buckley LJ and p. 392 *per* Denning MR. For an account of the detailed procedure in an application for an indemnity (as to joinder or parties, etc.), see Boyle [1976] JBL 18.

[106] *Smith v Croft* [1986] 1 WLR 580. Applied in *Re Charge Card Services Ltd* [1986] 3 WLR 697 in a creditor's application for costs in a winding-up. Cf. *Jaybird Group Ltd v Green* [1986] BCLC 319 (decided in 1981). Here a less restrictive approach was taken. The criterion applied was that of an honest, independent and impartial board of directors.

plaintiff, in applying for a *Wallersteiner* order for costs, to show that it is genuinely needed. Even when an order is granted, it is appropriate to leave some proportion of the costs to be borne by the plaintiffs, since otherwise there would be no incentive for the plaintiff to prosecute the action effectively. This might ultimately result in the action being dismissed for want of prosecution.

Walton J conceded that in an application for a *Wallersteiner* order it was not appropriate to conduct an interim trial. However, the court is obliged to assess (in the light of both the agreed and the disputed facts) whether the action should be allowed to continue at the company's expense. The test to be applied was that of the standard of care exercised by the prudent businessman in the conduct of his own affairs. On the facts of the case, Walton J held the action had little chance of success. He noted that it was being brought against the wishes of the majority of independent shareholders. He therefore decided that it would be unjust to grant the plaintiffs an indemnity for the costs down to discovery of documents which had been asked for.[107] While this decision was well warranted by the facts of the case, its spirit is a very different one from that of the Court of Appeal in *Wallersteiner*. It may well tend to further discourage the bringing of derivative actions by minority shareholders, even where serious abuse has occurred.

In *Wallersteiner v Moir (No. 2)*,[108] the Court of Appeal held that legal aid was not available to a shareholder bringing a derivative action on the ground that section 25 of the Legal Aid Act 1974 defines 'person' in a way which excludes a body of persons corporate or unincorporated.[109] Buckley LJ expressly reserved the question, however, that legal aid might be available in one limited class of case. This is where the company has only two or three shareholders, 'a company of a kind sometimes described as a quasi-partnership,' and is, apart from any property which may be recoverable in the action, of very little financial substance;[110] Buckley LJ here makes the further assumption that the plaintiff's resources are such that it would make him eligible for legal aid if he were suing on a cause of action of his own.[111]

15.10 Shareholders' actions to enforce rights against the company

Where a minority shareholder seeks a remedy *against* the company under any of the exceptions to the rule in *Foss v Harbottle*, then the special rules which apply to the 'derivative' type of representative action, described at 15.8, above, do not apply. Whenever he seeks to enforce a right which he enjoys together with other shareholders, or

[107] Walton J held that since the company should be in a position to lay the relevant facts before the court before any order as to costs was made against it, the application before the Master should normally be heard *inter partes* and the company should see all the affidavits and exhibits unless they were covered by legal professional privilege or some other good reason for withholding such evidence: [1986] 1 WLR 580 at pp. 587–8.

[108] Above.

[109] See, in particular, the judgment of Buckley LJ in [1975] QB 373 at p. 400, which pursues this question in greater depth than the other judgments.

[110] ibid. at pp. 400–1.

[111] The majority of the Court of Appeal refused to accept the argument of the Master of the Rolls in favour of the American 'contingency fee' system; nor did they regard it as possible to introduce it in the case of derivative actions by relaxing the Law Society's practice rules.

some class of them, he may sue in the representative form.[112] However, a representative action is not obligatory in such cases. He may instead sue simply in his own name.[113] In either event, the normal remedy against the company will be to seek an injunction[114] or bring an action for a declaration.[115] Where the representative form of proceedings is employed the 'clean hands' doctrine may apply to the conduct of the plaintiff.[116] The plaintiff in such an action has the right to control the conduct of proceedings, as *dominus litis* until judgment.[117]

In shareholders' actions *against* the company it is not necessary to join the directors as parties, unless some form of relief is sought against them in addition to the remedy against the company. However, in such an action it is possible to seek relief by way of injunction against the company while joining the directors as co-defendants in order that relief may be claimed against them for the company's benefit.[118] In such an action the two forms of relief sought should arise out of a series of related transactions. The court will not allow what is in substance a derivative suit to be brought in the guise of a representative action in tort (e.g. the tort of conspiracy).[119]

15.11 Proceedings in the company's name

The proper persons to give instructions for the commencement of an action to enforce any right of the company, or to obtain redress for a wrong done to the company, or to recover its property, are the directors; and the company itself is the only proper plaintiff in such an action,[120] though it cannot appear in person, either as plaintiff or defendant, and, except in the county court,[121] can only be represented by counsel.[122] Whether before or in a liquidation the company's name alone should appear as plaintiff, it being improper to add the directors or liquidators as plaintiffs unless some relief is claimed by them in their individual capacity.

Although the directors are the proper persons to give the instructions for commencing such an action, it was long ago held that effect should be given to the wishes of a majority of the shareholders when they desire that proceedings should be taken to protect the company's rights, and that an action may be commenced in the company's name as plaintiff by such a majority, or even in case of urgency by one or more shareholders who

---

[112] Under RSC Order 15, rule 12. See e.g. *Pender v Lushington* (1877) 6 Ch D 70; *Mosely v Koffyfontein Mines Ltd* [1911] 1 Ch 73, affirmed *sub nom. Koffyfontein Mines v Mosley* [1911] AC 409 (HL).

[113] *Simpson v Westminster Palace Hotel Co.* [1860] 8 HLC 712; *Sidebotton v Kershaw, Leese & Co. Ltd* [1920] 1 Ch 154 (CA).

[114] *Wood v Odessa Waterworks* (1889) 42 Ch D 636; *Pender v Lushington* (1877) 6 Ch D 70.

[115] *Edwards v Halliwell* [1950] 2 All ER 1064 (CA); *Sidebottom v Kershaw, Leese & Co. Ltd* [1920] 1 Ch 154 (CA); *Greenhalgh v Arderne Cinemas Ltd* [1951] Ch 286 (CA). A shareholder may now seek a judgment in an action against his company: section 111A of the Companies Act 1985.

[116] *Burt v The British Nation Life Insurance Association* (1859) 4 De G & J 158. But cf. *Mosely v Koffyfontein Mines* [1911] 1 Ch 73 (CA), an action to restrain future illegal acts.

[117] See above as to the 'derivative' type of action. This principle applies to any representative action.

[118] See *Russell v Wakefield Waterworks Co.* (1875) LR 20 Eq. 474 at pp. 481–2; *Bagshaw v Eastern Union Rly* (1849) 7 Hare 114, affirmed 2 Mac. & G 389; *Hogg v Cramphorn* [1967] 2 Ch 254.

[119] *Gray v Lewis* (1873) 8 Ch App. at p. 1050; *Russell v Wakefield Waterworks Co.* (1875) 20 Eq. 474 at p. 479; *Duckett v Gover* (1877) 6 Ch D 82; *Burland v Earle* [1902] AC 83 at p. 93 (AC); *Prudential Assurance v Newman Industries (No. 2)* [1982] Ch 204; *Heron International v Lord Grade* [1983] BCLC 244 at pp. 281–3.

[120] *Prudential Assurance v Newman Industries (No. 2)* [1982] Ch 204.

[121] *Charles P. Kinnell & Co. v Harding Wace & Co.* [1918] 1 KB 405 (CA).

[122] *Frinton & Walton UDC v Walton & District Sand Co.* [1938] WN 31; *Tritonia v Equity & Law Life Assurance Society* [1943] AC 584 (HL (Sc.)).

believe that they have the support of a majority, and subsequently obtain the sanction of a resolution of the company.[123] An interim injunction may be obtained in such an action before their sanction has been procured. But if it ultimately appears that the majority is not in favour of the proceedings,[124] the name of the company as plaintiff will be struck out.[125]

In *Breckland Group Holdings Ltd v London & Suffolk Properties*,[126] a shareholder was restrained from continuing a legal action in the company's name where the articles provided that actions in the company's name could be commenced only with the consent of two particular directors. The shareholder who brought the action argued unsuccessfully that the directors would have to agree to take proceedings as this was obviously in the company's best interests.[127]

PART 2: A STATUTORY REMEDY FOR MINORITIES

15.12 Power of the court to grant relief on a petition alleging unfair prejudice

The Cohen Committee[128] designed what used to be section 210 of the Companies Act 1948 as a procedure to meet the specific problems of minority oppression. It was realised that a 'just and equitable' winding-up under what is now section 122 (1) (*g*) of the Insolvency Act 1986,[129] though it might be kept in reserve, was usually inappropriate, and a derivative action was frequently unavailable owing to the restrictive nature of the *Foss v Harbottle* rule. The Jenkins Committee,[130] when it came to review section 210, found its provisions restrictive in various respects. It made a number of proposals which were originally enacted in section 75 of the Companies Act 1980. The most important of these changes is that the basis on which a court may grant a petition is no longer that of oppression but that of 'unfair prejudice'. These provisions are now contained in Part XVII (sections 459 to 461) of the Companies Act 1985, as amended by the Companies Act 1989.

Section 459 (1) allows a member[131] to apply to the court by petition for an order under the section. The ground on which he may petition (and on which the court must be

---

[123] *Pender v Lushington* (1877) 6 Ch D 70; *Imperial Hydropathic Hotel Co. v Hampson* (1883) 23 Ch D 1 (CA); *La Compagnie de Mayville v Whitley* [1896] 1 Ch 788 (CA); it seems difficult to reconcile these cases with *Salmon v Quin & Axtens* [1909] AC 422 (HL), and *Automatic Self-Cleansing Filter Co. v Cunninghame* [1906] 2 Ch 34; but they have been often followed. See also *Marshall's Valve Gear Co. v Manning* [1909] 1 Ch 627.

[124] If such approval is obtained the action may proceed in the company's name: *Danish Mercantile Co. Ltd v Beaumont* [1951] Ch 680 (CA). This decision of the Court of Appeal was followed in *Alexander Ward & Co. Ltd v Samyang Navigation Co. Ltd* [1975] 1 WLR 673 (HL. Sc.)).

[125] *Silber Light Co. v Silber* (1878) 12 Ch D 717: *East Pant Du Mining Co. v Merryweather* (1864) 2 H & M 254; *Duckett v Gover* (1877) 6 Ch D 82. Where it is intended to bring a genuine minority action (i.e. under one of the exceptions to *Foss v Harbottle*) an action should not be commenced in the company's name: *Alexander v Automatic Telephone Co.* [1900] 2 Ch 56 at p. 69 *per* Lindley MR (CA).

[126] (1988) 4 BCC 542. See also 13.11, above.

[127] For further details on procedure, especially motions to strike out the company's name and security for costs under section 726 of the Companies Act 1985, see *Gore-Browne on Companies* (Jordans, 44th edn, loose-leaf), 28.11.1 and 28.11.2.

[128] Cmnd 6659, para. 60 (1945).

[129] As to which, see 15.17, below.

[130] Cmnd 1749 (1962).

[131] This may theoretically include a passive majority – it is not necessarily restricted to a minority member (see *Re Baltic Real Estate Ltd (No. 1)* [1993] BCLC 499, cf. *Re Baltic Real Estate Ltd (No. 2)* [1993] BCLC 503).

satisfied that the petition is well founded)[132] is as follows: that the company's affairs are being or have been conducted in a manner which is unfairly prejudicial to the interests of its members generally or of some part of the members (including at least himself) or that any actual or proposed act or omission[133] on its behalf is or would be so prejudicial.[134]

15.13 The concept of unfair prejudice

This still remains a rather elusive concept. It is perhaps better characterised as a general standard to guide the courts as to what kind or degree of misbehaviour or mismanagement should justify the court, on hearing a petition under section 459 of the Companies Act 1985, exercising its wide powers of intervention under section 461. There is a school of thought[135] that the courts should regard their 'jurisdiction' under section 459 in the widest possible way but that they should preserve an unfettered discretion in deciding, in particular cases, whether the interests of a petitioning member have in fact been unfairly prejudiced. Indeed some would contend that this is the only explanation that can be given to the wide spectrum of judicial dicta which preface particular discussions of the question of whether unfair prejudice has been established to the satisfaction of the court in the way section 459 requires.

If this indeed were the state of the authorities interpreting this section, it would be a most unsatisfactory state of affairs for legal advisers and their clients throughout Britain, whenever the affairs of small companies produce an inevitable incidence of what perhaps can be best described as the corporate equivalent of marital breakdown. The argument for a wide jurisdiction with an almost unlimited judicial discretion within that jurisdiction is that in that way it is possible to obtain the maximum justice in particular cases. This can be achieved in the light of a multiplicity of varying factors concerning the capital structure, management arrangements and business activity of each particular company whose affairs are being considered by the court. This may be an ideal approach from the point of view of a chancery judge and/or counsel specialising in this area of company law, who are well aware of the course of judicial practice illustrated by many unreported decisions. Others more remote from Lincoln's Inn and the Strand may need at least some conceptual guidance as to the meaning of 'unfair prejudice' so that disputes may be settled between the parties and their solicitors without the expense of litigation.

Fortunately, some decisions have grappled with this central issue, and it is now possible to formulate some general propositions as to what the courts mean by the term 'unfair prejudice' and the related phraseology in section 459 (1).

The following passage from the judgment of Slade J,[136] later cited with approval by Nourse J in *Re R. A. Noble (Clothing) Ltd*,[137] speaks pretty well for itself.

> I do not think it necessary or appropriate in this judgment to attempt any comprehensive exposition of the situations that may give rise to the court's jurisdiction under

---

[132] See section 461 (1). See *Re a Company* [1987] 1 WLR 589.

[133] See *Re Kenyon Swansea Ltd* [1987] BCLC 514.

[134] The procedural rules to be followed are now set forth in a statutory instrument, the Companies (Unfair Prejudice Application) Proceedings Rules 1986 (SI 1986 No. 2000).

[135] See Vinelott J, in 6 Co. Law 21 at p. 31 (1985) (the LSE moot).

[136] *Re Bovey Hotels* (31 July 1981, unreported). As Nourse J pointed out, the 'case went to the Court of Appeal but there was no appeal against that finding'; see [1983] BCLC 273, 291. The passage quoted in the text was cited with approval by Ralph Gibson LJ in *Re a Company ex parte Nicholas* [1992] BCC 895 at p. 910 (CA). See further *Re Saul D. Harrison & Sons plc* [1995] 1 BCLC 14.

[137] [1983] BCLC 273 at pp. 290–1. See also *Re Sam Weller Ltd* [1990] BCLC 82 at pp. 85–90.

section 75. Broadly, however, I would say this. Without prejudice to the generality of the wording of the section, which may cover many other situations, a member of a company will be able to bring himself within the section if he can show that the value of his shareholding in the company has been seriously diminished or at least seriously jeopardised by reason of a course of conduct on the part of those persons who have had de facto control of the company, which is unfair to the member concerned. The test of fairness must, I think, be an objective, not a subjective one. In other words it is not necessary for the petitioner to show that persons who have had de facto control of the company have acted as they did in the conscious knowledge that this was unfair to the petitioner or that they were acting in bad-faith; the test I think is whether a reasonable bystander observing the consequences of their conduct would regard it as having unfairly prejudiced the petitioner's interests.

Thus, it is readily apparent that the abandonment of the term 'oppressive' (in the old section 210 of the 1948 Act) and the judicial gloss put upon it[138] has been given its intended effect by the judiciary. 'Bad faith' and 'lack of probity' (and their associated burden of proof) are now irrelevant. Similarly, the use or threatened use of majority shareholders' voting power is not a requirement. The term 'unfair prejudice', whether analysed as a 'standard' or a 'concept', is a relatively more objective one which is concerned with running the company in a way that is clearly unfair in its consequences to the complaining shareholder, even if the respondents can claim to have acted in the best of good faith. While it is clear that the judge still has a considerable discretion as to how this concept is applied to the widely varying sets of circumstances in those corporate disputes that lead to section 459 petitions, this does not increase the discretionary elements which already existed under the old section 210; still less does it make the new standard or concept 'more subjective'.

It is, however, clear that the petitioner does not have to establish the infringement of a shareholder's right given by some other aspect of company law. The concept of unfairness cuts across the distinction between acts which do or do not infringe rights attaching to shares.[139] It has also been judicially observed[140] that unfairness is a familiar concept employed in ordinary speech – often by way of contrast to infringement of legal rights. The court may pay regard to wider equitable considerations. For example, in a 'quasi-partnership' type company, the court may take account of legitimate expectations of members.[141] On the other hand the plain infringement of a shareholder's right (e.g. to

---

[138] See *Gore-Browne on Companies* (Jordans, 44th edn, loose-leaf), 28.13 for a summary of the old case-law on section 210.

[139] In *Re a Company (No. 008699 of 1985)* [1986] 2 BCC 99, 024; see also *McGuinness v Bremner plc* [1988] BCLC 673, Ct of Sess. The conduct complained of in a section 459 petition must relate to the manner in which the affairs of the company are conducted. In *Nicholas v Soundcraft Electronics* [1993] BCLC 360 (CA), the non-payment of debts owed by a holding company to its subsidiary (where this was an attempt to keep the group afloat in financial difficulties) was held not to constitute unfair prejudice in the conduct of the subsidiary's affairs. It does not include acts of a shareholder carried out in a personal capacity outside the course of the company's business: *Re a Company (No. 001761 of 1986)* [1987] BCLC 141.

[140] ibid., *per* Hoffmann J. Seemingly 'popular' speech is now a better guide than the dictionary definition given in *Gore-Browne on Companies* 28.13: that which is not just, unbiased, equitable, legitimate. See Vinelott J in the 'LSE Moot' in 6 Co. Law 21 at p. 31 (1985).

[141] *Re Kenyon Swansea Ltd* [1987] BCLC 514. Cf. *Re Postgate and Denby (Agencies) Ltd* [1987] BCLC 8, see also *Re a Company ex parte Schwartz (No. 2)* [1989] BCLC 427 and *Re Elgindata Ltd* [1991] BCLC 959.

be given accurate accounting information as prescribed in the Companies Act 1985) could also be the basis of an allegation of unfair prejudice.[142] This might well succeed even though the persistent denial of such a right could not be shown to have the consequence that the value of his shareholding could be shown to have been 'seriously diminished (or at least seriously prejudiced) by reason of a course of conduct' etc. As Slade J indicated (in the passage cited earlier) this is an element in what must normally be shown in order to establish unfair prejudice but that is 'without prejudice to the generality of the wording of section 459'.

A question that was raised by most commentators[143] on section 459 is how far a breach (or breaches) of directors' fiduciary duties may be of assistance in establishing unfair prejudice. Or, to put it another way, to what extent is section 459 of use in circumventing the limitations of the 'fraud on a minority' exception to the rule in *Foss v Harbottle*? The passage cited earlier from *Re Bovey Hotel Ventures Ltd*[144] and adopted with approval in *Re R. A. Noble Clothing Company*[145] indicates that de facto control by those against whom unfairly prejudicial conduct or acts (or indeed omissions) is alleged is sufficient.[146] In three cases which took the form of applications to strike out petitions under section 459 (on the basis that there was no case in law for the respondents to answer) the allegations in the petition referred to various breaches of duty by directors. Hoffmann J (who heard all three applications),[147] in rejecting these applications to strike out, clearly regarded allegations of breach of fiduciary duty as capable of establishing unfair prejudice to minority shareholders in a private company or a small unlisted public company.

The contention that the facts (e.g. a crude misappropriation of assets by a majority shareholder) would have readily warranted the bringing of a derivative action will not bar a petition under section 459.[148] Moreover a breach of directors' fiduciary duties not to mislead shareholders when making statements supporting one of two rival takeover bids is capable (at a later full hearing of a section 459 petition) of establishing unfair prejudice.[149] Where the petitioners were fraudulently induced to sell their shares in a private company to a small public company (as part of a manifestly dishonest scheme), Hoffmann J refused to strike out a petition merely on the ground that the matters complained of constituted wrongs to the petitioner as defrauded vendors of their former private company's shares and as a wrongfully dismissed managing director (as regards one petitioner) of that company. Once again it was held that the interests of a member are not limited to his strict legal rights since the use of the word 'unfairly' in section 459 enabled the court to have regard to wider equitable considerations.[150]

The developments described above are encouraging for shareholders in private

---

[142] See, e.g. *Re a Company ex parte Shorter* [1990] BCLC 384. Compare *Re a Company ex parte Schwartz* [1989] BCLC 427. See further *Re a Company ex parte Harries* [1989] BCLC 383, where an old allotment in breach of statutory pre-emptive rights was found to be evidence of unfair prejudice.

[143] e.g. *Gore-Browne on Companies*, 28.13.

[144] Unreported.

[145] [1983] BCLC 273.

[146] See *Re a Company* [1987] BCLC 141; *Re a Company ex parte Nicholas* [1992] BCC 895 (CA); and *Re BSB Holdings Ltd* [1993] BCLC 246.

[147] *Re a Company* [1986] 1 WLR 281; *In Re a Company* [1986] BCLC 382; *In Re a Company* [1986] BCLC 376. See also *Re a Company ex parte Burr* [1992] BCLC 724 and *Re Ghyll Beck Driving Range Ltd* [1993] BCLC 112.

[148] See [1986] 1 WLR 281 at p. 284.

[149] *In Re a Company* [1986] BCLC 382.

[150] *In Re a Company* [1986] BCLC 376; *McGuinness v Bremner plc* (1988) SLT 891.

companies, but there is less encouraging news in respect of public listed companies with widely dispersed shareholders. It is in this type of company, of course, that the restricting aspects of 'fraud on a minority', and especially wrongdoer control,[151] prevent shareholders' derivative suits having much impact on the still serious problem of corporate abuse. In *Re Carrington Viyella plc*,[152] in a petition in respect of a publicly listed company, it was held by Vinelott J that failure to obtain shareholders' approval for the chairman's long-term contract of employment, as required by section 319 of the Companies Act 1985,[153] did not amount to unfairly prejudicial conduct within section 459 (1).[154] Other section 459 cases involving public companies[155] have rejected petitions principally on the ground that there is no room in this context for allegations of failure to meet legitimate expectations outside what is contained in the company's public documents, i.e. its memorandum and articles, prospectus or listing agreement, etc. It was arguable that the previous wording of section 459, which referred to 'the interests of some part of the members (including at least himself)', made relief under the section more difficult in the case of public listed companies, on the grounds that the alleged unfair prejudice had to differentiate or discriminate between the interests of classes or groups of shareholders. Whatever the force of this argument,[156] the current wording of section 459 (1), as revised by the Companies Act 1989[157] – 'unfairly prejudicial to the interests of its members generally or some part of its members' – has removed this particular difficulty, and it can no longer be an answer to a section 459 petition concerning a public company where the majority remains passively indifferent, that the unfair prejudice has been suffered by all shareholders alike (or all but a handful who are also the wrongdoers). There is no evidence that the Jenkins Committee, in reforming the old section 210, intended to exclude such companies from the wide discretion it proposed should be conferred upon the court by what is now Part XVII of the 1985 Act.

Another aspect of the enforcement of directors' duties by means of a petition under section 459 which remains unclear is the director's duty of care. It would seem that the Jenkins Committee[158] intended that the reformed statutory remedy might be used in this regard, although the courts decided otherwise[159] in the case of the old section 210. Where serious mismanagement causes real economic harm to the company's business (and therefore to the value of the members' interest) the general conceptual developments examined earlier should enable the courts to hold that unfair prejudice has been established. The terminology in section 459 (1) (referring to 'any actual or proposed act or omission of the company including an act or omission on its behalf' where this 'is or would be so prejudicial') should be of assistance here. Once again, however, a petition in

---

[151] See 15.5, above.

[152] (1983) 1 BCC 98, 951; see 4 Co. Law 164 (1983).

[153] See 14.15, above.

[154] It was also held that the failure of a controlling shareholder to comply with an undertaking given to the Secretary of State for Trade and Industry in order to avoid a reference to the Monopolies Commission did not affect the rights of the petitioning shareholders; this finding is wholly understandable.

[155] *Re Blue Arrow plc* [1987] BCLC 585, *Re Ringtower Holdings plc* (1989) 5 BCC 82.

[156] It was accepted in *Re a Company* [1988] 1 WLR 1068 but rejected in *Re Sam Weller and Sons Ltd* [1990] Ch 682.

[157] See Schedule 19, para. 11. The wording now mirrors that in section 27 of the Insolvency Act 1986, which gives a remedy to members and creditors unfairly prejudiced when a company is in administration; see 17.28, below.

[158] Cmnd 1749 (1962) paras. 207–8.

[159] *Re Five Minute Car Wash Service* [1966] 1 WLR 745.

the case of a public listed company may present greater difficulty. In *Re Elgindata Ltd*[160] Warner J was of the view that the court would ordinarily be very reluctant to treat managerial decisions as unfairly prejudicial conduct but that it would be open to the court in an appropriate case to find that serious mismanagement of a company's business could constitute unfair prejudice. Disagreement between the parties as to whether a particular managerial decision was commercially sound is clearly not enough. Shareholders realise that the value of their shares will depend upon the measure of competence in management. A breach by a director of his duty of care and skill must, however, be distinguished from the quality of management turning out to be poor. An example of unfair prejudice might be 'where the majority shareholders, for reasons of their own, persisted in retaining in charge of the management of the company's business a member of their family who was demonstrably incompetent'.[161]

15.14 'Member *qua* member'

It was a clear distinction between the old remedy under section 210 of the Companies Act 1948 and the remedy of just and equitable winding up (as reinterpreted by the House of Lords in *Ebrahimi v Westbourne Galleries Ltd*)[162] that a petitioner had to complain in his capacity as 'member *qua* member' under section 210[163] but not, at any rate in the case of a 'quasi-partnership', under what is now section 122 (1) (*g*) of the Insolvency Act 1986. 'It is obvious that in a small private company it is legalistic to segregate the separate capacities of the same individual as shareholder, director or employee. His dismissal from the board or from employment by the company will inevitably affect the real value of his interest in the company expressed by his shareholding'.[164] However, in the first fully reported case (on what was then section 75 of the Companies Act 1980) Lord Grantchester QC appeared to apply the 'member *qua* member' test to section 75:

> To my mind, in passing section 75 of the 1980 Act, Parliament did not intend to give a right of action to every shareholder who considered that some act or omission by his company resulted in unfair prejudice to himself. In argument, an example was advanced of a shareholder who objected to his company carrying out some operation on land adjoining his dwelling house, which resulted in that house falling in value. It is not difficult to envisage an act or omission on the part of the company rendering an asset of a shareholder, other than his share, of lesser value. In my judgment section 75 is to be construed as confined to 'unfair prejudice' of a petitioner '*qua* member'; or to put it another way, the word 'interests' in section 75 is conferred to 'interests of the petitioner or member'.[165]

While the specific examples given (and the facts of the case so far as this passage was

---

[160] [1991] BCLC 959.

[161] *Per* Warner J in *Re Elgindata Ltd* [1991] BCLC 959 at p. 993, applied in *Re Macro (Ipswich) Ltd* [1994] 2 BCLC 354.

[162] [1972] AC 360. See 15.17, below.

[163] See e.g. *Re Five Minute Car Wash Service* [1966] 1 WLR 745.

[164] *Gore-Browne on Companies* (Jordans, 44th edn, loose-leaf), 28.13, cited by Lord Grantchester in *Re a Company* [1983] Ch 178.

[165] [1983] Ch 178. See *Re JE Cade & Son Ltd* [1992] BCLC 213, where it was held that the interests that the petitioner was trying to protect were his interests as a freeholder of a farm and not as a member of the company. See also *Jaber v Science and Information Technology Ltd* [1992] BCLC 764.

germane to his decision) make this attempt to define the 'interests' of members understandable, this approach could put an undue restriction upon what is now section 459 of
the Companies Act 1988 in other situations. In other decisions the phrase 'interests of
some part of the members' has been more liberally interpreted so as to free it from this
particular shackle on the old section 210. In one case, in which the company was 'a classic
example of a quasi-partnership', Vinelott J strongly expressed the view obiter (and has
amplified it extrajudicially[166]) that the introduction of the term 'interests' allows the court
to avoid the 'member *qua* member' approach and take account of the same 'interests'
(granted the need to prove unfair prejudice) as in a just and equitable winding-up. More
recently Hoffmann J[167] observed that 'the interests of a member who had ventured his
capital in a small private company might include the legitimate expectation that he would
continue to be employed as a director – so that his dismissal would be unfairly prejudicial
to his interests as a member.' This was related to other allegations of unfairly prejudicial
behaviour and linked to the wider principle that 'the interests of a member are not
necessarily limited to his strict legal rights.'[168]

There is not yet general agreement on this question, however. Even in the case of a
'quasi-partnership' type of company, dismissal from employment and a position on the
board will not necessarily establish unfair prejudice. This is made clear by Nourse J in *Re
London School of Electronics*.[169] This case concerned a company which provided courses of
study in electronics in conjunction with City Tutorial College Ltd (CTC), the majority
shareholder. The petitioning minority shareholder's complaint was that the two individuals who owned the shares in CTC had resolved at a board meeting of the London
School of Electronics (LSE) to transfer substantially all of the LSE students to CTC (and
to register all new students for the electronics course with CTC) on the grounds that that
was necessary to quality for recognition by an American university as a degree course.
The petitioner was subsequently removed from his office as director. The petitioner had
then set up a rival establishment and taken away a number of pupils enrolled at the LSE.
The following passage in the judgment of Nourse J indicates when dismissal may provide
evidence of unfair prejudice:

> In my judgment it was CTC's decision to appropriate the B.Sc. students to itself which
> was the effective cause of the breakdown in the relationship of mutual confidence
> between quasi-partners. Furthermore, that was clearly conduct on the part of CTC
> which was both unfair and prejudicial to the interests of the petitioner as a member of
> the company. It is possible, although I do not so decide, that CTC would have been
> entitled to relieve the petitioner of his teaching duties before June 1983. It is even
> possible, although it is much less likely, that CTC, had it gone through the appropriate
> formalities, could have properly removed the petitioner as a director of the company.
> But none of that is to say that CTC was entitled to take the extreme step of determining
> to deprive the petitioner of his 25 per cent interest in the profits attributable to the B.Sc.
> students.

In another sense, the unfair prejudice remedy is not confined to members. Section 459 (2)

---

[166] *Re a Company* [1983] BCLC 151 and 6 Co. Law 21 at p. 30 (1985).
[167] *Re a Company* [1986] BCLC 382.
[168] For a discussion on this aspect of 'unfair prejudice' see 15.13, above.
[169] [1986] Ch 211. See also *Re a Company (No. 004377 of 1986)* [1987] BCLC 94.

allows those to whom shares have been transferred[170] or transmitted by operation of law to petition. Section 460 also gives such a right to the Secretary of State (after powers of investigation have been used), but this has been almost totally ignored by the Department of Trade and Industry.[171]

As will be seen below, in regard to members a section 459 petition is often combined with a petition for a just and equitable winding-up. It has long been established that a contributory's winding-up petition may not be brought if he has no tangible interest. This prevents such petitions where the company is insolvent. It has been held[172] that this also bars a petition under section 459. It is not entirely clear why this should always be so. Thus the victim of unfair prejudice might still wish his shares bought by a wealthy respondent protected from the company's creditors by limited liability.

15.15 The 'alternative remedy'

What is now section 125 (2) of the Insolvency Act 1986 requires the court, on hearing a winding-up petition presented by members of the company as contributories on the ground that it is just and equitable, to grant a winding-up order 'if it is of the opinion (a) that the petitioners are entitled to relief either by winding up the company or by some other means and (b) that in the absence of any other remedy it would be just and equitable that the company should be wound up'. The section then emphasises this second point with the addition of this rider: '... but this does not apply if the court is also of the opinion both that some other remedy is available to the petitioners and that they are acting unreasonably in seeking to have the company wound up instead of pursuing the other remedy.'

This 'alternative remedy' provision, as it is usually called, has now become even more important since section 459 of the Companies Act 1985 has become a remedy of a more inclusive nature than the old section 210, and since it obviously furnishes a more satisfactory range of remedies which contrast favourably with the stark and 'sledge-hammer' outcome of a successful petition under what is now section 122 (1) (*g*) of the Insolvency Act 1986.[173] There will still of course be cases where it is not possible to petition successfully under both of these statutory minority remedies. Thus in *London School of Electronics*,[174] it was held that there was no overriding requirement (in a petition under what is now section 459 of the Companies Act 1985) that it should be just and equitable to grant relief or that the petitioner should come to court with clean hands. However, the misconduct of a petitioner might still be relevant in a number of ways. The two most obvious are that it might render the conduct of which the petitioner complained, even if prejudicial, not unfair. Secondly, even if the treatment (by the respon-

[170] The use of the term 'transferred' in section 459 (2) does not permit those with an equitable interest in shares (who are not registered as shareholders) to petition: *Re a Company (No. 007838 of 1985)* (1986) 2 BCC 98, 952. Those who are in no sense members cannot petition: *Re a Company* [1986] BCLC 391.

[171] See *Gore-Browne on Companies* (Jordans, 44th edn, loose-leaf), 28.14.

[172] *Re Commercial and Industrial Insulation Ltd* [1986] BCLC 191; as to a winding-up order, see *Re Chesterfield Catering Ltd* [1977] Ch 623.

[173] See *Practice Direction (Companies Court: Contributories Petition)* [1990] 1 WLR 490. This draws practitioners' attention to the undesirability of including as a matter of course a petition for winding up as an alternative to an order under section 459. This should be done only if a winding-up is the relief that the petitioner prefers or if it is considered that it is the only relief to which he is entitled.

[174] [1986] Ch 211, 233. See 15.14, above.

dents) of the petitioner was still found to be unfair and prejudicial, it might affect the relief granted by the courts. The 'clean hands' doctrine clearly applies to a just and equitable winding-up petition. However, the Privy Council has held that even if the petitioning minority shareholder has been partly responsible for the breakdown in the relationship between the parties, if his conduct was not the cause of the breakdown he will not be prevented from obtaining a winding-up order on the just and equitable grounds.[175]

In a petition for a just and equitable winding-up,[176] unfair prejudice does not have to be shown. Moreover, it is not necessarily part of the petitioner's case that the respondents have acted unjustly or inequitably. Thus where petitions under both section 459 of the Companies Act and section 122 (1) (g) of the Insolvency Act are presented, the court may, as Nourse J did in *Re R. A. Noble (Clothing) Ltd*,[177] dismiss the former petition and grant the latter.

Where, however, the petitioner (whether or not he has petitioned under both sections) could succeed under either remedy, the importance of section 125 (2) of the Insolvency Act 1986 and the 'alternative' remedy principle will come into play. Thus section 125 (2) will point the court firmly in the direction of section 459 (and its ampler and more appropriate remedial solutions) whenever the petitioner can establish 'unfair prejudice' to the satisfaction of the court. The 'alternative remedy' need not be section 459 as such. A reasonable offer to buy out the petitioner's shares at a fair price (with appropriate expert valuation) may suffice. In *Re a Company*,[178] Vinelott J observed that the jurisdiction under what is now section 125 (2) is discretionary. The court would be at least entitled to refuse to make a winding-up order if satisfied that the petitioner was persisting in asking for such an order, and that it would be unfair to the other shareholders to make that order having regard to any offer they made to the petitioner to meet his grievance in another way. The petitioner was also held to have acted unreasonably in refusing to accept the respondent's offer to purchase his shares at a valuation. The date when the adequacy of the respondent's offer has to be determined is the date of the hearing and not that of the presentation of the petition. 'It is as much an abuse of the process of the court to persist in a petition which, because of a subsequent offer, is bound to fail as it would be to present a petition which on the facts existing at the time of presentation is bound to fail.'[179] This gives the respondents, faced with a petition under section 122 (1) (g) every incentive to negotiate an adequate offer to buy out the petitioner by means of a fair and independent valuation, i.e. where no price can be agreed. To make sure the respondent continued to show sincerity until the completion of the 'buy-out', Vinelott J decided not to dismiss the petition outright. It was merely 'stood over' to enable the parties to agree the terms of submission to an arbitration or valuation by an expert. When agreement was reached 'the matter could be mentioned to the court and the petition stayed'. If there was any disagreement, Vinelott J continued, he would 'then hear further argument'.

Whenever possible, it would seem, a winding-up order with all its potential for the destruction of an otherwise viable business and with harsh consequences for the innocent employees will be denied whenever a viable alternative remedy is available. In the case before Vinelott J (referred to above), the court rejected the argument that in a small quasi-partnership type company the petitioner is entitled to reject an alternative 'buy-out'

---

[175] *Vujnovich v Vujnovich* [1990] BCLC 227 (PC).

[176] See 15.17, below.

[177] [1983] BCLC 273.

[178] *Re a Company* [1983] 1 WLR 927.

[179] Applying *Bryanstone Investment Co. v De Vries (No. 2)* [1976] 2 WLR 41.

remedy on the ground that (as in partnership law) he is entitled to a share of 'partnership' assets on their realisation. The only qualification to this proposition admitted by Vinelott J was that where the petitioner (excluded from a quasi-partnership despite the underlying assumption of a right to participate) has always insisted on a winding-up as the only remedy, then the argument that he was entitled to that remedy might have succeeded. On the facts of this case that was not so. From the time of exclusion from participation, the petitioner had indicated a willingness to sell to his co-shareholders at a fair price to be negotiated.

The principle so firmly stated in these first-instance decisions on the 'alternative remedy' has been reviewed by the Court of Appeal in *Virdi v Abbey Leisure*.[180] Where a petitioner is entitled in principle to a just and equitable winding-up, an offer by the respondent majority shareholders to buy his shares, under a provision in the articles, at a fair value to be agreed by an accountant, could reasonably be refused by the petitioner. The trial judge was held to be wrong in the exercise of his discretion under section 125 (2), in deciding to strike out the petition. The Court of Appeal accepted that an accountant acting under the procedure in the articles would value them on a discounted basis as a minority holding. The petitioner was entitled to insist on his normal right to a pro rata valuation, which would result from an order for a just and equitable winding-up. Balcombe LJ[181] observed that the courts have shown a general inclination (under both sections 459 and 122 (1) (*g*)) towards a valuation on a pro rata basis. Balcombe LJ also stressed that in a just and equitable winding-up based on the principles laid down by the House of Lords in *Ebrahimi v Westbourne Galleries*,[182] 'legal rights and obligations conferred or imposed on shareholders by the constitution of the company may be subject to equitable considerations'. This freed the petitioner from his obligation under the articles.[183]

In a number of cases[184] the courts have stressed that, where there is an irretrievable breakdown which is the fault of neither petitioner nor respondent, pre-emptive rights provisions in the articles should be sought rather than a petition under section 459 on the ground of unfair prejudice. Where the court concludes that unfair prejudice to the petitioner could not be established at a full hearing, this is obviously right. However, some decisions go further than this on motions to strike out unfair prejudice petitions. These would bar a petitioning minority shareholder from complaining about unfair prejudice if no attempt has been made to use the machinery provided by the articles for determining the fair value of the party's shares.[185] In view of the Court of Appeal's observations in *Virdi v Abbey Leisure*,[186] these decisions would appear to be open to question where the

---

[180] [1990] BCLC 342. The Court of Appeal also held that the discretion of the trial judge exercised under section 125 (2) could be reviewed by the Court of Appeal not only on ground of principle but on the ground of whether the petitioner had acted reasonably.

[181] ibid. at p. 350. Balcombe LJ referred in particular to *Re Bird Precision Bellows Ltd* [1984] BCLC 395.

[182] [1973] AC 360. See 15.17, below.

[183] [1990] BCLC 342 at p. 350.

[184] *Re R. A. Noble (Clothing) Ltd* [1983] BCLC 273; *Re a Company* [1986] BCLC 362; *Re a Company* [1987] BCLC 94. See further *Re a Company ex parte Kremer* [1989] BCLC 365, where such a petition was struck out on this basis. See likewise, *Re Castleburn Ltd* [1991] BCLC 89. But contrast *Re a Company ex parte Harries* [1987] BCLC 383 at p. 398.

[185] See Hoffmann J in *Re a Company* [1987] BCLC 94 at p. 102, cited by the same judge in *Re a Company ex parte Kremer* [1989] BCLC 365 at p. 368. Admittedly this is qualified in respect of cases of 'bad faith or plain impropriety or where the articles provide for some arbitrary or artificial method of valuation'.

[186] [1990] BCLC 342.

provision in the articles allows only for a discounted minority holding basis of valuation if, under a successful section 459 petition, a pro rata basis would be appropriate. The observations of the Court of Appeal are applicable to unfair prejudice petitions even though the case itself concerned a just and equitable winding-up.[187]

15.16 The remedies available to the court: section 461

To the original remedies[188] available to the court under section 210 of the Companies Act 1948, new specifically procedural remedies were added in 1980 on the basis of the Jenkins Committee's proposals. These were that the court may 'require the company to refrain from doing or continuing an act complained of by the petitioner or to do an act which the petitioner has complained it omitted to do' and it may 'authorise civil proceedings to be brought in the name of or on behalf of the company by such person or persons and in such terms as the court may direct'.[189]

It is not surprising that in the case of most successful petitions (and there were few of them under the old section 210) the remedy sought by the petitioners, and granted by the court, is that of purchase of the minority's shares by the majority. As a solution to intra-corporate disputes in small private companies this is still the most attractive choice among the remedial solutions offered by section 461. It is likewise not surprising that there have been a number of decisions in the reports (and others unreported) on the related questions of the method of valuing the minority's shares and the date on which that valuation should be made.

In *Re Bird Precision Bellows*[190] Nourse J considered the legal basis for valuing the minority's shares where a 'buy-out' order is made. He emphasised that there was no rule that the price of a minority holding in a small private company be fixed on a pro rata basis (according to the value of the shares as a whole), or, alternatively, that the price should be discounted to reflect the fact that the shares were a minority holding. He indicated, however, that the court would employ the pro rata basis where the shares had been acquired on the incorporation of a quasi-partnership company, and it was thus expected that the shareholders would participate in the conduct of the affairs of the company.[191] The valuation would be on a discounted basis where, in an exceptional case, the minority had acted so as to deserve exclusion. This would also apply where the shares were allotted or later acquired as an investment in a private company. Nourse J's decision is one of the few cases that has been taken to the Court of Appeal. There the court confirmed Nourse J's exercise of his discretionary power while emphasising the wide nature of the first

---

[187] See *Re a Company ex parte Harries* [1989] BCLC 383 at p. 398 *per* Peter Gibson J, who anticipated the Court of Appeal in *Virdi v Abbey Leisure* [1990] BCLC 342. See also *Re a Company ex parte Holden* [1991] BCLC 597.

[188] These are a wide power to 'make such order as it thinks fit for giving relief in respect of the matters complained of' and further powers to order the complainants' shares be bought by the company (with a consequent reduction of capital) or by the majority from the minority (or vice versa). The court has power to give this relief against an ex-shareholder: *Re a Company* [1986] BCLC 68. There is also a power to 'regulate the conduct of the company's affairs in the future' and to alter the articles and memorandum. See *Gore-Browne on Companies* (Jordans, 44th edn, loose-leaf), 28.17.

[189] See section 461 (2).

[190] [1984] Ch 419.

[191] This would also apply, in such a company, where the minority were ordered to purchase the majority's shares. If a company's articles provide machinery for a sale of the minority shareholder's shares, and a fair means of assessing the value of the shares, a member seeking to sell his shares on a breakdown of relations with other shareholders should not ordinarily be entitled to complain of unfair conduct if he has made no attempt to use the machinery provided: *Re a Company* [1987] 1 WLR 102.

instance court's power once unfair prejudice was shown.[192] The Court of Appeal emphasised that the overriding consideration[193] is that the valuation must be fair and equitable between the partners. The specific power (in what is now section 461 (2) (*d*)) 'to provide for the purchase of the shares of any member of the company by other members' is subject to the wide discretion in section 461 (1): 'make such order as it thinks fit for giving relief in respect of the matters complained of'. The Court of Appeal affirmed, but did not reopen, Nourse J's exercise of this discretion since it was a matter for the court of first instance rather than an appellate court. However, the court accepted that in a quasi-partnership case the 'pro rata' solution was a proper exercise of the judge's discretion.[194] By implication they also accepted Nourse J's observation that in other cases the discounted minority interest method would be more appropriate.[195]

The same overriding requirement in valuing shares (that the price should be fair) will govern the choice of date for this purpose. Various dates have been chosen (e.g. the date of the unfair prejudice, the date of the petition,[196] the date when the valuation is made,[197] or the date of a consent order that shares should be purchased 'at such a price as the court should therefore determine'). The petitioner's own conduct, though not precluding a finding of unfair prejudice in his favour, may affect the date chosen by the court in exercising its discretion.[198] In the appropriate case, however, fairness may sometimes require that the shares be valued at a date earlier than the petition.[199]

The additional powers conferred by section 459 (2) (*b*) and (*c*), (referred to earlier), allowing civil proceedings to be brought, have not yet been much invoked. However, in one case, which went to the Court of Appeal, the court hearing the petition appointed a receiver and manager,[200] permitted civil proceedings in the name of the company against certain of its creditors and ordered the cancellation of an issue of shares. The Court of Appeal[201] made certain further orders as to how the litigation should be controlled and conducted, while rejecting the argument that the original petitioner was not a suitable person to leave in charge of such litigation. The court also decreed that the

---

[192] [1986] 2 WLR 158 (CA).

[193] i.e. after the court is satisfied that unfair prejudice has been established.

[194] This was the basis applied by the same judge in another 'quasi-partnership' case, *Re London School of Electronics* [1986] Ch 211.

[195] The same principles apply where the court has to exercise its powers on the basis of a consent order made after an earlier hearing with a provision for the matter of valuation to be settled by a judge. This was what had happened in *Re Bird Precision Bellows*. The court also held that the consent order did not constitute an agreement that interest should be awarded. There was no other basis on which interest could be awarded before the principal sum (the valuation) was determined.

[196] *Re London School of Electronics* [1986] Ch 211. In *Virdi v Abbey Leisure Ltd* [1990] BCLC 342 the Court of Appeal noted the general inclination of the courts towards a pro rata basis of valuation. Cf. *Howie and Others v Crawford* [1990] BCC 330.

[197] i.e. the date of the Master's certificate.

[198] See *Re London School of Electronics* [1986] Ch 211 where Nourse J considered a choice between the date of presentation of the petition and the date of valuation. He chose the former because of the petitioner's behaviour. See also *Re Cumana Ltd* [1986] BCLC 430 (CA).

[199] *Re O. C. Transport Services Ltd* [1984] BCLC 251. Here by any later date the value of the petitioner's shares had been influenced by the reorganisation of its capital to allow another company to take the benefit of its unused capital allowances. See also *Re a Company* [1983] 1 WLR 927.

[200] See also *Re a Company (No. 00596 of 1986)* [1987] BCLC 133.

[201] In *Cyplon Developments Ltd* (CA) 3 March 1982 (*Lexis* transcript). See also *Re Whyte* (petitioner) 1984 SLT 330, where the court interdicted the holding of a meeting because the resolution to be passed would have removed a managing director from a committee responsible for company litigation. The effect of the resolution would have been to put the litigation under control of the defendants.

debts of various creditors connected with the company (including the appellants and the respondents) 'be made subordinate to the outside creditors'.

The power of the court under section 461 (2) (*c*) to 'authorise civil proceedings to be brought in the company's name' has not yet shown its full potential. If the concept of 'unfair prejudice' in section 459 is to encompass grave corporate abuse (including serious negligent mismanagement) in public listed companies, it may become a more commonly sought remedy. Such proceedings would essentially amount to a thinly disguised derivative action[202] with the statutory concept of 'unfair prejudice' rather than the *Foss v Harbottle* concept of 'fraud on a minority' determining the issue of access to an action in the company's name or for its benefit. The simple wording of section 461 (2) (*c*) leaves unanswered a number of questions as to the conduct and control of civil proceedings permitted under section 461.[203] For example, could the court exercise its discretion, in an appropriate case, to allow 'pro-rata recovery' where to require the proceeds of an action to be restored to the company would only benefit the wrongdoers left in control of the company? Another important question is whether the company would be responsible for the costs of an unsuccessful litigation permitted by the court (or the costs awarded in an action which succeeded but the defendant could not pay). In other words would the petitioner, put in charge of such proceedings, be at least as well protected as if he had the benefit of a *Wallersteiner* order[204] in a derivative action? Even if that is a fairly safe assumption, this would still not meet the point that the petitioner under section 459 must hazard the risk of costs at least until the stage when the issue of unfair prejudice is determined.[205] To that extent a derivative action, even in the case of a small private company, will be more attractive assuming that the difficulties of establishing 'fraud in a minority' can be overcome. The issue of costs can be resolved (at least to a particular stage in the litigation) at an early stage in an application before the Master.[206]

It may be fairly observed that a justifiable assertion by a minority shareholder of a serious breach of directors' duties (especially the duty of care) may fall between the alternative remedies of a derivative action on the one hand and a section 459 petition on the other. This is much more likely to be the case where a public listed company is concerned. There is still a strong case for the introduction of a statutory derivative suit on the model of that introduced into many jurisdictions in Canada (including the Federal jurisdiction).[207] Broadly this would allow the question of *locus standi* to be determined in a preliminary application. The court would have to be satisfied that the applicant was

---

[202] See *Re a Company* [1986] 1 WLR 281 at p. 284. Such relief (i.e. court proceedings in the name of the company to recover sums improperly paid out by the company) was refused where an administrative receiver had already been appointed: *Re a Company* [1992] BCC 542.

[203] See *Gore-Browne on Companies* (Jordans, 44th edn, loose-leaf), 28.16.

[204] See, however, *Smith v Croft* [1986] 1 WLR 580 where Walton J gave a rather restricted interpretation to *Wallersteiner v Moir (No. 2)* [1975] QB 373 (CA); see further, 15.9, above.

[205] As to the award of costs where unfair prejudice is established and the petitioner's shares are ordered to be purchased, see *Re Elgindata Ltd (No. 2)* [1993] BCLC 119 (CA).

[206] *Smith v Croft* [1986] 1 WLR 580 implies that an interim order for costs will only be given where it is genuinely needed (e.g. the plaintiffs cannot afford to sue) and even then some proportion of the costs must be borne by the plaintiffs.

[207] Canadian Business Corporations Act 1974/75/76, section 232; Alberta Business Corporation Act 1981, section 232; Ontario Business Corporation Act 1982, section 245, British Columbian Company Act 1979, section 225, Saskatchewan Business Corporation Act 1978, section 232, Manitoba Corporation Act 1976, section 232, New Brunswick Business Corporation Act 1981, section 104.

acting in good faith and had, on a prima facie basis, a reasonable cause of action on behalf of the company.[208]

The other approach to statutory reform is the simpler solution contained in Article 16 of the draft Fifth Directive. That solution, based in German and French law, would give *locus standi* to those holding 10 per cent of the share capital. As under the Canadian legislation, shareholder ratification or approval is no longer a bar to minority litigation.[209]

Such a solution combined with the existing practice of *Wallersteiner* orders, would certainly redress the balance in favour of the minority shareholder. There is no evidence that this has affected business confidence in Canada (where somewhat less generous court orders can be made). However, as in Ontario, where Canada's first statutory derivative remedy was introduced, legal practitioners who act for large companies and other representative business organisations (like the CBI and the Institute of Directors) are likely to resist any change of the kind discussed above.

15.17 Just and equitable winding up as a minority shareholder's remedy

The preceding treatment of Part XVII of the Companies Act 1985 (petitions on the ground of unfair prejudice) sought to relate that type of relief to the alternative (but much older) remedy of a contributory's (i.e. a member's) petition for a just and equitable winding-up under what is now section 122 (1) (*g*) of the Insolvency Act 1986. It was seen that the concept of a 'quasi-partnership' type of company (which was first developed by the House of Lords[210] in restating the principles applicable to just and equitable winding up), has in recent years been applied in the context of petitions under section 459. Another important link between the two statutory remedies is the 'alternative remedy' requirement now contained in section 125 (2) of the Insolvency Act 1986.[211] This is an important factor in the exercise of judicial discretion, whether or not the petitioner combines a petition under section 459 of the Companies Act 1985 with one under section 122 (1) (*g*) of the Insolvency Act 1986. In *Ebrahimi v Westbourne Galleries*[212] the House of Lords reviewed the nature and scope of the 'just and equitable' ground. It was empha-sised that this ground should not be confined to special categories of situation. The facts of the case were as follows. *A* and *B* established a business as retailers of Persian carpets. *A* provided most of the initial finance. Although no agreement as to the nature of the

---

[208] See Hadden, Forbes and Simmonds, *Canadian Business Organisation Law* (Butterworths, Toronto 1984), pp. 265–75; Bruce Welling, *Corporate Law in Canada: The Governing Principles*, (Butterworths, Toronto 1984), pp. 502–19.

[209] See A. J. Boyle in Hopt and Teubner (eds.), *Corporate Governance and Directors' Liabilities* (Walter de Gruyter, 1985), pp. 261–81.

[210] *Ebrahimi v Westbourne Galleries Ltd* [1973] AC 360, discussed below.

[211] See 15.15, above.

[212] [1973] AC 360 (HL (E)). The House of Lords was influenced by a number of Commonwealth decisions where the principles governing just and equitable winding up had been developed on similar lines. See in particular *Re Straw Products Pty Ltd* [1942] VLR 222 at p. 223 and *Re Wondoflex Textiles Pty Ltd* [1951] VLR 467 at p. 458 cited in the speech of Lord Wilberforce. See also *Tench v Tench Bros. Ltd* [1930] NZLR 403; *Re Sydney and Whitney Pier Bus Service Ltd* [1944] 3 DLR 468; and *Re Concrete Column Clamps Ltd* [1953] 4 DLR 60, which were also referred to by Lord Wilberforce. See also *Re Tivoli Freeholds* [1972] VR 445. For further examination of the implications of the House of Lords' decision, see Chesterman (1973) 36 MLR 129 and Prentice 89 *Law Quarterly Review* 107 (1973). See Prentice, ibid., pp. 123–4, on the application of the principle to directors' refusal to transfer shares and on this see Lord Cross of Chelsea's speech.

business existed it was clearly such as to create a partnership between *A* and *B*. After some years the partners transferred the business into a company and each received 500 shares of £1 each. Subsequently, *A*'s son, *C*, became a shareholder, receiving 100 shares from each of *A* and *B* by way of transfer. *A*, *B* and *C* were the only directors of the company. All three members worked full-time for the company and all profits were distributed in the form of directors' remuneration. Dividends were never paid. *A* always regarded *B* as a mere employee of the business. Relations deteriorated between *A* and *C* on the one hand and *B* on the other hand. The deterioration culminated with the removal of *B* from the board pursuant to what was then section 184 of the Companies Act 1948 (now section 303 of the 1985 Act)[213] and regulation 96 of the 1948 Table A.

Plowman J held that whilst *B* had been lawfully removed from the board pursuant to the provisions of the Act and of the company's articles, such removal constituted an 'abuse of power and a breach of the good faith which partners owe to each other' in so far as the removal represented the exclusion of *B* from all participation in the business. The Court of Appeal reversed that decision and held that the lawful removal of a 'quasi-partner' from the board is not a ground for winding up unless the petitioner establishes that the power of removal was not exercised 'bona fide in the interests of the company', or that the grounds for the exercise of the power were such that no reasonable man could consider that the removal was in the interests of the company. The Court of Appeal held that the petitioner had not established grounds for winding up.

The House of Lords unanimously reversed the Court of Appeal decision and ordered winding up. It is clear that the effect of the House of Lords' decision is to extend the range of circumstances in which an order may be made on the just and equitable ground. The extent of the extension is still not entirely clear. Lord Wilberforce and Lord Cross of Chelsea delivered the only reasoned speeches. Although the case on its facts involved exclusion from participation in management, the observations made are of general significance in relation to the just and equitable ground. Lord Wilberforce also emphasised that references to 'quasi-partnerships' are confusing in the context of section 122 (1) (*g*) except in so far as they recognise that concepts of probity, good faith and mutual confidence produced by the law of partnership are relevant to the exercise of the power to wind up on the just and equitable ground.

Lord Wilberforce emphasised that the mere fact that the exclusion of a director from participation in a company accords with the powers conferred by section 303 of the Companies Act 1985 and the articles of a company is not conclusive. The effect of section 122 (1) (*g*) of the Insolvency Act 1986 is to enable the court 'to subject the exercise of legal rights to equitable considerations; considerations, that is, of a personal character arising between one individual and another, which may make it unjust, or inequitable, to insist on legal rights, or to exercise them in a particular way'.[214] Lord Wilberforce declined to define in an exhaustive manner the circumstances where the court would effect such a 'subjection'. He confined himself to a description of the type of situation which would typically give rise to the subjection of the legal rights or powers to the equitable considerations.

He stated that such a situation:

... may include one or probably more of the following elements: (i) an association

---

[213] See 13.7, above.
[214] [1973] AC at p. 379. See *Clemens v Clemens Bros.* [1976] 2 All ER 268 at p. 282 for an application of this passage outside a just and equitable winding-up. *Sed quaere.*

formed or continued on the basis of a personal relationship, involving mutual confidence – this element will often be found where a pre-existing partnership has been converted into a limited company; (ii) an agreement, or understanding, that all, or some (for there may be 'sleeping' members), of the shareholders shall participate in the conduct of the business; (iii) restrictions upon the transfer of the members' interest in the company – so that if confidence is lost, or one member is removed from management, he cannot take out his stake and go elsewhere.[215]

On the facts, Lord Wilberforce found the special underlying obligation of the petitioner's fellow members in good faith, or confidence, that so long as the business continued he should be entitled to management participation. Lord Wilberforce emphasised two factors: first the principal individual respondent made it clear that, notwithstanding the clear nature of the petitioner's status, he regarded the petitioner not as a partner but as an employee; and secondly, the petitioner by reason of his expulsion lost his right to participate in profits by way of directors' remuneration and was unable to dispose of his interest without the consent of the individual respondents. Finally, Lord Wilberforce rejected the contention that the petitioner must show *mala fides* in the sense of proving that his removal was not bona fide in the interests of the company or was a step which no reasonable man could conclude to be in the interest of the company.

The primary importance of the decision of the House of Lords is to reject the view that the petitioner must prove that his exclusion was not bona fide in the interests of the company or such that no reasonable man could consider it to be in the interests of the company. The decision established, on a positive note, that the court possesses jurisdiction under section 122 (1) (*g*) to order winding up where the circumstances disclose some underlying obligation in good faith and confidence that the petitioner should participate in management so long as the business continues. Expulsion justifies the assertion of that jurisdiction at least where the expulsion results in the loss of participation in profits and leaves the party expelled as a locked-in shareholder.[216]

The application of the above principles to situations *not* involving expulsion remains to some degree uncertain.[217] The position also remains uncertain where a (private) company has adopted the increasingly uncommon practice of distributing profits by way of dividend. However, it does not appear that an exclusion either from participation in management or from participation in profits is essential. Any course of dealing which produces a breakdown in mutual confidence may well suffice to justify the making of a winding-up order under section 122 (1) (*g*),[218] unless that breakdown in mutual confidence is referable to the conduct of the complainant shareholders.[219] It is also possible that retention of profits which excludes members from participation by way of dividend

---

[215] [1973] AC at p. 398.

[216] See *Lewis v Haas* 1971 SLT 57 (Ct of Sess.) and *Re Davis & Collett* [1935] Ch 593.

[217] An example of the application of the principle in *Westbourne Galleries*, above, in the context of a joint venture company is *Re A. B. C. Chewing Gum* [1975] 1 WLR 579.

[218] See e.g. *Jesner v Jarrard Properties Ltd* [1993] BCLC 1032 (Ct of Sess.). See also *Re Pauls Federated Merchants Ltd* (unreported) 30 July 1976, where Brightman J applied the *Westbourne* decision to a company which was not a quasi-partnership.

[219] Cases such as *Re Yenidje Tobacco Co.* [1916] 2 Ch 246 (CA); *Re Sailing Ship Kentmere Co.* [1897] WN 58, and *American Pioneer Leather Co.* [1918] 1 Ch 556 must now be interpreted not merely as cases establishing that deadlock in management justifies a winding-up order, but as illustration of the wide concept of section 122 (1) (*g*) established in *Westbourne Galleries*, above.

will justify a winding-up order where this defeats the members' expectations and leaves the petitioner unable to realise the full value of his shares.[220]

An important issue is the relationship between the just and equitable winding-up and the unfair prejudice remedies. As seen earlier in this chapter, there are some circumstances where one of these remedies may be available and the other will not be, but there are other circumstances, of which the situation exemplified in the *Westbourne Galleries* case is probably a classic example, where both remedies may be available. The issue of which remedy might 'prevail' has been examined in 15.15, above.

15.18 Earlier cases consistent with *Westbourne*

There are other English and Scottish cases decided before *Westbourne* which can still be regarded as consistent with it. A company was wound up where there were only three shareholders, each holding one-third of the capital, and an article directed that if one shareholder offered his shares to the others and they refused to purchase, the company should be wound up. In this case the winding-up was on the ground that it was just and equitable, and that though the article was not binding on the court it formed a reason for holding that the company ought to be wound up.[221] In another case there were only two shareholders, each of whom was a director, one holding a single share, and the other the remainder of the issued capital: namely 1,501 shares. The latter having usurped the whole powers of the company, the former, though holding one share only, successfully petitioned for a winding-up order.[222]

15.19 Loss of 'substratum'

The court will wind up a company even within a year of its formation, although it may be solvent, if it appears that it has become impossible to carry on the business for which it was formed.[223] Thus where the mine which a company was formed to work could not be found,[224] or the patent it was to work was not granted,[225] or the bulk of its property had been sold and its capital exhausted,[226] or there was no reasonable probability of obtaining the benefit of the contract it was formed to carry out,[227] a winding-up order was made. The *substratum* of the company was also held to have vanished where a bank had ceased to carry on banking business[228] or the mine which the company was working proved worthless,[229] or a company formed to amalgamate three syndicates for speculating in seats for the Diamond Jubilee proposed, after losing money over that speculation, to do other financial business,[230] or a single steamship company had lost its only ship and proposed with a small sum of cash to carry on business as a charterer of ships.[231] The sale by the company of the only business it has ever carried on, even if the carrying on of that

---

[220] *Re a Company, ex parte Glossop* [1988] 1 WLR 1068.

[221] *In re American Pioneer Leather Co.* [1918] 1 Ch 556.

[222] *Thomson v Drysdale* 1925 SC 311.

[223] This principle was first suggested in the case of *Suburban Hotel Co.* (1867) 2 Ch App. 737.

[224] *Re Haven Gold Mining Co.* (1882) 20 Ch D 151.

[225] *Re German Date Coffee Co.* (1882) 20 Ch D 169.

[226] *Re Diamond Fuel Co. (No. 2)* (1879) 13 Ch D 400 (CA).

[227] *Re Blériot Manufacturing Aircraft Co.* (1916) 32 TLR 253.

[228] *Re Crown Bank* (1890) 44 Ch D 634.

[229] *Re Red Rock Mining Co.* (1886) 61 LT 785.

[230] *Re Amalgamated Syndicate* [1897] 2 Ch 600.

[231] *Pirie v Stewart* 1904, 6 F 847 (Ct of Sess.).

particular business was stated in its memorandum as the first object, will not justify an order being made under this paragraph if, under its memorandum, it has power to resume that or any other kind of business.[232]

Compulsory acquisition of the property of a company for the purposes of nationalisation will not apparently render it in any case immediately liable to be wound up under section 122 (1) (*g*).[233] In some of the earlier cases the court has paid attention to what appears to be the most important object of the company appearing in its memorandum.[234] In others this has not been decisive.[235] It is, however, clear that the memorandum must be construed on a question of this kind in the same way as it would be construed for any other purpose.[236]

15.20 Fraudulent and illegal companies

A company may also be wound up on the just and equitable ground where the company was in its inception fraudulent and hopelessly embarrassed by actions for rescission, and where a winding-up is the best means of recovering money from the promoters,[237] or where the company never had a real foundation and was a mere 'bubble',[238] or is formed to carry on an illegal business, such as dealing in lottery bonds.[239]

The court will not, however, wind up a company because it is not prosperous,[240] or its chance of success small,[241] unless the company passes a special resolution for liquidation; thus except where the company is insolvent the mere fact that it has passed an ordinary resolution that it be wound up, and that the directors be directed to present a petition therefore, will not justify the making of an order.[242] A contributory whose shares are fully paid up must establish that he has a tangible interest in the winding-up. To do this the petition must show a prima facie probability that the company is solvent and consequently there will be substantial assets for distribution.[243]

---

[232] *Re Kitson & Co.* [1946] 1 All ER 435; *Re Taldua Rubber Co.* [1946] 2 All ER 763; *Galbraith v Merito Shipping Co.* 1947 SC 446. In the first of these cases Lord Greene MR suggested that if after selling its business a company was obviously unable, e.g. for lack of capital, to carry on any business which under its memorandum it had power to carry on, this might afford a ground for a winding-up order: [1946] 1 All ER at p. 440. He also suggested that different considerations might arise if the main business which the company was originally intended to carry on was never acquired on incorporation, so that it did not start its career in the way the original shareholders bargained for (ibid. at p. 438). See also *Re Eastern Telegraph Co.* [1947] 2 All ER at p. 111, where Jenkins J stated that this case was not one of the contemplated objects failing *ab initio*.

[233] *Re Eastern Telegraph Co.* [1947] 2 All ER 104.

[234] *Re Red Rock Mining Co.* (1889) 61 LT 785; *Re Coolgardie Consolidated Gold Mines* (1897) 76 LT 269; *Stephens v Mysore Reefs (Kangundy) Mining Co.* [1902] 1 Ch 745.

[235] With the words only slightly differing from those in the cases cited in the previous note, Warrington J held that other mines were within the original contemplation of the company: *Pedlar and Road Block Gold Mines* [1905] 2 Ch 427; and see *Campbell v Australian Mutual Provident Society* (1908) 77 LJPC 117.

[236] *Re Kitson & Co.* [1946] 1 All ER 435. See *Butler v Northern Territories Mines of Australia* (1907) 96 LT 41; see also *Cotman v Brougham* [1918] AC 514 (HL).

[237] *Re Thomas Edward Brinsmead & Sons* [1897] 1 Ch D 406 (CA); compare *Re Diamond Fuel Co.* (1879) 13 Ch D 400 (CA); and *Re General Phosphate Corp.* [1893] WN 142.

[238] *Anglo-Greek Steam Co.* (1866) LR 2 Eq. 1; *Re West Surrey Tanning Co.* (1886) LR 2 Eq. 737; *Re London and County Coal Co.* (1867) LR 3 Eq. 355.

[239] *Re International Securities Corp.* (1908) 99 LT 581, where Swinfen-Eady J also held that the company was conducted in a fraudulent manner.

[240] *Re Langham Skating Rink Co.* (1877) 5 Ch D 669 (CA); *Re Suburban Hotel Co.* (1867) 2 Ch App. 737.

[241] *Re Kronand Metal Co.* [1899] WN 15. See, however, *Davis v Brunswick (Australia) Ltd* [1936] 1 All ER 299.

[242] *Re Anglo-Continental Produce Co.* [1939] 1 All ER 99.

[243] *Re Expanded Plugs Ltd* [1960] 1 WLR 514; *Re Othery Construction Co.* [1966] 1 WLR 69.

PART 3: THE DEPARTMENT OF TRADE AND INDUSTRY'S POWERS TO INVESTIGATE COMPANIES AND THEIR SECURITIES

15.21 Introduction

Under the Companies Act 1985[244] the Department of Trade and Industry is given powers to appoint inspectors to investigate the affairs of a company.[245] The Department may also conduct its own investigations into a company's affairs by more informal enquiries. As the result of its own investigations, or as the result of the publication of a report by inspectors, the Department has the power to bring proceedings on behalf of the company or to petition for a winding-up order. The account of the Department's powers of investigation, etc., in the following pages excludes the more extensive powers of supervision and control in respect of insurance companies. The Department of Trade and Industry has the power to appoint inspectors to investigate the ownership of a company. The Department may also appoint inspectors to investigate share dealings which are in contravention of certain provisions of the Companies Act 1985.[246]

15.22 Investigation of the affairs of the company

As regards the investigation of the affairs of a company,[247] the Department of Trade and Industry is obliged to appoint an inspector if the court orders the Department to do so.[248] Section 431 (2) (*c*) provides that the Department may appoint inspectors 'in any case, on the application of the company'. The Department may at its discretion appoint an inspector on the application of a specified number of minority shareholders.[249] This application must be supported by evidence showing that the applicant or applicants have good reason for requiring the investigation. In addition security for the costs of the inquiry, not exceeding £5,000, must be provided. The maximum amount of the security may be further increased by statutory instrument. These powers have been very little used.[250]

---

[244] These provisions of the Act have been amended by Part III of the Companies Act 1989. The references in this part of this chapter to the 1985 Act are to it as so amended.

[245] The powers conferred by Part XIV of the Companies Act 1985, as amended by the Companies Act 1989, apply to registered companies. As to unregistered companies, see Schedule 22 of the Companies Act 1985, as amended by section 71 of the 1989 Act.

[246] i.e. sections 323, 324 and 328 (restrictions on share dealings by directors and their families, etc.) See also section 446.

[247] An inspector, appointed under either section 431 or 432 to investigate the affairs of a company, has the power, if he thinks it necessary, to investigate the company's holding or subsidiary company 'or a subsidiary of its holding company or a holding company of its subsidiary'. This applies to any body which *is* a subsidiary, etc., or which 'has at any relevant time *been*', etc.: Companies Act 1985, section 433. For the statutory definition of the relationship of holding and subsidiary company, see section 736. See further 1.13.1, above.

[248] Section 432 (1).

[249] Section 431 (2) (*a*) and (*b*). The applicants must consist of not less than 200 members of the company or of members holding not less than one-tenth of the shares issued in the case of a company having share capital. In the case of a company not having share capital the applicants must consist of not less than one-fifth in number of the persons on the company's register of members.

[250] It will be seen that this is linked with the Department's power to obtain repayment of the expenses of an inspection.

The Department may also appoint an inspector under section 432 (2)[251] if there are circumstances suggesting any of the following:

(1) that the company's business is being conducted with intent to defraud its creditors or the creditors of any other person, or otherwise for a fraudulent or unlawful purpose or in a manner which is unfairly prejudicial to some part of its members, or that any actual or proposed act or omission of the company (including any act or omission on its behalf) is or would be so prejudicial, or that it was formed for any fraudulent or unlawful purpose; or

(2) that persons concerned with its formation or the management of its affairs have in connection therewith been guilty of fraud, misfeasance or other misconduct towards it or towards its members; or

(3) that its members have not been given all the information with respect to its affairs which they might reasonably expect.

A new provision inserted in section 432 by the Companies Act 1989 allows the Secretary of State to appoint inspectors under section 432 (2) on terms that 'any report that may be made is not for publication'.[252]

Although more use has been made of what is now section 432, prior to the 1967 Act the Department had been inclined only to exercise its discretion in cases where notoriety in the press had already caused serious public concern. This cautious policy had been defensible to the extent that the mere announcement of a Department of Trade and Industry inspection can do a company's business reputation irreparable harm on The Stock Exchange and elsewhere before any abuse is proven. On the other hand this reaction of the business community may in part reflect the limited use of this power in the past.

To overcome this difficulty the Department was given new powers in the Companies Act 1967 to obtain the information it needs more quickly and informally. These additional powers[253] enable the Department to compel the production of any books and papers it may specify. The Department may lay any information before a justice of the peace to obtain a warrant giving power to enter and search premises for the books and papers they require.[254] Penalties are also provided for the destruction of documents and for furnishing false information.[255]

The rules of natural justice have been held not to apply to the discretion exercised by the Department of Trade and Industry in appointing inspectors to investigate the affairs of a company.[256] So long as the Secretary of State is acting within his powers[257] and is in good faith, his decision cannot be challenged. His decision does not imply there is any

---

[251] Section 432 (3) allows the Department to appoint an inspector where the company is in course of a voluntary liquidation.

[252] See section 432 (2A).

[253] Companies Act 1985, section 447.

[254] Section 448. See section 449, which provides for security of information obtained under section 447 and for the permitted disclosure of this information in certain cases (e.g. examination of persons by inspectors appointed to conduct an investigation, or with a view to bringing criminal proceedings).

[255] ibid., sections 450 and 451. The 1985 Act also confers powers on inspectors, approved by the Department to conduct a formal investigation, to enable them to compel the attendance of witnesses: sections 434 and 436.

[256] *Norwest Holst v Secretary of State for Trade* [1978] 3 WLR 73 (CA).

[257] In the *Norwest* case the inspector had been appointed under what is now section 432 (2) (*c*), but this decision would apply to any other statutory discretion to appoint inspectors or to take proceedings.

case against the company or its management and he cannot be made to reveal the evidence which has led him to act. The Secretary of State may appoint inspectors to investigate matters which may also be the subject of criminal proceedings.[258] It has also been held that an inspector appointed to make an informal investigation under section 447 cannot be cross-examined (in subsequent winding-up proceedings) either as to his reasons for investigating under section 447 or as to why he thought it in the public interest that the company be wound up under section 440.[259]

It has been held that the court will not exercise powers of review (on the basis of orders of prohibition and certiorari under RSC Order 53) in the case of officers of the Department of Trade and Industry exercising powers under section 447. The principle of bias did not apply to an investigation under section 447, since under this section the officers are exercising a police function and not a judicial or quasi-judicial function. However, a complainant may be entitled, on the ground of unfairness, to an order quashing a notice under section 447 (2) (requiring the production of documents relating to the company's finances) on the basis that the notice is unreasonably and excessively wide.[260]

15.23 The conduct of proceedings by inspectors

The Court of Appeal has held[261] that although the proceedings before inspectors are not judicial or quasi-judicial,[262] but are of an administrative nature, yet the characteristics of the proceedings require the inspectors to act fairly. In this sense the rules of natural justice apply. Thus, if they were disposed to condemn or criticise anyone in a report, the inspectors must first give him a fair opportunity to correct or contradict the allegation against him. For this purpose an outline of the charge will usually suffice. So long as the inspectors acted fairly they were not subject to any set rules procedure. The Court of Appeal held that directors were not entitled to refuse to answer questions put to them by the inspectors until they were shown the transcripts of evidence and the documents used against them, and had been allowed to cross-examine witnesses. The inspectors were held to have acted fairly, and in accordance with rules of natural justice,[263] by undertaking that no one would be criticised in the report without first being told in general terms of the allegation against him and being afforded an opportunity to give an explanation. The inspectors were prepared to make known the purport of the relevant evidence and documents. The directors' refusal to give evidence on these terms was unjustified.

Where an officer or agent of the company or other body corporate refuses to answer questions which are put to him by inspectors, the latter may 'certify the refusal under their hand to the court'.[264] The House of Lords has held that an officer or agent of the

---

[258] *Re London United Investments plc* [1992] BCLC 285 (CA).

[259] *Re Golden Chemical Products Ltd.*, *The Times*, 8 December 1979, *per* Deputy Judge Michael Wheeler QC.

[260] *R v Secretary of State for Trade, ex parte, Perestrello* [1980] 3 WLR 1.

[261] *Re Pergamon Press Ltd* [1970] 3 WLR 792 (CA), affirming the decision of Plowman J [1970] 1 WLR 1075. See also *Maxwell v Department of Trade and Industry* [1974] 1 QB 523 (CA).

[262] See *Re Grosvenor and West End Railway Terminus Hotel Co. Ltd* (1897) 76 LT 732; *Hearts of Oak Assurance Co. Ltd v Attorney-General* [1932] AC 322 (HL).

[263] The Court of Appeal referred, as to the rules of natural justice, to *Russell v Duke of Norfolk* [1949] 1 All ER 109; *Ridge v Baldwin* [1964] AC 40 (HL); *Wiseman v Borneman* [1969] 3 WLR 706 (HL); *R v Gaming Board for Great Britain, ex parte Benaim* [1970] 2 QB 417 (CA).

[264] Companies Act 1985, section 436 (2). The same procedure applies to a refusal to produce to the inspectors any book or document which it is the duty of such an officer to produce under section 434 or 435, or to a refusal 'to attend before inspectors when required so to do'.

company examined by the inspectors is entitled to refuse to answer questions on the ground that the answers would incriminate him. But if such a witness does so, the matter may be referred to the court under section 436 (2).[265] The issue of self-incrimination is one which the court not the inspectors should decide.[266]

It has been seen that an investigation is not a judicial enquiry, and the proceedings should be conducted in private. However, it has been held that the inspector is entitled to the assistance of anyone whose presence is reasonably necessary, and that a person examined could not object to the presence of a shorthand writer.[267] Parties involved in the investigation may be represented by counsel.[268]

15.24 The inspectors' report and subsequent proceedings

A copy of any report of inspectors appointed to investigate into the affairs of a company is admissible in any legal proceedings as evidence of the opinion of the inspectors in relation to any matters contained in the report.[269] Moreover, section 434 (5) of the Companies Act 1985 provides that an answer given by a person to a question put to him under the powers conferred by section 434 (as to the conduct of investigations by inspectors) may be used in evidence against him.[270]

15.25 The power to examine on oath and obtain documents

Section 434 (3) of the Companies Act 1985 gives an inspector power to examine any person on oath and to administer an oath accordingly. Section 434 (1) imposes a duty on all officers and agents of the company to produce documents, attend before the inspectors and give assistance in connection with the investigation. Section 434 (2) amplifies this duty. It provides that if the inspectors consider that a person other than an officer or agent of the company (or other body corporate) is, or may be, in possession of any information concerning its affairs, they may require that person to produce to them any books or documents[271] in his custody or power. They may also require such a person to attend before them and otherwise to give them all the assistance, in connection with the investigation, which he is reasonably able to give (and it is the duty of such a person to comply). In certain circumstances section 435 (1) gives inspectors power to request disclosure of documents relating to the bank accounts of directors (or past directors) of the company or other body corporate whose affairs are being investigated. This may apply where the director maintains (or has maintained) a bank account of any descrip-

---

[265] The power conferred by section 436 now extends to 'any person'. See 15.25, below.

[266] See further *Gore-Browne on Companies* (Jordans, 44th edn, loose-leaf), 28.23 as to the right to refuse to disclose information given to the company's bankers and those entitled to 'professional legal privilege'. See also *Re London United Investments* [1992] BCLC 285, in which the Court of Appeal held that the privilege against self-incrimination is not a basis for refusing to answer questions.

[267] *Re Gaumont-British Picture Corp.* [1940] 1 Ch 506.

[268] See *McClelland, Pope and Langley Ltd v Howard* [1968] 1 All ER 569n. As to the Department of Trade and Industry's decision to publish a report and furnish it to various interested parties, see the Companies Act 1985, sections 437 and 441. See *Gore-Browne on Companies*, 28.24.

[269] Companies Act 1985, section 441 (1). The report is certified by the Secretary to be a true copy of such report (and it must be received in evidence etc.).

[270] See e.g. *R. v Seelig* [1991] BCLC 869; *Re London United Investments plc* [1992] BCLC 285. See further as to the use of evidence so obtained in subsequent proceedings, *Gore-Browne on Companies*, 28.25.2. The power to obtain evidence under section 434 applies also to investigations into the ownership of the company under section 442, and to an investigation into share dealings under section 446.

[271] i.e. in relating to the company or other body corporate.

tion, whether alone or jointly with another person, and whether in Great Britain or elsewhere. However, this can only be done if the inspectors have reasonable grounds to believe that the following types of payment have been paid into, or out of, the account. These are of three types:

(1) Emoluments or part of the emoluments of his office as such director, particulars of which have not been disclosed in the accounts of the company or other body corporate for any financial year contrary to paras. 24 to 26 of Schedule 5.

(2) Any money which has resulted from, or been used in, the financing of various types of transaction, arrangement or agreement which are in breach of various provisions listed by section 435 (2).

(3) Any money which has been in any way connected with any act or omission, or series of acts or omissions, which constituted misconduct (whether fraudulent or not) on the part of that director towards the company or body corporate or its members.

15.26 Civil proceedings by the Department of Trade and Industry

The Department may now act on the basis of its powers to obtain documents and other information from the company without a formal investigation by the Department's inspectors. It still retains the power to take proceedings after receiving an adverse report by an inspector.

The Department can bring any action the company itself might bring if it appears that such proceedings ought to be brought in the public interest.[272] The Department's power to petition for a winding-up likewise depends on its opinion of what is in the public interest.[273] Again the Department may act not only on the basis of an inspector's report, but under its new power to obtain information without a formal public inquiry. Where it was sought in ordinary civil proceedings (as opposed to a winding-up petition, as to which see below) to use an inspector's report, it was held inadmissible since it contained only opinions. If the inspector's opinions (contained in their report) were referred to in an affidavit to be used in interlocutory proceedings, they may be struck out as containing inadmissible evidence.[274]

In a winding-up petition by the Department, where the accuracy of an inspector's report is not disputed, the court may act on the basis of the report although it is supported only by the affidavit of a Department official.[275] Where allegations against a company and its officers are contested, the Department must support the petition 'by evidence of true evidential value.'[276] A challenge to a report (on which a petition by the Secretary of State is based) means 'a challenge by someone with knowledge of the facts coming along and saying the inspectors' report is wrong, and being willing to put forward an affidavit

---

[272] Section 438 (1).

[273] See now section 124 (4) (*b*) of the Insolvency Act 1986. See section 124A as to the reports and statutory sources of information on the basis of which the Secretary of State may conclude that it is expedient in the public interest that a company should be wound up. These provisions were substituted for section 440 of the Companies Act 1985 by section 360 of the Companies Act 1989. A voluntary liquidation will no longer inhibit the exercise of this power: *Re Lubin Rosen and Associates Ltd* [1975] 1 WLR 122.

[274] *Savings and Investment Bank Ltd v Gasco Investments (Netherlands) B.V.* [1984] 1 WLR 271.

[275] *Re Allied Produce Co.* [1967] 1 WLR 1964; *Re Travel & Holiday Club* [1967] 1 WLR 71.

[276] *Re A. B. C. Coupler Engineering Co.* [1962] 1 WLR 1236. As to the evidence admissible in a compulsory winding-up brought by the Department of Trade, see *Re Koscott Interplanetary (UK) Ltd* [1972] 3 All ER 82.

and be cross-examined, and to be judged in the witness box on the evidence which he puts forward in contradiction of the inspectors' report'.[277] Even if the report is challenged in the above sense, it ought to be treated as prima facie evidence and it ought to be left to the judge in any case, having read the report and having seen the witnesses, to make up his own mind whether it is just and equitable to wind up the company.

> The whole machinery of the inspector's report was evolved in order to enable the Secretary of State to present a winding up petition where he considers the public interest so demands. It would be unfortunate if, once the Secretary of State has reached that conclusion on proper grounds based on the inspector's detailed report, the court should go right back to square one and start again as though the inspector had never come on the scene at all.[278]

The Department also possesses the power to seek relief under section 460 of the Companies Act 1985, if it appears to the Department that the affairs of a company are being conducted in a manner unfairly prejudicial to some part of the members. Here the Department is not required to have regard to the public interest, and it may seek to enforce this minority shareholders' remedy either in addition to or instead of a winding-up petition.[279]

15.27 Expenses in investigations and proceedings by the Department

One of the attractions for shareholders in seeking the intervention of the Department of Trade and Industry, under section 432 of the Companies Act 1985, is that the expenses of the investigation and any consequent proceedings brought by the Department must be defrayed in the first instance by the Department.[280] The Department is entitled to repayment of these expenses if the report of the inspector results in a successful prosecution in a criminal court, or a judgment in a civil court, to the extent specified in an order made in those proceedings.[281] In addition a company for whose benefit civil proceedings have been brought by the Department is liable to repay the expenses 'to the amount or value of any sums of property recovered by it as a result of those proceedings'.[282]

Where the Department appoints an inspector 'otherwise than of the Department's own motion' the company can also be made to contribute from its own resources to the

---

[277] *Re Armvent Ltd* [1975] 3 All ER 441 at p. 446 *per* Templeman J.
[278] ibid.
[279] See 15.14, above.
[280] Section 439 (3); but see section 439 (5).
[281] Section 439 (2).
[282] Section 439 (3). Any amount for which the company is liable under section 439 (3) is a first charge on the sums or property recovered. But in the case of a civil action brought on behalf of the company, the Department is required to indemnify the company against costs or expenses incurred by the company in connection with the proceedings: section 438 (2). Thus the company may have to contribute from the proceeds accruing to it from a successful action, but it cannot be prejudiced by an unsuccessful action. It has been held that 'the amount or value of any sums recovered by the company' (as limiting what it may be liable to pay to the Department under section 439 (3) (*b*)) includes the costs recovered by the company: *Selangor Rubber Estates Ltd v Cradock (No. 4)* [1969] 2 WLR 1773. However, the Department's duty to indemnify the company for the expenses of litigation includes costs ordered to be paid by the company to other parties: *Selangor United Estates v Cradock (No. 1)* [1967] 1 WLR 1168 at p. 1173.

costs of inspection and subsequent proceedings. Thus where, under section 432 (1), the court orders an inspection, the Department has no choice in the matter, and it is only fair that the company should be liable 'except so far as this Department otherwise direct'. But shareholders who apply under section 431 are also liable to repay the Department 'to such extent (if any) as the Department may direct', even though here it is not compelled to appoint an inspector.[283] Where minority shareholders do not make a formal request under section 431, but confine themselves to persuading the Department to act 'of its own motion' under section 432 (2), the Department has no power to make the minority or the company contribute to the expenses of an inspection. Thus if the Department chooses to act under section 432 (2), it will only recover its expenses in the event of successful proceedings resulting from the inspector's report. There is provision for rights of contribution as between any of the parties who may become liable to repay the Department's expenses.[284] What the Department cannot recover must of course be paid by public funds.[285]

15.28 The Department's power to investigate the ownership of shares

Under section 442 of the Companies Act 1985, the Department of Trade and Industry has power to investigate the ownership of shares of a company. Where it appears to the Department that there is good reason so to do, it may appoint one or more competent inspectors to investigate and report on the membership of any company and otherwise with respect to the company for the purpose of determining the true persons who are or have been financially interested in the success or failure (real or apparent) of the company, or are able to control or materially influence its policy.[286]

Where an application for an investigation under the section is made to the Department of Trade and Industry with respect to particular shares or debentures of a company, in the case of a company having a share capital, either by not less than 200 members or by members holding not less than one-tenth of the shares issued, or in the case of a company not having a share capital, by not less than one-fifth in number of the persons on the register of members, then the Department is to appoint an inspector to conduct the investigation unless it is satisfied that the application is vexatious. Where inspectors are appointed, their terms of appointment must include any matter insofar as the Secretary of State is satisfied that it is reasonable to be investigated.[287] Section 442 (3C) permits the Secretary of State to proceed instead under section 444 where he deems it more appropriate. The Secretary of State may, before appointing inspectors, require the applicants to give security up to an amount not exceeding £5,000 for the payment of the costs of the investigation.[288]

Subject to the terms of an inspector's appointment, his powers are to extend to the investigation of any circumstances suggesting the existence of an arrangement or

---

[283] Section 439 (5).
[284] Section 439 (9); and see section 439 (8).
[285] Section 439 (10).
[286] Section 442 (1).
[287] Section 442 (3), (3A).
[288] This amount may be increased by the Secretary of State by order: see section 442 (3B).

understanding which, though not legally binding, is or was observed or likely to be observed in practice and which is relevant to the purposes of his investigation.[289]

Where it appears to the Department that there is good reason to investigate the ownership of any shares in or debentures of a company but that it is unnecessary to appoint an inspector for the purpose, under section 442 they may require any person whom they have reasonable cause to believe to have or to be able to obtain any information as to the present and past interests in those shares or debentures and the names and addresses of the persons interested and of any persons who act or have acted on their behalf in relation to the shares or debentures to give any such information to the Secretary of State.[290]

15.29 Power to impose restrictions on shares or debentures

Part XV of the Companies Act 1985 gives the Department of Trade and Industry power to impose restrictions on shares[291] 'in connection with an investigation' under section 442 or 444 (investigation of the ownership of a company).[292] The Department may invoke these powers where it appears to it that there is difficulty in finding out the relevant facts about any shares (whether issued or to be issued). In that event the Department may by order direct that the shares shall be subject, until further order, to the restrictions imposed by section 454.

So long as any shares are directed to be subject to the restrictions imposed by Part XV of the Act, the following provisions of section 454 (1) shall apply:

(1) any transfer of those shares, or in the case of unissued shares any transfer of the right to be issued with them and any issue of them, is void;
(2) no voting rights are exercisable in respect of those shares;
(3) no further shares are to be issued in right of those shares or in pursuance of any offer made to their holder;
(4) except in a liquidation, no payment shall be made of any sums due from the company on those shares whether in respect of capital or otherwise.

Section 454 (2) and (3) contain provisions which amplify the effect of these restrictions. Where shares are subject to the restrictions imposed in (1) above, any agreement to transfer the shares, or in the case of unissued shares the right to be issued with the shares, is void.[293] Where shares are subject to the restrictions imposed in (3) and (4), any

---

[289] Section 442 (4). With the necessary modifications, certain of the provisions governing an investigation of the company's affairs by inspectors are applied to investigations under section 442 of ownership of shares. These provisions are section 433 (1) (power to investigate related companies), section 434 (production of documents, etc.), section 436 (obstruction of inspectors) and section 437 (inspector's report).

[290] Section 444 (1). See further, *Gore-Browne on Companies* (Jordans, 44th edn, loose-leaf), 28.28.1.

[291] Part XV applies to debentures as well as to shares: section 445 (2).

[292] This power can also be invoked under Part VI of the Companies Act 1985. See section 216. See *Re Geers Gross plc* [1987] BCLC 253. and *Re F. H. Lloyd Holdings plc* (1985) 1 BCC, 99, 407 as to the application of these provisions to foreign shareholders; see also *Re Richards plc (No. 1)* [1989] BCLC 566, *(No. 2)* [1989] BCLC 766 and *(No. 3)* [1989] BCLC 771.

[293] 'Except an agreement to sell shares on the making of an order under section 456 (3) (*b*).' See the amendment of section 454 (2), (3) by the Companies Act 1989, Schedule 19, para. 10. 'Sale' means a sale for cash, not an exchange of shares: *Re Westminster Property Group plc* [1985] BCLC 188 (CA).

agreement to transfer any right to be issued with *other* shares in right of those shares or to receive any payment on those shares (otherwise than in a liquidation) is void.[294]

Where the Department of Trade and Industry makes an order directing that shares shall be subject to such restrictions, or refuses to make an order directing that shares cease to be subject thereto, any person aggrieved may apply to the court for an order directing that the shares be no longer subject to the restrictions.[295] If the order was made by the court under section 216 (1) (non-disclosure of shareholding), the application may be made by the person aggrieved or by the company.[296]

Section 456 (3) states the conditions on which the court, or the Secretary of State, may make an order that shares shall cease to be subject to the restrictions imposed by section 454. These are that the court or, as the case may be, the Secretary of State, is satisfied that the relevant facts about the shares have been disclosed to the company, and no unfair advantage has accrued to any person as a result of the earlier failure to make disclosure. Alternatively an order under section 456 (3) may be made if the shares are to be transferred and the court (in any case) or the Secretary of State (if the order is made under section 210 or 445) approves the sale. Section 456 (4) gives the court a power to order the sale of shares on the application of the Secretary of State (unless the restrictions were imposed by the court under section 216) or the company. On such an application the court may also order that the shares shall cease to be subject to the restrictions imposed. Where shares are sold by an order made under section 456 (4), the proceeds of sale, less the costs of sale, shall be paid into court for the benefit of the persons who are beneficially interested in the shares. Such persons may apply to the court for payment of the whole[297] or part of the proceeds. On an application under section 457 (1) the court must order the payment to the applicant of the whole of the proceeds of sale (together with any interest) or, if any other person had a beneficial interest in the shares at the time of their sale, such proportion of those proceeds (and interest thereon) as is equal to the proportion which the value of the applicant's interest in the shares bears to the total value of the shares.[298]

15.30 Powers to investigate share dealings

Under section 446 of the Companies Act 1985 the Department of Trade and Industry is given power to appoint 'one or more competent inspectors' if it appears to the Department that circumstances suggest a contravention of section 323 (dealing by directors in options for quoted securities of their company) or of section 324 and Schedule 13 (obligation of directors to notify their company of interests in the securities of their company).[299] Such inspectors are to carry out such investigations as are requisite to establish whether or not contraventions have occurred, and to report the results of their investigation to the Department. In making such an appointment the Department may

---

[294] Except on an agreement to transfer any such right on the sale of the shares on the making of an order under section 456 (3) (*b*). See the amendment of section 454 (2), (3) by the Companies Act 1989, Schedule 19, para. 10.

[295] Section 456 (1) and (2).

[296] *Re Lonrho plc* [1988] BCLC 53.

[297] This is subject to any order as to costs for the benefit of the applicant made under section 457 (3).

[298] Section 457 (2).

[299] This includes the extension (under section 325) of section 324 to spouses and children of directors. As to section 323, see 14.19, above, and s to section 324, 13.22, above.

limit the period of the inspector's investigation or confine it to shares or debentures of a particular class (or both).[300]

The powers given to inspectors to obtain documents relating to a company, and to examine its officers and agents on oath, by sections 434 to 436, with some modifications, apply to investigations into share dealings under section 446.[301] As it applies to an investigation under section 446, the reference to 'any other body corporate whose affairs are being investigated under section 433 (1)' (in sections 434 to 436) is to have substituted for it a reference to 'any other body corporate which is, or has at any relevant time been, the company's subsidiary or holding company'. The powers given by sections 434 to 436 are also to apply (for the purposes of an investigation under section 446) to the following classes of individual:[302]

(1) any individual who is an authorised person within the meaning of the Financial Services Act 1986;
(2) any individual who holds a permission granted under para. 23 of Schedule 1 to that Act;
(3) any officer (whether past or present) of a body corporate which is so authorised or permitted;
(4) any partner (whether past or present) in a partnership which is so authorised or permitted;
(5) any member of the governing body or officer (whether past or present) of an unincorporated association which is so authorised or permitted.

Section 446 provides that inspectors appointed under it may (and must if so directed by the Department) make interim reports to the Department, and on the conclusion of their investigation they must make a formal report.[303] The Department may cause such a report to be published.[304] The expenses of an inspection under section 446 must be defrayed by the Department of Trade and Industry out of moneys provided by Parliament.[305]

[300] Section 446 (2).
[301] Section 446 (3).
[302] Section 446 (4) as amended by the Financial Services Act 1986, Schedule 16, para. 21.
[303] Section 446 (5).
[304] Section 446 (5). A report may be written or printed as the Department may direct.
[305] Section 446 (7).

16 Takeovers and Mergers

16.1 Introduction

This chapter is concerned with the legal machinery for merging and reconstructing companies. Some of this machinery is contained in legislation,[1] but the bulk of it is to be found in the City Code on Takeovers and Mergers and the Rules Governing the Substantial Acquisitions of Shares.[2] This self-regulatory body of rules, under the auspices of the Panel on Takeovers and Mergers, does not have the full force of law in the sense of being established by legislation, but has nonetheless proved to be a fairly effective mechanism for policing takeovers and mergers. In addition to the City Code, the *Listing Rules* made by The Stock Exchange require detailed information to be disclosed in the document making a takeover bid about the character of the offeror and the precise terms of the offer, and listed companies must notify the Exchange of a number of matters relating to a takeover or merger or consequent upon it.[3]

Takeovers and mergers have other important dimensions which are beyond the scope of this book. For example, they may lead to a reference by the Department of Trade and Industry to the Monopolies and Mergers Commissions under Part V of the Fair Trading Act 1973, or to the European Commission for offers with a Community dimension under Article 86 of the Treaty of Rome.[4] There are also taxation implications for the offeror and the shareholders of the offeree,[5] and there are employment law consequences under the Acquired Rights Directive, as implemented by the Transfer of Undertakings (Protection of Employment) Regulations 1981.[6]

16.2 The Takeover Panel and its administration of the Code

When the machinery of the Panel was reconstituted in March 1969, it became a purely supervisory body and the day-to-day administration of the Panel's business was taken over on a full-time basis by the Panel's Executive – consisting of the Director-General, the Deputy Director-General(s), the Secretary and their staff reporting directly to the Chairman.[7] The day-to-day business of the Panel, which the Panel Executive administers, consists chiefly of monitoring all takeover and merger transactions to ensure as far as possible that the proposals and the manner of their execution conform to the spirit and to the detailed provisions of the Code, on the basis that such rulings are subject to reference

---

[1] Principally the Companies Act 1985 and the Insolvency Act 1986.

[2] The most recent version of this loose-leaf code was published in 1993. It is regularly updated.

[3] For detail, see *Gore-Browne on Companies* (Jordans, 44th edn, loose-leaf), 29.26.

[4] For a brief introduction, see *Gore-Browne on Companies*, 29.25.

[5] See *Gore-Browne on Companies*, 30.12 to 30.28.

[6] See, e.g. McMullen, *Business Transfers and Employee Rights* (Butterworths, 2nd edn, 1992).

[7] The Chairman and Deputy Chairman are nominated by the Governor of the Bank of England and the bodies represented on the Panel are: the Association of Investment Trust Companies, the Association of British Insurers, the Confederation of British Industry, The National Association of Pension Funds, The Stock Exchange, the Institute of Chartered Accountants in England and Wales, the Association of Unit Trusts and Investment Funds, the British Bankers' Association, the British Merchant Banking and Securities Houses Association, the Investment Management Regulatory Organisation, and the Securities and Futures Authority.

to the full Panel. The Director-General or his Deputies are available at all times to give rulings on points of interpretation of the Code. They will endeavour to give these rulings as promptly as is necessary to ensure the free functioning of the takeover and merger business. Companies and their advisers are encouraged to consult the Panel's Executive on points needing clarification either by telephone or by meetings at short notice.

The main functions of the full Panel in its supervisory role are to consider progress reports of the Director-General and matters of policy, which it does at regular quarterly meetings, and to hear

(1) appeals against rulings of the Director-General;
(2) references by the Panel's executive;
(3) disciplinary cases; and
(4) cases of exceptional importance where the Chairman is of the opinion that the Panel should be fully informed.

The Code incorporates a section describing the procedure that will be followed when the full Panel's decision is required. In general, proceedings are informal and private, consistent with ensuring that all parties are given a fair hearing. Principals (whether companies, individuals or their advisers) present their case in person, without representation by lawyers. All parties are usually present at the hearing and see the papers submitted to the Panel by each other party unless, exceptionally, evidence is of a commercially confidential nature, when the full Panel may be prepared to hear evidence in the absence of some or all of the other parties concerned.

If there appears to have been a breach of the Code, the Panel Executive invites the person concerned to appear before the full Panel for a hearing. He is informed by letter of the nature of the alleged breach and of the matters which the Director-General will present. If any other matters are raised at the hearing he is allowed to ask for an adjournment. If the Panel finds that there has been a breach, it may have recourse to private reprimand or public censure or, in a more flagrant case, to further action designed to deprive the offender temporarily or permanently of his ability to enjoy the facilities of the securities markets. The Panel may refer certain aspects of a case to the Department of Trade and Industry, The Stock Exchange or another appropriate body. No reprimand, censure or further action will take place without the person concerned having forty-eight hours to serve notice of appeal to the Appeal Committee of the Panel. However, it is the Panel's policy, in the case of important or controversial matters, to publish its conclusions and the reasons for them. In this manner its own activities are subject to public scrutiny.

There is a right of appeal[8] to the Appeal Committee where the Panel both finds a breach of the Code and proposes to take disciplinary action, and in a case where it is alleged that the Panel has acted outside its jurisdiction or where the Panel refuses to recognise or ceases to recognise a market-maker or fund-manager as an exempt market-maker or fund manager. An appeal may also lie with leave of the Panel against decisions which, although not strictly of a disciplinary nature, inflict in the view of the Panel serious

---

[8] The Court of Appeal has held that decisions of the Panel and its Appeal Committee are in principle open to judicial review but in the particular case an application for judicial review was rejected; *R v Panel on Take-overs ex parte Datafin plc* [1987] QB 815. Sir John Donaldson MR indicated that the relationship between the Panel and the court should be historic rather than contemporaneous. The court should allow contemporary decisions to take their course, considering the complaint and intervening, if at all, later and in retrospect by declaratory orders. See also *R v Panel on Take-overs and Mergers, ex parte Guinness plc* [1990] 1 QB 146.

hardship on an individual or company. No appeal, however, lies against a finding of fact or against a decision of the Panel on the interpretation of the Code.

The Appeal Committee do not normally hear new evidence. If the Appeal Committee consider there may be material new evidence which could not have been presented to the Panel, then they would normally remit the matter to the Panel for further consideration. Proceedings before the Appeal Committee are conducted in a similar way to those before the Panel.

If an appeal is upheld, the appellant is consulted on the form of statement (if any) which should be published. If an appeal is dismissed, the findings of the Panel are published and any steps decided upon by way of penalty implemented.

16.3 The sanctions available to the Panel

The Panel is not a statutory body and its decisions do not have the force of law. Furthermore, it is no answer on a failure to consult the Panel Executive that a legal opinion has been obtained on the interpretation of a rule.[9] It has to be recognised that the City Code is a voluntary one; this has advantages in that the General Principles and Rules contained in it may go beyond, or be at least in advance of, anything which could be laid down in legislation and may be more readily adapted to changing circumstances as well as more quickly and flexibly administered. But voluntary rules inevitably suffer from the disadvantage that they depend in the main upon voluntary observance and often lack explicit sanctions which can be enforced. It is for this reason that the Panel – and, indeed, all the Institutions associated with it – attach the highest importance to a loyal observance of the Code and to support for the Panel's rulings by all concerned. This duty to observe the Code rests particularly, of course, upon directors of companies affected. But shareholders as well should recognise that if they wish their investment generally to be protected by orderly markets and integrity on the part of those whose conduct may affect them, there may be occasions when in spite of some short-term disadvantage they should accept and support the operations of the Code.

Although the Panel is not a statutory body and its decisions do not have legal force, its decisions remain fully effective unless and until they are set aside by a court of competent jurisdiction. It is acknowledged by government and other regulatory bodies that those who seek to take advantage of the facilities of the securities market in the United Kingdom should conduct themselves in matters relating to takeovers in accordance with the best business standards and so according to the Code. Therefore, for those who do not do so, by way of sanction, the facilities of those markets may be withheld. In particular, the Securities and Investments Board (SIB) and the self-regulating organisations (SROs) recognised under the Financial Services Act 1986 may require that those subject to their jurisdiction should not act in takeovers for any person who does not appear likely to comply with those standards. Moreover, if a person authorised by SIB or an SRO to carry on an investment business fails to comply with the Code or a ruling of the Panel, that may lead to the withdrawal of authorisation. The European Commission is also empowered to suspend concentrations and to impose fines and penalties in appropriate circumstances.

In 1987 the Department of Trade and Industry (DTI) arranged a formal review of the framework for the working and authority of takeovers. It was decided that the Panel

[9] See the Panel's statement in Mooloya Investments Ltd and Customagic Manufacturing Company Ltd (20 July 1978).

would continue in its current form to administer, as a self-regulatory body, takeover activity in the United Kingdom. Nevertheless it does operate within a legal framework. Following the 1987 review, the Panel is designated under section 18 of the Financial Services Act 1986 as an authority to receive restricted information from the SIB, The Stock Exchange and information acquired by the DTI under 'books and papers' inspections pursuant to section 447 of the Companies Act 1985.[10] The Panel is similarly designated under the Banking Act 1987 to receive information from the Bank of England. The SIB and relevant SROs require practitioners to co-operate with Panel inquiries and investigations. The DTI have their own far-reaching investigative powers[11] and the Panel can request that they should be invoked.

16.4 The scope and form of the Code

The Introduction to the Code states that those who wish to take advantage of the facilities of the securities markets in the United Kingdom should conduct themselves in matters relating to takeovers according to the Code and that such persons are required to observe the spirit of the Code. Types of transaction which are explicitly stated in the Code as being subject to its regulations, in addition to self-evident takeover transactions, include partial offers and offers by a parent company for shares in its subsidiary. Certain other transactions where control[12] of a company is to be obtained or consolidated also fall within the area to which the Code applies, including transactions effected by way of schemes of arrangement[13] and reverse takeovers. The Code does not apply to offers for non-voting non-equity capital.

Whether or not the Code applies to a particular company is determined by the characteristics of the company which is the offeree or potential offeree, or in which control may change or be consolidated. The Code applies to offeree public companies, listed or unlisted, which are resident in the United Kingdom, the Channel Islands or the Isle of Man.[14] In addition to applying to all public companies, it governs private companies which have filed a prospectus for the issue of equity share capital during the preceding ten years, whose shares have been listed within that period, or in whose equity share capital dealings have been advertised in a newspaper regularly for a continuous six-month period within those years.

The provisions of the Code fall into two distinct categories. Firstly, there are the General Principles, of which there are ten. These are intended to be 'general principles of conduct to be observed in takeover and merger transactions'. They are a 'codification of good standards of commercial behaviour and should have an obvious and universal application'. The second and larger part of the Code consists of Rules (of which there are now thirty-eight).[15] Some of these 'are no more than examples of the application of the general principles whilst others are rules of procedure designed to govern specific forms of takeover and merger transactions practised in the United Kingdom'.

The Code emphasises that a legalistic and literal interpretation should not be given to

[10] See Chapter 15.
[11] ibid.
[12] See Introduction to the Code, paras. 3 and 4.
[13] i.e. under sections 425 to 427 of the Companies Act 1985. See 16.16 to 16.20, below.
[14] The Code also applies to Irish companies listed on The Stock Exchange.
[15] There are also Notes to the Rules which are intended to furnish a more detailed guidance as to how the Rules are to operate.

any part of the Code. It is framed 'in non-technical language and is, as a measure of self-discipline, administered and enforced by the Panel, a body representative of those using the securities markets and concerned with the observance of good business standards and not the enforcement of the law'.

16.5 The Principles of the Code

The Code first of all states its guiding philosophy. This is that the 'spirit as well as the precise wording' of the General Principles and the Rules be observed. Furthermore, 'the General Principles and the spirit of the Code will apply in areas or circumstances not explicitly covered by any Rule.' It is conceded that (in accordance with the principles of company law) boards of directors and their advisers have a duty to act in the best interests of their shareholders. But the General Principles and the Rules inevitably impinge on the freedom of action of boards and persons involved in takeover and merger transactions. This applies to the board and advisers of both the offeror and offeree companies. However, 'there are limitations in connection with such transactions on the manner in which pursuit of these interests can be carried out'. The Principles indicate those areas where the Code impinges on the traditional freedom of action of boards in takeover battles or agreed mergers.[16]

A number of the Principles are concerned with fair treatment of shareholders, including equal treatment of different classes of shares, as well as among members of each class. Thus, 'rights of control must be exercised in good faith and the oppression of a minority is wholly unacceptable', and all shareholders of the same class of an offeree company shall be treated similarly by an offeror.[17]

General Principle 10 indicates where the acquisition of a degree of control by a person (or persons acting in concert)[18] will necessitate a general offer to all other shareholders. A similar obligation may arise where control is consolidated.[19]

The Code[20] imposes a general duty on the directors of both offeror and offeree companies, when advising their shareholders not to have regard to their personal or family shareholdings or to their personal relationships with their companies. It is shareholders' interests as a whole, together with those of employees and creditors, which should be considered.[21]

A number of the Principles of the Code are concerned with the adequacy of information (and opinions) given to the shareholders of an offeree company. General Principle 4 requires that shareholders must be given sufficient information and advice to enable them to reach a properly informed decision and must have sufficient time to do so. No relevant information may be withheld. General Principle 2 is concerned that there should be equality of information available to all shareholders. Neither the offeror, the offeree company nor their advisers may furnish information to some shareholders which is not available to all. As to the standard of accuracy required, any document or

---

[16] See *Gore-Browne on Companies* (Jordans, 44th edn, loose-leaf), for text of the Principles at 29.7.

[17] General Principles 1 and 8. This of course expresses the gist of a similar principle of company law. In other respects, however, the Principles and Rules go further than existing company law.

[18] As to 'persons acting in concert', see the 'Definition' section to the Code. See further, 16.6 at footnote 32, below.

[19] This Principle is elaborated by Rule 34. See 16.9, below. There is an obligation on the person acquiring such control to ensure that it will be possible to implement such a general offer.

[20] General Principle 9.

[21] This, broadly speaking, also reflects the requirements of company law; see Chapter 14.

advertisement addressed to shareholders containing information or advice from the board of an offeror or an offeree company (or their advisers) must, as in the case of a prospectus, be prepared with the highest standard of care and accuracy.[22]

The Code also requires 'every endeavour to prevent the creation of a false market in the share of an offeror or offeree company'.[23] There are also Principles dealing with the frustration of a bona fide offer by the board of an offeree company[24] and requiring that an offeror be able to implement an offer once it has been announced.[25]

16.6 The Rules

The scope of a book of this nature does not permit a full account of the thirty-eight Rules of the Code (and their attendant Notes). These make up the bulk of the Code. The Rules are intended to regulate the whole process by which a takeover bid (or agreed merger) is conducted, from its initial launch to its (hopefully) successful completion. There are detailed provisions regulating the preliminary stages. These include the approach to the board of the offeree[26] company and the announcement of the offer or approach.[27] The General Principles of the Code will govern the offeree board's consideration of the offer. It should be observed that the Code requires the offeror to give evidence of financial (and other) ability to implement the offer.[28] Furthermore, where the offer comes within the statutory provisions for possible reference to the Monopolies and Mergers Commission, it must contain a term stating that it will lapse if there is a reference to the Commission by the Secretary of State for Trade and Industry before the closing date for the offer, or the date (whichever is later) when it is declared unconditional.[29]

Besides the Rule governing the timing and contents of offer announcements,[30] the Code makes elaborate provision as to the information that must be given to the shareholders of the offeree company.[31] This includes the shareholding by the offeror company in the offeree company.[32] It also includes shareholding in the offeror (in the case of a securities exchange offer) and (in any event) shares in the offeree in which the directors of the offeror are interested. A similar disclosure must be made as to shareholdings owned or controlled by persons 'acting in concert'[33] with the offeror. It likewise applies to holdings owned or controlled by any persons who, prior to the posting of the offer document, have irrevocably committed themselves to accept the offer.[34] There is also provision for disclosure of directors' service contracts in respect of the offeree company. This applies in the case of documents sent to shareholders of the offeree

---

[22] General Principle 5.

[23] General Principle 6.

[24] General Principle 7.

[25] General Principle 3.

[26] Rule 1.

[27] Rule 2.

[28] Rule 2.5.

[29] See Rule 9.4 and Rule 12.

[30] Rule 2. Rule 2 stresses the importance of secrecy prior to an announcement.

[31] See Rules 23–27.

[32] Rule 24.3.

[33] The term 'persons acting in concert' is widely used throughout the Code and is thus defined in the Definitions which preface the Code.

[34] Rule 25.3 imposes a parallel duty on the offeree company in respect of a document advising its shareholders on an offer.

company (by the board of the offeree) which recommend either acceptance or rejection of an offer.[35]

The Code makes provision for profit forecasts and for asset valuations.[36] The policy expressed by the Code is that information concerning profit forecasts may be vital to the shareholders' assessment of the merits of a takeover proposal. General Principle 5 requires that takeover documents must be prepared with the same standard of care as if the document were a prospectus. However, whereas in a prospectus it is the proper practice to make a conservative estimate of profits (so as not to inflate the price of securities offered for sale), in a takeover document it may mislead shareholders to err on the conservative side in estimating profits. In any event, since there are obvious hazards in such forecasting, Rule 28 lays down precise and stringent requirements as to the preparation of forecasts. Directors are required to state the assumptions, including commercial assumptions, upon which they base their profit forecasts. Although such forecasts are the sole responsibility of the directors making them, the accounting bases and assumptions must be reported on by the offeror's auditors (or reporting accountants) as well as by its merchant bank or other financial adviser mentioned in the offer document. This is not required where the forecast is made by an offeror offering solely cash.[37]

It may be noted that, though the common law as to misrepresentation is ill adapted to provide a remedy for predictions (e.g. profit forecasts) or opinions (e.g. asset valuations), the law of contract, being concerned with the enforcement of promises, is more apt for such purposes. Since an offer document will, as its name indicates, produce a contract between the offeror company and the shareholders in the offeree who accept its terms, legal redress will be available in the case of a misleading forecast (or unsound valuation) which events show to be widely inaccurate. 'The Panel recognises that legal responsibility may arise from statements made in takeover documents. If legal proceedings are initiated or threatened in such circumstances the Panel will normally suspend its own enquiries'.[38]

Rule 29 also stipulates that where a valuation of assets is given in connection with a takeover offer, the board of the offeror should be supported by the opinion of a named independent valuer and the basis of the valuation clearly stated.[39]

A number of Rules in the Code relate to what has been termed the 'mechanics of the formal offer'.[40] These concern such matters as what is permissible in respect of the revision and extension of offers, and as to the withdrawal of acceptances. Provision is made as to how and when an offer may be declared unconditional. It should be noted that copies of all offer documents (and other announcements or documents bearing on a takeover) must be lodged with the Panel at the same time as they are dispatched to their intended recipients.[41]

---

[35] Rule 25.4. In the offer document itself it should be stated (except in the case of an offeror offering solely cash) whether the offeror's directors' emoluments will be affected by a successful acquisition of the offeree: Rule 24.4.

[36] See Rules 28 and 29.

[37] Rule 28.3.

[38] See the Panel's Report for the year ending 31 March 1978, p. 13.

[39] Rule 29.2.

[40] i.e. Rules 30–34.

[41] Rule 19.3.

16.7 Partial offers

In Rule 36 the Code tries to curtail any unfairness to shareholders that may arise from 'partial offers'. Although such offers for less than 100 per cent of a company's shares (or a class thereof) may sometimes be justified, Rule 36 states that the Panel's consent is required for *any* partial offer and it then lays down guidelines as to how and when that consent may be given. In the case of an offer which would result in the offeror holding shares carrying less than 30 per cent of the voting rights[42] of a company, consent will not normally be given. Where the result will be control of between 30 per cent and 100 per cent, such consent will not normally be given if the offeror (and 'persons acting in concert') have acquired shares in the offeree company during the previous twelve months. Where an offer is made which would result in the offeror holding shares carrying 30 per cent or more of the voting rights, a comparable offer must be made to each class. Acquisition of 30 per cent of the voting rights is also critical in 'triggering' an obligation under Rule 9 to make an extended offer to other voting shareholders. In the case of a partial offer which could result in the offeror holding over 50 per cent (but less than 100 per cent) of the voting rights of the offeree, the precise number of shares offered for must be stated. The offer may not be declared unconditional as to acceptance unless acceptances are received for not less than that number. Any offer which would result in the offeror holding shares carrying 30 per cent or more of the voting rights must be conditional, not only on the specified number of acceptances being received, but also on approval by 50 per cent of the voting rights not held by the offeror and persons not acting in concert with it.[43]

Today partial offers are rarely made *ab initio*. Instead a tender offer under the Substantial Acquisition Rules (discussed later)[44] is made. Rule 36 also provides for partial offers which are intended to increase a holding to a higher level. Here it will have more relevance.

16.8 Restrictions on dealings

The wider context of the regulation of insider dealing has been considered earlier in this book.[45] The City Code was early in this field in so far as insider dealing in the context of a takeover bid or merger is concerned. The main restriction is found in Rule 4. This forbids persons who are privy to the intention to make an offer (or to the preliminary negotiations) from dealing in the securities of the offeree company from the time when there is reason to suppose that an approach is contemplated until the issue of a press announcement (or the termination of the previous discussions). Furthermore, no such dealings shall take place in the securities of the offeror except where the proposed offer is not deemed price-sensitive. Rule 4 also imposes a general injunction of confidentiality upon anyone privy to such information making recommendations to any other person as to dealing in the relevant securities.

[42] These are defined by the Code as 'all the voting rights attributable to the share capital of a company which are currently exercisable at a general meeting'. However, the Panel should be consulted where rights exercisable only in restricted circumstances have in fact been exercisable for a long time, or it may be considered that the shares in question have voting rights for the purpose of the Code.

[43] See *Gore-Browne on Companies* (Jordans, 44th edn, loose-leaf), 29.20 as to the possibilities of waiver by the Panel, and as to how Rule 36 applies to different classes of shares.

[44] See 16.11, below.

[45] See 14.21, above.

Rule 5 restricts the speed with which, just before and during an offer, voting shares and rights over voting shares of a company may be acquired by a person, or those acting in concert with him, whose aggregate holding of shares and rights over shares would thereby rise to or through 30 per cent of the voting rights in that company. It also restricts acquisitions of voting shares and rights over shares by a person whose aggregate holding would thereby rise from a level between 30 and 48 per cent by more than 1 per cent in any twelve-month period. Acquisitions having either of these effects are not permitted before the announcement of a firm intention to make an offer, unless the acquisition immediately precedes and is conditional upon such an announcement being made with the public recommendation of the board of the offeree company.

However, once a takeover proposal is announced, all parties may (subject to certain other provisions of the Code) deal subject to daily disclosure to The Stock Exchange, the Panel and the press.[46] This disclosure must be made on a daily basis (whether on or off the market and at whatever price) in respect of purchases of shares in the offeror or offeree. The basic freedom to purchase is posited on the basis that it is 'undesirable to fetter the market'. However, the Code implicitly recognises that this philosophy of the unfettered market may well give an unfair advantage to the offeror and those acting in concert with it.[47] Thus Rule 6.2 requires that if the offeror (or any person acting in concert) purchases securities during the offer period at above the market price (being the then current price of the offer), the offer must be increased to not less than the highest price paid for the security so acquired.[48]

In certain cases Rule 11 requires that offers in respect of a class of shares shall either be in cash or be accompanied by a cash alternative.[49] This obligation applies, first of all, where shares of any class (under offer in the offeree company) are purchased[50] for cash by the offeror (and any person acting in concert) where the shares purchased carry 15 per cent or more of the voting rights exercisable at a class meeting of that class. The shares in question must have been bought during the offer period or within the twelve months prior to its commencement. The Panel may give its consent to dispense with this obligation. Additionally the panel may also dispense the offeror from paying the highest price (under Rule 11) in a particular case.[51]

16.9 The mandatory offer to the remaining shareholders

Rule 9 exists to prevent the problem of the 'locked in' minority shareholder arising. It is also designed to discourage acquisition of de facto control by stealth. In certain circum-

---

[46] See Rule 8.1. This obligation applies not only to the 'parties to a takeover or merger transaction' but to their 'associates' – not only where they deal for their own account but also where 'associates' deal for the account of investment clients. (See Rule 8.2) Disclosure of dealing by major shareholders (within the meaning of the Companies Act 1985) is also required. 'Associates' is elaborately defined in the definition section of the Code; see *Gore-Browne on Companies*, (Jordans, 44th edn, loose-leaf), 29.10.

[47] Rule 8.3 and Rule 16 (special deals with favourable conditions).

[48] Immediately after the purchase it must be announced that a revised offer will be made in accordance with Rule 6. Where practical, disclosure must be made of the number of securities purchased and the price paid. As to the 'highest price', etc. see also Rule 7, which deals with purchases of offeror shares prior to purchases of offeree shares and partial offers and 'whitewashes'. Rule 7.1 also requires an immediate announcement to be made if the offer has to be amended where purchases give rise to obligations under Rules 6, 9 and 11.

[49] This must be valued at not less than the highest price paid (excluding stamp duty and commission) for the shares of that class purchased during the offer period and within twelve months prior to its commencement.

[50] e.g. through the market or by private purchase.

[51] Rule 11.2. See the note thereto as to the 'relevant factors' that the Panel will take into account.

stances this Rule requires an existing offer to be extended to the remaining shareholders hitherto excluded from it. Rule 9 applies where any person *acquires*, whether by a series of transactions over a period of time or not, shares which (taken together with shares held or acquired by persons acting in concert with him) carry 30 per cent or more of the voting rights of a company. Rule 9 also applies where any person, together with persons acting in concert, *holds* not less than 30 per cent but not more than 50 per cent of the voting rights, and such a person or any person acting in concert, acquires in any period of twelve months additional shares carrying more than 1 per cent of the voting rights. In either of these situations, those concerned must extend an offer[52] to the holders of any class of equity share capital whether voting or non-voting. This offer must also be made to the holders of any class of voting non-equity share capital in which such person or persons acting in concert with him hold shares.[53]

The Code contains other provisions to curb rapidly repeated takeover bids or improper defensive tactics by the offeree company. Thus it prevents those who have made an offer, which has lapsed or been withdrawn, from making another offer within the next twelve months for the same company, except with the permission of the Panel.[54]

Rule 21 is designed to amplify further General Principle 7. The latter condemns any action by the board of an offeree company which is designed to frustrate a bona fide takeover bid unless such action has the approval of the shareholders in general meeting. Rule 21 is concerned with the issue of any authorised (but unissued) shares or the issue or grant of options in respect of such shares, or convertible debentures. The board of the offeree company may not issue such securities during the course of the offer, or even before the date of the offer if the board has reason to believe that a bona fide offer is imminent, unless the approval of the shareholders in general meeting is obtained. There is a similar prohibition on the sale, disposal or acquisition of 'assets of material amount' and on 'entering into contracts otherwise than in the ordinary course of business'.[55]

16.10 Assessing the Code's effectiveness

Whatever the criticism levied at an earlier stage in their development,[56] the Code on Takeovers and Mergers, and the Panel which administers it, are now generally regarded as a successful example of self-regulation. The Code is sometimes held up as a model that might be followed in other areas of City activity which are in need of more effective

[52] The offer so extended must comply with the condition set out in Rule 9.5; e.g. it must be in cash or be accompanied by a cash alternative. Such offers must be conditional upon the offeror having received acceptance in respect of shares which, together with the shares acquired or agreed to be acquired before or during the offer, will result in the offeror, etc. holding shares carrying more than 50 per cent of the voting rights. See Rule 9.3.

[53] Offers for different classes of equity capital must be comparable. Here the Panel must be consulted in advance. This rule is complex in its varied applications. It has an extensive Note giving detailed interpretation, in particular as to 'persons acting in concert'.

[54] Rule 35. This also applies on an acquisition of shares of the offeree company which may result in an obligation to make an offer as required by Rule 9. See also Rule 35.2 (partial offers) and 35.3 (delay of six months before acquisition above the offer price).

[55] Rule 21 does not apply to contracts to issue shares, etc. already entered into. In special circumstances the Panel may give its consent to dispense with this rule.

[56] See Davies, *The Regulation of Takeovers and Mergers* (Sweet & Maxwell, 1976), pp. 39–46 for criticism of the 1974 version of the Code. Much of this is still true as regards enforcement and sanctions. See also McCrae and Cairncross, *Capital City* (Eyre & Methuen, 2nd edn 1985), pp. 150–7.

self-regulation.[57] It is certainly so regarded by the senior staff of the Panel[58] and by the City institutions who have to live with the Code and the Panel's rulings. It can be argued that the Code admits of regular and rapid amendments in response to the lessons of experience. It is not staffed by civil servants with a bureaucratic mentality, but by those knowledgeable of the problems of effective regulation of takeover bids. Further, the Panel has built up wide support from all the City and governmental bodies concerned.

In 1987 the Secretary of State for Trade and Industry instigated a full review of the powers and personnel and rules of the Panel. Although it was considered that some measures could be provided which would strengthen the regulation of takeovers, it was decided that the Panel would continue as a self-regulatory body. It was felt overall that the Panel had, in general, worked effectively in ensuring fair treatment for all shareholders, regardless of whether takeovers succeed or fail. A self-regulatory system was preferred to a statutory underpinning, which would be slower and would encourage more formal litigation through appeals against the Panel's decisions.

Nevertheless the unofficial status of the Panel's Executive has drawbacks when it has to investigate abuses. This encouraged the Panel to withdraw from the field of policing 'insider dealing' and to welcome sanctions imposed by the criminal law. A lack of the power to subpoena witnesses, and the inhibiting effect of the laws of defamation, are said to curb the effectiveness of the Panel as an investigatory body. However, this has not in general hindered it in seeking compliance with the administration of the Code and in resolving disputed interpretations. Further, it now appears that the Panel enjoys qualified privilege in the conduct of investigations into alleged breaches of the Code.[59] However, the publication of critical reports may still be inhibited by the law of defamation and contempt.

Most of the criticisms that have been made about the unsatisfactory nature of the sanctions available to the Panel are still valid. At one end of the scale (suspension of listing or of dealing in shares or the termination of the careers of professionals, such as stockbrokers) the sanctions are heavy-handed and clumsy. They may also damage the interests of innocent shareholders not involved in any breach of the Code. At the other end of the scale, there is the sanction of public censure of individuals or institutions. Such a sanction, where very substantial financial advantages are at issue, may seem feeble, especially in the case of those who will not need to maintain the goodwill of the Panel in the future. Yet the Panel still resorts to such censure even where it has found culpable (if not deliberate) breaches of important rules of the Code.[60]

16.11 The Substantial Acquisition Rules

Certain much-discussed abuses which have occurred in the last few years have shown both the strengths and the limitations of the Panel and the other self-regulatory bodies. The problem of what are known as 'dawn raids' seems in the end to have produced a

---

[57] See L. C. B. Gower, *Review of Investor Protection* (Cmnd 9125, 1984) at 9.09–9.11.

[58] For a review of the 5th edition of the Code by Peter Lee, Deputy Director of the Panel, see 2 Co. Law 99 (1981).

[59] See *Graff v Shawcross, Macdonald and Frazer*, 10 October 1980. See 2 Co. Law 33 (1981). Caulfield J's observations were obiter, but they would apply to investigations by other self-regulatory bodies, such as The Stock Exchange.

[60] See 3 Co. Law 132 (1982) for an illustration of a decision of the Panel's Executive, upheld by the Appeal Committee, in connection with a breach of Rules 31 and 32. On occasion the parties voluntarily agree to pay a sum of money to charity.

reasonably effective response. The practice of making a 'dawn raid', by rapid and organised early trading to acquire a substantial interest in a target company, first attracted widespread comment in the case of the acquisition of Consolidated Gold Fields by Anglo-American Trust.[61] Frequently such raids were carried out through a complex web of subsidiaries and associates acting, often, through foreign nominees. The principal objection to this practice is that it favoured the interests of large institutional investors (e.g. pension funds), who were able to make a rapid response to a purchasing raid and so gain (at a favourable price) an advantage from which the small individual investor was excluded. The Department of Trade and Industry refused the opportunity to legislate for new disclosure provisions,[62] and encouraged the self-regulatory bodies to cope with the problem. At the prompting of the Panel and The Stock Exchange, the Council for the Securities Industry (which has since ceased to exist) produced a set of rules to curb the more blatant forms of market raid.[63]

The Substantial Acquisition Rules are rules which restrict the speed with which a person (and any person acting with him) may increase to between 15 and 30 per cent his holding of voting rights in a company resident in the United Kingdom, the shares of which are listed or otherwise traded on The Stock Exchange. They are issued on the authority of the Panel and are administered by the Panel Executive. They do not apply to a person whose acquisitive action or intention is such as to make him subject to the Code.

The Rules provide that a person who proposes to acquire shares which would result in his holding 15 per cent or more, but less than 30 per cent, of the then exercisable voting rights in a relevant company may do so only:

(1) by acquiring less than 10 per cent of the voting rights within a period of seven days, unless the only acquisition within the seven-day period is from a single shareholder;

(2) by means of a tender offer whereby he advertises a firm offer to make such an acquisition if shares are tendered to him by a date at least eight days after it is advertised; or

(3) by acquiring shares immediately prior to and conditional upon the announcement by the person making the acquisition of a firm intention to make an offer for the company (whether or not the posting of the offer is subject to the fulfilment of any condition) which is publicly recommended by the board of the offeree company.

In a tender offer, the buyer makes a firm offer to purchase a specified number of shares at a fixed price or up to a maximum price. In a maximum price tender, he indicates the maximum price which he is prepared to pay and invites shareholders to tender at that price or at any lower price. He then accepts all shares tendered at the price (the striking price) at which his needs are met which may be at or below the maximum price. The striking price is paid for all tenders which are accepted (subject, if necessary, to pro rata scaling down or balloting of shares tendered at the striking price). If the tender is not fully satisfied, the maximum price applies. In a fixed price tender, if the tenders exceed the number of shares sought, they will be scaled down pro rata. The Council of The Stock

---

[61] See 1 Co. Law 66 at pp. 218 and 303 (1980).

[62] It contended that the problems of appropriate drafting and effective administration of legislation once drafted were too great to overcome the problems of defining and locating 'concert parties' acting through foreign nominees. However, what is now the Companies Act 1985 has improved the disclosure provisions in respect of 'concert parties' and increased the power to 'freeze' dealings in suspect shares under the 1985 Act. See 10.9.7 and 15.29, above.

[63] 'Rules Governing Substantial Acquisitions of Shares', 11 December 1980. See 2 Co. Law 2 (1981). The Council of The Stock

Exchange permits maximum price tender offers, but not fixed price tender offers, to be made on The Stock Exchange. The Substantial Acquisition Rules permit either type of tender offer to be made outside The Stock Exchange.

The Rules set out the information which must be included in the advertisement announcing a tender offer. They also provide that a person who, as a result of an acquisition, comes to hold 15 per cent or more of the voting rights in a company must publicly disclose his total holding (distinguishing between acquisitions and holdings of shares and rights over shares and specifying the nature of any rights concerned) by 12 noon on the business day following the acquisition. He must thereafter similarly disclose any further acquisitions which increase his holding to and beyond any whole percentage figure above 15 per cent of the voting rights.

Rule 37 of the Code concerns the impact upon corporate control where the powers to redeem and purchase a company's shares under powers in the Companies Act[64] are exercised. It may require the directors of the company and those acting in concert with them to make a general offer. Rule 37 provides that when a company redeems or purchases its own voting shares, a resulting increase in the percentage voting rights (carried by the shareholders or the directors and persons acting in concert with them) will be treated in principle as an acquisition for the purposes of Rule 9 (i.e. will require a mandatory offer). However, subject to prior consultation the Panel will normally waive this obligation to make a general offer if there is an independent vote of the shareholders and certain other procedures are followed.[65]

16.12 Reconstruction and amalgamation under section 110 of the Insolvency Act 1986

It is possible for a company to carry out a sale of its undertaking in two distinct ways: the sale of the undertaking may be effected (a) before liquidation, under powers contained in the memorandum, but this is only possible when a liquidation is not in immediate contemplation; or (b) in contemplation of, or after the commencement of, a voluntary liquidation, under the powers now contained in sections 110 and 111 of the Insolvency Act 1986.[66]

However, a power in the memorandum to sell its undertaking (i.e. (a)) may not be used to enable the company to avoid compliance with the provisions of section 111 (examined below). In reversing earlier decisions[67] which upheld such a course, the Court of Appeal[68] held that the proper function of the memorandum was to deal with the objects of the company during its corporate life and not after that life has come to an end. Thus it is not part of the corporate objects to define the distribution of assets in a winding-up (including a section 110 reconstruction).

---

[64] Under Part III, Chapter VII of the 1985 Act. See 6.17 *et seq.*, above.

[65] See Appendix I, 'Whitewash Guidance Note'. See also Rule 37.3 (Redemptions or Purchases of Offeree Company Shares) and Rule 37.4 (Redemptions or Purchases of Offeror Shares). Rule 38 is concerned with dealings by connected exempt market-makers.

[66] These provisions now apply to both a members' and a creditors' voluntary winding-up. See section 110 (3). See Chapter 17, below as to voluntary winding up.

[67] See *Gore-Browne on Companies* (Jordans, 44th edn, loose-leaf), 30.3. If such a power is appropriately drafted it may allow the sale of the company's undertaking not only for cash but for shares, ibid.

[68] *Bisgood v Henderson's Transvaal Estates* [1908] 1 Ch 743.

16.13 Procedure under sections 110 and 111

The procedure under section 110 of the Insolvency Act 1986 is as follows: the company[69] will usually go into a members' voluntary winding-up,[70] and pass a special resolution authorising the liquidator to sell the undertaking under section 110. These powers may also be given to a liquidator in the case of a *creditors'* voluntary winding-up. Here the sanction of the court or the liquidation committee must be sought.[71] However, the sale can take place before winding up and authority can then be given to distribute shares. The authority may be general, or may be confined to a specified sale, to be made in accordance with a scheme of reconstruction or a draft agreement submitted to the meeting. To avoid unpleasant mistakes, it is advisable that the resolution authorising the sale of the property should be submitted simultaneously with the winding-up resolution, so that if the former is not carried the latter may also be dropped: otherwise the company will find itself in liquidation without any scheme for selling its business.[72] Both the voluntary winding-up and the authority for a sale require a special resolution; but they may be passed together at the same meeting.[73] Express notice of each resolution must, however, be given to the shareholders, specifying that a sale is intended under section 110,[74] and if the directors derive any special advantage a notice which does not disclose this fact is insufficient.[75] But it is no objection to a scheme of reconstruction that it openly gives a bonus to directors.[76]

Where a draft agreement for sale is prepared, the special resolution may refer to and approve it, and no other scheme of reconstruction is necessary. But power should be taken for the agreement to be carried out with or without modifications.[77]

16.14 Rights of dissenting shareholders

If any member of the company[78] being wound up who has not voted for the special resolution expresses his dissent from the resolution in writing, addressed to the liquidator and left at the registered office of the company[79] not later than seven days after the

---

[69] For the purposes of section 110 the 'transferor company' (i.e. the one put into voluntary liquidation) must be a registered company. But the transferee company may be a 'company within the meaning of this Act or not': section 110 (1). However, the transferee must be a company and not an individual. See *Gore-Browne on Companies* (Jordans, 44th edn, loose-leaf), 30.6.1.

[70] The resolution sanctioning the sale may be either before, concurrent with, or after the resolution for voluntary winding up: section 110 (6).

[71] See Insolvency Act 1986, section 110 (3) (*b*).

[72] *Cleve v Financial Corp.* (1874) 16 Eq. 363; *Clinch v Financial Corp.* (1869) 4 Ch App. 117; *Thomson v Henderson's Transvaal Estates* [1908] 1 Ch 765 (CA).

[73] See section 110 (6).

[74] *Imperial Bank of China v Bank of Hindustan* (1868) 6 Eq. 91; *In re Irrigation Company of France, ex parte Fox* (1871) 6 Ch App. 176 at p. 193.

[75] *Kaye v Croydon Tramways* [1898] 1 Ch 358 (CA); *Tiessen v Henderson* [1899] 1 Ch 861; *Clarkson v Davies* [1923] AC 100 (PC).

[76] *Southall v British Mutual Life Association* (1871) 6 Ch App. 614. As to payments made to directors for loss of office (or retirement), see the provisions of section 313 of the Companies Act 1985, discussed at 14.20, above.

[77] As to the forms of consideration the liquidator may give to the transferee company's shareholders, see the wide terms of section 110 (2) and (4).

[78] This includes the executors of a deceased member, even if the articles declare that they shall not have the rights of a member till they are registered: *Llewellyn v Kasintoe Rubber Estates* [1914] 2 Ch 670 at p. 679 (CA).

[79] In the case of a Rhodesian company, under similar words in the Colonial Ordinance, Warrington J held that a notice actually served on the liquidator in England and not left at the registered office was sufficient, and that the liquidator could waive service at the office: *Brailey v Rhodesia Consolidated* [1910] 2 Ch 95.

passing of the resolution, he may require the liquidator either to abstain from carrying the resolution into effect or to purchase his interest[80] at a price which, if not settled by agreement, shall be determined by arbitration.[81] In such an arbitration the dissentient has to prove the value of his interest. If a person who ought to be, but is not, on the register of members gives notice of dissent, the court may, on making an order for rectifying the register, declare that it shall relate back, so as to render the notice of dissent effective.[82] If the liquidator elects to purchase a dissenting member's interest, the purchase money must be paid before the company is dissolved, and be raised by the liquidator in such manner as may be determined by special resolution: section 111 (3). Articles used often to provide that shareholders dissenting shall not have the rights given them by this section, or that the value of their interests shall be determined in some way other than by arbitration under the Act. But such provisions are invalid, for the articles cannot negate a provision in the statute for the benefit of the whole body,[83] and they are not an agreement settling the price within the meaning of section 111 (4).[84] If the company being wound up is in difficulties, the value of the interest of such members is, of course, very small. These safeguards for dissenting shareholders in section 111 of the Insolvency Act 1986 apply to the case of section 110 in a members' voluntary liquidation. Where section 110 is used in a creditors' voluntary winding-up, section 111 has no application.[85]

Schemes of reconstruction under section 110 may be upset by a dissentient minority on the ground that some of the provisions are an infringement of the rights of the minority, which the majority cannot impose upon them.[86] If proceedings are taken to set aside a sale to another company after the agreement for sale has been executed, the purchasing company must be made a defendant to the action,[87] and if the method of distributing the purchase consideration can be severed from the provisions for sale, the sale may stand good, leaving the proper distribution of the shares to be made according to the rights of the members of the vendor company.[88] The resolution for winding up is not invalidated by reason of its being coupled with an invalid resolution dealing with the distribution of the purchase consideration.[89]

The arrangement for a sale under section 110 can provide for the manner in which the consideration is to be paid, but cannot determine how it is to be distributed among the members of the vendor company, as this must be done in strict accordance with their rights.[90] It will be seen that this introduces a serious difficulty where there are either preference or other shares having special rights in the distribution of surplus assets. If one

---

[80] The notice must in terms state both alternatives for the liquidator to choose from, or it will be inoperative: *Re Demerara Rubber Co.* [1913] 1 Ch 331; *Re Union Bank of Kingston-upon-Hull* (1880) 13 Ch D 808.

[81] Section 111 (2), (3) and (4).

[82] *Re Sussex Brick Co.* [1904] 1 Ch 598 (CA).

[83] *Payne v Cork Co.* [1900] 1 Ch 308; *Bisgood v Henderson's Transvaal Estates* [1908] 1 Ch 743 at p. 758 (CA).

[84] *Baring-Gould v Sharpington Combined Pick and Shovel Syndicate* [1899] 2 Ch 80 (CA).

[85] See section 111 (1).

[86] As to the provisions which may lawfully be inserted in a scheme of reconstruction under section 110 (e.g. as to time limits for members to apply for shares and as to the disposal of shares unapplied for), see *Gore-Browne on Companies* (Jordans, 44th edn, loose-leaf), 30.5–30.6.2.

[87] *Doughty v Lomagunda Reefs* [1903] 1 Ch 673 (CA).

[88] *Wall v London and Northern Assets Corporation* [1898] 2 Ch 469 (CA).

[89] *Thomson v Henderson's Transvaal Estates* [1908] 1 Ch 765 (CA); *Cleve v Financial Corp.* (1873) 16 Eq. 363.

[90] *Griffith v Paget* (1877) 5 Ch D 894 and 6 Ch 514; *Simpson v Palace Theatre* [1893] WN 91; affirmed by Court of Appeal (1893) 9 TLR 470.

million shares of £1 each are to be distributed, and the rights of the holders of preference shares to the extent of £200,000 are that they shall be paid in full the amount of such shares before any repayment is made to the holders of ordinary shares, who shall say how many shares in the new company would be equivalent to a payment in full of the amount of the preference shares?

It is often attempted to meet the difficulty by giving holders of preference shares in the old company preference shares in the new; but this will not prevail over the rights of any of the old company's preference shareholders who insist on getting the full value of their shares before the old company's ordinary shareholders get anything.

The result is that in companies where there are preference shares a reconstruction under section 110 alone is not possible unless either there is power in the articles of association to meet the circumstances of the case, or the preference shareholders consent unanimously,[91] or those who do not consent to the proposed distribution also dissent from the whole scheme, so as to be paid out under section 111.[92]

16.15 The protection of creditors

If after a voluntary winding-up of a company has been commenced an order is made within one year for winding it up, the special resolution is not valid unless sanctioned by the court: section 110 (6). This sanction cannot be given in the voluntary winding-up. It will only be effective if given when the company is in compulsory liquidation.[93] When a scheme is unfair or improper this may be a ground for the court making a compulsory order on the application of dissatisfied shareholders;[94] but, 'generally speaking, the only persons who could raise this question or ask for an order ... would be the creditors'.[95]

If creditors of the company, instead of proving in the liquidation and having their claims met in the ordinary way, accept securities in the transferee company, then they have the power, under section 110 (6), to impeach any arrangement which proves unsatisfactory to them within this twelve-month period.[96] This means that a scheme under section 110 may remain liable to be impeached for this period.[97]

16.16 Duties of the liquidator under sections 110 to 111

The liquidator must apply the funds which he receives from the new company in paying the costs of the liquidation and any debts which the old company is bound to pay, and in buying out dissentient members. If anything remains, it must be distributed among the

---

[91] Note that the court does not draw the inference that shareholders not represented at the meeting have consented: *Re North-West Argentine Rly* [1900] 2 Ch 882.

[92] Such a scheme has, however, been brought before the Court of Appeal under what is now section 425 of the Companies Act 1985, so as to bind the preference shareholders: *Sorsbie v Tea Corp.* [1904] 1 Ch 12 (CA). However, this case conflicts with other decisions on the relationship between sections 110 and 425.

[93] *Re Callao Bis Co.* (1889) 42 Ch D 169 (CA).

[94] *Re Consolidated South Rand Mines* [1909] 1 Ch 491.

[95] See footnote 93, above.

[96] *Re City & County Investment Co.* (1879) 13 Ch D 475 (CA).

[97] In *Re New Flagstaff Mining Co.* [1889] WN 123 the company itself applied to the court for a supervision order.

members of the old company according to their rights.[98] If the cash which the liquidator receives is not sufficient for the above purposes, he must raise cash by selling or mortgaging the shares or other property which he receives from the new company. The shares remaining over he will distribute among the members of the old company who have not been bought out.

The contract for sale usually provides that the purchasing company shall take over all the assets and pay all the liabilities of the old company, so that the business of the old company can be wound up at once; but such an arrangement does not relieve the liquidator of the old company from the obligation of seeing that the debts are duly paid before the old company is dissolved: to leave everything to the new company is 'a gross dereliction of duty by the liquidator',[99] and if he fails to pay income tax due from the company he will be personally liable to the Crown for the amount.[100]

If a liquidator makes a mistake in distributing the purchase shares, and has none left to correct his mistake, the court cannot upon a summons give damages against him.[101] Whether in an action damages could be recovered is doubtful.

As regards the new company, the same considerations will apply as in the case of a purchase from ordinary vendors, and the usual provisions will apply concerning the filing of contracts with the Registrar of Companies.[102]

Upon a reconstruction being carried out into effect the liquidator should wind up the old company with all possible speed, and, after making up his accounts, should call and advertise the meeting or meetings for receiving those accounts as provided in what is now section 94 of the Insolvency Act 1986. He should then make a return to the Registrar of the meeting or meetings having been held, and at the end of three months from the registration of the return the company is dissolved,[103] subject, however, to the power of the court to reopen the dissolution.[104] The importance of this is that sometimes claims arise for damages, or on other grounds, which, if the company were still in existence, might give rise to great difficulties. The liquidator will have to pay all the debts of which he knows;[105] but claims for damages may arise unexpectedly, and if the shares of the new company have been distributed there is nothing to meet such claims. A contract between the old and the new companies that the new will satisfy the liabilities of the old company cannot be enforced against the new company by creditors of the old for their own benefit, unless it has been made part of a scheme sanctioned under section 425 of the Companies Act 1985.[106]

---

[98] If the real value of the assets received by the transferee company exceeds the nominal amount of the shares issued by it, then the transferee company must transfer a sum equal to the amount in value to the share premium account: *Henry Head & Co. v Ropner Holdings* [1952] Ch 124. See sections 131 to 132 of the Companies Act 1985 for relief from section 130. See 6.15, above.

[99] *Pulsford v Devenish* [1903] 2 Ch 625; *Argyll's v Coxeter* (1913) 29 TLR 355; *In re Aidall* [1933] 1 Ch 323 at p. 327 (CA).

[100] *Re New Zealand Joint Stock Corp.* (1907) 23 TLR 238.

[101] *Re Hill's Waterfall Co.* [1896] 1 Ch 947.

[102] See also 6.10, above.

[103] Section 201 of the Insolvency Act 1986.

[104] See section 110 (6) and 16.15, above. Sections 106 and 201 will govern the final meeting and dissolution, where it is a *creditors'* voluntary liquidation.

[105] The liquidator will be personally liable, however, if he does not secure the payment of claims of which he has notice: *Pulsford v Devenish* [1903] 2 Ch 625; *Re New Zealand Joint Stock Corp.* (1907) 23 TLR 238; *In re Aidall* [1933] 1 Ch 323 at p. 327 (CA).

[106] *Craig's Claim* [1895] 1 Ch 267 (CA).

The decisions[107] by the courts on the relationship between section 425, which provides for an alternative procedure for a reconstruction, as described in 16.17 below, and section 110 of the Insolvency Act 1986 are difficult to reconcile. However, they appear to require that when a 'so-called' scheme is really a sale and transfer of assets under section 110, then that section must be complied with and cannot be evaded by petitioning for a scheme of arrangement under section 425.[108] However, this proposition is open to question as an unwarranted restriction on the powers conferred on the court by sections 425 to 427 of the Companies Act 1985.[109]

16.17 Procedure under section 425 of the Companies Act 1985

A reconstruction can be carried out in pursuance of a compromise or arrangement under section 425, which applies not only as between the company and the creditors or any class of them, but as between the company and the members or any class of them. This section provides that where any compromise or arrangement[110] is proposed between a company[111] and its creditors or any class of them, or between the company and its members or any class of them, the court may, on the application[112] of the company, or any creditor or member of the company, or the liquidator, order a meeting of the creditors or class of creditors, or of the members or class of members, as the case may be, to be called. If at the meeting so ordered a majority in number representing three-quarters in value of the creditors or class of creditors, or members[113] or class of members, present either in person or by proxy, agree to the compromise or arrangement, and it is also sanctioned by the court, it will be binding on all the creditors or the class of creditors, or on the members or class of members, as the case may be, and on the liquidator and the contributories of the company.

An order under the section is of no effect until an office copy has been delivered to the Registrar for registration, and a copy of every order must be annexed to every copy of the memorandum issued after the order has been made, or in the case of a company not having a memorandum, of every copy so issued of the instrument constituting or defining the constitution of the company: section 425 (3).

---

[107] See *Sorsbie v Tea Corp.* [1904] 1 Ch 12 (CA); *Re General Motor Cab Co.* [1913] 1 Ch 377 (CA); *Re Sandwell Park Colliery* [1914] 1 Ch 589; *Re Guardian Assurance Co.* [1917] 1 Ch 431 (CA).

[108] See the judgment of Astbury J in *Re Anglo-Continental Supply Company* [1922] 2 Ch 723. Where there are preference shares and this creates difficulties in making a distribution under section 110 of the Insolvency Act 1986, then a scheme under section 425 of the Companies Act 1985 has been upheld. See the *Tea Corp.* and *Sandwell Park* cases cited in the footnote above.

[109] For a further discussion of this question, see *Gore-Browne on Companies* (Jordans, 44th edn, loose-leaf), 30.7.

[110] This includes a reorganisation of the share capital by the consolidation of shares of different classes or by the division of shares into shares of different classes or by both those methods: section 425 (6).

[111] 'Any company liable to be wound up under the Act': section 425 (6).

[112] *Ex parte* by originating summons under RSC Order 102, rule 5 (England).

[113] As to the approval of members in the case of a company limited by guarantee, see *Re N.F.U. Development Trust Ltd* [1972] 1 WLR 1548. Brightman J held that in such a company each member had in law the identical financial stake in the company. Thus a three-quarters majority of those present and voting satisfied the requirements of section 425 (2).

16.18 The information required by section 426

The Companies Act 1985 imposes certain requirements, by section 426, as to giving information in relation to schemes under section 425. Section 426 provides that where a meeting is convened under section 425 there shall

(1) with every notice summoning the meeting which is sent to a creditor or member, be sent also a statement explaining the effect of the scheme and in particular stating any material interests of the directors of the company, whether as directors or as members or as creditors of the company or otherwise, and the effect thereon of the scheme, in so far as it is different from the effect on the like interests of other persons,[114] and

(2) in every notice summoning the meeting which is given by advertisement, be included either such a statement or a notification of the place at which and the manner in which creditors or members entitled to attend the meeting may obtain copies of the statement.[115]

Where the scheme affects the rights of debenture holders, the statement must give the like explanation as respects the trustees[116] of any deed for securing the issue of the debentures as it is required to give as respects the company's directors.[117]

Where there has been a failure to include an explanatory statement in an advertisement or to indicate where copies might be obtained, the fact that no prejudice is suffered as a result of the omission does not enable the court to dispense with the requirements of section 426. Fresh meetings with proper notice are necessary.[118]

Where the material interests of directors change, after the notices required by section 426 have been sent out, there is, strictly speaking, no requirement under that section for information about this later change to be sent to those who have already received notice under this section. Nevertheless the court will take any change in directors' material interests into account in deciding whether to confirm a scheme under section 425. The court will have to be satisfied that no reasonable shareholder would change his decision on how to act on the scheme if the changes had been disclosed.[119]

The practice is to apply by originating summons for an order to convene the requisite meetings,[120] and if the appropriate majorities are obtained to apply by petition to the court for its sanction to the scheme.

The responsibility for determining what creditors or members are to be summoned to any meeting, as constituting a class, rests upon the applicant. If the meeting is incorrectly convened or constituted, or an objection is taken to the presence of any particular creditors as having interests completing with the others, the objection must be taken on

---

[114] As to what is sufficient disclosure of the interests of the directors see: *Rankin & Blackmore* 1950 SC 218; *Peter Scott* 1950 SC 507; *Coltness Iron Co.* 1951 SLT 344; *City Property Investment Trust Corp. Ltd* 1951 SLT 371.

[115] They are entitled to have a copy free of charge: section 426 (5).

[116] See *Second Scottish Investment Trust Corp. Petitioners* 1962 SLT 392.

[117] As to the sanctions imposed upon the company and officers in default for failure to comply with section 426, see section 426 (6). There is also an obligation on directors and trustees for debenture holders to give the necessary particulars as to their interests: section 426 (2) and (4).

[118] *Scottish Eastern Investment Trust* 1966 SLT 285.

[119] *Re Minster Assets plc* [1985] BCLC 200; *Re Jessel Trust Ltd* [1985] BCLC 119.

[120] A copy of the proposed statement under section 426 should form part of the evidence in support of the summons. This, of course, applies to proceedings in England.

the hearing of the petition for sanction, and the applicant must take the risk of the petition being dismissed.[121]

The classic test of what is a class for the purposes of what is now section 425 was laid down by Bowen LJ in *Sovereign Life Assurance Co. v Dodd*:[122] 'it must be confined to those persons whose rights are not so dissimilar as to make it impossible for them to consult together with a view to their common interest.' In *Re Hellenic & General Trust Ltd*,[123] a majority of the ordinary shares of a company were owned by a wholly owned subsidiary whose holding company sought to acquire all the sub-subsidiary's shares under a section 425 scheme. Templeman J held that there was a sufficient community of interest between the holding and the subsidiary companies so that the latter was to be regarded as being in the purchasers' camp rather than in the vendors'. Consequently there was a sufficient difference of interest from that of the dissenting minority shareholders for two separate class meetings to be required. As in fact only one class meeting had been held for all the ordinary shareholders the scheme under section 425 could not be confirmed. It must be observed that this seems a rather strained interpretation of Bowen LJ's dictum, of which it has been said that the 'emphasis here is on rights, which are not dissimilar, and the rights in question must surely be against the company in respect to the shares or debts in question. Extraneous interests should surely be disregarded'.[124] Moreover, Templeman J's decision does not accord with previous English and Commonwealth decisions that the members of a single class of shares (or debenture holders or unsecured creditors, as the case might be) should, for the purpose of organising meetings, be treated as one class even though there are clear conflicts of interest between them.[125] However, if different amounts are paid on shares, or certain shareholders have paid amounts in advance of calls, this makes various classes of shareholders, and separate meeting must be called.[126]

In sanctioning a scheme the court may ignore the fact that a class has not consented if it be proved that upon an immediate distribution of the assets none would be available for that class.[127] The power of the court to sanction a scheme is a discretionary one, as to which see 16.22, below.

At meetings held in pursuance of section 425 proxies are allowed, and foreign creditors must be taken into account.[128] The treatment of foreign creditors must depend on the terms of the scheme, and the conduct of meetings in this as in other respects is governed entirely by the court's directions. The court may allow the result of proxies to be communicated by telex or cable from distant places.[129] A form of proxy is settled in chambers for use at such meetings; the shareholder signing it cannot, when the company

---

[121] *Practice Note* [1934] WN 142 (England).

[122] [1892] 2 QB 573 at p. 583.

[123] [1976] 1 WLR 123 at pp. 125–6.

[124] This quotation is from a note by J. A. Hornby in 39 MLR 207 at p. 208 (1976).

[125] See *Re Alabama, New Orleans, Texas and Pacific Junction Rly* [1891] 1 Ch 213; *Re Holders Investment Trust Ltd* [1971] 2 All ER 289. See also the Australian and South African cases discussed by Hornby in 39 MLR 207; *Re A. W. Allen Ltd* [1930] VR 251; *Re Chevron (Sydney) Ltd* [1963] VR 249; *Re Jax Marine Pty Ltd* [1967] 1 NSWR 145; *Re Landmark Corp. Ltd* [1968] 1 NSWR 759; *Rosen v Bruyns* 1973 (1) SA 815 (T). This simply means that a scheme under section 426 (or other statutory provisions) will not fail simply for not having separate meetings. The court may still refuse to sanction it on other grounds.

[126] *Re United Provident Assurance Co.* [1930] 2 Ch 477.

[127] *Sorsbie v Tea Corp.* [1904] 1 Ch 12 (CA); *Re Oceanic Steam Navigation Co.* [1939] Ch 41.

[128] *Re Queensland National Bank* [1893] WN 128.

[129] *Re English, Scottish and Australian Bank* [1893] 3 Ch 385 (CA).

is in liquidation, leave the decision to his proxy,[130] but when the company is not in liquidation he may use any proper form of proxy, whether lodged before the meeting or not.[131] Directors who, pursuant to the order of the court, get proxies for or against a scheme are bound to use them.[132] A proxy appointing a person to act for a shareholder at a class meeting and to vote either for or against a scheme of arrangement empowers the holder to vote against a resolution to defer the consideration of the scheme.[133] Meetings of shareholders not convened exactly in accordance with the directions of the court may be held good, if in the result a sufficient number of the shares are accounted for,[134] but it is most advisable to comply strictly with the directions.

If there are debentures to bearer or share warrants, the holders must produce them at the meeting, or otherwise prove their title to be treated as debenture holders before the vote is taken.[135]

16.19 The court's powers under section 427

Section 427 of the Companies Act 1985 confers upon the court certain additional powers which it may exercise on an application under section 427 for the court's sanction for a compromise or arrangement. A common use of these powers enables what is broadly the equivalent of an amalgamation under section 110 of the Insolvency Act 1986 to be carried out under sections 425 to 427.[136] Indeed, for the powers given by section 427 to be employed, it must be shown to the court that the compromise or arrangement has been proposed for the purposes of, or in connection with, a scheme 'for the reconstruction of any company or companies or the amalgamation of any two or more companies'. It must further be shown that under the scheme the whole or any part of the undertaking or the property of any company concerned in the scheme is to be transferred to another company. Section 427 (2) terms the first-named company the 'transferor company' and the second the 'transferee company'. Where these conditions are met, the court may either by the order sanctioning the compromise or arrangement or by any subsequent order make provision in respect of any of the matters which are set out below.

In contrast with an amalgamation under section 110 of the Insolvency Act 1986, a scheme carried out under sections 425 to 427 has the advantage of effectively over-riding[137] the objections of dissenting shareholders and creditors. The problem of preference shareholders' entitlement and the difficulties of the arbitration procedure to settle the claims of dissenting shareholders do not arise. Furthermore, dissenting creditors may not threaten the validity of a scheme by seeking to put the company into compulsory liquidation within one year, as may occur in a transfer of assets under section 110 (6). On the other hand, the procedure under section 425 will inevitably entail court proceedings (in respect of the meeting ordered by the court and its subsequent sanction of the

---

[130] *Re Magadi Soda Co.* [1925] WN 50.

[131] *Re Dorman, Long & Co.* [1934] Ch 635. The judgment in this case contains an exhaustive exposition of the law relating to proxies and will repay careful study.

[132] See footnote 130, above.

[133] *Re Waxed Papers* (1937) 156 LT 452 (CA).

[134] *Re Anglo-Spanish Tartar Refineries* [1942] WN 222.

[135] *Re Wedgwood Coal Co.* (1877) 6 Ch D 627.

[136] As to the relationship between section 110 of the Insolvency Act 1986 and sections 425 to 427 of the Companies Act 1985, see 16.16, above.

[137] The appropriate consents required by section 425, as well as the sanction of the court, having been obtained.

scheme). Under section 110, no application to court may be made unless shareholders or creditors have some ground to challenge the transfer of assets by the liquidator.

The matters as to which the court can make provision under section 427 of the Companies Act 1985 are as follows:

(1) the transfer to the transferee company of the whole or any part of the undertaking and of the property or liabilities of any transferor company;

(2) the allotting or appropriation by the transferee company of any shares, debentures, policies, or other like interests in that company which, under the compromise or arrangement, are to be allotted or appropriated by that company to or for any person;

(3) the continuation by or against any transferee company of any legal proceedings pending by or against any transferor company;

(4) the dissolution, without winding up, of any transferor company;

(5) the provision to be made for any persons who, within such time and in such manner as the court directs, dissent from the compromise or arrangement;

(6) such incidental, consequential, and supplemental matters as are necessary to secure that the reconstruction or amalgamation shall be fully and effectively carried out.

Section 427 (4) states that where an order under the section provides for the transfer of property or liabilities, that property is, by virtue of the order, transferred to and vests in the transferee company, and those liabilities are by virtue of the order, transferred to and become the liabilities of, the transferee company. Any property, if the order so directs, vests freed from any charge which is by virtue of the compromise or arrangement to cease to have effect. The expression 'property' includes property, rights and powers of every description,[138] and the expression 'liabilities' includes duties, but not a duty to serve under a contract of personal service.[139]

The normal procedure under the section is first to obtain an order under section 425 sanctioning the scheme.[140] Then application will be made in chambers under section 427 in accordance with RSC Order 102, rule 7 (2) (*b*), to which the transferee company should be a party.[141]

16.20 The Companies (Mergers and Divisions) Regulations 1987

The Companies (Mergers and Divisions) Regulations 1987[142] implement Council Directive No. 78/855/EEC, which concerns mergers of public limited liability companies, and Council Directive No. 82/891/EEC, which concerns the division of public limited

---

[138] Such property and rights do not include the rights of the transferor company under contracts of service with its employees: *Nokes v Doncaster Amalgamated Collieries* [1940] AC 1014 (HL); and do not include rights to carry forward losses and wear and tear allowances for income-tax purposes: *United Steel Companies v Cullington* [1940] AC 812 (HL). Nor does section 427 (2) extend to the rights, duties or powers of an executor: *Re Skinner (deceased)* [1985] 1 WLR 1043.

[139] Section 427 (6). *Nokes v Doncaster Amalgamated Collieries*, above. Section 427 (5) requires a copy of the court order to be delivered to the Registrar for registration within seven days of the court making the order.

[140] Where the scheme provides for one company assuming the liabilities of another, a meeting of the creditors of the latter is not necessary: *Clydesdale Bank*, 1950 SC 30.

[141] *Practice Note* [1939] WN 121 (England).

[142] SI 1987 No. 1991.

liability companies. Both the mergers and the divisions in question involve the transfer of the undertaking, property and liabilities of public companies ('transferor companies') to other public companies or, in some cases, companies, whether or not public, formed for the purpose of the merger or division ('transferee companies').

The transfer of the undertaking, etc. of the transferor company must be in exchange for shares in the transferee company with or without additional cash payment. In British company law these mergers or divisions take place under sections 425 to 427 of the Companies Act 1985. To comply with the directives, the regulations amend the Act by inserting a new section 427A and a new Schedule 15A. Section 427A provides that, in the case of mergers or divisions within the scope of the regulations, sections 425 to 427 shall have effect subject to the provisions of that section and Schedule 15A. A court may only sanction a compromise or agreement under section 425 if it complies with Schedule 15A.

The main requirements of Schedule 15A[143] are that three-quarters of each class of the shareholders of the transferee companies involved at a meeting agree, and that the draft terms of the merger or division are drawn up by the directors of the companies involved and published by the Registrar of Companies. There is also provision for directors' reports containing special information and the reports of independent experts containing specified information. All these documents and the relevant company accounts must be made available to shareholders.[144]

16.21 Composition with debenture holders and other creditors

Under the powers given by section 425 of the Companies Act 1985, if the requisite majority of debenture holders agree to forgo their security, and accept preference shares in the new company in exchange for their debentures in the old company, their decision, if confirmed by the court, will be binding upon the minority who oppose the exchange,[145] and an agreement whereby a new company agrees to purchase all the assets and pay a composition to the creditors will be enforced, even though a large sum may be subsequently offered by another person.[146] Since the Insolvency Act 1986 came into force it is very likely that a scheme of reconstruction affecting the rights of creditors (secured or otherwise) will have been preceded by the appointment of an administrator under Part II of the 1986 Act. One of the purposes for which an administration order can be made is the sanctioning of a scheme of arrangement under section 425 of the Companies Act 1985.[147]

A company can effect compromises or arrangements with its creditors without going into liquidation, for section 425 applies to companies not in the course of being wound up, as well as to companies which are being wound up. The result is that with the sanction of the court any compromise or arrangement between the company and its creditors, or

[143] See *Gore-Browne on Companies* (Jordans, 44th edn, loose-leaf), appendix to Chapter 30 at pp. 30.039–30.048.

[144] Section 427A and Schedule 15A do not apply where the company in respect of which the compromise or arrangement is made is being wound up. See further, *Gore-Browne on Companies*, 30.11.B and 30.11.C.

[145] *Re Empire Mining Co.* (1890) 44 Ch D 402; *Re Alabama, New Orleans, etc. Rly Co.* [1891] 1 Ch 213 (CA); *Follit v Eddystone Granite Quarries* [1892] 3 Ch 75 at p. 85.

[146] *Re Oriental Bank* [1887] WN 109 at p. 112.

[147] See section 8 (3) (*c*) of the Insolvency Act 1986. As to administration, see Part 3 of Chapter 17. Where there is an estimated deficiency for creditors affected by section 425, subordinated creditors can be excluded from the scheme: *Re British Commonwealth Holdings plc* [1992] BCC 58.

any class of such creditors, may be made binding on all such creditors or class of creditors and the company, provided that it has been submitted to a meeting of the creditors or class of creditors summoned under the direction of the court and approved by a majority in number representing three-quarters in value of such creditors or class of creditors present either in person or by proxy. If the company is in liquidation, the compromise or arrangement may be made binding on the liquidator and contributories, and any compromise or arrangement between the company and its members, or any class of its members, may equally be made binding.

In the case of the reconstruction of a company, if the creditors of the old company are to be paid in full at once, their consent need not be asked to a reconstruction; but if they are to accept a composition, or to take shares or debentures in the new company in satisfaction of their claims, or to accept deferred payment, their consent must be obtained to a scheme of composition.

16.22 The rights of dissenting shareholders and creditors

The sanction of the court to the scheme is essential,[148] and in determining whether such sanction should be given, the duties of the court are twofold: first, to see that the resolutions are passed by the statutory majority, and secondly, to see whether the proposal is such that an intelligent and honest man, a member of the class concerned and acting in respect of his interest, might reasonably approve.[149] But though shareholders acting honestly are usually much better judges of what is to their commercial advantage than the court can be, this proposition is of little value when it is proved that the majority of a class have voted or may have voted in the way they did because of their interests as shareholders of another class.[150]

A scheme will not be sanctioned if the terms of the scheme are such that it does not qualify as a 'compromise or arrangement' between the company and its members within section 425. These words 'compromise' and 'arrangement' imply some element of accommodation on each side and are not apt to describe a total surrender of the rights of one side. Where in a scheme concerning a guarantee company the rights of members were being expropriated without any compensating advantage, such a scheme was held by Brightman J not to be capable of being sanctioned under section 425: 'The word "compromise" implies some element of accommodation on each side. It is not apt to describe total surrender. A claimant who abandons his claim is not compromising it. Similarly, I think the word "arrangement" in this section implies some element of give and take. Confiscation is not my idea of arrangement.'[151] Brightman J also found that the scheme was unreasonable, that is one which 'properly examined, no member voting in the interests of members as a whole could reasonably approve'.[152]

---

[148] After the resolutions approving the scheme have been passed, in meetings summoned by the court under section 425, the company presents a petition to the court for its sanction under RSC Order 102, rule 5 (1) (*h*). The petition need not state that the company is carrying on business: *Re Great Universal Stores Ltd* [1960] 1 WLR 78. The procedure differs in detail in Scotland.

[149] *Re Alabama, New Orleans, etc., Rly Co.* [1891] 1 Ch 213 (CA); *Re English, Scottish & Australian Chartered Bank* [1893] 3 Ch 385 (CA); *Re Dorman, Long & Co.* [1934] Ch 635; *Re National Bank* [1966] 1 WLR 819.

[150] *Carruth v Imperial Chemical Industries* [1937] AC 707, at p. 769 *per* Lord Maugham (HL); *Re National Bank*, above. See *In re Holders Investment Trust Ltd* [1971] 1 WLR 583.

[151] *Re N.F.U. Development Trust Ltd* [1972] 1 WLR 1548 at p. 1555. The dictum of Bowen LJ in *Re Alabama, etc. Rly Co.* [1891] 1 Ch 213 at p. 243 was applied.

[152] ibid.

It has nevertheless been held, in *Re Savoy Hotel Ltd*,[153] that a scheme is an 'arrangement' between the company and its members (for the purposes of section 425) even though the applicant (which was not the company) sought to acquire all the company's A and B shares[154] (other than those already held) in exchange for shares in the applicant or cash sums. As a matter of jurisdiction this 'arrangement' was within section 425 since the scheme would affect the contractual relationship between the company and its members by requiring the company to register the applicant in the place of the existing share-holders as the holders of the company's shares. Nevertheless, Nourse J held[155] that the court had no power to sanction the scheme since the company itself had not given its consent to the scheme through a decision either of its board or of the company in general meeting. The judge's reasoning turns largely on the legislative history of section 425 and a slender line of judicial dicta. The application before Nourse J was for the summoning of separate meetings of the A and the B shareholders.[156] He refused to exercise his discretion to order such meetings where the much greater number of A shareholders could override the advantage that weighted voting would normally give to the B shareholders. The reason given was that this would circumvent the essential requirement of the company's consent. A sounder basis for the decision might have been that the court had no power to circumvent the special voting rights attached to the B shares. It should still have been possible, following earlier authority,[157] to hold separate meetings for the two different classes of shares. The scheme, however, could only effect a transfer of that class of shares which at its own meeting gave the degree of consent required by section 425. Admittedly this would still have had the effect of defeating the object of the scheme proposed by the applicant.

It has been held[158] that it is not a valid objection to a scheme under section 425 that its aim in essence was a purchase by an outsider of all the issued shares of the company, and that this was attempting to do under sections 425 to 427 what should have required approval by 90 per cent of the shareholders under Part XIII A of the Companies Act 1985 (as to which see 16.23, below). The latter gives dissenting shareholders the right to be bought out. Plowman J refused to accept that what was then section 209 of the 1948 Act thus limited the court's jurisdiction under what is now section 425: 'In the first place, it seems to me to involve imposing a limitation or qualification either on the generality of the word "arrangement" under section 206 [section 425 of the 1985 Act] or else on the discretion of the court under that section. The legislature has not seen fit to impose such a limitation on terms and I see no reason for implying any.'[159] Plowman J maintained that these two statutory methods of amalgamation involved different considerations and

---

[153] [1981] 3 All ER 646.

[154] The holders of the A shares owned approximately 97 per cent of the company's total equity, but only 51 per cent of the votes. The holders of the B shares owned only 2.3 per cent of the equity but were entitled to 48 per cent of the votes. Moreover, 65 per cent of the B shares (carrying 31 per cent of the votes) were owned, either beneficially or as trustee, by the company's board.

[155] [1981] 3 All ER 646.

[156] Note that his decision as to the sanction of the court was not as to the merits of the scheme (since these had not yet been submitted to the meetings of shareholders affected or voted upon). Instead, in refusing to order any meetings, he held that as a matter of law the scheme was incapable of sanction by the court.

[157] As to the practice in holding meetings where different classes of shares are concerned, see 16.17, above.

[158] *Re National Bank* [1966] 1 WLR 819.

[159] ibid. at p. 829. In *Re Hellenic and General Trust* [1976] 1 WLR 123 at pp. 127–9, Templeman J reached a different conclusion while attempting to distinguish *National Bank* on its facts. For a critique of the decision in *Hellenic*, see *Gore-Browne on Companies* (Jordans, 44th edn, loose-leaf), 30.26.

approaches to reconstructions. Under Part XIII A the scheme need never come to court unless the minority bring it. If they do, they have the burden of demonstrating unfairness. In this respect there is good reason for requiring a small majority.

If the resolution has been passed by the statutory majority, but members of the class sufficient to have prevented the obtaining of the statutory majority appear on the hearing of the petition and oppose it, such opposition will be ignored if the change of mind was induced by a misleading circular: *quaere* whether a change of mind not so induced would be regarded.[160]

16.23 Compulsory acquisition of shares under Part XIII A of the Companies Act 1985

Part XIII A[161] amended the law on compulsory acquisition of shares. It substituted nine new sections for three sections (428 to 430) in the Companies Act 1985. The reform of these provisions had been long delayed, having originally been proposed by the Jenkins Committee[162] in 1962. The new restatement on Part XIII A is almost entirely based on a memorandum by the Law Society's Standing Committee on Company Law.[163]

One of the more obvious flaws in the old legislation was that, on a literal interpretation, it allowed class rights to be overridden where an offeror obtained a nine-tenths level of acceptances from the shareholders of a company as a whole, even though the terms of the offer might be much more attractive to one class than to another. Such behaviour would of course have been a breach of the Code on Takeovers and Mergers. It will be seen that section 429 prevents this happening. Even now, however, there is no definition of a 'class of shares' for the purposes of Part XIII A. Its meaning is simply assumed. What is meant by a 'class of shares' or a 'class right' has never been entirely clear since it is not defined in the Companies Act 1985 and, until fairly recently, this has been true of the case law. The decision in *Cumbrian Newspaper Group Ltd v Cumberland and Westmorland Herald Newspaper and Printing Co.*[164] makes the matter more complex than earlier commentators had thought.[165] Scott J held that rights given to certain individual shareholders (e.g. to nominate a director to the board or a right of pre-emption over the company's shares) are to be regarded as class rights and are therefore protected by the class rights protection provisions of the Companies Act 1985,[166] even if the rights are given to individuals and do not attach to any particular shares. Nevertheless, a distinction may have to be drawn, so far as Part XIII A is concerned, since it refers to 'a class of shares' and not to 'class rights' or 'rights attached to any class of shares'. The term 'a class of shares' accords better with the more traditional concepts of class rights. This requires a distinct class, or classes, of shares to be differentiated from each other by distinctive rights attaching to a particular type of share. These rights usually relate to voting, dividend or capital rights but, so long as they are attached to identifiable shares, could include particular rights of another kind.

160 *Re Waxed Papers* (1937) 156 LT 452. Compare *Re National Bank* [1966] 1 WLR 819, where the non-disclosure of the bank's accounts was held entirely proper under the law applicable to banks at that time.

161 Inserted by Schedule 12 to the Financial Services Act 1986.

162 Cmnd 1762, para, 294.

163 November 1984. This was given the approval of the Law Reform Committee of the Senate of the Inns of Courts and the Bar. See Milman 6 Co. Law 129 (1985).

164 [1986] 3 WLR 26.

165 See Polack [1986] CLJ 399, and the criticisms in 7.7.1, above.

166 i.e. sections 125 and 127.

This concept of 'class of shares' would seem much more appropriate to the purpose and scope of Part XIII A of the Companies Act 1985.

It will be seen that a number of features in Part XIII A are better adapted than the old law to contemporary takeover practice (e.g. in giving a choice of consideration to the offeree). The solutions adopted tend to imitate those of the Code on Takovers and Mergers.

16.24 The power of compulsory acquisition

Section 428 of the Companies Act 1985 provides the defined meaning for the purposes of Part XIII A of a number of terms used in sections 429 to 430E. The most important of these terms is that of 'takeover offer' in section 428 (1). It is only takeover offers coming within this definition which will confer on the offeror the power of compulsory acquisition of a dissenter's shareholdings conferred by sections 429 and 430.[167] For the purposes of these provisions, then, a 'takeover offer' means an offer to acquire all the shares, or all the shares of any class or classes in a company, *other than* those which at the date of the offer are already held by the offeror.[168] It is further required that it is an offer on terms which are the same in relation to all the shares to which the offer relates or, where those shares include shares of different classes, in relation to all the shares[169] of each class. Where the 'bidder' invites offers with the intention of accepting them, this does not amount to a 'takeover offer' as defined by section 428 (1).[170]

The powers conferred by section 429 distinguish between two types of takeover offer. This is indicated by the definition in section 428 (1), which refers to an offer to acquire all the shares, *or* all the shares of a particular class or classes. Section 429 (1) deals with 'a case in which a takeover offer does not relate to shares of different classes'. In that case, if the offeror has, by virtue of acceptances of the offer, acquired or contracted to acquire not less than nine-tenths in value of the shares to which the offer relates, he may give a section 430 notice leading to compulsory acquisition of those shares that he had not acquired. In the case of a takeover offer which relates to shares of different classes, he must obtain (by virtue of acceptance of the offer, etc.) nine-tenths in value of the shares of any class of shares to which the offer relates.[171] Thus, if the offeror wishes to acquire all the shares in a company with several classes of shares, it must achieve the appropriate level of acceptance *vis-à-vis* each class. It can, of course, use the powers conferred by sections 429 and 430 in the case of any class of shares where it does achieve that level of acceptances.

Section 429 (3) imposes a four-month 'deadline' as the maximum period from the date of the offer allowed for acceptances after which notices starting the process of compulsory

---

[167] This is equally true of a minority shareholder's right to be bought out by the offeror under sections 430A and 430B. These provisions are discussed at 16.26, below. This definition excludes the possibility of 'partial bids' that a loose interpretation of the earlier section arguably allowed.

[168] Substantial consideration rather than 'technical consideration' or a contract under seal. See section 428 (5).

[169] 'Shares' primarily means shares which have been allotted on the day of the offer. However, a takeover offer may include among the shares to which it relates all or any of the shares that are subsequently allotted before a date specified in, or determined in accordance with, the terms of the offer: section 428 (2). The terms offered in relation to shares must be the same in relation to all the shares, or, as the case may be, all the shares to which the class relates: section 428 (3). A limited variation is allowed to meet the requirements of foreign law: section 428 (4).

[170] *Re Chez Nico (Restaurants) Ltd* [1992] BCLC 192 of pp. 203–4.

[171] Section 429 (2).

acquisition cannot be given.[172] It is also provided that no such notice may be given after the end of the period of two months beginning with the date on which the offeror has acquired, or contracted to acquire, shares that satisfy the nine-tenths minimum. Practice in making takeover offers, and the need to comply with the Code on Takeovers and Mergers, are likely to keep the exercise of these powers well within the statutory periods allowed for.

Subject to certain safeguards, section 429 allows an offeror to acquire shares during the offer period *otherwise* than under the offer. Clearly there is a need to protect those who have sold their shares under the offer. Section 429 (8) makes sure that the 'side purchases' permitted do not give those who have sold to the offeror (other than by acceptance of the terms of the offer) a better bargain. It, first of all, permits such purchases where the 'acquisition consideration'[173] does not exceed the value of the consideration specified in the terms of the offer. Alternatively, such purchases are permitted if the terms of the offer are subsequently revised so that, when the revision is announced, the value of the 'acquisition consideration' at the time of acquisition (or a contract to acquire) no longer exceeds the value of the consideration specified in those terms. If either of these conditions is met, the shares so purchased 'count' towards the nine-tenths level of acceptances required by section 429 (1) and (2). If not, they are of course excluded from this calculation.

Section 430D allows joint offers to be made 'by two or more persons'.[174] So far as they acquire, or contract to acquire, the necessary shares under the takeover offer, the offerors do so jointly. However, so far as they acquire shares apart from the offer (i.e. within the limits allowed by section 429 (8)), they may do so jointly or separately.[175] Section 430E makes special provision for the acquisition of shares by the 'associates' of the offeror. (This elaborately defined term is discussed later.) It was seen that for the purposes of sections 429 and 430, a takeover offer must extend to all the shares, or all the shares of any class or classes in a company. For this purpose, however, shares held or contracted for by associates of the offeror are not to be counted. Thus the offeror must obtain nine-tenths acceptances from the remainder of the shares (or class of shares as the case may be) without counting on shares acquired (or contracted for) by the offeror's associates to make up the required level of acceptances.[176] This applies to acquisitions at the time when the offer is made as well as shares obtained subsequently. An exception is made for shares acquired during the offer period by associates of the offeror which satisfy the same

---

[172] As to the formal requirements for the offeror giving a section 429 notice, see section 429 (4) to (5). Criminal sanctions are provided for failing to send a copy to the company: section 429 (6) and (7). Section 429 (4) requires the statutory declaration at or about the same time as the first section 429 notice is served. In *Re Chez Nico (Restaurants) Ltd* [1992] BCLC 192 at p. 205, this provision was held to be directory and not mandatory and was not intended to nullify the whole procedure. On the facts, the failure to comply with the procedure for fourteen days would not affect the right to acquire the shares. Section 429 (5) does not require that the section 429 notice be signed personally. It may be signed by an authorised agent such as a solicitor: ibid.

[173] This is defined as the valuable consideration for which they were acquired or contracted to be acquired. See section 429 (8) (*a*).

[174] Although the definition of the 'offeror' in section 428 (8) refers to the 'person making a takeover offer', it is clear from section 430E (8) that an offeror may be an individual. In practice offerors, whether single or joint, are likely to be registered companies.

[175] Section 430D (2). See sections 430D (3) and (7) for the consequential changes made to the other provisions in Part XIII A in the case of joint offerors.

[176] Section 430E (1).

conditions[177] that must be satisfied by an offeror acquiring shares otherwise than by acceptance of the takeover offer.

The term 'associates'[178] is widely defined[179] to include nominees of the offeror, companies in the same group as the offeror,[180] and bodies corporate in which the offeror is substantially interested.[181] It also includes any person[182] who is a party to an agreement with the offeror for the acquisition of shares, or in an interest in shares. This must amount to an 'acquisition agreement' within section 204 of the Companies Act 1985.[183] Where an offeror is an individual, his 'associates' include his or her spouse and any minor child or stepchild.[184]

The powers of compulsory acquisition conferred by Part XIII A apply to shares of any kind, but obviously not to debentures. However, convertible securities are to be treated as shares in the company if they are convertible into shares or rights to subscribe for shares.[185] It is possible for the terms of a takeover offer to make provision for their revision and for acceptances on the previous terms to be treated as acceptances on the revised terms. Section 428 (7) provides that for the purposes of Part XIII A the revision of such terms is not to be regarded as the making of a fresh offer. The date of the offer remains the date on which the original offer was made.

16.25 The 'price' payable to those whose shares are compulsorily acquired

Once a valid notice under section 429 of the Companies Act 1985 is given to those whose shares the offeror is entitled to acquire, the offeror then becomes both entitled and bound to acquire those shares on the terms of the offer. One of the improvements in the new Part XIII A is that it deals with the situation where the terms of the original offer gave those who accepted its terms a *choice* of consideration. Here any notice under section 429 must give particulars of the choice. The holder of the shares to be acquired must be given six weeks to make his choice in a formal written communication. The notice must also provide for the eventuality of the holder failing to make a choice. It must specify which consideration will apply in that event.[186] The fact that the terms of the original offer set a time-limit or other conditions as to the choice of consideration to be made by shareholders accepting the offer will not prevent those whose shares are to be compulsorily acquired under section 429 from still retaining that choice.[187] Special provision is made for the situation where a non-cash consideration is chosen by the holder of the shares and the offeror is no longer able to provide it. Here the consideration shall be taken to consist

---

[177] i.e. in section 429 (8) (*a*) and (*b*). See section 430E (2). See above.

[178] This is a term used in the Code on Takeovers and Mergers where it is likewise widely defined.

[179] See section 430E (4) to (8).

[180] See section 430E (5).

[181] Section 430E (6). Two criteria are used: the company or its directors are accustomed to act in accordance with the offeror's directions or the offeror has one-third or more of the voting power at general meetings.

[182] Or a nominee of such a person.

[183] See 10.9.6, above. See Section 430E (7) as modifying section 204 (5) and (6).

[184] Section 430E (8).

[185] See section 430F. As to how such securities should be treated in respect of the class share to which they belong, see section 430F (2).

[186] Section 430 (3).

[187] Section 430 (4).

of an amount of cash payable by the offeror which at the date of the notice is equivalent to the chosen consideration.[188]

Six weeks from the end of the section 429 notice the offeror must begin to complete the process of compulsory acquisition by sending a copy notice to the company, and must pay or transfer to the company the consideration for the shares to which the offer relates. This must (in the case of registered shares) be accompanied by an instrument of transfer executed on behalf of the shareholder by someone appointed by the offeror. On the receipt of this the company must register the offeror as holder.[189] Any sums received by the company in this process are to be held in trust for those whose shares have been acquired.[190]

16.26 The right of minority shareholders to be bought out

Where an offeror, whether in a bid for all the shares of a company or in a bid for a class or classes, has obtained acceptance of the offer (whether by acquisition or contract to acquire) by nine-tenths of the shareholders (or those of the class or classes concerned), then those who have not been acquired may demand to be bought out.[191] The shares already held (i.e. acquired or contracted to be acquired) by the offeror 'count' towards the nine-tenths level of acceptance required to 'trigger' the dissenting shareholder's right to be bought out. It was seen that these shares do not 'count' in order to 'trigger' the offeror's right compulsorily to acquire the shares.[192]

Once a dissenting shareholder has exercised his rights, the offeror is entitled and bound to acquire the dissenter's shares 'on the terms of the offer or on such terms as may be agreed'.[193] Where the takeover offer gave a choice of consideration to those who accepted its terms, this choice is preserved for dissenting shareholders who exercise their rights to be bought out.[194] If the parties cannot agree on the terms of the offer, then either side may apply to the court. The terms may then be 'such as the court thinks fit'.[195] Unlike the equivalent jurisdiction where the offeror compulsorily acquires shares, there is no guidance from reported judicial decisions. It may be noted, however, that the court here has no power to prevent the shareholder having his shares bought. It can only change the terms. It would appear that there has been very little need for this form of relief, but together with the right to be bought it forms a useful protection when minority shareholders are 'locked into' a company under the overwhelming control of the offeror.

---

[188] Section 430 (4). This solution also applies where the consideration was to be provided by a third party who is no longer bound or able to provide it (e.g. a put option from a merchant bank). This in effect legislates the decision in *Re Carlton Holdings* [1971] 1 WLR 918.

[189] Section 430 (5) and (6). As to bearer shares and shares to be allotted, see section 430 (7) and (8).

[190] Section 430 (9). Provision is made as to appropriate banking of such sums, and as to what enquiries and other steps must be taken where those entitled cannot be traced. See section 430 (10) to (15).

[191] Section 430A (1) and (2). As to the notice of the rights to buy which an offeror must give the dissenters, the time allowed for the exercise of their rights and the sanctions for failure by the offeror to comply, see section 430A (3), (4), (6) and (7).

[192] Where the offeror can and does exercise his rights to acquire the shares of those who have not accepted the offer, they cannot exercise the right to be bought out: section 430A (5).

[193] Section 430B (2).

[194] Section 430B (3). Similar provision is made as in the case of an offeror compulsorily acquiring shares where the consideration is not in cash and the offeror is no longer able to provide it, etc. See section 430B (4).

[195] Section 430C (3).

16.27 Applications to the court by dissenting shareholders

As in earlier legislation which Part XIII A of the Companies Act 1985 replaces, there is a provision for dissenting shareholders who are not happy to have their shares compulsorily acquired, or at least with the terms on which this is being done, to apply to court. This application must be made within six weeks of when the notice to acquire the shares (under section 429) is given.[196]

The court may be asked to do two things. It may order that the offeror shall not be entitled and bound to acquire the shares. This is the same power as existed under the earlier legislation.[197] Thus the case-law in respect of application under this earlier legislation may still be relied upon.[198] It is thus explored in the pages that follow. Section 430C (1) also allows the court to 'specify terms of acquisition different from those of the offer'. This allows the court more flexibility in meeting the claims of the applicant. It may encourage more judicial intervention than is evidenced by the reported cases. However, the same factors that have made Chancery Division an awkward forum in which to examine the true merits of a takeover bid will still apply. These include judicial reliance on the nine-tenths level of acceptance as indicating that sound commercial judgment must be behind the decision of such a large majority. There is also the difficulty for dissenting shareholders in matching the means, access to expert advice, and internal corporate information that the offeror will have at its command. Nevertheless, the necessity for a public hearing where dissenters apply to the court will place some restraint upon those who frame the terms on which a successful takeover offer is made. Where this has not been contested by the offeree company (or another bidder), this may be all the more necessary.

There are two other new provisions in section 430C which may prove useful. The court has always tended to encourage applicants by the award of costs even when their application fails. Section 430C (4) now enjoins this as a general rule, unless the application has been unnecessary or vexatious, or there is unreasonable delay or other misconduct in the prosecution of the application. The Court of Appeal has considered the meaning of 'vexatious' in section 430C (4). In allowing an appeal against the judge's decision that an application under section 430C (1) was vexatious the court[199] found that there were sufficient grounds[200] for it to consider the fairness of the offer. This meant that the application was not so obviously unsustainable or impossible of success as to amount to an abuse of the process of the court. There is also a new power for the court to deal with the problems of 'untraceable shareholders'.[201] Where the offer needs additional acceptance to make up the nine-tenths level required, the court may make an order authorising that such untraced shareholdings be treated as acceptances. The section contains obvious safeguards to prevent abuse. Thus reasonable enquiry must have been made to trace the shareholders, and the consideration must be shown to be fair and reasonable. This imposes a tougher and more objective standard than the courts usually apply in appli-

---

[196] Section 430C (1). If an application to court is pending, the power to acquire is suspended: section 430C (2).

[197] See section 428 (4) in the original provisions of the Companies Act 1985.

[198] That will not of course be true of decisions upon the 'procedural' aspects of Part XII A, in so far as changes have been made.

[199] *Re Britoil plc* [1990] BCC 70.

[200] The offeree board's original defence document put a value on the shares 40 per cent above the offer. The later recommendation of the offer by the board did not come to the applicant's attention.

[201] Section 430C (5).

cations under this section. There is, finally, an overriding requirement that the court must conclude that such an order is just and equitable, having regard in particular to the number of shareholders who *have* been traced but who have not accepted the offer.

It is well established that there rests upon dissenting shareholders a heavy onus of proof if they are to show that a scheme which holders of 90 per cent of the shares have accepted, is unfair. In *Re Sussex Brick Co*,[202] Vaisey J observed that it was not sufficient for the applicant to set out in his affidavit certain criticisms which undoubtedly show that a good case could be made 'for the formulation of a better scheme, of a fairer scheme, of a scheme which would have been more attractive to the shareholder, if they could have understood the implications of the criticisms'. The courts are clearly influenced by the high proportion of shareholders who must assent to a scheme under what is now section 430C. Vaisey J, in *Re Sussex Brick Co.*, said that it was difficult to 'predicate unfairness' where the good faith of the transferee company is not challenged and there is no case of any intentional misleading of the offeree shareholders. A dissenter under section 430C is faced with the very difficult task of showing that 'he, being the only man out of step in the regiment, is the only man whose views should prevail'. These principles were followed by Plowman J in *Re Grierson, Oldham & Adams Ltd*,[203] where the fact that holders of 99 per cent of the shares had approved the scheme, and that the price offered was slightly above the market price,[204] was held to indicate that there was no unfairness. In estimating whether a 'fair value' is being paid for the shares, the market price is a good indication of such value. The real value of the transferor company and its assets to the transferee company is not as a rule to be taken into account.[205] The new power in section 430C (1) enabling the court to specify different terms of acquisition may now encourage more judicial scrutiny.

Where the Part XIII A procedure was misused to expropriate a minority shareholder in a small private company, the Court of Appeal allowed his application.[206] There two shareholders who already held 90 per cent of the shares set up a company as a vehicle through which to compulsorily acquire the shares of the remaining shareholder. However, it does not follow that the approving shareholders must always be wholly independent of the transferee company. This is merely a factor to be taken into account by the court in exercising its discretion, the weight to be given to it depending on the circumstances of the case.[207]

It has recently been held that the court will be much more inclined to exercise its jurisdiction under section 430C where the bidder is *not* an outsider, but a director and shareholder in the target company and it is shown that the information made available to dissenting shareholders falls far short of what should have been provided. In *Re Chez Nico (Restaurants) Ltd*,[208] Browne-Wilkinson VC supported this statement of principle by adverting to various disclosure provisions in the City Code on Takeovers and Mergers

---

[202] [1961] Ch 289n following *Re Hoare & Company* [1933] 150 LT 374; *Re Evertite Locknuts* [1945] Ch 220; *Re Press Caps Ltd* [1949] Ch 434 (CA).

[203] [1968] Ch 17.

[204] See also *Re Sussex Brick Co.* [1961] Ch 289n.

[205] *Re Press Caps Ltd* [1949] Ch 434 (CA); *Re Grierson, Oldham & Adams Ltd* [1968] Ch 17.

[206] *Re Bugle Press Ltd* [1961] Ch 270 (CA).

[207] See *Sammel v President Brand G. M. Co.* (1969) (3) SA 629, at pp. 677–691.

[208] [1992] BCLC 192 at pp. 206–12.

which had not been complied with.[209] There had also been a failure to comply with the restrictions on advertising contained in section 57 of the Financial Services Act 1986.[210]

Under the Part XIII A procedure there is no provision (equivalent to section 426 in a scheme under sections 425 to 427) requiring information to be given to the shareholders to whom the offer is made. It would appear that the lack of full disclosure will not necessarily amount to unfairness.[211] In *Gething v Kilner*,[212] however, Brightman J accepted that the directors of an offeree company owe a duty towards their own shareholders which 'clearly includes a duty to be honest and a duty not to mislead'. Any minority shareholder in an offeree company could properly complain if they were being wrongfully subjected to the power of compulsory purchase, conferred by section 429 on the offeror company, as a result of a breach of the above-mentioned duty by the board of the offeree company in recommending the offer. The minority shareholders would have to show bad faith or conduct so unreasonable as to amount to bad faith.

---

[209] ibid. at p. 209. The court indicated that the liability considered in *Coleman v Myers* [1977] 2 NZLR 225 might also have applied; as to this, see 14.3, above.

[210] ibid. at pp. 210–11.

[211] *Re Evertite Locknuts* [1945] Ch 220; Roxburgh J in *Re Press Caps* [1948] 2 All ER 638 held that an order for discovery will not be made on an application by originating summons under what is now section 430C in the absence of special circumstances. But see *Coni v Robertson* [1969] 1 WLR 1007. This latter decision was followed in *Re Lifecare International plc* (1990) BCLC 227 on the basis that the position applicable at the time of *Re Press Caps* has been changed by what is now RSC Order 24, rules 3 and 8. In *Lifecare* the discovery sought related to the professional advice given to the board of the offeree company. It did not call for 'an extensive investigation of the company's affairs'. Cross-examination was also allowed on the expert evidence submitted by affidavit.

[212] [1972] 1 WLR 337.

17 Corporate Reconstruction and Insolvency

PART 1: GENERAL

17.1 Introduction

There are a number of options for a company which is experiencing serious financial difficulties. The first is to continue to trade despite the underlying difficulties, in the hope that the crisis will prove to be temporary and capable of being quickly resolved. This may only be possible for so long as the company is able to pay its debts as they fall due or, to the extent that it is not, the creditors are prepared to tolerate late payment. If the financial difficulties are more serious, the company may try to come to some formal arrangement with its creditors regarding the repayment of its debts but, for a company with a large number of creditors, reaching agreement with all of them may not be practicable. There are now a number of statutory procedures which a company can invoke to bind all of its creditors to a voluntary arrangement which has been agreed with some of them. Schemes of arrangement under section 425 of the Companies Act 1985, which require the approval of the court, are considered in 16.17 to 16.22 above. The other main procedure is the voluntary arrangement scheme contained in the Insolvency Act 1986.

The Insolvency Act 1986, together with the Insolvency Rules 1986,[1] also governs administration and liquidation. Administration and liquidation are similar procedures, to the extent that they both involve the appointment of a qualified insolvency practitioner to a company and the displacement of the company's existing board of directors from their management function. A company can resolve to go into liquidation (or to be wound up, liquidation and winding-up being synonymous terms) or can be forced compulsorily into liquidation by order of the court. Commonly, although not necessarily, it would be creditors of the company who would seek a winding-up order. An administrator can only be appointed by order of the court. The persons who can apply for an administration order include the company itself, and also its creditors.

Where liquidation and administration differ most significantly is in their intended purpose. Liquidation of a company involves the cessation of its business, the realisation of its assets, the payment of its debts and liabilities, and the distribution of any remaining assets to the members of the company. At the end of a liquidation, a company is wound up and ceases to exist. Administration, in contrast, is designed primarily as a rescue procedure aimed at facilitating the survival of the company's business either in whole or in part; but, if that is not possible, the administration process is also available to secure a more advantageous realisation of the company's assets than would be possible on a winding-up; and administration can also be used to bolster a voluntary arrangement between a company and its creditors.

---

[1] SI 1986 No. 1925. References in this chapter to 'rules' are to the Insolvency Rules 1986 unless otherwise indicated. The Insolvency Rules apply to compulsory liquidations and, with some modifications and limitations, to creditors' voluntary liquidations. They have only limited application to members' voluntary liquidations.

The administration procedure was first introduced by the 1980s insolvency legislation[2] and its enactment resulted largely from recommendations made by a committee under the chairmanship of Sir Kenneth Cork. The Cork Committee was appointed by the Department of Trade and Industry in 1977 to review insolvency law and practice and, in its report,[3] the Committee identified the absence of a statutory procedure to assist ailing but basically sound companies as one of the key deficiencies of insolvency law at that time.

The Insolvency Act 1986 also regulates some aspects of the receivership process. Receivers are persons appointed by secured creditors in order to realise their security. Under the Act a distinction is drawn between 'administrative receivers' and other receivers. Administrative receivers are, broadly, receivers appointed under floating charges on the whole or substantially the whole of the chargor company's property. The role of administrative receivers is considerably more important than that of other types of receiver. Since it is a remedy for secured creditors, receivership is considered in Chapter 9 but certain aspects of the procedure which are regulated by the Insolvency Act are mentioned in this chapter.

Insolvency law is a subject in its own right and it is not appropriate in a company-law textbook to attempt to provide much more than an overview of the various insolvency procedures and the ways in which they are regulated by the insolvency legislation. Specific aspects of insolvency law, in particular, the manner in which transactions entered into in the twilight period of the company's solvency are liable to be held void or set aside, merit closer examination.

17.2 The definition of insolvency

There are two principal tests of insolvency: a company is insolvent if it is unable to pay its debts as they fall due ('cash flow' insolvency); it is also insolvent if its liabilities exceed its assets ('balance sheet' insolvency). Under the Insolvency Act 1986,[4] a company may be compulsorily wound up where the court is satisfied that it is insolvent in either of these senses; where it is demonstrated that a company is or is likely to become insolvent in either of these senses, this may also lead to the appointment of an administrator.[5]

Failure to pay a debt which is due and not disputed amounts to evidence of cash flow insolvency.[6] Thus a company which has a policy of late payment of bills could find itself

---

[2] The reforms were first enacted in the Insolvency Act 1985. This was replaced by the Insolvency Act 1986, which consolidated the earlier Insolvency Act and also certain other provisions (including some in the Companies Act 1985) relevant to insolvency. The principal factors underlying the legislative reforms and consolidation of insolvency law in 1985 and 1986 are discussed in Fletcher, 'The Genesis of Modern Insolvency Law – An Odyssey of Law Reform', [1989] JBL 365.

[3] *Insolvency Law and Practice*, (1982), Cmnd. 8558.

[4] Sections 122 and 123.

[5] Section 8; other conditions must also be satisfied in order for an administrator to be appointed: see para. 17.14 below.

[6] *Taylor's Industrial Flooring Ltd v M&H Industrial Flooring Ltd* [1990] BCLC 216, [1990] BCC 44 (where the Court of Appeal held that an order could be granted even though the petitioner had not previously served a statutory demand); *Cornhill Insurance plc v Improvement Services Ltd* [1986] 1 WLR 114, (1986) 2 BCC 98, 942; *Re a Company* (No. 006273 of 1992) [1992] BCC 794 (presentation of winding-up petition not restrained despite company's cross-claim for a larger amount). At the hearing of a petition where a genuine cross-claim is raised by the company, the court has a discretion whether to dismiss the petition or make a winding-up order: *Re Portman Provincial Cinemas Ltd* (1964) 108 SJ 581; *Re LHF Wools Ltd* [1970] Ch 27; *Re FSA Business Software Ltd* [1990] BCC 465; *Re Leasing and Finance Services Ltd* [1991] BCLC 29, [1991] BCC 29.

the subject of a petition for a winding-up or administration order. Such a petition will not be struck out at an early stage as a form of improper pressure and an abuse of the process of the court, because, as Staughton LJ explained in *Taylor's Industrial Flooring*,[7] creditors, not late payers, are more worthy of insolvency law's protection:

> Many people today seem to think that they are lawfully entitled to delay paying their debts when they fall due or beyond the agreed period of credit, if there is one ... This can cause great hardship to honest traders, particularly those engaged in small businesses recently started. Anything which the law can do to discourage such behaviour in my view should be done.

The position is different if there is a bona fide dispute about a debt. A petition based on a disputed debt may be struck out as an abuse of process.[8]

Balance sheet insolvency for the purpose of winding-up or administration petitions is defined as an excess of liabilities over assets, and contingent and prospective liabilities must be taken into account in the assessment. Prospective liabilities include an obligation to repay a loan in a year's time.[9] Contingent liabilities are distinguishable from prospective liabilities in that a prospective liability is a binding liability which has not yet matured, whilst a contingent liability is a liability which may never mature because it is dependent on an event which may or may not occur.[10] An example of a contingent liability is the liability of a guarantor under a guarantee.

Prospective and contingent liabilities must be 'taken into account' in determining whether there is balance sheet insolvency. In *Re a Company (No. 006794 of 1983)*[11] it was held that taking into account contingent liabilities does not mean simply adding up the principal amount of those liabilities and deducting the total from the assets, but rather involves considering whether, and if so when, they are likely to become present liabilities. An examination of the likelihood of contingent liabilities becoming present liabilities also takes place when liabilities are admitted for proof in a winding-up and, at that stage, contingent liabilities may be discounted to reflect the fact that they are uncertain. The Insolvency Act 1986 does not specify how contingent liabilities (and indeed prospective liabilities which are not yet certain in amount) are to be valued for the purpose of the balance sheet insolvency test but, presumably, some guidance would be had from the practice of admission of such liabilities for proof on winding-up.

The balance sheet insolvency test also requires valuation of assets. Valuation, however, is not an exact science and different valuers might well disagree about the value of an asset. A particular difficulty is that the Act does not indicate whether the assets are to be valued on the basis of the company's business being sold as a going concern or on the basis of the assets being broken up and sold separately; the former basis would usually be expected to produce a higher figure.

The company's assets include any unpaid capital unless this has been declared reserve

---

[7] [1990] BCC at 51.

[8] *Re a Company* (No. 003079 of 1990) [1991] BCLC 235, [[1991] BCC 683.

[9] *Byblos Bank SAL v Al Khudhairy* (1986) 2 BCC 99, 550 at pp. 99, 562.

[10] *Re British Equitable Bond and Mortgage Corp Ltd* [1910] 1 Ch 574; *Winter v IRC* [1961] 3 All ER 855; *Stonegate Securities v Gregory* [1980] Ch 576, in particular at p. 579 *per* Buckley LJ.

[11] [1986] BCLC 261. Although this case concerned an earlier statutory provision, the reasoning would still seem to be applicable.

capital under section 120 or 124 of the Insolvency Act 1986;[12] but the prospect of acquiring future assets from continued trading or from other sources is ignored.[13]

17.3 The regulation of insolvency practitioners

Until the reforming legislation of the 1980s it was possible to act as a liquidator or receiver without holding any relevant professional qualifications or having any previous experience. This could be exploited by unscrupulous persons to their own advantage, because the controllers of a company could elect to put the company into liquidation and appoint a sympathetic liquidator who, through ignorance, inexperience or complicity, would agree to the sale of the company's business at a low price to another company controlled by the same persons. This stratagem allowed the controllers to continue the business free from the burden of existing debts; meanwhile the creditors of the old company were left with claims which, in all probability, would never be paid.

Under the Insolvency Act 1986, it is an offence for an unqualified person to act as in insolvency practitioner in relation to a company.[14] Apart from the Official Receiver, who is regulated as an officer of the court, all liquidators, provisional liquidators, administrators, administrative receivers and supervisors of voluntary arrangements act as insolvency practitioners.[15] The principal way[16] of obtaining the appropriate qualification is through membership of one of the recognised professional accountancy bodies[17] or of the Law Society.[18] Specific restrictions prevent undischarged bankrupts, persons disqualified under the Company Directors Disqualification Act 1986 and persons subject to the mental health legislation from acting as insolvency practitioners,[19] and there are also bonding requirements.[20] Only individuals may act an insolvency practitioners.[21]

PART 2: VOLUNTARY ARRANGEMENTS

17.4 The use of voluntary arrangements

The Insolvency Act 1986 provides a procedure for voluntary arrangements between a company and its creditors and members. A voluntary arrangement approved by the majority of creditors and members of a company in accordance with the Act can be made

---

[12] *Re Bristol Joint Stock Bank* (1890) 44 Ch D 703; *Re European Life Assurance Society* (1870) LR 9 Eq 122; *Re Suburban Hotel Co.* (1867) 2 Ch App. 737.

[13] *Re European Life Assurance Society*, above; but the prospect of acquiring further assets before future liabilities are due will be relevant where the court is exercising a discretion: *Byblos Bank SAL v Al-Khudhairy*, above at pp. 99, 562.

[14] Section 389.

[15] See also section 388.

[16] The Secretary of State can also grant direct authorisations: section 392. This function can be (but, as yet, has not been) delegated to a 'competent authority'.

[17] Guidance notes issued by the accountancy bodies (and also by the Secretary of State) indicate that 'independence' is a further requirement. If, e.g., one of the partners of an individual who is otherwise qualified to act as an insolvency practitioner has in the previous three years been the auditor of a company, that individual is not qualified to act as an insolvency practitioner in relation to that particular company.

[18] Section 390 (2). See generally Part XIII and the Insolvency Practitioners Regulations 1990 (SI 1990 No. 439).

[19] Section 390 (4).

[20] Section 390 (3) and the Insolvency Practitioners Regulations 1990.

[21] Section 390 (1).

binding on all of them. The procedure governing voluntary arrangements is less formal than that governing the other Insolvency Act rescue procedure, namely, administration. In practice, however, 'stand alone' voluntary arrangements are relatively uncommon when compared to the overall number of insolvencies. More common are voluntary arrangements combined with administrations,[22] although the number of these compared to administrative receiverships and liquidations is still small. One important factor which may explain why the 'stand alone' voluntary arrangement procedure has not been more widely used[23] is the absence of a moratorium on creditors' rights. The company is not given a breathing space in which to try to come to an arrangement with its creditors. Whilst negotiations are ongoing, individual creditors can continue to press for payment and can commence or continue proceedings for that purpose; secured creditors can enforce their security; landlords, suppliers of goods on hire purchase and others who have supplied goods to the company on credit terms can continue to exercise their contractual rights. The administration procedure does provide a moratorium and it is for this reason that a voluntary arrangement is often combined with that procedure.

Case-law has highlighted a significant flaw in the voluntary arrangement procedure which arises from the wording of the relevant Insolvency Rules. A voluntary arrangement which is duly approved in accordance with the Rules is binding on all of the creditors who had notice of and were entitled to vote on it (whether or not they chose to vote). It has been held that creditors with unliquidated or unquantified claims are only entitled to vote where they reach a bilateral agreement with the chairman of the creditors' meeting as to the value of their claims, and that the chairman cannot bring them within the arrangement simply by unilateral valuation.[24] If this is correct, this greatly undermines the utility of the voluntary arrangement procedure, because it means that creditors with unliquidated or unquantified claims cannot be bound without their consent.

Another difficulty inhibiting the use of the voluntary procedure is that it can be extremely difficult for a company to raise new finance during the period whilst a voluntary arrangement is being negotiated. Also, a knowledge gap has been identified: directors know little about the voluntary procedure and few insolvency practitioners have direct experience of its operation.

The Insolvency Act voluntary arrangement procedure is now under review by the DTI.[25] What follows is simply a brief overview of the procedure as it is set out in the Insolvency Act 1986 and Insolvency Rules.

17.5 The proposal and who can make it

A voluntary arrangement is based upon a proposal to the company and its creditors for a composition in satisfaction of its debts or a scheme of arrangement of its affairs. The

---

[22] Section 8 (3) (*b*) specifies the approval of a voluntary arrangement as one of the purposes for which an administration order may be made.

[23] See generally, *The Insolvency Act 1986. Company Voluntary Arrangements and Administration Orders. A Consultative Document.* (DTI, October 1993) and comments by Rajak (1993) 9 IL&P 111; Penn [1994] JIBL 3; Wood (1993) 4 PLC 4.

[24] *Re Cranley Mansions Ltd, Saigol v Goldstein* [1994] BCC 576. See also *RA Securities Ltd v Mercantile Credit Co. Ltd* [1994] 2 BCLC 721 at p. 727.

[25] The DTI published a consultative document in October 1993: see footnote 23. A further consultative document, *The Insolvency Act 1986. Revised Proposals for a New Company Voluntary Arrangement Procedure,* was published in April 1995.

proposal must provide for some person to act as trustee or otherwise to supervise its implementation. That person is referred to as the 'nominee' and must be a licensed insolvency practitioner.[26] The effect of the appointment of a nominee is that control of the implementation of the proposal is not retained by the directors, but passes to an insolvency practitioner.

The proposal may be made:

(1) by the directors of the company (where there is no administration order in force and the company is not being wound up);
(2) by the administrator, where an administration order is in force; and
(3) by the liquidator, where the company is being wound up.[27]

17.6 Commencement of the procedure

The nominated person is required to make a report to the court stating whether he considers that the proposal should be considered at meetings of creditors and of the company.[28] To assist the nominee in preparing this report, there is an obligation on the directors, or on the administrator or liquidator where either of them was responsible for the making of the proposal, to provide the nominee with detailed information about the proposal and about the company's affairs.[29] The requirement for a report to the court is dispensed with where an administrator or liquidator designates himself as the nominee and, in this case, the matter proceeds directly to the convening and holding of meetings of creditors and of the company.[30]

The role of the court at this stage of the voluntary arrangement procedure is largely administrative. It is not required to approve the nominee's report or to vet the proposal. One power that the court does have is to nominate a substitute nominee: where a report to the court is required but the designated nominee fails to submit one, the court may be asked by the person intending to make the proposal for a direction that the nominee be replaced by another person who is qualified to act as an insolvency practitioner in relation to the company.[31] In practice, however, the nominee would usually have worked quite closely with the proposers of the voluntary arrangement and would be expected, barring an exceptional change of circumstances, to be willing to act.

17.7 Meetings of the creditors and of the company

The nominee must then summon meetings of the creditors and of the company.[32] These meetings are required to decide whether to approve the proposed voluntary arrangement.[33] The meetings may modify the proposal, including with regard to the replacement of the nominee by another insolvency practitioner,[34] but the modifications must not

---

[26] Section 1 (2).
[27] Section 1.
[28] Section 2. The period for submitting this report is twenty-eight days or such longer period as the court may allow.
[29] Section 2 (3) and rules 1.2–1.9 (directors' proposal) and rule 1.12 (administrator's or liquidator's proposal).
[30] Section 3 (2).
[31] Section 2 (4).
[32] Section 3. Where the nominee is not the liquidator or administrator, the summoning of meetings is subject to directions from the court: section 3 (1). The procedural aspects of the meetings are governed by the Insolvency Rules, Part 1, Chapter 5.
[33] Section 4.
[34] Section 4 (2).

be so extensive as to change the character of the proposal so that it is no longer a composition in satisfaction of the company's debts or a scheme of arrangement in respect of its affairs.[35] Also, the meetings are specifically prohibited from approving any proposal which would interfere with the rights of a secured creditor or of a creditor whose debt is afforded preferential status by the Insolvency Act, unless the secured creditor or, as the case may be, preferential creditor concurs.[36]

Both the creditors' meeting and the company meeting must approve the proposal (with modifications, where relevant) for it to become effective. The detailed procedure governing the summoning of these meetings, chairmanship, entitlement to vote, requisite matters and other organisational matters is set out in the Insolvency Rules.[37] Broadly, for an arrangement to become effective, it must attract the support of more than three-quarters in value of the creditors present in person or by proxy and voting on the resolution at the creditors' meeting[38] and of more than one-half of the members present in person or by proxy and voting at the company meeting.[39] The result of the meetings must be reported by the chairman to the court and to the persons who were sent notice of the meetings.[40] If the arrangement has been approved, the chairman's report must also be sent to the Registrar of Companies.[41]

17.8 The effect of the approval of the voluntary arrangement

When both the creditors' meeting and the company meeting approve the proposed voluntary arrangement, either with the same modifications or without modifications, then:[42]

(1) the voluntary arrangement takes effect as if made by the company at the creditors' meeting; and

(2) binds every person who in accordance with the Rules had notice of, and was entitled to vote at, the meeting (whether or not he was present or represented at the meeting) as if he were a party to the voluntary arrangement.[43]

The court may, if the company is being wound up or an administration order is in force, stay the winding-up or discharge the administration order and give such directions with respect to the conduct of the winding-up or the administration as it thinks appropriate for facilitating the implementation of the approved voluntary arrangement.[44]

17.9 Implementation of the proposal

When a voluntary arrangement is approved the nominee becomes the supervisor of the voluntary arrangement.[45] The supervisor's role is to carry out the functions conferred on

---

[35] Section 4 (2).
[36] Section 4 (3) and (4).
[37] Rules 1.13–1.21.
[38] Rule 1.19.
[39] Rule 1.20.
[40] Section 4 (6) and rule 1.24.
[41] Rule 1.24 (5).
[42] Section 5.
[43] It is not binding on creditors who are not entitled to vote at the meeting: *Re Cranley Mansions Ltd, Saigol v Goldstein* [1994] BCC 576.
[44] Section 5 (3), subject to the qualification in the next following subsection.
[45] Section 7 (2).

him by the arrangement.[46] The directors, or, where relevant, the administrator or the liquidator, must immediately do all that is required for putting the supervisor into possession of the company's assets which are included in the arrangement.[47]

17.10 The role of the court after the proposal has been approved

A specific right to challenge the decision to approve a voluntary arrangement is conferred on certain persons by section 6. The challenge may be based on the substantive ground that the arrangement unfairly prejudices the interests of a creditor, member or contributory of the company, or may relate to material irregularities at or in relation to either of the meetings. The persons with standing to bring a claim under section 6 are those who were entitled to vote at either of the meetings, the nominee or a replacement nominee, and the company's liquidator or administrator.[48] The challenger must move swiftly, because an application under section 6 may not be made after the period of twenty-eight days beginning with the first day on which the results of the creditors' and company meetings were reported to the court.[49] Any irregularity at or in relation to a meeting does not invalidate the approval given by that meeting unless it is challenged successfully under section 6.[50]

Where the court is satisfied that one or other of the grounds is made out, it may revoke or suspend approvals given by meetings and may give directions for the summoning of further meetings, either to consider a new proposal from the person who made the original proposal or to reconsider the original proposal.[51] The court itself has no power to devise a new proposal for consideration at creditors' and company meetings.

The supervisor has a general right to apply to the court for directions in relation to any particular matter arising under the voluntary arrangement, and may also apply to the court for a winding-up order or an adminstration order to be made.[52]

Any of the company's creditors or any other person who is dissatisfied by any act, omission or decision of the supervisor can apply to court. The court can confirm, reverse or modify the supervisor's act or decision, give him directions or make such other order as it thinks fit.[53]

The court may also appoint substitute supervisors.[54]

17.11 Completion of the voluntary arrangement

Not more than twenty-eight days after the final completion of the voluntary arrangement,[55] the supervisor must notify all creditors and members of the company who are

---

[46] Section 7 (2).

[47] Rule 1.23 (1).

[48] Section 6 (2).

[49] Section 6 (3).

[50] Section 6 (7).

[51] Section 6 (4). If the original proposer fails to put forward a new proposal in accordance with the court's direction, the court must revoke the direction and revoke or suspend the earlier approvals: section 6 (5). The court may also give supplemental directions: section 6 (6).

[52] Section 7 (4). An example of such an application is *Re FMS Financial Management Services Ltd* (1989) 5 BCC 191.

[53] Section 7 (3).

[54] Section 7 (5) and (6).

[55] Unless the court extends the period as is permitted by rule 1.29 (4).

bound by the arrangement of that fact and must provide them with an account of receipts and payments.[56] A copy of the notice and account sent to the creditors and members must also be sent to the Registrar of Companies and to the court.[57]

PART 3: ADMINISTRATION

17.12 The role of administration

The administration procedure is relatively new having been first introduced by the Insolvency Act 1985. The relevant provisions are now contained in Part II of the Insolvency Act 1986.

The background to the introduction of the administration procedure emerges from Chapter 9 of the Cork Committee's report.[58] The Committee identified one aspect of the floating charge which it considered to have been of outstanding benefit to the general public and to society as a whole, namely the power to appoint a receiver and manager of the whole property and undertaking of a company. The Committee noted that such receivers and managers were usually given extensive powers to carry on the business of the company. In some cases they had been able to restore an ailing enterprise to profitability and return it to its former owners, and in others they had been able to dispose of whole or part of the business as a going concern. In either case, the profitable parts of the business were preserved and this was of advantage to the employees, the commercial community and the general public. The Committee observed that none of these steps was possible in the absence of a floating charge and concluded that, in a significant number of cases, companies with potentially viable businesses were closed down and forced into liquidation for want of a floating charge under which a receiver and manager could have been appointed. Accordingly, it recommended the introduction of the administration procedure to fill this lacuna in the range of available insolvency procedures.

The Government, in *A Revised Framework for Insolvency Law*,[59] accepted the need for the enactment of an administration procedure. There appeared to be a slight change of emphasis in this document, because, whereas the Cork Committee had envisaged a role for administration where there was no floating charge or the holder of the floating charge did not want to appoint a receiver, the Government noted that receivership might not be a complete remedy for the further reason that a receiver acted principally in the interests of the charge-holder, but there could be circumstances in which it would be desirable for the affairs of a company in financial difficulties to be conducted by an independently appointed insolvency practitioner. In the event, however, the enacted procedure closely resembles the Cork Committee's model, because the holder of a floating charge on the whole, or substantially the whole, of the company's assets can veto the appointment of an administrator and instead appoint his own administrative receiver. An administrative receiver's primary obligation is to the person who appointed him but he owes certain obligations to other parties. An administrative receiver must be a qualified insolvency practitioner and this serves to minimise the risk that he will fail to discharge these obligations.

---

[56] Rule 1.29 (1) and (2).
[57] Rule 1.29 (3).
[58] *Insolvency Law and Practice* (1982), Cmnd. 8558.
[59] 1984, Cmnd. 9175.

The veto enjoyed by holders of floating charges inhibits the use of the administration procedure, and the number of administrations in comparison to administrative receiverships and liquidations is quite low.[60] On occasions, however, holders of floating charges have held back from appointing administrative receivers and have consented to administration. One type of case where this has happened is in relation to the collapse of large, multinational enterprises involving assets and creditors scattered worldwide; a court-appointed administrator can be seen to be better placed to command support on an international basis than a privately appointed administrative receiver. Another is in relation to companies with businesses which are not entirely commercial, such as football clubs, where there seems to be some reluctance on the part of lenders to be specifically identified as the persons responsible for imposing an insolvency procedure.

Apart from the inhibiting effect of the floating charge holder's veto, low usage of the administration procedure has also been attributed to other factors.[61] Certain aspects of the procedure have been seen to be time-consuming and costly and there may be insufficient creditor involvement. An administrator can remove the directors of the company from office and this may deter them from initiating the procedure. The directors may also be deterred by the fact that the administrator is required to make reports on them to the Secretary of State for the purposes of the Company Directors Disqualification Act 1986. On the other hand, in a series of helpful decisions the courts have emphasised that the purpose of the administration procedure is to facilitate efficient corporate rescues and, by adopting a purposive construction of the legislation, the judges have done much to minimise delay and costs. Some difficulties still remain and the Government has commenced a review of the adminstration procedure in conjunction with its review of voluntary arrangements.

17.13 The moratorium

One of the most important features of the administration procedure is the moratorium. The commencement of the administration procedure by the presentation of a petition for an administration order[62] imposes a freeze on proceedings or executions against the company and its assets. This provides a breathing space during which the company has an opportunity to make arrangements with its creditors and members for the rescheduling of its debts and the reorganisation and restructuring of its affairs.[63]

17.14 When can an administration order be made?

The court may make an administration order if two matters are established.[64]

(1) It is satisfied that the company is, or is likely to become, unable to pay its debts

---

[60] The DTI's consultative document published in October 1993 (footnote 23, above) notes that in the previous three years only 447 administration orders were made in England and Wales compared with 21,597 administrative receiverships, 40,052 creditors' voluntary liquidations and 26,120 compulsory liquidations. For a review of the operation of the administration procedure in its early years see Homan, *Administrations under the Insolvency Act 1986: The Result of Administration Orders made in 1987*, for the Research Board of the Institute of Chartered Accountants of England and Wales.

[61] DTI consultative document, October 1993 (footnote 23, above).

[62] Section 10.

[63] The operation of the moratorium throughout the administration is modified in respect of market charges, that is charges arising out of dealings in securities. The modifications of the law of insolvency in respect of market charges are made by Part VII of the Companies Act 1989.

[64] Section 8 (1).

within the technical meaning given to that expression by section 123 of the Insolvency Act. In addition to situations of cash flow and balance sheet insolvency, section 123 deems a company to be unable to pay its debts –

(a) if a creditor who is owed a sum exceeding £750 then due has served a written demand on the company requiring it to pay the amount due and the company has failed to pay such sum for a period of three weeks or to secure or compound for it to the reasonable satisfaction of the creditor; or

(b) if execution or other process issued on a judgment or other court order in favour of the creditor of the company is returned unsatisfied in whole or in part.

(2) It considers that the making of an administration order would be likely to achieve one of the purposes specified in section 8 of the Act.

These purposes are:

(a) the survival of the company and the whole or any part of its undertaking as a going concern;

(b) the approval of a voluntary arrangement under Part 1 of the Act;

(c) the sanctioning under section 425 of the Companies Act 1985 of a compromise or arrangement between the company and any of its creditors or its members; and

(d) a more advantageous realisation of the company's assets than would be effected on a winding-up.[65]

The Act requires the administration order to specify the purpose or purposes for which it is made. In many cases, more than one purpose will be specified since there may be grounds for believing that one or other of the purposes is likely to be achieved but only further investigation will reveal which of the purposes is more appropriate. In many cases the purposes set out in both paras. (2) (a) and (d) above will be specified since there may be a good chance of a rescue operation that will allow control of the company to be restored to the company's directors, but if that aim cannot be achieved it may be possible to sell the company's assets as a going concern, which is likely to produce a more advantageous realisation of assets than on a winding-up (when the company would only have the limited right to continue trading for the beneficial purposes of its winding-up).

It is now established that it is sufficient for the court to consider that there is a real prospect of the specified purpose or purposes being achieved.[66] A higher standard requiring the evidence to show that the purpose or purposes will more probably than not be achieved was favoured in a few early cases[67] but that standard, which would have hindered the development of the new procedure, has now been universally rejected in favour of the less rigorous test.

An administration order cannot be made:[68]

---

[65] Section 8 (3) of the Insolvency Act 1986.

[66] *Re Harris Simons Construction Ltd* [1989] 1 WLR 368, [1989] BCLC 202, (1989) 5 BCC 11; *Re SCL Building Services Ltd* (1989) 5 BCC 746, [1990] BCLC 98; *Re Primlaks (UK) Ltd* [1989] BCLC 734; *Re Rowbotham Baxter Ltd* [1990] BCLC 397, [1990] BCC 113; *Re Chelmsford City Football Club (1980) Ltd* [1991] BCC 133; *Re Arrows Ltd (No 3)* [1992] BCLC 555.

[67] *Re Consumer and Industrial Press Ltd* [1988] BCLC 177, (1988) 4 BCC 68; *Re Manlon Trading Ltd* (1988) 4 BCC 455.

[68] Section 8 (4). An administration order may now be made against a bank: Banks (Administration Proceedings) Order 1989 (SI 1989 No. 1276).

(1) if a resolution to wind up the company has been passed or a winding-up order has been made (in relation to a company which is not already in voluntary liquidation by virtue of the passing of a winding-up resolution); or

(2) in relation to an insurance company.

17.15 Who can make the application and how is it made?

An application to the court for an administration order is made by petition, which can be presented either by the company or its directors, or by a creditor or creditors (including any contingent or prospective creditor or creditors) or by all or any of those parties, together or separately.[69] The reference to 'the directors' does not necessarily mean that all of the directors must join in the petition; provided there has been a formal board resolution to apply for administration, it becomes the duty of all of the directors to implement the decision and any director has authority to present the petition.[70]

The petition, the form of which is laid down in the Insolvency Rules,[71] must be accompanied by a supporting affidavit stating the deponent's belief that the preconditions to the making of an administration order are satisfied and giving details of the company's financial affairs, including particulars of security over its property and, where relevant, of actual appointments of administrative receivers or of the existence of powers of appointment.[72] If the petition is presented by the company or its directors, this affidavit must be made by one of the directors or by the company secretary.[73] If the petition is presented by creditors, the affidavit must be made by a person acting under authority from all of them.[74]

Rule 2.2 is concerned with independent reports. It provides for the preparation of a report by an independent person to the effect that the appointment of an administrator is expedient. This independent report may be exhibited to the affidavit in support of the petition. Although rule 2.2 is worded in permissive rather than mandatory terms, the practice grew up of treating the rule 2.2 report as indispensable. A corrective to this practice was finally made by a Practice Statement issued by the Vice-Chancellor in January 1994.[75] The Practice Statement emphasises that the primary aim of the administration procedure is the facilitation of the rescue and rehabilitation of insolvent but potentially viable businesses, and that this aim should not be frustrated by the costs of obtaining an order. It states that, in a normal case, what the court needs is not an elaborate report but rather a concise assessment of the company's situation and of the prospects of an administration order achieving one or more of the specified purposes. It accepts that there may be straightforward cases in which the report can be dispensed with altogether because it would provide little assistance.

---

[69] Section 9 (1). Under section 74 of the Financial Services Act 1986, regulatory bodies can petition for the administration of authorised persons. The Bank of England can seek an administration order in respect of an authorised institution: Banks (Administration Proceedings) Order 1989 (SI 1989 No. 1276).

[70] *Re Equiticorp International plc* [1989] 1 WLR 1010, [1989] BCLC 594, distinguishing *Re Instrumentation Electrical Services Ltd* [1988] BCLC 550, where Mervyn Davies J had held in relation to a winding-up petition that all of the directors had to join in the petition, on the grounds that there had been no formal board resolution in that case.

[71] See generally rule 2.4.

[72] Rule 2.3.

[73] Rule 2.1 (2).

[74] Rule 2.1 (3).

[75] [1994] 1 All ER 324, [1994] 1 WLR 160, [1994] BCC 35.

17.16 Service and notification of the petition

The courts have taken a similarly helpful attitude with regard to the requirements for publication of the petition prior to the hearing.[76] The basic rule is that the petition, once issued, must be served on various persons[77] including, in particular, any person who has appointed an administrative receiver of the company or who has power to do so. The purpose of serving the petition on a person who is entitled to appoint an administrative receiver is to enable him to consider in good time whether he wants to veto the administration. The Insolvency Rules stipulate that the petition must be served not less than five days before the date fixed for the hearing, but the court can,[78] and have in practice proved to be willing to,[79] abridge this period in suitable cases. If the person entitled to appoint an administrative receiver consents in advance to the making of an administration order, the court will dispense altogether with the need to serve the petition on that person.[80]

In circumstances where there is a need for urgent action, the courts have even been prepared to grant an administration order before the petition is presented, against an undertaking to do so.[81] An example of the type of situation where there may be a need to act quickly is where the directors, mindful of potential wrongful trading liability, refuse to continue to carry on the business of the company, but the nature of the business is such that a hiatus pending the appointment of an administrator would be fatal to the chances of eventual recovery and any person entitled to appoint an administrative receiver has consented to the administration.[82] In *Re Chancery plc*[83] the petition was actually presented but the directors sought an administration order on the same day before any formal service could be effected. Harman J, although at pains to emphasise that the case was exceptional, granted the order because the company was a bank and a delay of even a few days could cause a loss of confidence and a run on the bank; and, if the bank had tried to continue to trade normally, the directors would be at risk of wrongful trading, difficulties would be caused to customers and various commercial arrangements would be put at risk.

17.17 Effect of presentation of the administration petition

After a petition for an administration order has been presented:[84]

(1) no resolution may be passed or order made for the winding-up of the company;

(2) no steps may be taken to enforce any security over the company's property[85] or to

---

[76] Wheeler, 'Insolvency Act 1986 Part II–A Look at Current Judicial Attitudes', (1991) 7 *Insolvency Law and Practice* 69.

[77] Section 9 (2) and rule 2.6.

[78] Rule 12.9.

[79] *Re a Company* (No. 00175 of 1987) [1987] BCLC 467; *Re Gallidoro Trawlers Ltd* [1991] BCLC 411, [1991] BCC 691.

[80] As e.g. in *Re Vosper Shiprepairers Ltd*, 7 February 1987 (unreported).

[81] e.g. *Re Cavco Floors Ltd* [1990] BCLC 940, [1990] BCC 589; *Re Sharps of Truro Ltd* [1990] BCC 94 (where an ex parte administration order was later discharged). But use of an expedited procedure is exceptional: *Re Rowbotham Baxter Ltd* [1990] BCC 113.

[82] *Re Cavco Floors*, above.

[83] [1991] BCLC 712, [1991] BCC 171.

[84] Section 10 (1).

[85] 'Security' in sections 10 and 11 extends to a landlord's rights of re-entry under a lease: *Exchange Travel Agency v Triton Property Trust* [1991] BCLC 396.

repossess goods in the company's possession under any hire-purchase agreement[86] except with the leave of the court and subject to such terms as the court may impose; and

(3) no other proceedings[87] and no execution or other legal process[88] may be commenced or continued and no distress[89] may be levied against the company or its property except with the leave of the court and subject to such terms as the court may impose.

Thus the moratorium begins to bite from the time the petition is presented. This is intended to ensure that the status quo is maintained and the company's business and assets are protected pending the outcome of the hearing. The operation of the moratorium is qualified in one case: if the petition for an administration order is presented at a time when there is an administrative receiver of the company, the moratorium only applies from the time when the appointor of the administrative receiver consents to the making of the order.[90]

The presentation of a petition for an administration order does not prevent: (a) the presentation of a winding-up petition (the two petitions may be heard together to allow the court to grant the most appropriate order); or (b) the appointment of an administrative receiver and the exercise by that receiver of all of his powers and functions.[91]

17.18 Hearing of the petition

Where the court is satisfied that there is an administrative receiver of the company it must dismiss the petition unless it is also satisfied that:[92]

(1) the appointor of the administrative receiver has consented to the order; or

(2) if an administration order were made, any security by virtue of which the receiver was appointed would be liable to be released or discharged under sections 238 to 240 of the Insolvency Act 1986 (which are concerned with transactions at an undervalue and preferences) or would be avoided under section 245 of the Act (which is concerned with certain floating charges).

As yet, there is no reported test case on the 'trial within a trial' envisaged by the second of these options. A challenge to the validity of a security could raise difficult questions of

---

[86] Defined by section 10 (4) as including conditional sale agreements, chattel leasing agreements and retention of title agreements.

[87] The proceedings in question are legal proceedings or quasi-legal proceedings such as arbitration: *Bristol Airport v Powdrill* [1990] Ch 744, [1990] 2 All ER 493, [1990] 2 WLR 1362, [1990] BCLC 585, [1990] BCC 130. This can include applications to industrial tribunals: *Carr v British International Helicopters Ltd* [1993] BCC 855. An application to court under section 404 of the Companies Act 1985 to register a charge out of time is not caught, but the court should exercise its discretion under that section against granting leave where it is clear that insolvent liquidation is inevitable: *Re Barrow Borough Transport Ltd* [1990] Ch 227, [1989] 3 WLR 858, [1989] BCLC 653. The revocation of Civil Aviation Authority licences is not a 'proceeding' for this purpose: *Air Ecosse v CAA* (1987) 3 BCC 492.

[88] A 'legal process' requires the assistance of the court and therefore the service of a notice making time of the essence is not within this category: *Re Olympia and York Canary Wharf Ltd* [1993] BCC 154; *McMullen & Sons Ltd v Cerrone* [1994] BCC 25. Cf. *Exchange Travel Agency v Triton*, above.

[89] The essential feature of distress is that the assets distrained are seized and detained by the distrainor: *Bristol Airport v Powdrill*, above.

[90] Section 10 (3).

[91] Section 10 (2).

[92] Section 9 (3).

law which might not be easy to resolve quickly but, as there is usually a need for quick action in relation to companies in financial difficulties, the court might be unwilling to embark on a lengthy inquiry. Whether, if it did inquire and did decide that the security was vulnerable and therefore that the appointment of an administrative receiver under it was not a bar to the appointment of an administrator, that decision would be binding in the context of a full trial of the issues under sections 238 to 240 or 245 is also unclear.

Apart from the requirement to dismiss the petition where there is an administrative receiver, the court has a general discretion to dismiss it or adjourn the hearing or make an interim order[93] or any other order that it thinks fit.[94] *Re Imperial Motors (UK) Ltd*[95] illustrates the approach of the court in exercising this discretion. A secured creditor petitioned for an administration order on the ground that this would effect a more advantageous realisation of the company's assets than would be effected in a winding-up. The petition was presented without the consent of the company and was opposed by its directors. The company was insolvent in a cash flow sense but appeared to be solvent in the balance sheet sense. Hoffmann J held that the task of the court was to balance the interests of the petitioning creditor in achieving a more advantageous realisation against the interests of the company, its shareholders and its management in not having the business taken out of their hands and sold to a third party. The court was also required to balance the interests of the company's various creditors. Hoffmann J accepted[96] that since the petitioning creditor was a secured creditor, and as such stood to lose much less than the company's unsecured creditors, its interests weighed lighter in the scales than other creditors; also, the petitioner was already adequately secured by its security without the intervention of a court of law, but an administration order would have a potentially disastrous effect on a director who had guaranteed the company's liabilities and was one of its unsecured creditors. All of these factors pointed to the conclusion that the risks in making the order outweighed those of refusing it; and, accordingly, no order was made.[97]

The opposition of the majority in value of the creditors does not necessarily preclude the making of an administration order[98] but it is a relevant consideration because it affects the question whether creditors are likely to support the administrator's proposals for achieving the administration purpose or purposes.[99] This factor may point towards the conclusion that a winding-up order would be more appropriate than administration.[100]

---

[93] On interim orders see *Re a Company (No. 00175 of 1987)*, above and *Re Gallidoro Trawlers*, above.

[94] Section 9 (4).

[95] [1990] BCLC 29.

[96] Applying the decision of Peter Gibson J in *Re Consumer and Industrial Press Ltd*, above.

[97] *Re Business Properties Ltd & Ors* (1988) 4 BCC 684 was another case of cash flow insolvency but balance sheet solvency. The essence of the dispute was a breakdown in the relationship between the various members of the company. In Harman J's view in these circumstances winding-up was a more appropriate remedy than administration.

[98] A court could sanction the implementation of the administrator's proposals even though they have not been approved by the creditors' committee: *Re Maxwell Communications Corporation plc* [1992] BCLC 465 at p. 467.

[99] *Re Arrows (No. 3)* [1992] BCLC 555, [1992] BCC 131.

[100] *Re Arrows (No. 3)*, above. See also *Re Land and Property Trust Co Ltd (No. 2)* [1991] BCLC 849.

17.19 Effect of the administration order

When an administration order is made, the administrator, who must be a qualified insolvency practitioner, takes office. It is possible for the court to appoint joint administrators. Any winding-up petition is dismissed and any administrative receiver of the company must vacate office.[101] The moratorium that first began to bite when the petition for the administration order was presented continues in place with the added limitations that no order may be made for the winding-up[102] of the company and no administrative receiver may be appointed.[103] A receiver who is not an administrative receiver (that is a receiver of part only of the company's property) is not required automatically to vacate office but may be required to do so by the administrator.[104]

The directors of the company do not vacate office on the making of an administration order but their powers of management pass to the administrator.[105] The administrator has very wide powers to manage the company's business and to deal with its assets in order to achieve the purpose or purposes specified in the administration order. Thus the administrator may allow the company to continue to trade, to dispose of its assets and to commence or continue legal proceedings. The administrator has the power to remove directors and to appoint any person to be a director, whether to fill a vacancy or otherwise.[106] He can also call meetings of members and of creditors,[107] and has a general power to apply to the court for directions in carrying out his functions.[108]

A person dealing with an administrator in good faith and for value is not concerned to inquire whether the administrator is acting within his powers.[109] There are, nevertheless, various disclosure obligations which are designed to ensure that persons who have an interest in the company or who have dealings with it are aware of its new status.[110] In particular, every invoice, order for goods or business letter which is issued by or on behalf of the company or the administrator after the making of an administration order, being a document on or in which the company's name appears, must also contain the administrator's name and a statement that the affairs, business and property of the company are being managed by the administrator.[111]

17.20 Relaxation of the moratorium

With the leave of the court or with the administrator's consent, security may be enforced, goods may be repossessed, other proceedings, execution or legal processes may be commenced or continued, and distress may be levied notwithstanding the existence of

---

[101] Section 11 (1). Section 11 (4) provides for payment of the administrative receiver's remuneration, expenses and any indemnity to which he may be entitled. Section 11 (5) relieves him of his obligations in respect of preferential debts.

[102] Where administration is to be followed by winding up, the administration order must first be discharged: *Re Charnley Davies Business Services Ltd* (1987) 3 BCC 408.

[103] Section 11 (3).

[104] Section 11 (2).

[105] Section 14 (1) and Schedule 1.

[106] Section 14 (2) (*a*).

[107] Section 14 (2) (*b*).

[108] Section 14 (3).

[109] Section 14 (6).

[110] Section 21 and rule 2.10.

[111] Section 12.

the administration order.[112] There have been a number of test cases in which the courts have had an opportunity to spell out their approach to the granting of leave. However, as the procedure becomes more established and the attitude of the court to requests for leave becomes more settled, administrators may be expected to deal with most requests themselves, with applications to court being reserved for particularly difficult or novel matters. This is certainly how the courts have envisaged the further development of the leave procedure.

The leading authorities are the decisions of the Court of Appeal in *Bristol Airport plc v Powdrill*[113] and *Re Atlantic Computer Systems plc (No. 1)*.[114] The former case arose from the administration of Paramount Airways Ltd. Among the airline's unsecured creditors were Bristol and Birmingham airports. Both airports, claiming a right of detention under the Civil Aviation Act 1982, sought leave to retain aircraft leased by Paramount which were parked on their runways. On the facts, the Court of Appeal held the interest of Paramount under the lease of the aircraft amounted to property,[115] that the right under the Civil Aviation Act was a 'security'[116] over the company's property' and that the exercise of the right of detention was a 'step taken to enforce security', thus bringing the situation squarely within section 11 and making it necessary to obtain leave or consent. The Court of Appeal then held that the first-instance judge had properly taken into account the relevant factors and properly exercised his discretion in refusing leave. Particularly telling factors against the airports were that none of the company's aircraft was on their runways at the commencement of the administration, aircraft only arriving there subsequently because of the administrator's decision to continue the business; the airports had acquiesced in the administrator's proposal to sell the business as a going concern, which detention of the aircraft would prevent; and the airports had benefited financially from the continuation of the business by the administrator because they had received payment of substantial fees. In other words, having supported the administration when it suited them, the airports could not later seek to enforce a right which was inconsistent with the achievement of the purpose of the administration.[117]

Although the facts of the case were slightly unusual, the Court of Appeal in *Powdrill* accepted that its reasoning would extend to a case where the holder of ordinary possessory lien[118] or similar right was requested by an administrator to give up the chattels subject to the right. Refusal to comply with the request would amount to a step taken to enforce security and would fall within section 11. The Court of Appeal accepted that it would be practically inconvenient and costly for the holder of every lien to have to apply to court for leave in accordance with section 11 irrespective of the amounts involved but, despite expressing some misgivings,[119] thought that these potential difficulties would be mitigated in practice by the fact that, especially in matters involving small amounts, the administrator and the holder of the lien could simply agree the matter

---

[112] Section 11 (3).

[113] Above.

[114] [1992] Ch 505, [1992] 1 All ER 476, [1992] 2 WLR 367, [1991] BCLC 606, [1990] BCC 859.

[115] Section 436 defines property very broadly.

[116] 'Security' is defined by section 248 as including a 'lien or other security'.

[117] [1990] Ch at p. 767 *per* Browne-Wilkinson V-C.

[118] Under section 246 liens and similar rights on the company's books, papers or other records are unenforceable against 'office-holders', a category which includes administrators. On lien-holders see also *Re Sabre International Products Ltd* [1991] BCLC 470.

[119] Staughton LJ at p. 772 considered that 'the effect of section 11 should be kept carefully under review'.

between themselves without the intervention of the courts. As for the argument that, in a case where the parties could not reach agreement, the holder of the lien would have to hand over the chattels when requested in order to avoid being in contempt of court but, by so doing, would lose the possessory right, the Court of Appeal thought it unlikely that, in the light of their ruling, administrators would insist on chattels being given up before the holder of the lien had had an opportunity to apply for leave; but the court observed that, if an administrator did so insist, the holder of the lien would not be in contempt of court or otherwise at fault in refusing to give up possession provided that, at the same time, he was making every effort to obtain the leave of the court.

Browne-Wilkinson V-C, giving the leading judgment, emphasised the need for a purposive approach to the interpretation of the statutory provisions governing administration so as to achieve the aims for which that procedure was introduced, namely, either the restoration of the financial health of the company or the sale of its business as a going concern. The courts could not distort the meaning of words used by Parliament, but if the words used were capable of bearing more than one meaning it was legitimate to adopt the meaning which gave effect to, rather than frustrated, the statutory purpose.

Re Atlantic Computer Systems plc (No. 1) decided the narrow point that where a company in administration has leased goods and then sub-leased the goods to customers, those goods nevertheless remain in the possession of the company for the purposes of section 11. The facts therefore fell within the scope of section 11 and the Court of Appeal granted leave to lessors and security holders to recover their property and to enforce their security. The wider significance of the case is that, despite some reluctance to lay down guidelines in case they would be treated as rigid rules rather than guidelines, the Court of Appeal did take the opportunity to set out in general terms the approach of the court to applications under section 11 for leave to assert proprietary, including security, rights.[120] The Court of Appeal regarded as a compelling point in favour of providing guidance the fact that it could assist administrators in deciding whether to grant consent themselves and thus help to make applications to court for leave the exception rather than the rule.

The guidelines provided by *Re Atlantic Computers* are substantially set out below. The underlying principle is that an administration for the benefit of unsecured creditors should not be conducted at the expense of those who have proprietary rights except to the extent that this may be unavoidable.

(1) The onus is on the applicant to establish a case for leave to be granted.
(2) The moratorium is intended to assist in the achievement of the purpose for which the administration order was made. If granting leave to the applicant is unlikely to impede that purpose, leave should normally be given.
(3) In other cases, the court should balance the legitimate interests of the applicant and the legitimate interests of the other creditors of the company.[121]
(4) In carrying out the balancing exercise great importance is normally to be given to the proprietary interest of the applicant. In general, so far as possible the

---

[120] Nicholls LJ, delivering the judgment of the court, also reflected that the range of circumstances in which leave could be sought would vary almost infinitely thus making guidelines inadequate, and noted that first-instance judges in the Commercial Court had more practical experience of the procedure than the members of the Court of Appeal.

[121] For an example of the operation of this balancing process, see *Re Meesan Investments Ltd (Royal Trust Bank v Buchler)* (1988) 4 BCC 788; [1989] BCLC 130.

administration procedure should not be used to prejudice those who were secured creditors or lessors at the commencement of the administration.[122]

(5) It will normally be sufficient ground for the grant of leave if significant loss would be caused to the applicant by the refusal. But if substantially greater loss would be caused to others by the grant of leave, or loss which is out of all proportion to the benefit which leave would confer on the applicant, that may outweigh the loss to the applicant caused by a refusal.

(6) In assessing the respective losses the court will have regard to matters such as: the financial position of the company; its ability to pay rental arrears and continuing rentals (or, in the case of security, to meet its obligations under its loans); the administrator's proposals; the period for which the administration order has been in force and is expected to remain in force; the effect on the administration if leave is given and on the applicant if it is refused; the end result sought to be achieved by the administration; the prospects of that result being achieved; and the history of the administration so far.

(7) In considering these suggested consequences it will often be necessary to assess how probable they are.

(8) Other factors, such as the conduct of the applicant, may also be relevant.[123]

(9) The above conditions will also apply to a decision to impose terms if leave is granted.[124] They will also apply to a decision whether to impose terms as a condition for refusing leave.[125] An example of refusal to grant leave on terms is provided by *Re Meesan Investments*, where leave to enforce security was refused but the administrator was ordered to return to court in two months' time if the secured property had not been sold by then. The guidelines envisage refusal on terms becoming a common phenomenon.

(10) On applications to enforce security, an important consideration will often be whether the applicant is fully secured. If he is, delay in enforcement is likely to be less prejudicial than in cases where his security is insufficient.

(11) Unless the issue can be easily resolved, it is not appropriate on a leave application for the court to resolve a dispute about the existence, validity or nature of a security which the applicant seeks leave to enforce. The court needs to be satisfied only that the applicant has a seriously arguable case.

Wrongful refusal by an administrator to allow an owner of goods to repossess them could render the administrator liable to pay compensation.[126]

---

[122] Significantly the airports in the Paramount Airways litigation were not in that position.

[123] As in the Paramount Airways litigation.

[124] Section 11 (3) (*c*) and (*d*) provide for the granting of leave on terms.

[125] There is no provision in section 11 entitling the court to refuse leave on terms but this result can be achieved by the court giving directions to the administrator, for instance under section 17 or in response to a section 14 (3) application by the administrator, or in exercise of its control over the administrator as an officer of the court. It can also be achieved indirectly by ordering that the applicant shall have leave unless the administrator is prepared to do a particular thing or to take a particular step in the conduct of the administration.

[126] *Barclays Mercantile Business Finance Ltd v Sibec Development Ltd* [1992] 2 All ER 195, [1992] 1 WLR 1253, [1993] BCLC 1077, [1993] BCC 148. The basis of this jurisdiction is the administrator's position as an officer of the court. Whether an administrator could be liable for conversion was left open.

17.21 Power to deal with charged property

In many cases, in order to achieve the purpose or purposes laid down in the administration order, the administrator will need to be able to use or dispose of all the company's
property, including that part of it which is charged to a third party, for example the
company's bankers. Many trading companies will have granted fixed and floating
charges to their bankers although the making of the administration order, in a case where
there is a floating charge covering the whole or substantially the whole of the company's
property, presupposes that, in the absence of a defect in the security, the floating charge
holder has consented to the making of the administration order.

Section 15 of the Insolvency Act 1986 gives the administrator certain powers to deal
with property charged to third parties and chattels owned by third parties but in the
company's possession irrespective of the wishes of the chargees or owners. Section 15 of
the Act makes a distinction between, on the one hand, assets subject to a fixed charge (or
to hire-purchase agreements),[127] and, on the other, assets subject to a floating charge.

In the case of assets subject to a floating charge, the administrator is given power to
dispose of such assets or otherwise exercise his powers in relation to them as if the assets
were not subject to the floating charge. Accordingly, the administrator can deal with such
assets and dispose of them as he sees fit without reference to the floating charge holder
and without being fettered by any contractual restrictions contained within the floating
charge, for example a negative pledge clause.

The reference in section 15 to a floating charge means a charge which, as created, was
a floating charge.[128] Accordingly, the crystallisation of the floating charge prior to the
administration order would not prevent the administrator having these wide powers.

Where the administrator disposes of floating charge assets the holder of the floating
charge is given the same priority in respect of any of the company's property directly or
indirectly representing the assets disposed of as he would have had in respect of the assets
subject to the floating charge. Accordingly, if the administrator, for example, sells plant
and machinery subject to the floating charge the proceeds of the sale will fall within the
floating charge and the holder of the charge will be entitled to the same priority as against
third parties (for example holders of subsequent floating charges) in respect of the
proceeds as he had in respect of the plant and machinery disposed of.

The administrator, it should be noted, is not required to pay the claims of preferential
creditors out of floating charge assets coming into his hands. In the event that the
company goes into liquidation upon the discharge of the administration order, then the
preferential creditors will have claims in the winding-up. The preferential claims will then
be quantified by reference to the date on which the administration order was made.[129]

As regards assets subject to a fixed charge (as created) or goods which are in the
possession of the company under a hire-purchase agreement the administrator may
apply to court in accordance with section 15 (2) for an order authorising him to dispose of
the property. The court may make such an order if it is satisfied that the disposal (with or
without other assets) of the fixed charge assets or goods acquired on hire purchase would
be likely to promote the purpose, or one or more of the purposes, specified in the
administration order. The court order will authorise the administrator to dispose of the

---

[127] This term includes conditional sale agreements, chattel leasing agreements and retention of title
agreements: section 15 (9).

[128] Sections 15 (3) and 251.

[129] Section 387 (3) (*a*).

assets or goods as if they were not subject to the fixed charge or, as the case may be, as if the owner's rights under the hire-purchase agreement were vested in the company. Section 15 (5) provides that the court must make it a condition of any such order that:

(1) the net proceeds of the disposal; and
(2) a sum equalling the deficit between the net proceeds of disposal and the net amount which would be realised by a sale of the assets in the open market (presupposing a willing vendor)

must be applied towards discharging the sums secured by the fixed charge or payable under the hire-purchase agreement.

Thus, if the administrator sells all of the company's property, including assets which are subject to a fixed charge, in order to comply with the terms of the section 15 court order, he must apply the net proceeds of sale (together with a further sum, if necessary, to make up the open market value of the fixed-charge assets disposed of) towards discharging the fixed charge.

The operation of section 15 was considered in *Re ARV Aviation Ltd*[130] where, with a view to achieving the administration purpose of a more advantageous realisation of the company's assets than would be effected on a winding-up, an administrator had provisionally agreed to sell all of the company's undertaking and assets as a going concern. One creditor, which held a fixed charge on part of the company's assets, opposed the proposal and the administrator therefore sought leave under section 15 (2) to sell those assets as if they were not subject to the creditor's security.

Knox J held that the task of the court in leave applications was to balance the prejudice that would be felt by the secured creditor by the making of an order against the prejudice that would be felt by those interested in the promotion of the administration purpose, in this case the unsecured creditors, if it were not made. From the facts, it appeared that not making the order could result in the loss of the sale, and that, in that event, the business could not be continued because there would be no money from which to pay employees' salaries. On the other hand, it seemed that if the sale went through it would generate more than enough to repay the sum secured by the objecting creditor's security, including interests and costs. On balance, therefore, Knox J concluded that this was a suitable case for the making of an order.

The view that the court takes of the open-market value of the assets which the administrator seeks leave to sell is extremely important because it is this amount which the administrator is required to discharge as a condition of obtaining leave. In *ARV Aviation* Knox J proceeded on the assumption that the purpose of this condition was to protect to the maximum practicable extent the secured creditor.[131] Evidently with a view to achieving this purpose, Knox J held that the granting of leave under section 15 could be a two-stage process, with the open-market valuation being assessed some time after the making of the order granting the administrator leave to dispose of the assets.

Leave under section 15 may be sought in circumstances where the administrator and the secured creditor[132] are unable themselves to agree on a valuation; but such a dispute is not an essential prerequisite of the jurisdiction under the section.[133] Where a secured

[130] (1988) 4 BCC 708, [1989] BCLC 664.
[131] *Mutatis mutandis*, the same underlying purpose would exist where the administrator seeks leave to dispose of goods in the possession of the company under a hire-purchase agreement.
[132] Or supplier of goods on hire purchase, as the case may be.
[133] *Re ARV Aviation Ltd*, above.

creditor consents to the sale of the charged assets,[134] the administrator may not use the mechanism of section 15 to retain the proceeds of the sale but must deal with these proceeds in accordance with the terms on which the secured creditor has agreed to release its security.[135]

Where assets are subject to more than one fixed charge and the court makes an order authorising the disposal of such assets, the proceeds of sale must be applied towards discharging the sums secured by the securities in their order of priority.[136]

17.22 Status of the administrator

The administrator acts as the company's agent.[137] Under general principles an agent is not liable under a contract which he makes on behalf of his principal. Accordingly, an administrator would not be personally liable on any contract entered into by him in the course of acting as administrator, except in so far as the contract otherwise provides. However, in a suitable case, the court may oblige the administrator to comply with a contractual obligation of the company by granting an injunction.[138]

In acting as the company's agent in contractual matters, the administrator will commit a breach of duty if he fails to observe the limits imposed by the company's objects clause.[139] If the administrator has acted honestly and reasonably, under section 727 of the Companies Act 1985 the court may relieve him from liability for this breach of duty.[140]

Although the normal rule is that an agent is not personally liable on his principal's contracts, the Insolvency Act makes special provision for the payment of debts and liabilities incurred during the administration under contracts entered into by the administrator.[141] The special provision also applies to debts and liabilities incurred during the administration under contracts of employment adopted by the administrator after the first fourteen days from his appointment.[142] The nature of the provision is that a statutory charge, ranking in priority to the administrator's statutory charge for his own remuneration and expenses[143] and to any floating charge, is imposed on the company's property in respect of the said debts and liabilities.[144] Strictly these statutory charges only arise when the administrator vacates office but the ordinary practice is for administrators to meet obligations, including salaries and other payments due to employees, as they arise during the continuance of the administration.

It is central to a procedure intended to facilitate the recuperation of the financial health of a struggling business that, if at all possible, business continuity be maintained. Until the matter was litigated in the course of the administration of Paramount Airways Ltd

---

[134] Or a supplier of goods on hire purchase consents to the sale of those goods.

[135] *Re Newman Shopfitters (Cleveland) Ltd* [1991] BCLC 407.

[136] Section 15 (6).

[137] Section 14 (5).

[138] *Astor Chemicals Ltd v Synthetic Technology Ltd* [1990] BCLC 1, [1990] BCC 97.

[139] *Re Home Treat Ltd* [1991] BCLC 705, [1991] BCC 165.

[140] *Re Home Treat*, above.

[141] Section 19 (5).

[142] ibid. Note that the statutory charge is limited to debts and liabilities incurred while he was administrator.

[143] This statutory charge is conferred by section 19 (4). On what falls within the category of administration expenses, see *Re Atlantic Computers*, above.

[144] Section 19 (5).

(litigation which reached the House of Lords and which is reported as *Powdrill v Watson*)[145] the standard practice of administrators who chose to continue businesses was to inform employees that, despite the continuation of the business, their contracts would not be adopted and that no personal liability would be assumed by the administrators in respect of them. The underlying aim of this practice was to take the employees' contracts outside the scope of the statutory charge and hence ensure that payments arising from them did not rank in priority to the administrators' own remuneration and expenses.

In *Powdrill* the House of Lords held that this practice was ineffective. The mere assertion of non-adoption was judged to be without legal effect because adopting was a matter not merely of words but of fact. If administrators continued after the fourteen-day grace period to employ staff and to pay them in accordance with the terms of their previous contracts, they would be held to have inevitably adopted those contracts. Accordingly, as well as payments due in respect of services actually rendered by employees during the course of, and for the benefit of, the administration, sums in respect of wages accruing during contractual notice periods or in respect of damages payable for failure to give such notices, as well as pension contributions in respect of these periods, were entitled to the 'super priority' afforded by section 19 (5).

The outcome of the Paramount Airways litigation caused considerable consternation amongst insolvency practitioners who argued that it undermined the 'rescue culture' because administrators would be reluctant to retain employees with a view to continuing the business if this meant that they might not be able to recover their own remuneration and expenses, the company's resources having been exhausted by payments to employees. Lord Browne-Wilkinson, delivering the only reasoned opinion in the House of Lords, accepted this argument but felt compelled to conclude that the legislation could not be construed so as to avoid this unfortunate result. However, because of the furore caused by the earlier decision of the Court of Appeal (which was to broadly the same effect as that of the House of Lords, although with one variation with respect to holiday pay entitlements) the Government had already been galvanised into reviewing the position before the House of Lords gave its ruling. In March 1994 a new Insolvency Act was hurriedly enacted to clarify the position. The Insolvency Act 1994 amends the Insolvency Act 1986 with effect from 15 March 1994, but contracts of employment adopted prior to that date remain governed by the unamended section 19 as interpreted by the House of Lords in *Powdrill*.

Under the amendments introduced by the Insolvency Act 1994, liabilities to pay sums by way of wages or salary[146] or by way of contribution to an occupational pension scheme which are in respect of services rendered after adoption of the contract are 'qualifying liabilities' and, as such, they are entitled to the priority afforded by the statutory charge. Payments in respect of services rendered before the adoption of the contract are to be disregarded.[147] Payment in lieu of contract notice and damages for breach of contract are not payments in respect of services rendered after adoption and

---

[145] [1995] 2 All ER 65, [1995] 2 WLR 312. the decision of the Court of Appeal ([1994] 2 All ER 513), which wass varied by the House of Lords with respect to holiday pay entitlements, is noted Fletcher (1994) 15 Co. Law 145; Davies (1994) 23 ILJ 141.

[146] The position regarding wages and salary payable during sickness or holiday is clarified by section 19 (9) and (10) (as amended).

[147] Section 19 (8) as amended.

thus would not be qualifying liabilities under the amendments introduced by the Insolvency Act 1994.[148]

An administrator may incur liability in tort as an agent and, as an officer of the court, is subject to the rule in *ex parte James*[149] which requires him to do the fullest equity.[150]

17.23 Duties of the administrator

The first duty of the administrator is to take into his custody or under his control all the property to which the company is or appears to be entitled.[151] Where the administrator seizes or disposes of property which does not belong to the company, then, provided that at the time of such seizure or disposal he believed and had reasonable grounds for believing that his actions were justified, he is not liable to any third party in respect of resulting loss or damage except to the extent that it was caused by his own negligence.[152]

Secondly, the administrator must manage the affairs, business and property of the company.[153] In the initial period of the administration, the administrator must discharge this management obligation subject to any directions from the court. Once the creditors have approved the administrator's proposals, the administrator must manage in accordance with those proposals.[154]

17.24 The administrator's proposals

The formulation of proposals is an important stage in the administration procedure. Within three months after the making of the administration order[155] (or such longer period as the court may allow) the administrator must produce proposals for the achievement of the purpose or purposes specified in the administration order.[156] A statement of the proposals must be sent to all creditors (so far as their addresses are known) and also to the Registrar of Companies.[157] Members must also be informed of the proposals, either by being sent a copy of the statement or by publication of a notice informing them of their right to apply for a copy free of charge.[158] A copy of the statement of proposals must also be laid before a meeting of the company's creditors.[159]

Forthwith on appointment, the administrator must[160] require certain persons, in particular the officers of the company, to submit a statement of affairs giving details of *inter alia* the company's assets, debts and liabilities and of creditors and of securities held

---

[148] It is clear that under the general law, damages for breach of contract are not 'wages or salary': *Delaney v Staples* [1992] 1 AC 687 at pp. 692–3, [1992] 1 All ER 944, [1992] 2 WLR 451, [1992] ICR 483.

[149] (1874) LR 9 Ch App. 609.

[150] In *Powdrill*, above, the rule in *ex parte James* was applied by the Court of Appeal to require the administrator to pay interest on the sums payable to employees.

[151] Section 17 (1).

[152] Section 234 (3) and (4).

[153] Section 17 (2).

[154] Section 17 (2).

[155] The report must be made within three months and not at the end of the three months: *Re Charnley Davies Business Services Ltd* (1987) 3 BCC 408.

[156] Section 23 (1).

[157] Section 23 (1).

[158] Section 23 (2).

[159] Section 23 (1) (*b*).

[160] This is a mandatory obligation on the administrator: section 22 (1). But he can release individual persons from their obligation to comply: section 22 (5) (*a*).

by them.[161] The information produced is likely to be of considerable assistance to the administrator in the drawing-up of his proposals.

17.25 The meeting of the creditors

The meeting of the creditors convened to consider the administrator's proposals has limited powers. It can accept the administrator's proposals in toto but any modification favoured by the meeting can only be incorporated into the proposals with the administrator's consent.[162] If the administrator and the creditors cannot reach agreement, the matter must be referred back to the court. The court may order the discharge of the administration order and make such consequential order as it thinks fit, or adjourn the hearing conditionally or unconditionally or make an interim order or any other order that it thinks fit.[163] This can include allowing the administration to proceed despite the creditors' opposition.[164]

Where agreement is reached, the administrator must again report the outcome to the court and must also inform creditors and the Registrar of Companies.[165] Thereafter, for the duration of the administration, the administrator must make periodic reports to creditors.[166] The administrator's role after the proposals have been approved is to manage the company in accordance with the proposals. Ordinarily any proposed substantial revisions to the proposals must be put to the creditors at a creditors' meeting[167] but it has been held that the court has jurisdiction[168] itself to authorise deviation from the original proposals in an exceptional case, for example where the delay involved in convening a meeting could be fatal to the chances of success of the revised proposal.[169] If revised proposals are not approved, the administrator can continue to follow the old proposals, or, if his experience leads him to conclude that each of the purposes specified in the original administration order is incapable of achievement, he might apply to court under section 18 for the administration order to be discharged or varied so as to specify an additional purpose.

17.26 The committee of creditors

Where the administrator's proposals are approved at a creditors' meeting, the meeting may also decide to establish a creditors' committee. The function of the creditors' committee is to assist the administrator in discharging his functions.[170]

17.27 Cases where urgent action is required

The structure of the Insolvency Act 1986 envisages the administrator managing the day-to-day conduct of the company's affairs for the period during which he is making

---

[161] Section 22. They must comply within twenty-one days of being given notice of the requirement by the administrator unless the administrator extends the period: section 22 (4) and (5) (*b*).

[162] Section 24 (2).

[163] Section 24 (5).

[164] *Re Maxwell Communications Corp* [1991] BCC 465 at p. 467.

[165] Section 24 (4) and rule 2.30.

[166] Rule 2.30.

[167] Section 25.

[168] Under section 14.

[169] *Re Smallman Construction Ltd* (1988) 4 BCC 784, [1989] BCLC 420.

[170] Section 26 and rules 2.32 *et seq.*

investigations and inquiries with a view to formulating the proposals for the achievement of the administration purposes; but, before any radical steps are taken to achieve those purposes, the creditors are to be given an opportunity to consider and review what the administrator proposes to do. Underlying this structure is the assumption that, in return for the moratorium imposed by the administration procedure, creditors are to have an important say in the conduct of the administration.

What this standard scheme ignores, however, is the possibility of circumstances arising in which the company's interests dictate that the administrator should act very quickly, perhaps even before there is an opportunity to convene a meeting of the creditors. If, for example, the administrator is offered a generous price for the business conditional upon the sale being concluded in accordance with a tight timetable which does not allow for the holding of a creditors' meeting, what can and should the administrator do? Under sections 14 and 17 of the Act the administrator has wide powers even before his proposals are approved by the creditors, but do they extend to selling off the company's business prior to the holding of the creditors' meeting?

One of the earlier administrations was of the Charnley Davies group of companies. The administrator had some difficulty in reconciling the need for urgent action and the timetable of events envisaged by the legislation, and this gave the courts an opportunity to consider the matter. First, in an unreported decision, Vinelott J held that the administrator's powers under sections 14 and 17 were sufficiently wide to allow him to sell off the business of various companies in the Charnley Davies group before the creditors' meeting and that this sale did not require the sanction of the court.[171] However, in *Re Charnley Davies Business Services Ltd*[172] Harman J described the administrator's disposal of these businesses without complying with the statutory duty to put proposals before the creditors as 'regrettable' because it undermined the scheme of the Act. Harman J's criticism is echoed in cases arising from other administrations where the courts have indicated that, although an expedited procedure is possible, it should be regarded as exceptional since it cuts across the normal order of events contemplated by the legislation.[173] The safest course for an administrator faced with this dilemma is to apply to court under section 14 or 17 for directions as to how to proceed. Where the company's assets are subject to fixed charges, the administrator may be required to apply to court in any event in order to obtain an order authorising disposal of these assets.[174]

A particular problem which can result from following an expedited procedure is that this may mean the administrator has effectively achieved the purpose or purposes set out in the administration order before the meeting of creditors. What, if anything, is left for the creditors to approve? In *Re Charnley Davies Business Services Ltd*[175] Harman J held that the meeting of creditors convened under section 23 was only competent to consider the administrator's proposals for achievement of the administration purpose or purposes and that it could not alternatively consider a proposal to wind up the company. However,

---

[171] 21 January 1987, unreported.

[172] Above.

[173] *Re Consumer & Industrial Press Ltd (No. 2)* (1988) 4 BCC 72; *Re NS Distribution Ltd* [1990] BCLC 169 (sale of a single asset distinguished from sale of the whole undertaking).

[174] Section 15. This will also apply to goods in the company's possession under a hire-purchase agreement. The courts will not, barring exceptional circumstances, make a section 15 order in respect of a material part of the company's assets before the proposals have been approved by the creditors: *Re Consumer and Industrial Press Ltd (No. 2)*, above.

[175] Above.

since there were no administration purposes left to consider, Harman J adopted the exceptional course of discharging the administration before the section 23 meeting had been held[176] and of appointing the administrator as the liquidator of the various group companies.

17.28 Protection of the interests of creditors and members

At any time when an administration order is in force a creditor or member of the company may apply to the court by petition for an order under section 27 of the Insolvency Act 1986 on the ground that the company's affairs, business and property are being or have been managed by the administrator in a manner which is unfairly prejudicial to the interests of its creditors or members generally or of some part of its creditors or members (including at least himself) or that any actual or proposed act or omission of the administrator is or would be so prejudicial. This is an important provision which allows aggrieved creditors (and members) whose rights of action are otherwise suspended to seek relief from the court if they can show that the administrator is not maintaining a proper balance between the interests of creditors (or members) in his conduct of the administration.

On such an application the court may make such order as it thinks fit for giving relief in respect of the matters complained of, or adjourn the hearing conditionally or unconditionally, or make an interim order or any other order that it thinks fit.[177] An order under section 27 may, in particular:[178]

(1) regulate the future management by the administrator of the company's affairs, business and property;

(2) require the administrator to refrain from doing or continuing an act complained of by the petitioner or to do an act which the petitioner has complained he has omitted to do;

(3) require the summoning of a meeting of creditors or members for the purpose of considering such matters as the court may direct;

(4) discharge the administration order and make such consequential provisions as the court thinks fit.

However, an order under section 27 must not prejudice or prevent the implementation of a voluntary arrangement approved by the creditors or any compromise or arrangement sanctioned under section 425 of the Companies Act 1985 or, where the application for the order under section 27 of the Act has been made more than twenty-eight days after the approval of any proposal or revised proposals put forward by the administrator, the implementation of those proposals or revised proposals.[179]

Thus far the one reported decision under section 27 is that of Millett J in *Re Charnley Davies Ltd*[180] where it was held that the administrator had not acted negligently in the timing or the manner of the sale of the business of various companies in the Charnley Davies group, In a dictum which could limit the scope of this remedy in later cases,

---

[176] He also extended the period for holding this meeting to relieve the administrator of the personal liability that would otherwise have been incurred for the failure to hold the meeting within three months of the making of the administration order.

[177] Section 27 (2).

[178] Section 27 (4).

[179] Section 27 (3).

[180] [1990] BCLC 760, [1990] BCC 605.

Millett J commented that an allegation of negligence only does not constitute an allegation of management in a manner which is unfairly prejudicial to the creditors and that, accordingly, it does not fall within the scope of section 27.

17.29 Discharge of the administration order and vacation of office

The administrator may apply to court at any time for the administration order to be discharged or to be varied so as to specify an additional purpose.[181]

The administrator must make an application for the discharge or variation of the administration order if it appears to him that the purpose, or each of the purposes, specified in the administration order either has been achieved or has become incapable of achievement or if he is required to do so by a meeting of the company's creditors.[182]

The court is given a wide discretion on the hearing of the administrator's application to discharge or vary the administration order and may make such consequential provision as it thinks fit, or adjourn the hearing conditionally or unconditionally or make an interim order or any other order it thinks fit.[183]

An office copy of the order discharging or varying an administration order must be sent to the Registrar of Companies.[184]

The administrator may be removed from office by order of the court.[185] Under the Insolvency Rules, an administrator may also resign by giving notice but only on grounds of ill health, because he intends ceasing to be in practice as an insolvency practitioner or because there is some conflict of interest or change of personal circumstances which precludes or makes impracticable the further discharge by him of the duties of administrator.[186] The administrator is only entitled to resign on other grounds with leave of the court.[187]

The administrator is required to vacate office if he ceases to be qualified to act as an insolvency practitioner in relation to the company or if the administration order is discharged.[188]

A person who has ceased to be the administrator of a company obtains a release at such time as the court may determine (except in the case of a person who has died when the release is obtained at the time at which notice is given to the court indicating that the administrator has ceased to hold office). The release discharges the administrator from all liability both in respect of acts or omissions of his in the administration and otherwise in relation to his conduct as administrator.[189] However, the provisions as to release do not prevent the court from exercising its powers under section 212 of the Act which allows an order to be made for misfeasance against an administrator on the application of the Official Receiver, the liquidator or any creditor or contributory of the company.

---

[181] Section 18 (1) of the Insolvency Act 1986.
[182] Section 18 (2).
[183] Section 18 (3).
[184] Section 18 (4) and see section 18 (5).
[185] Section 19 (1).
[186] Rule 2.53 (1).
[187] Rule 2.53 (2).
[188] Section 19 (2).
[189] Section 20.

17.30 The administrator as an 'office-holder'

The Insolvency Act 1986 gives certain rights and privileges to categories of insolvency practitioners defined as 'office-holders'. An administrator is within the definition of an office-holder for certain purposes.

As an office-holder, an administrator can attack transactions which took place prior to his appointment on the grounds that they amount to transactions at an undervalue, preferences, extortionate credit transactions, vulnerable floating charges or transactions defrauding creditors. These special powers are also enjoyed by liquidators and are considered further below.[190] Unlike a liquidator, an administrator does not have standing to bring proceedings for fraudulent or wrongful trading.

Suppliers of gas, electricity, water and telecommunications services cannot make it a condition of continuing the supply that the administrator pay outstanding charges. This protection is given to the administrator as an office-holder. However, the supplier can require the administrator to give a personal guarantee in respect of any new supplies.[191]

The powers which an administrator, as an office-holder, enjoys in relation to investigating the conduct of the company's affairs prior to his appointment are the same as those enjoyed by a liquidator. They are considered further below.[192]

PART 4: THE COMPULSORY LIQUIDATION OF COMPANIES

17.31 Compulsory winding-up

We now turn to consider the liquidation or, as it is also called, the winding-up of companies. The first type of winding-up procedure is the compulsory liquidation, which entails the presentation of a petition requesting that the court make a winding-up order and appoint a liquidator. All companies incorporated under the Companies Act 1985 and the statutes which it replaced are subject to the winding-up jurisdiction of the court under the Insolvency Act 1986.[193] Oversea companies registered under the branch registration regime[194] or the place of business regime[195] may also be compulsorily wound

---

[190] Part 7, below.

[191] Section 233.

[192] Part 7, below.

[193] Section 117 of the Insolvency Act 1986 deals with the respective jurisdictions of the High Court and County Court.

[194] Oversea Companies and Credit and Financial Institutions (Branch Disclosure) Regulations 1992 (SI 1992 No. 3179).

[195] Companies Act 1985, Part XXIII.

up, as may unregistered companies[196] including foreign companies which carry on business in Great Britain but which are not registered.[197]

Under section 11 of the Insolvency Act 1986, upon the making of an administration order any petition for the winding-up of the company must be dismissed by the court. During the currency of an administration order no winding-up order can be made.[198]

17.32 Grounds for a compulsory winding-up order

Section 122 of the Insolvency Act 1986 sets out the grounds upon which a company may be wound up by the court.[199] Each of the grounds laid down in the section will be considered in turn.

Ground A: 'The company has by special resolution resolved that the company be wound up by the court.'

Nothing further need be said about this ground.

Ground B: 'Being a public company which was registered as such on its original incorporation, the company has not been issued with a certificate under section 117 of the Companies Act 1985 (public company share capital requirements) and more than a year has expired since it was so registered.'

As to section 117, see 2.7, above.

Ground C: 'It is an old public company, within the meaning of the Consequential Provisions Act.'

The Companies Consolidation (Consequential Provisions) Act 1985, section 1 defines 'old public company' for these purposes. An old public company is a company limited by shares or by guarantee having a share capital in respect of which the following conditions are satisfied:

(1) the company either existed on 22 December 1980 or was incorporated after that date pursuant to an application made before that date;

(2) on that date or, if later, on the day of the company's incorporation the company was not or (as the case may be) would not have been a private company within section 28 of the Companies Act 1948; and

---

[196] Defined for this purpose by section 220 of the Insolvency Act 1986. See *Re Witney Town Football and Social Club* [1993] BCC 874; *Re Normandy Marketing Ltd* [1993] BCC 879.

[197] The court must be satisfied that there is a sufficient connection with the jurisdiction. It has been held that this does not necessarily have to be the presence of assets in the jurisdiction: *Re Real Estate Development Co.* [1991] BCLC 210; *Re a Company (No. 00359 of 1987)* (also reported as *International Westminster Bank plc v Okeanos Maritime Corp*) [1988] Ch 210, [1987] 3 All ER 137, [1987] 3 WLR 339, [1987] BCLC 450; *Re Eloc Electro-Optieck and Communicatie BV* [1982] Ch 43, [1981] 2 All ER 1111, [1981] 3 WLR 176. See also *Banque des Marchands de Moscou v Kinderley* [1951] 1 Ch 112 (CA); *Re Compania Merabello San Nicholas SA* [1973] Ch 75; *Re Allobrogia Steamship Corp* [1978] 3 All ER 423. There must be a reasonable possibility that the winding-up order would benefit those applying for it and the court must be able to exercise jurisdiction over one or more persons interested in the distribution of the company's assets.

[198] The correct procedure where liquidation is to follow administration is for the administration order to be discharged before the winding-up order is made: *Re Charnley Davies Business Services*, above.

[199] These are the general grounds. There are also special grounds which apply in particular circumstances, e.g. section 124A (petition by the DTI on grounds of public interest), and section 92 of the Banking Act 1987 (Petition by Bank of England against authorised institutions or former authorised institutions).

(3) the company has not since that date or the day of the company's incorporation (as the case may be) either been re-registered as a public company or become a private company.

This ground enables those companies which have not complied with the requirements as to re-registration to be wound up. It is envisaged that the Secretary of State would be responsible for petitioning to have such companies wound up.

Ground D: 'The company does not commence its business within a year from its incorporation or suspends its business for a whole year.'

Whether or not a company has commenced its business or suspended it is essentially a question of fact. However, questions may arise over the construction of the company's objects clause in its memorandum of association in determining whether for the purposes of the section the business of a company has been commenced or suspended.[200] If evidence is placed before the court that a company's business will be commenced or resumed within the foreseeable future the court may exercise its discretion and refuse to make an order.[201] If a company suspends merely part of its business it does not run the risk of being wound up on this ground unless that part may fairly be said to represent 'substantially the whole' of the company's business.[202] There is some overlap between this ground and the so-called 'just and equitable ground' discussed below and those cases where the substratum of the company has vanished. As to the latter, see 15.19, above.

Ground E: 'Except in the case of a private company limited by shares or by guarantee, the number of members is reduced below two.'

In determining the number of members, past members who may still be liable to contribute in a winding-up and the representatives of deceased members may not be counted.[203]

Ground F: 'The company is unable to pay its debts.'

This is the most common ground upon which petitions are presented. Section 123 of the Insolvency Act 1986 contains the definition of inability to pay debts. The cash flow and balance sheet tests of insolvency are also tests of inability to pay debts for this purpose. In addition, a company is deemed unable to pay its debts:

(1) if a creditor (by assignment or otherwise) to whom the company is indebted in a sum exceeding £750 then due has served on the company, by leaving it at the company's registered office, a written demand (in the prescribed form) requiring the company to pay the sum so due and the company has for three weeks thereafter neglected to pay the sum or to secure or compound for it to the reasonable satisfaction of the creditor; or

(2) if, in England and Wales, execution or other process issued on a judgment, decree

---

[200] *Re Eastern Telegraph Co.* [1947] 2 All ER 104.

[201] *Re Railway Warehousing Co.* (1867) 36 LJ Ch 827 but see *Re Tumacacori Mining Co.*, (1874) LR 17 Eq. 534 where an order was made despite the fact that a majority of the members opposed the order, the court holding that they were acting unreasonably.

[202] *Re Norwegian Titanic Iron Co.* (1866) 35 Beav. 223; *Re New Gas Co.* (1877) 5 Ch D 703 (CA); *Re Patent Bread Machinery Co.* (1866) 14 LT 582; *Re Kronand Metal Co.* [1899] WN 14.

[203] *Re Bowling and Welby's Contract* [1895] 1 Ch 663 (CA).

or order of any court in favour of a creditor of the company is returned unsatisfied in whole or in part; or

(3) if, in Scotland, the induciae of a charge for payment on an extract decree, or an extract registered bond, or an extract registered protest, have expired without payment being made; or

(4) if, in Northern Ireland, a certificate of unenforceability has been granted in respect of a judgment against the company.

The trade creditors of a company very often serve statutory demands upon it to bring pressure on the company to pay their debts. This practice can prove to be more effective than issuing a writ which the company knows may not come to trial for some time. However, there is a risk in proceeding in this way. If the company disputes the debt and the court accepts that the dispute is genuine,[204] it may be held to be an abuse of process to proceed by way of statutory demand instead of by writ[205] and the creditor may be held liable to indemnify the company for its costs.[206] Also, the company may be able to resist the making of a winding-up order by establishing that its failure to pay resulted otherwise than from neglect, for example where it can show that the demand was never received.[207]

If a debt is disputed in part but the part of the debt which is indisputable is above the statutory minimum a petition can still validly be presented.[208] If a creditor makes a statutory demand for more than was actually due, provided the amount that was due was more than £750, any winding-up order made by the court on the basis of the demand remains valid.[209]

The deeming provisions set out in (1)–(4) above provide convenient methods where by the petitioner is able to establish to the court that a company is unable to pay its debts within the meaning of section 123. A company can also be shown to be unable to pay its debts if it fails to pay an undisputed[210] debt when payment is demanded ('cash flow insolvency'). An advantage that this ground has over the statutory demand procedure is that the creditor does not have to wait three weeks before applying to court. Being able to act swiftly against a company in financial difficulties can be extremely important, especially where there is a risk of the directors of the company deliberately dissipating its assets in the period before control is taken out of their hands, or of assets being absorbed into a secured creditor's floating charge.[211]

The test of cash flow insolvency does not in terms require the unpaid debt to amount to more than £750 and this therefore appears to be a further advantage over the statutory demand procedure. This apparent advantage has been limited in practice. Where the

---

[204] *Re Janeash Ltd* [1990] BCC 250 (no genuine dispute).

[205] *London Wharfing Co.* (1866) 35 Beav. 37; *Re Brighton Club Co.* (1865) 35 Beav. 204; *Re London and Paris Banking Corp* (1875) 19 Eq. 444; *Re Gold Hill Mines* (1883) 23 Ch D 210; *Mann v Goldstein* [1968] 1 WLR 1091; *Stonegate Securities Ltd v Gregory* [1980] Ch 576.

[206] *Re a Company (No 0012209 of 1991)* [1992] 2 All ER 797, [1992] 1 WLR 351, [1992] BCLC 865 followed in *Re a Company (No. 00751 of 1992)* [1992] BCLC 869.

[207] *Re London and Paris Banking Corp* (1875) 19 Eq. 444; *Re a Company* [1985] BCLC 37; and see *Re Cannon Screen Entertainment Ltd* [1989] BCLC 661.

[208] *Re Tweeds Garage Ltd* [1962] 1 Ch 406; *Re Trinity Insurance Co. Ltd* [1990] BCLC 235; *Taylor's Industrial Flooring Ltd v M&H Plant Hire (Manchester) Ltd* [1990] BCC 44, [1990] BCLC 216.

[209] *Cardiff Coal Co. v Norton* (1867) 2 Ch App. 405. On costs in these circumstances, see *Re a Company (No. 008122 of 1989) ex parte Transcontinental Insurance Services Ltd* [1990] BCLC 697.

[210] *Taylor's Industrial Flooring* was distinguished in *Re a Company (No. 0010656 of 1990)* [1991] BCLC 464, where the debt was disputed.

[211] *Taylor's Industrial Flooring*, above.

petitioner succeeds in establishing a ground on which a winding-up order may be made, it has been said that he has a prima facie right to a winding-up order or that he is entitled to the order *ex debito justitiae*[212] but this prima facie 'right' is subject to certain settled exceptions. The courts do not want the winding-up procedure to be used as a mechanism for the collection of small debts and, as a result, the practice of the courts is to refuse a petition based on a debt of less than £750 unless there are special circumstances such as where it is supported by other creditors.

Another established exception, which applies even where the petition is based on a debt of more than £750, is where other creditors in the same class[213] oppose the making of the winding-up order. In this case the court will usually have regard to the majority of the creditors and will refuse the petition if it is opposed by the majority.[214]

A specific case where there can be a difference of opinion between groups of creditors is where some creditors favour a compulsory winding-up whilst others are content for the company to be wound up voluntarily. This situation is discussed at 17.50, below.

Ground G: 'The court is of the opinion that it is just and equitable that the company should be wound up.'

This is in effect a remedy for minority shareholders and is examined at 15.17–15.20, above.

17.33 Persons who may present a petition

Section 124 of the Insolvency Act 1986 provides that a petition for the winding-up of a company may be presented to the court by all or any of the following whether acting together or separately:

(1) the company;
(2) the directors of the company;
(3) any creditor or creditors of the company (including any contingent or prospective creditor or creditors);
(4) any contributory or contributories.

A petition presented by the directors does not require the approval of the shareholders. In *Re Instrumentation Electrical Services Ltd*[215] Mervyn Davies J held that all the directors had to join in the petition. The position may be different where the decision to seek a winding-up is embodied in a formal board resolution, because it is the duty of all directors to implement such resolutions.[216]

An administrative receiver is expressly empowered by the Act[217] to present or defend a

[212] *Bowes v Hope Life Insurance etc. Co.* (1865) 11 HLC 389; *Re Western of Canada Oil Lands and Works Co.* (1873) 17 Eq. 1 at 6; *Re Chapel House Colliery Co.* (1883) 24 Ch D 259.

[213] *Re Crigglestone Coal Co. Ltd* [1906] 2 Ch 327 (unsecured creditors in different class from secured creditor for this purpose), *Re Leigh Estates (UK) Ltd* [1994] BCC 292. See section 195 which provides for the holding of meetings to ascertain the wishes of creditors (or contributories) on matters relating to the winding up of the company.

[214] *Re Chapel House Colliery Co.*, above; *Re Uruguay Central and Hygueritas Rly Co. of Monte Video* (1873) 11 Ch D 372; *Re St Thomas's Dock Co.* (1876) 2 Ch D 116.

[215] (1988) 4 BCC 301.

[216] See *Re Equiticorp International plc* (1989) 1 WLR 1010 (directors' petition for an administration order).

[217] Section 42 and Schedule 1, para. 21. Whether a receiver who is not an administrative receiver has this power depends upon the construction of the debenture under which he was appointed: *Re Emmadart Ltd* [1979] 1 Ch 540. For an example of an administrative receiver's petition see *Re Television Parlour plc* (1988) 4 BCC 95.

petition for the winding-up of the company over which he has been appointed. An administrator also has this power.[218]

A contributory, which means, broadly, any present or past member of the company, is not entitled to present a winding-up petition unless either: (a) the number of members is reduced below two; or (b) the shares in respect of which he is a contributory, or some of them, were originally allotted to him, or have been held by him and registered in his name, for at least six months during the eighteen months before the commencement of the winding-up or devolved on him through the death of a former holder. The term 'contributory' is considered further at 17.56, below.

A contributory who has not paid calls upon his shares will only be permitted to petition in very special circumstances[219] and will usually be required to pay the amount of his unpaid calls into court.[220] The company's articles of association cannot take away the right of a member to petition for the company's winding-up.[221]

In practice most petitioners will be creditors of the company. A creditor may petition whether he is secured or unsecured.[222] The creditor may be the original creditor of the company or an assignee of the debt.[223] Difficulties arise where a creditor has taken an assignment of part of a debt and wishes to present a petition. Because he is only a creditor of the company in equity he is unable without the concurrence of the original creditor to make a valid demand for the debt to be paid. If he cannot obtain the concurrence of the owner of the residue of the debt he will have to proceed on a basis other than non-compliance with a statutory (or other) demand.

A contingent or prospective creditor of the company is also entitled to petition.[224]

17.34 The hearing of the petition

Section 125 of the Insolvency Act 1986 states that the court, on hearing the petition, may:

(1) dismiss it;
(2) adjourn the hearing conditionally or unconditionally;
(3) make an interim order;
(4) make any order that it thinks fit;
(5) make a winding-up order.

The court cannot refuse to make a winding-up order on the basis only that the company's assets have been mortgaged to an amount equal to or in excess of those assets or that the company has no assets.

---

[218] Section 14 and Schedule 1, para. 21. The clerk of the magistrates' court, the Secretary of State and the Bank of England are other persons who can petition for winding-up on various grounds: sections 124, 124A and section 92 of the Banking Act 1987. Note also the power of the Official Receiver to petition for the winding-up of a company which is being wound up voluntarily: section 124 (5).

[219] The holder of share warrants to bearer, who is not the original allottee, cannot present a petition: *Re Wala Wynaad Co.* (1882) 21 Ch D 849; see also *Re Patent Steam Engine Co.* (1878) 8 Ch D 464 (company neglected to register persons who established their title to shares for more than six months: held they were entitled to petition); *Re Gattopardon Ltd* [1969] 1 WLR 61; *Re a Company* [1894] 2 Ch 349.

[220] *Re Crystal Reef Gold Mining Co.* [1892] 1 Ch 408.

[221] *Re Peveril Gold Mines* [1898] 1 Ch 122 (CA).

[222] The secured creditor does not invalidate his security; *Moor v Anglo-Italian Bank* (1879) 10 Ch D 681; *Re Borough of Portsmouth etc. Tramways Co.* [1892] 2 Ch 362; *Re Great Western Coal Co.* (1882) 21 Ch D 769; *Re Cambrian Mining Co.* [1881] WN 125.

[223] *Re Paris Skating Rink Co.* (1877) 5 Ch D 959 (CA); *Re Montgomery Moore Syndicate* [1903] WN 121.

[224] *Re Dollar Land Holdings plc* [1993] BCC 823; *Tottenham Hotspur plc v Edennote plc* [1995] 1 BCLC 65.

If a petition has been presented by the members of a company as contributories on the ground that it is just and equitable that the company should be wound up, the court, if it is of the opinion (a) that the petitioners are entitled to relief either by winding up the company or by some other means; and (b) that in the absence of any other remedy it would be just and equitable that the company should be wound up, may make the order. However, if the court is of the opinion that some other remedy is available to the petitioners and that they are acting unreasonably in seeking to have the company wound up instead of pursuing that other remedy, it may refuse to make the order.[225]

Once made, a winding-up order operates in favour of all creditors and contributories of the company as if made on the joint petition of a creditor and a contributory.[226]

17.35 Commencement of the winding-up

On the making of a winding-up order the commencement of the liquidation relates back to the time at which the petition was presented. However, if before the presentation of the petition the company has passed a resolution for voluntary winding-up, the winding-up of the company is deemed to have commenced at the time that resolution was passed (whether it was for a members' or creditors' voluntary liquidation).[227] The relation back is important because of some of the results which follow upon the commencement of the winding-up, such as its effect upon dispositions of the company's assets.

17.36 The effect of a winding-up order on dispositions of assets

Section 127 of the Insolvency Act 1986 states:

In a winding-up by the court, any disposition of the company's property, and any transfer of shares, or alteration in the status of the company's members, made after the commencement of the winding-up is, unless the court otherwise orders, void.[228]

In *Re French's (Wine Bar) Ltd*[229] the company had contracted to sell its assets, comprising mainly a lease and the goodwill of the business, prior to the commencement of its winding-up. Vinelott J held[230] that the completion of the contract did not constitute a disposition of the company's property within what is now section 127, because that section relates only to property in which the company is beneficially interested. The company had entered into an unconditional contract to sell the property and the contract was specifically enforceable. Accordingly the beneficial interest in the property had passed to the purchaser before the commencement of the winding-up.

Vinelott J cautioned that it did not follow that the completion of any contract would in all circumstances fall outside the section. If, for example, the contract was conditional or voidable by the company, the waiver of the condition or the confirmation of the contract

[225] Section 125 (2). See 15.15, above.
[226] Insolvency Act 1986, section 130 (4).
[227] Section 129 of the Insolvency Act 1986. The time will be noted on the petition itself by the court when it is presented. The section also states that 'unless the court, on proof of fraud or mistake, directs otherwise, all proceedings taken in the voluntary winding up are deemed to have been validly taken.'
[228] This section does not apply to dispositions giving rise to market charges: section 175 (4) of the Companies Act 1989.
[229] [1987] BCLC 499, (1987) 3 BCC 173.
[230] Citing *Re Gray's Inn Construction Co. Ltd* [1980] 1 All ER 814, [1980] 1 WLR 711 and *Re Margart Pty Ltd, Hamilton v Westpac Banking Corp* (1984) 9 ACLR 269, [1985] BCLC 314 (realisation of floating charge security).

might amount to a disposition, as might the variation of contractual terms. Vinelott J stated that in practice, unless a contract was plainly specifically enforceable and there was no possible dispute, it would be prudent to seek the court's approval for completion.

The operation of section 127 in relation to payments into and out of a company's bank account has generated some case-law. The simplest view is that all such payments are dispositions of property[231] but the cases do not fully support this view. It is established that any payments into an overdrawn account are dispositions of the company's property for the purposes of section 127.[232] The argument that a payment into an account which is in credit is also a disposition within section 127[233] was considered and rejected in *Re Barn Crown Ltd*,[234] where such a payment was characterised as amounting simply to an adjustment of entries in the statement recording the account between the bank and the company. In respect of payments out of an account, *Re Gray's Inn Construction*[235] supports the proposition that a withdrawal from an overdrawn account is a disposition of the company's property, but the point was there conceded by counsel. Against the view that this is a disposition it may be argued that a withdrawal from an overdrawn account merely increases the company's liability to its bank and does not involve the disposition of any of its property.[236] A withdrawal from an account which is in credit is widely regarded as a disposition of the company's property because this has the effect of reducing the value of the company's claim against its bank.[237]

The safest course for anybody dealing with a company which has a petition on file is for an application to be made to the court for a validating order. The court can make such an order even before the hearing of the winding-up petition.[238] The court can authorise particular dispositions or the general continuance of trading (including, for that purpose, the continued operation of the company's bank accounts). The court can validate prospective dispositions or grant retrospective validations. In *Re Gray's Inn Construction*[239] it was held[240] that the bank was entitled to have validated retrospectively payments in and out of the account before it became aware of the petition. Buckley LJ stated that 'a disposition carried out in good faith in the ordinary course of business[241] at a time when the parties are unaware that a petition has been presented may, it seems, normally be validated by the court unless there is any ground for thinking that the transaction may involve an attempt to prefer the disponee in which case the transaction would probably

---

[231] *Re McGuinness Bros (UK) Ltd* (1987) 3 BCC 571 at p. 574.

[232] *Re Gray's Inn Construction Ltd*, above; *Re McGuinness Bros (UK) Ltd*, above.

[233] This argument, which derives some support from dicta in *Re Gray's Inn Construction Ltd*, and *Re McGuinness Bros (UK) Ltd*, above, is explained in Goode, *Principles of Corporate Insolvency Law*, (Sweet & Maxwell, 1990) at pp. 187–8.

[234] [1994] 4 All ER 42, [1994] BCC 381.

[235] Above.

[236] Goode, op. cit. at pp. 189–90. Compare *Pennington's Corporate Insolvency Law* (Butterworths, 1991), p. 99.

[237] Goode, op. cit. at pp. 188–9; Pennington, op. cit. at p. 99. But note the Australian cases cited in *Re Barn Crown* which hold that there is no disposition of a company's property where its bank meets cheques drawn on an account which is in credit.

[238] *Re AI Levy (Holdings) Ltd* [1964] Ch 19.

[239] [1980] 1 All ER 814, [1980] 1 WLR 711.

[240] Citing *Re Wiltshire Iron Co.* (1868) LR 3 Ch App. 443; *Re Neath Harbour Smelting and Rolling Works* (1887) 56 LT 727, 729; *Re Liverpool Civil Service Association* (1874) LR 9 Ch App. 511; see also *Re Clifton Place Garage Ltd* [1970] Ch 477, approving *Re Steane's (Bournemouth)* [1950] 1 All ER 21; *Re TW Construction* [1954] 1 WLR 840.

[241] See also *Denney v John Hudson & Co. Ltd* [1992] BCLC 901. Expenditure incurred in defending an unfair prejudice petition is not incurred in the ordinary course of business where the essence of the claim is a dispute between shareholders: *Re Crossmore Electrical and Civil Engineering Ltd* (1989) 5 BCC 37.

not be validated'. It was also accepted that dispositions which did not reduce the value of assets (such as sales of assets at full value or for more than they were worth) would normally be validated. In general the court, in considering whether to grant the validating order, will consider whether the disposition would be for the benefit of the company's creditors.[242] A disposition which allows one pre-liquidation creditor to receive payment in full whilst other creditors are limited to the dividends that they will receive in the liquidation will only be sanctioned where this will benefit the creditors as a whole.[243]

Section 127 does not in itself afford a statutory remedy towards the recovery of property disposed of after the commencement of the liquidation. Recourse must be had to the rules for the tracing of property and, accordingly, no claim will be upheld against a bona fide purchaser for value without notice.[244]

Section 127 states that every transfer of shares or alteration in the status of the company's members made after the commencement of the winding-up is void unless the court orders otherwise. No transfer can be effected without registration of that transfer in the register of members of the company. The register cannot be rectified without leave of the court. Nevertheless, as between the vendor and purchaser of shares under a contract equitable rights arise which are not affected by this section, and the purchaser can claim through his vendor any payments made in the liquidation in respect of the shares, and the vendor may, when calls are made (but not before), enforce his right to indemnity.[245]

17.37 The provisional liquidator

At any time after the presentation of a petition and before a winding-up order is made the court has power upon the application of any person who was entitled to present a petition to appoint a provisional liquidator.[246]

The powers of a provisional liquidator will be set out in the order of the court appointing him. Typically a provisional liquidator's powers will be limited to 'taking possession of, collecting and protecting the assets of the company, such assets not to be distributed or parted with until further order'.

The purpose of appointing a provisional liquidator is to preserve the status quo pending the hearing of the petition by the court.

Either the Official Receiver[247] or any other qualified insolvency practitioner may be appointed provisional liquidator. If a winding-up order is subsequently made or the petition is dismissed, the provisional liquidator's appointment terminates and if appropriate a liquidator will be appointed by the court or the creditors and contributories as described below.[248]

---

[242] *Re AI Levy (Holdings) Ltd*, above. See also *Re a Company (No. 007523 of 1986)* (1987) 3 BCC 57; *Re Sugar Properties (Derisley Wood) Ltd* (1987) 3 BCC 88; *Re Tramway Building & Construction Co. Ltd* [1988] Ch 293, [1988] 2 WLR 640, (1987) 3 BCC 443; *Re Webb Electrical Ltd* (1988) 4 BCC 230; *Re Rafidain Bank* [1992] BCC 376.

[243] *Re Gray's Inn Construction*, above.

[244] *Re J. Leslie Engineering Co. Ltd* [1976] 1 WLR 292.

[245] See sections 550 and 567 of the Companies Act 1985 and section 160 (2) of the Insolvency Act 1986; *Re Onward Building Society* [1891] 2 QB 463 (CA); *Re Hughes–Hallet v Indian Mammoth Mines* (1883) 22 Ch D 561.

[246] Insolvency Act 1986, section 135.

[247] If the Official Receiver is appointed the applicant is also required to deposit a sum with the Official Receiver to cover his remuneration and expenses; Insolvency Rules 1986, rule 4.27.

[248] See 17.38, below.

17.38 Appointment of the liquidator

On a winding-up order being made by the court the Official Receiver becomes the liquidator of the company and continues in office until another person is appointed as liquidator by the creditors or contributories of the company.[249] The Official Receiver will normally summon separate meetings of the company's creditors and contributories so that they may choose another person to act as liquidator of the company in his place.[250] The creditors and contributories may both resolve at those meetings to nominate a person to be a liquidator of the company. The liquidator will be the person nominated by the creditors. Where creditors do not resolve to nominate a liquidator the person nominated by the contributories fills that office.[251] In the event that the creditors and contributories resolve to nominate different persons, it is open for any creditor or contributory to apply to the court within seven days of the date of the creditor's nomination to determine who should be liquidator. On such an application the court has power to order that the contributories' nominee some other person be liquidator of the company or that there be a joint appointment with the creditors' and the contributories' nominees acting as joint liquidators.[252]

Where a winding-up order is made immediately upon the discharge of an administration order or during the currency of a voluntary arrangement under Part I of the Insolvency Act 1986, the court may upon the making of the order appoint the person who has ceased to be administrator or the continuing supervisor of the voluntary arrangement to be the liquidator. In this event the Official Receiver does not become liquidator of the company and there is no need to summon meetings of the creditors and contributories.[253]

If there is any vacancy in the office of liquidator this is filled by the Official Receiver until a further appointment is made.[254]

17.39 The liquidator's status

As in the case of directors, it is not easy to state succinctly yet accurately the position occupied by a liquidator. In several cases there will be found statements to the effect that he is a trustee for the creditors, or, in the case of a solvent company, for the contributories. Thus, Lord Selborne says, 'The hand which receives the calls necessarily receives them as a statutory trustee for the equal and rateable payment of all the creditors',[255] and James LJ speaks of the assets as being 'fixed by the Act of Parliament with a trust for equal distribution among the creditors'.[256] The House of Lords has confirmed that a liquidator

---

[249] Section 136 (2). The appointment arises 'by virtue of his office'. The Official Receiver is a civil servant and should not be confused with an administrative receiver.

[250] Section 136 (4), (5). If the Official Receiver decides not to call meetings of creditors and contributories he must give notice of his decision to the court and to the company's creditors and contributories who may compel him to summon such meetings.

[251] Section 139 (3).

[252] Section 139 (4).

[253] Section 140.

[254] Section 136 (3).

[255] *Re Black & Co.'s Case* (1872) 8 Ch App. 254, at p. 262 (CA).

[256] *Re Oriental Inland Steam Co.* (1874) 9 Ch App. 557 at p. 551 (CA). See also *Re Flack's Case* [1894] 1 Ch 369; *C.I.R. v Olive Mill* [1963] 1 WLR 712; *Re Movitex Ltd* [1992] 2 All ER 264, [1992] 1 WLR 303, [1992] BCLC 419, [1992] BCC 101 (position of trustees and beneficiaries considered by way of analogy in determining whether creditors were entitled to an order for the inspection of books and records).

is not a trustee in the strict sense, while also holding, in the context of a taxing statute, that when a company enters liquidation it ceases to be 'the beneficial' owner of its assets.[257] But it must not be inferred that all the results follow which would ensue if the liquidator were a trustee in the full sense of the word; and in particular it is to be noted that the property in the assets remains vested in the company and does not pass to the liquidator. But the court may on the application of the liquidator by order direct that all or any part of the property belonging to the company or held by trustees on its behalf shall vest in the liquidator by his official name: section 145 of the Insolvency Act 1986. When a liquidator makes a contract he does so in the name of the company; thus if he employs a solicitor in the company's business he is not personally liable for the costs.[258] A liquidator

> ... is a person having a prima facie right to costs [out of the estate], but he is not in the ordinary sense a trustee. He is a person appointed by the court to do a certain class of things; he has some of the rights and some of the liabilities of a trustee, but is not in the position of an ordinary trustee. Being an agent employed to do business for a remuneration, he is bound to bring reasonable skill to its performance.[259]

Similarly Romer J has said 'In my judgment the liquidator is not a trustee in the strict sense.'[260]

It is clear that the liquidator occupies a fiduciary position.[261] As such, he must avoid conflicts between his interests and his duties[262] and must not make a secret profit out of his position. It may be safely asserted that the liquidator has all the duties an agent would have; but it is suggested that he is liable only to the company and not directly, prior to its dissolution, to third parties, even though they be creditors or contributories, for negligence apart from misfeasance or personal misconduct.[263] If, however, the liquidator 'has misapplied or retained or become liable or accountable for any moneys or property of the company, or been guilty of any misfeasance or breach of trust in relation to the company', he can be brought to account by any creditor or contributory on a summons under section 212 of the 1986 Act, but this will not enable a contributory who has accidentally been omitted in a distribution of assets to proceed by summons against the liquidator to obtain his due proportion of the assets.[264] A liquidator who pays an unfounded claim against the company, though acting honestly in the transaction, is guilty of a misfeasance, and is not protected by section 30 of the Trustee Act 1925.[265] A high standard of care and diligence is required from a liquidator. But even where he is held liable, the court may relieve him in part.[266]

---

[257] *Ayerst v C. & K. (Construction) Ltd* [1975] 3 WLR 16 (HL).

[258] *Re Anglo-Moravian Co.* (1875) 1 Ch D 130 (CA).

[259] *Per* Cotton LJ in *Re Silver Valley Mines* (1882) 21 Ch D 381 at p. 392 (CA).

[260] *Knowles v Scott* [1891] 1 Ch 717 at pp. 721, 723. As to the possibility of recovering damages against a liquidator for neglect of statutory duty (even though there is no evidence of wilful default), see *Gore-Browne on Companies* (Jordans, 44th edn, loose-leaf), 32.5.

[261] *Silkstone and Haigh Moore Coal Co. v Edey* [1900] 1 Ch 167.

[262] *Re Corbenstoke Ltd (No. 2)* [1990] BCLC 60, (1989) 5 BCC 767.

[263] *Knowles v Scott* [1891] 1 Ch 723.

[264] *Re Hill's Waterfall Estate and Gold Mining Co.* [1896] 1 Ch 947.

[265] *Re Windsor Steam Coal Co.* [1928] 1 Ch 609; [1929] 1 Ch 151 (CA); *Re Home and Colonial Insurance Co.* [1930] 1 Ch 102 (England).

[266] *Re Home and Colonial Insurance Co.* [1930] 1 Ch 102. A liquidator who does a specific act after seeking and obtaining the approval of the court cannot be liable in negligence: *Highland Engineering Ltd and Another v Anderson and Others* 1979 SLT 122.

The liquidator represents creditors and contributories alike, and should bear an even hand between them.[267] He should afford reasonable assistance and facilities to persons seeking information to enforce their rights,[268] but in cases of litigation he usually requires parties desiring access to the books and documents of the company to obtain an order for inspection under section 155 (1) of the 1986 Act. This provides that the court may make an order for inspection of the books and papers of the company by creditors and contributories, and any books or papers of the company may be inspected accordingly but not further or otherwise. Orders under section 155 (1) are rarely granted.[269] The section does not restrict any statutory right of a government department or person acting under its authority: section 155 (2).

The liquidator, being an officer of the court, will be directed to deal fairly:[270] for example, he may be ordered to repay moneys paid to him under a mistake of law. Instances of this rule may also be found in cases under the Bankruptcy Acts.[271]

When a liquidator contracts he does so as agent of the company, but he should, to avoid personal liability, make it clear that he contracts as liquidator of the company concerned and without personal liability.

Where a liquidator has properly carried on the business of the company after his appointment, the post-liquidation creditors are entitled to be paid out of the assets of the company, in priority to its creditors at the commencement of the winding-up.[272]

If a company holds property as a constructive trustee and enters liquidation, the liquidator does not automatically become a trustee of such property. He becomes a trustee, if at all, only when he deals with the property. He is not liable if he bona fide fails to realise that its property is subject to a trust.[273]

17.40 Duties and powers of a liquidator

Once made, a winding-up order operates in favour of all creditors and contributories of the company.[274]

The liquidator's primary duty is to collect in and realise the assets of the company and then to distribute the proceeds amongst the creditors of the company and, if any surplus remains, to the members in accordance with their rights. The fundamental tenet governing the making of distributions in a liquidation is that the free assets of the company must be distributed rateably among the company's unsecured creditors. If the assets of the company are insufficient to meet all of the unsecured debts, such debts abate equally. This method of distribution is known as the pari passu rule. The pari passu rule, which also applies to voluntary liquidations, is subject to a number of qualifications or exceptions.[275]

---

[267] *Re Palmer Marine Surveys Ltd* [1986] 1 WLR 573; *Re P. Turner (Wilsden) Ltd* [1987] BCLC 149.

[268] *Re Sir John Moore Gold Mining Co.* (1879) 12 Ch D 325 at p. 328 (CA).

[269] *Re Brazilian Sugar Factories* (1887) 37 Ch D 83; *Re DPR Futures Ltd* [1989] 1 WLR 778, [1989] BCLC 634, (1989) 5 BCC 603.

[270] *Re Regent Finance and Guarantee Corp.* [1930] WN 84.

[271] See e.g. *Ex Parte James* (1874) 9 Ch App. 6099 (CA)); *Ex parte Simmonds* (1885) 16 QBD 308 (CA); *Scranton's Trustee v Pearse* [1922] 2 Ch 87 (CA).

[272] *Re National Arms and Ammunition Co.* (1885) 28 Ch D 474 at p. 481 (CA); *Re Great Eastern Electric Co.* [1941] Ch 241.

[273] *Competitive Insurance Co. Ltd v Davies Investments Ltd* [1975] 1 WLR 124.

[274] Section 130 (4).

[275] See Part 6, below.

As soon as a winding-up order is made the powers of the directors to manage the business of the company are terminated. To allow these to continue would be inconsistent with the liquidator's duty and power to collect in the assets of the company for the collective benefit of all of the creditors.

The liquidator has a range of specific duties and powers. He must take into his custody or bring within his control all the property to which the company is or appears to be entitled.[276] He can require any person who has in his possession or control any property, books or papers or records to which the company appears to be entitled to deliver up the same to him.[277] In exercising the powers conferred on him by the Insolvency Act 1986 to collect in the assets of the company, the liquidator is an officer of the court and is subject to its control.[278] If the liquidator mistakenly seizes property owned by a third party, he will not incur any liability for having seized or subsequently disposed of the property, provided he had reasonable grounds for believing that he was entitled to make the seizure. This protection, which is afforded by section 234 (3) and (4), does not extend to any loss or damage resulting from the seizure or disposal which is caused by the liquidator's negligence. In the event of the liquidator's entitlement to make a seizure being disputed, the court can resolve the dispute.[279]

Section 167 and Schedule 4 of the Act set out the powers of a liquidator in a compulsory winding-up. These are divided into powers which may be exercised with the sanction of the court or the liquidation committee[280] and powers which are exercisable by the liquidator without such sanction. The powers which can only be exercised with the appropriate sanction include conducting litigation and carrying on the business of the company so far as is necessary for the beneficial winding-up of the company. Amongst the things which a liquidator can do without sanction are selling the company's property and raising money and giving security on the company's assets. A person who deals for value and in good faith with a liquidator need not be concerned whether any requisite consent from the liquidation committee or the court has been obtained by the liquidator.[281]

Certain specific powers relating to the holding of meetings, settling of lists, making of calls, proving of debts and other matters in the administration of a compulsory liquidation are formally vested in the court by the Act but are delegated to the liquidator by the Insolvency Rules.[282]

Where the liquidator intends to carry on the business of the company he may only do so where this is necessary for the beneficial winding-up of the company. This limitation on his power reflects the fact that the primary objective of liquidation is the orderly winding-up of a company and the distribution of its assets to its creditors rather than rescue and rehabilitation. Necessity in this context has been described as mercantile necessity as opposed to absolutely compelling force.[283] On this basis something which is highly expedient for the beneficial winding-up of the company would be permitted; where a liquidator has a reasonable expectation of selling the business as a going concern

---

[276] Section 144.
[277] Section 234 and rule 4.185.
[278] Rule 4.181.
[279] *Re London Iron & Steel Co. Ltd* [1990] BCLC 372, [1990] BCC 159.
[280] See para. 17.41, below, for a brief description of the status and function of the liquidation committee.
[281] Rule 4.184.
[282] Section 160 makes provision for delegation.
[283] *Re Wreck Recovery Co.* (1880) 15 Ch D 353.

(which usually results in a much higher price being paid by a purchaser than on a sale on a break-up basis)[284] the liquidator may thus be allowed to carry on the business with this objective in mind. In cases of doubt the liquidator can always apply to the court for guidance; he is allowed to apply to court for directions in relation to any matter arising during the course of the liquidation.[285]

The prudent liquidator will always have regard to the wishes of the majority of those with the most substantial interest in the assets of the company.[286] The liquidator has power to summon general meetings of creditors and contributories to ascertain their wishes in respect of any particular aspect of the conduct of the liquidation. If the holders of more than one-tenth in value of the creditors or contributories request a liquidator to summon such meeting he is duty-bound to do so.[287] If any person is aggrieved by an act or discretion of the liquidator he may apply to the court for an order reversing or modifying that act or decision. The court has power to make any order it thinks fit on such an application.[288]

17.41 The liquidation committee

A liquidation committee may be established under section 141 of the Insolvency Act 1986. Either the liquidator or one-tenth in value of the creditors may summon general meetings of the company's creditors and contributories for the purpose of determining whether a liquidation committee should be established.[289]

The liquidation committee will consist of at least three and not more than five creditors of the company elected at the creditors' meeting which decides to establish the liquidation committee.[290] Where the company is being wound up by the court but the grounds upon which the order was made do not include the inability of the company to pay its debts, up to three contributories may become members of the liquidation committee.[291] Once the liquidation committee has been duly constituted the liquidator has a duty to keep it informed in respect of matters arising out of the conduct of the winding-up and to supply it with information.[292] Meetings of the liquidation committee must be held either when required by a creditor member of the liquidation committee or upon such dates as the liquidation committee may resolve to hold the same. The liquidator or his nominee (who must be an insolvency practitioner or someone from his firm who is experienced in insolvency matters) acts as chairman at any meeting of the liquidation committee.[293] The purpose of the liquidation committee is not only to sanction the exercise by the liquidator

---

[284] Tax losses may be available to the purchaser of a business sold on a going-concern basis.

[285] Section 168 (3).

[286] The liquidator should not deny those solely concerned in the outcome of the liquidation the opportunity even of throwing good money after bad; *Re Agricultural Industries* [1952] 1 All ER 1188.

[287] Section 168 (2); see also section 195, which states that the court may have regard to the wishes of creditors and contributories in all matters relating to a winding-up and may direct that such meetings shall be held if it thinks fit.

[288] Section 168 (5).

[289] Section 141.

[290] Rule 4.152.

[291] ibid. A person may not be a member of the liquidation committee in his capacity as both a creditor and a contributory: rule 4.152 (4). For the procedure followed where the creditors decide not to form a liquidation committee, see rule 4.154.

[292] Rule 4.155.

[293] Rules 4.156 and 4.157.

of the powers conferred upon him but also to perform the function of a watchdog to ensure that the liquidator carries out his function in a proper manner.

The members of the liquidation committee will be privy to a good deal of information which could be used for their own benefit. The Insolvency Rules contain certain safeguards[294] which are intended to ensure that members of the liquidation committee and persons associated with such members do not take advantage of their position in order to obtain a benefit for themselves at the expense of the general body of creditors. No transaction whereby any such member or associate receives out of the company's assets any payment for services or goods, obtains a profit, or acquires any assets from the company may be entered into other than with the leave of the court or with the sanction of the full liquidation committee (which must first satisfy itself that full value will be given). In matters of urgency or where the transaction is in respect of the performance of a contract in force before the date upon which the company went into liquidation, no leave or consent need be obtained prior to the transaction. However, in this case an application must be made to the court for leave to enter into the transaction without undue delay after the event. If a transaction is entered into in breach of these require- ments the court may upon the application of any person interested set the transaction aside and make such order to protect the general body of creditors as it thinks fit. The order may require a person in breach of the Rules to account for any profit obtained from the transaction and to compensate the company for any loss occasioned.

In two circumstances the functions of the liquidation committee are to be vested in the Secretary of State.[295] The first is where the Official Receiver is the liquidator of the company. The second is where there is no liquidation committee (e.g. where the creditors and contributories decide not to have one) but the liquidator is a person other than the Official Receiver.

17.42 Ceasing to act as liquidator

Section 172 of the Insolvency Act 1986 deals with the removal and resignation of a liquidator from office.

A liquidator may be removed from office only by one of the following methods:

(1) an order of the court;[296]
(2) a resolution of a general meeting of the company's creditors summoned specifi- cally for that purpose;
(3) where the liquidator was appointed by the Secretary of State, by a direction of the Secretary of State.

There are restrictions on the power of the creditors to remove a liquidator who is the Official Receiver or who was appointed by the court.[297]

A liquidator may resign only in certain prescribed circumstances. Rule 4.108 of the Insolvency Rules 1986 sets these out. The liquidator may only resign following the

---

[294] Rule 4.170.

[295] Section 141 (4), (5). The Secretary of State has the functions vested in him 'except to the extent that the rules otherwise provide'.

[296] *Re Corbenstoke Ltd (No. 2)* [1990] BCLC 60, (1989) 5 BCC 767 (removal from office on grounds of conflict of interests and duties).

[297] Section 172 (3).

procedure laid down in the rule on the grounds of ill health or if he intends to cease to practise as an insolvency practitioner or if there is some conflict of interest or change in personal circumstances which precludes or makes it impracticable for him to discharge his functions as liquidator of the company.

A liquidator who wishes to resign will need to summon a meeting of the creditors of the company for the purposes of receiving his resignation, and give notice of his intention to resign to the Official Receiver. If the creditors' meeting resolves to accept the resignation it will take effect as from the date the Official Receiver files with the court a copy of the notice of resignation.[298] The liquidator may apply to the court for leave to resign if the creditors' meeting resolves not to accept his resignation.[299]

In certain circumstances a liquidator must vacate his office. If a liquidator ceases to be qualified to act as an insolvency practitioner in relation to the company in question, for example if the specific bond required by the Act becomes invalid, he automatically vacates office.[300] Where a final meeting is held and the liquidator's report on the completion of the winding-up is received, the liquidator vacates office as from the date he gives notice to the court and the Registrar of Companies that the final meeting has been held.[301]

The time when a liquidator will obtain his release depends upon the manner in which he vacates office.[302] Where the liquidator has obtained his release he is discharged from all liability both in respect of acts and omissions during the course of the winding-up and otherwise in relation to his conduct as liquidator. However, the Insolvency Act 1986 specifically provides that nothing contained in any release will prevent a misfeasance summons being issued under section 212 of the Act.

PART 5:
THE VOLUNTARY LIQUIDATION OF COMPANIES

17.43 Introduction

The most common type of winding-up procedure is the voluntary winding-up. It is voluntary in the sense that the procedure has to be initiated by the company itself (although, of course, a company does have power to present a petition).[303] A creditor cannot compel a company to wind itself up voluntarily.

There are two types of voluntary liquidation both of which are considered below. If the company's directors are able to swear a declaration of solvency the liquidation will be a members' voluntary liquidation. In this type of liquidation all creditors will be paid in full. If there is no declaration of solvency the liquidation will be a creditors' voluntary liquidation in which the creditors may not be paid in full.

---

[298] Rule 4.109.
[299] Rule 4.111.
[300] Section 172 (5).
[301] Section 172 (8).
[302] Section 174 and rules 4.121 and 4.123–4.125.
[303] See 17.33, above.

17.44 Resolutions for voluntary winding-up

Section 84 of the Insolvency Act 1986 sets out the circumstances in which a company may be wound up voluntarily:

(1) when the period (if any) fixed for the duration of the company by the articles expires, or the event (if any) occurs, on the occurrence of which the articles provide that the company is to be dissolved, and the company in general meeting has passed a resolution requiring it to be wound up voluntarily;

(2) if the company resolves by special resolution that it be wound up voluntarily;

(3) if the company resolves by extraordinary resolution to the effect that it cannot by reason of its liabilities continue its business, and that it is advisable to wind up.

Once a resolution has been passed under (1), (2) or (3) above a copy of it must be filed with the Registrar of Companies within fifteen days.[304]

It is unusual nowadays for the articles of association of a company to provide for the company's duration to be limited or for it to be wound up on the occurrence of any specified event. If there are such provisions in the articles it is the directors' duty to call a general meeting for the purposes of considering a resolution that the company be wound up.

A resolution under para. (3) will only be passed when it is intended that the liquidation is to be a creditors' voluntary winding-up.

17.44.1 *Commencement of a voluntary liquidation*

A voluntary winding-up (whether members' or creditors') is deemed to commence at the time the resolution under section 84 is passed by the members in general meeting.[305]

17.44.2 *Consequences of resolution to wind up*

Once a resolution has been passed a company must cease to carry on its business except in so far as continuance may be deemed necessary for its beneficial winding-up.[306] Any transfer of shares in the company not made to or with the sanction of the liquidator or any change in the status of the company's members will be void.[307]

Notice of the resolution must be given by advertisement in the *London Gazette* within fourteen days.[308]

The Act provides that the corporate existence and the powers contained in the memorandum of association continue, notwithstanding anything in its constitution, until such time as the company is finally dissolved.[309] This provision is, obviously, necessary to ensure the liquidator has the ability to wind up the company in an orderly manner.

17.45 The declaration of solvency

If the directors of a company propose to recommend to the members that the company be wound up voluntarily in a members' voluntary liquidation, they will also have to

---

[304] Sections 84 (3) and 194.

[305] Section 86. Where a resolution is passed at an adjourned meeting it is treated as having been passed at the time it was actually passed, not at any earlier date: section 194.

[306] Section 87 (1).

[307] Section 88.

[308] Section 85.

[309] Section 87 (2).

consider whether or not they can swear a statutory declaration of the company's solvency. Only if a majority of directors consider the swearing of a statutory declaration to be possible will they be able to recommend such course of action to the members.

The statutory declaration of solvency must state[310] that the directors have made a full inquiry into the company's affairs and that they have formed the opinion that the company will be able to pay its debts in full, together with interest at the official rate[311] within such period not exceeding twelve months from the commencement of the liquidation as may be specified in the declaration. In addition the declaration must contain a statement of the company's assets and liabilities as at the latest practicable date before the making of the declaration.[312]

The directors must swear the declaration of solvency within the five weeks immediately preceding the passing of the resolution to wind up. If the declaration is to be sworn on the same day as the meetings to consider the resolutions to wind up it must be sworn before the resolutions are actually passed.[313] A copy of the declaration must be sent to the Registrar of Companies within fifteen days of the commencement of the liquidation.[314]

A director must not decide to join in the swearing of a declaration of solvency lightly. The Insolvency Act 1986 provides that any director making a declaration of solvency, without having reasonable grounds for the opinion that the company will be able to pay its debts in full together with interest at the official rate within the period specified in the declaration, will be liable to imprisonment or a fine or both.[315] There is a presumption that a director did not have reasonable grounds for his belief that the company would be able to so pay its debts if in fact the debts are not paid within the period specified in the declaration.[316] The Act imposes criminal liability in this respect to ensure that directors do not swear declarations of solvency and proceed by way of members' voluntary liquidation in which control rests substantially with the members and not with the creditors, who may be more interested in making a thorough investigation into the directors' conduct of the business. This is particularly important in the case of a private company where the directors have majority shareholdings and therefore would have the power to appoint a friendly liquidator (although the liquidator must be a qualified insolvency practitioner even in a members' voluntary winding-up).

If a declaration of solvency is not sworn the liquidation must proceed as a creditors' voluntary winding-up.

Under section 95 of the 1986 Act, a liquidator in a members' voluntary liquidation is under a duty to summon a meeting of the creditors of the company within twenty-eight days if he forms the opinion that the company will be unable to pay its debts in full (together with interest at the official rate) within the period specified in the directors' declaration of solvency. In addition the liquidator must draw up a statement of affairs to submit to the creditors when their meeting is held. Under section 96 the date of the first meeting of the creditors is deemed to be the date upon which the winding-up becomes a creditors' voluntary liquidation (and the provisions of the Act apply accordingly). The creditors at that meeting may nominate a liquidator, who, if different from the members'

---

[310] Section 89 (1).
[311] For the 'official rate' see section 189 (4).
[312] Section 89 (2) (*b*); see also *De Courcy v Clement* [1971] Ch 693.
[313] Section 89 (2) (*a*).
[314] Section 89 (3).
[315] Section 89 (4).
[316] Section 89 (5).

nominee, will take over the conduct of the liquidation subject to the right of any director, creditor or member, to apply to the court for an order to the contrary. This right is discussed in 17.46, below.

17.46 Appointment of a liquidator

In a members' voluntary winding-up the company in general meeting has the power to appoint one or more liquidators. On the appointment of a liquidator all of the powers of the directors cease, except in so far as the members or the liquidator sanction their continuance.[317] If a vacancy occurs the company in general meeting may fill it.[318]

In a creditors' voluntary winding-up the procedure for appointing a liquidator is more complex. Under section 98 of the Insolvency Act 1986 the company, having decided to wind itself up because of its inability to pay its debts, has a duty to summon a meeting of its creditors on a day not later than fourteen days after the day upon which the members' meeting to consider the resolution is to be held.[319] Notices of such meeting must be sent to creditors not less than seven days before the date upon which the meeting is to be held and notices placed in the *London Gazette* and two local newspapers.[320] Both the members and the creditors at their respective meetings may nominate a person to be liquidator. If there are different nominees the creditors' choice prevails.[321] Where there are different nominees any director, member or creditor may apply to the court during the seven days after the creditors' nomination for an order either directing that the members' nominee shall become liquidator (or joint liquidator with the creditors' nominee) or that some other person shall be liquidator.[322] The creditors have power to fill any vacancy in the office of liquidator.

On the appointment of a liquidator in a creditors' voluntary winding-up the directors' powers cease except in so far as the liquidation committee (or if there is no liquidation committee the creditors) sanction their continuance.[323]

Under section 108 (1) of the 1986 Act the court has a power to appoint a liquidator in any voluntary winding-up if 'from any cause' there is no liquidator acting.

A liquidator in a voluntary winding-up must be a qualified insolvency practitioner. A liquidator in a voluntary winding-up is not an officer of the court but, otherwise, the status of the liquidator is as discussed at 17.39, above, in relation to compulsory windings-up.[324]

---

[317] Section 91.

[318] Section 92. The members' ability in this respect is expressly made subject to any arrangement with the company's creditors.

[319] Section 98.

[320] The notice must give the name and address of a qualified insolvency practitioner who will provide information on the company's affairs and state a place where lists of the company's creditors will be available: section 98 (2).

[321] Section 100 (2).

[322] Section 100 (3).

[323] Section 103; see also 17.48, below, for certain limitations on the powers of liquidators; see 17.47, below, for a discussion of the liquidation committee.

[324] *Re TH Knitwear (Wholesale) Ltd* [1985] Ch 275.

17.47 The liquidation committee

In a creditors' voluntary winding-up the creditors may resolve to form a liquidation committee to exercise the functions conferred on it by the Insolvency Act 1986.[325] The committee may consist of up to five creditors and, if the creditors do not object, five members of the company. If the creditors object to the members' nominees having the right to sit on the committee, such nominees cannot act as members of the committee unless the court so directs.[326]

17.48 Powers and duties of a voluntary liquidator

The fundamental duty of a voluntary liquidator is the same as that of a liquidator in a compulsory winding-up. He must collect in and realise the assets of the company, apply the proceeds in satisfaction of the company's debts and liabilities and distribute any remaining proceeds to the members of the company in accordance with their rights under the memorandum and articles.[327] The pari passu rule applies with respect to distributions.

In a voluntary winding-up the liquidator has the same specific powers as are conferred on a liquidator in a compulsory winding-up by section 167 and Schedule 4 of the Insolvency Act 1986. Where sanction is required to exercise a particular power, it can be given by an extraordinary resolution of the company in a members' voluntary winding-up; in a creditors' voluntary winding-up the liquidator may obtain the requisite sanction from the court, the liquidation committee or (if there is no liquidation committee) from the creditors.[328] Although the matters requiring sanction in the case of a compulsory winding-up include conducting litigation and carrying on the company's business, a liquidator in a voluntary winding-up can exercise both of these powers without formal sanction.[329]

A voluntary liquidator also has the power to settle lists of contributories, make calls, pay debts, adjust the rights of contributories and to deal with other matters connected with the administration of the liquidation.[330]

In a creditors' voluntary winding-up the timing is such that it is possible for the members to nominate a liquidator before a meeting of the creditors has been held, giving them an opportunity to decide who should fill that office. Before the 1986 Act came into force there was a procedure, known as 'Centrebinding' after the case of *Re Centrebind*[331] in which it first came before the courts, whereby members could exploit this to their own advantage.

The 'Centrebind' procedure enabled a company to be put into creditors' voluntary liquidation very quickly by resolution of the members, but with no opportunity at an early stage for creditors to be involved and in particular to nominate their own liquidator. The liquidator appointed by the members therefore effectively had a free hand to deal with the assets until the creditors' meeting was eventually held. If notices had not been sent out by the company, as required by the Companies Act, the creditors might not even

---

[325] For the role of a liquidation committee in a compulsory winding-up see 17.41, above.
[326] The court may direct other persons to act as members of the liquidation committee: section 101 (3).
[327] Sections 107 and 165 (5).
[328] Section 165.
[329] Section 165 (3).
[330] Section 165 (4).
[331] [1967] 1 WLR 337.

have known that the company was in liquidation. The liquidator nominated by the company in *Re Centrebind* was held to be able to exercise all the powers of a liquidator, including the power to pass good title to assets prior to any creditors' meeting being held. The liquidator nominated by the members could therefore dispose of the assets of the company and the interests of the creditors could be damaged by his actions taken prior to the creditors having the opportunity to vote him out of office. Prior to the 1980s insolvency legislation, attempts were made to cure this loophole by the legislature[332] but these proved unsuccessful.

Section 166 of the Insolvency Act is intended to stamp out this practice. In a creditors' voluntary liquidation the liquidator nominated by the members may not exercise his powers prior to the first meeting of creditors without the sanction of the court except where the exercise of his powers is:

(1) to take into custody or under his control all the property to which the company is or appears to be entitled;

(2) to dispose of perishable goods and other goods the value of which is likely to diminish if they are not immediately disposed of; and

(3) to do all such other things as may be necessary for the protection of the company's assets.

If the liquidator fails to recognise the restrictions imposed by section 166 he is liable to a fine. This section, together with the requirement for any liquidator to be a qualified insolvency practitioner, should prevent the abuses which arose out of the Centrebind procedure.

Under section 112 the liquidator or any contributory or creditor may make an application to the court to determine any question arising in the winding-up of the company including the exercise of certain powers of the liquidator. The court may make such order as it thinks just in the circumstances.[333]

Finally, where in the case of a voluntary winding-up no liquidator has been appointed or nominated by the company the directors shall not exercise any powers except with the sanction of the court or (in the case of a creditors' voluntary winding-up) so far as may be necessary to call a meeting of creditors or prepare a statement of affairs in accordance with the Act. The directors may, however, exercise their powers in the circumstances described in (2) and (3) above. Again failure to have regard to these limitations on the exercise of powers will result in a fine.[334]

17.49 Ceasing to act as a voluntary liquidator

Section 171 of the Insolvency Act 1986 states that a liquidator in a voluntary winding-up may only be removed:

(1) by an order of the court; or

(2) in the case of a members' voluntary winding-up by a resolution of the company in general meeting passed at a meeting summoned for that purpose; or

---

[332] See section 106 of the Companies Act 1981.

[333] *Re Movitex Ltd*, above, is an example of an application made by creditors under section 602 of the Companies Act 1985 (which was replaced by section 112 of the Insolvency Act 1986). Scott LJ, with whom the other members of the Court of Appeal agreed, assumed, without deciding, that a post-liquidation debt would not provide the desired *locus standi* for such an application.

[334] Section 114.

(3) in the case of a creditors' voluntary winding-up by a resolution of the company's creditors passed at a meeting summoned for that purpose.

Where the liquidator has been appointed by the court under section 108[335] the meetings summoned in (2) and (3) above may only be called if the liquidator agrees, the court directs or one-half of the members (on the basis of their voting rights) or creditors (value), as the case may be, requires.[336]

A voluntary liquidator vacates office automatically if he ceases to be a person qualified to act as an insolvency practitioner in relation to the company or when the final meetings of members and creditors (in the case of a creditors' voluntary liquidation) have been held and notice of the same has been given to the Registrar of Companies.[337]

Under section 108 of the 1986 Act the court retains power on cause being shown to remove a voluntary liquidator, and appoint another in his place. A court using this power may appoint an additional liquidator or replace a retiring liquidator.[338] An applicant must show course why the liquidator should be removed.[339] The cause may lie in some unfitness or unsuitability of the liquidator, whether this be personal or arising from the particular circumstances of the case, for example some conflict of interest.[340] In *Re Keypak Homecare* a liquidator was removed because of his relaxed and complacent conduct of the liquidation although there was no evidence of misconduct or conflicts of interest.

In a voluntary liquidation the liquidator may resign in the prescribed circumstances, which are the same as in a compulsory winding-up.[341] The Insolvency Rules 1986 provide that in the case of a creditors' voluntary liquidation a liquidator whose resignation is not accepted by the creditors may apply to the court for leave to resign.[342] The procedures in this respect are broadly speaking the same as in the case of a compulsory winding-up.

The time at which a voluntary liquidator obtains his release depends on the manner in which he vacates office.[343] The release operates to discharge the liquidator from all liability in respect of acts and omissions in the course of his winding-up and otherwise in relation to his conduct as liquidator. It does not give him immunity from misfeasance proceedings under section 212 of the 1986 Act.[344]

17.50 The relationship between voluntary liquidation and other insolvency-related procedures

The fact that a company is being wound up voluntarily does not prevent any creditor or contributory from presenting a petition to the court requesting a winding-up order.[345]

---

[335] See 17.46, above.

[336] Section 171 (3).

[337] Section 171 (4) and (5).

[338] *Re Sunlight Incandescent Gas Lamps Co.* [1900] 2 Ch 728; *Re Sheppey Portland Cement Co.* [1892] WN 184.

[339] *Re Keypak Homecare Ltd* [1987] BCLC 409, (1987) 3 BCC 558.

[340] *Re Sir John Moore Mining Co.* (1879) 12 Ch D 325 (CA); *Re Adam Eyton* (1887) 36 Ch D 299 (CA); *Re London Flats* [1969] 1 WLR 711; *Re Charterland Goldfields* (1909) 26 TLR 132.

[341] See 17.42, above.

[342] Rule 4.111. In a members' voluntary winding-up the meeting of members must accept the resignation: rule 4.142.

[343] Section 173.

[344] Section 173 (4).

[345] Section 116.

Where, however, the petition is presented by a contributory the court must be satisfied that the rights of the contributories will be prejudiced by the continuation of the voluntary winding-up and that some benefit would accrue from making a winding-up order.[346]

Where a creditor presents a petition, he is not required to show that he would be prejudiced by the continuance of the voluntary liquidation.[347] However, although a creditor is entitled *ex debito justitiae* between himself and the company to a winding-up order,[348] as between himself and the other creditors the court will normally give effect to the wishes of the majority.[349] The majority, both in number and value, is considered but the majority in value is more significant than the numerical majority.[350] As Diplock LJ stated in *Re JD Swain Ltd*:[351]

> For the wishes of the petitioner to overrule those of the majority of the creditors there must be some reason why the wishes of the majority should be overridden ... [the petitioner must] show some reason why the remedy under the voluntary winding-up is not an adequate remedy for him.

In *Re Lowestoft Traffic Services Ltd*[352] Hoffmann J noted that the decision whether to grant the winding-up order lay in the court's discretion and that, in exercising this discretion, the court would consider a range of matters including: the number, value and quality of the creditors for and against the petition; the possible or probable motives of these creditors; and general principles of fairness and commercial morality. Because it is a matter of discretion, it may not be strictly correct to speak of an onus of proof on the petitioner to demonstrate to the court reasons why the order should be made[353] but if no such reasons are put before the court this may result in the discretion being exercised against the making of a winding-up order.

If a company has already been dissolved under the voluntary liquidation[354] the creditor or contributory will be unable to present a petition because the court will have no jurisdiction to make a winding-up order.[355]

It is possible in the light of the fact that liquidators must be qualified insolvency practitioners that there will be a decrease in the number of applications made for compulsory winding-up orders where a voluntary liquidation is on foot. The most common ground upon which such orders were formerly made was the misconduct of the liquidator or his failure to pursue a course of investigation where this was merited by the conduct of the business prior to the voluntary liquidation.[356]

---

[346] *Re National Company for the Distribution of Electricity* [1902] 2 Ch 34.

[347] Older cases (e.g. *Re New York Exchange* (1888) 39 Ch D 415 (CA); *Re Russell Cordner & Co.* [1891] 2 Ch 171; *Re Medical Battery Co.* [1894] 1 Ch 444) emphasised that point, but the need to show prejudice was removed by the Companies Act 1929.

[348] *Re James Millward & Co.* [1940] Ch 333.

[349] Section 195.

[350] *Re HJ Tomkins & Sons Ltd* [1990] BCLC 76. See also *Re William Thorpe & Son Ltd* (1989) 5 BCC 156.

[351] [1965] 1 WLR 909 (CA) at p. 915B adopted by Harman J in *Re Medisco Equipment Ltd* [1983] BCLC 305.

[352] [1986] BCLC 81, (1986) 2 BCC 945.

[353] *Re Lowestoft Traffic Services Ltd*, above; *Re Marine Surveys Ltd* [1986] 1 WLR 573; *Re Falcon RJ Developments Ltd* [1989] BCLC 437, (1987) 3 BCC 146.

[354] 17.61, below.

[355] 17.31, above.

[356] *Re Varieties* [1893] 2 Ch 235; *Re London and Hull Soap Works* [1907] WN 254.

Where there is a petition pending for an administration order during the period beginning with the date of the presentation of the petition and ending with the making of the order or the dismissal of the petition or whilst an administration order is current, no resolution may be passed for the winding-up of a company.[357]

The fact that there is a voluntary arrangement in force under Part I of the Insolvency Act 1986 does not prevent a company from being wound up voluntarily. However, where a company is in the course of being wound up, the power to make a proposal under section 1 of the 1986 Act rests with the liquidator and not the directors of the company.

The fact that an administrative receiver has been appointed over the assets of the company does not prevent the company from being wound up voluntarily.

PART 6: THE CONDUCT OF LIQUIDATIONS

17.51 Introduction

In this part we explore some of the most important aspects of both compulsory and voluntary liquidations. We have already noted in general terms the liquidator's fundamental duty to collect in and realise the assets of the company and to apply the proceeds in discharging the debts and liabilities of the company in accordance with the pari passu rule. Any remaining surplus belongs to the members of the company and must be distributed to them in accordance with their rights under the company's memorandum and articles. Closer examination, however, reveals that the liquidator's duty is far more complex than this summary may suggest. This part highlights the main areas of complexity.

17.52 Creditors' claims

A liquidator need only apply the company's assets in payment of creditors' debts and liabilities which have been admitted to proof in the liquidation. If a creditor in a compulsory liquidation fails to submit a proof, or for some reason his claim is not admissible to proof, the liquidator cannot, in normal circumstances,[358] take it into account in making distributions.[359] In a voluntary winding-up (whether members' or creditors') the liquidator may require creditors to submit proofs.[360]

Admissibility to proof in both compulsory and voluntary liquidations is governed by Part 4, Chapter 9 of the Insolvency Rules. All debts and liabilities, including contingent debts and debts due in the future, can be proved, provided the company is subject to them at the date when it goes into liquidation or becomes subject to them after the date of the liquidation by reason of obligations previously incurred.[361] A debt or liability need not be fixed or liquidated in amount.[362] Where a claim is contingent or for some reason is not capable of being ascertained exactly, a just estimate of that claim has to be made by the liquidator.[363] In the event of a creditor disputing the liquidator's valuation, the court may

---

[357] Sections 10 (1) and 11 (3).

[358] Note rule 4.67 (2) which provides for an exceptional case where, by order of the court, a debt which has not been the subject of a proof may be treated as if it had been proved for the purpose of paying a dividend.

[359] Rule 4.73 (1) and (3).

[360] Rule 4.73 (2) and (3).

[361] Rule 13.12 defines 'debt' and 'liability'.

[362] ibid.

[363] Rule 4.86.

be asked to determine the matter.[364] If circumstances change, for example if a contingency is fulfilled, estimated proofs can be revised.[365]

The position with regard to secured creditors and the submission of proofs is as follows. Generally speaking, the liquidation of a company does not affect a secured creditor's rights (subject to what is said below about the priority of preferential claims over the claims of the holder of a floating charge and the invalidation of certain security interests). The secured creditor is free to realise his security without reference to the liquidator. Thus, where the value of the security is more than sufficient to discharge the debt or the security is a floating charge on all of the company's assets the secured creditor may simply choose to enforce his security outside the liquidation. It is possible for a secured creditor voluntarily to surrender his security and prove for his debt as if he were unsecured[366] but there can be few circumstances in which it would be advantageous for a creditor to give up his security in this way.

If a secured creditor realises his security but the amount so realised is insufficient to discharge the debt, he may prove for the balance in the liquidation.[367] A secured creditor also has the option of valuing his security and submitting a proof for the balance. In that case the liquidator can offer to redeem the security at the value stated in the proof,[368] which he may well choose to do where he considers that the value stated in the proof is less than the value which the assets subject to the security could fetch on a disposal, although, because there is some scope for the secured creditor to revise the value stated in his proof,[369] the matter may then become one for negotiation between the liquidator and the creditor.

A secured creditor, part of whose secured claim is preferential, may, if he realises his security, appropriate the proceeds of the realisation to the non-preferential element of his claim in a liquidation.[370]

17.53 Proof of debts and rights of set-off

Where, before a company goes into liquidation, there have been mutual credits, mutual debits or other mutual dealings between the company and any creditor of the company proving in the liquidation, an account must be taken of what is due from each party to the other in respect of the mutual dealings, and the sums due from one party must be set off against the sums due from the other. If, after the operation of the set-off, there is still a balance owing from the company to the creditor, that balance is the amount provable by the creditor in the liquidation. Alternatively, if the result of the operation of the set-off is that an amount remains owing to the company from the creditor, the creditor must pay that amount to the liquidator and it is part of the company's assets available for distribution.[371]

Thus, the result of the operation of a right of set-off is that, to the extent of the amount set off, the creditor in effect obtains repayment of the amount owing to him from the

---

[364] Section 168 (3) and (5) and rule 4.83.

[365] Rule 4.86.

[366] Rule 4.88 (2). Note rule 4.96 which deems a secured creditor to have voluntarily surrendered (unless the court grants relief) if he omits to disclose his security in his proof.

[367] Rule 4.88 (1).

[368] Rule 4.97.

[369] Rules 4.84 and 4.95.

[370] *Re William Hall (Contractors) Ltd* [1967] 2 All ER 1150, [1967] 1 WLR 948.

[371] Rule 4.90.

company in priority to the company's general creditors. From the company's viewpoint, the amount of assets available to repay its general creditors is reduced by the amount of the debt which the creditor is allowed to set off but, in turn, the company is spared the trouble and potential expense involved in suing the creditor for the amount owing to it to the extent that this is diminished by the set-off. The operation of set-off is said to facilitate proper and orderly administration of insolvent estates.[372] It has also been described as a method of doing justice between the parties;[373] it is considered that it would be unjust for a creditor to have to pay the whole of the debt which he owes to the company while, in respect of the amount which the company owes to him, he is only allowed to prove for a dividend in the company's liquidation.[374] In practice, it is creditors who most obviously benefit from the operation of set-off but, because its purpose is wider than simply the benefiting of one particular party and extends to ensuring the proper administration of insolvent estates, set-off is regarded as mandatory and it is not possible to contract out of the relevant provisions of the Insolvency Rules.[375]

The conditions governing the availability of set-off in liquidation are, first, that there must be debts, credits or dealings between the company and the person seeking to assert a right of set-off and, second, that these debts, credits or dealings must be mutual. The interpretation of these conditions has spawned a considerable amount of case-law.[376] In brief, mutual debts are liquidated amounts owing from each of the parties to the other. 'Mutual credits' is a wider term than 'mutual debts,'[377] and means credits which will eventually result in money claims such as where one party, who is indebted to the other, supplies the other party with property on the basis that the property is to be resold and the proceeds handed over.[378] Mutual dealings are arrangements in which the parties extend credit to each other in respect of individual sums, with the intention, express or implied, that at some point the individual sums will be brought into account and set off against each other.[379] Each claim must result in a liability to pay money; for example, a claim to the return of goods cannot be set off against a money debt.[380] 'Mutual dealings' is the widest term and could encompass both mutual debts and mutual credits.

The requirement for mutuality means that a joint debt cannot be set off against a several debt. For the same reason, money held by the company for a specific purpose or on trust cannot be set off against a debt owed to the company.[381] In *MS Fashions Ltd v*

---

[372] *National Westminster Bank Ltd v Halesowen Presswork & Assemblies Ltd* [1972] AC 785, [1972] 1 All ER 641, [1972] 2 WLR 455; *Re Maxwell Communications Corp. plc (No. 3)* [1993] 1 All ER 737, [1993] 1 WLR 1402, [1993] BCC 369.

[373] *Forster v Wilson* (1843) 12 M&W 191 at pp. 203–4.

[374] *Stein v Blake* [1994] Ch 16, [1993] 3 All ER 225, [1993] 3 WLR 718, [1993] BCLC 1478, [1993] BCC 587 (a bankruptcy case, but the principle is the same).

[375] *National Westminster Bank Ltd v Halesowen*, above.

[376] See generally, Wood, *English and International Set-off* (Sweet & Maxwell, 1989); Derham, *Set-off* (Clarendon Press, 1987); and Derham, 'Some Aspects of Mutual Credit and Mutual Dealings' (1992) 108 LQR 99.

[377] *Palmer v Day & Sons* [1895] 2 QB 618.

[378] *Rolls Razor Ltd v Cox* [1967] 1 QB 552, [1967] 1 All ER 397, [1967] 2 WLR 241.

[379] *Rolls Razor v Cox*, above.

[380] *Eberle's Hotels & Restaurant Co. v Jones* (1887) 18 QBD 459.

[381] *Ex parte Caldicott* (1884) 25 Ch D 716; *Re City Equitable Fire Insurance Co. Ltd (No. 2)* [1930] 2 Ch 293; *Young v Bank of Bengal* (1836) 1 Moore Ind App. 87; *National Westminster Bank v Halesowen*, above.

BCCI SA[382] mutuality was found to exist in a tri-partitive situation. BCCI, a bank, went into liquidation and was owed money by various companies. These debts had been guaranteed by the companies' directors, the directors being described as 'principal debtors' in the documentation, and, as security, the directors had deposited sums with the bank. The Court of Appeal held that the liability of the directors as principal debtors and the liability of the bank for the deposits[383] could be set off against each other so that the effect of the set-off was automatically to reduce or extinguish the indebtedness of the companies to the bank.

There is some uncertainty regarding the operation of set-off in relation to contingent debts.[384] In *Carreras Rothmans Ltd v Freeman Mathews Treasure Ltd*[385] Peter Gibson J held that a debt which was contingent at the time when a company went into liquidation could not be the subject of a set-off. He distinguished a wholly contingent debt from a liability which was certain but uncertain in amount because its quantification depended on future events: a liability of uncertain amount could be set off. In *Re Charge Card Services Ltd*[386] Millett J conducted an extensive review of the authorities and, from this, concluded that, as well as debts which were contingent in amount only, wholly contingent debts which could be proved in the liquidation could be set off, provided that they resulted from mutual credits or mutual dealings and had been quantified by the time that the claim to set off was made.

Both of these cases concerned section 31 of the Bankruptcy Act 1914 which has now been replaced for companies by rule 4.90 of the Insolvency Rules. The Cork Committee favoured the approach later adopted in *Re Charge Card Services Ltd*, that is, that debts which were contingent in either existence or amount could be the subject of set-off provided the amount could be quantified when the claim was made.[387] The Committee recommended that the position should be confirmed by statute but rule 4.90 fails to clarify the uncertainty thrown up by the cases.

A secured debt may be set off against an unsecured debt; the existence of a security does not destroy mutuality.[388] However, a creditor who relies on his security to enforce his debt does not prove in the liquidation and is not subject to set-off.[389]

---

[382] [1993] Ch 425, [1993] 3 All ER 769, [1993] 3 WLR 220, [1993] BCLC 1200, [1993] BCC 360. Compare *Re Bank of Credit and Commerce International SA (No. 8)* [1994] 3 WLR 911, [1994] BCC 462, where mutuality was not established, because the third parties who had deposited money with BCCI as security for loans made to various companies had not undertaken personal liability for the companies' debts.

[383] This was held not to be money held for a special purpose such as to destroy mutuality.

[384] An additional complication to that discussed in the text is that arising form the rule against double proof (a rule which is illustrated by *Barclays Bank Ltd v TOSG Trust Fund Ltd* [1984] AC 626, [1984] 1 All ER 1060, [1984] 2 WLR 650): a contingent claim, such as one arising under a guarantee, may not be admissible to proof for that reason and, if it is not provable, it will also not be capable of being the subject of set-off.

[385] [1985] Ch 207, [1985] 1 All ER 155, [1984] 3 WLR 1016.

[386] [1987] Ch 150, [1986] 3 All ER 289, [1986] 3 WLR 697, [1987] BCLC 17, (1986) 2 BCC 99, 373 (affirmed [1988] 3 All ER 702, [1988] 3 WLR 764, but on grounds not relevant to this point).

[387] *Report of the Review Committee on Insolvency Law and Practice*, Cmnd 8558 (1982), paras. 1352–7.

[388] *Ex parte Barnett* (1874) LR 9 Ch App. 293; *Hiley v Peoples Prudential Assurance Co.* (1938) 60 CLR 468.

[389] *Re Norman Holding Co. Ltd* [1990] 3 All ER 757, [1991] 1 WLR 10, [1990] BCLC 1, [1991] BCC 11.

17.54 The company's assets

The liquidator must get in and realise the company's assets.[390] Assets which are not beneficially owned by a company fall outside the scope of its liquidation and are not available to meet the claims of its general body of creditors. Instead, the persons who are beneficially entitled to the property are entitled to invoke equitable claims, such as tracing rights, to recover their property.

The decision of the House of Lords in *Barclays Bank Ltd v Quistclose Investments Ltd*[391] demonstrates how creditors may be able to take advantage of the fact that trust assets fall outside the normal rules governing distribution of assets in liquidation. Rolls Razor Ltd was a company in serious financial difficulties but it had managed to declare a dividend. Lacking available funds to pay the dividend, and being unable to raise them from its bank, the company entered into an arrangement with Quistclose, whereby Quistclose agreed to lend the money on condition that the company would use it only to pay the dividend and, if that could not be done, that it would return the money to Quistclose. The House of Lords held that this arrangement amounted to a relationship of a fiduciary character or trust in the form of a primary trust to pay the dividend and, if that failed, a secondary trust in favour of Quistclose. It was further held that the primary trust had failed[392] and that Quistclose was entitled to recover the money.

The Quistclose trust is a device which has been upheld in a number of later cases.[393] For insolvency law purposes, the main issue raised by the Quistclose trust is the question of policy, namely, whether the law should recognise and give effect to this interest, given that it occurs in transactions which, in economic terms, are often indistinguishable from secured loans; unlike a secured loan, a Quistclose trust does not require registration, and hence disclosure, at Companies House. The same policy question can arise where assets are sold to a company on credit terms which provide that title to the assets will not pass until debts owing from the company to the supplier have been paid for in full.[394] Like a charge, a retention of title clause also achieves the effect of giving credit to the company whilst at the same time allowing the creditor to protect its position with a proprietary interest; but because the creditor's interest is retained in its own property rather than taken on property of the company, legally it is not a charge and does not require

---

[390] Sections 144 and 148 (compulsory liquidation). The duty is not spelt out in relation to a voluntary liquidator in a voluntary winding-up but a liquidator must necessarily collect in the assets of the company in order to be able to fulfil his duty (section 107) to distribute the proceeds amongst those who are entitled.

[391] [1970] AC 567, [1968] 3 All ER 651, [1968] 3 WLR 1097. On the 'Quistclose Trust' see Goodhart & Jones, 'The Infiltration of Equitable Doctrine into English Commercial Law' (1980) 43 MLR 489; Millett, 'The Quistclose Trust: Who Can Enforce It?' (1985) 101 LQR 269; Rickett, 'Different Views on the Scope of the *Quistclose* Analysis: English and Antipodean Insights' (1991) 107 LQR 608; Bridge, 'The Quistclose Trust in a World of Secured Transactions' (1992) 12 OJLS 333.

[392] Although, as Goodhart & Jones, op. cit. point out at p. 494, n 28, it is arguable whether this was in fact the case unless it is accepted that there were also other conditions attached to the loan. Millett, op. cit. suggests that the primary purpose for which the loan was made available was to ensure the survival of the company, a purpose which certainly failed.

[393] These include *Re Northern Developments Holdings Ltd* (unreported); *Carreras Rothmans Ltd v Freeman Mathews Treasure Ltd*, above; *Re EVTR Ltd* [1987] BCLC 464, (1987) 3 BCC 389; cf. *Re Multi-Guarantee Co. Ltd* [1987] BCLC 257.

[394] This is the simplest type of retention of title clause. Suppliers sometimes insert more elaborate clauses into their supply contracts, whereby title is also claimed to the proceeds of resales or to goods manufactured from those supplied. More elaborate clauses have tended not to be regarded favourably by the courts. See further 9.30, above.

registration; in the event of liquidation leading to a breach of the terms on which the assets were supplied, the creditor can simply assert its proprietary claim to the assets supplied.

Various review bodies have criticised the law in this area on the grounds that it appears to be concerned more with form rather than substance.[395] Retention of title provisions have attracted more attention than Quistclose trusts, with the most widely supported suggestion being that such provisions should be brought within the scope of revised law relating to security interests. Despite calls for reform stretching back over a number of decades, however, the Government has shown little enthusiasm for extensive reform in this area.[396]

A decision regarding trust property which is debatable on technical as opposed simply to policy grounds is that of Megarry J in *Re Kayford Ltd*.[397] This case involved customers of a mail-order company who paid in advance, either in whole or in part, for the goods that they ordered. The company, which was concerned about its financial position, took advice and, on the basis of that advice, declared itself trustee of these pre-payments and paid them into a separate account. Unlike *Quistclose*, the initiative to create the trust came from the company rather than from its customers. Nevertheless, Megarry J held that the trust was effective and that the customers had first claim on the money.

The technical difficulty with *Re Kayford* is that it is difficult to avoid the conclusion that the company was doing anything other than creating a trust of its own property, namely, the pre-payments made to it. The argument that the money was impressed with a trust from the time when it was received from the company, although accepted by Megarry J, is not altogether convincing when it is remembered that the customers knew nothing of the trust and that it was declared by the company itself. If, in reality, the company was declaring a trust of its own property, the act would be vulnerable as a preference, that is an act whereby a company sought to improve the position of particular creditors in the event of its liquidation. On policy grounds, on the other hand, the decision in *Re Kayford* has much to commend it since it affords protection to the general public, who would not themselves normally be expected to think of invoking Quistclose trusts. Megarry J himself noted that the position might well have been different in relation to trade creditors, presumably because he considered such creditors to be reasonably capable of protecting themselves.[398] However, in *Re Lewis of Leicester Ltd*,[399] a *Re Kayford*-type trust created by a company in favour of licensees who held concessions within the company's department store (ie commercial businesses) was upheld, the court expressly ruling that the creation of the trust did not constitute a transaction at an undervalue or a preference, nor did it infringe the pari passu principle.

---

[395] *Report of the Committee on Consumer Credit* (1972) Cmnd 4596; *Report of the Review Committee on Insolvency Law and Practice* (1982) Cmnd 8558; Diamond, *Review of Security Interests in Property*, (1989). See also, Bridge, 'Form, Substance and Innovation in Personal Property Security Law' [1992] JBL 1.

[396] See Chapter 9.

[397] [1975] 1 All ER 604, [1975] 1 WLR 279.

[398] The Cork Committee at paras. 1048–56 of its report (Cmnd 8558) expresses support for the decision in *Re Kayford*.

[399] Unreported, 13 January 1995.

17.55 The order of payment of debts and liabilities and the *pari passu* rule

Although the pari passu rule is a fundamental tenet of insolvency, there are a number of ways in which the principle of pari passu distribution is qualified.[400] We have already seen how the operation of insolvency set-off can in effect allow one creditor to be paid in advance of other creditors, which cuts across the pari passu rule, and how trust assets fall entirely outside the ambit of the pari passu rule. Other important illustrations of the qualified nature of the pari passu principle are the position of secured creditors (who may, subject to the special rules discussed below governing debts secured by a floating charge, enforce their security outside the liquidation) and the ranking of liquidation costs and expenses and of preferential debts.

The precise order of application of funds in a liquidation is:[401]

(1) costs and expenses of the liquidation including the liquidator's remuneration;
(2) preferential debts;
(3) ordinary debts;
(4) deferred debts;
(5) any balance remaining is distributed to members in accordance with their entitlements under the company's memorandum and articles.

17.55.1 Preferential debts

Preferential debts are payable in priority to all other unsecured debts.[402] They rank equally among themselves after the expenses of the winding-up and must be paid in full, unless the assets are insufficient to meet them, in which case they abate in equal proportions.[403] Also, whilst preferential debts rank behind debts secured by fixed charges, so far as the assets of the company available for payment of general creditors are insufficient to meet them, they have priority over the claims of debentures secured by, or the holders of, any floating charge created by the company and must be paid accordingly out of any property comprised in or subject to that charge.[404] The fact that the floating charge may have crystallised prior to the commencement of the winding-up does not deprive the preferential debts of this special priority, because it is expressly provided by section 251 that a floating charge for this purpose means a charge created as such.

Schedule 6 of the Insolvency Act 1986 sets out the categories of preferential debts. They include up to twelve months' unpaid PAYE and social security contributions, up to six months' unpaid VAT and up to four months' back-pay to employees and former employees (subject to a prescribed maximum limit per employee which currently stands at £800) as well as unpaid holiday pay and contributions to state and occupational pension schemes.

The 1980s insolvency legislation reduced the categories of preferential debts quite considerably. Previously, corporation tax, income tax, capital gains tax and rates also ranked as preferential debts and the period for which VAT was treated as preferential was twelve months rather than six as it is now. The Cork Committee recommended a

---

[400] Oditah, 'Assets and the Treatment of Claims in Insolvency' (1992) 108 LQR 459.
[401] Sections 107 and 115 (voluntary liquidations) and 143 and 156 (compulsory liquidations) and section 175 and rule 4.218 (both types of liquidation).
[402] Section 175 (1).
[403] Section 175 (2) (*a*).
[404] Section 175 (2) (*b*).

reduction in the categories of preferential debts,[405] noting that the cardinal principle of pari passu distribution was often denied effect because of the large number of preferential debts. The Committee also considered that difficulties in settling the preferential claims of the Inland Revenue, particularly with regard to income tax and corporation tax, were occasioning serious delays which worked against the ideal aim of expeditious adminis-tration of insolvent estates.

Where a company is being wound up by the court and a person has distrained upon goods of the company within three months of the winding-up order being made, those good (or the proceeds of their sale) are treated as having been charged for the benefit of the company with the preferential debts, to the extent that the company's available assets are insufficient for meeting the preferential debts.[406]

17.55.2 *Liquidation expenses*

Liquidation expenses rank before preferential debts but behind debts secured by fixed charges. Since preferential debts enjoy a priority over debts secured by a floating charge, the logical position would be that liquidation expenses also rank before debts secured by floating charges. In respect of floating charges which crystallise only upon liquidation, it is clearly established that this is the position[407] but, until recently, there was some doubt where the floating charge had crystallised prior to the liquidation. In *Re Portbase Ltd*[408] Chadwick J held that, irrespective of the time of crystallisation, liquidation expenses ranked before debts secured by floating charges, as well as before preferential debts. He distinguished earlier authority to the contrary[409] on the grounds that it was concerned with older legislation which did not provide, as section 251 now does, that a floating charge under the Act means a charge which, when created, was a floating charge.

Since liquidation expenses enjoy 'super priority' the range of expenses encompassed within this category is especially important. Rule 4.218 of the Insolvency Rules defines the various expenses payable out of the assets and, subject to the court's power under section 156 to order otherwise in a compulsory liquidation,[410] the order in which they are payable. The liquidator's own remuneration is included in the list of liquidation expenses. Also more or less automatically included (although in theory the matter is in the discretion of the court) are continuing rent or hire-purchase charges in respect of land or goods in the possession of the company which the liquidator continues to use for the purposes of the liquidation.[411]

---

[405] Chapter 32, *Report of Review Committee on Insolvency Law and Practice* (1982) Cmmd 8558.

[406] Section 176.

[407] *Re Barleycorn Ltd* [1970] Ch 465, [1970] 2 WLR 898; *Re MC Bacon (No. 2)* [1991] Ch 127, [1990] 3 WLR 646, [1990] BCLC 607.

[408] Also reported as *Mond v Taylor* [1993] Ch 388, [1993] 3 All ER 829, [1993] 3 WLR 14. But note the reference in *Re MC Bacon* [1991] Ch at p. 138 to a floating charge which is uncrystallised at the date of liquidation.

[409] *Re Christonette International Ltd* [1982] 3 All ER 225, [1982] 1 WLR 1245.

[410] Note also section 112 which provides generally for the reference to court of matters arising from voluntary liquidations. Rule 4.218 applies to creditors' voluntary winding-ups.

[411] *Re International Marine Hydropathic Co.* (1884) 28 Ch D 470; *Re Lundy Granite Co.* (1871) LR 6 Ch App. 462; *Re Oak Pits Colliery Co.* (1882) 21 Ch D 322; *Re Atlantic Computer Systems plc* [1992] Ch 505, where the earlier authorities and the general principle are reviewed.

17.55.3 Deferred debts

As among ordinary unsecured debts, the pari passu rule generally prevails. However, section 74 (2) (*f*) creates a category of deferred debt: any sum due to a member of a company (in his character of a member) by way of dividends, profits or otherwise is not deemed to be a debt of the company, payable to that member in a case of competition between himself and any other creditor not a member of the company; but such sum may be taken into account for the purpose of the final adjustment of the rights of the contributories among themselves.

Whether a creditor can by contract choose to opt out of the pari passu rule and defer his debt to other debts of the company was, until recently, unclear.[412] The difficulty with such subordination arrangements was perceived to be that the pari passu rule might fall to be regarded as a mandatory rule. On one interpretation, this view was supported by the decision of the House of Lords in *British Eagle International Air Lines v Compagnie Nationale Air France.*[413]

British Eagle, an airline operator, was in liquidation. Prior to its liquidation, it had participated in a clearing house system operated by IATA. The purpose of the system was to free the operators from having to claim against each other; it operated on the basis that each month, each member would tot up its debits and credits as against other members of the system and would then pay to or claim through IATA as the case might be. At the time of its liquidation, British Eagle was indebted to a number of the members of the clearing-house system but it was owed money from Air France. Its liquidator sought to claim the sum owing from Air France. Under the clearing-house contractual system, this debt could be set off against the debts owing from British Eagle but the arrangement lacked the mutuality required for the operation of set-off under the insolvency legislation. The House of Lords, by a narrow majority, held that the insolvency legislation prevailed over the clearing-house arrangement and that, accordingly, Air France was not entitled to claim a set-off.

The position that Air France sought to claim for itself was better than that to which it was entitled under the insolvency legislation: Air France sought to give effect to a contractual right of set-off in circumstances where it was not entitled to an insolvency set-off. The nature of a subordination agreement is rather different, in that the creditor who agrees to be subordinated seeks a worse, rather than a better, position than that to which he is entitled under the insolvency legislation. This provides a ground for distinguishing the decision in *British Eagle*.

Another perceived obstacle to effective subordination under English insolvency law was the decision of the House of Lords in *National Westminster Bank Ltd v Halesowen*.[414] In this case, insolvency set-off was held to be mandatory. Significantly, the contractual arrangement considered by the House of Lords could have denied a creditor the benefit of the right of set-off to which it was entitled under the insolvency legislation; like a subordination agreement the arrangement, if it had that effect as a matter of contract, would have undermined rather than improved the creditor's position.[415] Although

---

[412] The question produced much literature, a sample of which includes Wood, *English and International Set-Off* (Sweet & Maxwell, 1989), Chapter 17; Johnson, 'Debt Subordination: The Australian Perspective' (1987) 15 ABLJ 80; Johnson, 'Contractual Debt Subordination and Legislative Reform' [1991] JBL 225.

[413] [1975] 2 All ER 390, [1975] 1 WLR 758, applying *Ex parte Mackay* (1873) 8 Ch App. 643, 647.

[414] [1972] AC 785, [1972] 1 All ER 641, [1972] 2 WLR 455.

[415] On the facts, the House of Lords held that the agreement in question did not have the effect of excluding set-off.

Halesowen was concerned strictly with set-off, it was thought to be susceptible to the wider interpretation that any arrangement which would operate so as to effect a distribution of assets otherwise than in accordance with the statutory scheme was void on the basis of public policy, irrespective of whether it produced an advantage or disadvantage for any of the contracting parties.[416]

However, in *Re Maxwell Communications Corp. plc (No. 3)*[417] Vinelott J, following Australian and South African authority,[418] held that a contractual subordination arrangement was effective. *British Eagle* was distinguished on the basis that it was a case where the creditor had sought to achieve a better position than is possible under the pari passu principle. *Halesowen* was distinguished because it was concerned with set-off and did not apply by analogy to the pari passu principle. Vinelott J considered that it was important, particularly at a time when insolvency increasingly had international ramifications, for English law to give effect to contractual subordination arrangements in the same way as other jurisdictions.

17.56 Contributories

Under section 74 of the Insolvency Act 1986 every present and past member is liable to contribute to the assets of the company on winding-up and is therefore a contributory.[419] Section 74 then limits the amount of the contribution that can be required of a contributory. Consistent with the principle of limited liability, no contribution can be required from any present or past member of a limited company in excess of the amount unpaid in respect of the shares held, or previously held. No contribution can be required from a past member who ceased to be a member one year or more before the commencement of the winding-up.[420] Past members are, in addition, only liable to contribute where present members appear to be unable to make the contributions required of them and furthermore are not liable to contribute in respect of debts or liabilities contracted by the company after they ceased to be members.[421]

17.57 Distribution of remaining assets

The liquidation process may result in a surplus remaining after the expenses, costs and debts have been paid in full, although it would be comparatively rare for this to happen. Where there is a surplus, the question arises as to its distribution. Section 107 of the Insolvency Act 1986 provides that in the case of a voluntary liquidation, remaining assets are to be distributed among the members according to their rights and interests in the company. The equivalent provisions governing compulsory liquidations are sections 143 and 154, which provide for the distribution of remaining assets among the persons entitled to them.

The distribution of any surplus must take into account the rights conferred on the

---

[416] *Carreras Rothmans Ltd v Freeman Mathews*, above; *Re Orion Sound Ltd* [1979] 2 NZLR 574 not following *Re Walker Construction Company Ltd* [1960] NZLR 523.

[417] [1993] 1 All ER 737, [1993] 1 WLR 1402, [1993] BCC 369.

[418] *Horne v Chester & Fein Property Developments Pty Ltd* 11 ACLR 485; *Re Carbon Developments (Pty) Ltd* [1993] 1 SA 493.

[419] Contributory being defined by section 79 as meaning any person who is liable to contribute. This category does not include persons who are ordered to make a contribution as a result of liability for fraudulent or wrongful trading: section 79 (2).

[420] Section 74 (2) (*a*).

[421] Section 74 (2) (*b*)–(*c*).

members by the terms of the company's memorandum and articles of association but, leaving aside any special provisions made by these documents, the position is as follows. Where there are shares having a preference as to capital, the amount paid on those shares must be repaid before any amount is paid to those whose rights are deferred, such as the holders of ordinary or deferred shares in the company. It now seems to be generally accepted that the annexation to preference shares of the right to receive back their capital on a winding-up in priority to ordinary shares is an exhaustive delimitation of the capital rights attaching to the preference shares, so that their holders are excluded from any participation in any surplus after all capital has been returned.[422]

Where, however, all the shares rank equally among themselves and the same amount has been paid up on each of them, the surplus is distributed in repayment of the capital paid up on those shares rateably, according to the number of shares. If more has been paid up on some shares than on others, equalisation must first be achieved, usually by paying back the amount which exceeds that which has been paid in respect of all of the shares.[423]

If all capital has been repaid but there still remains a surplus then, unless the articles otherwise provide, it is divisible amongst the shareholders in proportion to the nominal amount of the share capital held by them respectively, and not in proportion to the amount paid up on their shares.[424] Where there has previously been a reduction of capital, the shares rank only at the reduced amount.[425]

PART 7:
SPECIAL POWERS OF LIQUIDATORS AND OTHER OFFICE-HOLDERS IN INSOLVENCY PROCEEDINGS

17.58 A liquidator's ability to disclaim property

Section 178 of the Insolvency Act 1986 gives a liquidator the power by giving notice to disclaim any onerous property notwithstanding that he has taken possession of it, endeavoured to sell it or otherwise exercised rights of ownership in relation to it. This is a potentially very important power to rid a company in liquidation of assets which are subject to liabilities, thus rendering retention undesirable from the point of view of a beneficial realisation of the assets of the company for the benefit of the creditors generally. For the purposes of the section, 'onerous property' means any unprofitable contract and any other property of the company which is unsaleable or not readily saleable or is such that it may give rise to a liability to pay money or perform any other onerous acts.

A notice of disclaimer under the section cannot be given by the liquidator in respect of any property, if the person interested in that property has applied in writing to him (or his predecessors) requiring the liquidator to decide whether or not he will disclaim and the liquidator has not given notice of intention to disclaim within twenty-eight days (or such longer period as the court may allow upon his application).[426]

---

[422] See 7.4.2, above; *Scottish Insurance Cor. v Wilsons & Clyde Coal Co.* [1949] AC 462.
[423] *Re Exchange Drapery Co.* (1888) 38 Ch D 171.
[424] *Birch v Cropper* (1889) 14 App. Cas. 525.
[425] *Re Espuela Land and Cattle Co. (No. 2)* [1909] 2 Ch 187.
[426] Section 178 (5).

Once effectively made, the disclaimer operates to determine as from its date the rights, interests and liabilities of the company in respect of the property disclaimed. It does not, however, except in so far as is necessary for the purpose of releasing the company from any liability, affect the rights or liabilities of any other person interested in that property.[427]

Under section 178 (6) of the 1986 Act any person sustaining loss or damage in consequence of a disclaimer is deemed a creditor of a company to the extent of the loss or damage sustained and may prove for that loss or damage in the winding-up of the company.

Under section 179 a disclaimer in respect of any leasehold property does not take effect until such time as a copy of the disclaimer has been served on every person claiming under the company as underlessee or mortgagee and either:

(1) no application is made under section 181 (see below) in respect to that property within fourteen days; or

(2) where such an application under section 181 has been made the court directs that the disclaimer shall take effect.

Under section 181 of the Act, which applies not only to disclaimers of leasehold property but also to disclaimers of any other onerous property, any person who has an interest in the disclaimed property or who is under any liability in respect of it (not being a liability which would be discharged by the disclaimer[428]) may apply to the court for an order to have the disclaimed property vested in it. Where the application is made by a person who is under a liability in respect of the disclaimed property, the court will not make the order unless it considers it would be just to do so for the purposes of compensating that person.

The court cannot make an order under section 181 vesting leasehold property in any person claiming under the company as underlessee or mortgagee except on terms making that person:

(1) subject to the same liabilities and obligations which the company was subject to under the lease at the commencement of the winding-up; or

(2) if the court thinks fit, making the person who has the property vested in it subject to the same liabilities and obligations as that person would be subject to if the lease had been assigned to him at the commencement of the winding-up.

Where either an underlessee or mortgagee is unwilling to accept a vesting order on the above terms the court can order that the property be vested in any person who is liable as guarantor or surety (whether alone or jointly with the company) to perform the lessee's covenants under the lease.[429]

Section 168 (5) allows persons who are aggrieved by an act or decision of a liquidator to apply to court; the court may confirm, reverse or modify the act or decision complained

---

[427] Section 178 (4).

[428] An original lessee of a lease which has been assigned remains liable for the rent notwithstanding disclaimer by the assignee's liquidator: *Warnford Investments Ltd v Duckworth* [1979] Ch 127; *WH Smith Ltd v Wyndham Investments Ltd* [1994] BCC 699; *Hindcastle Ltd v Barbara Attenborough Associates Ltd* [1994] 3 WLR 1100 (leave to appeal to the House of Lords granted [1995] 1 WLR 385). But disclaimer of a lease releases a guarantor from liability for the current lessee's obligations under the lease: *Stacey v Hill* [1901] 1 KB 660; *Re No. 1 London Ltd* [1991] BCLC 501, [1991] BCC 118; *Re Yarmarine (IW) Ltd* [1992] BCLC 276, [1992] BCC 28.

[429] Section 182 (3). For the procedural requirements as to disclaimer see rule 4.187 *et seq.*

of, and make such order in the case as it thinks just. *Re Hans Place Ltd*[430] was an attempt to use this provision to challenge a liquidator's decision to disclaim a lease. The court held that it did have jurisdiction to consider the complaint but that it could only interfere where the liquidator had acted in bad faith or had made a perverse decision.

17.59 Office-holders

Office-holders are given certain special powers under the insolvency legislation. Who an office-holder is depends on the power in question, but the category can include administrators, administrative receivers (but not other receivers), supervisors of voluntary arrangements, liquidators and provisional liquidators.

17.59.1 *Utilities*

Suppliers of gas, electricity, water and telecommunications services cannot make it a condition of continuing the giving of the supply that the office-holder pay outstanding charges, but the supplier can require the office-holder to give a personal guarantee in respect of any new supplies.[431] For this purpose administrators, administrative receivers, supervisors of voluntary arrangements, liquidators and provisional liquidators all count as office-holders.

17.59.2 *Transactions at an undervalue*

An administrator or a liquidator, as an office-holder, has the power to make an application to court in respect of transactions at an undervalue.[432] If the application is successful, the court must make such order as it thinks fit for restoring the position to what it would have been if the company had not entered into the transaction.[433]

The Insolvency Act 1986 defines a transaction[434] at an undervalue as one where:

(1) the company makes a gift to a person or otherwise enters into a transaction with a person on terms that provide for the company to receive no consideration; or

(2) the company enters into a transaction with a person for a consideration the value of which, in money or money's worth, is significantly less than the value, in money or money's worth, of the consideration provided by the company.

The first limb of the definition envisages a total absence of any consideration passing to the company, while the second limb covers the case where there is some mutual consideration but significantly differing in amounts. The second limb was considered in *Re MC Bacon Ltd*[435] where Millett J made the following observations:

(1) a comparison must be made between the value obtained by the company for the transaction and the value of the consideration provided by the company;

(2) both values must be measurable in money or money's worth;

(3) both values must be considered from the company's point of view.

---

[430] [1993] BCLC 768.

[431] Section 233.

[432] Section 238.

[433] Section 238 (3).

[434] The term 'transaction' is defined in section 436 of the Act to include 'a gift, agreement or arrangement'.

[435] [1990] BCLC 324, [1990] BCC 78. Millett J's analysis of the provision was adopted by Balcombe LJ in *Menzies v National Bank of Kuwait SAK* [1994] BCC 119, and by Sir Christopher Slade in *Agricultural Mortgage Corpn plc v Woodward* [1995] 1 BCLC 1 (both cases on section 423 of the Insolvency Act).

Millett J held that the granting of a debenture by a company in return for its bank forbearing from calling in its overdraft and continuing to make advances was not within the scope of the second limb of the definition of a transaction at an undervalue. In granting the debenture the company had parted with nothing of value: the granting of the debenture meant that assets of the company were appropriated for the payment of a debt, but those assets were not depleted or diminished in value. Further, the consideration which it received in return was not something which was capable of being valued in monetary terms.

This reasoning would seem to be equally applicable to the giving of a guarantee, other than a guarantee which is caught by the first limb as being granted as a gift or for no consideration. A guarantee creates a contingent obligation but does not normally deplete or diminish the company's assets (although conceivably it could be treated as having that effect where, at the time when the guarantee is given, it is certain or virtually certain that it will be called upon). Whether a transaction is within the section is tested at the time when it is entered into,[436] so that if a guarantee, when given, is not within its scope later payment under that guarantee should not amount to a transaction at an undervalue.

Re MC Bacon thus limits the scope of office-holder's power in respect of transactions at an undervalue quite considerably. Where it may prove to be most useful is in relation, first, to gifts made by a company prior to its administration or liquidation and, second, to cases where the company has sold assets for considerably less or, as the case may be, bought assets for considerably more than their true worth.[437]

There is one way in which a transaction which would otherwise amount to a transaction at an undervalue can be saved. The court may not make an order in respect of a transaction at an undervalue if it is satisfied that: (a) the company entered into the transaction in good faith and for the purpose of carrying on its business; and (b) at the time when it did so, there were reasonable grounds for believing the transaction would benefit the company.[438] Good faith, propriety of purpose and reasonableness must all be established to the satisfaction of the court; if any of these elements is missing, the transaction remains vulnerable.

There is a time limit on the power of an administrator of liquidator to attack a transaction at an undervalue. The transaction must have taken place at a 'relevant time'.[439] There are two elements to the definition of 'relevant time'. First, the transaction must be entered into within a specified period before the onset of the administration or liquidation. The transaction at an undervalue must take place either at a time within the period of two years ending with the onset of the administration or liquidation, or at a time between the presentation of a petition for the making of an administration order and the making of such an order on that petition. For these purposes, the onset of the administration or liquidation is as follows:

(1) the date of the presentation of the petition on which an administration order is made, in the case of a company in administration or in liquidation where the company went into liquidation immediately upon the discharge of an administration order; or

---

[436] Sections 238 (2) and 240.

[437] Factual situations similar to those which arose in *Re Halt Garage (1964) Ltd* [1982] 3 All ER 1016 and *Aveling Barford Ltd v Perion* [1989] BCLC 626 may now be vulnerable as transactions at an undervalue.

[438] Section 238 (5).

[439] Section 240.

(2) the date of the commencement of the winding-up in a case where the company is otherwise in liquidation. The commencement of the winding-up will be[440] either the passing of the resolution for voluntary winding up or the presentation of a winding-up petition (except in the case where the winding-up petition follows a resolution to wind up when the winding-up is deemed to commence at the date of the resolution).

Secondly, it is only a relevant time for the purposes of the provisions relating to transactions at an undervalue if, at the time, the company is unable to pay its debts within the meaning of section 123 of the Act or if it becomes unable to pay them within the meaning of that section in consequence of the transaction. This requirement, however, is deemed to be satisfied, unless the contrary is shown, where the transaction in question is entered into by the company with a person who is connected with the company.[441]

The court is given a very wide power to make such order as it thinks fit for the purpose of restoring the position to what it would have been if the company had not entered into the transaction. Without prejudice to the generality of this discretion, the Act gives the court powers to make various orders, details of which are set out at 17.59.4 below.

The court also has power to set aside transactions at an undervalue in applications brought under section 423.[442] There is no time limit on applications under this section and, as well as liquidators and administrators, supervisors of voluntary arrangements and victims of transactions[443] have standing to seek an order under this section although, if the company is in administration or liquidation, a victim must obtain the leave of the court.[444] Whoever brings the claim, it is treated as made on behalf of every victim of the transaction.[445] The court can only make an order under this section where it is satisfied that the transaction was entered into by the company for the purpose of putting assets beyond the reach of any person who is making, or may at some time make, a claim against the company or of otherwise prejudicing the interests of such a person in relation to the claim which he is making or may make.[446] The need to establish this purpose inhibits the use of the power contained in this section.[447]

17.59.3 *Voidable preferences*

An administrator or liquidator may apply to the court for an order on such terms as the court thinks fit, for restoring the position to what it would have been if the company had not given a preference.[448] A company gives a preference to a person if:

---

[440] Sections 86 and 129.

[441] Section 240 (2). For the definition of a person connected with the company, see sections 249 and 435.

[442] A transaction at an undervalue for this purpose is defined by section 423 (1). So far as companies are concerned, the definition is the same as that under section 238.

[443] A litigant in proceedings against a company who has a chance of success in those proceedings can be a 'victim' for this purpose: *Pinewood Joinery v Starlem Properties Ltd* [1994] BCC 569. See also *Re Ayala Holdings Ltd* [1993] BCLC 256 and *Agricultural Mortgage Corpn. plc v Woodward*, above (application by mortgagee).

[444] Section 424 (1) (a).

[445] Section 424 (2).

[446] Statutory predecessors of this section, which also applies to individual insolvents, can be traced back to 1571. See *Arbuthnot Leasing International Ltd v Havelot Leasing & Ors (No. 2)* [1990] BCC 636; *Menzies v National Bank of Kuwait SAK*, above; *Chohan v Saggar* [1994] BCC 134; *Agricultural Mortgage Corpn. plc v Woodward*, above.

[447] Section 425 specifies orders which can be made in respect of a transaction defrauding creditors (such specific provision to be without prejudice to the general power of the court).

[448] Section 239.

(1) that person is one of the company's creditors or a surety or guarantor for any of the company's debts or other liabilities; and
(2) the company does anything or suffers anything to be done which (in either case) has the effect of putting that person into a position which, in the event of the company going into insolvent liquidation, will be better than the position he would have been in if that thing had not been done.

These elements of the definition of preference must be determined objectively: a preference arises in the event that the objective effect referred to occurs. However, the court may not make an order to reverse the preference unless the company which gave the preference was influenced in deciding to give it by a desire to put the recipient in a better position in an insolvent liquidation than he would have been in if the preference had not been given.

A desire to prefer is narrower than intention in that a person may be held to have 'intended' the necessary consequences of his acts even though he does not desire them to happen: to be held to have desired it, the company must be shown positively to have wished to improve the creditor's position in its insolvent liquidation. A company is 'influenced' by a desire to prefer where it is a motivating factor, but it need not be the only or the predominant one.[449]

Where the preference is given to a person connected with the company (otherwise than by reason only of being its employee) at the time that the preference was given then the company is presumed, unless the contrary is shown, to have been influenced in deciding to give the preference by the requisite desire.

A company may be held to have given a preference by giving an unsecured creditor a security over the company's assets. However, in a case such as *Re MC Bacon*, where the debenture was granted to avert the calling-in of the company's overdraft and the immediate liquidation which would have followed if the bank had withdrawn its support, the requisite desire to prefer may not be established. Another example of a possible preference is the decision to pay some debts but not others: the creditors whose debts are paid are obviously placed in a much better position than those who remain unpaid and who become subject to the moratorium in administration or, as the case may be, become obliged to prove for their debts in the company's liquidation.

The fact that something has been done in pursuance of an order of the court does not prevent that thing from constituting the giving of a preference. This provision is intended to prevent, for example, the company submitting to a judgment against itself by the person to be preferred and then arguing that it had no choice in giving the preference because of the judgment.

The preference can only be reversed by court order if it was given at a relevant time. This means, in the case of a preference given to a person who is connected with the company (otherwise and by reason only of being its employee), a period of two years ending with the onset of the administration or liquidation. In the case of a preference which is not given to a person connected with the company then the relevant period is six months ending with the onset of the administration or liquidation. In addition, the time between the presentation of a petition for the making of an administration order and the making of such order is a relevant time. It will only be a relevant time, however, if the company is unable to pay its debts within the meaning of section 123 of the Act or

---

[449] *Re MC Bacon*, above; *Re DKG Contractors Ltd* [1990] BCC 903; *Re Beacon Leisure Ltd* [1991] BCC 213, [1992] BCLC 565; *Re Fairway Magazines Ltd* [1992] BCC 924, [1993] BCLC 643.

becomes unable to pay its debts within the meaning of that section in consequence of the preference (but there is no presumption as to such inability even in relation to connected persons).

The same definition of the onset of the administration or liquidation applies as in the case of transactions at an undervalue.

17.59.4 *Court orders in respect of transactions at an undervalue and preferences*

The court is given a very wide discretion to make orders for the purpose of restoring the position to what it would have been if the company had not entered into the transaction or preference. Without prejudice to the generality of this discretion the court is also given the power to make the following orders:[450]

(1) to require any property transferred as part of the transaction, or in connection with the giving of a preference, to be vested in the company;

(2) to require any property to be so vested if it represents in any person's hands the application either of the proceeds of sale of property so transferred or of money so transferred;

(3) to release or discharge (in whole or in part) any security given by the company;

(4) to require any person to pay, in respect of benefits received by him from the company, such sums to the administrator or liquidator as the court may direct;

(5) to provide for any surety or guarantor whose obligations to any person were released or discharged (in whole or in part) under the transaction, or by the giving of the preference, to be under such new or revived obligations to that person as the court thinks appropriate;

(6) to provide for security to be provided for the discharge of any obligation imposed by or arising under the court order, for such an obligation to be charged on any property and for the security or charge to have the same priority as a security or charge released or discharged (in whole or in part) under the transaction or by the giving of the preference; and

(7) to provide for the extent to which any person whose property is vested by the order in the company, or on whom obligations are imposed by the order, is to be able to prove in the winding-up of the company for debts or other liabilities which arose from, or were released or discharged (in whole or in part) under or by the transaction or the giving of the preference.

An order relating to a transaction at an undervalue or a preference may affect the property of, or impose any obligation on, any person, whether or not he is the person with whom the company in question entered into the transaction or, as the case may be, the person to whom the preference was given. However, such an order:

(1) must not prejudice any interest in property which was acquired from a person other than the company and was acquired in good faith and for value, or prejudice any interest deriving from such an interest; and

(2) must not require a person who received a benefit from the transaction or preference in good faith and for value to make a payment to the administrator or liquidator, except where that person was a party to the transaction or the payment

---

[450] Section 241.

is to be in respect of a preference given to that person at a time when he was a creditor of the company.[451]

Section 241 (2A), inserted by the Insolvency (No. 2) Act 1994, amplifies the concept of good faith in this context. A person who has notice of the relevant surrounding circumstances and of the relevant proceedings, or who was connected with, or an associate of, either the company in question or the person with whom the company entered into the transaction or to whom the company gave the preference, is presumed, unless the contrary is shown, not to be in good faith. The relevant surrounding circumstances are the fact that the company entered into the transaction at an undervalue or, as the case may be, the circumstances which amounted to the giving of a preference by the company in question.[452] A person has notice of administration proceedings if he has notice of the fact that a petition has been presented or an order has been made; and a person has notice of liquidation if he has notice of the fact that a petition has been presented or of the fact that the company has gone into liquidation.[453]

The proceeds of an action to set aside a preference are held by the office-holder for the benefit of its general creditors and do not fall within the scope of a floating charge on its assets.[454] The reasoning underlying this is that the power to attack a preference is granted only to the liquidator and administrator and is not available to the company itself; therefore the proceeds of an action in respect of a preference cannot be the subject of a charge granted by the company on its assets and they are held separately by the administrator or liquidator for the benefit of unsecured creditors.[455]

The Act[456] specifically states that the provisions relating to transactions at an undervalue and preferences apply without prejudice to the availability of any other remedy, even in relation to a transaction or preference which the company had no power to enter into or to give. Accordingly, the ultra vires doctrine is unaffected.

17.59.5 *Extortionate credit transactions*

A liquidator or administrator may apply to the court in respect of an extortionate credit transaction which was entered into within three years of the date of the administration order or, as the case may be, the company went into liquidation.[457]

A transaction is extortionate if, having regard to the risk accepted by the person providing the credit:

(1) the terms of it are or were such as to require a grossly exorbitant payment to be made (whether unconditionally or in certain contingencies) in respect of the provision of the credit; or

(2) it otherwise grossly contravened ordinary principles of fair dealing.

---

[451] Section 241 (2), as amended by the Insolvency (No. 2) Act 1994.

[452] Section 241 (3) as amended by the Insolvency (No. 2) Act 1994.

[453] Section 241 (3A) and (3C), as inserted by the Insolvency (No. 2) Act 1994. See also section 241 (3B), which deals with the situation where liquidation follows immediately upon the discharge of an administration order.

[454] *Re Yagerphone* [1935] 1 Ch 392. This ratio in the case was that payment of a debt due to an unsecured creditor prior to crystallisation bound the debenture holder but Bennett J's obiter statement as to the application of the proceeds recovered on a preference claim is widely regarded as correct: see *Re MC Bacon Ltd (No. 2)* [1991] Ch 127 at p. 137.

[455] Wheeler, 'Swelling the Assets for Distribution in Corporate Insolvency' [1993] JBL 256.

[456] Section 241 (4).

[457] Section 244. These provisions follow closely the terms of sections 137–9 (inclusive) of the Consumer Credit Act 1974.

It is to be presumed, unless the contrary is proved, that a transaction is extortionate.

An order in respect of an extortionate credit transaction may contain one or more of the following, as the court thinks fit:

(1) provision setting aside the whole or part of any obligation created by the transaction;

(2) provision otherwise varying the terms of the transaction or varying the terms on which any security for the purposes of the transaction is held;

(3) provision requiring any person who is or was a party to the transaction to pay to the office-holder any sums paid to that person, by virtue of the transaction, by the company;

(4) provision requiring any person to surrender to the administrator or liquidator any property held by him as security for the purposes of the transaction; and

(5) provision directing accounts to be taken between any persons.

The power to attack any transaction as being extortionate may be exercised concurrently with any other powers exercisable in relation to that transaction.

17.59.6 *Avoidance of floating charges*

Floating charges created by the company within a specified period prior to the commencement of the administration or the liquidation (a 'relevant time') will be invalid[458] except to the extent of the aggregate of:

(1) The value of so much of the consideration for the creation of the charge as consists of money paid or goods or services supplied to the company at the same time as, or after, the creation of the charge. The value of any goods or services supplied by way of consideration for a floating charge is deemed to be the amount in money which at the time that they were supplied could reasonably have been expected to be obtained for supplying the goods or services in the ordinary course of business and on the same terms (apart from the consideration) as those on which they were supplied to the company.[459]

(2) The value of so much of that consideration as consists of the discharge or reduction, at the same time as, or after, the creation of the charge of any debt of the company.[460]

(3) The amount of such interest (if any) as is payable on the amount falling within para. (1) or (2) in pursuance of any agreement under which the money was so paid, the goods or services were so supplied or the debt was so discharged or reduced.

The phrase 'at the same time as' which is used in section 245 was considered by the Court of Appeal in *Re Shoe Lace Ltd*.[461] Not following authorities on a statutory prede-

---

[458] Section 245.

[459] Section 245 (6).

[460] This would appear to reverse the decision in *Re Destone Fabrics Ltd* [1941] Ch 319. Section 245 preserves (contrary to the recommendations of the Review Committee on Insolvency Law and Practice, 1982, Cmnd 8558, paras. 1561–2) the decision in *Re Yeovil Glove Co. Ltd* [1965] Ch 148, whereby in respect of a floating charge created in favour of a bank to secure an overdrawn account, if payments are made into the account after the creation of the charge, these will, under the rule in *Clayton's Case* (1816) 1 Mer 572, go to reduce the pre-charge indebtedness, so that cheques drawn on the account after the creation of the charge will be money paid to the company thereafter and the charge will therefore be valid to this extent.

[461] [1993] BCC 609 (also reported as *Power v Sharp Investments Ltd*).

cessor to section 245,[462] the Court of Appeal held that whether the consideration for the charge was given at the same time as the creation of the charge is a mechanical issue determined solely by the clock, subject only to *de minimis* delays.

In *Re Fairway Magazines Ltd*[463] the company was indebted to its bank and this debt was personally guaranteed by one of its directors. As part of a series of measures designed to keep the company alive, the director lent sums of money to the company which, at his request, were paid directly into the company's overdrawn bank account. A debenture was granted to the director as security for these advances. The effect of paying the borrowed money into the company's bank account was to reduce the director's personal liability under the guarantee. This led to a corresponding reduction in the amount for which the director would be required to lodge a proof in the liquidation of the company in respect of his payments under the guarantee. Instead, to the extent of the reduction of his exposure as an unsecured creditor, the director became a secured creditor.

Mummery J held that payments made by the director which were paid into the company's bank account were not in substance paid to the company for its benefit, since the effect of the payments was merely to substitute a secured debt for an unsecured debt. Therefore the arrangement was avoided by section 245 because the payments were not 'paid ... to the company' as required by section 245 (1) (*a*).[464]

A floating charge is created at a relevant time if:

(1) in the case of a floating charge created in favour of a person who is connected with the company it is created at a time in the period of two years ending with the onset of insolvency;

(2) where the floating charge is not created in favour of a person connected with the company, it is created at a time in the period of twelve months ending with the onset of insolvency; or

(3) in any case it is created at a time between the presentation of a petition for the making of an administration order in relation to the company and the making of such an order on that petition.

In addition, in a case where the floating charge is created in favour of a person who is not connected with the company then the company must at that time be unable to pay its debts within the meaning of section 123 of the Act or become unable to pay its debts within the meaning of that section in consequence of the transaction under which the charge is created.

The definition of the onset of the insolvency for the purpose of section 245 is the same as for transactions at an undervalue.

---

[462] e.g. *Re Columbian Fireproofing Co. Ltd* [1910] 2 Ch 120 and *Re F & E Stanton Ltd* [1929] 1 Ch 180, which had held that a delay between the creation of the charge and the giving of consideration would not bring a charge within the scope of the section if the person seeking to uphold the charge could establish a good reason for the delay.

[463] [1992] BCC 924, [1993] BCLC 643.

[464] *Re Orleans Motor Co. Ltd* [1911] 2 Ch 41; *Re Matthew Ellis Ltd* [1993] Ch 458; *Re GT Whyte & Co. Ltd* [1983] BCLC 311.

17.60 Other powers

The Insolvency Act 1986 contains various powers which office-holders and other insolvency practitioners[465] can call upon to assist them in their task of collecting in the assets of the company for the benefit of the creditors. The powers are extensive: in *Re British & Commonwealth Holdings plc (No. 2)*[466] Woolf LJ described the powers contained in Part IV of the Act as 'a remarkable armoury of summary weapons with which to assist "office-holders" ... to perform their functions'.

The relevant powers include the following:

(1) Power to require the submission of a statement of affairs. This can be required by the nominee under a proposed supervisory arrangement,[467] an administrator,[468] an administrative receiver[469] and the Official Receiver in a compulsory winding-up.[470] In a creditors' voluntary winding-up a statement of affairs must be laid before a meeting of the creditors.[471] The persons required to produce the statement of affairs are those who were connected with the conduct of its affairs, including, in particular, its past and present officers.[472]

(2) A power to get in the company's property. Under section 234 of the Act, where a person has in his possession or control any property, books, papers or records to which the company appears to be entitled, the court may require that person to pay, deliver, convey, surrender or transfer the same to the office-holder. An office-holder for this purpose means an administrator, an administrative receiver, a liquidator or a provisional liquidator.

(3) Under section 235 the following persons can be compelled to give to the office-holder any information concerning the company and its promotion, formation, business dealings or affairs generally and may be required to attend on the liquidator at such times as he may reasonably require. The persons who have this duty to co-operate with the office-holder are:

    (a) those who are or have at any time been officers of the company;

    (b) those who have taken part in the formation of the company at any time within one year before the effective date (ie, broadly, the date of the administration, administrative receivership or liquidation)

    (c) employees of the company (including persons employed under a contract for services) within a year before the effective date who, in the office-holder's opinion, are capable of giving information;

    (d) those who within a year before the effective date have been officers or

---

[465] Nominees under voluntary arrangements and the Official Receiver are not generally regarded as office-holders, but the Official Receiver is an office-holder for the purposes of sections 235 and 236.

[466] [1992] Ch 342, [1992] 2 All ER 801, [1992] 2 WLR 931, [1992] BCLC 641, [1992] BCC 165 and 172; affirmed (*sub nom British and Commonwealth Holdings (Joint Administrators) v Spicer and Oppenheim* [1993] AC 426, [1992] 4 All ER 876, [1992] 3 WLR 853, [1993] BCLC 168, [1992] BCC 977.

[467] Section 2 (3).

[468] Section 22.

[469] Section 47.

[470] Section 131.

[471] Section 99. By section 95 (3) this requirement also applies where a members' voluntary winding-up is converted to a creditors' voluntary winding-up.

[472] Where a members' voluntary winding-up converts to a creditors' voluntary winding-up, the duty falls on the liquidator: section 95 (3).

employees of another company which itself was within that period an officer of the company in insolvency.

(e) in the case of a company being wound up by the court, any persons who acted as administrator, administrative receiver or liquidator of the company.

If a person fails in his duty to co-operate under section 235 he is liable to a fine. In addition to those who are office-holders under section 234, the Official Receiver is also an office-holder in this case.

(4) Power to apply to court for an examination of certain persons.[473] The office-holders who have this power are administrators, administrative receivers, liquidators and provisional liquidators, and also the Official Receiver. Examinations under this power, which is conferred by section 236, are private. In compulsory liquidations the Official Receiver also has power to apply to court for public examinations.[474]

The court may on the application of an office-holder under section 236 summon to appear before it any officer of the company, any person known or suspected to have in his possession any property of the company or supposed to be indebted to the company, or any person whom the court thinks capable of giving information concerning the promotion, formation, business dealings, affairs or property of the company.[475] If necessary the court can issue warrants for arrest and for seizure of documents, money or goods.[476]

The power under section 236 is directed to enabling the court to assist the office-holder to discover the truth of the circumstances connected with the affairs of the company and its business, in order that the office-holder may discharge his functions as effectively as possible.[477] The court's power to make an order under the section is not limited to information needed to 'reconstitute the state of the company's knowledge', that is information to which the company was entitled from its officers or servants, past or present, as a matter of contract or fiduciary duty.[478] The decision whether to make an order lies in the court's discretion and, in coming to its decision, the court must balance the reasonable requirements of the office-holder against any possible oppression of the person to be examined: a proper case for an order is one where the office-holder reasonably requires to see documents to carry out his functions and the production does not impose an unnecessary and unreasonable burden on the person required to produce them in

---

[473] Section 236.

[474] Section 133. See *Re Wallace Smith Trust Co. Ltd* [1992] BCC 707. This power has extra-territorial effect: *Re Seagull Manufacturing Co. Ltd* [1993] Ch 345, [1993] 2 All ER 980, [1993] 2 WLR 872, [1993] BCLC 1139, [1993] BCC 241. Note *Re Campbell Coverings Ltd (No. 2)* [1954] Ch 225 where it was held that the power to apply for a public examination applies to voluntary liquidations. In *Bishopsgate Investment Management Ltd v Maxwell* [1993] Ch 1, [1992] 2 All ER 856, [1992] 2 WLR 991, [1992] BCC 222, the point was not decided but the Court of Appeal accepted that a public examination might be available in a voluntary liquidation by virtue of section 112. There is no privilege against self-incrimination in public examinations.

[475] Section 236 (2).

[476] Section 236 (5).

[477] *Re Gold Co.* (1879) 12 Ch D 77; *Re Imperial Continental Water Corp.* (1886) 33 Ch D 314; *Re North Australian Territory Co.* (1890) 45 Ch D 87; *Re Rolls Razor Ltd* [1968] 3 All ER 698; *Re Esal (Commodities) Ltd* [1989] BCLC 59, (1988) 4 BCC 475; *Joint Administrators of Cloverbay v BCCI SA* [1991] Ch 90, [1991] 1 All ER 894, [1990] 3 WLR 574, [1991] BCLC 135; *British & Commonwealth Holdings plc v Spicer & Oppenheim*, above.

[478] *British & Commonwealth v Spicer & Oppenheim*, above.

the light of the office-holder's requirements.[479]

The privilege against self-incrimination is impliedly abrogated by sections 235 and 236[480] but, if criminal charges have already been brought, the court may disallow questioning under section 236 if it would be oppressive for the person who is to be examined.[481] Statements made in a section 236 examination, or in pursuance of a requirement imposed by or under the Act or the Insolvency Rules, may be used in evidence against the maker or against any other person who concurs in the making of the statement.[482]

(5) Unenforceability of liens on company documents. Under section 246, where a company is in administration or liquidation or a provisional liquidator has been appointed, any lien or other right to retain possession of any books, papers or other records of the company is unenforceable against an office-holder (here meaning an administrator, a liquidator or a provisional liquidator) to the extent that its enforcement would deny possession of any books, papers or other records to the office-holder. The only exception to this is where a person has a lien on documents which gives title to property and the documents are held as such. For example, anybody who has a charge on title deeds by way of deposit would not be compelled to surrender possession of those deeds to an office-holder under this section.[483]

17.61 Dissolution of companies

Section 201 of the Insolvency Act 1986 deals with the dissolution of a company which has been wound up voluntarily. Where the liquidator has filed his final accounts and returns,[484] the Registrar of Companies will put these on the company's file. On the expiration of three months from the registration of those returns the company is deemed to be dissolved. The court has power, on the application of the liquidator or any other interested party, to make an order that the dissolution of the company takes place at some later date if the court thinks fit.[485]

In a compulsory winding-up the Official Receiver, if he is the liquidator of the company and believes that the realisable assets are insufficient to cover the expenses of the winding-up and that no further investigation of the company's affairs is required, may apply to the Registrar of Companies for the early dissolution of the company.[486] If the Official Receiver gives such a notice this is registered by the Registrar of Companies. At the expiry of three months from the date of registration of the notice the company is dissolved. Where a notice has been given by the Official Receiver in this respect, any

---

[479] ibid. See also *Re North Australia Territory Co.* above, at p. 93; *Re Bletchley Boat Co. Ltd* [1974] 1 WLR 630; *Re Brook Martin & Co. (Nominees) Ltd* [1993] BCLC 328.

[480] *Re Jeffrey S Levitt Ltd* [1992] Ch 457, [1992] 2 All ER 509, [1992] 2 WLR 975, [1992] BCLC 250, [1992] BCC 137; *Re AE Farr* [1992] BCLC 333, [1992] BCC 150; *Re Bishopsgate Investment Management Ltd*, above; *Re Arrows Ltd (No. 4)* [1994] BCC 641.

[481] *Re AE Farr Ltd*, above; *Re Arrows Ltd* [1992] BCLC 1176, [1992] BCC 446 (orders granted even though person to be examined had been charged).

[482] Section 433; *Re Arrows Ltd (No. 4)*, above; *Re Adviser (188) Ltd ex parte Trachtenburg* [1993] BCC 492; *Re Headington Investments Ltd ex parte Maxwell* [1993] BCC 500.

[483] *Re SEIL Trade Finance Ltd* [1992] BCC 538 where, as well as share certificates and leases, charging documents were held to be documents giving a title to property.

[484] Section 94 (members' voluntary); section 106 (creditors' voluntary).

[485] Section 201 (3).

[486] Section 202 (2).

creditor or contributory of the company or any administrative receiver may apply to the Secretary of State for a direction if he considers that:

(1) the realisable assets of the company are sufficient to cover the expenses of the winding-up;
(2) the affairs of the company do require further investigation; or
(3) for any other reason the early dissolution of the company is inappropriate.[487]

The Secretary of State may give directions enabling the winding-up of the company to proceed as if the Official Receiver had not given a notice requiring the early dissolution of the company to the Registrar of Companies. His powers in this respect include the power to make a direction deferring the date at which the dissolution of the company is to take effect.[488]

Where in a compulsory winding-up no application is made by the Official Receiver for an early dissolution, the provisions of section 205 of the Insolvency Act 1986 apply. When the liquidator has filed his final returns or the Official Receiver has filed a notice stating that he considers the winding-up to be complete, the Registrar of Companies will register those returns or the notice as the case may be. At the end of a three-month period beginning with the date of that registration the company is dissolved.[489]

Again, the Official Receiver or any other person interested in the company's dissolution may apply to the Secretary of State for a direction deferring the date of the dissolution.[490]

When a company is dissolved its corporate existence ceases. It no longer has any officers or agents who can be served with notices or other proceedings on behalf of the company. It is not infrequently the case, however, that there are persons who have grievances or claims involving the company which they still wish to enforce.

Under section 651 of the Companies Act 1985 on the application of the liquidator of the company or any other person appearing to be interested the court may make an order declaring the dissolution to be void.[491] This power will be exercised where, upon a reconstruction, the new company, after agreeing to satisfy the liability of the old company,[492] has failed to perform its obligations and the old company has been dissolved. Note, however, that the order, if made, will not validate any purported corporate activity of the company carried out prior to the making of the order.[493] It has been stated that ordinarily the purposes of restoring a company to the register are to enable the liquidator to distribute an overlooked asset or a creditor to make a claim which he has not previously made.[494] The jurisdiction can be used to put a creditor in a better position than he would otherwise have been in.[495]

Generally such applications must not be made after the end of the period of two years

---

[487] Section 203 (2).
[488] Section 203 (3).
[489] Section 205 (2).
[490] Section 205 (3), with a right of appeal to the court if the Secretary of State refuses to grant a deferral.
[491] Note also the power given to the Registrar of Companies to strike a defunct company off the register by section 652. Creditors and members who object may apply to the court for the company to be restored to the register: section 653. On the effect of restoration to the register see: *Allied Dunbar Assurance plc v Fowle* [1994] BCC 422.
[492] *Re Spottiswoode, Dixon and Hunting* [1912] 1 Ch 410.
[493] *Morris v Harris* [1927] AC 242 (HL).
[494] *Re Forte's Manufacturing Ltd* [1994] BCC 84 at p. 87 *per* Hoffmann L.J.
[495] ibid.

from the date of dissolution of the company, but applications for the purpose of bringing proceedings against the company for damages for personal injuries or under the Fatal Accidents Act 1976 may be brought at any time subject to any applicable limitation periods.[496]

Once a company is dissolved all property and rights whatsoever which may still be vested in or held on trust for the company immediately before its dissolution (including leasehold property, but not including property held by the company on trust for any other person) are deemed to be *bona vacantia*[497] and vest in the Crown, subject to its right to disclaim. Section 656 of the Companies Act 1985 lays down the conditions upon which such disclaimer may be made by the Crown.

---

[496] Section 651 (4) and (5). The court has power to direct that the period between the dissolution of the company and the making of the order under the section shall not count for limitation purposes: section 651 (6).

[497] Section 654 of the Companies Act 1985.

Index